ANTIQUES
Handbook
& Price Guide
2024~2025

First published in Great Britain in 2024 by Miller's, a division of Mitchell Beazley, imprints of
Octopus Publishing Group Ltd, Carmelite House, 50 Victoria Embankment, London, EC4Y 0DZ
www.octopusbooksusa.com

An Hachette UK Company
www.hachette.co.uk

Distributed in the US by Hachette Book Group
1290 Avenue of the Americas, 4th and 5th Floors, New York, NY 10104

Distributed in Canada by Canadian Manda Group
664 Annette St., Toronto, Ontario, Canada M6S 2C8

Miller's is a registered trademark of Octopus Publishing Group Ltd
www.millersguides.com

ISBN: 978-1-78472-943-1

Set in Frutiger

Printed and bound in the United Arab Emirates

1 3 5 7 9 10 8 6 4 2

Publisher Alison Starling
Editor Scarlet Furness
Proofreader Julie Brooke
Indexer Hilary Bird
Designer Ali Scrivens, T J Graphics
Senior Production Manager Peter Hunt

Photographs of Judith Miller page 7, by Chris Terry

Page 1: A bronze figure, "Dancer," by Josef Lorenzl (1892-1950), on an onyx base, signed "LORENZL" on base in the bronze.
ca. 1925 23in (58.5cm) high $10,000-12,500 L&T
Page 3: A Delft lobed dish, painted with a portrait of King William, with the initials "KW," the rim with a border of tulips and other
flowers, blue painter's numeral on the base. ca. 1690 8¾in (22cm) wide $1,600-2,100 WW
Page 4 from left to right: A rare pair of Derby or Staffordshire leopards, the leopardess originally leaning over two cubs (one cub now
lacking) and cleaning one with her tongue, her companion recumbent with mouth open, each raised on a rocky base painted a rich blue
and defined around the lower perimeters with gilding. ca. 1840 1½in (4cm) high $1,500-1,900 WW
A 19thC French marble mantel clock, with perpetual calendar, by Henri Marc, Paris, with visible escapement and striking movement
signed and numbered "38518," the dial above a gilt-metal panel containing a calendar dial with moon phase and day, date, and month
subsidiary dials. 19¼in (49cm) high $3,100-4,300 GORL
A George IV silver teapot, by George Burrows II, London, part-fluted with a gadrooned rim, domed hinge cover, scroll handle, on a circular
foot. 1821 10in (25.5cm) wide 18¾oz $625-750 WW
A Jaeger-LeCoultre stainless steel wristwatch, "Reverso Classique" model no. 252.8.86, manual wind movement, silver-colored dial with
Arabic numerals in black, inner railroad seconds track also in black, blued steel sword hands, stainless steel case with ribbed sections
on top and bottom, model and serial numbers on the back, on a signed "JLC" tan ostrich strap with signed deployant clasp, no box or
papers. ca. 2014 1½in (3.5cm) high $3,100-3,500 L&T
A Lalique butterscotch glass "Chardons" vase, no. 929, molded "R. LALIQUE." 1922 7¼in (18.5cm) high $6,000-7,500 L&T
A Christian Dior fuschia pink medium "Lady Dior" purse, cannage quilted lamb leather, "DIOR" charm, gold-tone hardware, date code
"15-BO-0113," with detachable strap, authenticity card, dust bag, and box. 2013 9¼in (23.5cm) wide $2,900-3,300 CA
A Chinese Qing Dynasty coral red Chinese side-fastening women's three-quarter-length robe, bordered with cream silk, with summer
flowers, hydrangeas, and Peking knot peonies with butterflies, damage on the collar. ca. 1850 42½in (108cm) long $5,000-6,000 DN
An early Artifort "Groovy" chair, by Pierre Paulin (1927-2009, French), model no. F-580, painted aluminum with purple
upholstery, unmarked. 1960s 26½in (67.5cm) high $2,000-2,700 FRE

ANTIQUES
Handbook
& Price Guide

2024~2025

Judith Miller with
John Wainwright

MILLER'S

CONTENTS

LIST OF SPECIALISTS

CERAMICS

John Axford
Woolley & Wallis
51-61 Castle Lane
Salisbury SP1 3SU

Ed Crichton
Lacy Scott & Knight
10 Risbygate St
Bury St. Edmunds IP33 3AA

Clare Durham
Woolley & Wallis
51-61 Castle Street
Salisbury SP1 3SU

Will Farmer
Fieldings
Mill Race Lane
Stourbridge DY8 1JN

Alexander Hallett
Sworders
Cambridge Road
Stansted Mountfitchet
Essex CM24 8GE

Nic Saintey
Bearnes Hampton
& Littlewood
St Edmund's Court
Okehampton Street
Exeter EX4 1DU

FURNITURE

Lennox Cato
1 The Square, Edenbridge
Kent TN8 5BD

Douglas Girton
Lyon & Turnbull
33 Broughton Place
Edinburgh EH1 3RR

Guy Schooling
Sworders
Cambridge Road
Stansted Mountfitchet
Essex CM24 8GE

ASIAN

**John Axford &
Jeremy Morgan**
Woolley & Wallis
51-61 Castle Street
Salisbury SP1 3SU

Dan Bray
Gorringes
15 North Street, Lewes
East Sussex BN7 2PE

Rachel Holland
Fieldings
Mill Race Lane
Stourbridge DY8 1JN

Adrian Rathbone
Kinghams
10-12 Cotswold Business Village
Moreton-in-Marsh GL56 0JQ

Lee Young
Dore & Rees
Vicarage Street
Frome BA11 1PUA

Ling Zhu
Eskenazi
10 Clifford St
London W1S 2LJ

CLOCKS

Paul Archard
Campbell & Archard
www.qualityantiqueclocks.com

SILVER

Duncan Campbell
Dore & Rees
Vicarage Street
Frome BA11 1PUA

Alastair Dickenson
128-130 High Street,
Godalming, Surrey, GU7 1AB

JEWELRY

Trevor Kyle
Lyon & Turnbull
33 Broughton Place
Edinburgh EH1 3RR

Gemma Redmond
Gemma Redmond Vintage
www.gemmaredmondvintage.com

TOYS

Kayleigh Davies
Fieldings
Mill Race Lane
Stourbridge DY8 1JN

SPORTING

Graham Budd
Graham Budd
PO Box 47519
London N14 6XD

TRIBAL

Alex Tweedy
Lyon & Turnbull
33 Broughton Place
Edinburgh EH1 3RR

Waddington's
275 King Street East,
Toronto, Ontario
Canada M5A 1K2

DECORATIVE ARTS

Wayne Chapman
Lynways
www.lynways.com

Will Farmer
Fieldings
Mill Race Lane
Stourbridge DY8 1JN

Michael Jeffrey
Woolley & Wallis
51-61 Castle Street
Salisbury, SP1 3SU

John Mackie
Lyon & Turnbull
33 Broughton Place
Edinburgh EH1 3RR

Mike Moir
M & D Moir
www.manddmoir.co.uk

David Rago
Rago Arts
333 North Main Street,
Lambertville, NJ 08530 USA

MODERN DESIGN

Sarah Delves
Bags of Glamour
Hampshire, UK

John Mackie
Lyon & Turnbull
33 Broughton Place
Edinburgh EH1 3RR

David Rago
Rago Arts
333 North Main Street,
Lambertville, NJ 08530 USA

HOW TO USE THIS BOOK

Running head Indicates the subcategory of the main heading.

Page tab This appears on every page and identifies the main category heading as identified in the table of contents on pages 4-5.

Essential Reference Gives key facts about the factory, maker, or style, along with stylistic identification points, value tips, and advice on fakes.

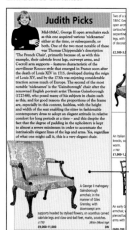

Judith Picks Items chosen specially by Judith, either because they are important or interesting, or because they are good investments.

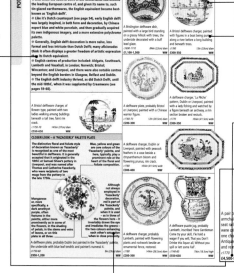

Closer Look Does exactly that. We show identifying aspects of a factory or maker, point out rare colors or shapes, and explain why a particular piece is so desirable.

The object The antiques are shown in full color. This is a vital aid to identification and valuation. With many objects, a slight color variation can signify a large price differential.

Caption The description of the item illustrated, including, when relevant, the period, the maker or factory, medium, the year it was made, dimensions, and condition. Many captions have **footnotes** that explain terminology or give identification or valuation information.

The price guide These price ranges give a ballpark figure of what you should pay for a similar item. The great joy of antiques is that there is not a recommended retail price. The price ranges in this book are based on actual prices, either what a dealer will take or the full auction price.

Source code Every item has been specially photographed at an auction house, a dealer, an antiques market, or a private collection. These are credited by code at the end of the caption, and can be checked against the Key to Illustrations on page 589.

INTRODUCTION

In 1979, as its cofounder, Judith Miller penned the Introduction to the first *Miller's Antiques Handbook and Price Guide*. Nearly 45 years and numerous editions on, Judith was all set to introduce you to this, the 2024-2025 Guide. Sadly, however, this was not to be, and following her unexpected death last year it falls to me—her husband and her writing partner for the last 32 years—to welcome you on Judith's behalf.

You should know that, despite her passing, Judith's extensive knowledge of and passion for antiques still runs right through this new edition, not only because of the numerous sections she personally completed page by page, but also because of the many discussions she had while mapping out the rest to best reflect the state of the market. She had discussions with me and with her long-time colleagues and friends from not only the BBC "Antiques Roadshow" but also throughout the antiques trade—auctioneers and dealers alike. Many thanks are due to all these specialists (who are listed on the facing page) and, for their introductory insights into the major collecting markets, additional thanks go to: Clare Durham (Porcelain and Pottery); Will Farmer (Pottery and Decorative Arts); Rachel Holland (Asian); Douglas Girton (Furniture); and David Rago (Modern Design).

Of course, the Guide's completion—especially given the huge volume of all-new images (more than 8,000) and accompanying information—would not have been possible without the Miller's team at Octopus Publishing, and I want to extend both personally and on Judith's behalf heartfelt thanks to all of them, and especially Scarlet Furness (Editor) and Ali Scrivens (Designer at TJ Graphics), for really stepping up to the plate and delivering under logistically and emotionally testing circumstances.

While the main collecting fields are, as noted above, addressed within their individual introductions, there are two overriding trends Judith wanted to highlight at the outset. First is the on-going expansion of Internet transactions by collectors, dealers, and auction houses alike—thereby further enlarging the "antiques shop window," and making buying and selling less-restricted by geographic location. Second, and showing increasing traction, especially among younger buyers, is the "green" factor—the belief that recycling, for example, a 200-year-old solid wood chest that is good for another 200 years, is both more ethical and more financially astute than buying a just-made, short-shelf-life, MDF equivalent.

To take best advantage of buoyancy in the market, and to best insulate against downturns, Judith also wanted to reemphasize at the outset her factors to focus on when buying or collecting. Look for "Quality of Design," "Quality of Construction," and "Quality of Decoration." Look for "Good Condition." Look for "Good Provenance"—of both Maker and Owner (original and/or subsequent)—and "Look for Rarity," too. Dotted throughout the following pages you will find around

1951-2023

40 artifacts from diverse collecting fields that Judith specifically chose and commented on—"Judith Picks"—to illustrate the enduring importance of these focal points. Above all, however, and aside from adding "Always Buy the Best You Can Afford," for pleasure and enjoyment's sake: "Always Buy What You Really Like!"

Underpinning all this is, of course, "Knowledge," or the acquisition of it. That was Judith's mission in the first Guide just as, 45 years on, it was and is with this one: to empower you with greater knowledge of that huge antiques market out there, and the many hidden treasures still awaiting recognition. As to the latter, just two days before writing this, the BBC website ran a feature on an anonymous-looking little vase purchased a couple of years ago from a local store for the princely sum of $10, and thereafter sat in a corner of the owner's downstairs bathroom—until, that is, a more knowledgeable relative dropped by, and not long after what turned out to be a small Chinese Ming Dynasty vase sold at auction for $4,200. Judith would have loved that!

John Wainwright

THE PORCELAIN MARKET

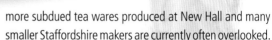

It has taken some time, but the "eccentric" prices witnessed during and immediately after the global pandemic appear to have subsided, and the porcelain market is now looking much more like it was pre-pandemic. Namely, serious collectors continue to dominate the top of the market in all areas, competing for the rarest items of the highest quality, while what was once classed as the middle market has been dropping steadily. For example, English blue-and-white porcelain, once such a stalwart of auction houses, have become increasingly unfashionable, and common patterns now tend to be grouped together at auction. There are, however, exceptions, notably the rarest patterns and shapes—especially pre-1755—and documentary and dated examples, with condition becoming less of an issue where uniqueness is concerned. Also, factories with a smaller output—for example, Vauxhall and some of the Liverpool concerns—have proved more popular and maintained a steady market.

In general, 18thC figures have been struggling to achieve the prices they sold for ten, or even five, years ago. But bucking the porcelain market precedent of tending to favor smaller things, large Derby and Bow figures have been in demand, especially among American buyers. Figures by the less common factories have held their own, and animal and bird subjects also continue to attract collectors across the board.

As for Regency porcelain, buyers tend to demand perfection and lean toward the highly decorative. The Flight and Barr partnerships at Worcester, for example, continue to attract strong interest, especially where shell- or feather-decorated pieces are involved. In contrast, the more subdued tea wares produced at New Hall and many smaller Staffordshire makers are currently often overlooked.

Experiencing an arguably surprising resurgence are Royal Worcester wares, some of which are selling for prices substantially exceeding those of five years ago. Fruit-painted wares are commanding high prices, supported by an eager market in the Far East but still hotly contested in the UK. Larger, more ornamental, pieces are especially desirable, but tea wares also find buyers. Pieces by earlier artists, including Charles Baldwyn, Harry Davis, and the Stintons, have also been increasing in popularity.

The market for European Continental porcelain in the UK has yet to regain its footing due to post-Brexit logistics complicating shipping for items easily found elsewhere in Europe; but buyers will still throw their hats into the ring for statement and rare pieces. Sèvres continues to prove popular, especially the colored grounds of the 18thC, but prices have marginally dampened compared to two or three years ago. Prices for Meissen have improved on those from recent years but are still some distance from the headier prices of a decade ago—especially the fine figures of J. J. Kändler. Indeed, pricewise many late-19thC Meissen figures have been dominating those produced 150 years earlier, and Continental buyers now appear to be more focused on statement and decorative pieces.

In conclusion, I'd say that with long-term collectors in most areas being focused on the top end of the market, there are now plenty of affordable opportunities for new collectors to establish themselves.

Clare Durham, Associate Director & Head of British and Continental Ceramics, Woolley & Wallis

Top Left: A Flight & Barr Worcester porcelain inkstand, with swan-neck handle, a pounce pot, two inkwells, and a cover, painted with feathers within gilt line borders, incised "B" mark, two covers lacking, wear to gilding, one inkwell cracked on the rim.

ca. 1800   *7in (18cm) wide*
$750-875   **TEN**

Above: A pair of Minton pâte-sur-pâte vases and stands, by Marc Louis Solon, enameled with putti courting, the narrow panels with flowers inscribed "Passionnement," "Pas de tout," "Beaucoup," and "Un Peu," on an ivory ground within gilt borders, by Alfred Evans and J. Marrow, signed "M L Solon" on one panel and "L Solon" on another, each signed underneath "J Marrow & A Evans," the bases with gilt factory marks and marked "Manufactured for Phillips," green "SMS" monogram.

1889   *9¾in (24.5cm) high*
$25,000-31,000   **WW**

PORCELAIN

A late-18thC Berlin cabinet saucer, painted with forget-me-nots and titled "Ulm" in black, within a gilt floral border on a deep blue ground, blue scepter mark.

5¼in (13.5cm) diam

$125-250   **WW**

A pair of late-19thC Berlin porcelain vases and covers, painted with 18thC figures in landscapes, scepter marks in underglaze blue, some minor surface wear and scratching.

20in (51cm) high

$3,700-4,300   **TEN**

A Berlin porcelain coffee cup, painted en grisaille with a portrait of Catherine II of Russia, the gilt diaper rim suspended with laurel.

2½in (6.5cm) high

$375-500   **CHEF**

A large 19thC KPM Berlin porcelain plaque, painted with "The Penitent Magdalene" after Pomeo Gerolamo Batoni, signed "A Jahn," impressed "KPM" and scepter mark.

15½in (39.5cm) wide

$3,700-5,000   **WW**

A mid-19thC KPM Berlin porcelain plaque, painted with the "Ecstasy of Saint Cecilia" after Raphael, impressed scepter mark and "KPM SZ 227-158," in a giltwood and gesso frame, frame with repairs.

9¼in (23.5cm) high

$1,700-2,200   **TEN**

A mid-19thC KPM Berlin porcelain plaque, painted with a girl reclining on a sofa, in a giltwood and gesso frame, plaque with surface scratching, frame with some repair and loss.

7¾in (19.5cm) wide

$2,000-2,500   **TEN**

A mid-19thC KPM Berlin porcelain plaque, painted with a girl in Turkish costume, in a landscape with a ruined temple beyond, impressed scepter, "KPM" and "F5" marks, in a giltwood and gesso frame, frame with wear.

10½in (26.5cm) high

$1,500-2,000   **TEN**

A mid-19thC KPM Berlin porcelain plaque, painted with a girl wearing a blue shawl, impressed scepter and "KPM" mark, in a giltwood and gesso frame.

The composition of this plaque appears to derive from "The Penitent Magdalene" by Correggio; more faithful versions of this 16thC work are known on KPM plaques.

7¾in (19.5cm) wide

$1,050-1,200   **TEN**

A late-19thC porcelain plaque, in KPM style, impressed "324," in a giltwood and gesso frame, pinhead-size flat chip to her hair, frame with extensive repairs.

8¼in (21cm) high

$750-875   **TEN**

ESSENTIAL REFERENCE—BOW PORCELAIN

Porcelain wares from the Bow factory, which was founded in London ca. 1744 by Thomas Frye and Edward Heylyn, were relatively inexpensive and initially very popular. However, during the course of the 1760s, the factory gradually declined and it eventually closed in 1776.

● Bow porcelain is white and chalky in appearance, with an irregular surface and granular texture, while its glassy glaze had a grayish-green hue. The predominant colors in the Bow decorative palette were blues, yellows, and purples.

● Inspired by Asian designs, most early Bow wares were either plain blanc-de-Chine or decorated in underglaze blue. Later enameled wares were based on the famille rose palette or Kakiemon designs.

● Bow figures were press molded, making them heavier and less fine than those slip cast at, for example, the Chelsea or Derby factories.

● Early Bow is, in general, unmarked, but from ca. 1765 an anchor and dagger mark was applied, painted in red enamel.

A pair of mid-18thC Bow cream boats, "Desirable Residence" pattern, interior with Taoist symbols and a diaper pattern rim, each marked with a faint blue painted "21."

5½in (14cm) wide

$525-625 **L&T**

A pair of Bow blue-and-white plates, "Broken Scroll" pattern, with flowering peony and holey rockwork, painted "15" and "16" on the bases.

ca. 1750-55 8in (20.5cm) diam

$375-500 **WW**

A Bow white-glazed cup, of U-shaped form, molded with flowering prunus, between molded handles.

ca. 1754-55 2¾in (7cm) high

$625-750 **WW**

A Bow porcelain pickle stand, modeled as three deep shells, on a molded base applied with further shells, some minor restoration.

ca. 1755 8¼in (21cm) wide

$700-800 **TEN**

A Bow porcelain coffee cup, with crabstock handle, painted in famille rose style, with foliage and rockwork, small chips in the foot rim, some glaze pitting.

ca. 1755 2¼in (5.5cm) high

$450-550 **TEN**

A Bow porcelain coffee can, with crabstock handle, painted in famille rose style, some minor wear, slight glaze pitting, minor staining.

ca. 1755 2¼in (5.5cm) high

$500-625 **TEN**

A rare Bow blue-and-white pickle dish, of early leaf shape, painted with a willow tree on sloping rocks, with small birds in flight above, the underside molded with veining.

ca. 1755-58 4¼in (10.5cm) wide

$800-950 **WW**

A Bow blue-and-white dish or pudding bowl, painted with two figures standing before pagodas and rockwork in a Chinese island landscape, the rim with flowering branches, painter's numeral 17.

ca. 1755-58 6½in (16.5cm) diam

$875-1,100 **WW**

A Bow blue-and-white mug, "Dragon" pattern, painted with a sinuous beast encircling the body amid stylized cloud scrolls, further cloud motifs on the inside rim, a grooved strap handle, workman's "12" on the base, some chipping, extended firing crack.

ca. 1755-58 6in (15.5cm) high

$1,050-1,200 **WW**

PORCELAIN

A Bow miniature blue-and-white coffee cup and saucer, naively painted with a fruiting grapevine.

ca. 1760   *3in (7.5cm) diam*

$375-500   **WW**

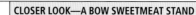

Raised on peg feet, the stand comprises a column in the center embellished with small inverted scallop shells and supporting three radiating scallop formlike dishes beneath a fourth atop column. Scallop shells the have been a recurringly popular form and motif in the decorative arts since Greek antiquity.

The Asian-style imagery is painted in underglaze blue and, typical of Bow, the glaze itself is soft and has a slightly blue tint, and a tendency to pool around the base.

Set within cell diaper borders, the dishes are decorated with a pagoda landscape pattern. Of Chinese inspiration, it is typical of mid-18thC Bow porcelain—to the extent that, in the 1750s, Bow's East London factory was referred to as "New Canton."

A Bow tiered sweetmeat or pickle stand.

ca. 1750   *5¼in (13.5cm) high*

$375-500   **WW**

A Bow porcelain cream boat, painted in famille rose style, with a Chinese boy picking fruit from a tree, chip on spout, some wear and scratching.

ca. 1760   *4¼in (11cm) wide*

$450-500   **TEN**

A rare Bow blue-and-white bowl, painted with a landscape scene, with figures conversing on bridges and beside pagodas, the interior with a figure fishing from an island, the foot inscribed "I*S. 1772," rim crack.

1772   *6in (15.5cm) diam*

$1,100-1,500   **WW**

A rare Bow white-glazed figure of Erato, by the Muses Modeller, depicted sitting with Cupid, the base applied with roses and a small quiver of arrows, small losses.

ca. 1750-52   *6¼in (16cm) high*

$5,000-6,200   **WW**

A Bow figure of Flora, standing beside a tall urn of flowers, some restoration to her hands and the base.

ca. 1755-58   *9½in (24cm) high*

$500-625   **WW**

A Bow figure of "Water," from the "Elements" series, modeled as Neptune standing before a dolphin, the end of the dolphin's tail lacking in the firing.

ca. 1756-58   *7¾in (19.5cm) high*

$700-800   **WW**

A Bow figure of Ceres, emblematic of Earth from the "Four Elements" series, standing before a recumbent lion, the low pad base applied with further flowers.

ca. 1758-60   *7¾in (19.5cm) high*

$950-1,050   **WW**

A rare Bow figure of "Winter," from the "Standing Rustic Seasons" series, modeled as an old man warming his hands before a flaming brazier, some good restoration.

ca. 1760   *9in (23cm) high*

$1,050-1,200   **WW**

A Bow figure of a musician, playing a fife and a drum over one shoulder, small losses.

ca. 1760   *6¾in (17cm) high*

$375-500   **WW**

A pair of Bow figures of dancers, raised on pierced scrolled bases with turquoise and gilt detailing, red anchor and dagger marks, and blue crescent marks, some restoration.

ca. 1760-65   *7½in (19cm) high*

$1,000-1,100   **WW**

A pair of Bow figures of vintners, modeled as a boy and his companion standing barefoot among leaves and flowers.

ca. 1765   *6¾in (17cm) high*

$700-800   **WW**

CLOSER LOOK—A PAIR OF BOW COMMEDIA DELL'ARTE FIGURES

Bow followed the commercially successful example of Chelsea in copying Meissen figures, and although they don't have the elegance and sophistication of Chelsea figures, they do display a distinctive, rustic charm of their own.

The pair of dancing figures, Columbine on the left, Harlequin on the right, are characters from a traditional form of Italian theater known as Commedia dell'Arte, which first appeared in decorative ornament in the late 16thC.

The bright colors on later Bow figures, often combined with a strong underglaze blue, resulted in to highly decorative ornaments that sold particularly well at the time.

A Bow figure of "Autumn," from the "Adolescent Seasons" series, modeled as a youth, some losses in the bocage.

ca. 1765   *7¾in (19.5cm) high*

$375-450   **WW**

A Bow figural group of "Summer" and "Autumn," from the "Adolescent Seasons" series, some restoration.

ca. 1765   *9¾in (24.5cm) high*

$500-625   **WW**

Because Bow figures were press molded, they were noticeably heavier than, for example, the figures made at Chelsea, which were slip cast from the mid-1740s on.

A rare pair of Bow figures of Harlequin and Columbine dancing, from the "Commedia dell'Arte" series, red and gold anchor and dagger marks, some repairs.

ca. 1765-70   *7in (18cm) high*

$1,900-2,500   **WW**

A rare matched pair of Bow candlestick figures of the "Dutch Dancers," the bases before a flowering tree stump, supporting a candle sconce.

ca. 1765-70   *10¼in (26cm) high*

$700-800   **WW**

A Bow figure of "Autumn," from the "Rustic Seasons" series, sitting on a harvesting basket, red anchor and dagger mark, minor faults.

ca. 1765-70   *6½in (16.5cm) high*

$300-450   **WW**

A Bow flowerpot, some small losses and repairs.

ca. 1765   *5½in (14cm) high*

$625-750   **WW**

PORCELAIN

ESSENTIAL REFERENCE—BRISTOL PORCELAIN

In ceramics, the port city of Bristol is best known for its pottery. In contrast, porcelain production in Bristol was on a smaller scale, more short lived, and essentially confined to three factories.

● The first was established ca. 1748-49 by, and named after, a Quaker, Benjamin Lund. It produced blue-and-white porcelain similar to that made at the Limehouse factory in London (one of whose proprietors had joined Lund in Bristol), but it was more durable due to its secret ingredient: Cornish soapstone, a good substitute for petuntse (china clay). In 1752, Dr. John Wall and William Davis of the Worcester factory, realizing the potential of soapstone, purchased Lund's factory, along with its secret "hard paste" formula, and Worcester went on to become Britain's most successful 18thC porcelain factory.

● The second factory had originally been established as Cookworthy's in Plymouth, but it was moved to Bristol in 1770 and its ownership was subsequently transferred to Richard Champion. From 1774 until 1781, when it was sold to a number of Staffordshire potters, Champion's factory produced a harder and whiter porcelain than other 18thC English soft-paste porcelains, and its cold, glittering glaze clearly distinguished it from the wares of Bow, Chelsea, Worcester, and Derby. Early wares looked to Asian porcelain for style, but under Champion it was Meissen and the French factories that provided the primary inspiration—most notably for tea and coffee services.

● The third Bristol factory, the Walter Lane Pottery, successfully made nonporcelain earthenware from 1682 until the 1880s, but it briefly—ca. 1845-50—added some porcelain to its output.

A Bristol mask pitcher, painted with bouquets of European flowers and single scattered sprigs, the spout modeled as the head of a bearded man, small chip on the spout.
ca. 1773-75　　　*7in (18cm) high*
$800-950　　　　　　**WW**

A Bristol teapot and cover, painted in green camaïeu, with flower garlands and scattered sprigs around, the spout with Rococo molding.
ca. 1772-75　　　*7in (18cm) wide*
$625-750　　　　　　**WW**

A Champions Bristol porcelain leaf-shaped pickle dish, painted with a spray of flowers and scattered sprigs, cross and "17" mark in blue, broken into two pieces, with numerous sections of small loss on the left edge, all professionally restored.
ca. 1775　　　*3¾in (9.5cm) wide*
$550-700　　　　　　**TEN**

A Bristol chocolate cup with cover and stand, painted with flowers suspended from gilt lines, beneath basket weave molded borders, blue "X5" marks, small chip on the cover's rim.
ca. 1775　　　*6½in (16.5cm) diam*
$875-1,000　　　　　**WW**

A Bristol coffeepot and cover, painted with flowers, the rims with puce foliate bands interlaced with wide green ribbons, restoration on the cover.
ca. 1775　　　*8½in (21.5cm) high*
$875-1,000　　　　　**WW**

A Bristol quatrefoil sauce tureen with cover and stand, possibly painted by Henry Bone, with garlands of flowers suspended from interlaced blue and lilac ribbons, blue "X" and gilt "6" marks, the cover's finial restored.
ca. 1775　　　*8in (20.5cm) wide*
$3,100-3,700　　　　**WW**

A rare Bristol armorial pitcher, painted with the arms of Pye of Faringdon, a shaped shield of Ermine with a bend of indented gules, within a puce Rococo border, the crest a cross crosslet between wings.

The two most likely members of the Pye family for whom this pitcher might have been made are Admiral Sir Thomas Pye (ca. 1708/9-85), who served during the American Revolution, and Henry James Pye (1745-1813), a member of Parliament for Berkshire and Poet Laureate from 1790.
ca. 1775　　　*5¼in (13.5cm) high*
$1,900-2,500　　　　**WW**

A rare Bristol chocolate cup with cover and stand, painted in sepia, with portraits of Classical figures within berried leafy swags suspended from wide gilt borders.
ca. 1775-80　　　*6in (15cm) diam*
$1,700-2,000　　　　**WW**

A Bristol teapot and cover, painted in polychrome enamels, with sprays of fuchsia and rose, yellow "X 18" mark on the underside, a little chipping on the spout.
ca. 1775-80　　　*8½in (21.5cm) wide*
$700-800　　　　　　**WW**

ESSENTIAL REFERENCE—CHELSEA

Flemish silversmith Nicholas Spirimont founded the Chelsea factory in London ca. 1744. Spirimont focused on luxury porcelain wares, targeted at "the Quality and Gentry." Chelsea's different phases of production can be defined by the factory's changing marks of identification.

● During the early or first phase, Chelsea wares—mostly small-scale tableware such as pitchers, beakers, teapots, and salts—were marked with an incised triangle. In terms of form and decoration, these wares were influenced by Spirimont's past as a silversmith and the French Rococo style.

● Wares from the second phase—the Raised Anchor Period (ca. 1749-52)—bore a raised anchor mark of identification and were in part inspired by Asian Kakiemon shapes and by Meissen designs.

● In the third phase—the Red Anchor Period (ca. 1752-56)—the factory changed its porcelain formula, and these wares were finished with a clear bluish glaze. It was also during this period that Chelsea began to produce its distinctive Rococo style tureens in the shapes of fruit, vegetables, and animals.

● During the fourth phase—the Golden Anchor Period (ca. 1756-69)—Chelsea's wares, inspired by Sèvres porcelain, became more elaborate in form and decoration. A new, thick blush glaze was also introduced, and wares were often painted in a brighter palette and often gilded.

● In ca. 1769, the Chelsea factory was purchased by William Duesbury, owner of the Derby porcelain factory.

A Chelsea fable teapot and cover, painted by Jefferyes Hamett O'Neale, with a depiction of the "Fox Who Had Lost His Tail," the solo fox encouraging three others to cut off their brushes, in a continuous landscape with birds, the cover decorated with a moth and flowers, a red anchor mark on the underside of the handle, some good restoration.

ca. 1752-55   *7¾in (19.5cm) wide*

$10,000-12,000   **WW**

A Chelsea dish, "Hob in the Well" pattern, painted in the Kakiemon palette, red anchor mark, broken and restored.

ca. 1752-55   *12¼in (31cm) diam*

$190-250   **WW**

A very rare Chelsea blue-and-white plate, painted after a Kakiemon design, with two long-tailed birds, broken and cleanly restored.

ca. 1754-55   *9in (23cm) diam*

$3,700-5,000   **WW**

A Chelsea figure of "Winter," modeled by Joseph Willems, as a bearded man in an overcoat and fur-lined hat, holding a basket of hot coals, red anchor mark, some chipping.

ca. 1755   *5in (12.5cm) high*

$1,050-1,200   **WW**

A Chelsea dessert plate, "Brocade" pattern, in the Imari palette, with sprays of flowering chrysanthemum.

ca. 1752-58   *9¼in (23.5cm) diam*

$625-750   **WW**

A Chelsea botanical plate, painted with a carnation spray, a bud, and other flower and leaf sprays, brown anchor mark.

ca. 1756   *8¼in (21cm) diam*

$700-800   **WW**

A Chelsea teabowl and saucer, painted in Meissen style, with small flower sprays, moths, and flying insects, brown anchor mark on the saucer.

ca. 1758-60   *5¾in (14.5cm) wide*

$750-875   **WW**

A pair of Chelsea fruit dishes, painted with fruit, including cherries, pears, gooseberries, and plums, amid large moths, brown anchor marks, short rim cracks.

ca. 1758-60   *12in (30.5cm) wide*

$375-500   **WW**

A Chelsea silver-shaped porcelain dish, painted with exotic birds, anchor mark in brown, minor wear in the enamels, some glaze pitting.

ca. 1760   *8¼in (21cm) wide*

$700-800   **TEN**

A pair of Chelsea figures of a hunter and his companion, some damages.
ca. 1758-65   10½in (26.5cm) high
$1,000-1,100   **WW**

A Chelsea dessert dish, painted on the well with a spray of fruit, the rim with four panels of exotic birds, flanked by gilt moths, gold anchor mark, some restoration on the rim.
ca. 1760   11½in (29cm) wide
$250-370   **WW**

Judith Picks

What do I really like about this 18thC porcelain plate, made at the Chelsea factory during its "Gold Anchor" period (ca. 1756-69)? Well, first and foremost I love its utterly splendid decoration, in which exceedingly pretty sprays of polychrome flowers have been hand painted on a very refined pale blue ground, and then further contrasted against five sumptuous dark blue ground cartouches, each gilt framed and embellished with gilded birds, flowers, and foliage. It's a Rococo masterpiece, and, in addition, it comes with some intriguing and desirable provenance—it is similarly molded and shares a number of decorative characteristics with the much-lauded "Mecklenburg-Strelitz" service ordered from the Chelsea factory in 1762 by King George III and Queen Charlotte for her brother Duke Adolphus Frederick IV of Mecklenburg-Strelitz, part of which survives in Buckingham Palace to this day.

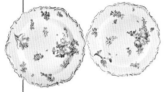

A pair of Chelsea polychrome plates, painted with flowers, within a gilt and turquoise C-scroll border, gold anchor marks, some surface wear, each with a shallow rim chip.
ca. 1760   9in (23cm) diam
$875-1,000   **DN**

A pair of Chelsea figural candlestick figures, Cupid and girl swathed in flowers, on Rococo scroll bases, girl with gilt gold anchor mark.
ca. 1760-65   9½in (24cm) high
$625-750   **CHOR**

A Chelsea plate, polychrome painted with floral sprays on a pale blue ground and gilded with exotic birds and foliage on a dark blue ground, gold anchor mark, some historic fritting and burst bubbles in the gilding.
ca. 1765   9½in (24cm) diam
$1,250-1,500   **DN**

A Chelsea porcelain "busto" emblematic of "Autumn," discoloration on the base and a surface chip suggesting restoration.

For a similar set of four "bustos of heathen gods and godesses" from the red anchor period with similarly modeled plinths, see F. Severne Mackenna, "Chelsea Porcelain the Red Anchor Wares" (1951), plate 54, figure 108.
ca. 1765-69   4in (10cm) high
$550-700   **CHEF**

A Chelsea-Derby coffeepot and cover, painted with flowers, some chipping on the foot.
ca. 1765-70   10½in (26.5cm) high
$375-500   **WW**

A Chelsea-Derby vase, supported by three female terms rising from lion paw feet, gilded with butterflies and applied with flowers on a mazarin blue ground, on a base painted with landscape panels, double gold anchor mark, one handle repaired, the cover lacking.

The shape was copied from a print in Joseph-Marie Vien's "Suite de Vases" of 1760. The shape was made at Chelsea prior to its takeover by the Derby porcelain factory in 1770.
ca. 1770   9¼in (23.5cm) high
$1,000-1,250   **WW**

A Chelsea-Derby two-handle butter tub with cover and stand, painted with scattered roses, marks in gilt, rubbing in the gilding, only the stand is marked.
ca. 1770   6in (15cm) diam
$450-500   **CHEF**

A 19thC English porcelain scent bottle, after Chelsea or Charles Gouyn, modeled as a chicken with three chicks, the largest chicken's head forming the stopper, some restoration.
3in (7.5cm) high
$375-450   **WW**

ESSENTIAL REFERENCE—DERBY

A porcelain factory was founded ca. 1748 in Derby by Frenchman André Planché. In 1756, it was bought by John Heath and William Duesbury, previously decorators at Chelsea. In 1770, they also bought out the Chelsea factory and operated together as Chelsea-Derby until 1784. In 1811, the company was acquired by Robert Bloor, who managed the factory until its closure in 1848.

- Early Derby soft-paste porcelain is fine grained, its glaze either grayish white or grayish green. Its early wares were mostly figures—pastoral and allegorical subjects, often left in white. During the 1750s and 1760s, Derby figures were typically Rococo in style and stood on scrolled bases.
- After 1756, Derby's range expanded to include tureens, baskets, and other tableware. Its tea wares often cracked in use, so surviving examples are rarely found today.
- After the acquisition of Chelsea, the porcelain paste became a pure white and the glaze a clear blush. New designs included landscapes, detailed, naturalistic flowers, and exotic birds. Many patterns were loose copies of Chelsea or Sèvres designs.

A Derby blue-and-white chestnut basket and cover, painted in the interior with a pagoda landscape, the exterior molded with latticework and applied with flowering branches, firing crack in the base.

ca. 1765　　*7½in (19cm) diam*

$625-750　　　　WW

A Derby blue-and-white plate, decorated with a patterned censer of Asian flowers, including peony and chrysanthemum.

ca. 1765-70　　*8in (20.5cm) diam*

$550-700　　　　WW

A Derby dry-edge figure emblematic of "Taste," probably modeled by André Planché, with a sitting lady holding an apple, a basket of fruit under her left arm, enameled with famille rose flower sprays, some good restoration.

See Peter Bradshaw, "18th Century English Porcelain Figures," Antique Collectors Club (1981), page 176.

ca. 1752-55　　*6¼in (16cm) high*

$2,500-3,100　　　　WW

A near pair of Derby sweetmeat figures, modeled as a lady and gentleman sitting on rocky outcrops holding a shell, painted with flowers, male figure restored with cracks in the base, female figure restored with some losses in the applied flowers on the base.

ca. 1757-58　　*7in (18cm) high*

$1,100-1,250　　　　TEN

A rare Derby figural group of Isabella with a Gallant and Jester, after a Meissen group of "The Hypochondriac" by J. J. Kändler, the young lovers canoodling before flowering bocage, attended by Harlequin, minor faults.

ca. 1760　　*11in (28cm) high*

$1,700-2,200　　　　WW

A pair of Derby figures of a harvester and his companion, small losses.

ca. 1760-65　　*10½in (26.5cm) high*

$500-625　　　　WW

A rare and large Derby allegorical figure of "Smell," modeled as a boy sitting on a flower-encrusted stump, some restoration.

ca. 1765　　*10½in (26.5cm) high*

$500-625　　　　WW

A Derby figure of Mercury, wearing a winged hat and holding a caduceus, some damages and restoration.

ca. 1760-65　　*13½in (34cm) high*

$190-310　　　　WW

A large Derby figure of John Wilkes, on a plinth, atop of which is a scroll inscribed "Bill of Rights," with a putto to his right, holding a Phrygian cap on the end of a stick and supporting a book titled "Lock [sic] on Gov't," minor losses.

John Wilkes (1725-97) was an English politician and radical journalist whose criticism of the King in his magazine "The North Briton" earned him a warrant for his arrest for libel in 1763. Citing parliamentary privilege, he was cleared of the charge and went on to become Lord Mayor of London in 1774.

ca. 1765-70　　*12in (30.5cm) high*

$500-625　　　　WW

A Derby figure of "Europe," from the "Four Quarters of the Globe" series, personified as a girl wearing a coronet, the base with attributes relating to the Arts and Science, some restoration, her scepter lacking.

ca. 1760-65   8¾in (22cm) high

$375-500   WW

A Derby figural group of three putti, encircling a tree with two dogs, one with a bird and a cage, two others playing instruments, some losses and restoration.

ca. 1780   10in (25.5cm) high

$125-250   WW

A pair of Derby figures, from the "Four Quarters of the Globe" series, emblematic of America and Europe, the former with a foot on an alligator, the latter holding a cornucopia of fruit, bases titled "Amerika" and "Europa," some damages and restoration.

A series of adult models of the "Four Quarters of the Globe" was first created by J. J. Kändler at Meissen about 1745 and adapted a few years later by Meyer, using children instead. Meyer's series was copied at Chelsea, and it is likely that this Derby series was derived from the Chelsea figures instead of the German originals.

ca. 1800   8½in (21.5cm) high

$375-500   WW

A pair of Derby "Spectacle" baskets, painted with fruits, butterflies, and insects, one of the baskets badly restored, with three broken and glued circles.

ca. 1760-65   8¼in (21cm) wide

$500-625   CHEF

A Derby coffeepot and cover, of baluster form, painted in famille rose enamels, with flowering Asian branches issuing from rockwork, the cover with a floral finial.

ca. 1765-70   9¾in (24.5cm) high

$500-625   WW

Judith Picks

The provenance of this pair of leopards may be slightly uncertain; they may well have been made at Derby, or possibly in Staffordshire, and they were probably modeled by George Cocker (1794-1868), an English sculptor who modeled porcelain figures at various points in time for not only the Derby factory, but also Coalport, Worcester, Minton, and various Staffordshire potteries. Over and above those ambiguities, however, I simply like them. In their posture and expression, they are endearingly modeled, both individually and as a pair, and while the rich deep blue and gold coloring of their bases may be far from naturalistic, its opulence somehow enhances the more realistically painted but highly exotic wildlife (in mid-19thC Great Britain) they support.

A pair of Derby campana vases, painted, one with a fisherman before two figures on an arched bridge, the other with figures launching a boat beneath Classical ruins.

ca. 1820   12¾in (32.5cm) high

$1,600-2,200   WW

A pair of Crown Derby vases and covers, painted by James Rouse Sr., one side with arrangements of fruit, including peaches, pears, cherries, and grapes, the reverses with panels of flowers, gilt crowned factory marks, signed underneath "Painted by J. Rouse Sen'r, Derby," some restoration.

ca. 1875-80   9¾in (24.5cm) high

$1,000-1,100   WW

A rare pair of Derby or Staffordshire leopards, the leopardess leaning over two cubs (a third cub now lacking), cleaning one with her tongue, her companion recumbent with mouth open, each raised on a rocky base painted a rich blue and defined around the lower perimeters with gilding.

ca. 1840   5½in (14cm) wide

$1,500-1,900   WW

PORCELAIN

Mostly of the soft-paste type, porcelain was produced ca. 1754-1804 by a number of factories in the port city of Liverpool. A great variety of flat and hollow wares, and some figures, were made, and while most of the production was underglaze blue-and-white porcelain, some over- and underglaze transfer-printed wares and overglaze polychrome-enameled pieces were made, too. The Liverpool factories included:

- Richard Chaffers & Co. (ca. 1754-65)—Soapstone-type porcelain; mainly Asian designs; resembles Worcester; Philip Christian took over on Chaffers' death and produced similar designs until 1778.
- Samuel Gilbody (ca. 1754-60)—Enameled porcelain.
- William Reid (1756-61)—Underglaze blue Asian designs.
- James Pennington and Co. (1769-ca. 1800)—Three branches of the family, under James, John, and Seth, worked from different sites in the city; wares included underglaze and transfer-printed.

A Richard Chaffers Liverpool Imari sauceboat, molded with Rococo scrolls and a shell motif on the spout, with bamboo and Asian flowers beside an ornamental fence, the interior rim with flower panels.

ca. 1757-59   *7in (18cm) wide*
$450-550   **WW**

A Richard Chaffers Liverpool coffeepot and cover, painted in famille rose enamels, with bamboo and flowering chrysanthemum, some restoration on the edge of the cover.

ca. 1758-60   *9½in (24cm) high*
$625-750   **WW**

A Richard Chaffers Liverpool blue-and-white coffee can or small mug, painted with trees in a Chinese landscape, the reverse with a small hut on an island before cannonball rocks, small chip inside the rim.

ca. 1758-60   *2½in (6.5cm) high*
$250-370   **WW**

A Richard Chaffers Liverpool blue-and-white saucer dish, painted with a figure in a boat mooring up at an island with trees, in the distance a low hut on a further island, rim flaws.

Saucer dishes are an uncommon product of the Chaffers factory.

ca. 1758-60   *7½in (19cm) diam*
$500-625   **WW**

A Richard Chaffers Liverpool porcelain teabowl and saucer, painted in underglaze blue with willow and peony in a fenced garden, minor surface wear, small rim frit.

ca. 1760
$450-500   **TEN**

A Richard Chaffers Liverpool blue-and-white beaker, "Jumping Boy" pattern, painted with a Chinese boy in a garden beside a maiden sitting beneath a tree, four-character script mark.

ca. 1760   *2½in (6.5cm) high*
$750-875   **WW**

A Richard Chaffers Liverpool blue-and-white teapot and cover, "Two Men Bowing" pattern, with figures in a Chinese island landscape, some restoration on the cover.

ca. 1758-60   *7¾in (20cm) wide*
$250-370   **WW**

A rare Richard Chaffers Liverpool tureen with cover and stand, in imitation of Derby and Bow, painted with a pagoda beneath trees in a Chinese landscape, within peony and flowering branches, the flowers echoed on the cover, surmounted by a fruit knop.

ca. 1760-65   *8¾in (22cm) wide*
$1,000-1,100   **WW**

A Richard Chaffers Liverpool blue-and-white leaf pickle dish, painted with a butterfly, with three further insects around it, tiny rim chip.

ca. 1760-64   *4¼in (11cm) wide*
$375-500   **WW**

Judith Picks

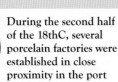

During the second half of the 18thC, several porcelain factories were established in close proximity in the port city of Liverpool. Most notable were the factories owned by Samuel Gilbody (from ca. 1754-60), three branches of the Pennington family (from 1769-ca. 1800), and Richard Chaffers (from ca. 1754-65, then continued by Philip Christian until 1778). It was Chaffers who, in 1756, bought the secret formula of the Worcester factory's soapstone porcelain recipe, and as a result was able to produce

pleasingly thin but durable tea wares, its underglaze blue decoration largely inspired by the blue-and-white patterns found on Chinese porcelain and, indeed, in some instances truly difficult to distinguish from Worcester equivalents. This Chaffers' teabowl and saucer is a particularly nice example, in which the clarity of painted imagery is underpinned by characteristically light and bright underglaze blue, nicely contrasted with darker blue elements, and sealed under a complementary and subtle, bluey-gray-tinted glaze.

A documentary Richard Chaffers Liverpool blue-and-white teabowl and saucer, painted with a bird on a flowering peony branch within a lattice border, the reverse of the teabowl inscribed "Mary Touchet," the underside of the saucer with the same name and the date "1764."

1764   *5in (12.5cm) diam*

$1,900-2,500   **WW**

A Samuel Gilbody Liverpool figure of "Spring," modeled as a putto carrying a basket of flowers, left in the white.

ca. 1756-60   *4½in (11.5cm) high*

$1,200-1,350   **WW**

A rare Samuel Gilbody Liverpool set of figures of the "Four Seasons," each modeled as a putto, "Spring" with a basket of flowers, "Summer" a sheaf of corn, "Autumn" garlanded in grapes, and "Winter" dressed in a fur-lined robe, some small damages and restorations.

ca. 1756-60   *5in (12.5cm) high*

$7,000-8,000   **WW**

A John Pennington Liverpool porcelain potted meat pot, painted in underglaze blue with a chinoiserie landscape, minor surface wear.

ca. 1770   *3½in (9cm) wide*

$750-875   **TEN**

A John Pennington Liverpool porcelain salt, reeded and feather molded, with an underglaze blue dash border and flower spray in the center, minor staining, scratching, misfiring, and crazing.

ca. 1775   *3¼in (8.5cm) wide*

$700-800   **TEN**

A Pennington's Liverpool miniature blue-and-white coffee cup and saucer, painted with a low hut beneath a gnarled tree and rockwork, restoration in the cup's handle and the saucer.

ca. 1775   *3½in (9cm) diam*

$300-450   **WW**

A Liverpool blue-and-white mug, probably John Pennington, painted with flowers, including chrysanthemum, heartsease, and convolvulus, the reverse with a butterfly and a further flying insect beside a flower posy, the scroll handle with molded leaf terminal and thumbrest.

ca. 1765-75   *10¾in (27.5cm) high*

$1,900-2,500   **WW**

A rare William Reid Liverpool blue-and-white saucer, "Cross-Legged Chinaman" pattern, painted with a figure sitting beneath a willow tree, with another figure fishing beside.

ca. 1758-60   *4¾in (12cm) diam*

$700-800   **WW**

ESSENTIAL REFERENCE—LONGTON HALL

William Littler (1724-84) founded the Longton Hall factory in Staffordshire ca. 1749. His first soft-paste porcelain recipe had a thick, semiopaque white glaze that earned the nickname "snowman class" for early Longton Hall figures. However, by ca. 1752, Littler had improved the recipe to produce porcelain that could be molded thinly, making it ideal for the forms, such as fruit, vegetables and, especially, leaves, that dominated the factory's characteristic and brightly painted dishes, pitchers, and tureens.

- **The factory's figures show the influence of Meissen, and they are similar to those produced at Bow and Derby.**
- **Meissen-style flowers in Longton Hall decoration are often attributed to an artist known as the "trembly rose painter," although many artists painted in this manner.**
- **The variable quality of Longton Hall porcelain—sometimes the body contains "moons" (tiny air bubbles that appear as pale spots against a strong light)—along with heavy kiln losses led to bankruptcy.**
- **After the factory's closure in 1760, Littler moved to Scotland, where he later opened a new porcelain works at West Pans, near Musselburgh.**
- **No mark was used on Longton Hall wares, and pieces with a crossed "L" mark in blue formerly attributed to the factory are now known to come from Littler's later venture at West Pans.**

A rare Longton Hall blue-and-white saucer, with an unusual deep trembleuse well, painted with the "Folly" pattern of an obelisk beside bulrushes in a country landscape, small chip on the foot rim.
ca. 1754-58   5¼in (13.5cm) diam
$1,900-2,500   WW

A Longton Hall blue-and-white lettuce leaf sauceboat, formed of overlapping leaves, painted with a Chinese pagoda landscape, the interior with a flower spray, the handle formed of a gnarled branch issuing small gourds and flowers, two small foot rim chips.
ca. 1755   7in (18cm) wide
$1,000-1,100   WW

A rare Longton Hall blue-and-white trembleuse saucer, molded and decorated in French porcelain style, with a lambrequin border around a fluted band enclosing a quatrefoil gallery, painter's mark on the base, short rim crack.
ca. 1755-58   5in (12.5cm) diam
$500-625   WW

A Longton Hall figure of "Winter," from the "Rustic Seasons" series, modeled as a bearded gentleman in a fur-lined hat and lilac overcoat, warming his hands before a flaming brazier, a few small chips.

This figure was derived from Meissen and also produced at Chelsea around the same time as Longton Hall.
ca. 1758-60   4½in (11.5cm) high
$625-750   WW

A pair of Longton Hall Rococo-molded vases and covers, painted in polychrome enamels with flowers around and within frilled scrolls, the covers modeled as a profusion of flowers including tulip, carnation, and narcissus, small losses.
ca. 1758-60   9¾in (25cm) high
$700-800   WW

A rare Longton Hall commemorative mug, printed in black, probably by Sadler, Liverpool, with a portrait of William Pitt, flanked by Britannia and Liberty with Fame above, signed in reverse in the print with "G Smith Sculpt," some restoration on the rim.
ca. 1760   5in (12.5cm) high
$3,700-5,000   WW

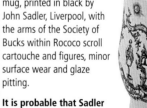

A Longton Hall porcelain mug, printed in black by John Sadler, Liverpool, with the arms of the Society of Bucks within Rococo scroll cartouche and figures, minor surface wear and glaze pitting.

It is probable that Sadler bought undecorated Longton Hall mugs during the latter years of the factory and some may have been printed after the closure of the factory. Signed examples of this print are found on similar mugs as well as creamware, enamels, and delft tiles. The engraving is attributed to Jeremiah Evans, who signed and engraved the invitation for the Liverpool Lodge in 1770.
ca. 1760   5in (12.5cm) high
$1,400-1,900   TEN

ESSENTIAL REFERENCE—LOWESTOFT

The Lowestoft factory, in Suffolk, was founded by Robert Browne and three other partners in 1757.

- **It made phosphate porcelain, similar to Bow, with a tendency to discoloration. The glaze is of either a greenish or grayish tone.**
- **In the factory's first decade, it made wares decorated in underglaze blue, influenced by Worcester and by Chinese blue-and-white ceramics.**
- **From the mid-1760s, overglaze colors and underglaze blue printing were introduced. The factory also began to produce figures, especially of dogs, cats, and sheep.**
- **The Lowestoft factory closed in 1800.**

A Lowestoft blue-and-white mug, painted with a Chinese lady sitting in a landscape, holding a parasol and resting one foot on a low stool, a young attendant bringing her a cup of tea, the interior rim with a paneled lattice border, painter's numeral 5, probably for Robert Allen.

ca. 1761-62   *3¾in (9.5cm) high*
$4,300-5,000   **WW**

A rare Lowestoft blue-and-white butter tub with cover and stand, with Hughes-type molding, possibly painted by Richard Phillips, with Asian landscape panels, the stand with a more extensive pagoda landscape, painter's numeral 4 on the tub's foot rim.

See Geoffey A. Godden, "Lowestoft Porcelains," Antique Collectors Club (1985), page 67, plate 61, where the author points out the upside-down flowers on one side of the tub, due to an inverted mold.

ca. 1762-65   *7in (18cm) wide*
$1,900-2,500   **WW**

A Lowestoft tea canister and cover, with Hughes-type molding, reserving panels painted with bridges and boats in island landscapes, the shoulder with a floral sgraffito border, the cover broken and reattached.

ca. 1762-65   *3¾in (9.5cm) high*
$3,100-3,700   **WW**

A Lowestoft blue-and-white coffee cup, painted with a rare pattern of willow trees over low pagodas in an island landscape, painter's numeral 3 and 7 on the foot.

ca. 1765   *2½in (6.5cm) high*
$500-625   **WW**

A Lowestoft blue-and-white sauceboat, probably painted by Robert Allen, with long-tailed birds among flowering Asian branches, painter's numeral 5, cracked.

ca. 1764-66   *7½in (19cm) wide*
$500-625   **WW**

A Lowestoft blue-and-white sauceboat, possibly modeled by James Hughes, painted with a version of the "Fisherman and Billboard Island" pattern, the interior with flowering branches, the molding on the spout with the date "1765," painter's numeral 4 inside the foot.

1765   *7½in (19cm) wide*
$1,400-1,700   **WW**

A rare Lowestoft blue-and-white hors d'euvre dish, with eight compartments around a well, the center painted with a figure crossing a bridge beside a hut, the external compartments with stylized floral sprays, painter's numeral 5 inside the foot rim, several small rim chips.

ca. 1765   *7¼in (18.5cm) diam*
$8,000-9,500   **WW**

A rare pair of Lowestoft blue-and-white cider mugs, painted with birds in flight between flower sprays, the shoulders and rims molded with a stiff leaf design on a seeded ground, painter's numerals on the inside foot rim.

ca. 1765   *3½in (9cm) high*
$8,000-9,500   **WW**

A large Lowestoft porcelain teapot or punch pot and cover, painted in underglaze blue with a three-story pagoda in landscape, within scroll borders, painter's mark in underglaze blue, hairline cracks.

ca. 1765-70   *7¾in (20cm) high*
$375-500   **TEN**

A Lowestoft blue-and-white tea or chocolate cup, painted with a hut beside a fence, the reverse with a hut on an island, with an unusual molded handle.

The larger size of this cup might indicate that it was a breakfast cup. Handled cups of this shape were rarely made at Lowestoft.

ca. 1765-70   *1¾in (4.5cm) high*
$250-370   **WW**

PORCELAIN

A very rare and important documentary Lowestoft blue-and-white pitcher, painted by Richard Phillips, with an unusual scene of a figure tending three lines of herrings being hung and smoked over two burning fires, flanked by a three-masted fishing smack and a smaller rowing boat, inscribed "John Cooper 1768," the interior rim with a formal border, the handle's terminal inscribed "RP," painter's numeral 3 on the foot rim, broken and reattached.

The rarity and considerable value of this Lowestoft mug is substantially attributable to its painter, the Lowestoft factory artist Richard Phillips—the terminal of its handle bears his initials, "RP," and its foot rim bears the painter's numeral, "3," with which he is associated; the only other recorded piece bearing Phillips' initial or signature is in Norwich Castle Musuem. However, precedent confirms the subject matter was also a contributory factor: historically, the highest prices for Lowestoft have been for those pieces painted in underglaze blue with scenes from around the town and along the local coastline, with the latter including local industries, such as fishing and shipbuilding.

1768   *4¼in (11cm) high*

$28,500-35,000   **WW**

A Lowestoft blue-and-white tea canister, "Dragon" pattern, painted with two scaly beasts chasing flaming pearls, the sloping shoulders with stylized cloud bursts, open crescent mark, the cover lacking.

ca. 1765-75   *4in (10cm) high*

$1,500-1,900   **WW**

A Lowestoft tankard, decorated in the Mandarin style with Chinese figures in a fenced garden, cracks in the base and rim, scratching and rubbing in the glaze.

ca. 1770   *5¼in (13.5cm) high*

$500-625   **CHEF**

A rare Lowestoft figure of a pug dog, on a flat shaped base, left in the white, base chip, with a small collection of fragments and kiln wasters.

See Geoffrey A. Godden, "Lowestoft Porcelains," Antique Collectors Club (1985), page 132, plate 165, for a polychrome model with head turned to the left, suggesting that these were made in pairs. Sitting figures were more common, but wasters with this flat base have been found at the factory site.

ca. 1765-70   *2in (5cm) high*

$3,700-5,000   **WW**

A Lowestoft feeding cup, painted with flowering plants beside a fence, the top half covered and painted with a flower spray, long rim crack.

ca. 1770   *3¼in (8.5cm) high*

$625-750   **WW**

A Lowestoft porcelain teabowl and saucer, painted in underglaze blue and overpainted in colors, painter's numeral 3 in underglaze blue, hairline cracks in teabowl, flat rim chip, short hairline crack in saucer.

It has been suggested that this may be an experimental use by the factory of polychrome enamels and so possibly the earliest recorded piece of polychrome Lowestoft.

ca. 1770

$550-700   **TEN**

A Lowestoft blue-and-white butterboat, painted with cannonball rocks before a hut on an island with a tree, the rim with a lattice border, the underside molded with leaf floral feet, short rim crack.

ca. 1770-75   *2¾in (7cm) wide*

$190-250   **WW**

A documentary Lowestoft blue-and-white teabowl and saucer, painted with bamboo and chrysanthemum, rootwork, and a fence, within a lattice border, each piece inscribed on the underside with "Mary Crowfoot 1778."

1778   *4¾in (12cm) diam*

$3,700-5,000   **WW**

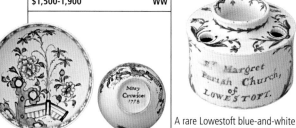

A rare Lowestoft blue-and-white inkwell, attributed to Robert Allen, inscribed "St Margret Parish Church of Lowestoft" within a foliate cartouche, the reverse with insects around a flower spray, the shoulder with further flower sprigs around three small holes encircling a well in the center with everted rim, a hole in the base.

ca. 1790   *2¾in (7cm) diam*

$7,000-8,000   **WW**

A rare Lowestoft blue-and-white birth tablet, inscribed on one side for "Maryann Lifin born November 4 1790," the reverse painted with a dove holding a twig in its beak, on a branch, pierced with a small suspension hole.

The Liffin family were connected to the Lowestoft factory through Mary Redgrave (Jr.), an artist at the factory who married John Liffin in 1785 and died in May 1795 at the age of 33. Mary's death is commemorated on the reverse of another birth tablet for Martha Liffin, born August 17, 1794. Baptism records at St. Margaret's Church show a Mary Ann Liffin baptized on November 7, 1790, as the daughter of John Liffin and Mary Redgrave. Her sister, Martha, was baptized on August 18, 1794. Mary Liffin never married and, when Martha was widowed in 1841, she went to live with Mary, where she remained until the latter's death in October 1861 at the age of 70. Mary is buried at the north side of St. Margaret's churchyard.

1790   *3in (7.5cm) diam*

$10,000-11,000   **WW**

ESSENTIAL REFERENCE—MEISSEN

True hard-paste porcelain was first developed in Europe in 1708 by Johann Friedrich Böttger and Walther von Tschirnhausen. Böttger, an alchemist famed for his claims that he could create gold, had been ordered by Augustus the Strong, Elector Prince of Saxony and King of Poland, to assist the scientist von Tschirnhausen with his porcelain experiments. By 1710, Augustus the Strong was able to establish the Meissen factory near Dresden—it was Europe's first hard-paste porcelain factory.

- The factory prospered under J. G. Höroldt, a chemist who was also appointed chief painter in 1720. Johann Joachim Kändler joined as chief modeler in 1733 and was responsible for producing many of Meissen's most striking figures.
- Early decoration was highly influenced by Asian designs, and copies and fusions of Japanese Kakiemon and Chinese famille verte wares were produced. From these emerged a new style of exotic floral decoration known as "Indianische Blumen" (Indian flowers), so called because much of Asian porcelain was imported by the East India Companies.
- From the 1730s, European themes, such as harbor scenes, cityscapes, and hunting and battle scenes, also became popular, and wares began to be made in the newly fashionable Rococo style, embellished with scrolled bases and painted in pastel colors. With this, a more naturalistic floral decoration developed, known as "Deutsche Blumen" (German Flowers), which was then replaced, in turn, by a looser representations of scattered flowers known as "Manierblumen" (Mannered Flowers).
- In the 19thC, Meissen, which still produces today, made pieces in numerous and diverse styles, including Neoclassical and the Gothic, Classical, and Rococo revivals.
- Meissen's forms and decoration have been much copied by other manufacturers over the years, as have on occasions its distinctive "crossed swords" identification marks.

A Meissen sugar or spice box and cover, in the Imari palette, blue crossed swords mark, three small firing cracks in the rim of the cover.
ca. 1725   *4¼in (11cm) wide*
$1,900-2,500   DN

A Meissen teabowl and saucer, painted in the Imari style, blue crossed swords and painter's "S" marks, slight rubbing in gilding.
ca. 1730
$1,000-1,100   DN

A Meissen soup plate, "Dulong" pattern, painted with grapes, the molded rim with panels of animals, birds, and flowers, blue crossed swords mark, small foot rim chip.
ca. 1740   *9½in (24cm) diam*
$200-250   WW

A Meissen bowl, molded with a band of stiff leaves, painted with sprays of "Deutsche Blumen" and single flowers, blue crossed swords mark, broken and repaired.
ca. 1740   *6¼in (16cm) diam*
$150-220   WW

A Meissen silver-gilt-mounted porcelain tankard, with chinoiserie flowers among rockwork, the mounts repoussé with acanthus and scrolls, silver hallmarks for Dresden, wear in gilding, minor surface wear in enamels, hairline cracks in base.
ca. 1740   *8¾in (22cm) high*
$3,100-3,700   TEN

A pair of Meissen Kakiemon porcelain soup plates, "Koreanischer Löwe" pattern, crossed swords mark in underglaze blue, minimal surface wear.
ca. 1740   *9in (23cm) diam*
$875-1,000   TEN

A Meissen Kakiemon teabowl and saucer, with flowering prunus and bamboo, small factory fault in the saucer, wear in the enamel, tiny niggles on the foot rim.
ca. 1740   *5in (12.5cm) diam*
$750-875   CHEF

A Meissen model of a parrot, modeled by J. J. Kändler, blue crossed swords mark, section of twig growing from the stump missing, one leaf chipped, beak restored.
ca. 1740   *5½in (14cm) high*
$2,500-3,700   DN

A pair of mid-18thC Meissen vases or urns, molded with flowers, painted with flower sprays in puce and green camaïeu, with shell handles, blue crossed swords, and dot marks.
9½in (24cm) high
$1,250-1,700   WW

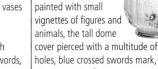

A Meissen sugar caster or sifter, molded with floral swags issuing from cherub masks, painted with small vignettes of figures and animals, the tall dome cover pierced with a multitude of holes, blue crossed swords mark, chipping in the flange.
ca. 1760   *7in (18cm) high*
$700-800   WW

PORCELAIN

The cover is painted with scattered sprigs of pink and red flowers, typical of mid-18thC Meissen, and topped with a crocuslike finial.

Here, painted in a predominantly green palette, the scenes on the body of the teapot are examples of "fêtes galantes," a mid-18thC style of decoration that depicted fashionably dressed men and women in romantically rural landscapes. Often inspired by the paintings of the French artist Jean-Antoine Watteau (1684-1721), such scenes are often described as "Watteau-esque."

The handle is molded in the shape of a wishbone, a delicate curvaceous form in-keeping with aesthetics of the Rococo style.

Enhanced with delicate painted and gilt plant forms, the spout is molded in another curvaceous form—that of a mythical serpent.

A Meissen teapot and cover, painted with Watteau-esque scenes of figures in garden settings, with wishbone handle and serpent spout, blue crossed swords mark, firing flaw in base, minor chips in the cover.

ca. 1760-70   *7¾in (20cm) wide*
$625-750   **WW**

A pair of Meissen bouquetiere figures, modeled by J.J. Kändler, the tops pierced for flowers, restoration to her basket and feet, and to the flower in his hat, slight wear to gilding.

ca. 1765   *7¾in (20cm) high*
$3,700-4,300   **CHEF**

A Meissen Academic Period porcelain ecuelle and cover, decorated with lovers in a landscape, on a molded wrythen ozier ground, crossed swords mark struck out, some losses in flower decoration, finial reattached, some wear in gilding.

ca. 1770   *8¾in (22cm) diam*
$700-800   **TEN**

A Meissen coffee can, painted with a fox eating a bird, crossed swords mark in blue, factory fault in the handle, rubbing on the rim.

ca. 1770   *2¾in (7cm) high*
$375-500   **CHEF**

A Meissen figure of a young Bacchus, wearing a stag pelt, raising a gilt goblet, wearing a grapevine wreath, and with a further basket of grapes by his feet, incised crossed swords in a triangle mark, incised "1696," several small chips.

ca. 1770   *6in (15cm) high*
$450-550   **WW**

A 19thC Meissen porcelain figural group representing "Architecture," the three putti about an entablature, one holding a rule, another a chisel, the third a scroll, crossed swords mark in underglaze blue, some professional restoration, some gilt wear on the base.

9in (23cm) high
$1,200-1,350   **TEN**

A pair of 19thC Meissen wine coolers, each painted with a landscape scene of figures trading and loading boats in a harbor, divided by narrow gilded columns with a foliate design, the sides applied with satyr mask handles, blue crossed swords and star marks, one incised "E174."

4¼in (10.5cm) high
$4,300-5,600   **WW**

A mid-19thC Meissen armorial tureen and cover, after an earlier model by J. J. Kändler, of elaborate double-wall form, painted with landscape panels within applied floral garlands, the cover applied with medallions painted with the arms of Saxony and flanked by putti, the finial formed as a crown, blue crossed swords mark, incised "b136," impressed "99," some losses.

10in (25.5cm) wide
$15,000-20,000   **WW**

A pair of mid-19thC Meissen figures of a shepherd and shepherdess, each figure with a sheep by his or her feet, on rocaille scroll bases, underglaze blue crossed swords mark, incised "5," painted "26," impressed numbers.

10½in (26.5cm) and 9¾in (25cm) high
$875-1,000   **L&T**

A 19thC Meissen figure of Count Brühl's Tailor, after the model by J. J. Kändler, modeled on a billy goat, which holds a flat iron in his mouth, the tailor brandishing scissors, two kids sitting in a half barrel strapped to his back, blue crossed swords mark, some restoration.

Heinrich von Brühl was a Polish-Saxon statesman and diplomat with a famed reputation as a dandy and profligate. Frederick II of Prussia is reported as having said of him, "Brühl had more garments, watches, laces, boots, shoes, and slippers than any man of the age. Caesar would have counted him among those curled and perfumed heads that he did not fear."

9¼in (23.5cm) high

$550-700   WW

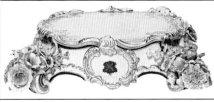

A 19thC Meissen stand, possibly for a clock, applied with flowers and decorated with gilt foliate scrolls, blue crossed swords marks, minor restorations.

6¾in (17cm) wide

$375-500   WW

A Meissen model of a fisherman, crossed swords mark in underglaze blue.

6¾in (17cm) high

$500-550   CHEF

A large 19thC Meissen mantel clock and stand, modeled with four putti emblematic of the Four Seasons, applied with flowers and leaves, around the clock dial with an ouroboros, the triangular stand painted and applied with flowers, blue crossed swords marks, incised "2179" on the base, some damages.

23in (58.5cm) high

$3,700-5,000   WW

A 19th/20thC Meissen coffee cup and saucer, painted with "Purpurmalerei" scenes of figures, a couple walking with a child and a gentleman mounting a horse, above gilt foliate scrollwork, blue crossed swords marks.

5in (13cm) diam

$500-625   WW

A 19thC Meissen eyebath, painted with flower sprigs, blue crossed swords mark.

1¾in (4.5cm) high

$150-200   WW

A pair of mid- to late-19thC Meissen figures of a shepherd and shepherdess, on Rococo bases, blue crossed swords marks, incised "1," painted "42.," impressed "69."

10¾in (27.5cm) and 10¼in (26cm) high

$1,000-1,100   L&T

A late-19thC Meissen porcelain model of a jay, after the model by J. J. Kändler, crossed swords mark in underglaze blue, minor losses on extremities.

16¼in (41cm) high

$2,500-3,700   TEN

A late-19thC Meissen porcelain figure, modeled as a young boy, standing against a "ruined" marble column, crossed swords mark, incised "F34," indistinctly inscribed.

6in (15cm) high

$190-250   HT

A late-19thC Meissen porcelain figure, modeled as a young girl allegorical of Autumn, crossed swords mark, incised "F21," inscribed "16."

5½in (14cm) high

$190-250   HT

PORCELAIN

A late-19thC Meissen figural group of Europa and the Bull, incised "2697," single cancellation mark.

9in (23cm) high

$750-875 CHOR

A late-19thC Meissen figural group, "The Broken Egg," after the model by M. V. Acier, modeled as a lady and companion, an upturned basket of eggs at her feet and Cupid kneeling before them, crossed swords mark in blue, small losses, small chips in the flowers.

9in (23cm) high

$800-950 CHEF

A Meissen figural basket, with a lady supporting a pierced basket, crossed swords mark, restoration in the basket handles and foot, firing crack in the base.

11¾in (30cm) wide

$500-625 CHEF

A late-19th/early-20thC Meissen figural group of two putti with a monkey and a crib, after the 18thC model by J. C. Schönheit, crossed swords mark in blue, incised model no. "H.89," the thumb of the cherub is missing.

6¼in (16cm) high

$500-625 CHEF

A Meissen figural group, a courting couple with a pug dog, crossed swords mark in underglaze blue, incised "778," restoration in the bocage.

ca. 1900 *6in (15.5cm) wide*

$375-500 CHEF

Two Meissen figures, one modeled as a winged young girl holding a fan, the other of Cupid as George and the Dragon, crossed swords marks in blue.

ca. 1900 *8¾in (22cm) high*

$1,400-1,700 CHEF

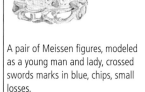

A pair of Meissen figures, modeled as a young man and lady, crossed swords marks in blue, chips, small losses.

ca. 1900 *5in (13cm) high*

$550-600 CHEF

A Meissen porcelain figure, by Julius Konrad Hentschel, modeled as a young boy riding a hobbyhorse, wearing a newspaper hat, crossed swords mark in underglaze blue, incised "W120" and painter's "33," dated, minor surface wear.

This figure, known as the "Child with Paper Hat," is one of the "Hentschel Kinder" modeled by Julius Konrad Hentschel between 1904 and 1907, capturing the joys of childhood.

1905 *6¾in (17cm) high*

$1,900-2,500 TEN

A pair of late-19th/early-20thC Meissen porcelain figures of parakeets, crossed swords marks in underglaze blue, small losses, restoration.

11in (28cm) and 11½in (29cm) high

$3,700-4,300 TEN

A late-19th/early-20thC Meissen porcelain figural group, depicting an 18thC couple, crossed swords mark in underglaze blue, vase lacking cover, some minor losses in extremities.

8½in (21.5cm) high

$875-1,000 TEN

ESSENTIAL REFERENCE—NANTGARW

In 1813, William Weston Young and William Billingsley, the latter previously a decorator at Derby, established a porcelain factory at Nantgarw, in Wales. Soon after, in 1814, the company moved to Swansea and merged with Lewis Weston Dillwyn's Cambrian Pottery, but in 1817 Dillwyn left the business, and Billingsley and Young returned to Nantgarw and reopened the factory there. In 1819, it was purchased by Coalport and remained open until 1823.

- Nantgarw porcelain was so fine that it was very difficult to fire, and a large proportion was lost in the kiln. Usually, it is also very translucent and almost pure white when held to the light; the glaze tends to be thick and smooth.
- The factory primarily made tea wares and flatware, while its large hollow wares are very rare.
- Cofounder William Billingsley was particularly known for his flower painting.
- The factory's wares tend to be impressed "NANT-GARW CW," with the "CW" standing for China Works.

A Nantgarw muffin dish and cover, from the Hensol Castle service, impressed "NANT-GARW CW" mark, some regilding on the rim.
ca. 1818-20   *8¼in (21cm) diam*
$500-625   **WW**

A Nantgarw bowl and an eggcup stand, from the Hensol Castle service, decorated by Pardoe, impressed "NANT-GARW CW" mark.
ca. 1818-20   *11in (28cm) wide*
$700-800   **WW**

A rare pair of Nantgarw duck or goose eggcups, from the Hensol Castle service, decorated with a sprig design in blue and gilt.
ca. 1818-20   *2½in (6.5cm) high*
$950-1,050   **WW**

A Nantgarw breakfast cup and saucer, from the Hensol Castle service, decorated by Pardoe.
ca. 1818-20   *6¾in (17cm) diam*
$375-450   **WW**

A pair of Nantgarw dessert plates, decorated in London, with sprays of flowers, the rims with C-scroll molding, gilt dentil rims, impressed "NANT-GARW CW" marks.
ca. 1818-20   *9¾in (25cm) diam*
$750-875   **WW**

A pair of Nantgarw spill vases, decorated in London, probably in the Sims workshop, with sprays of flowers, the interior rims with formal paneled gilt designs.
ca. 1818-20   *4½in (11.5cm) high*
$3,100-3,700   **WW**

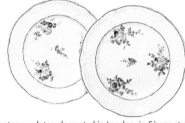

A pair of Nantgarw plates, decorated in London, in Sèvres style, impressed "NANT-GARW CW" marks and gilt Mortlocks marks.

Mortlocks was a firm of London china dealers and were patrons of both the Sims workshop and that of Robins & Randall.
ca. 1818-20   *9¾in (25cm) diam*
$300-375   **WW**

A Nantgarw cabinet plate, decorated in London, probably in the Sims workshop, with painted flower arrangement, including rose, stocks, and passionflower, impressed "NANT-GARW CW" mark.
ca. 1818-20   *9¼in (23.5cm) diam*
$1,200-1,350   **WW**

PORCELAIN

A Nantgarw cabinet cup and saucer, decorated in London, probably in the Sims workshop, and a large teacup in the same pattern.

ca. 1818-20   5½in (14cm) diam

$750-875   **WW**

A Nantgarw cabinet cup and saucer, probably painted in London, each piece with diagonally placed sprays of garden flowers, a little gilt wear.

ca. 1818-20   5¼in (13.5cm) diam

$500-625   **WW**

A Nantgarw cup and saucer, probably decorated in London, with sprays of flowers, with a gilt border of diaper and other panels, the cup with an inverted heart-shaped handle.

ca. 1818-20   5½in (14cm) diam

$550-600   **WW**

A Nantgarw taperstick, painted with flower sprays, including rose and narcissus, the handle broken and cleanly reattached.

ca. 1818-20   1¾in (4.5cm) diam

$1,000-1,100   **WW**

A Nantgarw dessert dish, possibly decorated in London, with roses, auricula, forget-me-nots, and strawberries, impressed mark.

ca. 1818-20   11¼in (28.5cm) wide

$250-370   **WW**

CLOSER LOOK—A NANTGARW CUP AND SAUCER

Although architectural forms, notably arches, ground the pattern, most of the imagery on the gilded saucer/stand comprises repeat plant-form motifs, more stylized toward the rim and in the partly obscured center, more naturalistic under the arches.

A pair of Nantgarw plates, painted in William Pollard style, with flowers and fruit, including primroses, forget-me-nots, convolvulus, heather, and strawberries, impressed marks.

ca. 1818-20   9in (23cm) diam

$1,900-2,500   **WW**

Gilded with plant-form embellishments en-suite with the saucer/stand, the partly obscured cup handle is in the form of a serpent— a decoratively curvaceous shape also well suited to its function.

The hand-painted landscape panel on the cup, which incorporates a figure on a bridge and a castle in the background, is of excellent quality, and while it may have been painted at the Nantgarw factory in Wales, it could well have been sent to independent painters in London for decoration.

A Nantgarw muffin dish and cover, from the Spence-Thomas service, painted by Thomas Pardoe, with flowers, including auricula, rose, stocks, convolvulus, and tulip, the cover with a gilt acorn finial.

ca. 1818-20   8½in (21.5cm) diam

$8,500-10,000   **WW**

A Nantgarw cabinet cup and saucer, the cup with landscape panel, the saucer with formal predominantly plant-form patterns, a crack in the latter.

ca. 1818-20   6in (15cm) diam

$1,050-1,200   **WW**

ESSENTIAL REFERENCE—SWANSEA

Having established a porcelain factory in Nantgarw in 1813 (see page 29), founders William Weston Young and William Billingsley moved production to Swansea a year later, in 1814, and merged with the Cambrian Pottery.

● Swansea pieces were made from a highly translucent soft-paste porcelain, of which three variations have been identified: "glassy," "duck egg," and "trident."

● Many shapes and designs were in the contemporary and fashionable French style.

● Talented painters who worked there included Thomas Pardoe, William Pollard, and David Evans, all of whom specialized in floral patterns (as did William Billingsley), and Thomas Baxter (who went on to work for Worcester), who primarily painted figures and landscapes.

● Although commissions came in from local dignitaries, and members of the aristocracy from farther afield, costly production inconsistencies eventually led to Young and Billingsley abandoning the Swansea venture in 1817 and returning to Nantgarw.

A Swansea miniature cabinet cup and stand, painted with landscapes of sailboats and buildings beside water, within gilt seaweed borders, small chip on the cup's rim.

ca. 1815-17   4¾in (12cm) diam
$450-500   WW

A pair of Swansea dishes, "Marquis of Anglesey" pattern, painted in London, with flowers, including primrose, narcissus, rose, chrysanthemum, and convolvulus, impressed "SWANSEA" marks, one riveted.

ca. 1815-17   9¼in (23.5cm) diam
$500-625   WW

A Swansea chamberstick, painted by Evans or Pollard, with wild flowers, including heather, primrose, dog rose, and wild strawberry, red "SWANSEA" mark, crack in the drip pan.

ca. 1815-17   5in (12.5cm) diam
$450-550   WW

A Swansea inkwell, probably painted by David Evans, with flowers, including tulip, rose, heather, buttercup, and strawberry, the interior with three quill holders around a drum with liner, the liner and one quill holder restored.

ca. 1817-20   5¼in (13.5cm) diam
$550-700   WW

A Swansea miniature cabinet cup and stand, probably painted by Henry Morris, with flowers and marble plinths, between gilt foliate scroll borders, faint red script mark on the saucer.

ca. 1815-17   4in (10cm) diam
$3,100-3,700   WW

A Swansea miniature model of a watering can, painted by William Pollard, with wild flowers, including speedwell, dog rose, heather, and primrose, the spout with a pierced watering rose, the handle restored.

ca. 1817-20   3¼in (8.5cm) high
$450-550   WW

A pair of Swansea cabinet cups and saucers, decorated in London, probably in the Sims workshop, each cup and saucer with vases of flowers, within gilt scroll borders.

ca. 1815-17   6¼in (16cm) diam
$1,900-2,500   WW

A Swansea cabaret or petit dejeuner set, decorated with pink roses between gilt borders with rose hip sprays, comprising a square tray, coffeepot and cover, cabinet cup and saucer, sucrier and cover, breakfast teabowl and saucer, and a candlestick, red "SWANSEA" mark on one saucer.

ca. 1815-17
$3,700-4,300   WW

A near pair of rare Swansea tureens and covers, painted by Henry Morris, with wild flowers, including buttercup, heather, dog rose, and forget-me-nots, the sides with lion-head masks, small damages and repairs.

ca. 1815-20   7¾in (19.5cm) high
$2,500-3,100   WW

PORCELAIN

ESSENTIAL REFERENCE—SÈVRES

The Sèvres porcelain factory was founded in Vincennes in 1740 and was known as the Vincennes factory until it moved to Sèvres in 1756. It became one of the most important porcelain manufacturers in Europe during the second half of the 18thC, and well beyond.

- The Sèvres factory initially flourished under Jean-Jacques Bachelier, who was appointed its art director in 1751.
- The factory's early wares were primarily inspired by Meissen, with typical decorative features being sprays of small flowers painted with a palette of soft colors. Rococo shapes and patterns were also introduced in the early 1750s.
- The crossed "L" mark of the royal cipher was adopted in 1753, while the factory was still at Vincennes, and King Louis XV bought the Sèvres factory in 1759.
- The factory lost its royal patronage as a result of the French Revolution (1789-99), and, at the beginning of the 19thC, it almost went bankrupt before gradually recovering.
- During the course of the 19thC, Sèvres' output became extensive again, and especially notable among numerous and diverse wares were porcelain services decorated with landscapes and portrait cameos rendered in colorful enamels and inspired by historical-revival styles that included the Rococo, Neoclassical, and Classical revivals.

A Vincennes or early Sèvres dish or stand, painted with flowers, within gilt floral and hatched panel cartouches.
1756-57   *9¼in (23.5cm) wide*
$500-625   **WW**

A Sèvres ice cup stand or plateau de tasse à glaces and three ice cups, painted with flower sprays, blue interlaced "L" marks, the stand with a letter "F" date code for 1758-59.
ca. 1758-70   *9in (23cm) wide*
$1,500-1,700   **WW**

A Sèvres biscuit figure of a boy, sitting on a tree stump and playing the flageolet.
ca. 1760   *4½in (11.5cm) high*
$375-500   **WW**

A Sèvres cabinet cup and stand, painted with barrels being brought ashore, small surface chip on the rim of the saucer.
                  5¼in (13.5cm) diam
$4,300-5,000   **CHEF**

A large Sèvres hexafoil stand or plateau à pots à jus, painted with flowers and fruit, including pink and yellow roses and grapes, the rim with a bleu celeste border with gilt foliate scrolls, interlaced blue "L" mark and painter's mark "PTX."

The Artists' Ledgers at Sèvres record a quantity of stock pieces decorated with fruit and flowers in the well and with bleu celeste grounds. Such stock pieces are thought to have been adapted for the Duchess of Manchester Service of 1783, which bears very similar decoration in the wells.
ca. 1775-85   *11¼in (28.5cm) wide*
$450-550   **WW**

A Sèvres ormolu-mounted vase and cover, losses in mount.
ca. 1765   *9in (23cm) high*
$450-550   **WW**

A Sèvres porcelain miniature teacup and saucer, painted in Ambroise Michel style, with exotic birds, painted marks, the saucer with scratching in the blue ground and small pit marks in the glaze, the cup with minor scratching.
ca. 1765
$2,200-2,700   **TEN**

A Sèvres saucer or soucoupe, possibly painted by Jean-Charles Sioux l'aîné, in overglaze blue enamel, crowned blue interlaced "L" mark, indistinct painter's mark.
ca. 1770   *5¼in (13.5cm) diam*
$190-250   **WW**

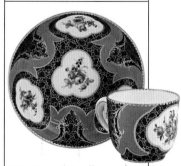

A Sèvres porcelain coffee cup and saucer, the porcelain 18thC, the decoration later, painted with flowers, painted marks in blue, minor surface and gilt wear.
$1,050-1,200   **TEN**

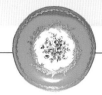

A Sèvres octofoil dish, later decorated in imitation of the service for Prince Henry of Prussia, the well painted with a flower spray, blue interlaced "L" mark, painter's mark.

A service with this decoration was presented to Henry of Prussia by King Louis XVI when the prince visited the French Court in 1784. A true example is in the collection of the Musée National de la Céramique, Sèvres (MNS 15.054).

1775   *8½in (21.5cm) diam*
$1,250-1,600   **WW**

A matched pair of Sèvres bottle coolers or seau à demi-bouteille, later decorated with fruit and flowers, blue interlaced "L" marks, date codes, and painter's marks, one cracked.

ca. 1775-80   *6¾in (17cm) high*
$700-800   **WW**

A Sèvres saucer or soucoupe, the well painted by Armand Léandre, with a solitary figure holding a staff and standing beneath tall trees surveying a distant view, the underside rim with a continuous gilt leaf band, blue interlaced "L" mark, enclosing date letter "HH," above painter's mark "LA."

1785   *5¾in (14.5cm) diam*
$800-950   **WW**

CLOSER LOOK—A SÈVRES COFFEE CAN AND SAUCER

Neoclassicism had become fashionable in France by the late 1770s, and is immediately evident in the portrait medallions on the saucer (or soucoupe), which were inspired by Roman equivalents in frescoes uncovered during excavations of archaeological sites, such as at Pompeii.

While, to some extent, the profusion of delicate and pretty polychrome flowers on the saucer recall the earlier Rococo style, the configuration of many of them as garlands reflects, like the portrait medallions, the Neoclassical taste.

The primary decoration on the coffee can (or gobelet litron) is the sword-wielding, female personification of "Justice," one of the Classical Roman "Virtues"—the others include "Fortitude," "Prudence," "Temperance," "Patience," "Humility" and "Chastitiy." This motif is echoed in the medallion centered in the saucer.

A Sèvres coffee can and saucer, painted with Neoclassical figural and floral imagery, the can titled in blue on the underside, the saucer with a gilt interlaced "L" mark, restored.

ca. 1780   *5¼in (13.5cm) diam*
$700-800   **WW**

A pair of Sèvres cabinet cups and stands, the cans painted with two named oval panels, Madame du Barry and Madame Victoire, slight wear and discoloration in gilding.

5in (12.5cm) diam
$1,600-2,200   **CHEF**

A Sèvres sauceboat, from the Comte d'Aranda service, painted with flowers and fruit, blue interlaced "L" mark with date letters "jj," painter's mark for Bouillat and gilt "HP" mark for Henri-Martin Prévost, tiny restored chip on one handle.

The Comte d'Aranda was the Spanish Ambassador Extraordinary and Plenipotentiary to France from September 12, 1773, to September 23, 1787, and this service was a gift to him at the end of his ambassadorship.

The gift is recorded in "Journal des Présents du Roi" on September 16, 1787, as "une Service de porcelaine Sèvres," costing 43,428 livres. See David Peters, *Sèvres Plates and Services of the 18th Century*, Vol. IV, French Porcelain Society, no. 87-7 for a full discussion of this service.

1786   *9¼in (23.5cm) wide*
$3,700-4,300   **WW**

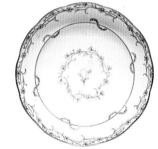

A Sèvres dish, from the Guirlande de Barbeaux service, painted with a centered pink rose encircled by cornflowers, overglaze crowned blue interlaced "L" mark, date letters "KK," and a fleur-de-lis painter's mark for Taillandier, some wear.

The Guirlande de Barbeaux service was first ordered for Louis XVI in 1783, and deliveries were staggered up until 1790. See David Peters, *Sèvres Plates and Services of the 18th Century*, Vol. III, French Porcelain Society, no. 83-2 and 85-2. According to Peters, the small compotiers are listed in a document with dessert plates and small baskets and so may have been designed to be used together. Four are believed listed in the 1787 supplement. This would appear to be the only recorded example of this size and shape.

1787   *7in (18cm) diam*
$625-750   **WW**

A Sèvres porcelain coffee can and saucer, the porcelain 18thC, the decoration later, painted with exotic birds in landscape, painted marks in blue, firing flaws.

$1,050-1,200   **TEN**

A late-18thC Sèvres miniature teapot and cover or théière litron, painted on one side with a colorful bird, the reverse with flowers, interlaced blue "L" mark and painter's mark of sixteenth notes.

4¾in (12cm) wide
$1,250-1,600   **WW**

PORCELAIN

A pair of Sèvres plates, the wells painted by Vandé (fils), with flowers and gilt barley, the rims with gilt leaves, flanked by flowers, blue interlaced "L" mark, painter's mark "V d."

The plates can be attributed to a service purchased by Madame Lefebvre, née Le Clerq, a Paris marchand-mercier, in 1794. The decoration is described as "souvenirs différents" which David Peters matches to plate design no. 148 (see David Peters, "Sèvres Plates and Services of the 18th Century," Vol. V, French Porcelain Society, page 1027), the description of which corresponds to these plates.

ca. 1794   *9½in (24cm) diam*

$875-1,000   **WW**

A Sèvres tray or stand, painted with a basket of flowers including tulip, rose, auricula and lilac, resting on a marble shelf, blue interlaced "L" mark, enclosing "OO" date code, painter's mark "B," some later decoration, a chip to one handle and restoration to the other.

1791   *9¾in (24.5cm) wide*

$500-550   **WW**

A pair of Sèvres comports, gilt with a flower head within formal leaf borders, the rim painted with floral meander within gilt line borders, bases inscribed "21 Mai.B.T.," printed marks in blue, minor surface wear.

ca. 1820   *10¾in (27cm) wide*

$2,700-3,500   **TEN**

A set of nine Sèvres porcelain plates, gilt with a monogram, printed marks in green for 1870 and red for 1875, very minor gilt wear.

ca. 1870   *9¾in (24.5cm) diam*

$3,100-3,700   **TEN**

A pair of Sèvres porcelain and ormolu mounted vases and covers, by Louis-Constant Sévin (1821-88), painted with Classical frieze of children, the covers mounted with Classical figures, the mounts stamped "LC," some "jeweled" beads are missing.

11½in (29cm) high

$2,500-3,700   **CHEF**

A pair of Sèvres vases, with two panels, one painted with Watteau-esque scenes, the opposing panels with rustic scenes of cottages in a landscape, some damage.

6¼in (16cm) high

$450-550   **CHEF**

An early- to mid-19thC sucrier and cover, in Sèvres style, painted with birds on branches, blue interlaced "L" mark and "OO" date code.

1791   *4¼in (10.5cm) high*

$450-500   **WW**

A pair of 19thC porcelain vases and covers, in Sèvres style, painted with exotic birds in landscape and with sprays of flowers, one vase broken and repaired around base of body, crack to foot, some minor wear.

15in (38cm) high

$875-1,000   **TEN**

A tête-à-tête tea service, in Sèvres style, with panels painted with King Louis XVI, Queen Marie Antoinette and the Royal children, comprising a tray, teapot and cover, sucrier and cover, cream jug, and two cups and saucers, some damage.

tray 11¾in (30cm) wide

$1,700-2,200   **CHEF**

ESSENTIAL REFERENCE—EARLY WORCESTER (1751-74)

The Worcester factory was founded in 1751 by a group of 15 gentlemen, merchants, and craftsmen, including Dr. John Wall, who managed it until 1774.

- In 1752, the factory bought out Benjamin Lund's Bristol factory (see page 14), and the consequent fusion of technical expertise and a soft-paste porcelain formula containing soapstone, which made it able to withstand boiling water, resulted in a sophisticated range of products, notably increasingly fashionable tea and coffee wares.
- Early Worcester wares were invariably thinly potted, most were on the small side—few are more than 6in (15cm) high—and many shapes were derived from silverware precedents.
- Most early Worcester pieces were blue and white—the imagery being painted in underglaze blue. Polychrome-enameled pieces were also produced, especially those with chinoiserie patterns, which were painted with bold colors derived from both the Chinese famille rose and famille verte palettes.
- While Worcester was one of the pioneers of overglaze transfer printing, in 1760 it began to switch to more durable underglaze printing.
- From the 1760s onward, early period Worcester was marked with a crescent in underglaze blue, which was copied at Lowestoft and should not be confused with the "C" of Caughley.

A Worcester blue-and-white teabowl and saucer, "Cormorant" pattern, painted with a bird perched on rocks beside flowering peony branches, a small fisherman in the distance, differing workman's marks.

ca. 1754-56   *4¾in (12cm) diam*

$1,000-1,250   **WW**

A Worcester blue-and-white coffee cup and saucer, "Gazebo" pattern, painted with a small hut protruding from crossed rocks, a figure in a boat in the foreground, workman's marks.

ca. 1755-58   *4½in (11.5cm) diam*

$950-1,050   **WW**

A Worcester porcelain finger bowl stand, "Cormorant" pattern, workman's mark in underglaze blue, minor surface wear, glaze pitting and scratches.

ca. 1756   *6in (15cm) diam*

$700-800   **TEN**

A Worcester porcelain leaf-molded dish, "Rose and Floral Sprays" pattern, workman's mark in underglaze blue, minor surface wear, chips in the foot rim, some glaze pitting.

ca. 1758   *8¼in (21cm) wide*

$550-700   **TEN**

A rare and small Worcester blue-and-white teapot and cover, "Mansfield" pattern, tiny chip on the spout.

ca. 1755-58   *5¾in (14.5cm) wide*

$750-875   **WW**

A rare and early Worcester blue-and-white junket dish, molded with basket weave, reserving three landscape panels in the "Neighbours" pattern, the shaped rim with flowers and moths, workman's mark.

ca. 1758   *9in (23cm) wide*

$1,500-2,000   **WW**

A Worcester blue-and-white potting pot, "Mansfield" pattern, the interior with a single floral sprig, workman's mark.

ca. 1756-60   *6¼in (16cm) diam*

$550-700   **WW**

A miniature Worcester blue-and-white teapot and cover, "Prunus Root" pattern painted on one side, the reverse with a flowering spray, workman's marks on the base and inside cover.

Miniature Worcester wares painted with the "Prunus Root" pattern are believed to have been produced for the Dutch market.

ca. 1758-60   *4½in (11.5cm) wide*

$950-1,050   **WW**

A Worcester blue-and-white coffeepot and cover, "Mansfield" pattern, workman's mark, chips in the knop and spout.

ca. 1760   *8¾in (22.5cm) high*

$450-550   **WW**

A Worcester porcelain honey pot and cover, "Mansfield" pattern, crescent mark in underglaze blue, minor surface wear, small firing blemish on the rim of the pot.

ca. 1765   4¾in (12cm) high
$800-950   TEN

A Worcester blue-and-white sauceboat, "Mission Church" pattern, one side painted with a bridge beside a pagoda, the reverse with a figure in a boat beside an island, open crescent mark.

ca. 1765   8½in (21.5cm) wide
$700-800   WW

A Worcester blue-and-white chamber pot, "Bouquets" pattern, printed with floral sprays and sprigs, the interior with the "Primula" print, hatched crescent mark.

ca. 1770   9in (23cm) wide
$500-625   WW

A Worcester porcelain sauceboat, "Hundred Antiques" pattern, painted in underglaze blue, pseudo Chinese porcelain mark, minor surface wear.

The "Hundred Antiques" pattern is not uncommon but is predominantly found on dessert plates and dishes and occasionally on sauce tureens; sauceboats are much more uncommon.

ca. 1775   8¾in (22cm) wide
$700-800   TEN

CLOSER LOOK—A WORCESTER MUG

After 1752, when Worcester bought Benjamin Lund's factory in Bristol, and with it his secret porcelain formula that included Cornish soapstone, Worcester's porcelain, notably its teapots and mugs, was able to withstand contact with boiling water without cracking—in marked contrast to the porcelain of most of its contemporary British counterparts.

Transfer printed in overglaze black enamel (a technique that Worcester invented), this "Rural Lovers" scene, featuring a milkmaid with cows and her companion leaning against a tree, was taken from a 1760 Francis Vivares print in the style of Thomas Gainsborough.

The engraved plates used to print the "Rural Lovers" scene on the mug were made by Robert Hancock (1730-1817) who had become draftsman and engraver to the Worcester Porcelain Works ca. 1756, and continued working there until 1774.

A Worcester mug, black transfer printed, with a "Rural Lovers" scene on one side and a "Milking Scene" on the reverse.

ca. 1760-65   6in (15cm) high
$450-550   WW

A documentary Worcester blue-and-white mug, "Rock Strata" pattern, inscribed with the name "Jno Griffith," open crescent mark, one secured crack.

ca. 1780   4½in (11.5cm) high
$250-370   WW

A Worcester mug, printed in black, from a design by Robert Hancock, with the arms of the Grand Lodge and the motto "Amor Honor Et Justitia Sit Lux Et Lux Fuit," amid Masonic emblems, with figures on the left.

ca. 1760-62   4¾in (12cm) high
$800-950   WW

A Worcester Masonic printed mug, by James Ross, printed in black, with the arms of the Grand Lodge of England and other Masonic emblems, three figures on one side, the whole flanked by two brick obelisks surmounted by globes.

James Ross was apprenticed to Robert Hancock in 1765 and the copper plate for this print, signed by him, is in the Dyson Perrins Museum in Worcester.

ca. 1765-70   6in (15cm) high
$1,000-1,100   WW

An early Worcester pickle or sweetmeat dish, of scallop shell form, painted in Kakiemon enamels with a ho ho bird in flight, above bamboo and flowering branches.

ca. 1753-54   5¼in (13.5cm) wide
$1,100-1,250   WW

A rare and early Worcester sauceboat, of curled leaf shape but molded with panels of flowers and leaves, painted with the "Stag Hunt" pattern, the handle formed as a stalk.

ca. 1755-56   8¾in (22cm) wide

$1,250-1,700   **WW**

Judith Picks

Although I've long and generally most admired the blue-and-white porcelain produced during the Worcester factory's early period (1751-70), I must confess that from time to time I come across one of the less common polychrome painted pieces from that era that jumps straight to the top of my "gosh, I really really want that" list. This Worcester mug with a "Beckoning Chinaman" pattern is a particularly good example of that. The predominantly verte and rose palette is nicely employed, enhancing a crisply painted chinoiserie composition (probably inspired not only by Chinese originals, but also some of the Meissen factory's chinoiserie patterns). It is, however, in the delightful expression on the Chinaman's face, and in the delicate sense of movement in not only him, but also the bird in flight and elements of the foliage, that the utterly charming appeal of the painting really lies.

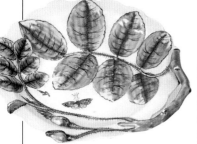

A Worcester sweetmeat dish, "Blind Earl" pattern, small niggles on foot rim, small firing faults on the surface, restoration on the rim.

ca. 1758   6¼in (16cm) wide

$750-875   **CHEF**

A Worcester cream pitcher, of low Chelsea ewer shape, molded and decorated with a band of acanthus leaves, painted with flowers, the interior rim with a puce scroll band, small rim fault.

ca. 1760   4¼in (11cm) wide

$500-625   **WW**

A Worcester lettuce leaf dish, "The Magician" pattern, with two Chinese figures watching a third standing beside a low table and garden seats, a butterfly above.

ca. 1760-65   8½in (21.5cm) wide

$375-500   **WW**

A Worcester bell-shaped mug, "Beckoning Chinaman" pattern, the figure crooking his finger toward a bird in flight, the reverse with a floral spray.

ca. 1758   4in (10cm) high

$950-1,050   **WW**

A Worcester teapot and cover, painted in Kakiemon enamels, with flowering branches, square seal mark.

ca. 1765-75   7¾in (19.5cm) wide

$700-800   **WW**

A Worcester teapot and cover, "Queen Charlotte" pattern, with Asian flowers in the Imari palette, blue crescent mark, the cover possibly associated.

ca. 1765   7¼in (18.5cm) high

$700-800   **WW**

A Worcester plate, decorated in the workshop of James Giles, scratching in the enamel, wear in the gilding.

ca. 1765   8¾in (22cm) diam

$300-450   **CHEF**

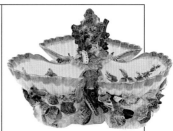

A Worcester porcelain pickle stand, with a centered shell handle flanked by three scallop shells, painted with flower sprays, some hairline cracks and minor losses.

ca. 1770   6in (15cm) wide

$625-750   **TEN**

ESSENTIAL REFERENCE—WORCESTER PORCELAIN 1783-1862

After cofounder and manager Dr. John Wall retired in 1774, the Worcester factory was managed by another partner, William Davis, until it was bought by its London agent, Thomas Flight, in 1783.

- Subsequent factory name changes over the next 80 years, as follows: Flight (1783-92); Flight & Barr (1792-1804); Barr, Flight & Barr (1804-13), and Flight, Barr & Barr (1813-40).
- During the same time period as above, two additional Worcester factories emerged: one founded by Humphrey Chamberlain and his son ca. 1786; the other founded by Thomas Grainger, a former Chamberlain employee, ca. 1806.
- While Grainger's factory operated, under various guises (including Grainger, Lee & Co.) until 1902, Chamberlain's merged with Flight, Barr & Barr to form Chamberlain & Co. in 1840.
- In 1852, Chamberlain & Co. was itself taken over by Henry Kerr and Richard William Binns, who together managed the factory for ten years, until 1862. In that year Kerr left, and Binns continued to manage the factory alone, reforming and renaming it, and from then until today it is most commonly referred to as Royal Worcester (see page 40).

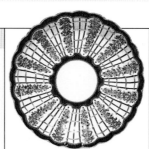

A Worcester saucer dish, a version of the "Hop Trellis" pattern.
ca. 1770   7¼in (18.5cm) diam
$450-550   WW

A Worcester fluted coffee cup and saucer, a version of the "Scarlet Japan" pattern.
ca. 1770   5¼in (13.5cm) diam
$700-800   WW

A Worcester fluted milk pitcher, "Chequered Tent" pattern, in the Kakiemon palette, square seal mark.
ca. 1768-72   4¼in (11cm) high
$750-875   WW

A Worcester punch bowl, printed in black with the "The Fox Hunt," after a painting by James Seymour, the interior rim with flower sprays, some wear.
ca. 1770-75   8¼in (21cm) diam
$550-700   WW

A Worcester Barr, Flight & Barr porcelain inkstand, with swan-neck handle over three inkpots and covers in a lobed base, incised "B" and script mark, some damage and repair.
ca. 1800   7in (18cm) wide
$625-750   TEN

A Barr Worcester inkstand, with a mythical serpent handle, painted with feathers between gilt Greek key borders, incised "B" marks, the covers lacking.
ca. 1800-05   7in (18cm) wide
$1,500-2,000   WW

A Flight & Barr Worcester porcelain inkstand, with swan-neck handle, a pounce pot, two inkwells, and a cover, painted with feathers within gilt line borders, incised "B" mark, two covers lacking, wear in gilding, one inkwell cracked in the rim.
ca. 1800   7in (18cm) wide
$750-875   TEN

A pair of Barr, Flight & Barr chocolate cups with covers and stands, painted with colorful feathers, owls on ribbon swags, incised "B" marks and script marks on the covers and stands, one cup broken and cleanly repaired.
ca. 1810   6½in (16.5cm) high
£1,700-2,200   WW

A pair of Flight, Barr & Barr vases, painted by Thomas Baxter, with a sitting Classical lady, one with a script mark in brown enamel.
ca. 1815   3½in (9cm) high
$1,900-2,500   WW

A Chamberlain Worcester plate, "Princess Charlotte" pattern, border probably painted by George Davis with exotic birds, black script mark with a foliate cartouche.

Princess Charlotte Augusta was the only legitimate child of George IV and ordered a service of this pattern to celebrate her marriage to Prince Leopold of Saxe-Coburg-Saalfield. She died in childbirth in November 1817 and was greatly mourned by the family and public alike. In 1814, she had appointed Chamberlain as her porcelain manufacturer and was a significant patron, ordering several services in the three years before her death, including this one, which included some 144 plates alone.

ca. 1816-17   *9¼in (23.5cm) diam*
$190-250   **WW**

A Flight, Barr & Barr basket, painted with a girl carrying a basket along a clifftop path, with seagulls and boats behind her, titled beneath "The Fisherman's Daughter," on four paw feet, script factory mark.

ca. 1825   *9¾in (25cm) wide*
$500-625   **WW**

A pair of Flight, Barr & Barr ewers and covers, the covers painted with flowers, including tulip, rose, and convolvulus, finials formed as a sitting sphinx, script marks, one cover restored.

ca. 1825   *5¼in (13.5cm) wide*
$875-1,000   **WW**

A late-19thC Royal Worcester nautilus vase, gilt decorated with a lizard.

8¾in (22cm) high
$190-250   **WHP**

A Royal Worcester Aesthetic Movement tazza, with a swallow among bullrushes.

1874   *7in (17.5cm) high*
$190-250   **WHP**

A Royal Worcester vase and cover, shape no. 1481, decorated by Edward Raby, with a floral design, signed "ER," printed marks, the finial reattached.

1892   *18½in (47cm) high*
$700-800   **WW**

A Royal Worcester vase, "Ivory Blush," with floral sprays.

1898   *15½in (39.5cm) high*
$250-310   **WHP**

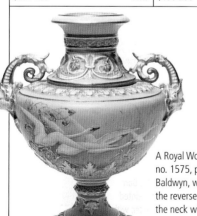

A Royal Worcester vase, shape no. 1575, painted by Charles Baldwyn, with four swans in flight, the reverse with swallows in flight, the neck with foliate scrolls, the handles issuing from mythical masks, signed, printed mark, cover lacking.

1901   *8¾in (22cm) high*
$5,000-6,200   **WW**

A Royal Worcester vase, painted by Charles Baldwyn, with swans in flight, signed, repaired.

1901   *6¼in (16cm) high*
$2,000-2,500   **CHOR**

PORCELAIN

ESSENTIAL REFERENCE—ROYAL WORCESTER

Evolving from a long series of Worcester porcelain factories (see pages 35 and 38), Royal Worcester was formed in 1862. Best known for its vases and figures, it survives to this day.

● In 1902, when the nearby Grainger porcelain factory (see page 38) closed, many of Grainger's employees transferred to Royal Worcester. They included a number of highly skilled painters, notably the Stinton family.

● In 1905, Royal Worcester purchased the Hadley factory— Hadley had become the chief modeler at Royal Worcester in 1870 before setting up his own studio in 1875 and then his own factory in 1897. In 1906, the Hadley workforce, molds, and designs were moved to the Royal Worcester factory.

● In the 1920s and 1930s, Royal Worcester experienced financial problems and was largely kept afloat by the collector Charles Dyson Perrins, who bought the company in 1934 and became its chairman.

● Having become a public company in 1954, and come under common ownership with Spode in 1976, the Royal Worcester brand was purchased in 2009 by the Portmeirion Pottery and its factory in Severn Street, Worcester, was closed.

A Royal Worcester vase and cover, shape no. 1572, painted by R. T. Rea with four swans in flight, scroll handles with mask terminals, signed, puce mark.
1908   *12in (30.5cm) high*
$3,700-4,300   **HT**

A Royal Worcester porcelain vase, by William Powell, painted with cranes watering at a desert oasis, signed, printed mark in puce, minimal surface wear and scratching.
ca. 1909   *9in (23cm) high*
$2,200-2,700   **TEN**

A Royal Worcester porcelain vase, by Harry Stinton, painted with highland cattle in a misty landscape, signed, printed mark in green, minor surface wear.
1909   *6in (15cm) high*
$625-750   **TEN**

A Royal Worcester porcelain vase, by Harry Davis, painted with sheep in a misty landscape, signed, printed mark in green, minor surface wear.
1909   *5½in (14cm) high*
$875-1,000   **TEN**

A Royal Worcester porcelain ewer, by John Stinton, painted with highland cattle in a misty landscape, signed, printed mark in puce, minor surface wear.
1910   *9¾in (25cm) high*
$1,500-2,000   **TEN**

A pair of Royal Worcester porcelain vases, by Ernest Barker, painted with sheep in misty landscapes, signed, printed marks in puce, minor surface wear.
1912   *3¼in (8.5cm) high*
$750-875   **TEN**

A Royal Worcester urn and cover, shape no. 2366, painted by Harry Stinton, with highland cattle, signed, puce mark.
1912   *8½in (21.5cm) high*
$800-950   **HT**

A pair of Royal Worcester vases, shape no. 1410, painted by Walter Powell with two storks at an oasis in a landscape, signed, puce mark.
1912   *11¼in (28.5cm) high*
$1,700-2,200   **HT**

A Royal Worcester porcelain coffee cup and saucer, by Harry Stinton, painted with highland cattle in a landscape, signed, printed marks in puce, minor surface wear.
1916-17
$250-310   **TEN**

A Royal Worcester porcelain vase, by John Stinton, painted with highland cattle in a landscape, signed, printed mark in puce, minimal surface wear.
1919   *6in (15cm) high*
$1,250-1,700   **TEN**

A Royal Worcester cabinet cup and saucer, decorated with fruit, cup signed "H. Everett."

5¾in (14.5cm) diam

$625-750 **WHP**

A Royal Worcester porcelain vase, by John Stinton junior, painted with highland cattle in a misty landscape, signed, printed mark in puce, possibly originally with cover, minimal surface wear and scratching.

ca. 1920 *8½in (21.5cm) high*

$1,700-2,200 **TEN**

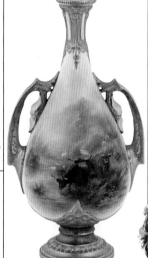

A Royal Worcester porcelain twin-handle vase, by John Stinton Jr., painted with highland cattle in a misty landscape, signed, printed mark in puce, pinhead-size area of gilding missing from upper rim, some minimal surface wear and scratching.

ca. 1929 *10¼in (26cm) high*

$1,500-2,000 **TEN**

A Royal Worcester porcelain vase, by Harry Stinton, painted with cattle in a highland landscape, signed, printed mark in puce, minor surface wear.

1924 *4¾in (12cm) high*

$450-550 **TEN**

A Royal Worcester porcelain bottle vase, by Harry Stinton, painted with highland cattle in a misty landscape, signed, printed mark in puce.

1926 *5½in (14cm) high*

$625-750 **TEN**

A matched pair of Royal Worcester dishes, by Harry Ayrton and John Freeman, painted with fruit on a mossy bank, signed, printed marks in puce and black, minimal wear.

1928 and later *7in (18cm) wide*

$1,250-1,700 **TEN**

A Royal Worcester shallow dish, decorated with ripe fruits, signed "Freeman."

6¾in (17cm) wide

$750-875 **WHP**

A Royal Worcester dish, painted by Thomas Lockyer, signed, printed mark in puce, minimal surface wear.

1931 *12½in (32cm) wide*

$3,100-4,300 **TEN**

A matched pair of Royal Worcester porcelain dishes, by Reginald Austin and Horace Price, printed marks, some surface wear, one with adhesive plate hanger on reverse, with scratches.

ca. 1932 *10¾in (27.5cm) wide*

$3,100-3,700 **TEN**

A Royal Worcester dish, by Thomas Lockyer, signed, printed mark in puce, hairline crack in rim, minor crazing, small crack in the apple.

1932 *12½in (32cm) wide*

$2,200-2,700 **TEN**

A rare pair of Samuel Alcock porcelain hedgehogs, with rough clay spines.

See D. G. Rice, "English Porcelain Animals of the 19th Century," Antique Collectors Club (1981), page 173, where he describes hedgehogs in porcelain as very rare.

ca. 1835   *3in (7.5cm) wide*

$3,700-4,300   **WW**

A Baddeley-Littler porcelain leaf-shaped pickle dish, minor surface wear, one misfired glaze bubble on the handle, another on the reverse rim.

ca. 1785   *4½in (11.5cm) wide*

$800-950   **TEN**

A late-18thC Buen Retiro figure of a Chinese sage, Chinese characters written on a tablet he holds to his chest, blue fleur-de-lis mark, some faults.

9¾in (24.5cm) high

$625-750   **WW**

A Caughley blue-and-white plate, "Bridge and Windmill" pattern, blue "S" mark, broken and reattached.

Founded in Caughley, Shropshire, in the 1750s as the Salopian China Manufactory, Caughley produced soft-paste porcelain until it was purchased by the Coalport factory in 1799. Pieces included a range of tableware, homeware, and miniature "toys," primarily in blue and white, but occasionally with gilded or enameled decorative details, with designs essentially emulating Chinese porcelain, but also with a French influence in later decades. The "Bridge and Windmill" pattern on this plate is one of Caughley's best-known patterns—others being "Fisherman" and "Willow," both of which were later adopted by other factories, including Worcester.

ca. 1780   *9in (23cm) diam*

$190-250   **WW**

A Caughley blue-and-white spoon tray, "Bright Sprigs" pattern, impressed "Salopian" mark.

ca. 1782-92   *6¼in (16cm) wide*

$250-370   **WW**

A Caughley blue-and-white coffeepot and cover, "Rock and Willow" pattern, "S" mark, some chipping.

ca. 1775   *9in (23cm) high*

$1,900-2,500   **WW**

A Coalport vase and cover, probably painted by William Cook, with flower sprays, including lily, dahlia, auricula, lilac, and rose, the neck and shoulders draped with gilt rope twists, blue "CBD" monogram marks for Coalbrookdale.

ca. 1850   *15½in (39.5cm) high*

$1,900-2,500   **WW**

A garniture of three Coalport vases, painted, possibly at Mansfield, with a landscape scene in sepia monochrome, with further landscape panels within formal gilt borders on a yellow ground, the pair of smaller vases similarly decorated, some restoration on the cover.

ca. 1800-20   *10¾in (27.5cm) high*

£1,800-2,400   **WW**

A late-19thC Coalport part dessert service, each piece painted with a centered gilt medallion and a Scottish landscape, comprising 18 plates and a pair of tazza, stamped "ENGLAND COALPORT A. D. 1750."

8¾in (22cm) diam

$800-950   **L&T**

A pair of 20thC Coalport porcelain bowls, decorated with still lifes of fruit on a mossy bank, on three scroll feet, printed marks in blue.

10¾in (27cm) diam

$450-500   **TEN**

A Copeland ewer, attributed to Daniel Lucas Jr., of oenochoe form, painted with Italianate landscapes, the handle issuing from female masks, green printed mark, body crack on one side.

ca. 1850   15¼in (38.5cm) high

$2,500-3,100   **WW**

A rare 19thC Copeland butter tub, cover, and dish, copying the 1771 Sèvres service for Madame du Barry, decorated with "DB" monograms in gilt and flowers, the rims with vases and flowers, probably painted by Charles Bayford Brough, blue "CB" monograms, pseudo Sèvres marks, gilt marks for Thomas Goode & Co, paper labels for Grand Prize, Paris 1889.

Copeland produced, through Thomas Goode, specific commissions that sometimes included reproductions of known Sèvres services. These usually featured the interlaced "L" mark seen on the butter tub here.

10½in (26.5cm) wide

$375-500   **WW**

A 19thC Royal Copenhagen biscuit porcelain figure of Mercury, after the 1818 statue by Bertel Thorvaldsen, blue waves mark.

11in (28cm) high

$450-550   **WW**

A late-19thC Fischer & Mieg Bohemian plaque or tray, painted with a German scene of a couple introducing their baby to two ladies, signed "C Bauer," titled beneath "Der Besuch [The Visit], F. Defregger," impressed "F&M" mark.

Franz von Defregger's painting "The Visit" was executed ca. 1875 and is displayed at the Neue Pinakothek in Munich.

12in (30.5cm) diam

$500-625   **WW**

A miniature Cozzi figure of a lady, probably emblematic of the Arts, the base broken and reattached.

ca. 1775   2¾in (7cm) wide

$450-550   **WW**

A Doccia soup plate or shallow bowl, "Tulipano" pattern.

ca. 1775   9¼in (23.5cm) diam

$250-370   **WW**

A Du Paquier teabowl and saucer, painted in sepia monochrome, restoration.

ca. 1725-30   5in (12.5cm) diam

$190-250   **WW**

A German porcelain figure of a Turkish boy with small dog, possibly Frankenthal, iron red loop mark, has been off at the ankles and glued.

ca. 1770   4½in (11.5cm) high

$300-450   **DN**

A Höchst figure of Mars, modeled in warlike pose, left in the white, blue wheel mark, incised letters.

ca. 1765   5¼in (13.5cm) high

$250-370   **WW**

A Limbach figure of a harpist, "LB" monogram mark, slight wear in enamels.

ca. 1780   4¾in (12cm) high

$375-500   **DN**

PORCELAIN

A Ludwigsburg porcelain teacup and saucer, painted with landscapes, crowned interlaced "C" in underglaze blue, saucer with rim chip, flake and large chip on foot rim.
ca. 1760
$120-190   **TEN**

A Ludwigsburg figure of a woman with pheasant, blue interlaced "C" mark, woman's neck and the neck of the pheasant restored.
ca. 1770   *6½in (16.5cm) high*
$375-500   **DN**

A Ludwigsburg figural group of a courting couple, sitting beneath a tree, the tree broken off and reattached, some chipping in his hat.
ca. 1770   *8¾in (22cm) high*
$500-625   **WW**

A Mennecy pitcher, painted with floral bouquets, including tulip and rose, the crabstock handle issuing from applied berries and leaves, incised "DV" mark.
ca. 1760   *5in (13cm) high*
$875-1,000   **WW**

A pair of Minton porcelain moon flasks and covers, in Chinese cloisonné style, one with faint impressed marks, some cracks.
ca. 1880   *14½in (37cm) high*
$1,000-1,250   **TEN**

A pair of Minton vases and covers, painted with roses, vetch, and sweet pea, impressed marks and date codes.
1869   *13¼in (33.5cm) high*
$1,000-1,100   **WW**

Judith Picks

I picked out this plaque because it is a very impressive example of the pâte-sur-pâte (or "paste-on-paste") technique, which, used in China in the 18thC, was introduced to Europe in the mid-19thC. Pâte-sur-pâte involves gradually building up the design in layer upon layer of slip to stand in low relief against a flat ground, then carving it to resemble a cameo and finally glazing it for protection. Although multicolor examples were produced, most are just two colors, usually white on a darker ground. This white on olive green plaque was designed and made for Minton by the French-born porcelain artist Marc Louis Emmanuel Solon (1835-1913). After studying at the École des Beaux Arts in Paris, Solon began his career at the Sèvres factory. In 1870, during the Franco-Prussian War, he moved to Stoke-on-Trent, England, and joined Mintons Ltd., where he became a leading exponent of pâte-sur-pâte. In terms of both subject matter and style, Solon drew primarily for inspiration on Classical Greek and Renaissance sculpture, as well as 17thC and 18thC paintings. As can be easily imagined from this example, his work commanded high prices in the late 19thC, as it does today.

A pair of Minton pâte-sur-pâte vases and stands, by Marc Louis Solon, enameled with putti courting, the narrow panels with flowers inscribed "Passionnement," "Pas de tout," "Beaucoup," and "Un Peu," on an ivory ground within gilt borders, by Alfred Evans and J. Marrow, signed "M L Solon" on one panel and "L Solon" on another, each signed underneath "J Marrow & A Evans," the bases with gilt factory marks and marked "Manufactured for Phillips," green "SMS" monogram.

1889   *9¾in (24.5cm) high*
$25,000-31,000   **WW**

A Minton pâte-sur-pâte plaque, by Marc Louis Emmanuel Solon, worked in white slip on an olive ground, centered on Cupid standing at an anvil flanked by a kneeling solider and maiden of Classical antiquity, and further flanked by six putti, minor firing flaws and surface wear.
1872   *14¼in (36cm) wide*
$5,500-7,000   **TEN**

A Paris cabinet plate, of Egyptian interest, probably decorated by Dagoty, in sepia monochrome, with two figures sitting before the Medinet Habu temple of Ramesses III at Thebes, titled in gilt on the underside "Temple de Thèbes à Médjinet-âbou."

The scene on the plate derives from Vivant Denon's drawing of 1799, published in 1802, depicting figures before the temple.
ca. 1805   *8¾in (22cm) diam*
$2,500-3,700   **WW**

A Dagoty Paris porcelain cabinet plate, of Egyptian interest, painted in sepia monochrome, with two figures standing at the foot of the Sphinx of Gaza, titled "Le Sphinx" in gilt on the underside, "Dagoty à Paris" mark.

The scene on this plate derives from Vivant Denon's print of the Sphinx being measured by members of the Academy of Egypt.
ca. 1805   *8¾in (22cm) diam*
$1,900-2,500   **WW**

A Dihl et Guérhard Paris porcelain plate, painted with a shepherdess wading through a stream and carrying a lamb, with other sheep and goats beside, signed "Duchesne," printed black mark, small rim chip.

ca. 1800   9½in (24cm) diam

$700-800   WW

A Plymouth putto figure of "Autumn," wearing a grapevine diadem, possibly later decorated, heavily peppered.

ca. 1770   5½in (14cm) high

$700-800   WW

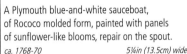

A Plymouth blue-and-white sauceboat, of Rococo molded form, painted with panels of sunflower-like blooms, repair on the spout.

ca. 1768-70   5¼in (13.5cm) wide

$700-800   WW

A Plymouth figure of a female musician, with flowering branches and playing the mandolin, restored.

ca. 1770   6in (15cm) high

$375-500   WW

A Plymouth figure of "Europe," from the "Four Continents" series, modeled as a Classical maiden standing before a horse and trophies of war, some restoration.

This series was first produced at Vauxhall and is thought to have been brought to Plymouth by the former Vauxhall mold maker named Hammersley.

ca. 1768-70   13in (33cm) high

$2,200-2,700   WW

A Plymouth figure of "Asia," from the "Four Continents" series, modeled as a Classical maiden standing before a recumbent camel, some restoration.

ca. 1768-70   12½in (32cm) high

$2,200-2,700   WW

A Plymouth coffeepot and cover, painted with flowering branches, some restoration on the cover.

ca. 1770   9½in (24cm) high

$750-875   WW

A Plymouth salt or sweetmeat stand, on a bed of seaweed, coral and further shells around a coral spray in the center, gilt tin mark, some small faults.

ca. 1768-70   8½in (21.5cm) wide

$750-875   WW

A 19thC Prague figure of a beggar musician, after J. J. Kändler's model at Meissen, impressed "Prag" mark.

5in (12.5cm) high

$190-250   WW

A pair of late-19thC Samson pigeon bonbonnières, after Meissen, the hinged metal mounts each decorated with a coat of arms, pseudo blue crossed swords mark on one, one restored.

2in (5cm) high

$250-370   WW

A Samson porcelain armorial punch bowl, decorated in 18thC Chinese style, slight wear on gilding.

11¾in (30cm) diam

$450-500 — CHEF

A 19thC Samson famille rose eggshell porcelain ruby-backed dish, copying a Yongzheng original, finely painted with a beautiful young woman sitting amid vases and antiques attended by two boys, the border with three floral panels on a pink cell ground.

8in (20.5cm) diam

$1,000-1,100 — WW

A 19thC Samson Imari five-piece garniture, in Japanese style, decorated with birds in flight in peonies and chrysanthemums.

18¼in (46.5cm) high

$3,100-4,300 — WW

A Union Porcelain Works ice water pitcher, designed by Karl L. H. Muller, printed marks and incised "UPW," wear in gilding.

A pitcher of the same model is in the collection of the Metropolitan Museum of Art, New York, and another is in the collection of the Brooklyn Museum, New York.

ca. 1876   9¾in (24.5cm) high

$7,500-8,500 — DOY

A Spode porcelain pastille burner, pattern no. 1166, painted with flowers, painted marks in red, minor wear in gilding.

ca. 1815   4¼in (10.5cm) high

$700-800 — TEN

A late-19thC American Union Porcelain Works New York glazed and biscuit porcelain "Century Vase," molded with a profile portrait of George Washington, with bison-head handles, black specking in biscuit areas.

Designed by Karl L. H. Mueller, the "Century Vase" was created for the U.S. Centennial Exhibition in Philadelphia in 1876.

12¾in (32.5cm) high

$7,500-8,500 — DOY

ESSENTIAL REFERENCE—VAUXHALL

In ca. 1752, Nicholas Crisp established a small porcelain factory in Vauxhall, London.

- **Vauxhall's primary output was blue-and-white porcelain, its forms and decoration being influenced by Chinese export porcelain and Meissen wares.**
- **Vauxhall's underglaze blue can often look inky, wet-looking, and smudged.**
- **The factory also experimented with polychrome glaze printing, and all glazes may sometimes be "peppered" in appearance.**
- **The Vauxhall factory closed in 1764.**

A Vauxhall porcelain saucer, painted in Chinese Imari style, with a figure crossing a bridge in a river landscape, minor surface wear.

ca. 1755   4¾in (12cm) diam

$300-450 — TEN

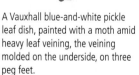

A Vauxhall blue-and-white pickle leaf dish, painted with a moth amid heavy leaf veining, the veining molded on the underside, on three peg feet.

ca. 1755-58   3¼in (8.5cm) wide

$625-750 — WW

A Vauxhall blue-and-white bowl, painted with a Chinese figure fishing from a sampan, in a landscape scene, two foot rim chips.

ca. 1755-60   5in (12.5cm) diam

$625-750 — WW

A Vauxhall blue-and-white teabowl and saucer, painted with a European gentleman and his companion sitting beneath a tree beside a three-bar gate, with birds in flight, some chipping in the teabowl's foot rim.

ca. 1758-60   4½in (11.5cm) diam

$4,300-5,000 — WW

A Vauxhall blue-and-white plate, painted with a peony spray beneath a weeping willow, rim chip.

ca. 1756-60   *8¾in (22cm) diam*

$700-800   **WW**

A Vauxhall blue-and-white cream pitcher, painted with a Chinese boy offering a flower to a Chinese lady carrying a tray.

ca. 1756-64   *3in (7.5cm) high*

$1,250-1,600   **WW**

A Vienna porcelain campana vase, painted with "Diana Im Barde" and other Classical figures, titled in red, printed marks in blue, minimal gilt wear.

ca. 1900   *21¼in (54cm) high*

$5,000-6,200   **TEN**

A pair of Vienna porcelain vasiform vases, painted with Classical figures, one with a finial reglued, both with gilt wear.

ca. 1890   *9¾in (25cm) high*

$1,000-1,250   **TEN**

A pair of Vienna covered vases, decorated with Classical scenes.

14in (35.5cm) high

$1,700-2,200   **WHP**

A Vienna vase or tureen and cover, the porcelain ca. 1805, later decorated with mythological scenes, the cover with scenes of putti, titled on base "Ravissement de Helena" and "Enlevement d'Europe," blue shield mark, some staining on the cover.

15¾in (40cm) wide

$1,250-1,900   **WW**

An English porcelain blue-and-white sauceboat, attributed to Wirksworth, painted with Chinese riverscapes.

Founded ca. 1772 in Wirksworth, Derbyshire, the small Wirksworth ceramics factory traded until 1777, when the building, raw materials, molds, and finished wares were sold off. During its brief existence, it produced both earthenware and porcelain of a bone ash composition, with decoration of the latter, such as on the sauceboat here, mostly decorated with fashionable Chinese scenes rendered in underglaze blue.

ca. 1775   *7¾in (19.5cm) wide*

$1,250-1,700   **WW**

An English porcelain figure of a lion, his thick mane detailed in crumbed clay, impressed "347" on the base.

ca. 1820-30   *4in (10cm) high*

$700-800   **WW**

An English porcelain plaque, in Thomas Bott style, painted in Limoges enamels, with a bust portrait of a girl after Jean Baptiste Greuze, some surface scratching.

Having worked in Birmingham in a glass factory and as a portrait painter, Thomas Bott joined the Worcester factory in 1852, where he developed the technique of imitating Limoges enamels on porcelain. His work was exhibited at the 1855 Paris Exposition and the 1862 London International Exhibition.

ca. 1860   *9½in (24cm) high*

$1,250-1,700   **TEN**

An English porcelain antislavery dish, printed with an African woman cradling a child, the molded rim with Biblical verses regarding labor and oppression.

ca. 1830-50   *9¾in (24.5cm) wide*

$625-750   **WW**

THE POTTERY MARKET

Although this is a generalization, the market for pottery made prior to the last quarter of the 19thC appears to be a little more dynamic thus far, post-COVID-19, than its porcelain equivalent. Certainly in the UK, in-person, presale viewings have enjoyed something of a revival in some, albeit not all, auction houses, and in a few places are almost back to pre-COVID-19 levels—perhaps indicating that the desire to look closely, touch, and feel before bidding remains a prerequisite for some, especially "old-school," collectors.

This is not to say that purely Internet viewing and bidding—supported by increasingly clearer photography and faster streaming—are not still expanding (and not just in the pottery market) and have not facilitated a commensurate increase in, for example, cross-Atlantic transactions. The latter, however, is in marked contrast to the trade between the UK and Europe post-Brexit. As Clare Durham at auctioneers Woolley & Wallis observed: "European buyers now find it much more difficult to ship from the UK, so will only put themselves through it for rarities and items they will not be able to find elsewhere; essentially, pricewise, the lower and middle sections of the cross-Channel market have been hit by red tape."

Looking more specifically at the major collecting categories within the market, English delft is performing reasonably well across the board, with a real resurgence in apothecary vessels (drug jars). Interest in Dutch Delft is not as marked, although statement pieces, such as big garnitures, are selling strongly. In contrast, faience has been struggling lately and, post-COVID-19, maiolica has been unpredictable and not what it was—basically, pieces have to be really excellent examples to do well.

Collecting fields performing quietly but steadily, and much the same post- as pre-COVID-19, include creamware, pearlware, Prattware, and transfer-printed wares—with a notable demand in the latter for large chargers and soup tureens. There is a similar continuity of performance with Wedgwood, with the rare dry-bodied stoneware pieces attracting particularly good money. Much the same could be said of stoneware in general, with the top end of that market doing well. In the USA, redware of exceptional quality and condition, and with outstanding provenance, can still command very high prices—for a particularly splendid example, see the Pennsylvania redware charger on page 71. In contrast, prices for mocha ware in the USA have, in general, decreased over the last couple of years, most notably for lower-end and middle-market pieces.

Going forward, Will Farmer at Fieldings Auctioneers recently observed that for a while now in interior design the tide has been turning against Minimalism. One phenomena indicative of this is a revival of a 19thC Victorian decorative convention in which multiple artifacts are displayed in carefully considered groupings—a practice once described as "the art of placement." As Will added: "I"ve seen some new, really splendid multiple-piece displays, ranging from Wedgwood Jasperware to a huge and attention-grabbing pack of sitting Staffordshire spaniels!" In terms of interest and demand, especially among new, younger collectors, this is already proving to have healthy consequences not only for the pre-late-19thC pottery market, but also for pottery produced more recently—see the sections on Decorative Arts (page 514) and Modern Design (page 572).

Top Left: A Staffordshire model of a Medici lion, of Obadiah Sherratt type, base titled "The Roran [sic] Lion," base cracked.

ca. 1825   *13½in (34cm) wide*

$5,500-7,000   **WW**

Above: A Bristol delft plate, "Farmyard" pattern, sponged and painted in shades of iron red, ocher, blue, and manganese with a cockerel and trees, some wear on the rim.

ca. 1730   *8in (20.5cm) diam*

$3,700-5,000   **DN**

POTTERY

ESSENTIAL REFERENCE—ENGLISH DELFT

Production of tin-glazed earthenware was initiated in England ca. 1567 by two emigrant Dutch potters from Antwerp. By the mid-17thC, when the town of Delft in the Netherlands had become the leading European center of, and given its name to, such tin-glazed earthenwares, the English equivalent became best known as "English delft."

● Like it's Dutch counterpart (see page 54), early English delft was largely inspired, in both form and decoration, by Chinese export blue-and-white porcelain, and then gradually acquired its own indigenous imagery and a more extensive polychrome palette.

● In general, English delft decoration is more naive, less formal, and less intricate than Dutch Delft; many aficionados think it often displays a greater freedom of artistic expression than its Dutch equivalent.

● English centers of production included: Aldgate, Southwark, Lambeth, and Vauxhall, in London; Norwich; Bristol; Wincanton; and Liverpool. There were also notable centers beyond the English borders in Glasgow, Belfast, and Dublin.

● The English delft industry thrived, as did Dutch Delft, until the mid-18thC, when it was supplanted by creamware (see pages 59-60).

A Bristol delftware charger, of Bowen type, painted with two ladies walking among buildings beneath a tall tree, faint rim crack.

ca. 1750-70   14½in (37cm) diam
$700-800   **WW**

CLOSER LOOK—A "FAZACKERLY" PALETTE PLATE

The distinctive floral and foliate style of decoration known as "Fazackerly" is recognized as one of the most beautiful in delftware. It is generally accepted that it originated in the 18thC at Samuel Shaw's pottery in Liverpool and was named after Thomas and Catherine Fazackerly, who were recipients of two mugs from the pottery in the late 1750s.

Blue, yellow, and green are core colors of the "Fazackerly" palette and, here, typically play a prominent role at the heart of the floral and foliate composition.

Manganese or, specifically, a dark amethyst purple, often features in the palette, either more prominently, such as in some of the flowers, in the shading of the petals, in the stems and veins of leaves, or, as on this plate, in all three.

Although not always employed in "Fazackerly" decoration, red is part of the "Fazackerly" palette, and when it is used—as in three of the flowers here—it invariably draws the eye and irradiates the greens—the two colors enhancing each other's saturation when in close proximity.

A delftware plate, probably Dublin but painted in the "Fazackerly" palette, the underside with blue leaf tendrils and painter's numeral 4.

ca. 1750-60   9in (23cm) diam
$1,200-1,500   **WW**

A Brislington delftware dish, painted with a large bird standing on a grassy hillock with trees, the underside decorated with a buff lead glaze.

ca. 1690-1710   8¾in (22cm) diam
$1,400-1,900   **WW**

A Bristol delftware charger, painted with figures in a boat being punted along a river before a long building and beneath trees.

ca. 1760   13in (33cm) diam
$375-450   **WW**

A delftware plate, probably Bristol or Liverpool, painted with a Chinese warrior figure.

ca. 1760-70   12in (30.5cm) diam
$250-370   **WW**

A delftware charger, "La Pêche" pattern, Dublin or Liverpool, painted with a lady fishing and watched by a figure beneath an archway, a rim section broken and reattached.

ca. 1770   16¼in (41.5cm) wide
$375-450   **WW**

A delftware charger, Dublin or Liverpool, painted with peacock feathers in a vase beside a chrysanthemum bloom and flowering prunus, rim crack.

ca. 1760   16¼in (41.5cm) wide
$375-500   **WW**

A delftware charger, probably Lambeth, painted with flowering plants and rockwork beside an ornamental fence, restored.

ca. 1780   14¼in (36.5cm) diam
$250-370   **WW**

A delftware puzzle jug, probably Lambeth, inscribed "Here Gentleman Come try your skill, I'le hold a wager if you will, That you Don't Drinke this liquor all, Without you spill or lett some Fall."

ca. 1740-60   7¼in (18.5cm) high
$700-800   **WW**

A Liverpool delftware tile, painted with swans and a harborside scene, later mounted on a wood board.
ca. 1750-75   *5¼in (13.5cm) wide*
$250-370   **WW**

A pair of delft armorial plates, possibly Liverpool, decorated with a crest, losses in the enamel, niggles around the rim, pitting in the glaze.
ca. 1730   *8½in (21.5cm) wide*
$1,500-2,000   **CHEF**

A Liverpool delftware tile, painted with a lady sitting before a stone balustrade, mounted on a later wooden board, restoration in one corner.
ca. 1755-75   *5in (12.5cm) wide*
$1,050-1,200   **WW**

An English delft punch bowl, probably Liverpool, inscribed in blue "Success to the British Arms," glaze chips, crack in the rim and foot rim.
ca. 1760   *10¾in (27.5cm) diam*
$1,900-2,500   **TEN**

A pair of delftware plates, "La Pêche" pattern, Liverpool or Dublin, painted with a lady fishing and watched by a figure beneath an archway, small filled chips.

This design, commonly seen on Caughley and Worcester porcelains, is copied from a design by Jean Pillement, engraved by P. C. Canot and published in 1759. It was then published in the second edition of "The Ladies Amusement" the following year.
ca. 1770   *7in (18cm) wide*
$550-700   **WW**

A pair of delftware chargers, probably Liverpool, painted with flowering peony issuing from holey rockwork.
ca. 1760   *13¾in (35cm) diam*
$210-275   **WW**

Two London delftware manganese bin labels, of coat hanger form, one inscribed "CONSTANCIA," the other "MADEIRA."

Constantia was a South African dessert wine that was widely exported to Europe during the 18thC and 19thC. It is referenced in Jane Austen's *Sense and Sensibility*, when Mrs. Jennings recommends a glass of "finest old Constantia wine" to cure Marianne's broken heart.

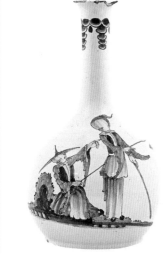

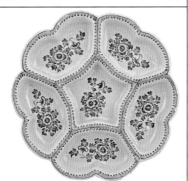

An English delft guglet or water bottle, probably Liverpool, painted with two chinoiserie figures and flowers, with chips and glazed fritting.
ca. 1760   *9½in (24cm) high*
$800-950   **TEN**

A London delft pickle tray, probably Lambeth High Street, painted with flowers, small area of old restoration and hairline cracks in rim, glaze flakes.
ca. 1750   *8¾in (22cm) diam*
$500-625   **TEN**

ca. 1770-80   *5¼in (13.5cm) wide*
$3,100-3,700   **WW**

POTTERY

A London delftware plate, with a centered geometric flower-head design, several small rim chips.
ca. 1700　　　　*8¼in (21cm) diam*
$550-700　　　　**WW**

A London delftware charger, painted with a maiden on a rocky outcrop and attended by a young shepherd, beneath a tree and a ruined archway.

The figures are copied from an engraving by Charles Albert von Lespiliez after François de Cuvilliés in "Morceaux de Caprice." See Frank Britton, "London Delftware," Jonathan Horne (1987), page 161, for a similar example and the print it derives from.
ca. 1770　　　　*13½in (34.5cm) diam*
$450-550　　　　**WW**

A London delftware milk tureen or broth bowl and cover, painted with Asian flowers, the interior molded with a pierced straining compartment.
ca. 1690　　　　*11in (28cm) wide*
$1,000-1,100　　　　**WW**

A delftware tulip charger, probably London, painted with tulips and other flowers, glaze chipping on the reverse, retouching on the rim.
ca. 1690　　　　*12¼in (31cm) diam*
$3,700-4,300　　　　**WW**

Two London delftware drug or apothecary jars, painted with a cartouche surmounted by a shell, flanked by putti holding flower stems, one inscribed "UNG. ALB. C.," the other "UNG: CAERUL," some glaze loss and stabilizing.

Unguentum album was an ointment made from white lead, egg white, and oil of roses, used in the treatment of burns. Unguentum caeruleum (The Blue Ointment) was made from mercury, hog's lard, and turpentine and was thought to guard against venereal disease.
ca. 1740-50　　　　*7½in (19cm) high*
$3,700-5,000　　　　**WW**

A London delft drug jar, the body with a vacant winged angel cartouche.
ca. 1700　　　　*7¾in (19.5cm) high*
$625-750　　　　**CHEF**

A London delftware drug or apothecary jar, painted with two peacocks and leaf sprays flanking the head of Apollo, above a cartouche inscribed "C. SALVIAE," beneath with an angel and floral garlands, the base drilled.

Salvia (sage) is high in antioxidants and continues to be used in the treatment of a number of digestive ailments. It is also thought to be effective in counteracting the effects of memory loss and depression.
ca. 1680　　　　*7in (18cm) high*
$7,000-7,700　　　　**WW**

A delftware tile, probably London, painted with a chinoiserie design of a figure in a landscape.
ca. 1750-75　　　　*5in (12.5cm) wide*
$450-550　　　　**WW**

A Vauxhall delftware plate, painted with a basket of fruit and flowers, riveted crack.
ca. 1710-20　　　　*11½in (29.5cm) diam*
$190-250　　　　**WW**

A Vauxhall delftware plate, painted with a flower band within a swagged and tasseled border.
ca. 1720-30 *9in (23cm) diam*
$190-250 **WW**

A delftware plate, with two figures crossing a bridge over a canal lined with trees.
ca. 1760-80 *9in (23cm) diam*
$120-190 **WW**

A pair of delftware plates, painted with flowers on the rim around a centered sprig.
ca. 1770-80 *9¼in (23.5cm) diam*
$150-200 **WW**

A delftware plate, painted with a Chinese lady sitting in an interior.
ca. 1760-70 *7in (18cm) diam*
$300-375 **WW**

A delftware plate, painted with a couple in court dress promenading through a landscape beneath trees, a church visible in the distance, some rim chipping.
ca. 1720-30 *10in (25.5cm) diam*
$190-250 **WW**

A delftware dry drug jar, painted with a cartouche inscribed "E:E,SCORD:C:OP," beneath two putti holding flowers and flanking a shell, glaze flaking and restoration.

Electuary of Scordium (water germander) with opium had a variety of uses in the treatment of diseases, such as smallpox, measles, and other "pestilent" diseases.
ca. 1760 *7½in (19cm) high*
$375-450 **WW**

A delftware flower brick, painted with Asian flowers, restoration on one corner.
ca. 1770 *6in (15cm) wide*
$500-625 **WW**

A mid-18thC delftware Biblical tile, painted with Saul on the road to Damascus, depicted falling from his horse (Acts 9: 3-6), glaze chip on the upper edge.
5in (12.5cm) wide
$250-370 **WW**

An English delftware puzzle jug, inscribed with a poem.
7in (18cm) high
$800-950 **CHOR**

POTTERY

ESSENTIAL REFERENCE—DUTCH DELFT

Dutch potters were making tin-glazed earthenware—originally often in imitation of maiolica (see page 57) from Spain and Italy—as early as the late 15thC. The attribution "Delft" derived from the city that was the most important center of production during the second half of the 17thC, although others included Amsterdam, Delftshaven, Gouda, and Haarlem.

● The industry expanded rapidly from the mid-17thC, when supply-line problems with Asia disrupted the import of Chinese porcelain, and Dutch potters looked to fill the gap in the market. One consequence of this is that the form and decoration of earlier Dutch Delft pieces is often Chinese in style.

● Gradually, however, Dutch Delt developed a style of its own, not only in terms of imagery—such as Biblical scenes, local city and rural landscapes, and European flora and fauna—but also with the addition of colors, such as purple, red, yellow, green, and black to the original blue-and-white palette.

● By the mid-18thC, many Dutch Delft factories had gone out of business, largely due to competition from rapidly expanding European porcelain production, as well as the development of more durable and refined earthenware, notably creamware (see pages 59-60).

A Delft vase, painted with three fan-shaped panels with Chinese figures, trees in landscapes, some repairs on the neck and foot, the cover lacking.
ca. 1660-80   *9¼in (23.5cm) high*
$625-750   **WW**

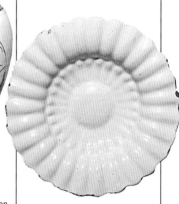

A Delft dish, molded with bands of fluting around a centered well, left in the white, some glaze chipping.
ca. 1680-90   *13in (33cm) diam*
$625-750   **WW**

A Delft lobed dish, painted with a portrait of King William, with the initials "KW," the rim with a border of tulips and other flowers, blue painter's numeral on the base.
ca. 1690   *8¾in (22cm) diam*
$1,600-2,100   **WW**

A Delft plate, with the initials "AC" above the date "1692," within a cartouche of griffins and a mask beneath a crown, rim crack.
1692   *8¾in (22cm) diam*
$750-875   **WW**

A late-17thC Delft charger, painted with Christ upon the cross between sponged trees, two riveted cracks.
14¼in (36cm) diam
$300-375   **WW**

A late-17thC Delft vase, decorated in Chinese Transitional style, with peacocks and other birds, "GK" monogram mark, probably for Ghisbrecht Cruyck, the cover lacking.
6½in (16.5cm) high
$190-250   **WW**

A Delft lobed dish, painted with a Chinese figure, the rim with figures in garden settings.
ca. 1690-1700   *13½in (34cm) diam*
$250-370   **WW**

A Delft dish, decorated in Chinese style, with a figure on the back of a camel, a figure standing beside, in a Chinese island landscape.
ca. 1690-1700   *15¾in (40cm) diam*
$625-750   **WW**

A late-17th/18thC Dutch Delft garniture of five vases and covers, possibly De Dissel or later De Griecksche A, decorated in a chinoiserie manner, the covers with Fo dog finials, painted "D/7" marks, chips, one vase with shoulder cracks.
14½in (37cm) high
$7,500-8,500   **DN**

A mid-18thC Delft charger, painted with two birds flanking a vase of flowers, the rim with five leaf panels, blue "AB" monogram mark.

17in (43cm) diam

$625-750 **WW**

A mid-18thC Delft charger, painted with two finches.

13½in (34.5cm) diam

$300-375 **WW**

A mid-18thC Delft charger, painted with an aquatic bird.

13½in (34.5cm) diam

$150-220 **WW**

A mid- to-late-18thC Delft sauceboat, painted with flower sprigs over faint bianco-sopra-bianco latticework.

7¾in (19.5cm) wide

$200-250 **WW**

Judith Picks

This really is a truly splendid 19thC Delft plaque. The balance of colors from the polychrome palette—dark and pale blues, green, yellow, a burnt red, a manganese brown, and black—is pleasingly harmonious, and the caged-bird subject matter delightful or wistful, depending on your sensibilities. Above all, however, the painter has skillfully achieved a separation of the senses that lies at the heart of the best trompe l'oeil work. Translated from the French as "trick of the eye," trompe l'oeil is a method of decorative painting in which light, shade, and perspective are employed to give flat-painted images a three-dimensional appearance. The technique goes back to Greek and Roman antiquity, and coincidently scrolling acanthus leaf motifs of Classical Roman inspiration appear on the lower side of the cage. That pleasing ambivalence, however, lies in the bigger picture: We can keep confirming by touch that the bird-cage plaque is two-dimensional, yet when we look and look again it remains convincingly three dimensional.

A late-18thC Delft albarello, with a cartouche inscribed "OE SYPI: HUN:," surmounted by a stag, a little chipping.

Oesypus humida is wool fat or lanolin that continues to have a variety of practical uses as a greasing agent, protective coating, and moisturizer.

5¼in (13.5cm) high

$375-500 **WW**

An 18thC Delft jardinière, painted on one side with a figure fishing beneath trees, the reverse with travelers in a landscape, with mask handles, small pierced hole in the base.

5½in (14cm) high

$375-450 **WW**

One of a pair of 18th/19thC Delft or faience tulipières, of fan shape, each with seven separate openings heavily molded with a leaf design, applied with S-scroll handles, some damages.

15¼in (38.5cm) high

$5,500-7,000 the pair **WW**

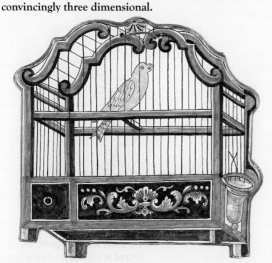

A 19thC Delft trompe l'oeil bird cage plaque, painted with a yellow canary perched within a cage.

10¼in (26cm) wide

$1,100-1,350 **L&T**

A pair of 19thC Delft figures of horses, red "APK" monograms after Koeks, some damages and repairs.

8in (20.5cm) wide

$500-625 **WW**

A Frankfurt faience dish, painted with figures in a Chinese garden setting.

ca. 1670   *13½in (34.5cm) diam*
$210-275   **WW**

A French faience albarello, with a cartouche inscribed "Conf. flor. Urticae" beneath a basket of flowers, base broken out and reattached.

Urtica is the Latin name for the common stinging nettle, which has a variety of medicinal and culinary uses, although the leaves and roots are more commonly used than the flowers.

ca. 1690-1740   *5½in (14cm) high*
$150-250   **WW**

A German faience pewter-mounted tankard, painted with buildings within a crowned foliate scroll cartouche, the pewter cover inscribed "JHG 1778," blue "CCC/P" mark on the base.

1778   *8in (20.5cm) high*
$500-550   **WW**

A German faience pewter-mounted jug or enghalskrug, restoration to the handle, the mount later.

ca. 1690   *12¾in (32.5cm) high*
$140-190   **WW**

A faience dish, probably Portuguese, painted with a bird perched beside a large building.

ca. 1690-1700   *11½in (29cm) diam*
$190-250   **WW**

A mid-18thC Savona faience drug or apothecary jar, inscribed "U. egiptiac," panel on the shoulder enclosing the initials "DR," rim section lacking.

Egyptian ointment contained copper acetate, vinegar, and honey and was used in the treatment of ulcers.

7in (18cm) high
$190-310   **WW**

A mid-18thC French faience dish, painted with a lady in a court dress, flanked by plants, minor chipping.

8¾in (22cm) diam
$250-310   **WW**

A late-19th/early-20thC faience cistern and cover, mounted with two birds, painted with figures sitting at a table, the cover with a cherub.

27½in (70cm) high
$190-250   **CHEF**

ESSENTIAL REFERENCE—MAIOLICA

The term "maiolica" refers to tin-glazed earthenware made in Italy (since at least the 13thC), which distinguishes it from tin-glazed earthenware made in France, Germany, Spain, and Scandinavia, where it is known as "faience" or "fayence," and from tin-glazed earthenware made in the Netherlands, known as "Dutch Delft," and in England, known as "English delft."

● The term "maiolica" is probably derived from the Tuscan name for the island of Majorca, via which Hispano-Moresque wares from Spain were shipped to Italy from the 14thC.

● While unusual and striking shapes are often one of the attractions of Italian maiolica—such as coffeepot-like wet drug jars, urnlike vases, and intricately reticulated plates—the overriding appeal, especially from the 16thC on, resides primarily in the artistic skills of the decorator and the warmth and vibrancy of the palette employed, not the form.

● Favored subjects for decoration included mythical, Classical and Biblical scenes, and portraits, many derived from the works of famous contemporary artists.

A Caltagirone maiolica albarello, painted with flowering branches, on a blue ground between concentric bands, rim crack, some glaze loss.

ca. 1660-80   *10½in (26.5cm) high*
$1,050-1,200   **WW**

A Caltagirone maiolica albarello, painted with a flower garland between bands of scrolling foliage, rim crack.

ca. 1680   *7½in (19cm) high*
$550-600   **WW**

A late-16th/early-17thC maiolica charger, Italian Urbino or French Nevers, painted with Amphitrite and Cupid, reserved on a broad grotteschi ground.

19in (48.5cm) diam
$20,000-25,000   **DN**

An Italian maiolica syrup or wet drug jar, titled "UNG to BASILICO" with a landscape panel, with a double-strap coiled handle, some glaze wear and chipping.

ca. 1700   *8¼in (21cm) high*
$625-750   **WW**

A North Italian maiolica charger, with a putto carrying fruit and standing on a large dog, the rim with a fabric swag design, raised on a low foot.

ca. 1720   *12½in (32cm) diam*
$700-800   **WW**

A pair of 18thC North Italian maiolica wet drug jars, each inscribed, one "Syr:de:Limon," the other "Syrup:de:Cicor.C:Rabnbl," chips on edges and body cracks.

8in (20.5cm) high
$800-950   **DN**

A Montelupo maiolica pitcher, painted with an owl, in a panel on a ground of foliate motifs, with a strap handle and pinched spout, some glaze wear and chipping.

ca. 1500s   *6½in (16.5cm) high*
$1,600-2,200   **WW**

A Montelupo maiolica albarello, painted with Saint Paul with a banner inscribed "Si: Acetoso."

This jar would have contained dried sorrel, which had a variety of uses, including reducing swelling, treating bacterial infections, and as a diuretic.

ca. 1550-80   *6¾in (17.5cm) high*
$625-750   **WW**

A late-17thC Montelupo maiolica charger, painted with a woman standing and winding yarn from a drop spindle, some rim sections broken out and restored.

12½in (32cm) diam
$800-950   **WW**

An Italian maiolica armorial albarello, probably Naples, inscribed in blue with "BENEDETTA. LAX," on a scroll amid leafy branches, above a shield, with a tree and the initials "D I," repaired rim chip.

Benedicta (Benedetta) laxativa is a laxative electuary made from turpeth root and other ingredients.

ca. 1720   *7¾in (20cm) high*

$750-875   **WW**

A late-17thC Savona maiolica albarello, painted with figures in a European landscape, inscribed "Conf: Hamec," the shoulder bearing the initials "F.R," lighthouse mark, some chipping.

Hamech's Confection was a purgative preparation reputedly named after an Arab physician. Among other ingredients, it contained rhubarb, senna leaves, agaric, and colocynth.

8in (20.5cm) high

$375-500   **WW**

A 17th/18thC Sicilian maiolica albarello, painted with a portrait of a saint, with a halo behind his head, some chipping.

10½in (26.5cm) high

$550-700   **WW**

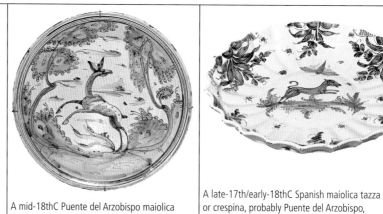

A mid-18thC Puente del Arzobispo maiolica charger, painted with a young deer between trees, short rim crack, chip on the underside.

14¼in (36.5cm) diam

$550-700   **WW**

A late-17th/early-18thC Savona maiolica plate, painted with a putto carrying a tray of fruit within floral sprays, large lantern mark on the underside, a little rim chipping.

12½in (32cm) diam

$375-450   **WW**

A 17th/18thC Sicilian maiolica albarello, painted with a soldier wearing a peaked helmet, reserved on a ground of fruiting branches, repaired chip on the foot rim.

10¼in (26cm) high

$500-625   **WW**

A late-17th/early-18thC Spanish maiolica tazza or crespina, probably Puente del Arzobispo, painted with a dog beneath a large flying insect, on a circular foot, cracked.

12in (30.5cm) wide

$150-220   **WW**

A Seville maiolica pitcher, painted with a figure on horseback blowing a bugle, a long-tailed bird in the horse's path, damages.

ca. 1770-80   *14in (35.5cm) high*

$700-800   **WW**

A 19thC Spanish Manises maiolica plate, painted with tall buildings on a dense foliate ground, drilled in the rim.

8in (20.5cm) wide

$70-100   **WW**

A creamware teapot and cover, possibly William Greatbatch, painted on one side with a stag hunt scene, the reverse with a Chinese figure fishing, the foot, shoulder, and rims with gadrooned decoration highlighted in gilt, some damages and restoration.

ca. 1765-70 *7¼in (18.5cm) wide*

$550-700 **WW**

A William Greatbatch creamware mug, probably enameled in the Leeds workshop of Rhodes & Robinson, with a Chinese figure smoking in a garden and waited on by an attendant, the rim with a cell diaper border in black and red, applied with a large grooved handle, three small chips.

ca. 1770 *6¼in (16cm) high*

$1,000-1,100 **WW**

A late-18thC Staffordshire creamware punch pot and cover, transfer printed by Thomas Fletcher, Shelton, the prints titled "Conjugal Felicity" and "Gretna Green, or the Red-Hot Marriage/Oh! Mr. Blacksmith ease our Ruins/And tie us fast in Wedlocks Chains," one print signed, some restoration.

The firm of Thomas Fletcher & Co. was in business in Shelton, Staffordshire, from ca. 1796-1800.

8¾in (22cm) high

$250-370 **BE**

A commemorative Liverpool creamware pitcher, printed on one side with a figure holding aloft the head of an aristocrat beside a guillotine, titled "The Martyr of Equality," the reverse with four figures outside a tavern, titled "The British Hero or Arts yield to Arms," minor faults.

ca. 1793 *8¾in (22cm) high*

$700-800 **WW**

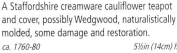

A Staffordshire creamware cauliflower teapot and cover, possibly Wedgwood, naturalistically molded, some damage and restoration.

ca. 1760-80 *5½in (14cm) high*

$300-375 **BE**

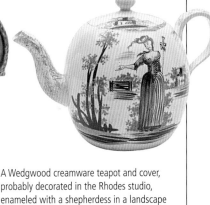

A Wedgwood creamware teapot and cover, probably decorated in the Rhodes studio, enameled with a shepherdess in a landscape with a gate and building, some restoration and glaze spotting.

ca. 1770-80 *6in (15cm) high*

$550-700 **BE**

A Whieldon-type creamware figure of a lioness, sitting on her haunches with her head turned to the right and her tail tucked beneath her body, minor faults.

ca. 1780 *2½in (6.5cm) high*

$200-275 **WW**

A Whieldon-type creamware teapot and cover, the globular body decorated in washed stripes of yellow, green, and manganese.

ca. 1780 *5½in (14cm) wide*

$150-220 **WW**

A Whieldon-type creamware figure of a dog, recumbent on a low base with head turned, an incised "X" on the interior, chip on the base.

ca. 1780-90 *4in (10cm) wide*

$550-700 **WW**

POTTERY

A late-18thC creamware pitcher, "Harvest" pattern, printed on one side with harvesters celebrating before the village inn and giant haystacks, the reverse with a scene of "Faith, Hope and Charity," beneath the spout with the initials "J & C B," some staining, some restoration on the foot.

8in (20.5cm) high

$190-250　　　　　　　**WW**

A late-18thC Masonic creamware pitcher, transfer printed and painted in colors, with the Masonic arms and figures on each side and above, inscribed "the world in pain, the secret to gain of and free and accepted mason," the reverse with a ship and "our ships hearts of oak are our men, we always are ready steady boys steady, we'll fight and we'll conquer again and again."

$300-375　　　　　　　**DUK**

CLOSER LOOK—A CREAMWARE MUG

The satirical imagery refers to the notorious early-19thC "Mary Anne Clarke scandal." A mistress of Prince Frederick, Duke of York and Albany, Mary had been set up by him with a lavish lifestyle he could not afford. The scandal broke when, in 1809, she admitted to the House of Commons that, to make ends meet, she had sold army commissions with his knowledge. Here, she is depicted instructing her servants to burn all the ledgers and contracts that recorded these illegal transactions.

The body of this early-19thC creamware mug benefits from improvements made to the creamware "recipe" during the second half of the 18thC by potters, such as Enoch Booth, Thomas Whieldon, and William Greatbatch, and the entrepreneurial industrialist Josiah Wedgwood; it became significantly stronger, lighter, whiter, and more impervious to liquids than its predecessors.

A creamware mug, printed and hand colored with politically satirical imagery, one long crack.

ca. 1809　　　　　　*5in (12.5cm) high*

$4,500-5,000　　　　　　　**WW**

A commemorative creamware frog mug, printed with a naval engagement scene titled "Lord Nelson engaging the Combined Fleets of Cape Trafalgar," the interior with a large gray-glazed frog climbing up the side, some restoration on the rim and foot.

ca. 1805　　　　*6in (15cm) high*

$500-625　　　　　　　**WW**

An 18th/early-19thC creamware model of a dog, his head cocked to one side, wearing a wide collar, some clean repairs on the base and forelegs.

6in (15cm) high

$250-370　　　　　　　**WW**

A late-18th/early-19thC creamware melon tureen with cover and ladle, the base resting on a large leaf, the cover formed as the upper half of the melon, the ladle of pierced cinquefoil form with a heart-shaped terminal.

9¾in (25cm) wide

$800-950　　　　　　　**WW**

A commemorative creamware mug, after James Gillray, printed in black and hand colored, with a satirical scene of a glutton slicing into roast beef, entitled "British Slavery," flanked by Britannia and a scroll.

Gillray's anti-Gallican cartoon, published by Hannah Humphries on December 21, 1792, contrasted the excesses of the French revolutionaries as compared to the dignity of the Englishman, albeit obsessed by tax. See David Drakard, "Printed English Pottery," Jonathan Horne (1992), pages 168-69.

A creamware revolving inkstand, printed with views, including Warwick Castle.

ca. 1810　　　*5in (12.5cm) high*

$375-500　　　　　　　**CHEF**

ca. 1815

$375-500

5¾in (14.5cm) high

　　　　　　　WW

A commemorative creamware mug, celebrating the coronation of King George IV, printed in black, with a portrait of the King within the inscription "George the fourth, Born Aug 12 1762, Succeeded to the Throne Jan 29th 1819, Crowned July 19th 1821."

1821　　　*3in (7.5cm) high*

$950-1,050　　　　　　　**WW**

A Staffordshire pearlware theatrical character pitcher, possibly Rockingham, modeled as John Liston in his role as Paul Pry, wearing a yellow top hat impressed with his famous line "Hope I Don't Intrude," some restoration on the hat.

ca. 1825-30   *5½in (14cm) high*

$375-450   **WW**

A Staffordshire pearlware figural group of Romulus and Remus, on a titled mound base, with acanthus scrolls.

ca. 1800   *7½in (19cm) wide*

$450-500   **CHOR**

A Staffordshire pearlware bust of John Milton, the poet, with a melancholy expression, wearing a fringed pink robe over a claret jacket with embroidered collar, raised on a socle base, titled on the reverse.

ca. 1810-20   *11½in (29.5cm) high*

$300-450   **WW**

A 19thC Staffordshire pearlware meat dish or charger, printed and colored with a family sitting at a table in a garden, an attendant struggling with a windswept umbrella, within a bold border reserving four panels of flowering plants and four smaller of birds on a rich coral ground.

21¼in (54cm) wide

$1,000-1,100   **WW**

An antislavery pearlware sucrier, probably Wedgwood, bat printed with kneeling figures in chains, with a mother and her baby and verse "This Book teli Man not to be cruel, Oh that Massa would read this Book."

ca. 1830   *6in (15cm) wide*

$450-550   **PW**

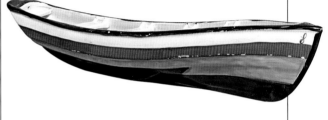

A Yorkshire pearlware model of a "Coble" boat, painted on the exterior with stripes of orange, green, and black, the interior modeled with four seat struts.

"Coble" boats are traditional open fishing boats found on the North East coast of England. Models of this type were thought to have been made for boat owners to display in their windows, advertising their boats for hire. The colors on the model matched those of the boat itself.

ca. 1820-40   *16¼in (41.5cm) long*

$1,900-2,500   **WW**

A late-18thC English pearlware pitcher, inscribed "William Walklate/ One nother Jug and then 1785," painted with floral sprays, star crack, chip on foot rim.

7¾in (20cm) high

$500-550   **BE**

A commemorative pearlware pitcher, printed with a scene entitled "View of La Guillotine or the modern Beheading Machine at Paris, By which Louis XVI late King of France was Beheaded Jan. 21 1793," two figures watching as the King lies prone beneath the blade, chip on the foot rim.

ca. 1793   *6¼in (16cm) high*

$2,500-3,700   **WW**

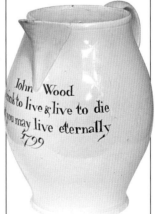

A late-18thC pearlware pitcher, the ovoid body inscribed "John Wood Drink to live & live to die/That you may live eternally/1799."

9½in (24cm) high

$450-550   **CHEF**

A pearlware bust of Voltaire, after the 1718 painting by Nicolas de Largillière, on a waisted and marbled socle, impressed title on the reverse.

ca. 1790-1800   *6in (15cm) high*

$950-1,050   **WW**

A pearlware fox head stirrup cup, naturalistically modeled with ears erect and teeth slightly bared, its features detailed in polychrome enamels.

ca. 1800   6¼in (16cm) long

$2,000-2,500   **WW**

A pearlware wall pocket, of cornucopia form, molded with cattle and goats before a church, some restoration.

ca. 1800   8in (20.5cm) high

$250-370   **WW**

A pearlware puzzle jug, the flattened moon flask body molded with a sun motif, decorated with colorful bands, the neck with three apertures beneath a pierced rim, the handle modeled with a terminal figure, some restoration.

ca. 1800   11½in (29cm) high

$375-500   **WW**

A pearlware fox head stirrup cup, naturalistically modeled with ears laid back and mouth slightly open, a little glaze chipping, faint rim crack.

ca. 1800   5½in (14cm) long

$500-625   **WW**

A pearlware watch stand, modeled as a long-case clock flanked by two figures wearing black crowns, one holding a bunch of grapes, the other a lyre and an orb, the clock case painted with flower sprays, some good restoration.

ca. 1800-10   9in (23cm) high

$190-250   **WW**

An early-19thC pearlware plate, probably Yorkshire, painted in Pratt colors with an urn of flowers.

9¾in (25cm) diam

$190-250   **BE**

An early-19thC pearlware mug, with mocha decoration of black and brown banding, initialed "IL."

4in (10cm) high

$500-550   **BE**

An early-19thC antislavery pearlware nursery mug, printed with verse from a William Cowper poem "Forced from home and all its pleasures, Afric's coast we left forlorn, to increase a stranger's treasures, O'er the raging billows bourne."

2¼in (6cm) high

$2,500-3,100   **PW**

An early-19thC pearlware sponge-decorated model of a chest-of-drawers, possibly Northeast England, repaired.

6½in (16.5cm) high

$4,300-5,000   **DN**

A mid-19thC English blue-and-white pearlware frog mug, transfer printed with a lake scene.

5¾in (14.5cm) high

$120-190   **BE**

A Swansea pearlware cabaret set, comprising a twin-handle oval tray, teapot and cover, sucrier and cover, slop bowl, milk pitcher, and teacup and saucer, painted by William Weston Young, with views of the Marino residence (Vivian family), Swansea Bay and Mumbles in Wales, gilded by Thomas Pardoe, tray repaired, bowl with hairline crack, small chip repair on cover of sucrier.

ca. 1805   tray 15in (38cm) wide

$8,500-10,000   **JON**

A Prattware watch stand, modeled as a long-case clock flanked by a boy and girl, the case molded and enameled in typical palette with Classical scenes, minor faults, with a later Metoda pocket watch.

ca. 1800   *10½in (26.5cm) high*
$700-800   **WW**

A Prattware figure of "Winter," modeled as a boy pulling his cloak about his shoulders, decorated in blue, yellow, green, and ocher.

ca. 1800   *7¾in (19.5cm) high*
$190-310   **WW**

A Prattware plaque, molded in high relief with two recumbent lions, their coats decorated with dots in blue, manganese, and ocher, their manes and tails detailed in brown, the integral frame painted blue.

ca. 1800   *11¼in (28.5cm) wide*
$1,000-1,100   **WW**

A Prattware figure of a lion, recumbent on a low rocky base with head turned, its coat decorated in patches of ocher and brown.

ca. 1800   *4in (10cm) wide*
$300-450   **WW**

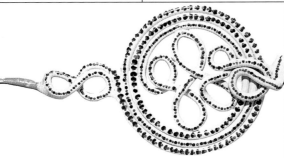

A Prattware novelty pipe, formed of elaborate coils of clay, decorated in blue and ocher dots, some restoration.

ca. 1800   *11¾in (30cm) wide*
$250-370   **WW**

A Staffordshire Prattware oval plaque, with two recumbent lions in ocher and brown glaze, two suspension holes on the top rim, and a later suspension hole near the lower rim.

ca. 1800   *11½in (29cm) wide*
$375-500   **L&T**

A Prattware figure of Flora or "Spring," wearing Classical drapery.

ca. 1800   *9in (23cm) high*
$250-310   **BE**

A Ralph Wood Pratt-type pearlware Bacchus and Pan pitcher, molded with Bacchus holding a cornucopia with a fish-head spout, sitting on a barrel back-to-back with the young Pan, with brown mottled leopard handle, painted in blue, ocher, and green, unmarked.

ca. 1810   *11½in (29cm) high*
$625-750   **HT**

A Dixon Austin & Co. Prattware watch stand, modeled as a long-case clock flanked by two children in Classical dress, the case molded and painted with further figures, decorated in a typical palette of blue, green, yellow, and ocher, impressed mark on the top of the base, small amount of restoration.

ca. 1820   *11in (28cm) high*
$500-625   **WW**

A late-16th/17thC German Frechen stoneware Bellarmine or Bartmannskrug, decorated with three oval roundels of stylized flower heads, the spout applied with a bearded mask.

8¼in (21cm) high

$1,200-1,350 WW

A German Frechen stoneware Bellarmine or Bartmannskrug, applied with a crisply molded stylized floral roundel, the neck with a grimacing face mark.

ca. 1650 *9in (23cm) high*

$500-625 WW

A 17thC German stoneware armorial Bartmann jug or Bellarmine, decorated with a panel with a quartered coat of arms, the neck with a grimacing bearded face mask, repair on the neck.

13in (33cm) high

$700-800 WW

A 17thC German stoneware armorial Bartmann jug or Bellarmine, impressed with a coat of arms, the neck with a mask, chip on the handle, wear, small niggles on the foot rim.

7¾in (20cm) high

$500-625 CHEF

A 17thC German salt-glazed stoneware jug, of "Cardinal Bellarmine" type, molded in relief with a typical Bellarmine mask and three armorial panels.

Salt-glazed stoneware jugs made in Europe in the 16thC and 17thC and bearing at the neck stamped images of the head of a bearded man were widely referred to as "Bartmann" jugs (from the German word "Bartmann," meaning "bearded man"). However, in some quarters, they became known as being of the "Cardinal Bellarmine" type. Always painted with a prominent beard in contemporary portraits, Cardinal Robert Bellarmine (1542-1621) was an Italian Jesuit, a professor of theology, a Cardinal of the Catholic Church, Archbishop of Capua, and the man appointed by the Church to summon Galileo to tell him to desist from promoting the then-revolutionary Copernican theory that the sun, not Earth, was the center of the universe. As a leading advocate of the Catholic or Counter-Reformation, and having been responsible for sending some "heretics" to be burned at the stake, Bellarmine was detested by many Protestants. Accounts of Protestants defiantly and symbolically smashing Bellarmine bottles and jugs after drinking alcohol from them are probably not apocryphal!

19¾in (50cm) high

$7,500-8,500 DN

A German stoneware Bartmannkrug, with bearded face mask, above a circular seal.

16½in (42cm) high

$375-500 CHOR

A London salt-glazed stoneware mug, possibly Fulham or Mortlake, with a cherub riding a lion and hunting scenes, the Sheffield plated rim initialed, cracks and chip on rim.

5¼in (13.5cm) high

$625-750 CHOR

A 19thC Westerwald stoneware jug, incised with formal flower scrolls between checkered borders, with a hinged pewter cover bearing faint inscribed initials.

15in (38cm) high

$120-190 WW

A 19thC stoneware whisky flask, molded with Masonic insignia, inscribed "ALEXANDER MILNE / MILL / OF / ALLOTHAR / UDNY," the neck has been off and glued, losses.

11½in (29.5cm) high

$500-625 CHEF

An early-19thC Staffordshire transfer-decorated covered serving dish, "Highbury College, London," by Adams, Tunstall, with molded handles, lid with molded knop.

11¾in (30cm) wide

$110-150

SK

A James & Ralph Clews blue-and-white transfer-ware meat dish, from the "Indian Sporting" series, after Spode, with figures leashing hounds for the hunt, the rim with exotic animals, impressed mark.

ca. 1818-34   18¾in (47.5cm) wide

$550-700   **WW**

A Thomas & Benjamin Godwin pottery drainer, "View of London," transfer printed with a view of the Thames River and Blackfriars Bridge, a sailing barge and other vessels in the foreground, St. Paul's cathedral beyond.

ca. 1830

13½in (34cm) wide

$700-800   BE

A meat plate, "Bewick Stag" pattern, probably Minton, the border with vignettes of exotic and other animals, rim chips, fritting on rim.

ca. 1820   20½in (52cm) wide

$375-450   **CHOR**

CLOSER LOOK—A TRANSFER-WARE PLATE

Developed in the mid-18thC to replace more time-consuming and expensive hand painting, transfer printing gradually became more sophisticated, especially, as here, in the nuances and gradations of shade in the underglaze blue.

While polychrome decorated pieces were made during this period, most transfer-printed wares were blue and white, partly because they were easier to produce, but also because underglaze cobalt blue was, in contrast to overglaze enamels, the color best suited to withstanding the heat of a pottery kiln.

It was during the Peninsula War (1808-14) that Arthur Wellesley (1769-1852) cemented his military reputation, was elevated to the peerage (Viscount of, and then Duke of, Wellington in, respectively, 1809 and 1814), and became a national hero—a status then further and substantially enhanced by his victory over Napoleon at the Battle of Waterloo (1815).

The plate documents three important battles fought against the French during the Peninsula War: Vimiera (1808) in Portugal, and Talavera (1809) and Albuera (1811) in Spain, the first two under the direct command of Arthur Wellesley.

A small blue-and-white transfer-ware plate, "Lord Wellington and Peninsular Campaign Battles," with centered portrait, the names of three battles, and associated scenery around the rim.

ca. 1811   4½in (11.5cm) diam

$500-625   WW

An Enoch Wood & Sons transfer-ware plate, "The 1812 War with America," for the American market, printed with a naval scene titled "Commodore MacDonnough's Victory," the border with seashells, faint impressed mark on the underside.

Thomas MacDonough was commander of the Lake Champlain squadron and overcame the British navy on September 11, 1814.

ca. 1820-30   7¾in (19.5cm) diam

$100-150   WW

A blue-and-white transfer-ware pitcher, "Duke of Wellington and Lord Hill," printed with named equestrian portraits, flanking a drum and other military trophies, small filled rim chip.

ca. 1814   6in (15cm) wide

$500-625   WW

A transferw-are saucer, "1815 Waterloo," printed with soldiers before the building at Hougoumont, indistinctly named "Waterloo," the border with named and dated portrait medallions of Wellington and Blücher, the underside impressed with an anchor and "F 4 B," small rim chip.

ca. 1815   5¼in (13.5cm) diam

$110-150   WW

POTTERY

A transfer-ware dish, "Queen Caroline," printed with the Royal party on a boat before the Villa D"Este, titled "Her Majesty's Residence on the Lake of Como."

ca. 1820   *4¼in (11cm) diam*

$200-250   **WW**

A transfer-ware pitcher, "1820 Royal Divorce Proceedings," printed on one side with a profile portrait of Queen Caroline, the reverse with a quotation from Shakespeare's "King Henry VIII," Act III, Scene I, the rim with Union flowers.

ca. 1820   *5¾in (14.5cm) diam*

$500-625   **WW**

A pair of transfer-ware plates, "1820 George III In Memoriam," each printed with a portrait, one of George III, the other of Queen Caroline, within borders of rose, thistle ,and shamrock, the Caroline plate chipped and restored.

ca. 1820   *10¼in (26cm) diam*

$450-550   **WW**

A Staffordshire transfer-decorated coffeepot, decorated with an Asian scene and floral motifs.

ca. 1830   *9¼in (23.5cm) high*

$250-310   **SK**

A Staffordshire historical covered vegetable dish, "Landing of Lafayette," large repaired break on base.

11¾in (30cm) wide

$250-370   **POOK**

A Staffordshire historical reticulated bowl and undertray, "Landing of Lafayette."

12¾in (32.5cm) wide

$3,000-3,700   **POOK**

A Staffordshire historical blue platter, "Welcome Lafayette," several small rim repairs.

10½in (26.5cm) wide

$3,200-3,700   **POOK**

A Staffordshire historical blue teapot, "Landing of Lafayette," handle reattached, edge of lid rest ground down, glaze burn on tip of spout.

8½in (21.5cm) high

$1,600-2,500   **POOK**

A Staffordshire historical blue transfer-decorated sugar bowl, "Boston State House."

6in (15cm) high

$120-200   **SK**

A Staffordshire salt-glazed bottle vase, the body sprigged with birds perched on floral branches.

ca. 1740 8½in (21.5cm) high

$750-875 WW

A Staffordshire salt-glazed double-lip sauceboat, of silver shape, the handles with dolphin spouts, molded with panels of flowers, hair crack on rim.

ca. 1750 7in (18cm) wide

$1,200-1,250 BE

A Staffordshire white salt-glazed cream pitcher, molded with panels of figures, birds, animals, and heraldic motifs, faint internal hair crack on base, minor glaze flaws.

ca. 1750-60 3½in (9cm) high

$550-700 BE

A Staffordshire salt-glazed coffeepot and cover, painted with flowers, short rim crack, the cover's finial broken and reattached.

ca. 1760-65 8½in (21.5cm) high

$750-875 WW

A late-18thC Ralph Wood figure of Jupiter, holding a staff on his shoulder, an eagle standing by his foot, impressed "Ra Wood Burslem" on the base, some restoration.

11¼in (28.5cm) high

$550-700 WW

A pair of Staffordshire figures, each modeled as a black-and-white whippet.

7¾in (20cm) high

$9,500-10,500 WHP

A Staffordshire figural group of "The Dandies" or "Dandy and Dandizette," minor damages.

ca. 1800-10 8in (20.5cm) high

$875-1,000 WW

A large Staffordshire spill vase group, with two cattle and figures standing before flowering bocage and flanking a large hollow tree, a musician sitting at the base of the tree playing a flageolet to two ducks, one cow being milked by a figure sitting beside.

ca. 1820 12½in (32cm) wide

$5,000-6,200 WW

A Staffordshire figural group, "Tithe Pig," with three figures beneath bocage, a couple handing a baby and a piglet to the village parson, some restoration.

ca. 1820 7½in (19cm) high

$300-450 WW

A Staffordshire model of a Medici lion, of Obadiah Sherratt type, base titled "The Roran [sic] Lion," base cracked.

ca. 1825   *13½in (34cm) wide*

$5,500-7,000   **WW**

An early- to mid-19thC Staffordshire figural group of a performing animal troupe, with an organ grinder beside a dancing bear, the trainer holding out his hat for donations, some chipping.

Different arrangements of this group exist, sometimes with the inclusion of a monkey on the back of a dog.

6in (15cm) high

$550-600   **WW**

A pair of Staffordshire greyhounds, each with a gilt collar and hare.

9¼in (23.5cm) high

$450-550   **CHOR**

A 19thC Staffordshire model of a sitting nun, after Bow in imitation of Meissen, reading from a Bible, firing dust pickup, restoration on the hands and book, small firing imperfections on the edges.

6in (15cm) high

$300-375   **FLD**

A 19thC Staffordshire model of a cat, both ears restored, firing flaws, scuff marks, some crazed lines.

10¾in (27.5cm) high

$1,100-1,250   **FLD**

A 19thC Staffordshire earthenware fox head stirrup cup, chips, some wear on the enamels.

5½in (14cm) long

$450-550   **BELL**

A 19thC Staffordshire pottery hound head stirrup cup, some flaking on the brown enamel, chip on the rim.

5½in (14cm) long

$150-220   **BELL**

A pair of 19thC Staffordshire pottery lion and lamb groups, each big cat sitting on its haunches with head turned, a small lamb tucked behind its forepaws.

10½in (26.5cm) high

$1,900-2,500   **WW**

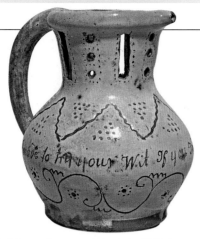

A rare North Devon slipware puzzle jug, incised "This jug I made to try your wit, If you the Licqor out can Geet 1796" between stylized scrolls and zigzag designs, the neck pierced with holes, decorated in a cream slip with small green splashes.

1796   *6¼in (16cm) high*
$2,000-2,500   **WW**

A 19thC Barnstaple slipware cider jug, with flowering sprays on a treacle ground, some glaze loss, surface chip.

12¾in (32.5cm) high
$4,300-5,000   **WW**

A slipware charger, in Thomas Toft style, the center with King William and "God Save The King."

19¾in (50cm) diam
$1,250-1,900   **CHEF**

A Welsh Claypits Pottery slipware dish, decorated in white and brown slips under a lead glaze, with a woodsman wielding his ax, the reverse incised "1882."

1882   *10¼in (26cm) diam*
$190-250   **BE**

A 19thC Welsh slipware pottery miniature chest-of-drawers, attributed to the Buckley Pottery, with six drawers, inscribed "WILLm Hampson 1884."

See J. M. Lewis, "The Ewenny Potteries," National Museums and Galleries of Wales (1982), page 2.

1884   *11in (28cm) wide*
$2,200-2,700   **BE**

An early Donyatt slipware puzzle jug, with sgraffito decoration of stylized tulips and other flowers, inscribed "Fill me full, drink of me while you would" above "1754" and the initials "SW," some glaze loss.

1754   *8in (20.5cm) high*
$1,250-1,700   **WW**

A Donyatt slipware puzzle jug, with sgraffito decoration of stylized tulips and other flowers, inscribed with a two-line stanza and "1790" in two places, the neck pierced with eight small holes, a repair on the spout.

1790   *8¼in (21cm) high*
$1,500-2,000   **WW**

A Donyatt slipware cream pitcher, with sgraffito decoration of birds and stylized motifs, inscribed "1805."

1805   *3½in (9cm) high*
$1,050-1,200   **WW**

A Staffordshire redware teapot and cover, applied on each side with a bird holding a branch in its beak, the cover probably associated.
ca. 1760-70   *6in (15cm) wide*
$150-220   **WW**

An early-18thC Elers-type redware miniature teapot and cover, with leafy branch sprigging.
                                    2¾in (7cm) diam
$625-750   **HT**

An early-18thC Elers-type redware mug, the lower bulbous body with leafy branch sprigging.
                                 3¾in (9.5cm) high
$1,050-1,200   **HT**

An early-18thC Elers-type redware mug, with leafy branch sprigging within turned reeded bands, with contemporary unmarked silver rim.
                           3½in (9cm) high
$750-875   **HT**

An early-18thC Elers-type redware mug, the lower section with leafy branch sprigging, with contemporary unmarked silver rim.
                              3¾in (9.5cm) high
$1,900-2,500   **HT**

An early-18thC Elers-type redware miniature teapot and cover, the cover and body with leafy branch sprigging.

Also called "dry-bodied stoneware," this fine red stoneware was first produced in England in the late 17thC by John Dwight, who patented wheel-thrown red stoneware vessels in 1684. They were copied by the Dutch Elers brothers, who moved to Staffordshire and continued to produce the red stoneware by slip casting until about 1700. There was a hiatus in production between ca. 1700 and ca. 1750, when many Staffordshire potters, including Josiah Wedgwood, began to produce both wheel-thrown and molded dry-bodied stoneware vessels. The engine-turned pieces date from after 1760.
$700-800   **HT**

An elaborate 19thC French redware bowl and cover.
                           10¾in (27.5cm) high
$300-375   **POOK**

A Lester Breininger redware sitting figure of Lester, with lamb and dog.
                           8½in (21.5cm) high
$750-875   **POOK**

A Bucks County, Pennsylvania, redware bowl and cover, attributed to David Haring, the lid with applied fruit, on a reticulated base, with rope-twist handles, several repaired breaks.
ca. 1830   *8¼in (21cm) diam*
$1,000-1,100   **POOK**

A 19thC miniature Pennsylvania redware bowl, with manganese sponge decoration on a green ground, impressed "John Bell" on underside.

3½in (9cm) diam

$1,250-1,700   **POOK**

A 19thC Pennsylvania redware butter tub, minor glaze flakes on rim.

8¾in (22cm) diam

$625-750   **POOK**

A 19thC Pennsylvania redware sitting dog, clutching a basket of fruit in its mouth, incised "18" under base, repaired break on base.

4¾in (12cm) high

$1,900-2,500   **POOK**

A 19thC Berks County, Pennsylvania, redware plate, attributed to Dryville, with multicolor slip tulip decoration, very minor edge flakes.

8in (20.5cm) diam

$1,900-2,500   **POOK**

A 19thC Pennsylvania redware bowl and cover, attributed to John Nice, Montgomery County, with yellow slip dot decoration, a few rim chips.

5¼in (13.5cm) diam

$3,700-5,000   **POOK**

An early-20thC miniature redware pitcher, attributed to Henry Schofield Jr., Rock Springs, Maryland, with stamped snowflakes around the mid-body.

3¼in (8.5cm) high

$550-600   **POOK**

A 19thC Shenandoah Valley redware jar, with mottled glaze, some glaze wear on rim.

4¼in (11cm) high

$1,250-1,700   **POOK**

ESSENTIAL REFERENCE—A 19TH C REDWARE CHARGER

Primarily a utilitarian form of earthenware made from clay with a high iron content that, when fired, turn a reddish-brown color, redware was originally made in Europe, but it became particularly popular in North America, initially during the Colonial era, because such clay was abundant there and the products affordable.

- Being porous, redware needed to be waterproofed for food storage, cooking in, dining on, and drinking from, and typically this was done using lead-based glazes, while decorative imagery was either incised into the clay's surface, sometimes employing a "sgraffitio" technique with a thin layer of slip to reveal the red clay beneath, or applied, using contrasting colors of glaze and slip.
- John Pride, of Salem, Massachusetts, is documented in the mid-17thC as the first American redware potter by name.
- Although redware was mostly supplanted by stronger and more refined stoneware and whiteware during the mid-19thC, production continued into the 20thC, most notably in regions of North Carolina, Virginia, and Pennsylvania.
- The splendid "bird-on-branch," slip-decorated example featured here is Pennsylvanian, dates to the 19thC, and was probably made in one of the Quaker-owned potteries operating in Montgomery and Bucks counties. The considerable price it achieved recently at auction is, of course, explained by the quality of the decoration, and the fact that it's in very good condition (with no evident damage or repairs), but it is also due in no small part to it's historical-cultural importance and provenance—in particular well-documented previous sales at auction from eminent private collections in the 1940s, 1950s, 1990s, and in 2014.

A 19thC Pennsylvania redware charger, with yellow slip bird-on-branch decoration.

13¼in (33.5cm) diam

$31,000-43,000   **POOK**

A Mocha mug, with brown bands, repairs, bottom sprayed.

Mocha refers to a type of slip-decorated earthenware or pearlware originating in late-18thC England and spreading to early North America.

6in (15cm) high

$200-250   **POOK**

An early-19thC Mocha mug, in-the-making base rim chip.

5¾in (14.5cm) high

$550-700   **POOK**

A 19thC yellowware Mocha bowl, with "Seaweed" decoration.

8in (20.5cm) diam

$300-375   **POOK**

A 19thC Mocha pitcher, with marbleized body, handle with staple repairs, small rim flakes on spout, hairline cracks.

7½in (19cm) high

$800-950   **POOK**

A 19thC Mocha bowl, with "Earthworm" decoration, restored.

4¾in (12cm) diam

$100-150   **POOK**

A 19thC Mocha mug, with "Seaweed" decoration and applied crown, some glaze exfoliation.

6½in (16.5cm) high

$190-250   **POOK**

A 19thC Mocha pepperbox, with "Earthworm" decoration, repaired base rim and collar.

4¼in (11cm) high

$875-1,000   **POOK**

A pair of 19thC Mocha pepperboxes, with "Cat's-Eye" decoration, flakes on collar, hairline cracks, base rim firing chip.

4½in (11.5cm) high

$450-550   **POOK**

A Mocha pitcher, several flakes on spout and rim, hairline cracks.

5¾in (14.5cm) high

$250-370   **POOK**

A creamware "Step" Toby jug, with a clay pipe held between his teeth, a foaming jug of ale on one knee, a dog between his feet, restoration.

ca. 1780-85   9½in (24cm) high

$875-1,000   **WW**

A creamware "Step" Toby jug, his clay pipe resting along his right arm, a jug on his left knee, his mouth slightly agape to reveal a missing front tooth, some chipping.

ca. 1780-85   9¾in (24.5cm) high

$1,400-1,700   **WW**

CLOSER LOOK—A RALPH WOOD TOBY JUG

Not all Toby jugs are male! This is Martha Gunn (1726-1815), a famous "dipper"—an operator of a bathing machine, which, being enclosed, allowed for ladies to bathe in the sea while preserving their modesty from potential onlookers.

Martha, who worked as a bathing machine attendant in Brighton from her youth to her late 80s, was a favorite of George Prince of Wales, later Prince Regent and King George IV—hence the Prince of Wales feathers on her hat.

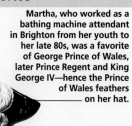

The manganese color splashed on her apron, and also used for her hair and on her hat, is, like the green of her dress, strongly associated with the decorative palette of the Wood family Staffordshire potters: Ralph (1715-72), his son Ralph (1748-95), and his grandson Ralph (1774-1801).

A Wood-type Toby jug, a foaming jug of ale resting on one knee, a repair on his hat.

ca. 1790-1800   9¾in (24.5cm) high

$200-250   **WW**

A creamware Wood-type Toby jug, holding an empty jug titled "ALE," his unusually large hat decorated in manganese, some restoration.

ca. 1790   9¾in (24.5cm) high

$2,500-3,700   **WW**

The origins of the name "Toby" for Toby jugs is ambiguous; it might reference Sir Toby Belch in Shakespeare's "Twelfth Night," or Toby Fillpot, an infamous drinker from the popular 18thC song "The Brown Jug." Either way, and male or, as here, female, all Toby jugs are depicted holding a vessel containing alcohol.

A Ralph Wood Toby jug of Martha Gunn, sitting wearing a hat and an apron over a dress, and holding a gin bottle and glass, raised on a stepped base, some restoration.

ca. 1780   10¼in (26cm) high

$2,500-3,700   **WW**

A Wood-type Toby jug, some restoration on his hat and base.

ca. 1790   10¼in (26cm) high

$625-750   **WW**

A Ralph Wood Toby jug, sitting with an empty round-bellied jug on his knee, his long-stemmed pipe by his right foot, restoration on his hat.

ca. 1790   9¾in (24.5cm) high

$1,250-1,700   **WW**

A Ralph Wood Toby jug, of "Mold 51" type, sitting with a foaming jug of ale and holding a small glass in his right hand, restoration on his hat.

ca. 1790   10in (25.5cm) high

$1,000-1,100   **WW**

POTTERY

A creamware Wood-type Toby jug, with an empty jug on one knee, his clay pipe at his side, some restoration.
ca. 1785-90   *10in (25.5cm) high*
$300-450   **WW**

A rare Prattware Toby jug, "Thin Boy," sitting with a patterned jug resting on his left knee, wearing a striped coat over a yellow vest and ocher breeches.
ca. 1790-1800   *8¾in (22cm) high*
$6,000-7,700   **WW**

A Prattware Toby jug, "Convict," sitting with a foaming jug of ale on his left knee, in typical colors with small arrows on his coat, over a patterned vest, blue breeches, and striped stockings, his cheeks ruddied with ocher.
ca. 1800   *9¾in (24.5cm) high*
$500-625   **WW**

A Prattware Toby jug, sitting with a foaming jug of ale on one knee.
ca. 1800   *9¼in (23.5cm) high*
$220-270   **WW**

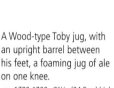
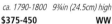

A Wood-type Toby jug, with an upright barrel between his feet, a foaming jug of ale on one knee.
ca. 1790-1800 *9¾in (24.5cm) high*
$375-450   **WW**

An early-19thC Staffordshire pottery Toby jug, the "warty faced" sitting subject clasping a pipe and jug of ale.
9½in (24cm) high
$190-250   **SWO**

An early-19thC pearlware Toby jug, decorated in colored enamels.
9¾in (24.5cm) high
$800-950   **TEN**

A 19thC Staffordshire pottery Toby jug, colored in enamels.
11¾in (30cm) high
$550-700   **TEN**

A pair of late-19thC Minton majolica Toby jugs, one modeled as a man in 18thC dress, impressed marks, numbered "1140," date mark for 1867, the other modeled as a lady holding a fan and wearing a shawl, impressed factory marks, date mark for 1868.
11in (28cm) and
1867 and 1868   11¼in (28.5cm) high
$750-875   **L&T**

A Wedgwood & Bentley black basalt portrait medallion of Augustus, Viscount Keppel, impressed lower case mark.

ca. 1780 4in (10cm) high

$700-800 BE

A late-18th/19thC Wedgwood Jasperware portrait plaque of Captain James Cook, modeled by John Flaxman, titled, impressed mark, in a hardwood frame.

This portrait was modeled by Flaxman in 1784, probably after the Royal Society model by Lewis Pingo. See David Bindman ed., "John Flaxman," Royal Academy of Arts (1979), page 54, no. 28, for more details.

4½in (11.5cm) high

$750-875 WW

A Wedgwood sage Jasperware two-handle vase and cover, vasiform, decorated with Classical figures.

11½in (29cm) high

$375-500 CHOR

A rare Wedgwood gelatin mold and core, the core painted with flowers, impressed mark.

ca. 1790 9¾in (24.5cm) high

$3,100-3,700 CHEF

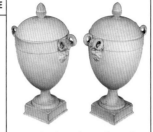

A pair of early-19thC Wedgwood Neoclassical white Jasper vases and covers, with acorn finials and horned Bacchus handles.

9½in (24cm) high

$2,000-2,500 CHOR

A Wedgwood rosso antico vase and cover, with Bacchic mask handles, the sides sprigged with dancing figures.

10¾in (27cm) high

$625-750 CHOR

A late-19thC Wedgwood Jasperware Portland vase, decorated with the myth of Pelius and Thetis, the underside with a portrait of Paris, impressed upper case mark, damage on foot rim.

10¼in (26cm) high

$250-370 BE

Judith Picks

The "Sydney Cove Medallion" is of considerable importance in the history of not only ceramics, but also the beginning of European settlement in Australia, and its origin can be traced back to Captain James Cook's discovery of the continent 1770. Following the American Revolution in 1776, Britain became particularly eager to expand its territories elsewhere, in part to alleviate increasing overcrowding in British prisons. Under instruction from the British government, Captain Arthur Phillip and the "First Fleet" initially landed at Botany Bay in January 1778, and soon after established the first settlement and penal colony on the Australian continent at nearby Sydney Cove (now Sydney Harbour).

In November 1788, Phillip sent samples of minerals and white clay found in the vicinity of Sydney Cove to Sir Joseph Banks—President of the Royal Society, and who had also accompanied Captain Cook in 1770. The minerals were forwarded to various scientists, and the clay to his friend, fellow Royal Society member and entrepreneurial industrialist, Josiah Wedgwood, to investigate its potential for ceramic production.

The medallions made from it were manufactured at Wedgwood's Etruria factory in 1789. Designed by Henry Webber and modeled by William Hackwood, they are molded in bas-relief with Classical scenes depicting "Hope" encouraging "Peace," "Art," and "Labor" to work for the prosperity of the new settlement. The original medallions ranged in color from pale biscuit to, as in the example here, a dark brown, almost black, hue. Two series were produced from the sample: the first was sent to Governor Arthur Phillip in Sydney Cove, while recipients of the second batch included Wedgwood's friend, the physician, philosopher, poet, and slave-trade abolitionist, Erasmus Darwin, whose grandson Charles went on to publish "On the Origin of Species" in 1859.

A rare ceramic "Sydney Cove Medallion," by Josiah Wedgwood, the original issue, modeled from dark brown unglazed earthenware, with Classical figures emblematic of "Hope", "Peace", "Art," and "Labor", on the shores of a bay with ships in the distance, inscribed "ETRURIA/1789" below the scene in raised letters, the reverse impressed "MADE BY/IOSIAH WEDGWOOD/OF CLAY/ FROM/SYDNEY COVE."

1789 2¼in (5.5cm) diam

$60,000-75,000 L&T

A pair of Wedgwood Jasperware vase and covers, "Dancing Hours" pattern, decorated with Classical maidens dancing and holding garlands, with grotesque mask handles, impressed mark on one, one with a break in the pedestal and a chip on the lid, the other with an old break in the handle.

9½in (24cm) high

$625-750 FLD

POTTERY

A Talavera or Puente del Arzobispo pitcher, inscribed "UNICORNIUM," beneath the handle inscribed "1570," some foot chipping and general crazing.

Throughout the 16thC, belief in unicorns was commonplace, and their horns were thought to have magical properties and to guard against poison. Elizabeth I of England had a unicorn horn cup from which to drink. Philip II of Spain had 12. In fact, the horns were probably those of the narwhal.

9¼in (23.5cm) high

$375-500   **WW**

A 17th/18thC Hispano-Moresque luster dish, with a cockerel, small drill hole in the rim.

7¼in (18.5cm) diam

$375-500   **WW**

A large Mexican Talavera de Puebla vase, with stylized eagle motifs, cracked.

ca. 1720   *16¼in (41.5cm) high*

$700-800   **WW**

A commemorative Somerset Donyatt Pottery puzzle jug, incised through yellow slip glaze with stylized leaves and flowers, inscribed with initials and dated, significant areas of glaze flaking.

1789   *8¾in (22cm) high*

$1,900-2,500   **DN**

A pair of late-18thC Scottish glazed pottery spaniels, unmarked.

8½in (21.5cm) high

$375-500   **L&T**

An 18thC pottery fox head stirrup cup.

4¾in (12cm) long

$160-250   **CHEF**

A plaster model of the Portland vase, probably late 18thC, attributed to James Tassie from a mold taken by Giovanni Pichler, molded with figural decoration, the base with a roundel of a figure in a Phrygian cap, the whole decorated in a brown lacquer.

The Italian gem engraver, Giovanni Pichler, took a mold of the Portland vase ca. 1780, which was subsequently used by James Tassie to produce a number of casts. A number of factors date it to the late 18thC. First, the inclusion of the roundel on the base, which was removed in 1786; second, the visible fracture lines that are not present in copies taken after 1845, when the vase was broken and restored. The unevenness of the rim and handles is another feature present in earlier casts and not in the later Wedgwood and 19thC examples.

10in (25.5cm) high

$750-875   **WW**

A silver-mounted Jasperware mug, with four Classical maidens emblematic of the "Four Seasons," the silver mount with hallmarks for Thomas Law, Sheffield, 1796.

ca. 1796   *5in (12.5cm) high*

$450-550   **WW**

A Turner & Co. Jasperware antislavery medallion, with a kneeling chained figure, inscribed "Am I Not a Man and Brother," under a mica covering, impressed mark, broken and restored.

ca. 1805   *1½in (4cm) high*

$1,100-1,500   **WW**

A rare pair of early-19thC Sewell & Donkin Newcastle-upon-Tyne lusterware quintal vases, impressed marks, a few small chips.

7¼in (18.5cm) high

$1,500-2,000   **WW**

A 19thC Jasperware cheese bell and stand, with Classical figures between trees.

10½in (26.5cm) wide

$190-250   **WW**

A Parian bust of Vice Admiral Horatio Nelson (1758-1805), modeled by Joseph Pitts after a drawing by John Whichelo, inscribed under the base "by JOSH PITTS. SC. LONDON 1853 Model'd under the direction of Admiral Sir William Parker K.C.B. from the Painting by Wichell [sic] in his possession."

9¼in (23.5cm) high

$3,100-3,700   **CHEF**

A Copeland Parian figure of "The Bride," modeled by Raphaelle Monti for the Crystal Palace Art Union, a diaphanous veil clinging to the contours of her face, incised and impressed marks, small chip on one flower.

ca. 1861   *14¼in (36.5cm) high*

$750-875   **WW**

A Victorian Parian figure of the Venus de Medici, after the antique, a dolphin and cherub at her side, no maker's mark.

30¼in (77cm) high

$875-1,000   **TEN**

A Parian bust of Benjamin Disraeli, 1st Earl of Beaconsfield, unmarked, the socle base lacking.

ca. 1875-80   *17½in (44.5cm) high*

$375-450   **WW**

A late-19thC Dunmore Pottery bust of Sir Walter Scott, in treacle-color glaze, impressed "DUNMORE" on the reverse.

19¾in (50cm) high

$2,200-2,700   **L&T**

An Edwardian silver-mounted earthenware mug, printed with a portrait of Briggs Priestley (1831-1907), MP for Pudsey 1885-1900, an education philanthropist for Leeds and Bradford, retailed by E. Senior, Leeds Road, Bradford, the silver by Watson & Gillot, Sheffield, 1905.

4½in (11.5cm) high

$120-190   **HT**

THE ASIAN MARKET

It is important not to lose sight of the fact that the Asian market spans not only many cultures, countries, and economies, but also a multitude of decorative artifacts—as diverse as Chinese porcelain tea wares, Japanese bronze vases, Tibetan wooden Buddhas, Indian stone carvings, and Mughal jewelry, to name but a few. When you also factor in diversities of style relating to different dynastic or historical periods, it comes as no surprise that there are many "micromarkets" operating under the Asian umbrella and that, ergo, these can often to varying degrees buck more general economic leanings.

However, with that caveat in mind, there are some overarching trends well worthy of mention. Perhaps first and foremost among these is that both buyers and sellers alike continue to become more knowledgeable of the different collecting fields. This is in marked contrast to the first and second decades of the 21stC, when crazy prices were often paid—sometimes too low, when the importance of many pieces was not recognized, but more often too high, when offered by newly affluent, new-to the-market, and highly competitive Chinese buyers intent on reclaiming their heritage from the West. This new and growing discernment—part of which has involved collectors becoming far more knowledgeable about the fakes and reproductions out there—has had the overall effect of calming or steadying the market. This is not to say that when the right piece comes onto the market, a bidding war at auction cannot still push the boat out pricewise—see, for example, the Imperial Qianlong "Bat and Crane" tianqiuping ("heavenly globe vase") at $2,000,000-2,500,000 on page 108!

So, against this background of steady momentum and growth in the Asian market, in general, what is worthy of particular note? Well, it would be remiss not to point out that ongoing international strengthening of the ban on the sale of ivory (with some certified exemptions)—such as the strengthening of the UK Ivory Act of 2018 with a further Act in 2022—has had a further major impact on, for example, the once-thriving markets in Japanese okimono and netsuke. In terms of Japanese artifacts in total, however, this has been partly offset by what appears to be a healthy and ongoing demand for cloisonné and mixed-metal wares. Nevertheless, overall (and in marked contrast to its heady, financially super-buoyant days back in the 1980s) the Japanese market remains overshadowed by the strength of its Chinese counterpart.

Within the latter, and over the last year or so, there appears to have been a slight drop-off in celadon and other monochrome glazed porcelain compared to more exotic glazes, such as flambé and sang de boeuf, while early pieces of Yuan Dynasty and Ming Dynasty blue and white appear currently favored over Kangxi equivalents. In general, however, at the time of writing, no one area appears to be hotter than any other. Indeed, given that during the last year top-selling lots have included a jade seal, a huanghuali chair, and a famille rose-enameled bowl, it would seem that the old truism still holds firm: It's not the type of artifact, it's its quality, its rarity, and its (well-documented) provenance that really count.

Rachel Holland, Director & Asian Art Specialist, Fieldings Auctioneers

Top Left: An early-20thC Japanese Meiji/Taisho Period silver okimono of a Minogame, the mythical turtle with seaweed growing from the top of its shell and trailing behind it, signed "Ryubundo zo," and with a junjin silver mark below.

9¾in (24.5cm) wide

$4,300-5,000   **WW**

Left: A Chinese famille rose "Dragon" vase, six-character Guangxu mark and of the period, with three large iron-red and gilt five-clawed dragons, chasing pearls amid cloud scrolls and flames, the neck with a key fret and ruyi border, the shoulder with a band of lotus and "shou" characters.

1875-1908   *26in (66cm) high*

$50,000-62,000   **WW**

ASIAN CERAMICS

CHINESE REIGN PERIODS AND MARKS

Imperial reign marks were adopted during the Ming Dynasty, and some of the most common are illustrated here. Certain emperors forbade the use of their own reign mark, to avoid the disrespect of a broken vessel bearing their name being thrown away. This is where the convention of using earlier reign marks comes from—a custom that was enthusiastically adopted by potters as a way of showing their respect for their predecessors.

It is worth remembering that a great deal of mperial porcelain is marked misleadingly, and pieces bearing the reign mark for the period in which they were made are, therefore, especially sought after.

EARLY PERIODS AND DATES

Xia Dynasty	ca. 2070-1600 BC	Three Kingdoms	221-280	The Five Dynasties	907-960
Shang Dynasty	ca. 1600-1046 BC	Jin Dynasty	265-420	Song Dynasty	960-1279
Zhou Dynasty	ca. 1046-221 BC	Northern and Southern Dynasties	420-581	Jin Dynasty	1115-1234
Qin Dynasty	221-206 BC	Sui Dynasty	581-618	Yuan Dynasty	1279-1368
Han Dynasty	206 BC-AD 220	Tang Dynasty	618-906		

EARLY MING DYNASTY REIGNS

Hongwu	1368-98	Zhengtong	1436-49
Jianwen	1399-1402	Jingtai	1450-57
Yongle	1403-24	Tianshun	1457-64
Hongxi	1425	Chenghua	1465-87
Xuande	1426-35		

MING DYNASTY MARKS

Hongzhi
1488-1505

Zhengde
1506-21

Jiajing
1522-66

Wanli
1573-1619

Chongzhen
1628-44

QING DYNASTY MARKS

Kangxi
1662-1722

Yongzheng
1723-35

Qianlong
1736-95

Jiaqing
1796-1820

Daoguang
1821-50

Xianfeng
1851-61

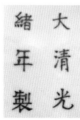
Tongzhi
1862-74

Guangxu
1875-1908

Xuantong
1909-11

Hongxian
1915-16

A Chinese Tang Dynasty pottery model of a horse, with a saddle on its back, the head partly covered with a chesnut glaze, with a modern detachable hair tail and a wood stand.

22in (56cm) high

$6,000-7,500   **WW**

A Chinese Tang Dynasty pottery model of a horse, probably late 7th/early 8thC, Luoyang area, Henan province, with traces of painted decoration.

11in (28cm) high

$3,700-5,000   **CHEF**

CLOSER LOOK—A CIZHOU WARE WINE JAR

The bulbous, broad-shoulder shape of the vase instantly conveys a sense of the sturdiness characteristic of Cizhou wares.

As here, slip painting, in black or dark brown, was the most common method of applying decorative imagery to Cizhou wares, although other techniques, notably sgraffitio, were also sometimes employed.

Prior to applying the slip-painted imagery, the fired clay body of the jar was typically coated with a boldly contrasting white or cream-color slip.

Chinese scholars were a popular subject for figural decoration, and are here accompanied by equally stylized imagery, much of it of botanical origin.

A Chinese Yuan Dynasty Cizhou ware wine jar, "Guan," with two scholars, leaves, and scrolls, horizontally banded.

1279-1368   *13in (33cm) high*

$12,500-15,000   **CHEF**

A Chinese Tang Dynasty Changsha ware ewer, with two conjoined fish motif, small chips, rim restored.

ca. 618-906   *7½in (19cm) high*

$625-750   **CHEF**

A Chinese Tang Dynasty pottery sancai groom, with traces of original pigment, base replaced, with inventory number, some damage.

24in (61cm) high

$3,100-3,700   **DN**

A Chinese Jin/Yuan Dynasty Cizhou jar, painted with a crane, deer, and hare in bracketed reserves beneath a shoulder band of flower heads and tendrils, loss of glaze around the foot rim through firing.

6in (15cm) high

$1,900-2,500   **CHEF**

A Chinese Longquan celadon jug, probably Northern Song Dynasty, the body of six panels, four carved with wispy foliage, reeded handle and curved spout, sign of sea washing on the glaze.

8¼in (21cm) high

$6,000-7,000   **CHEF**

ESSENTIAL REFERENCE—LONGQUAN

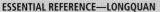

- The kilns of the city of Longquan, located in the Chinese province of Zhejiang, are best known for their celadon wares.
- "Proto-celadons," usually of brown or yellowish hues, were made at various locations in China as early as the Eastern Han (AD 25-220) and Three Kingdoms (220-265) dynasties.
- Wares with the classic jadelike bluish, blue-green, and olive green hues were initially produced at Longquan during the Northern Song Dynasty (960-1127), but really flourished under the Southern Song (1127-1279).
- As well as being made for domestic consumption, they were also exported throughout East and Southeast Asia and the Middle East (eventually reaching Europe via the Islamic world).
- After the development of blue-and-white porcelain, in Jingdezhen in the early 14thC, celadon gradually went out of fashion, both domestically and abroad, although there were some antiquarian revivals in subsequent centuries.

A Chinese Longquan celadon vase, probably Song Dynasty, covered overall with an even glaze of sea green tone.

9½in (24cm) high

$19,000-25,000   **WW**

A Chinese Ming Dynasty Longquan celadon incense burner and cover, with mythical "luduan" beast, the body incised with flame motifs, with a wood box and cover.

4¼in (11cm) high

$2,500-3,700   **WW**

ASIAN CERAMICS

A carved Longquan celadon barbed dish, carved with a fruiting tree, firing flaws, long crack from rim to center.

17in (43cm) diam

$3,700-5,000 DN

A 15th/16thC Chinese Longquan celadon-glazed dish, carved with calligraphy, with foliage and barbed rim, some minor surface scratching.

12½in (32cm) diam

$4,300-5,600 TEN

A rare Chinese Kangxi carved celadon brush pot, "Bitong," decorated with a landscape of pagodas, willow, pine, rocks, and figures and in a sampan, the base with a six-character Xuande mark, with a wood stand.

1662-1722 *6¾in (17cm) wide*

$31,000-37,000 WW

A celadon dish, the center with flower heads, additional flowers and scrolls around, barbed rim, some scratches.

22in (56cm) diam

$5,000-6,200 DN

An 18thC Chinese carved celadon bottle vase, "Danping," decorated with meandering lotus scrolls below stiff leaves, key frets, and petals, with a wood stand.

20½in (52cm) high

$12,500-17,500 WW

An 18thC Chinese celadon vase, with blossoms amid foliage, under bands of stiff leaves and ruyi heads, a lappet border encircling the foot.

17¼in (44cm) high

$25,000-31,000 WW

A Chinese Qing Dynasty celadon-glazed brush pot, the four sides each with a line of poem in underglaze blue, and seals in Tang Ying style, base drilled with two holes.

5¾in (14.5cm) high

$6,000-7,500 DN

A Chinese celadon jardinière, six-character Guangxu mark and of the period, suffused with a network of crackles.

1875-1908 *9¾in (24.5cm) wide*

$6,000-7,500 WW

A Chinese Yueyao molded bowl, probably Song Dynasty (10-12thC), with two phoenixes among peonies, the rim without glaze, some marking knocks from the kiln.

7in (18cm) diam

$1,250-1,700 CHEF

A Song Dynasty Qingbai wine pot, carved with foliate motifs and combed wisps, restored, no lid.

960-1279 *7in (17.5cm) high*

$2,500-3,700 CHEF

A 17th/18thC Chinese blanc-de-Chine figure of Guanyin, the goddess sits wearing flowing robes, with downcast eyes.

5¼in (13.5cm) high

$2,500-3,700 WW

A rare pair of Chinese Kangxi white-glazed figures of horse water droppers, with accented manes, tails, and forelocks, one with open hole in center of mane and one with open hole in back, pricked ears, with legs bent as if about to stand, right-hand horse with both ears restored, hairline crack in base, firing blemishes in glaze, scratches and small chip on mane, left-hand horse with one ear missing, one ear restored, large piece glued to top of mount but original piece reattached, tail reglued.

Compare with a related pair of piebald horses, illustrated by William R. Sargent in "The Copeland Collection," Peabody Museum Salem (1991), no. 20, pages 63-65; Fitzwilliam Museum, Cambridge, for a pale yellow-glazed single version, accession no. "C.2-1962"; The British Museum, accession no. "Franks 504"; and also those from the Nelson Rockefeller collection.

6in (15cm) wide

$37,000-43,000 DN

A Chinese Kangxi biscuit-glazed water dropper, of a boy on a buffalo, glazed in green and yellow with black details, inscribed "686," minor surface scratches and firing blemishes.

4¾in (12cm) wide

$5,000-6,200 DN

Two Chinese Kangxi gilt-bronze-mounted biscuit-glazed water dropper models of horses, glazed in eggplant with accented tails, manes, and forelocks, on gilt-metal bases, both with holes in the back and open mouths, one horse with right foreleg off and glued back, and both ears missing, the other with one ear missing, both with small chips.

4¼in (11cm) wide

$15,000-19,000 DN

CLOSER LOOK—A PAIR OF PARROTS

A similar pair of turquoise-glazed Kangxi parrots are recorded as being supplied to Marie Antoinette for display at Versailles.

These Kangxi porcelain birds were decorated in turquoise with accented beaks and claws, but other examples were produced in blanc-de-Chine and various polychrome combinations.

The 18thC fashion for importing Chinese porcelain birds and creating metal mounts to turn them into candelabra was primarily promoted by entrepreneurial French decorative art dealers (often described as "marchands-merciers"), such as Lazare Duvaux and Simon-Phillippe Poirier.

The gilt-metal candelabra mounts are finely cast. The intertwined branches supporting the candle sconces are naturalistic and incorporating charming little details, notably a little lizard.

A fine pair of Chinese gilt-metal-mounted biscuit porcelain parrot candelabra, the porcelain Kangxi (1662–1722), the mounts French ca. 1740-60, the right-hand parrot with long body crack in the glaze, some crazing in the glaze and loss on the beak, the left-hand parrot with some firing cracks and blemishes.

8¾in (22cm) high

$110,000-140,000 DN

A fine Chinese Imperial lemon yellow-enameled bowl, six-character Yongzheng mark and of the period, with deep rounded sides rising to a slightly flared rim, the exterior covered with an opaque enamel of even lemon yellow tone, the interior and rim glazed white, with a wood stand.

1723-35 3¼in (8.5cm) diam

$200,000-250,000 WW

A Chinese stem bowl, six-character Yongzheng mark and of the period, the exterior covered with a deep copper-red glaze, thinning slightly around the base of the bowl and flaring rim.

1723-35 6in (15cm) wide

$17,500-20,000 WW

An 18thC Chinese bottle vase, covered with a mottled, cobalt blue glaze, thinning to white at the mouth rim and stopping at the foot.

16in (40.5cm) high

$3,100-4,300 WW

An 18thC Chinese Yixing teapot and cover, the cover with a lion dog and a revolving ball finial, the spout with a metal mount, the cover with a two-character mark "Yi Mao."

8in (20.5cm) wide

$750-875 WW

An 18thC Chinese flambé-glazed bottle vase, covered with a mottled deep red glaze.

9¾in (24.5cm) high

$3,100-3,700　　**WW**

A near pair of 18thC Chinese flambé-glazed vases, in lustrous blue glazes with streaks of milky blue and flecks of violet to mushroom gray.

10¾in (27.5cm) high

$8,500-10,000　　**WW**

A Chinese coral-ground and gilt-decorated Ingot-shaped dish, six-character Jiaqing mark and probably of the period, the interior painted with a lotus, with butterflies and bats amid peaches and blooms.

5¾in (14.5cm) wide

$5,500-7,000　　**WW**

A large 18th/19thC Chinese flambé-glazed vase, with a red speckled glaze, with a mushroom tone, with lavender and violet on the rim.

23¼in (59cm) high

$1,000-1,100　　**WW**

A Chinese Qing Dynasty copper red-glazed waterpot, the body modeled with an inverted rim.

4in (10cm) wide

$1,900-2,500　　**WW**

A 19thC Chinese lime green-glazed brush pot, "Bitong," with two horses beneath a willow tree and prunus branches in a rocky landscape, the base with a four-character Qianlong mark.

5in (13cm) high

$2,000-2,500　　**WW**

A Chinese green-glazed and incised "Dragon" bowl, Qing Dynasty or later, with two dragons pursuing flaming pearls, amid flames and clouds above a band of crashing waves, with a six-character Daoguang mark.

4¼in (11cm) diam

$5,000-5,600　　**WW**

A Chinese Archaistic Guan-type beaker vase, "Gu," Qing Dynasty or later, in a bluish-gray glaze, suffused with a dark and russet crackle.

7¾in (19.5cm) high

$1,900-2,500　　**WW**

A Chinese late-Qing Dynasty blue-ground "Dragon" bottle vase, with three five-clawed dragons contesting a flaming pearl.

17¼in (44cm) high

$3,100-4,300　　**WW**

A 19thC Chinese Qing Dynasty green-glazed vase, bulbous body with a short foot and long neck, covered overall in a bright green crackled glaze, the base covered in a crackled glaze with ivory tinge.

7¾in (19.5cm) high

$1,700-2,200   **L&T**

A Chinese Yixing brush pot, "Bitong," Qing Dynasty or later, decorated in low relief with different colors of slip, with a figure on a sampan approaching a dwelling beneath trees, the base stamped with an artist's mark reading "Yang Jichu."

6¼in (16cm) wide

$3,100-4,300   **WW**

Judith Picks

Unglazed, reddish-brown stoneware made from locally sourced clay has been produced by potteries in and around Yixing, in the Chinese province of Jiangsu, since the late Ming Dynasty (1368-1644). Pronounced "yeeshing," Yixing is perhaps best known for its teapots, which were initially popular from the early 16thC with the intellectual and artistic classes in China, but from the mid-17thC they were, along with other Yixing stonewares, exported to Europe. Their popularity in the latter was evidenced—given imitation is the sincerest form of flattery—by the fact that in the last quarter of the 17thC Dutch Delft potters began to produce redware equivalents, as did some of the Staffordshire potteries. In terms of decoration, some Yixing teapots were left plain, while others were decorated in relief—like the splendid example here—with garden or landscape scenes, or images of flora and fauna. Their appeal, however, went beyond form and decoration: after you've used a Yixing stoneware teapot for many years, and only ever washed it out with water, it will have gradually absorbed the flavour and aroma of the tea and you can therefore make a new brew simply by pouring boiling water into the empty pot!

A Chinese Imperial powder blue-ground gilt-decorated bottle vase, six-character Guangxu mark and of the period, decorated with floral and animal roundels, with "shou" characters, with borders of ruyi heads and lappets.

1875-1908   *15in (38cm) high*

$12,500-17,500   **WW**

A Chinese Qing Dynasty inscribed Yixing teapot, decorated with a pavilion and landscape scene on one side, a poetic calligraphic inscription on the other, the base impressed with a six-character Qianlong mark, very minor wear.

4¾in (12cm) high

$12,500-17,500   **DN**

A Chinese lime green-ground "Dragon" bowl, six-character Tongzhi mark but later, with two scaly dragons chasing flaming pearls.

6in (15cm) diam

$1,000-1,100   **WW**

A Chinese late-Qing Dynasty powder blue-ground and gilt-decorated vase, "Hu," painted with a monkey climbing up a fruiting peach tree above pines, shrubs, and bamboo, the reverse with a spotted deer and a pair of cranes in a rocky landscape, with mythical beast handles, the base with a Qianlong mark.

13½in (34.5cm) high

$7,000-8,000   **WW**

A pair of Chinese Imperial pink-enameled bowls, six-character Xuantong marks and of the period.

1909-11   *6½in (16.5cm) diam*

$5,000-6,200   **WW**

A Chinese Ge-type bottle vase, Qing Dynasty or later, with a crackle glaze.

10in (25.5cm) high

$2,500-3,100   **WW**

A 16thC Chinese bowl, painted with hibiscus amid leafy scrolls, the base with a four-character mark "bing chen nian zhi."

5¾in (14.5cm) diam

$2,500-3,100 WW

A 16thC Chinese Ming Dynasty bowl, painted with dragons chasing a flaming pearl, smashed and riveted, with a few missing pieces.

14¼in (36cm) diam

$700-800 DN

A Chinese Wanli blue-and-white jar, painted with ducks in a lotus pond, and with birds in flight between lappets and ruyi head bands.

1573-1619 *5¼in (13.5cm) high*

$2,500-3,700 WW

A 16th/17thC Chinese brush and ink holder, the top with four apertures with foliage, the side painted with birds perched on floral branches, the base with a "shou shan fu hai" mark.

5¼in (13.5cm) diam

$7,000-8,000 WW

A pair of Chinese Wanli "Boys" dishes, each painted with three boys at play in a fenced garden forming "shou" characters, in front of rockwork, the undersides painted with lingzhi sprigs.

1573-1619 *3¾in (9.5cm) diam*

$5,000-6,200 WW

CLOSER LOOK—A JIAJING/EARLY WANLI DISH

There are eight "shou" roundels around the perimeter of the dish. They symbolize longevity which, in Chinese philosophy and culture, is one of the most important aspirations in life.

The sitting figure in the center of the scene is Shoulao (also known as Shouxing). Invariably depicted with a long beard and a pronounced bald head, he is the Chinese god of longevity.

Attending to Shoulao, and making offerings to him, are four (two on each side) of the "Bar Xian," the Eight Immortals. This legendary group of Chinese heroes who fight together to vanquish evil and individually represent male, female, the elderly, the young, the rich, the noble, the poor, and the humble.

The longevity theme of the decorative imagery is further underpinned by the inclusion of flora and fauna also symbolic of it. These include a spotted deer, a crane, a tortoise, a peach gourd, and a pine tree.

A 16th/17thC Chinese Jiajing/early Wanli dish, decorated with immortals making offerings to Shoulao, who holds a ruyi scepter with a crane, with a pine tree, a deer in the foreground, with eight "shou" roundels, two long hairline cracks, area of rim unglazed.

16¾in (42.5cm) diam

$22,000-27,000 DN

A Chinese porcelain Kraak-type bowl, painted with Chinese figures at pursuits beside duck ponds, flanked by formal floral designs in the Iznik manner, cracked and riveted.

ca. 1635-50 *14¼in (36cm) diam*

$1,600-2,000 WW

A Chinese late-Ming Dynasty incense burner, painted with a landscape, on three animal mask feet, the rim with flowers and complex diaper.

6¼in (16cm) wide

$2,500-3,700 WW

A Chinese Ming Dynasty "Lotus" bowl, painted with four lotus flower heads on a branch, the well with a peony branch.

6¼in (16cm) diam

$3,100-4,300 WW

ESSENTIAL REFERENCE—TRANSITIONAL WARES

Porcelain described as "Transitional" was produced in or near Jingdezhen, in the Jiangxi province in southern China, during and for some time after the transition from the Ming to the Qing dynasties. In terms of specific dates, it's generally considered to have begun with the death of the Wanli emperor in 1620, spanned the "official" transfer from the Ming Dynasty to the Qing Dynasty in 1644, and ended with the arrival of Zang Yingxuan as director of the factories at Jingdezhen in 1683. In commercial and artistic terms, it is the period during which the Ming Dynasty lost, and the Qing Dynasty had yet to regain, imperial control of the Jingdezhen factories. One consequence of the latter was that, in the absence of imperial patronage, the potters and other associated craftsmen at Jingdezhen had to turn their hands to producing for the ordinary domestic market and, more significantly, the newly emerging export markets, most notably Japan and the Netherlands. The consequences of the latter were a gradual and increasing adoption of forms, shapes, and decorative imagery from European and other Asian vocabularies of ornament.

A Chinese Transitional Period "Figural" jar, painted with a dignitary and his attendants in a fenced garden, with willow and plantain trees and rockwork, below a band of stylized leaf lappets.

The subject is a ceremony called the "Jia Guan Jin Jue," which commemorates an official's promotion to the rank of nobility.

ca. 1640   *7½in (19cm) high*
$37,000-50,000   **WW**

A rare Chinese Transitional Period "Romance of the Western Chamber" beaker vase, painted with figures illustrating a scene from "Xi Xiang Ji," depicting Zhang Sheng and Fa Pen in a fenced garden, the middle section with a dignitary and a male attendant, the base inscribed with a cursive "ST 1658."

"The Romance of the Western Chamber" is one of the most famous Chinese dramatic works. It was written by the Yuan Dynasty playwright Wang Shifu and is set during the Tang Dynasty. It tells the story of a young couple consummating their love without parental approval.

ca. 1640   *18¼in (46.5cm) high*
$70,000-80,000   **WW**

A Chinese Transitional Period "Boys" bottle vase, painted with three boys playing in a garden, the neck with flowers.

ca. 1650   *8¾in (22cm) high*
$6,000-7,500   **WW**

A Chinese Transitional Period brush pot, painted with a sitting scholar and attendant in his studio by the lotus pond, cracked and glued, one large rim chip.

6¾in (17cm) high
$8,500-10,000   **DN**

A Chinese Transitional Period porcelain vase, painted with a bird perched on branches issuing from rockwork, extended firing fault to rim, some surface wear.

8¾in (22cm) high
$1,500-1,900   **TEN**

A Chinese underglaze blue and copper red "Figural" dish, six-character Kangxi mark and of the period, with a star-shaped panel of a lady daydreaming of her beloved, against a powder blue ground.

Dream scenes are rare on Chinese porcelain. A Chongzhen (1628-44) dish in the Shanghai Museum, painted with Simau dreaming of a young woman singing, is illustrated by A. White, Chen Xiejun and Wang Qingzheng in "Seventeenth Century Jingdezhen Porcelain from the Shanghai Museum and the Butler Collections," Scala (2006), pages 124-25, as well as a similarly painted Shunzhi (1644-61) dish on pages 130-31.

A Chinese Imperial "Dragon and Carp" basin, six-character Kangxi mark and of the period, painted with a ferocious three-clawed dragon emerging from turbulent waves above two carps and a smaller fish, broken and repaired, with loss.

1662-1722   *16¾in (42.5cm) diam*
$50,000-56,000   **WW**

A Chinese Kangxi "Scholar" brush pot, "Bitong," painted in inky cobalt blue, with a sitting scholar contemplating in a rocky landscape with bamboo and pine shrubs, his attendants preparing tea, with a narrow chevron and freestyle dotted borders.

1662-1722   *5½in (14cm) high*
$31,000-37,000   **WW**

A Chinese Kangxi erotic wine cup, painted with a couple in an amorous embrace amid furnishings and a plantain tree, the base with a six-character Chenghua mark.

1662-1722   *2½in (6.5cm) wide*
$22,000-27,000   **WW**

1662-1722   *13in (33cm) diam*
$25,000-37,000   **WW**

ASIAN CERAMICS

A Chinese Kangxi underglaze-blue and copper red brush pot, "Bitong," painted with two panels, one containing a flowering prunus branch, the other with orchids growing from rocks, the base with a ribbon-tied lozenge mark in a recessed glazed circle.

1662-1722   *7½in (19cm) wide*
$60,000-75,000   **WW**

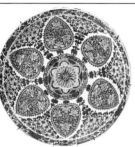

A pair of Kangxi dishes, for the Islamic market, with petals on a scrolling blue ground about a centered floral medallion, stylized flower mark, with fritting and rim chips.

18½in (47cm) diam
$16,000-20,000   **DN**

CLOSER LOOK—A KANGXI LANDSCAPE VASE

The porcelain produced in Jingdezhen after Emperor Kangxi reorganized the kilns there in 1683 is markedly more refined than earlier wares; as here, the potting is economical and neatly trimmed, and the glaze is pleasingly thin and glassy.

Typically for this period, the underglaze blues range dynamically from a silvery hue to an almost purple tone.

Landscape designs during the Kangxi Period (1662-1722) mostly convey—as here, with mountains in the background—a sense of craggy remoteness.

Also characteristic is the inclusion of a sampan on the river being guided away from the idyllic rural island retreat with a canopy of trees and a partly obscured pavilion.

A Chinese Kangxi "Landscape" vase, painted with an idyllic watery landscape, with figures in a sampan, pavilion, and gnarled trees, distant mountains, the neck with floral sprigs, the base with a Chenghua mark.

1662-1722   *17in (43cm) high*
$60,000-75,000   **WW**

A Chinese "Red Cliff" vase, six-character Kangxi mark and of the period, two sides with the two "Odes to the Red Cliff" by the Song Dynasty poet Su Dongpo (1037-96), the other two sides painted with the poet going to the famous site with his friends, the reduced neck with sprays of bamboo.

A number of "Red Cliff" vases were produced in the Jingdezhen kilns around the 1690s and painted with images deriving from woodblock prints. See "Transactions of the Oriental Ceramic Society," vol. 49, M. Butler, *Chinese Porcelain at the Beginning of Qing*, pages 34-35, no. 38-40, for similar "Red Cliff" vases.

1662-1722   *16½in (42cm) high*
$20,000-25,000   **WW**

A 17thC Chinese porcelain jar, painted with chrysanthemums within formal borders, cracks, scratches, wood cover reglued with sections of loss.

9in (23cm) high
$1,250-1,600   **TEN**

A Chinese double gourd vase, possibly 16thC but probably later, painted in inky blue, with flower foliage and Buddhist emblems, extensive wear on the surface.

21in (53.5cm) high
$3,700-5,000   **DN**

A Chinese Kangxi porcelain jar and cover, painted with foliage and landscape, restored.

23½in (60cm) high
$6,000-7,500   **TEN**

A Chinese Kangxi porcelain jar, painted with deer and birds in a mountainous river landscape, later hardwood cover and stand, lacking original porcelain cover, surface wear, glaze pitting.

14¼in (36cm) high
$11,000-12,500   **TEN**

A Chinese Kangxi porcelain bowl, painted with scrolling lotus, six-character reign mark in underglaze blue, badly broken and professionally restored.

7½in (19cm) diam
$3,700-5,000   **TEN**

A pair of Chinese porcelain vase table lamps, the porcelain Kangxi, the ormolu mounts 19thC French, with fan-shaped panels and treasures, floral sprays, and flowering branches, beneath ruyi and flower-head shoulders, with an oil lamp cover, now fitted for electricity.

27½in (70cm) high

$5,500-7,000   **WW**

A Chinese Kangxi "Antiques" brush pot, "Bitong," decorated with Archaic vessels and precious objects, the reverse with lines of calligraphy and a seal mark, the base with a six-character Jiajing mark.

1662-1722   5¼in (13.5cm) high

$11,000-14,000   **WW**

A Chinese Kangxi "Dragon and Phoenix" brush pot, "Bitong," with a dragon and phoenix in pursuit of a sacred pearl amid flames, the base with an artemisia leaf mark.

1662-1722   5¼in (13.5cm) high

$11,000-14,000   **WW**

A Chinese Kangxi mallet-shaped "Scholar" vase, painted with a scene of a scholar with his attendants in a fenced garden, below bands of ruyi heads, chevrons and sawtooth designs.

1662-1722   10¼in (26cm) high

$14,000-17,000   **WW**

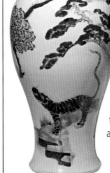

A Chinese Kangxi blue-and-white, celadon, and underglaze copper red vase, painted and carved with a scene of a tiger looking up at a ferocious dragon emerging from clouds, with pine trees and rocks on the reverse.

1662-1722   17¼in (44cm) high

$11,000-14,000   **WW**

A Chinese Kangxi double gourd vase, decorated with rose blooms and bamboo emerging from craggy rocks, the reverse with butterflies, the base with a six-character Chenghua mark.

1662-1722   8½in (21.5cm) high

$7,000-8,000   **WW**

A pair of Chinese Kangxi "Phoenix Tail" vases, painted with Buddhist lions, precious objects, and some of the Hundred Treasures, one vase with old restoration on foot and underside of base.

18¼in (46.5cm) high

$25,000-37,000   **DN**

A Chinese Kangxi "Celebration" dish, painted with figures in celebration of the promotion of an official, with a poem on the right detailing this, the base with a six-character Xuande mark, hairline crack, three rim chips.

8¼in (21cm) diam

$9,500-10,500   **DN**

A Chinese Kangxi vase, painted with landscapes and precious objects, including vases and a qin instrument, the neck inscribed with a poem and two seals, Jiajing mark, hairline crack, firing blemishes.

16¾in (42.5cm) high

$14,000-17,000   **DN**

A Chinese Kangxi Gu-shaped vase, painted with scholars in a mountainous river landscape with trees, birds, clouds, and fishermen, the center section painted with lotus pods, lotus flowers, and peony, the rim with glaze chips, minor frits on foot rim, formerly mounted as a lamp.

17¾in (45cm) high

$25,000-37,000   DN

A Chinese Kangxi "Phoenix Tail" vase, painted with a dignitary receiving an official, with attendants and soldiers in a pavilion, with plantain trees, the neck with a dignitary, a crane, and attendants, the reverse painted with a pine tree and a rock, neck hairline crack, chips in rim.

17½in (44.5cm) high

$25,000-31,000   DN

A Chinese Kangxi "Lotus" bowl, painted in the interior with a lotus spray, with a frieze on the exterior, demi-lotus flowers on the interior rim, the base inscribed with a Chenghua mark, minor scratches in the glaze.

8in (20.5cm) diam

$5,000-6,200   DN

An 18th/19thC Chinese lavender-ground, underglaze blue, and copper red vase, painted with blossoming prunus and bamboo, the reverse with poetic inscriptions and seal marks, with openwork handles with bats suspending ruyi heads, the base with a Qianlong mark, ormolu mounted.

16¼in (41cm) high

$15,000-17,000   WW

A Chinese late-Ming/early-Qing Dynasty porcelain bowl, with four groups of fruit and ruyi clusters divided by "shou" characters, firing flaws.

6in (15cm) diam

$450-550   CHEF

A Chinese Kangxi "Ladies" vase, painted with four ladies in conversation, with a table and musical instrument, neck ground down, cracks.

9¾in (24.5cm) high

$4,300-5,000   DN

A Chinese Kangxi porcelain plate, painted with figures in an interior, within a broad lotus-and -cale border with four panels of figures reclining in gardens, six-character reign mark in underglaze blue, minor surface wear.

8in (20.5cm) diam

$2,100-2,500   TEN

A Chinese Kangxi "Eight Lucky Horses" porcelain jar, the horses in a playful manner, with landscape frieze, restored to rim, poor regluing throughout.

1662-1722   *8¾in (22cm) high*

$2,100-2,500   CHEF

A Chinese Kangxi Gu-shaped vase, decorated with lion head masks, the neck and foot decorated with stiff leaves.

1662-1722   *8¾in (22cm) high*

$4,300-5,000   WW

A Chinese Kangxi "Peacock" dish, painted with a peony sprig, enclosed by chrysanthemum, lotus, peony, and camellia blooms, the rim painted with four peacocks, the underside with Buddhist emblems, with a lingzhi spray mark on the base.

1662-1722 *21¾in (55.5cm) diam*

$7,500-8,500 **WW**

A Chinese Kangxi "Flowers and Bird" vase and cover, decorated with birds, peony, magnolia, chrysanthemum, and camellia, the shoulder painted with auspicious objects, the cover similarly decorated.

1662-1722 *23½in (60cm) high*

$5,000-6,200 **WW**

A Chinese Kangxi teapot and cover, with a figure in a landscape scene, scholars' objects and antiques below a cracked-ice border with prunus blossoms, the spout and handle with cloud scrolls, with a metal chain.

1662-1722 *7¼in (18.5cm) high*

$2,500-3,700 **WW**

A Chinese Kangxi vase, painted with birds flying among branches of flowers and rockwork.

1662-1722 *22¼in (56.5cm) high*

$4,300-5,000 **WW**

A Chinese Kangxi cup, with ladies holding musical instruments, with flowerpots, four-character Chenghua mark on the base, small cracks in the rim and base.

3¼in (8.5cm) high

$750-875 **DN**

A pair of Chinese Kangxi "Master of the Rocks" dishes, decorated with a landscape scene with characteristic rockwork and a pine tree, with a figure walking toward a building or beside a lake, both rims with glaze fritting.

10in (25.5cm) diam

$14,000-17,000 **DN**

A Chinese Kangxi "Eight Immortals" bowl, with the Eight Immortals in scrolling clouds, the base inscribed with a Chenghua mark, crack in the rim, some firing blemishes.

6in (15cm) diam

$2,500-3,700 **DN**

A Chinese Kangxi ginger jar, painted with six scholars on riverbanks among pine, blossoming trees, and rockwork, old chips on the rim, one firing flaw, some blemishes.

8¼in (21cm) high

$11,000-12,000 **DN**

A Chinese Kangxi fishbowl, the exterior powder-blue with traces of gilt, the outer rim with iron red floral-and-cloud scroll band, the inside with four large fish with smaller fish and weeds in green, black, iron red, and yellow enamels, exterior gilding worn, some surface scratches.

23½in (60cm) diam

$21,000-25,000 **DN**

ASIAN CERAMICS

A Chinese Kangxi "Deer and Crane" Yen Yen vase, decorated with cranes and spotted deer by a pine tree and craggy rocks, under swirling clouds.

1662-1722   *14¾in (37.5cm) high*

$5,000-5,600   **WW**

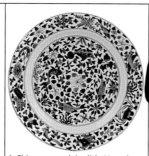

A Chinese porcelain dish, Xuande reign mark but Kangxi, painted with fish among foliage, within a border of fish, foliage, auspicious objects, and shellfish, six-character reign mark, broken in two and reglued, hairline crack in the border, rim chips, and glaze fritting.

10¾in (27cm) diam

$875-1,000   **TEN**

A Chinese vase, probably Kangxi, decorated on the shoulder with an Archaistic design of dragon mask and ring handles, the base with a four-character Chenghua mark.

7¾in (20cm) high

$7,000-8,000   **WW**

A Chinese teapot and cover, probably Kangxi, painted with flower heads on scrolling tendrils, the handle molded with Archaistic dragons.

6in (15cm) high

$1,250-1,900   **WW**

Judith Picks

In addition to the aesthetics of shape and form, pattern, and color, to me one of the great appeals of Chinese ceramics is that in many instances the decorative imagery employed is a form of storytelling. For example, the imagery on this Kangxi basin is derived from the "Yang Jia Jiang," or the "Generals of the Yang Family"—a series of stories and plays from Chinese folklore which date to the Song Dynasty (960-1279). They recount the bravery and unflinching loyalty of a military family, the Yangs, who sacrificed themselves to defend their country against the Khitan-ruled Liao Dynasty (907-1125) and the Tangut-ruled Western Xia (1038-1227). In this scene, Mu Guiying, a legendary heroine from the stories and a symbol of a brave, persevering, and loyal woman, is depicted capturing the young and handsome Yang Zongbao and demanding a marriage proposal from him.

A Chinese Kangxi "Yang Jia Jiang" basin, painted with warriors and figures carrying banners under a tree, the cavetto with further soldiers, the reverse with floral sprigs and ruyi heads, with a six-character Chenghua mark.

1662-1722   *12½in (32cm) diam*

$2,500-3,700   **WW**

A Chinese Yongzheng vase, "Meiping," painted with a band of mallow meander with blossoms separated by leaves, the shoulder with cranes dancing amid foliage.

1722-35   *13¾in (35cm) high*

$110,000-140,000   **DN**

An 18thC Chinese blue-and-white "Landscape" scroll bowl, painted with figures in a mountainous river landscape with tiered pavilions and trees, all below a band of spirals, with a reticulated wood stand.

24in (61cm) wide

$55,000-70,000   **WW**

A Chinese Qianlong export dish, with a herring, small areas of rim fritting, pitting in the body.

9½in (24cm) wide

$1,600-1,900   **CHEF**

One of a pair of Chinese "Dragon and Phoenix" bowls, Qianlong mark and of the period, with flaming pearls and clouds, with minyao six-character seal marks on bases, rim chips, hairline cracks.

8¾in (22cm) diam

$1,500-1,900 the pair   **DN**

An 18thC Chinese mug, from the collection of Augustus the Strong, painted with a river landscape with distant pagodas.

3¾in (9.5cm) high

$1,200-1,350   **WW**

A Chinese Jiaqing porcelain bidet, painted with a river landscape, with a wave border, spout missing, some wear and glaze flakes.

24in (61cm) long

$800-950   **TEN**

A Chinese Jiaqing bottle vase, painted with a figure in a lakeland and mountainous landscape, the neck with the "fu lu shou" symbol.

7½in (19cm) high

$5,000-5,600   **DN**

A 19th/20thC Chinese vase, "Zun," painted with lotus meander, the neck with elephant handles, the base with a six-character Qianlong mark, some minor blemishes.

17¾in (45cm) high

$21,000-25,000   **DN**

A 19thC double gourd vase, decorated with a dragon.

13½in (34cm) high

$2,500-3,700   **CHEF**

A Chinese Daoguang "Boys" bowl, painted with two boys playing games, divided by ruyi heads, the interior with a flower head and scrolling tendrils, the border with "fu" characters, the base with a four-character mark reading "Fuhai cang zhen."

1821-50   *6¾in (17cm) diam*

$2,500-3,700   **WW**

A 19thC Chinese Qing Dynasty vase and cover, large-scale rim chip on edge of cover.

14½in (37cm) high

$5,000-5,600   **DN**

A 19thC Chinese Qing Dynasty punch bowl, the interior with a dragon in clouds, the exterior with figures, vases, and birds in branches, the base with a six-character Kangxi mark, small chip on foot rim.

15in (38cm) diam

$3,700-5,000   **DN**

A Chinese Qing Dynasty bowl, in Ming Dynasty style, with a formal design of lotus flower heads and scrolling leaves.

10¾in (27.5cm) diam

$1,900-2,500   **WW**

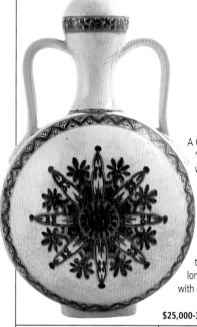

A Chinese Qing Dynasty "Pilgrim" flask, "Bianhu," with a motif of plant scrolls, with eight branches around the heart housing the yin and the yang, the neck with foliage scrolls, the handles with ruyi head terminals, rim restored, long cracks in body, glaze with grazing.

14¼in (36cm) high

$25,000-31,000   **DN**

A pair of 19thC Chinese "Sanduo" vases, painted with lotus flower heads on leafy scrolling foliage, with bands of peaches, pomegranates, and finger citrons.

26½in (67.5cm) high

$2,200-2,700   **WW**

A Chinese porcelain ginger jar and cover, in Kangxi style, painted with precious objects, on a cracked-ice and prunus ground, some minor surface wear.

11¾in (30cm) high

$1,900-2,500   **TEN**

A pair of Chinese porcelain jars and covers, in Kangxi style, painted with flower sprays, with foliate lappet borders, some minor surface wear and glaze pitting.

8¾in (22cm) high

$3,700-5,000   **TEN**

A late-19thC Chinese export jardinière, decorated with prunus, with a diaper and key border, slight pitting in the interior.

10¼in (26cm) high

$1,900-2,500   **CHEF**

A 19thC Chinese Qing Dynasty porcelain vase, with flowering blossoms, rockwork, and birds, Kangxi mark but later, rim chip with crack.

12in (30.5cm) high

$250-370   **CHEF**

A Chinese late Qing Dynasty vase, decorated with Li Jing, Hong Fu Nü, and Qiu Ran Ke beneath a tree, the base with Guangxu mark.

13½in (34cm) high

$1,000-1,100   **WW**

A Chinese vase, "Yuhuchunping," probably 20thC, with plantain trees and bamboo in a fenced garden, with a band of leaves and scrolling tendrils, the base with a Tongzhi mark.

11¼in (28.5cm) high

$1,000-1,250   **WW**

A 20thC Chinese figure of Budai, the corpulent figure wearing open robes decorated with floral scrolls, with an impressed "Wei hong tai zao" mark on the base.

Budai was a 10thC nomadic Chinese monk who, following the subsequent spread of Chan Buddhism, also came to be venerated in Japan, Korea, and Vietnam. Named after the bag he carried his few possessions in—"budai" means "cloth sack"– he is invariably depicted as being overweight, with a large belly, and either smiling or laughing—hence his nickname: the "Laughing Buddha." Believed by some to be an incarnation of Maitreya, the "Buddha of the Future," and especially adored by children, he was essentially a symbol of contentment and abundance.

9¾in (24.5cm) wide

$6,000-7,500   **WW**

A Chinese "Qilin" vase, in Kangxi style, probably 20thC, painted with three scaly mythical beasts, each with bulging eyes, mouths agape, and emitting wisps of flames.

18¼in (46.5cm) high

$1,500-2,000   **WW**

ESSENTIAL REFERENCE—FAMILLE VERTE

The term "famille verte" was first employed in France during the mid-19thC, and literally translates as "green family."

● It is used to describe the polychrome enamel palette dominated by shades of green (most notably "apple" green), which first appeared on Chinese porcelain ca. 1680, during the Kangxi Period (1662-1722).

● A development from the "wucai" ("five colors") style of decoration, it typically also included less dominant reds, yellows, blues, eggplant (or aubergine, basically a subdued shade of purple), and sometimes also black or gold.

● Superseded in popularity by the famille rose palette in the mid-18thC, famille verte wares are still produced in the 21stC, albeit Kangxi examples continue to be the most desirable.

A pair of Chinese Kangxi famille verte "Sui Tang Yan Yi" rouleau vases, with An Lu Shan and other figures, before the Tang Xuanzong emperor at a desk in a pavilion with his attendants, the reverse with rocks, trees, and distant mountains, the necks with "shou" characters beneath bands of ruyi heads.
1662-1722   18in (45.5cm) high
$60,000-75,000   **WW**

A Chinese Kangxi famille verte porcelain basin, with birds in flowering peony and rockwork, cloud scroll borders, and cell rim, with foliate panels, two areas of rim restoration.
13½in (34.5cm) diam
$1,600-1,900   **TEN**

A Chinese Kangxi famille verte porcelain brush pot, with a lakeland scene, with a figure in a pavilion watching a punt, a large chunk has been out the side and crudely reglued back.
1662-1722   5¾in (14.5cm) high
$5,000-6,200   **CHEF**

A Chinese Kangxi famille verte plate, with insects and flowers, within a band of ruyi scepter heads, the base inscribed with a "zhuo cun zhai" mark in a double circle, the rim with nibbles, a chip, and a crack, wear in the enamel.
10in (25.5cm) diam
$7,000-8,000   **DN**

A Kangxi famille verte wucai dish, with the legendary figure Jiang Ziya fishing on a riverbank, visited by King Wen of Zhou and his military entourage seeking his help, the border with precious objects, the underside with a conch shell mark.
1662-1722   13½in (34.5cm) diam
$12,500-15,000   **WAD**

A Chinese Kangxi famille verte porcelain basin, with a foliate roundel, the border with panels of objects, rim chips and fritting, long crack in the well.
11in (28cm) diam
$625-750   **TEN**

A Chinese Kangxi famille verte Yen Yen vase, with a pheasant crouching on rockwork among peony blooms, with insects and birds flying above, the neck with peony and chrysanthemum around rocks, with iron red bands on the rim, shoulder, and foot.
1662-1722   16in (40.5cm) high
$3,700-5,000   **WW**

A Chinese Kangxi famille verte vase, with a gnarled flowering prunus branch issuing from rockwork and perched with a magpie, butterflies, and insects, with hardwood cover and stand, minor wear.
8¾in (22cm) high
$6,000-7,500   **DN**

A Chinese Kangxi famille verte "Prunus" bowl, painted with leafy flowering branches, the interior with floral sprays, the base with a fangding mark.
1662-1722   8¾in (22cm) diam
$2,100-2,500   **WW**

A Chinese famille verte brush pot, "Bitong," Kangxi or later, painted with the deity of examinations, Kui Xing, standing on the head of an ao emerging from crashing waves and florets, holding a calligraphy brush, the reverse inscribed with calligraphy, with a wood stand.
5in (12.5cm) high
$2,500-3,700   **WW**

An 18th/19thC Chinese Qing Dynasty famille verte model of Budai, holding a peach, unglazed interior, wood base, some surface crazing and cracks in glaze.

7½in (19cm) high

$5,000-6,200   **DN**

An 18th/19thC Chinese famille verte bowl, painted with scholars, the interior with a sitting figure, with apocryphal six-character Chenghua marks, cracked in half and glued, with two further cracks, wear in enamel.

8¾in (22cm) diam

$1,250-1,500   **DN**

A pair of Chinese Qing Dynasty famille verte "Dragon Boat" rouleau vases, with figures on terraces and the riverbank overlooking the dragon boat carrying the Sui emperor Yang along the canal, below bands of Taoist Immortals, mythical beasts, and auspicious objects.

31¼in (79.5cm) high

$50,000-56,000   **WW**

A Chinese Qing Dynasty porcelain famille verte vase table lamp, with a powder blue glaze, painted with figures, birds, deer, a rock, and a tree, with gilt mons on the neck, on a gilt-metal base.

17¼in (43.5cm) high

$1,500-1,700   **WW**

A 19thC Chinese famille verte "Bird and Flower" dish, with a bird perched on a flowering branch of prunus, with bamboo below and a gilt moon above, the rim with blooms in cell diaper, formal flower heads and cartouches with Precious Things, the reverse with sprays of peony.

10½in (26.5cm) diam

$20,000-22,000   **WW**

A pair of 19thC Chinese Qing Dynasty famille verte vases, painted on each side with figures, scratches on surface.

15¾in (40cm) high

$8,500-10,000   **DN**

A 19thC Chinese famille verte "Dragon" brush pot, "Bitong," painted with five dragons, colorful cloud scrolls and flames, with a recessed glazed circle in the base.

8¾in (22cm) wide

$1,900-3,100   **WW**

A Chinese late Qing Dynasty famille verte porcelain fishbowl, internally painted with goldfish among weeds, externally with shaped panels of courtly figures, on an associated hardwood and marble-top stand, badly cracked.

ca. 1900   *18in (46cm) high*

$700-800   **CHEF**

A Chinese famille verte vase, painted with two magpies perched on a pine trunk, with blossoming prunus trees emerging from jagged rocks, signed by the artists on one side and the base with "jiang xi jing de zheng" mark, dated, minor wear in the enamel.

1956   *13½in (34.5cm) high*

$37,000-50,000   **DN**

A Chinese Yongzheng famille rose "Sanxing" brush pot, "Bitong," painted with figures from Chinese mythology, including Shoulao holding a peach, Fu Xing, Lu Xing, and their attendants, with a gnarled pine tree on the reverse, the base with a recessed glazed circle and a Chenghua mark.

1723-35   *4¾in (12cm) high*

$19,000-25,000   **WW**

CLOSER LOOK—A FAMILLE ROSE "IMMORTALS" VASE

The decorative imagery was applied with the distinctive overglaze enamel famille rose palette. Dominated by shades of pink—here, paler in the landscape scene and darker in the border decoration—and also including various combinations of other, in general, soft hues, notably yellow, green, blue, and white, the style of decoration was introduced around the beginning of the 18thC.

Aside from the geometric key fret patterns in blue around the shoulder and base of the vase, the border decoration closely framing the landscape is composed of repeat lappet and ruyi head motifs. The lappets imitate the decorative hanging folds or flaps around a garment or headdress; the ruyi heads the ornate and often flowerlike heads found on ceremonial scepters.

The figures are flanked and overhung by pine trees, which in traditional Chinese culture symbolize longevity, integrity, and perseverance.

Accompanied by an attendant, the figure on the right is Magu, a Taoist deity or Immortal ("xian"), who is associated with the elixir of life and is also a symbolic protector of women.

A Chinese famille rose "Immortals" vase, six-character Qianlong mark and of the period, with a landscape and three scenes depicting Magu on a log raft in gentle waves, standing amid pine trees and rocks, and with a deer and an attendant, all framed by ruyi head and key fret borders encircling the shoulder and base, all beneath scrolling foliage on a ruby red ground and a band of stylized lappets with interlocking kui dragons, the base glazed turquoise, the neck reduced.

1736-95   *8¾in (22cm) high*

$50,000-62,000   **WW**

A pair of Chinese famille rose porcelain chargers, in Yongzheng style, with dignitaries and attendants in a fenced garden with trees and rockwork, artemisia leaf mark, much rim gilding now lacking, minor scratches.

14½in (37cm) diam

$3,700-5,000   **TEN**

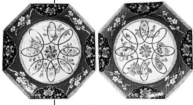

A pair of 18thC Chinese ruby-ground famille rose dishes, with flower heads with floral sprays and geometric bands, the cavettos and rims with prunus branches and peonies, and scrolling chrysanthemum.

8¼in (21cm) wide

$3,100-3,700   **WW**

A pair of Chinese Qianlong/ Jiaqing famille rose cockerels, with their heads turned and cockscombs raised.

For a related pair, dated to 1775, see M. Cohen and W. Motley, "Mandarin and Menagerie," Cohen & Cohen (2008), page 228.

11½in (29.5cm) high

$7,000-8,000   WW

A Chinese Qing Dynasty famille rose brush pot, one side with Shoulao in a boat, the other side with figures below deities in a floating pavilion, with flower branches and rockwork, the base with a six-character Qianlong mark.

5in (12.5cm) high

$8,000-9,500   WW

A Chinese Qianlong famille rose "Western Chamber" vase, one side with the scene from "Romance of the Western Chamber," the other side with a landscape scene with pavilions, the base with a Qianlong mark in iron red, fitted as lamp, drilled in the base, neck restored.

15¼in (39cm) high

$5,000-6,200   DN

An 18thC Chinese en grisaille and gilt-decorated famille rose coffee cup and saucer, of young farmers, their rams and distant equestrian figures in a watery landscape.

4¼in (11cm) diam

$3,100-3,700   **WW**

An 18thC Chinese famille rose punch bowl, the interior with a kingfisher on a peony branch, with a floral border, the exterior with butterflies flying amid roses and magnolia.

13¼in (33.5cm) diam

$5,000-6,200   **WW**

An 18thC Chinese famille rose brush pot, "Bitong," decorated with landscape scenes, plants, and calligraphic inscriptions.

5in (13cm) high

$10,000-11,000   **WW**

Judith Picks

The historical background to this truly splendid vase, which bears a Jiaqing seal mark, is that Jiaqing was the fifth emperor of the Qing Dynasty (1644-1911/12). During his reign (1796-1820)—claimed upon the abdication of his father, the emperor Qianlong (reigned 1736-95)—he attempted to restore the deteriorating state of the empire, in part by banning the importation of opium into China. Somewhat indecisive, and with power effectively remaining in the hands of his father's corrupt court official, Heshen, he was far from successful. Although attempts toward the end of his reign to refill a treasury largely emptied by rampant corruption bore some fruit, it did little to improve the characteristic impropriety and ineffectiveness of the government.

Equally, but more positively characteristic of Jiaqing's reign, is the decorative composition of the vase. Rendered in the famille rose palette, it features stylized wandering vines set on a white ground and paired with animals to create a bold but intricate aesthetic. Each element of this imagery is typically chosen for its auspicious significance, for example: pomegranates, a fruit brimming with seeds, represent fertility, familial happiness, and the wish for many children; dragons, in the form of the handles, symbolize strength and good luck; and lingzhi, also luck but longevity, too. The latter, translated as "divine branch" and usually identified with the fruiting body of the lingzhi fungus (part of the Polyporacae family), contributes significantly to the overall theme of wellness and fruitfulness and, in combination with the pair of songbirds also depicted, suggests that this vase may well have been originally given as a wedding gift.

A Chinese famille rose vase, Jiaqing seal mark and probably of the period, the dragon and lingzhi shoulder handles flanked by a ruby-ground lotus and floral shoulder pattern, the body with song birds among fruiting pomegranates, minor scratches.

12¼in (31cm) high

$50,000-62,000   **CHEF**

An 18thC Chinese famille rose Canton enamel tea service, with Magu and He Xiangu with an attendant ascending into heaven accompanied by a phoenix, comprising two plates, teapot stand, bowl, teapot with an associated cover, milk pitcher, 11 saucers, 5 teabowls and 6 coffee cups, stress cracks in the enamel, some old restoration.

plate 8¾in (22cm) diam

$41,000-47,000   **DN**

A Chinese Qianlong famille rose porcelain "Tobacco Leaf" dish, with scattered leaves and flower sprays, chips, wear in gilding.

17½in (44.5cm) wide

$1,100-1,350   **TEN**

A Chinese Imperial famille rose ruby-ground medallion bowl, six-character Jiaqing mark and of the period, the exterior with four gilt-bordered roundels with peonies, peaches, hollyhocks, and pomegranates, divided by lotus scrolls, the interior with a flower basket encircled by fruiting flower branches, with lingzhi and auspicious emblems in underglaze blue.

1796-1820   *5¾in (14.5cm) diam*

$60,000-75,000   **WW**

A Chinese Imperial famille rose "Bajixiang" turquoise-ground incense burner, six-character Jiaqing mark and of the period, enameled with the Eight Buddhist Emblems and lotus scrolls, below a band of ruyi heads and a key fret border.

1796-1820   *11in (28cm) wide*

$19,000-25,000   **WW**

ASIAN CERAMICS

A Chinese Imperial famille rose ruby-ground bowl, six-character Daoguang mark and of the period, with four gilt-bordered medallions with peonies, peaches, hollyhocks, and pomegranates, with stylized lotus flower heads on scrolling tendrils, the interior with a flower basket, with fruiting floral sprays and lingzhi in the cavetto.

1821-50   *6in (15cm) diam*

$55,000-60,000   **WW**

A pair of Chinese famille rose ruby-ground "Lanterns" bowls, six-character Daoguang marks and of the period, the sides with four roundels with vases with "Lanterns of Abundance," and antiques and auspicious objects, each roundel divided by lotus blossoms on leafy stems, the interiors in shaded tones of cobalt blue with stylized centered medallions, encircled by large lanterns with suspending tassels in the cavettos.

In Chinese culture, lantern decorations are typically associated with festivals and auspicious occasions, such as weddings. Ears of grain accompanied by a lantern represents wugu fengdeng and is a wish for a bumper harvest of the five grains. The symbol of an elephant carrying a vase is a pun on taiping youxuang and signifies peace, stability, and happiness.

1821-50   *6in (15cm) diam*

$170,000-200,000   **WW**

A Chinese Daoguang famille rose porcelain "Bitter Melon" bowl, with a butterfly and fruiting tendrils, six-character reign mark, faint hairline crack in rim.

This dish-shaped fruit is probably a bitter melon, which is a symbol of fertility.

6in (15cm) diam

$750-875   **TEN**

A 19thC Chinese Canton porcelain famille rose vase, with figures on a bridge above water, with figures in boats or riding on clouds or bats, applied with chilong on the shoulders, with lion-dog handles.

25in (63.5cm) high

$700-800   **WW**

A Chinese famille rose porcelain charger, Qianlong reign mark but not of the period, with peony and lilies, with incised scrollwork and scattered sprigs, reign mark in red, some minor wear.

16¼in (41cm) diam

$1,600-1,900   **TEN**

A mid-19thC Chinese Canton famille rose metal-mounted vase and cover, depicting court scenes, supported by fan-shaped and circular panels of courtesans, with butterflies and flowers, rubbing on gilding, small chips, rim damage.

24½in (62cm) high

$3,700-4,300   **CHEF**

A 19thC Chinese famille rose vase, painted with a riverscape scene, the rim inscribed in ink with the names of five different scenic sites in Jiangxi province, with wood base, minor wear.

14½in (37cm) high

$7,000-8,000   **DN**

A pair of mid-19thC Chinese Canton famille rose vases, with dignitaries, ladies, and actors, birds and insects amid flowers, with ruyi scepter handles, on a celadon ground.

23½in (59.5cm) high

$7,000-8,000   **WW**

A Chinese famille rose yellow-ground "Floral" bowl, six-character Xianfeng mark and of the period, with lotus, chrysanthemum, peonies, cherry blossoms, and orchids.

1851-61   *6¾in (17cm) diam*

$31,000-37,000   **WW**

A pair of 19thC Chinese Canton famille rose "Figural" vases, panels with dignitaries at tables with courtly figures and warriors, the smaller panels with scholars, ladies, and attendants, with fruits and floral sprays, butterflies, auspicious objects, and vases, the shoulders with chilong and mythical creatures.

24¾in (63cm) high

$2,500-3,700 WW

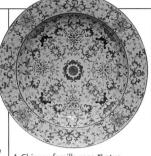

A 19thC Chinese famille rose "Lady and Phoenix" vase, with a beauty in a fenced garden by rockwork and flower branches, with a phoenix in flight, with a six-character Qianlong mark.

8¾in (22cm) high

$1,400-1,600 WW

A Chinese famille rose "Lotus and Bats" dish, six-character Jiaqing mark but probably later, the interior painted with five iron red bats encircling a gilt swastika roundel, surrounded by peaches, pomegranates, and Buddha's-hand (a type of citron) above lotus blooms, with pink bats and double fish.

14¾in (37.5cm) diam

$3,700-5,000 WW

A pair of Chinese famille rose vases and covers, painted with flowers and foliage, with wood stands, cracks, firing blemishes.

22in (56cm) high

$2,700-3,700 DN

A late-19thC Chinese Canton famille rose vase, with court scenes, birds, and butterflies, on a gilt ground with green scrollwork and enameled with butterflies and flowers, crack in neck, rubbing in gilding and enamel.

24¾in (63cm) high

$1,000-1,100 CHEF

A Chinese famille rose "Dragon" vase, six-character Guangxu mark and of the period, with three large, iron red-and-gilt five-clawed dragons, chasing pearls amid cloud scrolls and flames, the neck with a key fret and ruyi border, the shoulder with a band of lotus and shou characters.

1875-1908 *26in (66cm) high*

$50,000-62,000 WW

Judith Picks

Incense—the word derives from the Latin "incendere," meaning "to burn"—is essentially composed of aromatic plant materials, often combined with essential oils, which when burned release fragrant smoke into the air. Whether simply as an air deodorant, insect repellent, for aromatherapy, or for enhancing meditation or religious worship, incense has been employed since antiquity by civilizations around the globe. In China, its use can be traced back to Neolithic times; it gradually became more widespread in the Xia (ca. 2070-1600 BC), Shang (ca. 1600-1046 BC), and Zhou (ca. 1050-221 BC) dynasties, and expanded to almost all classes of Chinese society during the Song Dynasty (960-1279), when it was also elevated to the status of one of the "Four Arts of the Chinese Scholar" (the other three being painting, flower arranging, and making tea).

Just as the herbs and other plants used for incense varied considerably (in China, cassia, cinnamon, styrax, and sandalwood were much favored), so did the vessels—the incense burners, or censers—used to burn it in. Made from materials as diverse as base or precious metals, stone, bamboo, earthenware, or porcelain, they ranged in shape from the simplest of dishes or pots, to animal or bird forms, representations of mountains, and models of boats. However, among the most prized were those raised on legs, whether three or four, compartmented, and elaborately decorated—such as in the 19thC Chinese censer shown here, embellished in the famille rose palette with symbolic imagery from the Chinese vocabulary of ornament.

A 19thC Chinese famille rose incense burner with cover and stand, on four mythical beast legs, the sides painted with Buddhist lions and antiques, bats, and clouds, "shou" characters and geometric designs, the pierced cover with a lion dog.

19in (48.5cm) high

$5,000-6,200 WW

A pair of 19thC Chinese Canton famille rose garden seats, with figures in landscapes and on terraces, with cash motifs, between molded studs and gilt-ground borders with floral sprays, bats and auspicious objects, with wood stands.

26¾in (68cm) high

$12,500-15,000 WW

A late-19thC Chinese Canton famille rose bowl, with courtesans, birds, and flowers, reserved on a gilt-ground body with green scrollwork and enameled with butterflies, flowers, and birds, on a hardwood pierced stand, rubbing in the enamel.

13½in (34cm) diam

$1,900-2,500 CHEF

ASIAN CERAMICS

A Chinese famille rose "Peony" bowl, six-character Guangxu mark and of the period, with peony blooms with leafy branches issuing from rockwork, the reverse with two warblers in flight.

1875-1908   *7¾in (20cm) diam*

$2,500-3,700   **WW**

A 19thC Chinese famille rose jardinière, painted with birds and peonies, wear and scratches.

22¾in (58cm) diam

$1,700-2,000   **DN**

A Chinese Guangxu famille rose plate, with exotic birds perched on flowering prunus branches, the base with a six-character Guangxu mark, minor firing blemishes.

9½in (24cm) diam

$1,700-2,100   **DN**

A pair of large 19thC Chinese Canton famille rose vases, with dignitaries, ladies, and attendants, with butterflies among flowers, fruits, and leaves, each with applied chilong on the shoulders, the necks with lion-dog handles.

23¾in (60.5cm) high

$8,000-9,500   **WW**

A late-19th/20thC Chinese Qianjiang famille rose porcelain brush pot, with landscape and calligraphy, chips on rim, wear in surface decoration.

11in (28cm) high

$5,000-5,600   **TEN**

A Chinese famille rose figure of Buddha Shakyamuni, Qing Dynasty or later, sitting in dhyanasana, his hands in dharmachakra mudra, robes with bats amid swirling clouds, floral sprays, and scrolling tendrils.

10¼in (26cm) high

$5,500-7,000   **WW**

A Chinese late-Qing Dynasty famille rose millefleur "Dragon" vase, four-character mark in iron red on base, both dragon horns restored, one eye lacking.

9¾in (24.5cm) high

$750-875   **DN**

A pair of Chinese famille rose porcelain alcove vases, with pierced lug handles, with figures at various pursuits, on a foliate, bird, and insect ground.

25in (63.5cm) high

$3,100-3,700   **HT**

A Canton Qing Dynasty famille rose punch bowl, with figures and foliage, the yellow-ground border with bats and scrolling foliage, restored break in rim, star crack on base.

15¼in (39cm) diam

$950-1,050   **CHOR**

A near pair of Chinese late-Qing Dynasty famille rose moon flasks, "Baoyueping," with equestrian warriors and dignitaries and a pair of pheasants amid peony and magnolia branches, with Xuande marks.

19¾in (50cm) and 18¾in (47.5cm) high

$7,000-8,000   **WW**

A Chinese late-Qing Dynasty famille rose, coral red-ground vase, with figures enjoying daily life, the body with incense burners and lotus scrolls picked out in gold.

10¾in (27.5cm) high

$3,100-3,700   **WW**

A Chinese late-Qing Dynasty/Republic Period blue-ground famille rose medallion "Lovers" bowl, the interior with Niulang and Zhinu, on a bridge of magpies amid swirling clouds, the exterior with further scenes from the folktale, the base with a six-character Daoguang mark.

The romantic legend of the two lovers Niulang and Zhinu is an ancient Chinese love story that has been told since the Han Dynasty. Zhinu was a weaver girl and Niulang a cowherd, and their love was forbidden, so they were banished to opposite sides of the Heavenly River (symbolizing the Milky Way). Once a year, on the seventh day of the seventh month of the lunar calendar, a flock of magpies would form a bridge to reunite the lovers.

6in (15cm) diam

$3,700-4,300   **WW**

A 20thC Chinese famille rose vase, painted on one side with the bearded painter Ni Zan and his attendant cleaning a wutong tree in a fenced garden, the base with a mark "Yang he tang zhi."

10¾in (27.5cm) high

$5,000-6,200   **WW**

A Chinese Republic Period famille rose vase, with a lady and her attendant holding a flower basket in a landscape setting, the shoulder inscribed with a poem, the base with an apocryphal Qianlong mark.

9¾in (24.5cm) high

$19,000-25,000   **DN**

A pair of Republic Period famille rose millefleur vases, "Shiliuzun," of pomegranate form, with lotus, peonies, chrysanthemums, daylilies, hydrangeas, and poppies, with marks that read "Ju Ren Tang zhi."

8¾in (22cm) wide

$15,000-20,000   **WW**

A Chinese Republic Period blue-and-white and famille rose "Figural" bowl, with three medallions, each with a figure enjoying daily life, the base with a four-character mark "Ju Ren Tang zhi."

"Ju Ren Tang zhi" can be translated as "The Hall where Benevolence Resides."

4in (10cm) diam

$3,700-4,300   **WW**

A Chinese famille rose "Boys" bottle vase, Republic Period or later, with five boys playing in a garden, with five cockerels, chrysanthemum and peony branches, intertwining bamboo and double gourd vines, the base with a six-character Guangxu mark.

16in (40.5cm) high

$3,700-5,000   **WW**

A pair of Chinese famille rose porcelain vases, by Zhai Xiao Xiang, with birds on blossoming branches, on a celadon ground with inscriptions and seal marks, four-character marks in red, with presentation boxes and certificate signed by the artist.

Zhai Xiao Xiang is one of just eight senior masters currently working in Jiangdezhen, and the only one still painting in the traditional Imperial style. He is senior master at the Art Porcelain Factory, which is the direct descent of the Qing Imperial Factory.

ca. 1996   *13½in (34cm) high*

$3,100-3,700   **TEN**

CLOSER LOOK—A KANGXI BITONG BRUSH POT

Like the majority of the pieces decorated with the doucai palette, this Bitong (an artist's or scholar's brush pot) is small, refined, and very well made.

The decorative technique employed with the doucai (contrasted colors) palette involved tracing the outline in underglaze blue, glazing and firing the pot, then applying the other colors as overglaze enamels before a final firing, which gives the colors a jewel-like effect.

The small object being presented to the official by the scholar is a "jue," which is a traditional Chinese vessel used to serve warm wine during ceremonies.

The scene shows a ceremony called "jia guan jin jue," which takes place when an official—here, the figure in the center—is promoted to the ranks of the nobility.

A Chinese Kangxi doucai "Figural" brush pot, "Bitong," painted with scenes of a scholar offering a jue and a book to an official in a fenced garden, divided by stylized "shou" characters, the base with a recessed glazed circle.
1662-1722   *7in (18cm) wide*
$50,000-62,000   **WW**

A Chinese Kangxi/Yongzheng doucai dish, with a narrative scene, glaze loss, hairline crack, small chips around the foot rim.
12½in (32cm) diam
$9,500-10,500   **RMA**

A doucai "Mythical Horse" dish, Yongzheng mark.
8in (20.5cm) diam
$375-500   **WAD**

A pair of Chinese doucai "Pomegranate" dishes, Yongzheng marks and of the period, painted with leafy shrubs, pomegranates, grapes, and plums, the undersides similarly decorated with fruiting sprays.
1723-35   *7¾in (20cm) diam*
$25,000-31,000   **WW**

A Chinese doucai ogee bowl, Qianlong mark and of the period, with ruyi heads, the cavetto with floral motifs, the reverse with a lotus flower meander, each bloom supporting one of the Eight Buddhist Emblems, filled rim chip.
8¾in (22cm) diam
$21,000-25,000   **DN**

An 18th/19thC Chinese doucai "Mandarin Ducks" plate, Chenghua mark, minor superficial baking flaw, small filled rim chip.
7¾in (19.5cm) diam
$11,000-12,000   **RMA**

An 18th/19thC Chinese doucai "Lotus Scroll" bottle vase, Qianlong mark, top rim with a hairline crack and one rust spot, some losses in the overglazed enamel.
14¼in (36cm) high
$12,500-15,000   **RMA**

A 19thC Chinese doucai "Lotus and Bats" bowl, with iron red bats suspending swastika motifs, with lotus, lingzhi, ruyi heads, scrolling tendrils, Jiaqing mark, with a wood stand.
5¼in (13.5cm) diam
$2,500-3,700   **WW**

A pair of Chinese Qing Dynasty doucai "Lotus" bowls, with lotus blooms on leafy tendrils above a band of lappets, with Qianlong marks, with wood stands.
4¾in (12cm) diam
$12,500-17,500   **WW**

A 19th/20thC Chinese doucai and famille rose vase, enameled with carps leaping from waves and surmounted by bats, with two peach trees, Buddhist emblems on iron red clouds, Chenghua mark, hairline crack, firing imperfections.
9¾in (24.5cm) high
$550-700   **ROS**

A Chinese Tianqi/Chongzhen wucai ko-akae horse dish, spots of glaze loss, small chips, baking flaw on rim.

5½in (14cm) diam

$875-1,000   RMA

A Chinese wucai "Dragon" bowl, Jiajing mark and of the period, enameled in eggplant, yellow, green, black, and red, with two sketchily drawn dragons amid flames above waves and rockwork, the interior with a dragon roundel, the base with a three drill-hole collector or inventory mark.

The three drilled holes in the base is a practice that appears to have been common in Islamic countries. The pattern of three dots drilled in the shape of a triangle is found on 54 Ming Dynasty porcelain pieces in the Topkapi Saray Museum, Istanbul. The exact meaning of the holes remains unclear, although they appear to be collector or inventory marks.

See R. Krahl, "Chinese Ceramics in the Topkapi Saray Musuem Istanbul," I, Sotheby's (1986), pages 125-38, where non-Chinese marks and inscriptions are discussed in detail by Nurdan Erbahar.

1522-66   *7in (17.5cm) diam*

$125,000-190,000   WW

A Chinese Transitional Period wucai "Phoenix" jar, with a phoenix on rockwork, with prunus and peonies, with a border of floral branches.

ca. 1640   *11in (28cm) high*

$2,200-2,700   WW

A Chinese Transitional Period wucai "Figural" vase and cover, with a dignitary, an official, and attendants on a garden terrace, with pine shrubs and rocks, domed cover similarly decorated with three boys at play.

ca. 1650   *15in (38cm) high*

$10,000-11,000   WW

A pair of Chinese Shunzhi wucai "Journey to the West" vases, "Gu," with scenes from "Xi You Ji," depicting Tang Sanzang, Sun Wukong, Zhu Bajie, Sha Wujing, with ladies on a garden terrace, with chrysanthemums, peonies, and fruiting branches.

1644-61   *19½in (49.5cm) high*

$30,000-37,000   WW

A pair of Chinese Transitional Period wucai "Galloping Horses" vases and covers, some glaze loss and overspraying, retouching, hairline cracks.

16in (40.5cm) high

$7,500-8,500   RMA

A Chinese Transitional Period wucai "Phoenixes" vase, hairline crack from base caused by a baking flaw.

7½in (19cm) high

$1,250-1,700   RMA

A 17thC Chinese wucai "Pheasant" vase, the pheasant perched on rockwork among peony blooms, bamboo, and magnolia branches, the base unglazed.

10¼in (26cm) high

$5,000-6,200   WW

A 17thC Chinese Transistional Period wucai vase, with ladies and attendants with a group of boys, neck reduced and now fitted as a lamp, body cracks.

vase 11¾in (30cm) high

$8,500-10,000   DN

ESSENTIAL REFERENCE—WUCAI

Meaning "five colors," wucai decoration involved using a palette of three overglaze enamels, red, green, and yellow, applied to the outlines of a design established on a white porcelain body in black cobalt or underglaze blue.

● It is almost certainly no coincidence that the adoption of this palette was due in no small part to the fact that the number five in Chinese (pronounced "wu") was associated with the five basic elements: earth, water, fire, wood, and metal—the foundations of the world.

● Wucai originally referred to the Chinese porcelain wares decorated with this palette during the Ming Dynasty, especially the reigns of the Jiajing (1522-66), Longqing (1567-72), and Wanli (1573-1619) emperors. However, it was also revived at intervals during the Qing Dynasty (ca. 1644-1911).

A Chinese Kangxi wucai garlic-mouth "Dragon" bottle vase, with a scaly three-clawed dragon chasing a flaming pearl, with its tail coiled around the neck, with a border of lappets on the mouth rim.

1662-1722   *12in (30.5cm) high*

$14,000-17,000   **WW**

A pair of Chinese Yongzheng wucai "Tian" jars and covers, with flower heads in eggplant, green, red, black, and ocher, with bands of lappets, the bases with tian marks.

1723-35   *3½in (9cm) wide*

$50,000-62,000   **WW**

A Chinese Imperial wucai "Dragon and Phoenix" bowl, Yongzheng mark and of the period, painted with one green and one red five-clawed dragon, divided by phoenixes amid flowers and foliage, beneath a border of the Bajixiang, the interior with an iron red dragon amid green waves.

1723-35   *6in (15cm) diam*

$80,000-90,000   **WW**

A pair of Chinese Imperial wucai "Dragon and Phoenix" bowls, Daoguang marks and of the period, each with one green and one iron red five-clawed dragon chasing flaming pearls, divided by phoenixes, beneath bands of the Bajixiang, the interiors with further dragons in iron red.

1821-50   *6¼in (16cm) diam*

$37,000-50,000   **WW**

A wucai "Dragon and Phoenix" bowl, Daoguang mark and of the period, with two pairs of dragons and phoenixes among floral bush, the interior with a coiling dragon chasing a flaming pearl.

6¼in (16cm) diam

$5,500-7,000   **L&T**

A 19thC Chinese wucai vase, with floral design, chips on the rim.

9¾in (24.5cm) high

$1,250-1,700   **RMA**

A 19th/20thC Chinese wucai vase, with narrative design.

10½in (26.5cm) high

$3,100-3,700   **RMA**

A Chinese late Qing Dynasty wucai sleeve vase, painted with a scene from "The Three Kingdoms."

10in (25.5cm) high

$1,900-2,500   **ROS**

A Chinese Kangxi charger, in Imari style, with the arms of Thomas Pitt, for the American market.

This charger is attributed to a documentary service with the arms of Pitt, one of the three earliest Chinese pieces decorated with British arms and the first true service of plates and dishes. Made for Thomas "Diamond" Pitt, notorious rebel private trader in India and later East India Company Governor of St. George, Madras. His son, Thomas Pitt Lord Londonderry, and grandson, William Pitt the Elder, Earl of Chatham and Prime Minister, both had fine and unique services.

12¾in (32.5cm) diam

$3,700-5,000   RMA

A Chinese Yongzheng armorial plate, with the arms of Blonkebijle, for the Dutch market, small chips.

See J. Kroes, "Chinese Armorial Porcelain for the Dutch market," CBG (2007), page 162, no. 71, for a large dish from this service, "with one other known piece: a teapot … today in the Ostfriesische Teemuseum in Norden, Germany. … This porcelain is a good example of a souvenir service which would have been made for Jan Blankebijle as a memento of his stay in China in 1733."

ca. 1733   *8¾in (22cm) diam*

$1,250-1,700   RMA

A Chinese Qianlong armorial plate, with the arms of Van Reverhorst, for the Belgian market, hairline rim crack.

ca. 1745   *9in (23cm) diam*

$2,000-2,500   RMA

A Chinese Qianlong 21-piece armorial tea service, with the arms of Van der Cruyce, for the Belgian market.

teapot 7¼in (18.5cm) wide

$14,000-19,000   RMA

A rare Chinese Qianlong export part dinner and tea service, with the arms of the Taswell family, comprising 16 dinner plates, 7 soup bowls, 4 plates, 5 serving dishes, soup tureen stand, tea cannister and cover, sugar bowl, 2 cups, teabowl, 3 saucers, and a coffee cup, minor wear and rubbing on gilding, small rim chips, cracks.

The Taswell family had been merchants in the City of London from Elizabethan times. The Reverend Dr. William Taswell (1652-1731), who in 1666 had been page to the Dean of Westminster, witnessed the Great Fire of London and later wrote a vivid account of the event. This Chinese armorial service was made ca. 1755 for Dr. Taswell's son, William Taswell (1708-77), Rector of Wotton-under-Edge in Gloucestershire. In his will, dated October 3, 1775, he specifies that "all such China in my possession as shall be found marked with my family's arms" was to go to his son George Taswell, at the time serving the East India Company in India as colonel of "The Madras Terribles."

ca. 1755   *serving dish 16in (40.5cm) wide*

$7,500-8,500   DN

An 18thC famille rose armorial punch bowl, with the arms and motto of the Dundas family, with two cartouches of the Dundas family arms and crest above the motto "ESSAYEZ," with floral bouquets and insects, the interior with a gilt ruyi scepter border, restored.

13in (33cm) diam

$800-950   L&T

A Chinese Qianlong armorial bottle vase, the neck with breaks and repairs, chip on foot.

10¾in (27cm) high

$1,000-1,500   RMA

A pair of Chinese Republic Period famille rose armorial "Geese" tureens and covers, each modeled as a goose with a raised head, folded wings, and with webbed feet tucked under their bodies, each with a coat of arms on their breasts, with inscriptions that read "A D Villaleal 1675."

13¼in (33.5cm) high

$19,000-25,000   WW

A Chinese famille rose armorial porcelain saucer dish, with the arms of Lambert over a scroll with the motto "SEGUITANDO.SI.GIUNGE," with two three-plumed crests and two flower sprays, old cracks, former staple repair removed and professionally repaired.

For a discussion of the service see D.S. Howard, "Chinese Armorial Porcelain," Faber & Faber (1974), page 206, where it is noted that Sir John Lambert, a wealthy London merchant and director of the South Sea Company, was created Baronet in February 1711 and died in February 1723, to be succeeded by his son, Sir John, 2nd Baronet. It has been the unvaried tradition that this service was made for the 1st Baronet, although armorially there is no reason why the service could not have been made for Sir John's son. This service is, therefore, the earliest dateable example of the new famille rose enamels being used on Chinese porcelain influenced by European originals. The order for the service possibly having been despatched in 1720 or 1721, before the full effect of the bursting of the South Sea Bubble was felt.

ca. 1722   *16½in (42cm) diam*

$1,900-2,500   TEN

ASIAN CERAMICS

A Chinese Wanli brush and ink holder, with five apertures separated by flower heads in underglaze blue and iron red, with floral and cloud designs, the base with a mark "wan fu you tong," the enamels possibly later.

1573-1619　　*1½in (3.5cm) high*
$5,500-6,000　　**WW**

A pair of Chinese gilt-metal-mounted porcelain Yen Yen vases, the porcelain Kangxi, the European metal mounts later, with the "Eight Horses of Mu Wang," and with cranes and deer on a celadon ground, vases with reduced necks and minor wear, mounts with extensive wear.

20in (51cm) high
$16,000-19,000　　**TEN**

A mid-17thC Chinese Ko-Sometsuke water jar and cover, "Mizusashi," for the Japanese market, with peacocks, butterflies, and flower sprays issuing from rockwork, the cover with peony flowers and scrolling tendrils, the base inscribed "Da Ming Chenghua nian zhi," with a tomobako wood box.

This rare type of Chinese export piece was probably made to order for Japanese merchants and practitioners of the tea ceremony at the end of the Ming Dynasty, and developed at a time when demand from the imperial Chinese court was waning.

7¼in (18.5cm) wide
$2,500-3,700　　**WW**

A pair of Chinese Kangxi glazed biscuit Buddhist lion joss-stick holders, in ocher, green, and eggplant, a cub climbing up one leg and a rotating brocade on the other, female with chip on tail.

3½in (9cm) high
$4,300-5,000　　**DN**

CLOSER LOOK—A QIANLONG DRAGON BOWL

Porcelain, such as this dragon bowl, made during the earlier years of the reign of the fourth Manchu Dynasty emperor, Qianlong (1736-95), are almost invariably of a refined, traditional, and aesthetically pleasing form.

Repeat floral and foliate motifs abound in the Chinese vocabulary of ornament, especially as border decoration around the rim, shoulder, or foot of a vessel. While sometimes naturalistic, they can also be stylized, sometimes to the extent of botanical anonymity, such as the overlapping petals here.

Symbols of cosmic energy, high achievement, good fortune, and prosperity, among many other attributes, the two dragons on the bowl—one green with blue scales, the other (not shown) iron red with black—are depicted chasing flaming pearls. The pearls are not only symbolic of the moon, but also of wisdom and, ergo, the dragon's continual pursuit of it.

A rare Chinese blue-ground polychrome "Dragon" bowl, with two dragons, one in green enamel, the other iron red, racing through green, yellow, and iron red flames in pursuit of flaming pearls above a band of overlapping petals, with a dragon medallion in green in the interior, the base with six-character Qianlong seal mark, star crack in the well.

1736-95　　*5½in (14cm) diam*
$37,000-50,000　　**DN**

A Chinese Kangxi blue and copper red "Phoenixes" vase, "Gu," with flowers in different stages of bloom among leafy stems, surrounded by eight phoenixes in flight, the base with a beribboned lozenge mark.

1662-1722　　*17in (43cm) high*
$19,000-25,000　　**WW**

A Chinese Imperial blue-glazed silver and gilt "Bat and Crane" vase, "Tianqiuping," Qianlong seal mark and of the period, with bats and flying cranes holding the Eight Taoist Emblems, "Anbaxian," amid clouds, the base with underglaze blue six-character seal mark on a white ground, hairline crack on rim, some wear on gilding, scratches, inside of neck with old dirt.

This vase is a magnificent example of Imperial Qianlong porcelain. The name of this shape of vase in Chinese is tianqiuping, "heavenly globe vase," because in Chinese iconography heaven is a sphere. Hence, the large globular body of such vases provides an ideal reference to heaven. The vase is remarkable for its highly unusual enameling techniques, with a striking and exceptionally rare palette of gold and silver against a vivid blue ground, which gives the vase a brilliance of tone. The rich cobalt blue on the vase is sometimes referred to as "sacrificial blue." This name derives from the use of vessels bearing this color glaze during sacrifices at the Imperial Altar of Heaven. It is extremely unusual to see blue vases painted in both gilding and slightly raised silver. The rarity of painted silver on porcelains suggests that the medium may have been difficult to control. An example of a moon flask with similar technique is on display at the Shanghai Museum. This vase is a testament to the creativity of craftsmen working during the Qianlong Period in exploring and perfecting enameling techniques to cater to the emperor's taste for the innovative and the exotic while remaining rooted in antiquity. Such a vase would require at least three firings in the kiln for the three different glazes and enamels. First at above 2,200°F for the cobalt blue, then at a lower temperature for the turquoise green on the interior of the vase, finally the gold and silver enamels in a special kiln designed for enamels. T'ang Ying succeeded Nien His-yao as commissioner at Huai An and superintendent of the Imperial Factories in 1736. He is recorded as overseeing the making of enameled silver (mio yin). The exceptional quality, monumental size, and imposing presence of this tianqiuping, as well as its fine and auspicious decoration, would have rendered it suitable for prominent display in one of the halls of the Qing palace. As a devout Buddhist, the Qianlong emperor was also a follower of Taoism with the wish for long life. There are sliver cranes holding an emblem for each of the eight immortals associated with Taoism—including a flower basket, a flute, a fan, and castanets—on the vase's body. The flying cranes and bat also carry auspicious messages for longevity and prosperity.

24¼in (61.5cm) high
$2,000,000-2,500,000　　**DN**

A rare Chinese Qianlong vase, painted in rich copper red with lotus flowers growing from meandering leafy scrolls, all between bands of ruyi heads, lappets, and double underglaze-blue lines.

1736-95   *12in (30.5cm) high*

$8,000-9,500   **WW**

An unusual Chinese export rectangular serving dish, the porcelain Qianlong, painted with a harbor scene of cloth traders offering their merchandise to prospective buyers, on the left a panel is inscribed "AVP," relating to a cloth trader from Leiden, with Latin motto, the borders in underglaze blue, the decoration probably period but unrecorded and a variant of the earlier 1740-50 plates painted in the Netherlands with the same trading scene, but these additionally featuring the arms of the City of Brussels, some wear on gilding, some firing blemishes, very minor rim frits.

ca. 1780   *11¾in (30cm) wide*

$2,500-3,700   **DN**

A fine Chinese Imperial "Dragon" jar and cover, six-character Qianlong mark and of the period, painted in rich tones of green enamel, with two five-clawed dragons striding amid wispy clouds and flames in pursuit of flaming pearls, beneath a border of the Eight Buddhist Emblems, Bajixiang, around the shoulder and a band of lotus lappets encircling the base, the cover decorated with a writhing dragon chasing a flaming pearl above a ruyi head border, with a paper label inscribed: "Green & white jar; from Peking Oct.6 1879. Arrived Shales and unpacked Dec. 12. 1879. very good.," with a wood stand.

Provenance: From the collection of Admiral Robert Coote CB (1820-98), and thence by descent. Admiral Coote enlisted in the Royal Navy in 1833. He was made commander of HMS "Volcano" from 1845, HMS "Victory" from 1860, HMS "Gibraltar" from 1864, and HMS "Arethusa" from 1867. In 1874, he was appointed commander in chief of Queenstown and served as commander in chief of the China Station between 1878 and 1881.

1736-95   *8in (20.5cm) high*

$250,000-310,000   **WW**

An exceptional and rare pair of Chinese Imperial yellow-ground Tibetan-style ewers, "Penba Hu," six-character Jiaqing marks and of the period, with the Eight Buddhist Emblems, Bajixiang, arranged in two registers among lotus blooms on intertwining tendrils, framed by gilt borders, bands of ruyi head, and stylized lappets, the interiors of the mouths and the bases decorated with turquoise.

See Chen and Wang "Treasures from the Snow Mountains: Gems of Tibetan Cultural Relics," Shanghai Museum (2001) page 158, no. 74, for a similarly shaped gold ewer; see also Kerr, "Chinese Ceramics: Porcelain of the Qing Dynasty," V&A (1986), pages 114-15, no. 101, for a Qianlong Buddhist ewer, and page 101 for a Qing famille rose example; see the Simon Kwan Collection, Decoration and Meaning in Chinese Porcelain, Smithsonian Institution for a Daoguang marked pair.

1796-1820   *7¾in (20cm) high*

$370,000-430,000   **WW**

A Chinese sgraffito and en grisaille brush pot, "Bitong," six-character Qianlong mark and of the period, painted with idyllic mountainous landscapes, set against a light sea green ground incised with lotus scrolls.

1736-95   *3½in (9cm) high*

$3,700-5,000   **WW**

ESSENTIAL REFERENCE—BAJIXIANG

The word "Bajixiang" refers collectively to the "Eight Auspicious Symbols" introduced to China with Tibetan Buddhism during the Yuan Dynasty (1279-1368). Employed in the decorative arts to promote peace and blessings they are, and stand for, the following virtues:

- The Wheel of Dharma ("lun"): Knowledge.
- The Conch Shell ("luo"): Thoughts of the Buddha.
- The Victory Banner ("san"): Victorious battle of the Buddha's teaching over all hindrances.
- The Parasol ("gai"): Protection, and also spiritual power.
- The Lotus Flower ("hehua"): Purity and enlightenment.
- The Treasure Vase ("guan"): Inexhaustible treasure and wealth.
- The Pair of Golden Fish ("yu"): Conjugal happiness and freedom from restraint.
- The Endless Knot ("panchang"): Harmony.

A Chinese iron red "Bat" saucer dish, Jiaqing mark and of the period, with bats symbolizing long life, the underside rim with three bats, the center with minyao six-character seal mark, slight wear on rim gilding, minor scathes, small firing blemishes.

9in (23cm) diam

$5,000-6,200   **DN**

A Chinese pink-ground Gu-shaped "Bajixiang" vase, Qianlong mark but probably later, with lotus flowers and foliage, the design incorporating the Bajixiang, the interior and base turquoise.

10¾in (27.5cm) high

$16,000-20,000   **WW**

ASIAN CERAMICS

An 18th/19thC Chinese robin's-egg glazed tripod censer, with taotie-headed elephant leg tripod, with two dragons, a solid gilt elephant handle, associated wood cover with stone lingzhi finial.

10¼in (26cm) high

$1,050-1,200   **CHEF**

A 19th Chinese "Eight Immortals" vase, painted with the Eight Immortals and attendants, the base inscribed with Jiaqing mark in iron red, cracked and restored.

27¾in (70.5cm) high

$17,500-20,000   **DN**

A pair of early-19thC Chinese Qing Dynasty coral-ground bowls, turquoise-glazed interior, reserves depicting mythical persons, children, maidens, and scholars, with Qianlong seal marks but later, rim gilding rubbed.

5in (13cm) wide

$1,500-1,700   **CHEF**

A pair of Chinese Imperial iron red and underglaze blue "Sea Creatures" bowls, six-character Daoguang marks and of the period, with sea creatures, haishou, on a ground of froth-capped, iron red waves between key fret and dentil borders, the interiors with medallions of winged creatures leaping in a similar wave ground, each with a wood stand.

1821-50   *8¼in (21cm) diam*

$75,000-80,000   **WW**

A 19thC Chinese famille noire "Dragon" rouleau vase, with five-clawed dragons above crashing waves, divided by a black-enameled ground with chrysanthemum flower heads on leafy stems, with a band of small cartouches containing the four arts of the Chinese scholar.

21¾in (55cm) high

$4,300-5,000   **WW**

A 19thC Chinese porcelain triple gourd vase, painted in underglaze blue, with scrolling lotus on a yellow ground, glaze loss, scratching.

24in (61cm) high

$4,300-5,000   **TEN**

A 19thC Chinese Qing Dynasty porcelain moon flask, with dragons on the shoulder, the front and reverse panels with precious objects and a phoenix among peonies, Qianlong seal mark but later.

17½in (44.5cm) high

$1,500-1,700   **CHEF**

A Chinese Qing Dynasty porcelain rouleau vase table lamp, with a powder blue glaze, with gilt figures in a garden pavilion.

18¼in (46.5cm) high

$625-750   **WW**

A 19thC Chinese porcelain cricket cage, pierced and molded with dragons chasing the flaming pearl, with openwork lattice, missing stopper, minor wear.

8¼in (21cm) long

$3,200-3,700   **TEN**

A Chinese Imperial yellow-ground "Dragon" saucer dish, six-character Guangxu mark and of the period, with two dragons leaping toward a sacred pearl, the underside with four cranes in flight, with a fitted box.

1875-1908   *5in (13cm) diam*
$5,500-6,000   **WW**

A 19thC Canton export garden stool, with figures, butterflies, and flower foliage, wear on surface, cracked.

                          18¼in (46.5cm) high
$1,250-1,700   **DN**

A Chinese iron red "Dragon" dish, six-character Guangxu mark and of the period, with two ferocious scaly dragons in pursuit of a flaming pearl, clouds, and flames, the underside with two dragons.

1875-1908   *13½in (34.5cm) diam*
$5,000-6,200   **WW**

A Chinese late Qing Dynasty "Buddhist Lions" brush pot, "Bitong," painted with a lion dog with its paws on its pup, with flamelike hair and bushy tail.

                          4½in (11.5cm) high
$4,300-5,600   **WW**

A late-19th/early-20thC Chinese porcelain sang-de-boeuf vase table lamp, with later brass mounts.

                          11½in (29.5cm) high
$625-750   **WW**

A late-19th/20thC Chinese Republic Period porcelain teapot and cover, with a fruit knop, with winter landscapes and calligraphy, Cheng Men seal marks in red, minor wear.

                          7in (18cm) wide
$1,100-1,350   **TEN**

A late-19th/early-20thC Chinese porcelain crane table lamp, on a wood base.

                          13¾in (35cm) high
$300-450   **WW**

A Chinese Canton porcelain garden barrel seat, pierced with coin motifs, with fighting dragons, the ground of saya-gata, minor scratches.

ca. 1910   *18¾in (47.5cm) high*
$2,500-3,700   **CHEF**

A Chinese late-Qing Dynasty plaque, by Re Huanzhang, in Qianjiang style, with one bird perched on prunus branch, signed by the artist, minor wear on enamel.

                          10¾in (27cm) diam
$22,000-27,000   **DN**

A Chinese Republic Period scraffiato bottle vase, with lotus foliage, the base inscribed with an apocryphal four-character Qianlong nianzhi mark.

12½in (31.5cm) high

$5,000-6,200   **DN**

A Chinese Republic Period porcelain model of Putai, the jovial god holding a rosary, slight factory firing smudges in enamels.

ca. 1920-30   *10¾in (27cm) high*

$8,500-10,000   **CHEF**

A Chinese Republic Period porcelain saucer dish, with six doves by a tree near a fence, black ruyi head repeat border, puce seal mark, apocryphal Qianlong mark, two rim chips.

10¾in (27.5cm) diam

$700-800   **CHEF**

A Chinese Republic Period porcelain imitation cloisonné model of a Tibetan ewer, "Duomuhu," with lotus amid scrolling tendrils, spout painted with two phoenixes, the handle as a stylized dragon, the cover with a lion-dog finial, the base with Qianlong mark.

19½in (49.5cm) high

$2,500-3,100   **WW**

A 20thC Chinese en grisaille and gilt-decorated vase, with a "Journey to the West" scene, depicting Wei Zheng holding a sword standing beside the chained three-clawed dragon, the base with a mark "Yanghe tang zhi."

8¼in (21cm) high

$11,000-12,000   **WW**

A Chinese Republic Period porcelain "Dragon" bottle vase, the neck with Eight Buddhist Emblems, with two dragons below, Jiaqing seal mark but later, wear in gilding.

16in (40.5cm) high

$1,400-1,700   **CHEF**

A pair of Chinese porcelain vases, Qianlong marks but Republic Period, the duck-egg blue ground with floral scrolls, seal mark in blue.

10½in (26.5cm) high

$1,200-1,350   **CHEF**

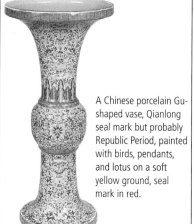

A Chinese porcelain Gu-shaped vase, Qianlong seal mark but probably Republic Period, painted with birds, pendants, and lotus on a soft yellow ground, seal mark in red.

14¾in (37.5cm) high

$800-950   **CHEF**

A Chinese Ko-Akae-style small dish, "Mukozuke," Qing Dynasty or later, made for the Japanese market, with two fishermen on a sampan, the base with an underglaze blue Wenguang (literary "luster") seal mark.

5¼in (13.5cm) wide

$500-750   **WW**

ESSENTIAL REFERENCE—SATSUMA

Although a leading center of ceramic production from the 16thC, the town of Satsuma became synonymous with the highly decorative wares made for export from the mid-19thC. Also produced in the town of Kyoto, Satsuma wares comprised distinctive, cream-color earthenwares with finely crackled glazes and thickly applied enameled and gilded decoration. Typical forms included incense burners ("koro"), vases, wine or sake ewers, bowls, covered jars, and figures. Typical decorative imagery included paneled scenes of people engaged in everyday activities, well-known landmarks, such as Mount Fuji, and indigenous Japanese flora and fauna, all surrounded by ornate borders. Displays at international exhibitions and fairs made Satsuma wares popular in the West. The quality of craftsmanship ranges from exceptionally high to poor, with the latter often the case with pieces originally made for sale in Western department stores.

A pair of 19thC Japanese Meiji Period Satsuma "Shimazu Mon" vases, on elephant feet.

The neck of these vases is decorated with the mon (family crests) of the Shimazu family on both sides. They were the feudal lords of the province of Satsuma. The Shimazu family controlled the production of pottery in Japan from the end of the 16thC, when a family member returning from an invasion of Korea brought with him 17 skilled Korean potters. They built kilns and produced ceramics for the exclusive use of this powerful family. This workshop continued throughout the 17thC and 18thC.

15¾in (40cm) high

$3,100-3,700 RMA

A pair of 19thC Japanese Meiji Period Satsuma vases, Kinkozan mark, one with loss on the dragon's horn, superficial wear.

18¼in (46.5cm) high

$2,500-3,700 RMA

A 19thC Japanese Meiji Period Satsuma vase, by the Yasuda Company, with figures, birds, and flowers, one side with Momotaro riding on a horse and accompanied by his armor-clad dog, monkey, pheasant, and rabbit brothers-in-arms, two oni from Onigashima (Demon Island), the reverse painted with a horse rider and an attendant fleeing from other warriors, the base with the Shimazu mon, the Yasuda trademark, and a mark for Nihon and possibly Unzan.

13¾in (35cm) high

$2,200-2,700 WW

A 19thC Meiji Period Satsuma vase, by Kaizan, one side with beauties and children in a mountainous river landscape, wearing ornate garments and one holding an open fan inscribed "Kyoto Kaizan," the reverse with armor-clad warriors, with mon, stiff leaves, key fret, flower heads, and other formal designs, signed "Kaizan sei" under the Shimazu mon.

18in (45.5cm) high

$6,000-7,500 WW

A 19thC Japanese Meiji Period Satsuma cup, by Kinkozan, with a beauty observing farmers at work, a water mill behind them, signed "Kinkozan," and impressed "Kinkozan zo."

3in (7.5cm) diam

$250-370 WW

A 19th/20thC Japanese Meiji Period Satsuma sugar bowl and cover, by Kinkozan, with Immortals and attendants, beauties, and children, with bamboo-shaped handles decorated with gilt karakusa scrolls and hanabishi mon, inscribed to the base "Kinkozan zo."

5in (12.5cm) high

$500-625 WW

A Japanese Meiji Period Satsuma dish, by Kinsui, for the Kinkozan Workshop, with travelers by a pavilion on the shores of a river, the figures wearing ornate garments, one beauty and her companion with wide-brimmed hats, another traveler a samurawashi (monkey trainer) with his pet by his side, red seal mark for Kinsui, the reverse with a stamped mark for Kinkozan zo.

ca. 1900 7¾in (20cm) diam

$1,000-1,100 WW

A pair of 19th/20thC Japanese Meiji Period Satsuma vases, by Kinkozan, with a family in an interior wearing rich Heian-style garments, the reverse with an Immortal and his armor-clad attendants, all reserved with mythical creatures, inscribed "Kinkozan zo."

18in (45.5cm) high

$1,050-1,200 WW

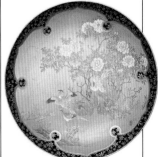

A Japanese Meiji Period Satsuma dish, by Kinsui, for the Kinkozan Workshop, with three birds by a chrysanthemum and with further blooms, red seal mark for Kinsui, the reverse with mark for Kinkozan zo.

ca. 1900 8in (20.5cm) diam

$875-1,000 WW

A late-19th/early-20thC Japanese Meiji Period Satsuma vase, by Kinkozan, with beauties and children in gardens, and two men behind them, wearing elegant garments, the reverse with chickens among chrysanthemums, morning glories, daisies, and wisteria, with two fanciful birds in flight above, the base with an impressed mark and gilt seal, both reading "Kinkozan zo."

9¼in (23.5cm) high

$3,100-4,300   WW

A Japanese Meiji Period Satsuma pottery vase, with a peacock amid rocks and peonies, bearing a Shimazu mon and inscribed "Satsuma ... (?)," some damage.

22in (56cm) high

$875-1,000   DN

A Japanese Meiji Period Satsuma pottery vase, by Yabu Meizan, with a cockatoo perched on the branch of a magnolia tree, gilt seal on base "Yabu Meizan," slight rubbing on the gilding.

5¾in (14.5cm) high

$3,100-3,700   DN

A Meiji Period Satsuma vase, gankou (the flight formation of geese) against a dark sky with a moon, inscribed "Nihon, Kyoto, Kinkozan Sei" (Japan, Kyoto, made by Kinkozan).

16in (40.5cm) high

$450-550   L&T

A Satsuma vase, with waves and dragons on the body, painted and slip decorated with figures.

24½in (62.5cm) high

$1,250-1,900   L&T

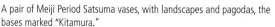

A pair of Meiji Period Satsuma vases, with landscapes and pagodas, the bases marked "Kitamura."

9¾in (24.5cm) high

$450-550   L&T

A Japanese Meiji Period Satsuma vase, with figures in a landscape, with dragons, stamped mark on base, small chip on rim.

1868-1912   *12¼in (31cm) high*

$950-1,050   SWO

A Japanese Meiji Period Satsuma vase, with figures under cherry blossoms or in a courtyard of a temple, with a tablet reading "Kinkozan," Kageyama seizo mark, gilt losses, surface scratches.

1868-1912   *9¾in (24.5cm) high*

$2,500-3,700   SWO

A Japanese Meiji Period Satsuma vase, with a cockerel and chicken by bamboo, pigeons by a fence, or a bird in a maple tree, signed with seals "Shisui" and "Kinkozan zo," gilt losses on edges.

1868-1912   *6in (15cm) high*

$1,900-2,500   SWO

A Japanese Meiji Period Satsuma vase, with landscapes and figures by a pond under a blossoming tree, signed "Shozan seizo," gilt losses on rim.

1868-1912   *9½in (24cm) high*

$2,200-2,700   **SWO**

A Japanese Meiji Period Satsuma incense burner and cover, "Koro," with mandarin ducks in a lake among florets, the cover with a chrysanthemum finial, signed "Raisan."

1868-1912   *3¼in (8.5cm) diam*

$1,600-2,000   **SWO**

CLOSER LOOK—A SATSUMA TEMPLE JAR

The large finial on the cover is a sitting figure of Kannon, the Buddhist goddess of Mercy. Her origins are in the Indian deity Avalokiteshvara, and the equivalent Chinese deity Guanyin, for which the Japanese word is Kannon.

The figural handles are in the form of a pair of "karako"—the literal translation of the word being "Tang children." Symbolizing the innocence and joy of childhood, they are usually depicted playing and, as here, with a distinct hairstyle that's knotted at the top and shaved on both sides of the head.

In marked and deliberate contrast to the karako handles, the body of the jar is decorated with intense and dynamic scenes of samurai warriors engaged in battle—imagery that would have appealed to the Western markets for which the jar was exported to. The decorative palette is classic Satsuma/Kyoto, being polychrome enameled and gilded over cream-color earthenware and with a finely crackled glaze.

The elaborately carved, four-legged, hardwood stand with a marble inset is from Canton and, like the jar it supports and displays, made specifically for export to the West.

A Meiji Period Kyoto Satsuma earthenware temple jar and cover, with a sitting figure of Kannon (Avalokiteshvara) as the cover finial, and two karako (Tang Chinese children) holding rings tied with silk tassels as handles, the body with scenes of samurai engaged in battle, with a 19thC Canton export marble-inset hardwood stand.

ca. 1900   *44in (112cm) high*

$1,900-2,500   **WAD**

A Japanese Meiji Period Satsuma vase, with a lady playing cards with two children, the reverse with egrets in a river, signed "Kinkozan zo" and a stamped seal.

1868-1912   *5in (12.5cm) high*

$1,900-2,500   **SWO**

A Meiji Period Satsuma vase and cover, by Okamoto Ryozan, for the Yasuda Company, with ladies and children engaged in kitsuke (kimono preparation), courtesans with cherry blossoms, two sparrows mid-flight, signed on the base "Ryozan" with the Yasuda Company trademark and the Shimazu mon.

ca. 1900   *7½in (19cm) high*

$3,100-4,300   **WAD**

A Meiji Period Satsuma tripod censer and cover with toad finial, with six Chinese sages and their attendants, with gourd handles.

1868-1912   *13in (33cm) high*

$1,100-1,350   **WAD**

A pair of small Meiji Period Satsuma "Figural" vases, signed.

1868-1912   *7in (17.5cm) high*

$160-220   **WAD**

A Japanese Meiji Period gilt Satsuma tripod incense burner, "Koro," with dragon handles, with court ladies, officials, emperor, monk, and samurais, a Buddhist lion dog on the cover, Satsuma mark.

9¾in (24.5cm) high

$250-370   **ROS**

A pair of Meiji Period Satsuma trumpet vases.

1868-1912   *23½in (60cm) high*

$1,900-2,500   **WAD**

ASIAN CERAMICS

A pair of Meiji Period Satsuma dark green-ground "Samurai" vases.

1868-1912   *17¼in (44cm) high*
$625-750   **WAD**

A Meiji Period Satsuma box and cover, with two daimyo and a samurai, the interior with sparrows and peony blossoms.

1868-1912   *8¾in (22cm) diam*
$500-625   **WAD**

A pair of 20thC Japanese Meiji Period Satsuma vases, by Taizan, with sparrows, with borders of brocade patterns, mon, and other formal designs, signed "Dai Nihon Taizan sei."

12¼in (31cm) high
$750-875   **WW**

A Japanese Taisho Period Satsuma "Peacock and Peony" bowl, the base signed "Koshida."

The Taisho Period (1912-26) in Japanese history corresponds to the reign of the Taisho emperor Yoshihito (1879-1926). It followed the Meiji Period and represented a continuation of Japan's rise on the international scene.

9¾in (24.5cm) diam
$190-250   **WAD**

A Japanese Edo Period Shoki Imari dish, with a mountainous river landscape, rocky outcrops, sailboats, and moon, with crenellations on the rim, the underside with concentric rings.

ca. 1640-50   *7½in (19cm) diam*
$3,100-4,300   **WW**

A pair of late-17th/early-18thC Japanese Edo Period Imari vases and covers, with ho ho in a flowering landscape separated by large ribbon-tied leaf sprays, the domed lids surmounted by a gilt karashishi finial, some damage and surface crazing, hairline cracks, wear on gilding.

19in (48cm) high
$3,700-5,000   **DN**

Two Japanese Edo Period Imari tureens and covers, with flowering sprays of chrysanthemum, prunus, peony, and other flowers, between bands of maple, paulownia leaves, and lappets, the covers with 16-petal chrysanthemum flower heads on the knop.

ca. 1700   *13in (33cm) wide*
$11,000-12,000   **WW**

A Japanese Edo Period Imari charger, with the shochikubai (the Three Friends of Winter), prunus, bamboo, and pine issuing from a vessel, the cavetto and rim with peonies and two ho ho birds in flight, the underside with flowering sprays.

ca. 1700   *21in (53.5cm) diam*
$4,300-5,600   **WW**

Two Japanese Edo Period Imari figures of beauties, each holding the hem of her garment and with her hair elegantly held up with a comb, one wearing a robe painted with chrysanthemum by a stream, the other with pine and branches of plum.

Tall figures, such as this pair of Edo Period beauties, were popular decorative artifacts in European courts during the late-17thC and early-18thC, especially in the Netherlands. Known in Japan as "bijin," which literally translates as "beautiful person," graceful Japanese ladies, such as these, were also often referred to in the West as "Kanbun beauties"— after the Kanbun era (1661-73), during which they first became popular. While this pair is decorated in the Imari palette, they were also produced in Kakiemon colors.

ca. 1700   22¾in (58cm) high
$8,000-9,500   WW

A Japanese Edo Period Imari tureen and cover, with vases of flowers, the background with figures in a mountainous river landscape, the rims with borders of stylized flowers and formal designs.

ca. 1700   19¼in (49cm) high
$8,000-9,500   WW

A pair of Japanese Edo Period Imari vases and covers, with prunus, peonies, and figures observing birds between borders of leaves and flowers, both covers topped with a shishi on a rocky outcrop.

ca. 1700   24in (61cm) high
$2,500-3,700   WW

An early-18thC Japanese Edo Period Imari vase and cover, with prunus, chrysanthemum, and peony issuing from rocky outcrops, with a border of lappets, the shoulder with tendrils and chrysanthemum flower heads, the neck with open fans.

27½in (70cm) high
$7,000-7,500   WW

A mid- to late-18thC Japanese Edo Imari barber's bowl, with flowering prunus, within a lattice border with standing figures and flowers, minor surface wear.

11in (28cm) diam
$300-375   TEN

An 18thC Japanese Edo Period Imari dish, with two pairs of shishi and fenhuang birds, around a centered bamboo and peony roundel, rim cracks, two blisters, gilding wear.

21½in (54.5cm) diam
$700-800   CHEF

An 18thC Japanese Edo Period Imari charger, with a centered peony in a vase, within a border of kiku and two spotted shishi, crack across the reserve, some glaze bubbling and clotting.

21¼in (54cm) diam
$1,000-1,100   CHEF

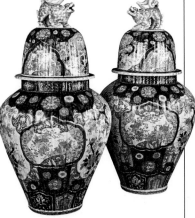

A pair of late-19thC Imari vases, ribbed, with covers surmounted by shishi dogs.

30¼in (77cm) high
$5,000-6,200   CHEF

ASIAN CERAMICS

A Japanese Edo Period tenmoku and blue-and-white dish, the upper section in mottled chocolate brown tenmoku glaze and the fences below rendered in underglaze blue, with old kintsugi gold lacquer repairs.

See O. Impey, "The Early Porcelain Kilns of Japan: Arita in the First Half of the Seventeenth Century," Clarendon (1996), no. 48d, where this dish is illustrated. Also, see "Ko_imari: A Catalog of Hizen Porcelain from the Nezu Museum's Yamamoto Collection," page 72, no. 274, for a related dish with the same decoration of snow-covered brushwood fences.

ca. 1660-70   *6in (15cm) wide*
$5,000-6,200   **WW**

A Japanese Edo Period molded dish, "Mukozuke," with three cranes and flowers, with gintsugi silver lacquer repair.

Provenance: Formerly the Tryhorn Collection. Donald Tryhorn (1942-2007) of Kingsbridge, Devon, collected a large number of 18thC and 19thC European ceramics, including examples of Bow, Bristol, Plymouth, Chantilly, and St Cloud porcelain, with a particular focus on Kakiemon wares. His collection also featured early Japanese pieces, such as this one.

ca. 1655-80   *5½in (14cm) diam*
$7,000-8,000   **WW**

A Japanese Edo Period Arita tankard, with peony, leafy branches, and buds, a band of karakusa scrolls below the rim and on the handle, the 19thC silver hinged cover with two heraldic birds, the reverse with punch marks and a shield-shaped hallmark enclosing the letter "V" and with a crown above (a 19thC Dutch mark for foreign silver).

See M. A. Pintos de Matos and R. Kerr, "Tankards and Mugs," Jorge Welsh (2016), page 118, fig. 36A, where this very mug is illustrated and discussed.

ca. 1660-80   *8¾in (22cm) high*
$1,250-1,500   **WW**

A 17thC Japanese Edo Period Arita shallow bowl, with a barbed rim, painted in Kraak style with a scholar stargazing by a plantain tree, with floral sprays, with a landscape border, Xuande mark.

9¼in (23.5cm) diam
$750-875   **WW**

A Japanese Edo Period Nabeshima dish, with a bamboo basket with chrysanthemum, leafy sprays, and fruits, the cover falling on one side, the reverse with three beribboned clusters of shippo-tsunagi (cash), with a combed foot.

Provenance: From the collection of Dr. Oliver Impey (1936-2005), and Dr. Jane (Mellanby) Impey (1938-2021). According to Oliver Impey's archive, this is a "v.good" example, and "shards of this pattern have been found at the Okawashi kiln site."

ca. 1700-20   *7¾in (20cm) diam*
$8,000-9,500   **WW**

A late-17thC Japanese Edo Period Arita dish, leafy sprays in the well, the cavetto with chrysanthemum and peonies, the rim with waves, the reverse with scrolling tendrils and a mark reading "Da Ming Chenghua nian zhi."

Provenance: From the collection of the late Gas Kimishima, wood-fire potter and specialist in the ancient kilns of Japan. Kimishima established his studio in England and built his own anagama kiln in Tring, Hertfordshire.

12½in (31.5cm) diam
$375-500   **WW**

A pair of 17th/18thC Japanese Edo Period Arita saucer dishes, with a Dutchman next to his camel, one with a hairline crack.

7in (18cm) diam
$6,000-7,500   **RMA**

A Japanese Arita porcelain dish, with a carp leaping up a waterfall amid overhanging pines, the reverse with shishi and ribbons, marked on the base "Fuki Choshun" (Wealth, Nobility, Longevity, and Youth), light surface wear.

ca. 1700   *20¼in (51.5cm) diam*
$625-750   **DN**

An early-18thC Japanese Edo Period Arita "Hare" dish, superficial crazing and rim chips.

8½in (21.5cm) diam
$1,500-2,000   **RMA**

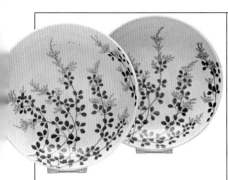

A pair of 18thC Japanese Edo Period Nabeshima dishes, with grasses and foliage, with three flower sprays and leafy tendrils on the reverse, raised on feet painted with a comb design.

6in (15cm) diam

$2,000-2,500   WW

An 18thC Japanese imitation Chinese Swatow export bowl, the exterior decorated with flowers, the interior with imitation "Da Qing" seal mark, the base with a spurious Chenghua mark.

6in (15cm) diam

$375-500   WAD

A Japanese Meiji Period Arita porcelain vase, with panels of landscape and birds among foliage.

22¾in (58cm) high

$300-375   TEN

A pair of 18thC Japanese Edo Period ai-Kakiemon "Deer" plates, one with hairline crack on the rim.

8¼in (21cm) diam

$950-1,050   RMA

A 19thC Japanese Meiji Period Seto vase and cover, with shishi and an eagle.

47¼in (120cm) high

$2,500-3,700   RMA

A Japanese Meiji Period double gourd vase, painted with a landscape, neck with old sprayed restoration.

17in (43cm) high

$450-550   DN

An 18thC Japanese Edo Period armorial plate, with barbed rim.

8¾in (22cm) diam

$1,250-1,900   RMA

A 19thC Japanese pierced jardinière, pierced with two tiers of chrysanthemum and peonies between columns in the shape of bamboo, inside with a metal container.

15¼in (38.5cm) high

$250-370   ROS

An early- to mid-20thC Japanese Arita vase.

30¾in (78cm) high

$750-875   WAD

ASIAN CERAMICS

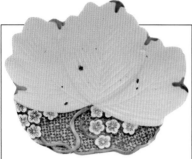

A mid-17thC Japanese Edo Period dish, the well with a large leaf, with prunus blossoms and tendrils, the reverse with foliage and flowers, the foot with comb pattern.

6½in (16.5cm) wide

$7,500-8,500   **WW**

A pair of Japanese Edo Period Kakiemon porcelain beakers, with stylized flowering tendrils, minor surface wear.

ca. 1680

2¼in (6cm) high

$2,500-3,700   **TEN**

A pair of 17thC Japanese Edo Period Ko-Kutani bowls.

3½in (9cm) diam

$875-1,000   **RMA**

A 17thC Japanese Edo Period Kakiemon rooster, comb restored, superficial wear.

A 17thC Japanese Edo Period Ko-Kutani "Lobster and Fish" dish.

9¼in (23.5cm) diam

$1,900-2,500   **RMA**

A late-17thC Japanese Edo Period Kakiemon basin, with floral design, minor superficial wear.

10¼in (26cm) diam

$2,200-2,700   **RMA**

8¼in (21cm) high

$12,500-15,000   **RMA**

A late-17thC Japanese Ko-Imari bottle vase, probably Edo Period, in Ko-Kutani style, with a rooster, a hen, and their chick, glaze lines, chips on foot rim.

9¾in (24.5cm) high

$3,700-5,000   **RMA**

A late-17th/early-18thC Japanese Arita dish, with two exotic birds amid the branches of The Three Friends (Pine, Prunus, and Bamboo), with a "Batavian" brown rim, the base with six spur marks, glaze wear and scratches.

9½in (24cm) diam

$7,000-7,500   **DN**

A late-17th/early-18thC Japanese Edo Period Ko-Imari sake bottle, "Tokkuri," with scrolling flowers, blossoming trees with bamboo, and wisteria.

7½in (19cm) high

$625-750   **WAD**

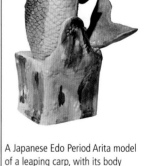

A Japanese Edo Period Arita model of a leaping carp, with its body contorted and its mouth open, the scales with cobalt blue and details in red paint.

See M. Cohen and W. Motley, "Mandarin and Menagerie," Cohen & Cohen (2008), pages 134-35, no. 8.1, for two comparable leaping carp.

ca. 1710

11¾in (30cm) high

$1,500-2,000   **WW**

ESSENTIAL REFERENCE—MEIJI PERIOD

The Meiji Period extended from October 23, 1868, to July 30, 1912, and corresponds to the reign of Emperor Meiji.

● It was an era when Japan moved from being an isolated feudal society at risk of colonization by Western powers to a modern, industrialized nation-state and emerging great power, influenced by Western ideas.

● The wholesale adoption of radically different ideas resulted in profound changes; it affected Japan's social structure, internal politics, economy, military, and foreign relations.

● The country's rapid modernization was not without its opponents. During the 1870s, many disaffected traditionalists from the former samurai class rebelled against the government, most famously Saigō Takamori, who led the Satsuma Rebellion.

● The Meiji Period was succeeded by the Taisho Period, following the accession of Emperor Taisho.

A Japanese Meiji Period Kutani porcelain bowl and cover, with painted and gilt chrysanthemums, the interior with dragon and foliage, minor wear.

6¾in (17cm) diam

$300-375 TEN

An Edo Period Arita porcelain stem cup, with "One Hundred Horse" design, with a male Immortal riding a phoenix in flight, the stem decorated with calligraphy in gilt.

ca. 1800-30 6¼in (16cm) diam

$450-550 L&T

A Japanese Meiji Period Kutani "Former Ode on the Red Cliffs" calligraphy cup, signed "Ze Ko Do San Jin," with original wood box.

1868-1912 7in (18cm) high

$450-550 WAD

A 20thC Japanese Kakiemon dish, with flower heads and rolling waves, signed "Imaizumi Imaemon."

8¾in (22cm) diam

$250-370 WAD

A rare Japanese Edo Period tripod porcelain box and cover, probably 18thC, possibly Seto ware, legs molded as small boys, embellished with geese in flight above snow-covered branches, with details in underglaze blue on the deep chocolate brown ground, the knop modeled as three uchiha fans.

6¼in (16cm) wide

$5,000-6,200 WW

A Japanese Edo Period Arita "Daffodil" dish.

7in (18cm) diam

$625-750 WAD

A pair of 20thC Japanese Showa Period Nabeshima dishes, with ho ho in flight, with trailing feathers above peonies issuing from rockwork, signed "Imaemon," probably for Imaizumi Imaemon XII (1897-1975).

8½in (21.5cm) diam

$500-625 WW

An 18th/19thC Japanese Edo Period Kutani dish, with mandarin ducks, scrolling clouds above, red Y-shaped diaper, the reverse with prunus branches, a green and black fuku mark.

12½in (32cm) diam

$3,700-4,300 WW

A 19th/20thC Japanese Meiji Period tripod vase, by Makuzu Kozan (1842-1916), in puce with three medallions and a band of clouds below, the panel with scenes of yokai, the oni and other monsters depicted holding banners and weapons while running haphazardly, on a sayagata (key fret) ground, the base inscribed "Makuzu gama Kozan sei."

4½in (11.5cm) high

$950-1,050 WW

A Japanese Republic Period wucai-style bucket, for the Chinese market, Wanli mark.

11in (28cm) high

$250-370 RMA

ESSENTIAL REFERENCE—CHINESE CLOISONNÉ

- Cloisonné is an ancient technique for decorating metalware. It involves soldering or otherwise attaching silver or gold wire to the surface of an object to form compartments—"cloisons" in French, hence the name. Different color enamels or inlays are then applied within the compartments, with the silver or gold wire perimeters remaining visible and keeping the compartments separate.
- The cloisonné technique reached China in the 13th/14thC, possibly from the Middle East, and possibly from Byzantium. The earliest datable pieces are from the reign of the Xuande emperor (1425-35) and display a wide range of styles from the Chinese vocabulary of ornament, suggesting considerable experience in the technique by this time; it is probable that further expertise arrived with a wave of refugee Byzantine craftsmen fleeing the fall of Constantinople in 1453.
- By the beginning of the 18thC, the Kangxi emperor had established a cloisonné workshop among the many other imperial factories working in the decorative arts.
- Characteristic colors include cobalt blue, dark green, red, yellow, white, and pink—the latter first appearing in the 18thC—and are often contrasted against a turquoise-color ground.

A Chinese cloisonné bowl, possibly 16thC, with flower foliage, with a six-character Xuande mark, wear in the gilding.

3¾in (9.5cm) diam

$7,500-8,500   **DN**

A 16thC Chinese Ming Dynasty cloisonné bowl, with lotus heads and Buddhist emblems below scrolling foliage, the interior decorated with a carp, with lacquer stand, enamels around the foot with later filling.

9½in (24cm) diam

$6,000-7,500   **DN**

A 17th/18thC late-Ming/early Qing Dynasty cloisonné enamel "Grapes" tripod incense burner, with grapes, foliage, and tendrils, with gilt highlights.

2¾in (7cm) high 12oz

$15,000-20,000   **L&T**

A 17th/18thC Chinese cloisonné enamel and gilt-bronze baluster vase, with lotus, other flowers, scrolling tendrils, and leaves, overall wear.

7¾in (19.5cm) high

$7,500-8,500   **GORL**

A Chinese cloisonné enamel dish, Ming Dynasty or later, with lotus amid tendrils.

4¾in (12cm) diam 8½oz

$2,200-2,700   **WW**

An 18th/19thC Qing Dynasty cloisonné enamel stupa, of Tibetan style, with lotus lappets, scrolling tendrils with beads, and mythical beast heads, opening to a side with a silk padded shrine set within a niche and lotus throne, topped with a hardstone-inlaid sun-moon finial and pinnacle.

12¼in (31cm) high 59⅝oz

$22,000-27,000   **L&T**

An 18th/19thC Qing Dynasty cloisonné enamel "Lotus" elephant head tripod censer, with a gilt-bronze roundel with a dragon and phoenix chasing a flaming pearl, with lotus in tendrils, the mouth rim and the edge of the base with gilt mount, with Qianlong mark.

19in (48cm) diam

$25,000-31,000   **L&T**

An 18th/19thC Qing Dynasty cloisonné enamel foliate charger, with a mythical qilin and a flying phoenix in a garden scene, the cavetto with cranes and deer, the underside with Eight Buddhist Emblems, the base with six lotus flowers, with a six-character Kangxi mark.

19in (48.5cm) diam

$8,500-10,000   **L&T**

CLOSER LOOK—A CLOISONNÉ ENAMEL LANDSCAPE VASE

The neck is decorated with Archaistic cicada lappets and ruyi head borders, which are echoed on the foot.

This is classic Chinese landscape decoration, with human figures, flora and fauna (some mythical), mountains, pavilions, and a river running through—a related "Landscape" vase is illustrated on page 153 in "The Complete Collection of Treasures of the (Beijing) Palace Musuem," 43, "Metal-Bodied Enamel Ware," Commerical Press Ltd. (2002).

"Cong" vases are of a visually distinct form; the square-section outer part encloses a tubular inner section, with the latter usually extending above the former in the form of a neck and a foot. The earliest "Congs" were produced by the Liangzhu culture ca. 3400-2250 BC. It has been speculated that the shape of the "Cong" may symbolize "the unity of heaven (the circle) and Earth (the square)."

An 18thC Chinese cloisonné enamel "Landscape" vase, of "Cong" form.

15¾in (40cm) high

$100,000-110,000   **WW**

A pair of 18th/early-19thC Chinese cloisonné enamel double gourd wall vases, with two gilt "da ji" characters with bats and cloud scrolls.

8½in (21.5cm) high

$3,700-4,300 **WW**

A pair of early-19thC Chinese Qing Dynasty cloisonné enamel vases, with French ormolu mounts, decorated with flowers and butterflies, the bases with lion pelts and paw feet.

15¾in (40cm) high

$12,500-15,000 **WW**

A 19thC Chinese cloisonné enamel bottle vase, with two birds perched on flower branches emerging from rockwork.

17in (43cm) high

$625-750 **WW**

A pair of 19thC Chinese cloisonné models of water buffalo, the underside of each pierced with a cash motif, each with a wood stand.

4½in (11.5cm) wide 7⅛oz

$1,250-1,500 **WW**

A Chinese cloisonné vase, with two dragons among clouds, with gilt lion-head handles, apocryphal Wanli mark, firing holes to surface.

12¼in (31cm) high

$22,000-27,000 **DN**

A Chinese Qing Dynasty cloisonné enamel "Lotus" vase, "Meiping," with flower heads and tendrils, with ruyi-shaped cartouches.

6½in (16.5cm) high 102¼oz

$2,500-3,100 **WW**

A pair of Chinese cloisonné enamel qilin, with cast and engraved gilt-metal heads, tails and hooves, with carved stands.

12½in (32cm) wide

$625-750 **HT**

A Chinese cloisonné enamel garlic-mouth vase, Qing Dynasty or later, with lotus in bloom among seed pods, curly leaves and millet above crashing waves, with a ruyi border on the mouth rim.

14in (35.5cm) high 104¾oz

$1,900-2,500 **WW**

A 19th/20thC late-Qing Dynasty/Republic Period cloisonné enamel "Millefleur" vase, the base with workshop mark "De Xing Cheng Zao" (Made by De Xing Cheng).

11¼in (28.5cm) high 24oz

$1,900-2,500 **L&T**

A Chinese Archaistic cloisonné enamel bell, "Bianzhong," probably 20thC, with taotie masks, kui dragons, zoomorphic and floral designs, the finial with gilt-bronze serpent flanges.

9½in (24cm) high 81⅛oz

$3,700-4,300 **WW**

A pair of late-20thC Chinese cloisonné vases, with birds, butterflies, and flowers, on carved hardwood stands.

40½in (103cm) high

$2,000-2,500   **WW**

A Canton enamel wine pot and cover, with panels of flowers below a dark green geometric border, unmarked.

6½in (16.5cm) high

$2,500-3,100   **HT**

A pair of Canton enamel saucers, one painted with a flowering bulb and moths, the other with flowering prunus, both with a metal "button" cast with a dragon, the bases painted with a dragon.

4½in (11.5cm) diam

$950-1,050   **HT**

A Canton enamel wine pot and cover, with flowers below a landscape, unmarked.

6½in (16.5cm) high

$750-875   **HT**

A pair of Canton enamel saucer dishes, with figures in mountainous river landscapes with prunus, the bases painted with a dragon, the border painted with three dragons.

8¼in (21cm) diam

$3,700-5,000   **HT**

A Canton enamel supper set, with a center dish and seven outer fan-shaped sections, painted with flowers, birds, and insects.

10½in (26.5cm) diam

$1,250-1,500   **HT**

A Chinese Qing Dynasty Canton enamel European-subject ewer and cover, painted with a couple drinking and a child by a gnarled tree, with attendants, the cover with a flower head.

7¾in (19.5cm) high

$3,700-4,300   **WW**

A Chinese Qing Dynasty champlevé enamel archer's ring, with pierced "shou" characters, on a gilt-metal ground.

Archaeological digs have revealed that archer's rings have been used in Asia since the Neolithic Period (ca. 10,000-2200 BC). Made from materials as diverse as wood, bone, stone, metal, ceramics, and leather, they were originally designed to fit over the tip of the thumb—they are also known as thumb rings—to protect the pad of the thumb against abrasion from the bowstring when drawing, holding, and releasing it. While elongated shaped rings, similar in profile to the pad of the thumb itself, were the most common form, during the course of the Qing Dynasty (ca. 1644-1911), they were gradually superseded by cylindrical thumb rings which, unlike their predecessors, fitted over the primary thumb joint and allowed the bowstring to be hooked around the base of the cylinder. The Qing Dynasty ring shown here is an example of the latter, and its elaborate decoration, which includes pierced "shou" characters, is also indicative of it being of a type that wasn't usable but was instead ceremonial and/or a symbol of status—its surface being so ornamented that it would interfere with the release of the bowstring. Such rings were often displayed hanging from cords on a belt instead of being worn on a thumb.

1½in (3.5cm) diam 1¼oz

$3,100-3,700   **WW**

A Chinese Qing Dynasty Canton enamel shell-shaped box, the silver-mounted lid painted with figures and huts in a mountainous watery landscape, the sides and interior painted with fruits, flowers and insects.

4¼in (10.5cm) diam

$1,400-1,500   **WW**

A pair of Chinese gold- and silver-inlaid bronze "Tiger and Boar" weights, probably Western Han Dynasty, depicting a snarling tiger pouncing on a boar.

2¼in (6cm) wide 24¾oz

$1,900-2,500 **WW**

A 16thC Chinese Ming Dynasty gilt-bronze vessel, "Gui," by Hu Wenming, with twin dragon handles, with Buddhist auspicious animals within bandings of dragons and butterflies, with incised four-character seal of Hu Wenming, general rubbing.

The incised four-character seal on the "Gui" is that of Hu Wenming. From Songjiang, in Jiangsu province, Wenming is widely acknowledged as being among the most skilled and gifted metalworkers of the late 16thC and early 17thC (the late Ming Dynasty). Most of his pieces were objects made for (and much desired by) scholars, notably incense burners and brush pots. Decoratively, they are characterized by densely worked backgrounds and mostly covered with flora and/or fauna cast in high relief, although this example also includes some of the Eight Buddhist Emblems ("Bajixian"—see page 109). The shape of this incense burner was inspired by an Archaic prototype dating to either the Shang (ca. 1600-1046 BC) or Zhou (ca. 1064-221 BC) dynasties.

7in (18cm) wide

$14,000-16,000 **CHEF**

A pair of Chinese Ming Dynasty Archaistic bronze altar vases, with leiwen panels and pixiu-head ring handles, some damage.

9in (23cm) high 44⅛oz (each)

$1,000-1,100 **GORL**

A Chinese Ming Dynasty Archaistic bronze vase, "Gu," with Archaistic scrolls and taotie masks, several dents.

7½in (19cm) high 33½oz

$450-550 **GORL**

A Chinese Kangxi parcel-gilt quatrefoil-section ewer and cover, cast with vases of flowers and qin qi shu hua, the four arts of the Chinese scholar, the handle modeled as a gnarled branch, the spout as a tapering section of bamboo, the neck with auspicious objects, above gilt ruyi heads, the cover with a gilt Buddhist lion dog.

See The Victoria & Albert Museum, London, no. M.69:1,2-1955 for a related vessel dated to ca. 1680.

1662-1722 *7½in (19cm) high 20⅜oz*

$12,500-15,000 **WW**

A Chinese Archaistic bronze censer, probably 17thC, with loop handles, cast with taotie, wear and scratches.

6¼in (16cm) wide

$875-1,000 **TEN**

A 17thC Chinese parcel-gilt bronze "Mythical Beast" incense burner, "Gui," cast with winged dragons flying between qilin and a leonine mythical beast, crashing waves, the rim and foot cast with phoenixes, flowers, and leaf scrolls, the handles as mythical beasts, the base with mark "yun jian Chu Chen Ming zhi."

8¾in (22.5cm) wide 67oz

$37,000-43,000 **WW**

A 17thC Chinese embossed copper and gilt-bronze incense burner, "Gui," with mythical creatures between key fret bands inlaid in silver, the handles cast as dragon heads, the base with a six-character "yun jian Hu Wen Ming zhi" mark.

7¾in (20cm) wide 24½oz

$10,000-11,000 **WW**

A 17thC late-Ming/Qing Dynasty bronze tripod censer, the base with "Xuan De Wu Nian Zhi Zao" (Made in the Fifth Year of Xuande Reign).

7¾in (19.5cm) wide 97⅝oz

$10,000-11,000 **L&T**

A 17thC Chinese parcel-gilt bronze "Falcon" incense burner, with a hinged cover on its back.

10¾in (27cm) high 47⅝oz

$22,000-27,000 **WW**

A 17th/18thC Chinese "Shi Sou" silver-inlaid bronze "Dragon" vase, with dragons chasing flaming pearls above breaking waves, the handles cast as animal masks, the base with a two-character "Shi Sou" mark.

12in (30.5cm) high 74oz

$1,250-2,500 **WW**

A 17th/18thC Chinese bronze vase, inspired by the Archaic bronze "Zhi," with two elephant-head handles, the body cast with flowers and fruits.

9in (23cm) high

$6,000-7,500 **DN**

A 17thC Chinese Archaistic parcel-gilt bronze Gu-shaped vase, with taotie masks on a leiwen ground, with pendant leaves on the neck.

11¼in (28.5cm) high 52⅞oz

$2,500-3,700 **WW**

A 17th/18thC Chinese bronze censer and stand, the original base cast with an apocryphal Xuande mark, some wear and marks.

7¾in (19.5cm) wide 105⅜oz

$19,000-25,000 **DN**

A 17th/18thC Chinese Archaistic parcel-gilt bronze tripod incense burner, "Ding," with three stylized taotie masks, on a leiwen ground divided by three vertical flanges.

13¾in (35cm) wide 176⅜oz

$37,000-43,000 **WW**

A late-17th/18thC Chinese inlaid bronze two-handle censer, "Gui," with scrollwork and taotie masks against scrolls, kui dragon handles.

23½in (60cm) wide

$10,000-11,000 **CHEF**

A Chinese Archaistic bronze "Jue," Qianlong mark and of the period, with kui dragons among key fret, raised on flared legs.

1736-95 *7in (17.5cm) high 49⅜oz*

$11,000-14,000 **WW**

A Chinese bronze gold splash vase, probably 18thC, with mask handles, small rim dents.

12¼in (31cm) high

$7,000-8,000 **LC**

An 18thC Chinese Imperial copper alloy censer, "Ding," with gilt lion-mask handles, cover lacking, some wear.

4¾in (12cm) wide 10⅞oz

$1,100-1,250 **GORL**

An 18thC Chinese bronze censer, cast Archaistic two-character Xuande mark, dents, later polished.

4¾in (12cm) diam 68¾oz

$6,000-7,500 GORL

A Chinese Qing Dynasty bronze censer, the base with Xuande mark, polished, three very small old copper patches.

7in (18cm) wide 49oz

$25,000-31,000 DN

An 18th/19thC Qing Dynasty bronze tripod censer, the base cast with "Kang Xi Liu Shi Nian Zhi" (Made in the Sixty Year of Kangxi Reign).

7in (18cm) wide 46¾oz

$20,000-25,000 L&T

An 18th/19thC Qing Dynasty Archaistic parcel-gilt bronze vessel, "Lei," the shoulders with Archaistic taotie motif, the lower body with kui dragon pattern, flanges, plantain leaves with phoenix motif, flanked with elephant-head handles.

13½in (34.5cm) high 190½oz

$4,300-5,600 L&T

An 18th/19thC Chinese bronze censer and stand, "Ding," cast Archaistic four-character Xuande mark, two dents, repair on rim.

7¼in (18.5cm) wide 30oz (without stand)

$1,000-1,100 GORL

A Chinese Qing Dynasty Archaistic bronze vase, "Hu," with masks and inlaid details, with geometric waves, the handles cast as mythical beasts, the base with scripts, wear and encrustation.

15½in (39.5cm) high 176⅜oz

$31,000-37,000 DN

A Chinese Archaistic bronze vase, cast with stylized clouds on a "seal" ground, below a row of six lappet panels, eight-character mark on base.

13¼in (33.5cm) high

$1,250-1,500 HT

A Chinese Qing Dynasty bronze censer, the base with a six-character Xuande mark, polished surface and loss of original patina.

2¼in (6cm) high 11¾oz

$5,000-6,200 DN

A Chinese Qing Dynasty gilt-bronze incense burner, the base with a four-character mark that reads "yu tang qing wan."

8¼in (21cm) wide 74oz

$1,000-1,100 WW

A Chinese Qing Dynasty bronze tripod censer, incised with a Xuande mark, surface polished, patch of restoration.

7½in (19cm) wide 53½oz

$3,700-5,000   DN

A Chinese bronze vase, probably late-Qing Dynasty, with pine and peach trees, bats and cranes, the neck with birds and flowers and elephant-mask handles, the base with a Qianlong mark.

13in (33cm) high 317½oz

$5,000-6,200   WW

A Chinese gilt-decorated "Bronze Imitation" Archaistic vase, "Pou," probably Republic Period, with kui dragons and mythical beast masks divided by flanges, the shoulder with four mask handles, the base with four-character Qianlong mark.

5¾in (14.5cm) high

$2,500-3,100   WW

Judith Picks

Shangqing, also known as Lingbao Tianzun, and also the Heavenly Lord of Spiritual Treasures, is one of the Sanqing—the other two being Yuqing and Taiqing. The Sanqing, also known as the Three Purities, are regarded as the most important deities in the Taoist pantheon. So, the subject of this figural sculpture is far from anonymous and represents a significant strand of spirituality and belief. Undoubtedly, that contributes hugely to the desirability and value of the figure, but there are also other qualities that reinforce them. Among these are the very high quality of the modeling and casting, and the subtly lustrous and particularly pleasing brown and gilt-brown patina. However, for me—and above all—it is the meditative serenity and sheer contentment that the sculptor has captured in Shangqing's expression and posture.

A Chinese late-Ming Dynasty gilt and lacquered bronze figure of Shangqing, the sitting deity wearing loose flowing robes decorated with cloud scrolls and geometric designs, with his hand held in front of his chest, his face with a serene expression, with his hair arranged in a topknot, framed by elongated earlobes and strands of a long beard, raised on a three-legged stand decorated with fierce animal masks.

25¾in (65.5cm) high 635oz

$80,000-95,000   WW

A Chinese Ming Dynasty parcel-gilt bronze figure of Guanyin, the bodhisattva sitting in dhyanasana, her right hand held in vitarkamudra, with a double lotus wood stand.

8¼in (21cm) high 56⅛oz

$1,250-1,900   WW

A Chinese Ming Dynasty bronze sitting figure of a dignitary, with a wood stand.

9¾in (24.5cm) high 34⅜oz

$1,500-1,900   WW

A Qianlong cast and repoussé gilt-bronze figure of Chaturbhuja Lokeshvara, sitting in padmasana, front hands in anjali mudra before the chest, back-left hand holding a lotus stem and right in karana mudra, with a five-leaf crown with a chignon topped with a Buddha's head, heavily jeweled.

6¾in (17cm) high 20⅝oz

$6,000-7,500   L&T

An 18thC Chinese gilt-copper repoussé model of Amitayus, sitting in dyhanasana, the base with a double vajra.

7in (18cm) high 19½oz

$1,900-2,500 WW

A Chinese gilt-bronze figure of Buddha, in Ming Dynasty style, on a lotus petal dais.

18in (46cm) high

$3,100-3,700 CHEF

A 19thC parcel-gilt and silvered copper figure of Buddha, sitting in dhyanasana upon a double lotus throne.

6¼in (16cm) high 26½oz

$1,400-1,700 WW

A 19thC Qing Dynasty gilt-bronze figure of Milarepa, cast sitting on a double lotus throne in lalitasana, the sage wearing a loose robe with his upper body exposed, his meditative face looking slightly to the right with gently tilted head, right arm resting on right thigh with palm raised, left hand set with a kapala tucked on the lap, the base sealed with a plaque incised with double-vajras, lower back of the throne engraved with Tibetan inscriptions.

Most often depicted with a hand raised to his ear in a listening gesture, Milarepa was a hermit yogi and poet, who was known and much respected by the Tibetan people. As a renowned poet, his listening gesture symbolizes his unique way of imparting Buddhist's wisdom through songs. The skull cap or kapala vessel is a reminder of the impermanence of life, and the inevitability of death, which through the practice of Buddhism, one can achieve enlightenment and be released from Samsara.

7¾in (19.5cm) high 50¾oz

$190,000-250,000 L&T

A Chinese Six Dynasties silver repoussé "Tiger" bowl, with a ferocious tiger with lotus petals, the border with five animals amid leafy scrolls, with a metal stand.

4¾in (12cm) diam

$4,300-5,600 WW

A Chinese silver and parcel-gilt vase, "Hu," probably Qing Dynasty, with chilong amid lingzhi, the neck with bats and lingzhi, the borders with swastikas, ruyi heads, lappets, and flower scrolls, with a four-character Qianlong mark.

15in (38cm) high 127oz

$19,000-25,000 WW

A Chinese Qing Dynasty export silver tankard, by Cheng Ji, Canton, with scholars at leisure among trees, rockwork, and pavilions, a dragon-form handle, with initials "MCSS," with a two-character maker's mark "Cheng Ji" in Chinese.

Cheng Ji, an artisan operating in Canton (Guangzhou) from the early- to mid-19thC, produced only tankards and stemmed goblets. He is known to have made items on a regular basis for the two Canton retail merchants HOACHING, and his mark is still, in general, known as "GOTHIC K."

ca. 1850-60

5in (12.5cm) wide 9⅞oz

$3,100-3,700 L&T

A Chinese Qing Dynasty "Shi Sou"-style zitan silver and gold wire-inlaid incense stick holder, with poetic inscriptions, with prunus and pine beside rockwork, the base with a seal mark "yu tang."

6½in (16.5cm) high

$12,500-15,000   **WW**

A late-19thC Chinese silver goblet, with vine and grape decoration, with marks for "Wang Hing," "90," and with Chinese characters.

11¼in (28.5cm) high 22¼oz

$1,200-1,350   **WW**

A Chinese silver card case, with dragons and a cartouche, the reverse and sides with a bird and cherry blossom, marked "Wang Hing," "90," and with Chinese characters.

4in (10cm) long 2¾oz

$625-750   **WW**

A Chinese Qing Dynasty export silver "Bamboo" tankard, by Lee Ching, Canton and Shanghai, incised with a bamboo groove issuing from low piles of rocks visited by insects, marked "LC" and "Quan."

ca. 1830-95   *3¾in (9.5cm) high 5⅞oz*

$750-875   **L&T**

A Chinese silver mug, with two dragons and a pearl cartouche, simulated bamboo handle, initialed, gilt interior, with Chinese characters and "Luenwo, Shanghai."

ca. 1900   *4¼in (10.5cm) high 7⅞oz*

$1,000-1,100   **WW**

A Chinese silver bowl, the body with a dragon, cherry blossom scroll handles, marked "WA" twice and with Chinese characters.

9½in (24cm) wide 18⅝oz

$700-800   **WW**

A pair of Chinese silver bowls, with birds and cherry blossom, with Chinese characters and "WA."

5¼in (13.5cm) diam 14½oz

$500-625   **WW**

A cased Chinese late-Qing Dynasty/Republic Period export silver three-piece tea service with sugar tongs, by Sheng Chang, Canton, with bamboo grooves with butterflies, marked "Shen Chang," "90," and a retail mark "CL" for Cheong Lam (Cheng Lin).

ca. 1875-1930   *teapot 6in (15cm) high 20⅜oz*

$7,000-8,000   **L&T**

ESSENTIAL REFERENCE—JAPANESE CLOISONNÉ

● While cloisonné enamel ware became widely appreciated in Japan in the late-16thC (centuries after China—see page 122), the development of Japanese cloisonné manufacturing did not really begin until the early-19thC.

● Its introduction is credited to a former samurai, Kaji Tsunekichi (1803-83) of Nagoya, in Owari province. Like many other samurai, he was forced to find ways to supplement his official stipend and ca. 1838, having purchased a piece of Chinese cloisonné and closely examined how it was made, he produced his first cloisonné dish. He based most of his designs on the motifs and color palettes of Chinese precedents.

● By the mid-1850s, Tsunekichi had taken on pupils and, by the late-1850s, he had been appointed official cloisonné maker to the daimyo (feudal chief) of Owari.

● One of Kaji Tsunekichi's pupils was Hayashi Shōgorō (d.1896), a craftsman celebrated for the fact that many of his pupils taught, in turn, many of the later Japanese masters of cloisonné enameling. Among the former was Tsukamoto Kaisuke (1828-87), and among the latter, Hayashi Kodenji (1831-1915), who established an independent cloisonné workshop in Nagoya in 1862; equally worthy of mention among the late Japanese masters is Namikawa Sōsuke (1847-1910), who in 1896 was appointed Imperial Craftsman to the court of Emperor Meiji.

A pair of Japanese Meiji Period cloisonné enamel vases, with birds and flowering rose branches, the base with white daisies.

46¾in (118.5cm) high

$6,000-7,500   HT

A 19thC Japanese Meiji Period red Ginbari cloisonné vase, with chrysanthemum flowers, scrolling clouds, with metal mounts on the rims.

9¼in (23.5cm) high

$1,250-1,500   WW

A pair of 19thC Japanese Meiji Period cloisonné vases, with sparrows in flight, chrysanthemum blooms and daisies, with formal designs and flower heads on the rims, with impressed marks of a single character in a five-petal flower.

7½in (19cm) high

$2,500-3,100   WW

A Japanese Edo/Meiji Period cloisonné vase and cover, with panels enclosing a chicken, on a background of leafy tendrils, flowers, and geometric textile-weave panels.

ca. 1860-70   22¾in (57.5cm) high

$450-550   WW

A pair of 19thC Japanese Meiji Period cloisonné vases, with birds flying and perched among prunus in gold and silver wires, the rims with borders of lappets and stylized flower heads, both with silver mounts, stamped "jungin" underneath.

14½in (37cm) high

$7,500-8,500   WW

A pair of 19thC Japanese cloisonné vases, with ho ho birds and writhing dragons chasing flaming pearls of wisdom, with medallions enclosing butterflies and chidori plovers in flight, the rims with metal mounts.

9¾in (25cm) high

$750-875   WW

A pair of 19thC Japanese Meiji Period cloisonné vases, with butterflies flying among flowering peonies, the necks with writhing dragons in scrolling clouds, the design rendered in silver, gold, and brass wires.

12½in (32cm) high

$500-625   WW

A pair of 19thC Japanese Meiji Period cloisonné vases, with birds of prey on branches of prunus, with bands of lappets above the feet and under the rims.

15¼in (38.5cm) high

$800-950   WW

A 19th/20thC Japanese Meiji Period cloisonné vase, by Ota Kichisaburo, with two doves on a flowering prunus tree, the base with an impressed mark reading "O Kichi" for Ota Kichisaburo.

6in (15cm) high

$750-875   WW

A 19th/20thC Japanese Meiji/Taisho Period cloisonné vase, by Tamura I/Ota Shunjiro (1864-1931), with three birds in flight before branches of bamboo, the design rendered in gold wires, the rims with metal mounts, the base stamped "Tamura zo."

5in (12.5cm) high

$700-800   **WW**

A 19th/20thC Japanese Meiji Period cloisonné vase, by Hayashi Kodenji (1831-1915), with chrysanthemum, peonies, daisies, dandelions, a maple tree with a stream, rendered in silver and gold wires, marked "Aichi Hayashi saku" with the stamped lozenge seal of Hayashi Kodenji.

7in (18cm) high

$1,900-2,500   **WW**

A Japanese Meiji Period silver-wire cloisonné vase, in the manner of Hayashi Kodenji, with shrubs and trees, unmarked, small scuffs, wear.

6in (15cm) high

$500-625   **GORL**

A 19th/20thC Japanese Meiji Period cloisonné vase, by Hayashi Kodenji (1831-1915), with two sparrows in flight with daisies and bamboo, with silver mounts, signed with the lozenge mark of Hayashi Kodenji.

9¾in (24.5cm) high

$2,500-3,700   **WW**

A Japanese cloisonné enamel and gilt-bronze-mounted jardinière, with qilin and a ho ho bird, the mounts European, possibly restored.

17¾in (45cm) wide

$1,000-1,100   **CHEF**

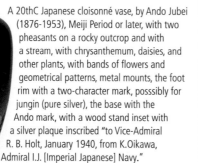

A Japanese Meiji Period cloisonné incense burner, "Koro," by Namikawa Yasuyuki (1845-1927), with two birds flying toward flowering branches of prunus, the sakura blossoms and buds in shades of pink, with silver and shakudo mounts and cover, the base with the four-character mark for Kyoto Namikawa in silver wires.

It appears that this mark was used for the best pieces produced by Namikawa Yasuyuki's workshops, and possibly for those made for international exhibitions.

ca. 1910-15   *3¾in (9.5cm) high*

$7,500-8,500   **WW**

A 20thC Japanese Taisho/Showa Period cloisonné vase, by Hayashi Tanigoro (active 1895-1935), with silver mounts, impressed "SILVER," with mark "Hayashi Tani" for Hayashi Tanigoro.

6¾in (17cm) high

$1,000-1,100   **WW**

A 20thC Japanese cloisonné vase, by Ando Jubei (1876-1953), Meiji Period or later, with two pheasants on a rocky outcrop and with a stream, with chrysanthemum, daisies, and other plants, with bands of flowers and geometrical patterns, metal mounts, the foot rim with a two-character mark, posssibly for jungin (pure silver), the base with the Ando mark, with a wood stand inset with a silver plaque inscribed "to Vice-Admiral R. B. Holt, January 1940, from K.Oikawa, Admiral I.J. [Imperial Japanese] Navy."

Provenance: The collection of Vice Admiral Reginald Vesey Holt, CB, DSO, MVO, (1884-1957). The vase was gifted by Admiral Koshiro Oikawa (1883-1958), the Japanese Naval Minister during World War II.

9¾in (24.5cm) high

$3,100-3,700   **WW**

A pair of 20thC Japanese Meiji/Taisho Period cloisonné vases, with poppies and other flowers, some petals rendered in foil, both with a stamped flower mark for Tsukamoto Hikokichi.

7in (18cm) high

$375-500   **WW**

A mid-20thC Japanese silver-wire cloisonné-enamel baluster vase, by Ando, decorated with Archaistic birds, scrolls, and lappets, Ando mark on base, plated rims, one scratch.

10¼in (26cm) high

$500-625   **GORL**

A 19thC Japanese Meiji Period silvered bronze okimono of a cockatoo, by Mitani, the feathers with highlights in gilt and the eyes, beak, and claws in shakudo, signed in a gilt rectangular plaque underneath "Mitani sei."

See L. Bordignon, "The Golden Age of Japanese Okimono," ACC (2010), pages 244-45, where another okimono of a cockatoo by Mitani is illustrated.

7¾in (19.5cm) high

$16,000-20,000   WW

ESSENTIAL REFERENCE—OKIMONO

Unlike netsuke, which originally had a specific and functional purpose (see page 152), Japanese okimono are small decorative objects that were always intended purely for display (often in a toconoma alcove or a butsudan altar). Although usually larger than netsuke, okimono are crafted from a similar range of materials, notably wood, ivory, ceramic, or metal, and depict subjects as diverse as humans, deities, flora and fauna, and mythological beasts. One subcategory of okimono is jizai okimono: articulated figures often made from bronze or iron. Some okimono were designed as a collection or group of objects intended to be displayed together as an ensemble.

A 19thC Japanese Meiji Period bronze okimono of a hawk, by Hidemitsu/Shuko, the raptor naturalistically depicted, perched on a rocky outcrop emerging from silvered waves, its wings stretched as if to take flight, with some details rendered in gilt and shakudo, the underside of its tail feathers signed in a double seal for Kazumasa Ishida and Hidemitsu/Shuko Kansei (supervised by Hidemitsu/Shuko).

Kazumasa Ishida had a workshop in Tokyo and was a member of the Tokyo Chukin Kai (Tokyo Cast Metal Association).

28¼in (72cm) high

$10,000-11,000   WW

A Japanese Meiji Period bronze model of a sword fittings master craftsman, by Miyao Eisuke, the sitting artist chasing a bronze tsuba, signed, with original gilt-lacquered wood stand, some damage.

7in (18cm) high

$2,500-3,700   GORL

A 19thC Japanese Meiji Period bronze okimono of a tiger and crocodile, the ferocious-looking feline pouncing over the back of the reptile, eyes inlaid in glass, on a wood base, the tiger with a mark for Masamitsu.

20¾in (53cm) wide

$2,500-3,700   WW

A 19thC Japanese Meiji Period bronze okimono of a bear cub and tiger, the feline attacking the small bear, the distressed cub attempting to defend itself.

8½in (21.5cm) wide

$1,250-1,500   WW

A 19thC Japanese Meiji Period bronze vase, by Moriguchi, in gold and silver nunomezogan with thatched pavilions in mountainous river landscapes, seal mark for Kyoto Moriguchi.

5¼in (13.5cm) high

$1,000-1,100   WW

A 19thC Japanese Meiji Period bronze dish, the well with a silver crane wading in lotus leaves and flowers, the cavetto with geometric designs and the three mitsuba-aoi mon (three hollyhock leaves crest) used by the Tokugawa clan, the reverse with a two-character mark.

9½in (24cm) diam

$800-950   WW

A 19thC Japanese Meiji Period bronze okimono of Daruma, the Father of Zen Buddhism, depicted standing, on a scroll-shaped stand.

12¼in (31cm) high

$1,000-1,100   WW

A 19thC Japanese Meiji Period silver-inlaid bronze vase, with a pheasant on prunus, with a wood stand.

6½in (16.5cm) high

$500-625   WW

A 19th/20thC Japanese Meiji Period jizai okimono model of a crab, with a three-character signature.

8¾in (22cm) wide

$2,500-3,700   WW

A Japanese parcel-gilt bronze of a samurai, possibly by Miyao Eisuke, standing holding his tanto, the sheath, and Wakasashi, with inro, sword snapped off halfway.

11½in (29.5cm) high

$3,100-3,700   CHEF

A Meiji Period "Chrysanthemum" double-skin silver bowl, representative of an Imperial Chrysanthemum, stamped with a two-character mark "jungin" on the base for "pure silver."

11in (28cm) diam 69½oz

$6,000-7,500   L&T

A Meiji Period patinated bronze vase, with draping branches bearing blossoming flowers, applied in silver shakudo and gold takazogan mixed metals.

9½in (24cm) high 69¾oz

$1,900-2,500   L&T

A pair of 19th/20thC Japanese Meiji Period bronze incense burners and covers, "Koro," with tigers and writhing dragons, lids with a tiger.

13¼in (33.5cm) high

$250-310   WW

A pair of late-19thC Japanese Meiji Period parcel-gilt bronze vases, by Hashimoto Isshi I or II, with birds and flowers, a writhing dragon and bird-shaped handles, each with a band of gold splashes on the neck and inscribed with a poem, "Bush warblers are singing and flitting between the branches of plum trees, as if they are embroidering a hat with designs of plum blossom," and the other, "The guards are idle at the moment, however, the scent of plum flowers is carried though the fence by the wind," signed "Hashimoto" for Hashimoto Isshi I (1820-96) or II (active ca. 1903).

See R. E. Haynes, "The Index of Japanese Sword Fittings and Associated Artists," Ellwangen, (2001), page 400, where both Isshi I and II are discussed. Hashimoto Isshi I came from Omi province and later worked in Edo by order of the Shogun, before returning to Kyoto in 1863. The author notes that he "became a retainer of the Hirohata kuge family and was allowed to wear a sword." His son Yoshitaro, later becoming the second Isshi, worked in the same style as his father, so, because of this, it can be difficult to differentiate their works.

30in (76.5cm) high

$5,000-6,200   WW

A 19th/20thC Japanese bronze okimono of Amida Buddha, Meiji Period or later, sitting in the dhyanasana meditative pose, with his hands held in the mida no join mudra, on a lotus throne.

20¾in (53cm) high

$1,000-1,100   WW

A late-19th/early-20thC Japanese Meiji Period silver-inlaid bronze vase, with leafy branches of bamboo, the side with a two-character signature.

9¾in (24.5cm) high

$3,700-4,300   WW

CLOSER LOOK—A GENRYUSAI SEIYA ANIMAL GROUP

Genryusai Seiya (1868-1912) was one of the foremost bronze sculptors of the Meiji Period, and specialized in animal subjects, especially elephants. His early death, at the age of 44, means there are far fewer examples of his work than there would have been had he lived to a ripe old age. Underpinned by his compositional skills, this further enhances the desirability of his pieces.

Surface texture plays an important role in the composition: the rougher skin of the elephant contrasts with the smoother, sleeker skin of the tigers—the former contributing to a sense of muscular solidity, the latter to agility and speed.

Much of the attraction of the sculpture resides in the sense of dynamic, albeit violent, movement in both the individual figures and the overall composition.

The group sculpture retains its original wood base, which harmoniously complements the cast bronze figures in terms of both color and patination.

A Japanese Meiji Period cast bronze group, by Genryusai Seiya, the elephant being attacked by two Siberian tigers, the tusks inlaid in ivory, with a foundry seal on the belly, with original wood stand.

12¾in (32.5cm) wide

$1,250-1,900   DN

A 19th/20thC Japanese Meiji Period gold and silver-inlaid bronze vase, with a songbird on magnolia, with daisies and lotus leaves, seal mark for "Dai Nihon Tokyo Saito seizo."

11¾in (30cm) high

$2,500-3,100   WW

A pair of 19th/20thC Japanese Meiji Period bronze incense burners and covers, "Koro," signed "Mori Homei."

16½in (42cm) high

$500-625   WW

A 20thC Japanese Meiji/Taisho Period inlaid bronze vase, with three cranes in flight before a mountain, possibly Mount Fuji, signed and inscribed with a dedication mentioning Tokyo Denki (Tokyo Electric Industry Association), with a wood stand.

11¾in (30cm) high

$500-625   WW

A 19th/20thC Japanese Meiji/Taisho Period bronze okimono of a puppy, by Takahashi Ryoun, two-character mark for Ryoun.

Ryoun was a famous bronze artist living in Tokyo at the turn of the century. He was a special member of the Tokyo School of Fine Arts, and he exhibited at the Exposition Universelle in Paris in 1900, where he received several awards for the quality of his artworks.

6in (15cm) high

$1,500-1,900   WW

A 19th/20thC Japanese Meiji Period bronze okimono of Hotei, the God of Good Fortune, leaning against his treasure sack, signed "Juko" on the back.

8¼in (21cm) wide

$450-550   WW

A Japanese Showa Period bronze okimono of two sumo wrestlers, the base dated and signed "Inosuke Yamaguchi."

1966   *14¼in (36cm) high*

$875-1,000   WW

An early-20thC Japanese Meiji/Taisho Period silver okimono of a Minogame, the mythical turtle, with seaweed growing from the top of its shell and trailing behind it, signed "Ryubundo zo," and with a junjin silver mark below.

9¾in (24.5cm) wide

$4,300-5,000   WW

A Meiji/Taisho Period bronze okimono of a tiger, its eyes of inlaid glass with black pupils, marked "Tamemitsu."

24¾in (63cm) wide 194oz

$1,250-1,500   L&T

A 20thC Japanese Meiji/Showa Period bronze okimono of Prince Shotoku, Shotoku Taishi depicted as a youth on a rocky outcrop, a falcon on his left arm, the back with calligraphy, possibly with a signature for artist Hata Shokichi (1882-1966).

Prince Shotoku Taishi (574-622) was a semi-legendary Crown Prince and Regent to the Empress Suiko during the Asuka Period (538-710). He became an important political and cultural leader modernizing the government administration. He also promoted Buddhism and is sometimes regarded as one of its founders in Japan.

9¾in (24.5cm) high

$1,250-1,500   WW

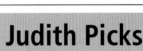

Judith Picks

While it will not be to everyone's taste, I must confess to really liking the very dynamic, yet smooth, streamlined, and overtly modern aesthetic of this 20thC samurai figure. I also like the fact that, in contrast, it represents something much older: legend has it that the Japanese Shogun Hideyoshi once gifted a famed spear to one of his generals, Masanori. One day, a samurai from the Kuroda clan, Mori Tahei—the subject of this sculpture—arrived with a message for the general, who, on receiving it, invited Mori Tahei to take a drink with him. Initially, Mori Tahei refused, but General Masanori offered him any gift of his choice if he would accept some sake. Eventually, Mori Tahei agreed, drank the sake, and then claimed the famed spear. This, in turn, gave rise to the popular song "Kuroda Bushi," which includes the lines: "Drink, drink sake. If you drink it, you will win the best spear in Japan. And if you drink enough to win it, you are a true Kuroda samurai!"

A 20thC Japanese modern silvered- and parcel-gilt bronze okimono of Mori Tahei, the samurai standing, holding his spear and sake cup, with a seal mark on the back, possibly for Junichiro Hanwaka.

14¾in (37.5cm) high

$500-625   WW

ASIAN WORKS OF ART

A Tibetan late-Qing Dynasty copper repoussé figure of Buddha, sitting in dhyanasana upon a lotus throne, with one hand held in dhyana mudra, the other touching the ground in bhumisparsha mudra.

28¾in (73cm) high 634⅞oz

$5,000-6,200   WW

A 16th/17thC Tibetan gilt-copper repoussé fragment depicting Padmapani, the bodhisattva stands on a lotus platform on an elephant beneath a mythical beast, the panel with red cold-painted pigments.

13½in (34cm) high

$3,700-4,300   WW

A 17thC Sino-Tibetan gilt-bronze Buddha, sitting in dhyanasana upon a double lotus throne, the left hand in dhyana mudra, the right hand in karana, draped in monk's robes covering one shoulder and falling in folds at the legs, the chest bare except for a wan emblem, the full face with bud lips and heavy-lidded eyes below an urna, ears pierced and elongated, the hair covered in tight curls and surmounted by an usnisa, obvious wear in gilding, some green verdigris on underside.

5in (12.5cm) high 34⅛oz

$7,500-8,500   DN

An 18thC Tibetan gilt-bronze sitting figure of Buddha Shakyamuni, on a double lotus throne, lacking bowl, wear in gilding.

3¾in (9.5cm) high 12⅞oz

$2,500-3,100   GORL

A large 18thC Thai bronze standing figure of Buddha, picked out in red lacquer and gold, with a wood stand.

33¾in (86cm) high 564⅜oz

$5,000-6,200   WW

A Thai bronze core-on-clay standing Buddha, Ayutthaya style.

17¼in (44cm) high

$750-875   CHEF

An 18thC Himalayan parcel-gilt iron vajra, the eight-prong vajra with bulbous center section flanked by a band of four faces, framed by beaded rims and lappets.

In Buddhism and Hinduism, "vajra" means "a thunderbolt or mythical weapon," especially one weilded by the god Indra.

10in (25.5cm) long 23½oz

WW

ESSENTIAL REFERENCE—THE SWAT VALLEY

By the 5thC, Buddhism had been thriving for over 600 years in Gandhara and the Swat Valley in Northern Pakistan.

● Strategically located on the ancient Silk Road, the Swat Valley was an especially vibrant center of Buddhist art, financed by the extensive trade that flowed through the Khyber and Karakorum passes.

● The art was primarily sculptural in form, and gave rise to the term "Swat Valley sculpture," which encapsulates both a geographic area and a time period, namely and respectively: the far Western Himalayan regions inclusive of the Swat Valley, Gilgit, and Baltistan, from the 6thC to the 9thC.

● Although not extensive, the iconographic subjects of Swat Valley sculpture included most important Buddhist deities.

● Here, the sitting Buddha is cast in copper alloy, the most common metallic material for Swat Valley sculptures,

and is covered in a dark brown and touch of forest green patina. Finely modeled, it is a classic rendition of Buddha Shakyamuni, shown sitting on a throne supported on a single lotus base. Its large lotus petals are bulbous, polished, and smooth and contrast with the rippling folds of Shakyamuni's robe. Shakyamuni holds the hem of this robe with his left hand—a gesture widely employed in sitting Swat Valley Buddhas, and extending the style from earlier Gandharan stone images. It is also interesting to note that within the peaceful demeanor of his face, the cavity in Shakyanumi's eyes suggest that they might have been originally inlaid with silver—a common embellishment in Swat Valley figures to celebrate Buddha's enlightened nature.

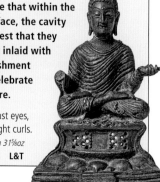

An 8thC Swat Valley copper-alloy figure of Shakyamuni, cast sitting in padmasana on a lotus throne, with downcast eyes, prominent lips and nose flanked by a pair of large pendulous ears, the head and domed ushnisha covered with tight curls.

6in (15cm) high 31⅝oz

$16,000-20,000   L&T

ESSENTIAL REFERENCE—JADE

As a decorative medium, jade has a long history in China, and traditionally it has been prized almost as much as gold. Carved into jewelry and ceremonial or decorative items, examples have been unearthed dating to as long ago as ca. 4000 BC.

- **Technically, jade refers to two separate minerals: nephrite and jadeite, although objects carved from other stones that are similar in appearance are also sometimes referred to as jade.**
- **The majority of Chinese jades are fashioned from nephrite, which was mined in Eastern Central Asia. Its color can vary from creams and whites to greens and blacks, while pieces made from jadeite can include green, white, and flecks of red in close proximity.**
- **Ming Dynasty jades tend to be carved from different color stones and have a soft polished finish, while Qing Dynasty jades are often white and almost translucent.**
- **It's a generalization, but heavier, more elaborate pieces are probably of more recent origin. Having said that, jade is notoriously difficult to date.**
- **Because jade is brittle and easily scratched, condition is a significant factor when it comes to desirability and value. That said, the jade market is fairly unpredictable and it's not uncommon for Chinese jades to go to auction with low estimates, but then to sell for (sometimes much) more than expected.**

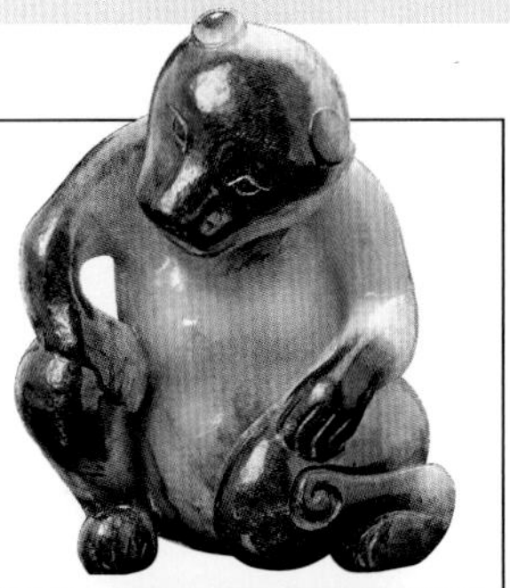

A white jade with russet skin carving of a sitting bear, Han Dynasty or later, alerted bulging eyes, pricked ears, strong jaw incised with details, the stone of white color with russet patches and lines.

The relaxed posture and playful attitude resembles the Ellsworth bear, a gilt-bronze sitting bear dated to the Western Han Dynasty (206 BC-AD 8) and formerly in the collection of Robert Hatfield Ellsworth. Such relaxed naturalism in the asymmetrical pose, informal manner, and somewhat whimsical presentation finds an antecedent in a small jade bear in Harvard's Grenville L. Winthrop Collection (object no. 1943.50.310) that dates to the Warring States period (475-221 BC).

3in (7.5cm) high

$16,000-20,000 L&T

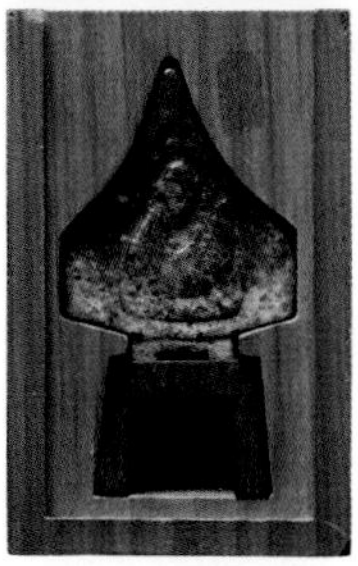

A Six Dynasties yellowish-brown jade carving of a Stele, the leaf-shaped aureole containing a worn image of the Buddha, the reverse bearing an incised inscription with the last name "Gao" (first name not legible), title "Zhongjun Sima" (Central Minister of the Army) under the King of Lanling, of the donor and a date corresponding to 484 (the second year of Yongming, Qi Dynasty), with sandalwood stand and storage box.

220-589 *2¼in (6cm) high*

$60,000-75,000 WAD

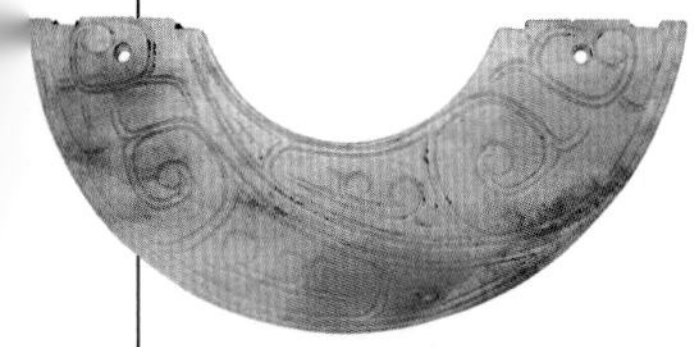

A Chinese yellow and russet jade "Dragon" huang, possibly Zhou Dynasty, carved with a motif representing an abstract dragon body, with a small hole in each end.

4½in (11.5cm) wide

$12,500-15,000 WW

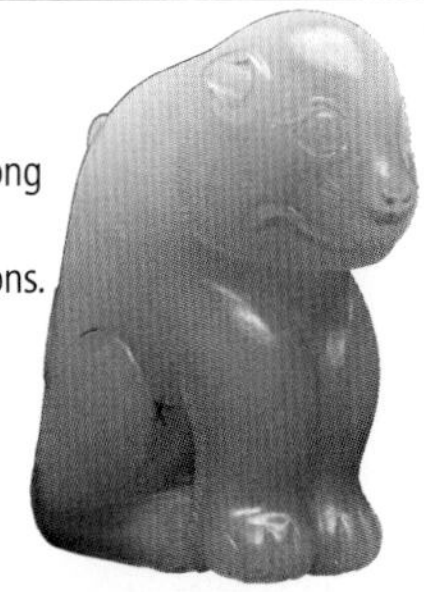

A Chinese pale celadon jade feline, probably Song Dynasty, features and fur detailed with incised lines, pale tone stone with minor russet inclusions.

Provenance: From the private collection of Roger Bluett (1925-2000), and thence by descent. Roger Bluett took over the dealership buisness founded by his grandfather, Leonard Bluett, in 1884. He and his partner Brian Morgan introduced a number of innovations, including being the first dealers to publish scholarly catalogs, and turned it into one of the greatest London dealerships in Chinese art of its day. His clients included King Gustav VI Adolf of Sweden (who granted Bluett's his royal warrant and was a regular visitor), and museums, including the British Museum and the Victoria & Albert and New York Metropolitan museums.

2in (5cm) high

$25,000-31,000 WW

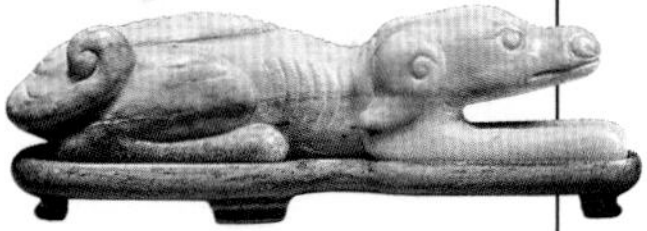

A Chinese carved jade model of a dog, Ming Dynasty or possibly earlier, the hound in shades of white and brown, hardwood stand, natural flaws in jade.

3¼in (8.5cm) wide

$8,500-10,000 DN

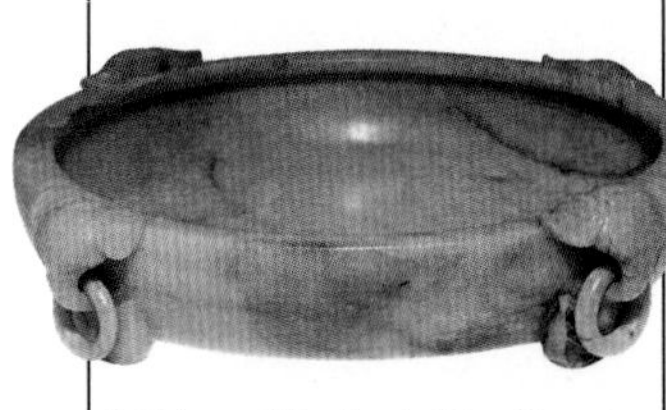

A Chinese Ming/early-Qing Dynasty mottled celadon jade brush washer, with four elephant-mask handles with loose rings, the stone a pale green color with russet veins, some darker areas and cloudy white inclusions.

11in (28cm) wide

$8,000-9,500 WW

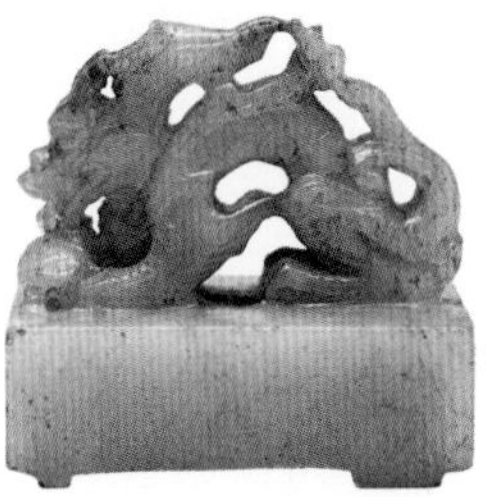

A Chinese mottled celadon jade "Dragon" seal, Ming Dynasty or later, the finial carved as a dragon and a tortoise, the rectangular seal face carved with a single character.

1½in (4cm) wide

$70,000-75,000 WW

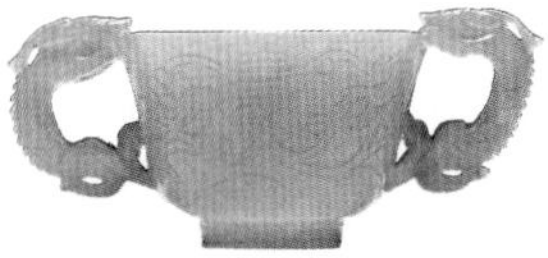

A 17thC Chinese pale celadon jade "Chilong" cup, carved with two shou with flower heads with pierced chilong loop handles, the stone of pale grayish-green tone with some cloudy white inclusions.

5in (12.5cm) wide

$7,000-8,000 WW

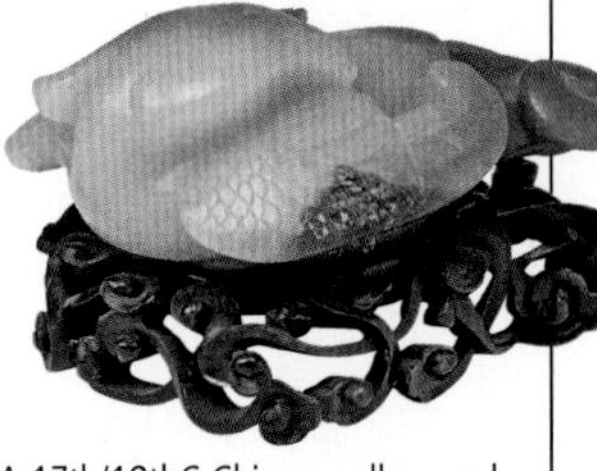

A 17th/18thC Chinese yellow and russet jade carving of a bird, with a curling plume rising above its neck, the stone of a yellowish-green tone with dark brown and russet inclusions, with a wood stand.

3¾in (9.5cm) wide

$25,000-31,000 WW

ASIAN WORKS OF ART

ESSENTIAL REFERENCE—THE QIANLONG EMPEROR

The fifth emperor of the Qing Dynasty, Qianlong, reigned from 1736-95. A very capable and cultured ruler, Qianlong was an avid historian, a passionate collector of antiques, and an author of poetry and prose. The poetic inscription on this pale celadon jade Archaistic vase is attributed to him, and is dated to the "yisi" year (1785). It translates into English as: "This precious jade comes from Hetian and has been carefully carved into a gu-shaped vase. Modern designs are too vulgar to use, and so instead I have imitated an archaic style. It is a rare shape with taotie mask designs. The vase was once used as a drinking vessel during the Shang and Zhou dynasties, whereas I now use it to enjoy flowers."

Of the two seals on the vase, the one that reads "hui xin bu yuan" translates as "enlightened mind not far," and the other that reads "de chong fu" translates as "sign of virtue within."

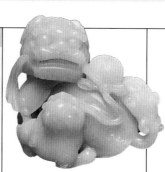

A Chinese Qianlong pale celadon jade Buddhist lion group, the lion dog with her head turned to look at her puppy playing with a brocade ball, ribbons held in their mouths, the celadon stone with russet markings.
1736-95   5½in (14cm) wide
$80,000-95,000   **WW**

A Chinese Qianlong spinach green jade vase, carved in relief with a lotus scroll design, flanked by a pair of pierced flower-head and acanthus-leaf handles with loose rings, the dark green stone with darker flecks and cloudy inclusions.
1736-95   12¾in (32.5cm) high
$55,000-60,000   **WW**

A rare Chinese Imperial pale celadon jade Archaistic vase, fanggu four-character Qianlong Yu Wan mark and of the period, the center section with elaborate taotie masks set between bands of plantain leaves on the trumpet neck and spreading base, the interior incised with a poem and two seals that read "hui xin bu yuan" and "de chong fu," the stone with slight cloudy inclusions and russet veining, with a four-character mark reading "Qianlong yu wan" on the base.
8in (20.5cm) high
$430,000-560,000   **WW**

A Chinese Qianlong pale celadon jade incense burner and cover, carved with lotus petals, with three openwork chrysanthemum handles, lotus-formed domed cover, wood stand.
1736-95   4¾in (12cm) wide
$43,000-50,000   **WW**

A Chinese celadon jade group of two cats, probably Qianlong, with a hardwood stand and presentation box, minor surface flaws.
1½in (4cm) wide
$750-875   **TEN**

A Chinese Qianlong pale celadon and brown jade model of a "Monkey and Infant," with a wood stand, chips on two toes.
1736-95   5in (12.5cm) high
$22,000-27,000   **DN**

An 18thC Qing Dynasty spinach jade Archaistic "Cong" vase, with three sections, the middle section with taotie head with large horns, the upper and lower sections with a cicada motif flanked by four divisions, each side of the vase with tree entangling chi dragons, the base inscribed with a six-character "Da Qing Qianlong Fanggu" (Made in imitation of antiquity in the Qianlong reign of the Great Qing Dynasty).

The use of the fanggu mark, meaning "imitating antiquity," was used during the Qianlong reign on Archaistic jade vessels. This vase, with its Archaic jade inspired "Cong" form and design of taotie mask, embodies the artistic pursuit of fanggu. Compare to a related Archaistic spinach green jade square Gu vase and a gong vessel with chi dragon decoration, both with Qianlong fanggu mark and of the period, from the Qing Court Collection, in the National Palace Museum, Taipei, museum no. Gu Yu 248 and 732.
12½in (32cm) high
$50,000-56,000   **L&T**

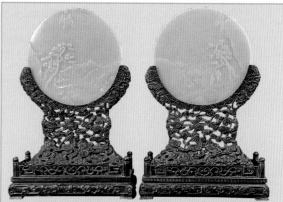

A pair of Qianlong pale celadon jade table screens with zitan stands, one with a sitting elderly scholar by the riverbank with his attendant amid lush pine trees issuing from craggy rocks, the reverse with a pine tree amid jagged cliffs with a small sampan berthing underneath, the other table screen with an elder scholar walking on stick in conversation with a young boy under pine trees near waterfalls, the reverse with an elder scholar playing a qin musical instrument on a sampan passing by pine trees growing on the riverbank, each plaque with a two-part zitan wood stand, with bats flying between ruyi head clouds, further supported on a stand with fenced border.
1736-95   19in (48cm) high
$100,000-110,000   **L&T**

CLOSER LOOK—A JADE CARVING

The water buffalo is a symbol of great potency in Chinese culture. Underpinning the rural economy, it is emblematic of strength, endurance, hard work, and prosperity. Along with the mythical qilin lying next to it, they represent a harmonious link between the natural and mythical animal worlds.

The qilin is a legendary hooved, one-horn chimerical creature from Chinese mythology. Often depicted with dragonlike features, and in modern times sometimes equated with the Western mythological unicorn, the qilin is most commonly associated with the imminent arrival, or passing, of a sage or an illustrious ruler.

The carving makes particularly skillful and dynamic use of the gradations of color—from black to blue to white—that can be found, as here, in some pieces of jade.

A Qianlong jade carving of a water buffalo and a qilin, formed from a single stone as a white qilin entwined with a black crouching buffalo, with a wood stand.

The history of the Song Dynasty records that a buffalo gave birth to a qilin, which was considered as a symbol of fortune by the emperor.

1½in (4cm) wide

$6,000-7,500   **DN**

A pair of Chinese Qianlong/Jiaqing white jade dishes, the semitranslucent stone of even tone, with minor paler inclusions.

7½in (19cm) diam

$55,000-70,000   **WW**

An 18th/19thC Chinese white jade plaque, with three sitting immortals and two acrobats, with leaves and tendrils surmounted by a lotus flower, the reverse with a fish leaping from waves, a rock, and two cranes, with a wood stand, attachment holes in the back.

3¼in (8.5cm) wide 3oz

$25,000-31,000   **GORL**

An 18th/early-19thC Chinese Qing Dynasty white and russet jade "Marriage" bowl, "Zhadou," worked as a bat with outstretched wings suspending a ring, the interior with peaches, the exterior with two of the Bajixiang emblems and xi characters, one natural crack through the body.

5½in (14cm) diam

$17,500-20,000   **DN**

A Chinese Qing Dynasty Archaistic greenish-yellow jade bi disk, with a chilong facing a smaller chilong, the reverse with Archaistic scrolling motifs, the stone of a honey brown tone with russet and celadon inclusions, with a wood stand.

5in (12.5cm) high

$9,500-10,500   **WW**

A Chinese Qing Dynasty spinach jade censer, carved with key fret dragons, with dragon head handles, the stone of mottled dark green tone with pale green, black, and white inclusions, natural flaws in jade.

8¼in (21cm) diam

$11,000-14,000   **DN**

A Chinese Qing Dynasty white jade incense holder, with scholars in a mountainous landscape, with key fret borders, knocks on the rims.

7½in (19cm) high

$14,000-17,000   **DN**

A pair of 19thC Chinese celadon jade doves, with hardstone eyes, with gold wire decorated hardwood stands.

9in (23cm) high

$10,000-11,000   **WW**

A Chinese Qing Dynasty carved spinach green jade brush pot, "Bitong," with a rocky landscape with pine, wutong trees, and bamboo, with scholars and attendants in pavilions and beside a river, stone of deep green tone with darker inclusions.

6¾in (17cm) high

$19,000-25,000   **WW**

A Chinese Qing Dynasty celadon jade carving, with a lady holding a fan and leaning on a door, the reverse with a plantain tree and pierced rocks, stone with natural inclusions and cracks.

9½in (24cm) high

$5,000-6,200   **DN**

A 19thC Chinese Qing Dynasty Archaistic jade bowl, with fo dog-scroll handles, the bowl with two shou characters, on a wood stand, foot rim chip.

5in (13cm) wide

$2,200-2,700   **CHEF**

A Chinese Qing Dynasty white jade pendant, carved as a gnarled flowering prunus trunk, with a phoenix on one side.

2¼in (5.5cm) high

$8,000-9,500   **WW**

A Chinese yellow jade "Bajixiang" bowl and cover, Qing Dynasty or later, carved as a lotus flower head, the petals enclosing the Eight Auspicious Buddhist Emblems and two Amitabha Buddhas, with bats in flight amid ruyi-shaped clouds, the pale stone with russet inclusions.

5½in (14cm) diam

$12,500-15,000   **WW**

A 19th/20thC Chinese celadon jade model of a deer, holding a branch of lingzhi fungus, some natural brown inclusion in the jade, with a wood stand.

7¾in (20cm) wide

$5,000-6,200   **DN**

A Chinese celadon jade vase and cover, Qing Dynasty or later, with scroll handles, and a bat and chrysanthemums.

6in (15cm) high

$3,700-5,000   **WW**

A Chinese Qing Dynasty lobed jadeite Gu-shaped vase, in Mogul style, with flowers growing from leafy stems, the icy green stone with milky white, lavender, and darker inclusions.

14¼in (36cm) high

$37,000-43,000   **WW**

A 19th/20thC jadeite "Dragonfly and Lotus" brush washer, as a lotus leaf growing from a stem that forms the base, further carved with a dragonfly in flight between lotuses, the translucent stone of a mottled tone with emerald green, apple green, and white inclusions, with a wood stand.

3½in (9cm) wide

$14,000-17,000   **L&T**

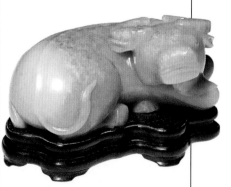

A Chinese celadon jade buffalo, Qing Dynasty or later, the tail sweeping over its haunches, the stone of a pale tone with patches of russet, with a wood stand.

6¼in (16cm) wide

$6,000-7,500   **WW**

A Chinese pale celadon jade carving of Guanyin, Qing Dynasty or later, depicted sitting in dhyanasana upon a beaded double lotus throne, with her hands held in dhyana mudra, wearing a crown.

2¾in (7cm) high

$2,500-3,700   **WW**

A Chinese late Qing Dynasty spinach green jade bowl, in Mughal style, the base with a six-character Qianlong mark.

7¾in (20cm) wide

$3,700-4,300 **WW**

A Chinese late-Qing Dynasty/Republic Period jadeite Archaistic incense burner and cover, "Fangding," with kui dragons, the sides with two panels, one inscribed "yu lin bao ding," the base with a Qianlong mark, the cover with two Buddhist lion dogs and a puppy.

11½in (29cm) high

$23,500-26,000 **WW**

A Chinese late-Qing Dynasty/Republic Period white jade figure of Magu, with her right hand holding a tray with the Three Abundances (sanduo), a peach, a pomegranate, and a Buddha's hand (or finger citron), with a silver wire-inlaid wood stand.

6in (15cm) high

$7,000-8,000 **WW**

A Chinese late Qing Dynasty/Republic Period celadon jade horse, the stone of grayish green with white and russet speckles.

7¾in (20cm) wide

$10,000-11,000 **WW**

A Chinese celadon jade vase and cover, possibly Republic Period, with three chilong, Archaic-style handles, the green stone with mottled inclusions and flecks of brown.

7½in (19cm) high

$6,000-7,500 **DN**

A Chinese mottled celadon jade "Dragon" seal, Qing Dynasty or later, with a crouching horned dragon, the seal face carved with six characters.

3¾in (9.5cm) wide

$16,000-19,000 **WW**

A Chinese yellow jade bactrian camel, Qing Dynasty or later, the yellowish-green jade with minor dark speckles and inclusions.

4in (10cm) wide

$1,250-1,900 **WW**

A Chinese pale celadon jade brush washer, Qing Dynasty or later, with animal-mask handles.

6in (15cm) wide

$1,000-1,100 **WW**

A Chinese late-Qing Dynasty/Republic Period jadeite tripod incense burner and cover, with lappets and stiff leaves, the sides and domed cover with handles with loose rings, the hollow finial formed as a chrysanthemum.

10¼in (26cm) high

$8,000-9,500 **WW**

A 20thC Chinese spinach jade-type horse, in Ming Dynasty style.

16½in (42cm) wide

$1,900-2,500 **CHEF**

A Chinese amethyst-color glass bottle vase, four-character Qianlong mark and of the period, the rim with a metal fitting.

1736-95

14¼in (36.5cm) high

$2,100-2,700　　WW

An 18th/19thC Chinese glass "Anbaxian" bowl, carved with beribboned Taoist emblems, the opaque glass of a bright egg-yolk yellow color.

6in (15cm) diam

$800-950　　WW

A Chinese Qing Dynasty pale turquoise glass seal, the finial formed as a qilin, raised on a tall oval plinth, the seal face with three characters that read "dou fu xuan."

2in (5cm) high

$20,000-25,000　　WW

A Chinese Qing Dynasty blue overlay glass snuff bottle, with a gourd vine, on a dove gray ground.

2¾in (7cm) high

$1,400-1,700　　WW

A Chinese Beijing ocher glass vase, probably 19thC, unmarked, small rim chips, minor marks on body, minor wear on base rim.

6¼in (16cm) high

$625-750　　LC

A Chinese Beijing green glass vase, probably 19thC, unmarked, marks, scratches, wear on base rim.

7¾in (20cm) high

$500-625　　LC

A small 18thC Chinese overlay glass snuff bottle, in a pale celadon-color glass with a brown skin imitating jade, with green prunus overlay sprays, with a malachite-color stopper.

2¼in (5.5cm) high

$2,500-3,700　　WW

An 18th/19thC Chinese imitation baroque pearl glass snuff bottle, the pearlized body with an enameled silver collar, below a gilt-bronze neck, with a coral stopper.

2¼in (5.5cm) high

$4,300-5,000　　WW

ESSENTIAL REFERENCE—SNUFF

Fermented, dried, ground (to a fine powder), and flavored tobacco, snuff was "discovered" some 500 years ago in the Americas by Christopher Columbus, who encountered the Caribs inhaling it as a stimulant and as a remedy for ailments, such as toothache. Transported back to Europe, it was taken up by royalty and the aristocracy as a fashionable luxury—its medicinal properties now also valued for the alleviation of gout.

● Almost certainly introduced to China by Portuguese merchants during the mid- to late 16thC, it was originally smoked there in pipes, prior to the establishment of the Qing Dynasty, when smoking it became illegal but ingesting it through the nose was allowed, because, as in Europe, it was considered to be a remedy for various illnesses, which now also included stomach disorders.

● Also as in Europe, the taking of snuff increasingly became a social ritual and, through the evermore exquisite snuff bottles used to carry it about, a symbol of status and wealth.

● By the end of the first decade of the 20thC, in both the East and the West, taking snuff had been supplanted by an even more addictive method of consuming tobacco: cigarette smoking. Since then, the use of snuff has been largely confined to a relatively small number of "connoisseurs."

A Chinese Qianlong cinnabar lacquer snuff bottle, one side with a scholar and pupil, the other side with fruits being offered on a tray, later green aventurine quartz stopper, some wear.

3¼in (8.5cm) high

$2,500-3,100   **DN**

A Chinese agate snuff bottle, four-character Qianlong mark and probably of the period, the stone with irregular striations and streaking in white, gray, and pink.

1¾in (4.5cm) high

$1,900-2,500   **WW**

A Chinese cinnabar lacquer snuff bottle, two-character Qianlong mark and of the period, with a scene of a figure within a mountainous landscape, with pine and wutong, with a chrysanthemum bud stopper.

1736-95   *2¼in (6cm) high*

$625-750   **WW**

A Chinese Qing Dynasty carnelian agate snuff bottle, with areas of reddish-brown and creamy crystalline inclusions, suggesting the yin-yang symbol.

1750-1850   *2¼in (5.5cm) high*

$190-250   **TEN**

A Chinese Qing Dynasty underglaze red and blue snuff bottle, with a fisherman under a willow tree, with five rows of calligraphy in underglaze blue, firing blemishes to glaze.

3¼in (8.5cm) high

$7,000-7,500   **DN**

A Chinese Qing Dynasty miniature porcelain calligraphic snuff bottle, with incised details and highlighted in black enamel, wood stand, light surface wear.

2½in (6.5cm) high

$1,900-2,500   **DN**

A 19thC Chinese dendritic agate snuff bottle, the honey-color stone with green/gray inclusions, possibly representing reeds in water, with gilt-metal-mounted carnelian stopper, surface wear.

2½in (6.5cm) high

$500-625   **TEN**

A 19thC Chinese dendritic agate snuff bottle, with mask and ring handles, imitation coral stopper, surface wear.

3¼in (8.5cm) high

$250-370   **TEN**

CLOSER LOOK—A YE ZHONGSAN SNUFF BOTTLE

The vast majority of Chinese glass snuff bottles have a glass, as here, or hardstone stopper in a color that contrasts the body of the bottle.

It's not unusual for the decoration on glass snuff bottles to include the artist's signature—in this case, it is for Ye Zhongsan (1869-1945)—and a date of manufacture, in this case 1888. Ye Zhongsan lived and worked in Beijing and is regarded as one of the four most prominent "inside painters" of the late Qing Dynasty.

A traditional Chinese art form, "inside painting" involves manipulating a specialized curved brush through the neck of a snuff bottle to paint an image in reverse on the inside. It will be viewed the other way around from the outside of the bottle. Not surprisingly, it requires absolute precision from the artist.

Neither zebra nor white polar bears, nor lions (as on the unseen reverse of the bottle) are indigenous to China, so it is more than likely that this snuff bottle was intended for export.

A Chinese interior-painted glass snuff bottle, by Ye Zhongsan (1869-1945), one side painted with a zebra and a white bear, the reverse with a lion, with a signature of "Ye Zhongsan" and dated wuzi year.

1888　　　　　　　　　　　　　　　　*2¼in (6cm) high*

$1,600-2,000　　　　　　　　　　　　　　　　**WW**

A Chinese carved agate snuff bottle, Qing Dynasty or later, with figures beside a pavilion and a pine tree, the reverse with a landscape scene, the stone with dark speckles and russet inclusions.

4in (10cm) high

$1,900-2,500　　　　　　**WW**

A Chinese Qing Dynasty moss agate snuff bottle, the stopper in green glass imitating jade, some chips.

2¾in (7cm) high

$550-700　　　　　　　　**TEN**

A 19thC Qing Dynasty carved cinnabar lacquer "Eight Taoist Emblems" snuff bottle, with bats and tassels, the stopper carved with flower petals resembling a blossoming chrysanthemum, the base lacquered in black, and incised with a two-character Qianlong mark in seal script.

2½in (6.5cm) high

$875-1,000　　　　　　**L&T**

A Chinese interior-painted glass snuff bottle, one side painted with a watery landscape scene, the other side with vases and rockwork, dated the guisi year.

1893　　　　　　*2½in (6.5cm) high*

$1,700-2,000　　　　　　**WW**

A Chinese porcelain snuff bottle, modeled as a lady, probably Republic Period, her right foot forming the stopper, with a Daoguang mark on her back.

4¼in (10.5cm) wide

$625-750　　　　　　**WW**

A Chinese late-Qing Dynasty/ early-Republic Period cinnabar snuff bottle, with an Archaistic dragon among clouds, turquoise matrix stopper, with incised apocryphal four-character Xuande mark.

2¾in (7cm) high

$625-750　　　　　**DN**

A 20thC Chinese blue-and-white snuff bottle, attributed to Wang Bu, one side painted with an insect and convolvulus, and with the seal for Wang Bu, the reverse with iris and butterflies, the base with a mark reading "Jiangxi ciye gongsi."

2½in (6.5cm) high

$1,500-2,000　　　　　**WW**

A Chinese Qing Dynasty carved and pierced rhinoceros horn on stand, openwork pierced with five immortals, one with a boy attendant, another with an ape, among pine, magnolia, and plum branches enriched with gourds and fruits, rim chip, old drying cracks, scuffs.

ca. 1880
32¼in (82cm) high
$31,000-37,000   **CHEF**

A Chinese Qing Dynasty carved hardwood brush pot, "Bitong," carved to simulate natural knots in the wood, with prunus and pine branches.

8in (20.5cm) wide
$5,000-6,200   **WW**

A 17th/18thC Chinese bamboo wrist rest, carved in relief with Tieguai Li beside a sampan, beneath a pine tree, rocks, and a waterfall.

9½in (24cm) high
$2,200-2,700   **WW**

A 19thC Qing Dynasty bamboo carving of Magu with deer, the female immortal riding a deer, her left hand holding lingzhi fungus, right arm with a vase, the deer's mouth with a lingzhi fungus, turning back to an attendant presenting a cup on a tray.

5¼in (13.5cm) high
$5,500-7,000   **L&T**

A 19thC Qing Dynasty bamboo root carving of a type of citron known as Buddha's hand, with a leaf and an attendant fruit, the bamboo of a smooth patina, with a wood stand.

12½in (31.5cm) wide
$1,900-2,500   **L&T**

A 19thC Qing Dynasty carved bamboo "Lady" wrist rest, of tile shape, with a lady appreciating a scroll painting, with the title "Shi Nu Tu" (Painting of a Lady) and "year of Geng Yin," with a "Shou Zhi" seal.

7¼in (18.5cm) high
$625-750   **L&T**

A Chinese Qing Dynasty carved bamboo "Landscape" brush pot, "Bitong," with a mountainous landscape, with two groups of scholars and a fisherman, with pavilions, pine trees, and bamboo groves, the reverse with a poem by Zhi Nie, dated wu yin year.

5¼in (13.5cm) high
$10,000-11,000   **WW**

A 16thC Nepalese rhinoceros horn "Vishnava" bowl, the shallow yoni-shaped body with Vishnu on a lotus base within a mandorla, his left hand holding a scepter, the right raised in a gesture of blessing, the exterior with various incarnations of Vishnu.

5¾in (14.5cm) long 5¼oz
$9,500-10,500   **CA**

A pair of 19th/20thC Japanese Meiji Period bamboo brush pots, with river landscapes, with figures enjoying daily pursuits in pavilions and others in boats, with Mount Fuji towering above them.

5in (12.5cm) high
$250-370   **WW**

ESSENTIAL REFERENCE—WOOD

Sometimes stained, painted, or lacquered, sometimes embellished with metal, horn, or bone, and sometimes left "au naturel," diverse species of wood were used by Asian sculptors, carvers, and cabinetmakers. Many of these woods—for example, bamboo, boxwood, burlwood, and sandalwood—were also familiar to Western craftsmen, but some, even to this day, remain more "exotic." Notable among these are:

- Agarwood: Also known as aloeswood, it is a dark, dense, resinous, and fragrant wood used for not only small carvings but also in incense and perfume. It is formed in the heartwood of Aquilaria trees when they become infected with a type of mold and produce a dark, aromatic, and protective resin in response.
- Huanghuali: Classed in the 1990s as a "vulnerable species," it is a fragrant species of rosewood endemic to China and so sometimes referred to as "Chinese rosewood." It is especially, but by no means exclusively, associated with furniture made from the late-Ming to the early-Qing dynasties.
- Zitan: Also a species of rosewood, it is exceptionally slow-growing, extremely dense, and relatively rare. Blackish purple to blackish red in color, its fine grain makes it especially suitable for intricate carving.

A Chinese Ming Dynasty wood figure of Bodhisattva, wearing loose long-flowing robes, the face finely carved in a contemplative expression with downcast eyes, traces of pigment remaining, wood with cracks, both hands damaged and lost.

56¾in (144cm) high
$110,000-120,000 **DN**

A Chinese Qing Dynasty carved and painted wood model of eight-armed Avalokiteshvara, the life-size temple figure with hands displaying a different mudra, she stands enrobed and bejeweled wearing a crown, paintwork flaking.

81in (206cm) high
$6,000-7,500 **CHEF**

A Chinese Qing Dynasty lacquer and gilt sandalwood Buddha, the robe open at the chest, with an opening in the back showing the wood inside his chest, the tightly curled hair in blue, chip in lacquer, minor losses and small cracks in wood, some wear.

17¼in (44cm) high
$17,500-22,000 **DN**

A Chinese Qing Dynasty carved and lacquered wood figure of Guanyin, her left hand clutching a scroll, with downcast eyes, and her hair arranged in a high chignon.

21¼in (54cm) high
$625-750 **WW**

A Chinese Qing Dynasty boxwood figure of Guanyu, the back of the figure signed "huang bing xun," minor stains.

12½in (32cm) high
$10,000-11,000 **DN**

A pair of Chinese carved wood and polychrome-lacquered Bodhisattvas, Qing Dynasty or later, the figures standing barefoot in robes and wearing elaborate necklaces, the hair drawn up to a topknot within a foliate crown, each centered by an Amitabha, with glass inset eyes, standing on lotus bases.

Each Bodhisattva wears a crown bejeweled with a small Amitabha icon, also known as Amida or Amitayus—the definition of boundless light. As a bestower of longevity, they are believed to be a celestial buddha who rules over the Pure Land in the West of the universe. Devotion to the Amitabha came to the foreground in China about AD 650 and from there spread to Japan.

51¼in (130cm) high
$12,500-15,000 **CHEF**

A Chinese Qing Dynasty burlwood carving of a deer, standing by a withered tree.

9¼in (23.5cm) high
$500-625 **WW**

An 18thC Qing Dynasty huanghuali carved "Prunus" libation cup, on gnarled prunus branches with blossoming flowers, buds, and leaves, the interior inlaid with a silver lining.

3¾in (9.5cm) high

$1,900-2,500 **L&T**

A Chinese Qing Dynasty zitan mallow-shaped box and cover, with reeded and molded rims, on a shallow foot.

4¼in (10.5cm) wide

$5,000-6,200 **WW**

A Chinese Qing Dynasty huanghuali brush pot, "Bitong," the grain ranging from dark brown to honey colors, with a recessed circular plug in the base.

9¾in (24.5cm) wide

$19,000-25,000 **WW**

A Chinese Qing Dynasty lapis lazuli boulder carving, one side carved in relief with two scholars and an attendant crossing a bridge, framed by wutong trees, pine trees, and rocky mountains, the summit inscribed with a poem of six lines, gilt characters, the reverse with a mountainous landscape, with a wood stand.

The Qianlong emperor is believed to have written the poem in the yuhai year (1755), describing the painting of Lin Jing Wei Yin Tu by Ming Dynasty painter Wen Zhengming.

9¼in (23.5cm) wide

$25,000-37,000 **WW**

A Chinese Qing Dynasty huanghuali brush pot, "Bitong," with 21 rounded reeds, the rim tilting inward, the base with a replacement plug.

8in (20.5cm) wide

$7,500-8,500 **WW**

A 19thC Qing Dynasty agarwood "Pine Tree" brush pot, carved with small figures in a village setting surrounded by large pine trees, the reverse incised with a poem, including a line of Qianlong Bing Wu year, mounted with hardwood, the interior covered in lacquer.

7¼in (18.5cm) wide

$2,500-3,700 **L&T**

A Chinese late-Qing Dynasty/Republic Period huanghuali brush pot, with a young boy atop a water buffalo, and a boy cuddling a buffalo cub, some cracks.

6½in (16.5cm) high

$5,000-6,200 **DN**

A 19th/20thC Chinese late-Qing Dynasty coral branch carving, with long-tailed birds, prunus blossom and leaves, on a hongmu wood stand, small losses.

15¾in (40cm) high

$3,100-3,700 **CHEF**

An early-20thC Chinese coral carving of an immortal maiden, playing a mandolin, with blossom sprays, on a wood stand inlaid with a silver-color wire.

9½in (24cm) high 12¾oz

$875-1,000 **CA**

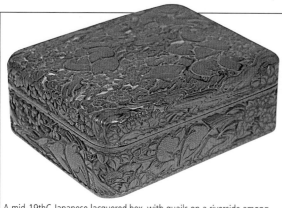

A mid-19thC Japanese lacquered box, with quails on a riverside among chrysanthemums, peonies, and other foliage, the interior and base lacquered black.

5in (12.5cm) wide

$2,500-3,700　　CHEF

A 19thC Japanese Edo/Meiji Period lacquered wood portable shrine, "Zushi," the doors opening to the Amida Triad comprising of Amida Buddha, Kannon Bosatsu, and possibly Seishi Bosatsu, with clouds, reishi heads, and flowers, inscriptions on the base.

9¾in (24.5cm) high

$300-450　　WW

A 19thC Japanese Edo/Meiji Period lacquered wood portable shrine, "Zushi," the doors opening to a Buddhist guardian deity, probably Kōshin-shinkō, the god with six arms and three eyes, holding a bow and arrow, a sword, and a halberd, another hand grasping the hair of a human figure in prayer, probably the soul of a worshipper.

20¾in (52.5cm) high

$3,100-4,300　　WW

A 19thC Japanese Meiji Period wood okimono of a tanuki, by Koichi, the racoon dog sitting on its haunches, inscribed "Koichi" underneath.

1½in (4cm) high

$800-950　　WW

A 19thC Japanese Meiji Period Noh mask of Hannya, carved in wood and painted in polychrome over gesso.

"Noh" is a traditional form of Japanese dance theater that has been performed since the 14thC, albeit in embryonic form it emerged many centuries earlier than that. Primarily based on tales from traditional Japanese literature, and often including a supernatural being transformed into human form as a hero narrating the story, Noh makes considerable use of not only costumes but also masks. While emotions are conveyed by the actors using stylized conventional gestures, the masks they wear symbolize or represent particular roles, such as ghosts, deities, or demons. The fearsome Meiji Period Noh mask shown here represents Hannya, a jealous, angry, and vengeful female demon.

10¼in (26cm) high

$250-370　　WW

A 19thC Japanese Edo/Meiji Period lacquered wood carving of Tenjin, the Shinto God of Learning, his robes with chrysanthemum and paulownia mon, the base with lines of calligraphy.

18in (46cm) wide

$500-625　　WW

A 19th/20thC Japanese wood tray for incense, shaped as a lotus leaf, with a crab resting, the wood carved to imitate the leaf's coarseness, with an inscribed fitted tomobako box.

18in (45.5cm) wide

$2,500-3,700　　WW

A Japanese Meiji Period wood plaque, by Ishikawa Komei (1852-1913), with a plump rat gnawing on small seeds, inscribed with three lines of calligraphy reading "Meiji Mizunoe-ne Gantan, Gyonen Rokuju-ichi-sai" (New Year's Day, in the year 1912 of the Meiji Period), signed "Komei" underneath and with a seal reading "Ishi" (for Ishikawa), with two metal hooks on the top, with a fitted tomobako wood box.

Ishikawa Komei was recognized as one of the greatest artists of the Meiji Period. Born in Asakusa, Tokyo, he grew up in a family of miya-bori (sculptors of wood carvings for Shinto shrines). In 1891, he was appointed as Teishitsu Gigeiin (Imperial Craftsman), and then became professor at the Tokyo School of Fine Art. His work was exhibited in Japan and overseas, and he received many awards for his works, both in his own country and internationally. His sculptures were admired at the Philadelphia Centennial Exposition (1876), the Paris Expositions Universelles (1889 and 1900), Chicago's World's Columbian Exposition (1893), and the Japan-British Exhibition (1910). Komei died on July 30, 1913, a year after he carved this plaque, when he was at the apotheosis of his career.

1912　　12½in (32cm) diam

$12,500-15,000　　WW

A Japanese Taisho Period wood okimono of a rabbit, with two lines of calligraphy that read "Taisho juninen shunjitsu, Ryusen to" (Carved by Ryusen, on a spring day in Taisho 12th).

1923　　8¾in (22cm) wide

$1,050-1,200　　WW

ESSENTIAL REFERENCE—LACQUERING AND JAPANNING

The decorative technique of lacquering involves the application of numerous layers of colored varnish, made from the sap of the "Rhus vernicifera" tree, onto primarily wood, but also leather or fabric; common colors include black, red, eggplant, and cream. When dry, the layers form a smooth, hard, waterproof crust, which can be decoratively carved in relief, often to reveal underlying, contrasting color layers.

- First made in China in about the 4thC BC, lacquer wares later proved a very popular European import.
- However, by the mid-17thC, given the relatively high cost and scarcity of lacquer, and the ever-expanding demand for Asian pieces, a European imitation was developed, which was known as "japanning."
- Made from shellac, seed lac, or gum lac deposited by the insect "Coccus lacca," it was dissolved in alcohol before being applied in numerous coats.
- Unlike lacquer, however, the shellac was water permeable and relatively weak, and thus to imitate the depth of relief possible with real lacquer it was necessary to build up raised areas using a mixture of sawdust and gum arabic, and also to surface embellish with gilt chinoiserie designs.

An 18th/19thC Japanese Edo Period six-case tsuishu red lacquer inro, with scholars and attendants in luxuriant gardens, with clouds above, with an agate ojime.

4¼in (11cm) high

$1,000-1,100   WW

A 19thC Japanese Edo/Meiji Period single-case gold and black lacquer inro, by Kajikawa Bunryusai, with a kubi furi tora (bobbing-head tiger toy) and a den-den daiko (double-ended drum), the reverse with bamboo, in gold takamakie and with raden mother-of-pearl inlays.

3in (7.5cm) wide

$800-950   WW

An 18th/19thC Japanese Edo Period guri lacquer four-case inro, with formal designs, with an en suite netsuke.

2¾in (7cm) high

$250-370   WW

A 19thC Japanese Edo Period three-case gold, silver, and black lacquer inro, by Yoyusai Hara (1768-1845), with chidori (plovers) in flight above pines, signed on the base "Gyonen nanaju-san o, Yoyusai" (Yoyusai, an old man of seventy-three), with a white glass ojime.

2½in (6.5cm) high

$750-875   WW

A 19thC Japanese Edo/Meiji Period three-case gold lacquer inro, in gold and silver hiramakie, kirikane and takamakie, with a farmer in a rice field with six geese in flight, the man holding a pole with a letter attached to it, with a coral ojime.

The decoration on this inro may refer to the story of Sobu (Su Wu in Chinese), an official of the Han emperor Wu, often depicted fastening a letter to the leg of a goose to send messages home while held captive by the Huns.

2¼in (6cm) high

$625-750   WW

A 19thC Japanese Meiji Period two-case inro, in gold and silver takamakie and kirikane lacquer, with a writhing dragon on one side and clouds on the other, with a coral ojime.

2¾in (7cm) diam

$1,000-1,100   WW

A 19thC Japanese Edo/Meiji Period five-case gold, silver, and black lacquer inro, by Koma Koryu, in hiramakie and takamakie with cranes, the base signed "Koma Koryu saku," with a glass ojime.

3½in (9cm) high

$1,700-2,000   WW

ESSENTIAL REFERENCE—INRO

An "inro" is a small, boxlike container traditionally used by Japanese men to store small personal items, such as seals, ink and brushes, or medicines, about their person when wearing a traditional, pocketless kimono.

● One of a number of different types of container collectively known as "sagemono," inro were hung on a cord from a sash around the waist of a kimono and secured at the sash by a togglelike clasp known as a "netsuke" (see page 152).

● Most inro are made from either wood or paper and are most commonly decorated with lacquered designs, although metal foils and ivory or bone inlay can also be employed.

● Some examples, especially the oldest ones, are comprised of more than one compartment, often taking the form of a nest or stack of boxes held together externally by cord runners, which are loosened (to open the boxes) or tightened (to close them) by sliding a small "ojime" bead up or down the cords.

A 19thC Japanese Edo/Meiji Period three-case gold lacquer inro, by Jitokusai, in hiramakie, gold and silver takamakie, and kirikane, with a man pulling a boat in tall grasses, a silver moon above, details in raden (mother-of-pearl inlays), signed "Jitokusai saku" underneath, with a glass ojime.

The design on this inro may be inspired by the print entitled "Hikifunegawa" (Hikifune River) by Utagawa Hiroshige. Hikifune means "towboat." Canals around Edo (Tokyo) were first used for irrigation, and later for the transportation of goods and passengers.

2¾in (7cm) high

$1,100-1,250　　WW

A 19thC Japanese Meiji Period three-case silver inro, with butterflies, with an en suite ojime.

3¼in (8cm) high

$1,700-2,000　　WW

An 18thC Japanese Edo Period gold lacquer mirror box and cover, with mitsu-tomoe (commalike swirls) in gold fundame hiramakie lacquer, on a roiro-nashiji ground.

5in (12.5cm) diam

$500-750　　WW

An 18thC Japanese Edo Period gold lacquer letter box and cover, "Fubako," in gold and silver hiramakie and kirikane on a nashiji ground, with prunus behind rocky outcrops, with a stream and clouds, two silk cords in metal rings on the sides, the paulownia kiri mon decorating the mounts.

8¾in (22cm) wide

$1,000-1,100　　WW

A Japanese negoro lacquer tray, probably 19thC Edo or Meiji Period, with red, black, and ocher striations, the abstract patterns evoking fantastical landscapes, with a tomobako wood box.

16¼in (41.5cm) wide

$3,700-5,000　　WW

A 19thC Japanese Meiji Period lacquer incense box and cover, "Kogo," in gold and silver takamakie, hiramakie, with silver inlays on the nashiji ground, with a stream among rocks, prunus, and pine, with two characters reading "tsuki o" (the moon), possibly a reference to "Tale of Genji," and with ai go mon crests for the Tokugawa clan.

3¼in (8.5cm) wide

$1,400-1,600　　WW

A 15thC Chinese carved black tixi lacquer bracket-lobed dish, with layers of black, red, and ocher, with a center motif of a ruyi-shaped floret, with two concentric bands of ruyi clouds.

5¼in (13.5cm) diam

$6,000-7,500　　WW

A 15th/16thC Chinese cinnabar lacquer box and cover, with two deer beside a wutong tree and chrysanthemums, with mantis and butterflies in flight, the box with blossoms growing from leafy foliage on the underside.

3¾in (9.5cm) diam

$8,500-10,000　　WW

A 17th/18thC cinnabar lacquer box and cover, with a solitary monk carrying a large sack behind his back, encircled by key fret and lotus petals.

2½in (6.5cm) diam

$7,000-8,000　　WW

A 17th/18thC Chinese carved red tixi lacquer box and cover, with swirling ruyi scrolls exposing layers of red, black, and ocher.

2¼in (6cm) diam

$3,100-3,700 **WW**

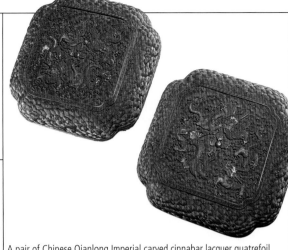

A Chinese Qianlong cinnabar lacquer foliate box and cover, with a flute tied with a brocade sash, surrounded by five flying bats, on tempestuous waves.

1736-95 *6in (15cm) wide*

$3,700-5,000 **WW**

A pair of Chinese Qianlong Imperial carved cinnabar lacquer quatrefoil "Dragon" boxes and covers, with three dragons leaping from turbulent waves in pursuit of flaming pearls, the sides and covers carved with waves.

See "Carving of the Subtle Radiance of Colors: Treasured Lacquerware in the National Palace Museum," National Palace Museum (2008), page 133, no. 132, for a similar cinnabar lacquer box of this design.

1736-95 *9in (23cm) wide*

$37,000-50,000 **WW**

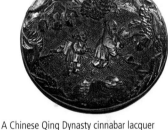

An 18thC Chinese cinnabar lacquer tray, with a diaper-ground center panel, and borders of key fret, cell diaper, and swastika designs.

7in (18cm) wide

$2,500-3,100 **WW**

A Chinese Qing Dynasty lacquer box and cover, with chrysanthemum flower heads and swastikas, the cinnabar-color ground with black outlines and yellow borders.

17¼in (43.5cm) wide

$3,700-4,300 **WW**

A Chinese Qing Dynasty cinnabar lacquer "Scholars" box and cover, lacquered on metal, with scholars and attendants in a rocky landscape, two figures beneath wutong branches, three standing under a pine tree.

3¼in (8.5cm) diam 8⅞oz

$1,900-2,500 **WW**

A 19thC Chinese three-color cinnabar lacquer box and cover, with a bowl containing flaming pearl, leaves, coins, and fylfots, and with Shoulao with a crane and deer.

7½in (19cm) diam

$750-875 **WW**

An 18th/19thC Chinese cinnabar lacquer vase, with scholars and boys in mountainous river landscapes, small losses.

9¾in (24.5cm) high

$550-600 **GORL**

A 19thC Chinese export black lacquer work box, with figural scenes in gardens and pavilions, the interior fitted with ivory accessories.

CITES certification no. 785YXHAQ

14¼in (36cm) wide

$750-875 **L&T**

ASIAN WORKS OF ART

ESSENTIAL REFERENCE—NETSUKE

Traditional Japanese clothing—initially the "kosode" and later the "kimono"—did not have any pockets in which to store small personal belongings, such as money, pipes, and tobacco. Instead, the latter were housed in small containers, collectively known as "sagemono." These could be in the form of leather or cloth pouches, or woven baskets, or small boxes known as "inro" (see page 150), all of which were hung on cords from the sash around the waist of the kimono. The fastener that secured the cords to the top of the kimono sash was a carved, buttonlike toggle called a "netsuke" ("ne," meaning "root," and "tsuke," meaning "attached"). Initially just functional objects, netsuke gradually evolved—especially during the Edo Period (1603-1867)—into increasingly intricate and sophisticated objets d'arts.

Typical materials employed to fashion netsuke include ivory (now illegal), horn (some of which is now illegal), pottery and porcelain, nuts, cane, and wood (mostly hardwoods), while subject matter is exceptionally diverse and wide ranging, and includes human figures, deities, mythical creatures, flora and fauna, domestic artifacts, and geometric and abstract imagery.

For would-be collectors, a 2010 memoir by the British ceramic artist Edmund de Waal, entitled "The Hare with Amber Eyes," is highly recommended reading. The book traces the history of a collection of 264 netsuke—some by well-known craftsmen—that were taken to France in the late-19thC and purchased by a wealthy art collector who was a member of the Jewish Ephrussi family. After subsequently being transferred to a branch of the family in Vienna, they were hidden during the Holocaust (when the family's other possessions were stolen by the Nazis), and were returned to Japan in 1947, when a surviving family member went to live in Tokyo.

An 18th/19thC Japanese Edo Period wood netsuke of a sleeping farmer, probably Kyoto School.

1½in (3.5cm) high

$1,000-1,100 WW

An 18thC Japanese Edo Period wood netsuke of Chokaro Sennin, grimacing with exertion as he lifts a gourd over his shoulders, a coat of mugwort leaves on his back.

3¼in (8cm) high

$500-625 WW

An 18th/19thC Japanese Edo Period wood netsuke of General Gentoku, the armor-clad warrior depicted riding his horse Tokiro.

Gentoku was a Chinese emperor, and one of the Three Heroes of the Han Dynasty (along with Kan'u and Chohi). He is often depicted riding his horse as he escapes from a castle besieged by his brother-in-law.

1¾in (4.5cm) wide

$625-750 WW

An 18thC Japanese Edo Period wood netsuke of a sennin, the Immortal clutching his walking stick.

4in (10cm) high

$500-625 WW

An 18th/19thC Japanese Edo Period wood netsuke of two monkeys, clambering upon a rocky outcrop, with a branch of pine on the side, the base signed "Genryosai."

1¾in (4.5cm) wide

$5,000-6,200 WW

A 19thC Japanese Meiji Period wood netsuke of a snail, its shell with a radiating pattern of lines with dark staining, the animal emerging from its shell, signed "Masanao" (for Masanao of Yamada, Ise province).

1½in (4cm) wide

$10,000-11,000 WW

A 19thC Japanese Meiji Period boxwood netsuke of two toads, one on the back of the other, their eyes inlaid in horn, the belly of the larger toad signed "Masanao" (for Masanao of Yamada, Ise province).

1¾in (4.5cm) wide

$5,000-6,200 WW

A 19thC Japanese Meiji Period tooth netsuke of Kiyohime on the Dojoji Bell, the witch's snakelike body coiling around the tall bell, holding a T-shaped striker.

2¼in (5.5cm) high

$1,400-1,600 WW

A 19thC Japanese Meiji Period narwhal tusk netsuke, carved as a tiger on bamboo.

1½in (3.5cm) wide

$1,500-1,700 WW

A 19thC Japanese Meiji Period boxwood netsuke, carved as two rats on peanuts, their eyes inlaid in dark horn, signed "Masanao" underneath with kao (for Masanao of Yamada, Ise province).

1½in (4cm) wide

$1,900-2,500 WW

A 19thC Japanese Meiji Period boxwood netsuke of a frog, by Issai, its eyes inlaid in horn, squatting on a waraji (straw sandal), the looped thong forming the himotoshi, signed.

2in (5cm) wide

$1,400-1,600 WW

A 19thC Japanese Meiji Period wood netsuke of two monkeys, carved as an adult and its young, signed "Masanao" (for Masanao of Yamada, Ise province).

1½in (4cm) wide

$2,000-2,500 WW

A 19thC Japanese Meiji Period wood netsuke, of six monkeys with a double gourd, a seventh with a hammer and chisel to force the cucurbit open, a two-character mark underneath.

1½in (4m) high

$700-800 WW

A 19thC Japanese Edo Period red wood netsuke of a mermaid (ningyo), probably Nagoya, inscribed "Tadatoshi" in ukibori in a reserve underneath.

See M. T. Coullery and M. S. Newstead, "The Baur Collection: Netsuke," Collections Baur (1977), page 115, no. C224, for another example of a mermaid by Tadatoshi. The authors explain that in Japanese folklore, ningyo are lovely creatures, well-disposed toward humans and believed to share the secrets of the sea by listening to the murmurs of seashells. Eating one would give you immortality.

1¾in (4.5cm) wide

$6,000-7,500 WW

A 19thC Japanese Edo/Meiji Period boxwood netsuke of a horse, the mount with scrolling designs and a ribbon around its chest.

2½in (6.5cm) wide

$2,500-3,700 WW

A 19thC Edo/Meiji Period boxwood netsuke of a shishi, the lion dog sitting on its haunches.

2in (5cm) wide

$1,250-1,500 WW

A 19thC Japanese Edo/ Meiji Period bamboo sashi netsuke of a shishi, by Morikawa Toen (1820-94), the mythical beast on a double lotus throne, inscribed "Shosoin, hoko, heigoro no shishi baku, Morikawa Toen" (copy of an incense burner handle with lion dog at the Shosoin Treasure House by Morikawa Toen) with kao.

Morikawa Toen was known for his Nara ningyo (dolls) sculptures and as a Noh actor. His work was admired by the Daimyo of Tosa, the magistrate of Nara, who awarded him with names from Japanese mythology. The imperial household also became his patron.

4in (10cm) high

$1,900-2,500 WW

A 19thC Japanese Meiji Period red lacquer manju netsuke, with a scaly dragon among scrolling clouds, on a dense diaper ground.

1¾in (4.5cm) wide

$500-625 WW

A 20thC Japanese wood netsuke of a Portuguese merchant, Showa Period or later, signed "Shosai."

3½in (9cm) high

$375-500 WW

An early-19thC Chinese Qing Dynasty Imperial "Dragon" robe, "Jifu," made for a consort to the emperor, with nine gold five-clawed dragons, including one gold dragon hidden by the overflap, with flaming pearls among ruyi-shaped clouds, with the side-facing dragons clasping the pearl of wisdom, the ground is interspersed with coral-colored bats, above lishui water and wave design with the eight auspicious emblems, borders, cuffs, and neck brocade embroidered with the classic dragon pattern, with original blue damask silk lining with a peony and butterfly design, some wear, some staining.

See Linda Wrigglesworth and Gary Dickinson, "Imperial Wardrobe," Bamboo (1990), page 23, plate 12, for a painted book plate referencing the 1759 regulations, and also page 192, where it is stated that the extra dragon band at the elbow was not present on robes that were not for the first rank consort. Hence, this yellow may be seen as golden yellow for a second or third rank consort. See the rank table on the same page. Female yellow robes did not display the 12 symbols until later in the 19thC. Compare with a Manchu woman's robe in Robert D. Jacobsen, "Imperial Silks in the Minneapolis Museum Institute of Arts," Vol. 1, pages 138-39.

58¼in (148cm) long
$70,000-80,000   DN

A Chinese Qing Dynasty crepe silk Han women's robe, with the Dragon Boat Festival that takes place on the fifth day of the fifth month of each lunar year, the front and back of the robe show mandarins walking across bridges with bird cages, small children swimming in the river, boats filled with people cheering alongside the grand blue dragon boats with oarsman rowing to win the race, other boats depict intimate scenes of concubines being rowed to mysterious pavilions, and fishermen and families enjoying the festivities of the day.

ca. 1820   *39¾in (101cm) long*
$31,000-37,000   DN

A Chinese deep satin silk women's side-opening robe, edged with ribbon borders, with flowers embroidered in Peking knot and satin stitch, with butterflies above waves with coral silk Peking knot peonies, staining on lining.

ca. 1830   *42¼in (107cm) long*
$1,250-1,600   DN

A Chinese Qing Dynasty coral red Chinese side-fastening women's three-quarter length robe, bordered with cream silk, with summer flowers, hydrangeas, and Peking knot peonies with butterflies, damage in the collar.

ca. 1850   *42½in (108cm) long*
$5,000-6,200   DN

A Chinese satin silk "Dragon" robe, "Longpao," with nine five-clawed dragons flying among clouds and auspicious symbols, the dragon eyes are seen chasing the pearl of immortality, with billowing water and waves, lishui decorate the hemline, with auspicious symbols bouncing upon the waves surrounding the mountains of the immortals.

Probably worn by a court mandarin attending the ceremony at the temple of heaven, when the gold would glitter against the rising sun and elevate the mandarin to immortal status.

ca. 1860   *57¾in (147cm) long*
$7,000-8,000   DN

A Chinese Qing Dynasty women's side-fastening jacket, with ten gold thread roundels, with precious scholarly objects and vases of flowers, butterflies, and exotic birds.

ca. 1870   *41¼in (104.5cm) long*
$6,000-7,500   DN

A late-19thC Chinese Qing Dynasty crimson silk marriage robe, with mauve Peking knot flowers, a green, white, mauve, and blue lishui hem, with mountains, waves with flowers, and auspicious emblems, above which gold-work dragons and phoenixes chase flaming pearls, minor stains, a few loose threads.

41in (104cm) long
$1,500-1,700   DN

A 19thC Chinese Qing Dynasty Manchu gauze courtier's summer riding robe, with twinned dragon roundels, with button flap below so the robe can be opened to let the rider sit astride the horse, minor stains.

54¼in (138cm) long

$3,100-3,700   DN

A Chinese late-Qing Dynasty silk summer robe, with peony blossom, Buddha's hand (or finger citrons) and other auspicious objects.

40¼in (102cm) long

$1,250-1,700   WW

A Chinese late-Qing Dynasty kesi "Dragon" robe, with sky dragons, three dragons, and Buddhist emblems on the back, with gilt-thread details, above the terrestrial diagram and lishui stripe at the hem.

50in (127cm) long

$4,300-5,000   CHEF

A Chinese late-Qing Dynasty silk "Nine Dragon" robe, with dragons in gold couched thread, Buddhist symbols, and cloud scrolls above breaking waves.

56¾in (144cm) long

$5,000-6,200   WW

A Chinese late-Qing Dynasty silk and kesi gauze "Dragon" summer robe, with nine dragons amid clouds and auspicious objects above rocks, waves, and lishui stripes, some alterations.

$3,100-3,700   GORL

An early-20thC Chinese embroidered silk formal court "Dragon" robe, "Chaofu," with five-clawed sky dragons chasing pearls over lishui stripes above mountains, the pleated skirt with dragon roundels.

86½in (220cm) long

$8,000-9,500   CHEF

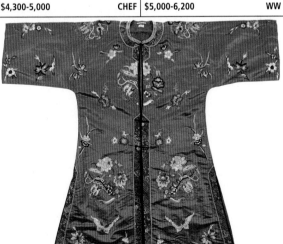

A Chinese Republic Period export satin silk front-opening jacket, with flowers, butterflies, and blossoms, edged with the "Hundred Boy" design, some fading.

ca. 1920

43¾in (111cm) long

$250-370   DN

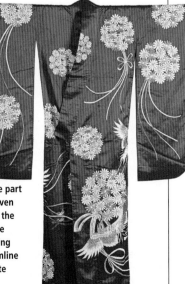

A Japanese late Taisho Period wedding kimono, "Furisode," decorated with large white embroidered cranes, and floral mons tied with silver tasseled thread chords, minor tears in silk.

These robes were expensive to make and were part of the dowry of the bride given by her family. This robe was the outmost kimono worn by the bride during the long wedding ceremonies; the padded hemline and long length would create a resplendent vision.

ca. 1920

$1,250-1,900   DN

ASIAN WORKS OF ART

A Chinese Qing Dynasty kingfisher feather headdress, with mythical creatures, butterflies with spring-mounted antennae, swallows, and stylized flower heads, with kingfisher feathers, simulated pearls, and a carved jadeite Buddha in a pagoda.

8¾in (22cm) wide

$2,500-3,100   **WW**

A Chinese Qing Dynasty kingfisher feather "Shuangxi" headdress, with nine phoenixes, each with geometric pendants suspended from their mouths, with shuangxi and shou characters, dragons and phoenixes contesting a flaming pearl, with simulated pearls and color hardstones.

9in (23cm) wide

$1,500-2,000   **WW**

A Chinese Qing Dynasty/Republic Period kingfisher feather headdress, with two four-clawed dragons and a flaming pearl, with phoenixes, bats, insects, and foliage, the back with the Eight Taoist Emblems, with semiprecious stones, simulated pearls.

7½in (19cm) wide

$2,500-3,100   **WW**

A Chinese Qing Dynasty/Republic Period kingfisher feather opera headdress, with spring-mounted butterflies, with two scaly dragons on each side, with red pompoms, simulated pearls, glass stones, and beads.

10¼in (26cm) wide

$1,400-1,600   **WW**

A Qing Dynasty Qianlong Imperial silk brocade "Dragon" throne cushion cover, with a five-clawed gilt dragon above the terrestrial diagram, flanked by two five-clawed golden dragons amid auspicious clouds and above waves, hardwood frame.

It was customary in China that the silk furnishing fabrics for the emperor's palaces, staterooms, and private apartments should be of minghuang—"bright yellow" silk and, indeed, the same color was used for costumes worn by the emperor, the dowager empress, the empress, and first rank imperial concubine on formal occasions.

This particular shade of yellow was created from the flowers of the pagoda tree, and, because the color was reserved for the imperial family alone, it has become associated in China with all things imperial for more than 1,000 years. The color was chosen because the emperor represented the daytime sun on Earth.

The symbol of the emperor was the dragon, an ancient association, of which the "five-clawed" dragon was the most superior, and the palace furnishings were universally decorated with an uneven number of five-clawed dragons, since uneven numbers represented the yang, or male, principle, while even numbers represented the yin or female principle.

Three different techniques could be used to create the silk furnishings: embroidery, brocade, or tapestry (kesi), of which embroidery and brocade were the ancient traditional Chinese techniques. Within subsections of brocade weaving, the most highly complex is "lampas," which lets the light fall on silk threads, usually woven vertically in the background and horizontally on the design, creating an almost three-dimensional effect, and interwoven to produce a strong fabric. It was used almost exclusively for palace brocade weaving.

The panel presented here embodies all such requirements for an imperial textile and was created especially for the emperor's throne cushion.

31½in (80cm) wide

$10,000-12,000   **L&T**

A Chinese imperial satin silk throne cushion, Daoguang or Xianfeng, with a five-clawed dragon chasing the pearl of wisdom and two running dragons, all above a lishui water and wave pattern, with lotus flowers, leaves, and auspicious bats, with eight auspicious symbols and clouds surrounding the dragons, originally tailored.

31½in (80cm) wide

$14,000-17,000   **DN**

A 19thC Qing Dynasty silk "Lotus" elbow cushion, with lotus flowers hanging below a bat and bianqin (a traditional Chinese percussion instrument), the top and bottom similarly decorated with four bats encircling a blossoming flower.

Solid cushions like this, for resting the elbows and forearms, were put on large thronelike chairs and on the raised heated platforms used for sitting in North China. The graded blues and reds of the embroidery silks and the yellow color of the background material indicate that they may have originally been in one of the imperial palaces.

10¾in (27cm) wide

$3,700-5,000   **L&T**

A Chinese Qing Dynasty embroidered silk "Dragon" panel, with four dragon roundels, bats, cloud scrolls, and other auspicious things.

56in (142cm) wide

$300-450   **WW**

ASIAN FURNITURE

A pair of Chinese export exotic hardwood side chairs, possibly huanghuali.

ca. 1740   41in (104cm) high

$3,700-5,000   DN

Judith Picks

What on Earth, you might well ask, is a pair of mid-18thC English side chairs doing in a section on Asian furniture? Well, I decided to go off-piste and include them here to illustrate just how influential and, indeed, fashionable the Asian—in this case Chinese—vocabulary of ornament was in Europe during the late 17thC and 18thC. With their squared cabriole legs, the chairs are unmistakeably English, but their distinctive tall back splats and top rails are inspired in terms of form by Chinese chairs of the Qing Dynasty (ca. 1550-1600) known as "guan mao shi yi," which translates as "shaped like an officer's hat" and references the curved top rail shaped like a milkmaid's or oxen's yoke. Sometimes, and misleadingly, referred to in Great Britain as "India backs," the Asian input is further and significantly enhanced by the decorative finish, which is in imitation of the colors and motifs employed in Chinese lacquerwork, and known in Europe as "Japanning" (see page 149, "Essential Reference—Lacquering and Japanning").

A pair of mid-18thC black lacquer side chairs, decorated with flowers and utensils, with a yoke top rail above an "India back" splat and later padded drop-in seat, five ears replaced.

44in (112cm) high

$2,500-3,700   DN

A pair of late-18th/early-19thC Chinese export padouk and marquetry side chairs, the splats inlaid with a dog-and-crown armorial, marks, knocks.

37¾in (96cm) high

$5,000-6,200   DN

A pair of 18th/19thC Chinese hardwood armchairs, probably elm, marks, splits.

48½in (123cm) high

$1,250-1,600   DN

A pair of 19thC Chinese hardwood armchairs, carved with dragons and scrolls, on claw-and-ball feet, some damage.

$2,500-3,700   CHOR

A 19th/20thC Chinese huanghuali horseshoe-back folding chair, "Jiao Yi," splat with a quatrefoil panel, with a curling dragon above a qilin among clouds and lingzhi, the rattan seat over a frieze carved with chilong dragons, the footrest with a huangtong plaque.

41¾in (106cm) high

$5,000-6,200   CA

A 19th/20thC Chinese hardwood open armchair, with mother-of-pearl carved as auspicious objects, butterflies, and flowering leafy stems, the back with a circular panel inset with marble, above a seat also inset with marble, the front frieze carved as stems inlaid with mother-of-pearl carved as cash symbols, peonies, and leafy stems.

39½in (100.5cm) high

$1,700-2,200   CA

A 19th/20thC Chinese carved wood chair, on four feet with bat-form terminals, and aprons incised with kui dragons, the backboard with a similar pattern below a figurative panel, with rectilinear scrolls extending outward to form the arms.

32¼in (82cm) high

$1,900-2,500   CA

ASIAN FURNITURE

A Chinese late-Qing Dynasty hardwood open armchair, the splat with geometric panels, flanked by openwork square scrolls.

35½in (90cm) high

$950-1,050   **WW**

A pair of Chinese wood chairs, each back with an S-shaped splat carved with stylized scrolls, the legs with stepped stretchers with further scrolls.

30¾in (78cm) high

$1,900-2,500   **CA**

A pair of Chinese hardwood horseshoe-back chairs, each centered with a backsplat carved with a "shou" character-shaped medallion.

29in (73.5cm) high

$375-500   **CA**

One of a pair of Chinese Qing Dynasty yoke-back armchairs, "Guanmaoyi," the "official's hat" top rail with swept-back ends, the curved back splat carved with two panels of deer, bamboo and pine, some wear and cracks.

41¾in (106cm) high

$1,000-1,100 the pair   **DN**

A pair of Republic Period jadeite-inlaid horseshoe-back chairs, in Ming Dynasty style.

41½in (105.5cm) high

$1,900-3,100   **CHEF**

A pair of Chinese huanghuali armchairs, each with dragon rails above the back splat, slight wear.

ca. 1950s   36½in (93cm) high

$2,500-3,100   **DN**

A Chinese Qing Dynasty elm settee, with carved and pierced panels decorated with dragons and leaves, with a rattan seat.

67¼in (171cm) wide

$1,500-1,900   **WW**

A Chinese Qing Dynasty padouk settee, the openwork scroll back centered with a carved "shou" character, with an apron with a pair of chilong dragons.

78¼in (199cm) wide

$1,900-2,500   **WW**

A Chinese hardwood bench or window seat.

ca. 1900   45¼in (115cm) wide

$375-500   **TEN**

A 17thC Chinese Ming Dynasty walnut "heitaomu" altar table, "Qiaotouan," probably from Shanxi province, the plank top terminating in tall everted flanges, originally lacquered red with traces of this on most surfaces, the bottom of one slab foot has been replaced.

Although in the West tables of this form are known as altar tables, the Chinese term "Qiaotouan" only refers to the fact that the ends are raised. According to the Palace Museum, Beijing, tables of this scale would have stood at the center of a main hall or against the side walls in one of the important rooms in the Imperial Palace, on which decorative objects would have been displayed.

154in (391cm) wide

$14,000-16,000   **DN**

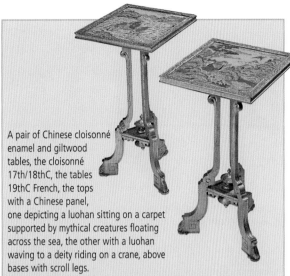

A pair of Chinese cloisonné enamel and giltwood tables, the cloisonné 17th/18thC, the tables 19thC French, the tops with a Chinese panel, one depicting a luohan sitting on a carpet supported by mythical creatures floating across the sea, the other with a luohan waving to a deity riding on a crane, above bases with scroll legs.

The "arhats," or "luohan" in Chinese Buddhism, are seen as the original followers of Gautama Buddha, or arhat. They have reached the state of Nirvana; they are now free of all worldly cravings and their role is to protect Buddhism until the arrival of Maitreya, an enlightened Buddha predicted to appear on Earth many centuries in the future. In the earliest Indian depictions, only 4 disciples were shown, but over time this number rose to 16, and by the Tang or Five Dynasty periods in China there were 18, a tradition that continues into modern Chinese Buddhism. The symbolism of the two plaques included in these tables show a luohan welcoming the Mother of the West, and the other shows four demons carrying a luohan over the Bitter Sea.

25¼in (64cm) high

$55,000-70,000   **WW**

A Chinese Kangxi hongmu altar table, the top with raised scroll ends, the frieze carved with cloud spandrels, on splayed trestle legs pierced with panels, enclosing ruyi head-shaped cloud motifs.

1662-1722   *43in (109cm) wide*

$10,000-11,000   **WW**

A Chinese Qing Dynasty hardwood altar table, the single-panel top enclosed within fluted edges, on an open paneled waist and decorated apron, with legs of square section with hoof feet, some repairs.

59in (150cm) wide

$12,500-15,000   **DN**

A 19thC Chinese Qing Dynasty hardwood and marble center table, minor cracks and losses in wood.

36¼in (92cm) diam

$4,300-5,000   **DN**

A 19thC Chinese huanghuali side table, the top inset with red marble, the frieze carved and pierced with trailing flowers with a center tablet, on four block legs, with claw-and-ball feet.

47in (119.5cm) wide

$5,500-7,000   **HT**

A Chinese Qing Dynasty hardwood low table, the frieze carved with ruyi clouds and linked circle designs, with humpback side stretchers at the base.

47¾in (121cm) wide

$1,250-1,900   **WW**

A Chinese hardwood altar table, the cleated top above a pierced frieze, with scrolled ends, some scratches.

ca. 1900   *49½in (126cm) wide*

$3,100-3,700   **DN**

A Chinese late-Qing Dynasty hardwood scroll table, the frieze with lotus foliage and flowers, with a glass top.

74½in (189cm) wide

$7,000-8,000   **WW**

A Chinese late-Qing Dynasty hardwood low "Kang" table.

30in (76cm) wide

WW

$375-500

A Chinese late-Qing Dynasty hardwood "Kang" table, the shaped frieze carved as scrolls and flower heads, on cabriole legs.

30in (76cm) wide

WW

$500-625

A Chinese late-Qing Dynasty hardwood scroll table, the pierced frieze of formal scrolls and tied cash designs.

82¼in (209cm) wide

WW

$1,900-2,500

A 19thC Chinese cedar and elm scroll table, in Ming Dynasty style, with a pair of similar benches, originally lacquered.

65in (165cm) wide

WW

$1,000-1,100

A Chinese late-Qing Dynasty hardwood altar table, the top with an openwork geometric scroll frieze, on square legs, joined by frame end supports.

54¾in (139cm) wide

WW

$2,500-3,700

A pair of 19thC Chinese hardwood vase stands, each top with a recessed band, above a frieze with carved scrolls and flower heads, stamped "876" and "879" on the stretchers.

12½in (31.5cm) high

WW

$1,500-1,700

A late-19thC Chinese hardwood table, inlaid with mother-of-pearl with leaves and flowers, the top inset with white marble, above a carved frieze.

25¾in (65.5cm) wide

WW

$950-1,050

A late-19thC Chinese hardwood stand, the top inset with a marble panel, with fret carved decoration, on reeded supports with scroll feet.

31¼in (79.5cm) high

WW

$375-500

A late-19thC Chinese hardwood table, the top inset with a marble panel, above curved legs united by an undertier.

27¼in (69.5cm) diam

WW

$750-875

A 19th/20thC Japanese Meiji Period gold and black lacquer writing table, "Bundai," the top with 13 cranes in gold takamakie, hiramakie, and nashiji, with details in red lacquer, the legs with a silver and gold diaper design enclosing four-petal flower mon, the metal mounts with scrolling tendrils.

25½in (64.5cm) wide

WW

$625-750

A late-18th/early-19thC Chinese export lacquer cabinet-on-stand, the doors enclosing a stepped arrangement of architectural recesses and drawers, with four cabriole legs with claw-and-ball feet, part of a Chinese character seal visible on the underside, scratches, knocks.

57½in (146cm) high

$6,000-7,500   **DN**

A 19thC Chinese carved hardwood display cabinet, with carved and pierced scrolling, foliate, and floral decoration.

38½in (98cm) wide

$1,250-1,500   **WW**

A 19thC Chinese hongmu cabinet, carved with grapevines on the sides, the panels of the lower cabinet with a pair of dragons, minor cracks and slight warping, missing door latch.

82in (208cm) high

$2,500-3,700   **DN**

A Chinese Qing Dynasty elm cupboard, the body of paneled construction, with a pair of doors with a locking bar, enclosing shelves, and two drawers.

67in (170cm) high

$1,250-1,500   **WW**

A pair of Chinese Qing Dynasty jichimu round-corner cabinets-on-stands, "Yuanjiaogui," the upper sections each with a pair of doors enclosing shelves and two drawers, the stands with two drawers above pierced undertiers.

67in (170cm) high

$3,700-4,300   **WW**

A Chinese hardwood cabinet, late Qing Dynasty and later, with two paneled doors opening on each side, revealing shelves, the front set with 12 panels decorated with figures and pagodas, and inset with ivory details.

Ivory Act certification no. RCCGQHMW

57¾in (147cm) high

$1,400-1,600   **WW**

A Chinese Republic Period hardwood cabinet-on-stand, with glazed door, the stand with two shelves, one leg with cracks.

73¼in (186cm) high

$1,200-1,350   **DN**

ASIAN FURNITURE

A Chinese export black lacquered table cabinet, the pair of doors enclosing various drawers, with a gilt- and mother-of-pearl-decorated body.

15¼in (39cm) wide

$450-550　　　　　　　　　　　WHP

An early-18thC Chinese coromandel lacquer and japanned ebonized chest, the hinged cover depicting japanned birds and flowers, the front with coromandel panels with birds and flowers, with metal corner straps and side handles.

47¾in (121cm) wide

$1,900-2,500　　　　　　　　　　L&T

A mid- to late-18thC padouk and parquetry-inlaid bureau, probably Chinese export, the drop front opening to pigeonholes and drawers, centered by a cupboard door, some marks and scratches.

39¼in (100cm) wide

$1,500-1,700　　　　　　　　　　DN

An 18th/19thC Chinese padouk and brass-mounted chest, some marks, no key.

31in (79cm) wide

$3,100-4,300　　　　　　　　　　DN

A late-19thC Chinese lacquered cabinet, copper- and brass-mounted with gilt-lacquered birds in flowering trees on the top, front, and sides, the interior with 14 drawers, all with foliate decoration, with further bird and shrub decoration on the inside of the doors, on a later perspex base, scratches, no keys.

29¼in (74cm) wide

$3,700-5,000　　　　　　　　　　LC

A 19thC Chinese export camphor wood and brass-banded chest, on modern casters.

37¾in (96cm) wide

$625-750　　　　　　　　　　L&T

A Chinese Qing Dynasty huanghuali picnic box, the two removable compartments with a shallow tray enclosed by a lid with a gilt-metal locking rod, the carrier with a square-section handle.

11½in (29cm) wide

$4,300-5,600　　　　　　　　　　WW

Judith Picks

At not much over a foot (30cm) wide, the sumptuously decorative front of this truly splendid drop-front Namban cabinet certainly punches well above its weight!

From the mid- to late 16thC, Japanese lacquerware made for Western markets became known as Namban (which translates as "Southern Barbarian") lacquer. Sometimes also spelled Nanban, it references the epithet given by the Japanese to foreigners from Portugal—trading with whom had been given considerable impetus, in 1580, when Pope Gregory XIII granted Portugal exclusive rights to maritime trade east of the Red Sea to as far as 17 degrees east of the Moluccas (today's eastern Indonesia). Japan, thus, became one of the new sources for exotic luxury goods that could be imported to Europe for profit. Moreover, while lacquered chests and other objects inlaid with mother-of-pearl had previously been sourced by the Portuguese from Gujarat, the undoubted superiority—in terms of both design and craftsmanship—of the Japanese equivalents rapidly increased both the volume and the profitability of the trade.

An early Japanese Momoyama Period Namban cabinet, for the export market, with a hinged drop front opening to reveal nine drawers, the door and sides decorated with panels enclosing many fans embellished with geometric designs and flowering branches of prunus, scrolling tendrils, and ume-bachi mon, in between borders of chevrons and other formal patterns, the decoration in a multitude of raden (mother-of-pearl) inlays and gold and black lacquer, the inside with further mother-of-pearl inlays and gilt decoration depicting panels of flowering prunus and peony, the copper fittings and side loop handles with designs of melons, flowers, and tendrils, with a key.

ca. 1580-1620　　　　　　*14¾in (37.5cm) wide*

$15,000-19,000　　　　　　　　　　WW

A 17th/18thC Japanese Edo Period export gilt and black lacquer cabinet, with two hinged doors, depicting an extensive landscape, with temples and pavilions in the hills, the right door painted with buildings reminiscent of Kiyomizudera and Kinkaku-ji in Kyoto, the sides with peonies and bamboo, all in gold and silver hiramakie on the black roiro lacquer ground, the front doors decorated on the inside with two pairs of cranes and opening to eight drawers and two smaller doors with lock plates, the drawers embellished with birds, flowers, and pavilions in landscapes, with a built-in stand and raised again on an associated European stand with chinoiserie decoration.

40¼in (102cm) wide

$4,300-5,600 WW

A 19thC Japanese cabinet, gilt decorated, carved, and inlaid with figures, birds, and animals within landscapes, with seven hinged and sliding doors, and three drawers on a plinth base.

54in (137cm) wide

$4,300-5,000 WHP

A 19thC Japanese Meiji Period gold and black lacquer cabinet, "Kodansu," with a pair of hinged doors and a drawer below, the interior with seven drawers of various sizes, the exterior with ships sailing on lakes, with cranes flying above and Mount Fuji in the distance, the panels framed by borders or geometric patterns, the reverse of the doors with birds of prey and the inner drawers with cranes in flight.

21¼in (54cm) wide

$5,500-7,000 WW

A Japanese Meiji Period carved hardwood, parcel-gilt, and ivory-inlaid shodhana, the pediment as a dragon above a molded frieze decorated with flowers, above an arched niche and 11 quarter panels with figures across a landscape, surrounding a center cinnabar arched bridge, the base with heavily carved foliage, minor losses in the carved decoration.

Ivory Act certification no. 581K5VBE

1868-1912 *81½in (207cm) high*

$6,000-7,500 TEN

An early-20thC Japanese hardwood and bone display cabinet, the pagoda top with figures in a temple flanked by boats, with a removable temple finial, with three shelves below, flanked by carved dragon supports, on a molded stand with dragon head-carved legs and casters.

86½in (220cm) high

$3,100-4,300 TEN

A Japanese Edo Period lacquer jewelry box, for the export market, of architectural form, the top sliding to reveal a secret compartment, the two small doors on the front concealing six drawers, the exterior with flowers, figures at rest, houses in lush landscapes, and scrolling tendrils, in silver and gold hiramakie, takamakie, and nashiji lacquer on the black roiro ground, with some petals and leaves inlaid with mother-of-pearl and metal, the inside of the lid with a mirror and a design of a pavilion on stilts, with rocky outcrops and trees in hiramakie and kirikane, with pilasters on the corners and the metal mounts embellished with flowers, the edges with geometric borders inlaid with mother-of-pearl.

See O. Impey and C. Jörg, "Japanese Export Lacquer (1580-1850)," Hotei (2005), pages 170-72, where comparable boxes are illustrated and discussed. They are described as jewel boxes in pictorial style.

ca. 1640-90 *13½in (34.5cm) wide*

$5,000-6,200 WW

A 17thC Mughal Gujarat ivory-inlaid rosewood table cabinet, the hinged flap inlaid in the front with lions beneath trees and in the interior with four figures below trees, enclosing 21 drawers around a deep center drawer, the drawer fronts inlaid with foliage and birds, the drop front a little hard to open/close, tiny losses in ivory, back and drop hinges are replacements.

29½in (75cm) wide

$43,000-50,000 CHOR

Judith Picks

It took me a while to avert my gaze after I first set eyes on this Qing Dynasty screen. Certainly the simple, stepped rectilinear aesthetic of its characteristically blackish-purple, fine-grained zitan wood (a species of rosewood) frame does what all the best frames do: make you briefly admire them, before focusing your attention on what's within them—and that certainly didn't disappoint either! The composition is quintessential Chinese: an idyllic and typically symbolic scene, set against a gently flowing river (of life), and on and

under a "wutong" (or "Chinese Parasol" tree—symbolizing "yin," the nurturing female element of life). The primary focus, however, are the birds, which include magpies, cranes, and mandarin ducks, and a pair of phoenixes—a classic Chinese interplay of the natural and the spiritual, and of reality and myth. There is, of course, much to admire in just the artistic techniques displayed, especially the exquisite use of mother-of-pearl, jade, semiprecious stones, and wood inlay.

An 18th/19thC Qing Dynasty stone-inlaid "Phoenixes" screen, inlaid with mother-of-pearl, jade, soapstone, semiprecious stones, and wood, with birds, including magpies, cranes, and mandarin ducks, worshipping two phoenixes perching under a wutong tree, with zitan frames and gilt-bronze hanging mount.

43in (109cm) wide

$25,000-31,000 **L&T**

A Chinese coromandel lacquered wood four-leaf screen, probably Ming Dynasty, with birds, including pheasants, egrets, and mandarin ducks, amid craggy rocks and flower branches, with poetic inscriptions and four seals, one reading "Ding Yan" and two others "Gao Qizhuo," above four smaller panels, each with a mythical beast, the inscription is a poem which reads "Pomegranates begin to ripe/Every plant hurries to beautify itself/All animals gather in groups."

91¾in (233cm) wide

$14,000-17,000 **WW**

A late-19th/early-20thC Chinese lacquer two-leaf screen, in Coromandel Coast style, with figures, landscapes, and buildings.

72in (183cm) high

$375-500 **WW**

A Chinese late Qing Dynasty black lacquer four-leaf screen, inlaid with soapstone and bone, with 18 luohan in groups or individually, in landscapes, the lower panels with fruit, birds, and flowers, the reverse painted with birds amid foliage and antique vases.

70¾in (180cm) wide

$375-500 **WW**

A Chinese late-Qing Dynasty painted marble eight-leaf screen, one side with celebration scenes, the other with mountain landscapes, both sides with calligraphy panels, each panel including a wood frame, breaks in most of the marble panels.

30¼in (77cm) high

$550-700 **DN**

An early- to mid-20thC Chinese lacquer and parcel-gilt eight-leaf screen, with figures in gardens with pavilions and lakes, the reverse in polychrome with birds, branches, and flowers.

83¾in (213cm) high

$5,000-6,200 **DN**

A Chinese Republic Period famille rose miniature four-leaf screen, each panel with a porcelain plaque painted with a scholar and a boy standing by a tree, one with a rock, in a wood frame, with friezes of scrolling foliage.

23¼in (59cm) wide

$2,200-2,700 **WW**

A Chinese late-Qing Dynasty/Republic Period famille rose table screen, with a scholar and attendants among bamboo and rockwork, the scholar holding a sprig of chrysanthemum and a stalk, within a hardwood frame, carved with scrolls and shaped panels.

30in (76cm) high

$2,500-3,700   **WW**

A 19thC Qing Dynasty hardwood table screen, with variegated black, white, and gray dali marble panel, in a hardwood stand, with shaped aprons with a narrow marble panel.

11½in (29cm) high

$1,500-1,700   **L&T**

A Chinese cloisonné enamel-, hardstone- and mother-of-pearl-mounted table screen, with a pierced and carved wood stand, possibly reproduction, one foot lacking.

16½in (42cm) high

$1,250-1,500   **GORL**

A Chinese late-Qing Dynasty carved and giltwood temple display panel, with a palace scene, with historical figures, equestrian warriors, scholars, and court figures, with rocky wooded landscapes with mythical animals, three panels above with crustaceans, fish, and pheasants, the narrow side panels with inscriptions, small parts lacking.

87in (221cm) wide

$3,100-3,700   **CHEF**

A Chinese late-Qing Dynasty hardwood stand or easel, with hinged legs, the front with a panel carved with rocks and breaking waves, the center support carved as a bat.

14¾in (37.5cm) wide

$25,000-31,000   **WW**

A Korean mother-of-pearl-inlaid lacquer table screen, probably Koryo Dynasty, 12thC, with a panel painted to imitate striated dream stone, carved on both sides with seal script calligraphy, mounted with inlaid mother-of-pearl on one side with four cranes among clouds, and with fans and shells on the reverse.

8¾in (22cm) wide

$2,500-3,700   **CA**

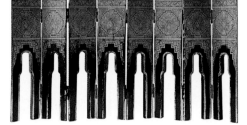

A pair of Chinese Yongzheng hexagonal armrests, with reticulated panels of kui dragons and "shou" characters set against a cell diaper ground, beneath a border with scattered bats, swirling clouds, "shou" roundels, surrounding a center medallion of a coiled dragon.

1723-35   *10¼in (26cm) wide*

$25,000-31,000   **WW**

A Burmese black gilt-lacquer folding screen, 19thC or later, with eight panels carved in the lower part with an arch, and with a bird and scrolling foliate borders.

11½in (29cm) high

$625-750   **CA**

THE FURNITURE MARKET

The ups and mostly downs of the traditional antique "brown" furniture market have been well documented, not least within these pages, over the past 15 years or so. In some respects, not that much has changed. There is, however, very good reason to think that the tide really is shifting: interiors magazines and style gurus are now trumpeting the death of the modern "gray" interior—which most traditionalists have viewed as a particularly unfortunate history- and character-canceling trend, and one reminiscent, in its decorative inappropriateness, of the "nouveau" interior designer Mrs. Beaver in Evelyn Waugh's "A Handful of Dust," when remodeling the walls and furnishings of a room at Hetton Abbey—a neo-Gothic ancestral country estate—with of all of things: chromium plating!

Social media is undoubtedly a driving force in this shift, and the likes of Instagram and Pinterest are now full of sumptuous images of rooms where minimalism is banished, color rules, and antique furniture and decorative artifacts play a starring role. The English country house "look," in particular, is stronger now than it has been for some time, with a creative mixing of colors and patterns producing eclectic but visually pleasing interiors with no slavish adherence to individual periods. Within this, one specific development has been a market revival in "country" or vernacular furniture. It is not uncommon, for example, for a simple, but warmly worn scumble-painted period press cupboard to sell for more than its finer Georgian mahogany counterpart. So, perhaps the new rule is: There are no rules! Well, maybe, but what we can definitely take from this is that momentum is building—perhaps not for a full-blown renaissance, but at the least for a welcome renewal of interest in traditional furniture.

Another significant change in the furniture market is the rapid shift to online selling. Post-global pandemic, the vast majority of sales are now generated by online platforms, be they auctioneer websites, aggregate auction sites, or dealer websites, with fewer bricks-and-mortar antiques stores around than 20 years ago. Auctioneers now regularly sell to empty salerooms—a once inconceivable prospect—and wave their gavels to faceless bidders sitting at computers or on smart devices around the world. Generally speaking, prices are still lagging behind any growth in the market, but you should expect to pay more for the best pieces, whether buying at auction or from a dealer. Demand for the unusual, rare, and pedigree pieces is high, while the abundant supply of more mundane antique furniture is keeping prices at a level that makes them good value for money. In any event, do your research, whether you intend to buy at auction or from a dealer's store or website, ask questions and always buy the best you can afford.

Looking ahead, the "green" element to buying antique furniture is a key point and should be an incentive to everyone. As we all become more aware of our carbon footprint, the case for buying something made 200 years ago that is still functional and beautiful, instead of something recently made overseas, shipped halfway around the world, and with a life expectancy of ten years, has never been stronger!

Douglas Girton, Head of Fine Furniture and Works of Art, Lyon & Turnbull

Top Left: A 19thC Victorian walnut, ebonized, and marquetry credenza, the top above a centered door, inlaid with a musical trophy and foliate scrolls, flanked by glazed cabinets, enclosing shelves, on a base with toupie feet, with gilt-metal mounts.

65¼in (165.5cm) wide

$2,200-2,700   L&T

Above: A mahogany four-poster bed, early 19thC and later, in the manner of George Hepplewhite, the tester painted with flower sprays and ribbon-tied drapery swags, surmounted by acorn finials, hangings by Colefax and Fowler, possibly made out of parts from multiple beds.

86½in (220cm) long

$16,000-20,000   DN

FURNITURE

UK PERIOD	US PERIOD	FRENCH PERIOD	GERMAN PERIOD
Elizabethan *Elizabeth I (1558-1603)*		**Renaissance** *(to ca. 1610)*	**Renaissance** *(to ca. 1650)*
Jacobean *James I (1603-25)*			
Carolean *Charles I (1625-49)*		**Louis XIII** *(1610-43)*	
Cromwellian *Commonwealth (1649-60)*	**Early Colonial** *(1620s-1700)*	**Louis XIV** *(1643-1715)*	**Renaissance/ Baroque** *(ca. 1650-1700)*
Restoration *Charles II (1660-85)* *James II (1685-88)*			
William and Mary *(1689-94)*	**William and Mary** *(1690-1720)*		
William III *(1694-1702)*			
Queen Anne *(1702-14)*	**Queen Anne** *(1720-50)*	**Régence** *(1715-23)*	**Baroque** *(ca. 1700-30)*
Early Georgian *George I (1714-27)* *George II (1727-60)*	**Chippendale** *(1750-90)*	**Louis XV** *(1723-74)*	**Rococo** *(ca. 1730-60)*
		Louis XVI *(1774-92)*	**Neo-classicism** *(ca. 1760-1800)*
Late Georgian *George III (1760-1811)*	**Early Federal** *(1790-1810)* *American Directoire (1798-1804)* *American Empire (1804-15)*	**Directoire** *(1792-99)*	**Empire** *(ca. 1800-15)*
		Empire *(1799-1815)*	
Regency *George III (1811-20)*	**Later Federal** *(1810-30)*	**Restauration** *(1815-30)* *Louis XVIII (1814-24)* *Charles X (1824-30)*	**Biedermeier** *(ca. 1815-48)*
George IV *(1820-30)*			
William IV *(1830-37)*		**Louis Phillipe** *(1830-48)*	**Revivale** *(ca. 1830-80)*
Victorian *Victoria (1837-1901)*	**Victorian** *(1840-1900)*	**2nd Empire** *(1848-70)*	
Edwardian *Edward VII (1901-10)*		**3rd Republic** *(1870-1940)*	**Jugendstil** *(ca. 1880-1920)*

A mid- to late-17thC Yorkshire joined oak armchair, Leeds, the top rail carved with foliage and scrolls, the fielded back carved with tulips and initialed "A.H.," with down-curved arms on bobbin-turned supports.

46¼in (117.5cm) high

$1,250-1,500   HT

A 17thC oak wainscot armchair, the scrolled and carved top rail over a foliate-carved back panel, on turned front legs, joined by a peripheral stretcher.

37¾in (96cm) high

$1,900-2,500   CHEF

A Charles II oak child's highchair, 17thC and later, the arched back carved with lunettes and a leaf panel, the apron carved with scrolling foliage.

$750-875   WW

A late-17thC Flemish carved walnut and caned high-back open armchair, the crest rail carved with cherubs supporting a basket of flowers and flanked by serpents, caned paneled back, flanked by pierced cherubs amid vine leaves, over curving foliate-carved and scrolling arms, restored.

48½in (123cm) high

$625-750   CHOR

A late-17thC Anglo-Dutch ebonized fruitwood side chair, with molded sparred back and C-scroll carved cresting, with scrolled legs, joined by a pierced and molded arched-front stretcher and turned baluster stretchers, marks, knocks, woodworm.

54¾in (139cm) high

$550-700   DN

A 17thC Charles II carved walnut and caned armchair.

46¾in (119cm) high

$750-1,000   L&T

A 17thC Charles II oak armchair, the two-panel back with scroll-carved cresting and carved stylized foliate scrolls, above a chip-carved seat, on ring-turned forelegs joined by peripheral stretchers.

48in (122cm) high

$1,250-1,600   L&T

A 17thC oak wainscot armchair, the scroll- and foliate-carved top rail above a paneled back carved with a stylized flower and tulips, on bobbin-turned legs joined by peripheral stretchers.

44in (112cm) high

$800-950   L&T

An oak child's chair, 17thC and later, the scrolled pediment back above a carved floral panel, on bobbin-turned front legs and stretcher.

44in (112cm) high

$3,700-4,300   CHEF

FURNITURE

A late-17thC Charles II walnut side chair, with a caned back and seat, with boy-head finials flanking a carved crown-and-thistle surmount.

$500-625 WW

A matched pair of high-back chairs, in 17thC style, with pierced crown crestings, above vacant cartouches with turned uprights.

51¼in (130cm) high

$1,000-1,250 TEN

An 18thC Georgian oak settle, the triple-panel back fitted with a center hinged panel for use as a table, above a hinged plank flanked by open arms, on a paneled box base.

73½in (187cm) wide

$3,100-3,700 L&T

An 18thC Georgian oak settle, the back with three over five panels, above a seat with a hinged compartment, flanked by open arms, on a box base.

77½in (197cm) wide

$2,500-3,100 L&T

A George III oak three-panel settle, on slight cabriole front legs and square-section back legs, united by back and side stretchers.

39¾in (101cm) wide

$700-800 CHEF

An early-19thC late-Georgian pine settle, the three over four panel back with a shaped hood and enclosed arms, above a loose plank seat, on a box base.

63in (160cm) wide

$1,600-2,000 L&T

A late-19thC carved oak hall bench, the three-panel carved back depicting naturalistic lions and foliate carving, the armrests with lion-head terminals.

96in (244cm) wide

$625-750 CHEF

A late-19th/early-20thC late Victorian hall settle, with turned spindle decoration and fielded panels, the base with a hinged drop front revealing a shelf.

49¾in (126.5cm) wide

$500-625 WW

A 20thC elm and ash two-seat hoop-back settle, in Georgian style, with a spindle back above a shaped double saddle seat, on turned legs joined by twin crinoline stretchers.

46¾in (119cm) wide

$2,700-3,200 L&T

A pair of mid- to late-18thC George III Thames Valley elm and sycamore Windsor chairs.

35in (89cm) high

$3,100-3,700

DN

A Thames Valley ash, fruitwood, and elm comb-back armchair, the vase-shaped splat flanked by spindles, on turned front and back legs, united by an H stretcher, signs of restoration throughout.

ca. 1775   *41¾in (106cm) high*

$1,400-1,700

CHEF

An 18thC George III provincial elm and ash armchair, the yoke-shaped top rail above a pierced vasiform splat, over a wide overstuffed seat, flanked by scrolling open arms.

36½in (93cm) high

$550-700

L&T

A Thames Valley fruitwood and elm shawl-back armchair, the bowed top rail above a vase-shaped splat, flanked by spindles over a molded elm seat, raised on turned legs and an H stretcher.

ca. 1800   *43¼in (110cm) high*

$1,000-1,100

CHEF

A set of four George III elm and beech stick-back armchairs, with saddle-shaped seats and cabriole front legs, united by an H stretcher.

37in (94cm) high

$7,000-8,000

CHEF

A late-18th/early-19thC folk art primitive ash and elm child's Windsor armchair, probably Welsh, with traces of original green painted decoration.

$500-625

WW

A harlequin set of seven late-18th/early-19thC Regency ash and yew Windsor kitchen chairs, the stick backs with a pierced center splat decorated with an urn, with elm seats.

$500-625

WW

An ash Windsor chair, attributed to Gillows, with hoop back and a molded saddle seat constructed from sycamore or beech, with traces of green paint beneath, general wear.

ca. 1800   *36½in (93cm) high*

$750-875

SWO

A set of six late-George III mahogany country dining chairs, in Sheraton style, each with a vertical splat back, above a solid seat and chamfered legs.

ca. 1800-10

$950-1,050

WW

A Vale of York ash and elm stick-back Windsor armchair, hooped top rail, barrel-turned and split lath underarm supports, on turned tapering splayed legs, joined by an H stretcher, remnants of old paint.

44½in (113cm) high

$500-625   **HT**

A set of eight early-19thC yew and elm stick-back armchairs, with solid saddle-shaped seats, on turned supports united by crinoline stretchers.

35½in (90cm) high

$8,500-10,000   **CHEF**

An early-19thC Welsh primitive ash Windsor armchair, with a burl elm thick plank seat, with traces of original painted decoration.

$2,200-2,700   **WW**

An early-19thC yew and elm stick-back armchair, with a saddle-shaped seat, on turned legs united by a crinoline stretcher, some worm.

39in (99cm) high

$700-800   **CHEF**

A near pair of early- to mid-19thC fruitwood and elm stick-back armchairs, on ring-turned legs.

$375-500   **WW**

An early-19thC Regency fruitwood country armchair, with a curved elm seat.

$120-190   **WW**

A 19thC folk art primitive ash Windsor armchair, probably Welsh, the stick back above an elm seat, with traces of original green painted decoration.

$1,900-2,500   **WW**

Two Victorian yew low-back Windsor armchairs, one with an elm seat, the other probably alder.

ca. 1840

$950-1,050   **WW**

A mid-19thC Victorian painted child's Windsor chair, possibly West Country, with a stick back above a solid seat.

$200-250   **WW**

A Victorian elm "Oxford" Windsor armchair, by Stephen Hazell, the underside of the seat with branded initials "SH."

Stephen Hazell was a maker of Windsor chairs who worked from premises in South Parade, Summertown, north Oxford. Listed in contemporary trade directories as a "maker of Windsor chairs and cane chairs," he first advertised his services as a "Turner and Chair-Maker" in 1846. In the 1870s, the business was passed on to his son, Stephen Charles Hazell, who continued manufacturing chairs until 1892. Among a number of notable commissions for Hazell chairs include those produced for the Reading Rooms of Oxford's Bodleian Library.

ca. 1850-70

$250-370   **WW**

Five of a set of eight George II walnut chairs, each with a shaped rectangular back, with a slender foliate-carved surround and surmounted by a floral- and foliate-carved terminal, each herringbone-banded vase splat above a drop-in seat covered with an 18thC floral needlework panel, on acanthus-carved cabriole legs, joined by stretchers and terminating in carved lion-paw feet, splits, various repairs and replacement elements.

This is a particularly distinctive set of George II walnut chairs: They incorporate an unusual combination of features that do not appear to be clearly identifiable with the work of either a particular maker or, indeed, region. For example, while their idiosyncratic paw feet have affinities of form with well-documented groups of contemporary Irish chairs (and tables), the scrolls in the inside of the paws appear to be without parallel in Irish furniture. Moreover, their turned and square H stretchers are in marked contrast to the more prevalent flat H stretchers found on Irish chairs of the second quarter of the 18thC. Other atypical elements of the design include the herringbone bandings on the splats, the finely carved foliate moldings surrounding the backs, and the gadrooned splat shoes. Altogether, these features make a significant contribution to the chairs' desirability and price.

A pair of George I dining chairs, with solid vase-shaped splats, on front cabriole legs with hoof feet and splayed back legs, united by a waved H stretcher, knocks, scratches, old repairs, minor worm.

40¼in (102cm) high

$700-800   CHEF

ca. 1730

$50,000-62,000 the set

40½in (103cm) high

DN

A set of eight George II walnut and parcel-gilt dining chairs, with repeating eagle motifs, each vertical splat with the crest of the Altieri family of Rome, the six stars surmounted by a galero, mantle, and tassels, each with cabriole legs terminating in claw-and-ball feet, with a pair of later 19thC chairs to match, splits, repairs, evidence of worm, fabirc worn.

This set of eight walnut and parcel-gilt dining chairs, along with two mahogany examples en suite, bear the arms of the Altieri family from Rome. The broad proportions of these chairs, with their waisted upright back posts, solid shaped baluster splat, compass seat, and cabriole legs, are typical of high-quality "banister back" chairs of the 1730s. The arched crest rail has evolved from the milkmaid's yoke found in Chinese prototypes. The chair's back is slightly bent to ergonomically fit the back of the sitter. The introduction of the "India back"—India or Indian being used to denote all of South and Southeast Asia—also sometimes called a "bended," "crook'd," or "sweep" back chair is considered "the most radical and far-reaching design innovation of the eighteenth century" (A. Bowett, "Early Georgian Furniture 1715-1740," Woodbridge/2009, page 156). The back of the splats of the present chairs have been chamfered to "lighten" their appearance. These chairs are highly unusual for the carved decoration on the "shoe" (where the splat joins the back of the drop-in seat) and the stylized claw-and-ball feet.

Provenance: Formerly the Messel family collection in the dining room at 104 Lancaster Gate, the London family home of British stage director and artist, Oliver Messel (1904-78).

ca. 1730

$11,000-12,000

41in (104cm) high

DN

A pair of Irish George II mahogany chairs.

ca. 1750

$3,100-3,700   DN

Three of a set of six mid-18thC George II mahogany dining chairs, after a design by Thomas Chippendale, each with serpentine top rail above a pierced and interlaced "Gothic" splat, on leaf-carved cabriole legs, with claw-and-ball feet, two chairs with original corner blocks.

39¼in (100cm) high

$5,000-5,600 the set   DUK

A set of six early-George III mahogany dining chairs, with a serpentine top rail carved with leaves, tassels, and frills, above a pierced and interlaced splat, the drop-in seat on leaf- and cabochon-carved cabriole front legs, with claw-and-ball feet.

ca. 1760-70

$7,500-8,500   WW

A set of eight early-19thC Regency mahogany dining chairs, the bar top rail with Greek key-style carving, above an X splat with a center floral roundel, the saber legs with reeded decoration, the front rails with a Ronald Phillips label, reference no. "12160."

$3,100-3,700   WW

A set of eight early-to-mid-19thC Regency dark-stained beech dining chairs, comprising two armchairs and six side chairs, each with a rosewood curved tablet top rail inlaid with floral marquetry, above a caned seat with later padded seat, on saber legs.

33½in (85cm) high

$1,250-1,900 DUK

A set of eight mid-19thC early Victorian mahogany dining chairs, by Gillows, comprising two armchairs and six side chairs, each with a curved tablet top rail above a horizontal splat, the front legs with brass caps and casters stamped "Cope & Collinson Patent," the front seat rail stamped "GILLOW."

33¾in (86cm) high

$7,000-8,000 DUK

A set of six Victorian walnut and parcel-gilt dining chairs, by Gillows, in French style, with molded frames, with leaf decoration, stamped "Gillow" and with initials "G.R."

ca. 1860-70

$875-1,000 WW

A set of 12 mahogany dining chairs from RMS "Majestic," early 20thC and later, from either the First Class or the À La Carte restaurant, each inlaid with stringing, the top rail above an Empire-style pierced splat, the outswept arms with flower-head finials, on reeded front legs and an X stretcher.

RMS "Majestic" was built and launched in Germany in 1914 as SS "Bismarck." The largest ship in the world until SS "Normandie" was launched in 1935, she was later handed to the Allies as part of Germany's war reparations, following which she was bought by the White Star Line and renamed RMS "Majestic." There were two restaurants on board—First Class and À La Carte—and, by repute, it was the latter that was actually favored by First Class passengers. When the economic depression of the early 1930s deepened, it was perhaps, therefore, ironic that of the two the À La Carte was closed, and its chairs put into storage, to be subsequently purchased by the eminent photographer and designer Cecil Beaton, who had often crossed the Atlantic on RMS "Majestic." In 1930, Beaton had leased Ashcombe House, in Wiltshire, from R. W. Borley, on the understanding that he would make improvements—subsequently overseen by Austrian architect Michael Rosenauer. On completion, Beaton, an exceptionally well-connected society host, regularly held large dinner parties there—guests included Salvador Dalí, Rex Whistler, and Oliver Messel—for which long runs of dining chairs would have been essential. When Beaton's lease on Ashcombe ended in 1945, it was reoccupied by the Borley family until 1993, and during a clearance of the outbuildings prior to it being sold, this set of chairs was "rediscovered." Kept by the family, they came onto the market just recently, for the first time since Beaton bought them back in the 1930s.

$4,300-5,600 the set WW

A set of 12 late-19thC carved mahogany dining chairs, of Chippendale design, the shell carved top rails above C-scroll and interlaced pierced splats, on square fluted forelegs joined by an H stretcher.

38¼in (97cm) high

$1,500-1,700 TEN

A pair of late-17thC Anglo-Dutch walnut side chairs, the backs with foliate cresting above foliate-carved and pierced vasiform splats, on bellflower-carved scrolled legs joined by shaped stretchers.

48¾in (124cm) high

$550-700 L&T

A George I walnut and marquetry side chair, in the manner of James Moore.

There are several closely dated analogues for this style of leg and foot, particularly a set of chairs (ca. 1725) at Houghton Hall, Norfolk, and a closely dated set (probably before 1726) made for Chicheley Hall, Bedfordshire, and now at Montecute, Somerset.

ca. 1720 *43¾in (111cm) high*

$3,100-3,700 DN

A pair of early George III mahogany side chairs, each with an arched back, on molded and chamfered front legs.

ca. 1760

$375-500 WW

A pair of late-17th/early-18thC William and Mary oak side chairs, each with a scroll-carved top rail, above a vase-shaped splat back and a solid seat.

$200-250   **WW**

A pair of early-18thC Scottish Queen Anne laburnum side chairs, the shaped top rails above vasiform splats and drop-in seats with wavy seat rails, on block and turned legs joined by stretchers.

39¾in (101cm) high

$550-700   **L&T**

A pair of early-18thC South Yorkshire oak side chairs, the arched splats carved with masks, scrolls, and stylized leaves, mounted with acorn pendant finials, on turned and block legs joined by stretchers.

42¼in (107cm) high

$800-950   **L&T**

A pair of Irish George II mahogany side chairs, with curved solid vase-shaped splats, with scrolled decoration, on shell-capped cabriole front legs and scroll trefid feet.

ca. 1740-50

$1,000-1,100   **WW**

A pair of 18thC George III mahogany side chairs, the shaped top rails above pierced and foliate-carved interlaced splats, on straight chamfered legs joined by stretchers.

37½in (95cm) high

$800-950   **L&T**

A pair of early-19thC provincial elm side chairs, with turned spindle backs.

34¾in (88cm) high

$2,500-3,100   **L&T**

A pair of early-19thC Italian mahogany and marquetry side chairs, in the manner of Giuseppe Maggiolini, Milan, each inlaid with a cartouche decorated with fleur-de-lis, flanked by winged cherubs, flowers, and leaves, with brass moldings above a leaf-and-flower-carved splat.

$875-1,000   **WW**

A set of fourteen 19thC walnut and upholstered side chairs, in Louis XV style, on cabriole legs, with 18thC embroidered silk and velvet damask loose covers.

$7,000-8,000 the set   **WW**

A pair of late-19thC Italian green japanned side chairs, probably Venetian, in 18thC style, each painted with flowers, Rococo motifs, and figures, with a cane seat.

$950-1,050   **WW**

A pair of 20thC upholstered side chairs, in Georgian style, on square tapered legs joined by H stretchers.

39in (99cm) high

$1,000-1,100   **L&T**

FURNITURE

An early-18thC George II provincial oak corner armchair, the curved arm rail above twin vasiform splats and squared baluster supports, on square chamfered legs joined by stretchers.

35¾in (91cm) high

$1,050-1,200　　　L&T

A George II oak corner chair, the curved top rail terminating in recessed coaster-style ends, on turned and vase-shaped supports, cabriole legs and an X stretcher, damage and repairs.

33in (84cm) high

$190-250　　　LC

An 18thC George III mahogany corner chair, the curved back rail with scrolled terminals, on chamfered straight legs with brass casters.

32in (81cm) high

$550-700　　　L&T

An 18th/19thC Anglo-Chinese exotic hardwood corner chair.

37in (94cm) high

$5,000-6,200　　　DN

ESSENTIAL REFERENCE—SGABELLO

A sgabello—the word is derived from "scabellum," the Latin for "stool"—is a form of backstool or armless chair that originated in Italy during the Renaissance.

- Their component parts were essentially rudimentary: two plank-form legs united front-to-back by a single stretcher and supporting a wood seat with a plank-form back.
- However, curvaceously shaped, and often elaborately carved with decorative motifs and/or family crests, sgabellos (or "scabelli," in Italian) were mainly designed not for comfort (their seats were solid wood) but instead to impress guests.
- As such, they were usually employed in entrance halls, or in long, gallery-like rooms ("portegos," in Italy) mainly employed for displays, celebrations, and hospitality.
- Especially associated with Venice and the city-states of Tuscany, their popularity gradually spread throughout Europe during the 16thC and 17thC, and they enjoyed a number of fashionable revivals during the 18thC and 19thC.

A pair of mid-18thC George III oak hall chairs, the backs centered by a painted armorial of a stag, the Collingwood family crest, undersides stamped "CFA," splits, armorials worn.

38¼in (97cm) high

$1,900-2,500　　　DN

A set of eight George III oak hall chairs, of sgabello form, the stylized shield-shaped backs above shaped seats and supports, joined by curved stretchers, the seat front supports with vacant recess.

ca. 1780　　　*37¾in (96cm) high*

$3,700-5,000 the set　　　DN

A pair of George II mahogany, satinwood, and line-inlaid hall chairs, of sgabello form.

ca. 1750　　　*39in (99cm) high*

$1,250-1,900　　　DN

A set of three late-18thC George III mahogany hall chairs, in the manner of Ince & Mayhew, with fluted oval backs, each with a crest of an armored arm holding a dagger.

37in (94cm) high

$2,000-2,500　　　DUK

A set of three late-18thC Georgian oak armorial hall chairs, the vasiform backs decorated in an oval reserve, with a polychrome crest for the Shee family, above curved seats with recessed panels, on trestle bases.

38½in (98cm) high

$2,500-3,100　　　L&T

A pair of early-19thC Regency mahogany hall chairs, each later painted with a rampant lion crest.
$375-450 WW

A pair of Regency mahogany hall chairs.
ca. 1815 *35½in (90cm) high*
$2,500-3,700 DN

A pair of early-19thC Regency mahogany hall chairs, attributed to Gillows, with carved scallop shell backs, with an eagle-head crest, above a solid seat and molded front saber legs.
$1,900-2,500 WW

A pair of early-19thC Regency mahogany armorial hall chairs, the backs carved with plantain leaves, centered with painted armorials inscribed "FLIGHT" above a coronet and eagle, on square tapered legs.
35½in (90cm) high
$500-625 L&T

A late-19thC Black Forest "Bull" hall chair, the back carved with a bull mask, over a "hair" seat, on carved legs with hoof feet.
38½in (98cm) high
$5,000-6,200 L&T

One of a pair of late-19th/early-20thC Austrian ebonized hall chairs, by Jacob & Josef Kohn, scratches, marks, possible later reinforcement, some worm.

Jacob Kohn (1791-1866), along with his son Josef Kohn (1814-84), founded Jacob & Josef Kohn in 1849. Kohn would later rise to become one of the leading furniture makers in Austria–Hungary, becoming one of the leading competitors of Gebrüder Thonet. Kohn designed many pieces with artists of the Wiener Werkstätte, including Josef Hoffmann.
35¾in (91cm) high
$19,000-25,000 the pair DN

A Regency mahogany hall seat, scratches, knocks, cracks, wear.
ca. 1825 *60¼in (153cm) wide*
$2,500-3,100 DN

A Victorian mahogany hall bench.
ca. 1860 *56¼in (143cm) wide*
$1,900-2,500 DN

A mahogany and simulated rosewood hall seat, early to mid-19thC and later, in the manner of Gillows, with foliate carved C-scroll-shaped supports, wear and rubbing.

The form of the legs on this seat are similar to designs by Thomas King that feature in Anglo-Indian and Ceylonese furniture of the period.
54in (137cm) wide
$3,700-5,000 DN

FURNITURE

A late-18thC George III mahogany bowfront window seat, with scroll ends, on molded tapering legs united by a curved stretcher.

40¾in (103.5cm) wide

$625-750 WW

A late-18thC George III mahogany window seat, with scroll ends, on tapering legs and block feet.

31¾in (80.5cm) wide

$500-625 WW

A Victorian walnut and parcel-gilt window seat, by Holland & Sons, with scroll ends, a molded frame, and on cabriole legs, stamped "Holland & Sons."

ca. 1860 *43¼in (110cm) wide*

$1,000-1,100 WW

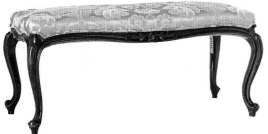

A Victorian mahogany-framed dressing stool or window seat, with a serpentine-shaped seat rail carved with acanthus leaves, on scrolled cabriole legs, some bruising.

ca. 1870 *43¼in (110cm) wide*

$1,000-1,100 TEN

A Victorian mahogany window seat, with scroll ends, on turned legs.

51¼in (130cm) wide

$500-625 CHEF

A 19thC mahogany window seat, the scrolled arms above a bowfront seat rail, raised on square tapered legs, on spade feet.

60¼in (153cm) wide

$950-1,050 CHEF

A late-19thC carved mahogany window seat or stool, in George III style, on carved cabriole legs, with claw-and-ball feet, legs have been darkened.

43¼in (110cm) wide

$500-625 TEN

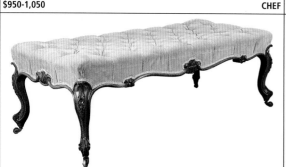

A late-Victorian walnut stool, with a scroll-and-shell-carved seat rail, on leaf carved cabriole legs, with brass toes and casters.

57in (145cm) wide

$875-1,000 HT

An early-20thC French walnut or stained beech dressing stool or window seat, the close-nailed overstuffed seat above a molded seat rail, on acanthus carved cabriole legs, joined by arched stretchers, framework repolished/stained.

43¼in (110cm) wide

$1,700-2,200 TEN

An oak joined stool, 17thC and later, the top with an ovolo-molded edge above nulled carved rails with a shaped lower edge, on turned and stiff-leaf-carved supports, with a nulled and leaf-carved stretcher.

20½in (52cm) high

$500-625   **CHEF**

A George I walnut stool, the bifurcated legs with acanthus-carved knees terminating on pad feet, marks, knocks, old worm, old repairs.

ca. 1715   *20½in (52cm) wide*

$1,900-2,500   **DN**

A George II elm stool, with a later needlework drop-in seat, on cabriole legs and pad feet.

ca. 1730   *20in (51cm) wide*

$1,000-1,100   **WW**

A Regency simulated satinwood and polychrome painted stool, decorated with flowers, the beechwood painted to simulate satinwood, cracks, seat torn, worm, paintwork with some craquelure.

ca. 1820   *56¼in (143cm) wide*

$1,250-1,500   **DN**

A pair of George II walnut stools, with shaped friezes, on shell-capped cabriole legs and pad feet, one with an applied "Apter-Fredericks" trade label.

ca. 1735-40   *19¼in (49cm) wide*

$20,000-25,000   **WW**

A pair of mid-19thC Victorian rosewood footstools, the molded rails with gilt beading, on turned and gadrooned feet with casters.

14½in (37cm) wide

$1,250-1,600   **TEN**

A mid-19thC French giltwood stool, in Louis XV style, the serpentine seat above a pierced and carved base decorated with leaves and flowers, with a shaped X stretcher.

15¾in (40cm) high

$1,000-1,100   **WW**

An early-Victorian rosewood-framed dressing stool, the overstuffed seat on a C-scroll frame, joined by a spiral turned stretcher.

ca. 1850   *27¼in (69cm) wide*

$450-550   **TEN**

A pair of 19thC walnut stools, in George II style, both with rails stamped "1861," restored.

23½in (60cm) wide

$2,200-2,700   **DN**

A 19thC carved giltwood stool, in George II style, the overstuffed seat above a molded acanthus carved seat rail centered by scrolled shells, on cabriole legs with vacant cartouches and scrolled toes.

32in (81cm) wide

$1,100-1,350   TEN

A mid-19thC rosewood adjustable piano stool, on claw feet.

$90-100   WHP

A Victorian walnut foot stool, on four thick cabriole legs.

31½in (80cm) wide

$625-750   DN

A Victorian walnut stool, upholstered by Gisbert Rentmeister, with scroll-and-leaf-carved rails, on cabriole legs and scrolled feet, with ceramic casters.

57½in (146cm) wide

$1,000-1,100   HT

A late-19thC Victorian walnut stool, in William and Mary style, on turned legs united by an X stretcher, on brass casters.

25in (63.5cm) wide

$375-500   WW

A pair of late-19th/early-20thC carved mahogany stools, in George II style.

24in (61cm) wide

$1,500-2,200   DN

ESSENTIAL REFERENCE—METAMORPHIC FURNITURE

Dual-purpose pieces of furniture are sometimes described as "mechanical," but more often as "metamorphic"—an adjective derived from the noun "metamorphosis," meaning a change in the form or nature of a thing into a completely different one. For example, the George III stool shown here is "metamorphic," because, by opening up and pulling out some hinged (mechanical) components, it can be transformed into a set of library steps—and vice versa. The fashion for metamorphic furniture really gathered momentum in the mid-18thC in France, when a succession of German-born cabinetmakers, notably Jean-Henri Riesener and David Roentgen, sent a number of exquisitely made pieces to the courts of Louis XV and Louis XVI (with Roentgen becoming Master Cabinetmaker to Marie Antoinette). The rest of Europe soon followed suit, and numerous and diverse designs subsequently appeared during the late-18thC and 19thC, including: tables and chairs into library or bedside steps; chests-of-drawers into writing desks; chairs into tables; bedside cupboards into washstands; and commodes that looked like bedside cupboards or chests-of-drawers. Perhaps most notable among a number of post-19thC innovations in this field have been the cabinets that "turn into" record players or cocktail bars.

A George III mahogany and rosewood meamorphic stool and set of library steps, attributed to Gillows.

ca. 1800   *35½in (90cm) high*

$1,600–2,000   DN

A 19thC leather upholstered mahogany stool.

62¼in (158cm) wide

$1,000-1,250   CHEF

FURNITURE

A set of four early-18thC Régence giltwood fauteuils à la reine, wear on the gilt surfaces, woodworm.

42in (106.5cm) high

$55,000-60,000   DN

A pair of early-18thC Louis XIV giltwood fauteuils, old woodworm, tack marks, old knocks and chips.

45¼in (115cm) high

$125,000-150,000   DN

A George II carved walnut open armchair, attributed to James Moore, possibly adapted in the 19th/20thC, marks, knocks, old worm.

ca. 1730   42in (106.5cm) high

$11,000-14,000   DN

An Anglo-Chinese export child's commode chair, in George II style, possibly padouk or hongmu, with an aperture for a chamber pot, on cabriole front legs.

ca. 1740

$3,700-5,000   WW

An early-18thC North European oak and fruitwood wing armchair, leather upholstered, later 19thC alterations, scratches, marks, worm.

47in (119.5cm) high

$1,000-1,250   DN

A George II walnut armchair, the shaped top rail above a vase-shaped center splat, scroll arms, on cabriole legs with shell motifs, on pad feet.

38¼in (97cm) high

$1,000-1,100   DUK

A pair of mid-18thC Anglo-Chinese export padouk armchairs, in Irish style, with scroll top rails, above a pierced and interlaced splat back carved with bird heads, on leaf-and-rosette-carved cabriole front legs and claw-and-ball feet.

This pair of armchairs were constructed in China, probably Canton or Macau for an English client, possibly an East India Company official.

$25,000-37,000   WW

A mid-18thC Irish George II mahogany open armchair, scratches, scuffs, worm.

38½in (98cm) high

$3,100-3,700   DN

A mid-18thC George II mahogany library armchair, marks, restorations, some movement in the joints.

39in (99cm) high

$3,100-3,700   DN

FURNITURE

Judith Picks

Mid-18thC, George II open armchairs, such as this one, acquired various nicknames at the time, subsequently, or both. One of the two most notable of these was Thomas Chippendale's description "The French Chair," primarily because of, as with this example, their cabriole front legs, outswept arms, and C-scroll arm supports. These features are characteristic of the curvilinear Rococo style that emerged in France soon after the death of Louis XIV in 1715, developed during the reign of Louis XV, and by the 1730s, was enjoying considerable traction across much of Europe. The second of the most notable nicknames is the "Gainsborough" chair, after the renowned English portrait artist Thomas Gainsborough (1727-88), who posed many of his subjects in chairs such as this. He did so for good reason: The proportions of the frame are, especially in this context, faultless, with the height and width of the seat enabling the sitter in fashionable contemporary dress to adopt an elegant attitude in relative comfort for long periods at a time. This was despite the fact that the degree of padding in the upholstery is kept to almost a severe minimum to accentuate the intrinsically elegant lines of the legs and arms. Yes, regardless of what one might call it, this is an elegant chair.

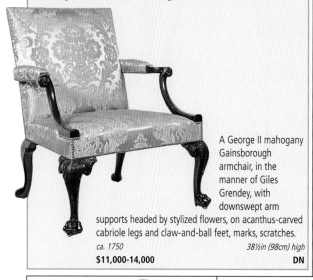

A George II mahogany Gainsborough armchair, in the manner of Giles Grendey, with downswept arm supports headed by stylized flowers, on acanthus-carved cabriole legs and claw-and-ball feet, marks, scratches.
ca. 1750   38½in (98cm) high
$11,000-14,000   **DN**

Two of a set of four mid-18thC George III painted open armchairs, each with cartouche-shaped back and serpentine seat, on cabriole legs, with traces of earlier layers of decoration.
36½in (93cm) high
$3,100-3,700 the set   **DUK**

An early-George III mahogany library armchair, possibly Irish, Chippendale period, outswept arms with flower-head terminals and molded supports, the dished, overstuffed seat above cabriole front legs and swept and slightly twisted back legs, carved with vines, anthemions, and flower heads, on scroll feet.
ca. 1760
$19,000-25,000   **WW**

An Italian giltwood armchair, knocks, scratches, restorations, worm.
ca. 1760   37¾in (96cm) high
$1,250-1,500   **DN**

An early-George III mahogany open armchair, with molded top rail and pierced ladder back, the outswept arms with foliate molding.
37¾in (96cm) high
$750-875   **CHEF**

A pair of George III mahogany library armchairs, with arched padded backs above padded arms, with show-wood supports carved with foliate scroll and stiff leaf, on square chamfered and molded legs, replacement elements.
ca. 1760   38½in (98cm) high
$14,000-16,000   **CHEF**

An early-George III library armchair, with a serpentine back, padded seat and armrests, the arms carved with Rococo leaf scrolls, on cabriole front legs and brass roller castoes.
ca. 1760-70
$2,500-3,100   **WW**

A George III carved mahogany Gainsborough open armchair, in the manner of Wright & Elwick.
ca. 1765   40½in (103cm) high
$3,100-3,700   **DN**

A pair of George III mahogany cockpen armchairs, in Chinese Chippendale style, one seat rail stamped "VIII," suggesting that this pair were originally part of a longer set of chairs, one chair with a paper label for "Launa & Co Antiques Washington DC," some worm, repairs, and reinforcements, small losses.
ca. 1770   37¾in (96cm) high
$5,500-7,000   **DN**

A Louis XV beech-frame fauteuil, the molded frame and shaped arms decorated with rocaille and floral carving, on cabriole legs, historic repairs.

40½in (103cm) high

$2,000-2,200 **CHEF**

A Louis XV beech-frame fauteuil, the molded frame and shaped arms decorated with rocaille and floral carving, on acanthus-capped cabriole legs, worm, repairs, dry splits in the legs.

37in (94cm) high

$5,500-6,000 **CHEF**

A mid-18thC George III mahogany armchair, on cabriole legs headed by fan motifs.

34¾in (88cm) high

$550-700 **DUK**

A George III mahogany open armchair.

ca. 1780 *36½in (93cm) high*

$1,900-2,500 **DN**

A pair of George III mahogany Gainsborough armchairs, later seat rails, cracks, worm, repairs throughout.

ca. 1780 *42¼in (107cm) high*

$5,000-6,200 **DN**

A George III mahogany armchair, in French Hepplewhite style, depicting figures dancing and a pair of deer, with scrolling flower-and-leaf borders.

ca. 1780-90

$625-750 **WW**

A rare 18thC Anglo-Chinese export padouk armchair, in Irish style, with scrolled crest rail, the pierced and interlaced splat carved with bird heads, drop-in seat, on leaf- and rosette-carved cabriole front legs, with claw-and-ball feet.

Such chairs were commissioned by European clients and made by cabinetmakers in Canton or Macau—part of a long tradition of the decorative arts and furnishing items made in China to European designs but constructed in a Chinese manner. The high quality of this chair would indicate a wealthy client, perhaps an East India Company official. The splat design echoes Irish examples noted in The Knight of Glin and James Peill, "Irish Furniture," Yale (2007), page 213, figures 38 and 39, while for further information on Chinese cabinetmaking, see Carl L. Crossman, "The Decorative Arts of the China Trade," ACC (2004), pages 220-34.

39in (99cm) high

$2,500-3,700 **DUK**

An 18thC Italian painted and parcel-gilt armchair, the frame carved with scrolls and leaves, on hoof feet.

$1,250-1,500 **WW**

A pair of George III mahogany armchairs, in the manner of John Linnell, old repairs, upholstery with minor wear.

ca. 1790 *36in (91.5cm) high*

$2,500-3,700 **DN**

FURNITURE

An 18thC fruitwood open armchair, the top rail with paper scrolled ears, above a pierced vase-shaped splat and outswept scroll arms, drop-in seat, with cabriole front legs on claw-and-ball feet.

38¼in (97cm) high

$875-1,100   **CHEF**

A set of 12 late-George III satinwood armchairs, with painted faux ebony decoration, with pierced back center rails over a cane seat, on ring-turned tapering front legs.

34in (86.5cm) high

$5,000-6,200   **DUK**

A set of three George III giltwood open armchairs, gilding rubbed, one chair with front leg damage, chips, missing paintwork.

$3,700-4,300   **CHOR**

A George III mahogany elbow chair, with a serpentine rosette-carved front rail, on fluted tapering legs, structurally weak, legs restored, front seat rail reinforced.

35½in (90cm) high

$1,000-1,100   **CHEF**

A George III mahogany elbow chair, in Hepplewhite style, the shield-shaped back with carved ribbon and flower-head decoration between scrolling arms, on square tapered front legs with bellflower detail, on spade feet.

36½in (92.5cm) high

$700-800   **CHEF**

A George III mahogany "Cockpen" chair, in the Chinese pattern, in the manner of Thomas Chippendale, restoration and repairs, movement in arms.

35in (89cm) high

$1,600-2,000   **LC**

A George III mahogany armchair, with scroll-end crest rail, pierced splat, shepherd's crook arms, on cabriole legs carved with scallop shells, with claw-and-ball feet, scratches, marks, worm.

40¼in (102cm) high

$1,100-1,350   **DN**

An early-19thC Regency mahogany armchair, the curved top rail inlaid with brass stringing and a rosewood panel, with scroll arms and carved leaf decoration.

$500-625   **WW**

A set of four ebonized, parcel-gilt and painted armchairs, ca. 1810 and later, in the manner of John Gee, two stamped "T S" the other "G," marks, knocks, looseness in joints, signs of repairs.

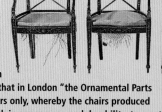

This set of ebonized and parcel-gilt open armchairs illustrates the fashion in the latter part of the 18thC for japanned (painted) furniture. In 1793, an advertisement of William Peat in the Edinburgh Evening Courant noted that in London "the Ornamental Parts of Japanned Work … are practiced by Japanners only, whereby the chairs produced from that Capital are found to be superior, both in appearance and durability, to any that have hitherto done here." Thus, cabinet- and chairmakers seemingly outsourced decorative work. This is reinforced by Thomas Sheraton in his "The Cabinet Dictionary" (1803), who affirmed that chair painting was a specific branch of the decorator's art. In this example, foliate scrolls, floral sprays, and grisaille panels depicting putti, possibly inspired by the work of Jacob de Wit (1695-1754), were applied to the ground paint of chairs that were intended for a parlor or drawing room. Such furniture generally harmonized with the color palette of the rooms for which it was acquired. Although most painted furniture was finished in the decorator's workshop, some pieces were the work of middle-class and aristocratic women, who were described in "Pride and Prejudice" by Jane Austen as accomplished, for they all "paint tables, cover screens and knit purses."

34¼in (87cm) high

$11,000-12,000   **DN**

An early-19thC Regency mahogany armchair, in the manner of Gillows, the curved scroll and reeded top rail above a roundel-decorated horizontal splat, with shepherd's crook arms, and X-shaped supports united by a turned stretcher, the front rail stamped with workman's initials "ET."
$1,400-1,600 WW

A Regency oak Spanish chair, in the manner of Gillows, light wear.
41in (104cm) high
$1,900-2,500 CHEF

A late Regency mahogany library chair, split, knocks, historic worm, repairs.
40¼in (102cm) high
$1,250-1,500 CHEF

A pair of George IV giltwood armchairs, in the manner of Morel and Seddon, the front recessed casters stamped with a coronet and "B S & P PATENT."
ca. 1830 39¾in (101cm) high
$5,000-6,200 DN

A William IV yew and burl yew armchair, attributed to Gillows, in George II style, chips, marks, arm joints opening, a dip in the center.
ca. 1830 35¾in (91cm) high
$5,000-6,200 DN

A William IV mahogany and leather adjustable armchair, the wings detachable on brass fittings, the front seat rail sliding out to a hinged leather-upholstered leg rest.
ca. 1830 45¾in (116cm) high
$1,250-1,500 DN

A George IV mahogany library armchair, on reeded front legs with brass casters and splayed back legs.
41¾in (106cm) high
$2,000-2,500 CHEF

A pair of William IV mahogany and plum pudding mahogany armchairs, attributed to Gillows, marks, repairs, minor separation in joints.
ca. 1830
36¼in (92cm) high
$5,000-6,200 DN

A William IV caned rosewood library armchair.

33¾in (86cm) high

$750-875   CHEF

A William IV mahogany library armchair, decorated with carved leaves and lappets, with a drop-in seat, on brass caps and ceramic casters.

ca. 1830-35

$750-875   WW

A pair of 19thC giltwood and gesso fauteuils, in Louis XV style, with a serpentine-shaped seat rail, on cabriole legs decorated with flower heads and acanthus leaves, the underside inscribed "Noel 1846."

33in (84cm) high

$1,100-1,350   TEN

One of a pair of carved beech and needlework upholstered Gainsborough armchairs, in George III style, probably early to mid-19thC.

39¾in (101cm) high

$3,100-3,700 the pair   DN

A Victorian rosewood framed open armchair, the C-scroll- and acanthus-carved top rail with spiral turned supports, with reeded handgrips, on turned legs joined by a spiral turned H stretcher, small repairs.

ca. 1860   52in (132cm) high

$375-500   TEN

A 19thC carved mahogany library armchair, in George III style, acanthus-carved arm supports, on carved cabriole legs, with claw-and-ball feet.

43in (109cm) high

$1,250-1,600   TEN

A pair of Victorian mahogany-framed open armchairs, with scrolled top rails and shell-form scrolled splats, on cabriole forelegs with casters, slight wear, legs scuffed.

ca. 1870   37½in (95.5cm) high

$800-950   TEN

A late-19thC carved mahogany library armchair, in George II style, with acanthus-carved arm supports above an overstuffed seat, on carved cabriole legs, some scuffs/general faults.

41¼in (105cm) high

$3,100-3,700   TEN

A set of four 19thC carved and painted fauteuils, in Louis XV style, the C-scroll-carved top rail and molded frame with padded back support, arms, and an overstuffed serpentine-shaped seat rail, on molded cabriole legs with carved feet, worm holes, losses in the carved details.

37in (94cm) high

$3,100-3,700   TEN

A Victorian mahogany armchair, by WM. A. & S. Smee, with a gilt-metal manufacturer's label on the underside.

ca. 1880

$700-800   WW

A pair of 19thC fauteuils, in Louis XV style, painted en grisaille and parcel gilt, various losses, slight movement in joints and arm supports.

39in (99cm) high

$3,100-3,700   **TEN**

A 19thC mahogany reclining armchair, the hinged ladder back with four angles adjusted by a movable bar, on front cabriole legs, with lion-paw feet and brass casters.

39in (99cm) high

$1,500-1,700   **CHEF**

A pair of late-19thC Italian walnut open armchairs, in Baroque style, the molded arm supports decorated with flowerbells and terminating in acanthus-carved handgrips, with a shell-carved seat rail, on carved claw forelegs.

44in (112cm) high

$1,100-1,350   **TEN**

One of a pair of 19thC satinwood open armchairs, in George III style, in the manner of Gillows.

37in (94cm) high

$3,100-3,700 the pair   **DN**

A 19thC goncalo alves library armchair, with scrolled top rail, on turned front legs headed by roundels and terminating in brass casters.

34¾in (88cm) high

$625-750   **CHEF**

A late-Victorian mahogany swivel desk chair, with a horseshoe-shaped back and circular seat, on four scrolled legs and casters.

34¼in (87cm) high

$3,700-5,000   **CHEF**

A Victorian mahogany library armchair, the back surmounted by pair of ball finials over a spindle back.

37in (94cm) high

$950-1,050   **CHEF**

An early-20thC carved mahogany and upholstered Gainsborough armchair, in George II style, chips, rubbing, some worm.

40½in (103cm) high

$1,250-1,500   **DN**

An early-20thC carved mahogany and leather upholstered open armchair, in George III style, in the manner of Wright & Elwick, minor chips.

39¼in (100cm) high

$1,500-1,900   **DN**

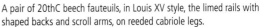

A pair of 20thC beech fauteuils, in Louis XV style, the limed rails with shaped backs and scroll arms, on reeded cabriole legs.

38¼in (97cm) high

$800-1,000   **DUK**

FURNITURE

A Louis XV beech-frame bergère armchair, by Louis Delanois, with floral carving on the show frame, on cabriole legs, stamped "L. DELANOIS" under the shaped front seat rail.

Born in Savignies, France, Louis Delanois (1731-92) was a menuisier working in the late Rococo style. Notably today, he is considered an active precursor of the Louis XVI style. Delanois moved to Paris in the 1750s to train as a joiner. He was awarded master qualification in 1761 and then set up his own business. In 1777, he moved away from the furniture trade into lumber and property, however, this resulted in bankruptcy by the early 1790s. Among his most notable patrons were the Count of Artois, Madame du Barry, the King of Poland, and the Duke of Dorset. Delanois was involved in the furnishing of the Palais Bourbon for the Prince de Conde from 1770 to 1777, and from 1768 to 1770 he worked for Madame du Barry on her palaces at Louveciennes and Versailles.

37¾in (96cm) high

$5,000-5,600

CHEF

A pair of Regency mahogany and caned library bergère armchairs.

ca. 1815   *39in (99cm) high*

$5,000-6,200   **DN**

A Regency mahogany bergère, the caned back and sides within a reeded frame, with padded arms supported by ring-turned columns, on turned and tapered legs and brass casters.

34¾in (88cm) high

$5,000-6,200   **CHEF**

A Regency mahogany library bergère armchair, the caned back and sides within a reeded frame, with padded arm supports, on reeded front legs, and outsplayed back legs, on brass wheel casters.

35½in (90cm) high

$3,700-5,000   **CHEF**

A Regency mahogany library bergère armchair, a brass aperture in one arm where a reading stand once sat, repairs and replacements.

ca. 1815   *36¼in (92cm) high*

$4,300-5,600   **DN**

A pair of early-19thC Regency mahogany bergères, with curved gondola backs and scrolled top rails, above caned backs and seats, on turned and tapered legs.

The backs of chairs, such as these Regency bergères, are usually referred to as "gondola" backs and, indeed, chairs with such backs are also often referred to as "gondola" chairs. Of concave form, and with side rails that curve down to the seat, which sometimes not only define the sides of the back but also serve as the arms of the chair, they take their name from the gondola boats that ferry the canals of Venice, the prows and sterns of which have similar curvilinear profiles. Although chair backs with such profiles date back to antiquity, the term "gondola back" only emerged around the turn of the 19thC, and is especially, albeit not exclusively, associated with Empire and Regency styles of furniture.

30¾in (78cm) high

$2,500-3,700   **L&T**

A pair of early-19thC Regency ebonized and parcel-gilt bergères, the squared caned scroll backs with reeded top rails above ball mounts, on fluted saber legs, with brass caps and casters.

37in (94cm) high

$6,000-7,500   **L&T**

An early-19thC Regency mahogany bergère.

39¾in (101cm) high

$2,500-3,100   **L&T**

A Regency mahogany library bergère armchair, minor old splits and chips, one caster lacking two screws.

ca. 1820   *38½in (98cm) high*
$4,300-5,600   **DN**

A Regency mahogany bergère armchair.

37¾in (96cm) high
$1,000-1,100   **CHEF**

A mid-19thC French bergère armchair, in Louis XV style, the gray painted frame with floral and foliate carving, the back and seat upholstered with Flemish verdure-style floral tapestry.

$1,900-2,500   **WW**

A mid- to late-19thC mahogany library bergère armchair, in Regency style.

$500-625   **WW**

A 19thC French giltwood and painted bergère, the giltwood frame carved with rocaille and flower heads, on cabriole legs.

40½in (103cm) high
$550-700   **L&T**

A 19thC French giltwood bergère, in Louis XVI style, with a leaf-molded frame.

$700-800   **WW**

A 19thC caned mahogany library bergère armchair, wear.

42¼in (107cm) high
$1,250-1,500   **CHEF**

A pair of early-20thC Edwardian black lacquer "Chinese" bergères, with chinoiserie decoration with gilt details, depicting figures and pagodas in mountainous landscapes.

39¼in (100cm) high
$4,300-5,000   **L&T**

A pair of 20thC mahogany library bergère armchairs, in Regency style, breaks and losses in caned panels.

36¼in (92cm) high
$8,500-10,000   **DN**

A George I walnut and upholstered wing armchair.

ca. 1720   *45¾in (116cm) high*

$1,250-1,900   **DN**

A George II carved walnut wing armchair, movement in the joints, worm.

ca. 1740   *44½in (113cm) high*

$2,500-3,700   **DN**

A George II walnut wing armchair, probably Irish, previously with casters, evidence of worm.

ca. 1750   *44in (112cm) high*

$5,500-7,000   **DN**

A George III mahogany wing armchair, the serpentine-headed padded back with shaped sides over outscrolling arms, on square-section front legs and splayed back legs, light wear on frame.

45¾in (116cm) high

$1,500-1,900   **CHEF**

A Regency rosewood library armchair.

ca. 1820   *41in (104cm) high*

$3,700-4,300   **DN**

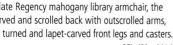

A late Regency mahogany library armchair, the curved and scrolled back with outscrolled arms, on turned and lapet-carved front legs and casters.

35in (89cm) high

$2,500-3,700   **CHEF**

A George IV rosewood and leather upholstered library armchair, in the manner of Gillows, minor chips and splits, old worm.

ca. 1825   *39¾in (101cm) high*

$5,000-5,600   **DN**

An early-19thC George IV painted and parcel-gilt tub armchair, the lyre-form frame carved with acanthus scrolls, on foliate-carved reeded tapered legs, with brass casters.

32¾in (83cm) high

$2,700-3,500   **L&T**

A William IV rosewood and leather library armchair, scuffs, restorations, worm.

ca. 1830   *39¾in (101cm) high*

$3,100-3,700   **DN**

A William IV mahogany button-back armchair, the rounded back over outscrolling acanthus-carved arms, on turned and lapet-carved front legs, with brass casters.

40½in (103cm) high

$1,500-2,000   **CHEF**

A pair of mid-19thC Victorian mahogany armchairs, by Mackenzie & Crosbie, Edinburgh, covered in original buttoned leather, on turned and tapering forelegs with casters, the underside labeled "Mackenzie & Crosbie Manufacturers Edinburgh."

35½in (90cm) high

$8,500-10,000   **TEN**

A pair of mid-19thC mahogany armchairs, the feet with recessed brass casters, some repairs, worm.

38½in (98cm) high

$3,100-4,300   **DN**

A pair of mid-19thC early-Victorian oak library armchairs, in the manner of A. W. N. Pugin, marks, knocks, gilt wear.

Several elements suggest that these chairs are by, or are strongly influenced by, the work of A. W. N. Pugin. The decorative upholstery nails reflect Pugin's belief that decorative elements must relate to the practical use of an object.

37½in (95cm) high

$1,900-2,500   **DN**

A mid-19thC walnut-framed armchair, with carved ram-head mask handles.

$1,600-2,000   **CHOR**

A late-19thC Victorian armchair, by Cornelius V. Smith, on turned forelegs with casters, stamped and numbered "91638."

33½in (85cm) high

$12,000-13,500   **TEN**

Judith Picks

They say imitation is the sincerest form of flattery. I think they may be right! This pair of truly extravagant yet elegant chairs was made around the turn of the 20thC, but fashioned in the Empire style: a form of Neoclassicism in the French decorative arts that originally flourished some 100 years earlier (ca. 1800-15), during the periods known as the Consulate and First French Empire. Taking its name from the French emperor Napoleon (aka Napoleon Bonaparte), it was intended to idealize Napoleon's leadership and achievements, and in so doing marked a return to ostentatious richness after the more austere and minimalist form of Neoclassicism of the preceding Directoire style. These chairs encapsulate that: from their ancient Egyptian thronelike forms (inspired by Napoleon's military campaigns in Egypt and their accompanying archaeological excavations) to classic Empire-style motifs, such as six-pointed stars (on the upholstery fabric), and the mythical winged lions (the ebonized arms supports) to the gilt finish on the exposed areas of the frames. The fact that they remain desirable some 120-plus years after they were made would, therefore, also seem to indicate that imitation is not only the sincerest form of flattery, but also perhaps the most enduring!

A pair of late-19th/20thC giltwood and ebonized armchairs, in Empire style, gilding and paintwork rubbed/flaking.

36¾in (93.5cm) high

$5,000-6,200   **DN**

FURNITURE

A 19thC mahogany wing armchair, in George II style, on shell-carved cabriole front legs, on claw-and-ball feet.

46in (117cm) high

$1,250-1,600 **CHEF**

A late-19thC late-Victorian upholstered armchair, the rear legs stamped and numbered "B654."

35in (89cm) high

$7,000-8,000 **TEN**

A matched pair of late-Victorian horsehair and gray-upholstered deep-sitting armchairs, in the manner of Howard & Sons.

33in (84cm) high

$6,000-7,500 **TEN**

A late-19th/early-20thC deep-seated armchair, by Howard & Sons, covered in Howard & Sons fabric, on shell-carved and acanthus cabriole forelegs, with claw-and-ball feet, rear leg stamped "Howard & Sons Ltd, Berners Street, 5988559," scuffs on the legs.

34¼in (87cm) high

$7,500-8,500 **TEN**

A near pair of armchairs, by Howard & Sons, the rear legs stamped "1829/5572 HOWARD & SONS LTD BERNERS ST" and "185?/5576 HOWARD & SONS LTD BERNERS ST," back two casters stamped "Howard & Sons Ltd," front two are later replacements, legs heavily knocked.

28¾in (73cm) high

$3,700-5,000 **CHEF**

A late-19thC deep-sitting armchair, in the manner of Howard & Sons, on square tapering legs, with brass capped feet and casters.

34¾in (88cm) high

$2,200-2,700 **TEN**

A late-19th/early-20thC upholstered armchair, in George III style.

39in (99cm) high

$1,000-1,100 **TEN**

A late-19th/early-20thC feather-filled armchair, by Howard & Sons, the rear leg stamped "Howard & Sons Ltd, Berners Street" and numbered "1965 5683," front leg section of wood missing.

34¼in (87cm) high

$6,000-7,500 **TEN**

ESSENTIAL REFERENCE—HOWARD & SONS

London-based makers of custom-made furniture, Howard & Sons were founded in 1820 and, as Howard Chairs Ltd., are in business to this day.

- They were established by cabinet manufacturer John Howard in Leman Street, who, joined by his son George, relocated to Great Alie Street in 1829 and opened a showroom and upholstery workshop in Red Lion Street in 1832.
- Officially becoming John Howard & Sons in 1848, it began trading as "Cabinet Maker, Upholsterer, and Decorator" from premises at 22 Berners Street—acquiring additional workshop space in not only Berners Street, but also nearby Fitzroy Square and Charlotte Mews as the business flourished.
- Subsequent developments recognized the high quality of its work during the second half of the 19thC and included gold and silver medals at the 1862 Crystal Palace Exhibition, and later at the Exposition Universelle in Paris and the Exposition Internationale d'Anvers in Antwerp, culminating in the award of a Royal Warrant in 1901.
- Much of its success can be attributed to its robustly made, durable, and exceptionally comfortable spring-upholstered furniture, for which it remains best known, and of which the chair shown here is one of many surviving examples.

A late-19thC armchair, by Howard & Sons, on shell- and scroll-carved forelegs with pad feet, the rear leg stamped "HOWARD & SONS LTD/ BERNERS ST" and "620 7403."

37in (94cm) high

$6,000-7,500 **L&T**

A late-19th/early-20thC walnut wing armchair, in George I style, the front legs carved with flower heads, on claw-and-ball feet.

$1,600-2,000   WW

A pair of late-19th/early-20thC feather-filled armchairs, in the manner of Howard & Sons, one rear leg stamped "4824," the other "4901."

31½in (80cm) high

TEN

An early-20thC Edwardian armchair, by Howard & Sons, with Howard floral and red stripe lining fabric, on mahogany square tapering front legs and brass casters, stamped "Howard & Sons Ltd London," back leg stamped "12529 9866 Howard & Sons Ltd Berners St.," with later loose covers.

$7,000-8,000   WW

An early-20thC Edwardian walnut wing armchair, by Howard & Sons, in William and Mary style, on Braganza-style front feet and with an X stretcher, one rear leg stamped "523011," the other "Howard & Sons Ltd. Berners St."

$2,500-3,700   WW

A walnut and embroidery-upholstered sofa.

ca. 1710 and later   *74in (188cm) wide*

$1,900-2,500   DN

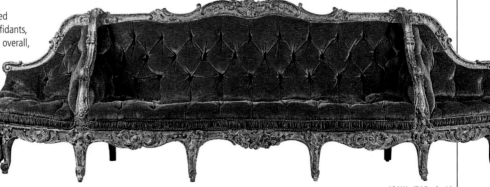

A mid-18thC Continental carved giltwood sofa or canapé à confidants, the frame molded and scrolled overall, the crest rail above a deep-buttoned padded back, the seat rail set with a rocaille cabochon, flanked by scrolled acanthus between and above each cabriole leg with a scrolled foot, wear, knocks, later gilding, worm, repairs.

124½in (316cm) wide

$50,000-62,000   DN

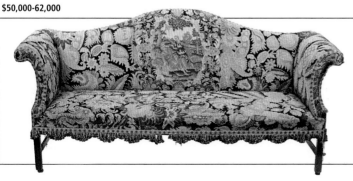

A mid-18thC saddleback sofa, with scroll arms, on square legs and stretchers, with leather barrel casters.

90½in (230cm) wide

$3,700-5,000   CHOR

A mid-18thC walnut chair-back settee, later upholstered in two-tone damask, knocks, abrasions.

79¼in (201cm) wide

$4,300-5,600

DN

A Louis XVI giltwood sofa or canapé, upholstered in woven gray-brown silk fabric, reinforcements, later gilding.

ca. 1780   *92½in (235cm) wide*

$43,000-50,000

DN

A George III mahogany sofa, with arched padded back and outscrolled armrests, on square legs with brass caps and casters, joined by square stretchers, marks, knocks, scratches.

ca. 1780   *90¼in (229cm) wide*

$25,000-31,000

DN

A Louis XVI cream-painted and parcel-gilt canapé.

ca. 1800   *62¼in (158cm) wide*

$1,500-2,000   DN

A pair of Regency painted settees, decorated with green lines and bellflower swags on a cream ground, on turned and fluted front legs, redecorated.

63in (160cm) wide

$4,300-5,600   DUK

An early-19thC Regency mahogany, ebony-strung and gilt-metal-mounted scroll-end sofa, on turned baluster supports, with brass capped toes and casters.

75¼in (191cm) wide

$800-950   TEN

A Regency simulated rosewood and parcel-gilt frame sofa, with scroll ends and a molded back, on reeded legs and casters.

85in (216cm) wide

$1,250-1,900   CHEF

A George IV bird's-eye maple, carved oak, and upholstered sofa.

ca. 1830   *87in (221cm) wide*

$5,500-7,000   DN

A William IV mahogany framed sofa, with scrolled ends and a carved show frame decorated with shamrocks, rosettes, and acanthus leaves.

90½in (230cm) wide

$1,600-2,000   CHEF

An early-19thC mahogany framed settee, the shaped arms with turned column supports, on three tapered and fluted front legs, with brass casters, repairs.

60¼in (153cm) wide

$1,400-1,700   **CHEF**

A mid-19thC giltwood sofa, in Louis XV style, the molded frame carved with leaves, flowers, and C scrolls, with button upholstery.

84¾in (215cm) wide

$625-750   **WW**

A Victorian walnut-framed sofa, with overstuffed back support, above a serpentine-shaped seat rail, on carved cabriole legs with casters.

ca. 1865   *70in (178cm) wide*

$625-750   **TEN**

A Victorian Chesterfield sofa, with rounded back support and arms above an overstuffed seat, on turned, ebonized, and parcel-gilt tapering forelegs with casters, some marks/discoloration on the upholstery.

ca. 1870   *83in (211cm) wide*

$4,300-5,000   **TEN**

A 19thC mahogany framed three-seater library sofa, the molded frame with downswept arms, padded back support, sides, and seat, on husk-decorated forelegs, with brass capped feet and casters.

69¼in (176cm) wide

$6,000-7,500   **TEN**

A 19thC carved mahogany and upholstered sofa, in George II style, of camelback form, some chips, knocks, and scuffing.

77¼in (196cm) wide

$5,000-6,200   **DN**

A Victorian two-seater sofa, by Howard & Sons, the drop ends with adjustable heights, on barley twist supports joined by stretchers.

63in (160cm) wide

$5,000-6,200   **CHOR**

A Victorian mahogany and button-upholstered double chaise, on turned front legs with casters.

$190-310   **WHP**

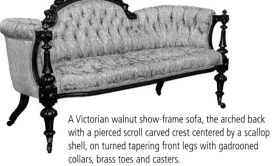

A Victorian walnut show-frame sofa, the arched back with a pierced scroll carved crest centered by a scallop shell, on turned tapering front legs with gadrooned collars, brass toes and casters.

66½in (169cm) wide

$625-750   **HT**

FURNITURE

A late-19thC humpback sofa, in George III style, with rounded arms and close-nailed overstuffed seat, on acanthus carved forelegs, with claw-and-ball feet, general scuffs and faults in the carved decoration.

74¾in (190cm) wide

$2,200-2,700   **TEN**

A late-19thC mahogany settee, in Hepplewhite style, with turned column arm supports with acanthus-carved detail, on square tapered legs and spade feet.

56¼in (143cm) wide

$550-700   **CHEF**

A late-19th/early-20thC Chesterfield sofa, on squat bun front feet and square rear legs, with later casters.

81in (206cm) wide

$1,400-1,700   **CHEF**

An oak paneled country house corner seat, well weathered, a little worm, losses.

each section 72¾in (185cm) wide

$2,500-3,700   **CHEF**

An early-20thC Edwardian mahogany sofa, by Howard & Sons, in George II style, with scroll arms, on shell-and-leaf-carved cabriole legs and claw-and-ball feet, with later iron casters, stamped "18227 7231 Howard & Sons Berners St.," with a printed paper label numbered in pencil "11364 2678."

76½in (194cm) wide

$7,500-8,500   **WW**

A feather-filled three-seater country house sofa, in Howard style, on mahogany tapering legs, with brass capped toes and casters.

77¼in (196cm) wide

$2,200-2,700   **TEN**

A 20thC feather-filled three-seater sofa, in Howard style, on mahogany tapering forelegs, with brass capped feet and casters.

72½in (184cm) wide

$3,700-4,300   **TEN**

A 20thC three-seater sofa, in Howard style, on short tapered front legs and casters, one caster slightly loose.

83¾in (213cm) wide

$2,500-3,100   **CHEF**

ESSENTIAL REFERENCE—KNOLE SOFAS

With a deep seat, arms or sides the same height as the back, and with four (usually acornlike) finials for winding ropes or tassels around to secure the sides upright to the back (and from which they can be lowered to be flush with seat level if desired), Knole sofas are undoubtedly one of the most visually distinctive types of upholstered seating. Their form or shape is inspired by a setteelike sofa that was made ca. 1640 and originally used as a throne wide enough to seat both a monarch and his or her consort side-by-side. Upholstered in crimson velvet with gold braid trim, the original is still located (and on display) at Knole—from which it, and all subsequent examples, take their name. Located in Kent, Knole is predominantly Jacobean in style but dates back to the mid-15thC.

A 20thC tapestry Knole sofa, upholstered in 18thC Flemish verdure tapestry, tapestry worn and faded.

65in (165cm) wide

$6,000-7,500   **DN**

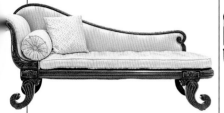

An early-19thC Regency carved mahogany chaise longue, with scrolled armrest and squab cushion above a molded seat rail, on scrolled and reeded legs, faults on the carved decoration, formerly raised on casters.

74¾in (190cm) wide

$1,400-1,700   **TEN**

An early-19thC Regency ebonized chaise longue, head and foot boards with leaf- and acanthus-carved facings, raised on lobed and reeded short tapered legs with brass casters, the casters stamped "COPE AND COLLINSON/ PATENT."

73½in (187cm) wide

$2,500-3,700   **L&T**

An early-19thC Regency chaise longue, on stained, turned and tapered legs ending in brass casters.

59¾in (152cm) wide

$750-1,000   **L&T**

A William IV carved mahogany chaise longue, with molded and acanthus-decorated scrolled frame, on turned and reeded legs, formerly on casters.

ca. 1830   *71¼in (181cm) wide*

$700-800   **TEN**

A mid-19thC early Victorian bird's-eye maple day bed, in the manner of Holland & Sons, the seat rails stamped "bq" and twice stamped "VQ," one caster loose.

73½in (187cm) wide

$1,250-1,500   **DN**

A mid-19thC Victorian mahogany chaise longue, the shaped back with buttoned upholstery, above a long serpentine seat, raised on cabriole legs with ceramic casters.

64¼in (163cm) wide

$750-875   **L&T**

A Victorian satin birch chaise longue, with overstuffed back support above a plain seat rail, on baluster turned legs, with brass and ceramic casters.

ca. 1870   *69¼in (176cm) wide*

$300-375   **TEN**

A 19thC French giltwood chaise longue, in Louis XVI style, with a carved giltwood frame and loose squab cushion.

88½in (225cm) wide

$950-1,050   **L&T**

A late-19thC Victorian ebonized and marquetry-inlaid chaise longue, the pierced armrest and frame inlaid with trailing leaves, on splayed legs.

This chaise longue is believed to have been designed by Owen Jones (1809-74) and manufactured by Jackson and Graham, ca. 1840-85.

71¼in (181cm) wide

$43,000-50,000   **TEN**

A late-17thC oak refectory table, the four-plank cleated top above a guilloche-carved frieze, on four turned ball-and-fillet legs.

110¼in (280cm) long

$19,000-25,000　　　　　　**CHEF**

A joined oak refectory table, the four-plank top with cleated ends.

ca. 1720　　　　*77½in (197cm) long*

$1,900-2,500　　　　　　**TEN**

An oak refectory table, 17thC and later, the two-plank top over a lunette- and leaf-carved frieze, on baluster turned legs, on squat bun feet.

90½in (230cm) long

$1,700-2,000　　　　　　**CHEF**

An 18thC oak farmhouse kitchen table, of three-plank boarded construction, one foot retipped.

89in (226cm) long

$1,900-2,500　　　　　　**TEN**

A Gothic Revival oak refectory table, possibly German, one side with two drawers, on two shaped supports joined by a stretcher.

76¼in (193.5cm) long

$3,100-3,700　　　　　　**DUK**

A Franco-Flemish walnut draw-leaf refectory table, probably 19thC, in 17thC style, with iron mounts, the pull-out top with cleated ends, with a center tablet on both sides, one with the date "1702," the other with the initials "DVMT," the frieze with punched decoration, on carved scroll-and-flower-turned legs.

66in (167.5cm) long

$2,500-3,700　　　　　　**WW**

An Italian walnut trestle table, in Renaissance style, the top over a pair of urn-shaped end supports, with carved fruit and vase decoration.

96½in (245cm) long

$5,000-6,200　　　　　　**CHEF**

A 20thC oak refectory table, the three-plank cleated top above a carved frieze and turned legs.

76¾in (195cm) long

$3,700-5,000　　　　　　**CHEF**

A mid-18thC Irish George II mahogany drop-leaf hunt dining table, the hinged single-plank leaves supported by a twin gate-leg action, the underside of one leaf stenciled "HODGES DUBLIN," marks, knocks, replacement elements, repairs.

"Hunt" tables acquired their name in the 18thC from usage. Of large size yet fairly portable—because of their relative light weight and drop-leaf sides—they could be easily moved from the dining or breakfast rooms of large country houses to outside their entrances, where gathering horse riders could imbibe fortifying beverages from them before embarking on a hunt. Depending on the time of year and the weather, the riders would sometimes also dine sitting around them on their return. However, "hunt" tables also had another name, especially in Ireland and again from usage. Being of almost identical width, a coffin bearing the body of a deceased relative would be placed on the center plank of the table for a short period prior to burial, during which time a vigil and various other funerary rituals, known as a "wake" in Ireland, could be observed— hence the alternative name: a "wake" table.

93¾in (238cm) long

$5,500-7,000   DN

A George III mahogany D-end dining table, 18thC and later, with center drop-flap section, the ends on square tapering legs, scratches, marks, adaptations, worm.

ca. 1780   *124in (315cm) long*

$4,300-5,600   DN

An early-19thC Regency mahogany extending dining table, with two D ends, the center section with two drop leaves.

171¼in (435cm) long

$4,300-5,600   DUK

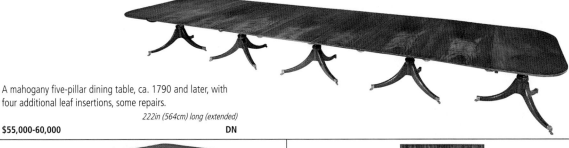

A mahogany five-pillar dining table, ca. 1790 and later, with four additional leaf insertions, some repairs.

222in (564cm) long (extended)

$55,000-60,000   DN

A mahogany triple-pillar extending dining table, ca. 1815 and later, with two additional leaf insertions.

130¼in (331cm) long (extended)

$5,000-6,200   DN

An early-19thC Regency mahogany extending dining table, attributed to Gillows, with four additional leaves supported by a telescopic frame, on ribbed tapering legs, with brass caps and casters.

125¼in (318cm) long (extended)

$7,500-8,500   WW

An early-19thC William IV mahogany dining table, in the manner of Gillows, the D-end sections sliding on a telescopic frame, with two original leaves with reeded edge, on turned and reeded tapering legs, with brass capped toes and casters, scratches.

109½in (278cm) long (extended)

$3,700-5,000   TEN

FURNITURE

ESSENTIAL REFERENCE—GILLOWS OF LANCASTER

One of the most prestigious furniture manufacturing companies of the 18thC and 19thC, Gillows of Lancaster was founded in the Lancashire town that gave it half its name in ca. 1727 by a local joiner, Robert Gillow (1703-72).

● By the mid-18thC, the company had firmly established its reputation for making fine-quality furniture, much of which was superbly crafted from mahogany that Robert Gillow was able, through part-ownership of a ship, to import directly from the West Indies.

● In 1757, Robert Gillow entered into an equal partnership with his son, Richard Gillow (1733-1811), and the company became known as Robert Gillow & Son.

● In 1768, Robert Gillow retired and left his share of the company to his other son, Robert Gillow II, and in the mid-1770s the brothers' cousin Thomas Gillow (1736-79) established a London saleroom for their furniture.

● By the late-18thC, Gillows had introduced several new forms of furniture, including the Davenport desk (see page 274), and now a byword for quality, their furniture was referenced in novels by Jane Austen and Thackeray and, subsequently, in a Gilbert and Sullivan opera.

● By 1814, the company had been taken over by a partnership, Redmayne, Whiteside and Ferguson, that continued to use the Gillow name.

● In 1897, Gillows absorbed fellow furniture manufacturers Collinson & Lock, and in 1903 it merged with S. J. Waring & Sons of Liverpool to become Waring & Gillow.

● Having branched out into fitting luxury cruise liners during the first half of the 20thC, Waring & Gillow were taken over by Great Universal Stores in 1953, and its Lancaster workshops closed down.

● In 1980, it merged with Maple & Co., to become Maple, Waring & Gillow, and eventually became, in 1990, part of the Allied Maples Group.

A George IV mahogany extending dining table, attributed to Gillows, Lancaster, conforming to Gillows' "Imperial" dining table design, with four additional leaf insertions, marks, knocks.

In 1813, Gillows supplied a similar "Set of mahogany Imperial dining tables on stout twined [sic] reeded legs and brass socket casters" for Broughton Hall, Yorkshire, at a cost of 50 guineas. Prior to this, Richard Gillow had taken out a patent in 1800 for an extending table, known as the "Patent Imperial dining-table" (see M. Jourdain, "Regency Furniture 1795-1830," Country Life, 1965, pages 64-65, figure 130).

ca. 1825   *141in (358cm) long (extended)*
$3,700-5,000   **DN**

An early-19thC mahogany extending dining table, with two D ends and a center gate-leg section, on ring-turned and tapered legs.

106¾in (271cm) long
$1,250-1,700   **CHEF**

A Victorian mahogany dining table, with a winder to accommodate five additional leaves, on five lobed and ribbed tapering legs, with brass caps and casters, with a leaf cabinet and two winders.

ca. 1870-80   *167in (424cm) long (extended)*
$12,500-15,000   **WW**

A late-Victorian mahogany and ebonized extending dining table, with seven additional leaves, on five turned baluster legs with ebonized rings and fluted terminals, some scratches and light wear.

191¼in (486cm) long (extended)
$7,500-8,500   **CHEF**

A 20thC mahogany and ebony-strung extending dining table, Jupe style, the pivoting top with eight additional leaves, on a center column support, with molded socle and four turned spindle supports and quadripartite base, with brass cast hairy paw feet.

86½in (220cm) diam (extended)
$11,000-14,000   **TEN**

An early-20thC mahogany triple-pillar dining table, in Regency style, the top with a reeded edge, on turned stems and splay legs, inlaid with stringing and foliate-decorated sabot and casters, with two additional leaves.

136¼in (346cm) long
$1,900-2,500   **WW**

A George III padouk pembroke or breakfast table, in the manner of Thomas Chippendale, the frieze drawer fitted with a baize inset slide, above divided compartments.

ca. 1760   *35½in (90cm) wide (open)*

$7,500-8,500   **DN**

A George III mahogany breakfast table, with a single-piece oval tilt-top with kingwood crossbanding, on a turned stem and four reeded splay legs with brass casters.

ca. 1790   *64½in (164cm) wide*

$7,500-8,500   **WW**

A Regency rosewood and crossbanded breakfast table.

52in (132cm) wide

$1,000-1,100   **CHEF**

An early-19thC Regency mahogany breakfast table, inlaid with ebonized stringing, the tilt-top with reentrant corners, with leaf-carved and ribbed scroll legs, terminating in brass sabot and casters.

57½in (146cm) wide

$500-625   **WW**

An early-19thC Regency rosewood breakfast table, the tilt-top inlaid with stringing and partridgewood banding, on a faceted stem, with brass caps and casters.

60in (152.5cm) wide

$700-800   **WW**

An early-19thC Regency mahogany and rosewood breakfast table, the banded tilt-top with brass line inlay, above a bead molded frieze, on a tapered square column and quadripartite base, with outscrolled legs ending in leaf-cast brass caps and casters.

50in (127cm) diam

$1,400-1,700   **L&T**

An early-19thC William IV rosewood breakfast table, the tilt-top on a faceted baluster column and tripartite base, with disk feet with casters.

51¼in (130cm) diam

$875-1,000   **L&T**

A 19thC Irish mahogany circular breakfast table, by Strahan, Dublin, the solid panel top with reeded edge, on a fluted center column and reeded downswept legs, with brass caps and casters.

63¾in (162cm) diam

$3,100-3,700   **ADA**

A William IV mahogany "Jupe's Patent" extending dining table, by Johnstone, Jupe & Co., the radially segmented circular top comprising eight sections with two sets of additional leaves, on a baluster pedestal and four leaf-carved outscrolling legs ending in carved paw feet with brass casters, the internal mechanism with a center brass capstan engraved "JUPE's PATENT," the frieze with an ivory trade label inscribed "JUPE's PATENT/ JOHNSTONE, JUPE, & CO. NEW BOND ST. LONDON," the larger leaves with brass caps on the points.

In March 1835, Robert Jupe, an upholsterer based at 47 Welbeck Street, Cavendish Square, London, applied for a patent on an "improved expanding table" that was "so constructed that the sections composing its surface may be caused to diverge from a common centre and that the spaces caused thereby may be filled up by inserting leaves or filling pieces." From 1835-40, Jupe was in partnership with John Johnstone of New Bond Street and the company traded under the name Johnstone, Jupe & Co. The partnership dissolved after 1840, and each man set up on his own, each selling tables with Jupe's patent mechanism but under different trade names, Jupe under his own name and Johnstone with a new partner Jeanes. Beautifully engineered, the genius of Jupe's mechanism was that it enabled the table's radial top to expand with minimal effort to accommodate two different sets of eight leaf inserts, enabling the table to transform into three different sizes. Pedestals and bases could be tailored to the wishes of the buyer, from fairly plain to more exuberantly carved examples. Other closely related Jupe tables are on record, all with the distinct leaf-carved quadripartite base and lion-paw feet. Although of the same design, many are marked with various combinations of Jupe and Johnstone's company names, an interesting detail as the partnerships changed within such a short period. See C. Gilbert, "Pictorial Dictionary of Marked London Furniture 1700-1840," Routledge (1996), figure 535.

ca. 1835-40 / 88½in (225cm) diam (extended)

$200,000-250,000 / **L&T**

A 19thC William IV mahogany breakfast table.

63½in (161cm) wide

$875-1,000 / **L&T**

An early Victorian rosewood breakfast table, the tilt-top on a baluster-turned stem and tripod legs, carved with leaves, scrolls, and cabochons, the block stamped "3795."

ca. 1850 / 48in (122cm) diam

$500-625 / **WW**

A mid-19thC early-Victorian mahogany breakfast table, the tilt-top with a molded edge, on a faceted baluster column and quadripartite base, with flat bun feet with casters.

55½in (141cm) wide

$1,400-1,700 / **L&T**

A Victorian figured walnut and tulipwood-banded breakfast table, the molded top with boxwood stringing and Tunbridge parquetry-decorated panels, on a platform base with turned spindle supports, carved cabriole legs with acanthus-carved scrolling toes and casters.

ca. 1870 / 52¾in (134cm) wide

$1,250-1,600 / **TEN**

A 19thC oak breakfast table, the top with an alternating rope twist-and-rosette-carved frieze, on an octagonal column and quatreform base, with lion-paw feet.

72in (183cm) diam

$1,250-1,600 / **CHEF**

A Victorian dining table, the top with segmented radial veneers, over a carved column support, on four acanthus-capped cabriole legs, with scrolled feet, top is later, kingwood veneered, base with repairs and dry cracks, mechanism adapted to accomodate the top.

61¾in (157cm) diam

$1,000-1,250 / **CHEF**

An early-19thC fruitwood farmhouse table, the four-plank cleated top above end frieze drawers, on square tapering supports, scratches and marks.

89¼in (227cm) long

$2,500-3,700 / **CHEF**

A 19thC French cherry and fruitwood farmhouse kitchen table, the top above a frieze drawer, on square tapering legs.

78¼in (199cm) long

$2,000-2,500 / **WW**

A William III fruitwood gate-leg dining table.
ca. 1700   *56¾in (144cm) wide*
$2,200-2,700   **DN**

A George II Cuban mahogany gate-leg table, the top raised on slender cabriole legs, with a carved scroll at the tops and pointed pad feet, historic repair on one leg.
ca. 1740   *61in (155cm) wide*
$950-1,050   **CHEF**

An early-to-mid-18thC burl elm and fruitwood gate-leg table, marks, knocks, scratches, replacements, old worm.
50½in (128cm) wide (open)
$11,000-12,500   **DN**

An 18thC oak gate-leg table, the oval twin flap top above a single end drawer, on turned baluster supports.
41in (104cm) wide
$250-370   **CHEF**

An 18thC elm and oak gate-leg table.
46½in (118cm) wide (open)
$450-550   **CHEF**

A late-17thC Continental carved walnut center table, probably Italian, the carved scrolling foliate supports terminating in bearded masks, marks, knocks, some warping and bending in the top.

Elaborately carved walnut center tables such as this are typical of the exuberant Mannerist style that had its origins in Florence, Tuscany, and Fontainebleau, France, in the mid-16thC, and which remained popular in some areas of Continental Europe until the second half of the 17thC. Essentially an extension of, and a play on, some of the architectural and decorative conventions of Classical Antiquity— particularly Roman—that had been rediscovered and reestablished during the Renaissance, Mannerism was typified by forms and motifs such as swags, cartouches, strapwork, caryatids, and, as on this table, grotesques, scrolling leaves, and flowers. There are stylistic variations between regions and during different time periods— Mannerists in Northern Europe, for example, wove in elements of the late Flamboyant Gothic style, often to bizarre effect. However, one essential quality that almost all variants had in common was, as evident in this center table, a strong sense of theatricality.
46in (117cm) wide
$50,000-62,000   **DN**

A George II mahogany center table, the later verde antico marble top above a plain frieze, with ovolo and leaf moldings, on scroll- and cabochon-carved cabriole legs, with scroll toes.
ca. 1750   *38½in (98cm) wide*
$7,000-8,000   **WW**

A George III mahogany center table, late-18thC and later, in Chinese Chippendale style, the square-section legs with Greek key-style blind fretwork decoration and fretwork brackets, on block feet.
65¼in (166cm) wide
$5,000-6,200   **WW**

FURNITURE

An oak draw-leaf dining or center table, 17thC and later, marks, scratches.

111½in (283cm) long (extended)

$1,400-1,600 DN

A Regency rosewood and brass-banded drum table, the top above eight alternating frieze drawers and dummy drawers, on a faceted tapering column and outswept legs, with brass toes and casters.

36¼in (92cm) diam

$4,300-5,000 DUK

A Regency rosewood and giltwood center table, early 19thC and later, the tilt-top with a frieze applied with husks and paterae, the stem decorated with palmettes, on winged scroll feet and casters.

48in (122cm) diam

$2,500-3,700 WW

A Regency figured and carved mahogany center table, in the manner of Gillows, marks, dents, minor repairs.

This table incorporates many stylistic elements and the quality of craftsmanship synonymous with the celebrated firm of cabinetmakers Gillows of Lancaster. An example of this is the unusual scrolled feet, which are closely related to those on the Lytham Hall sideboard table that were carved by Gillows in 1832.

ca. 1820 *54in (137cm) diam*

$15,000-19,000 DN

A George IV cream-painted and parcel-gilt center table, in the manner of Morel & Seddon, with an Italian pietra dura top.

A center table by Morel & Seddon incorporating related decoration is held in Windsor Castle (Royal Collection Trust, RCIN 33462).

ca. 1830 *39¼in (100cm) diam*

$7,500-8,000 DN

An early-19thC Regency mahogany drum table, the top with a bead-molded frieze with four real and four dummy drawers, on a turned column support and outswept legs, ending in scroll cast brass casters.

45in (114cm) diam

$1,400-1,700 L&T

ESSENTIAL REFERENCE—ROSEWOOD

Due to decades of overexploitation, strict trading restrictions have now been placed on more than 300 different species of the rosewood tree by CITES (the Convention on International Trade in Endangered Species of Wild Fauna and Flora). This worrying state of affairs wasn't a consideration back in the 19thC, when this substantial George IV rosewood and gilt-metal-mounted center table was made.

- **The most highly prized of those species was the wood of the Dalbergia nigra, otherwise known as Brazilian rosewood— with darkly streaked figuring and a distinctive sweet smell that endures for many years (hence the name rosewood), it was used prolifically throughout Europe and North America in the early 19thC.**
- **Other prized rosewoods include: Dalbergia latifolia, known as Indian (or East Indian) rosewood; Dalbergia maritime, from Madagascar, known as "bois de rose" and prized for its distinctly reddish hue; Dalbergia oliveri, from Southeast Asia; and various other South American species, such as Guatemalan, Panama, and Honduran rosewood.**
- **Rosewood is closely related to a number of other species of wood under the large Dalbergia genus, which were also highly prized by cabinetmakers. These include African blackwood, cocobolo, kingwood, and Brazilian tulipwood.**

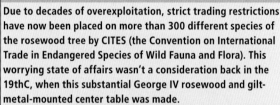

A Victorian pollard oak center table, in the manner of Richard Bridgens, splits, old veneer repairs, vacant screw holes suggest the feet have moved position.

ca. 1840 *26in (66cm) wide*

$1,600-1,900 DN

A mid-19thC Louis Philippe ebony and brass marquetry center table, with gray variegated marble top, the brass marquetry engraved.

39¼in (100cm) diam

$5,000-6,200 DN

A mid-19thC George IV rosewood and gilt-metal-mounted center table, the hinged tilt-top above a pedestal and concave-side-shaped plinth, on scrolled feet and brass casters.

63in (160cm) diam

$2,500-3,700 DUK

A mid-19thC Dutch ebonized, marquetry, and bone-inlaid center table, the top inlaid with birds among floral cartouches, conforming spandrels, and decorations in the borders, above a blind frieze drawer, the legs similarly inlaid and headed by gilt foliate collars, marks, knocks, old splits.

50½in (128cm) wide

$8,500-10,000 DN

A pietre dure and specimen marble-top table, the marble top mid- to late-19thC Florentine, the base 19thC, likely associated, centered by a musical tondo with a lapis lazuli border, on a breccia di Seravezza ground with marble specimens, the rosewood base decorated with gilt-metal mounts, repairs and restorations, later gilding.

29¼in (74cm) high

$12,500-16,000 DN

A mid-19thC Anglo-Indian solid padouk center table, shrinkage in the top, small repairs.

42¼in (107cm) diam

$750-875 CHEF

A mid- to late-19thC carved oak center table, in 17thC style.

44½in (113cm) wide

$1,250-1,600 DN

A 19thC Italian walnut and ivory-inlaid center table, the inlaid ebonized border incorporating birds and animals, carved and inlaid initials "H" and interlaced "D's throughout, the carved frieze above bulbous end supports and a center stretcher, with trestle ends.

57in (145cm) wide

$4,300-5,000 CHOR

A French ash and mahogany center table, with parquetry top and ebonized wood inset with Japanese lacquer panels.

ca. 1880

29½in (75cm) high

$1,100-1,350 L&T

A Victorian walnut and floral marquetry center table, the circular tilt-top banded and radially veneered with a center floral roundel and floral outer border, the stem with cabochon banding, on a scroll- and flower-carved tripod base, with rocaille feet and inset casters.

55in (139.5cm) diam

$2,200-2,700 HT

A French ormolu, Japanese lacquer-mounted, ebony, ebonized, and hardwood center table, by Henry Dasson, Paris, after Adam Weisweiler, the frieze drawer released by two push catches, the underside stamped "HENRY DASSON," one leg with herm mount stamped "HD," fine cracks, loss of veneer on legs.

ca. 1880

33in (84cm) wide

$50,000-56,000 DN

A 19thC French marble-top giltwood center table, the top above an egg-and-dart molded rim, with pierced shell and foliate frieze, on a carved baluster column, on down scrolling legs with figural sphinxes.

32¾in (83cm) high

$1,200-1,350 CHEF

A 19thC Spanish walnut and inlaid center table, the top with inset 12 x 12 checkerboard, the frieze with two short drawers on two sides.

58¾in (149cm) wide

$4,300-5,000 **DN**

A 19thC Italian walnut and marquetry center table, in the manner of Giuseppe Maggiolini, Milan, inlaid with birds, grotesque masks, cornucopiae, stag heads, scrolling leaves, dragons, urns, and flowers, with frieze drawers.

68in (172.5cm) wide

$1,600-2,000 **WW**

A 19thC Italian walnut center table, in Renaissance style, with a marquetry top on an arcaded base, with carved mythical beast supports.

61¾in (157cm) wide

$1,100-1,250 **DUK**

A 19thC North Italian ebonized and marquetry inlaid center table, the top inlaid with flowers, acanthus scrolls, and mother-of-pearl, framed by an ivory-decorated border of leaves and flowerbells, with two frieze drawers in the end sections, flanked by carved lion masks, on cabriole legs, joined by a stretcher and small shelf.

46in (117cm) wide

$1,500-1,900 **TEN**

A late-19thC Victorian satinwood, marquetry, and parcel-gilt center table, in the manner of Holland & Sons, the gilt-brass handle to release the top stamped "COPE & COLLINSON" and "REGISTERED OCTR 31ST 1856 No389T," wear in the parcel-gilt border.

41¾in (106cm) diam

$7,500-8,000 **DN**

A 19thC mahogany center table, with later specimen marble top inlaid with a geometric stylized flower-head design, on a spiraled column pedestal, on four acanthus-leaf and scroll carved legs.

39¼in (99.5cm) diam

$2,200-2,700 **CHEF**

A French fruitwood and marquetry center table, dated, sunbleached, old stains, veneer lifting and repairs.

1891 *42¾in (108.5cm) diam*

$1,900-2,500 **DN**

A French mahogany and ormolu-mounted center table, in Louis XVI style, with bleu tarquin marble top.

ca. 1900 *29¼in (74.5cm) high*

$3,700-4,300 **DN**

A 20thC French ormolu-mounted and breche violette marble center table, in Louis XVI style, with a frieze drawer, repaired cracks.

51¼in (130cm) wide

$9,500-10,500 **DN**

A George III rosewood and brass-inlaid library writing table, attributed to George Oakley, the frieze drawer lock stamped "GR PATENT," scratches, cracks, worm.

George Oakley (d. 1840) worked in partnership with various cabinetmakers, including George Shackleton and George Seddon, producing furniture in the Grecian taste and specializing in "Buhl" inlay (see "Dictionary of English Furniture Makers 1660-1840," Routledge, 1986, pages 658-60).

ca. 1810   *41¼in (105cm) wide*
$5,000-6,200   **DN**

A George III mahogany drum library table, with a revolving top and drawers, scratches, cracks.
ca. 1790   *41¾in (106cm) diam*
$5,000-6,200   **DN**

An early-19thC Regency rosewood library table, with two frieze drawers, above simulated rosewood scrolled lyre-shaped end supports with saber legs, brass paw feet and casters.
50½in (128cm) wide
$700-800   **TEN**

An early-19thC Regency mahogany library table, with a pair of cedar-lined frieze drawers, on reeded swept legs.
59¾in (152cm) wide
$3,700-4,300   **WW**

An early-19thC Regency amboyna- and rosewood-banded library table, attributed to Gillows.
48in (122cm) wide
$4,300-5,600   **DN**

An early-19thC Regency mahogany and ebony-strung library table, with a gilt tooled leather top and six frieze drawers.
54¼in (138cm) wide
$3,100-3,700   **DN**

A Regency mahogany library table, with three frieze drawers with brass drop handles and dummy drawers opposite, on reeded end supports with downswept legs and brass toes and casters, stamp for "R. Taylor & Sons, Great Dover Street, Boro."
51in (129.5cm) wide
$1,000-1,100   **HT**

A mahogany library writing table, in the manner of Gillows, with two frieze drawers, on turned and reeded legs with brass capped toes and casters, scuffing to legs.
ca. 1820   *53½in (136cm) wide*
$1,600-2,000   **TEN**

A Regency rosewood and brass-inlaid library table, in the manner of John McLean, marks.
ca. 1820   *62½in (158.5cm) wide*
$9,500-10,500   **DN**

A William IV walnut and burl walnut center or library table, by Gillows, the craftsman John Barrow, with a fixed top, stamped "GILLOWS.LANCASTER" on drawer, with pencil inscription on underside for John Barrow, sun fading.

Both John Barrow, the craftsman, and his father, William, worked for Gillows; John worked there from ca. 1825-60. From 1826, he served a seven-year apprenticeship to Leonard Redmayne, for which he was paid 7s per week after two years' service.

ca. 1830   56¼in (143cm) wide
$7,500-8,500   DN

A George IV figured mahogany library table, the flame mahogany quadruple book-matched top above two frieze drawers, backplate is missing, small restorations.

ca. 1825   61½in (156cm) wide
$2,200-2,700   DN

A William IV rosewood library table, attributed to Gillows, the frieze with concealed drawers on the ends and one side, mahogany-lined drawers, brass recessed casters on the scroll-carved feet, chips, staining, knocks.

ca. 1835   57½in (146cm) wide
$3,100-4,300   DN

A William IV rosewood library table, on solid turned rosewood "barley twist" legs and stretchers.

This mid-19thC library table is fashioned in a style that gained considerable traction in Britain from the latter years of the reign of George IV (1820-37) and well into the reign of Queen Victoria (1837-1901). Initially promoted as a "revival of domestic Gothic" by architects, such as Anthony Salvin (1799-1881), it became essentially a fusion of Tudor-Elizabethan, Jacobean, and early Stuart forms, sometimes collectively referred to as Jacobethan, especially in the decorative arts. Well suited to furniture, barley twist legs and stretchers were instantly evocative of a style and time that preceded by some distance the more rectilinear forms of the Neoclassicism that had been fashionable for the preceding 70 years or so. So, it was not surprising that Jacobethan was also sometimes promoted as being in the "antiquarian" taste—especially by purveyors of fine furniture, who, to add a little alternative exoticism as a selling point to potential British buyers, also referred to tables such as this as "Portuguese" library tables—their basic style and form having been enduringly fashionable in that country since the 16thC.

ca. 1835   58¼in (148cm) wide
$8,500-10,000   DN

A William IV satinwood library table, attributed to Gillows, the blind drawers opened by a recess in the underside with no handles by design, one drawer stamped "COX," some rubbing.

ca. 1835   42¼in (107cm) wide
$3,700-5,000   DN

A mid-19thC George IV mahogany library table, with two real and two dummy drawers, on lyre end supports, with a turned pole stretcher, with block supports and scrolled feet.

                        54¾in (139cm) wide
$4,300-5,600   TEN

A Victorian amboyna, walnut, and gilt-metal-mounted library table, attributed to Johnstone and Jeanes, veneered and with gilt-metal mounts, with concealed frieze drawers on one side, knocks, gilt lacquering worn.

ca. 1860   48½in (123cm) wide
$9,500-10,500   DN

A mid- to late-19thC Victorian mahogany library writing table, with four molded frieze drawers, on turned and reeded legs, with turnip feet and casters.

                        60¼in (153cm) wide
$1,250-1,500   TEN

A Victorian burl walnut drum library table, the frieze with four real and four dummy drawers with turned-wood handles, on a faceted tapering stem and concave platform, with bun feet and casters.

                        48in (122cm) diam
$3,100-3,700   HT

One of a pair of mid-18thC Louis XV carved giltwood console tables, with shaped brocatello marble tops, repair, flaking, losses, old holes.

35½in (90cm) wide

$5,500-7,000 the pair DN

A mid-18thC Italian carved giltwood console table, possibly Piedmont, with a portasanta marble top, scratches, repairs, later elements.

39in (99cm) wide

$5,000-6,200 DN

An 18thC carved pine eagle console table, with a probably later fior di pesco marble top, marks, scratches.

The use of an eagle as a support for a table was popularized in England by William Kent (1685/6-1748). The inspiration for many of Kent's designs came from the decade he spent in Italy, from 1709-19. More specifically, his design for an eagle table support was probably derived from drawings by Giovanni Giardini, published by Disegni Diversi (1714).

41¼in (105cm) wide

$4,300-5,000 DN

Judith Picks

Simply the price they recently sold for clearly indicates that I am not the only one who thinks this pair of George III demilune console tables is really special. Much of their desirability resides in the high standards of craftsmanship evident in their construction and nicely understated decoration. Indeed, it is this latter quality that really resonates with me. The tables seem to encapsulate that seismic transformation in aesthetics, style and, of course, fashion, that took place around the mid-18thC. Gone are the overly extravagant curvilinear forms and decorative embellishments of the later Rococo style to be replaced, as here, with the more rectilinear and symmetrical forms and motifs of a Neoclassical style that drew its inspiration from a decorative vocabulary rooted in Greco-Roman antiquity. Of course, there's also the attribution of their manufacture to Thomas Chippendale: They bear design similarities—notably the linked paterae marquetry pattern on the frieze—to an iconic library table by Chippendale, made for Harewood House, commissioned by Edwin Lascelles, 1st Baron Harewood, and now in the collection at Temple Newsam, Leeds. As provenance goes, that's about as "blue-chip" as it gets!

A pair of George III satinwood and marquetry demilune console tables, attributed to Thomas Chippendale, the tops inlaid with fan medallions and bands of leaves and anthemion, enclosed by narrow borders of anthemion and leaves separated by inlaid dot banding, the edges in Greek key, above friezes inlaid with floral paterae between carved leaf-tip molding and Vitruvian scroll inlay, the legs headed by carved elliptical paterae and inlaid with pendant husk trails, ending in crisp laurel-leaf carved square toupie feet.

ca. 1760

45¼in (115cm) wide

$100,000-125,000 L&T

A French Louis XVI mahogany and ormolu-mounted console desserte, in the manner of Adam Weisweiler, late 18thC and later, with a breche violette breakfront marble top, above three frieze drawers with concealed button mechanisms and scrolling leaf and rosette rinceaux mounts, centered with a Classical mask and a basket of fruit and flowers, on fluted Doric columns, the galleried undertier inset with conforming marble, on toupie feet, possibly remounted.

89½in (227.5cm) wide

$25,000-31,000 WW

A Regency rosewood and gilt-metal-mounted console table, attributed to George Bullock, with a green marble top, minor lifting of veneers with some repairs, mounts with wear.

ca. 1815

37¾in (96cm) wide

$6,000-7,500 DN

A mid-19thC Anglo-Indian ebony Buddhist "Moonstone" console table, Ceylon, with a center stupa flanked by dolphin heads issuing waves, above carved concentric bands of flames in the outer ring, a band of elephants, bulls, horses and lions, swans, and foliage, including the lotus, the apron of Buddha surrounded by foliage.

"Moonstone," an approximate English translation of "sandakada pahana," is characteristic of Sri Lankan architecture and is usually found before doorways and at the bottom of flights of steps. It is believed to symbolize the cycle of Samsara in Buddhism and is first found in architecture of the Anuradhapura Kingdom (377 BC-AD 1014).

52¾in (134cm) wide

$12,500-15,000 WW

FURNITURE

One of a pair of 19thC French giltwood console tables, in Louis XV style, each with a red and gray veined marble top, on a serpentine base with a scrolling apron with foliate swags, on scrolling legs, the stretcher with acanthus.

44½in (113cm) wide

$3,700-4,300 the pair　　**WW**

A pair of 19thC cream and pale blue painted console tables, in George III style, with Jasper veneered tops, chips, splits, repairs, painted surface applied later.

48in (122cm) wide

$5,500-7,000　　**DN**

A mahogany console table, in Empire style, the black marble top over a long frieze drawer, on scrolling supports with gilt acanthus-leaf mounts, with a platform undertier.

48in (122cm) wide

$1,400-1,700　　**CHEF**

A 19thC cream painted and parcel-gilt console table, in Louis XVI style, the gray veined marble top above a pierced foliate carved frieze, on shell-and-scroll-carved supports and scroll feet, with a shaped undertier, chips, painted surface is later.

38¼in (97cm) wide

$1,100-1,250　　**DN**

A 19thC giltwood console table, in Louis XVI style, the green veined marble top above a frieze pierced with latticework, on stop-fluted square-section and baluster legs carved with foliage, scratches, marks, worm.

49¼in (125cm) wide

$3,700-4,300　　**DN**

A 19thC giltwood console table, in Rococo style, the pierced leaf and scroll support with a red and gray marble top, one foot broken, wear, signs of restoration and gluing, gilding is very rubbed.

38½in (98cm) wide

$1,400-1,700　　**CHEF**

A pair of late-Victorian satinwood and marquetry console tables, in the manner of Edwards & Roberts, inlaid with urns and ribbon-tied husk swags, with tops above a frieze drawer.

ca. 1890 1900　　25¼in (64cm) wide

$4,300-5,000　　**WW**

A gilt mahogany console table, in Louis XV style, later serpentine breccia marble top, above a pierced frieze centered by an open cartouche of C scrolls, on cabriole legs formed of C scrolls, with foliage, regilt.

39¾in (101cm) wide

$2,500-3,700　　**DUK**

ESSENTIAL REFERENCE—OLIVER MESSEL

Born in London in 1904, Oliver Hilary Sambourne Messel was educated at Westminster School and Eton, and then at the Slade School of Fine Art at University College London.

- Initially a portrait painter, he soon went into costume and set design, initially for the theater, and then for ballet and film, and numerous accolades ensued, including Tony Awards and, in 1959, a nomination for an Academy Award (an "Oscar").
- In 1953, his career took a further turn when he was commissioned to design the decor for a suite at London's prestigious Dorchester Hotel. A lavishly ornate fusion of Baroque, Rococo, Modernist, and Fantasy styles, it, like many other suites he designed for the hotel, has been restored and preserved as part of Britain's National Heritage.
- These commissions, along with dabbling in retail design (for a shoe store in London's Bond Street), proved a stepping stone into his final and equally successful career: designing, building, and transforming residential homes, including, in many instances, designing the furnishings for them.
- Based in the Caribbean, primarily on the islands of Barbados and Mustique, his commissions came largely from wealthy friends (his nephew was Antony Armstrong-Jones, Lord Snowdon, who had married Princess Margaret).
- Fusing Baroque and Classical styles with indigenous materials and building techniques, his work was memorably described by the architect Barbara Hill as "converting quite ordinary houses into wonderlands."
- Oliver Messel died in Barbados in 1978 at the age of 74.

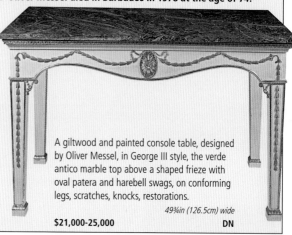

A giltwood and painted console table, designed by Oliver Messel, in George III style, the verde antico marble top above a shaped frieze with oval patera and harebell swags, on conforming legs, scratches, knocks, restorations.

49¾in (126.5cm) wide

$21,000-25,000　　**DN**

A George III mahogany serpentine serving table, in the manner of Thomas Chippendale, with slides on each side.

ca. 1780   65¾in (167cm) wide

$7,500-8,500   **DN**

A George III mahogany serpentine serving table, inlaid with stringing, the fan-inlaid top with a center oval panel, above a fluted frieze fitted with three drawers, on paneled and stop-fluted legs.

ca. 1790   55in (139.5cm) wide

$2,500-3,700   **WW**

A George III mahogany and marquetry serving table, in the manner of Ince & Mayhew.

ca. 1790   90in (228.5cm) wide

$15,000-17,000   **DN**

A George III mahogany serving table, in the manner of George Smith.

This sideboard-table, with its bacchic lion tablets above tapering and reed-enriched legs that terminate in lion paws, relates closely to an 1804 design published in George Smith's "Collection of Designs for Household Furniture and Interior Decoration," J. Taylor (1808), plate 92.

ca. 1805-10   78in (198cm) wide

$12,500-15,000   **DN**

An early-19thC Regency mahogany serving table, the top with a rear gallery with anthemions, gadrooned edge on the top, on four fluted tapering columns, on a solid base with a deep incurved center recess.

This solid mahogany serving table, or sideboard, is a typical example of the substantial pieces of furniture fashionable in the early 19thC for the adornment of dining rooms in grand houses being furnished in the Classical style, and in this instance probably in the more austere Grecian taste. Similar examples, in overall form, decorative detail, or both, can be found in George Smith's "Collection of Designs for Household Furniture and Interior Decoration," J. Taylor (1808) and, much later, in Henry Whitaker's "Practical Cabinet Maker and Upholsterers Treasury of Designs," Peter Jackson (1847).

105½in (268cm) wide

$1,900-2,500   **DUK**

A Regency mahogany and ebonized hall or serving table.

ca. 1820   102in (260cm) wide

$25,000-31,000   **DN**

A George IV mahogany serving table, with a frieze drawer, on scroll front legs.

ca. 1825   70¾in (179.5cm) wide

$1,000-1,250   **WW**

One of a pair of 19thC Irish carved mahogany serving tables, in George II style, scratches, scuffing, cracks.

62in (157.5cm) wide

$12,500-16,000 the pair   **DN**

An early-19thC mahogany breakfront serving table, in the manner of Gillows, with later red painted faux marble inset top, on acanthus carved reeded tapering legs.

96¾in (246cm) wide

$1,900-2,200   **CHEF**

A mid-17thC oak credence table, probably Somerset, extensive restoration, old worm holes.

36¼in (92cm) wide

$1,250-1,500 CHOR

A Charles II walnut side table, marks, old worm, repairs and replacements.

This table is a rare and sophisticated survival being constructed entirely from "walnut tree" instead of the more commonly found oak examples.

ca. 1660 *35in (89cm) wide*

$10,000-11,000 DN

A late-17thC William and Mary olivewood and walnut side table, the oyster-veneered top and frieze drawer with holly banding.

26¾in (68cm) wide

$3,000-3,700 WW

A late-17thC William and Mary oak side table.

34¾in (88cm) wide

$625-750 L&T

A late-17th/early-18thC William and Mary oak side table, with a frieze drawer, on ring-turned baluster legs.

33½in (85cm) wide

$700-800 WW

An oyster-veneered and line-inlaid side table, late-17thC and later, the top above a frieze with a drawer, on cabriole legs with pad feet, losses, replaced veneers, worm, later handles and lock.

31in (79cm) wide

$1,250-1,500 DN

A George II red walnut side table, with a later marble top above a plain frieze, on cabriole legs and pad feet.

ca. 1740 *45in (114.5cm) wide*

$3,700-4,300 WW

A carved giltwood and gesso side table, ca. 1725 and later, with a portoro marble top, marble pitting and chips, lacking one lion paw.

29in (73.5cm) wide

$11,000-12,500 DN

A mid-18thC Louis XV walnut side table, the serpentine Siena marble top above a pierced foliate frieze, on cabriole legs and inscrolled feet.

58¼in (148cm) wide

$6,000-7,500 DUK

A mid-18thC oak and crossbanded side table, later fittings and handles, one back leg repaired, worm.

35¾in (91cm) wide

$1,050-1,200   DN

A George III mahogany silver table, in Chinese Chippendale style, the galleried top above a blind fret and pendant frieze, with pierced tapering legs, on guttae feet with leather roller casters.

ca. 1770   *32in (81.5cm) wide*

$3,100-3,700   WW

ESSENTIAL REFERENCE—FRANÇOIS LINKE

Born in 1855 in the Bohemian village of Pankraz (now Jitrava, the Czech Republic), François Linke served his apprenticeship under a master cabinetmaker and, having visited Paris in 1875, returned permanently in 1877. By 1881, he had set up workshops in Faubourg St. Antoine, begun supplying furniture for makers, such as Jansen and Krieger, and rapidly became known for exceptional craftsmanship, especially in wood carving, marquetry, and bronze. However, what really established his reputation was the gold medal he won for his exhibits at the Paris Exposition Universelle in 1900.

Following Linke's success at the Exposition, orders flooded in (notably from the King of Belgium, the President of France, and many leading industrialists and bankers), and his workshops expanded into Place Vendôme. All this was underpinned by the exceptionally high quality of his furniture and the exuberantly refreshing quality of its style. Like many contemporaries, he looked back for inspiration to the 18thC Rococo furniture of Louis XV and the Neoclassical of Louis XVI, but, unlike his contemporaries, he did not just try to accurately reproduce it. Instead, he invested it with a new vitality: for example, the curvilinear forms of Louis XV Rococo were seamlessly fused with the energetic flowing lines of contemporary Art Nouveau to create a style one critic described as "entièrement nouveau" ("entirely new").

Orders for Linke's furniture continued to pour in prior to and after World War I—the commission to furnish King Faud's Ras El Tin Palace in Alexandria being possibly the largest single furniture commission ever, eclipsing even Versailles. Active until the mid-1930s, Linke died in 1946.

A French mahogany and ormolu-mounted side table, by François Linke, in Louis XV/Transitional style, the marble top above a reeded tablet, decorated with satyrs flanked by flower garlands and ribbons, signed "F Linke," on fluted tapering legs with brass capped feet, scratches and small chips.

25½in (65cm) wide

$15,000-19,000   TEN

A giltwood side table, in George II style, in the manner of William Kent, the marble slab top above a rusticated frieze, centered by a large raised shell, on carved legs with scrolling foliate knees, carved fetlocks and paw feet.

58½in (148.5cm) wide

$75,000-90,000   WW

An 18thC Georgian oak side table, the top with a molded edge above a single long drawer, on square straight legs, joined by peripheral stretchers.

27¾in (70.5cm) wide

$1,500-1,900   L&T

A pair of late-18thC George III mahogany side tables, the demilune tops above friezes carved with drapery swags.

48in (122cm) wide

$3,100-3,700   L&T

A late-18thC Georgian painted mahogany demilune side table, with later decoration, the associated back panel centered by a painted reserve with putti, the whole painted with flower garlands, paterae, trophies, portrait medallions, leaf fronds, and bellflower trails, converted from a fold-over table.

35¾in (90.5cm) wide

$1,900-2,500   L&T

A late-18th/early-19thC George III painted pine lady's kidney-shaped side table, with gilt edging and bands of harebells, the hinged top with a rising silk firescreen, above a gilt-brass wirework panel with a pair of doors above a drawer, on splay legs and brass casters.

25¼in (64cm) wide

$1,250-1,500   WW

A George IV rosewood, specimen marble and gilt-metal-mounted side or writing table, attributed to Gillows, a frieze drawer on one side.

ca. 1825   *42¾in (108.5cm) wide*

$5,000-6,200   **DN**

A pair of George IV mahogany side tables, with later pierced three-quarter galleried superstructures on turned brass supports, above a frieze drawer, on reeded tapering legs with brass caps and casters.

45in (114cm) wide

$5,000-5,600   **CHEF**

A Regency painted pine side table, early 19thC and later, with a pair of frieze drawers, on faux bamboo legs.

36in (91.5cm) wide

$1,900-2,500   **WW**

A walnut side table, in George II style, the quarter-veneered top with cross and feather banding, on shell-capped cabriole legs and claw-and-ball feet.

29¼in (74.5cm) wide

$625-750   **WW**

A mahogany and crossbanded side table, attributed to Gillows, Lancaster, the two-drawer frieze of burl walnut, cross stretcher with the center modeled as a pineapple, stamped "Gillow" on the drawer.

ca. 1850s   *47¾in (121cm) wide*

$550-700   **WHP**

A late-19thC carved mahogany side table, in the manner of Thomas Chippendale, spandrels with some old breaks and repairs.

43¾in (111cm) wide

$1,900-2,500   **DN**

A late-19thC Classical Revival giltwood side table, with faux marble top, over a carved frieze with rosettes and pharaoh mask motif, on ebonized and gilt tapered legs.

43in (109cm) wide

$950-1,050   **CHEF**

A late-19thC mahogany side table, in Chippendale style, the marble inset top above a blind fret-carved frieze, on internally chamfered legs with fret-carved corner brackets.

38¼in (97cm) wide

$500-625   **CHEF**

One of a pair of late-19th/early-20thC mahogany side tables, in Chinese Chippendale style, with an egg-and-dart carved edge, on blind fret bracketed chamfered legs and block feet.

52¼in (133cm) wide

$3,700-4,300 the pair   **WW**

ESSENTIAL REFERENCE—TEA

All manner of paraphernalia is associated with drinking tea in Great Britain, and you will find them scattered throughout this Price Guide—from ceramic teapots, cups, and saucers to wood and metal tea caddies to the wood tea tables on this page, and many more besides. But what of the tea itself? Well, the fact that for over hundreds of years tea has fueled trade on a global scale, been subject to punitive taxation, and triggered wars between nations clearly elevates it beyond the status of just a refreshing libation.

While tea drinking began in China some 5,000 years ago, and had been introduced to Japan and Tibet in the 3rdC AD by Buddhist monks, it wasn't until the early-17thC that tea was exported in any quantity to Europe, initially under sail to the Netherlands by the Dutch East India Company. However, tea drinking in Britain did not begin until the mid-17thC, when Catherine of Braganza, who had acquired the taste in her native Portugal, married King Charles II and introduced it to the English aristocracy. It's subsequent popularity, and the British East India Company entering the increasingly profitable tea-trading market, was to have profound political consequences. Perhaps chief among the latter was the infamous Boston Tea Party of 1773, in which North American colonists threw chests of East India Company tea into Boston Harbor in protest against the Tea Act of 1773, which allowed the company, unlike the colonists, to sell tea from China without paying the high tax on it—an event that would trigger the American Revolution, the subsequent loss of Britain's colony and, ultimately, the foundation of the United States.

A George II mahogany folding tea table, old splits, chips, repairs, some replacements.
ca. 1750   29¼in (74cm) wide
$2,200-2,700   DN

A mid-18thC mahogany tea table, the shaped fold-over top above a single frieze drawer, on lappet-carved tapered legs with pad feet, light scratching, cock beading knocked off but present, some reenforcement in the underside.
30in (76cm) wide
$1,200-1,350   CHEF

A mid-18thC George III mahogany tea table, the hinged top carved with a ribbon-and-rosette border, above a frieze drawer.
32¾in (83.5cm) wide
$625-750   DUK

A late-18thC late George III mahogany tea table, the fold-over top above a frieze with a center table, inlaid with grain veneers, on tapered legs and spade feet, the whole outlined with line inlay.
36½in (93cm) wide
$1,000-1,250   L&T

A pair of early-19thC mahogany tea tables, attributed to William Trotter, Edinburgh, the fold-over tops outlined with bead molding, on waisted and lotus-clasped squared supports, on shaped quadripartite bases with bun feet.

William Trotter was born into a family of merchants in 1772, descended on the maternal side from the family of John Knox. He became a member of The Merchant Company in 1797, and, by 1809, he was sole proprietor of the firm Young & Trotter. Often regarded as the most eminent of all Scottish cabinetmakers, his success was in part due to his appreciation for his client's taste. Using the finest quality materials, Trotter developed a distinctive Regency style typically characterized by bold carving, bead molding, and reeded legs.
38½in (98cm) wide
$11,000-12,000   L&T

A mid-19thC George IV mahogany fold-over tea table, with plain frieze and gadrooned border, on a turned vasiform support with reeded saber legs, brass capped toes, and casters.
35¾in (91cm) wide
$1,000-1,100   TEN

A mid-19thC early-Victorian rosewood fold-over tea table, with hinged leaf, quadripartite base and compressed feet, with recessed casters.
37in (94cm) wide
$450-500   TEN

A late-18thC George III satinwood Pembroke table, the twin-flap top above a frieze end drawer.

41¾in (106cm) wide

$1,000-1,250 DUK

A George III satinwood Pembroke table, inlaid with stringing and amaranth banding, the top above a frieze drawer at each end.

ca. 1790 *22¼in (56.5cm) wide*

$700-800 WW

A late-18thC George III mahogany and satinwood Pembroke table, in the manner of Henry Hill, Marlborough, the top inlaid with concentric ovals, above a frieze drawer on one end and a dummy drawer opposing.

39in (99cm) wide (open)

$1,600-2,000 L&T

A George III satinwood and marquetry Pembroke table, attributed to Ince & Mayhew, lock is a Victorian replacement.

ca. 1790 *39¼in (100cm) wide (open)*

$4,300-5,000 DN

A George III burl yew, sycamore, and tulipwood metamorphic Pembroke table, in the manner of Ince & Mayhew, the sliding top opening to reveal a compartment, drawers and pigeonholes operated by a pully mechanism in the underside, one side fitted with a frieze drawer and three dummy drawers, veneer cracks, slightly faded hue.

ca. 1790 *40¼in (102cm) wide (open)*

$4,300-5,000 DN

A George III mahogany and satinwood Pembroke table, in the manner of Gillows, the top with a sycamore panel marquetry inlaid with a ribbon and flowers, the ground of radiating panels divided by boxwood stringing, with a satinwood and kingwood border, above a frieze drawer.

ca. 1790 *39¼in (99.5cm) wide*

$4,300-5,000 WW

A Regency mahogany Pembroke table, the top with a single end drawer, with column support on hipped and splayed legs, with brass paw caps and casters.

40½in (103cm) wide

$500-625 CHEF

A satinwood and giltwood Pembroke table, in Sheraton style, in the manner of Wright & Mansfield, the top with a center panel, painted en grisaille with Aurora in her chariot, in the manner of Angelica Kauffman, with a border painted with roses, above a frieze drawer.

ca. 1860-70 *36in (91.5cm) wide*

$625-750 WW

A George III rosewood and line-inlaid sofa table, attributed to Gillows, the top banded in casuarina oak (partridgewood), two frieze drawers on each side, later reinforcing.

The elegant high arched braces beneath the top of this sofa table are characteristic of Gillows designs and make an elegant alternative to the more common cross stretchers.

ca. 1800   *61in (155cm) wide*
$11,000-12,000   **DN**

A Regency rosewood, satinwood crossbanded, and line-inlaid sofa table.

ca. 1815   *59¼in (150.5cm) wide (open)*
$1,900-2,500   **DN**

An early-19thC Regency mahogany sofa table, the top with drop leaves above a frieze drawer, on a column support with quadripartite base and reeded saber legs, with brass hairy paw feet and casters.

37in (94cm) wide
$1,050-1,200   **TEN**

A Regency satinwood, ebony, and brass-inlaid sofa table, with one frieze drawer and one dummy drawer on each side.

ca. 1815   *60¼in (153cm) wide*
$2,500-3,100   **DN**

A Regency rosewood and brass marquetry sofa table.

ca. 1820   *69¼in (176cm) wide (open)*
$2,200-2,700   **DN**

A Regency burl yew-banded, exotic hardwood, and ebonized sofa table, with two frieze drawers opposing dummy drawers.

ca. 1820   *59½in (151cm) wide*
$3,100-3,700   **DN**

An early-Victorian burl wood sofa table, the top above two frieze drawers, stamped "James Winter Wardour Street," light scratching on the top, slight warpage in ends.

67¼in (171cm) wide (open)
$5,000-6,200   **CHEF**

CLOSER LOOK—A MID-19THC SOFA TABLE

The inlaid and polychrome painted decoration draws on imagery and motifs from the Classical vocabulary of ornament, including portrait medallions, swags, and garlands of flowers, and scrolling acanthus leaf borders.

Although the table was made in the mid-19thC, it is essentially a revival of a form first associated with the reign of George III (1760-1820) and the "overlapping" English Regency (1811-20).

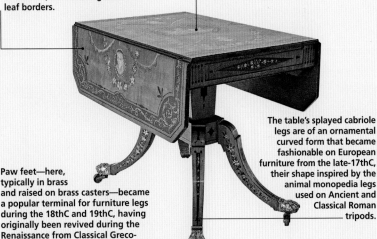

The table's splayed cabriole legs are of an ornamental curved form that became fashionable on European furniture from the late-17thC, their shape inspired by the animal monopedia legs used on Ancient and Classical Roman tripods.

Paw feet—here, typically in brass and raised on brass casters—became a popular terminal for furniture legs during the 18thC and 19thC, having originally been revived during the Renaissance from Classical Greco-Roman prototypes.

A mid-19thC satinwood sofa table, in George III style, polychrome painted with Classical decoration, the drop leaves above two frieze drawers, the cabriole legs terminating in brass capped hairy paw feet and casters.

43¼in (110cm) wide
$3,100-3,700   **TEN**

A George I walnut and feather-banded card table, with a baize inset surface, old worm, old veneer repairs, replacement elements.

ca. 1720   *33in (84cm) wide*

$3,700-5,000   **DN**

A George II figured walnut and feather-banded folding card table, with concertina action, minor wear, replacements include the baize surface.

ca. 1730   *40¼in (102cm) wide*

$3,700-5,000   **DN**

A George II concertina-action card table, possibly padouk, on shell-, leaf-, and scroll-carved cabriole legs and pad feet.

ca. 1740   *36in (91.5cm) wide*

$1,400-1,600   **WW**

A mid-18thC Irish George II mahogany folding card table, the top faded and stained, repairs, later elements.

33in (84cm) wide

$1,900-2,500   **DN**

A George III amboyna concertina-action card table, the hinged top with outset corners enclosing baize and candlestands, the frieze on cabriole legs with pad feet.

39½in (100.5cm) wide

$6,000-7,500   **TEN**

A pair of late-18thC George III mahogany and marquetry card tables, with D-shaped hinged tops inlaid with a shell at the rear edges.

33in (84cm) wide

$2,500-3,700   **DUK**

A pair of George III mahogany demilune card tables, with molded fold-over tops, on patera-headed turned, tapered, and fluted legs, fading, old scratches on one, water damage on the other, light worm.

38¼in (97cm) wide

$5,500-6,000   **CHEF**

An 18thC Dutch mahogany and marquetry concertina card table, the top inlaid with an urn of flowers, birds, and butterflies, baize-lined playing surface, with sunken counterwells and candlestands, each inlaid with a playing card.

30¼in (77cm) wide

$1,900-2,500   **WW**

A George III coromandel card table, with burl yew banding.

ca. 1800   *35¾in (91cm) wide*

$2,500-3,700   **WW**

A Regency burl yew and rosewood-banded combination games table, attributed to Gillows, the top with a sliding section with a marquetry checkerboard on the reverse, enclosing a marquetry backgammon board in the recess, flanked by a short cedar-lined frieze drawer on each side, restorations and repairs.

ca. 1815 — 35¾in (91cm) wide

$8,500-10,000 — DN

A pair of early-19thC Regency rosewood card tables, with crossbanded tops and friezes with scrolled leaf marquetry, inlaid with boxwood stringing, on twin turned columns, platform bases, and scrolled feet.

35¾in (91cm) wide

$2,500-3,700 — DUK

An early-19thC Regency rosewood card table, inlaid with brass stringing, with gilt-bronze mounts of rosettes and anthemion motifs.

35½in (90cm) wide

$1,400-1,600 — WW

An early-19thC Regency mahogany card table, inlaid with ebonized stringing, the fold-over D-shaped top on twin gate supports, above a frieze with a stylized Greek key motif.

35¾in (91cm) wide

$1,050-1,200 — WW

A pair of Regency rosewood and simulated rosewood card tables, with kingwood and brass banding, with swivel tops and painted stems, interior baize is later.

ca. 1815 — 36¼in (92cm) wide

$3,700-5,000 — DN

A pair of mid-19thC Napoleon III scarlet tortoiseshell and brass marquetry card tables, in the manner of André-Charles Boulle, one table premiere-partie marquetry, the other contre-partie, each with a rotating hinged top, with an ebony and brass marquetry border, all sides of both friezes with Boulle marquetry, set with gilt-metal masks, chips, tortoiseshell losses, some later brass pins, baize is later.

35½in (90cm) wide

$8,000-9,500 — DN

A French ebonized, red tortoiseshell, and brass-inlaid fold-over card table, in Louis XV style, in the manner of André-Charles Boulle, the frieze centered by a mask, on cabriole legs, with caryatid mounts and sabots.

ca. 1860 — 34¼in (87cm) wide

$1,050-1,200 — TEN

A Victorian satinwood combination games table, the top with an oval painted Georgian gentleman within a game, the fold-over top with a card table with four counterwells over a built-in roulette wheel with playing surface, on square tapered and fluted legs, with brass casters.

44½in (113cm) wide

$4,300-5,000 — CHEF

A Victorian amboyna, walnut, and gilt-metal-mounted fold-over card table, with quarter-veneered and bone-inlaid top, the supports inset with blue-and-white Jasper mounts, the stretcher with a gilt-metal urn, on capped feet and ceramic casters, scratches on the top, faults in the veneers.

ca. 1880 — 35¾in (91cm) wide

$1,900-2,500 — TEN

A George II mahogany games and tea table, the triple top with counterwells and candlestands, above a frieze drawer, on shell-capped cabriole legs and claw-and-ball feet.

ca. 1740-50   32in (81cm) wide
$1,900-2,500   WW

A late George III mahogany games table, the top with lift-out center section, enclosing a well with backgammon board and pieces, with two small drawers on each side, on square-section fluted legs, on block feet with casters, damage and losses.

                                              48in (122cm) wide
$3,700-5,000   LC

An early-19thC Regency rosewood and brass-inlaid games and worktable, with pierced brass gallery and sliding games board, enclosing a boxwood and ebony chess set, above two drawers with lion-mask handles, a gathered sliding workbox below, weak structure/legs, old repairs, scratches on the top.

                          24¾in (64cm) wide
$1,050-1,200   TEN

An early-19thC Scottish Regency burl yew, ebony, and ebonized games table, the fold-over top with a baize playing surface, above a tablet-centered frieze, on a square baluster support and quadripartite platform, on lobed feet with brass casters.

                                36¼in (92cm) wide
$1,250-1,600   L&T

A mid-18thC George II burl walnut games table, with quarter-veneered and crossbanded hinged leaf, the rear legs expanding on a scissor-action frame, on square chamfered legs, splits, veneer losses, mold decay on legs.

                                    34¾in (88cm) wide
$2,500-3,100   TEN

An early-19thC Regency mahogany games and sofa table, in the manner of John McLean, the twin-flap top with a center slide, with removable leather-lined games tray with a backgammon board on one side and a chessboard on the other, with four drawers below, on X-frame end supports with inward-facing bronze paw feet, repairs on feet.

A games table of ca. 1800 with removable slide and reeded X-frame legs, by John McLean (fl. 1770-1814), is at Saltram, Devon, and a writing table at Berrington Hall, Herefordshire.

                                53¾in (136.5cm) wide
$4,300-5,600   DUK

A late-18thC George III mahogany Pembroke games table, inlaid with stringing and burl yew banding, reversible top inlaid with a checkerboard revealing a backgammon board and wells for games pieces.

                                  33¾in (85.5cm) wide
$1,200-1,350   WW

A Regency combination brass-inlaid rosewood writing and games table, the top with three-panel tooled leather writing surface, the center sliding section with chessboard inlay on the reverse, sliding to reveal a backgammon board.

                                    33¾in (86cm) wide
$1,500-1,900   CHEF

A Regency rosewood and gilt-metal-mounted writing and games table, attributed to Gillows, with leather inset top and center sliding section, the reverse leather inset and with a marquetry checkerboard, enclosing backgammon, the locks curved in form to match the table ends, cracks, repairs, repolishing of top, veneer losses, escutcheons possibly later.

ca. 1820   28¾in (73cm) wide
$5,500-7,000   DN

A George III mahogany worktable, in the manner of Thomas Shearer, inlaid with stringing and satinwood banding, the top with an oval flame mahogany panel, above a frieze drawer, originally with divisions and a bag slide.

ca. 1780 28¼in (71.5cm) high
$1,250-1,600 WW

A George III satinwood worktable, Sheraton period, the top inset with a leather writing surface and rising screen, the side drawer with divisions for pen and ink, with ivory handles, the front with a pull-out slide, the left side with a silk-lined pull-out work bag.

ca. 1790 23in (58.5cm) wide
$750-875 WW

A George III satinwood and inlaid worktable.

ca. 1790 20¾in (53cm) wide
$875-1,000 DN

A late George III mahogany worktable, inlaid with stringing, the top with bird's-eye maple panels and banding, with two frieze drawers, one with divisions and with a bone escutcheon.

ca. 1800 28¼in (72cm) high
$500-625 WW

An early-19thC late George III satinwood, ebony-strung, and crossbanded worktable, with bowfront drawer and sliding fabric workbox below.

24¾in (63cm) wide
$500-625 TEN

A late George III mahogany lady's reading and worktable, with slides on each side, a frieze drawer, and a work bag, on brass casters.

ca. 1800-10 30¾in (78cm) high
$375-500 WW

An early-19thC Regency rosewood worktable, with molded hinged lid and a later fabric-lined interior, on a baluster support with carved socle, quadripartite base, acanthus-carved scrolled toes, and casters.

29½in (75cm) high
$700-800 TEN

An early-19thC late-George III mahogany and brass hexagonal tripod worktable, the hinged top opening to a void interior, with column support and outswept legs, with brass caps and casters.

30in (76cm) high
$800-950 L&T

A Biedermeier mahogany worktable, with flame-veneered hinged top, the fitted interior with nine lidded compartments with ivory handles, the base with scroll corbels and a cupboard, on flattened bun feet.

Ivory Act certification no. CABXCX4Y

ca. 1840-50 30¾in (78cm) high
$1,000-1,100 WW

FURNITURE

ESSENTIAL REFERENCE—GILES GRENDEY

Born in Wotten-under-Edge, Gloucestershire, in 1693, Giles Grendey was apprenticed in 1709, made free of the Joiners' Company in 1716, and, by 1726, was hiring his own apprentices.

- Working as a "Cabinet-Maker and Chair Maker" out of a workshop in St. John's Square in Clerkenwell, London, he was elected to the Livery of the Joiners' Company in 1729, and 37 years later in 1766, at the age of 72, was elected its Master. By 1779, he had moved to Palmer's Green, then just north of London, and he died there at the age of 87 in 1780.

- During the course of his long career, Grendey employed numerous craftsmen at his workshop and supplied both high-quality pieces for prestigious patrons as well as well-made but simpler furniture for less wealthy clients. He was also renowned for his export business, mostly to Spain.

- He famously supplied, for example, a suite of red japanned furniture to the Spanish Duke of Infantado, for his castle at Lazcano, which comprised at least 77 pieces—the largest suite of English furniture ever recorded. One of the reasons he was one of the best-known cabinetmakers of his time was that, unlike most cabinetmakers of the period, he sometimes labeled his furniture.

- Of course, labels come off, so a Grendey label on a piece of furniture nowadays causes considerable excitement in salerooms and among dealers. Unfortunately, however, genuine Grendey pieces that can be firmly attributed are extremely rare.

A George II walnut lowboy, in the manner of Giles Grendey, repairs, old worm.

The carved shell and bellflower motif to the cabriole legs on this piece is seen on the legs of tables and chairs by Giles Grendey.

ca. 1730   31in (79cm) wide
$5,000-5,600   DN

A George II walnut and feather-banded lowboy, repairs and replacements, old worm.
ca. 1740   30in (76cm) wide
$4,300-5,000   DN

A mid-18thC American New England oak lowboy, with stylized oak leaves carved on the legs.
28¼in (72cm) wide
$1,900-2,500   DN

An early-18thC George I walnut kneehole dressing table, with quarter-veneered and feather banded top, above a long drawer over a kneehole recess with an apron drawer and cupboard, flanked by banks of three short drawers.
21½in (54.5cm) wide
$7,000-8,000   L&T

A mid-18thC George II walnut cross- and feather-banded kneehole dressing table, the quarter-veneered molded top above a center drawer, flanked by eight drawers around a cupboard door, on later bracket feet.
36½in (93cm) wide
$1,100-1,350   TEN

A George III mahogany, rosewood crossbanded and boxwood-strung kneehole dressing table, the top above a pull-out brushing slide and long frieze drawer, with wavy-shaped kneehole drawer below, flanked by six small drawers all around a center cupboard door, on bracket feet, top slightly misshapen with some splitting, handles replaced, front foot section is detached.
ca. 1780   36¼in (92cm) wide
$1,500-1,900   TEN

An 18thC George III mahogany dressing table, the molded top above a long frieze drawer, center kneehole with a cupboard and apron drawer, flanked by three drawers on each side.
36½in (93cm) wide
$700-800   L&T

A late-18thC George III mahogany dressing table, inlaid with boxwood stringing, the twin hinged top revealing an interior with four lidded compartments and two pin cushions.
28¾in (73cm) wide
$250-370   WW

An 18thC George III mahogany dressing table, the top with a molded edge above two short drawers and a long drawer, on chamfered square tapered legs.
38¼in (97cm) wide
$1,700-2,100   L&T

A George IV mahogany dressing table, the top with a three-quarter gallery, above a pair of frieze drawers, with paneled trestle ends, on lobed bun feet and sunken brass casters.

ca. 1830 *48in (122cm) wide*

$1,000-1,100 **WW**

A late-19thC mid-Victorian satin birch dressing table, by G. Trollope & Sons, the kidney-shaped leather-lined top above a frieze drawer carved with foliage and a shell, on cabriole legs joined by a shaped undertier, on hoof feet, the drawer with label printed "G. TROLLOPE & SONS," inscribed "CAB.SK. / 877."

Advertised as cabinetmakers, paper hangers, upholsterers, and house agents, Trollope & Sons was active from 1787-1890.

46in (117cm) wide

$950-1,050 **DUK**

A Victorian walnut dressing table, the molded top with three frieze drawers, above carved baluster supports with a turned stretcher, on scrolled legs with brass casters, stamped "EDWARDS & ROBERTS."

48in (122cm) wide

$500-625 **CHEF**

A 19thC Victorian mahogany dressing table, the top with a three-quarter gallery above three frieze drawers and an arched apron, on turned and tapered legs ending in brass caps and casters.

53½in (136cm) wide

$1,500-1,900 **L&T**

A George II mahogany tripod table, the tilt-top on a baluster-turned stem, on scroll-carved legs, with paw feet.

ca. 1750 *36½in (92.5cm) diam*

$1,500-1,900 **WW**

A George II mahogany tripod table, the tilt-top revolving on a birdcage, with a stop-fluted column, on foliate-capped cabriole legs and claw-and-ball feet.

ca. 1750 *29½in (75cm) diam*

$4,700-5,200 **WW**

A George II mahogany tripod occasional table, the tilt-top with a piecrust molded edge revolving on a birdcage, with a ribbed stem, on shell-capped cabriole legs, with claw-and-ball feet.

ca. 1755 *28¼in (72cm) diam*

$4,300-5,600 **WW**

A mid-18thC George II mahogany tripod dumb-waiter on a vase-shaped shaft and tripod base, with carved claw feet and recessed brass casters.

42½in (108cm) high

$1,600-1,900 **DUK**

A George III mahogany tripod table, the base possibly 19thC, with unusual handle holes, the tray top molding with a brass string, repairs, marks, chips, section of brass string missing.

ca. 1760 *29½in (75cm) high*

$3,100-4,300 **DN**

A George III mahogany tripod table, with a piecrust molded edge, marks, chips, repairs.

ca. 1760   *26½in (67cm) high*

$1,900-2,500   **DN**

A George III padouk and needlework-inset birdcage tripod table, with gros and petit point woolwork of figures by boats, the base rosewood, scratches, restorations, repairs.

ca. 1760   *37½in (95cm) wide*

$2,500-3,100   **DN**

A George III mahogany dish-top tripod table, on a baluster-turned support, with cabriole legs and pad feet.

ca. 1780   *26¾in (68cm) diam*

$550-700   **TEN**

An 18thC George III mahogany tripod wine table, the tilt-top on a ring-turned column.

31in (79cm) high

$500-625   **L&T**

A George III mahogany dish-top tripod table, with a spiral and part-wrythen turned baluster support, with cabriole legs and pad feet, scratches, repair on one leg.

ca. 1800   *28¼in (72cm) high*

$800-950   **TEN**

An early-19thC Regency yew wood tripod wine table, the tilt-top raised on a baluster column and umbrella tripod base, with spade feet.

28¾in (73cm) high

$1,400-1,600   **L&T**

An early-19thC Regency rosewood and brass-mounted tripod table, in the manner of Louis Le Gaigneur, with a crossbanded top, the stem applied with acanthus leaves.

28¼in (72cm) high

$1,050-1,200   **WW**

An early-19thC Regency kingwood and brass-mounted tripod games table, in the manner of Louis Le Gaigneur, the top with satinwood banding and inlaid with a checkerboard, the stem applied with acanthus leaves.

28¼in (72cm) high

$1,100-1,350   **WW**

A Victorian walnut tripod table, by Holland & Sons, the top inlaid with a satinwood band, on a barley twist stem, the scrolling tripod base with a centered turned finial, stamped "Holland & Sons" twice.

ca. 1860   *28¾in (73cm) high*

$375-500   **WW**

A mid-18thC George III mahogany spider-leg table, on turned block legs joined by stretchers, the underside labeled "Property of Earl of Lonsdale."

23½in (60cm) wide

$875-1,000   TEN

A George III mahogany spider-leg table, chips, losses, later elements.

ca. 1780   29¼in (74cm) wide

$500-625   DN

A late-18thC George II mahogany drop-leaf corner table, with hinged top, plain frieze, on turned legs and pad feet.

25½in (65cm) wide

$700-800   L&T

An early-19thC Austrian mahogany and gilt-metal-mounted occasional table, the glazed top with a pen and ink Neoclassical border, around an engraving after Louis de Boullogne the younger, "Venus at the Forge of Vulcan," with a frieze drawer, scratches on glass top, water marks, worm, losses in veneer.

27¼in (69.5cm) wide

$11,000-14,000   DN

A pair of George IV rosewood and satinwood occasional tables, attributed to Gillows, satinwood bentwood undertiers.

ca. 1825   28¼in (71.5cm) high

$7,000-8,000   DN

An Anglo-Indian carved rosewood pedestal occasional table, with a center satinwood inset, possibly later, repairs.

ca. 1825   28¾in (73cm) high

$1,600-2,000   DN

An early-19thC late George III oak cricket table, with a boarded top.

32in (81cm) diam

$700-800   WW

A Maltese pietra dura and specimen marble armorial table top, by Joseph Darmanin, the Irish base by Robert Strahan, inlaid in various marbles with the arms of General Robert Edward King, 1st Viscount Lorton of Boyle (1773-1854), on a yellow marble ground containing fossils, the underside with a paper label inscribed "J. Darmanin & Sons/Marble Workers/Monumental & Mosaic Slabs/and other ornamental work/Strada Levante No 45/Malta," set into an Irish carved rosewood base with foliate decoration on the rim, on a scrolling tripod base carved with floral swags, stamped "I 906 / Strahan" on the frame, the underside with a paper label inscribed "Robert Strahan, Cabinet Maker, Upholstered, Auctioneer & Undertaker, 24 Henry Street."

The interesting and impressive provenance associated with this table contributes significantly to its considerable value, especially in comparison to far more "anonymous" equivalents. In the early 19thC, its original owner, Viscount Lorton, commissioned the eminent architect John Nash to design and supervise the construction of his new residence, Rockingham House, in County Roscommon, Ireland. Nash's plans arrived in 1809 and, after a few amendments, construction began in 1810. Despite Nash being dismissed near the end of 1811, and responsibility for overseeing the work then falling to the clerk of works, John Lynn, on its completion in 1817, the house was considered by many to be Nash's finest house in Ireland. The final bill for the decoration and furnishing of the house, submitted by Lynn in 1817, was considerable, with more than £5,700 (at least $680,000 in today's money) having been spent on furniture alone! This table wasn't among those original pieces. However, it was acquired by Lord Lorton himself on one of the two Grand Tours of Continental Europe he undertook—possibly the first in 1825, but more likely, judging by the style of the rosewood base, the second in 1836, and it remained in the house, primarily in the billiard room, until its demolition in 1957.

As to the table's maker: Giuseppe Darmanin had established his business in Malta in the early 19thC, and his sons joined the firm in the late 1820s or 1830s. Darmanin used the anglicized Joseph (J) Darmanin to better cater for the steady flow of British Grand Tourists heading, through Malta, to North Africa, the Levant (eastern Mediterranean), and India. By 1851, the firm's reputation had become so well established that it represented Malta that year at the Great Exhibition in London, where it was awarded an "Honorable Mention" in the judges report for the excellence of its workmanship.

top ca. 1825-36, base ca. 1837-40   35½in (90cm) diam

$25,000-37,000   WW

A William IV mahogany occasional table, the specimen top inlaid with radiating sections, on a fluted column with carved acanthus terminal above a triform base, on scrolled feet.

26in (66cm) diam
$3,700-5,000   **CHEF**

A William IV verre églomisé and giltwood tilt-top occasional table, the top with reverse painting of floral sprays, above a lappet-carved stem and triform base ending in scrolled feet, knocks, later painting, movement in joints, some worm.

ca. 1835   *29½in (75cm) high*
$1,400-1,700   **DN**

A pair of mahogany lamp tables, early-19thC and later, the fixed tops on ribbed stems and brass casters.

28¾in (73cm) high
$1,500-1,700   **WW**

An early-Victorian cedar occasional table, of Naval interest, made from wood from the wrecked schooner "Columbine," the underside with a printed paper label outlining the circumstances of the shipwreck.

ca. 1838-40   *28¾in (73cm) high*
$500-625   **WW**

A set of four early-19thC late-Georgian mahogany nesting tables, the tops with a cock-beaded edge, above ring-turned legs, on trestle bases joined by curved stretchers.

29½in (75cm) high
$875-1,000   **L&T**

An early-19thC quartetto nest of satinwood occasional tables, with ebonized stringing, the beaded tops with kingwood banding, on ring-turned legs.

27¼in (69cm) high
$1,400-1,600   **WW**

A mid-19thC Victorian mahogany coaching table, with a hinged top, on scroll supports with turned stretchers.

39½in (100.5cm) wide (open)
$625-750   **WW**

A 19thC French mahogany and gilt-metal-mounted kidney-shaped bijouterie table, the hinged top with a bevel glass insert, on square supports and an undertier, on cabriole legs ending in sabots.

30¾in (78cm) high
$625-750   **L&T**

A Victorian specimen wood occasional table, with ebonized decoration, the top inlaid with a parquetry star.

ca. 1870   *18½in (47cm) high*
$500-625   **WW**

A Victorian Gothic oak occasional table, in the manner of Julius Yacoby, the top inlaid with interlaced star parquetry, on pierced trefoil, leaf, and berry column supports united by a cruciform stretcher, on ceramic casters.

Julius Yacoby was listed in Kelly's "Post Office Directory" of 1877 as an "Art Furniture Manufacturer, Cabinet Maker, Specialist for Carved oak Furniture … Parquet Flooring Manufacturer." He exhibited at the International Exhibition in Paris in 1867.

ca. 1870-80

27¼in (69cm) high

$800-950 WW

A late-19thC Victorian gilt and gesso bijouterie table, with rockwork and C-scroll molding, on molded cabriole legs with scrolled toes, cracking in the gesso, gilding restored, small losses in the carved decoration.

30¾in (78cm) wide

$1,400-1,700 TEN

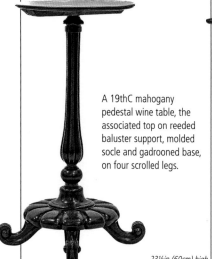

A 19thC mahogany pedestal wine table, the associated top on reeded baluster support, molded socle and gadrooned base, on four scrolled legs.

23½in (60cm) high

$750-875 TEN

A late-19thC mahogany silver table, in George II style, the molded serpentine-edged top above a pierced frieze, on claw-and-ball feet.

31in (79cm) wide

$500-625 WW

A late-19thC French kingwood and ormolu-mounted table ambulant, in Louis XV/Transitional style, the brèche de Saint-Maximin marble top above a parquetry frieze, on cabriole legs, with foliate mounts and sabots, marble top with repair.

29½in (75cm) high

$800-950 TEN

An Edwardian mahogany-strung and crossbanded bookcase-table, with 24 volumes of "Punch Library of Humour," The Educational Book Co. Ltd.

17¾in (45cm) wide

$625-750 WHP

A late-19th/early-20thC Anglo-Indian shisham, brass, and ebony-inlaid occasional table, probably Lahore, with a center star and scrolling leaves and flowers, the top above carved and pierced panels.

20in (50.5cm) high

$875-1,000 WW

A pair of mid-20thC gilt-brass occasional tables, in Regency style, veneered with Indian rosewood, on casters.

25in (63.5cm) high

$1,900-2,500 WW

ESSENTIAL REFERENCE—LOW DRESSERS

The name "dresser" is derived from the French "dressoir," a medieval piece of furniture used either as a sideboard for serving food and wine, or in the service quarters for preparing and serving food and for storing dishes and utensils.

● Early dressers consisted simply of a side table with drawers supported on turned legs. Some of these had stretchers between the legs, and in the 16thC this base structure often became the framework for a low open shelf (or "potboard").

● From the early-17thC onward, alternatives began to appear in which, instead of an open shelf below the drawers, either cupboards were fitted, or a pair of cupboards at each side flanking additional drawers in the center.

● Around the middle of the 17thC, the fashion for not only eating off, but also displaying, decorative tin-glazed earthenware gathered momentum. This resulted in the "delft rack"—a tall superstructure of open shelves on which to display tin-glazed delftware—being added to the top of the dresser.

● Although dressers with or without this superstructure are technically all still dressers, in the furniture and antiques trades, those with it are, in general, referred to as dressers, while those without have, retrospectively, become low dressers.

A William and Mary oak dresser base.
ca. 1690   *78¾in (200cm) wide*
$6,000-7,500   **DN**

An oak dresser base, the top above three pine-lined drawers, on turned and block forelegs, some fading, scratches, old splits, decay in the backboards, metal strengthening.
ca. 1700   *77½in (197cm) wide*
$2,700-3,200   **TEN**

A mid-18thC George II oak dresser base, the rear legs with carved 17thC elements, marks, scratches, old repairs, fading.
71¾in (182cm) wide
$3,100-3,700   **DN**

A mid-18thC oak dresser base, the three-plank top over three molded drawers, on tapered front legs and pad feet, knocks, locks replaced, signs of restoration.
85½in (217cm) wide
$1,900-2,500   **CHEF**

A mid-18thC oak dresser base, the molded top over three drawers, above a shaped apron, on front tapered legs and pad feet, scratches, minor warping, historic worm, repairs.
79½in (202cm) wide
$1,250-1,900   **CHEF**

An oak potboard dresser base, 18thC in part, the top above three frieze drawers with brass backplate handles and escutcheons, on turned and block forelegs joined by a potboard, waxed finish, top with splits, faults and old decay in rear legs.
70in (178cm) wide
$3,700-5,000   **TEN**

An 18thC oak dresser base, the five drawers with scrolled inlay, on turned front legs, joined by stretchers.
50in (127cm) wide
$700-800   **WHP**

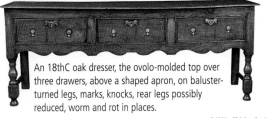

An 18thC oak dresser, the ovolo-molded top over three drawers, above a shaped apron, on baluster-turned legs, marks, knocks, rear legs possibly reduced, worm and rot in places.
84¼in (214cm) wide
$3,100-3,700   **CHEF**

An 18thC oak and elm dresser base, the molded top above three drawers over one smaller drawer, with a shaped apron, on cabriole legs with pad feet.
74in (188cm) wide
$2,200-2,700   **CHEF**

FURNITURE

An oak dresser, late-17thC and later, the molded cornice above four enclosed plate shelves flanked by arched recesses, the base with fielded panel doors and drawers, on stile feet.

81in (206cm) high

$1,400-1,700   **L&T**

An early- to mid-18thC Shropshire oak dresser, with three plate racks, above six drawers, the base with drawers and cupboard doors, one interior shelf a replacment.

82¼in (209cm) high

$3,100-3,700   **SWO**

An early-George III oak dresser, the architectural plate rack with fluted pilasters and pierced scroll corbels, the base with ten panel drawers and a pair of cupboard doors.

ca. 1760-70   *84¼in (214cm) high*

$7,000-8,000   **WW**

An 18thC elm dresser, the molded cornice above a boarded plate rack with display hooks, the bottom section with three drawers over two paneled cupboard doors.

74in (188cm) wide

$5,000-6,200   **CHEF**

A late-18thC George III oak and fruitwood banded dresser, the molded cornice above a frieze over three enclosed shelves, flanked by bowfront shelved niches over fielded panel cupboards and spice drawers, the base with three drawers, over four fielded panel doors and two drawers, on ogee bracket feet.

86½in (220cm) high

$4,300-5,000   **L&T**

A late-18thC George III oak dresser, the plate rack with three shelves, the base with three frieze drawers above paneled doors.

74¾in (190cm) wide

$1,400-1,600   **WW**

A late-18thC pale elm shelf-back dresser, with a shaped canopy on the plate rack, with three drawers and cupboards below.

4¾in (190cm) high

$950-1,050   **CHEF**

An 18thC oak dresser, later adapted, with a rack and four drawers, over drawers and cupboards, spice drawers are fixed open due to former store use.

89¼in (227cm) high

$950-1,050   **SWO**

A late-18thC George III oak and mahogany banded dresser, the dentil-molded cornice with a wavy frieze, above three shelves flanked by scalloped niche shelves and cupboards, the base with two drawers centered by a cupboard with shell paterae-inlaid doors and reeded quarter columns, on cabriole legs and pad feet.

82in (208cm) high

$1,400-1,700   **L&T**

A late-18thC George III Welsh oak dresser.

74½in (189cm) wide

$625-750   **WW**

A 19thC oak dresser, the breakfront base with two drawers over two dummy drawers, with two long drawers and doors, general wear.

81in (206cm) high

$625-750   **SWO**

An 18th/19thC oak Welsh dresser, the top with molded cornice above three shelves, flanked on each side by a niche shelf and paneled cupboard door, the lower section with three drawers over a shaped frieze, marks, wear.

95¾in (243cm) wide

$1,400-1,700   **CHEF**

An 18th/19thC French carved chestnut dresser, with a boarded plate rack above a foliate-decorated base, with two drawers and cupboard doors, splits, worm.

82¾in (210cm) high

$1,200-1,350   **SWO**

A 17thC oak livery cupboard, with a bog oak and holly chevron band and carved decoration.

60½in (153.5cm) high

$700-800   **WW**

A 17thC oak cupboard, with a pair of paneled doors, enclosing shelves.

62¾in (159.5cm) high

$950-1,050   **WW**

An oak livery cupboard, 17thC and later, the frieze and cornice with geometric and scrolling decoration, above doors carved with leaf and diamond motifs, the interior with hanging rail, iron hinges and hook latch, damage, worm, replacement back legs.

70in (178cm) high

$1,250-1,500   **LC**

An early-18thC joined and carved oak Westmorland livery cupboard, the doors carved with lunettes and flowers, the base with two real and two dummy drawers, carved stiles and muntins.

74¾in (190cm) high

$875-1,000   **TEN**

FURNITURE

An oak court cupboard, the carved frieze with S-scroll decoration bearing the date "1734," with a panel flanked by two doors, the lower section with two drawers and two cupboard doors.

50in (127cm) wide

$450-500 CHEF

An early-18thC oak livery cupboard, the cupboard doors enclosing a later brass hanging pole, the base with four dummy drawers above four real drawers, some deep scratches, later brasses, minor decay in base.

73¼in (186cm) high

$2,500-3,700 TEN

A mid-18thC Georgian mahogany standing corner cupboard, the cornice and blind fret frieze over a pair of doors, with twin arched fielded panels, the interior with a scallop shell, the base with a pair of paneled doors.

91¼in (232cm) high

$1,250-1,700 HT

A French Louis XVI kingwood and marquetry secretaire abattant, by François Bayer, with ormolu mounts and inlaid with woods, including purpleheart and fruitwoods, with latticework, panels of ribbon-tied musical trophies and an urn, the marble top above a frieze drawer and a hinged fall, the interior with six drawers and a later leather writing surface, the base with a pair of cupboard doors, enclosing a shelf.

François Bayer was made Maitre on the 5 December 1764.

ca. 1780 *54½in (138.5cm) high*
$5,000-6,200 WW

A George III oak cupboard.
ca. 1780 *74½in (189cm) high*
$1,900-2,500 DN

A Georgian oak cupboard, the double arch-top doors with three short and two long drawers below, drawer handles replaced.

52¾in (134cm) wide
$950-1,050 CHEF

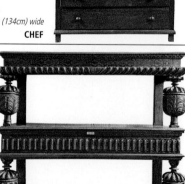

A carved and joined oak and marquetry inlaid court cupboard, early 17thC and later, with ivorine label "FROM THE BREADALBANE APARTMENTS, THE PALACE OF HOLYROOD HOUSE, movement in joints.

51¼in (130cm) wide
$2,500-3,100 TEN

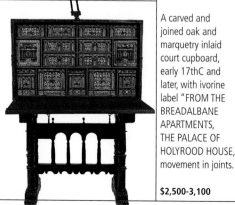

A mid-17thC Spanish walnut vargueno, the flap enclosing 15 drawers, the arcaded stand carved with masks, rust, scratches, one ivory drawer front roundel missing, the feet rotted in places.

44½in (113cm) wide
$8,500-10,000 CHOR

A mid- to late-19thC French ebonized, brass-inlaid and gilt-metal-mounted meuble d'appui, the Carrara marble top above a cupboard door, inlaid with acanthus scrolls and urns, with caryatid mounts.

44in (112cm) high

$700-800   **TEN**

An Italian walnut credenza/linen press, in Renaissance style, in the manner of Luigi Frullini (1839-97), Florence, the frieze with leaves and shell motifs above paneled doors with strapwork, a pair of fauns flanking a lion mask, with three figural terms, the interior with a shelf, the base with a drawer.

ca. 1880   *52¾in (134cm) wide*

$2,000-2,500   **WW**

A George II mahogany clothes press, in the manner of Giles Grendey, the doors enclosing three sliding trays, cracks, later elements, repairs, top sliding tray is missing.

The serpentine paneled doors and overall form of this clothes press relate to a clothes press bearing the trade label of Giles Grendey (see page 222), cabinetmaker of St. John's Square, Clerkenwell. See Ralph Edwards and Margaret Jourdain, "Georgian Cabinet-Makers," Country Life (1955), figure 51.

ca. 1750   *71½in (181.5cm) high*

$5,000-6,200   **DN**

A mid-18thC George II North Country mahogany linen press, in the manner of Gillows, with fielded panel doors, enclosing three later shelves, flanked by stop-fluted pilasters, above three long drawers, on ogee bracket feet.

73½in (186.5cm) high

$2,500-3,700   **WW**

An early George III mahogany linen press, Chippendale period, the dentil cornice above a pair of paneled doors enclosing four mahogany slides, above two short and two long drawers, on shaped bracket feet.

ca. 1770   *80¼in (204cm) high*

$2,500-3,700   **WW**

A George III figured mahogany clothes press, in the manner of Thomas Chippendale.

ca. 1780   *72¾in (184.5cm) high*

$5,000-6,200   **DN**

A George III mahogany linen press, the cornice above paneled doors enclosing slides, the lower section with three cock-beaded drawers, splits, doors slightly bowed, some cock beading replaced.

72in (183cm) high

$1,000-1,100   **CHEF**

A George III mahogany linen press, with dentil-molded cornice and fluted frieze, the doors enclosing an adapted interior for clothes hanging, the lower section with two short over two long drawers, with brass scroll handles, minor splits, possible repairs, feet are knocked and with restoration.

ca. 1800   *77¼in (196cm) high*

$1,900-2,500   **CHEF**

FURNITURE

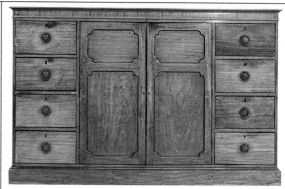

A matched pair of mid-19thC mahogany dwarf linen presses, each top above a pair of doors, one with five sliding trays, the other only one tray, with two drawers below.

50½in (128cm) high

$1,900-2,500   **TEN**

An early-19thC Regency mahogany and ebony banded linen press, the doors enclosing four sliding trays, flanked by eight deep drawers, scratches, small veneer losses.

74in (188cm) wide

$750-875   **TEN**

An early-19thC Regency mahogany linen press, attributed to Gillows, with reeded edge above panel doors, enclosing four oak-lined sliding trays, flanked by eight small drawers, fading, bruises, scratches, veneer losses, lock removed from center cupboard doors.

78in (198cm) wide

$3,700-5,000   **TEN**

An early-to-mid-19thC Dutch mahogany linen press.

83½in (212cm) high

$1,900-2,500   **DN**

A mid-19thC George IV mahogany linen press, the arched pediment centered by swags, dentil cornice and cupboard doors below, enclosing five oak-lined sliding trays, the base with two short over two long oak-lined drawers, later handles, faults, losses.

85½in (217cm) high

$1,250-1,500   **TEN**

A mahogany linen press, with associated late-18thC elements, the doors enclosing a hanging space, the base with two short and three long drawers.

87½in (222cm) high

$450-550   **DN**

A 19thC Dutch mahogany linen press, inlaid with stringing, satinwood banding, and Classical marquetry with ribbon-tied urns, the cornice with a giltwood figure of "Victory" and a pair of lion masks, the doors enclosing five slides, above two short and two long drawers.

91in (231cm) high

$1,700-2,200   **WW**

A 19thC Dutch mahogany and pine-lined press, the pediment above a panel with ebonized leaves and scrolls, molded cupboard doors with column supports with gilt-metal capitals, the base with three drawers.

98in (249cm) high

$1,700-2,200   **TEN**

ESSENTIAL REFERENCE—ARMOIRES

Like cupboards, linen presses, and wardrobes—to which they're closely related in terms of their basic structure—armoires are a form of carcass or case furniture.

- The French word "armoire" evolved from the Old French word "armarie," which, in turn, came from the Latin "armarium," meaning "a chest or cupboard for storing tools and arms."
- The armoire's initial existence as a weapons and tool store meant they were almost invariably of large and robust construction—characteristics that, for the most part, they retained after the transition to clothing storage.
- Most armoires are fronted with a pair of full-height doors—again a legacy of the ease of access required for weapons storage—but some examples have two pairs of half-height doors, and others, notably examples made in the Netherlands in the 18thC, have pairs of half- or two-thirds-height doors above drawers.
- Many armoires are of provincial (instead of city or urban) origin, and as such made of locally available instead of imported woods. Typical examples include cherry, chestnut, walnut, elm, and oak.
- While most city- or urban-made armoires, especially from the mid-18thC on, were fashioned in the prevailing decorative styles, such as Neoclassical or, later, Classical Revival, during the 18thC and 19thC, most provincial armoires retained the basic form established in the 17thC, onto which had been grafted mid-18thC Rococo motifs. This provincial style "fusion" remained popular long after the Rococo taste had been discarded in favor of Neoclassicism in the mid-18thC, and that "fashion-lag" is part of the charm of provincial armoires, in particular, and provincial furniture, in general.

An early-18thC paneled oak wardrobe, the doors with brass fittings, with a vacant interior, above two inlaid drawers, losses, splits, worm, damage on brass handle.

69¾in (177cm) high

$875-1,000 LC

A George III mahogany wardrobe, in the manner of Thomas Chippendale, the molded panel doors opening to a hanging rail, sun fading, cracks, veneer tears, later elements, some bowing.

ca. 1770 *80¾in (205cm) high*

$3,100-3,700 DN

A George III mahogany wardrobe, in the manner of Thomas Chippendale, with a later hanging rail, minor fading, later elements, one foot with carved front element detached but present.

ca. 1780 *79¼in (201cm) high*

$2,500-3,100 DN

A William IV mahogany wardrobe, with six drawers in the center flanked by hanging compartments, with cluster column pilasters, fitted with Bramah locks, splits, scratches, chips, knocks, molding replacements, casters later.

101¼in (257cm) wide

$2,000-2,500 CHEF

An early-20thC Edwardian mahogany breakfront compactum wardrobe, inlaid with stringing and satinwood banding, with interiors of brass rails and hooks, the base with a hinged compartment.

84¾in (215.5cm) high

$1,050-1,200 WW

An early-18thC Louis XIV ebony and brass-inlaid armoire, of "chapeau de gendarme" form, the glazed and fabric-lined doors enclosing shelves, later elements, old repairs on brass inlay, wear, marks.

96in (244cm) high

$25,000-31,000 DN

A late-18th/early-19thC North Italian walnut, ebonized and "Certazina" bone-inlaid armoire, possibly Tyrolean, worm, knocks, scratches, small losses, later elements.

The back with paper labels for "The Rt Hon the EARL OF DUICE, Date Rec 7/10 40, Depos No :- 7795, WALTER CARTER, MANCHESTER."

85½in (217cm) high

$11,000-14,000 DN

A 16thC chestnut coffer, the hinged top with molding, the interior with a lidded till, the front with a pair of strapwork panels flanking a stylized coat of arms with rampant lions above a sun motif, with a heart and a pair of lion heads.

57¾in (146.5cm) wide

$1,700-2,000   **WW**

A 17thC joined oak chest, the lid enclosing a vacant interior above a guilloche-carved frieze, the stiles carved as stylized flowers, with strapwork and carved panels below, on stile feet, carved "IM MB" and dated "1663," old decay, splits, hinges replaced, lock removed.

51¼in (130cm) wide

$875-1,000   **TEN**

A carved oak coffer, mid-17thC and later, in Gothic style.

52¼in (133cm) wide

$1,250-1,500   **DN**

An oak coffer, 17thC and later, with a triple-paneled lid above a strapwork frieze, with a center arched panel, flanked by flower heads and guilloche borders.

50in (127cm) wide

$550-700   **WW**

A late-17thC Italian Adige carved cedarwood, poker-work and ebonized chest, the underside of the hinged top with conforming decoration, some damage.

74in (188cm) wide

$2,500-3,700   **DN**

CLOSER LOOK—A 16THC GERMAN CHEST

The chest is assembled from planks of oak, a hard, coarse-grain, dense, and durable wood. Used in solid form since before the Middle Ages for the construction of provincial furniture, it is light yellowy-brown in color when cut, and subsequently darkens with age, staining, or both.

The basic pegged-tenon construction of the oak planks is further reinforced by "wrap-around" wrought iron straps secured by convex-head iron nails or studs driven into the wood—hence, the German name "stollentruhe" (stud chest) for carcass furniture, such as this, and of a type particularly associated with the Westphalia region of Germany.

In addition to their structural function, both the iron lockplate and "wrap-around" straps play a significant decorative role—the straps terminating in stylized floral "cinqfoils"; the lockplate radiating spade finials (often a symbol of nobility).

Carved with stylized, scrolling floral-foliate motifs, the long feet of the chest raise it well above floor level to protect the base of the chest and, ergo, its contents, from any damp present in the underlying (often stone) floor.

A 16thC German Westphalian oak and iron-mounted chest or stollentruhe, with floral strapwork mounts and carved scrolls on the front and feet, the lid revealing a vacant interior with a lidded till.

71½in (181.5cm) wide

$5,000-6,200   **WW**

A Charles II oak coffer, the twin-paneled top on pin hinges, with a till, the front with a frieze, above panels with carved lozenge decoration.

ca. 1680   *44½in (113cm) wide*

$625-750   **WW**

A boarded oak coffer, mid-17thC and later, the later lid above a thumbnail-decorated front, on cutout ends.

26¾in (68cm) wide

$300-375   **WW**

A 17thC oak coffer, later adapted and reduced in size, the hinged top over a chip-carved front panel, with flower motifs and a large iron lockplate.

26in (66cm) wide

$625-750   **L&T**

A 17thC West Country coffer, initialed "RL" and dated "1693," the front carved with flowering urns with scrolling borders, on a later terra-cotta lacquered ground, cut down, splits, repairs, alterations.

47¼in (120cm) wide

$1,050-1,200   **LC**

A late-17thC oak paneled coffer, the four-paneled hinged top with iron loop hinges, on stile feet.

55in (140cm) wide

$300-375   **CHEF**

An Italian walnut and polychrome painted cassone, 17thC and later.

65¼in (165.5cm) wide

$2,500-3,100   **DN**

An early-18thC carved oak coffer, with hinged top, the interior with candlebox, the front panels carved with architectural niches within foliate borders, on stile feet.

43in (109cm) wide

$750-875   **L&T**

An early-18thC West Country boarded elm coffer, the hinged lid above an arcaded front incised with flowers and the date "1714," on cutout ends.

44¼in (112.5cm) wide

$1,600-2,000   **WW**

An early-George III mahogany silver or blanket chest, the hinged lid with a caddy-molded edge, with a brass escutcheon and side brass carrying handles.

ca. 1760   49½in (125.5cm) wide

$1,400-1,600   **WW**

ESSENTIAL REFERENCE—EGYPTIAN REVIVAL

The decorative arts of Western civilization have witnessed a number of major revivals of interest in the architecture, art, and ornament of Egypt, which began during the Classical Roman era of Julius Caesar and Anthony and Cleopatra.

- The most notable of those revivals accompanied the archaeological excavations of Roman sites during the 18thC; the further discoveries made by French archaeologists traveling with the French emperor Napoleon's military campaigns against the British in Egypt around the turn of the 19thC; and, more than 100 years later, the discovery in 1922 of the Pharoah Tutankhamen's hitherto lost tomb.
- However, when recounting those huge, fashion-changing spikes of interest in all-things-Egyptian, it's easy to overlook some of the slightly less prominent but no less authentic or enduring manifestations of "Egyptiana" that have regularly surfaced in between.
- For example, Owen Jones, one of the 19thC's most influential designers (in both theory and practice), published his seminal work "The Grammar of Ornament" in 1858. A historical and global sourcebook, it included large sections on the Egyptian vocabulary of ornament and has never been out of print since.
- Seven years before publication, in 1851, Jones was appointed Superintendent of the Works of the Great Exhibition, and in 1852 joint Director of Decoration of the Crystal Palace. When this building was moved to Sydenham, Jones designed the Egyptian, Greek, Roman, and Alhambra courts for it, and the monumental centerpiece of the Egyptian Court incorporated decorative elements found on the Egyptian Revival coffer shown here—most notably the use of contrasting dark and light wood.
- As for inspiration and authenticity, the form and inlay of this Egyptian Revival coffer closely relate to those of an excavated jewelry chest and a cosmetics coffer from the 12th Egyptian Dynasty of ca. 1991-1778 BC.

An 18thC North Italian walnut cassone, the molded hinged top above a paneled front carved with foliage between panels, marks, scratches, worm, split in top, general wear.

67¼in (171cm) wide

$5,500-6,000   **DN**

An English Egyptian Revival coffer, in the manner of Owen Jones, walnut, sycamore, and ebony with brass fittings.

ca. 1870   28¾in (73cm) wide

$1,600-2,000   **L&T**

FURNITURE

A Charles II oak chest-of-drawers, with two short and three long geometrically molded and fielded drawers, on a plinth base and turned feet, scratches, splits, later elements, woodworm.

ca. 1670   *39¾in (101cm) wide*

$6,000-7,500   **DN**

A Charles II oak, walnut, and snakewood chest, in two halves, with applied split moldings, ivory rondels, and cedar moldings, with three drawers with geometric paneled fronts.

Ivory Act certification no. 2FCWBS8R

ca. 1680   *38½in (97.5cm) wide*

$3,100-3,700   **WW**

A late-17thC oak chest-of-drawers, in two parts, with two straight and two conforming two-as-one geometric molded drawers with applied mounts, old decay, splits, block feet are replacements.

41in (104cm) wide

$875-1,000   **TEN**

A William and Mary oak chest-of-drawers, basically 17thC, the top above four drawers with geometric moldings, handles replaced, minor restorations.

38½in (98cm) wide

$550-700   **DUK**

A late-17thC William and Mary walnut chest, with four drawers with paneled fronts.

34½in (87.5cm) wide

$1,600-2,000   **WW**

Judith Picks

Sometimes seemingly bad news isn't so bad after all. For example, the bun feet on this ca. 1690 William and Mary chest-of-drawers are not the originals—they are later replacements. However, in terms of both style and proportion, they are a good match, plus they show in their patina pleasing signs of age. The escutcheons and the handles also appear to be later replacements—they are of a slightly thinner gauge brass, and their gilding insufficiently dulled by age than might be expected of ca. 1690 originals. However, they fit what appear to be the original holes in the drawer fronts, and that brighter, fresher gilding does help to better convey what the chest would have looked like to its original owners. What is more, in my mind, all of the aforementioned does not in any way detract from the delightful proportions of the chest nor —especially—the wonderful oyster-veneered olivewood draw fronts. Developed in the late 17thC, oyster veneering involved slicing transversely across the end grain of smaller branches of wood (in this case olivewood, but walnut, kingwood, and laburnum were often used) to create thin veneers with a figuring and grain that resembled opened-out oyster shells—an eye-catching novelty ca. 1690, and just as eye-catching today.

A late-17thC William and Mary oyster-veneered olivewood chest, with holly and maple banding, the top inlaid with lobed rondel designs, above two short and three long drawers, on later bracket feet.

38¾in (98.5cm) wide

$3,100-3,700   **WW**

A William and Mary olivewood oyster-veneered chest-of-drawers, later elements throughout, old cracks, splits, marks, and staining.

ca. 1690   *37¾in (96cm) wide*

$15,000-22,000   **DN**

A William and Mary walnut chest-of-drawers, with floral and bird marquetry in ebony, walnut, and bone, veneer splits, marquetry losses, later elements, worm.

ca. 1690   *38½in (98cm) wide*

$4,300-5,000   **DN**

A William and Mary olivewood oyster-veneered chest-of-drawers, with holly line inlay, marks, scratches, old splits and chips, old repairs.
ca. 1690   *31½in (80cm) wide*
$12,500-15,000   **DN**

A William and Mary walnut and feather-banded chest-of-drawers, knocks, old splits, losses, worm, repairs, and replacements.
ca. 1690   *38¼in (97cm) wide*
$3,700-5,000   **DN**

A William and Mary figured walnut and feather-banded chest-of-drawers, knocks, scratches, repairs and replacements, worm.
ca. 1690   *37½in (95cm) wide*
$3,700-5,000   **DN**

A William and Mary walnut chest-of-drawers, in the manner of Gerrit Jensen, the sides with arched seaweed and bird marquetry, scratches, knocks, repairs, and replacements.
ca. 1690   *40in (101.5cm) wide*
$27,000-35,000   **DN**

An oyster-veneered chest-of-drawers, 17thC and later veneered, in William and Mary style, the top above two short and two long drawers, on later turned feet.
33½in (85cm) wide
$875-1,000   **TEN**

A Queen Anne walnut and feather-banded chest-of-drawers, of unusual compact proportions, repairs in moldings and veneers, later elements, worm.
ca. 1710   *26in (66cm) wide*
$5,500-6,000   **DN**

An early-18thC Queen Anne walnut chest, inlaid with boxwood stringing, the top above two short and three long drawers, on later bun feet.
39½in (100.5cm) wide
$950-1,050   **WW**

A George I walnut chest-of-drawers, the top with crossbanding, above two short and three long drawers, with brass swing handles and escutcheons, on bracket feet.
39¼in (100cm) wide
$1,600-2,000   **DUK**

A George I walnut bachelor's chest, with cross- and feather banding, the hinged fold-over top with a caddy-molded edge, above two short and three long graduated drawers, with engraved brass swing handles, on shaped bracket feet.
ca. 1720   *29¼in (74cm) wide*
$5,500-6,000   **WW**

A George II burl walnut bachelor's chest-of-drawers, the hinged top opening to a baize inset writing surface, and a hinged compartment opening to an inkwell above a small drawer, baize is later, various old repairs.

ca. 1730   *32¼in (82cm) wide*
$8,000-9,500   **DN**

A George II walnut, burl walnut, burl yew, and feather-banded bachelor's chest-of-drawers, of unusual small proportions, with brushing slide, repairs, splits, veneer losses, worm.

ca. 1730   *22¾in (58cm) wide*
$3,700-5,000   **DN**

A George II walnut bachelor's chest, crossbanded and inlaid with stringing, the fold-over top above two short and three long drawers, on bracket feet.

ca. 1735   *29in (73.5cm) wide*
$3,100-3,700   **WW**

A George II walnut chest-of-drawers, cracks, veneer repairs, worm, later elements.

ca. 1735   *33½in (85cm) wide*
$2,500-3,100   **DN**

A mid-18thC George II mahogany serpentine dressing chest, the top above four drawers, the top drawer fitted with divisions and compartments, between blind-fret-carved angles, on bracket feet, with later casters.

46¾in (119cm) wide
$1,500-1,700   **DUK**

A George II mahogany bachelor's chest, the hinged fold-over top above two short and three long graduated drawers, with brass ring pulls, on bracket feet.

ca. 1750   *34in (86.5cm) wide*
$2,100-2,500   **WW**

A mid-18thC Georgian mahogany chest, the top over two short and four long cock-beaded drawers, with swan-neck handles, flanked by fluted quarter columns, on bracket feet.

43¼in (110cm) wide
$1,400-1,600   **HT**

A George II mahogany bachelor's chest-of-drawers, with a hinged top, repairs, scratches, replacements, worm.

ca. 1750   *29in (73.5cm) wide*
$3,700-5,000   **DN**

A mid-18thC George II walnut chest-of-drawers.

30¾in (78cm) wide
$8,000-9,500   **DN**

FURNITURE

A mid-18thC George II mahogany chest-of-drawers, with brushing slide, losses, restorations, repairs, later elements.

31in (79cm) wide

$3,100-4,300 DN

A mid-18thC mahogany chest-of-drawers, the top above two short over three long cock-beaded drawers, flanked by blind-fret-canted corners, knocks, splits, repairs.

43¼in (110cm) wide

$1,250-1,500 CHEF

A George II red walnut chest, with two short and three long drawers, on bracket feet.

ca. 1750-60 *41¼in (105cm) wide*

$1,500-1,700 WW

Judith Picks

Dressing chests have become few and far between these days, so when this mid-18thC example came up for auction recently, it reminded me of just how much I like them. I do have one myself. I bought it 45 years ago and it's stayed with me, through five house moves, ever since. It's slightly earlier, larger, and more elaborate than this one—mine has a serpentine-profile top and drawer fronts—but in its essential top-drawer "dressing" components it's nearly identical. For any of you unfamiliar with these chests, I should point out that when you open the top drawer, the hinged, pull-up dressing mirror and the surrounding array of open-top and lidded compartments you see in this picture are not visible. Instead, they are completely concealed under a green- or red-baized (mine's green) slide. Left in-situ, the latter can serve as an additional worktop, but when the drawer is fully pulled out the slide can be pushed back into the carcass to reveal the dressing components below. Obviously, the mirror is very useful when dressing, as are the compartments for all the paraphernalia (brushes, makeup, jewelry, etc.) that goes with that. Ultimately, however, it isn't just the functionality of my dressing chest that has made me enduringly fond of it, it's also—and I guess I'm "speaking" on behalf of the inner child in me here—the thrill of all those secret compartments!

A mid-18thC Georgian mahogany chest, the caddy top over a slide and four graduated cock-beaded drawers, with brass drop handles, on bracket feet.

29¾in (75.5cm) wide

$700-800 HT

A George III mahogany chest-of-drawers, splits, fading, worm, backboard an old replacement.

ca. 1760 *29¼in (74.5cm) wide*

$3,100-3,700 DN

A George III mahogany serpentine chest-of-drawers, with a slide, the drawers flanked by stop-fluted columns, some replacement beading, worm, handles and escutcheons are later.

ca. 1770 *44in (112cm) wide*

$4,300-5,600 DN

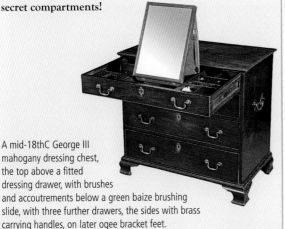

A mid-18thC George III mahogany dressing chest, the top above a fitted dressing drawer, with brushes and accoutrements below a green baize brushing slide, with three further drawers, the sides with brass carrying handles, on later ogee bracket feet.

34¼in (87cm) wide

$3,700-5,000 DUK

An early-George III mahogany chest, the caddy top above a brushing slide and four graduating drawers, on ogee bracket feet, scuffing on feet, replacement section on foot.

37¾in (96cm) wide

$2,100-2,500 CHEF

A George III mahogany and oak-lined bachelor's chest, the top above a pull-out brushing slide, with four graduated drawers, with pierced brass handles and escutcheons, on bracket feet, top drawer faded, scratches, splits, feet have later elements.

ca. 1780

$4,300-5,000　　　　　　　　*31½in (80cm) wide*

TEN

An 18thC French kingwood and crossbanded chest-of-drawers, the top over three long drawers, with later brass rope twist loop handles, veneer losses, splits, lifting, and repairs, knocks.

51¼in (130cm) wide

$1,100-1,250　　　**CHEF**

A George III mahogany bowfront chest, with a brushing slide above four graduated drawers, with lion-head brass handles, on outswept bracket feet.

37½in (95cm) wide

$1,500-1,900　　　**CHEF**

A walnut and boxwood ebony-strung and oak-side chest-of-drawers, 18thC elements, the quarter-veneered and crossbanded top above three short and three long oak lined drawers, on later bracket feet, split, restoration of the drawer linings, later backboards.

30¼in (77cm) wide

$1,600-1,900　　　　　　　　**TEN**

A late-18thC George III mahogany and oak-lined chest-of-drawers, the top above two short and three long graduated drawers, on bracket feet.

34¼in (87cm) wide

$1,400-1,600　　　　　　　　**TEN**

A late-18thC George III mahogany chest-of-drawers, the top above a pull-out brushing slide with three drawers below, ring marks, splits, later bracket feet, minor veneer lifting.

35¼in (89.5cm) wide

$1,500-1,700　　　　　　　　**TEN**

A late-18thC Dutch marquetry chest-of-drawers, the top quarter veneered with crossbanding, above two short and two long drawers, all with floral marquetry inlay.

38½in (98cm) wide

$1,000-1,100　　　　　　　　**DUK**

A late-18thC George III mahogany chest, with a brushing slide, above four graduated drawers.

34¼in (87cm) wide

$750-875　　　　　　　　**WW**

A George III mahogany chest-of-drawers, with two short and three long drawers, on bracket feet.

ca. 1790　　　　　　　　*32¼in (82cm) wide*

$1,400-1,600　　　　　　　　**WW**

A George III mahogany dressing chest, attributed to Gillows, with boxwood edging, the top drawer with a baize-lined slide revealing lidded compartments and divisions, above three long drawers, on slender French bracket feet.

ca. 1790   41½in (105.5cm) wide
$1,400-1,600   WW

A late-18thC George III mahogany serpentine chest-of-drawers.

43in (109cm) wide
$3,100-4,300   DN

A burl walnut and feather-banded chest-of-drawers, 18thC and later, in the manner of Giles Grendey, with a brushing slide.

33in (84cm) high
$4,300-5,600   DN

A late-18thC George III mahogany serpentine-fronted chest-of-drawers.

43¾in (111cm) wide
$2,500-3,100   DN

A late-18th/early-19thC Italian ebonized and marquetry secretaire chest, possibly Florence, the secretaire drawer with fittings, restorations, and repairs, some veneer lifting, worm, later elements.

55½in (141cm) wide
$4,300-5,600   DN

ESSENTIAL REFERENCE—WELLINGTON CHESTS

Essentially a form of chest-of-drawers, what soon became known as a Wellington chest was introduced in the 1820s and originally intended to house a collection of coins or similar precious artifacts. It acquired its name from the Duke of Wellington, whose successful campaigns against the French Emperor Napoleon, culminating in victory at the Battle of Waterloo in 1815, had made him a national hero. Wellington ordered one of the first of these chests, and commissioned it to have seven drawers, one for each day of the week. While many subsequent Wellington chests also had seven drawers, there were many variations in that respect, with some, such as the example shown here, having up to 12 drawers. Other variations include a secretaire drawer (sometimes of double-drawer height) in the middle. However, characteristics all Wellington chests have in common are that they're tall and narrow, have a plinthlike base, and have stiles (uprights, sometimes of columnar form) attached to each side of the drawers; one of the stiles (although occasionally both) is hinged to cover the drawer ends at one side, which enables the chest to be locked. While the majority of Wellingtons were in mahogany or rosewood, pollard oak, burl walnut, burl elm, and yew were also sometimes used.

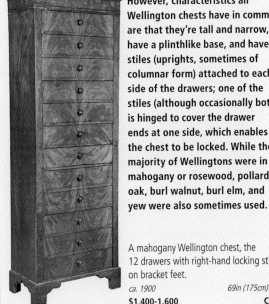

A Dutch marquetry bombé chest, with three drawers, veneer chips, splits, feet scuffed, drawer lock missing.

51¼in (130cm) wide
$550-700   CHOR

A late-19thC Victorian mahogany campaign chest, possibly Naval, with three drawers, the top one with a baize-lined slide with two brass apertures, with brass side-carrying handles.

28¾in (73cm) wide
$875-1,000   WW

A mahogany Wellington chest, the 12 drawers with right-hand locking stile, on bracket feet.

ca. 1900   69in (175cm) high
$1,400-1,600   CHEF

ESSENTIAL REFERENCE—COMMODES

Derived from the French word meaning "convenient" or "suitable," commodes first appeared in France toward the end of the 17thC, during the reign of Louis XIV. Essentially a replacement for the more rudimentary chest or coffer, their basic form comprised either a low cabinet or chest-of-drawers, raised on legs and used for storing personal items—mostly in boudoirs or bedrooms—but also in salons or drawing rooms. Throughout the 18thC and 19thC, numerous variations were conceived, both in terms of the ergonomics of their construction and their style and decoration, such as Rococo and Neoclassical. During the 19thC, the word "commode" also acquired a more specific meaning, namely: a bedside cabinet or chair enclosing a chamber pot (and in the United States it also became a colloquial synonym for a flush toilet).

An early-to-mid-18thC Italian walnut and inlaid commode, repairs, worm, handles and feet are later.

50in (127cm) wide

$2,500-3,100   **DN**

A Swedish kingwood, fruitwood, crossbanded, and parquetry bombé commode, in Louis XV style, the antique marble top above three drawers, with gilt-metal Rococo-style cast handles and escutcheons, scratches, ring marks, pitting, some veneer and wood losses.

ca. 1750

45¾in (116cm) wide

$6,000-7,500   **TEN**

A French Louis XV kingwood and ormolu-mounted serpentine bombé commode, attributed to Gilles Joubert (1689-1775), the rouge griotte marble top with a molded edge, above parquetry lattice panels and scrolling Rococo mounts, with two drawers, on cabriole legs with lion-paw feet, with alterations.

ca. 1755-60

49¼in (125cm) wide

$50,000-62,000   **WW**

A mid-18thC Austrian walnut and marquetry serpentine commode, fading on wood, later elements, old worm.

48¾in (124cm) wide

$3,700-5,000   **DN**

A mid- to late-18thC North Italian walnut, fruitwood, and parquetry commode, the top above two drawers, original brass handles and escutcheons, on square tapering legs.

40½in (103cm) wide

$8,500-10,000   **DUK**

A George III mahogany, tulipwood, and marquetry serpentine commode, in the manner of Pierre Langlois, the doors opening to a shelved interior.

The combination of the elegant bombé outline, marquetry, and gilt mounts seen on this piece are associated with the work of Pierre Langlois. A royal cabinetmaker of Huguenot origin, Langlois was known for producing fine English furniture in the French taste.

ca. 1770

44½in (113cm) wide

$6,000-7,500   **DN**

A George III mahogany breakfront commode, attributed to Wright & Elwick, the doors opening to shaped shelves.

ca. 1770   *40¼in (102cm) wide*

$8,500-10,000   **DN**

A George III mahogany and crossbanded serpentine-front commode, in the manner of Thomas Chippendale, scratches, losses, restorations, worm.

ca. 1770   *36½in (93cm) wide*

$1,600-2,000   **DN**

A Louis XVI walnut and gilt-metal-mounted commode, stamped "Jean Caumont," with a marble top, handles, and escutcheons with discoloration, signs of being refitted, losses.

Jean Caumont (b. 1739) was made Master in 1774, and was based in rue Traversiére, Paris. His documented oeuvre is considerable and eclectic. The Comte de Salverte describes this ébéniste extensively and mentions a Louis XVI giltwood console table stamped by Caumont in the Mobilier National, and a sécretaire á abattant in the collection of Mme. Demachy at the château d'Ognon (Comte de Salverte, "Les Ébénistes du XVIIIe siécle," Paris, 1953, page 52). Caumont played an active role in the revolution, and was elected juge de paix. He handed the leadership of his atelier over to his son in 1795 and was thereafter mainly engaged in politics (P. Kjellberg, "Le Mobilier Français du XVIIIe Siécle," Paris, 1989, page 169).

ca. 1780   *43¼in (110cm) wide*
$2,500-3,100   **DN**

A George III mahogany serpentine commode, losses, replaced crossbanding.
ca. 1780   *41¼in (105cm) wide*
$3,700-5,000   **DN**

A George III mahogany night commode, in the manner of Thomas Chippendale, areas of fading, handles and false escutcheons are period replacements.
ca. 1780   *33¾in (86cm) high*
$3,700-5,000   **DN**

A late-18thC North Italian walnut commode, the top above three drawers, on later legs.
51¼in (130cm) wide
$1,400-1,600   **DUK**

An 18thC French kingwood and marquetry commode, in Transitional style, with ormolu mounts and inlaid with flowers, fruit, and a landscape scene, the Siena brocatelle marble top above three drawers.
31¾in (80.5cm) wide
$2,500-3,700   **WW**

A Louis XVI mahogany and ormolu-mounted commode, with a marble top, cracks, repairs.
ca. 1785   *51½in (131cm) wide*
$16,000-20,000   **DN**

An 18thC parquetry commode, South German or North Italian, with three drawers, on squat bun feet, restoration, splits, worm, feet and handles are later.
51½in (131cm) wide
$1,700-2,000   **CHEF**

A George III satinwood commode, Sheraton period, inlaid with stringing and purpleheart panels, with a pair of bowfront paneled doors inset with painted flowers, enclosing a shelf, on square tapering legs and spade feet.
ca. 1790   *33in (84cm) wide*
$5,000-6,200   **WW**

FURNITURE

A late-18thC George III mahogany serpentine commode, the fluted corner pilasters with Corinthian capitals.

43¾in (111cm) wide

$3,700-5,000 DN

A late-18thC Italian walnut and tulipwood banded commode, the top above three drawers, on square tapering supports, no handles by design, the drawers would need to be pulled by a key, repairs, old worm.

45¼in (115cm) wide

$5,000-6,200 DN

A pair of Milanese walnut and marquetry inlaid commodes, in Neoclassical style, in the manner of Giuseppe Maggiolini, carcass and drawer construction is 20thC, each with marble slabs above three drawers inlaid with shells, leaves, and urns issuing flowers, one commode with later marble, minor splits, losses in the drawer fronts.

36½in (93cm) wide

$12,500-15,000 TEN

A pair of late-18th/early 19thC Continental walnut serpentine commodes, with marquetry marble tops, replacement veneers, worm, ebonized surround is worn, revealing underlying wood.

50¾in (129cm) wide

$9,500-10,500 DN

A late-18th/early-19thC North Italian walnut and marquetry commode, the top above three drawers with inlaid borders, ring handles, and brass escutcheons.

46¼in (117.5cm) wide

$1,500-1,700 DUK

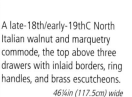

A late George III mahogany and plum pudding mahogany commode, with a brushing slide.

ca. 1810   40¼in (102cm) wide

$1,500-2,000 DN

An early- to mid-19thC French ormolu-mounted fruitwood bombé commode, in Louis XV style, the marble top above two drawers and sides with floral marquetry, on cabriole legs with scallop cast sabots.

42¼in (107cm) wide

$1,900-2,500 DUK

CLOSER LOOK—A FRENCH BOMBÉ COMMODE

Sitting on a commode of classic Louis XV-style bombé form, the serpentine profile, white vein marble top is a later replacement, but in-keeping with the original.

The painted decoration depicts a "fête galante," a French term used to describe a type of painting that first came to prominence with the work of artist Antoine Watteau in the second decade of the 18thC. It depicts groups of elegantly attired men and women, usually in parkland or a rural landscape, engaged in decorously amorous play.

The strongly figured, black-grain hardwood is best known as "kingwood" but is sometimes described as "palisander." Imported from the West Indies, it was originally much favored by French cabinetmakers during the Régence (1715-23) and the subsequent reign of Louis XV (1723-74).

The ormolu (gilt-bronze) mounts are typically cast in scrolling and intertwined acanthus leaf and other foliate forms. In France, decorative mounts such as this were cast by specialty "bronziers" and then gilded by "doreurs."

A French kingwood and ormolu-mounted bombé commode, made in the third quarter of the 19thC, in mid-18thC Louis XV style, the later marble top above a cupboard door painted with a "fête galante," small fritting on the top, some paint losses.

39¼in (100cm) wide

$37,000-43,000 TEN

An 18thC Italian commode, the top painted to simulate marble, the drawers lined with block-printed paper.

48in (122cm) wide

$3,100-4,300 **DN**

A 19thC Swedish marquetry commode, in Neoclassical style, the marble top over two drawers with gilt-metal mounts and marquetry, on square tapered legs, back leg and handles are replacements.

46in (117cm) wide

$25,000-31,000 **CHEF**

A 19thC Dutch marquetry and hardwood bowfront commode, inlaid with flowers and scrolls, with three drawers.

45¼in (115cm) wide

$2,100-2,500 **WW**

A 19thC French kingwood breakfront commode, in Transitional style, the marble top above two drawers with floral marquetry and brass mounts.

38½in (98cm) wide

$700-800 **CHEF**

An early-20thC mahogany, tulipwood, and specimen marquetry demilune commode, in George III style, in the manner of Robert Adam.

96in (244cm) wide

$7,000-8,000 **DN**

A late-19th/early-20thC Victorian satinwood commode, in Neoclassical style, the top painted with flower garlands, swags, and oval pendants, above two drawers and an apron.

43¼in (110cm) wide

$4,300-5,000 **TEN**

An early-20thC marquetry commode, in Louis XV style, the top over two drawers with floral marquetry and gilt mounts, on cabriole legs.

60in (152.5cm) wide

$2,500-3,700 **CHEF**

A 20thC tulipwood, palisander, and gilt-metal-mounted serpentine commode, in Louis XV style, with a marble top.

56in (142.5cm) wide

$1,900-2,500 **DN**

A pair of 20thC tulipwood and harewood serpentine commodes, in George III style, water marks, minor lifting in veneers, shrinkage cracks.

39in (99cm) wide

$6,000-7,500 **DN**

A joined oak chest-on-stand, the chest 17thC, the stand later, the top above three two-as-one drawers, on a stand with dummy drawers and turned legs, repairs, missing sections of wood.

46¾in (119cm) high

$1,000-1,100   **TEN**

A walnut cross- and feather-banded chest-on-stand, in Queen Anne style, the chest 17thC and later veneered, with four long drawers, the stand later, with three drawers.

51½in (131cm) high

$700-800   **TEN**

A William and Mary walnut chest-on-stand, late 17th/early 18thC and later, the stand fitted with three drawers, with later legs and stretchers.

62½in (159cm) high

$3,700-4,300   **WW**

A late-17thC walnut and feather-banded chest-on-stand, the cornice above two short and three long drawers, canted stiles, the base with two deep and one long drawer above an arched apron, splits, old decay.

64½in (164cm) high

$1,600-2,000   **TEN**

A late-17thC walnut, feather-banded and oyster-veneered chest, the top with tracery stringing above two short and two long drawers, the base with two drawers, on a stand with turned legs, repolished and recently restored, old decay.

51¼in (130cm) high

$2,500-3,100   **TEN**

An early-18thC Queen Anne walnut chest-on-stand, the top above two short and three long drawers, the stand with two short and one long drawer, on later bun feet.

53¼in (135cm) high

$3,700-4,300   **WW**

An early-18thC Queen Anne carved walnut high chest, the scroll bonnet with carved rosette terminals, centered by a flaming urn finial, the upper part frieze drawer over two short and three long drawers, the lower part with two short over three further short drawers, the center drawer carved with a matching concave shell, above an apron with a carved shell, raised on cabriole legs carved at the knees with shells.

89¾in (228cm) high

$3,700-4,300   **L&T**

A Queen Anne black lacquer and gilt chinoiserie chest-on-stand, early 18thC and later, sections of later painting, losses, restoration in chinoiserie, worm.

60¾in (154cm) high

$5,000-6,200   **DN**

An oyster-veneered walnut chest-on-stand, Queen Anne and later, with two short and two long drawers, the stand with spiral twist supports united by a wavy flat stretcher, restorations, veneer losses.

40¼in (102cm) high

$1,900-2,500   **CHEF**

A George I walnut chest-on-stand, repairs and later elements, woodworm throughout, discoloration on gilt-metal handles.

ca. 1730   *66¾in (169.5cm) high*

$5,000-6,200   **DN**

An early-18thC George II burl walnut and walnut chest-on-stand, the cornice above three short and three long crossbanded drawers, the stand with three short drawers around a shaped apron.

62¼in (158cm) high

$2,200-2,700   **L&T**

A George II walnut chest-on-stand, legs are later, repairs, worm.

ca. 1740   *61in (155cm) high*

$3,700-5,000   **DN**

A Georgian walnut chest-on-stand, early-18thC and later, cross- and feather-banded, with brass drop handles, molded cornice on banded quarter-veneered top, with two short over three long drawers below.

59½in (151cm) high

$950-1,050   **HT**

A mid-18thC walnut and boxwood-strung chest-on-stand, the top above three frieze drawers with three deep drawers below, with pierced brass handles and escutcheons, on a stand with three drawers above an arched apron, on later turned legs, veneers splits, old decay.

59½in (151cm) high

$1,700-2,000   **TEN**

A walnut chest-on-stand, mid-18thC and later, fitted with two short and three long herringbone-crossbanded drawers, the base with two further drawers, restored and adapted.

68in (173cm) high

$6,000-7,500   **DN**

A walnut chest-on-stand, mid-18thC and later, with three short and three long drawers, the stand base with three further drawers, on bun feet, losses, splits, restorations.

45in (114cm) high

$7,500-8,500   **DN**

A Charles II painted oak, mother-of-pearl, and bone-inlaid enclosed chest-of-drawers-on-chest, with a cushion frieze drawer above a deep drawer, the cupboard doors on the base enclosing three further drawers, splits, losses, alterations, and adaptions, later elements.

Dated to ca. 1660, this chest-of-drawers-on-chest was made during a particularly transitional period in the evolution of storage furniture. Some 100 years earlier, around the mid-16thC, the concept of the sliding pull-out drawer began to gather traction, especially in Spain and the Netherlands. Drawers did not, however, appear in Great Britain (where they were originally known as "drawing boxes") in significant numbers until the end of the 16thC, and then were only additions to traditional coffers and cabinets. By the middle of the 17thC, the purpose-built configuration of a two-part chest-on-chest comprising a shallow frieze drawer or drawers above a deep drawer, all raised on a cupboard base—like the example here—had become common. But it wasn't until around the turn of the 18thC that the chest-of-drawers with graduated drawers from top to bottom within a single carcass—the form we are most familiar with today—became the norm. Of course, underpinning this transition were considerable advances in woodworking techniques, to the effect that while chests-of-drawers in the late-16thC were largely still being made with joints secured by pegs and nails, and were thus the preserve of craftsmen known as "joiners," by the late-17thC far more sophisticated dovetail construction had become de riguer, and that was the preserve of the "cabinetmaker."

ca. 1660   *53½in (136cm) high*
$17,500-20,000   **DN**

A Queen Anne walnut and feather banded chest-on-chest, repairs and replacements, old worm.

ca. 1710   *70in (178cm) high*
$9,500-10,500   **DN**

A George I walnut and feather-banded chest-on-chest, the cornice above three short and three long oak-lined drawers, the base with a pull-out brushing slide, three drawers below, all between canted and fluted stiles, splits, some veneer losses.

ca. 1720   *73¼in (186cm) high*
$3,700-5,000   **TEN**

A George II burl walnut secretaire chest-on-chest, ca. 1730 and later, with cross- and feather banding and canted and fluted angles, the upper section with a cornice above three short and three long drawers, the lower section with a secretaire drawer fitted with pigeonholes, drawers, and secret drawers, above two short and two long drawers, with carved flower-head and swag handles and gilt-brass escutcheons.

70¾in (180cm) high
$6,000-7,500   **WW**

A George II walnut and feather banded chest-on-chest, repairs, old worm, later elements.

ca. 1730   *69¼in (176cm) high*
$6,000-7,500   **DN**

A George II walnut secretaire chest-on-chest, the drop drawer opening to drawers and pigeonholes, the handles and escutcheons of notable quality, feet are probably later, worm.

See Adam Bowett, "Early Georgian Furniture": "The chest on chest or double chest of drawers was a Georgian innovation, the earliest known … in a bill submitted by Gumley and Turing … to Kensington Palace in 1727. The coved sunburst decoration to the bottom of the drawer is usually an indication that the base is fitted with a secretaire. The cove was presumably an attempt to minimise damage to the base molding from a person sitting … at the secretaire."

ca. 1740   *67½in (171.5cm) high*
$6,000-7,500   **DN**

A mid-18thC George III mahogany chest-on-chest, the top above two short and three long drawers, the base with three drawers, on ogee feet, handles replaced.

59in (150cm) high
$1,250-1,500   **DUK**

A George III mahogany chest-on-chest, proably North Country, with two short and six long flame-figured drawers, flanked by stop-fluted quarter pilasters, on ogee bracket feet.

ca. 1770   *67in (170cm) high*
$2,500-3,700   **WW**

A George III mahogany chest-on-chest, the molded cornice above an arrangement of drawers.

ca. 1780   *73¼in (186cm) high*

$1,100-1,350   **DN**

A late-18thC George III mahogany and pine-lined chest-on-chest, the cornice above two short and three long drawers, between canted fluted stiles, the base of three drawers, on bracket feet.

70½in (179cm) high

$1,600-2,000   **TEN**

A late-18thC George III mahogany and pine-lined straightfront chest-of-drawers, the cornice above seven graduated drawers, between quarter-column fluted supports.

64½in (164cm) high

$1,050-1,200   **TEN**

A late-18thC George III mahogany pine-side chest-on-chest, the cavetto cornice above two short and three long drawers, between canted and fluted stiles, the base of three long drawers, recently restored, old splits.

69¼in (176cm) high

$4,300-5,000   **TEN**

A George III mahogany chest-on-chest, with a dentil cornice, above two short and three long drawers, the base with three drawers, all flanked by egg-and-dart molding, on ogee bracket feet.

67¾in (172cm) high

$4,300-5,000   **DUK**

A George III burl oak and mahogany chest-on-chest, the cornice above a parquetry chevron band, above two short and six long crossbanded drawers, with original brass handles.

ca. 1790-1800   *74in (188cm) high*

$1,900-2,500   **WW**

A late-18thC George III mahogany, boxwood, and rosewood crossbanded chest-on-chest, the cornice above two short and three long drawers, between canted fluted stiles, the base of four drawers.

69¾in (177cm) high

$1,400-1,600   **TEN**

A Channel Islands George III mahogany and marquetry chest-on-chest.

ca. 1800   *83½in (212cm) high*

$2,000-2,500   **DN**

A George II mahogany secretaire bookcase, in the manner of William Hallett, the waist fitted with pigeonholes and shelves above a hinged top.

ca. 1755   *89in (226cm) high*

$2,500-3,700   DN

A George III mahogany and satinwood-banded secretaire bookcase, the glazed doors enclosing adjustable shelves, the drop-front secretaire drawer enclosing a writing surface and drawers around a recess.

ca. 1790   *94in (239cm) high*

$7,000-8,000   DN

A George III mahogany breakfront secretaire bookcase, after designs by Thomas Sheraton, the glazed section with later glass shelves, the secretaire drawer with interior fittings, the drawers with fiddleback mahogany and a later green baize inset writing surface, the lower center section with sliding trays, small losses, cracks, splits in veneers.

ca. 1800   *99½in (253cm) high*

$6,000-7,500   DN

A George III mahogany secretaire bookcase, the cornice above a pair of astragal glazed doors enclosing shelves, the bottom section with a secretaire drawer with drawers, pigeonholes, and leather writing surface, above three long drawers, one glass panel cracked.

81½in (207cm) high

$500-625   CHEF

A Georgian mahogany secretaire bookcase, with rosewood banding and stringing, the arched pierced surmount over two astragal doors enclosing adjustable shelves, the secretaire drawer faced as two and opening to a divided interior with drawers and pigeonholes, two long drawers below, one deep and faced as two, oval brass drop handles, with a shaped apron, on splayed bracket feet.

ca. 1800   *103in (261.5cm) high*

$1,250-1,500   HT

An early-to-mid-19thC George IV mahogany breakfront secretaire bookcase, the top with five sections, the center double section and end sections with tablet pediments surmounted by bronze-painted balls, above a center pair of glazed doors enclosing three adjustable shelves, the narrow sections with 12 adjustable shelves, the center base section with two drawers above a secretaire drawer with rosewood knob handles, above a pair of doors, the recessed base sections with doors enclosing four drawers, the end sections headed by simulated drawers, restorations and replacements.

146in (371cm) wide

$10,000-11,000   DUK

A mid-19thC George IV mahogany secretaire bookcase, the upper section with glazed doors enclosing four adjustable shelves, above a secretaire drawer enclosing a fitted interior of pigeonholes and drawers, the base doors enclosing shelves, on later bracket feet, glazing with repair.

89in (226cm) high

$1,600-2,000   TEN

A Victorian mahogany, boxwood, ebony-strung, and satinwood-banded secretaire bookcase, in George III style, the broken bonnet pediment above a pair of glazed doors, enclosing adjustable shelves, the base with a secretaire drawer enclosing satinwood-veneered drawers and a writing surface, the base with two cupboard doors inlaid with Neoclassical urns.

92½in (235cm) high

$1,000-1,100   TEN

A George II mahogany bureau bookcase, the broken molded pediment and turned finial above a sunburst marquetry panel, the cupboard doors with later mirrors enclosing shelves, pigeonholes, and small drawers around a center arched cupboard door, with pull-out candle slides below, the drop enclosing a fitted interior, the base of four oak-lined drawers, on bracket feet, some molding losses, scratches.

ca. 1750   94½in (240cm) high
$2,500-3,100   TEN

A mid-18thC George III mahogany bureau cabinet, the upper section with two mirror doors enclosing a fitted interior of two adjustable shelves above pigeonholes and drawers, below an arched architectural cornice centered and flanked by turned giltwood ball finials, the base with two candle slides above a sloping drop front with molded bookrest and shaped lockplate, with pigeonholes and drawers around a center cupboard, the frieze with two lopers and three small drawers, above three long drawers.

94½in (240cm) high
$2,200-2,700   TEN

An 18thC Dutch walnut and marquetry bureau bookcase, the glazed doors opening to shelves, the lower part with a slope front opening to pigeonholes, drawers, and a sliding recess, over two short and two long drawers, the whole covered in flower-filled baskets, butterflies, and leaf trails.

93¼in (237cm) high
$5,000-6,200   L&T

A George III mahogany bureau bookcase, the broken arch pediment above a pair of astragal glazed cupboard doors enclosing shelves, the bureau base, with drop-front enclosing a fitted interior of pigeonholes, drawers, and a center cupboard, two short over three long drawers below, flanked by side carrying handles, cornice is later, replcements.

92½in (235cm) high
$1,200-1,350   CHEF

ESSENTIAL REFERENCE—JAMES MCBEY

This Moroccan bureau bookcase has a truly distinguished provenance: it formerly belonged to James McBey (1883-1959). McBey was a Scottish-born and largely self-taught artist and etcher who traveled to Morocco in 1912 and began to work in watercolors. In 1914, his poor eyesight prevented him from enlisting as a solider in World War I, but in February 1916 he was commissioned as a second lieutenant while employed with the Army Printing and Stationary Service. Due to his increasing success as a semiprofessional artist at this time, he was then appointed an official war artist to the Egyptian Expeditionary Force. After the war, during the 1920s, his etchings began to fetch prices at auction that had only hitherto been achieved by Old Masters. In 1929, McBey visited North America, and returned there in 1931 to marry Marguerite Loeb, a photographer from Philadelphia. In 1932, the couple bought a house on the Old Mountain, near Tangier in Morocco, and later bought a second property in Marrakesh, and it was while there that McBey purchased this bureau bookcase and brought it back to their house in Tangier.

A Moroccan painted pine bureau bookcase, late 19thC and later, scratches, losses, gilt wear, worm.

83½in (212cm) high
$5,500-6,000   DN

A Queen Anne walnut double-domed bureau cabinet, early 18thC and later, the mirrored doors enclosing drawers and recesses, the bureau drop enclosing drawers, pigeonholes, and a sliding section to a well, stains, feet later.

80¾in (205cm) high
$8,000-9,500   DN

A Queen Anne figured-walnut and feather-banded bureau cabinet, the mirror panel doors opening to pigeonholes, shelves, and drawers, the drop opening to pigeonholes and drawers, above a slide-covered well and a writing surface, the cabinet originally a bookcase, replacement elements.

ca. 1710   85½in (217cm) high
$6,000-7,500   DN

A mid-18thC polychrome painted and parcel-gilt bureau cabinet, later decorated, replacements, old worm.

82¾in (210cm) high
$3,700-5,000   DN

A late-18thC George III mahogany breakfront bookcase, the cornice above glazed doors with pointed arch astragals, enclosing adjustable shelves, the lower part with short frieze drawers over panel-molded doors enclosing further shelves.

102in (259cm) high

$3,700-5,000   L&T

An 18thC early-George III stripped pine breakfront bookcase, the broken arch pediment above a frieze, over glazed doors enclosing adjustable shelves, on a conforming base with doors centered by molded fan medallions, with shelves in the interiors.

91in (231cm) high

$8,000-9,500   L&T

An 18thC George III mahogany breakfront bookcase, the cornice above a pair of astragal glazed doors flanked by further doors, enclosing adjustable shelves, on a base with four molded panel doors, the center doors enclosing sliding trays, the outer doors enclosing drawers on one side and shelves on the other.

111in (282cm) wide

$4,300-5,000   L&T

A Regency rosewood and brass-inlaid breakfront library bookcase, in the manner of Thomas Hope, interior shelves are later.

ca. 1815

94½in (240cm) high

$7,000-8,000   DN

A Regency mahogany and ebony-inlaid breakfront library bookcase, in the manner of George Oakley, section of molding detached.

Although its manufacture is not attributable to George Oakley, the construction and style of this breakfront bookcase are certainly "in the manner" of his work. Born in 1773 (he died in 1841), Oakley became one of the most eminent "upholders and cabinetmakers" of his day, gradually acquiring a clientele that stretched through and beyond the upper echelons of society to the royal family. In 1799, he was awarded a Royal Warrant from Queen Charlotte, and in 1804 a foreign correspondent observed "all people with taste buy their furniture at Oakley's, the most tasteful of the London cabinetmakers." Especially notable among many notable commissions for Oakley's services include the work he did for the Prince Regent at Carlton House; the furniture he supplied for London's Mansion House; for the Cheere family of Papworth Hall, Cambridgeshire; and for Sir John Soane, first at Pitzhanger, then at the Bank of England, and also at Soane's house in Lincoln's Inn Fields, London. While Oakley neither stamped nor labeled his furniture, surviving pieces, notably at Papworth Hall and in the Royal Collection, have firmly established for posterity his distinctive, tremendously well-crafted, and undoubtedly luxurious style.

ca. 1815

112¼in (285cm) high

$16,000-20,000   DN

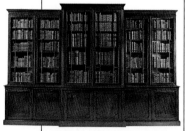

An early-19thC Regency mahogany breakfront library bookcase, the glazed and paneled doors enclosing adjustable shelves, cracks, restorations, later elements.

172¼in (437.5cm) wide

$12,500-15,000   DN

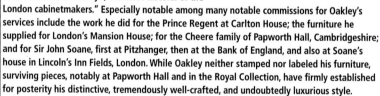

An early-19thC Regency mahogany breakfront bookcase, attributed to Gillows, Lancaster, the cornice above a frieze marked with flower heads, above glazed and mullioned doors with Bramah locks enclosing adjustable shelves, flanked by fluted pilasters with acanthus-carved capitals, the lower part with four panel doors, flanked and divided by fluted pilasters capped with acanthus scrolls and flower heads.

This bookcase relates to a group of furniture supplied by Gillows to the Langford-Brooke family of Mere Hall, Knutsford, Cheshire, in the first quarter of the 19thC. The pilasters with their acanthus capitals are typical of Gillows' designs of this period.

120½in (306cm) wide

$25,000-37,000   L&T

A Regency mahogany breakfront secretaire bookcase, early 19thC and later, the cornice over bar glazed doors, enclosing adjustable shelves, the secretaire drawer with eight internal drawers, above a pair of paneled doors, enclosing a shelf and tray, flanked by further cupboards, wear throughout.

84¼in (214cm) high

$2,500-3,100   SWO

A George IV mahogany breakfront bookcase, possibly Scottish, the cornice above Gothic lancet astragal glazed doors, enclosing adjustable shelves, the base with cupboard doors, enclosing shelves.

ca. 1820 102¼in (259.5cm) high

$5,000-5,600   **WW**

A 19thC William IV mahogany inverted breakfront bookcase, the egg-and-dart-molded cornice above a frieze marked with carved flower heads, above four glazed doors with adjustable shelves, the base with four molded panel doors, on a plinth base.

117¾in (299cm) wide

$12,500-15,000   **L&T**

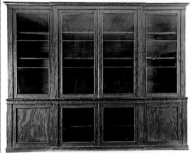

An early-Victorian mahogany breakfront bookcase, by M. Willson, London, the cornice above astragal glazed doors enclosing adjustable shelves, the base with a pair of paneled doors flanking a pair of glazed doors, with adjustable shelves, stamped "M. Willson 68 Great Queen Street, London."

According to the "Dictionary of English Furniture Makers 1660-1840," Thomas Willson of 68 Great Queen Street was a furniture broker/dealer in good-quality second-hand furniture and possibly makers or restorers. Mary and Matthew Willson worked at 68 Great Queen Street from 1830-54.

ca. 1840   130½in (331.5cm) wide

$6,000-7,000   **WW**

A 19thC mahogany breakfront bookcase, in George III style, the cornice above three astragal glazed doors enclosing adjustable shelves, above three cupboard doors, each enclosing a shelf.

91¼in (232cm) high

$700-800   **WW**

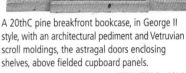

A 20thC pine breakfront bookcase, in George II style, with an architectural pediment and Vetruvian scroll moldings, the astragal doors enclosing shelves, above fielded cupboard panels.

87½in (222.5cm) high

$1,400-1,600   **WW**

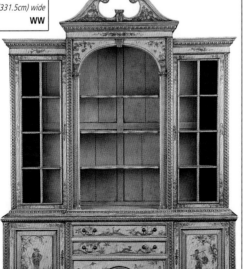

A 20thC chinoiserie lacquered bookcase, in George III style, the decoration of rural scenes, animals, and flowers, with a broken bonnet pediment over a center open-arched shelf, flanked by glazed cupboard doors, the bottom section with two cupboard doors and three long drawers.

91¾in (233cm) high

$7,000-8,000   **CHEF**

A 20thC walnut breakfront library bookcase, the pediment above four arched and glazed doors enclosing adjustable shelves, the base with four frieze drawers and arched cupboard doors below.

108¼in (275cm) wide

$2,700-3,500   **TEN**

FURNITURE

An unusual mahogany bookcase, ca. 1770 and later, in the manner of William Vile, with an inverted breakfront drawer arrangement, of one concealed shallow drawer above two short drawers, above one long drawer with dummy fronts, scratches, losses, worm, reconstructed with later materials.

The bold architectural form of this bookcase combined with the execution of the carved elements is related to known works by the Royal Cabinetmaker William Vile. The Groome Court library bookcase, made by Vile for Lord Coventry in the 1760s and currently held in the Victoria & Albert Museum, incorporates carved pilasters similar to those seen on this piece (accession no. W.76-1975). Another bookcase by Vile of related form, incorporating carved floral foliate swags, is held in the Royal Collection Trust (accession no. RCIN 252).

78¾in (200cm) high

$7,000-8,000　　　　　　　　**DN**

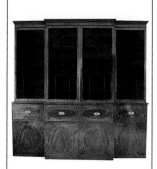

A late-18thC George III mahogany breakfront secretaire library bookcase, with a cornice over glazed doors, with plain Gothic arched glazed bars, the base with secretaire drawers over double cupboards, opening to interiors with shelves and four drawers.

109in (277cm) high

$3,700-5,000　　　　　　　**DUK**

A figured mahogany library bookcase, ca. 1815 and later, the cupboards opening to shelved interiors, the lower section incorporating ten fitted drawers, splits, losses, repairs, replacements, worm.

90in (228.5cm) high

$3,700-4,300　　　　　　　　**DN**

One of a pair of early- to mid-19thC George IV mahogany library bookcases, in the manner of Gillows, each with a top over a cornice carved with acanthus leaves and foliate bosses, above four glazed doors, each enclosing four adjustable shelves, flanked by fluted columns with leaf carved volutes.

95¾in (243cm) wide

$10,000-11,000 the pair　　　**DUK**

A mid-19thC Victorian mahogany breakfront library bookcase, the cornice above open and adjustable shelves, with scrolled supports, with cupboard doors below, flanked by smaller wings with further shelves.

152in (387cm) wide

$2,500-3,700　　　　　　　**TEN**

A late-19thC Victorian mahogany and marquetry library bookcase, by James Winter & Sons, inlaid with satinwood banding and boxwood stringing, the fret-carved bonnet pediment above three astragal glazed doors enclosing adjustable shelves, the base with three panel doors inlaid with Classical urns, leaves, and flowers, enclosing shelves, stamped "James Winter & Sons, 151,153,155 Wardour St. Soho, London."

99in (251.5cm) high

$3,100-4,300　　　　　　　**WW**

An early-20thC Edwardian mahogany breakfront secretaire library bookcase, by Edwards & Roberts, with fiddleback and flame veneers, inlaid with stringing and satinwood banding, with astragal glazed doors enclosing adjustable shelves, the secretaire fitted with pigeonholes, drawers, and a writing surface, above a pair of cupboard doors flanked by further cupboards, stamped "Edwards & Roberts."

102½in (260.5cm) high

$2,500-3,700　　　　　　　**WW**

A mahogany library bookcase, in George II style, of recent manufacture, with adjustable shelves in the top section and fixed shelves in the base.

94¾in (240.5cm) high

$5,000-6,200　　　　　　　**DN**

FURNITURE

A pair of George III mahogany concave open bookcases, unable to free stand, repairs, marks.

ca. 1810   52¼in (132.5cm) high

$2,500-3,700   **DN**

A pair of early-19thC Regency rosewood and brass open bookcases, each with a marble top above two adjustable shelves flanked by pilasters.

38in (96.5cm) high

$2,000-2,500   **WW**

A pair of Regency mahogany bookcases, in the manner of Gillows, with astragal glazed doors, the lower doors opening to shelved interiors, some chips and losses.

ca. 1820   94½in (240cm) high

$5,500-7,000   **DN**

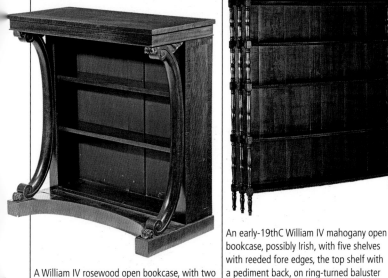

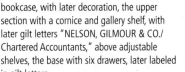

A William IV rosewood open bookcase, with two adjustable shelves, flanked by curved supports.

ca. 1830   37½in (95.5cm) high

$375-500   **WW**

An early-19thC William IV mahogany open bookcase, possibly Irish, with five shelves with reeded fore edges, the top shelf with a pediment back, on ring-turned baluster supports, on turned feet.

65¼in (166cm) high

$2,500-3,700   **L&T**

A 19thC Victorian Gothic Revival oak open bookcase, with later decoration, the upper section with a cornice and gallery shelf, with later gilt letters "NELSON, GILMOUR & CO./ Chartered Accountants," above adjustable shelves, the base with six drawers, later labeled in gilt letters.

82¼in (209cm) high

$3,700-5,000   **L&T**

A mid-19thC Victorian carved walnut open bookcase, minor old repairs.

102¾in (261cm) wide

$3,700-5,000   **DN**

An early-20thC Edwardian mahogany breakfront open bookcase, inlaid with stringing and satinwood banding, with adjustable shelves flanked by Corinthian column pilasters.

114in (289.5cm) wide

$1,050-1,200   **WW**

A late-18thC George III oak waterfall bookcase, with three graduated and sectioned tiers above a base drawer.

48in (122cm) high

$1,250-1,600 **L&T**

A pair of early-19thC North European painted pine waterfall bookcases, with graduated tiers above a base drawer, painted with leafy scrolls, on square tapered legs.

56¾in (144cm) high

$3,100-3,700 **L&T**

A William IV rosewood waterfall open bookcase.

ca. 1835 *62in (157.5cm) high*

$4,300-5,000 **DN**

A mahogany waterfall bookcase cabinet, the associated top section with three-quarter gallery and spindle supports, with two shelves below between reeded supports and a drawer, two cupboard doors below.

61in (155cm) high

$800-950 **TEN**

A Victorian mahogany, burl walnut, rosewood, and satinwood banded low bookcase, in two sections, with adjustable shelves and six lotus-carved pilasters, on gadrooned feet, formerly fitted with a superstructure.

ca. 1840 *159¾in (406cm) wide*

$3,700-5,000 **TEN**

A George II oak architectural bookcase or cabinet, ca. 1740 and later, in Neo-Palladian style, the dentilled cornice supported by large fluted Corinthian pilasters, cracks, repairs, inset sections, later elements.

92½in (235cm) high

$19,000-22,000 **DN**

A George II mahogany bookcase or cabinet, possibly Irish, the dentil-molded breakfront cornice above a band carved with oak leaves and acorns, centered by a male bust, possibly depicting Jonathan Swift, the pair of astragal glazed doors flanked by Ionic columns.

The carved male bust on the "keystone" terminal of the upper frieze of this bookcase or cabinet bears a strong resemblance to Jonathan Swift (1667-1745), the Anglo-Irish satirist and author of "Gulliver's Travels" and "A Tale of a Tub." A similar bust of Swift was executed by Michael Rysbrack. Swift would have been an appropriate subject for an Irish bookcase of this date.

ca. 1740 *82¾in (210cm) high*

$7,000-8,000 **DN**

A mid-18thC George II mahogany bookcase, in the manner of Thomas Chippendale, the panel doors opening to a shelved interior.

99½in (252.5cm) high

$5,000-5,600 **DN**

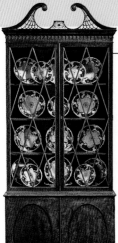

A George III mahogany bookcase, in the manner of William Bradshaw.

Little is known of the early life and training of the London-based cabinetmaker, "upholder" and "tapissier" William Bradshaw (ca. 1700-75). However, it is well-documented that he had premises in Frith Street from 1728-32, at 27 Soho Square and 59-60 Greek Street from 1732-55, and in Princes Street in Hanover Square from 1756-62. Working at intervals with various different partners, Bradshaw's wares were much desired, and over the years included a number of very prestigious clients. For example, ca. 1720 he supplied a suite of walnut furniture that included six chairs covered with Fulham tapestry to Lord Brownlow of Belton House, Lancashire. Other notable commissions, among many, included: the Watteau tapestries for the Cabal Room at Ham House, in Richmond, London; furniture (some japanned) for the 2nd Earl of Stanhope at Chevening, Kent; furniture, carpets, and tapestries for Longford Castle, Wiltshire; furniture for the 1st Earl of Leicester at Holkham Hall, Norfolk; and three couch beds for the 3rd Earl of Burlington at Chiswick Villa and Burlington House.

ca. 1780   *96½in (245cm) high*
$7,500-8,500   **DN**

An unusual George III mahogany and exotic hardwood bookcase, possibly Anglo-Chinese, scratches, chips, losses.

ca. 1800   *88¾in (225.5cm) high*
$11,000-14,000   **DN**

An early-19thC late George III mahogany bookcase cabinet, the cornice above glazed doors enclosing adjustable shelves, the base with two cupboard doors enclosing two shelves and two drawers.

95¼in (242cm) high
$750-875   **TEN**

A Regency mahogany bookcase, the broken triangular pediment with a center urn finial, above a pair of glazed doors enclosing adjustable shelves, over a pair of cupboard doors, old repairs in veneers.

104¼in (265cm) high
$3,100-3,700   **CHEF**

A Regency rosewood and brass bookcase, inlaid with scrolling leaves and arrowhead stringing, the cornice above a pair of astragal glazed doors, enclosing three shelves, above a pair of frieze drawers and silk doors, enclosing an adjustable shelf.

ca. 1815-20   *78in (198cm) high*
$1,900-2,500   **WW**

A mid-19thC William IV mahogany bookcase cabinet, the cornice above glazed doors enclosing adjustable shelves, with column supports, the base with two frieze drawers and cupboard doors, splits, later locks, repairs.

81in (206cm) high
$550-700   **TEN**

A late-19thC Victorian Gothic Revival ebonized and parcel-gilt bookcase, the cornice above glazed doors with Gothic tracery moldings, enclosing three shelves above pigeonholes, the base decorated with Asian figures, with four dummy drawers flanked by cupboard doors, some fine splits, shrinkage.

94½in (240cm) high
$3,700-5,000   **TEN**

A late-19thC Victorian satinwood bookcase, the top above glazed and paneled doors, with ebony and tulipwood lozenges.

59¾in (152cm) high
$1,050-1,200   **TEN**

FURNITURE

A late-17thC William and Mary walnut feather banded and quarter-veneered display cabinet-on-stand, the cornice above a frieze drawer and glazed doors, enclosing a fabric-lined interior and a shelf, the base with two drawers above later spiral-turned legs, splits, previous handle marks visible, wormholes.

67¾in (172cm) high

$2,500-3,700   **TEN**

A walnut display cabinet-on-stand, the cabinet early 18thC, the stand early 18thC and later.

80in (203cm) high

$2,500-3,100   **DN**

A 19thC Dutch walnut and marquetry display cabinet, the arched cornice with a rocaille-carved pediment, above glazed doors enclosing serpentine shelves, the base with two short over two long drawers, flanked by paneled sides, inlaid throughout with trailing flowers, cornucopia, and mother-of-pearl.

89in (226cm) high

$3,100-4,300   **TEN**

A late-19thC Sheraton Revival satinwood and giltwood serpentine display cabinet, in the manner of Wright & Mansfield, with flowers on an ebonized ground, with an astragal glazed door enclosing two glass shelves, above a paneled door.

76¼in (193.5cm) high

$2,500-3,700   **WW**

A pair of late-19thC French mahogany and gilt-metal-mounted display cabinets, in Louis XVI style, with marble tops and three-quarter pierced galleries, above pairs of glazed doors, enclosing interiors between fluted stiles, the bases with molded tops and paneled frieze drawers, on fluted tapering legs.

58¾in (149cm) high

$3,100-4,300   **TEN**

A French kingwood display cabinet, of vernis Martin style, the center panel painted with figures beside a lake, with glazed doors on the sides, the base fitted with a drawer, some splits.

60¾in (154cm) high

$3,700-4,300   **CHOR**

An Edwardian satinwood, marquetry, and painted display cabinet, in George III style, in the manner of Edwards & Roberts.

ca. 1905   81½in (207cm) high

$2,500-3,700   **DN**

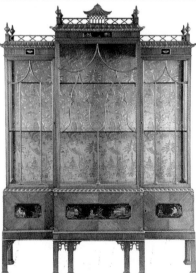

An early-20thC satinwood and parcel-gilt breakfront display cabinet, in Asian style, with black-and-gilt lacquer chinoiserie panels, the pagoda cornice with fret galleries and urn finials, above three astragal glazed doors enclosing glass shelves, above a pair of cupboard doors.

82in (208.5cm) high

$3,700-4,300   **WW**

A late-19thC French kingwood and ormolu-mounted vitrine, the marble top above a frieze with floral swags and satyr figures, above a center bevel glass mirror door with a blue Jasper plaque, the interior enclosing three adjustable plate-glass shelves, on cabriole legs with gilt foliate mounts and Rococo cast feet.

61½in (156cm) high

$8,500-10,000   TEN

A pair of late-19thC rosewood, kingwood, amaranth, and tulipwood-banded vitrines, in Louis XV/Transitional style, with one original and one later brocatelle marble top, the friezes and chiseled ormolu guilloche patterned moldings above a glazed door, with corners surmounted by acanthus leaves, with a parquetry-decorated panel below, flanked by conforming side panels above a leaf-cast base.

63in (160cm) high

$12,500-15,000   TEN

A kingwood, parquetry, and gilt-metal-mounted vitrine, in Louis XV/Transitional style, the marble top above a center glazed glass door, inset with a blue Jasper medallion and flanked by parquetry panels, stiles with musical trophies, ribbons, and urns, the interior with two glass shelves, on cabriole forelegs with foliate mounts and scrolled sabots.

ca. 1890   *59¾in (151.5cm) high*

$6,000-7,500   TEN

A late-19thC French kingwood, gilt-metal-mounted, and marquetry-inlaid vitrine, in Louis XV style, the cornice surmounted by an acanthus-pierced plume, above glazed doors with panels enclosing an interior with glass shelves, serpentine-shaped sides, on slender cabriole forelegs with foliate gilt mounts and sabots.

78¾in (200cm) high

$2,500-3,100   TEN

A French mahogany and gilt-metal-mounted vernis Martin vitrine, in Louis XVI/Transitional style, with a marble top, the doors with two painted panels, serpentine sides, side panels are not glazed, instead fitted with plastic.

The term "vernis Martin" is used for the lustrous lacquer substitute widely used in the 18thC to decorate furniture and personal articles, such as brisé fans and snuffboxes. The process of adding bronze or gold powder to green varnish was perfected by the Martin family, hence its name vernis Martin. Highly praised by Voltaire, it was developed to imitate East Asian lacquerware being imported into France during the reign of Louis XV.

ca. 1900   *63¼in (160.5cm) high*

$1,400-1,600   TEN

A 17thC olivewood oyster-veneered cabinet, on a later stand, the cornice above a long drawer, with a pair of doors below enclosing ten drawers surrounding a cupboard, which encloses a further three drawers and a removable shelving unit.

58¾in (149cm) high

$2,500-3,700   CHEF

A William and Mary oyster-veneered walnut cabinet, the doors opening to seven drawers around a cupboard, with three short drawers, above a long drawer on a later stand.

ca. 1690   *40½in (103cm) wide*

$4,300-5,000   DN

A late-17thC Dutch walnut and ebonized marquetry cabinet-on-stand, the top above seven drawers, with a center arched recess with three further drawers, the stand with a single frieze drawer.

61in (155cm) high

$2,100-2,500   CHEF

A 17thC Hispano-Moresque bone-inlaid cabinet, with 13 drawers and 3 deep drawers, carved with Islamic niches inlaid with geometric designs, on a 19thC Hispano-Moresque walnut table, with bobbin-turned legs, the side handles now absent, knocks, marks, one drawer with replaced handle.

35in (89cm) wide

$5,000-6,200   CHOR

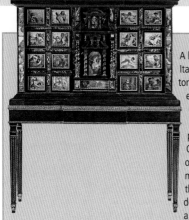

A late-17thC South Italian verre églomisé, tortoiseshell, rosewood, ebonized, and ebony cabinet, Circle of Luca Giordan, Naples, possibly by Domenico Coscia, of breakfront outline, the panels with mythological scenes, the center architectural door opening to a mirrored recess, on a late-18thC George III ebonized and parcel-gilt stand, cracks, losses, later elements, worm.

During the 17thC, 18thC, and early 19thC, just about everyone who went on the Grand Tour (a cultural tour of Continental Europe) would have marveled at the grand, exquisitely furnished Italian interiors they encountered. The cabinet-on-stand was an especially admired form, and examples were often commissioned locally by wealthy tourists and shipped back home. As to this particular example, the painted glass panels on the cabinet depicting mythological subjects resemble in style the work of Luca Giordano (1632-1705), although none of these particular designs have been specifically attributed to him. However, Giordano had a number of pupils, and it is probable that the most notable of them, Domenico Coscia, who became one of the most prolific verre églomisé artists of the late 17thC, was the painter.

57½in (146cm) wide

$16,000-20,000   **DN**

A late-17thC Italian walnut and marquetry cabinet, the cornice above an inlaid frieze Classical scene within an arch, above a paneled door, surrounded by 11 short drawers, on an associated 20thC stand base, with tapering hexagonal legs, losses, worm, the crest is bowed.

70in (178cm) high

$7,500-8,000   **DN**

A late-17th/early-18thC Indo-Portuguese teak, ebony, and ivory parquetry contador or cabinet-on-stand, Goa, with pierced gilt-metal copper handles and escutcheons, worm and splits.

A comparable cabinet-on-stand can be seen on page 59 of Amin Jaffer's "Luxury Goods from India: The Art of the Indian Cabinet-Maker," V&A (2002), in which Jaffer observes: "This cabinet is of a form that was much reproduced under Portuguese patronage in India. The pattern of stars and intersecting circles that adorns this cabinet is perhaps the most commonly reproduced motif … found on articles commissioned by the Portuguese. (However), the most distinctive feature of such furniture is the sculptural treatment of the legs, which are usually conceived as supporting figures. These assume a variety of human and animal forms. The most common are creatures with the upper body of a man or woman, and a scaled lower body like a sea serpent. Past scholars have identified these with nagas and naginis, Hindu snake divinities that are considered auspicious and are believed to provide protection from dangers, including snake bites."

54¼in (137.5cm) high

$31,000-37,000   **DN**

A late-17th/early-18thC Indo-Portuguese tortoiseshell, hardwood, and ivory table cabinet, Mughal, Gujarat, or Sindh, with leaf and flower panels and with parquetry banding, the hinged lid revealing a compartment above a pair of hinged doors enclosing ten drawers, the sides with brass carrying handles, the later cocus wood stand fitted with a drawer.

25¾in (65.5cm) wide

$14,000-17,000   **WW**

An early-18thC Flemish ebony, tortoiseshell, painted, and gilt-metal-mounted cabinet-on-stand, possibly Antwerp, each drawer front with allegorical scenes, the architectural molded doors opening to an ivory-inlaid and mirrored interior, splits in the ivory.

41in (104cm) wide

$14,000-16,000   **DN**

A rare 18thC South American Spanish Colonial tortoiseshell and mother-of-pearl cabinet-on-stand, "Mueble Enconchado," Mexico or Peru, with ebonized ripple moldings inlaid with brass and bone stringing and floral motifs, the top above seven drawers around a center cupboard, the door inset with a portrait of Saint Anthony of Padua, enclosing an interior fitted with a mirror, flanked by turned columns, the sides with hinged doors, enclosing a shelf, above two frieze drawers, on a later ebonized stand with spiral-twist supports.

During the 17thC and 18thC, the upper echelons of Colonial Latin American society spent enormous sums of money on sumptuous furnishings and works of art, produced both locally as well as in Europe and Asia. This cabinet is an example of the former and incorporates a Peruvian technique, known as "enconchado," practiced by ateliers in Lima. A type of marquetry that originated in the Spanish Philippines, it involved applying a complex mother-of-pearl inlay of floral motifs, arabesques, and geometric designs into a richly contrasting tortoiseshell ground. The prototype for these enconchado cabinets, which rapidly became popular, was made as a wedding gift for the granddaughter of the then Viceroy of Peru, and it can now be seen in the Dallas Museum of Art.

72in (183cm) wide

$20,000-25,000   **WW**

An 18thC black lacquer and gilt japanned cabinet-on-stand, the doors enclosing drawers, the exterior ebonized, possibly later, scratches, losses, splits, restorations, worm.

58¾in (149cm) high

$5,000-6,200   **DN**

An 18thC red japanned cabinet-on-stand, the chest with figures, birds, and pagodas, enclosing ten drawers, on a later gesso gilt stand, with double scroll legs on paw feet, splits, paint losses.

41¼in (105cm) wide

$5,000-5,600 **CHOR**

A French mahogany, bois satiné, tulipwood, and ormolu-mounted meuble d'appui, in Louis XVI style, the marble top above a center cupboard door with acanthus-scrolled metal mounts, centered by musical trophies, with parquetry decoration, on cabriole legs with foliate-cast mounts and claw feet, marble is modern.

ca. 1900 *39¾in (101cm) wide*

$4,300-5,000 **TEN**

A pair of 20thC satinwood and painted two-door side cabinets, the tops with flowers with a frieze drawer, above a pair of cupboard doors with painted musical trophies, on turned and tapering legs, veneer losses, one leg broken and glued.

32¾in (83cm) wide

$3,100-3,700 **CHEF**

A William and Mary burl walnut and marquetry cabinet-on-chest, the doors enclosing short and long drawers, later elements, veneer cracks and replacements, worm.

ca. 1690 *69½in (176.5cm) high*

$11,000-14,000 **DN**

A Queen Anne walnut cabinet-on-chest, the cornice above a pair of doors with cross- and feather banding, with eight feather-banded drawers around a center cupboard, the fittings removable to reveal four secret drawers fitted in the back and four small drawers in the back of the cupboard fitting, the lower section with four drawers, with feather banding and brass ring pulls, on later turned feet.

ca. 1710 *66½in (169cm) high*

$11,000-12,000 **WW**

An early-18thC George I walnut secretaire cabinet, with feather banding, the cornice above a mirrored door, enclosing a fitted interior of adjustable shelves, pigeonholes, and drawers, with a pair of hidden drawers, the base with a secretaire drawer with a fitted interior of pigeonholes and drawers, above three drawers with brass swing handles and escutcheons, evidence of side carrying handles.

77½in (197cm) high

$12,000-13,500 **WW**

An early-19thC Dutch walnut and marquetry inlaid side cabinet, the cornice above a pair of glazed doors enclosing three shelves, the base with two paneled doors inlaid with ribbon-tied trophies, the sides inlaid with scrolling foliage, losses, repairs.

97¾in (248cm) high

$2,500-3,700 **DN**

An 18thC corner cabinet, the cornice over a glazed cupboard door, with a pair of cupboard doors below, flanked by fluted pilasters, signs of restoration, worm, losses of paintwork, reconstructed at a later date.

80¾in (205cm) high

$1,000-1,100 **CHEF**

A 19thC Dutch marquetry floor-standing corner cabinet, the pediment surmounted by a carved flower over a single glazed door, the lower section with a single cupboard door decorated with flowers and exotic birds.

77¼in (196.5cm) high

$625-750 **CHEF**

FURNITURE

A late-16thC Augsburg marquetry table cabinet, with two cupboard doors enclosing 14 drawers, framing two architectural cupboard doors, profusely inlaid with densely scrolling foliage, monkeys, parrots, snails, squirrels, rabbits, and grotesque masks, knocks, splits, several drawer knobs replaced.

From the mid-16thC, cabinetmakers in the South German city of Augsburg specialized in table cabinets intended for the storage of small precious objects, such as exotic shells, medals, and jewelry. These luxury cabinets were often profusely decorated with colorful marquetry depicting fantastical ruins, strapwork, a variety of animals, birds, and insects, and a range of ornamental motifs drawn from contemporary German prints.

36½in (92.5cm) wide

$10,000-11,000   **CHOR**

A George III rosewood, satinwood-crossbanded, and marble-topped pier cabinet, attributed to Gillows, with columnar outset corners, the glazed doors enclosing a fixed shelf.

ca. 1800   *37in (94cm) wide*

$7,000-8,000   **DN**

ca. 1800   *44¼in (112.5cm) wide*

$5,000-6,200   **DN**

A 17thC South German marquetry cabinet, the cupboard door inlaid with a warrior on horseback surrounded by weapons and armor, enclosing cupboards and drawers decorated with architectural and ruinous landscapes.

28¼in (72cm) wide

$3,100-4,300   **CHEF**

A mid- to late-18thC George III mahogany side cabinet, the top above a pair of fluted panel doors centered by lion masks and flanked by large elliptical flower motifs, opening to a shelved interior, the side panels similarly carved, the plinth base with further carved leaf-tip molding.

The cabinet, with its robustly carved panels with deep undulating fluting, bears some similarites to a set of 12 gilt and painted stools made by John Linnell for Kedleston Hall for the 1st Lord Scarsdale. Other pieces by Linnell, with the same deep fluting but to designs by Robert Adam, can be found on a pair of dining room urns and pedestals at Osterley Park, made for Robert Child in 1767.

70¾in (180cm) wide

$11,000-12,500   **L&T**

A George III rosewood and gilt-metal side cabinet, in the manner of Marsh & Tatham, the doors with inset brass lattice panels, opening to a shelved interior, with solid cedar-lined frieze drawers above.

ESSENTIAL REFERENCE—CARVED CYPRESS & CEDAR

Intaglio carved and inked decoration, such as applied to the table cabinet shown here, was a popular embellishment for furniture made in the Northern Italian Alpine region, especially during the 16thC and early 17thC, and is particularly associated with the area around the Adige River. Biblical, historical, and literary scenes, often including or bordered by flora and fauna, were typical, as was the use of cedar or cypress wood—the latter not only because their relative softness made them relatively easy to carve, but also because of their warm natural coloring and pleasant scent, which provided a natural deterrent to woodworm. The scent also deterred moths, which made chests and boxes fashioned from cypress and cedar particularly useful for storing valuable textiles, and numerous house inventories throughout Europe record them, indicating that they were desirable objects traded far beyond their region of origin. Indeed, in Shakespeare's "Taming of the Shrew," the character Gremio brags of his cypress chests containing "arras counterpoints, costly apparel, tents and canopies, fine linen, Turkey cushions … and all things that belong to house or housekeeping."

An early-17thC North Italian Alto Adige cypress, cedarwood, and poker-work table cabinet, the top with a rising panel, over a pair of panel doors decorated in poker work and pen work, opening to a fitted interior with an architectural Neoclassical panel door, with three long and eight short drawers.

22½in (57cm) wide

$2,500-3,700   **L&T**

A Regency rosewood and brass marquetry side cabinet, attributed to Gillows.

The brass inlay ("buhl" or "boullework") and latticework paneling on this fine side cabinet are forms of ornamentation that featured prominently in many pieces of furniture made by the illustrious cabinetmakers Gillows of Lancaster (see page 200) during the second decade of the 19thC. Particularly notable examples include some pieces supplied in 1813 to William Powlett, the 2nd Baron Bolton, for Hackwood Park, Hampshire. Interestingly, the presence of brass inlay suggests production took place not at Gillows' Lancaster workshops, but in its London workshop—such metalwork being, at the time, a specialty trade associated with the London neighborhood encompassing St. Martin's Lane and Long Acre.

ca. 1815   *68in (173cm) wide*

$12,500-15,000   **DN**

An early-19thC Dutch Neoclassical mahogany, ebonized, fruitwood, and inlaid demilune side cabinet, the top above a pair of hinged swing-out drawers inset with black lacquer-style chinoiserie panels, above a pair of tambour doors, on tapered legs with brass feet.

37½in (95cm) wide

$2,200-2,700　　L&T

An ebonized, red tortoiseshell and brass-inlaid Boulle-style meuble d'appui, in Louis XV style, the marble top above a frieze drawer, with two cupboard doors below with oval panels, all between canted stiles with caryatid mounts, scratches, staining, signs of repair.

ca. 1850

45¼in (115cm) wide

$3,100-4,300　　TEN

A mid-19thC Victorian ebonized, pietra dura and gilt-metal-mounted side cabinet, the frieze with brass inlay, mounts, and a floral hardstone panel, above a center cupboard door mounted with hardstone reserves depicting fruits, flowers, and a bird, flanked by glazed doors enclosing shelves.

65¼in (166cm) wide

$6,000-7,500　　L&T

A Victorian rosewood serpentine side cabinet, with a mirror back, above a marble top and a pair of mirror doors enclosing a shelf, flanked by turned columns.

ca. 1850-60

57in (145cm) wide

$700-800　　WW

A 19thC Victorian rosewood side cabinet, the nero portoro marble top above a line-inlaid frieze over a center glazed door with pleated silk lining, and marked in the corners with foliate inlay, flanked by further glazed cupboards enclosing shelves.

72½in (184cm) wide

$1,600-2,000　　L&T

A late-19thC Victorian figured walnut, tulipwood crossbanded, and gilt-metal-mounted side cabinet, in the manner of Holland & Sons, the doors opening to a shelved interior.

65¾in (167cm) wide

$7,500-8,500　　DN

An early-20thC rosewood and parcel-gilt breakfront side cabinet, in Regency style, inlaid with stringing and banding, with three frieze drawers above pleated silk paneled doors, one drawer and two cupboards locked.

72in (183cm) wide

$950-1,050　　WW

A 20thC rosewood and parcel-gilt side cabinet, in Regency style, with a marble top, chips, parcel-gilt wear.

33¾in (85.5cm) wide

$2,500-3,700　　DN

FURNITURE

A pair of George III mahogany bedside commodes, drawers converted to vacant recesses, splits, marks.

ca. 1780   *30¾in (78cm) high*

$5,000-6,200   **DN**

A late-18thC George III mahogany and marquetry inlaid bedside commode, the tray top above two inlaid cupboard doors, a sliding commode drawer below.

29¼in (74cm) high

$700-800   **TEN**

A late-18thC George III mahogany tray-top bedside commode, the galleried top pierced with three handgrips, above a pair of crossbanded doors and a converted pull-out base.

31½in (80cm) high

$1,600-2,000   **WW**

A late-18thC George III mahogany tray-top bedside commode, the galleried top with three handgrips and Gothic quatrefoils, with a frieze drawer above a cupboard and a converted pull-out base.

31¼in (79.5cm) high

$1,600-2,000   **WW**

A pair of late-18thC George III mahogany bedside commodes, with bowfront tambour doors, one with a pair of crossbanded drawers below, the other with a deep drawer, on French bracket feet.

30¼in (77cm) high

$4,300-5,000   **L&T**

A George III mahogany night cupboard, the gallery top above a single tambour door, a single drawer below with a dummy handle.

30¼in (77cm) high

$700-800   **CHEF**

A George III mahogany bowfront night cupboard, the tray top above a tambour door and single boxwood-strung drawer below, shrinkage crack, one leg broken and repaired.

30¼in (77cm) high

$625-750   **CHEF**

A pair of 19thC Victorian walnut bedside cupboards, of bowfront outline, the tops above arch molded doors with carved foliate details.

29¼in (74cm) high

$2,200-2,700   **L&T**

A pair of 19thC Victorian satin birch bedside chests, each with four graduated drawers, on plinth bases.

28¾in (73cm) high

$1,900-2,200   **L&T**

FURNITURE

ESSENTIAL REFERENCE—CREDENZAS

A form of freestanding side cabinet or sideboard, the credenza originated in Italy during the Middle Ages. It acquired its name because in Italian "credenza" meant "belief" or "trust" (etymologically connected to the English word "credence"), and the act of "credenza" was the tasting of food and drink by a servant to test for poison prior to the master consuming it, and after a while the name of the act simply transferred to the piece of furniture where the food and drink was displayed prior to tasting and then serving at table.

● Credenzas became particularly popular not just in Italy, but also elsewhere in Continental Europe, especially France, and in Great Britain during the second half of the 19thC.

● Larger than chiffoniers, raised on a plinth base instead of feet, and with storage and/or display shelves fitted on each side of a center cupboard, the most desirable were of breakfront and/or serpentine profile and had glazed side panels.

● The form of the credenza, especially with its center cupboard door, lent itself to elaborate decoration, which ranged from pietre dure, marquetry, and boullework to porcelain panels.

● Traditionally, the end shelves, especially when fitted behind glazed doors, were lined with velvet—red being the most popular color—which accentuated the opulence of the surrounding decoration.

A mid-19thC early Victorian ebonized and parcel-gilt mirrored credenza, by Charles Nosotti, London, the top above two mirrored tiers with mirrored backs, divided by fluted columns with foliate capitals, the frame with applied gilt-gesso shell motifs, scrolls, and flowers, stencil maker's stamp on the reverse.

Charles Andrea Nosotti is listed as a carver, gilder, upholsterer, and cabinetmaker at 2 Dean Street, Soho, from 1835-40, although he appears to have set up a "looking glass manufactory" in 1831. Almost certainly born in Milan, his high standard of workmanship led him to exhibit a giltwood cabinet at the 1862 London Exhibition that he had made for the Countess of Waldegrave's drawing room at Strawberry Hill.

71¼in (181cm) wide
$4,300-5,600 **L&T**

A mid-19thC Victorian walnut and marble-top credenza and mirror, the mirror back with a blind-carved foliate border, over a marble top and twin cupboard doors with blind-carved reserves, flanked by corner shelves on each side.

106in (269cm) high
$3,700-4,300 **L&T**

A 19thC Renaissance Revival oak credenza, the superstructure with a shelf, surmounted by a pierced and carved cresting with a center cartouche flanked by dragons, on dragon shelf supports, the center of the lower part carved with an armorial flanked by mythical beasts and foliate scrolls, flanked by lion-mask pilasters, and on winged dragon supports, on an inverted breakfront plinth.

65¾in (167cm) high
$1,400-1,700 **L&T**

A 19thC Victorian walnut, ebonized, and marquetry credenza, the top above a center door, inlaid with a musical trophy and foliate scrolls, flanked by glazed cabinets, enclosing shelves, on a base with toupie feet, with gilt-metal mounts.

65¼in (165.5cm) wide
$2,200-2,700 **L&T**

A late-19thC Sheraton Revival satinwood credenza, the superstructure with a shelf, the base with a pair of doors painted with courting couples, opening to shelves, decorated with ribbon-tied flower garlands, swags, trophies, and husk trails.

42¼in (107cm) wide
$1,400-1,600 **L&T**

A Regency rosewood and brass-mounted chiffonier, in the manner of John Mclean, inlaid with brass marquetry and banding, the raised back with Gothic and geometric fret galleries with turned column supports, with two drawers above a frieze drawer and a pair of lattice and silk pleated doors, on gilt-brass-mounted feet.

ca. 1815   49¾in (126.5cm) high
$3,100-4,300 **WW**

An early-19thC French Empire mahogany chiffonier, the brass-galleried superstructure above a frieze drawer and a pair of silk pleated doors, flanked by columns.

48½in (123cm) high
$875-1,000 **L&T**

A mid-18thC George III mahogany sideboard, the crossbanded top above a center frieze drawer flanked by deep drawers, each side with a door in the rear, on tapering legs and spade feet.

76½in (194cm) wide

$2,000-2,200   DUK

A late-18thC Georgian mahogany and marquetry sideboard, crossbanded with stringing, the top over a frieze drawer with batwing paterae, flanked by a drawer and a lead-lined cellarette, both faced as a small drawer over a deep drawer.

60in (152.5cm) wide

$1,100-1,250   HT

A George III mahogany sideboard, with boxwood stringing and parquetry dogtooth banding, with four drawers.

ca. 1790-1800   *73in (185.5cm) wide*

$1,600-2,000   WW

A late-18thC Georgian mahogany and inlaid sideboard, the stage back with tambour doors, above a center drawer flanked by a cellarette drawer and pair of drawers, on tapered legs ending in block feet, outlined with stringing and with harebell and flowering urn inlay.

74in (188cm) wide

$1,250-1,500   L&T

A George III mahogany and marquetry sideboard, probably Irish, late 18thC and later, the crossbanded top with boxwood stringing, above a center frieze drawer, with a satinwood panel inlaid with a vase and flowers, flanked by a pair of decanter drawers, with pierced gilt-brass handles, with a crossbanded frame inlaid with a panel, the legs and brackets inlaid with flowering foliate motifs issuing from ewers.

83in (211cm) wide

$1,900-2,500   WW

A Scottish George III mahogany and crossbanded sideboard, with marquetry thistle decoration, fitted with a lead cellarette and ice box, splits.

ca. 1785   *48in (122cm) wide*

$3,100-3,700   CHOR

An early-19thC Scottish George III mahogany inlaid stageback sideboard, the superstructure with a sliding door compartment, above a concave base with two frieze drawers flanked by deep drawers, on square tapered legs ending in spade feet.

83½in (212cm) wide

$2,500-3,100   L&T

A 19thC Regency mahogany inlaid pedestal sideboard, with three frieze drawers, above cupboard doors outlined with stringing and bead molding, and inlaid with shell motifs, on bracket feet.

53½in (136cm) wide

$700-800   L&T

CLOSER LOOK—A VICTORIAN SIDEBOARD

At the apex of the mirror frame sits Britannia. Once a Roman warrior goddess, she became the personification of most of the British Isles after the Roman conquest in AD 43 and enjoyed a huge revival as such during the expansion of the British Empire in the Georgian-Victorian era. Accompanied by an emblematic lion (an animal found on the arms of England and Scotland), she sits above an oval medallion depicting ships at sea. This, combined with Britannia's trident, symbolize the Naval power that underpinned the Empire.

Additional figures and other military motifs are carved into the intertwined foliate forms of the mirror frame, and most prominent among the latter are scrolling acanthus leaves. A recurring motif in Classical architecture they, like Britannia, reinforce the link with the Roman Empire and antiquity.

The carved platform base is flanked by a pair of figural supports. Both Classical maidens, one holds a cornucopia overflowing with fruit, the other a branch of laurel leaves. Since Classical antiquity, the former, a goat's horn, has been a symbol of fertility and abundance, and the latter an emblem of renewal, resurrection, glory, and honor.

The center of the frieze is carved with a number of Masonic emblems denoting admirable qualities or virtues, such as temperance, fortitude, prudence, enlightenment, thrift, piety, and justice.

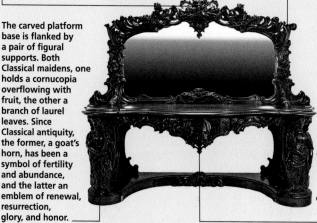

An imposing mid-19thC Victorian carved mahogany mirror-back sideboard, with later mirror plate, restored Britannia figure, acanthus scroll corner section missing.

109in (277cm) wide

$10,000-11,000   TEN

An 18thC walnut kneehole desk, with 12 drawers and a single door, the drawer fronts inlaid with pewter lines, within feather-banded edges.

ca. 1730   *42¼in (107cm) wide*

$550-700   **WHP**

A George II walnut and feather-banded kneehole desk, scratches, losses, restorations, replacements, worm.

ca. 1735   *29¼in (74cm) wide*

$1,400-1,900   **DN**

A George II mahogany desk, the open top fitted with six drawers, above a slide-out writing surface fitted with later leather and a hinged slope on a ratchet, above a pair of frieze drawers.

ca. 1740   *47½in (120.5cm) wide*

$1,900-2,500   **WW**

A George II burl oak kneehole desk, with a quarter veneer and feather-banded top, with seven oak-lined drawers around a center recess with a single cupboard door, veneer losses, alterations, and additions.

32¼in (82cm) wide

$5,000-6,200   **CHEF**

A George II mahogany kneehole desk, the caddy-molded top above eight drawers, surrounding a center cupboard door enclosing a shelf.

ca. 1750   *30in (76cm) wide*

$1,050-1,200   **WW**

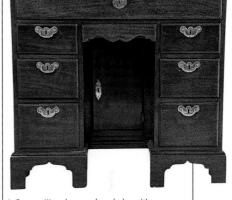

A George III mahogany kneehole writing desk, the molded and crossbanded hinged lid enclosing a fitted interior, with a writing slope and apertures for ink bottles and pen, a sliding drawer below flanked by six drawers around a center cupboard door, splits, scratches.

ca. 1770   *39in (99cm) wide*

$2,500-3,100   **TEN**

A George III mahogany desk, in the manner of Thomas Chippendale, on concealed brass casters, with a leather inset surface, scratches, losses, pitting, restorations, worm.

ca. 1770   *53½in (136cm) wide*

$8,500-10,000   **DN**

A late-18thC late George III mahogany and pine-lined partners' desk, the top with writing surface above three frieze drawers, on pedestal supports with six pine-lined drawers, some splits.

60¼in (153cm) wide

$1,050-1,200   **TEN**

A late-18thC George III mahogany kneehole desk, the blind fret lattice bracket feet with concealed casters, losses, handles are later.

33in (84cm) wide

$1,900-2,200   **DN**

FURNITURE

A George III mahogany partners' pedestal desk, with a tooled leather inset top, the center drawers on each side with baize inset hinge rests, scratches, old splits, cracks, later elements.

ca. 1800   *54¼in (138cm) wide*

$6,000-7,500   **DN**

A mid-19thC late Regency mahogany double-pedestal desk, the top with a leather writing surface above three frieze drawers, on pedestals, one side as drawers, the other with cupboard doors.

49in (124.5cm) wide

$1,000-1,250   **TEN**

A mid-19thC French mahogany and gilt-metal-mounted desk, in Empire style, the top with pierced brass three-quarter gallery above three drawers, with reeded borders and a tambour front enclosing a sliding work surface and drawers, the base with three dummy drawers above two long and two short drawers, all between anthemion, musical trophies, and husk-decorated gilt-metal mounts, the pull-out brushing slide with panels below.

57¾in (147cm) wide

$5,000-6,200   **TEN**

A Victorian oak double-pedestal partners' desk, the top with a leather writing surface above six frieze drawers, on pedestals with cupboard doors enclosing drawers, with scrolled and carved pierced supports and brackets, on sled bases with recessed casters.

ca. 1870   *54¼in (138cm) wide*

$2,500-3,100   **TEN**

A 19thC mahogany twin-pedestal desk, the top above nine drawers.

59½in (151cm) wide

$1,000-1,100   **WW**

A mid- to late-19thC Victorian satinwood and polychrome painted "Carlton House" desk, in George III style, the leather inset lifting to a ratcheted slope, scratches, splits.

52in (132cm) wide

$3,100-4,300   **DN**

A carved pine twin-pedestal partners' desk, in George III style, the writing surface above paneled ends with giant scallop shells and pendant husk chains, each side with nine drawers on a plinth base with egg-and-dart molding, in need of restoration, splits, three handles missing.

ca. 1900   *67¼in (171cm) wide*

$16,000-20,000   **TEN**

An Edwardian lady's writing desk, by Edwards & Roberts, the top with a tooled leather surface and three drawers, over two shaped pedestals, each with three graduated drawers, on splayed feet, stamped on the center drawer.

43in (109cm) wide

$950-1,050   **WHP**

An early-20thC Irish Edwardian mahogany and marquetry inlaid tambour-front cylinder desk, by J. Dooley & Sons, the top with a pierced brass three-quarter gallery and tambour molding on the verso, above a sliding cover enclosing seven satinwood drawers inlaid with flowerbells, above a sliding writing surface, with three drawers below.

36¼in (92cm) wide

$1,900-2,200   **TEN**

A George I walnut and cross- and feather-banded bureau, fitted beneath the drop with four drawers, on bracket feet, some veneer lifting, chips.

35¾in (90.5cm) wide

$1,900-2,500   CHOR

An early-18thC walnut and feather-banded bureau, originally the base of a bureau cabinet, the drop front enclosing pigeonholes over three drawers, four graduated drawers below, with brass escutcheons and later turned handles.

21¼in (54cm) wide

$3,100-3,700   HT

A diminutive burl walnut bureau, probably early 18thC, with cross -and feather banding, the hinged drop revealing pigeonholes, three drawers, and a later baize lined writing surface, above seven drawers and an apron with a drop center, on tapering legs, with brass side carrying handles.

18in (46cm) wide

$4,300-5,600   WW

A mid-18thC George II mahogany bureau-on-stand, the hinged drop revealing shaped and carved drawers around a center cupboard, above two short and one long cock-beaded drawer with brass swing handles, on cabriole legs, with brass side carrying handles.

28in (71cm) wide

$5,000-6,200   WW

A George II black lacquer and gilt chinoiserie decorated bureau, the drop front opening to an arrangement of small drawers and pigeonholes, centered by a small cupboard door.

ca. 1740   *43¼in (110cm) wide*

$6,000-7,500   DN

An Anglo-Chinese Qianlong huanghuali bureau-on-stand, the stand 18thC English, the drop-front revealing three drawers and a later lift-out surface enclosing a well, above a long drawer with brass handles, the side with brass carrying handles, on a Chinese Chippendale-style mahogany stand with a long drawer, with arcaded blind fretwork.

ca. 1750-60   *24½in (62.5cm) wide*

$3,700-4,300   WW

A mid-18thC Georgian burl walnut and feather-banded bureau, the drop front enclosing an interior with drawers and pigeonholes, centered by a cupboard, two short over three long drawers below, with brass drop handles.

33¼in (84.5cm) wide

$1,500-1,700   HT

A George III black lacquer and polychrome japanned bureau, with scenes of figures and pagodas in gardens, the hinged fall enclosing a fitted interior with pigeonholes and drawers around a center cupboard, all above two short and three long drawers, on bracket feet, damage and repair, paintwork is worn, later locks and handles, worm.

ca. 1780   *39in (99cm) wide*

$5,000-6,200   DN

A 19thC Dutch walnut and marquetry inlaid bureau, inlaid with flowers and leaves, the drop front enclosing a fitted interior with a sliding well, a center cupboard door, and small drawers, with pull-out lopers above three long drawers and an arched apron.

52in (132cm) wide

$4,300-5,600   TEN

A late-17thC North Italian cedar pine and poker-work escritoire, the back with mythical beasts and an inscription, the hinged drop decorated with a blindfolded cherub on a chariot, drawn by two lions, with an inscription in Latin that translates "He who has given to a worthy man receives a benefit from giving," the interior with drawers, pigeonholes, and cupboards, decorated with fountains, trees, and birds, the sides with scroll decoration, with gilt-brass side carrying handles, on a later stand.

44¾in (113.5cm) wide

$2,500-3,700   WW

A 19thC satinwood, tulipwood-banded, and brass-mounted bureau or cabinet, in George III style, in two sections, the pierced three-quarter gallery with silk grille doors below, the hinged writing slope enclosing a writing surface, ink bottles, and a compartment, a long frieze drawer below, with pull-out lopers.

50½in (128cm) high

$2,000-2,500   TEN

A mahogany and crossbanded bonheur du jour, by Hepplewhite, the superstructure with drawers and cupboards around a center recess, the lower section with a single long drawer fitted with an internal baize-lined slide, on square tapered legs.

ca. 1785   30in (76cm) wide

$3,100-4,300   CHEF

A Regency rosewood writing table, the top inset with tooled leather, with two frieze drawers with turned brass handles, on square tapering end supports, with scroll brackets joined by a pole stretcher, on a downswept trestle base with brass lion-paw toes and casters, stamped "A Solomon, 59 Great Queen Street, London."

39¼in (99.5cm) wide

$1,050-1,200   HT

A Regency rosewood writing table, in the manner of George Bullock, with a tooled leather-inset top and blind frieze drawer on one side.

ca. 1815   35¾in (91cm) wide

$2,500-3,100   DN

A William IV mahogany library or architect's table, the hinged top with brass arm hinges and two adjustable book or folio rests, one hinge stamped "HORNE PATENT," above a frieze drawer and two concealed folio recesses released by brass pins in the end supports, carved on all sides so that it can be placed in the center of a room.

ca. 1835   47¾in (121.5cm) wide

$2,500-3,700   DN

An early Victorian mahogany writing table, with two frieze drawers, one with a lock stamped "VR PATENT."

ca. 1840   48¼in (122.5cm) wide

$1,250-1,900   DN

A late-19th/early-20thC French tulipwood, parquetry, and gilt-metal-mounted bureau, in Louis XV style, the drop front opening to three small drawers above a slide-covered well and a baize-inset writing surface.

23¼in (59cm) wide

$1,900-3,100   DN

An early-19thC draftsman's mahogany table, the top with adjustable reading slope, flanked by storage compartments, one with fitted lift-out trays, the fascia with five dummy drawers above a kneehole.

35¾in (91cm) wide

$550-700 HT

A Victorian walnut and marquetry writing table, in Louis XV style, of kidney shape, with gilt-bronze mounts, the top inset with a gilt tooled-leather writing surface, inlaid with a pair of cornucopia and a basket of fruit and flowers.

ca. 1870 *45¾in (116cm) wide*

$1,500-2,000 WW

A mid- to late-19thC French tulipwood, specimen floral marquetry, and ormolu-mounted writing table, veneered on all sides, with a frieze drawer, old veneer repairs.

32¾in (83cm) wide

$3,700-5,000 DN

A 19thC French rosewood and ormolu bureau plat, in Louis XV style, with five drawers around the kneehole, opposing dummy drawers, the center drawer stamped "PARIS."

65¼in (166cm) wide

$3,700-5,000 DN

A 19thC mahogany gentleman's writing table, in the manner of Gillows, the top below a shell-carved shaped three-quarter gallery, with five drawers in the front and four dummy drawers in the reverse, with brass casters, wear, knocks, alterations.

50¾in (129cm) wide

$3,700-4,300 CHEF

A late-19thC French rosewood bureau plat, in Louis XV style, with ormolu mounts, the top with a gilt tooled leather writing surface, above three frieze drawers.

57in (145cm) wide

$1,200-1,350 WW

A late-19thC satinwood, tulipwood-banded, and polychrome-painted bonheur de jour, the superstructure above two cupboard doors, painted with panels flanking a ribbon decorated niche, the hinged leather writing surface and long frieze drawer decorated with ribbons and floral swags.

24in (61cm) wide

$1,500-2,000 TEN

A late-19th/early-20thC French kingwood and ormolu-mounted bureau plat, in Regencé style, after the model by Charles Cressent, the top inset with a gilt tooled tan leather writing surface, within a molded border and shell mounts to the corners, above three frieze drawers with substantial leaf cast handles interspersed with bearded male masks concealing secret drawers, with espagnolette chutes, the ends with satyr masks, on lion-paw feet.

This fine bureau plat is based on two known examples by the ébéniste Charles Cressent (1685-1768), who ranks with Boulle, Riesener, and Gouthiere as one of the most famous craftsmen of the 18thC. He was recorded as the official cabinetmaker to the Duc d'Orleans, who served as Regent to the young Louis XV from 1715-23. One of his specialities was the bureau plat, a new form of writing table thought to have been invented by André-Charles Boulle at the begining of the 18thC.

79½in (202cm) wide

$20,000-25,000 WW

A Victorian burl walnut writing table, the stepped back with five drawers and pierced brass gallery surmounts, two frieze drawers with brass drop handles, on twin turned fluted end supports.

48in (122cm) wide

$800-950 HT

ESSENTIAL REFERENCE—DAVENPORTS

An entry in the record books of the prestigious cabinetmakers Gillows of Lancaster (see page 200), made in the 1790s, states: "Captain Davenport, a desk," and it's this that is thought to be the first recorded example of the small writing cabinets that came to be named after the captain. Popular until around the end of the 19thC, davenports had a basic form that changed little, comprising a small chest-of-drawers with a desk compartment above. Pull-out drawers on one side, with dummy drawers opposite, were a common feature, as were feet with casters for ease of movement. However, there were numerous variations: the most fundamental being that earlier examples had a top section with a writing slope that slid forward when in use to accommodate the writer's legs, whereas from the mid-1840s most had the desk section fixed in the writing position, supported on brackets, thereby enabling a permanently recessed space for legs. Other variants included concealed drawers, real or dummy cupboard doors, wood or brass galleries, and pull-out candle sconces (rare). Decorative embellishments, such as elaborate carving or inlay work, also varied considerably; in general, earlier examples are understated, late Victorian ones often over-ornamented. Also, being small—usually no more than 18in (46cm) wide and deep prior to the 1830s, albeit broadening to around 24in (60cm) thereafter—davenports were primarily used by women.

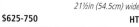

A Regency mahogany and ebony banded davenport, with lift-off slope section.

14¼in (36cm) wide

$700-800   BELL

An early-19thC burl yew swivel-top davenport, by C. Hindley and Sons, late Miles and Edwards.

19¾in (50cm) wide

$1,100-1,250   BELL

A George IV mahogany davenport, attributed to Gillows, the hinged slope with two drawers and a pull button mechanism for the pop-out hinged pen and ink compartment, with a pair of slides, the right side with a door enclosing four drawers.

ca. 1825   20¼in (51.5cm) wide

$750-875   WW

A George IV rosewood davenport, the sliding top with pierced brass gallery and side pen drawer, the slope enclosing an interior with drawers, four side drawers with turned wood handles.

21½in (54.5cm) wide

$625-750   HT

A mid-19thC early Victorian rosewood and satin birch davenport, of typical form with spiral column supports, with drawers on one side and dummy drawers opposing.

28in (71cm) wide

$450-550   L&T

A mid-19thC Victorian walnut davenport, with a hinged superstructure above a slope, on carved scrolled supports, with four drawers on one side and dummy drawers opposing.

21¾in (55cm) wide

$700-800   L&T

A Victorian burl walnut davenport, inlaid with stringing and burl banding, with a stationery compartment with a push-button mechanism, above a sloping hinged front, the interior with two drawers, the right side with a door enclosing four drawers.

ca. 1860-70   22in (56cm) wide

$500-625   WW

A Victorian walnut davenport, of serpentine form, with turned and carved baluster supports, and shaped drawers, splits, veneer wear.

ca. 1860   32¾in (83cm) high

$625-750   SWO

A Victorian rosewood davenport, the drop front opening to a maple-lined interior with drawers and pigeonholes, hinged ink drawer on the side over a slide, with four drawers below, conforming slide and four dummy drawers opposite.

23in (58.5cm) wide

$750-875   HT

A late-17thC carved giltwood mirror, possibly Dutch, the mirror plate surrounded by triumphal putti before symbols of war, surmounted by a Dutch royal crown with pearls and strawberry leaves, above a cypher that appears to depict "JWF" on two snarling lions, the apron with a sunrise medallion with the date "1711" inside a swag, repairs.

Stylistically, this carved giltwood is very much of the late 17thC and early 18thC. The monogram "JWF" on it possibly represents the initials of Prince Johan Willem Friso, who became the titular Prince of Orange in 1702. On coming of age in 1707, he became commander-in-chief of the Dutch troops during the War of the Spanish Succession, under the overall command of the Duke of Marlborough. A competent officer, Willem commanded the Dutch infantry at the Battle of Oudenarde (1708), the Siege of Lille (1708), and the Battle of Malplaquet (1709). However, on July 14, 1711, while traveling from the front in Flanders to meet the King of Prussia in The Hague, he drowned on a ferry that overturned in heavy weather. His son and heir, who was born six weeks after his death, grew up to become William IV, Prince of Orange.

57½in (146cm) high

$27,000-32,000 DN

An early-18thC George I giltwood and gilt-gesso girandole mirror, in the manner of James Moore, possibly supplied by Gerrit Jensen, the lower plate surmounted by a bevel plate in a scrolled gadrooned frame, surmounted by Prince of Wales feathers between confronted masks emerging from foliage, the apron centered by a shell between brass candle sockets.

When George I ascended the British throne in 1714, his son George Augustus became Prince of Wales and George Augustus's wife, Caroline of Ansbach, became Princess of Wales. The heraldic badge of the Prince of Wales—a plume of three white ostrich feathers (usually emerging from a gold coronet)—that surmounts this giltwood girandole mirror frame suggests that the mirror may well have once been part of a large consignment of furniture originally commissioned on behalf of either Prince George or Princess Caroline to furnish one of their private or state apartments. As to which of the latter, it could have been either for the ones in St. James's Palace or in Leicester House—today, the site of Leicester Square, and where the Prince and Princess lived after Prince George was expelled from his father's court in 1720.

63in (160cm) high

$28,500-32,000 DUK

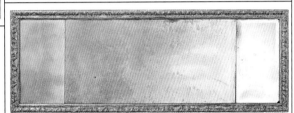

A George I gilt gesso mirror.
ca. 1720 43in (109cm) wide
$1,100-1,350 DN

A Régence carved giltwood mirror, inscribed "E. Caris, Faugeais, Chab," dated on reverse, cracks, gilding refreshed, worm, old glued repairs, replacement elements.
1719 82¾in (210cm) high
$27,000-32,000 DN

An early-18thC George I black and gilt japanned mirror, in the manner of Giles Grendey, the frame decorated with Chinese-inspired figures and scenes.
58¾in (149cm) high
$8,500-10,000 DUK

A George II giltwood and gesso wall mirror, mirror plate is a replacement, old small repairs.
ca. 1735 43in (109cm) high
$3,700-5,000 DN

A George II mahogany and giltwood wall mirror, the later plate within a shaped slip, the frame with applied leaves and a bonnet pediment centered with a carved ho ho bird.
ca. 1740 55in (140cm) high
$1,400-1,600 WW

An early-18thC Italian carved giltwood wall mirror, splits, repairs, mirror plate is later.
74in (188cm) high
$10,000-11,000 DN

A mid-18thC George II giltwood mirror, with a pierced foliate frame, surmounted by a cartouche of C scrolls, with pierced trefoil apron.
46¾in (119cm) high
$3,700-5,000 DUK

FURNITURE

A mid-18thC George II carved giltwood wall mirror, gilding refreshed, wear, losses.

55in (140cm) high

$8,000-9,300   **DN**

A Louis XV carved giltwood mirror, the crest centered with a musical trophy, some wear and loss in gildng, replacement elements.

ca. 1755   55in (140cm) high

$3,700-5,000   **DN**

A mid-18thC George II walnut and parcel-gilt mirror, the plate in a frame with scrolled cresting, centered by an eagle with open wings, with a shaped apron beneath.

46½in (118cm) high

$5,000-6,200   **DUK**

An early-George III giltwood mirror, Chippendale period, the plate probably later, inside a frame of foliate C scrolls, swags, and rocaille, beneath a Chinaman in a pagoda flanked by flowering urns, regilt.

ca. 1760   41in (104cm) high

$5,000-6,200   **WW**

A George III carved giltwood wall mirror, mirror plate and backboard are replacements.

ca. 1760   54in (137cm) high

$6,000-7,500   **DN**

A George III giltwood wall mirror, in the manner of Thomas Johnson, frame breaks and repairs.

Thomas Johnson's naturalistic and fanciful carving and ornament were popularized in the 1750s following the publication of his designs, including mirrors.

ca. 1760   63¾in (162cm) high

$7,500-8,500   **DN**

A late-18th/early-19thC carved giltwood mirror, in the manner of Thomas Chippendale, the plate within carved scrolling foliage, acanthus scrolls, and flowering branches, the arched C scroll carved cresting with eagles on rockwork, foliage, and acanthus leaves, the apron with acanthus and C-scroll carved clasp, repairs, plate is a replacement.

This mirror is an interpretation of a design for a pier glass by Thomas Chippendale (1718-79; see plate CLXIX for a related design published in Chippendale's "The Gentleman and Cabinet-Maker's Director," 3rd edition, 1763).

This mirror is from Flaxley Abbey in Gloucestershire, the interiors of which were designed by Oliver Messel (see page 210).

Because Messel was initially commissioned for the interiors of the morning room and drawing room, it seems probable that he incorporated this historic mirror from the original Crawley-Boevey family collection into his plan for Flaxley after it had been bought by Frederick Baden Watkins in the 1960s.

96in (244cm) high

$41,000-45,000   **DN**

An 18thC Italian Florentine carved giltwood wall mirror, the plate within a foliate and flower frame, divided by ribbon motifs.

55½in (141cm) high

$4,300-5,000   **TEN**

An early-19thC Regency giltwood mirror, the convex mirror plate in a reeded ebonized slip- and ball-mounted frame, surmounted by a carved dragon, with an acanthus pendant finial.

46in (117cm) high

$2,500-3,100   **L&T**

An early-19thC Florentine-type wall mirror, the giltwood fretwork surround enclosing a mirrored plate.

49½in (126cm) high

$2,500-3,100   **WHP**

A giltwood mirror, in the manner of William Kent, the plate in an egg-and-dart frame flanked with trailing foliage, surmounted by a shell flanked by C scrolls, the apron with a foliate spray.

59½in (151cm) high

$4,300-5,600   **DUK**

A 19thC Continental carved giltwood and gesso pier glass, the plate flanked by marginal plates, in a scrolling and floral decorated frame, the plume painted en grisaille with trailing leaves and C scrolls surrounding an urn issuing fruit.

75½in (192cm) high

$1,100-1,350   **TEN**

A scarlet tortoiseshell, engraved brass, and ormolu-mounted wall mirror, in the manner of André-Charles Boulle, in Louis XIV style.

ca. 1860   *54¼in (138cm) high*

$7,500-8,500   **DN**

A 19thC French gilt and silvered wood wall mirror, in Empire style, the later plate within a faux bois frame, with an eagle and leaf-branch surmount.

82in (208cm) high

$1,400-1,700   **WW**

One of a pair of 19thC North Italian giltwood mirrors, the aprons carved with female portrait masks wearing feathered headdresses, the shaped sides with female terms holding flowers and acanthus scrolls, the cresting with tasseled canopies suspending drapery swags and surmounted by two peasant figures wearing hats, resting on acanthus scrolls, mirror plates with splits, reinforcements.

The design is possibly inspired by the work of Jean Bérain (1640-1711), who featured a garlanded baldacchino in his representation of Pallas-Athena, flanked by two putti, Eros and Anteros, a scene symbolic of "Love's triumph."

41¾in (106cm) high

$5,000-6,200 the pair   **DN**

A mid- to late-19thC Swedish gilt-metal and engraved-glass pier glass, in Charles II style, decorated with scrolls and flowerbells, the scrolled pediment surmounted by an urn issuing flowers and foliage, flanked by repoussé-decorated flowers.

52¼in (133cm) high

$5,000-6,200   **TEN**

A 19thC gilt framed pier mirror, the plate below a verre églomisé panel depicting a barn within a woodland landscape, flanked by column pilasters.

29½in (75cm) high

$700-800   **CHEF**

A late-19thC Victorian gilt and gesso mirror, in Adam style, the plate within an egg-and-dart border, flanked by green Jasper relief-decorated medallions jointed by husks, the acanthus scrolling pediment centered by an urn.

48¾in (124cm) wide

$1,000-1,250   **TEN**

A late-18th/19thC carved giltwood overmantel mirror, in George III style, in the manner of Thomas Johnson, mirror plate with depletion, cracks in frame, wear, chips.

For a design by Thomas Johnson of a mirror of related form, incorporating similar pergola cresting and scrolls in the frame, see Elizabeth White, "Pictorial Dictionary of British 18th Century Furniture Design," Antique Collector's Club (1990), page 335.

90¼in (229cm) high

$16,000-20,000   DN

A 19thC carved giltwood mirror, in mid-18thC style, frame with cracks and splits.

58¼in (148cm) high

$6,000-7,500   DN

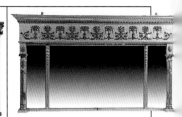

An early-19thC Regency giltwood and gesso triple overmantel mirror, the cornice with ball mounts, above a frieze depicting Apollo in a chariot pulled by lions.

56in (142cm) wide

$1,250-1,600   L&T

An early-Victorian giltwood and gesso overmantel mirror, with three plates flanked by cluster columns, the frieze decorated with palmettes interspersed with tazze of fruit.

ca. 1840-50   58¾in (149cm) wide

$500-625   WW

A mid-19thC George IV gilt and gesso triptych overmantel mirror, the frieze decorated with laurel leaves, with pilaster and acanthus supports, the mirror plate old but not original.

51¼in (130cm) wide

$700-800   TEN

A Victorian giltwood overmantel mirror, the plate within a bead and laurel frame, applied with cherubs, with a quiver, flaming torch, and floral wreath surmount.

ca. 1850-60   69in (175.5cm) high

$2,500-3,700   WW

A 19thC giltwood triple overmantel mirror, in George III style, the frieze centered by husk swags and a sunflower, the mirror plates flanked and divided by reeded columns.

56in (142cm) wide

$1,400-1,700   L&T

A Victorian giltwood and gesso overmantel mirror, the later plate within a naturalistic frame, centered on a fern leaf crest.

ca. 1860-80   60¾in (154cm) high

$1,700-2,200   WW

A 19thC giltwood landscape overmantel mirror, in George II style, with three plates within a leaf-molded frame, with applied scroll leaf and fruit garlands.

52¼in (132.5cm) wide

$800-950   WW

ESSENTIAL REFERENCE—CHEVAL MIRRORS

Cheval mirrors were first recorded in Paris in the 18thC at the court of Louis XVI. They were named "cheval," which is French for "horse," because they were mounted on a four-legged frame that, raised on casters, could be easily moved around a room.

● Being long and tiltable, the cheval mirror glass was able to provide a useful full-length reflection for someone getting dressed, and not surprisingly the design was quickly adopted in Great Britain and elsewhere in Continental Europe.

● While many decoratively restrained or understated cheval mirrors were produced, they did reach new heights of extravagance and luxury during the late 18thC and early 19thC, with typically opulent examples being mounted in gilt bronze with mythological deities, stars, and Classical reliefs, their mirror plates often arched and supported by Classical columns—a style copied throughout much of Europe, especially in Great Britain, Austria, and Germany, as well as in North America.

A George I walnut dressing table mirror, early 18thC and later, the plate in a molded slip, with a later fret surmount, the base fitted with four drawers flanking a cupboard.

30½in (77.5cm) high

$375-450   **WW**

An early-18thC George I walnut dressing table mirror, the arched plate in a gilt and molded slip, above a stepped box base fitted with five drawers.

26in (66cm) high

$375-450   **WW**

An early-18thC George II walnut and feather-banded dressing table mirror, the plate in a frame with turned brass finials, the base with three scroll-front drawers and a wavy apron.

25½in (65cm) high

$250-370   **WW**

A late-18thC George III mahogany dressing table mirror, the plate on scrolling supports, the serpentine box base with three drawers and inlaid with a shell motif.

24in (61cm) high

$800-950   **WW**

A George III mahogany dressing table mirror, inlaid with stringing, with bone rondels and escutcheon, with a shield-shaped plate above a serpentine box base.

ca. 1790-1800   *22¼in (56.5cm) high*

$250-370   **WW**

An early-20thC walnut dressing table mirror, in Dutch style, the swing mirror with a molded frame, the base with drop front and two long drawers above a shaped apron.

32¼in (82cm) high

$375-500   **CHEF**

An early-19thC Regency mahogany cheval mirror, the plate within a pivoting frame, with part wrythen-turned and reeded uprights joined by turned stretchers, on acanthus-carved cabriole legs, with brass paw feet and casters.

63¾in (162cm) high

$3,700-5,000   **TEN**

A Regency mahogany and ebonized cheval mirror, in the manner of Gillows, the engraved swing plate flanked by gilt-brass articulated candle arms.

ca. 1815   *67¼in (171cm) high*

$2,200-2,700   **DN**

A mid-19thC George IV mahogany cheval mirror, the mirror plate pivoting on reeded scrolled uprights, supporting pivoting brass candle arms.

61¾in (157cm) high

$2,000-2,500   **TEN**

A George III mahogany and brass-bound wine cooler, with a lead-lined interior, above handles and two brass straps.

ca. 1800   27¼in (69cm) high
$800-950   TEN

A George III brass-bound mahogany wine cooler, of coopered form, with brass side carrying handles and center rosette.

26¾in (68cm) wide
$1,400-1,600   CHEF

A Regency mahogany wine cooler, with reeded and canted sides.

30in (76cm) wide
$700-800   CHOR

A Regency mahogany cellarette, the hinged top enclosing a lead-lined interior, on hairy paw feet.

29½in (75cm) wide
$625-750   CHEF

A Regency mahogany and line-inlaid cellarette, the fitted and divided interior with a set of seven clear glass decanters and stoppers, knocks, repairs, worm.

ca. 1815   19¾in (50cm) high
$1,050-1,200   DN

An early-19thC Regency mahogany and crossbanded cellarette, with lion-mask loop handles and canted and reeded stiles.

29¼in (74cm) wide
$1,000-1,100   TEN

An early-19thC late Regency mahogany cellarette, with brass cast loop handles, on carved claw feet with recessed casters.

25¼in (64cm) wide
$700-800   TEN

A pair of Regency mahogany and brass-inlaid wine coolers.

ca. 1820   19¼in (49cm) high
$6,000-7,500   DN

A Victorian mahogany wine cooler, the lid surmounted by a fruit pediment, the lead-lined interior with metalwork dividers.

39in (99cm) wide
$800-875   WHP

A 20thC mahogany and gilt-brass wine cooler, in Regency style, lead lined, the paw feet with concealed casters.

45¾in (116cm) wide
$11,000-12,500   DN

A George III mahogany canterbury, with four curved divisions above a single drawer.

20¾in (53cm) wide

$625-750 **CHEF**

An early-19thC Regency rosewood canterbury, with four divisions and spindle supports above an open undertier.

17¼in (44cm) wide

$800-950 **L&T**

An early-19thC Regency mahogany canterbury, with three divisions with two solid dividers, enclosed by spindle gallery sides.

18in (46cm) wide

$450-550 **L&T**

A mahogany canterbury, in the manner of Lowndes, with five cross-framed dividers with a laurel wreath motif, with a single drawer below.

ca. 1820 *20in (51cm) wide*

$375-500 **CHEF**

An early-19thC Regency mahogany canterbury, with four dipped divisions above a frieze drawer, on brass casters.

19½in (49.5cm) wide

$800-950 **WW**

An early-19thC Regency mahogany canterbury, with three dipped divisions above a frieze drawer, on brass casters.

17¾in (45cm) wide

$375-500 **WW**

A George IV rosewood canterbury, with four sections and a center carrying handle above a single drawer.

22in (56cm) wide

$450-550 **CHEF**

A 19thC Dutch walnut and marquetry canterbury, with four divisions and urn finials in the corners, above a shaped undertier, with flowering urn marquetry throughout.

21¼in (54cm) high

$800-950 **L&T**

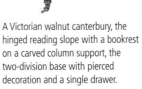

A Victorian walnut canterbury, the hinged reading slope with a bookrest on a carved column support, the two-division base with pierced decoration and a single drawer.

36½in (93cm) high

$1,000-1,100 **CHEF**

A late-Victorian walnut canterbury, with three divisions above a frieze drawer, on brass casters.

ca. 1890 *20½in (52cm) wide*

$250-310 **WW**

FURNITURE

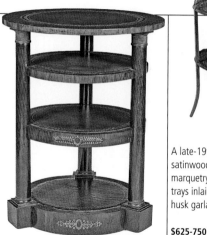

An early-19thC Regency rosewood, leather, and gilt-metal-mounted étagère, the tiers raised by columns with brass mounts.

33½in (85cm) high

$1,250-1,700　　　**L&T**

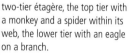

A late-19thC Sheraton Revival satinwood, rosewood, and marquetry étagère, with two trays inlaid with shell motifs and husk garlands.

32¾in (83cm) high

$625-750　　　**L&T**

A late-19thC chinoiserie-decorated two-tier étagère, the top tier with a monkey and a spider within its web, the lower tier with an eagle on a branch.

39¼in (100cm) wide

$800-950　　　**CHEF**

An early-20thC Edwardian brass, glass, and giltwood étagère, with three oval glass tiers, with giltwood supports, on toupie feet.

32¾in (83cm) high

$750-875　　　**L&T**

A 19thC Regency mahogany whatnot, in the manner of Gillows, with three tiers raised and divided by turned and tapered supports with finials.

31in (79cm) high

$625-750　　　**L&T**

An early-19thC Regency mahogany whatnot, the ratchet-adjusted top over three tiers and a base with drawers, outlined with faux bamboo molding.

36¼in (92cm) high

$700-800　　　**L&T**

An early-19thC rosewood four-tier whatnot, with two shelves on scrolled supports, each tier below with open slat divisions and turned X side braces.

76½in (194.5cm) high

$1,000-1,100　　　**HT**

An early-19thC William IV mahogany whatnot.

46¾in (119cm) high

$500-625　　　**L&T**

A mid-19thC Victorian ebonized and parcel-gilt whatnot, with a brass gallery above two tiers, the lower tier fitted as a canterbury, with a drawer in the base.

39in (99cm) high

$550-700　　　**L&T**

A mid-18thC George III mahogany dumbwaiter.

41¾in (106cm) high

$700-800　　　**WW**

A late-18thC George III mahogany dumbwaiter.

45¾in (116cm) high

$700-800　　　**WW**

A George III tole tray, black painted and inlaid with metal decoration, with a swag design inside two bands of ovals and flower heads.

ca. 1770   26¼in (66.5cm) wide

$500-625   WW

A George III mahogany and marquetry tray, with a brass balustrade gallery, inlaid with a center fan patera surrounded by urns and scrolling foliage.

ca. 1790   26¾in (68cm) wide

$800-950   WW

A George III mahogany and brass-bound tray, with twin molded handles and a later green felt base.

23½in (60cm) wide

$450-500   CHEF

An early-19thC German tôle peinte tray, in the manner of Stobwasser, black japanned with bands of gilt leaves and trophies, the center painted with a landscape scene with figures and horses, trees, and a town in the distance.

30¼in (77cm) wide

$500-625   WW

A George III mahogany and brass-bound tray.

ca. 1800   26in (66cm) wide

$450-550   TEN

An early-19thC English papier-mâché tray, by Clay, Covent Garden, London, decorated with butterflies amid foliage, with brass handles.

23½in (60cm) wide

$1,400-1,600   CHEF

A Victorian green lacquered papier-mâché tray, by W. Boulty & Son, London, painted and gilt with a peacock and exotic birds in flowering foliage, painted inscription verso.

ca. 1850   27¼in (69cm) wide

$1,200-1,350   WW

A 19thC tole tray, possibly French, with painted and gilt decoration of demonlike figures among gilt foliage, the border with a soldier, dragon, and insects.

15¼in (39cm) wide

$250-370   WW

A large Victorian painted papier-mâché tray, decorated with peacocks and flowers within a landscape to a gilt border.

31½in (80cm) wide

$700-800   CHEF

A George II red walnut candle stand.
ca. 1750   *20½in (52cm) high*
$5,000-6,200   **DN**

A George II mahogany wine table or candle stand, knocks, scratches, repairs.
ca. 1750   *22in (56cm) high*
$5,500-6,000   **DN**

An early-George III mahogany kettle stand, the top with a gallery, above a fluted tapering column with a foliate-carved baluster lower section, the legs with flower head-carved knees, on claw-and-ball feet.
ca. 1760   *18¾in (47.5cm) high*
$1,900-2,500   **WW**

A George III mahogany kettle stand, the hexagonal top with a sliding cup stand, restorations, repairs.
ca. 1760   *25½in (65cm) high*
$3,100-3,700   **DN**

A pair of 19thC cluster-column torchères, in George III style, with dish tops above tapering supports, on three cabriole legs with pad feet.
38½in (98cm) high
$1,000-1,100   **TEN**

A mahogany wine table, in George III style, the top over a turned column support, on three acanthus-capped cabriole legs and pad feet.
20¾in (53cm) high
$750-875   **CHEF**

An adjustable mahogany candle stand, in George III style, the top above an adjustable mechanism within a fluted column support.
31½in (80cm) high
$375-500   **CHEF**

A late-19th/early-20thC satinwood and marquetry music stand, in Georgian style, the lyre form music rest with brass "strings," inlaid with a musical trophy, flowers, and cornucopia, on an adjustable brass rod and faceted column.
54¾in (139cm) high
$1,600-2,000   **L&T**

An Edwardian brass and mahogany adjustable music or reading stand, by Carter, London, on a cast metal four-branch base.
$300-375   **WHP**

A George III mahogany and fretwork urn stand.
ca. 1780   26½in (67cm) high
$2,500-3,100   **DN**

A George IV mahogany and brass-mounted hall stand, in the manner of Gillows.
ca. 1830   82in (208cm) high
$1,000-1,100   **DN**

A William IV mahogany teapoy, the top with hinged lid enclosing a fitted six-compartment interior, above a turned and lapit-carved column on a quadripartite base, on lion-paw feet.
31½in (80cm) high
$450-500   **CHEF**

A pair of 19thC mahogany urn stands, in Chippendale style, the tops carved with foliate gadrooning, stylized leaves, and flower heads, on cabriole legs with foliate carving and scrolled feet.
21in (53.5cm) high
$5,000-6,200   **WW**

A 19thC satinwood jardinière stand, stretchers show signs of restoration, repair in one foot.
31in (79cm) high
$300-450   **CHEF**

A George III mahogany urn stand, the top above a drawer and undertier below, on internally chamfered square legs.
24¾in (63cm) high
$700-800   **CHEF**

A set of 19thC mahogany wall shelves, with pierced ends.
35in (89cm) wide
$250-370   **WW**

A mid-18thC George III mahogany and brass-bound plate bucket, of staved construction.
24½in (62cm) high
$875-1,000   **TEN**

A George III mahogany and brass-bound peat bucket, probably Irish.
ca. 1790-1800   15in (38cm) high
$1,600-2,000   **WW**

An early-19thC mahogany and brass-bound peat bucket, of navette shape.
7¾in (20cm) high
$1,000-1,100   **WW**

A mahogany and pine painted four-poster bed, ca. 1780 and later, later elements, including a modern headboard.

82¼in (209cm) long

$5,000-6,200 **DN**

A mahogany and upholstered four-poster bed, ca. 1780 and later.

85in (216cm) long

$5,000-6,200 **DN**

A carved mahogany four-poster bed, late-18th/early-19thC and later.

85¾in (218cm) long

$17,500-20,000 **DN**

An early-19thC French Empire walnut and parcel-gilt bed headboard, with a scrolling bird and ribbon crest above a coronet with initials "AM," flanked by Greek keys, with vasiform finials above further gilt urns, the bedstead with tapering and parcel-gilt fluted columns, flowerbud finials, and carved and gilt flower heads.

63½in (161cm) wide

$2,100-2,500 **WW**

A mahogany four-poster bed, early-19thC and later, in the manner of George Hepplewhite, the tester painted with flower sprays and ribbon-tied drapery swags, surmounted by acorn finials, hangings by Colefax and Fowler, possibly made out of parts from multiple beds.

86½in (220cm) long

$16,000-20,000 **DN**

A 19thC carved mahogany and painted four-poster bed, with later elements.

83in (211cm) long

£17,000-19,000 **DN**

A late-18th/early-19thC Swedish Gustavian painted pine daybed, with Classical carved paterae and leaf decoration, with drop ends and a pull-out seat.

78½in (199.5cm) wide

$3,700-4,300 **WW**

A late-19th/early-20thC Italian silvered double bed, the headboard carved with strapwork, lozenges, and flower heads centered by a scrolled shell, with conforming carved rails, on acanthus-carved cabriole legs.

83¾in (213cm) long

$1,400-1,700 **TEN**

A green-painted and chinoiserie-decorated bedstead, the headboard with exotic birds and stylized clouds, surmounted by a C-scroll pediment, with a panel decorated with buildings and a landscape, the footboard painted with gilt figures, buildings, and foliage.

1920s/30s *84¾in (215cm) long*

$1,400-1,700 **TEN**

A mid-18thC George II walnut tea caddy, the hinged top opening to three removable gilt-decorated tôle peinte compartments, no key.

7¾in (20cm) wide

$375-500   DN

A German kingwood and brass-mounted tea chest, attributed to Abraham Roentgen, the front with a pierced brass cartouche-shaped escutcheon, the interior with three brass canisters, the center one with a domed cover and a twin interior, the covers with star decoration, the base with a spring-operated secret drawer in the right-hand side released by a button hidden when the cover is closed, on bracket feet, with key, and a bright-cut Sheffield plate caddy spoon.

Abraham Roentgen (1711-93) was a German ébéniste. He was born in Müllheim, Germany, and learned cabinetmaking in his father's workshop; he then worked as an apprentice in The Hague before settling in London in 1731. He ran the Roentgen firm from 1742 until about 1800 along with his son, David. Abraham's work was characterized by superb marquetry and innovative designs, often incorporating hidden compartments, secret drawers, and mechanical and musical devices, and his work was desired by rulers throughout Europe. One of his most famous pieces is the Walderdorffer bureau, now in the Rijksmuseum, Amsterdam.

ca. 1750-60   8¾in (22cm) wide

$5,000-6,200   WW

A George III mahogany tea caddy, the twin canisters with hinged covers flanking a glass sugar bowl.

ca. 1780   14¼in (36cm) wide

$500-625   WW

A George III mahogany tea caddy, the cover opening to reveal three compartments and spoon fittings within, on bracket feet.

11½in (29cm) wide

$500-550   CHEF

A George III specimen parquetry and marquetry tea caddy, in the manner of George Hepplewhite, the hinged top with "EC" monogram engraved on a metal plate within a rosette relief, repairs and replacements, no key.

ca. 1790   4¾in (12cm) wide

$3,100-3,700   DN

A George III harewood and marquetry tea caddy, in the manner of Gillows, inlaid with scrolling Classical marquetry in the manner of designs by Robert Adam, with key, repairs and replacements.

ca. 1790   5¾in (14.5cm) wide

$1,900-2,500   DN

A George III tortoiseshell tea caddy, with a silver-colored ball finial and engraved plaque on front, with ivory stringing and bands, with key.

Ivory Act certification no. 3JYLG4GZ

ca. 1780-1800   5in (13cm) wide

$950-1,050   DN

A late-18thC George III satinwood and silver-mounted tea chest, with crossbanding, the interior with a pair of lidded canisters flanking a cut-glass sugar bowl, the underside of the lid with a monogrammed silver plaque, the hinges and feet with partial London hallmarks and maker's mark "GL."

10in (25.5cm) wide

$700-800   WW

A rare Georgian green tortoiseshell tea caddy, with ivory edging, a silver escutcheon and an engraved initial plate with a monogram.

ca. 1790   7½in (19cm) wide

$9,500-10,500   MGO

ESSENTIAL REFERENCE—FRUITWOOD FRUIT TEA CADDIES

Nowadays, tea is mostly bought in boxes of small, individual cup-size tea bags. In contrast, from the first half of the 17thC, when tea first appeared in Europe (initially from China), up until about the mid-20thC, tea was imported in large chests and sold loose. Therefore, a canister or a caddy was required to store the tea leaves prior to brewing.

- Various materials have been employed in their manufacture, from pottery and porcelain to silver and silver plate to glass, tortoiseshell, and wood, while shapes or forms have ranged from bottle- or jarlike canisters to box- or casketlike caddies.
- Among the most desirable, however, and especially in terms of their collectibility nowadays, were the caddies fashioned from various fruitwoods, such as apple, cherry, and pear, into the shape of various fruits (and some vegetables).
- The majority of these fruitwood fruit tea caddies were made during the late 18thC and early to mid-19thC, and typical fruits included apples, melon, and pears, while albeit rarer vegetable forms included pumpkins and eggplants. As well as their pleasing, tactile shapes, their desirability often also resides in the rich, deep, lustrous patina their polished wood surfaces gradually acquire over the passage of time.

A late-18thC German cherrywood tea chest, in the manner of Abraham Roentgen, the cover with line decoration and brass moldings, enclosing a pair of brass canisters and a two-section container in the center, each with star decoration, on brass winged hoof feet.

7¾in (20cm) wide

$875-1,000   WW

A George III mahogany and marquetry-inlaid tea caddy, boxwood strung, the hinged lid inlaid with an urn of flowers, the front with panels of flower vases, foil-lined two-division lidded interior.

7½in (19cm) wide

$625-750   SOU

A late-18thC George III fruitwood tea caddy, the lid and front applied with printed Classical scenes of figures, the interior with a lid with a turned bone handle.

5¼in (13.5cm) wide

$375-500   WW

A French "mulberry" tea caddy, burl maple body, with a pyramidal cover and a brass loop handle with a cut steel escutcheon, hinges, and lock, the interior with traces of foil lining.

ca. 1800   5½in (14cm) high

$1,000-1,100   WW

A George III quillwork or scrolled paper tea caddy, with string edging, floral and swag decoration, the hinged cover enclosing a single division interior with traces of foil.

ca. 1800   7in (18cm) wide

$625-750   WW

A treen fruitwood tea caddy, in the form of a pumpkin or squash, with remnants of green staining, with a stem finial, the interior with a weighted inner cover and foil lining.

ca. 1800   6½in (16.5cm) high

$5,500-7,000   WW

A late-18thC George III stained fruitwood tea caddy, in the form of a melon, with an ebonized acorn finial, with a void interior.

8¼in (21cm) high

$2,500-3,100   L&T

A late-18th/early-19thC treen fruitwood tea caddy, in the form of a pear, with a stem finial above an escutcheon, the hinged lid revealing an interior with traces of foil lining.

6¾in (17cm) high

$2,000-2,200   WW

A late-18th/early-19thC late George III mahogany and boxwood tea caddy, with line-inlaid borders, with brass lion-mask ring handles on the sides, opening to a cut-glass mixing bowl and a pair of lidded compartments.

13in (33cm) wide

$500-625   L&T

A late George III tortoiseshell tea caddy, with ivory stringing, restorations and old damages, no key.

ca. 1810 · 4¾in (12cm) wide

$625-750 DN

An early-19thC treen fruitwood tea caddy, in the form of an apple, with a stem finial, navette-shaped steel escutcheon, traces of foil lining.

4½in (11.5cm) high

$2,500-3,700 WW

A Regency rosewood tea caddy, the hinged cover opening to reveal twin lidded compartments, raised on brass ball feet.

7¾in (20cm) wide

$375-450 CHEF

A Regency tortoiseshell tea caddy, the hinged cover opening to reveal two lidded compartments and a center recess for a mixing bowl.

11½in (29cm) wide

$1,200-1,350 CHEF

An early-19thC Regency tortoiseshell tea caddy, inlaid with pewter stringing and boxwood edging, the interior with twin lidded divisions with ivory handles.

6¾in (17cm) wide

$2,100-2,500 WW

An early-19thC Regency tortoiseshell and mother-of-pearl tea caddy, with abalone banding, the interior with twin lidded divisions, with ivory banding and flattened bun feet.

5in (13cm) wide

$550-700 WW

An early-19thC Regency tortoiseshell tea caddy, the cover with pewter stringing, enclosing a twin lidded interior, with ivory edging and handles, on ivory flattened bun feet.

7in (18cm) wide

$1,500-1,900 WW

An early-19thC Regency tortoiseshell tea caddy, with a divided interior with ivory banded borders.

7¾in (19.5cm) wide

$800-950 L&T

An early-19thC fruitwood tea caddy, in the form of an apple, with a hinged cover, the stem loose.

4¼in (11cm) high

$450-550 CHEF

BOXES & TREEN

An early-19thC Regency sycamore tea caddy, painted with flowers with an oak leaf and acorn border, the interior with painted shell decoration on the underside of the cover and twin lidded divisions, with an ivory escutcheon.

9½in (24cm) wide

$550-700 WW

An early-19thC George IV amboyna tea chest, with a pair of canisters with hinged covers flanking a glass sugar bowl, on gilt-brass feet.

12in (30.5cm) wide

$625-750 WW

A pressed tortoiseshell and silver tea caddy, with a pagoda top and Gothic pressed tortoiseshell panels, on four sterling silver feet, by Edward, Edward junior, John & William Barnard, London.

ca. 1829 *7½in (19cm) high*

$17,500-20,000 MGO

Judith Picks

Having been born and brought up in Galashiels, in the Scottish Borders, I have a strong and enduring affection for Scottish arts and crafts. Having said that, I do not think any cultural bias is needed to appreciate both the artistic endeavor and the commercial success of Mauchlineware, of which this tea caddy is a nice example.

Still highly collectible today, Mauchlineware had its origins in the fine-quality wooden snuffboxes and tea caddies initially made in the late 18thC by Charles Stiven of Laurencekirk, Kincardineshire. Exquisitely decorated with hand-painted or pen-worked imagery, they proved so popular that other Scottish craftsmen—notably in the town of Mauchline—also began to make them. Although a decline in taking snuff forced many snuffbox makers out of business by the 1840s, a surge of interest in Scottish culture, and an attendant increase in tourism, in the mid-19thC afforded commercial opportunities that were seized upon by William and Andrew Smith of Mauchline, who rapidly diversified their output to produce a vast range of decorative but useful wooden objects as souvenirs for the tourists. From ca. 1850, they also substantially increased their output by using not only pen- and brushwork for decoration, but also transfer printing and, from ca. 1860, photographic images. Further growth then ensued by making these souvenirs for numerous other cities, towns, spas, and resorts throughout Great Britain, much of Europe, and the United States. In an industry that boomed well into the 1930s, the success of W. & A. Smith of Mauchline was such that even as other manufacturers sprang up around the country—most notably The Caledonian Box Work in Lanark—all such souvenirs, regardless of date or place of manufacture, or the geographic location of their decoration, became collectively known as Mauchlineware.

It is certainly an objectively impressive history, but why you might ask have I picked out this particular Mauchlineware tea caddy? Well, that is where a some bias has crept in: the front panel has a view of Abbotsford House on the banks of the Tweed River. Built by, and the home of, Sir Walter Scott in the early 19thC, it is not far from where I was born, and I have the fondest of memories of my parents often taking me their as a child ... oh, and also, albeit of much more recent nostalgia, the view on the lid is of Culzean Castle, overlooking the Firth of Clyde in South Ayrshire, where I filmed two episodes of the BBC Antiques Roadshow.

A Scottish Mauchlineware sycamore tea caddy, with a pen-work view of Culzean Castle, the front with a view of Abbotsford House, against a red textured ground, two-division interior, covers with ring handles, on gilt-brass ball feet.

ca. 1830 *8¾in (22.5cm) wide*

$190-310 SOU

A mid-19thC treen fruitwood tea caddy, in the form of a melon, naturalistically carved, with remains of green staining.

5½in (14cm) high

$375-500 WW

A French Napoleon III kingwood and parquetry tea chest, by Tahan, Paris, with lattice decoration in ebony and mother-of-pearl, with a brass rim, enclosing a pair of amaranth and brass-inlaid canisters, inscribed "TAHAN PARIS" on the lock.

ca. 1860 *10¼in (26cm) wide*

$1,200-1,350 WW

A 19thC shagreen tea caddy, with white metal mounts, the hinged cover enclosing a foil-lined interior.

4in (10cm) wide

$800-950 WW

A 20thC treen fruitwood tea caddy, in the form of an eggplant, with a screw-off calyx and stem on an inner lid.

5in (13cm) high

$550-600 WW

An early-Victorian rosewood dressing case, the lid with a brass plaque, the underside of the lid with a letter pouch, above a lift-out tray with divisions and fitted with glass bottles, jars, and boxes with silver lids hallmarked for London 1848, with mother-of-pearl handled utensils, above a base drawer.

ca. 1845-50   *10¾in (27.5cm) wide*

$625-750   **WW**

A mid-19thC Victorian brass-banded rosewood dressing box, the lid opening to a leather interior, stamped "Halstaff & Hannaford, Manufacturers, 228 Regent Street," the lid with a fold-out mirror, above a lift-out tray fitted with glass jars and boxes with plated covers, over a lower drawer with a writing slope and jewelry tray, the lock stamped "S Mordan & Co Makers."

11¾in (30cm) wide

$375-500   **L&T**

A mid-19thC coromandel wood and brass-lined dressing box, the hinged lid with a spring-loaded mirror, enclosing a fitted interior with mother-of-pearl tools and silver-plate-topped glass containers, over a drawer.

11¾in (30cm) wide

$700-800   **ECGW**

A cased silver-topped dressing table set, by Charles Boyton, London, the coromandel box by E. & E. Emanuel, Portsea, the underside of the lid with a lift-out mirror, with a fitted interior, with four cut-glass scent bottles, seven dressing table jars, and a shaving brush case, all with foliate decoration and crests, the slide-out drawer mechanism opening to reveal a previously fitted interior for a sewing set, box with wear.

1850   *11½in (29cm) wide*

$1,000-1,100   **SWO**

A Victorian silver-mounted traveling dressing table set, the mounts by Frances Douglas, London 1853, manufactured by Bayley, 17 Cockspur Street, London, with an initialed cartouche, comprising three scent bottles, four jars, four boxes, an inkwell, a vesta holder, and a small scent bottle, with a pull-out tray with a medicine spoon, by George Adams, and various silver, steel, and mother-of-pearl implements, including a ruler, a letter knife, a seal, two corkscrews, a dip pen, a pencil, and other items, the interior of the hinged cover with a mirror and stationery wallet, the front with a pull-out jewelry drawer, in a fitted brass-bound two-handled coromandel wood case, the top with a monogram.

12¼in (31cm) wide 8½oz

$1,000-1,250   **WW**

An amboyna silver-gilt dressing box, by Joseph Rodgers & Sons, Sheffield, cutler to her Majesty, the engraved silver-gilt lids by Thomas Johnson, London, the lid with a fold-down letter compartment with a removable mirror, with 13 cut-glass engraved sterling silver-gilt and pierced jars, the front with two drawers, with maker's label.

Unusually, the back five jars of this dressing box rise when the box is opened.

ca. 1854   *14¼in (36cm) wide*

$5,500-7,000   **MGO**

A Victorian silver-gilt-mounted traveling dressing table set, the mounts by Brownett & Rose, London 1860, retailed by Asprey, with foliate scroll decoration, with an initialed cartouche, with four scent bottles, two jars, four boxes, various manicure items, including a pair of tweezers, an ear cleaner, a file, a penknife, a corkscrew, a button hook, and two pairs of scissors (one later), the interior with a mirror, the front with a jewelry drawer, in a walnut case.

12½in (32cm) wide 8oz

$1,250-1,600   **WW**

A late-19th/early-20thC French carved fruitwood glove box, modeled as a miniature steam trunk with raised strapwork, handles and brass stud details, the lid with a pair of carved gloves.

12½in (32cm) wide

$1,100-1,350   **L&T**

An early-19thC satinwood hat-shaped workbox, fitted interior, including five ivory spool mounts and an ivory tape measure.

Ivory Act certification no. 2F8DSCV4

10in (25.5cm) wide

$250-370

CHOR

An early-19thC Napoleonic prisoner-of-war straw-work workbox, the hinged cover with a riverside view within a cartouche, the fitted interior with two drawers, one decorated with HMS "Victory," the other with a memorial urn, the cover inset with a mirror, further decorated with flowers, trophies, and a rural scene.

12½in (32cm) wide

$375-500

ROS

An early-19thC Regency rosewood and exotic hardwood ark-shaped workbox, with dogtooth banding, the center domed compartment enclosing a lift-out tray, flanked by a pair of lidded compartments, with brass lion-head handles and bun feet.

11¾in (30cm) wide

$300-375

WW

A Regency amboyna and rosewood workbox, inlaid with a center mother-of-pearl wreath with flower heads in the corners, the interior fitted with four mother-of-pearl and ivory spools and compartments.

Ivory Act certification no. 7K3JQ3A8

12¼in (31cm) wide

$500-625

CHOR

A Regency rosewood workbox, with a galleried top and inlaid mother-of-pearl, with a fitted drawer beneath, on bun feet.

14in (35.5cm) wide

$300-375

CHOR

A Regency rosewood sarcophagus-shaped workbox, with inlaid mother-of-pearl designs, with ring handles, the fitted interior with ivory spools and compartments.

Ivory Act certification no. 1DSGUNBS

$250-370

CHOR

A 19thC Trinity House walnut and marquetry workbox, with marquetry scenes of frigates, clippers, lighthouses, and steamboats, the interior with scrapwork pictures.

Trinity House in Deptford, London, was founded in 1514, when its first Master was Thomas Spert, sailing master of King Henry VIII's flagship, the "Mary Rose." Essentially, it is the authority responsible for the lighthouses, lightships, and other maritime navigational aids of England, Wales, the Channel Islands, and Gibraltar, as well as providing specialty navigators for ships trading in Northern European waters. It is also a maritime charity responsible for raising and distributing funds for the welfare of retired seamen and their families, and it is under that flag that "Trinity House" boxes, such as the example above, were produced.

The majority of them were made from around 1850 to 1880, by lighthouse and lightship keepers, who for the most part had a lot of spare time on their hands. Originally delivered to and sold from Trinity House, later on many keepers sold boxes directly to sailors and seamen as gifts for loved ones during their weeks, months, or more at sea. Made in the form of, for example, tea caddies, work/sewing boxes, money boxes, writing boxes, and simple storage boxes, nearly all are constructed from butt-jointed, nailed, and glued pine, which was then veneered in hardwoods, such as walnut, mahogany, and rosewood. Typical exterior decoration included marquetry, parquetry, and simple stringing, while favored decorative imagery included tea clippers, steamboats, lighthouses, flags, and stars; inside, velvet or paper linings were common, with the latter often in the form of ornate printed cardboard depicting either similar imagery to the exterior or, often, animals, fish, and birds.

13¼in (33.5cm) wide

$2,200-2,700

L&T

An early-19thC parquetry workbox, of geometric cube design, with inlaid mother-of-pearl roundels in the border, the fitted interior with mother-of-pearl and ivory spools and accessories.

Ivory Act certification no. DTBHJ45W

12in (30.5cm) wide

$450-500

CHOR

A 19thC Fernware stationery box, the interior with divisions.

8¼in (21cm) wide

$160-200

SOU

ESSENTIAL REFERENCE—KNIFE BOXES

Knife boxes first emerged in the 17thC—King Charles II of England is on record as gifting one to one of his mistresses. However, they did not really come into fashion until the second quarter of the 18thC and the reign of George II, when the convention of a dinner host providing their guests with cutlery, instead of them bringing their own, became firmly established among the wealthier classes.

- Often supplied in pairs as ornamental containers for expensive silver cutlery (initially, just knives, but eventually forks and spoons, too), their basic, serpentine-front form remained mostly unchanged until the 1780s, with early decorative differences primarily residing in their finish: either wood veneered or covered in silk-velvet or shagreen.
- Stylistic variations did, however, emerge—such as, during the 1760s, bowfront mahogany boxes with hinged slopes with drop handles and shaped bracket or claw-and ball feet.
- From the 1770s, increasingly lavish embellishments, such as crossbanding, feather banding, and parquetry work, also became more prevalent, while in the 1780s the Neoclassical vase-form knife box, or cutlery urn, emerged, designed to stand on pedestals or at each end of a sideboard.
- However, during the early 19thC, knife boxes and cutlery urns were gradually rendered increasingly redundant by sideboards with drawers fitted for cutlery storage.

A George III mahogany and string-inlaid knife box, the cover with flower head and stringing in the underside, enclosing the original fitted interior with stringing, with a drawer in the back.

ca. 1790-1800   *15¼in (38.5cm) high*
$190-250   **WW**

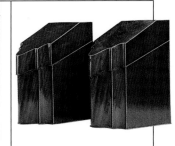

A pair of George III mahogany and boxwood line-inlaid knife boxes, the cover inlaid with a star motif and stringing in the underside, enclosing an original hinged fitted interior with line inlay, the front with a navette-shaped escutcheon.

ca. 1790-1800   *14in (35.5cm) high*
$1,250-1,900   **WW**

A George III mahogany knife box, the cover inlaid with a shell motif, enclosing a fitted interior and inlaid with a star and stringing in the underside, with a white metal shield-shaped escutcheon.

ca. 1790-1800   *14¼in (36.5cm) high*
$375-450   **WW**

A satinwood, mahogany, and pollard oak converted knife urn, George III and later, with refitted interior, on bun feet, top finial later.

Pollard oak is wood obtained from oak trees that have been "pollarded"—a technique that involves pruning branches of a tree to control its height and resulting in lumps or "burls" forming at the points of pruning. When cut these burls reveal a swirling figure in their grain much prized for decorative veneer work.

28in (71cm) high
$1,050-1,200   **CHEF**

A pair of Regency mahogany knife boxes, with pull-up lids above a matrix-lined interior, abrasions.

ca. 1820   *21½in (54.5cm) high*
$2,500-3,700   **DN**

A pair of late-18thC George III mahogany cutlery urns, with an urn finial, inlaid with boxwood and ebony stringing, with molded lifting covers enclosing fitted interiors.

23½in (60cm) high
$5,000-6,200   **DUK**

A rare pair of Georgian cutlery urns, made specifically for spoons, with turned finials, veneered in flame mahogany separated by checkered boxwood and ebony herringbone inlay, on square plinth bases on ogee bracket feet, with satinwood crossbanding and dogtooth inlay.

ca. 1820   *23½in (60cm) high*
$7,500-10,000   **MGO**

A George III oak candle box, carved with geometric motifs.

17in (43cm) high
$800-950   **LSK**

BOXES & TREEN

An early-19thC Regency red tôle peinte cheese coaster, possibly Pontypool, with gilt initials "RT" and foliate decoration, with blue-and-white painted flower heads on a red ground, with twin divisions, on brass roller casters.

16¾in (42.5cm) wide

$1,600-2,000 **WW**

A Regency mahogany cheese coaster, of dished form with center division, the split baluster lifts applied with roundels, the square base with brass barrel casters.

18½in (47cm) wide

$250-370 **HT**

An early-19thC Regency mahogany double magnum bottle holder or coaster, restorations.

15in (38cm) wide

$4,300-5,600 **DN**

Judith Picks

I played the Scottish card with the Mauclineware tea caddy I picked on page 290, and I make no apology for playing it again here. This lovely little early-19thC Scottish Regency carved mahogany coaster was made in Kelso, which lies on the confluence of the Tweed and Teviot rivers, in the historic county of Roxburghshire, just 17 miles (27 kilometers) from where I was born in Galashiels. I know Kelso, but the makers of this coaster—the Mein family—were long gone before I first visited. James Mein the Elder established the family firm as cabinetmakers and upholsters ca. 1784 and, when he died in 1830, his nephew, also called James Mein, took over the business until it went bankrupt in 1851. During its nearly 50-year existence, Mein developed a well-deserved reputation for its fine-quality furniture, to the extent that among the numerous well-heeled patrons it attracted were the 5th and 6th dukes of Roxburghe at Floors Castle, and the Earl of Haddington at Mellerstain.

An early-19thC Scottish Regency mahogany coaster, by James Mein, Kelso, with a fruiting vine border, on three leather and brass casters, stamped "MEIN KELSO 34185" on the underside.

7½in (19cm) diam

$625-750 **L&T**

A late-19th/early-20thC late-Victorian brass-mounted mahogany "Railway Wagon" table wine coaster, the mounts forming a wheeled carriage.

15¼in (39cm) long

$750-875 **L&T**

A late-19thC Norwegian folk art box and cover, the body with stamped and poker-work decoration, with hearts, flower heads, and square motifs.

17¾in (45cm) wide

$625-750 **WW**

A late-19thC Norwegian folk art painted pine box and cover, carved with scrolling and roundel decoration.

17½in (44.5cm) wide

$250-370 **WW**

An early-18thC Franco-Flemish burl walnut and gilt-brass coffre fort, with strapwork mounts and side carrying handles, with a hinged lid and drop fronts, the interior with two hinged compartments, two drawers, and four secret compartments.

25½in (65cm) wide

$11,000-12,000 **WW**

An early-18thC Franco-Flemish tortoiseshell and brass-mounted coffre fort, the tortoiseshell with a gilt foil backing, with trefoil strapwork mounts terminating in fleur-de-lis and side carrying handles, the hinged lid enclosing a vacant interior, with a steel lock.

12½in (31.5cm) wide

$8,000-9,500 **WW**

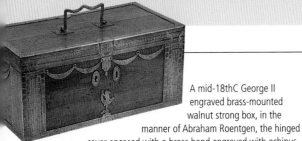

A mid-18thC George II engraved brass-mounted walnut strong box, in the manner of Abraham Roentgen, the hinged cover encased with a brass band engraved with echinus and dentil molding, each corner with Ionic pilasters against a stonework background, with foliate swags connecting the pilasters, the lower edge of the front face centered with the figure of Fortune, with two locks, the interior with a hinged panel in the cover, and a well with two divisions, possibly for tea caddies and a mixing bowl.

Furniture with engraved brass mounts was a distinctive feature of certain mid-18thC London makers, including Abraham Roentgen (see page 287). Roentgen's coreligionist in the London chapter of the Moravian Brotherhood and fellow furnituremaker, Frederick Hintz, made furniture with engraved brass plaques, too. Furniture by the Exeter maker John Channon is also characterized by engraved brass, fueling speculation that Roentgen, Hintz, and Channon may have worked together.

15¾in (40cm) wide

$5,000-6,200   DUK

A mahogany field surgeon's box, with a vacant brass initial plate, felt-lined interior, with all original equipment, the tools marked "Evans & Co London."

ca. 1840

15¼in (39cm) wide

$2,200-2,700   MGO

A mid- to late-19thC French gilt-metal-mounted amboyna and maple cigar humidor, the folding hinged cover enclosing a shelf over five sliding trays, with a steel and gilt-metal cigar cutter.

11½in (29cm) wide

$375-500   TEN

A Victorian coromandel decanter box, with four decanters and four liqueur glasses, one drinking glass replaced, glass chips.

9½in (24cm) wide

$625-750   CHEF

A matched pair of 19thC Trinity House marquetry boxes, one a rosewood money box, the other a walnut tea caddy, the lids and front panels with stained marquetry scenes of lighthouses, clipper ships, and steamboats, the other panels in bird's eye maple.

7in (18cm) wide

$2,500-3,700   L&T

A 19thC apothecary's mahogany cabinet, hinged cover, the drop front enclosing an interior of bottles, etc., some damage in wood.

10¼in (26cm) wide

$750-875   CHOR

An oak spice cupboard, late 17thC and later, the geometric molded door enclosing six drawers with turned brass handles, later wrought iron foliate hanging fittings.

14½in (37cm) wide

$800-950   HT

A late-17thC oak Bible box, the front carved with leaves and flower heads, with initials "E A," later mounted on a paneled oak stand.

29¼in (74.5cm) high

$375-500   WW

A rare collection of pipes, by Alfred Dunhill, the Queen Anne-style walnut cabinet with a cornice above a pair of doors, the 12 numbered drawers fitted to hold 366 Dunhill pipes, each stamped "Dunhill" and with a shape number.

ca. 1974-76

41in (104cm) wide

$60,000-75,000   WW

An early-19thC whitewood Tunbridgeware sewing box, with a colored aquatint view of "Priory Bridge Farm, Hastings."

ca. 1810   *3¾in (9.5cm) wide*

$375-500   **SOU**

A Tunbridgeware rosewood book stand, the top rail inlaid with a micromosaic border, the base inlaid with a mosaic panel depicting the State Apartments, Windsor Castle, within geometric and walnut-banded borders.

ca. 1840   *15¼in (38.5cm) wide*

$1,900-2,500   **SOU**

A Tunbridgeware and rosewood writing slope, the top with an image of Warwick Castle and flowers inside a floral border, the fitted interior with a velvet-lined slope, pen tray, lidded compartment, and two glass inkwells with Tunbridgeware covers.

ca. 1850-70   *10¾in (27.5cm) wide*

$250-370   **WW**

A 19thC Tunbridgeware rosewood lap desk, the slope with an abbey ruin enclosed by a rose border, opening to a fitted interior with Tunbridgeware inkwell caps, a page turner, and a cylindrical ruler.

17in (43cm) wide

$550-700   **L&T**

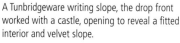

A Tunbridgeware writing slope, the drop front worked with a castle, opening to reveal a fitted interior and velvet slope.

Tunbridgeware is a form of decoratively inlaid woodwork, typically in the form of boxes, that is characteristic of Tonbridge and the spa town of Royal Tunbridge Wells in Kent in the 18thC and 19thC. The decoration typically consists of a mosaic of many tiny pieces of different colored woods that form a pictorial vignette.

15¼in (39cm) wide

$700-800   **CHEF**

A Tunbridgeware scent casket, the lid flanked by two glass side scent bottles.

9in (23cm) wide

$500-625   **CHEF**

A Tunbridgeware four-drawer table cabinet, the top inlaid with a thatched cottage, the doors with flowers.

8¼in (21cm) high

$875-1,000   **CHEF**

A Tunbridgeware writing box, with a view of Tonbridge Castle, waisted sides, the interior with a tooled red velvet writing surface, a pair of inkwells, and a dip pen, with lock and key.

ca. 1880   *12½in (32cm) wide*

$2,200-2,700   **MGO**

A 19thC Tunbridgeware rosewood stamp box, the lid with a micromosaic floral spray.

1½in (4cm) wide

£50-70   **SOU**

A 19thC miniature mahogany "Jupe's Patent" dining table, the top with eight triangular leaves, on a center baluster, four outer columns, and a cruciform base.

13¾in (35cm) diam

$3,100-3,700 **L&T**

A 19thC Pennsylvania miniature painted foot stool, with floral decoration, repaired break on one leg.

7¾in (19.5cm) wide

$6,000-7,700 **POOK**

A 19thC miniature rosewood and inlaid games table, the tilt-top inlaid with a rosewood and burl walnut parquetry chessboard.

4in (10cm) high

$750-875 **L&T**

A late-18thC olivewood miniature chest-of-drawers, probably Maltese, with three crossbanded long drawers.

20¾in (53cm) wide

$4,300-5,000 **CHEF**

An early-19thC New England miniature pine blanket chest.

21in (53.5cm) wide

$250-310 **POOK**

A late-18thC Pennsylvania miniature walnut blanket chest, with fitted interior and a side drawer.

10½in (26.5cm) wide

$2,000-2,500 **POOK**

A late-19thC miniature mahogany chest-of-drawers, Chippendale style, in the manner of Gostelowe.

17in (43cm) high

$1,250-1,700 **POOK**

A late-19thC French miniature satinwood and mahogany brass-mounted commode, in Directoire style.

12¼in (31cm) wide

$450-550 **L&T**

A mid-19thC Tunbridgeware miniature display case, the doors with floral panels, enclosing a decorated interior.

13¾in (35cm) high

$750-875 **L&T**

A 20thC miniature walnut bookcase-on-chest, in George II style.

14½in (37cm) high

$550-700 **L&T**

An early-20thC Viennese miniature gilt-metal and enamel salon suite, with figural backs and seats.

3¼in (8cm) high

$800-950 **JON**

An early-18thC laburnum snuff mull, engraved "GA" on underside, applied mounts on collar and base, the hinged lid with a cartouche with engraved motto "STARK LOVE & KINDNESS," crest of shaking hands and "ROB GIBB," unmarked.

2¾in (7cm) high

$1,100-1,350   **L&T**

A late-18th/early-19thC carved coquilla nut figural snuffbox, possibly French, with glass eyes, a hooked nose, the hinged lid in the form of his coattails.

3¾in (9.5cm) high

$1,250-1,700   **WW**

CLOSER LOOK—A COQUILLA NUT SNUFFBOX

The snuffbox is carved from a coquilla nut, which has a hard, dense shell and is the fruit of a Brazilian palm tree (Attalea funifera) that the Brazilians call "piassabe." It was first introduced into Europe in the mid-16thC and used for carving small objects.

In addition to being "Napoleonic" in its imagery, the box is also of a type known as a "Bugbear" box. Carved on one side, with only the back of his head visible from this view, is a bugbear, or boogerbear—a legendary creature comparable to the bogeyman—here, with colored glass eyes and a white metal mouth showing rows of teeth and a tongue.

The hinged box lid is carved in relief with figures of Napoleon (the French emperor) and a French Imperial Eagle on a pedestal. They may imply, given the "Bugbear" on the side, that the carver believed, as many did, that Napoleon and/or France was the bogeyman of Europe. Alternatively, given the inscription on the metal thumbpiece below, it might mean just the opposite?

The inscription "Aux Hellenes" on the metal thumbpiece on the lid may mean that the carver saw Napoleon, after his victories in Italy and his invasion of Egypt, as a possible savior and liberator of the Hellenes—i.e. the Greeks— from Ottoman Turkey.

An early-19thC carved coquilla nut "Bugbear" snuffbox, of Napoleonic interest, with an ink-inscribed label in the interior that reads "Given by Napoleon to Marshall Ney and given by Marshall Ney to a lady who gave it to my mother. C. Herbert Collis," small losses, splits.

3in (7.5cm) long

$4,300-5,600   **DAWS**

An early-19thC turned oak snuffbox, the pull cover with a metal button engraved "The oak of this Box was 656 years under Old London Bridge."

2½in (6.5cm) diam

$250-370   **SOU**

A Victorian novelty wood snuffbox, modeled as a dog head with bone teeth and tongue on show, glass eyes, the hinged lid with a scallop shell detail.

4in (10cm) wide

$1,500-1,900   **L&T**

A 19thC treen burrwood snuffbox, carved as a bearded man's face, inset with glass eyes, the reverse with sliding cover incised with Prince of Wales plumes and a thistle.

3½in (9cm) long

$700-800   **SOU**

A Victorian rootwood and pen-work snuffbox, with thistle detail on sides and vein detail on top, the hinged lid with a scene depicting the Robert Burns poem "Tam O'shanter," with a verse below.

5in (13cm) wide

$5,000-5,600   **L&T**

A 19thC silver-mounted novelty treen snuffbox, modeled as a monkey head, set with glass eyes, textured fur, the hinged cover with a plain thumbpiece, and applied with a snake motif, unmarked.

2¾in (7cm) wide

$1,250-1,700   **WW**

A 19thC treen bird snuffbox, with metal stud eyes, probably fruitwood.

4in (10cm) long

$120-160   **SOU**

An English fruitwood and horn-inlaid tobacco box, 17thC and later, the lid inlaid with a navette-shaped cartouche inscribed "MY BOXE IS FREE FOR YOU AND ME," centered by two pipes and a burning candle, the outer border with four shield-shaped panels each with a number, denoting 1651.

E. H. Pinto, in his book "Treen and Other Wooden bygones," states that these oval cedarwood boxes rimmed in horn and inlaid with bone "belong to a small and rare English group which all appear to have been made by one man between 1680 and 1710. They bear varied, but attractive inscriptions and dates; this one [in his collection] proclaims 'for you the best is not too good 1706'." If a box was good for keeping the pipe tobacco fresh, it would sometimes also be used for snuff, and boxes were sold by tobacconists for either purpose according to choice. It could also have been treated as a table box to be passed along to fill pipes at convivial functions. They were sometimes used for a free dip of tobacco on the counter of a tobacconist's shop, or at an inn where the landlord would keep the snuff freshly rasped, or the tobacco nicely moist, on a daily basis.

ca. 1651   *3½in (9cm) long*
$1,400-1,700   **CA**

A novelty boot snuffbox, with studwork and date on toe, minor chip.
1875   *2½in (6.5cm) high*
$190-250   **SWO**

A 19thC treen burlwood snuffbox, probably Scottish, the hinged top applied with a Victoria Two Penny red stamp, tinned interior.
4¼in (11cm) wide
$375-450   **JON**

A late-19thC Norwegian treen souvenir snuffbox, carved with scrolling flora and a Nisse (Norwegian goblin), the sides inscribed with a motto about the Nisse traveling from Dovrefjell to Kristiania for an exhibition in 1883.
3¾in (9.5cm) long
$375-500   **LSK**

A late-19thC treen frog or toad snuffbox, realistically carved with mother-of-pearl eyes and a hinged cover.
3¼in (8.5cm) long
$3,700-4,300   **WW**

A late-19thC Swedish treen dog snuffbox, with an ebonized finish, the hound with bone eyes and a hinged lid.
5½in (14cm) long
$250-370   **WW**

A 19thC novelty treen snuffbox, carved as a hand taking just a pinch of snuff, hinged cork-lined cover.
4¼in (11cm) high
$500-625   **WW**

A 19thC treen snuffbox, with engine-turned and engraved decoration.
2¾in (7cm) diam
$70-100   **CA**

A 19thC Scottish ram horn snuff mull, the horns united by a pewter box.
14½in (37cm) wide
$625-750   **SWO**

An 18thC Scandinavian burl birch tankard, the lid with leaping lion relief decoration.

8¼in (21cm) high

$625-750   **DN**

A 19thC Scandinavian chip-carved tankard, Norwegian or Danish, decorated with rondels of differing designs, the underside carved with a cross.

9¾in (24.5cm) high

$150-190   **WW**

A late-17th/early-18thC Irish treen willow lamhog, with an integral carved handle.

7in (18cm) high

$1,200-1,350   **WW**

An 18thC treen lignum vitae mortar, with a lignum vitae pestle.

8¾in (22cm) high

$625-750   **WW**

An 18thC treen lignum vitae mortar.

8¾in (22cm) high

$625-750   **WW**

A late-18th/early-19thC treen yew salt or spice pot and cover, with a molded lid, on a stepped foot.

8¾in (22cm) high

$500-625   **WW**

A late-18th/early-19thC turned lignum vitae mortar and pestle, the body turned with rings.

7in (18cm) high

$375-500   **CHEF**

A late-17th/early-18thC treen fruitwood mortar grater, possibly Laburnum, with an orb finial, the body with turned and notch decoration.

8in (20.5cm) high

$450-550   **WW**

A late-18th/early-19thC treen cocquilla nut nutmeg grater, the upper section with a grater, with turned and foliate decoration.

6in (15cm) high

$190-250   **WW**

An 18th/19thC treen primitive figural lever-action nutcracker, with the head of a man wearing a hat, with a flat face and nail eyes.

6in (15cm) high

$500-625   **WW**

A 19thC treen fruitwood caster or muffineer, with a pierced detachable cover.

7¾in (19.5cm) high

$300-450   **WW**

An 18thC treen lacewood snuff grater, the interior with a perforated iron plate.

6¼in (16cm) long

$625-750   **SOU**

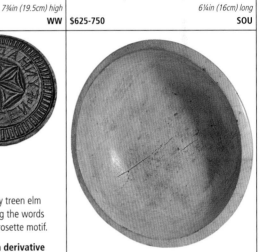

A 19thC sycamore dough bowl, each end with an iron band.

43½in (110.5cm) wide

$250-370   **WW**

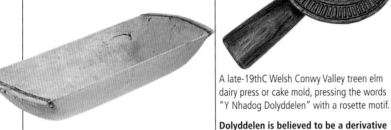

A late-19thC Welsh Conwy Valley treen elm dairy press or cake mold, pressing the words "Y Nhadog Dolyddelen" with a rosette motif.

Dolyddelen is believed to be a derivative of Dolwyddelan in Conwy, North Wales, and Y Nhadog a remote farming area nearby.

4¼in (10.5cm) diam

$250-370   **JON**

A 19thC treen sycamore dairy bowl, with banded decoration on the outside.

18in (46cm) diam

$300-375   **WW**

A 19thC treen dairy bowl, possibly ash, with banded decoration.

21in (53.5cm) diam

$250-370   **WW**

An early-19thC George III mahogany cheese coaster, with a scalloped rim and ring-turned handles, surface wear, one caster a replacement.

17¾in (45cm) wide

$250-310   **SWO**

A pair of treen "Brighton Bun" traveling candlesticks and snuffers, possibly zebrawood.

3¼in (8cm) diam

$375-500   **WW**

A late-18thC Welsh double-bowl love spoon, probably fruitwood, with piercework handle of center triskele (trisgel), flanking hearts and flowers, repeated piercework at terminal.

Traditionally given by a suitor to a young woman as a gift of romantic intent, decoratively carved wooden "love spoons" date back to at least the mid-17thC, and probably earlier. They are particularly associated with Wales, and the earliest known and authentically dated example from there is on display in the St. Fagan's National History Museum, near Cardiff. However, the tradition also extended to other countries, notably in Scandinavia, Germany, and parts of Eastern Europe. The primary purpose of the decorative carving was to convey various messages. Symbolic motifs included, for example: a cross for faith; bells for marriage; hearts and flowers for love; a wheel for support; a lock for security; and a triskele, often for prosperity and renewal. In addition, it was not unusual for an anchor motif to be included, not only as a sign of stability, but also if the spoon had been carved by a sailor while he was away at sea. However, the carving was also intended to reflect the skill of the carver and, therefore, to the eyes of a young woman's father, his potential competence to provide for her.

9in (23cm) long

$2,500-3,100   **JON**

A pair of William IV carved fruitwood vases, with lapit decoration, on circular plinths, shrinkage splits.

7¾in (19.5cm) high

$300-375   **LSK**

A mid-19thC Victorian treen sycamore four-section spice tower, the sections titled in gilt "Mace," "Cloves," "Nutmeg," and "Cinamon" (sic).

7½in (19cm) high

$150-220   **WW**

A Mauchlineware games box, by Striven, Laurencekirk, with title view "Castle from the mound, Edinburgh," with soldiers and women, opening to five sycamore hinged-lid boxes for cards/counters, each with initial "M," stamped mark.

Decorated with transferware scenes of landmarks, this Scottish wooden ware dates from about 1880 to 1900. It was sold throughout the United Kingdom, but great quantities were also exported to many parts of North America, Europe, South Africa, Australia, and elsewhere (see page 290).

12¼in (31cm) wide

$1,600-2,000   **JON**

A turned wood thimble box, in the form of a beehive set with a bee, with a silver thimble.

2¼in (6cm) high

$375-500   **CHOR**

An early-20thC folk art naive carved wood figure of an Asiatic lion, probably Indian, with shaped bone teeth and inset eyes, cracks.

23¼in (59cm) long

$300-375   **DAWS**

A 20thC oak letter box, the pitched roof above an inset brass "LETTERS" plaque and glazed door.

15¼in (39cm) high

$250-370   **CHEF**

A late-17th/early-18thC carved wood clogmaker's pattern sample, modeled as a toe cap with a geometric pattern, with studs and remnants of leather, on the verso with a suspension tab.

8¼in (21cm) long

$300-450   **SWO**

A Swiss Black Forest lindenwood bear, sitting with open mouth, painted details, glass inset eyes, and well-defined fur detailing.

19¼in (49cm) high

$8,500-10,000 **JON**

A late-19thC Black Forest carved wood hall stand, with a bear cub sitting on a tree trunk observed by the anxious mother bear below, the base with an umbrella/stick stand fitted with a pressed tin drip pan, on a heavily carved rocky base, "HS 5091" carved below the removable drip pan.

80¼in (204cm) high

$6,000-7,700 **DAWS**

A Black Forest carving, modeled as a bear standing, with glass eyes and a polychrome tongue.

13¾in (35cm) wide

$750-800 **WHP**

A late-19thC Black Forest carved bear piano stool, the adjustable seat carved with oak leaves and "INTERLAKEN," on a sitting bear with glass eyes.

19¾in (50cm) high

$3,700-4,300 **L&T**

A late-19thC Black Forest extending book stand, the hinged extending book ends carved as bears.

15¼in (39cm) wide

$250-370 **ECGW**

A late-19thC Black Forest carved tobacco jar music box, formed as a sitting bear, with hinged head and holding a honey pot, the base enclosing a Swiss musical mechanism.

12½in (32cm) high

$875-1,000 **ECGW**

A 19th/early-20thC Swiss Black Forest bear hall stand, the mother bear wrapped around the base of the tree, and bear cub playing in the branches, the base with a walking stick well.

80¾in (205cm) high

$3,700-5,000 **DN**

An early-20thC Black Forest carved stick and umbrella stand, modeled as a bear with outstretched arms.

33in (84cm) high

$1,500-2,000 **WHP**

A 20thC Black Forest bear side table, the top carved with oak leaf decoration, above a base carved as a sitting bear cub, old worm holes, crack in top.

43¼in (110cm) wide

$8,500-10,000 **DAWS**

BOXES & TREEN

An early-20thC Black Forest carved wood bear walking stick stand.

35½in (90cm) high

$1,900-2,500   ECGW

A late-19thC Black Forest carved lindenwood dog head inkwell, in the shape of a pug or boxer, with glass eyes and a leather collar.

3¾in (9.5cm) high

$450-550   WW

A late-19thC Black Forest wood desk stand, the foliate-carved stand with inkwells and carved with a pair of lions.

20¾in (53cm) wide

$500-625   CHEF

CLOSER LOOK—A BLACK FOREST SMOKER'S TABLE

In addition to its decorative role, the baby bear on the left serves as a finial handle on the hinged lid of a small compartment that, when lifted, triggers the mechanism of a Swiss music box concealed below.

The two baby bears on the right are the finial handles on the lid of a larger compartment intended for storing tobacco and other smoking paraphernalia.

Smoker's tables were a popular form of Black Forest carving in the late 19thC and early 20thC and, because of their size and shape, bears were almost invariably the animal of choice for the table support. Here, this bear holds the table aloft, but a common variation is a columnar support in the form of a tree trunk with a bear clambering up it.

This table was carved from oak and subsequently the wood was stained in graduated shades of a darker color. A commonly used alternative, however, was lindenwood—a classic wood for carving from the Middle Ages onward, especially in Central Europe but also the favored medium of the eminent English sculptor Grinling Gibbons (1648-1721).

An early- to mid-20thC Swiss Black Forest smoker's table, probably Brienz.

35in (89cm) high

$3,100-3,700   DN

A pair of Black Forest carved wood figures of partridges, with their offspring, on ivy carved naturalistic bases.

15in (38cm) high

$1,050-1,200   DAWS

A late-19th/early-20thC Black Forest lindenwood coat hook, in the form of a fox, with twin horn hooks.

11¼in (28.5cm) high

$700-800   WW

A late-19th/early-20thC Black Forest carved wood owl tobacco jar, hinged at the neck, small chip on cover, shrinkage crack in base.

12¾in (32.5cm) high

$3,700-4,300   CHEF

A late-19th/early-20thC Black Forest carved mantel clock, surmounted by a cockerel with a hen and chicks on the base, pendulum missing.

23¼in (59cm) high

$750-875   ECGW

An 18thC carved pine figure of an angel, traces of paint and gilt, break in arm, both wings have been off.

16¼in (41cm) high

$750-875   LSK

A Continental boxwood carving of Christ crucified, probably 17th/18thC, the armless figure pierced through the feet.

6¼in (16cm) high

$500-625   CHEF

A pair of carved figures, possibly 17thC, possibly limewood, of a knight and a maiden, the knight with clubs emblem on his shield and holding a sword.

15in (38cm) high

$625-750   DAWS

A carved oak figure of a monk, probably 18thC, fully robed, with losses, inlcuding both arms.

24¾in (63cm) high

$375-500   LSK

A carved and painted spread-winged eagle, by Wilhelm Schimmel, Cumberland Valley, Pennsylvania, with its original polychrome surface, with an unusual gilt body, chips on wings.

A German-born immigrant, Willhelm Schimmel (1817-90) was an itinerant wood-carver who traipsed the Cumberland Valley in Pennsylvania carving painted wooden birds and animals for local families in return for board and lodging—the latter almost invariably in lofts, barns, and other outhouses. An alcoholic with a violent temper, he also spent a lot of time in and out of jail—in 1869, for example, he was charged with "Assault with Intent to Kill" and "Assault and Battery," and was sentenced to a year in jail, a fine of 6 cents, plus costs. However, his highly distinctive and often dramatically colored carvings, especially of spread-winged eagles, such as the example here, nowadays either find their way into prestigious museums or change hands privately for multiple thousands of dollars—developments that have seen him come to be retrospectively regarded as one of the United States' premier folk artists.

6¼in (16cm) high

$43,000-50,000   POOK

A late-18th/early-19thC folk art carved and stained pine peg or bedpost doll, possibly American.

10¾in (27.5cm) high

$2,000-2,500   WW

A pair of 17thC English carved oak Romayne panels, depicting woodsmen, worm, later refinished.

17¾in (45cm) high

$4,300-5,000   SWO

A pair of mid-19thC Italian Venetian carved and painted monkey waiters, each with his tail wrapped around a tree trunk and holding out a platter.

56¾in (144cm) high

$14,000-17,000   WW

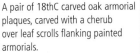

A pair of 18thC carved oak armorial plaques, carved with a cherub over leaf scrolls flanking painted armorials.

18½in (47cm) high

$3,700-4,300   LSK

A George III "Cornish" truncheon or mace, the head painted "III GR" beneath a crown on two sides, and "UP 1801" on the other sides.

1801   *22¾in (58cm) long*

$500-625   **WW**

An early-19thC wood truncheon, of tapering form, painted and gilt "IIII GR" above a royal crest, the date "1822," and "J. Smailes/ Constable."

1822   *22in (56cm) long*

$375-500   **WW**

An early-Victorian "Cornish" truncheon or mace, possibly military, painted and gilt "VR" beneath a crown, with a castle flanked by a pair of gilt keys, a Union Flag and a royal crest.

ca. 1840-50   *24in (61cm) long*

$375-500   **WW**

A 19thC American folk art carved bog oak walking stick, the head carved in the form of a snarling hound, with portraits of a governor and his wife.

42¼in (107cm) long

$1,500-2,000   **SWO**

An early-20thC carved mahogany suffragette walking stick, with the head of Emmeline Pankhurst, repairs.

Emmeline Pankhurst organized the UK suffragette movement, resulting in all women attaining the right to vote in 1928.

35¾in (91cm) long

$500-625   **SWO**

A 19thC satin birch walking cane, the automated handle modeled as a boxer dog, with small ivory details.

36½in (93cm) long

$300-450   **TOV**

A 19thC Yorkshire "Goose Wing" knitting sheath, with braided string handle, star-and-heart-carved waist and zigzag border.

9½in (24cm) long

$90-100   **JON**

A rhinoceros horn walking stick, with silver pommel, tapered to a white metal tip.

ca. 1890   *35¼in (89.5cm) long 17¼oz*

$3,100-3,700   **CHEF**

A rhinoceros horn walking stick, with black horn ferrule.

ca. 1890   *36in (91.5cm) long 10⅝oz*

$2,500-3,100   **CHEF**

A 19thC mahogany waste paper basket, the slatted open sides spaced by silhouette balusters, removable tin liner, on gilt lion-paw feet.

16¼in (41.5cm) high

$450-500   **HT**

A late-19thC mahogany waste paper basket, of pierced ladder rung form, old splits and cracks, repairs.

19in (48cm) high

$750-875   **DN**

A Georgian mahogany book tray, the shaped ends rising to a loop handle.

ca. 1800   *14¼in (36cm) wide*

$500-625   **HT**

A Regency rosewood and burl walnut book carrier, in the manner of Gillow, the sides with scrolled ends with gilt-metal foliate handles, with a base drawer.

ca. 1820   *16in (40.5cm) wide*

$875-1,000   **HT**

ESSENTIAL REFERENCE—TOLEWARE

The term "toleware" is used to describe any object fashioned from japanned (essentially varnished) and painted tinplate or pewter, and is derived from the French name for such products, "tôle peinte," which translates literally as "painted sheet metal."

● The basic metalworking technique involves fashioning thin sheets of iron or steel dipped in molten tin or pewter (an alloy of tin and copper) into diverse domestic and/ or decorative items. Typical examples include coffeepots, combs, tea caddies, teapots, trays, urns, sconces, and buckets.

● The basic decorative technique involved japanning or lacquering the objects with a varnish that varied in its specific ingredients from place to place, but was, in general, a mixture of linseed oil, driers, and colors. Subject matter for decorative imagery varied, but floral subjects were enduringly popular.

● Popular from the late 17thC to the late 19thC (albeit still made in small quantities today), the principal centers of production included Pontypool and Usk in Great Britain; Zeist and Hoorn in the Netherlands; Paris in France; and the Pennsylvania in the United States—examples from which are shown on this page.

A late-19thC folk art cedar box, with canoe handle and case, with applied antlers, axes, and stars.

11½in (29cm) wide

$3,700-5,000   **POOK**

An early-20thC folk art pig, the carved and painted head poking out of a pen with a shingled roof.

21in (53.5cm) high

$11,000-14,000   **POOK**

An early-20thC American carved figure of a cat, sitting on a brick wall with one raised paw and tail down, with inset glass eyes.

8¾in (22cm) high

$375-500   **SK**

A carved and painted wood folk art lion, by Jonathan Bastian.

Jonathan Bastian began carving wood 30 years ago. At a young age, he was surrounded and influenced by the Pennsylvania Dutch Arts and often spent hours playing in his father's woodworking shop.

12in (30.5cm) wide

$500-625   **POOK**

A 19thC red toleware coffeepot, wear, small repairs.

10½in (26.5cm) high

$2,000-2,500   **POOK**

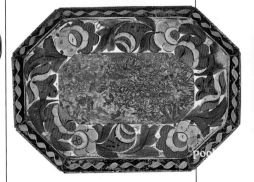

A 19thC Pennsylvania toleware tray, with floral decoration surrounding a crystallized center, sporadic paint loss.

12¼in (31cm) wide

$3,700-4,300   **POOK**

A 19thC toleware mug, with floral decoration.

5¾in (14.5cm) high

$2,500-3,100   **POOK**

A diminutive 19thC Pennsylvania toleware bread tray, with vibrant floral decoration.

7¼in (18.5cm) wide

$4,300-5,000   **POOK**

An unusual 19thC tin toleware haircomb, with red and yellow foliate decoration.

3¼in (8.5cm) wide

$1,400-1,700   **POOK**

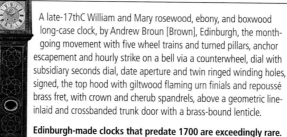

A late-17th/early-18thC walnut and marquetry long-case clock, by Fabian Robin, London, the brass eight-day movement with four turned and finned pillars, with an anchor escapement striking on a bell, the dial with a subsidiary seconds dial and a date aperture, signed "Fab Robin Londini Fecit," with cherub mask spandrels, the case inlaid with flowers and birds.

78¾in (200cm) high

$12,000-13,500 WW

A late-17thC William and Mary rosewood, ebony, and boxwood long-case clock, by Andrew Broun [Brown], Edinburgh, the month-going movement with five wheel trains and turned pillars, anchor escapement and hourly strike on a bell via a counterwheel, dial with subsidiary seconds dial, date aperture and twin ringed winding holes, signed, the top hood with giltwood flaming urn finials and repoussé brass fret, with crown and cherub spandrels, above a geometric line-inlaid and crossbanded trunk door with a brass-bound lenticle.

Edinburgh-made clocks that predate 1700 are exceedingly rare. Andrew Broun (or Brown; ca. 1651-1712) was apprenticed to Humphrey Milne on February 2, 1665. His apprenticeship was recorded thus "The second day of February 1665. The quilk day, Andro Broun, sone lawfull to umquihil Jon Broun, in Lang Newtone, is booked prentice to Umpra Milne, clock maker." Ten years later, he officially ended his apprenticeship after demonstrating his skill to a committee of clockmakers and became a freeman of the Hammermen's Incorporation. He then took on several apprentices and journeymen himself throughout his career. He became Captain of the City Guard in 1685 and Master of the Hammermen's Incorporation in 1689. In 1689 and 1690, he was elected Boxmaster (treasurer) of the Hammermen's Incorporation, and in 1696 he became a guild brother of Edinburgh. Although recorded as a highly capable maker, he apparently died penniless, with his son applying to the incorporation for financial assistance on his father's death.

John Smith, author of "Old Scottish Clockmakers from 1453 to 1850," states "In view of the long time he was in business – thirty-five years – it is remarkable how exceedingly scarce are specimens of his art, only three have come under our notice: one being the splendid clock in the lobby of the advocates library, another that was exposed for sale in the window of a dealer in Queen Street Edinburgh, both these two having cases of beautiful and chaste marquetry; and the third one in possession of a private party in Linlithgow."

97¼in (247cm) high

$31,000-37,000 L&T

A late-17th/early-18thC walnut long-case clock, by Peter Roger, London, the brass eight-day movement with five turned and finned pillars, the anchor escapement striking on a bell, the dial with a silvered chapter ring, with subsidiary seconds dial and date aperture, signed, with crown and boys spandrels, with two brass-cased weights and pendulum.

89½in (227.5cm) high

$3,700-4,300 WW

An early-18thC Queen Anne burl walnut eight-day long-case clock, the five-finned-pillar inside count-wheel bell-striking movement with anchor escapement regulated by seconds pendulum, the dial with ringed winding holes, foliate scroll and basket of flowers border-engraved calendar aperture, with subsidiary seconds dial, inscribed "John Kirton, London" flanked by dolphin cast mounts, in a case with architectural cornice, with pendulum, two weights, case key but no winder, movement not running, movement and dial not original.

A John Kirton is recorded in G. H. Baillie, "Watchmakers & Clockmakers of the World," Robert Hale (1966), as apprenticed in 1696 and gaining his freedom of the Clockmakers' Company in 1706.

88½in (225cm) high

$2,500-3,700 DN

A Queen Anne walnut eight-day long-case clock, by Charles Gretton, London, the five-finned pillar inside count-wheel bell-striking movement with anchor escapement regulated by seconds pendulum, the dial with calendar aperture in the center, signed, the case with Solomonic-twist three-quarter columns, brass-cased weights, pendulum, crank winder, case key, with 19thC marquetry decoration on door.

The life and work of Charles Gretton is thoroughly documented in Dennis Radage, Meinen Warner, and Laila Radage, "Charles Gretton: Through the Golden Age," Three O'Clock Publishing (2016). Charles Gretton was born in Clayplole, Lincolnshire, in 1648 and, by 1662, he had moved to London, entering into an eight-year apprenticeship under Humphrey Downing on June 30 of that year (turned over from Lionell Wythe). Humphrey Downing died in 1666, but it is thought that Gretton continued his apprenticeship under his widow, Cordelia, gaining his freedom of the Clockmakers' Company in 1672, and set up a business in Fleet Street. He was appointed an assistant of the Clockmakers' Company in 1889 and then warden in 1697; the same year he signed the "oath of allegiance." Gretton served as Master in 1700, and again in 1705/06. During his carreer, Charles Gretton took on many apprentices, including Henry Sully (freed April 1705) and Joseph Antram (freed October 1706), both of whom went on to become famous clockmakers in their own right. By the time of his death and internment at St. Dunstan's in the West, Gretton had become a wealthy and highly respected figure within the City of London as well as the clockmaking community.

ca. 1705

49½in (126cm) high

$3,700-5,000 DN

A Queen Anne eight-day long-case clock, by Charles Gretton, London, the five-pillar movement striking on a bell, the dial with female mask spandrels, with subsidiary seconds dial and date aperture, signed "Cha Gretton LONDON," in a walnut veneered case with caddy sliding hood.

87½in (222cm) high

$7,000-8,000 DUK

ESSENTIAL REFERENCE—JOHN & JOSEPH KNIBB

John Knibb was born in 1650 in Oxfordshire and apprenticed to his older brother, Joseph, in ca. 1664. When Joseph moved to set up in business in London (in a workshop probably inherited from his uncle, Samuel) in 1670, John took on Joseph's Oxford workshop and, by 1673, had gained Freedom of the City. Although throughout the last three decades of the 17thC John and Joseph worked in parallel, when the products from both workshops are examined, it becomes evident they had a close working relationship. When Joseph retired in 1697, he sold most of his workshop before moving to Buckinghamshire, where he did make a few more clocks prior to his death in 1711, whereas John continued in business until his death in 1722.

The movement of the clock by John Knibb shown here is fully latched and features a separate cock for the pallet arbor normally found on earlier clocks by Joseph with butterfly-nut pendulum regulation. However, the casting for the pendulum-hanging cock differs from those found on earlier clocks, and the use of an internal count wheel for striking hours certainly dates it toward the end of the century. Consequently, from these observations, one could plausibly speculate that the movement of this clock may have been acquired by John from Joseph's stock when he retired in 1697, or even on his death in 1711, before finishing and fitting with a dial. Also, despite being provincially (Oxford) made, the fine proportions of the case closely echo London work of the period, and certain features, such as the distinctive spherical finials with button-shaped caps (often seen on other long-case clocks by the Knibb family), set it aside from other provincial examples of the period.

An early-18thC Queen Anne ebonized long-case clock, by John Knibb, Oxford, the brass eight-day fully latched movement with five turned and finned pillars and inside count wheel, the anchor escapement striking on a bell, with a separate shaped cock for the pallet arbor and a cutout on the backplate for the pallets, with a long crutch, the dial with a silvered chapter ring with fleur-de-lis half-hour markers, with subsidiary seconds dial and date aperture, signed "John Knibb Oxon," the hood with a Knibb-type button capped giltwood center finial, flanked by conforming brass finials to the domed caddy top above a blind fret frieze, with integral columns with gilt-brass caps and plinths, the trunk with a concave molding and a lenticle on the door, with two brass-cased weights, pendulum, and case key.

94in (239cm) high

$22,000-27,000   WW

A mid-18thC George II walnut long-case clock, by Richard Greaves (d. 1741), Newcastle, the movement with anchor escapement and striking on bell, the dial with subsidiary seconds dial, with 24-hour moon-phase dial above, with gilt-brass dolphin mounts and foliate corner mounts, the door inlaid with a half sunburst, with two brass weights and a winding key.

83¾in (213cm) high

$3,100-4,300   DUK

A George I long-case clock, by Charles Gretton, London, the month-going five-pillar movement striking on a bell, the dial with corner spandrels of two cherubs holding a crown, subsidiary seconds dial and date aperture, the cartouche within the arch inscribed "Cha Gretton LONDON," in a walnut veneered case.

96in (244cm) high

$12,000-13,500   DUK

A walnut eight-day long-case lock, by Benjamin Gray, London, five-pillar movement with an anchor escapement and rack striking on a bell, dial strike/not strike selection lever above the 12, with seconds dial and date aperture, signed "Benj Gray, London," hood with later rebuilt caddy, woodworm, veneer lifting.

ca. 1730   93in (236cm) high

$2,500-3,700   TEN

A George II walnut eight-day long-case clock, the five-pillar rack- and bell-striking movement with anchor escapement regulated by seconds pendulum, the dial with calendar aperture and subsidiary seconds dial, the arch with herringbone border, engraved silver signature boss inscribed "William Creak, LONDON," flanked by dolphin cast mounts, with two weights, pendulum, crank winder, and two case keys, case may not be original for the movement and dial.

William Creak is recorded in G. H. Baillie, "Watchmakers & Clockmakers of the World," Robert Hale (1966), as a "fine maker" who worked in London from 1754-63. Other sources indicate that he was working from 1740-75 and his workshop was located in the Royal Exchange from 1754. Creak supplied musical and automaton clocks for export to the Middle East and China, and often incorporated similar complications into examples made for the domestic market.

ca. 1740   90¼in (229cm) high

$2,500-3,700   DN

A George III mahogany and satinwood eight-day long-case clock with tidal indication and moon phase, by William Tarleton, Liverpool, the four-pillar rack- and bell-striking movement with break-arch plates and escapement fitted with cranked crutch to provide impulse to the seconds pendulum, the dial with subsidiary calendar and seconds dials, and "HIGH/LOW" and with sector with scenes of coastal views, with disk annotated for the age of the moon and times of high water, with pendulum, two brass-cased weights, winder, and case key, repairs.

William Tarleton is recorded in G. H. Baillie, "Watchmakers & Clockmakers of the World," Robert Hale (1966), as a "watch-maker of repute" working in Liverpool 1763-1807. In 1798, Tarleton's business was taken on by his son-in-law Robert Roskell, who went on to establish one of the most important watchmaking workshops of the 19thC.

ca. 1775   93½in (237.5cm) high

$4,300-5,600   DN

A mahogany eight-day seven-tune musical long-case clock, by William Avenell, Portsmouth, five-pillar movement with an anchor escapement and striking on a bell, playing a musical tune on a nest of 12 bells every three hours, arch brass dial with a silvered Roman and Arabic chapter ring, dial center with seconds dial with figures in costume, date aperture and signed, arch with moon-phase aperture and above engraved with seven musical tune selections for "Brittons Strike Home/Fond Shepherd/104 Psalm/A Jigg/Patties Mill/A March/A Song," pagoda pediment, Corinthian capped columns, glass side panels.

ca. 1780   *93¼in (237cm) high*

$4,300-5,600   **TEN**

A mahogany eight-day long-case clock, signed Robert Lawson, Leigh, four-pillar movement with an anchor escapement and rack striking on a bell, dial with inner date ring, seconds dial, arch with moon-phase aperture and signed, bonnet-top pediment, flame mahogany trunk door flanked by fluted pilasters.

ca. 1780   *100in (254cm) high*

$1,900-2,500   **TEN**

A mahogany eight-day long-case clock, signed Barker, Wigan, four-pillar movement with an anchor escapement and rack striking on a bell, dial with inner date ring, seconds dial, arch with moon-phase aperture and signed, bonnet-top pediment, flame mahogany trunk door flanked by fluted pilasters.

ca. 1780   *96in (244cm) high*

$1,900-2,500   **TEN**

An 18thC Dutch walnut eight-day long-case clock, by Pieter Gib, Rotterdam, five-pillar movement with an anchor escapement, striking on the half hour and striking a larger bell for the hours, signed, dial center with seconds dial and date aperture, arch with moon-phase disk, hood with damages and losses.

95in (241cm) high

$2,500-3,100   **TEN**

A late-18thC Dutch mahogany and marquetry long-case clock, by Barent Dikhoff, Haarlem, the brass eight-day movement with four turned pillars and an anchor escapement striking on two bells, the dial with date and day of the week apertures, subsidiary seconds dial, the arch with a moon phase, with the four seasons spandrels, signed, the case with urns of flowers, birds, and a butterfly, with two brass-cased weights and pendulum.

84¾in (215.5cm) high

$1,900-2,500   **WW**

An 18thC George III mahogany chiming long-case clock, by John Prichard, London, the eight-day triple-chain movement striking a main steel bell and chiming on eight, graduated steel bells and brass play drum, subsidiary seconds dial and calendar aperture, the maker's name on the arch over further dials, "STRIKE/NOT STRIKE," "Brittons Strike Home/Correllies Gigg," [sic] and "CHIME/NOT CHIME."

95¼in (242cm) high

$4,300-5,600   **L&T**

A blue japanned long-case clock, 18thC and later, the later brass eight-day movement with an anchor escapement striking on a bell, the backplate stamped "Made in England," the dial signed "Izaac Rogers London," the case decorated in gilt with chinoiserie scenes.

78¾in (200cm) high

$3,700-5,000   **WW**

A black and gilt lacquered long-case clock, with eight-day bell-striking movement, the dial with subsidiary date dial, inscribed "Daniel Kedden, Little Britain, London," the arch with automaton panel inscribed "sic transit Gloria Mundi," the case with arch and molded cornice surmounted by three flaming torch finials, the blind fret-carved frieze with arched glazed door, the movement an early replacement, other later elements, losses.

100½in (255.5cm) high

$3,100-4,300   **DN**

A George III japanned long-case clock, by George Jefferys, Chatham, the brass eight-day movement with four turned pillars and an anchor escapement striking on a bell, the dial with subsidiary seconds dial and date aperture, with gilt Rococo spandrels and "STRIKE/SILENT" dial, signed, the faux tortoiseshell case with gilt highlights with chinoiserie scenes.

88½in (225cm) high

$1,050-1,200   **WW**

A mahogany musical long-case clock, by Robert Allam, London, 18thC and later, the brass three-train movement with five turned pillars, the anchor escapement striking on a bell and chiming on eight bells, the dial with a silvered chapter ring, with subsidiary seconds dial and date aperture, a "STRIKE/SILENT" dial in the arch, signed, the hood with a bird and orb finial, with pendulum, case, and winding keys.

93¼in (237cm) high

$1,900-2,500   **WW**

A Georgian long-case clock, by James Stevens, London, the silver dial with a secondary dial and date aperture, surrounded by brass spandrels, within a green case with a circular vision panel.

$550-700   **WHP**

An Irish mahogany long-case clock, by Dalrymple, Dublin, the eight-day movement with anchor escapement striking on a bell, enamel dial with Roman numerals and secondary dial, the case with carved cable edge banding.

85in (216cm) high

$625-750   **HT**

A 19thC ebonized, tortoiseshell, and brass Boulle marquetry long-case clock, in Louis XIV style, the eight-day movement striking a bell, the dial with enamel hour markers, surmounted by the figure of Chronos, the waisted bombé case with brass and tortoiseshell marquetry after Jean Berain.

90½in (230cm) high

$11,000-14,000   **L&T**

An Edwardian mahogany tubular bell-chiming long-case clock, triple weight-driven movement with an anchor escapement and quarter chiming with eight hammers striking eight tubular bells, and a further hammer striking another tubular bell for the hours, wavy-shaped brass dial with a seconds dial, three dials in the arch for "strike/silent," "chime/silent," and "Whittington/Westminster" selections, the case with leaf, scroll, and swag decoration, base with an inlaid basket of flowers and a scroll border, scratches and dents, movement not working.

107in (272cm) high

$8,500-11,000   **TEN**

A George III green lacquered musical bracket clock, by Robert Ward, London, the brass twin-fusee movement with a verge escapement striking on a single bell and chiming on eight bells, with twin repeat mechanisms for hours and minutes, a bob pendulum, the dial with a chapter ring, signed, "Chime/Not Chime" and "Song/Jigg" dials in the arch.

ca. 1760   23¼in (59cm) high
$5,500-6,000   WW

An 18thC French Régence Boulle marquetry bracket clock and bracket, by Le Faucheur, Paris, the movement with anchor escapement, outside count wheel and bell strike, dial with "LE FAUCHEUR A PARIS," the case surmounted by a youth, with a glazed door with a boy and a dog flanked by female busts, with a Boulle marquetry wall bracket with female masks.

36¼in (92cm) high
$3,100-3,700   L&T

A George III bracket clock, by Marriott, London, the engraved movement striking on a bell, secondary dial and "STRIKE/SILENT" dial, within an ebonized and gilt-metal-mounted case, with fretwork panels and brass bracket feet.

15¼in (39cm) high
$4,300-5,600   WHP

A George III bracket or table clock, by William Ward, Bloomsbury, London, the movement inscribed with the maker's name, foliate motifs, and striking on a bell, the silvered face with Roman numerals and a date aperture.

15¼in (39cm) high
$3,100-3,700   WHP

A George III mahogany bracket clock, twin-fusee movement with engraved backplate, converted to anchor escapement, the dial signed "John Grant, Fleet Street, London," "STRIKE/SILENT" in the arch, the case with brass handle and four pineapple finials.

19in (48cm) high
$2,000-2,500   CHEF

A George III ebonized bracket clock, with trip-hour repeat, the five-pillar, twin-chain fusee, bell-striking movement with anchor escapement regulated by lenticular bob pendulum, the dial signed "J. DUMBELL, PRESCOT," with pendulum and key for the rear door, but no front door key or winder.

This clock was probably made by Joseph Dumbell, who is recorded in G. H. Baillie, "Watchmakers & Clockmakers of the World," Robert Hale (1966), as working in Liverpool 1800-29.

ca. 1800   14in (35.5cm) high
$875-1,000   DN

An early-19thC Regency mahogany pagoda-top bracket clock, the twin-fusee eight-day movement striking on a bell, the case with foliate carving and scrolling spandrels.

21in (53.5cm) high
$625-750   WW

A George III mahogany bracket clock, the brass twin-fusee eight-day movement striking on a bell, the backplate with scrolling, flowering foliage, with a strike/silent dial in the arch, with pendulum.

ca. 1770-80   17¾in (45cm) high
$1,000-1,100   WW

A Regency brass-mounted ebonized quarter-chiming bracket clock with integral wall bracket, by John Thwaites & Co., the six-pillar triple-chain fusee movement chiming the quarters on eight bells and sounding the hour on a further larger bell, with anchor escapement regulated by lenticular bob pendulum, the backplate signed "John Thwaites & Co., Clerkenwell, London," the cream-painted Roman numeral dial signed "John Thwaites & Co. Clerkenwell, LONDON," with minute track on outer margin, the break-arch case with hinged carrying handle, with crescent-shaped scroll pierced brass fret, the sides with arched brass fish-scale frets, on a cavetto molded skirt base resting on original wall bracket, an ogee molded foot, with pendulum, winder, and two case keys, dial restored to a high standard, slight wear to case and bracket finish, brass strip on front has "sprung" slightly.

ca. 1813   25¼in (64cm) high
$5,500-7,000   DN

A Regency mahogany bracket clock, twin-fusee, bell-striking movement, dial signed "Wm Scott, London," the sides with ring handles and arched brass fret panels.

17in (43cm) high

$800-950 CHEF

An early-19thC Scottish Regency rosewood bracket clock, by Robert Bryson, Edinburgh, the twin-train movement striking the full hour on a bell, the signed dial with two winding holes.

17in (43cm) high

$1,000-1,250 L&T

A Regency brass-mounted mahogany bracket clock, in the manner of Thomas Hope Upjohn, the case possibly by Banting and France, London, the five-pillar, twin-fusee, bell-striking movement with trip-hour repeat and anchor escapement regulated by lenticular bob pendulum with holdfast to backplate, the dial signed "UPJOHN, 15 King William St., STRAND," the case in Romano-Egyptian style, no case key or winder, restorations.

The movement of this clock is probably by John and Thomas Upjohn, who are recorded in Brian Loomes, "Watchmakers & Clockmakers of the World, Volume 2," Robert Hale (1978), as makers "To His Majesty" and working in London 1828-32.

ca. 1825 *20¾in (52.5cm) high*

$5,000-6,200 DN

A George IV brass-inlaid mahogany quarter-chiming bracket clock and bracket, the six-pillar, triple-chain fusee movement chiming the quarters on a nest of eight bells and sounding the hour on a further larger bell, with anchor escapement regulated by lenticular bob pendulum, backplate signed "French, Royal Exchange, London," dial also signed, the case with a gilt-brass pineapple finial surmounting the Gothic arch, flanked by obelisk finials capped with pineapple finials, flanked by Corinthian columns, with pendulum, winder, and a case key, slight veneer shrinkage.

Santiago James Moore French is recorded in G. H. Baillie, "Watchmakers & Clockmakers of the World," Robert Hale (1966), as working from Royal Exchange and Sweetings Alley, London, ca. 1810-40.

ca. 1825 *41¼in (105cm) high*

$7,500-8,500 DN

An early-Victorian silvered brass-mounted ebonized bracket clock, with trip-hour repeat, the five-baluster-pillar, twin-chain fusee, bell-striking movement with anchor escapement regulated by lenticular bob pendulum, the backplate signed "James McCabe, Royal Exchange, London," the dial further signed "James McCabe, ROYAL EXCHANGE, London" and numbered "2515," with "STRIKE/SILENT" at 12, the case with a pineapple finial on the hipped "chamfer-top" superstructure, with pendulum, winding key, and two case keys.

James McCabe Jr., who succeeded his father of the same name, was one of the most successful British clock and watchmakers of the 19thC. He was apprenticed to Reid and Auld of Edinburgh and was admitted to the Clockmakers' Company as a Free Brother in 1822. Around this time, McCabe entered into a short-lived partnership with Strahan (probably Charles, who gained his freedom of the Clockmakers' Company in 1815). From 1826, James McCabe managed the business alone from 97 Cornhill, until 1838, when he was forced to temporarily relocate to 32 Cornhill due to a major fire at the Royal Exchange. The pasted paper label applied on the inside of the clock shown here indicates that it would probably have been supplied by McCabe to either the East India Company or the Government India Office. This suggestion is further supported by the silver-on-black appearance of the case, which would seem to follow Indian, not European, fashion.

A William IV Egyptian Revival mahogany bracket clock, the triple-fusee movement striking on eight bells, the silvered dial with seconds dial inscribed "Widenham London," case with brass string inlay and a sphinx finial.

22¾in (58cm) high

$1,400-1,700 DUK

A William IV carved and brass-inlaid mahogany bracket clock and bracket, the five-pillar, twin-fusee, bell-striking movement, with shoulder plates and anchor escapement regulated by lenticular bob half-seconds pendulum with holdfast at the center of the backplate, with signature "Turner, LONDON" and serial no. "591," the dial inscribed "TURNER, Fenchurch St., London," with original wall bracket, with case key but no winder.

ca. 1830 *27¼in (69.5cm) high*

$2,200-2,700 DN

ca. 1845 *19¾in (50cm) high*

$3,100-4,300 DN

CLOCKS

A 19thC ebonized "basket-top" bracket clock, in William and Mary style, brass twin-fusee movement, with an anchor escapement on a brass dial, the case with a pierced gilt-metal "basket" decorated with swags, fruit, and scrolls, with keys and pendulum.

15¼in (38.5cm) high

$7,000-7,500 WW

A mid-19thC brass-inlaid rosewood bracket timepiece, the four-baluster pillar, single-fusee movement with anchor escapement regulated by lenticular bob pendulum, the case with a pagoda-shaped pediment, with leaf carved detail on the canopy with canted silvered-brass fillet inset glazed front door, unsigned.

9¾in (25cm) high

$1,250-1,900 DN

A 19thC French red tortoiseshell and Boulle marquetry bracket clock and bracket, the twin-chain, eight-day movement by Honoré Pons with stamped numbers "92 66" and striking a gong, the dial with engraved seconds markers, in a case surmounted by a figure of a boy wearing a turban and sitting on a globe, with a Boulle marquetry bracket with exotic female masks.

35in (89cm) high

$2,200-2,700 L&T

A Victorian brass-mounted ebonized quarter-chiming bracket clock, by W. H. & S. Jackson, London, the six-pillar, triple-chain fusee movement chiming the quarters on a nest of eight bells and sounding the hour on a coiled gong, the going train with anchor escapement regulated by heavy disk-bob pendulum, the dial inscribed "W. H. & S. JACKSON, London, 242, F," with subsidiary "FAST/SLOW" regulation and "STRIKE/SILENT," case with a gilt pineapple finial, the door incorporating a winged cherub head and foliate scroll, light wear, key but no winder.

The partnership between William Henry and Samuel Jackson is recorded in Brian Loomes, "Watchmakers & Clockmakers of the World, Volume 2," Robert Hale (1978), as trading in London 1851-81.

ca. 1870 *27½in (70cm) high*

$1,700-2,200 DN

A late-Victorian burl walnut bracket clock, the eight-day recoil anchor movement with triple fusee and chain, quarter chime on eight bells and hour strike on gong, signed on backplate "Thwaites & Reed, London," the dial with 'SLOW/FAST' regulation ring.

18in (45.5cm) high

$3,700-5,000 DUK

A late-19thC French Boulle bracket clock and bracket, in Louis XV style, the movement stamped for C. Kuhling, the count-wheel bell-striking movement with anchor escapement regulated by sunburst mask cast pendulum, stamped "371, C, 9.10" over "C. KUHLING" on backplate, the dial with cockerel-inhabited Berainesque foliate strapwork cast center, the case with a figure of winged Fortuna and with martial trophy mounts at angles, the underside with an acanthus cast pendant mount terminating with a floral finial, with pendulum, case key, and winder, case cosmetically restored.

46¼in (117.5cm) high

$1,600-2,200 DN

A late-19thC oak bracket clock, the brass eight-day, three-train repeating movement chiming on eight bells and five gongs, with three subsidiary dials, with spandrels with leaves and flowers, the case with Jacobean foliage, flower heads, and masks, with key and pendulum.

22¾in (57.5cm) high

$2,200-2,700 WW

A late-19thC walnut and gilt-metal chiming bracket clock, in Persian style, the eight-day movement with gong strike and chiming on eight bells, dial with subsidiary "CHIME/SILENT" and "CHIME ON EIGHT BELLS/CAMBRIDGE CHIMES" dials on the arch, the top stamped "Rd45254."

17in (43cm) high

$2,200-2,700 L&T

A Victorian brass-mounted mahogany quarter-chiming bracket clock, the four-pillar, triple-chain fusee movement chiming a choice of two tunes at the quarters on eight bells and sounding the hour on a coiled gong, the going train with anchor escapement regulated by heavy disk-bob pendulum, backplate stamped "2995," the dial with "CHIME/SILENT," "FAST/SLOW," and "CHIME ON EIGHT BELLS/WESTMINSTER CHIME," the case with a gilt pineapple finial, unsigned.

ca. 1900 *30in (76cm) high*

$2,500-3,700 DN

TABLE 315

CLOCKS

An ebonized table clock, by Henry Younge, The Strand, twin fusee movement with turned pillars, dial with date aperture, winged mask spandrels, "strike/silent" arm on the backplate, pull repeat cord, on four gilt-brass feet, restored, pendulum holdfast is wrong.

ca. 1680   11¼in (28.5cm) high
$10,000-11,000   **CHEF**

A Charles II/James II ebony quarter-repeating table clock, of Knibb "Phase III" type, signed for Henry Merriman but attributed to the workshop of Joseph Knibb, London, the five-finned baluster-pillar, fully latched twin-fusee movement with verge escapement regulated by short bob pendulum, backplate signed "Henry Merriman, London," the strike train and quarter-repeat mechanism with typical "Knibb" scroll design sculpted steel feet to the two bell-stands, the square brass dial with Roman numeral chapter ring with fleur-de-lis half hour markers and Arabic five minutes within the narrow outer minute track, with "S/N" "Strike/silent" selection, and signed "Henry Merriman London," the case with later hinged scroll cast-brass handle, fruiting vine spray mounts, on stepped ogee molded shallow skirt base now with block feet.

ca. 1685-90   13½in (34cm) high
$31,000-37,000   **DN**

A William III gilt-brass-mounted ebony "basket-top" table clock, by John Moncreift, London, the six-finned pillar, twin-fusee, bell-striking movement with verge escapement regulated by short bob pendulum, the backplate signed "Jn'o Moncreift, London," the gilt-brass dial with scroll-bordered false bob and calendar apertures, within applied-silvered Roman numeral chapter ring with half-hour and Arabic five minutes markers, signed "Moncreift, London," "N/S" "Strike/silent" selection switch at 12, the case with Quare-type carrying handle over later 19thC pierced gilt-brass "basket" superstructure, with winged cherub masks flanked by putti, flanked by later 19thC pineapple finials, on molded skirt base with gilt-brass squab feet, formerly with pull-quarter repeat work, now removed, with winder but no case key, escape wheel has been repinioned.

ca. 1695   15¼in (38.5cm) high
$8,000-8,500   **DN**

ESSENTIAL REFERENCE—EARDLEY NORTON

Thought to have been born into a farming family from Rigsby, in Lincolnshire, Eardley Norton was apprenticed as a clockmaker in May 1743 to Robert Dawson of Alford. Subsequently, Norton moved to London, where he is listed as working at 49 St John's Street, Clerkenwell, from 1760. A member of the Clockmakers" Company (being freed in 1770), he remained so until his death in 1792. Notable accomplishments included his application in 1771 for a patent for a new type of striking mechanism for both clocks and watches. He was also one of few makers who utilized the "carriage-change system" to select tunes, whereby the entire bell and hammer assembly is moved along the barrel by a leaf spring, rather than the usual arrangement in which the barrel is shunted along beneath the hammers. He also enjoyed royal patronage, and his silver-mounted, four-dial astronomical clock (made in collaboration with James Ferguson FRS) commissioned by George III for Buckingham House (later Palace), still remains in the Royal Collection (RCIN 30432). On Norton's death, his business was taken over by the partnership of Gravell and Tolkien.

A rare mid-18thC George II gilt-brass-mounted ebonized quarter-striking table clock, by Henry Hindley, York, the six distinctive double baluster-turned-pillar, twin-chain fusee movement with arched plates enclosing greatwheels, the backplate engraved with scrolling foliage, signed "Hen. Hindley, of YORK" flanked by ho ho bird, lion and grotesque mask-inhabited strapwork, the arched brass dial with silvered Roman numeral dial with Arabic five minutes to outer track, signed "H. Hindley, York," "Strike quar's/Hr/ Silent" selection, subsidiary seconds dial flanked by female sphinx-inhabited scroll cast mounts, the bell-top case with brass carrying handle and pineapple finials, foliate scroll cast gilt upper quadrant frets and applied with female term mounts to uprights, the sides with arched brass fish scale sound frets, on a stepped ogee-molded skirt base.

19in (48cm) high
$17,500-20,000   **DN**

A George III gilt-mounted mahogany musical table clock, by Eardley Norton, London, the 11-pillar, triple-chain fusee movement playing a choice of 12 tunes through a pinned cylinder on 13 bells with 16 hammers, before sounding the hour on a larger bell, the going train with deadbeat escapement incorporating a lenticular bob pendulum, with signature "Eardley Norton London," dial signed "EARDLEY NORTON, LONDON," applied with "STRIKE/ SILENT" and "CHIME/NOT CHIME," with tune selection inscribed "MINUET" five times, "MARCH" three times, "GAVOT," "AIR," "DANCE," and "HORNPIPE," base applied with musical trophy, with pendulum, winder and case key, restoration.

ca. 1780   38in (96.5cm) high
$37,000-50,000   **DN**

A brass-mounted mahogany quarter-chiming table clock, by Matthew Dutton, London, five-pillar, triple-chain fusee movement chiming the quarters on six bells with six hammers and sounding the hours on a further larger bell, the going train with half-deadbeat escapement regulated by lenticular bob pendulum, backplate signed "Dutton, London" and numbered "340," the brass break-arch dial with white enamel disk with Roman numeral hour chapters and Arabic five minutes beyond the minute ring, "S/N" "Strike/silent" selection at 12 beneath subsidiary regulation dial, signed "Matthew Dutton, London," the break-arch case with brass handle and brass fillet moldings, the sides with brass diamond lattice sound frets, on a cavetto-molded skirt base with brass squab feet, with pendulum, winder, and case key, slight mellowing of brass, small veneer repair.

ca. 1800   17¼in (44cm) high
$22,000-27,000   **DN**

A late-George III mahogany table clock, the triple fusee movement chiming on eight bells and striking on a further bell, dial signed "Handley & Moore London," above a triple pad top break-arch case, refinishing on the case.

ca. 1820   18¼in (46.5cm) high

$2,500-3,100   **CHEF**

A William IV mahogany striking table clock, signed J. Huggins, London, twin-chain fusee movement with anchor escapement and rack striking on a bell, date dial, arch with "STRIKE/SILENT" selection, top with a pineapple finial, fish-scale pierced side sound frets, case with veneer cracks.

ca. 1830   20in (51cm) high

$3,100-4,300   **TEN**

A William IV rosewood striking table clock, signed Mitchell, Glasgow, twin-fusee movement with anchor escapement and rack striking on a bell, backplate engraved, signed "J&W Mitchell 80 Argyll Street Glasgow," strike/silent selection lever above 12, gadroon pediment.

ca. 1835   20½in (52cm) high

$1,000-1,100   **TEN**

A mahogany striking table clock, by Benjamin Reed, Plymouth, the twin-fusee movement with anchor escapement striking on a bell, the backplate signed, dial with "STRIKE/SILENT" dial and signature.

18½in (47cm) high

$1,250-1,900   **HT**

An ebony veneered and gilt-metal-mounted chiming table clock, by Penlington & Hutton, Liverpool, triple-chain fusee movement with anchor escapement, quarter chiming on eight bells and striking a gong for the hours, dial signed, slow/fast selection lever above 12, strike/silent selection lever at 3, pediment with carrying handle and acorn-shaped finials, acanthus leaf mounts.

ca. 1880   20in (51cm) high

$3,100-3,700   **TEN**

A Victorian ebonized and gilt-metal-mounted table clock, the triple-train movement chiming on eight bells and striking on a gong, the dial with silvered subsidiaries for chiming selection, "CHIME/SILENT," and "SLOW/FAST" regulation, chapter ring signed "Smith & Sons, Clerkenwell."

ca. 1887   26in (66cm) high

$3,100-3,700   **CHEF**

A rosewood and brass-inlaid quarter-chiming table clock, by Rood & Co., Burlington Arcade, triple-chain fusee movement with anchor escapement and quarter chiming on a nest of eight bells and striking the hours on a gong, "SLOW/FAST" and "CHIME ON EIGHT BELLS/ WESTMINSTER CHIMES," arched pediment with a pineapple finial and corner urn-shaped finials, Corinthian-capped columns.

ca. 1890   31½in (80cm) high

$2,500-3,100   **TEN**

A late-19th/early 20thC chinoiserie table timepiece, in 18thC style, A-frame, single-fusee movement with verge escapement, backplate with floral and scroll engraving and a later signature, bob pendulum, dial with a later inscription "Peter Wize London," date aperture, arch with moon-phase aperture, Asian-style decoration with figures, pagodas, and birds.

13¾in (35cm) high

$2,500-3,700   **TEN**

An Edwardian mahogany and gilt-metal-mounted table clock, the triple-train fusee movement chiming and striking on eight bells and a gong, arched dial with three subsidiaries above for "SLOW/FAST" regulation, "CHIME/SILENT," and "CAMBRIDGE CHIME/ WESTMINSTER CHIME."

28¼in (72cm) high

$2,500-3,700   **CHEF**

ESSENTIAL REFERENCE—CLARA

The rhinoceros depicted on this clock was called Clara. Raised from birth by Jan Albert Sichterman, a director of the Bengal region of the Dutch East India Company, she was sold in 1740, at about two years old, to Douwe Mout van der Meer, a retired Dutch East India Company captain. Two years after arriving with her in Rotterdam in 1741, der Meer embarked on a meticulously planned and brilliantly marketed tour of Europe with Clara, which essentially endured for some 15 years, until her death in 1758, and resulted in what became known as "rhinomania." Notable highlights among many included her five-month stay in Paris from winter 1749 to spring 1750, which was rapidly reflected in ladies' fashions, coiffures, poetry, commemorative pottery, and the creation of spectacular works of art. Probably the most impressive of the latter was painted from life in 1749 by Jean-Baptiste Oudry, who was commissioned by Louis XV to include Clara's likeness in a group of oil paintings of animals in the menagerie at the Royal Palace at Versailles. Clara was transported across Europe by water whenever possible, and where necessary by land in a specially designed carriage, the combined weight of which required six pairs of oxen or ten pairs of horses to pull it!

An important mid-18thC French Louis XV ormolu-mounted stained horn and patinated bronze musical mantel clock, the clock movement by François Beliard, the twin-barrel movement with silk suspension pendulum and count wheel striking on a bell, trip lever in the plinth housing the associated musical movement in a sarcophagus-shaped box, with fusee and spring-pin barrel playing music on 11 bells and 12 hammers, the dial with an Asian figure and inscribed "BELIARD/H.GER * DU ROY.," on a bellowing rhinoceros, on a naturalistic rocky base with eight scrolled feet, the ormolu stamped "ST GERMAIN."

$125,000-190,000   **DUK**

A late-18thC French Louis XVI white marble and ormolu mantel clock, by Folin l'Aîné, Paris, the brass eight-day, drum movement with an outside count wheel striking on a bell on the hour and half hour, the case surmounted by a cherub passing a basket of flowers to a young lady playing a lyre, with gilt swags beneath the dial and putti playing with a garland, with a pendulum and two keys.

Nicolas-Alexandre Folin was born ca. 1750 and was accepted into the guild as Master in 1789. He used the signature Folin l'Aîné "the elder" to distinguish himself from his brother, who was also a clockmaker. He was one of the top Parisian makers and specialized in high quality clocks. A superb skeleton clock of his is in the Getty Museum, Los Angeles.

16¾in (42.5cm) high

$3,700-5,000   **WW**

A French Directoire ormolu and Carrara marble portico mantel clock, by Lepine, the eight-day, brass drum movement with an outside count wheel and striking on a bell, the backplate inscribed and numbered, the dial by Barbichon, with the days of the week, signed "Lepine H.ger du Roi" and "Place des Victoires no.12," the temple case with an eagle surmount above urns of flowers and a gallery supported by Corinthian columns with laurel swags, with two female figures, representing "Justice" and "Fortitude," flanking war trophies.

Jean Antoine Lepine (1720-1814) began his horological career in Geneva, later moving to Paris, where he was apprenticed to André Caron, the king's clockmaker. He subsequently married Caron's daughter in 1756. He received his Maitre title in 1762 and soon after was appointed to the coveted position of Horologer du Roi for Louis XV. He subsequently served as watchmaker to Louis XVI and Napoleon I. He operated from premises in the rue Saint-Denis, and in 1789 he moved to 12 Place des Victoires. By this time, the day-to-day running of the business was handled by his son-in-law Claude-Pierre Raguet-Lepine. There are several clocks by Lepine in the British Royal Collection and according to C. Jagger, "Royal Clocks: The British Monarchy and its Timekeepers," Robert Hale (1983), Lepine was a favorite clockmaker of George IV, who is known to have bought a number of clocks from the firm.

ca. 1790-1800   *28¾in (73cm) high*

$8,500-10,000   **WW**

A French Directoire gilt- and patinated bronze and Carrara marble mantel clock, by Gaston Jolly, Paris, the circular eight-day, count-wheel, bell-striking movement with anchor escapement regulated by disk-bob pendulum with silk suspension, the white enamel Roman numeral dial signed "Gaston Jolly A Paris," the case modeled as an urn with floral surmount and decorated with an entwined serpent, gilt pendant finial on underside, raised on four tapered pierced lappet-leaf-molded supports incorporating female term upper terminals at the sides and outswept hoof feet, mounted on a stepped oval Carrara marble plinth base, with gilt engine-milled disk feet.

Francois-Pierre Gaston Jolly is recorded in Tardy, "Dictionnaire des Horlogers Francais," Paris (1971), as becoming a Master in 1794 and working from Pave St. Sauveur, Paris, 1810-20. He was a fine maker whose movements are often seen in cases by Pierre-Philippe Thomire, suggesting that there was some form of association between the two workshops.

ca. 1800   *23¼in (59cm) high*

$3,100-3,700   **DN**

CLOCKS

An early-19thC French Empire ormolu mantel clock, the dial signed "JAS. MURRAY/1 ROYAL EXCHANGE/LONDON," surmounted by an artist and his companion.

18in (46cm) high

$1,500-1,900 **L&T**

A mid-19thC ormolu eight-day mantel clock, with a silvered dial and silk escapement, an angel on each side embracing, on a marquetry base beneath a glass dome, glass dome is cracked, silk suspension broken.

26¾in (68cm) high

$2,500-3,700 **CHOR**

A French Boulle and gilt-metal-mounted striking mantel clock, by Miroy Fres Brevet, Paris, twin-barrel movement with outside count wheel striking on a bell, case with brass inlay and tortoiseshell veneers, case with small cracks, hand collet and pin are missing.

ca. 1880 *20¾in (53cm) high*

$1,050-1,200 **TEN**

A French ormolu and porcelain-mounted mantel clock, by Achille Brocot, twin-barrel movement striking on a bell, stamped with maker's mark "AB," original pendulum with bob stamped "9215," the porcelain panels depicting musical instruments and swag decoration.

ca. 1880 *15in (38cm) high*

$875-1,000 **TEN**

A 19thC French cloisonné and gilt-brass mantel clock, the cylinder eight-day movement stamped "S. MARTI ET CIE 1889, 12678 44," striking on a gong, with a mercury pendulum.

15¾in (40cm) high

$2,200-2,700 **L&T**

A 19thC French gilt- and patinated bronze figural mantel clock, the eight-day movement stamped "BT MARC PARIS 38804," striking on a bell, with the draped figure of Melpomene with her attributes leaning against a pillar.

27½in (70cm) high

$2,200-2,700 **L&T**

A 19thC French ormolu mantel clock, with a bell-striking drum movement, the dial flanked by two putti, the case surmounted by a Classical female figure and two putti, with inset porcelain painted with Vesta in a landscape, not ticking or striking.

22in (56cm) wide

$1,250-1,600 **CHEF**

A 19thC gilt-bronze case mantel timepiece, in the manner of Thomas Cole, the single-barrel movement with balance wheel escapement and rachet wind, compass finial above the three sides featuring a calendar, a thermometer panel and an engraved door, not currently ticking.

7in (18cm) high

$3,100-4,300 **CHEF**

A brass four-glass striking mantel clock, retailed by Martin, 5 Regent Street, London, twin-barrel movement striking on a bell, backplate stamped "GV" and numbered "3677," twin mercury-tube pendulum, recessed dial center with a visible "Brocot" escapement.

ca. 1890 *14¼in (36cm) high*

$1,400-1,600 **TEN**

A French ormolu striking mantel clock, twin-barrel movement with outside count wheel striking on a bell, backplate stamped with maker's mark "H&F Paris" and numbered "5787," dial with 12 Roman numeral enamel cartouches, surmounted by an urn, side lion-head masked ringed mounts, base with acanthus, scroll, and swag decoration.

ca. 1890   *24½in (62cm) high*

$3,700-4,300   **TEN**

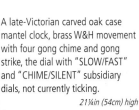

A late-19thC French bronze elephant-base mantel clock, the gong-striking drum movement marked "R & C Paris and London 587," the top with a moustached Asian-style figure holding an umbrella, on an elephant with trunk raised, hands broken, movement not working.

17¼in (44cm) high

$1,250-1,500   **CHEF**

A 19thC French marble mantel clock, with perpetual calendar, by Henri Marc, Paris, with visible escapement and striking movement, signed and numbered "38518," the dial above a gilt-metal panel containing a calendar dial with moon phase and day, date, and month subsidiary dials.

19¼in (49cm) high

$3,100-4,300   **GORL**

A green onyx and champlevé enamel striking mantel clock, retailed by Dantenez, Paris, twin-barrel movement striking on a gong, backplate stamped "Marti," champlevé enamel pendulum bob.

ca. 1900   *12¼in (31cm) high*

$375-500   **TEN**

A late-Victorian carved oak case mantel clock, brass W&H movement with four gong chime and gong strike, the dial with "SLOW/FAST" and "CHIME/SILENT" subsidiary dials, not currently ticking.

21¼in (54cm) high

$625-750   **CHEF**

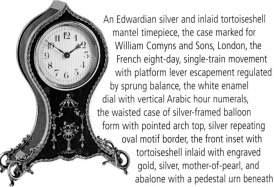

An Edwardian silver and inlaid tortoiseshell mantel timepiece, the case marked for William Comyns and Sons, London, the French eight-day, single-train movement with platform lever escapement regulated by sprung balance, the white enamel dial with vertical Arabic hour numerals, the waisted case of silver-framed balloon form with pointed arch top, silver repeating oval motif border, the front inset with tortoiseshell inlaid with engraved gold, silver, mother-of-pearl, and abalone with a pedestal urn beneath a canopy issuing floral trails below the dial, the sides with curved tortoiseshell panels inset within the silver frame, on delicate openwork scroll-cast feet with shaped apron between, the case hallmarked for London 1909, maker's "W.C." within an oval.

The Comyns family business of silversmiths was established by William Comyns in 1858. The firm initially traded from Soho in London but quickly expanded, taking on premises on Beak Street, off Regent Street. In 1885, William's two sons, Charles and Richard, joined the business, succeeding their father on his death in 1916. Charles died in 1925 and the firm was incorporated as William Comyns and Sons Ltd. in 1930, before being bought by Richard Copping on Richard's death in 1953. The Comyns family mainly specialized in producing small decorative wares for all price brackets, often produced using mechanical methods, such as die-stamping. The maker's mark on the current clock is recorded online (at silvermakersmarks.co.uk) as being registered in November 1890, and was in use until 1915.

1909   *6½in (16.5cm) high*

$1,600-1,900   **DN**

A French mantel clock, in Louis XV style, gong-striking Samuel Marti movement dated "1900," Boulle brass-inlaid waisted case, some damage.

1900   *14¼in (36cm) high*

$250-370   **CHEF**

An electric mantel clock, by the Eureka Clock Co. Ltd., the brass movement stamped "Patent no. 14614, No. 7006" and with fast/slow indicator, with a subsidiary seconds dial, in a mahogany case, with later battery fittings.

1906   *15in (38cm) high*

$3,100-4,300   **WW**

A "Pendule d'Officier" marble mantel timepiece, by Patek Philippe, Geneve, reference no. 1310, electronic battery-driven movement, signed, veined marble "pendule d'officier" form case, scroll and floral gilt-metal mounts, with Patek Philippe fitted box, guarantee, and instruction paperwork.

ca. 1980   *8¾in (22cm) high*

$7,500-8,500   **TEN**

An early-19thC Swiss brass capucine carriage alarm clock, eight-day movement, white enamel Roman numeral dial, housed in a rectangular case surmounted by a carrying handle incorporating a bell, movement restored, pendulum probably a replacement.

12¼in (31cm) high

$1,400-1,700 DN

A George IV gilt-brass carriage timepiece, by Grayhurst Harvey & Co., the brass chain-driven fusee movement with a horizontal escapement, the backplate inscribed "Grayhurst Harvey & Co, Strand and Regent Street, London, No. 8024," the silvered dial with Roman numerals and an engraved cornucopia of flowers in the center in a gilt scrolling foliate mount, the case with a scrolling frieze, column corners, beveled glass, and foliate scrolling handle.

ca. 1825   5¼in (13.5cm) high

$2,500-3,100 WW

A mid-19thC French gilt-brass carriage clock, the brass eight-day repeating movement with a platform lever escapement, striking on a bell, the backplate inscribed "Lepine a Paris," the enameled dial with Roman numerals, the "one-piece" case engraved with foliate decoration, with beveled glass, the shuttered back sliding upward, with a leather-bound traveling case.

6in (15cm) high

$1,500-1,900 WW

A brass engraved striking carriage clock, by Auguste, Paris, twin-barrel movement with a platform lever escapement, split bimetallic balance with an helical hairspring, outside count wheel striking on a bell, movement backplate numbered "133," enamel dial with Roman numerals and signed, elaborate scroll and floral engraved case with carrying handle, small corner chips in glass.

ca. 1860   6¾in (17cm) high

$1,500-1,900 TEN

A mid-19thC English gilt-brass carriage clock, in the manner of Thomas Cole, the brass movement with platform escapement chiming on three gongs, the silvered dial with Roman numerals and a foliate engraved center, inscribed "Arnold London" inside a gilt fretwork foliate mount, the shaped case with foliate engraving beneath a wreath swing handle on a stepped base with flower-bud finials in the corners and shuttered back, stamped "W Sluce" on back and underside.

Thomas Cole made clock movements for various clockmakers and retailers, including Arnold, Hancock, Hunt & Roskell, and Payne, but often did not sign his work. William Sluce is recorded as working on Bethnal Green Road, London.

7¾in (19.5cm) high

$8,500-11,000 WW

A French repeating carriage clock, unsigned bell-striking movement numbered "2248," the enameled dial with Roman numerals and moon hands, within an acanthus-scroll-engraved gilt surround, inscribed "C J Feilden February 16th 1860" below, the engraved gilt gorge case with platform lever escapement, with damaged travel case, movement does not currently run, strike, or repeat.

ca. 1860   6in (15cm) high

$800-950 CHEF

A mid-19thC Victorian gilt-brass carriage timepiece, by Matthew Thomson, London, the brass chain-driven, single-fusee movement with a horizontal escapement, the backplate inscribed "Mattw Thomson London, No. 133," the silvered dial with Roman numerals, subsidiary seconds dial, with a floral engraving in a gilt scrolling foliate mount, the case with fluted columns, with a scrolling case handle, together with a similarly decorated stepped rectangular base.

6in (15cm) high

$4,300-5,600 WW

A brass carriage timepiece, single-chain fusee movement with a platform lever escapement, floral engraved silvered dial with Roman numerals, elaborate floral and scroll engraved case, case sides and back door with fine engraved scenes of buildings, with boats and figures, top carrying handle, small scratches, slight discoloration and staining.

ca. 1870   6¼in (16cm) high

$1,700-2,200 TEN

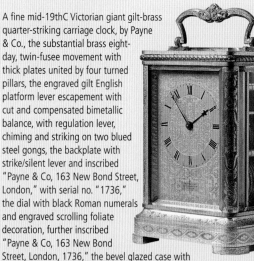

A fine mid-19thC Victorian giant gilt-brass quarter-striking carriage clock, by Payne & Co., the substantial brass eight-day, twin-fusee movement with thick plates united by four turned pillars, the engraved gilt English platform lever escapement with cut and compensated bimetallic balance, with regulation lever, chiming and striking on two blued steel gongs, the backplate with strike/silent lever and inscribed "Payne & Co, 163 New Bond Street, London," with serial no. "1736," the dial with black Roman numerals and engraved scrolling foliate decoration, further inscribed "Payne & Co, 163 New Bond Street, London, 1736," the bevel glazed case with rounded corners and finely engraved with scrolling and flowering foliate decoration, cast hinged handle.

William Payne is recorded as a watch and clockmaker at 62 South Molton Street in London from 1816. He moved to 163 New Bond Street in 1825.

9in (23cm) high

$30,000-33,000 WW

A small brass and silver-gilt striking and repeating carriage clock, signed Gay Lamaille, twin-barrel movement with a platform lever escapement and striking on a gong, backplate with maker's mark "GL" for Gay Lamaille and numbered "1313," blue enamel Arabic numeral chapter ring, carrying handle and repeat button, corners with Corinthian capped columns, discoloration, small glass chip, slight rubbing in the nine and ten numerals.

ca. 1890   *5½in (14cm) high*
$750-875   **TEN**

A brass engraved grande-sonnerie striking alarm carriage clock, twin-barrel movement with a platform lever escapement, two hammers striking on a bell, backplate numbered "2622," enamel dial with Roman numerals, alarm dial, carrying handle and repeat button, engraved swag decoration borders, underside with selection lever for grande/petite sonnerie/silent, small glass chips, dial cracked in one corner, movement needs servicing.

ca. 1890   *7in (17.5cm) high*
$1,250-1,500   **TEN**

A grande-sonnerie striking and repeating alarm carriage clock, by Chas Frodsham, 115 New Bond St., London, no. 20857, twin-barrel movement with a free-sprung, blued overcoil hairspring, split bimetallic balance, platform lever escapement signed by Frodsham, movement striking on two blued steel gongs and a smaller hammer for the alarm, movement backplate stamped with maker's mark "HJ" for Henri Jacot and numbered, enamel dial with Roman numerals signed and numbered, alarm dial, brass gorge case with carrying handle and repeat button, underside of the case with grande-sonnerie selection lever for full striking/silent/quarters, with original traveling case and winding key, case slightly discolor, balance, striking arm, alarm, repeat button, and movement all need attention, outer traveling case with wear.

7in (17.5cm) high
$3,700-4,300   **TEN**

A brass engraved striking carriage clock, twin-barrel movement with a platform lever escapement and striking on a bell, movement backplate numbered "2833," enamel dial with Roman numerals, case with scroll and floral engraving, carrying handle, scratches, glass chip, hairline crack in dial, platform escapement discolor.

ca. 1890   *7in (17.5cm) high*
$450-550   **TEN**

A French brass and champlevé enamel-mounted compendium carriage timepiece and barometer, the pillared case with red foliate champlevé enamel panels on all sides at top and bottom, conforming decoration in the dial masks, with thermometer in the front and compass on the top.

ca. 1890   *6in (15cm) high*
$1,100-1,500   **DUK**

A late-19thC French brass and champlevé enamel carriage clock, the brass eight-day repeating movement with a platform lever escapement, striking on a gong, the backplate stamped "7166," the enameled dial with Arabic numerals and floral swags, inscribed "Sharman D Neill, Belfast, Paris Make," inside a scrolling foliate frame, the case with enameled foliate decoration and a scrolling handle.

7½in (19cm) high
$2,500-3,100   **WW**

A carriage timepiece, fitted with a barometer, thermometer, and compass, within a brass and four-glass case.

6in (15cm) high
$375-450   **WHP**

A double carriage clock, with a barometer, compass, and visible escapement, in a brass and six-glass case.

10¼in (26cm) high
$625-750   **WHP**

A brass striking and repeating carriage clock, retailed by R. Wenrly & Co., Paris, twin-barrel movement with a platform lever escapement and striking on a gong, case borders with ivory, green, blue, and pink champlevé enamel, carrying handle and repeat button.

ca. 1890   *7½in (19cm) high*
$3,700-5,000   **TEN**

A late-19thC French eight-day hour-repeat carriage clock, half-hour striking on a gong, no. "10739," cream dial within a brass-mounted surround, the gilt-brass case with fluted pillars, light nibble in glass door verso, needs cleaning.

7¾in (19.5cm) high

$340-375 CHOR

ESSENTIAL REFERENCE—J. W. BENSON LTD

The firm of J. W. Benson has its roots in the partnership between brothers James William and Samuel Suckley Benson, who traded as watchmakers, goldsmiths, and silversmiths in Cornhill, London, from 1847 to 1855. After a while, James William Benson continued the business alone and opened premises at 33 Ludgate Hill, which quickly expanded into number 34l.

- By the 1860s, Benson was advertising his large store with an adjoining workshop specializing in not only the manufacture, but also the repair of, clocks and watches.
- J. W. Benson exhibited at numerous international exhibitions, including London 1862, Paris 1867, and at the 1885 "Invention Exhibition," where the firm unveiled its "Patent Dust and Damp Excluding Band for Watches."
- In 1872, J. W. Benson also opened a store on Bond Street and, after he died in 1878, the business continued to expand under his sons, Alfred and Arthur, with the opening of another store on Ludgate Hill; the award of a Royal Warrant from Queen Victoria in 1879; the acquisition of the celebrated silversmiths and goldsmiths Hunt & Roskill in 1889; and the opening of a steam-power factory in La Belle Sauvage yard in 1890.
- The business continued well into the 20thC and, although the factory was lost in a World War II bombing raid, its Bond Street store continued trading until taken over by Mappin & Webb in the 1980s.

A Swiss miniature gilt-brass minute-repeating carriage timepiece, retailed by J. W. Benson Ltd., London, the silvered eight-day, two-in-one, single-going barrel movement with platform lever escapement regulated by sprung bimetallic balance, sounding on two gongs, the backplate with trademark "RTP" monogram and "BREV (Swiss cross) DER" and no. "14007," the Roman numeral dial with retailer's signature "J. W. BENSON LTD, LUDGATE HILL, LONDON" and "SWISS MADE," the frosted gilt anglaise variant bevel-glazed bowfront case of "Mignonette No. 2" size, with hinged looped carrying handle, with fluted Corinthian columns at corners, on a caddy-molded skirt base, in original gilt-tooled green leather traveling case, with winding key, minor glass chips.

ca. 1900 *3½in (9cm) high (handle down)*

$3,100-3,700 DN

A French gilt-brass carriage clock, gong-striking movement with silvered platform lever escapement, cream annular ring dial, with engraved inscription on the top of "Annie August 27th 1912."

ca. 1900 *5½in (14cm) high*

$275-310 CHEF

A French miniature carriage timepiece, the white dial within a pierced foliate gilt surround, lacquered brass case with spiral-twist column corners, the backplate marked "Paris," wear in lacquer, glass crack in corner.

ca. 1900 *3½in (9cm) high*

$500-625 CHEF

A French champlevé-enameled gilt-brass bamboo-cased repeating alarm carriage clock, retailed by Chaude, Paris, the eight-day, two-train, gong-striking movement with silvered platform lever escapement, frontplate stamped "F V, 64," the rectangular gilt dial with blue-ground polychrome floral rosette champlevé enamel in center, Arabic hour numerals, inscribed "CHAUDE, 36 PALAIS-ROYAL 36, PARIS," subsidiary alarm setting dial, the case frame modeled to resemble sections of bamboo, each section champlevé enameled with further polychrome floral sprays on a mid-blue ground, with conforming hinged carrying handle, repeat button in leading edge, on angled bamboo T-shaped feet.

Bamboo-framed carriage clocks appear at auction relatively frequently, but those with champlevé-enameled decoration on the frame are particularly rare.

ca. 1900 *4½in (11.5cm) high*

$3,100-3,700 DN

A rare Edwardian Shibiyama insect-decorated silver carriage timepiece, the case marked for Reichenberg and Company, Chester, the French eight-day, single-train movement with platform lever escapement, the white enamel Roman numeral dial within a molded bezel incorporating canted insert in interior, the case with hinged C-scroll carrying handle over front and sides inlaid in mother-of-pearl, tortoiseshell, abalone, and other materials, with random crawling insects incorporating engraved legs and antennae, including a millipede apparently traversing the dial, on compressed bun feet, hallmarks for Chester 1906, rubbed maker's mark "R & Co."

The execution of Shibiyama decoration on this piece would have been undertaken by a specialty Japanese craftsman.

1906 *4½in (11.5cm) high (handle down)*

$1,900-2,500 DN

A George V silver desk carriage timepiece compendium with barometer, compass, and calendar, the case marked for John Manger, London, the Swiss-made eight-day movement with visible mainspring within a manually wound rotating drum applied on the backplate, hand setting wheel stamped "SWISS MADE, 496 (Swiss cross symbol) 497" on the winder, the left-hand side with a calendar comprising an aperture for month of the year (adjusted with a disk in the interior) within seven sections counting dates of the month and rotating, hallmarked for London 1916 and maker's "J.M," with original travel/display case gilt with a coronet for a duke or duchess over monogram "S.M."

1916 *2¾in (7cm) high (handle down)*

$3,100-4,300 DN

An early-18thC brass striking lantern clock, signed "Tho Sparrow, St Neots," two-train movement with a verge escapement and outside count wheel striking on a top-mounted bell, bob pendulum, signed, single hand, side and back panels are missing.

ca. 1720   *15¾in (40cm) high*
$1,700-2,200   **TEN**

A lantern clock with pin-and-hoop support, anchor escapement, with pendulum and weight, the support inscribed "John Bicknill of Cirencester, Fecit," hands possibly later, doors bent, one with new hinge plates.

16¼in (41cm) high
$1,900-2,500   **CHOR**

A brass skeleton clock, attributed to either Evans, Handsworth, or Smiths, Clerkenwell, large triple-chain fusee movement with a deadbeat escapement, four spoke wheels, quarter chiming on a nest of eight bells and striking the hours on a large gong, chapter ring, strike/silent lever above 12, later mahogany and glass outer case.

ca. 1860   *18½in (47cm) high*
$8,500-10,000   **TEN**

A brass skeleton mantel timepiece, single-chain fusee movement with anchor escapement, six spoke wheels, on a marble base, beneath a glass dome.

ca. 1870   *14¼in (36cm) high*
$2,000-2,200   **TEN**

A brass skeleton mantel timepiece, signed "Camerer Kuss & Co, 56 New Oxford St, London W.C," single-chain fusee movement with anchor escapement, five spoke wheels, passing strike on a top-mounted bell, signed, on a marble base, glass dome missing.

ca. 1880   *17¾in (45cm) high*
$1,050-1,200   **TEN**

A mid-19thC Victorian brass skeleton clock, the plates united by five double-screwed baluster pillars and enclosing twin-chain fusee trains, the going with anchor escapement regulated by half seconds lenticular bob pendulum, the strike train sounding the hours on a bell mounted above the plates, the silvered brass dial engraved "BROWN & Co., 18 QUEEN's-HEAD STREET, ISLINGTON, LONDON," on a Carrara marble base, with glass dome cover, with pendulum and winding key.

Brown & Co. are recorded in Brian Loomes, "Watchmakers & Clockmakers of the World, Volume 2," Robert Hale (1978), as working in London ca. 1881.

17¾in (45cm) high
$1,900-2,500   **DN**

A brass skeleton mantel timepiece, single-chain fusee movement with anchor escapement and passing strike on the hour, four spoke wheels, on an ebonized wood plinth, beneath a glass dome.

ca. 1890   *15in (38cm) high*
$500-625   **TEN**

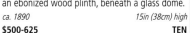

A brass skeleton mantel clock, twin-fusee movement with anchor escapement and rack striking on a top-mounted bell, on an ebonized base, glass dome missing.

ca. 1890   *15in (38cm) high*
$750-875   **TEN**

An epicyclic brass skeleton clock, by Dent, London, the single-fusee movement with skeletal dial, on an oval base, no. "61," with maker's label, on a mahogany stand with brass trimmed glass case, with winding key.

While this skeleton clock was made by Dent in the 1970s, it is based on a clock originally designed by W. Wigston and W. Strutt ca. 1820.

1970s   *14in (35.5cm) wide*
$1,700-2,000   **HT**

CLOCKS

A late-18thC black lacquered tavern clock, signed Levy Izaac, London, the A-frame, four-pillar, eight-day, weight-driven movement with anchor escapement, the gilt case with transfer of "The Country Tooth Drawer."

44in (112cm) high

$4,300-5,000 HT

A mid-19thC oak-cased hooded pantry clock with alarm, by Whitehurst, Derby, the four-pillar movement with anchor escapement, signed dial, with alarm dial and single iron hand.

25½in (65cm) high

$750-875 CHEF

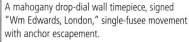

A mahogany drop-dial wall timepiece, signed "Wm Edwards, London," single-fusee movement with anchor escapement.

ca. 1860 *20in (51cm) high*

$375-500 TEN

A mid-19thC Victorian mahogany wall timepiece, with single-fusee movement, dial inscribed "THE SHIP TAVERN, LIME ST., E.C. 3," the case with a lion-mask crest issuing husk swags.

59¾in (152cm) high

$8,500-10,000 DN

A mahogany drop-dial wall timepiece, signed "G.Corsbie, Bath Place, New Road," single-fusee movement with anchor escapement.

ca. 1860 *17¼in (44cm) high*

$875-1,000 TEN

A mahogany drop-dial wall timepiece, signed "Jno Scott, Whitehaven," single-fusee movement, shaped movement plates, anchor escapement, dial signed, trunk with shell motif mounts, brass-inlaid trunk with pendulum window.

ca. 1870 *21¾in (55cm) high*

$750-875 TEN

A 19thC walnut and ebonized Vienna wall regulator, with a single winding hole over a single brass weight and grid pendulum, white enamel dial with Roman numerals, with an arched cornice.

68½in (174cm) high

$1,600-2,000 L&T

A mahogany wall timepiece, signed "J. Winterbottom, Oldham," single-fusee movement with anchor escapement, small cracks and scratches.

ca. 1870 *18in (46cm) diam*

$1,050-1,200 TEN

A mahogany drop-dial wall timepiece, signed "Broad, Wadebridge," single-fusee movement with anchor escapement, small scratches.

ca. 1880 *20¾in (53cm) high*

$500-625 TEN

A 19thC French ormolu cartel clock, in Louis XVI style, the brass drum movement with an outside count wheel and striking on a bell, stamped "Lay Fht, 2454 Pre Jouffroy 29," the case with an urn surmount and decorated with scrolls and laurel swags.

17in (43cm) high

$800-950 WW

A mahogany striking wall clock, signed "Wordley, London," twin-chain fusee movement with anchor escapement and striking on a bell, pendulum suspension spring is broken.

ca. 1890 *14¼in (36cm) diam*

$1,000-1,100 TEN

A 19thC mahogany fusee wall timepiece, the dial later marked "Samuel Jefferson London," pendulum spring broken.

14¼in (36cm) diam

$250-310 CHEF

A 19thC French ormolu cartel clock, in Louis XV style, the brass drum movement with an outside count wheel and striking on a bell, numbered "3625," the case with Rococo scrolls, leaves, and flowers.

19in (48.5cm) high

$700-800 WW

A mahogany wall timepiece, signed "Camerer Cuss & Co., 54/5 New Oxford St, London," single-chain fusee movement with anchor escapement, painted dial with Roman numerals, back with part of Camerer Cuss & Co. original label, small cracks, scratches.

ca. 1890 *10¾in (27.5cm) diam*

$750-875 TEN

A late-19th/early-20thC French minature ormolu cartel clock, the case molded in the Rococo style.

10¾in (27cm) high

$190-250 CA

A 19thC mahogany wall regulator, by Dent, four-pillar movement with deadbeat escapement, the dome-top glazed case with foliate carving below the dial.

69¼in (176cm) high

$2,500-3,100 CHEF

A late-19thC French ormolu cartel clock, the movement by Samuel Marti & Co., chiming on a bell, inscribed "Horl Ger Du Roy, a Paris."

20in (51cm) high

$450-550 DAWS

A 20thC mahogany-case dial clock, the single-chain fusee movement stamped "4121 Made by F. W. Elliot Ltd England 1938."

15in (38cm) diam

$300-375 WHP

CLOCKS

A Napoleon III gilt and patinated bronze clock garniture, by Charpentier & Cie., Paris, the brass eight-day drum movement striking on a bell, the backplate stamped "Charpentier de Bronzes, 200 A Paris," white marble Louis XVI-style case surmounted with two Classical figures, with a pair of figural six-light candelabra, each with a cherub on a rocky outcrop.

ca. 1870   clock 27¼in (69cm) wide
$3,700-4,300   WW

A 19thC Swiss Black Forest clock garniture, with a drum bell-striking movement, the case with a bird perched among foliage, marked "Auchalet 15809," with a pair of side ornaments, both with a glass trumpet vase.

20½in (52cm) high
$2,500-3,100   CHEF

A late-19thC French ormolu and porcelain clock garniture, by F. Barbedienne, the dial and drum movement signed "Ch. Boye," the urn-top case with cover and pair of female figural mounts, painted with a figural landscape scene, with a pair of matching five-socket candelabra.

21¼in (54cm) high
$14,000-17,500   CHEF

A 19thC French ormolu and porcelain mantel clock garniture, by Phillipe Mourey, Paris, in Louis XVI style, the twin-train movement with outside count wheel striking a bell, in an architectural case surmounted with an urn with a putto finial, the base with a floral roundel and frieze panels, bracket stamped "10 PH MOUREY 62," with a pair of ewers with songbirds, the bases also stamped "PH MOUREY."

14½in (37cm) high
$1,100-1,250   L&T

An English Egyptian Revival slate and marble clock garniture, the mantel clock with a twin-train movement striking a bell.

ca. 1880   obelisks 19¾in (50cm) high
$1,500-1,900   L&T

A 19thC French porcelain and gilt-metal clock garniture, the eight-day movement stamped "11427" and "A.1," striking a bell, the arched case with a porcelain urn finial and panel, painted in Sèvres style with a courting couple against a bleu celeste ground, with a pair of urns en suite, converted to lamps.

15¾in (40cm) high
$1,400-1,600   L&T

A late-19thC French Renaissance Revival gilt-metal and cloisonné enamel clock garniture, the twin-chain, eight-day movement stamped "JAPY FRÈRES" and "1004," with a bell strike, dial flanked and surmounted by putti, the arch case with a pointed finial, inverted breakfront base on toupie feet, with a pair of urns with figural handles.

20¾in (53cm) high
$4,300-5,600   L&T

A 19thC French red marble and gilt-metal garniture de cheminée, with a bell-striking drum movement marked for Barrard & Vignon, with a pair of matching candelabra.

clock 16¼in (41cm) high
$450-550   CHEF

A late-19thC Meissen porcelain clock garniture, the clock with an eight-day movement, the dial mounted with cherubs and encrusted with flowers, the stand painted with a Watteau-esque scene, the corners encrusted with flowers, with figural three-branch candelabra painted with flowers, crossed swords marks in blue.

22in (56cm) high

$4,300-5,600 **CHEF**

A late-19thC French gilt and patinated bronze, slate, and green marble figural clock garniture, by Japy Frères, the twin-train movement with an outside count wheel, in a case beside a figure of Minerva reading a book, the backplate stamped "Japy Frères" and numbered "622, 72," striking the full and half hours on a gong, the pendulum stamped "622," with a pair of urns en suite.

clock 21¼in (54cm) wide

$625-850 **L&T**

A 19thC French porcelain and gilt-metal clock garniture, the eight-day movement stamped "H. F. & CIE PARIS" and striking on a bell, the dial flanked by columns with a courting couple, the case with an urn finial, with a pair of urns en suite.

16½in (42cm) high

$875-1,100 **L&T**

A late-19thC French onyx, cloisonné, and brass clock garniture, with drum movement striking the half hours on a gong, with regulation and mercury pendulum, with vase side ornaments.

17in (43cm) high

$1,100-1,350 **SWO**

A late-19thC gilt-metal and "Pompadour" pink porcelain clock garniture, by Vincenti et Cie, the clock of urn-mounted Rococo form, the dial painted with figures and marked for the retailer J. Delaye, Grenoble, with a pair of six-sconce candelabra en suite, no pendulum, no bell.

23½in (60cm) high

$1,250-1,600 **DAWS**

A late-19thC French veined-marble clock garniture, with a portico clock and two urns.

19¼in (49cm) high

$625-750 **CHOR**

An early 20thC French gilt-metal and white marble mantel clock garniture, the twin-train brass movement striking a bell.

clock 13¾in (35cm) high

$500-625 **L&T**

An early 20thC French green onyx and champlevé enamel clock garniture, the eight-day movement with an enameled mercury compensating pendulum and chiming the hours on a coil gong, with a pair of matching Classical urns, clock needs attention to run.

18½in (47cm) high

$1,000-1,250 **DAWS**

An early- to mid-19thC French white and gray marble and gilt-metal-mounted portico clock, brass eight-day drum movement, flanked by foliate lyres and supported by shaped pillars with floral and rosette mounts.

15¾in (40cm) high

$950-1,050   **WW**

A French brass automaton windmill clock, by Andre Romain Guilmet, eight-day spring-driven movement, the sails powered by a separate movement in the base, a thermometer on both sides flanking the silvered thermometer and clock dials, the weathervane top above a tapering roof and faux stonework case on a marble base, some surface wear, weathervane and probably thermometers are replacements.

ca. 1890   18½in (47cm) high

$4,300-5,600   **CHEF**

Judith Picks

Everyone likes a good mystery, and I am certainly no exception to that! Illusionists' tricks that leave me thinking "How in heaven's name did that happen, how on earth did that work?" never fail to impress, and they have an appeal that easily transfers from the theater to the world of horology. Although their invention is often attributed to Jean-Eugene Robert-Houdin in the 19thC, the earliest "mystery" clocks date from the 17thC, albeit the principal period of mystery clock production was the 19thC and in France. They are so-called because there is no apparent connection between the pendulum and the movement, or no apparent connection between the movement and the hands—as with this elegant and classic example featuring a glass dial with a single hand, supported on a column and a sculpted base (containing the mechanism). A popular alternative comprised globe dials (with fake pendulums) held aloft by a bronze or spelter figure standing on a metal or marble base concealing a spring-driven mechanism. In either case, it is magic!

A mid-19thC French gilt and patinated bronze mystery clock, attributed to Jean-Eugene Robert-Houdin, Paris, two-train movement stamped "Brevet d'Invention, Boilviller A Paris" and "61," striking on a bell, glass dial, on a scrolling bracket supported by griffins, the case with a cherub among foliage, on a scrolling and shell foot.

16¼in (41.5cm) high

$7,500-8,500   **WW**

A gilt-brass congreve rolling ball clock, by Dent, London, single-fusee movement, chapter ring with seconds and calendar dials, on four pillars on a molded base with a mahogany plinth and green marble stand, with a glass case.

19½in (49.5cm) wide

$2,200-2,700   **HT**

A French striking movement bronzed spelter swinging mystérieuse clock, the movement stamped "Medaille d'argent, Brevette 1856," the female figure holding the spherical clock with ball counterweight, an aneroid barometer beside her, on a marble base, one old repair.

ca. 1900   35¾in (91cm) high

$1,900-2,500   **CHEF**

An early-20thC marble and pietra dura boudoir clock, retailed by John D. Harris Goldsmiths, Queen Square, Bath, with signed strut back, in original leather case.

7¾in (20cm) high

$375-450   **CHEF**

A rare 150th Year Anniversary "Atmos" clock, by Jaeger LeCoultre, Geneva, caliber 540 movement signed and numbered "600580," base with a large balance wheel, level bubble, beneath a glass dome, with original fitted Jaeger LeCoultre case, no. "0512."

ca. 1983   11½in (29cm) high

$5,000-6,200   **TEN**

An 18ct yellow gold full-hunter pocket watch, by T. F. Cooper, London, the white enamel dial with black Roman numerals and second-hand section, within an engine-turned case.

1¾in (4.5cm) diam 3⅛oz

$1,900-2,500 **WHP**

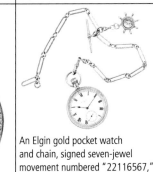

An 18ct-gold open-face pocket watch, by Edward Baker, cylinder-fusee movement, three-arm balance, signed, flat balance spring, white dial, two-piece hinged case, hallmarked London 1816, with winding key, movement not currently functioning, wear, small chips, tarnishing, scratches.

ca. 1816 *2in (5cm) diam 5oz*

$1,900-2,500 **DN**

A 14ct yellow gold open-face pocket watch, the white enamel dial with black Roman and Arabic numerals, within a plain case.

2in (5cm) diam 3⅜oz

$375-500 **WHP**

A gold-color keyless wind, full-hunter pocket watch, no. 203464, unsigned, lever movement, bimetallic split balance, overcoil balance spring, champagne dial, four-piece hinged case, the covers engraved with tessellated diamond decoration, stamped "14K 585" with a poinçon, no box or papers, movement, dial, and case with wear, hands with marks and tarnishing, back cover detached.

2in (5cm) diam 2½oz

$500-625 **DN**

An 18ct fob watch, unsigned three-quarter plate movement, white enamel dial with Roman numerals in black, outer railroad seconds track in black, open face, keyless wind, case with decorative engraving and center shield motif, with full 18ct-gold hallmarks for Birmingham

1894. *1½in (3.5cm) diam*

$875-1,000 **L&T**

An Elgin gold pocket watch and chain, signed seven-jewel movement numbered "22116567," white enamel dial with Roman numerals in black, sunken small seconds at six, railroad outer seconds track in black, open face, keyless wind, 9ct-gold case, with an Albert chain formed by oval and rounded rectangular links, marked "9.375," with a T-bar and anchor appendage, both also marked for 9ct gold.

1¾in (4.5cm) diam

$1,500-1,900 **L&T**

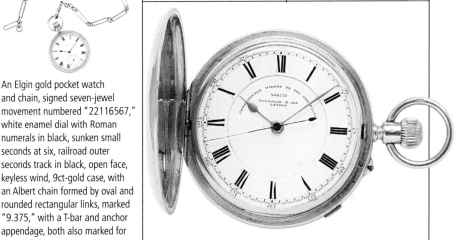

A chronometer pocket watch, by Reynolds & Son, movement numbered "566721" and signed, white enamel dial with Roman numerals in black, gold-color leaf hands, center seconds hand in black, full hunter, keyless wind, 18ct-gold case with full London hallmarks for 1900, case back with monogram "HI."

2¼in (5.5cm) diam

$2,500-3,100 **L&T**

A French gold-color keyless wind, open-face fob watch, no. 87908, cylinder movement, three-arm balance, flat balance spring, white dial, gold-color four-piece hinged case, the back cover engraved with flowers, scrolls, and engine-turned decoration, stamped with a poinçon, unsigned, with a gold-color floral brooch.

1¼in (3cm) diam

$375-500 **DN**

An 18ct-gold pocket watch, full hunter, keyless wind, unsigned ¾-plate movement, movement cover with inscription dated 1921, white enamel dial with Roman numerals in black, sunken small seconds at six, railroad outer seconds track in black, blued steel leaf hands, Birmingham hallmarks for 1919.

2in (5cm) diam

$1,700-2,200 **L&T**

A lady's 18ct-gold fob watch.

$750-1,000 **TEN**

A lady's 18k gold half-hunter pocket watch, with enamel dial.

1¼in (3cm) diam

$625-850 **CHOR**

A Baume & Mercier bracelet watch, model no. 15160.9, quartz movement, white dial with applied golf baton hour markers and date aperture at six, gold pencil hands, ribbed bezel, crown with Baume logo, the case back with model and serial numbers and personalized inscription dated 1989, on a square-link bracelet strap with signed "Baume & Mercier" clasp, the case marked "18K," additional links made into cufflinks, no box or papers.

1¼in (3cm) diam

$3,500-4,000   **L&T**

A Breguet white gold wristwatch, "Transatlantique chronograph XX Flyback," model no. 3820, black dial with Arabic numerals and date aperture at six, subsidiary dials at three, six, and nine for small seconds, 12-hour register and 60-minute register, respectively, outer seconds track, lume-filled index hands, center seconds hand with lume plot, bezel with count-up scale in black, case with European convention marks for 18ct white gold, case back with model and serial numbers, on a signed blue "Breguet" crocodile strap with signed clasp, in box, with outer box, no papers, with document from watchcentre.com.

ca. 2020   *1½in (4cm) diam*

$8,500-11,000   **L&T**

A lady's Chopard 18ct-gold watch, "Happy Sport," no. 276252-0001, the signed dial with Roman numerals at quarter intervals and five floating diamonds, cabochon ruby-set lugs and crown, with box, Chopard warranty certificate, and spare links.

ca. 2000   *1in (2.5cm) diam*

$4,300-5,000   **CHOR**

A De Witt chronograph wristwatch, "Twenty-8-Eight," model no. T8.POE.001, automatic movement, black dial with gold-color sections and Roman 12, 3, 6, and 9, dot inner seconds track, outer seconds track with Arabic numerals, skeleton hands, red 24-hour hand, textured bezel, titanium case with serial number, on a black alligator strap, with De Witt clasp, in box, with guarantee card.

De Witt is a Geneva-based watch manufacturer set up in 2003 by Jerome de Witt, and it currently makes around 1,000 watches per year.

1¾in (4.5cm) diam

$2,000-2,200   **L&T**

An Eberhard stainless steel wristwatch, "Champion," model no. 31044, automatic movement, black dial with stainless steel baton hour markers, date aperture at 3, subsidiary dials at 12, 6, and 9 for 30-minute register, 12-hour register and small seconds respectively, outer seconds track, crown with Eberhard logo, stainless steel case with model and serial numbers, on a black strap, with Eberhard clasp, in box, with outer box and papers.

1½in (4cm) diam

$750-1,000   **L&T**

A Girard-Perregaux chronograph wristwatch, "World Timer," model no. 49805, caliber 3387 auto movement signed "Girard-Perregaux," black dial with lume Arabic 12 and lume baton hour markers, date aperture between 1 and 2, subsidiary dials at 3, 6, and 9 for small seconds, 12-hour register and 30-minute register respectively, inner GMT bezel in blue and red, city names on outside, titanium case, exhibition case back with model and watch number, black rubber GP strap, "GP" deployant clasp, in boxes with papers.

1¾in (4.5cm) diam

$5,300-5,800   **L&T**

A Heuer square stainless steel wristwatch, "Monaco Automatic Chronograph," manual wind movement, dark gray-black dial with red hour markers, date aperture at six, rounded square 30-minute register at three, and 12-hour register at nine, outer seconds track in white, stainless steel hands with red inserts, red chronograph seconds hand, stainless steel case with tool no. "033" on back, on a stainless steel bracelet strap with signed "Heuer" clasp, no box or papers.

Heuer was founded in 1860 in St. Imier, Switzerland, by Edouard Heuer. It became TAG Heuer when it was bought by Techniques d'Avant Guarde in 1985. Originally known for creating some of the first dashboard timers in the early-1900s, Heuer soon became famous for its chronograph wristwatches, including the "Autavia" and "Carrera." These tool, or sports, watches were similar to their earlier dashboard timers, enabling wearers to time car races and calculate speed, among other functions. The "Monaco" is one of the brand's best-known models. First released in 1969, the watch refers to the Monaco Grand Prix and is easily recognized thanks to its distinctive square case. The watch was worn by Steve McQueen in the 1971 movie "Le Mans." It remains highly desirable to this day and has been re-released several times in the last 50 years.

1970s   *1½in (4cm) wide*

$6,000-7,500   **L&T**

A lady's TAG Heuer stainless steel wristwatch, "Formula 1," the dial with date aperture, within a diamond-set bezel on an articulated bracelet strap, with box and papers.

1½in (4cm) diam

$700-800   **WHP**

A TAG Heuer stainless steel wristwatch, "Aquaracer Caliber 7 GMT," model no. WAY201F, automatic movement, black dial with applied stainless steel-edge, lume-filled hour markers, date aperture at three, outer seconds track, blue and red GMT bezel, screw-down crown with TAG Heuer logo, with diver's helmet logo and model and serial numbers on the case back, stainless steel case, on a stainless steel bracelet strap with signed "TAG Heuer" foldover clasp, with additional links, in box, with outer box, warranty card, and booklet.

2021   *1¾in (4.5cm) diam*

$1,500-1,700   **L&T**

A Jaeger-LeCoultre stainless steel wristwatch, "Reverso Classique," model no. 252.8.86, manual wind movement, silver-color dial with Arabic numerals in black, inner railroad seconds track also in black, blued steel sword hands, stainless steel case with ribbed sections at top and bottom, model and serial numbers on back, on a signed "JLC" tan ostrich strap with signed deployant clasp, no box or papers.

ca. 2014   1½in (4cm) high

$3,100-3,500   **L&T**

A Jaeger-LeCoultre chronograph wristwatch, "Master Compressor," model no. 146.8.25, automatic movement, black dial with Arabic 12 and 9 and white wedge hour markers, 30-minute register at 3, 12-hour register at 9, outer seconds track and tachymeter scale, crown with "JLC" logo, stainless steel case with model and serial numbers, on a signed black crocodile strap with signed clasp, in box, with outer box and guarantee booklet.

1½in (4cm) diam

$4,300-5,000   **L&T**

A Jaeger-LeCoultre calendar wristwatch, "Master Compressor," model no. 148.2.60, automatic movement, black dial with Arabic 12, 6, and 9 in white and wedge hour markers, date aperture at 3, inner bezel with count-up scale in white and red, rose-color hands with lume inserts, center seconds hand with red arrowhead terminal, crowns with JLC logo, rose-color case with serial and model numbers, on a generic strap, in box, with outer box, no papers.

1½in (4cm) diam

$8,000-8,500   **L&T**

A World War II Lemania military wristwatch, the black dial with luminous Arabic numerals, center seconds and two subsidiary dials, reverse with arrow and numbered "0552/920-3305, 75812," on a later bracelet strap.

$2,500-3,100   **HT**

A Longines 9ct-gold bracelet watch, "Presence," ref. 25.182.675, no. 3981 156, caliber l156.4 quartz movement with six jewels, white dial, 9ct-gold case stamped with 9ct-gold common control mark, signed on movement, dial, and case, with an aftermarket 9ct-gold bracelet with ladder snap clasp, with Longines box, guarantee card, instruction booklet, Longines black leather strap with gold-plated pin buckle, light scratches.

1¼in (3cm) diam 1¾oz

$1,100-1,500   **DN**

A gentleman's Mont Blanc stainless steel automatic wristwatch, visible movement, the dial with day and date apertures and subsidiary dials, on a patent faux crocodile skin strap, with box.

1½in (4cm) diam

$1,400-1,700   **WHP**

An Omega steel wristwatch, "Seamaster Professional," quartz movement, blue dial with lume lot hour markers, date aperture at three, skeleton hands with lume terminals, center seconds hand, blue bezel with count-up scale, stainless steel case, on a stainless steel bracelet strap with signed "Omega" deployant clasp, in box, no papers.

1½in (4cm) diam

$1,700-2,200   **L&T**

An Omega De Ville stainless steel wristwatch, "Co-Axial Chronometer," model no. 42413402002001, automatic movement, silver-color dial with applied stainless steel Roman numerals, date aperture at three, beveled sword hands, center seconds hand, crown with Omega logo, stainless steel case, signed with serial number, on a generic black strap, with an Omega strap with signed buckle, no box or papers, in service case.

ca. 2014   1½in (4cm) diam

$1,400-1,700   **L&T**

A gentleman's Omega 18ct-gold wristwatch, manual winding movement, the silvered dial with gold baton indicators and blackened hands, plain gold case, dial and case signed "Omega," case with Swiss assay marks for 18ct gold and numbered "14453 61," with black leather strap, tarnished, glass scratched.

¾in (2cm) wide ¾oz

$220-275   **WW**

A Panerai chronograph wristwatch, "Luminor Daylight," model no. OP 6769, automatic movement, black dial with luminous hour markers, sunken subsidiary dials at three, six ,and nine for 30-minute register, 12-hour register and small seconds respectively, inner seconds track in white, stainless steel bezel with tachymeter scale in black, stainless steel case, the crown within a semicircular guard, on a signed Panerai black leather strap with signed deployant clasp, no box or papers, last serviced 2022.

2in (5cm) wide (including crown)

$4,300-5,000 L&T

A gentleman's Rolex gold bubbleback chronometer, "Oyster Perpetual," the pale champagne dial with applied gilt-metal Arabic numerals, center seconds hand, in a plain case, on a later stitched leather strap.

$2,700-3,100 HT

A gentleman's Rolex 9ct-gold chronometer, "Oyster Perpetual Superlative," the pale champagne dial with applied gilt-metal batons, center seconds hand, in a plain case, the reverse engraved with a presentation inscription dated 1964, on original stitched leather strap with 9ct-gold Rolex buckle (Edinburgh, 1956).

$3,100-3,500 HT

A Patek Philippe white gold calendar wristwatch, "Annual Calendar" model no. 5146G, caliber 315/299 automatic movement numbered "3420587," white dial with applied Arabic numerals and baton hour markers, sunken subsidiary dials at three and nine for months and days respectively, moon phase and date aperture at six, railroad outer seconds track in black, lume-filled hands, center seconds hand, the signed case with European convention mark for 18ct white gold, on a signed Patek Philippe crocodile strap with signed 18ct white gold deployant clasp, in box.

1½in (4cm) diam

$25,000-31,000 L&T

A Rolex stainless steel wristwatch, "Oyster Perpetual Air-king," model no. 114200, signed Rolex caliber 3130 automatic movement numbered "1895647," silver dial with applied Arabic 3, 6, and 9, coronet at 12, pink baton hour markers, stainless steel case, on a stainless steel Oyster bracelet strap with signed foldover clasp, in box, with outer box and booklet, no papers.

2007-08 *1½in (4cm) diam*

$4,200-4,700 L&T

A Rolex stainless steel wristwatch, "Oyster Perpetual Date GMT-Master," model no. 116710, signed Rolex caliber 3186 automatic movement, black dial with stainless steel-edge lume plots and baton hour markers, date aperture at three, outer seconds track, lume-filled Mercedes hands, center seconds hand with lume plot, green GMT hand with lume-filled pointer terminal, black ceramic bezel with 24-hour scale, stainless steel case, on a stainless steel Oyster bracelet strap with signed Rolex foldover clasp marked "7CT" on the interior, in box, with guarantee card and booklet.

2010 *1½in (4cm) diam*

$15,000-19,000 L&T

A Rolex bicolor wristwatch, "Oyster Perpetual Datejust," model no. 16233, signed Rolex caliber 3135 automatic movement, white dial with "ROLEX" in repeat, applied Arabic numerals in gold, date aperture at three, gold hands, center seconds hand, gold fluted bezel, stainless steel case with personal engraving, on a bicolor stainless steel and gold Jubilee bracelet strap, with signed Rolex foldover clasp numbered "62523H-18," no inner box, with outer box and papers.

ca. 1990 *1½in (4cm) diam*

$3,700-4,300 L&T

A Rolex bicolor wristwatch, "Oyster Perpetual GMT Master II," model no. 116713LN, signed caliber 3186 automatic movement, signed black dial with lume plot and baton hour markers, date aperture at three, Mercedes hands, gold bezel with black insert with 24-hour scale, stainless steel case, on a stainless steel and gold Oyster bracelet strap with signed clasp, in box, with outer box and guarantee card.

2008-09 *1½in (4cm) diam*

$14,000-16,000 L&T

A Vacheron Constantin wristwatch, manual wind, signed dial with applied Arabic 12 and 6, square hour markers, small seconds at 6, inner dot seconds track, pencil hands, on a generic mesh bracelet strap with foldover clasp, unmarked, no box or papers.

ca. 1950s *1½in (4cm) diam*

$4,300-5,000 L&T

A rare George II walnut mercury dial barometer, by John Hallifax, Barnsley, the engraved brass break-arch dial with radial foliate scroll-engraved center, the inner margin with annotations "Tempestous," "Rain Wind or Snow," "Changeable," "Fair or Frost," "Settle Fair or Frost," and "Very Dry," domed silvered boss signed "Jn:o Hallifax, Barnsley, Inv't & Fecit."

John Hallifax is recorded in Nicholas Goodison, "English Barometers 1680-1860," ACC (1999), as the son of the local vicar, born in Springthorpe, Lincolnshire, in 1694. The family name was originally Waterhouse but was changed by his grandfather during the previous century. John Hallifax moved to Barnsley and set up as a clockmaker after his father's death in 1711; he had seven children and was succeeded in his business by his fifth son, Joseph (1728-62), after his death in 1750. In addition to Joseph, his fourth son, George, also became a clockmaker in Doncaster, where he later twice served as mayor of the town. John's third son, Thomas, moved to London and became an eminent banker, also served as Lord Mayor, and became a member of Parliament. The regard in which John Hallifax was held is evident in the inscription on his tombstone, which reads: "Whose abilities and virtue few in these times have attained. His art and industry were such as his ingenious inventions will be a lasting monument of his merit – such as recommended him to the favour and esteem of all good men that knew him." This particular barometer belongs to a small series produced by John Hallifax during the second quarter of the 18thC. The glazed front panel over the dial is designed to be removable to enable adjustment while the instrument is being set up, but is then secured by screws to prevent tampering. The recording dial in the trunk allows for any changes in the pressure to be observed without having to touch the principal dial. Dial barometers by John Hallifax have traditionally been highly desirable, with examples residing in some of the most important collections of clocks and instruments as well as fine furniture and objects. One such example was offered at Christie's London in its sale of the "Samuel Messer Collection of English Furniture, Clocks & Barometers," December 5, 1991 (lot 12) where it achieved £32,000 ($39,700) hammer. More recently, another was sold at Tennants, Leyburn, in its "Autumn Catalogue Sale," November 18, 2010 (lot 1404) for £40,000 ($49,600).

ca. 1730   49in (124.5cm) high
$22,000-30,000   DN

A George III satinwood bowfront stick barometer, the silvered gauge inscribed "Willson & Dixey" beneath a painted urn finial, with a bone adjuster and an ebony urn reservoir cover.

ca. 1800   41¼in (104.5cm) high
$2,500-3,100   WW

A George III mahogany stick barometer, by George Adams, London, with a hygrometer and silvered register with vernier marked "G. Adams Fleet St., London," a long thermometer below, all within brass frames, turned cistern cover below, bonnet-top pediment set with an urn-shaped brass finial, damage in thermometer hinges, split in case, fading, repairs.

45¾in (116cm) high
$2,500-3,100   CHEF

A late-George III mahogany stick barometer, by Baptista Ronchetti, Manchester, silvered register signed "Bap'st Ronchetti, No.15 High St. Manchester," the exposed tube within a chevron banded border, turned cistern cover below, bonnet-top pediment with urn finial.

38½in (98cm) high
$500-625   CHEF

A Victorian mahogany bowfront stick barometer, the silvered gauge with vernier scale, inscribed "A Gilardoni, Bristol," the case with a bone adjuster and a thermometer, an ebonized urn cistern cover below, glass lacking.

ca. 1840   38¼in (97cm) high
$750-1,000   WW

A bowfront marine barometer, by J. B. Le Roy, Jersey, signed and with scales divided between 27-31, thermometer tube at front, gimbal ring mount and weighted brass reservoir, plain case with carved base.

ca. 1840   37in (94cm) high
$1,700-2,200   CM

A 19thC mahogany stick barometer, the angled pediment above a brass register, with a concealed tube and turned cistern cover below.

39in (99cm) high
$375-500   CHEF

A 19thC marine "Improved Sympiesometer," by Whyte Thomson, Glasgow, the plain case with signed ivorine barometer plates, with twin adjustment wheels, brass gimbal ring, the sympiesometer and thermometer mounted on silvered backplate, terminating in a brass clad weight, signature faded.

36in (91.5cm) high
$1,900-2,500   CM

An "Admiral Fitzroy" lifeboat station barometer, with enameled scales and top plate signed "Admiral Fitzroy's Barometer," with matched left and right scales divided 27-31, inscribed under "10am yesterday" and "10am to-day," left/right with adjustable indicators, oak case with thermometer tube and covered reservoir.

ca. 1880   39½in (100.5cm) high
$875-1,000   CM

SCIENTIFIC INSTRUMENTS

A large-George III mahogany celestial library globe, by J. & W. Cary, London, the 21in (53.5cm) sphere with label: "Cary's New and Improved CELESTIAL GLOBE on which Is carefully laid down the whole of the STARS and NEBULÆ, Contained in the ASTRONOMICAL CATALOGUE, of the Rev'd Mr. WOLLASTON, F.R.S. Compiled from the Authorities of FLAMSTEED, DE LA CAILLE, HEVELIUS, MAYER BRADELY, HERSCHEL, MASKELYNE &c. With an extensive number from the Works of Miss Herschel. The whole adapted to the year 1800, and the limits of each Constellation determined by a Boundry line/LONDON," supported in a turned mahogany tripod base with compass rose, some fading on globe, base compass missing indicator and glass.

1799   *52in (132cm) high*
$5,000-6,200   **WAD**

A George III terrestrial pocket globe, by Dollond, London, the 12 hand-colored gores overlaid with a Dollond cartouche, the decoration includes Anson's circumnavigation, Cook's last voyage of 1779, the Meridian of London, a four-point compass rose, the continents and regions of the world outlined in various colors, no northern coastline of North America and the Rockies named Stony Mountains, with two iron axis pins, the shagreen case lined with celestial gores and color green, dated.

1809   *2¾in (7cm) diam*
$15,000-19,000   **WW**

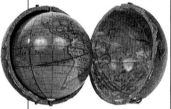

A Minshulls pocket globe, with applied retailers' cartouche, the globe of 12 hand-colored engraved gores, two metal axis pins rotating in its original simulated shagreen case, with interior of celestial gores, chips, scratches, axes a little rusty, some loose areas of covering on case.

ca. 1810   *3¼in (8cm) diam*
$3,700-5,000   **CHOR**

A Newton's "New Improved Terrestrial Pocket Globe," 1817 or later, in a modern wood case with domed cover, old repair.

3in (7.5cm) diam
$3,700-5,000   **CHEF**

A mid-19thC Victorian terrestrial library globe, 12in (30.5cm) sphere fitted with a brass scale, the horizon inscribed "engraved by Chas. Malby," raised on a turned and carved mahogany stand and tripod base, damage and repair with areas of loss and filler, overall distressed conditon.

34¾in (88cm) high
$875-1,100   **SWO**

A late-19thC American Andrews' terrestrial library globe, published by C. F. Weber & Co., Chicago, with 18in (45.5cm) sphere, supported within an early-19thC English mahogany tripod stand, marks, scratches, split, red wax spot infill, one bracket under horizon missing.

41¼in (105cm) high
$2,700-3,200   **DN**

An early-20thC "Geographia" terrestrial table globe and stand, the 10in (25.5cm) globe with railroads, steamer route distances, heights, and British territories in red, supported on a painted spelter figure of Atlas.

20½in (52cm) high
$625-850   **L&T**

An early-20thC "Husun Star" globe, by Henry Hughes & Son, London, 7in (18cm) globe with paper maker's label, brass meridian and horizon rings, housed in a stained pine case.

10¾in (27cm) wide
$1,500-1,900   **L&T**

An unusually large 20thC celestial globe, possibly Indian, Islamic brass, celestial sphere, the surface with various constellations depicted by mythological beasts and figures, many labeled, with graduated equatorial and ecliptic markers, with an axis through the celestial poles and through the horizontal plane, supported on a cast horizon ring, raised on four turned columns of tapering baluster form, the supports joined by a cruciform stretcher.

21¾in (55cm) high
$3,100-3,700   **SWO**

A possibly unique Wilson-type screw barrel microscope, recovered from the China Trade East Indiaman "Hartwell," wrecked in 1787, unsigned, the barrel with ½in (1.5cm) objective, sprung stage mounted on a tapering brass pillar with adjusting limb, on a square brass base with swivel mirror, along with a second eye-piece and objective lens, and two ebonized four-aperture slides, one with specimens, all within a later plexiglass display case.

This pattern of Wilson-type screw barrel has not been found in any national collections, and a letter accompanying this lot from Professor G. Turner, late of the Oxford Museum of the History of Science, confirms he has never located another example in this form.

ca. 1745   *3¼in (8.5cm) high*

$3,100-4,300   CM

An early-19thC Culpeper-type brass microscope, by Dolland, London, the tube body with S-scroll supports on the circular platform, inscribed "Dolland London," with an adjustable mirror hinged on a pair of uprights, on a stepped mahogany foot with a single drawer containing four additional lenses and three prepared bone slides, the fitted pyramidal case with a drawer containing other accessories.

Edward Culpeper (1670-1737) developed this style of microscope ca. 1728 and it proved so popular that versions were made by many other instrument makers throughout the 18thC and 19thC.

18in (46cm) high

$1,500-2,200   WW

Judith Picks

I find the science behind this microscope interesting (one of my Scottish "Highers" was in chemistry), but its subsequent history even more so! The design of the microscope originated with the English naturalist John Ellis (1710-76). It was designed so that the user could move the objective (object lens) to enable the person to follow the activity of small water creatures held by a glass watch on the stage. The first model was made for Ellis by John Cuff in 1752, but soon other makers were producing their own versions. With Peter Dolland's excellent reputation for lenses, it was soon being promoted by him as "Ellis's Aquatic Microscope" (for the not inconsiderable sum at the time of £2-12sh-6p!).

Subsequently, when Sir Joseph Banks (1743-1820) was offered the chance to accompany Captain James Cook on his voyage of discovery on the "Endeavour," he set about acquiring one of the finest collections of naturalist's instruments and accessories to take with him, and it included an Ellis Aquatic Microscope. It was recorded that "no people ever went to sea better fitted out for the purpose of Natural History, nor more elegantly," and of all the instruments, perhaps the most important were the "aquatic" microscopes in their original fish-skin cases, which were adaptable in practice not only for observations in marine biology (as originally intended by John Ellis), but also as early forms of dissecting microscopes for entomology and botany.

An Ellis-type aquatic microscope, by Peter Dollond, one of four taken by Joseph Banks aboard the "Endeavour" on Captain Cook's first voyage of discovery in 1768-71, with lacquered brass pillar thread-mounted into lid boss with concave mirror plate, circular specimen stage, two threaded eyepieces, support arm engraved over both sides "Joseph Banks/H.M.B. Endeavour," contained within a green plush-lined pocket case covered in black fish skin with securing hooks, case shrinkage and discoloration, the compartment dividers and support block are detached, losses, mirror lacks all silvering.

ca. 1768   *5in (12.5cm) high*

$50,000-62,000   CM

A barograph belonging to Sir Winston Churchill, seven pressure capsules on recording drum with clockwork mechanism, oak case mounted with brass bed plate, beveled glass cover, chart drawer, silver plate on front inscribed "THIS BAROGRAPH BELONGED TO/SIR WINSTON CHURCHILL/ AND HAS BEEN GIVEN BY/MRS M. K. GRANT TO THE/ROYAL NAVAL CLUB PORTSMOUTH/MARCH 1972," unsigned.

ca. 1920   *14½in (37cm) wide*

$12,500-15,000   CM

A "Service" microscope, by W. Watson, black lacquered finish, coarse/fine focusing, condenser and plano-concave mirror, with case, along with assorted prepared microscope slides in a mahogany and two cardboard boxes.

$150-190   TEN

A 3½in (9cm) refracting telescope, by Wray, London, the brass-mounted black painted body tube with sighting scope, mounted on a wood tripod stand, with stained wood box.

46in (117cm) long

$1,000-1,250   CHEF

A five-drawer telescope, by Negretti & Zambra, with a 2¼in (5.5cm) objective lens.

38½in (98cm) long

$100-125   TEN

A two-day marine chronometer, by Barrauds, London, four-pillar movement signed "Barrauds Cornhill LONDON 2/605," standard compensation balance with blued steel helical spring detent on standard escapement, the silvered dial signed "Barrauds LONDON 2/605," "UP/DOWN" aperture, blued steel hands, contained within a brass bowl with Barraud keyless winding, gimbal mounted in three-tier wood box with ivory number plate further inscribed, trade label for Reynolds & Son inscribed "Cloud Russell/8 Oxford Sq. cleaned July 1884," drop handles, minor fading, might be associated but no additional witness holes to middle tier, movement is stop/start, balance a little free.

ca. 1810 6in (15cm) wide

$3,000-3,500 CM

A one-day marine chronometer, by John Roger Arnold, no. 544, silvered dial with subsidiary seconds, typical brass gimbal mounted in mahogany case, with replacement ivory plate on the front, some marking/staining on the dial, winding key is probably a replacement.

This chronometer was originally supplied to the Admiralty in 1821. According to official records, it was used aboard the "Beagle" in 1837, although it just missed out on Charles Darwin's trip around the world on the same ship in 1831-36. It is last recorded in official use in 1887.

Ivory Act certification no. 8HQ5J5DB

ca. 1821

$8,500-12,500 CHEF

A two-day marine chronometer, by Litherland Davies & Co., Liverpool, the 3¼in (8.5cm) silvered dial signed and numbered "856/17955," standard balance with Poole's auxiliary, plain plates, helical spring, jeweled detent, contained within a bowl in a three-tier wood case with key, drop handles.

ca. 1841 7in (18cm) wide

$1,700-2,200 CM

A rosewood two-day marine chronometer, signed "John Brunton, 3 America Square, London," no. 513, single-chain fusee movement with a chronometer detent escapement, free sprung helical hairspring, split bimetallic balance with timing weights and screws, diamond end stone, movement contained in a gimbal, 4in (10cm) silvered dial with Roman numerals, seconds dial and 54-hour power reserve dial, three-tier brass-bound case with side carrying handles, front plaque signed and numbered, discoloration, scratches, movement needs cleaning.

Ivory Act certification no. GA6R9BBN

ca. 1860 7¼in (18.5cm) high

$1,600-1,900 TEN

A mid-19thC two-day marine chronometer, by Brockbank & Atkins, no. 1024, typical chain fusee movement, 3¼in (8.5cm) silvered dial with power reserve and seconds subsidiaries, signed on movement and dial, gimbal mounted in a mahogany box, with an ivory disk on the front.

Ivory Act certification no. 6DLFP2UE

6¾in (17cm) wide

$3,700-4,300 CHEF

A mahogany two-day marine chronometer, signed "J.W. Ray & Co, 17 So Castle St, Liverpool," no. 230, single-chain fusee movement with a chronometer detent escapement, free sprung blued helical hairspring, split bimetallic balance with timing weights and screws, diamond end stone, movement contained in a gimbal, 4in (10cm) silvered dial with Roman numerals and signed, seconds dial and 56-hour power reserve dial, three-tier brass-bound case with concealed side carrying handles, front plaque signed and numbered, seconds hand missing, case cleaned, top lid later, staining, scratches.

Ivory Act certification no. S9AD6VSS

ca. 1890 7¾in (20cm) high

$1,500-1,700 TEN

A mahogany two-day marine chronometer, signed "J.W. Ray & Co., 25 Cunliffe St, Liverpool," no. 232, single-chain fusee movement with a chronometer detent escapement, free sprung blued helical hairspring, split bimetallic balance with timing weights and screws, diamond end stone, movement contained in a gimbal, signed 4in (10cm) silvered dial with Roman numerals, seconds dial, and 56-hour power reserve dial, case with concealed side carrying handles, front plaque signed, inside case with cleaning/repair labels for 1940 and 1950, scratches, discoloration, and staining, top lid is missing, movement needs cleaning.

Ivory Act certification no. TQBD6QRV

ca. 1920 6¾in (17cm) high

$1,250-1,500 TEN

A 1:48 scale 24-gun sixth-rate warship of the 1741 "Establishment," possibly by a dockyard apprentice, the hull carved from the solid, finished in white below the waterline with black main wale and buff above, lower deck and stern gunports with hinges and rings, sweep ports, chain plates with deadeyes, boarding ladder, lion figurehead finished in gold paint, roundhouses, wooden anchors with bound stocks, stern with carved trumpeting cherub taffrail, wooden deck with fittings including bitts, belaying rails, with coiled ropes, belfry with canopy and bell, bound water cask, hatches with gratings, Venetian red capstan, rigged helm and inner bulwarks, guns in stepped wood carriages with trucks, swivel guns, companionways, and other details, bound masts with yards, fighting tops, standing and running rigging with blocks, and tackle with sheaths, loosely mounted on an ebonized cradle stand secured to a wood display base with plaque and brass pad feet.

A. H. Waite's "National Maritime Museum Catalogue of Ship Models to 1815," H.M.S.O (ca. 1970), page 95 reads: "The model is probably the work of an 18th century amateur craftsman but the proportions are reasonably good. Its general appearance, disposition of the gun-ports etc. suggests a 24 gun, 6th Rate of the 1741 Establishment, but the hull is a little too fine to represent an actual ship. The rigging is probably 19th century and although on the heavy side it is approximately correct for the period."

ca. 1745   *42in (106.5cm) wide*
$16,000-19,000   **CM**

A static display model for a large French frigate of 48 guns, possibly by a dockyard apprentice, the carved boxwood hull copper-sheathed below the waterline, ebonized wales, red lined gunports with brass guns, chain plates with deadeyes, female bust figurehead, carved quarter galleries and stern with fleur-de-lis, planked and pinned deck with fittings including belaying rails with pins, capstan, well deck with belfry, compass, doubled helm, glazed saloon lights, gratings, companionways, bound cutaway masts and bowsprit, loosely mounted on a wood cradle stand, rudder and guns may be later.

ca. 1800   *17in (43cm) wide*
$4,200-4,700   **CM**

A French prisoner-of-war boxwood model for a 74-gun ship, the hull carved with ebonized wales, brass guns with red port lids, ebonized warrior figurehead with spear, carved stern and quarter galleries, scored deck with ebonized strake, brass deck rings, well deck flanked by boats with one slung over, lined great cabin light, bound masts with yards, stuns'l booms, standing and running rigging, mounted on a raised straw-work display base, with associated straw-work display case with six mirrors and glazed drop front, on carved bone pad feet, brass carrying handle, case with mirror silvering wear and staining, evidence of old worm.

ca. 1810   *15in (38cm) wide*
$5,200-6,000   **CM**

A commemorative ship-in-bottle model of RMS "Lusitania," made by a survivor, carved in wood with waterline hull ebonized with gold-painted topsides, masts and funnels with cotton wool "Smoke," mounted on a blue molded sea with pilot cutter and tender fore and aft with townscape behind, with label inscribed "LUSITANIA/SUNK/4.5.1915/FRED JONES," the neck corked with twine grommet.

1915   *12in (30.5cm) wide*
$500-625   **CM**

A 1:48 scale waterline boardroom model of the MV "Landwade," built by Bartram & Sons Ltd. for Atlantic Shipping and Trading Co., 1960, modeled by Sunderland Model Making Co., with laminated and carved hull, ebonized deck with lined gray hold covers, masts rigged with derricks, superstructure with lined yellow decks with fittings as appropriate, funnel with logo, engine room lights, glazed bridge with binnacle over, comms mast, aerial, and other details, mounted on a molded and painted sea with maker's plate by stern, glazed cover and builder's plate, glass case with nibble.

50in (127cm) wide
$3,100-3,700   **CM**

A 1:48 scale builder's-style model of the RSS "Sir David Attenborough," built by Cammell Laird for the UK Research & Innovation Dept, 2021, modeled by W. Brogan, with box-section frames planked overall and complete with twin five-blade brass propellers and rudders, bow thrusters, Plimsoll markings, green decks with painted wood and metal fittings, coated wire deck rails, subsidiary vessels inset on davits, the stern with field trip research vessel "Boaty McBoatface" with davit and crane, stepped multisection glazed bridge with communication and navigation arrays and other details, mounted on display base with nameplate, within a plexiglass glazed wood case.

Built by Cammell Laird at a cost of £200m ($250m) and launched by the Duchess of Cambridge in 2018, the RSS "Sir David Attenborough" is the most advanced addition to the British Antarctic Survey's fleet. Unusually, it is her tender that briefly outshone her illustrious mother ship, when it had to be named "Boaty McBoatface" in deference to a public vote on naming the ship and which, as a result of a viral campaign, won the competition hands down. This model was constructed with unique access to the builder's plans and is one of a pair, the other being for the builder's use.

A 1:32 scale model of an Italian paredgia of ca. 1880, modeled by D.A. Brogden, the hull framed and planked with trennels, green below the waterline, decorative boot top over wale, planked deck arranged as for a working boat with details including capstan with three bars, partly opened hatches with visible cargo in marked sacks, fitted boat, coiled ropes, water casks, grapple anchor, open companionway, shaped tiller, masts with lateen rig, bowsprit and yard, mounted on a display base within a glazed wood case.

ca. 1981   *41½in (105.5cm) wide*
$1,900-2,200   **CM**

45in (114.5cm) wide
$10,000-12,500   **CM**

NAUTICAL ANTIQUES

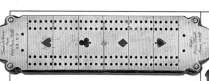

A cribbage board made from the USS "Constitution," the shaped wood section with a brass plate secured to the top, with filled emblems for the card suits, engraved "Timber & Brass from/Old Iron Sides/Capt. Issac Hull/Anno 1820."

12½in (32cm) wide

$2,500-3,100 CM

An American merchantman portrait figurehead, of a gentleman owner with lamb chop whiskers, high collar with neckerchief, pleated shirt, shawl collar vest and a cloak around his waist, the back with billet head, refinished.

ca. 1840 *33in (84cm) high*

$2,000-2,500 CM

A novelty marine-themed cast iron stick stand, probably French, modeled as a sailor on a fighting top with a "rope" stick container, supported by anchors, oars, and boat hooks, rock-form base initialed "H.F." with removable enameled drip tray.

ca. 1890 *28in (71cm) high*

$2,900-3,200 CM

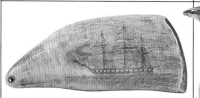

A noonday cannon dial, by Chevallier, Paris, the marble dial signed and inscribed on front "L'INGr. CHEVALLIER, OPTICIEN DU ROI. PLACE DU PONT NEUF. 15 A PARIS., latitude 39° 56," bronze gnomon, ignition lens on arc and cannon, on a later wood stand.

Jean Gabriel Augustin Chevallier (1778-1848) qualified as an engineer and moved to this address in Paris in 1820.

ca. 1820 *10½in (26.5cm) wide*

$1,700-2,100 CM

A 19thC sailor's scrimshaw decorated whale tooth, one side with a profile of a stationary whaler, the tip and root drilled.

The drilling suggests this might have once been a Fijian tabua (a presentation whale tooth, drilled and threaded onto a palm fiber cord).

7½in (19cm) wide 25½oz

$550-700 CM

The ship's bell from the SS "Sea Serpent," cast in silver bell metal and inscribed, lacks clapper.

Built by A. McMillan & Son Dumbarton for C. F. Leach, London, and registered at 902 imperial tons, on March 23, 1916, she struck a mine laid off Folkestone Pier and sunk with the loss of 14 lives, including the Master.

ca. 1898 *13in (33cm) high*

$1,600-2,000 CM

An early-19thC French Napoleonic prisoner-of-war spinning jenny, single character on a platform over a carved bone mechanism with handle, in a glazed dome.

7in (18cm) high

$375-500 CM

A Sunderland lusterware pitcher for the clipper ship "Great Australia," inscribed "The Great Australia Clipper Ship" and "The Unfortunate London," flanking a poem.

ca. 1870 *7½in (19cm) high*

$550-700 CM

A Kriegsmarine bulkhead clock, eight-day going barrel movement, the dial numbered "273" with KM mark, spade hands with sweep seconds, movement sticky, no key.

8in (20.5cm) diam

$3,100-3,700 CM

A 19thC Swiss cylinder music box, playing on 32 airs, within a walnut, ebonized, and marquetry case, label for "Marque de Fabrique" and numbered "44087."

22½in (57cm) wide

$1,000-1,100 WHP

A 19thC Swiss amboyna crank-wind cylinder music box, by Samuel Troll Fils, with nine bells in sight playing ten airs, some losses in teeth of comb.

26in (66cm) wide

$1,000-1,250 CHEF

A late-19thC French rosewood and marquetry music box, by J. Thibouville Lamy & Cie, the lid inlaid with lilies, the interior with a brass cylinder playing 12 airs, with a printed tune sheet, numbered "44543."

28½in (72.5cm) wide

$1,700-2,100 WW

A late-19thC Swiss music box, playing ten airs on a brass cylinder and nine bells, with engine-turned decoration and pagoda-topped hammers, the lever crank stamped "270832," the walnut case with kingwood crossbanding and ebonized details, with original title card.

25¾in (65.5cm) wide

$1,400-1,700 WW

A late-19thC Swiss music box, the cylinder playing ten airs as listed on the tune sheet and striking six bells, in an ebonized walnut case with floral marquetry sprays and kingwood banding.

24in (61cm) wide

$625-750 HT

A late-19thC musical snuff box, playing three airs, within a Bakelite-style molded case, titled "Port St Denis," complete with air sheet and key, stop/start not working, minor wear on case.

4¼in (10.5cm) wide

$480-520 SWO

A table-format interchangeable cylinder music box, most certainly by S. Troll, serial no. [**]114, gamme no. 34, 50, and 66, the three cylinders playing eight airs each, including operatic, waltz, dance, and patriotic titles, single-spring motor, butterfly governor, perpendicular weight-fly speed check, single section comb with three-quarter length zither attachment, on silvered reeded bedplate, finely pressed gilt maker's applique on rear runner, ebonized interior under dust lid, grained case with transfer above flush cylinder drawer plinth, domed veneered lid with floral inlay.

27in (68.5cm) wide

$550-625 TEN

A visible drum and bells music box, by P. V. F., no. 13664, playing eight patriotic and popular musical hall airs, single spring motor, with six drum hammer select and three fixed bell strikers on plain polished tuned buffet bells, reeded cast-gilt bedplate, single-section comb, ebonized interior under dust lid, color lithograph twin-column tune sheet, grained case with rosewood veneered lid with floral inlay, with restoration invoice from 1984.

18in (46cm) wide

$500-625 TEN

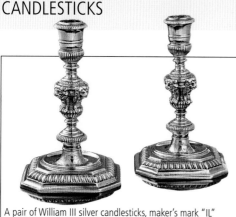

A pair of William III silver candlesticks, maker's mark "IL" with a coronet above, London, knop columns, applied with four lion masks, spool-shaped capitals, ropework borders, on raised square bases with canted corners and ropework decoration, each engraved with an armorial within foliate mantling, the undersides with scratch weights.

For the maker's mark, see "Jackson's," Ian Pickford Edition, Antique Collector's Club (1989), page 135.

1696   *6¾in (17cm) high 26⅞oz*
$7,500-8,500   **WW**

A George II silver taperstick, by James Gould, London, knop stem, spool-shaped capital, on a raised shaped square base.

1735   *4¼in (11cm) high 4oz*
$875-1,000   **WW**

A set of four George II silver candlesticks, by James Gould, London, knop baluster stems, fluted shoulders, spool-shaped capitals, on raised shaped square bases, each engraved with a crest.

The crest is that of Huddleston.

1739   *7¼in (18.5cm) high 67oz*
$5,200-6,000   **WW**

A set of four mid-18thC Irish candlesticks, by Robert Calderwood, Dublin, lobed shoulders, knop tapering columns, spool-shaped capitals, on raised shaped square bases, each engraved with a crest, possibly later rhodium plated.

ca. 1750   *7in (18cm) high 52oz*
$8,000-8,500   **WW**

A set of four George II silver candlesticks, by William Gould, London, shell-capped knop baluster stems, spool-shaped capitals, on raised shaped square bases with shell and scroll motifs, each engraved with an armorial.

The arms are probably those of Stewart/Stuart impaling another.

1742   *7¾in (19.5cm) high 62oz*
$3,100-3,700   **WW**

A George II silver taperstick, by William Gould, London, knop stem, shell shoulder, on a shaped square base with shell corners, engraved with a crest.

1751   *5in (12.5cm) high 5oz*
$625-750   **WW**

A set of four George II cast silver candlesticks, by John Cafe, London, knop columns, shell shoulders, spool-shaped capitals, detachable drip pans, on raised shaped square bases with shell corners.

1752   *8½in (21.5cm) high 68oz*
$3,100-3,700   **WW**

A pair of George II silver tapersticks, by John Cafe, London, knop columns, shell shoulders, spool-shaped capitals, detachable drip pans, on raised shaped square bases with shell corners.

1754   *5in (13cm) high 11¼oz*
$1,400-1,700   **WW**

A set of George III silver candlesticks, by John Carter II, London, tapering square baluster column stems, with fluted decoration, with Greek-key borders, ram-head and hoof supports, on raised square bases with medallions and ribbon-tied swags, each with an engraved armorial, stiff leaf borders, the sides numbered 1-4 and with scratch weights, with later filled bases.

1774   *11¾in (30cm) high*
$2,500-3,100   **WW**

A pair of George III cast silver candlesticks, by Robert Jones, London, knop tapering circular stems, gadroon borders, spool-shaped capitals, detachable unmarked drip pans, on raised stepped square bases with fluted and gadroon decoration, engraved with initials.

1778   *10¼in (26cm) high 44oz*

$2,500-3,100   **WW**

A matched set of four George III silver candlesticks, by John Parsons & Co., Sheffield, octagonal tapering columns and capitals, detachable drip pans, bright-cut borders, on raised circular bases, engraved with two different crests on the bases, all loaded.

The crests are probably that of Hawkshaw and another.

1790   *11¾in (30cm) high*

$2,200-2,700   **WW**

A pair of Italian silver candlesticks, possibly late 18th/early 19thC, gadroon borders, with Venice marks.

6½in (16.5cm) high 16oz

$500-625   **WW**

A 19thC Continental silver candlestick, possibly Austro-Hungarian, in Rococo Revival style, fluted drip pan, on a shaped circular base, marked "13."

11¼in (28.5cm) high 10⅞oz

$300-375   **WW**

A pair of Victorian cast-silver candlesticks, by Samuel Whitford, London, in George II style, knop baluster columns with foliate shoulders, spool-shaped capitals, ropework borders, on raised shaped square bases with anthemion motifs.

1856   *9¼in (23.5cm) high 38⅜oz*

$1,900-2,200   **WW**

A pair of late-Victorian silver dwarf candlesticks, by William Hutton and Sons, London, of Corinthian column form, beaded borders, on stepped square bases, inscribed.

1894   *5¾in (14.5cm) high*

$375-450   **WW**

A matched set of four silver candlesticks, by the Goldsmiths and Silversmiths Company, London, in mid-18thC style, shell-capped shoulders, spool-shaped capitals, on raised shaped square bases.

1928-29   *9¾in (24.5cm) high*

$1,250-1,700   **WW**

A set of four silver candlesticks, Birmingham, of Corinthian column form, weighted.

1964   *9¾in (25cm) high*

$1,000-1,250   **CHOR**

A late Elizabeth I/James I silver-mounted coconut cup, the coconut bowl mounted with three strap supports, the silver rim with engraved foliate decoration and engraved in single lobes "R M M September 14 1726," baluster stem, on a spread circular foot with engraved foliate scroll decoration, unmarked.

ca. 1600-20   7in (18cm) high
$9,500-10,000   **WW**

A James I silver wine cup, London, the bowl of tapering circular form, with a gilt interior, embossed foliate and scroll decoration on a matted background, tapering baluster stem, on a raised circular foot with chased decoration, maker's mark worn.

1613   7in (18cm) high 5¾oz
$7,000-7,500   **WW**

A George II silver mug, by John Eckford, London, with scroll handle, scratch initialed "B" over I*S," the front later initialed, on a raised circular foot.

1727   3¾in (9.5cm) high 7¼oz
$350-420   **WW**

A George II silver small baluster mug or tot cup, by George Jones, London, with a scroll handle, on a raised circular foot.

1733   2¾in (7cm) high 2¾oz
$1,500-1,700   **WW**

A George II provincial silver tumbler cup, by Richard Richardson, Chester, with a gilt interior.

1747   2in (5cm) high 2¼oz
$950-10,000   **WW**

A mid-18thC Irish silver two-handle cup and cover, by Samuel Walker, Dublin, with a center girdle, embossed with figural scenes in landscape settings, trailing vines, scrollwork, and foliate decoration, engraved with an armorial and later crest, the pull-off cover with a cone finial, on a raised circular base.

The crest is that of Massy.

ca. 1760   13¾in (35cm) high 63oz
$3,700-4,300   **WW**

A rare mid-18thC American Colonial silver half-pint mug, by Daniel Christian Fueter (1720-85), New York, of baluster form upon a spreading circular foot, acanthus-capped C-scroll handle, the underside engraved with initials "E A," then slightly later with "E J," forming a quartet in Roman script, with town mark and maker's mark "DCF."

Daniel Fueter was born in Berne, Switzerland, on April 14, 1720. He worked there as a silversmith until he took part in a conspiracy with the poet Samuel Henzi to overthrow the aristocratic government. In 1749, he was caught and sentenced to death, but he managed to escape to London, where he entered his maker's mark at Goldsmiths' Hall on December 8, 1753, with his address as "King's Road, Chelsea, next door to the Man In The Moon." Samuel Henzi was beheaded on July 17, 1749. Fueter's stay in London could not, however, have been for long as he was advertising as a silversmith in New York in May 1754 with the address of "Near the Brew-house, facing Oswego Market." In 1763, he relocated to Dock Street, New York, and on July 31, 1765, he took the oath of the Colonial Naturalization Act of 1740. By 1779, his son, Lewis Fueter, had taken over the running of the family business, because his father had returned to Berne.

ca. 1755   4in (10cm) high 6⅞oz
$4,000-4,700   **CA**

A mid-18thC Swedish silver beaker, by Nils Rydberg, Sater, with chased foliate decoration, engraved "S.A.K.S" in the cartouche, gilt interior and rims, on a circular fluted foot, the underside with initials, the front with a later inscription "Charles Edward Leathart Rae The Gift of his Grandmother Julia Rae upon his coming of Age. 1. July 1904."

ca. 1760   7in (18cm) high 13⅜oz
$500-625   **WW**

A George III silver mug, by Fuller White, London, with a leaf-capped scroll handle, on a raised circular foot, engraved with a ship and a mermaid and inscribed "Pray God prosper The Sally."

The sailing ship "The Sally," from Bristol, was used to ship port from Portugal to Bristol. In September 1769, it ran aground at Northam Burrows, Devon (later renamed "Westward Ho!"). The crew were rescued and its cargo was salvaged by a local landowner. Its remains can still be seen at low water.

1766   4¾in (12cm) high 11⅝oz
$1,900-2,200   **WW**

A pair of George III silver goblets, by Solomon Hougham, London, with engraved foliate decoration, gilt bowls, each engraved with a crest within a foliate cartouche, the reverse with a later crest, on raised circular stems and square feet.

1802   *6¼in (16cm) high 15¾oz*

$1,400-1,700   **WW**

A George IV silver christening mug, London, decorated with a band of fruiting vine, with a cornucopia handle.

1825   *5¼in (13.5cm) high 7½oz*

$300-450   **CHOR**

A George IV silver two-handle cup, by Emes and Barnard, London, probably 1827, of campana form, foliate capped scroll handles with rosette motifs, the body with a band of roses, thistles, and shamrock above foliate and leaf decoration, on a raised circular foot, with traces of gilding.

10¾in (27.5cm) high 63oz

$1,700-2,000   **WW**

An early-Victorian mug, by John & Henry Lias, London, with two bands of engine turning, with acanthus leaf sheathed loop handle.

1840   *4oz*

$125-190   **HT**

A pair of Victorian silver stirrup cups, by William Leuchars, London, the tapering cylindrical bodies forming the heads and wings of a griffin.

1883   *5½in (14cm) high 27¾oz*

$5,200-6,000   **DUK**

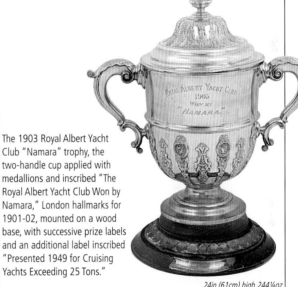

The 1903 Royal Albert Yacht Club "Namara" trophy, the two-handle cup applied with medallions and inscribed "The Royal Albert Yacht Club Won by Namara," London hallmarks for 1901-02, mounted on a wood base, with successive prize labels and an additional label inscribed "Presented 1949 for Cruising Yachts Exceeding 25 Tons."

24in (61cm) high 244¼oz

$21,000-25,000   **CM**

A large Edwardian silver two-handle trophy cup, by Charles Townley and John Thomas, London, retailed by F.B. Thomas and Co., with cut-card decoration and leaf-capped scroll handles, on a raised circular foot, inscribed "The 'Entente Cordiale' Cup, presented to The British Motor Boat Club by Mrs Walker Munro 1905, won by 1905 Aug 7 'Napier II' J. Scott Montagu, Lionel de Rothschild, 1906 Aug 6 'Yarrow Napier,' Lionel de Rothschild."

1904   *12¾in (32.5cm) high 150oz*

$8,500-10,000   **WW**

The Whitbread Round the World Race trophy, the silver two-handle covered cup inscribed on front "WHITBREAD ROUND THE WORLD RACE Organized by Royal Naval Sailing Association/ 2nd Overall on Corrected Time/ Presented by Royal Naval Club and Royal Albert Yacht Club," with Sheffield maker's marks for 1919-20.

17in (43cm) high

$2,500-3,100   **CM**

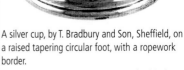

A silver cup, by T. Bradbury and Son, Sheffield, on a raised tapering circular foot, with a ropework border.

1931   *3½in (9cm) high 11oz*

$300-350   **WW**

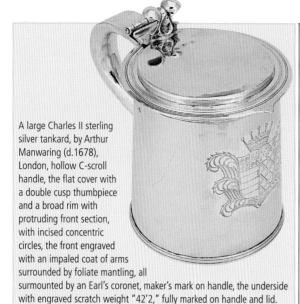

A large Charles II sterling silver tankard, by Arthur Manwaring (d.1678), London, hollow C-scroll handle, the flat cover with a double cusp thumbpiece and a broad rim with protruding front section, with incised concentric circles, the front engraved with an impaled coat of arms surrounded by foliate mantling, all surmounted by an Earl's coronet, maker's mark on handle, the underside with engraved scratch weight "42'2," fully marked on handle and lid.

The arms are that of Manners impaling Noel.

Arthur Manwaring was apprenticed to William Tyler, but was later turned over to Anthony Ficketts and became free on January 20, 1643. He spent much of his working life in financial difficulty, receiving financial aids from the Goldsmiths' Company's charities for poor goldsmiths several times. He received commissions from the Goldsmiths' Company and also appears to have produced work for other goldsmiths—in April 1666, for example, a cup and cover that was found by the wardens of the assay office to be below standard was "of Manwaring's making but marked by John Gibbs plateworker" (D. Mitchell, "Silversmiths in Elizabethan and Stuart London: Their Lives and Their Marks," Woodbridge: Boydell Press, 2017, page 228). This tankard, and another of 1671 by Mawaring in Queen's College, Oxford, are the only two Manwaring tankards recorded by Mitchell.

1677   *7¾in (19.5cm) high 45½oz*

$12,500-15,000   CA

A late-17thC Baltic parcel-gilt silver tankard, marked for Philip Luders (1694-1721), Narva, the cast cover decorated with a crest bearing wings, a figure, leaf scroll, and flowering plants, later engraved with a coronet and initials within a cartouche, on three leaf-chased and cast feet.

7½in (19cm) high 50½oz

$11,000-12,500   SWO

A Queen Anne Britannia silver tankard, with ivory insulators, later embossed with floral decoration around a monogrammed cartouche, the base engraved "Ex dono, Joanne Hall, Feb 10 1703," date and maker's mark indistinct, tarnished, spout may be later but contemporary due to London leopard head mark, signs of repair.

Ivory Act certification no. 8P6VPYA7

7in (18cm) high 27oz

$875-1,000   SWO

A George I silver tankard, by Richard Bayley, London, the domed cover with a fluted scroll thumbpiece, large scroll handle engraved "R S."

1717   *7¼in (18.5cm) high 26oz*

$500-625   DUK

A George II silver tankard, by Richard Bayley, London, the reeded girdle engraved with a crest, domed hinged cover with scroll thumbpiece, the scroll handle with a heart terminal.

1746   *7¾in (19.5cm) high 29⅝oz*

$1,900-2,200   DAWS

A George III silver tankard, by Thomas Wallis I, London, the domed hinged cover with a leaf and scroll thumbpiece, the scroll handle with a heart terminal, the three-quarter skirted body engraved with a monogram, dents, cover repair, center monogram rubbed.

1773   *7¾in (19.5cm) high 26oz*

$1,250-1,500   DAWS

A George III silver tankard, by John King, London, of baluster form, with center girdle, scroll handle, domed hinged cover with pierced thumbpiece, on a circular foot.

1777   *8¼in (21cm) high 22¾oz*

$1,500-1,700   WW

A George III silver tankard, maker's marks for John Schofield, London, the cover by John Edwards, London, 1905, with reeded bands, pierced thumbpiece, the cover with a ball finial, two pints measure, tarnished.

1785   *7¾in (19.5cm) high 28½oz*

$1,000-1,500   SWO

A Scottish George II silver bullet teapot, by John Main, Edinburgh, assay master Archibald Ure, leaf-capped scroll handle with insulators, one wood and one horn, chased foliate decoration, flush-hinged cover with a ball finial, on a raised circular foot, later initial.

ca. 1736 6in (15.5cm) wide 20¾oz

$1,100-1,350 WW

A George II bullet teapot, by Dougal Ged, Edinburgh, assay master Archibald Ure, crest in center for the Crawford family with motto "TUTUM TE ROBORE REDDAM" above, with engraved floral borders, straight spout and S-scroll handle, raised on circular stepped foot.

1736 6¼in (16cm) high 15¾oz

$3,100-3,500 L&T

A George III silver small or saffron teapot, by John Wakelin & William Taylor, London, later wood scroll handle and knop finial.

1785 3¾in (9.5cm) high 10¼oz

$1,100-1,350 WW

A George III silver teapot, by Andrew Fogelberg, London, of boat-shaped form, on four spherical feet.

1808 6¾in (17cm) high 15½oz

$375-500 WHP

A George IV silver teapot, by George Burrows II, London, part-fluted with a gadrooned rim, domed hinge cover, scroll handle, on a circular foot.

1821 10in (25.5cm) wide 18¾oz

$625-750 WW

A George III West Country silver teapot, Exeter, scroll handle with ivory insulators, flush-hinged domed cover, engraved with a crest, center girdle, on a circular foot, maker's mark worn.

Ivory Act certification no. VESSS8VZ

1826 9¾in (25cm) wide 19¼oz

$750-875 WW

A George IV silver teapot, by Richard Pierce and George Burrows II, London, of melon shape with rose finial, with ivory heat absorbers.

Ivory Act certification no. DB5SM6YP

1827 20oz

$375-500 CHOR

A Victorian silver teapot, by The Barnards, London, the hinged cover with a melon finial, scroll handle with ivory insulators, on a raised circular foot.

Ivory Act certification no. R6SMAUF2

1848 9¼in (23.5cm) wide 17oz

$400-475 WW

A Victorian silver teapot, by Army & Navy Cooperative Society Ltd. (Frederick Bradford Macrea), London, swirl fluted, with scroll handle and fluted spout.

1890 8¾in (22cm) wide 13½oz

$500-625 WW

An early-20thC silver teapot, by Viners, Sheffield, with gadrooned decoration.

1920 5½in (14cm) high 23oz

$625-750 WHP

A George I silver coffeepot, by Bowles Nash, London, faceted spout, scroll handle, domed hinged cover with a knop finial.

1721   *9¾in (24.5cm) high 28¼oz*

$2,700-3,100   **WW**

A George II silver coffeepot, by John Fossey, London, wood scroll side handle, faceted spout, hinged cover with a knop finial, on a spread circular foot, engraved with an armorial shield within foliate scroll mantling.

1736   *8in (20.5cm) high 20oz*

$1,600-1,900   **WW**

An Irish George II silver coffeepot, by Charles Leslie, Dublin, with chased foliate shell and strap-work border, leaf-capped faceted tapering spout with chased decoration, flat-chased cover with an urn finial, wood scroll handle, on a circular foot, engraved with an armorial within foliate scroll mantling, the reverse with a crest, the underside with a scratch weight "33:17."

The crest is that of Hansard of Lifford, Co. Donegal, impaling Eccles, Maddison, Marley, or Morris.

ca. 1740   *8¾in (22cm) high 34oz*

$8,000-9,500   **WW**

An 18thC Maltese Pinto Period silver coffeepot, maker's mark possibly "MP," embossed with shell scroll and trellis decoration, wood scroll handle with fluted rosettes, the domed hinged cover with a cone finial and scroll thumbpiece, on a circular foot, with a test scrape.

For similar examples, see Alaine Apap Bologna, "The Silver of Malta," MAG publications (1995), page 78, and J. Farrugia, "Antique Maltese Domestic Silver," Said International (1992), page 52.

ca. 1740   *8¾in (22cm) high 14⅝oz*

$27,000-31,000   **WW**

A Continental silver coffeepot, Paris, with embossed decoration of Classical ladies, the handle with ivory heat absorbers.

Ivory Act certification no. QPG5UMUG

1768-74   *19⅛oz*

$450-550   **CHOR**

A George III silver coffeepot, by John Robins, London, scroll handle, later embossed foliate decoration, flush-hinged fluted raised cover with an urn finial, on a raised oval foot.

1792   *12½in (32cm) high 27⅝oz*

$625-750   **WW**

A George IV silver coffeepot, by Thomas Ballam, London, in 18thC style, with embossed foliate scroll decoration, scroll handle, engraved with an armorial shield, domed cover with an acorn finial, beaded spout, on a raised circular foot with a gadroon border.

1824   *11½in (29cm) high 31⅛oz*

$875-1,000   **WW**

An Irish early-Victorian silver hot water ewer, Dublin, with embossed fruit and foliate scroll decoration on a matted background, leaf capped scroll handle, flush-hinged cover with a flower finial, on a circular foot, no apparent maker's mark, insulators removed.

1837   *9½in (24cm) high 26½oz*

$750-875   **WW**

A rare coffeepot, designed by Dr. Christopher Dresser for P&O, maker's marks for Elkington & Co., hinged lid, company device on front.

ca. 1870   *9in (23cm) high*

$1,000-1,100   **CM**

An Edwardian silver coffeepot, by Martin, Hall & Co., Sheffield, scroll handle, fluted decoration.

1907   *7¼in (18.5cm) high 12⅜oz*

$450-500   **WW**

ESSENTIAL REFERENCE—ARGYLES

The "argyle" (alternatively spelled "argyll") was invented in the 18thC, named after and initially made for John Campbell, 5th Duke of Argyll (1723-1806), who had complained that during the winter months the gravy at his table was invariably served cold, or at best luke warm, due to the length of time it took for a servant to bring it the considerable distance between the kitchens and the dining room in his house. The prototypes and early models of the vessel conceived to overcome this problem contained a separate internal compartment that could be heated with an iron rod to keep the gravy hot, but these gradually evolved into a much more efficient, internal double-walled chamber that could be filled with boiling water. Typically with a spout that emerges near the base of the vessel—which enabled the gravy to be drawn from underneath the layer of fat that settled on top of it—argyles were made in various shapes and sizes, but most bore a strong resemblance to a coffeepot. Indeed, many people used to confuse them for the latter and use them as such—to the point where many later examples were actually sold as individual coffeepots rather than gravy warmers.

An 18thC German silver kettle, Frankfurt, chased foliate scroll and rocaille decoration, the hinged handle with two warrior heads and with leather mounts, engraved with a crest, on a later 19thC unmarked circular stand, on three scroll wirework legs on three pad feet.

ca. 1780   10¾in (27cm) high 31oz
$750-875   **WW**

A William IV silver kettle-on-stand, by Robert Garrard, London, flush hinged cover with an ivory finial, silver-mounted ivory carrying handle, the stand with foliate supports, on four gnarl feet, with a burner, engraved with the Rothschild crest, with Ivory Act exemption certificate.

1836   15½in (39.5cm) high 102oz
$2,200-2,700   **WW**

A George III silver argyle, by William Lestourgeon, London, scroll handle, with a hinged water compartment, gadroon border.

1771   4¾in (12cm) high 11¾oz
$1,250-1,500   **WW**

A mid-Victorian Britannia standard spirit kettle, by Crichton Brothers, London, with an octagonal spout, scroll handle with turned oak insert, raised on four scroll branch legs, with burner intact.

1856   13in (33cm) high 61oz
$2,000-2,200   **L&T**

A Victorian silver kettle-on-stand, London, gadrooned decoration and engraved with the Elliot family crest, the stand on four foliate feet, with later burner, by Edward Barnard & Sons Ltd, London, 1897, maker's mark rubbed and illegible, tarnishing on kettle base.

1881   10¾in (27.5cm) high 29¼oz
$500-625   **SWO**

A Victorian silver kettle-on-stand, by Charles Stuart Harris, London, the stand with three scrolled feet, associated burner, minor dents and scratches.

1892   13½in (34cm) high 52⅜oz
$1,000-1,100   **SWO**

A late-Victorian presentation curling stone kettle-on-stand, by Walker & Hall, Sheffield, the kettle modeled as a curling stone with crosshatch wood handle, engraved on the body with winners, the stand formed as a cross, with circular disk engraved "THE GORDON TROPHY/ PRESENTED BY Mr. & Mrs. GORDON/FOR ANNUAL COMPETITION," the legs each modeled as two crossed brushes, all raised on four ball feet.

1899   9½in (24cm) high 45oz
$3,700-5,000   **L&T**

An Edwardian silver spirit kettle-on-stand, maker's mark "J D & S," Sheffield, semifluted with everted scallop shell, anthemion, and acanthus leaf rim, flat hinged domed cover, fixed overhead ebony handle, the circular stand raised on three leaf and flute supports on trefoil feet, the two chains with "keys," burner by Elkington, no date letter.

1902   12in (30.5cm) high 46oz
$1,000-1,100   **HT**

A Victorian three-piece silver tea service, by John Tapley, London, lobed with leaf-capped scroll handles, the teapot with ivory insulators, hinged cover with a flower finial, on four leaf-capped foliate and scroll bracket feet, each engraved with an armorial shield.

Ivory Act certification no. ZHT8S1MF

1838-40   *teapot 11¼in (28.5cm) wide 47¾oz*
$1,250-1,500   **WW**

A Victorian silver coffeepot, teapot, and sugar bowl, the coffeepot by Robert Hennell, London, sugar bowl maker's mark worn, London, and the teapot by Henry Wilkinson, Sheffield, all lobed with engraved decoration, the scroll handles with ivory insulators, on foliate capped scroll feet, each engraved with a crest and initials.

Ivory Act certification no. 989YGW7S

1840, 1854 ,and 1864   *coffeepot 8in (20.5cm) high 63oz*
$1,500-1,700   **WW**

A Victorian three-piece silver tea service, by The Barnards, London, paneled with engraved decoration, the teapot with scroll handle with ivory insulators, the hinged cover with a melon finial, on four pierced bracket feet.

Ivory Act certification no. 7N14YSLV

1853-54   *teapot 10in (25.5cm) wide 41oz*
$875-1,000   **WW**

A Victorian four-piece silver tea and coffee service, by George Angell, London, with bands of engraved decoration and smiling mask heads on the sides in low relief, the teapot and coffeepot with ivory heat absorbers on the handles.

Ivory Act certification no. DNBKRQUL

1865   *coffeepot 11½in (29cm) high 87⅜oz*
$2,700-3,100   **CHOR**

A Victorian three-piece silver tea service, by Edward & John Barnard, London, with foliate and scroll decoration, on grotesque mask-head-capped legs.

1857   *teapot 7¾in (19.5cm) high 61⅜oz*
$1,900-2,200   **CHOR**

A late-Victorian four-piece silver tea service, maker's mark "MW," Sheffield, of lobed quatrefoil form with ribbed decoration, the teapot inscribed "The Rev George Thompson by the Members of Newtown Cunningham Congregation on the occasion of his Removal to Omagh, May 1898."

1897   *52¼oz*
$700-875   **CHOR**

A late-Victorian three-piece silver tea service, by Cooper Bros, Sheffield, with everted scroll pierced quatrefoil rims, bright and wrigglework engraved with swags issuing from strapwork, the teapot with hinged domed cover with melon fluted mother-of-pearl finial, reeded angular handle with ivory stops, all engraved "D."

Ivory Act certification no. TQW9A8NS

1900   *teapot 11in (28cm) wide 47oz*
$1,250-1,500   **HT**

An Italian four-piece tea service, in Empire style, with stiff leaf-stamped rims, the teapot and hot water pitcher with hinged swept domed covers, all stamped "800."

teapot 9¾in (24.5cm) wide 46oz
$875-1,000   **HT**

A four-piece silver tea service, by S.B. & S. Ltd, Birmingham, the teapot inscribed to Mr. and Mrs. J. C. Fraser from Lieut. Col. and Mrs. E. J. Fergusson of Baledmund estate.

1920   *teapot 6in (15cm) high 46½oz*
$875-1,000   **CHOR**

A George III silver bombé tea caddy, by Pierre Gillois, London, with chased floral and foliate decoration, on four scrolled feet, the cover surmounted by a finial modeled as a squirrel, scratches, dents, rocks slightly, finial possibly later.

1765   *5¾in (14.5cm) high 8¼oz*
$700-800   SWO

A George III silver bombé tea caddy, by Emick Romer, London, the pull-off cover with a flower finial and gadroon border, on four pierced scroll bracket feet with shell motifs, engraved with an armorial and crest.

1769   *5¼in (13.5cm) high 8oz*
$1,100-1,350   WW

A George III oval tea caddy, London, all-over embossed floral shell and scroll decoration, vacant shield cartouche in the center of each side, the hinged lid with similar decoration and ivory finial, marked "W.S."

1790   *5½in (14cm) high 11¼oz*
$1,100-1,350   L&T

A William IV tea caddy, by Andrew Wilkie, Edinburgh, engraved scroll border on body, garland cartouche with italic "HF" in center, the hinged lid with a foliate engraved border and a knop rectangular finial.

1830   *5in (12.5cm) high 10½oz*
$2,100-2,500   L&T

An early-Victorian silver chinoiserie tea caddy and cover, maker's mark "WH," London, the lift-off cover with a cast recumbent figure, all-over chased with Rococo scroll, leaf and flower-head cartouche, with cast and applied scroll angles on the shoulders, raised on four outcurved supports.

1839   *6in (15cm) high 16oz*
$2,200-2,500   HT

A Victorian oval silver tea caddy, by Charles Stuart Harris, London, the hinged cover engraved with a monogram, the part-reeded body with original key, on a flared foot with reeded rim.

1884   *3¼in (8.5cm) high 11¼oz*
$500-625   DAWS

A silver tea caddy, by Mappin & Webb, London, in early 18thC style, slide-off top and pull-off cover.

1919   *5in (12.5cm) high 9oz*
$450-550   WW

An oval silver tea caddy, by the Goldsmiths and Silversmiths Company, London.

1925   *5¼in (13.5cm) wide 9½oz*
$300-375   CHOR

SILVER & METALWARE

ESSENTIAL REFERENCE—CADDY SPOONS

In Great Britain during the mid-18thC, the smaller tea canister for storing tea was gradually superseded by the larger, box-shaped tea caddy. It was easy to measure the loose tea leaves from the former, but the new caddies required a scoop—hence the creation of the caddy spoon. Early examples mostly had shell-shaped bowls—a form probably inspired by the practice of tea merchants using seashells to let wholesale customers sample the tea before buying. Indeed, until the mid-19thC, caddy spoons were commonly referred to as "caddy shells." From the second decade of the 19thC onward, other, increasingly more ornate, shapes were conceived. Many caddy spoons also featured deeply curved terminals, so they could be hooked over the rim of the caddy when not in use. The majority dated prior to the mid-19thC were made from thin sheet silver—silver being the preferred material not only because it and tea were equivalent luxuries, but also because it was thought to enhance, rather than detract from, the taste.

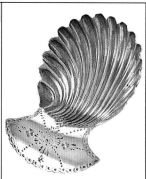

A George III silver caddy spoon, by Hester Bateman, London, shell bowl, the spread handle with bright-cut decoration.
1784   2¼in (5.5cm) long ¼oz
$400-475   **WW**

A rare Scottish provincial caddy spoon, by David Izat, Banff, the shaped handle with bright-cut engraved borders, large scalloped shell bowl, maker's mark "DI."
1794-99   3¼in (8cm) long ⅝oz
$750-875   **L&T**

A George III silver jockey's hat caddy spoon, by Joseph Taylor, Birmingham, with star and foliate decoration on a reeded background, the brim with a shield cartouche.
1799   2¼in (5.5cm) long ¼oz
$625-750   **WW**

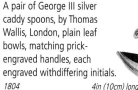

A pair of George III silver caddy spoons, by Thomas Wallis, London, plain leaf bowls, matching prick-engraved handles, each engraved withdiffering initials.
1804   4in (10cm) long
$170-220   **HT**

A George III silver-gilt leaf caddy spoon, by Elizabeth Morley, London, the leaf bowl with vein decoration, with wirework ring handle.
1805   2¾in (7cm) long
$250-310   **WW**

A George III silver caddy spoon, by Joseph Taylor, Birmingham, modeled as a right hand, with engraved decoration.
1806   2½in (6.5cm) long ¼oz
$300-375   **WW**

A George IV silver eagle's wing caddy spoon, by Joseph Willmore, Birmingham, the handle modeled as the eagle's head, with textured feather decoration.
1828   3in (7.5cm) long ⅜oz
$1,250-1,500   **WW**

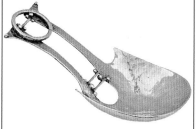

A white metal caddy spoon, attributed to Frances Macdonald McNair (1874-1921), with applied beading, marked "R" on verso.

Frances Macdonald and her sister Margaret were skilled in metalware, jewelry, and enameling. However, few executed pieces of their jewelry and silver are known. See G. & C. Larner, "The Glasgow Style," Paul Harris (1980), no. 43, for a similar silver caddy spoon.
ca. 1900   3in (7.5cm) long
$2,700-3,100   **L&T**

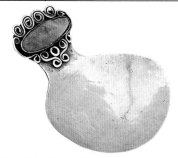

A Scottish white metal caddy spoon, in the manner of Mary Thew, set with an oval amethyst, unmarked.

Mary Thew was born in Hillhead, Glasgow, in 1876. She studied at the Glasgow School of Art from 1894-96. She was a member of the Glasgow Society of Lady Artists, and won the Lauder Award for a case of jewelry in 1925. She also exhibited at the Walker Art Gallery in Liverpool.
ca. 1910   2½in (6.5cm) long
$590-700   **L&T**

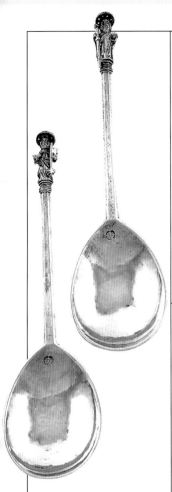

A 15thC diamond-point spoon, fig-shaped bowl, faceted tapering stem, the terminal with traces of gilding, maker's mark "B" in a pelleted punch, the reverse with a scratched mark.

ca. 1450-1500 6¼in (16cm) long 1oz

$11,000-14,000 WW

A fine Henry VIII silver Apostle spoon, The Master, by William Simpson, London, fig-shaped bowl, faceted stem, gilt finial, pierced nimbus, the reverse with scratch initials "G" over "IE."

1530 7in (18cm) long 1¾oz

$25,000-30,000 WW

A Henry VIII silver Apostle spoon, probably Saint Paul, by William Simpson, London, fig-shaped bowl, faceted stem, the finial with traces of gilding, pierced nimbus.

1534 7¼in (18.5cm) long 1⅝oz

$15,000-19,000 WW

A fine pair of Henry VIII silver Apostle spoons, Saint Peter and Saint James the Greater, by William Simpson, London, fig-shaped bowls, slight tapering stems, gilt finials with pierced nimbi.

1545 7½in (19cm) long 3¾oz

$40,000-45,000 WW

An Edward VI silver Apostle spoon, Saint James the Greater, London, fig-shaped bowl, faceted slight tapering stem, the finial with traces of gilding, pierced nimbus, maker's mark of a feather.

1547 7in (18cm) long 2⅛oz

$12,500-15,000 WW

A rare Mary Tudor wrythen knop silver spoon, London, fig-shaped bowl, tapering stem, the finial with traces of gilding, maker's mark of a cross with a pellet.

1556 6½in (16.5cm) long 1⅜oz

$14,000-16,000 WW

A pair of Elizabeth I seal-top silver spoons, London, fig-shaped bowls, faceted tapering stems, gilt finials, the reverse of the bowls with prick-dot initials "A.G" and "E.G," maker's mark of "W" within a sun.

1561 6¾in (17cm) long 3¾oz

$20,000-22,000 WW

A rare Elizabeth I provincial silver Apostle spoon, possibly Saint Matthew or Saint Thomas, by Thomas Pinder, York, fig-shaped bowl, faceted stem, gilt finial, with a rays-of-glory nimbus.

1585

$21,000-25,000 WW

A pair of Elizabeth I slip-top silver spoons, by Nicholas Bartholomew, London, fig-shaped bowls, faceted tapering stems, the reverse of the bowls scratch initialed "B" over "I.E," maker's mark of a crescent enclosing a mullet.

1596 6¼in (16cm) long 3⅛oz

$8,000-9,500 WW

A James I silver Apostle spoon, Saint Paul, probably by John Round, London, fig-shaped bowl, faceted tapering stem, the finial with a pierced nimbus, the reverse of the bowl with later initials.

1606 7in (18cm) long 2oz

$3,200-3,700 WW

A pair of Charles I seal-top silver spoons, by William Cary, London, fig-shaped bowls, faceted tapering stems, the gilt finials with scratch initials "I.W."

1640 7in (18cm) long 2¾oz

$3,200-3,700 WW

A pair of 17thC West Country silver Apostle spoons, Saint Peter and Saint James the Less, by William Corseley, Gloucester, fig-shaped bowls, faceted tapering stems, gilt initials, each nimbus prick-dot initialed "R*B," "1663" over "I*M," and "S*B" over "1663" over "I*M."

ca. 1663   *7in (18cm) long 2¾oz*
$8,000-8,500   **WW**

A George I basting spoon, London, "Hanoverian" pattern, no maker's mark.

1726   *13in (33cm) long 4oz*
$170-220   **HT**

A large George II silver basting spoon, by Jeremiah King, London, "Hanoverian" pattern, the reverse of the terminal with a crest, the reverse of the bowl with a plain heel.

1746   *16¾in (42.5cm) long 9⅜oz*
$1,600-1,900   **WW**

An important Scottish provincial masking/mote spoon, by Hugh Ross, Tain, the tapered upper section of stem with an urn finial, the lower scrollwork section with a pierced bowl with double drop heel, marked "HR" within an oval punch.

This extremely rare example of a Tain masking spoon seems to fit between the traditional Scottish masking spoon for stirring the tea in the pot, and the English mote spoon used to strain the floating leaves from the cup and clear blockages in the strainer/spout. Three of these spoons are known to survive—all are illustrated in "The Tain Silver Collection," Tain & District Museum, page 31. The last example sold is now within the Tain & District Museum Collection, no. 3283.

7½in (19cm) long ¾oz
$6,000-7,500   **L&T**

A George III silver soup ladle, maker's mark "RC," London, initialed "F."

1806   *6⅝oz*
$125-190   **CHOR**

A George III salt spoon, by William Pugh, Birmingham, the oval bowl riveted to a twisted tortoiseshell handle.

1808   *3¼in (8.5cm) long*
$70-100   **HT**

A George III silver basting spoon, by Paul Storr, London, "Old English Military Thread and Shell" pattern, the terminal with a crest.

The crest is that of Castleton, Chester, Farington, Glover, and others.

1817   *12¼in (31cm) long 5¾oz*
$700-800   **WW**

A William IV provincial silver soup ladle, by Barber, Cattle, and North, York, "Fiddle" pattern, oval bowl, the terminal with initials, town mark.

1830   *13½in (34.5cm) long 8oz*
$1,400-1,600   **WW**

A Scottish early-Victorian soup ladle, by J. McKay, Edinburgh, single struck "King's" pattern.

1838   *13in (33cm) long 7oz*
$170-220   **HT**

A set of six American silver serving spoons, by R. Wallace and Sons, foliate bright-cut engraved, the reverses engraved "1891," marked sterling.

10⅜oz
$170-220   **SWO**

A George II silver cream pitcher, by John Gorham, London, with a wavy-edge border, scroll handle, on three scroll-pad feet, scratch initialed "E.I."

1735   *3¾in (9.5cm) high 3½oz*

$500-625   **WW**

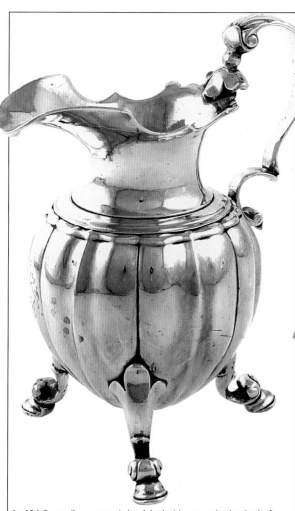

An 18thC cast silver cream pitcher, lobed with wavy-edge border, leaf-capped scroll handle, on three scroll-and-hoof feet, unmarked.

ca. 1740   *4¼in (11cm) high 5¾oz*

$1,000-1,250   **WW**

An 18thC silver cream pitcher, leaf-capped scroll handle, on three scroll legs with pad feet, marks worn.

4in (10cm) high 4½oz

$250-310   **WW**

A pair of George III silver sauceboats, London, gadroon borders, leaf-capped scroll handles, each on three shell-capped hoof feet, maker's mark partly worn "W?," signs of seam corrosion, fine surface scratches.

1762   *7¼in (18.5cm) wide 19oz*

$520-600   **WW**

A George III silver cream pitcher, by John Lambe, London, with embossed foliate and part-fluted decoration, engraved initials within a center foliate cartouche, scroll handle, on a raised circular foot.

1783   *4½in (11.5cm) high 2⅜oz*

$190-220   **WW**

A George III silver cream pitcher, by John Denziloe, London, of helmet form, with bright-cut decoration and initials, on a raised circular foot, later engraved "1785."

1785   *6in (15.5cm) high 4⅛oz*

$250-310   **WW**

A Victorian silver cream pitcher, London, with leaf-capped C-scroll handle, repoussé decorated body, on three outswept feet, maker's mark indistinct.

1875   *4½in (11.5cm) high 6oz*

$125-190   **WHP**

A Victorian silver cream pitcher, Chester, of helmet form, maker's mark "GH RH."

1897   *5¾in (14.5cm) high 3½oz*

$125-170   **WHP**

A late-18thC American silver pepper caster, by Eleazer Baker (1764-1849), Ashford, Connecticut, the pull-off domed lid surmounted by a bell-form finial, the lid with drill-pierced holes heightened with engraved panels of latticework, on a spreading circular foot, marked underneath "E.BAKER."

ca. 1785   *5in (12.5cm) high 3⅞oz*
$460-520   **CA**

A pair of Victorian novelty silver bird pepperboxes, by Jane Brownett, London, modeled in a standing position, pull-off pierced heads, with textured feathers.

1881   *2in (5cm) high 3⅞oz*
$650-720   **WW**

A Victorian novelty silver mouse pepperbox (also called a pepper pot), by Thomas Johnson, London, modeled in a standing position, textured fur decoration, with a pull-off oblong base.

1886   *3¼in (8.5cm) long 1oz*
$520-600   **WW**

A late-Victorian silver cow pepperbox, modeled in a standing position, with a pull-off pierced head, importer's mark for Berthold Muller & Son, London, 1900.

2¼in (5.5cm) wide 1oz
$300-375   **WW**

An Edwardian novelty silver rabbit pepperbox, by George Gillet, London, modeled in a sitting position, textured fur decoration, with a pull-off head.

1904   *2¼in (5.5cm) wide 2oz*
$775-850   **WW**

An Edwardian novelty silver teddy bear pepperbox, by H.V. Pithey & Co., Birmingham, modeled in a sitting position, with textured fur decoration.

1909   *1½in (4cm) high ¼oz*
$200-220   **WW**

A Norwegian novelty silver squirrel pepperbox, modeled eating in a sitting position, textured tail and ears, on a pull-off circular raised foot, marked "Sterling J. Tostrup Norway."

2½in (6.5cm) high ¾oz
$250-310   **WW**

A pair of 19thC circular silver salts, each on four scrolled acanthus feet, marks rubbed.

4¼in (11cm) diam 15¾oz
$375-450   **CHOR**

A pair of novelty silver fox salt and pepperbox, London, modeled in standing positions, with pull-off heads, maker's mark "G.I.P."

2002   *4in (10cm) long 8⅞oz*
$1,000-1,250   **WW**

A William III silver caster, possibly by William Bull, London, of lighthouse form, the bayonet-fitting pierced cover with fluted decoration and a fluted finial, on a raised fluted circular foot.

1701   *5¾in (14.5cm) high 4¾oz*
$875-1,000   **WW**

A George I octagonal sugar caster, by Mungo Yorstoun, Edinburgh, assay master Edward Penman, the pull-off cover pierced and engraved with scrolls, octagonal vase finial, on a stepped foot.

1716   *8½in (21.5cm) high 10¼oz*
$3,100-3,500   **L&T**

A set of George II silver casters, by Jabez Daniel, London, spirally fluted and gadrooned, crested, comprising a caster and a smaller pair.

7¾in (19.5cm) and
1755   6in (15cm) high 19⅛oz
$625-750   **CHOR**

A Victorian novelty silver owl mustard pot, by E. C. Brown, London, modeled in a standing position, textured feather decoration, the hinged cover set with red eyes, gilt interior.

1881   *3½in (9cm) high 3oz*
$1,600-1,900   **WW**

A Victorian Britannia silver sugar caster, by John & Frank Pairpoint, London, of lighthouse form, the bayonet-fitting pierced cover with knop finial, on a spread gadroon foot, some wear in marks, dents.

1893   *7¼in (18.5cm) high 11¼oz*
$160-200   **WW**

ESSENTIAL REFERENCE—QUEEN CHARLOTTE

Queen Charlotte (1744-1818), wife of King George III (1738-1820), was a well-known patron of the arts and, more specifically here, a collector of silver. Born Charlotte of Mecklenburg-Strelitz, when she married in 1761, she moved from her Royal residence in Northern Germany to St. James's Palace in London. In addition to giving birth to 15 children during her marriage, she also accrued a large collection of fine art and artifacts before passing away in 1818, at the age of 74. As an avid collector, her cypher can be found on many pieces—from simple wick trimmers to ornate tea services—spanning her lifetime in Great Britain. It is clear that the most eminent silversmiths of the day—notably Robert Garrard, Paul Storr, and John Emes, who created the silver-gilt caster shown here—were particular favorites of hers.

A George III silver-gilt caster, by John Emes, London, with Queen Charlotte's engraved cypher in a laurel wreath, foliate border on the rim, the domed screw-off lid with pierced detail and engraved floral detail, raised on a circular spreading foot with similar foliate border.

1798   *4¼in (11cm) high 2½oz*
$2,200-2,500   **L&T**

ESSENTIAL REFERENCE—CUTTING THE MUSTARD

Lavishly appointed table displays were a highlight of affluent Victorian dining, with sculptural centerpieces, floral displays, and comports overflowing with bonbons all considered essential accoutrements for a fashionable table. Cruets and condiment sets were also an important component, and many of the latter were often crafted in "novelty" forms, sometimes inspired by exotica from the far reaches of the British Empire. The chimpanzee mustard shown here is a splendid and particularly desirable example. A similar one, which forms part of the mustard manufacturer Coleman's archival collection, is referenced in their publication: "The Colman Collection of Silver Mustard Pots," Coleman Foods, Norwich (1979), page 90.

A scarce Victorian novelty silver and parcel-gilt mustard, by Richards & Brown, London, modeled as a chimpanzee sitting cross-legged wearing an Asian-style jacket and smoking a pipe, with spectacles and holding a beaker, all-over matted ground and engraved scroll and floral decoration, the hinged cover formed as a hat and with a spoon finial as the center plume, silver-gilt liner in interior, engraved on underside "W.B.E" and Victorian registration mark for February 26 (indistinct year).

1867   *4in (10cm) high 5oz*
$10,000-11,000   **L&T**

A pair of George II silver salvers, by William Peaston, London, with shell and scroll borders, each with a center crest within a cartouche.

1747 and 1748	*13½in (34cm) diam 91¼oz*

$2,100-2,500 CHOR

A George II silver snuffer tray, by William Cafe, London, shell and scroll border, scroll handle with a shell motif and a crest, on four shell feet, with a pair of George III silver scissor snuffers by John Booth, London, fluted decoration, engraved with a crest.

1757 and 1760	*8¼in (21cm) wide 16⅜oz*

$625-750 WW

A George III silver salver, by Hannam & Crouch, London, the piecrust border with scallop shell angles, raised on three stepped hoof feet.

1767	*12in (30.5cm) diam 26oz*

$625-750 HT

A rare pair of Scottish provincial salvers, by John Baillie, Inverness, slightly raised flared rim, the four corner bracket feet inswept following the shape of the rim, marked "I.B.," "INS," "X" (dots within angles).

Although not a well-recorded maker, the work of John Baillie of Inverness is universally of a high standard. It seems fair to say he was the most accomplished silversmith in Inverness in the mid-18thC and received many important commissions. His work is scarce, but from what survives we can see a maker of great quality receiving important and fashionable commissions. Like his contemporaries, he produced several fine quaichs of traditional form and these were probably a mainstay of his larger work. However, his true skill is seen in larger pieces, which would not have looked out of place coming from his Edinburgh contemporaries. He produced two hot milk pitchers, extremely rare for any Scottish silversmith, let alone provincially made (Aberdeen Art Gallery and Museum, no. 01365 and Inverness Art Gallery & Museum, no. 1978.260). Two pairs of mugs are also recorded, one within a private collection ("Exhibition of Scottish Silver," Royal Scottish Museum, August–September 1948, item no. 331), the other within the National Museums of Scotland collection, National Museum Scotland (MEQ 1575 and 1576). These salvers are the only recorded in Inverness silver by any maker and are of only a small handful of pairs of provincial examples extant.

5½in (14cm) wide 10oz

$8,500-10,000 L&T

A George III silver salver, London, pierced border with an outer beaded border, the center engraved with an armorial shield within husk-and-foliate mantling, on three pierced bracket feet, the reverse lightly inscribed "This Salver belonged to Jas Forster Knight (1751-1808). The Down House Blandford S. Mary. Arms of Forster of Bamborough Castle (Sic) See Hitchins History of Dorset, Editions I, II and III for Jas Forster and for Capt. James Forster Knight," overstamped with maker's mark of "J*S."

1777	*13½in (34cm) diam 35oz*

$875-1,000 WW

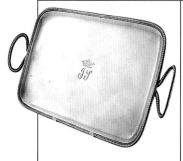

A small George III two-handle silver tray, by William Turton, London, beaded border and handles, with engraved initials and crest.

The crest is possibly that of Jemima Yorke, 2nd Marchioness Grey (1723-97).

1785	*9¾in (24.5cm) wide 6½oz*

$450-500 WW

A rare Scottish provincial tea tray, by Milne & Campbell, Glasgow, scalloped outline with molded rim, raised on four scrolling hoof feet, the reverse engraved "William Crawford born 1 Jany 1704, Elizabeth Gow born 15 Decr 1712—Married 5 August 1731—Died 21 May 1771, Died 5th June 1787," marked "M&C," Glasgow town mark "MC," "O."

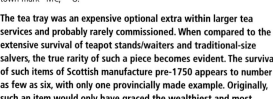

The tea tray was an expensive optional extra within larger tea services and probably rarely commissioned. When compared to the extensive survival of teapot stands/waiters and traditional-size salvers, the true rarity of such a piece becomes evident. The survival of such items of Scottish manufacture pre-1750 appears to number as few as six, with only one provincially made example. Originally, such an item would only have graced the wealthiest and most fashionable families and houses of Scotland.

14¼in (36cm) diam 35oz

$6,000-6,500 L&T

A George III silver meat platter, by John Wakelin & Robert Garrard, London, reeded border, with engraved armorial shield.

The armorial is that of Rous impaling Whittaker.

1794	*15¼in (38.5cm) wide 31¾oz*

$1,100-1,500 WW

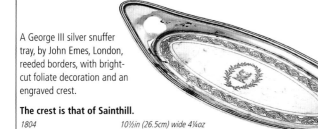

A George III silver snuffer tray, by John Emes, London, reeded borders, with bright-cut foliate decoration and an engraved crest.

The crest is that of Sainthill.

1804   10½in (26.5cm) wide 4¼oz
$190-250   **WW**

A George IV silver salver, by William Bateman, London, shell and scroll border, the center with chased foliate scroll decoration, on three paw feet, the underside with a scratch weight "57oz."

1824   14½in (37cm) diam 55¼oz
$1,250-1,500   **WW**

A small late-19thC American sterling silver salver, by Samuel Kirk and Co., Baltimore, Maryland, embossed foliage ovolo edge and a laurel rim, the field with engine-turned latticework pattern, centered with a vacant shaped circular cartouche, raised on four claw-and-ball feet, marked on the reverse "(1868-90)" and "11oz."

ca. 1880   8½in (21.5cm) diam 12oz
$410-450   **CA**

A Victorian silver twin-handle tray, by John Hunt & Robert Roskell, London, with twin loop handles, engraved with an alternating band of cannons and foliage and scrollwork, black marks on surface.

1881   29½in (75cm) wide 128oz
$2,900-3,100   **DN**

A 19thC Russian silver plate, probably by Grachev, St. Petersburg, acanthus leaf border, with initials.

1883   9¾in (24.5cm) diam 18½oz
$500-625   **WW**

A late-Victorian silver two-handle gallery tray, by Charles Stuart Harris, London, pierced foliate scroll gallery, inset handles, beaded border, the center engraved with a crest and motto.

The crest and motto are that of Ward.

1896   18in (45.5cm) wide 44¾oz
$1,500-1,900   **WW**

An Edwardian tray, by Walker & Hall, Sheffield, with arcade pierced gallery and two reeded scroll handles, engraved with scrolling acanthus enclosing a vacant panel and a Rococo cartouche engraved with the bust portrait of a young man in an open-neck shirt, and a shield cartouche engraved with the crest and motto of Leith "Persevere" below "Sigillum Oppidi de Leith," raised on four bun feet.

1902   24½in (62cm) wide 79oz
$1,900-2,200   **HT**

An Edwardian silver salver, by William Hutton and Sons, London, shell and scroll border, chased foliate scroll decoration, engraved with a crest, on three gnarl feet.

1905   12in (31cm) diam 35⅜oz
$875-1,100   **WW**

An Edwardian silver salver, by James Dixon & Sons Ltd., Sheffield, with extensive inscription on underside.

1908   12½in (32cm) diam 31¼oz
$550-700   **CHOR**

SILVER & METALWARE

A William III silver two-handle "Monteith" bowl, by Robert Timbrell, London, with alternate panels of plain and foliate decoration on a matted background, ropework borders, lion-mask drop-ring handles, detachable collar with a castellated scroll border with cherub heads, on a raised circular foot with a ropework border.

1698   *11in (28cm) diam 57oz*
$12,500-15,000   **WW**

A George I silver sugar bowl and cover, by William Fleming, London, with a pull-off cover, engraved with an armorial within foliate scroll mantling, on a raised circular foot.

The arms are that of C(o)oke impaling Shaw or Shawe.

1721   *3¾in (9.5cm) high 7⅞oz*
$2,100-2,500   **WW**

A Scottish George III silver sugar bowl, by Lothian and Robertson, Edinburgh, assay master Hugh Gordon, with a wavy-edge border, engraved with a crest and motto, on a raised circular foot.

1751   *5in (12.5cm) diam 8¾oz*
$500-625   **WW**

A late-Victorian silver trophy rose bowl, by S. & A. J. Fenton, Sheffield, chased and repoussé with panels of scrolling foliage enclosing two vacant cartouches, on a waisted socle and low domed foot, with two cast griffin scroll handles.

1891   *14½in (37cm) wide 33oz*
$2,000-2,200   **HT**

A late-Victorian silver trophy rose bowl, by William Hutton & Sons, London, the "Monteith" rim with cast and applied scrolls over straight fluting, enclosing two vacant oval cartouches, with two cast lion-mask angular-loop handles, on a low foot.

1898   *7in (18cm) high 34oz*
$1,700-2,000   **HT**

An Edwardian twin-handle silver bowl, by William Comyns, London, with paneled sides and planished finish.

1905   *13¾in (35cm) wide 54¼oz*
$1,400-1,700   **CHOR**

A pair of Egyptian silver bowls and covers, Al-Mansura, with engine-turned borders, the raised covers with flower finials, each with a Tughra mark.

1932   *6¾in (17cm) diam 30oz*
$1,500-1,900   **WW**

An American silver presentation bowl, engraved "Pennsylvania National Horse Show 1950, International Jumping Competition," marked sterling.

Provenance: The Trophy Cabinet of Peter Robeson, OBE—the "Godfather" of British Show Jumping.

10¾in (27.5cm) diam 38⅜oz
$700-875   **SWO**

A Charles II silver two-handle porringer, by Thomas King, London, embossed with a unicorn and lion within flowers and foliate decoration, with caryatid scroll handles, on a circular foot, later crest, the interior later gilded.

The crest is that of Hoghe of Cheshire.

1664   *4¼in (11cm) high 11oz*

$5,000-6,200   **WW**

A Charles II silver two-handle porringer, by Roger Stevens, London, with caryatid scroll handles, embossed with a running lion and another running animal, within foliate decoration.

1669   *7¾in (19.5cm) wide 14¼oz*

$6,500-7,200   **WW**

A Queen Anne silver two-handle porringer, possibly by Willoughby Masham, London, with part-fluted decoration below a ropework border, twisted ropework scroll handles.

1703   *3¼in (8cm) diam 2¾oz*

$800-950   **WW**

A George III provincial silver two-handle porringer, by John Langlands, Newcastle, with reeded scroll handles, the front initialed.

1757   *3¾in (9.5cm) high 6oz*

$300-375   **WW**

ESSENTIAL REFERENCE—QUAICHS

The word "quaich" is derived from the Scottish Gaelic word "cuach," meaning "cup," and is traditionally used to describe a shallow, twin-handle drinking cup or bowl. Most are made of wood, with some early ones being stave-built like barrels, but, in general, lathe turned and/or carved. However, other materials have been employed, including stone, horn, brass, pewter, and, as the examples here, silver. Although nowadays often awarded as commemorative prizes, and, therefore, not intended for actually drinking from, they are conventionally used for drinking liquor, such as whiskey or brandy, and in the 19thC the Scottish novelist and poet Sir Walter Scott was well known for dispensing drams from his collection of quaichs—one of which had been fashioned in wood from the elm tree that had been the Duke of Wellington's command post for most of the Battle of Waterloo in 1815.

A late-18thC American silver porringer, by Ezekiel Burr, Rhode Island, probably 1780s, with folded rim and pierced tab handle, with engraved monogram "JW."

8in (20.5cm) wide 8⅝oz

$1,050-1,250   **DAWS**

A Scottish provincial quaich, possibly by James Glen, Glasgow, the lugs each engraved "J McC" in a stylized border, "SCUOAB ASS" engraved on the body, on a circular foot, marked "IG" twice.

6in (15cm) wide 3¾oz

$1,250-1,500   **L&T**

A Scottish George III provincial silver two-handle quaich, by Alexander Stewart, Inverness, with plain lug handles, on a circular foot.

ca. 1800   *4½in (11.5cm) wide 2¼oz*

$2,200-2,700   **WW**

A Scottish provincial quaich, by Donald Fraser, Inverness, waisted lugs each engraved "JF" and "TF," the base inset with a Mary and William ½ crown coin, marked "DF."

4½in (11.5cm) wide 2⅜oz

$1,250-1,500   **L&T**

A George III silver entrée dish and cover, by Thomas Heming, London, gadroon border, foliate scroll handles, engraved with an armorial and crest, the pull-off cover with a later handle modeled as a coronet.

The armorial and crest are for Monson impaling Maddison, possibly for John, 2nd Baron Monson (1727-74).

1765   *11¼in (28.5cm) wide 39¾oz*
$1,700-2,000   WW

A pair of George III silver entrée dishes and covers, by John Wakelin & William Taylor, London, paneled with gadroon borders, the pull-off covers with gadroon borders and reeded ring handles, each engraved with an armorial and crest, the bases numbered "2" and "4," the covers numbered "1" and "3."

The armorial and crest are that of Gill impaling Lowndes.

1786   *12¼in (31cm) wide 85oz*
$4,700-5,200   WW

A pair of George III silver entrée dishes and covers, by Joseph Craddock & William Reid, London, with gadrooned, floral, and palmette cast borders, bayonet loop handles, crested and engraved with armorial cartouches.

The armorial and crest are that of Brice.

1817   *12½in (32cm) wide 150¼oz*
$3,100-3,500   CHOR

A silver entrée dish and cover, by Carrington and Co., London, gadroon border, the pull-off cover with a detachable handle.

1913   *10in (25.5cm) wide 40oz*
$875-1,100   WW

A pair of George III silver sauce tureens and covers, by John Robins, London, of navette form with reeded high-loop handles, on swept pedestals and oval feet, the swept covers with urn finials, covers and tureens both engraved on each side with an armorial.

1787   *10in (25.5cm) wide 32oz*
$1,900-2,200   HT

A pair of late-George III silver tureens and covers, by Richard Cooke, London, with cast and applied gadrooned rims, the domed lift-off covers each engraved on each side with the Royal coat of arms and motto over a further motto "Magistrates Indigat Virum," with cast acanthus- and scroll-capped handles, the base interiors further engraved with the Royal motto.

1802   *11½in (29cm) wide 113oz*
$3,700-4,300   HT

A pair of Irish George III regimental silver sauce tureens and covers, by James Le Bas, Dublin, retailed by West, with embossed foliate decoration, gadroon borders, cone finials, snake side handles issuing from masks, on foliate swirl-capped feet, each engraved with the 41st Regiment, heavily repaired.

1813   *11¾in (30cm) wide 67⅝oz*
$1,600-1,900   WW

A late-George III silver tureen and cover with liner, by William Burwash, London, with cast and applied gadroon, scallop shell and acanthus everted rim, domed cover engraved with an armorial, cast acanthus loop handle with nut fastening.

1816   *15in (38cm) wide 97oz*
$2,500-3,000   HT

A pair of George IV regimental silver two-handle soup tureens and covers, by Joseph Angell, London, with foliate, shell, and gadroon borders, reeded foliate handles, the domed pull-off covers with foliate capped snake handles, each on four foliate-capped paw feet, each engraved with the badge of the 69th Regiment, repairs, feet later filled.

1825   *16in (40.5cm) wide 296¼oz*
$6,000-7,500   WW

A George III silver swing-handle sugar basket, by Hester Bateman, London, pierced with slats and with engraved decoration, beaded borders, engraved with a crest, with a later clear glass liner, on a raised oval foot.

1785   *7in (18cm) wide 7¼oz*

$875-1,100   **WW**

A late-George III silver basket, London, with cast and applied gadrooned rim with anthemion angles, the overhead swing handle with circular box hinges, centrally engraved with an armorial, raised on a spreading foot, maker's mark mistruck (?E/F?).

1809   *14in (35.5cm) wide 48oz*

$1,050-1,250   **HT**

A Victorian silver basket, by Roberts & Belk, Sheffield, with cast and applied straight gadrooned rims enclosing a band engraved with Classical figures on a mat ground, overhead straight gadroon, scroll, and acanthus handle with circular box hinges, raised on a low oval spreading foot.

1869   *13in (33cm) wide 28oz*

$700-800   **HT**

A late-17thC silver counter box, with a pull-off cover, engraved decoration, unmarked.

ca. 1680   *1¾in (4.5cm) high 1½oz*

$625-750   **WW**

A 17thC German silver pomander, the screw-off cover with a hexafoil baluster finial, the body comprising six sections with the exterior engraved with panels of figures working in landscape settings, chased floral borders, openening to reveal six gilt sections, engraved decoration, each with a slide-off cover inscribed with various floral and herbal names, "Ruden," "Canel," "Rosen," "Rosmerin," "Schlog," and "Melgelken," on a domed circular foot, unmarked.

2¼in (5.5cm) high 2¼oz

$16,000-19,000   **WW**

A Dutch silver tobacco jar and cover, with laurel leaf garlands and lion-mask ring handles, the raised cover applied with foliate rosettes, with an urn finial and beaded border, on four bracket feet, with pseudo marks for Hendrik Vrijman, Rotterdam, 1780, also with a Rotterdam discharge and tax mark for Rotterdam 1795-1806, and a later tax mark, probably 19thC, the underside with initials "H.S."

5in (12.5cm) diam 19oz

$5,000-6,200   **WW**

A George III silver bougie box, by Henry Chawner, London, with a pierced hinged side handle, reeded borders, the pull-off cover with a hole for the wick and a crescent-shaped cutter.

1787   *2in (5cm) diam 2¼oz*

$450-500   **WW**

A late-Victorian silver stamp, sovereign, and cigar case, by Saunders & Shepherd, Birmingham, all-over engraved with scrolling foliage enclosing a roundel engraved with a monogram, hinged and with hanging loop.

1897   *3¼in (8.5cm) wide*

$220-275   **HT**

An Edwardian silver jewelry box, by Henry Matthews, Birmingham, the hinged cover embossed with a Classical courting scene surrounded by scroll foliate decoration, velvet and worn silk fitted interior, on four scroll padded feet.

1903   *7¾in (20cm) wide*

$420-475   **WW**

A George IV novelty silver-gilt monkey mustard pot and associated spoon, by John Bridge, London, modeled as a standing laughing monkey, his tail wrapped around his leg and with a pipe tucked into his belt, with later red eyes, and touching a coopered barrel with a pull-off cover with a cone finial, with a liner, on a rocky base set with a frog and foliage, the spoon with a pierced handle and vine leaf terminal, stamped "RUNDELL BRIDGE ET RUNDELL AURIFICES REGIS LONDINI."

spoon 1824, mustard pot 1825　　　　*4½in (11.5cm) high 24¾oz*

$12,500-15,000　　　　　　　　　　　　　　**WW**

A Victorian novelty silver owl inkstand, by George Richards & Edward Brown, London, modeled in a standing position, textured feather decoration, the hinged head set with red glass eyes and with a mouse in its beak, with a clear glass liner.

1861　　　　*3½in (9cm) high 3¾oz*

$2,000-2,200　　　**WW**

A Victorian silver centerpiece, by The Barnards, London, the center column modeled as two entwined palm trees, on a raised circular base mounted with a camel and two figures, one sitting holding a pipe, the other standing holding a staff, the base with foliate decoration, some leaves missing.

1861　　　*17in (43cm) high 79⅞oz*

$3,100-3,700　　　**WW**

A Victorian silver model of a dog, by Frederick Edmonds & Edward Johnson, London, modeled in a walking position on a scent.

1889　　　*7½in (19cm) wide 12¾oz*

$2,100-2,500　　　**WW**

An Edwardian Regimental presentation silver table cigar lighter, by the Goldsmiths and Silversmiths Company, London, the center baluster lighter with two holes for lighting rods, on a knop stem, engraved with the regimental badge of the 3rd Battalion The Welch Regiment, with two rampant goat supports, on an oblong base, mounted on a wood base.

1906　　　*9¼in (23.5cm) wide 32oz*

$4,000-4,300　　　**WW**

A silver statue of a horse, by Elkington and Co., Birmingham, modeled in a standing position with a saddle and bridle, on a rectangular base, mounted on a wood plinth, signed "G Halliday 1913."

1913　　　*13in (33cm) wide 90oz*

$4,600-5,000　　　**WW**

A Scottish novelty silver table bell, by Hamilton and Inches, Edinburgh, modeled as an old lady holding her dog, with a stick in her other hand, with a hinged head.

1931　　　*4¼in (11cm) high 16½oz*

$800-950　　　**WW**

A novelty silver dog napkin ring, by Horton & Allday, Birmingham, modeled as a sitting dog, fine surface scratches.

1931　　　*3¼in (8.5cm) wide ⅜oz*

$160-190　　　**WW**

A pair of silver models of grouse, by Edward Barnard & Sons Ltd, London, one slightly wobbly.

1978　　　*4½in (11.5cm) wide 17oz*

$2,200-2,700　　　**DN**

ESSENTIAL REFERENCE—WAX JACKS

Prior to the 18thC, tapersticks—essentially smaller versions of candlesticks—were used for holding a wax taper or a thin candle for melting sealing wax (for authorizing documents), and also for lighting tobacco pipes. However, from ca. 1700, tapersticks were gradually replaced by more ergonomically efficient wax jacks, such as the example shown here. Wax jacks featured a center rod or shaft (raised on a circular foot), around which the wax taper was coiled, its top end protruding through a hole in a small pan that incorporated a pincer to hold the taper in place—when the taper was lit, any resulting puddle of wax would form on the pan instead of drip down onto the surface of the table or desk below.

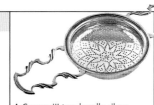

A George III two-handle silver lemon strainer, by William Plummer, London, with large foliate scroll side handles, the body with pierced decoration.

1761   9¾in (24.5cm) wide 3¾oz
$475-550   **WW**

A pair of George III silver asparagus tongs, by Thomas Northcote, London, the terminal with a crest.

The crest is that of Hansard.

1791   8¾in (22cm) long 3¼oz
$300-375   **WW**

A George III silver wax jack, London, the circular base with a ropework border, scroll handle, on three claw-and-ball feet, with a center column and hinged scissor-action wick holder, center flame finial nut, maker's mark possibly "C.B" with a mullet above, loose fitting finial nut.

1774   5in (12.5cm) high 5⅜oz
$625-750   **WW**

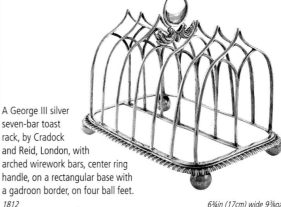

A George III silver seven-bar toast rack, by Cradock and Reid, London, with arched wirework bars, center ring handle, on a rectangular base with a gadroon border, on four ball feet.

1812   6¾in (17cm) wide 9⅜oz
$500-550   **WW**

An early-Victorian novelty silver tea infuser, London, modeled as a bed warmer with plain dot-pierced hinged cover, on a twisted baleen handle with a silver tip, maker's mark rubbed.

1845   5½in (14cm) long
$150-220   **HT**

A Victorian silver dog collar, by George Dyer, London, with a center plaque inscribed "JOLLIE," with a lock and key.

1885   1oz
$300-375   **WW**

A Victorian silver-gilt inkwell, by R. & S. Garrard & Co., London, in the form of a James I silver spice box, formed as a scallop shell with alternating plain and textured bands, the hinged cover opening to reveal an inkwell with a glass liner and a compartment, raised on four snail feet.

This inkwell is based on a James I spice box—the original with a maker's mark, triangle intersected, London, 1598—which was a gift from Lord Rothermere to the Honourable Society of the Middle Temple. This was part of an exceptional gift to the Temple in the 1930s. The Temple recently commissioned new cabinets befitting the collection and after some time were opened by Master Burnett in July 2021. On their website relating to the collection, the original spice box can be seen on the top shelf on the right.

1889   5½in (14cm) wide 17½oz
$875-1,100   **L&T**

An Edwardian regimental presentation novelty silver cigar cutter, by Henry Stuart Brown, London, modeled as an artillery shell, with a spring-action cutting section, on a rectangular base with punch stud decoration, on four ball feet, engraved with the regimental badge of the 3rd Battalion The Welch Regiment, and inscribed "Presented By 2nd Lieut. A. D Vaughan, March 6th 1907," some rust on mechanism.

1906   4¾in (12cm) high 5oz
$500-625   **WW**

An American silver hand mirror, by International Silver Co., the shaped beveled plate within a loop-handle mount, decorated on the reverse with rose heads and leaves.

ca. 1910   9in (23cm) high
$160-210   **SWO**

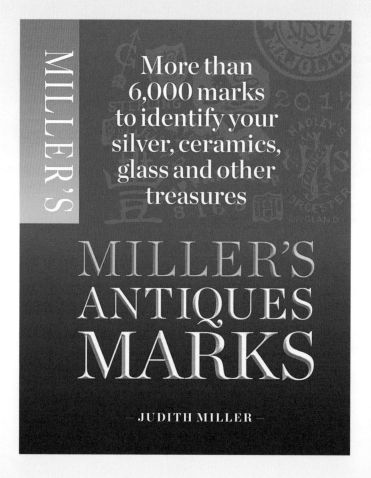

An early-19thC Old Sheffield plated two-handle wine cooler, part-fluted decoration, foliate-mounted side handles, foliate girdle, with detached collar and liner, on a circular foot.

ca. 1820   8¼in (21cm) high

$250-310   **WW**

A George IV wine cooler, London, the semi-ribbed campana pedestal urn with a cast fruiting vine band applied to a mat ground, on a single knop socle and stiff leaf cast circular foot, maker's mark "WE."

1821   8¾in (22cm) high 30oz

$1,000-1,250   **HT**

An early-20thC French 950 standard silver two-handle vase-shaped wine cooler, by Teytard Freres, the handles modeled as entwined serpents, with removable silver liner, repairs, scratches.

14in (35.5cm) high 69⅞oz

$1,700-2,000   **GORL**

A George III silver claret pitcher, by Peter & Ann Bateman, London, with grooves in girdle and engraved floral swags, the domed cover with a ball finial, the wood scrolled handle with acanthus-capped mounts, on a circular pedestal foot.

1793   13½in (34cm) high 27⅜oz

$950-1,050   **CHOR**

A mid-Victorian claret pitcher, possibly by William Smiley, London, the hinged cover with cast fruiting vine knop, naturalistic entwined twig handle, chased with a band of scrolling foliage enclosing a (now) vacant Rococo cartouche, on a low domed pedestal foot.

1860   11½in (29cm) high 21oz

$950-1,050   **HT**

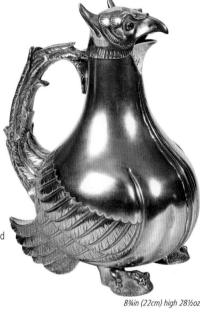

A Victorian silver claret pitcher, by George Fox, London, in the form of a standing griffin, with a hinged head set with red paste eyes, the cast scroll handle with applied feather decoration, the gilt body engraved with two crests, with simulated feathers in the lower half, on claw feet.

1884   8¾in (22cm) high 28½oz

$7,700-8,400   **DUK**

A late-19thC Anglo-Indian Raj Period silver claret pitcher or ewer, Bangalore, retailed by A. Bhicajee and Co., Bombay, the curved handle chased as a cobra, hinged domed lid of conforming shape surmounted by a figure of a snake charmer, the body with a center band of Swami pattern with nine gods upon their vehicles (vahana), such as Kalki upon a horse, Yama upon a water buffalo, Indra upon an elephant, Parvati upon a lion, Durga upon a tiger, Nirrti upon a man, Shiva upon Nandi the bull, Shiva as Bhairava upon a dog, and Agni upon a ram, each within shaped vignettes against a textured ground between borders of palmettes, the plain areas with traces of a satinized ground, stamped underneath "A. BHICAJEE&Co, BOMBAY, SILVER."

ca. 1890   11¾in (30cm) high 25¼oz

$6,000-7,500   **CA**

A silver claret pitcher trophy for the Royal Albert Yacht Club, with hinged lid, foliate scroll handle, the front with a coat of arms in a cartouche, a presentation inscription on the side, on a raised circular foot, unmarked.

ca. 1900   16in (40.5cm) high 73⅞oz

$3,000-3,500   **CM**

SILVER & METALWARE

A George II silver brandy pan, by George Greenhill Jones, London, with a turned wood handle.

1728   *6¾in (17cm) long 3oz*

$700-800   **WW**

A large George II silver brandy warmer, by George Bulman, Newcastle, the handle with a turned and ebonized fruitwood grip, dents, handle possibly repaired.

1739   *6¾in (17cm) diam 26⅞oz*

$2,200-2,700   **CHOR**

A George IV silver brandy pan on stand with burner, by Emes and Barnard, London, plain lip, turned wood baluster handle, the pull-off cover with a fluted wood finial with foliate mounts, circular stand, on three fluted scroll legs, with a burner, later burner cover.

1821   *9in (23cm) high 23oz*

$1,400-1,700   **WW**

A George III silver wine funnel, by Peter & Ann Bateman, London, reeded borders, plain side clip, tapering spout, maker's mark party worn, signs of repair, funnel has been cut down, fine surface scratches.

1798   *4¼in (11cm) high 2⅜oz*

$250-310   **WW**

A Scottish George III silver wine funnel, Edinburgh, reeded border, with three spike supports, maker's mark worn, possibly "F," with detachable unmarked cheesecloth ring.

5in (12.5cm) high 2¾oz

$400-475   **WW**

A George III silver wine funnel, by Thomas Robins, London, with thread border, crested.

1804   *6¾in (17cm) high 6½oz*

$250-310   **CHOR**

A George III silver wine funnel, by Elizabeth Morley, London, reeded border, plain side clip, tapering spout, with a cheesecloth ring.

1810   *5½in (14cm) high 3¼oz*

$300-375   **WW**

Judith Picks

Desirability in any context is never an entirely objective thing, and that certainly applies to antiques. Of course, objective factors always come into play: age, rarity, aesthetics, craftsmanship, etc, and any combination of them, are invariably relevant. However, there is often something else that transforms desirability from "oh, I really like that," to "oh gosh, I really love that" ... and that is very much the case for me with this little salmon-handle silver corkscrew. As to why, well it is quite simple really: it is nostalgia. As a small child growing up in the 1950s and early-1960s in the Scottish Borders, I vividly remember a local man, Freddie, knocking on our front door every Friday and selling my mother a whole salmon (one of a few my mother could chose from that were discretely hung on the inside lining of the large raincoat he always wore, regardless of the weather). Later that evening at supper, my father, having returned from work, and the salmon having been duly cooked, would always say, "gosh Bertha, this salmon is absolutely delicious, where did you get it?," and she would always reply, "from the fishmongers in town, Andrew." As I well knew, even as a little girl, it was a barefaced lie, and justified by my mother on the grounds that she did not want to upset my dad—he being an Elder of the Church—with the fact that he had just indirectly contributed to Freddie's ill-gotten gains! Basically, we lived close to the Tweed River, fishing from which required a license, and Freddie—a poacher—most certainly did not have one! Indeed, I learned in later life that he got caught red-handed, and in addition to a fine was slapped with an injunction that banned him from going within 50yds of the Tweed!

An Edwardian novelty silver corkscrew, by Henry Wells, Shrewsbury, Birmingham, the handle modeled as a salmon, with textured scale decoration, steel worm, in a fitted case.

1901   *4½in (11.5cm) wide*

$1,250-1,500   **WW**

A George III silver wine label, by Hester Bateman, London, of pierced urn form, with ribbon-tied swags and a pierced lower swag border, incised "BRANDY."

ca. 1790   2in (5cm) wide ¼oz
$300-375   WW

A George III silver wine label, by John Rich, London, of crescent and urn form, with pierced garlands and reeded borders, incised "WHITE WINE."

ca. 1790   2in (5cm) wide ⅜oz
$550-625   WW

A George III silver armorial wine label, by John McDonald, London, modeled as a walking dog, with engraved decoration, on a rectangular banner, incised "PORT."

ca. 1800   2¼in (5.5cm) wide ¼oz
$1,600-1,900   WW

A George III silver wine label, by William Fountain, London, with reeded border, incised "BOUSFIELD."

1815   1¾in (4.5cm) wide ¼oz
$550-625   WW

A George III silver wine label, by John Riley, London, with reeded border, incised "BRONTI."

1817   1½in (4cm) wide ¼oz
$375-450   WW

A George III silver wine label, by Edward Farrell, London, with a Bacchanalian cherub and vine decoration, pierced "BARSAC."

1817   2¼in (6cm) wide ⅝oz
$700-800   WW

A George IV provincial silver wine label, by James Barber and Co., York, with reeded border, the corners with shell motifs, incised and blackened "MADEIRA."

ca. 1820   1¾in (4.5cm) wide ¼oz
$300-375   WW

An early-19thC Scottish provincial silver wine label, by William Jamieson, Aberdeen, with canted corners and reeded border, incised "MADEIRA."

ca. 1830   1¾in (4.5cm) wide ¼oz
$250-310   WW

An early-19thC "Anti Corn Law League" silver wine label, by Mordan, with sheaves of corn, a bale of wool and a cornucopia, embossed "FREE," pierced "LISBON."

2¼in (5.5cm) wide ¼oz
$340-400   WW

SILVER & METALWARE

A George III silver meat dish and Old Sheffield plated cover, by Joseph Angell, London, gadroon and foliate shell border, engraved with an armorial and crests, the fluted domed cover with a foliate handle and gadroon and foliate border.

The arms are those of Hamilton quartering Kelso.

1816　　　　*22¾in (58cm) wide 101oz*
$3,200-3,700　　　　**WW**

A pair of George IV Old Sheffield silver-plated three-branch candelabra, by Matthew Boulton, Birmingham, elaborately cast on tapering reeded columns, on circular spreading feet, twin sun mark on the bases.

ca. 1820　　　　*25¼in (64cm) high*
$1,000-1,250　　　　**CA**

A pair of silver-plated candelabra, by Elkington, the three lights with detachable nozzles, shaped shell shoulders and foliate branches, conforming stems, raised on stepped square bases, with stag crest engraving, tarnishing throughout, one slightly unsteady.

1846　　　　*17in (43cm) high*
$500-625　　　　**SWO**

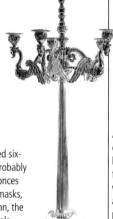

An Italian silver-plated six-light candelabrum, probably 19thC, the foliate sconces above winged satyr masks, tapering fluted column, the tripod base with female busts above bosses and lion-paw feet.

31in (78.5cm) high
$300-375　　　　**WW**

A Victorian silver-plated tea urn, with heavily chased floral decoration, floral and beaded borders, the pull-off domed lid with a knop floral finial, leaf-capped reeded handles, the spout with shell handle and ivory insulator, raised on a rounded square base, on four foliate capped paw feet, with detachable silver-plated heating rod holder.

CITES certification no. 75P5C8T4

17in (43cm) high
$475-525　　　　**L&T**

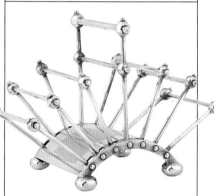

An electroplated letter rack, by Christopher Dresser (1834-1904) for Hukin & Heath, London, stamped "H&H/2555," with registration lozenge, dated.

1881　　　　*5in (12.5cm) high*
$1,700-2,000　　　　**L&T**

A 20thC silver-plated and frosted glass table lamp, cast as a composite column with ivy twisting around the fluted body, on a reeded domed base with scrolling foliate feet.

23¾in (60.5cm) high
$375-450　　　　**WW**

A 20thC silver-plated Corinthian column table lamp, on a rectangular base with laurel wreaths, a stag head crest and motto "Je Suis Prest" on one side, a monogram on the reverse, on a stepped foot.

24½in (62cm) high
$400-475　　　　**WW**

A pair of silver-plated table centerpieces, modeled after Pierre Jules Mene's "Two Whippets at Play," the palm trees each supporting a cut-glass bowl and three glass-lined hanging baskets.

21¾in (55cm) high
$1,500-1,700　　　　**CHOR**

A North European pewter ewer, possibly German, with a dragon-type handle and spout, domed cover, on a stepped circular foot, with banded decoration.

For a similar ewer in brass, see Victoria & Albert Museum, accession no. 539-1869.

ca. 1500   *11½in (29cm) high*

$800-950   **WW**

A 17th/18thC pewter goblet, bell-shaped bowl with a slightly flared rim, on a short stem and spreading foot, with banded decoration, touchmark on the base.

For a similar example in white brass, see Gentle and Field, "Domestic Metalwork 1640-1820," ACC Art Books (1999), page 280, figure 5.

3in (7.5cm) high

$550-625   **WW**

A silver-color metal egg-shaped urn, with flame finial on the cover, on a pedestal base, the ring handles each with a Georgian gold set memoriam ring.

$1,250-1,500   **CHOR**

A large 19thC Victorian copper braising pot and cover, fitted lid with center handle, with handles on the sides.

22½in (57cm) wide

$875-1,000   **L&T**

A late-19thC gilt-copper electrotype tankard, by Elkington Mason & Co., Birmingham, S-scroll handle, the hinged lid with a baby Bacchus finial, after a 17thC ivory tankard with silver mounts, representing the drunken Silenus, the underside inscribed "From the original ivory in the possession of Henry Bedford Esqr, executed by Elkington Mason & Co. 1348."

While first and foremost a commercial enterprise that produced electroplated artistic and domestic wares for retail to the general public, Birmingham-based Elkington, Mason & Co. (from 1861, just Elkington & Co.) also formed a relationship with the precursor of the Victoria & Albert Museum—the South Kensington Museum—to produce facsimile copies of museum artifacts for educational purposes. This, the Bedford tankard, was the third project between them, and is the only known example where the name of the owner was credited on the piece. Francis Bedford (1815-94) had loaned the 17thC tankard to the museum in 1854. He was the founder of the Photographic Society of London (later the Royal Photographic Society). Prince Albert had commissioned him to photograph items in the Royal Collection and had purchased an image of the tankard taken by Bedford, which still resides in the Royal Collections today—RCIN 29061112. Elkington made various options available for this tankard: from copper, to more expensive gilt or parcel-gilt.

ca. 1860   *11½in (29cm) high*

$1,600-1,900   **L&T**

A mid-19thC Victorian copper dog collar, with serrated borders, inscribed "B.Ryall Warminster," with padlock and key.

6¾in (17cm) diam

$410-475   **WW**

A pair of 19thC French cast iron urns, painted green.

25¼in (64cm) high

$2,700-3,000   **L&T**

A pair of large 19thC copper hot water urns, each fitted with twin handles and a tap.

27½in (70cm) high

$1,800-2,100   **L&T**

A late-19thC novelty brass crab inkwell, of naturalistic form, opening to reveal a single inkwell reservoir.

7¾in (19.5cm) wide

$1,400-1,600   **L&T**

SILVER & METALWARE

A large copper kettle, the swing handle stamped "John Kidd," Reading, Pennsylvania, minor dents.

ca. 1795   *14¾in (37.5cm) high*

$1,600-2,000   **POOK**

An exceedingly rare copper saucepan and lid, marker's mark for John Lay (1791-1844), York, Pennsylvania.

This is possibly the only known example.

14½in (37cm) diam

$14,000-17,500   **POOK**

A rare pewter beaker, bearing the touch of Simon Edgell, Philadelphia, Pennsylvania.

Fewer than 12 signed Edgell pieces are known. It may be the first marked American beaker. See Herr, "Pewter in Pennsylvania Churches," PA German Society (1995), figure 94.

ca. 1730   *4¼in (11cm) high*

$10,000-12,500   **POOK**

A pewter pint mug, bearing the touch of Robert Bonning (Bonynge), Boston, Massachusetts, the body engraved "The Gift of Mr. William Johnson to the Church in Southborough 1747."

4¾in (12cm) high

$11,000-14,000   **POOK**

A pewter canteen, bearing the touch of Johann Christoph Heyne, Lancaster, Pennsylvania.

Similar examples can be found in Laughlin, "Pewter in America," Barre (1971), figure 250, and Montgomery, "A History of American Pewter," Winterthur Museum (1973), page 195.

ca. 1770   *5½in (14cm) high*

$5,000-6,200   **POOK**

A pewter creamer, attributed to William Will, Philadelphia, with engraved monogram.

See Hamilton, "The Pewter of William Will," Winterthur Portfolio 7 (1972), figure 21.

ca. 1775   *4¼in (11cm) high*

$2,700-3,350   **POOK**

A very rare late-18thC Queen Anne pewter teapot, bearing the Love touchmark, Philadelphia.

Only a few Love teapots are known.

7¼in (18.5cm) high

$15,000-19,000   **POOK**

A pewter quart tankard, bearing the touch of Parks Boyd, Philadelphia.

Illustrated in "Pewter in American Life," Pewter Collectors Club (1984), page 30.

ca. 1805   *7½in (19cm) high*

$10,000-12,500   **POOK**

A pewter nursing bottle, bearing the touch of Thomas Boardman, Hartford, Connecticut.

Illustrated in Hornsby, "Pewter of the Western World," Schiffer (1998).

ca. 1840   *6½in (16.5cm) high*

$1,000-1,250   **POOK**

An enamel snuffbox, possibly Battersea, painted with a butterfly above flowers, including a pink rose, the corners with single sprays, including a tulip, the interior cover with a single butterfly, with gilt-metal mounts.

ca. 1755-60   2¾in (7cm) wide
$750-875   **WW**

A French enamel silver-mounted snuffbox, decorated with a raised gilt design of hearts enclosing single flower or fruit sprays, reserved on a pale yellow ground with pink striations, the silver with Paris marks, including a possible "TB" maker's mark, some cracking, repair on interior.

ca. 1765-75   2½in (6.5cm) wide
$375-500   **WW**

A large Bilston enamel snuffbox, possibly emblematic of "Travel," the cover depicting a figure sitting at a table before a stone column titled "Janus," a winged figure holding the staff of Asclepius, a ship visible in the background and a globe in the bottom right corner, the sides with floral panels reserved on a dark blue ground with raised white enameling, some good restoration.

ca. 1765   3¼in (8.5cm) wide
$375-500   **WW**

A polychrome enamel snuffbox, by J. F. Bautte & Cie, Geneva, with polychrome enameled flowers, birds, and figures in a scrolling foliate ground, the lid lip signed "J. F. BAUTTE & CIE A GENEVE" with unidentified control mark, heavy losses in the sitting figure on the cover and back edge, light scratches and wear.

J. F. Bautte & Cie was a celebrated Swiss jeweler and watchmaker, particularly known for its fine enamel work. The company found fame under Jean François Bautte (1772-1837), who was apprenticed into the enamel and jewelry trade from the age of 12 and, by the age of 20, was making his own pieces under the apprenticeship of watch case makers Jacques-Dauphin Moulinié and Jean François Blanchot in Geneva. Between 1804 and 1808, Bautte worked in partnership with Moulinié, after which Jean-Gabriel Moynier joined the partnership, and the company traded as Moulinié, Bautte & Moynier until 1821, when Mouliné retired. Between 1821 and 1826, the company traded as Bautte & Moynier. In the 1830s, Bautte traded under his sole name J. F. Bautte until his death in 1837, after which the company continued to trade under the direction of Bautte's son, Jacques, who continued to enjoy the patronage of many royal and asristocratic customers, including Queen Victoria.

ca. 1826-50   2½in (6.5cm) wide 1½oz
$4,300-5,000   **DN**

A rare Birmingham enamel "Combat" snuffbox, the top molded with a Cavalier spaniel pinning down a cat while in playful assault with a larger tabby cat, the dog's collar inscribed "Mr RC," the cover decorated with Venus on the back of a dolphin, being attended by Cupid, within a yellow and puce scrolled cartouche, some good restoration.

ca. 1765   3¼in (8.5cm) wide
$3,100-3,700   **WW**

A late-18th/early-19thC English enamel snuffbox, possibly London, molded with flutes and finely painted with flowers on a rich green ground, with elaborately turned gilt-metal mounts.

2½in (6.5cm) wide
$4,000-4,500   **WW**

A 19thC French gold and enamel snuffbox, set with an enamel miniature depicting The Three Graces festooning an urn, within a border of cushion-shaped diamonds, on an olive green guilloché enamel ground, the borders with green and white enamel decoration, the side panels spaced with urns, the base similarly decorated, partial French guarantee, maker's and décharge marks, with a fitted case stamped Garrard & Co.

3¼in (8.5cm) wide 6½oz
$16,000-19,000   **WW**

A 19thC French gold and enamel snuffbox, the lid set with a portrait of a lady in 18thC dress wearing pearls, possibly Marie Antoinette, within a dotted white border, on a ground of red guilloché enamel, the outer edge with a further border of white enamel and floral scrollwork in three-color gold, the sides and base of similar design, French assay and maker's mark, with a fitted case stamped Garrard & Co.

3¼in (8.5cm) wide 10⅝oz
$21,000-25,000   **WW**

A Staffordshire enamel patch box, in the form of a pocket watch (faux montre), the painted dial with two movable metal hands, the reverse painted with figures beside a tower in a harbor setting, within a polychrome scroll border, fitted with a metal suspension hook.

ca. 1770-80   2¼in (5.5cm) diam

$1,500-1,900   **WW**

A late-18thC English enamel patch box, inscribed to the top "A Trifle from Salisbury" within a pink and blue border, the sides in a pale pink, some restoration.

1½in (4cm) wide

$190-250   **WW**

A late-18thC Staffordshire enamel patch box, inscribed with the verse "Have Communion with few ... And speak evil of none," on a solid pink ground.

1½in (4cm) wide

$250-310   **HT**

A late-18th/early-19thC English enamel commemorative patch box, painted on the cover with a laurel wreath enclosing the inscription "British Gratitude to Nelson's Valour," reserved on a blue ground within a white bead border, restoration.

1½in (4cm) wide

$250-310   **WW**

An English enamel scent bottle, painted on two sides with courting couples within gilt scroll borders, reserved on a paneled ground of raised decoration over pink, white, yellow, and blue, with a gilt-metal scroll stopper, some good restoration.

ca. 1760-80   3½in (9cm) high

$625-750   **WW**

A South Staffordshire enamel scent bottle case, painted with small floral panels reserved on a green ground with flower-head motifs, the interior fitted with a small glass scent bottle and stopper.

ca. 1770-80   2¼in (5.5cm) high

$300-375   **WW**

A Bilston enamel double scent bottle case, decorated with raised flower sprays on a pink linen ground, the interior fitted with two narrow glass scent bottles with stoppers, minor restoration, chips, crack in base.

ca. 1770-80   2½in (6.5cm) high

$625-750   **WW**

An early-19thC Limoges enamel scent bottle, the black ground painted in white with gilt strapwork, the base seal engraved with a coronet and an initial, the hinged cover opening to reveal the original stopper, the silver mounts with traces of original gilding.

3¾in (9.5cm) high

$625-750   **HT**

A Victorian silver and enamel scent bottle, by Saunders and Shepherd, London, the front enameled with primroses, with a screw-off cover.

1889   2¾in (7cm) high 1oz

$400-450   **WW**

A Bilston enamel bonbonnière, modeled as a Cavalier spaniel recumbent on a green tasseled cushion, its coat decorated with black patches, the base painted with a lady sitting on a riverbank beneath a tree with a small dog on her lap.

ca. 1760-80   *2¼in (5.5cm) wide*

$625-750   **WW**

A Bilston enamel bird bonbonnière, modeled as a finch, with russet wings and a lilac breast beneath a black cap, the base decorated with a puce diaper pattern.

ca. 1760-80   *1¾in (4.5cm) high*

$800-950   **WW**

A South Staffordshire enamel bonbonnière and cover, naturalistically modeled and painted as an apple, minor repainting, surface cracks and scratches.

ca. 1770   *2¼in (5.5cm) high*

$375-450   **TEN**

A South Staffordshire enamel bonbonnière, naturalistically modeled as a peach, small chip, hairline cracks, cover with dent, possibly a manufacturing fault.

ca. 1770   *2in (5cm) high*

$375-450   **TEN**

A small enamel fruit bonbonnière, modeled as an apple, decorated with russet patches on a yellow ground, the underside painted with a brown stem.

ca. 1770-90   *1¼in (3cm) high*

$300-375   **WW**

A South Staffordshire enamel hinged box and cover, of egg form, with gilt-metal mounts, with decorated reserves of river scenes on a pink ground, hairline cracks, light wear.

1¾in (4.5cm) high

$275-325   **DN**

A late-18thC Staffordshire enamel box, of Lord Byron interest, painted with Sèvres-style floral bouquets, the lid interior with a butterfly, with a handwritten label on the underside "Given to my paternal Grandfather & Mother by Lord Byron about 1796."

2¼in (5.5cm) diam

$800-950   **SWO**

A Swiss gold and enamel octagonal hinged box, by J. F. Bautte & Cie, Geneva, decorated with red, green, white, and blue enamel flower heads and foliage in Ottoman style, stamped "BC" with a star above and an oval shape below within a lozenge-shaped punch, later mirror, chips, several knocks.

ca. 1826-50   *3½in (9cm) wide 3½oz*

$8,400-9,200   **DN**

A silver and enamel dressing table box, by the Adie Brothers, Birmingham, the hinged cover with purple enamel decoration, on four bracket feet, the interior velvet and silk lined.

1927   *5½in (14cm) wide*

$250-310   **WW**

A pair of large Staffordshire enamel candlesticks, with detachable sconces, decorated with panels of figures in harbor settings and beside Classical ruins, all within blue scroll borders, reserved on a deep pink ground.

ca. 1770   12in (30.5cm) high
$1,600-1,900   **WW**

A pair of South Staffordshire enamel vasiform cassolettes, with gilt goat-mask handles, the reversible tops as finials and candle nozzles, painted with figures in landscape on a green ground with blue and gilt scrollwork, on cylindrical columns, stepped square bases, and ball feet, one cover probably a replacement.

ca. 1770   11½in (29cm) high
$1,250-1,500   **TEN**

Three English enamel portrait plaques, relating to the American Revolution, printed in manganese with likenesses of Admiral Rodney, General Clinton, and Lord Cornwallis, each titled in a banner beneath the portrait, mounted in narrow metal frames with suspension rings.

Henry Clinton was commander-in-chief of North America from 1778-82; George Brydges Rodney was ordered to the West Indies in late 1779 by way of Gibraltar, where, in January 1780, he defeated the Spanish at the battle of Saint Vincent. Charles Cornwallis inflicted an embarrassing defeat on the American army in 1780 at the Battle of Camden, although he surrendered his army at Yorktown the following year after a series of disagreements with Clinton.

ca. 1780   3¼in (8.5cm) high
$1,900-2,200   **WW**

An English enamel plaque, of Masonic interest, painted with a goddess, probably Demeter, holding three ears of corn in one hand and a sacred heart in the other, with clasped hands below, in a narrow gilt-metal mount with a suspension ring.

ca. 1800   3in (7.5cm) high
$550-700   **WW**

An early- to mid-19thC Birmingham enamel plaque, printed and hand-colored with the profile portrait of a man with a long white beard, in a medallion inscribed "Grand Lodge of Modern Druids * Established at Walsall 1812," within an oak leaf wreath, restoration.

3¼in (8.5cm) high
$625-750   **WW**

An English School enamel portrait miniature of Queen Victoria, after Franz Xaver Winterhalter, in a gilt-metal frame with scrolling border.

ca. 1843   2in (5cm) high
$1,500-1,900   **CA**

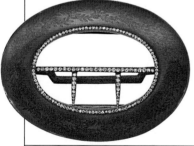

A Russian Fabergé silver-gilt, blue enamel, and diamond belt buckle, by Henrik Wigstrom, 88 Zolotniki, blue enamel over a foliate swag band ground, with a rose-cut diamond set border and clasp.

ca. 1900   3¼in (8.5cm) wide 1½oz
$6,000-7,500   **DN**

An early 20thC Russian gold, ivory, and red enamel small pipe, by Erik August Kollin, the gold bands engraved with foliate swags, the body with translucent red enamel and ivory screw fitting, surface scratches, no mouth piece.

Ivory Act certification no. 3GETT4K4

2¼in (5.5cm) long ½oz
$4,000-4,500   **DN**

An early 20thC French enamel, diamond, and tortoiseshell haircomb, the pale blue guilloché enamel with a white enameled border, with applied rose-cut diamond-set garlands interspaced by two pairs of rose-cut diamond and white-enameled tulip-shaped motifs between, stamped with French poinçons and numbered "1547," blonde tortoiseshell teeth, with a later Cartier Paris comb case, damage on box.

4in (10cm) wide 1⅝oz
$7,500-8,500   **DN**

A George III commemorative silver Battle of Trafalgar vinaigrette, by John Hart & Co., Birmingham, the hinged cover with engraved lozenge decoration and a center cartouche, opening to reveal a pierced and embossed silver-gilt grille with a scene of HMS "Victory" facing left, and embossed "Victory" and "Trafalgar, Octr 21, 1805."

1805   *1¼in (3cm) long ½oz*
$2,500-3,100   WW

A George III commemorative silver Nelson vinaigrette, by Matthew Linwood, Birmingham, with an engraved portrait of Nelson within an oval border, inscribed "England Expects Every Man Will Do His Duty," with reeded decoration, plain thumbpiece, the underside with a foliate motif, the hinged cover opening to reveal a pierced and embossed silver-gilt grille with scene of HMS "Victory" facing left, and chased "Victory" and "Trafalgar Ocr. 21. 1805."

1805   *1¼in (3cm) long ½oz*
$3,700-4,300   WW

A large George III silver military vinaigrette, by William Ellerby, London, with wriggle-work decoration, plain thumbpiece, the hinged cover opening to reveal a pierced and engraved silver-gilt grille, with flags, cannons and drums, and foliate decoration.

1805   *2in (5cm) wide ¾oz*
$500-625   WW

ESSENTIAL REFERENCE—BATTLE OF TRAFALGAR

Fought on October 21, 1805, just seven years after the Battle of the Nile (see right), the Battle of Trafalgar was a naval engagement fought between the British Royal Navy and the combined fleets of the French and Spanish navies during the Napoleonic Wars (1803-15). It was also, arguably, the most decisive victory in the entire history of war at sea.

As part of Napoleon's plans to invade England, the French and Spanish fleets combined to take control of the English Channel and provide Napoleon's Grande Armée safe passage to land on the English coast. To do this, the allied fleet under French admiral Villeneuve set sail from the port of Cadiz in the south of Spain on October 18, 1805. Three days later they encountered the British fleet under Admiral Lord Nelson, recently assembled to meet this threat, in the Atlantic along the southwest coast of Spain, at Cape Trafalgar.

Undaunted by having only 27 ships-of-the-line, compared to 33 in the combined French and Spanish fleets, Nelson brought the enemy to action in a ferocious battle that lasted less than three hours. Employing a brilliant strategy, which marked a significant departure from prevailing naval tactical orthodoxy, Nelson split the enemy line of battle in two places, isolating the rear from the French flag ship, "Bucentaure," resulting in the loss of 22 allied ships while the British lost none. However, the tactic had exposed the leading ships in the British lines to intense fire during their approach. Nelson's own, HMS "Victory," led the front column and was almost knocked out of action, while Nelson himself, highly visible on deck, was shot by a French musketeer firing from the mizzen of the French ship "Redoubtable"—a death that overshadowed the magnitude of a victory that resulted in the near-total destruction of French and Spanish sea power (the former taking many years to reassert itself; the latter never recovering).

A large George III commemorative silver-gilt Nelson vinaigrette, by Matthew Linwood, Birmingham, with an engraved portrait of Nelson within an oval border, inscribed "England Expects Every Man Will Do His Duty," with reed and dot decoration, the underside with a foliate motif, the hinged cover opening reveal a pierced and embossed silver-gilt grille with scene of HMS "Victory" facing right, inscribed "Victory" and embossed "Trafr. Octr. 21. 1805."

1805   *1½in (4cm) wide ⅞oz*
$8,500-10,000   WW

A George III commemorative silver Nelson vinaigrette, by John Shaw, Birmingham, with engraved foliate and wriggle-work decoration with a lozenge motif, the hinged cover opening to reveal a pierced and embossed silver-gilt grille with a scene of HMS "Victory" facing right within foliate decoration, embossed "Victory" and engraved "Immortal Nelson."

The majority of Nelson commemorative vinaigrettes were made by Matthew Linwood, so it is unusual to come across one made by John Shaw.

1805   *1¼in (3cm) wide ½oz*
$1,250-1,700   WW

ESSENTIAL REFERENCE—BATTLE OF THE NILE

Made in 1806, a year after Nelson's most famous victory at the Battle of Trafalgar in 1805 (see left), this vinaigrette retrospectively commemorates Nelson's earlier victory at the Battle of the Nile, in 1798. Having spent most of that summer cruising the Eastern Mediterranean looking for the French Fleet under Vice Admiral Brueys, the Royal Navy under Nelson (then a Rear Admiral) finally came upon it in a well-protected anchorage in Aboukir Bay, 15 miles west of Alexandria. It being late in the day when first sighted, Brueys assumed he had until the following morning to fully prepare for an attack. However, Nelson, with typical daring, amazed both his own captains as well as the French by ordering his ships directly into the bay. The decisive moment came just after 10 p.m., when the French flagship "L'Orient" blew up in a tremendous explosion and, when dawn broke, the French annihilation became readily apparent. With nine of their badly damaged ships captured and another four destroyed, it was a glorious victory for Nelson, and one of the greatest in British naval history.

A George III commemorative silver Battle of the Nile vinaigrette, possibly by John Brough, London, engraved with a recumbent lion and oval shield, initialed, the sides with Greek-key decoration, silver-gilt interior, with foliate decoration and an Egyptian Sphinx bearing the head of Napoleon Bonaparte.

1806   *1½in (4cm) wide ¾oz*
$3,000-3,500   WW

A George III silver military vinaigrette, by William Ellerby, London, with engine-turned decoration, plain thumbpiece, the hinged cover opening to reveal a pierced and engraved silver-gilt grille, with a flag, cannon and drums, and foliate decoration.

1808   *1½in (4cm) wide ¾oz*

$700-800   **WW**

A Scottish provincial vinaigrette, by William Jamieson, Aberdeen, hinged lid set with an agate, opening to a pierced silver-gilt grille with floral and foliate detail, marked "WJ," "ABD," "WJ."

1½in (4cm) wide

$1,500-1,900   **L&T**

A George III silver vinaigrette, by John Shaw, Birmingham, with engraved scales enclosing an initialed panel, the hinged cover opening to reveal a hinged foliate-engraved gilt grille.

1812   *1½in (4cm) wide*

$170-220   **HT**

A George III silver and parcel-gilt vinaigrette, maker's mark "O&S," Birmingham.

1818   *1¼in (3cm) wide*

$160-200   **WHP**

An early-19thC gold vinaigrette, modeled as a traveling case, the hinged cover with a carrying handle and inscribed "Souvenir," opening to reveal a pierced hinged grille.

ca. 1820   *¾in (2cm) wide ⅛oz*

$1,100-1,500   **WW**

A George IV silver and parcel-gilt vinaigrette, maker's mark "JW," Birmingham.

1823   *1in (2.5cm) wide*

$170-220   **WHP**

ESSENTIAL REFERENCE—THE ALL-SEEING EYE

Also known as the "Eye of Providence," the All-Seeing Eye is a symbol that depicts an eye, often (but not always) enclosed in a triangle and invariably surrounded by rays of light; it represents divine providence and the eye of God watching over humanity. In addition to being strongly associated with Christianity, especially since the Renaissance, the "Eye" has also featured in many national flags and numerous coats of arms around the world, notably in Eastern Europe and to a lesser extent in South America and Africa. Perhaps its most symbolically significant uses have been its inclusion in the original publication of France's "Declaration of the Rights of Man and of the Citizen" (1789) and, seven years prior to that, in 1782, on the reverse of the Great Seal of the United States—with the latter leading to its most prominent and enduring appearance: on the US one dollar bill. The reason for its inclusion in the engraved decoration on the 1829 vinaigrette shown here, however, is almost certainly because of its role, since 1797, in Freemason iconography—their belief being that all humanity's thoughts and deeds are always observed by the "Great Architect of the Universe," aka God.

A George IV silver vinaigrette, by Nathaniel Mills, Birmingham, bright-cut engraved with the All-Seeing Eye and "May it watch over you" within a foliate border, the hinged cover opening to reveal a foliate scroll pierced and engraved grille, the majority with original gilding.

1829   *1½in (4cm) wide*

$420-475   **HT**

A William IV silver-gilt "castle-top" vinaigrette, by Nathaniel Mills, Birmingham, depicting Abbotsford House, Melrose (home of Sir Walter Scott), with hinged lid and foliate pierced grille, engine-turned base with a rectangular cartouche engraved "CJE 7 April 1849."

1837   *1½in (4cm) wide*

$700-800   **JON**

An early-Victorian silver "castle-top" vinaigrette, by Gervase Wheeler, Birmingham, of bag form, the hinged cover with a scene of Windsor Castle, the cushioned sides with foliate decoration on a matted background, with a chain and finger ring, the underside with initials, the interior with a pierced silver-gilt foliate scroll grille.

1840   1¼in (3cm) wide ½oz
$625-750   **WW**

A Victorian silver vinaigrette, by Edward Smith, Birmingham, with wavy border, decorated scrolls and a center flower, with a pierced gilt interior.

1846   ⅝oz
$190-220   **CHOR**

A Victorian curly horn vinaigrette, the lid with embossed thistle decoration and collet set in the center with a citrine, opening to a silver-gilt pierced grill with loop and suspension chain, unmarked.

2¼in (6cm) long
$625-750   **L&T**

A Victorian silver vinaigrette, by Frederick Marson, Birmingham, decorated with floral swags, with the Scott monument verso.

1864   2in (5cm) wide ¾oz
$300-375   **CHOR**

A Victorian novelty horseshoe vinaigrette/flask and stamp case, by Henry William Dee, London, the hinged cover by Jenner and Knewstub, London, 1877, overstamped with maker's mark of Henry Dee, gold horseshoe inlay on both sides, one side opening to reveal a scent/water flask, stamp slit on the base, ring attachment, silver-gilt interior, the other side with a pierced and engraved foliate scroll grille, stamp case in the center, bottle stopper in a stuck position, worn motto on cover.

1879   2in (5cm) high 2⅛oz
$2,200-2,700   **WW**

CLOSER LOOK—A VICTORIAN VINAIGRETTE

Echoed in the gilt grid, the three (two unseen) thistle panels alternating with the Celtic knots around the base are motifs most commonly associated with Scottish decoration—especially following its adoption as the national emblem by James III, King of Scotland 1460-88.

Scottish and Celtic motifs abound in this Edinburgh-made vinaigrette—the gilt grill is engraved and pierced with thistles. They are set within plant- or ropelike interlacing around the circumference.

More interlacing is employed around the bottom of the base. Easily adapted to different-size spaces, it is a recurring motif in the Celtic Revival decoration that reemerged in the mid-19thC and remained widely popular well into the early 20thC.

The three (the other two out of view) large Celtic knot panels around the circumference of the egg-shaped base, symbolize union and love.

A Victorian vinaigrette, by J. M. Talbot, Edinburgh, with chased panels of alternating thistles and Celtic knots, the lower section with an interlaced border, the gilt interior with an engraved and pierced thistle grill.

1896   2¼in (5.5cm) high 1½oz
$3,000-3,500   **L&T**

A Victorian novelty silver flower vinaigrette, by Edward Stockwell, London, modeled as a carnation spray, with a center flower, bud, and stem, the hinged cover opening to reveal a hinged pierced silver-gilt grille, in a fitted velvet-lined case, retailed by Ortner and Houle, St. James Street, London.

1882   4¼in (11cm) long 2⅝oz
$5,200-5,700   **WW**

A Victorian vinaigrette, Birmingham, for the Scottish market, formed as a miniature curly horn snuff mull, engraved collar, hinged coned lid set with a hardstone-formed cross, the gilt interior with a pierced and engraved grill.

1899   2in (5cm) long ¾oz
$550-700   **L&T**

A mid-18thC cow horn snuff mull, the foot rim mounts with scalloped decoration, scroll mount on top, the hinged lid with scalloped hinge and thumbpiece, with applied cartouche in center.

2½in (6.5cm) high

$1,250-1,700   **L&T**

A rare mid-18thC Continental Jacobite enamel hidden portrait snuffbox, tartan decoration on hinged lid, body, and base, the interior lined with mother-of-pearl disks on base and inner lid, with an oil on copper half-length portrait of Prince Charles Edward Stuart.

2½in (6.5cm) diam

$8,000-9,500   **L&T**

A mid-18thC Jacobite enamel portrait snuffbox, with silver rims, the interior of the lid with a half-length portrait of Prince Charles Edward Stuart, after Sir Robert Strange.

2½in (6.5cm) diam

$12,500-15,000   **L&T**

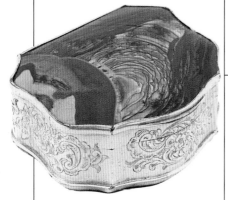

A German gilt-metal-mounted hardstone snuffbox and cover, engraved with Rococo scrolls and foliage, hardstone cracked, minor wear.

ca. 1760   *2½in (6.5cm) wide*

$375-450   **TEN**

An 18thC silver-mounted and lacquer snuffbox, inlaid with gold and silver scenes of a chateau and beehives, the underside of the base inlaid with a house.

4¼in (11cm) wide

$520-600   **WW**

A late-18thC gold and silver-mounted presentation tortoiseshell snuffbox, the cover and underside with a floral spray and radiating decoration, engraved mounts, the inside lip inscribed "From William Ford To His Friend The Honble Fitz Roy Stanhope," marks worn.

3¾in (9.5cm) wide

$875-1,000   **WW**

A Scottish provincial snuffbox, by Coline Alan, Aberdeen, with simple hinged cover, italic "AR" engraved on underside, marked "CA."

2¼in (5.5cm) high 3¼oz

$4,300-5,000   **L&T**

A late-18th/early-19thC George III white-metal-mounted cowrie shell snuffbox, the hinged cover with a coat of arms and initials "EG."

2½in (6.5cm) wide

$250-310   **ROS**

A late-18th/early-19thC gilt-brass-mounted tortoiseshell snuffbox, with engine-turned decoration, the gilt-brass-mounted interior inset with an enamel oval portrait depicting a gentleman with a wig and blue velvet jacket, with a shaped gilt-brass thumbpiece.

2¾in (7cm) diam

$450-500   **ROS**

A George III commemorative silver Nelson snuffbox, by John Shaw, Birmingham, with an engraved portrait of Nelson within an oval border, inscribed "England Expects Every Man Will Do His Duty," and with a banner "Trafalgar Oct 21. 1805," with reeded and dot decoration, the base with similar decoration and initials, plain thumbpiece, gilt interior.

1806   *2¼in (5.5cm) wide 1oz*

$3,100-3,700   WW

An early-19thC Continental gold snuffbox, with geometric engine-turned decoration, chased foliate scroll borders on a matted background, maker's mark "P.G."

1806   *2¾in (7cm) wide 1¾oz*

$1,900-2,200   WW

A late-George III silver snuffbox, by Phipps & Robinson, London, the hinged cover with scrolling foliate-engraved border, opening to a plain gilt interior.

1806   *2¾in (7cm) wide 3oz*

$190-220   HT

A George III 18ct-gold snuffbox, London, with chased foliate decoration on a reeded background, plain thumbpiece, maker's mark probably "T.H."

1807   *3in (7.5cm) wide 2¼oz*

$7,500-8,500   WW

A George III silver snuffbox, by William Weston, London, with wriggle-work decoration, center cartouche, plain thumbpiece, gilt interior.

1808   *2¼in (5.5cm) wide 1½oz*

$300-350   WW

A George III regimental silver table snuffbox, by A. J. Strachan, London, of drum form, with two flat flush-hinged covers engraved with a crown and a crest, the interior with two gilt compartments, engraved borders, the front engraved with the arms of the Cambridgeshire Regiment of Militia, on three lion-mask-capped paw feet.

1809   *3¾in (9.5cm) diam 11⅜oz*

$2,700-3,200   WW

A 19thC bronzed copper medal snuff box, of Napoleon interest, the lid decorated with a portrait bust of Napoleon, inscribed "Bonaparte Primus Consul Anno VIII," the base with Classical figures, along with a French silver and steel folding knife, scissor, and file tool, in the form of a Napoleon III coin, by Charles Louis Eloi Pernet, stamped "Eloi France."

2in (5cm) diam

$160-220   WW

A George III silver-gilt snuffbox, by Daniel Hockley, London, with engine-turned decoration, with a cast scene of an ancient Greek battle, foliate border, engraved crest on inside of hinged cover.

1810   *3¼in (8.5cm) wide 5¾oz*

$1,600-2,000   WW

A George III silver snuffbox, by Cocks & Bettridge, Birmingham, the hinged cover with engraved foliate decoration and a center cartouche, with bright-cut patterns on sides and base, plain thumbpiece.

1811   *2¼in (5.5cm) wide ⅞oz*

$250-310   WW

An early-19thC Continental tortoiseshell and piqué-work snuffbox, the pressed cover centered by hunting trophies in a landscape, the sides with hunting scenes.

3¼in (8.5cm) wide

$275-310   ROS

An early-19thC Scottish silver-mounted ram horn snuff mull, the lid with thistle-shaped hinge and a circular plaque engraved with Masonic set square and compass, the collar engraved "Jas Andrew 1820," unmarked.

3½in (9cm) long

$150-190   SOU

A George IV pollard oak snuffbox, the lid applied with a gilt-metal dog mount and foliate thumbpiece.

4in (10cm) wide

$250-310   TOV

An early-19thC French yew wood snuffbox, with yellow metal foliate borders, interior, and framework, inset in the hinged lid with a shell cameo depicting Poseidon holding a trident, unmarked.

3¼in (8.5cm) wide

$3,350-4,000   L&T

An early-19thC gold snuffbox, probably Swiss, engine-turned decoration, with a foliate three-color gold border, the cover with a vacant cartouche, the inside of the cover inscribed "Presented by A. J. Byron to his friend J MacGregor Mallock, M.D, Oct 1st 1826," marks partly worn.

A Captain A. J. Byrom, from the 16th Lancers, was present at the siege of Bhurtpore, Rajasthan, in 1826.

3in (7.5cm) wide 2⅞oz

$3,500-4,000   WW

An early-19thC German laquered papier-mâché snuffbox, attributed to Stobwasser, the lid painted with Cupid and Psyche, the interior titled in gilt "Amor and Psyche" and with red initials "St."

3¾in (9.5cm) diam

$450-550   WW

An early-19thC German laquered papier-mâché snuffbox, by Stobwasser, the lid painted with Venus and Cupid, the interior signed and numbered "Stobwassers Fabrik 3307," and titled "Schlafen de Venus."

3¾in (9.5cm) diam

$450-550   WW

An early-19thC German lacquered papier-mâché snuffbox, by Stobwasser, with a scene titled "La femme adultere," inscribed "A. Varotari, 3129" and stenciled "Stobwasser's Fabrik Braunschweig."

3½in (9cm) wide

$375-500   WW

A Victorian silver-gilt snuffbox, by John Tongue, Birmingham, the hinged cover with a raised scene of two hounds coursing, in a landscape setting, foliate and scroll border, the sides and base with engraved lattice decoration, foliate thumbpiece, the underside inscribed "F.LUNDI Newcastle on Tyne."

1838   2¾in (7cm) wide 2⅞oz

$550-625   WW

An early-Victorian silver engraved "castle-top" table snuffbox, by Edward Smith, Birmingham, heavy scroll foliate and engine-turned decoration, the hinged cover engraved with a view of Balmoral Castle, gilt interior, in a fitted case retailed by Garrard.

1838   4¼in (11cm) wide 9¼oz

$3,100-3,500   WW

A Victorian silver snuffbox, by Taylor & Perry, Birmingham, decorated with floral swags, dogs, and game animals, with a center cartouche, gilt interior.

1839   3¼in (8.5cm) wide 2¾oz

$220-275   CHOR

An early-Victorian silver snuffbox, by Francis Clark, Birmingham, engine-turned sides and base, the hinged cover with a foliate border.

1845   3¼in (8.5cm) wide 5¼oz

$750-875   WW

ESSENTIAL REFERENCE—GRACE DARLING

As a young woman of just 23 years old, Grace Darling assisted her father in saving the lives of nine people during the wreck of the SS "Forfarshire" on Big Harcar Rock, close to the Farne Islands off the coast of Northumberland, on September 7, 1838. Rowing out together in a simple coble boat (a traditional small open-top fishing boat), the pair fought through exceptionally rough seas, assisting numerous stricken passengers and returning them safely to Longstone. Such was Grace's subsequent fame, Queen Victoria—then still a young woman herself—sent her a personal gift of £50 ($60, a considerable sum in those days) in admiration of her heroic conduct at sea, while "The Times" newspaper of September 19, 1838, opined that "her actions formed an instance of heroism on the part of a female unequalled perhaps, and certainly not surpassed, by any on record."

An unusual early-Victorian commemorative silver Grace Darling snuffbox, by Nathaniel Mills, Birmingham, engraved with a panel depicting the heroine in a lifeboat rescuing sailors from a sinking ship, within deeply chased scrolling foliate borders, the base with engine-turned decoration, with a copy of "Grace Darling; or, The Heroine of The Fern Islands" by G. W. M. Reynolds, London (1839), tarnishing.

1838   2½in (6.5cm) wide 3oz

$5,000-6,200   GORL

A mid-19thC cow-horn snuffbox, with applied collar on body with inscription "HE THAT IS NAE FRIEND AT A PINCH, IS NO WORTH A SNUFF," the hinged lid with applied mounts, unmarked.

2in (5cm) high

$750-875   L&T

A 19thC novelty tortoiseshell and gold piqué-inlaid snuffbox, modeled in the form of a boat, with a hinged lid.

3¼in (8.5cm) long

$300-375   TOV

A 19thC Continental gold-mounted tortoiseshell snuffbox, probably German, the cover inlaid with flower sprays and two butterflies in four colors of gold, scroll thumbpiece.

2½in (6.5cm) wide

$625-750   ROS

A 19thC pressed composite and tortoiseshell circular snuffbox, the lid with a painted miniature depicting a shepherdess in a landscape.

3¼in (8.5cm) diam

$375-450   **TOV**

A rare Welsh folk-art horn snuffbox, in believed sheep horn, probably generational, with Masonic emblems, sgraffito decoration on base of farmhouse and "D P 1777 LATE TENANT of cae evan lloyd," the lid with "LLANVAIR BACH HOLYHEAD" and marriage initials "AP-AV" around an earlier scrolled monogram carved among a flowering vase, ax, and wheat sheaf, both sides featuring a Masonic square and compass, very minor losses in rim of lid.

3½in (9cm) wide

$1,250-1,500   **JON**

A 19thC novelty cow-horn snuff mull, modeled as a boot, with applied mount engraved "From a Friend TO JAMES CRUICKSHANK 1857," the hinged lid with applied crown and inscription, unmarked.

4in (10cm) long

$1,250-1,500   **L&T**

A 19thC Continental silver-gilt and silver-filigree snuffbox, probably Austro-Hungarian, mounted with filigree scroll decoration, gilt strap-work and foliate motifs, ropework border, marked "F" on the clasp, lacking feet.

2½in (6.5cm) wide 2¾oz

$300-375   **WW**

A Scottish Victorian Mauchlineware tartan snuffbox, painted with a loch scene on the cover, later titled on the interior.

ca. 1860   *3½in (9cm) wide*

$160-220   **WW**

A Victorian presentation book-form table snuffbox, by John Muirhead, Glasgow, the cover engraved with simulated tooling and a presentation inscription, reading "Presented to A Graham Esq. of Capellie, Captain of the 8th or Neilston Co R.R.V by the members of his Company, 30th December 1862," the spine engraved with soldiers at attention and crouched shooting with title "Chaucer" and a crest below, the base of the lower section engraved with a portrait of an officer, presumed to be Captain Graham.

1862   *6in (15cm) high 12¼oz*

$3,100-4,300   **L&T**

An early Victorian silver and micromosaic snuffbox, the micromosaic panel attributed to Giacomo Raffaelli (1753-1836), the silver box with a Rococo thumbpiece, engraved with scrolls and panels of differing machined decoration, the hinged lid with a circular micromosaic panel depicting the Doves of Pliny, with a bead outer border, the base inscribed "To S. Mc Culloch Esqr from Elizabeth Brown," the gilt-lined interior with Birmingham hallmarks for 1851 and maker's mark for Edward Smith.

4in (10cm) wide

$6,700-7,200   **WW**

ESSENTIAL REFERENCE—STOBWASSER

In 1740, in Lobenstein, master glazier Georg Siegmund Stobwasser (1717-76) and his wife had a son: Johann Heinrich Stobwasser. In 1757, after much experimentation, Johann Heinrich succeeded in producing a durable amber lacquer that enabled the family to establish a lacquerware factory in the town. Not a commercial success, the family moved to Braunschweig in 1763, attracted by numerous benefits offered by Duke Charles I of Brunswick to highly qualified artists and craftsmen as an inducement to settle in the city in the wake of the Seven Years' War. This new factory, located in Echternstrabe (the building still stands today), achieved a commercial breakthrough when the Braunschweig military ordered a large consignment of lacquered rifle stocks, bullet pouches, and drinking cups. However, it was when the Stobwassers started producing luxury goods, such as snuffboxes—such as the example shown here—that artistic acclaim and financial success really ensued.

Most of Stobwasser's exquisite lacquered artifacts were made of papier-mâché but also sometimes wood or sheet metal. As to decoration, they employed many well-known artists, notably Pascha Johan Friedrich Weitsch and his son Friedrich Georg, Christian Tuca, Hans Heinrich Jurgen Brandes, and Julius Carl Hermann Schroder. Subject matter ranged from landscapes, portraits (often of famous people), mythological or religious scenes, and also, occasionally, erotica. The growing demand across Europe for Stobwasser's exquisite wares enabled the family to open a branch in Berlin in 1772. After Georg Siegmund died in 1776, Johann Heinrich ran the factory on his own well into the 19thC, until his death in 1829. Subsequently, the factory continued in production until its eventual closure in 1863.

A 19thC papier-mâché snuffbox, by Stobwasser, painted with a young lady holding a wild bird, stamped in the interior and detailed "Lilis 2094."

2¼in (5.5cm) wide

$300-450   **TOV**

A Victorian silver double-sided "castle-top" card case, by Nathaniel Mills, Birmingham, the front with a scene of Windsor Castle, the reverse with a scene of Kenilworth Castle, within pierced foliate scroll decoration, in a fitted case retailed by Garrard.

1838   *3¾in (9.5cm) long 2⅝oz*
$1,000-1,250   **WW**

A Victorian silver double-sided "castle-top" card case, by Nathaniel Mills, Birmingham, the front with a raised scene of Windsor Castle, the reverse with a raised scene of Kenilworth Castle, within engine-turned tartan decoration, in a fitted case retailed by Garrard.

1838   *3½in (9cm) long 2⅛oz*
$1,000-1,250   **WW**

An engraved silver visiting card case, by Edward Smith, Birmingham.

1844   *3¼in (8.5cm) long*
$100-125   **CHOR**

A mid-19thC Persian lacquered visiting card case, painted in colors with gilt mythical beasts and peacocks, on a strawberry- and flower-strewn ground, with black velvet hinge, metal shield claspb and pale blue watered silk-fitted interior.

3¾in (9.5cm) wide
$150-190   **HT**

A 19thC gilt-metal-mounted agate card case, inlaid with a geometric design of varicolor agates, the mounts with engraved foliate decoration, with a seed pearl push-button clasp.

4¼in (11cm) long
$1,250-1,500   **WW**

A Gothic Revival silver-gilt and enamel card case, by Hillard and Thomason, engraved with stylized foliage panels and bands, in the manner of A. W. N. Pugin, set with center pale blue enamel heraldic panel on both sides, stamped mark "H & T Birmingham 1851."

1851   *3¾in (9.5cm) long 2½oz*
$625-750   **WW**

An Edwardian silver card case, by Deakin and Francis, Birmingham, with embossed foliate shell decoration on a matted background, with two vacant cartouches, in a fitted case.

1904   *4in (10cm) wide 2oz*
$300-375   **WW**

An embossed silver "castle-top" visiting card case, by Crisford & Norris Ltd, Birmingham, depicting Royal Windsor within a cartouche.

1906   *4in (10cm) wide*
$300-375   **CHOR**

An embossed silver visiting card case, by Crisford & Norris Ltd, Birmingham, depicting a collie dog sitting in a landscape.

1908   *4in (10cm) wide*
$250-310   **CHOR**

A Victorian silver and niello-work match safe, by Henry Dee, London, with a scene of a sitting man with a pipe and a man behind him, probably depicting Robinson Crusoe and Friday, the reverse with foliate decoration, the hinged cover opening to reveal a match compartment, striker, and lighting cord holder, with a turning wheel.

1872   *2in (5cm) long 1¼oz*
$1,500-1,900   **WW**

A 19thC Russian silver pocket combination vesta snuffbox, inlaid "Sergius" in rose gold, the gilt interior inscribed "This box was given to me by Prince Sergius Romanoffsky, Duc de Leuchtenberg, at Petersberg, December 1873. The Prince was killed in Bulgaria, October 1877 when serving on the staff with his cousin The Czarevitch," later engraved "Arthur Ellis, Grenadier Guards" on one end, the inside stamped "84 zolotnik" and St. Petersberg mark, lighter missing, vesta match strike rusted.

3¾in (9.5cm) wide 5⅝oz
$750-875   **SWO**

A Victorian novelty silver whistle match safe, by S. Mordan, London, with a ring attachment, hinged cover with a striker, engraved with a monogram.

1879   *2½in (6.5cm) long ¾oz*
$400-460   **WW**

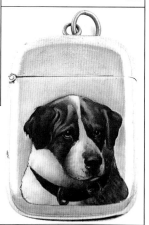

A Victorian silver and enamel match safe, by Sampson Mordan & Co., London, hinged cover with a ring attachment, the front enameled with a Saint Bernard dog.

1887   *2in (5cm) long ⅞oz*
$450-500   **WW**

A Victorian novelty silver and enamel match safe, probably by George Wilkinson, London, modeled as a fishing creel, the hinged cover polychrome-enameled with a landed pike, minor scratches.

1889   *1¾in (4.5cm) wide ⅝oz*
$1,500-1,900   **GORL**

A late Victorian silver and enamel match safe, by Minshull & Latimer, Birmingham, hinged cover with a ring attachment, the front enameled with a scene of a cricketer at the crease.

1900   *1¾in (4.5cm) long ¾oz*
$750-875   **WW**

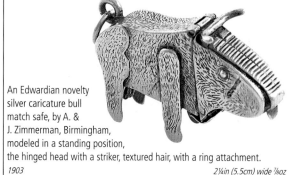

An Edwardian novelty silver caricature bull match safe, by A. & J. Zimmerman, Birmingham, modeled in a standing position, the hinged head with a striker, textured hair, with a ring attachment.

1903   *2¼in (5.5cm) wide ⅞oz*
$875-1,000   **WW**

An Edwardian 9ct-gold match safe, by Payton, Pepper & Sons Ltd, Birmingham, engraved foliate scroll decoration, with a ring attachment, the front with initials.

1912   *2in (5cm) long ¾oz*
$500-625   **WW**

A rare late-19thC Anglo-Indian Raj Period silver cigarette case, attributed to Heerappa Boochena, Poona, with an embossed hunting scene of a caparisoned elephant with a rider and two men in a houdah, one with a gun and the other a spear, all before a tiger set within a landscape, the reverse with chased Cutch-type foliate scrolls centered with a shaped vacant cartouche, push-button release, the interior with two attached silver retaining straps, unmarked.

ca. 1890   *3½in (9cm) wide 4oz*

$1,100-1,500   **CA**

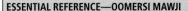

ESSENTIAL REFERENCE—OOMERSI MAWJI

Born the son of a cobbler in Gujarat (d.o.b unknown), and after initially specializing in leather engraving, Oomersi Mawji went on to become India's most esteemed silversmith of all time. By the 1860s he had become court silversmith to the Maharaos of Kutch and the Maharajas of Baroda, two of the most important Indian Royal courts. Working with his sons, Mawji's exceptionally fine quality pieces gradually also found admirers overseas, selling initially and primarily via Calcutta and Bombay. In 1878 they participated in the Exposition Universelle in Paris, subsequent to which their fame grew worldwide; in London Mawji silverware was retailed by Liberty & Co. After Oomersi died, ca. 1890, his sons continued the business, until it eventually ceased trading ca. 1930. Today, examples of Oomersi Mawji's exceptional work are in the collections of numerous museums around the world, including the Victoria & Albert Museum in London.

A late-19thC Austro-Hungarian gold and nephrite cigarette case, the hinged lid lined with gold, Austro-Hungarian assay marks.

3½in (9cm) long

$1,250-1,500   **WW**

A late-19thC German silver cigarette case, gilt interior, the cover enameled with a running hound and a horse and rider jumping a fence, stamped "M.Fleischmann," "800."

3¼in (8.5cm) long 2¾oz

$625-750   **WW**

An Indian silver cigarette box, by Oomersi Mawji, Bhuj, Cutch, with a scene of the Taj Mahal, within a chased foliate border, the reverse with foliate scroll decoration on a matted background, with an initialed cartouche, marked "OM" and "BHUJ."

4in (10cm) wide 5¼oz

$1,700-2,000   **WW**

A late-19thC Russian silver and niello-work cigarette case, Moscow, with a scene of the Eiffel Tower in Paris, within a foliate niello border, the reverse with similar decoration, unknown assay master.

1892   *3¼in (8.5cm) wide 3¾oz*

$500-625   **WW**

A Russian enameled silver cigarette case, the red guilloché-enamel lid with applied scrolled gilt corners and a double-headed eagle motif, polished blue stone clasp, opening to reveal a gilt interior with personal engraving, dents, gilt interior worn, surface scratches on enamel.

4in (10cm) wide

$750-875   **SWO**

A 9ct-gold military presentation match safe and cigarette case, 5th Battalion Yorkshire Regiment, by Sampson Mordan & Co. Ltd., Chester, the cigarette case of rounded square outline, the match safe of circular outline, each engraved with monogram, banner of the regiment, and "1907-1910" on one side, and crest and motto engraved above italic initials "ELPE."

"ELPE" was Eric Lea Priestly Edwards (1877-1914), a professional soldier who in the late 19thC had served in India with the British army, prior to being killed in action at the beginning of World War I, at the First Battle Aisne in 1914. In addition to this presentation match safe (or vesta case) and cigarette case, he is also remembered on the "Le Fert-sou-Jouarre Memorial" outside of Paris.

1909   *3¼in (8.5cm) wide 3⅛oz*

$2,000-2,200   **L&T**

An early-20thC Russian Fabergé silver cigarette case, molded with linear embossed decoration, with applied "LA" monogram and the Russian Imperial crest, both set with small diamonds, cut and polished rubies, the case secured with a cabochon garnet button, 84 zolotnik and Fabergé workshop mark, unidentified workmaster's mark, minor scratches, one interior elastic strap loose.

4¼in (11cm) wide 5½oz

$875-1,000 DAWS

An early-20thC Hungarian cigarette case, with ribbed design and a foliate border, with an oval cabochon sapphire thumbpiece, unmarked.

3¼in (8.5cm) wide 4¼oz

$4,300-5,000 L&T

A George V 9ct-gold cigarette case, by Stewart Dawson & Co. Ltd., Chester, with a Greek-key border, engine-turned decoration with an applied coronet.

1913 4in (10cm) wide 4oz

$2,400-2,700 L&T

A 9ct-gold cigarette case, by Deakin and Francis, Birmingham, with a crest and initials.

1930 3¼in (8.5cm) long 2⅞oz

$1,700-2,000 WW

A 9ct-yellow gold cigarette case, by the Adie Brothers, engine-turned pattern, push-button thumbpiece, opening to reveal the inscription "Richard August 6th 1937," Birmingham hallmarked "375," with maker's mark "ABrosLtd."

1936 4¼in (11cm) wide 4¾oz

$3,000-3,500 DAWS

An Edward VIII sterling silver-gilt and guilloché enamel long cigarette case, by Beddoes & Co., Birmingham, engine-turned decoration topped with translucent blue enamel, engine-turned reverse, push-button release, the gilt interior engraved "Kay from Leo, Grace, Sophie.," fully and part marked.

1936 6¼in (16cm) wide 5oz

$625-750 CA

A Cartier cigarette case, by Jacques Cartier, London, with gold rope-twist borders on each terminal, the hinged lid with a gold thumbpiece, signed "Cartier London" in interior, presented in a fitted red leather Cartier case.

1948 3¼in (8.5cm) wide 4¼oz

$1,100-1,350 L&T

A Russian Soviet silver cigarette case, Moscow, with embossed decoration of a solider holding the flag of the Soviet Union, with the Kremlin Clock in the background, push-button release with a collet-set cabochon-cut paste thumbpiece, gilt interior, the reverse engraved with an inscription, marked in the interior with 875 standard mark of 1927-58, with maker's mark.

1950 4¼in (11cm) long 6½oz

$800-950 WW

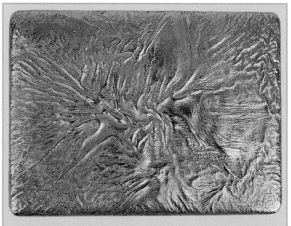

A 9ct-gold samorodok-style cigarette case, by Dunhill, London, signed by Bando, with slide-action spring-loaded opening, with date marks and "AD" for Alfred Dunhill, the cover marked "Dunhill London" with the signature of Bando, with leather box by Dunhill and silk sleeve, with two spare expandable cigarette containers.

Matteo Cellini became a famous Dunhill craftsman, having started at the company in 1919. His name was used by Dunhill as a "brand" up until the 1960s.

1966 5in (13cm) wide

$5,000-5,600 WW

A late-17thC William and Mary silver nutmeg grater, probably London, of teardrop form, each side with a hinged lid with standaway hinge, engraved with simple foliate sections, one side fitted with a serrated rasp, unmarked.

ca. 1690   *1½in (4cm) wide 1oz*

$750-875   **CA**

An 18thC English enamel nutmeg grater, the cover titled "A Trifle from Wisbich," over panels of flowers within enameled "jeweled" borders, on a pink ground, some discoloration, enamel loss in interior.

        1¾in (4.5cm) long

$1,400-1,700   **SWO**

A George III cylindrical silver nutmeg grater, by Richard Glanville, London.

1776   *2¾in (7cm) high 1½oz*

$500-625   **CHOR**

A George III nutmeg grater, possibly by William Key, London, formed as a Classical urn, with bright-cut floral decoration and a vacant oval cartouche with garland detail, folding out to the internal grater, raised on a square foot with canted edges.

1789 or 1809   *2¾in (7cm) high 1½oz*

$1,500-1,900   **L&T**

A George III provincial silver nutmeg grater, by George Lowe I, Chester, hinged cover and base, the interior with a steel grater, with an engraved crest on the cover.

1799   *1¾in (4.5cm) wide 1⅜oz*

$5,000-6,200   **WW**

A George III silver nutmeg grater, by Samuel Pemberton, Birmingham, the cover and base with engraved foliate decoration, the sides with bright-cut decoration.

1809   *1½in (4cm) wide ¾oz*

$1,000-1,250   **WW**

A George III silver nutmeg grater, by John Shaw, Birmingham, reeded decoration, the hinged cover with a vacant cartouche, opening to reveal a hinged grater.

1817   *1½in (4cm) wide 1¼oz*

$500-625   **WW**

A coquilla nut carved "Acorn" nutmeg grater, cracks, chips, lacks metal grater.

        2¼in (5.5cm) long

$125-150   **JON**

A George III silver filigree thimble, scent bottle, and tape measure, probably Birmingham, the screw-off thimble with scroll filigree decoration, the interior with a glass scent bottle, the reverse end with a tape measure.

ca. 1800   *2in (5cm) high*

$500-625   **WW**

An 18ct-gold thimble, London.

1812   *1in (2.5cm) high ⅛oz*

$250-310   **SWO**

A late-19thC gold thimble, maker's mark for René Lorillon, with textured and foliate decoration, French control mark, with fitted case.

1in (2.5cm) high

$500-625   **WW**

A coromandel sewing box, by Mechi, London, inlaid with engraved brass, mother-of pearl, and abalone, with a padded blue velvet interior, fully fitted with various sewing tools, including mother-of-pearl thread spools, thread winders, and mother-of-pearl-handle tools, with a needle book, lidded storage compartment and a pincushion.

ca. 1845

$3,700-5,000   **MGO**

A Victorian novelty sterling silver and enamel sewing companion, by Henry William Dee, London, of egg form with suspension loop, decorated in red and blue enamel with the motto of the Order of the Bath—"Tria Juncta In Uno"— the interior with a lift-out thread spool with thimble, fully and part marked on the exterior.

1868   *2in (5cm) high 2oz*

$450-550   **CA**

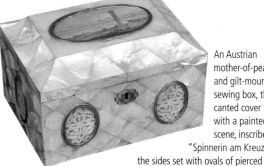

An Austrian mother-of-pearl and gilt-mounted sewing box, the canted cover with a painted scene, inscribed "Spinnerin am Kreuz," the sides set with ovals of pierced mother-of-pearl designs, the plush lined interior fitted with a Palais Royal sewing set.

9in (23cm) wide

$2,700-3,100   **CHOR**

A rare Victorian novelty sterling silver vinaigrette and sewing companion, by Thomas Johnson I, London, retailed by Walter Thornhill, formed as a dark lantern, with ring attachment and side clip, the front set in an Essex crystal in white with the name "MAUD," the hinged lid opening to reveal a pull-out unmarked silver-gilt sewing companion of a thread spool with an integral measuring tape, sat within a needle holder collar, the hinged base cap opening to reveal a pull-off pierced and engraved vinaigrette grille of a rosette, fully and part marked, stamped with registration lozenge, engraved on base "THORNHILL, 144 BOND ST."

1875   *2½in (6.5cm) high 4⅛oz*

$950-1,050   **CA**

A Scottish Victorian Mauchlineware spool box, in the form of a Pullman parlor car, the cover with a mountain landscape, the interior with a "Clark & Co Anchor Sewing Cottons" inscribed paper label.

ca. 1890   *6½in (16.5cm) wide*

$300-375   **WW**

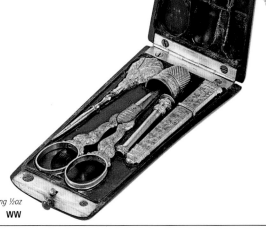

A late-19thC French five-piece two-color gold sewing étui, with chased foliate decoration, in a fitted ebony case, the cover with a shield cartouche with the initial "E," comprising a thimble, a pair of scissors, a pencil, a needle case, and a spike.

4½in (11.5cm) long ½oz

$1,100-1,350   **WW**

A small early-19thC needlework orphanage pincushion, decorated with an alphabet and numbers above a short verse on one side, diamond-form text on the opposing side, embroidered "Female orphan" on one end, with tassels on the corners.

2¼in (5.5cm) wide

$1,250-1,500   **L&T**

A late-Victorian novelty silver Christmas-style cracker-shaped pincushion and sewing box, by Gibson and Langman, London, the ends of the cracker with worn velvet pincushions, the center section with a hinged compartment, the cover mounted with a lady with a flute and a gentleman with a trumpet, marked with a registration number.

1898   6¾in (17cm) long 3⅜oz

$1,400-1,700   **WW**

An Edwardian novelty silver cow pincushion, by Levi & Salaman, Birmingham, modeled standing, wear in marks, repairs, pad is probably a replacement.

1906   2¼in (5.5cm) wide

$550-700   **WW**

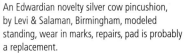

A novelty silver shoe pincushion, marks for Berthold Muller & Son, Chester, with repoussé decoration, missing pincushion.

1901   7½in (19cm) long 6¼oz

$250-310   **SWO**

An Edwardian novelty silver golf club pincushion, by Crisford & Norris, Birmingham, modeled as the head of a wooden club.

1908   2¾in (7cm) long

$800-950   **WW**

An Edwardian silver pincushion, by William Comyns, London, the lattice "buttoned" top enclosing a silk-covered pad, with rope-twist corners, purple velvet base.

1909   4½in (11.5cm) wide

$350-400   **HT**

A novelty silver lizard pincushion, by Crisford & Norris Ltd., Birmingham, no glass eyes, pad is a replacement.

1910   4¼in (11cm) long

$550-625   **WW**

OBJETS DE VERTU

A Montblanc "Meisterstück" Le Grand black fountain pen, with black resin cap and barrel, decorated with gilt banded highlights and pen clip, band on the cap marked "Meisterstück Mont Blanc," 18ct nib, with a Montblanc branded case and box.
$950-1,250   CA

An 18k yellow gold fountain pen, "Swan," by Mabie Todd & Co. Ltd., with engraved leaf cap, signed "Mabie Todd & Co. Ltd."
1935-36   5½in (14cm) long 1¼oz
$750-875   DRA

A Waterman "Red Ripple" no. 5 lever filler fountain pen, with rolled-gold clip and gold cap band, "BLUE/WATERMAN's" nib stamped marks.

See George Fischler, "Fountain Pens and Pencils," Schiffer (2008), page 71, for the illustrated set of no. 7 "Red Ripple" pens with color cap bands.
5in (12.5cm) long
$250-310   WW

A limited-edition fountain pen, "Torpedo G.M.T. World Time Zone," by Alfred Dunhill, brushed stainless steel, with engraved time zones on the body and numbers on an adjustable collar, "GMT" marked in red, marked "ALFRED DUNHILL," 18ct-white gold nib, marked "Dunhill M 18K-750."
6in (15cm) long
$300-375   CA

A Montblanc limited-edition fountain pen, "Catherine the Great," "Patron of the Arts" series 4810, no. 3496/4810, burgundy lacquer cap and barrel with gold-plated overlay and clip, medium yellow gold-color nib stamped "18K," piston filling system, inked, original Montblanc "Catherine the Great" box, "Catherine the Great" international service certificate, "Catherine the Great" outer card box and white card sleeve.
ca. 1997
$2,700-3,100   DN

A Montblanc limited-edition fountain pen, "Hommage à Alexander the Great," "Patron of the Arts" series 888, no. 354/888, green marbled lacquer cap and barrel with 18ct-gold overlay, the cap with a diamond-set clip, stamped with 18ct-gold common control mark, two-tone gold-color nib stamped "18K" and "750," piston filling system, inked, original Montblanc "Alexander the Great" box, "Alexander the Great" international service certificate, "Alexander the Great" outer card box and white card sleeve.
ca. 1998
$4,700-5,200   DN

A Montblanc limited-edition fountain pen, "Franz Kafka," "Writers" series, no. 01009/18500, with an unusual design that gradually shifts/metamorphoses from round to square from base to top, sterling silver clip and rings, 18k solid white-gold nib engraved with an insect (alluding to Kafka's "The Metamorphosis" of 1915).
2004
$625-750   CA

A 19thC Persian Qajar Dynasty lacquered papier-mâché qalamdan or pen box, painted and gilt with arabesques and botehs within line borders, the interior with gilt foliate decoration on a blue ground, with brass inkwells, steel scissors, and accessories.
11¼in (28.5cm) long
$450-550   WW

A Victorian four-piece silver-gilt pen and pencil set, by Brookes & Crookes, Sheffield, retailed by Leuchars and Son, London and Paris, comprising a pencil, a dip pen, a lead holder, and a letter knife, the handle with a hinged penknife, in a fitted case.
1880   letter knife 6½in (16.5cm) long 2oz
$450-500   WW

A Victorian novelty silver mechanical pencil, modeled as a flintlock gun, struck with maker's marks down the barrel, missing extension stud, hallmarks rubbed.

Purportedly manufactured in commemoration of the 1840 assassination attempt on Queen Victoria by Edward Oxford, who was sentenced for high treason at the Old Bailey.

ca. 1840   2½in (6.5cm) long
$220-275   SWO

A 9ct-gold mechanical pencil and pen, by S. Mordan & Co., three-section mechanical movement with a slide-action pen and pencil, with a ring attachment.

2½in (6.5cm) long
$250-310   WW

A late-19thC mechanical pencil, by S. Mordan & Co., the pencil with a foliate decorated barrel, stamped "S. MORDEN & CO.," with a flower-head slider, with a yellow paste seal inscribed "Forget me not," general wear.

3¼in (8.5cm) long ⅜oz
$300-375   DN

A Victorian gold mechanical pencil, by S. Mordan & Co., fluted with scroll and foliate mounts, the terminal with a plain hardstone matrix.

3½in (9cm) long ⁵⁄₁₆oz
$250-310   WW

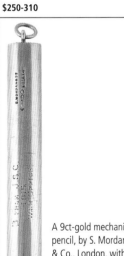

A 9ct-gold mechanical pencil, by S. Mordan & Co., London, with a suspension loop, engraved "B From J.S.C., 1915, War Office."

1912   3¼in (8.5cm) long ¼oz
$170-220   DN

An 18ct-gold "Gatling" mechanical pencil, by Asprey, London, design no. 632782, with a ring attachment, inscribed "J.A.C Feb 29, 1918."

This mechanical, or propelling, pencil was known as the "Gatling" pencil due to the resemblance of the internal lead storage chamber to a Gatling gun.

1915   3¾in (9.5cm) long ⅞oz
$625-750   WW

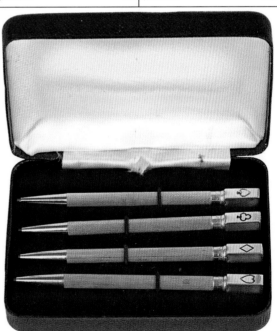

A set of four silver and enamel bridge pencils, engine-turned decoration, the finials enameled with the four playing card suits, marked sterling silver, in a fitted case.

$170-220   WW

A 9ct-gold mechanical pencil, by E. Baker & Son, Birmingham, engine-turned decoration, engraved "Christmas 1948" and "Raymond."

1947   4¼in (11cm) long ⅞oz
$170-220   DN

A 14k yellow-gold and enamel calendar pencil, with rotating stations to display dates, with graphite insert.

2¾in (7cm) long ⅞oz
$700-800   DRA

OBJETS DE VERTU

An English silver and horn cigar lighter, marks for "T W," London, date letter "e."

1900 *22in (56cm) long*

$1,000-1,100 **CA**

An Edwardian novelty silver cigar lighter, by Joseph Gloster, Birmingham, in the form of a golf ball, supported by three crossed golf clubs.

1908 *4¾in (12cm) high 2½oz*

$375-450 **DAWS**

A French gold, silver, and ruby lighter and lipstick case, each with a floral pattern gold case, set with cabochon rubies, with a square-cut ruby push-piece and ribbed silver ends, signed with French maker's mark for Numa Espezel.

1920s *2¾in (7cm) high 2⅞oz*

$1,000-1,250 **DRA**

A novelty silver hunting horn table lighter, by Carrington & Co., London.

1928 *9in (23cm) high*

$190-250 **WW**

Judith Picks

Never underestimate the impact that rarity can sometimes have on desirability and price. Founded in 1893 by Alfred Dunhill, the Dunhill company produced numerous cigar and cigarette lighters throughout the 20thC. Notable among many diverse types are its gold or silver "Rollagas" models and its Lucite side-paneled "Aquarium" lighters, and for some time now it is the latter that have become the most collectible.

Introduced in the 1950s, and gasoline instead of butane fueled, they were produced in four descending sizes—"giant," "half-giant," "Standard," and "Service"—with gold-, silver-, or chrome-plated lift arms and bases. It was, and is, however, their clear Lucite side panels hand carved with reverse intaglio and hand-painted aquatic imagery that made them look like nothing else. The work on the panels was carried out in an essentially cottage-industry-like manner by husband and wife team Allan and Margaret Bennett, in their home on the south coast of England—Mr. Bennett using dentistry tools to carve the design into the Lucite panels; Mrs. Bennett then back-painting them.

Most of the designs were of tropical fish in a tank. However, from time to time other subjects were produced—such as the lighter here depicting a pair of wading birds (and the reverse a single egret in white). Much rarer than fish Aquariums, they have suddenly become a lot more desirable, too, to the extent that while fish Aquariums tend to fetch $2,700-8,500, the wading birds Aquarium here recently soared past its preauction estimate and went for an eye-watering and bar-raising $20,000+.

A rare Cartier cigarette lighter, 18k white and yellow gold with a diamond-set edge, signed "by Cartier Paris" on the base and numbered "F61809."

2¾in (7cm) high

$2,500-3,100 **CA**

A German Petie camera lighter, by W. Kunik, red mottled enamel and bright plated metal body, with lighter and a removable 16mm Petie camera.

3¼in (8.5cm) high

$500-625 **DAWS**

A rare gilt-plated and lucite "Aviary" lighter, by Alfred Dunhill (1872-1959, British), electroplated gilt mounts, four Lucite panels, each deeply engraved in reverse intaglio technique and hand painted to create a three-dimensional effect, the front panel depicting two birds in pink, white, and black, the reverse with a single bird of paradise in white, with tree branches and tropical flowers, with vibrant greens and blues, base stamped "DUNHILL LIGHTER, MADE IN ENGLAND," damages.

4in (10cm) wide

$20,000-22,000 **CA**

An early-19thC Italian micromosaic plaque, Rome, worked in color tesserae with Pliny's Doves, some tesserae missing, one split.

2¼in (5.5cm) diam

$1,100-1,500 **TEN**

An early-19thC Italian micromosaic plaque, Rome, worked in color tesserae with a hound sitting beside a Classical altar, minor losses, some domestic paint spots.

2¼in (5.5cm) diam

$8,000-8,500 **TEN**

A 19thC micromosaic desk weight, Rome, the cartouche-shaped panel depicting a goldfinch on a branch.

6¾in (17cm) wide

$1,900-2,200 **L&T**

A late-19thC Italian Grand Tour micromosaic plaque of St. Peter's Square, Rome, depicting the Vatican and Bernini's Colonnade inside a blue and black border, in a later giltwood frame.

Initially undertaken by young aristocrats in the 17thC, the Grand Tour was a "cultural treasure hunt" throughout Europe and its antiquities. During the course of the 18thC and 19thC, the Grand Tour became popular with the newly affluent middle classes, and souvenirs—such as the micromosaic here—were produced to meet the demand of tourists, which, as early as the mid-18thC, had outstripped the availability of original artifacts.

6¾in (17cm) diam

$4,000-4,300 **WW**

A Maltese pietra dura armorial desk weight, by Joseph Darmanin, with a golden lion passant facing sinister above the motto "Fare Fac," on a black background, set into white marble, inscribed "Darmanin Fecit/1861" verso.

Malta was home to a number of marble workshops from the 17thC onward, initially founded by Italian craftsmen—the island had close historical links with Sicily and the southern Italian peninsula is only 50 miles away. The importation of the mosaic marble technique into Malta was primarily due to the patronage of the Knight Hospitallers of S.t John, based there from 1530 until 1798, who commissioned elaborate marble tombstones for themselves. Under British rule f rom 1800, the workshops began making marble items in the Italian style for the influx of wealthy British tourists, who had for many years previously shown an interest in buying marble slabs in Italy as souvenirs of the Grand Tour.

6in (15cm) wide

$625-750 **WW**

A mid-19thC French marble bust of Napoleon, the Emperor wearing his bicorn hat, looking slightly to his left, on a socle base.

17¾in (45cm) high

$4,000-4,300 **WW**

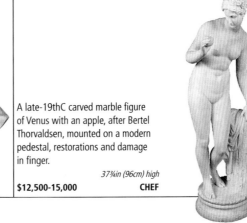

A late-19thC carved marble figure of Venus with an apple, after Bertel Thorvaldsen, mounted on a modern pedestal, restorations and damage in finger.

37¾in (96cm) high

$12,500-15,000 **CHEF**

ESSENTIAL REFERENCE—JEAN-VALENTIN MOREL

The celebrated French gold- and silversmith Jean-Valentin Morel (1794-1860) trained under his father and was also a student of Adrien Maximilian—maker of gold boxes to Louis XVI and Emperor Napoleon. Morel established his own business in 1818, registered his own mark in 1827, and specialized in high-quality inlay work and decorative hardstone vessels to satisfy the substantial demand for artifacts in not only the Renaissance style (as in the tazza shown here), but also the Baroque style.

From 1842-48, Morel worked in partnership with the French architect Henri Duponchel (1794-1868), establishing themselves as "Morel et Cie," and winning a gold medal at the Exposition des Produits de l'industrie of 1844, in Paris. However, their partnership ended acrimoniously and resulted in a lawsuit that prohibited Morel from working in Paris. After the revolution of 1848, Morel fled to London and established a workshop on New Burlington Street, registering his London mark in 1849, and employing more than 50 staff. In terms of accolades, the pinnacle of Morel's London career was his display of jewelry, silver, and numerous neo-Renaissance vessels at the Great Exhibition of 1851, for which he was awarded a prestigious Council Medal; among those vessels was a tazza similar to the one here, which was made by Morel for Maria Alexandrovna, wife of the future Czar Alexander II of Russia.

A French gold, enamel, and agate tazza, by Jean-Valentin Morel, in Renaissance style, the agate bowl with winged lion handles, raised on a strapwork, shell-, and leaf-decorated stem above a domed foot, stamped with Jean-Valentin Morel maker's mark "MV," with a compass and French eagle-head poincon de petite garantie.

ca. 1838-48   *4¼in (11cm) high*
$8,000-9,500   WW

An early-19thC Italian Grand Tour giallo antico marble tazza, the shallow oval bowl on a short molded stem and rectangular foot.

14¼in (36cm) wide
$1,100-1,500   WW

An Italian Grand Tour porphyry and white marble athenienne, mid-19thC and later, the green porphyry bowl with a gilt-bronze pinecone terminal, supported on three lion-head monopodia with paw feet around a gilt-bronze pinecone, on a concave white marble and Egyptian red porphyry triangular base.

16½in (42cm) high
$6,000-7,500   WW

A mid-19thC Grand Tour giallo antico marble tazza, in the manner of Benedetto Boschetti, the fluted dished top with angular handles and lion masks, raised on a spreading fluted foot and square base.

8¼in (21cm) wide
$1,500-1,900   L&T

A mid-19thC Italian Grand Tour rosso antico marble inkwell, after the Antique, in the form of a Roman bath, with lion-head masks on each side, on lion-paw feet, the wells with foliate carved domed covers, on a verde antico marble base, the covers possibly later.

The Roman original from the Baths of Caracalla is now a fountain in the Piazza Farnese in Rome.

7¾in (19.5cm) wide
$1,250-1,500   WW

A pair of late-19th/early 20thC French Maurin green marble and ormolu-mounted urns and covers, in Louis XVI style, each with flowering swag and laurel leaf decoration between a pair of ram heads, on knop socle bases and square plinths, the domed covers with flower-bud finials.

17in (43cm) high
$1,900-2,200   WW

A pair of late-19th/20thC Egyptian Revival marble obelisks, carved with numerous images, including Horus, and hieroglyphs highlighted in gilt, on black marble and gilt-brass plinths.

18½in (47cm) high
$875-1,000   WW

A pair of fossil specimen marble obelisks, each on four ball feet and a rectangular pedestal.

ca. 1900   *16¼in (41.5cm) high*
$700-800   WW

ESSENTIAL REFERENCE—BLUE JOHN AND BOULTON

In 1765, Matthew Boulton, engineer and entrepreneur, visited Paris to learn more about the ormolu workshops there and the wares they were producing to satiate the considerable and increasing Georgian demand for "antique"-inspired works of art. This visit resulted in Boulton and his partner John Fothergill establishing, in 1768, a new ormolu workshop at their premises in Birmingham—the primary role of which was to embellish the vases they were creating from various polished stones, the most popular being "blue john," a feldspar found only in a single seam in Derbyshire. Indeed, so popular were these blue john vases that, at around the same time, Boulton attempted to purchase or lease the blue john mines.

The design of the ca. 1775 blue john perfume burners shown here had been fine-tuned some five years earlier, in 1770, and can be found in Boulton and Fothergill's "Pattern Book 1," on page 171 (see Goodison, "Matthew Boulton Ormolu," Christie's, 1999, page 305, plate 278). The popularity of the design was essentially guaranteed after Boulton sold several to Queen Charlotte (see page 355), and they were eventually produced in a number of variations. The most popular were the perfume burners shown here, and the blue john candle vases with reversible covers. Other variations included ones with the vase or burner mounted on a lower socle, either in ormolu or white marble, combined with either white marble or porcelain for the ovoid body.

A fine pair of George III blue john and ormolu-mounted vase perfume burners, by Matthew Boulton and John Fothergill, each with a domed foliate cover with a flower-bud finial above a pierced rim, scrolling foliate handles with ram-head terminals and hung with laurel garlands, with ribboned oak-leaf swags, above a fluted socle, on a stepped square foot with an egg-and-dart border, in turn on a white marble waisted socle, with a guilloché cast ormolu band with scrolling ribbon and flower-head decoration.

ca. 1775 _9½in (24cm) high_

$110,000-125,000 WW

A rare early-19thC Grand Tour gilt and patinated bronze model of the Antonine Column, attributed to Wilhelm Hopfgarten and Benjamin Jollage, Rome, the column cast in low relief with war scenes and figures, surmounted by a figure of a Roman emperor, the plinth inscribed "Divo Antonino Aug Pio, Antoninus Augustus Et, Verus Augustus Filii" and decorated with funerary decursio, the other side with the apotheosis to the gods of the emperor and his wife, on an alabaster base.

34¼in (87cm) high

$11,000-12,500 WW

A 19thC blue john or crich fluorspar urn, with a turned "cover," on a pedestal base and a black stone square plinth, base broken with losses.

13in (33cm) high

$2,700-3,100 SWO

A 19thC blue john campana tazza, on a circular foot, the center pedestal possibly ebonized wood, chips, repairs.

3¼in (8.5cm) high

$1,100-1,500 TEN

A late-18th/early-19thC George III Derbyshire blue john urn, on a later socle and paneled plinth, with an Ashford black marble stepped base.

11½in (29cm) high

$7,500-8,500 WW

A late-19thC French Grand Tour bronze Warwick vase, the body cast with masks between entwined handles.

13¾in (35cm) wide

$750-875 WW

A 19thC blue john desk weight, of solid cubic form.

3½in (9cm) wide

$2,200-2,500 L&T

A 20thC gilt-bronze "Duval" urn, the body applied with crested roundels beneath a woven neck, with a pair of gilt cherubs sat on lion-head handles, the reeded base above a lappet knop and rim, on a square foot, fitted for electricity.

This urn is based on a model believed to have been originally designed by Pierre Duval Le Camus (1790-1854) for the gardens at the Palace of Versailles.

17½in (44.5cm) high

$1,600-1,900 WW

OBJETS DE VERTU

A Russian Lukutin factory lacquered papier-mâché box and cover, decorated with four peasants in traditional costume sitting around a table, one playing a balalaika, dated in Cyrillic, gilt imperial eagle mark, minor surface wear, dents, minor chips.

1869   *8¼in (21cm) wide*

$300-350   **TEN**

A late-19thC Russian Vishniakov factory lacquered papier-mâché tea caddy and cover, the hinged cover decorated with three horses drawing a troika in a snowy landscape, enclosing two lidded compartments, printed factory mark, minor wear, minor restoration, lacking key.

7in (18cm) wide

$300-375   **TEN**

A 20thC Russian Fedoskino factory lacquered papier-mâché box and cover, the hinged cover decorated with an officer of the 9th Kiev Hussars of His Majesty King Edward VII Regiment in full uniform from 1905, signed, inscribed on inside of cover, minor surface wear.

6¼in (16cm) long

$450-500   **TEN**

A 20thC Russian lacquered papier-mâché box and cover, the cover decorated with a stylized townscape, minor surface wear and scratching.

4¾in (12cm) long

$190-250   **TEN**

A late-17thC silver-gilt counter box, the pull-off cover engraved with a Tudor rose, the sides with cherubs and foliate decoration, unmarked.

ca. 1690   *¾in (2cm) diam ⅜oz*

$1,500-1,700   **WW**

An 18thC gold overlay bloodstone étui or scent bottle case, with overlaid pierced and embossed openwork decoration of birds and scrolls, hinged cover, the front with a push-button clasp, unmarked.

ca. 1770   *3¾in (9.5cm) high*

$1,900-2,200   **WW**

A George III gilt-metal-mounted tortoiseshell traveling writing nécessaire, with shell-cast thumbpiece, containing three glass bottles with Staffordshire enamel-mounted covers, a fob seal inscribed "JANE" and a pencil/pen with separate nib.

3½in (9cm) wide

$450-550   **TEN**

An Edwardian silver and tortoiseshell heart-shaped dressing table box, by William Comyns & Sons, London, hinged tortoiseshell cover with silver inlay and a garland border, velvet lined, on four foliate scroll feet.

1906   *4¾in (12cm) wide*

$275-310   **WW**

A cornelian oval seal, by Charles Brown (1749-95), after George Stubbs (1724-1806), the intaglio carved with "Horse Frightened by a Lion" (1770), signed in the stone "C. Brown F.," in a gold scroll mount with plain frame.

Charles Brown and his brother William were gem workers, both of whom exhibited at the Royal Academy. From 1786 until 1795, the brothers received numerous commissions from the Court of Catherine II, Empress of Russia, and approximately 200 cameos and intaglios remain in the Hermitage, St. Petersburg, to this day. This particular seal is one of two sold directly to Catherine. A gemstone specialist has suggested that this may be the original stone and that the one currently in the Hermitage was the second to be carved.

1½in (4cm) wide

$28,500-33,000 **HT**

A mid-19thC Russian porcelain egg, painted with a continuous band of flowers on a powder blue ground, gilt-lined top, previously mounted.

4¼in (11cm) high

$250-370 **SWO**

A late-19thC French Palais Royale glass and gilt-metal scent bottle holder, the spherical container with gilt floral decoration holding four scent bottles, on a socle base supported by a pair of figures among scrolling foliage and ribbons, on a shaped white glass base on scrolling twig legs and an oval giltwood plinth.

9¾in (25cm) high

$750-875 **WW**

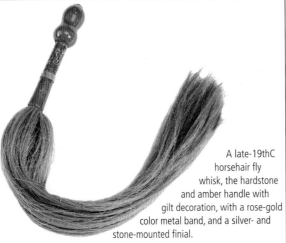

A late-19thC horsehair fly whisk, the hardstone and amber handle with gilt decoration, with a rose-gold color metal band, and a silver- and stone-mounted finial.

handle 7in (18cm) long

$3,100-3,700 **WW**

A late-19thC Russian sword stick, of tapered ebonized form, the silver-mounted handle with applied monogram, the hinged lid with applied Imperial Eagle, snuff compartment in lid, the whole handle pulling away to reveal a tapered stiletto blade.

1896 *37in (94cm) long*

$2,200-2,700 **L&T**

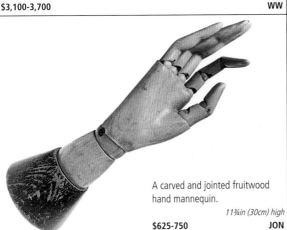

A carved and jointed fruitwood hand mannequin.

11¾in (30cm) high

$625-750 **JON**

Two late-19th/early 20thC optician's prosthetic glass eyes, with blue irises, one showing blood vessels, in fitted cases marked "G.T. Harvey & Co, Newcastle," with an outer cardboard box similarly marked.

$450-500 **WW**

A Russian icon of the Mother of God of Tenderness, probably 17thC, on a 14th/15thC panel, tempera on wood.

This is a very rare depiction of the Christ Child tightly holding His mother, with her finger pointing toward Him. A similar example with the pointing index finger, dated to 1314, is displayed in V. N. Lazarev, "The Russian Icon: From its Origin to the Sixteenth Century," Liturgical Press (1997), page 26.

12¼in (31cm) high

$25,000-31,000   SWO

ESSENTIAL REFERENCE—IONIAN ISLANDS SCHOOL

Also known as the "Heptanese School" (or the "School of the Seven Islands"), the Ionian Islands School succeeded the Cretan School as the foremost post-Byzantine Greek school of painting after Crete fell to the Ottoman Empire in 1669. From the 17thC to the 19thC, under successive Venetian, French and English occupation, the Ionian islands, centered on Corfu, offered Greek artists considerably more freedom than elsewhere in Ottoman-ruled Greece, and consequently artists migrated there in considerable numbers. Stylistically, the broad shift—already strongly evident in the Cretan School—was even farther away from (to the point of abandonment) strict Byzantine conventions and techniques, and farther toward Western styles. Notable earlier influences included Italian Baroque and Flemish painters, and later Italian and French Neoclassicists, while changing techniques and subjects included: three-dimensional perspective; oil on canvas as well as egg tempera on panel; and secular, not just religious, portraits and subjects. Highly influential throughout Greece (including Ottoman-occupied areas), the Ionian Islands School's impact waned from the mid- to late 19thC as the center of artistic Greek culture gradually transferred to Athens.

A mid-18thC Bulgarian icon of Saint Demetrios killing the Bulgarian czar Kaloyan, oil on gold ground.

3in (7.5cm) high

$375-500   CA

A mid-18thC Russian icon of Archangel Michael in triumph, oil on gold ground.

1½in (4cm) high

$3,500-4,000   CA

An icon of the Mother of God, probably 18thC, Greece or Balkans, flanked by Saint Haralampos, tempera and gold on wood, losses, warping, wear.

10¼in (26cm) high

$450-550   SWO

A Greek Ionian Islands School Tabernacle icon of Saint. Demetrius and the gladiator Lyaeus, tempera on panel, within a carved painted wood frame with two doors.

12¾in (32.5cm) high

$375-500   WW

A Greek Ionian Islands School Tabernacle icon of Saint George and the Dragon, below an upper section depicting Christ, tempera on panel, within a carved painted wood frame with two doors.

16in (40.5cm) high

$1,000-1,250   WW

A late-19thC Russian icon of the Mother of God of Bogolyubovo, the figure standing in three-quarter profile before various saints, tempera and gold on wood, panel bowed, paint loss, craquelure throughout, knocks.

17¾in (45cm) high

$625-750 SWO

A Russian School Menological icon for the month of June, tempera on panel.

14in (35.5cm) high

$2,500-3,100 WW

A large Russian icon of Saint Nicholas of Myra, flanked by Christ and the Mother of God, tempera and gold on wood, gilt losses, splits.

ca. 1900 *48¾in (124cm) high*

$3,500-4,000 SWO

A large Russian icon of the Mother of God, in the earlier Novrogod School style, from a Deisis, tempera on wood, with Tretyakov Gallery label and painted inventory numbers verso, chips, splits, knocks, probable overpainting, panel slightly warped, probably restored recently.

This icon was previously in the George R. Hann Collection. George Hann (1890-1979) was a pioneer of American aviation who assembled one of the world's finest private collections of icons, mostly in the 1930s, when the Soviet government released Russian treasures for sale abroad. Hann was committed to the study of the historical and religious significance of his collection, which was sold at Christie's the year after he died.

ca. 1900 *33in (84cm) high*

$15,000-19,000 SWO

A Romanian silver-plated icon of Saint John the Evangelist, sitting with an eagle, oil on wood, in a silver-plated relief mount, in a wood frame, losses, wear.

11¾in (30cm) high

$300-375 SWO

A late-19th/20thC brass and enameled icon, with a center winged figure, possibly Christ, surrounded by 18 saints in rondels, in an oak frame, possibly based on an icon in the Hagia Sophia.

6in (15cm) high

$300-375 WW

A Russian Orthodox silver-gilt-mounted icon, Moscow, stamped 84 Zolotniki mark, some losses.

1908-26 *8¾in (22cm) high*

$300-375 SWO

A wine glass, of probable Jacobite significance, the funnel bowl engraved with a crown and the initials "JS," raised on a plain stem above a folded foot.

ca. 1750   *6in (15cm) high*

$1,000-1,100   **WW**

A wine glass, of possible Jacobite significance, the round funnel bowl engraved with a sunflower spray, raised on a plain stem above a conical foot.

ca. 1760   *6in (15cm) high*

$750-875   **WW**

A Continental privateer wine glass, the drawn trumpet bowl engraved "J Barton/Success to the Unity," raised on a plain stem with a long teardrop above a folded conical foot.

More than one ship named "Unity" was involved in the American Revolution, and this glass probably relates to one of them.

ca. 1780   *6¾in (17cm) high*

$550-700   **WW**

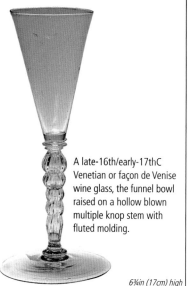

A late-16th/early-17thC Venetian or façon de Venise wine glass, the funnel bowl raised on a hollow blown multiple knop stem with fluted molding.

6¾in (17cm) high

$1,050-1,200   **WW**

A heavy baluster wine glass, the round funnel bowl with a solid base, rising from an inverted baluster stem over a folded conical foot.

ca. 1710   *6in (15cm) high*

$1,100-1,250   **WW**

A baluster wine glass, the bell bowl raised on a baluster stem, with triple-annulated center knop enclosing a long tear above a plain section and basal knop, over a folded conical foot.

ca. 1715   *6¾in (17cm) high*

$1,250-1,500   **WW**

A baluster wine glass, the generous bell bowl raised on a baluster stem, with two angular knops, each enclosing a single tear, above a folded conical foot.

ca. 1730-35   *6½in (16.5cm) high*

$1,050-1,200   **WW**

A wine glass, the funnel bowl rising from an eight-side pedestal stem, above a basal knop and folded conical foot.

ca. 1730   *6¼in (16cm) high*

$750-875   **WW**

A wine glass, the funnel bowl engraved around the rim with a formal foliate border enclosing flower heads, raised on a balustroid stem with an angular knop above a teared stem and basal knop, over a folded conical foot.

ca. 1740   *6in (15cm) high*

$500-625   **WW**

A large Jacobite wine glass, the bell bowl engraved with a rose and bud spray, above a double-knop air-twist stem and conical foot.

ca. 1755-60   *7¼in (18.5cm) high*

$2,100-2,500   **WW**

An armorial wine glass, of possible Jacobite significance, the round funnel bowl engraved with a coat of arms, of three poplar trees beneath the crest of a demi-savage holding a club, raised on an air-twist stem with shoulder and basal knops, over a conical foot.

ca. 1760   *6¼in (16cm) high*

$1,000-1,100   **WW**

A small wine glass, the round funnel bowl raised on an incised-twist stem, over a helmet foot.

ca. 1750-60   *6¼in (16cm) high*

$550-700   **WW**

A privateer wine glass, the bucket bowl engraved with a three-mast ship at sail, inscribed above "Success to the BETSY Privateer," raised on a multiseries opaque-twist stem over a conical foot.

The "Betsy" was a Liverpool ship under the command of William Watt. She was granted letters of marque on April 26 ,1758.

ca. 1758   *6¼in (16cm) high*

$19,000-22,000   **WW**

A Jacobite wine glass, the drawn trumpet bowl engraved with a flowering rose spray with two buds, an oak leaf, and the word "Fiat," raised on a dense air-twist stem above a conical foot.

ca. 1750-60   *6¼in (16cm) high*

$1,250-1,500   **WW**

A small Beilby wine glass, the ogee bowl enameled in white with diaper panels within Rococo scrolls, raised on an opaque-twist stem enclosing a gauze core, the bowl broken off and cleanly reattached.

ca. 1760   *5¾in (14.5cm) high*

$800-950   **WW**

A small color-twist wine glass, the ogee bowl raised on a stem with a red thread around a white gauze spiral, above a conical foot, stem repair.

ca. 1760   *5½in (14cm) high*

$625-750   **WW**

A Lynn wine glass, the rounded funnel bowl molded with three horizontal ribs, raised on a double-series opaque-twist stem over a conical foot.

For an Essential Reference on Lynn glass, see page 404.

ca. 1760   *5¾in (14.5cm) high*

$1,000-1,100   **WW**

An Admiral Byng wine glass, the round funnel bowl engraved with the officer hanging from a gibbet, flanked by the initials "A B," the reverse inscribed "JUSTICE," raised on an air-twist stem above a conical foot.

Admiral John Byng was a Royal Naval officer and an MP from 1751 until his death in 1757. During the Seven Years' War, Byng was sent to relieve a besieged garrison on the island of Minorca. With his ships in a poor state of repair, Byng opted to return to Gibraltar to see to his ships and await further promised resources. On his return to Britain, he was court-martialed for failing to "do his utmost" to prevent the loss of Minorca. Despite appeals to King George II for clemency, he was executed by firing squad on March 14, 1757—the engraving on the glass being symbolic rather than accurate. Byng was seen by many as a scapegoat for the Admiralty's inefficiency, and the execution in this way of such a high-ranking officer divided the country. His descendants continue to campaign for a posthumous pardon today.

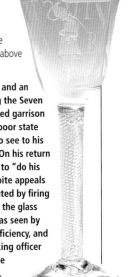

ca. 1763   *6¼in (16cm) high*

$2,200-2,500   **WW**

GLASS

A rare late-16th/early-17thC Venetian or façon de Venise tall latticino goblet, the slender tulip-shaped bowl rising from six graduating steps in the lower section, decorated in vetro a retorti, raised on a later metal foot.

14¾in (37.5cm) high

$7,000-7,500 **WW**

A heavy baluster goblet, the generous round funnel bowl raised on a baluster stem, with two bulbous knops over a folded conical foot.

ca. 1710   *8¾in (22cm) high*

$2,500-3,100 **WW**

A large goblet or ceremonial glass, the generous cup-shaped bowl raised on a knop air-twist stem.

ca. 1750   *8¾in (22cm) high*

$875-1,000 **WW**

A large wine goblet, the generous bowl gilded in the London atelier of James Giles, with a large stem of fruiting grapevine, raised on a multiple-series opaque-twist stem over a conical foot, yellow enameled collector's number on base.

ca. 1760-70   *7¼in (18.5cm) high*

$2,100-2,500 **WW**

A large mid-18thC Saxon ceremonial goblet, the deep round funnel bowl engraved on one side with two gentleman embracing while grapevine twines around them, inscribed in German "Aus reben wird ein liebes band" (Vines become a love bond), the reverse with a gentleman replacing the cover on a goblet held by his friend, inscribed in German "Am trincken wird ein freund er bannt" (A friend is stopped from drinking), raised on a hollow baluster stem, with a replacement wood foot.

15in (38cm) high

$1,100-1,350 **WW**

A large wine goblet, gilded in the London atelier of James Giles, with a spray of fruiting grapevine and two flower sprigs, raised on a knop faceted stem.

ca. 1770   *7in (18cm) high*

$1,050-1,200 **WW**

A large 18thC façon de Venise goblet, the rounded bowl engraved with stags between buildings and trees in a continuous landscape above molded gadrooning, raised on a pincered and twisted winged stem around a figure-eight applied with raspberry prunts, over an angular basal knop and folded conical foot, the foot cleanly broken and reattached.

9¼in (23.5cm) high

$450-550 **WW**

A pair of tall Bohemian glass goblets, the slightly flared octagonal forms cut with scenes of horses beneath trees in continuous landscapes, bearing monogrammed initials and "1886," raised on low faceted stems and thick feet.

1886   *8¾in (22cm) high*

$500-625 **WW**

A 19thC Bohemian goblet, in the manner of Moser, the round funnel bowl with a high scalloped rim, decorated with four applied opal cartouche panels decorated with alternating portraits and floral sprays, above a knop swept stem with matched opal-panel decoration, all on a fine gilt foliate scroll ground, minor wear.

Founded in 1857 by Ludiwig Moser (1833-1916), in the Karlsbad, Bohemia (nowadays Karlovy Vary in the Czech Republic), Moser a. s. started out as a glass polishing and engraving company—Loetz, for example, were one of the glassmakers who originally supplied it with blanks. However, Moser soon transitioned into a full-blown glass manufacturer of both utilitarian and art glass. Its work was of such universally praised quality that it won medals at the international exhibitions in Paris in 1879, 1889, and 1900, and Chicago in 1893; received a warrant to supply the Imperial Court of the Austrian Emperor in 1904; and in 1908 became a supplier to King Edward VII. Moser continued to make high-quality glass throughout the 20thC and is still in business to this day.

10¾in (27.5cm) high

$1,000-1,500 **FLD**

Judith Picks

If you already know what a "firing" glass is, then please bear with me—many people do not, and a while back I certainly did not either. So, "firing glasses" are essentially ceremonial liquor glasses of small, dramlike size—in the 18thC, when this particular glass was made, a dram equated to around one-eighth of a fl oz (3.5ml), but it is a measurement that has varied then and subsequently in both time and place. After a group toast had been raised and drunk by an assembled company, the glasses were then slammed down on the table in unison, producing a collective sound reminiscent of a volley of muskets—hence not only the name "firing," but also their being the precursor to the modern-day equivalent: the stemless and footless "shot" glass.

A rare portrait firing glass, one side engraved with the head and shoulders portrait of a man, possibly Bonnie Prince Charlie, the reverse with a dolphin within an eight-point star, raised on a plain stem above a thick foot.

ca. 1790   *4¾in (12cm) high*

$4,000-4,500   **WW**

A firing glass, of Masonic or other symbolic significance, the drawn trumpet bowl deeply engraved and gilded with the initials "GB" around crossed anchors beneath a crown, raised on a thick foot.

ca. 1760   *4in (10cm) high*

$875-1,000   **WW**

An Irish cordial glass, the small rounded funnel bowl raised on a thick plain stem, above a characteristic domed foot.

ca. 1740   *6¾in (17cm) high*

$700-800   **WW**

An Irish cordial glass, of Jacobite significance, the small rounded funnel bowl engraved with a rose spray, raised on a thick stem enclosing a long tear, above a basal knop and domed, folded foot.

ca. 1740-50   *6¾in (17cm) high*

$1,600-1,900   **WW**

A toasting glass or wine flute, the slender drawn trumpet bowl rising from a tall, opaque-twist stem, above a conical foot.

ca. 1760-70   *7in (18cm) high*

$375-500   **WW**

A Lynn ale glass, the long round funnel bowl molded with horizontal bands, raised on a double-series opaque-twist stem over a conical foot.

For an Essential Reference on Lynn glass, see page 404.

ca. 1760   *6¼in (16cm) high*

$1,250-1,500   **WW**

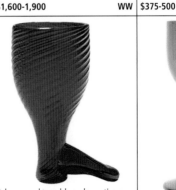

A large and rare blue glass stirrup cup, the wrythen-molded body tapering to a small foot, the whole of a rich cobalt tone.

ca. 1790-1800   *5in (12.5cm) high*

$250-310   **WW**

An 18thC drinking glass, the ovoid bowl above a solid plain stem and conical foot, all in deep green.

ca. 1750   *4¾in (12cm) high*

$190-250   **FLD**

A rare English beaker, the tall rounded funnel bowl deeply engraved with a formal motif of fruit and flowers around a trellis panel, raised on a short beaded knop and thick conical foot.

ca. 1750   *4¾in (12cm) high*

$2,500-3,100   **WW**

A ceremonial goblet or mixing glass, the generous bowl of baluster form, raised on a short knop above a folded helmet foot.

ca. 1750   *10½in (26.5cm) high*

$625-750   **WW**

A large glass ale mug or tankard, engraved with the initials "B/IM" within sprays of hops and barley, the wide strap handle with a scroll terminal.

ca. 1760   *7¼in (18.5cm) high*

$1,050-1,200   **WW**

ESSENTIAL REFERENCE—LYNN GLASS

In much the same way that "Bristol" is a term used to describe almost all blue, green, and amethyst glass made in Great Britain from the late 18thC to the mid-19thC, regardless of its place of origin (see page 407), "Lynn" glass is not restricted to glassware made in what is now Kings Lynn, formerly Lynn Regis or just Lynn, in Norfolk. Instead, it is used generically to describe glassware decorated with horizontal rings or banding, such as on the mid-18thC tumbler shown here. Despite being sometimes referred to as "Lynn molding," it is actually an applied or tooled finish—applied to the inner, outer, or both surfaces of the glass. There is also no definitional restriction on the number of rings—they range from a minimum of 3 to a (rarer) maximum of 12—nor on the uniformity of their spacing.

A large Lynn glass tumbler, the flared cylindrical body molded with concentric horizontal ribs.

ca. 1760-70   *5¾in (14.5cm) high*

$875-1,000   **WW**

A late-18th/early-19thC commemorative rummer, of antislavery interest, engraved on one side with a chained and kneeling figure titled "Am I Not a Man and Brother," the reverse with a verse "Health to the Sick, Honour to the Brave, Success to the Lover and Freedom to the Slave," on a short stem above a thick foot.

6½in (16.5cm) high

$8,000-9,500   **WW**

A ceremonial mixing rummer, engraved in the manner of James Giles, with the Bucrania pattern of bull heads and paterae between husk and leaf swags, engraved with the initials "GB" and "EB" and the date "1801."

1801   *8in (20.5cm) high*

$750-875   **WW**

A pair of early-19thC glass rummers, decorated by William Absolon, the deep bowls gilt with a sailing vessel beneath the partial inscription "Success to the S ...," the reverse of each with monogrammed initials beneath "A Trifle from Yarmouth," general wear on decoration.

5¾in (14.5cm) high

$875-1,000   **WW**

A "Sunderland Bridge" rummer, the bucket-shaped bowl engraved with a titled scene of a ship under the bridge, the reverse with a monogram, a basket of fruit, and flowers, minor manufacturing flaws.

ca. 1820   *7in (18cm) high*

$500-625   **TEN**

An early-18thC English wine bottle, of onion shape with a string rim, heavily iridescent from burial, two rim chips.

6in (15cm) high

$1,250-1,500 DN

An unusual early-18thC pale green tint wine bottle, of onion shape with a string rim, section of rim missing.

5¼in (13.5cm) high

$1,900-2,200 DN

An early-18thC English olive green tint sealed wine bottle, of onion shape with a string rim, applied with a seal with the crest for the 2nd Earl of Clarendon, section of rim missing.

6in (15cm) high

$2,700-3,100 DN

A bottle of wine from the Dutch East Indiaman "Vliegend Hert," wrecked in the Scheldt Estuary, 1735, recovered in 1991, the green glass onion bottle with protruding cork and twine binding, half full with original contents.

7in (18cm) high

$1,500-1,700 CM

A sealed wine bottle, of mallet form, applied with a circular seal inscribed "S.B 1767," minor manufacturing flaws.

1767   9¾in (25cm) high

$950-1,050 TEN

A small glass bottle or carafe, of possible Jacobite significance, the whole engraved with a rose spray and other six-petal flowers.

ca. 1760-70   6¼in (16cm) high

$1,250-1,500 WW

A blue glass decanter or carafe, the pear-shaped body of a deep cobalt hue, possibly gilded in the Giles atelier, with vertical bands of convolvulus twined around a rod, the neck applied with two rings, raised on a low circular foot.

ca. 1770-80   9¾in (25cm) high

$1,000-1,250 WW

A late-18th/early-19thC amethyst glass carafe, the heavy pear-shaped body gilt decorated with four vine tendrils beneath a neck ring.

7in (18cm) high

$250-370 WW

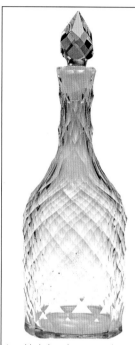

A molded glass decanter and stopper, with an allover diamond design, rising to a facet-cut neck and stopper.

ca. 1770-80   *10¼in (26cm) high*

$500-625   **WW**

A rare magnum decanter, of military interest, one side engraved "PLASSEY 1757" and "BUXAR 1764," the reverse with "THE HONOURABLE COMPANY," with a facet-cut stopper.

The battles of Plassey and Buxar were pivotal victories for the British East India Company during the Seven Years' War. The Battle of Plassey was under the direction of Major General Robert Clive, 1st Baron Clive.

ca. 1770   *14½in (37cm) high*

$2,200-2,500   **WW**

A rare magnum decanter, of Shropshire interest, finely engraved with a large cartouche of fruiting grapevine enclosing the inscription "RED WINE," around the top engraved "ALL FRIENDS ROUND THE WREKIN," the neck applied with annulated neck rings, with a flattened penny stopper.

The Wrekin is a large hill near Telford with an Iron Age hill fort at the top, but the term is also used to refer to the general area of East Shropshire. The toast engraved on this decanter is traditionally used in the county, especially at Christmas and New Year.

ca. 1770-80   *13in (33cm) high*

$1,500-1,900   **WW**

An Irish glass decanter and stopper, by Waterloo Glass Works, Cork, of Prussian shape, engraved with stylized flowers between ribbon bows above a band of vertical molded flutes, the neck applied with three rings, the flattened stopper with a trellis design, molded mark on base.

ca. 1820   *10¼in (26cm) high*

$950-1,050   **WW**

A decanter and stopper, by Salviati, with honeycomb molding rising to a spirally molded neck, with blue rigaree decoration and copper-color aventurine prunts.

ca. 1900   *14¾in (37.5cm) high*

$160-220   **WW**

A Victorian etched glass and silver claret pitcher, by William & George Sissons, Sheffield, the silver mounts repoussé decorated with a floral design, hinged cover with engraved phoenix and pierced thumbpiece, scroll handle, with star-etched bulbous body and star-cut base, on a silver circular foot.

1853   *9¾in (25cm) high*

$1,500-1,700   **MART**

A late-Victorian silver-mounted cut-glass claret pitcher, by E. Hutton, London, hobnail cut-glass body, the mounts with engraved decoration, fluted scroll handle, domed cover with a pierced thumbpiece, on a circular foot, engraved with a crest.

1882   *10½in (26.5cm) high*

$875-1,000   **WW**

A Victorian silver-gilt-mounted "rock crystal" cut-glass claret pitcher, by Charles Edwards, London, with panels of floral and foliate design, the silver-gilt mounts heavily chased and pierced, bearded-mask spout, domed cover with an urn finial, angular handle terminating in a mythical mask, on a petal-shape star-cut base.

1883   *12in (30.5cm) high*

$2,200-2,500   **MART**

A rare composite stem candlestick, with a baluster knop enclosing a row of tears, raised on a Silesian pedestal stem set into triple mereses over a basal teared knop, all over a panel-molded helmet foot.

ca. 1740   *8¼in (21cm) high*

$700-800   **WW**

A pair of cut-glass tapersticks, with flared sconces above hexagonal knops, raised on shaped domed feet, minor chips.

ca. 1790   *6in (15cm) high*

$500-625   **WW**

A pair of early-20thC Bristol blue glass candlesticks, with domed faceted bases.

12in (30.5cm) high

$375-500   **SWO**

An 18thC Spanish façon de Venise "Gemel" bottle or double cruet, comprising two joined flasks for oil and vinegar, each tapering to a curved neck decorated with trailed bands, raised on a circular folded foot.

6¾in (17cm) high

$125-190   **WW**

A rare blue glass salt, the shallow bowl molded with spiral ribs, raised on a knop stem over a wide foot.

ca. 1760-70   *2¾in (7cm) high*

$2,200-2,700   **WW**

A pair of 18thC Bristol green table salts, the round funnel bowls with hollow facet diamonds, on swept and stepped square bases.

ca. 1785   *3¼in (8.5cm) high*

$125-170   **FLD**

ESSENTIAL REFERENCE—BRISTOL GLASS

Although it would be perfectly logical to assume the term "Bristol" applied to glass made in the English port city of that name, it is, in fact, used generically to describe all blue, green, and (rarer) amethyst color glass produced in Great Britain from the end of the 18thC to around the middle of the 19thC. Moreover, only a few pieces are known to have been actually produced in Bristol: decanters, finger bowls, wine glass coolers, and perfume bottles, mostly blue—a color achieved by adding cobalt oxide to the batch—and signed "I Jacobs, Bristol." Jacobs was a gilder working in Bristol around the turn of the 19thC, and gilt decoration is a feature of many pieces of Bristol color glass, regardless of their geographic origin.

An Irish cut-glass bowl or centerpiece, of navette shape with turnover rim cut with bands of fluting, raised on a bobbin stem and fluted foot.

ca. 1820   *13¾in (35cm) wide*

$500-625   **WW**

A late Georgian Bristol blue pedestal bowl, of footed circular form, decorated with a pale blue rim over a dark blue ground.

4¼in (11cm) diam

$190-250   **FLD**

An Italian gilt-metal-mounted green glass vase, probably 17thC, the ovoid body lightly molded, of an emerald green hue, mounted with four winged masks over vertical straps between fleur-de-lis borders.

10½in (26.5cm) high

ca. ... *(see text)*

$1,250-1,500   WW

A blue glass vase, gilded in the London atelier of James Giles, the thistle shape with small flower sprays, including sunflower, rose, and honeysuckle, amid scattered leaf sprigs.

ca. 1770   6¼in (16cm) high

$125-170   WW

A pair of 19thC French Neoclassical glass and ormolu-mounted urns, each set with a scrolling handle on each side of the baguette-cut body, raised on faceted circular-to-square bases and paw feet, mounts tarnished in places.

11¾in (30cm) high

$3,100-3,700   SWO

A pair of early-19thC Anglo-Irish cut-glass vases and covers, with allover geometric cutting, on circular socles and square bases, chips on edges and feet.

12¼in (31cm) high

$550-700   TEN

A tall 19thC Bohemian glass vase, the slender green body applied with an opaque oval painted with the portrait of a young girl in traditional dress, reserved on a dense gilt convolvulus ground.

16½in (42cm) high

$375-500   WW

A Victorian cranberry glass epergne, the center trumpet with trailing decoration, enclosed by three smaller trumpets, with three further examples on spiral stems, all raised on a dished base with scalloped rim, chips and nibbles throughout.

ca. 1880   22in (56cm) high

$350-400   SWO

CLOSER LOOK—A PAIR OF BOHEMIAN GLASS VASES

The rims of the vases are "castellated" (or "crenellated"), an enduringly popular decorative conceit configured in the manner of castle battlements, and notably fashionable in the late 19thC and early 20thC during various Gothic-, Medieval-, and Baronial-style revivals.

Exquisitely painted on a contrasting white-overlay ground, within a gilt-bordered oval medallion, the floral sprays feature various postspring/prefall blooms, collectively known as summer flowers.

The vases are of slender baluster shape—a bulbous, columnar-like form that originally emerged ca. 14thC during the Renaissance, and was essentially inspired by the profiles of diverse vases of Greco-Roman Antiquity.

The gilt and scattered floral and foliate forms on the base of the stems and conical feet echo their counterparts surrounding the floral medallions above. The former are, however, set within elongated and splayed panels that are of a form popular in the contemporary and subsequent Art Nouveau style.

A pair of Bohemian white-overlay green glass vases, with gilt and painted decoration, some wear in gilding.

ca. 1880   14½in (37cm) high

$550-700   TEN

A Baccarat paperweight, with scattered millefiori and Gridel silhouette canes on white cheesecloth, with canes including stardust, ruffle, and shamrock, and a dog, horse, goat, rooster, elephant, and devil, date cane for 1847 with "B."

1847 3¼in (8.5cm) wide

$1,700-2,200 **FLD**

A 19thC French Baccarat paperweight, with a type III pansy with bud set in clear glass, the flowers with dark purple and yellow petals and stardust centers over a star-cut base.

ca. 1850 3¼in (8.5cm) wide

$250-310 **FLD**

A Clichy swirl glass paperweight, the radial opaque white and turquoise threads centering on a red and white pastry-mold cane, small scratches.

ca. 1850 2¾in (7cm) diam

$550-700 **MART**

A St. Louis "Clematis" glass paperweight, the swirling white latticinio ground supporting a flower with two rows of pointed pink petals around yellow stamens, short stem with five green leaves, natural flaws in glass, small scratches.

ca. 1850 2½in (6.5cm) diam

$375-450 **MART**

A St. Louis floral millefiori glass paperweight, double-white spiral latticinio cushion, set with six diamond star-shaped arrangements of canes in pastel shades of greens and pinks, centered on a large blue and yellow florette, minor manufacturing flaws.

3in (7.5cm) diam

$520-600 **MART**

A rare 19thC Baccarat Maltese cross/cruciform glass paperweight, the rich red ground set in the center with an opaque white cross, surrounded by a garland of white star-head florettes with green centers, small scratches.

2¾in (7cm) diam

$1,250-1,500 **MART**

A 19thC St. Louis miniature crown glass paperweight, decorated with six crown twists in lime green and red, alternating with latticino twists all radiating from a centered green, white, and pink cane.

1¾in (4.5cm) diam

$550-625 **MART**

A Baccarat millefiori mushroom glass paperweight, the center tuft tightly packed with colorful composite canes, the base encircled by a blue and white spiral torsade, star-cut base, small scratches.

ca. 1850 3in (7.5cm) diam

$800-950 **MART**

A 19thC Old English paperweight inkwell, possibly by Richardsons, with a concentric ruffle and cog cane-work canopy in red, white, and blue below a collar neck, with matched mushroom-form stopper with single large cane.

5½in (14cm) high

$220-275 **FLD**

A mid-17thC Commonwealth pewter trumpet candlestick, with banded decoration on the neck, drip tray and foot, with a "TC" touchmark on the collar.

5¼in (13.5cm) high

$2,500-3,100 WW

A pair of George II silver candlesticks, by John Cafe, London, on knop stems and stepped quatrefoil bases.

1749 *7½in (19cm) high 32oz*

$2,100-2,500 HT

A pair of early-19thC Regency gilt-bronze candlesticks, after a design by Cheney, London, with engine-milled decoration, on tripod eagle monopodia.

8½in (21.5cm) high

$625-750 WW

A pair of French gilt and patinated bronze candlesticks, with reeded stems, on laurel-leaf cast circular bases.

ca. 1820 *7in (18cm) high*

$750-875 L&T

A pair of early-19thC William IV bronze candlesticks, attributed to Thomas Abbott, the stems modeled as storks standing on naturalistic domed bases cast with shells.

15¾in (40cm) high

$550-700 L&T

An English Gothic Revival brass candlestick, set with jeweled cabochons.

ca. 1870 *48½in (123cm) high*

$450-550 L&T

ESSENTIAL REFERENCE—LE DIRECTOIRE

Exotic in both style and composition by today's standards, this pair of black and gilt, winged cherub-supporting urn candlesticks are from a period in France that was, in terms of decoration, significantly less extravagant than the periods that preceded and followed it. Comprising the last four years of the French Revolution (1795-99), when the French First Republic was directed by a five-member committee, it was known as "Le Directoire," and furniture and decorative artifacts made during it are described as being, ergo, in the Directoire style. Like the style that dominated the reign of Louis XVI before the Revolution, Directoire was Neoclassical, with its inspiration primarily drawn from the Classical Greco-Roman vocabulary of ornament. However, Directoire was a more austere, pared-down version of it than not only its predecessor but also its successor: the overtly grand and essentially imperial Roman-inspired Empire style ushered in by Napoleon Bonaparte after he overthrew the First Republic in 1799 and replaced it with the Consulate.

A pair of Directoire bronze and ormolu candlesticks, each urn-shaped nozzle supported by a standing cherub, on milled feet and square white marble plinths, one loose mount, chips in marble.

ca. 1795 *15¾in (40cm) high*

$1,400-1,600 SWO

A pair of French ormolu candlesticks, in Louis XV style, after a design by Juste-Aurele Meissonnier, the detachable sconces with rose-head details, on shafts of Rococo-style scrolling with a coronet set among the foliate scrolls, each on a spreading foot.

Juste-Aurele Meissonnier (1695-1750) was the leading and most extravagant pioneer of the Rococo style. He was born in Italy, the son of a silversmith and sculptor, but moved to Paris to work for the Royal Gobelins Manufactory. He received his warrant as master goldsmith from Louis XV in 1724. Described by one of his contemporaries as an "unruly genius, and what's more, spoiled by Italy," he produced designs for chairs, tables, lanterns, candlesticks, clocks, and even crucifixes. Meissonnier rendered three drawings of these candlesticks to show their exuberantly asymmetrical design. The drawings were engraved by Gabriel Huquier (1695-1772) and published in "Deuxieme Livre des oeuvres de J.A.Meissonnier: Livre de chandeliers de sculpture en argent" (1734-35). An almost identical pair of candlesticks can be seen in the Metropolitan Museum of Art, New York, accession no. 1999.370.1a.b,.2a,b.

12¼in (31cm) high

$3,100-3,700 WW

A pair of 19thC French ormolu three-light candelabra, in Louis XV style, each modeled with a cherub, supporting a branch issuing three flower-head nozzles, on Rococo scroll bases, the undersides with incised initials "EB."

15¼in (39cm) high

$450-500   WW

A pair of mid-19thC French bronze and gilt-metal three-light candelabra, in Empire style, each modeled as a winged figure standing on an orb, holding an urn with three scrolling candle holders, on cylindrical pedestals with engine-turned decoration and square feet.

25¾in (65.5cm) high

$1,900-2,200   WW

A pair of 19thC French gilt-metal and white marble three-branch candelabra, each surmounted by a figure of Pan sitting on a fluted circular boss, flanked by cornucopia branches and flower sockets, on tripod supports and circular bases with foliate scroll feet, one socket missing the liner, one figure of Pan slightly loose, minor surface scratching.

14¼in (36cm) high

$1,100-1,350   TEN

A pair of 19thC gilt-bronze and white marble-mounted twin-light candelabra, each modeled as a putto carrying flaming torches, the reeded column bases with gilt laurel wreaths and stepped bases.

17in (43cm) high

$500-625   CHEF

A 19thC gilt-bronze four-light candelabrum, in Empire style, the three branches around a center light with removable flame, on a fluted column and tripod base with lion-paw monopodia interspersed with lion-head masks.

23¼in (59cm) high

$1,500-1,900   WW

A pair of brass table candelabra, in Gothic Revival style, flimsy mounts.

29½in (75cm) high

$450-500   CHOR

A pair of large late-19thC French bronze and ormolu candelabra, with female figural stems supporting ten-light candelabra, on cockerel-mounted bases, loss in patina, slightly distorted in areas.

60in (152.5cm) high

$6,000-7,500   DN

An Edwardian silver four-branch five-light candelabrum, by Hawksworth Eyre & Co. Ltd., Sheffield, the Corinthian capitals issuing from acanthus-sheathed scroll branches, on a single pendant husk-stamped column, on a swept square foot stamped with Neoclassical-style urns with a gadrooned border.

1909   18in (45.5cm) high 44oz

$1,500-1,700   HT

A pair of George V silver dwarf twin-light candelabra, by R. Comyns, London, with baluster columns and scroll branches, with large center baluster finials, on circular feet, the underside inscribed "Presented to Edmund de Rothschild, by his friends at Exbury, Jan 2, 1937."

1936   7¾in (19.5cm) high

$1,000-1,250   WW

An early-19thC French Charles X bronze and parcel-gilt chandelier, with nine scrolled arms each supporting a candle sconce, the center surmounted by a Classical urn, the base with parcel-gilt flower buds, suspended on ornately linked chains.

39¼in (100cm) high

$3,000-3,500   **SWO**

A 19thC French gilt and bronze 15-light chandelier, the star-studded globe surmounted by a sitting maiden, issuing naturalistic branches, repairs in two arms.

22¾in (58cm) high

$1,000-1,250   **CHEF**

A large 19thC cut-glass 12-light chandelier, in George III style, the faceted ovoid compound baluster column with a ball, issuing a crown of shepherd crooks above two tiers of six faceted scrolling lights with flower-head drip trays, festooned allover with faceted beads, lusters, circular and tear-shaped drops, above a pendant base, with silvered metal, one arm broken, later fitted for electricity.

69¾in (177cm) high

$5,000-6,200   **WW**

A 19thC gilt-brass and crystal basket chandelier, the corona and ring band cast with thistles, roses, and shamrocks, hung with prim strands, converted to electricity.

31in (79cm) high

$950-1,200   **L&T**

A large giltwood 18-light chandelier, probably late 19th/early 20thC, in early-18thC French style, with S-scroll arms on two tiers, 6 lights above, 12 lights below, the whole on a spiral-turned floral stem.

93¾in (238cm) high

$15,000-19,000   **DN**

A late-19th/early-20thC French green glass and gilt-metal chandelier, with eight scrolling branches, decorated allover with fruit and trailing foliage, the body with gilt-heightened detail, surface wear.

26½in (67cm) high

$2,500-3,100   **SWO**

An early-20thC Bohemian blue and clear glass chandelier, for the Persian market, the center baluster issuing scrolling arms ending in dished bobeche and hurricane shades depicting various Qajar rulers, wear, chips, repairs.

51¼in (130cm) high

$8,000-9,500   **SWO**

An English brass chandelier, with period opalescent glass shades.

ca. 1910   *22in (66cm) diam*

$1,250-1,500   **L&T**

An early-20thC gilt-bronze, crystal, and Jasperware-mounted chandelier, in Regency style, the foliate cast frame hung with prism drops and swags, the center ring with ram masks and issuing four scrolling candle arms, mounted with oval green Jasperware plaques with Classical figures.

29½in (75cm) high

$2,000-2,400   **L&T**

A pair of 19thC Venetian gondola lanterns, black painted with parcel-gilt decoration, each surmounted by a crown, the four corner sections mounted with gilt urn finials, the joins with applied gilt flower heads, the gilt bases for mounting on poles.

49¼in (125cm) high

$2,500-3,100   CA

A 19thC Victorian silvered metal and leaded stained-glass pentagonal hall lantern, with leaded glass panels displaying armorial shields in a metal frame, with leaf scrolls, shields, fleur-de-lis, flowers, and shamrocks.

38¼in (97cm) high

$1,000-1,250   L&T

A 19thC French ebonized and gilt-copper hall lantern, with an oak-leaf and acorn corona, fitted with a later three-light fitting, with a pendant base.

30¼in (77cm) high

$2,500-3,100   WW

A late-19thC Victorian gilt-brass hexagonal hall lantern, with scroll supports above glass panels, four decorated with knights standing on plinths, the hinged door with a clenched fist handle.

20¾in (52.5cm) high

$1,000-1,250   WW

A late-19thC Victorian gilt-brass pentagonal hall lantern, the foliate corona above scrolling supports and floral swags, with serpentine panes.

20½in (52cm) high

$375-500   WW

A late-19thC French ormolu "Versailles" hall lantern, with an open crown surmount decorated with fleur-de-lis and issuing a chain, the octagonal faceted body with beveled glass panels, applied with shells and flower heads, with a single light fitting, the base with bearded male masks and a probably later cone pendant.

30½in (77.5cm) high

$1,250-1,600   WW

A late-19thC gilt-brass hexagonal hall lantern, the arched panes beneath an ogee top with suspension hoop and twisting chain, the base with swagged decoration.

12¼in (31cm) high

$500-625   WW

A large "Verdigris Leone" spherical lantern, in 19thC Italian style, formed from copper frames with a verdigris finish, decorated with gilt lion-head figures.

32¾in (83cm) high

$1,900-2,200   CA

A pair of 20thC tole-framed and glazed octagonal lanterns, in 18thC Italian style, with scrolling floral frames, black finish with paint loss in areas, one pane cracked, glass beveled.

45¼in (115cm) high

$1,900-2,200   DN

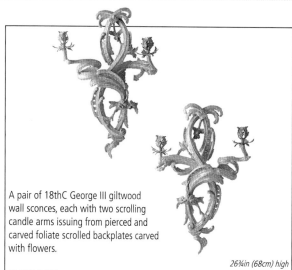

A pair of 18thC George III giltwood wall sconces, each with two scrolling candle arms issuing from pierced and carved foliate scrolled backplates carved with flowers.

26¾in (68cm) high

$1,900-2,200   L&T

A rare pair of mid-19thC French ormolu twin-light wall appliques, in Louis XV style, naturalistically cast as branches of oak leaves and acorns suspended from ribbon-tied drapes, later drilled and fitted for electricity.

24in (61cm) high

$10,000-12,500   WW

A pair of 19thC carved giltwood wall sconces, the cartouche-shaped backs centered by a cypher above a musical trophy and single scrolled candle arms, the backs flanked by wings and surmounted by a coronet.

22in (56cm) high

$3,700-5,000   L&T

A pair of 19thC French ormolu twin-light wall appliques, in Louis XVI style, after a design by Quentin-Claude Pitoin, in the manner of Jean-Charles Delafosse, each with a center flaming urn with swags above a ram head, with fluted columns and fruiting foliate terminals, flanked by a pair of sconces with stiff leaf decoration, with scrolling brackets and laurel swags, later adapted for electricity.

21¾in (55.5cm) high

$3,100-3,700   WW

A pair of late-19thC ormolu twin-light wall lights, in Louis XVI style, each with a ribbon and urn backplate.

15¼in (38.5cm) high

$375-500   WW

A pair of early-20thC Italian color glass, beaded and gilt-metal wall lights, with twin candle arms, hung with color glass drops in the form of fruits and leaves, fitted for electricity.

12½in (32cm) high

$750-1,000   L&T

A late-19thC plated standard oil lamp, the clear glass funnel and opaque glass shade above a bulbous knop, on a spiral column support, raised on three splayed legs and hoof feet.

63in (160cm) high

$500-625   CHEF

A Victorian brass standard lamp, of columnar form, surmounted by a cranberry glass reservoir and etched glass shade, on claw feet.

$100-125   WHP

A large 19thC Continental giltwood pricket standard lamp, in Baroque style, carved with shell motifs, C scrolls, and acanthus scrolls, on an ebonized tripartite base with bun feet, converted to electricity, with a pleated red silk shade.

51½in (131cm) high (excluding fitting)

$375-500   L&T

A pair of early-19thC Regency plaster torchère figures of Bacchus and Flora, in the manner of Humphrey Hopper, possibly after the bronze model by Pierre Garnier, Bacchus draped with a lion pelt and holding a gilt-brass wine cup, Flora standing beside a tree stump holding a ewer, each supporting a frosted glass storm lantern shade, mounted on gilt-bronze bases, on modern painted wood plinths.

figures 36½in (92.5cm) high

$2,500-3,100   **WW**

A pair of gilt-metal-mounted variegated pink marble table lamps, in George III style, as Corinthian columns, on stepped square bases and bracket feet, one column with resin infill from manufacture, metal dull, wear.

22½in (57cm) high

$750-875   **TEN**

A 19thC ruby glass paraffin lamp base, with lacquered brass mounts.

24¾in (63cm) high

$625-750   **L&T**

A copper and brass oil lamp, attributed to W. A. S. Benson, with copper petal and foliate decoration, on four feet, fitted with a glass chimney and a frilled Vaseline glass shade, the wick adjuster marked "Maple London," "Hinks Patent."

22¾in (58cm) high

$875-1,100   **CHOR**

A pair of large Regency bronze and gilt-bronze triform candlestick lamps, with pleated silk shades, converted for electricity.

19in (48cm) high

$1,400-1,700   **CHEF**

A pair of 19thC patinated bronze and gilt-metal lamps, converted from candlesticks, the flower-cast nozzles over tapering fluted lotus-cast stems, on circular bases with leaf decoration, with taupe pinch-pleated shades.

11½in (29.5cm) high (excluding fittings)

$2,000-2,200   **L&T**

A pair of large faux-bronze and ormolu table lamps, in Empire style, with reeded columns and triform bases, with cream pleated shades.

26½in (67cm) high

$550-700   **CHEF**

A Nelson's Column copper table lamp, by the Art Union of London, mounted on a wood base, stamped on base "ART-UNION OF LONDON, 1868."

In 1838, the Nelson Memorial Committee proposed a General Subscription for the purpose of erecting a national Nelson monument in London. William Railton won the design competition, and his Corinthian column decorated with bronze acanthus leaves cast from British cannon was finally completed in 1843. E. H. Baily's 18ft-high statue of Nelson, facing south, toward the Palace of Westminster, surmounted the 184ft-high granite column in November of the same year. The bas-reliefs of the four battle scenes around the base were added in 1854, and Landseer's lions were placed at the four corners in 1867.

1868   22in (56cm) high (excluding fitting)

$11,000-14,000   **L&T**

A pair of large early-20thC Italian gray marble lamps, carved with stiff leaves and bacchic masks, on square plinths with molded bases, fitted for electricity, with demi-drum shades.

38¼in (97cm) high (excluding fittings)

$2,200-2,500   **L&T**

JEWELRY

ESSENTIAL REFERENCE—THE STUART PERIOD

In Great Britain, antiques are often descriptively labeled, at least in part, according to which monarch was on the throne when they were made. Those made from 1603-1714, during the dynasty of the House of Stuart, can be described as "Stuart." However, more specific descriptions are sometimes employed to better reflect the stylistic impact that political and social upheavals of the period had on the decorative arts. These include:

- "Jacobean": 1603-25, the period when James VI of Scotland inherited the English crown on the death of Elizabeth I and became James I.
- "Caroline": 1625-49, the term derived from the Latin for Charles, and the period when Charles I was king; it overlaps with a subcategory—"Civil War," the period from 1642 when the Crown was at war with Parliament.
- "Interregnum": 1649-60, the term for the period following the execution of Charles I in May 1649, when England was ruled under various forms of republican government, including The Protectorate.
- "Carolean": 1660-85, also known as "Restoration," when Charles II was restored to the throne following the demise of The Protectorate.
- "William and Mary": 1689-1702, the reign of William III of Orange and Mary II (d. 1694)—the nephew and daughter of James II respectively, who went into exile during the "Glorious Revolution" of 1688.
- "Queen Anne": 1702-14, the reign of Queen Anne, daughter of James II, and the last of the Stuart monarchs.

A 17thC "Stuart Crystal" pendent brooch, the plaque with a hairwork center on a blue ground, applied with two putti holding a crown above a gilt-thread cypher, all beneath a faceted crystal, within a frame of split pearls and garnets in foiled closed-back settings, the reverse decorated with white, pink, and black enamel, suspended from a later surmount set with a baroque split pearl and three circular-cut garnets.

The type of jewels popularly known as "Stuart Crystals" were created as tokens of love, loyalty, and commemoration from the mid-17thC until the early 18thC. Initially created to commemorate the death of King Charles I and the Stuart monarchy, panels of woven hair, monograms, crowns, and initials in gold thread were set in gold or gilt beneath faceted rock crystal or paste covers to wear as rings or slides around the neck or wrist. Some of the more elaborate examples were embellished with coronets, hearts, skeletons, and winged putti decorated in polychrome enamel.

ca. 1680   1in (2.5cm) wide
$4,000-4,300   WW

An early-18thC "Stuart Crystal" and diamond mourning ring, set on the front with a coffin-shaped faceted rock crystal between rose-cut diamonds, the band carved with a skeleton and hourglass applied with black enamel, the interior inscribed "Let us share in joy and care," indistinct maker's mark, possibly "IC."

size J½
$6,000-7,500   WW

A rare gold, enamel, pearl, and diamond crucifix pendant, depicting Christ on the cross, a banner reading "INRI" above and the skull of Golgotha below, applied with white enamel en-ronde bosse, the cross with engraved wood grain applied with brown basse-taille enamel, accented with table-cut diamonds and suspending a pearl (untested), enamel losses.

ca. 1600   1¾in (4.5cm) long
$12,500-15,000   WW

A mid-17thC silver locket pendant, possibly French, glazed with faceted glass and containing paper scrolls, inscribed with the names of martyrs or saints, twisted-rope design border with a coral pendant, suspending from three silver chains.

$500-625

2in (5cm) long
WW

A rare "Stuart Crystal" mourning slide, set with a faceted section of rock crystal, covering a reclining skeleton on painted cardboard beneath entwined initials in gold wire, on a ground of woven hair, mounted in gold.

ca. 1690   1in (2.5cm) wide
$4,000-4,300   WW

A late-17th/early-18thC gold posy ring, lobed and engraved "Not for riches but for love."

ca. 1700   size L½ ¼oz
$3,100-3,500   JON

A 17thC rock crystal and enamel ring, set with seven graduated rose-cut rock crystals in cut-down collets, with black enamel decoration on the gallery, in closed-back yellow gold setting, with carved gold shoulders.

size S
$1,500-1,900   WW

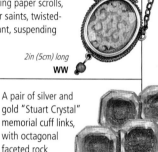

A pair of silver and gold "Stuart Crystal" memorial cuff links, with octagonal faceted rock crystal covers, over a fine twisted-wire monogram with a crown above, believed to be that of the Earls of Strathmore and Kinghorne, silver backs with gold conjoined hoop connections, one hinge broken, tarnished, and dirty.

Provenance: Formerly in the collection of Sir Timothy Colman KG. Sir Timothy Colman was married to Lady Mary Bowes-Lyon, niece of Elizabeth Bowes-Lyon, the Queen Mother. The family are descendants of King Robert II, the first Stuart King of Scots, who was a grandson of Robert the Bruce. Bowes-Lyon is the family name of the Earls of Strathmore and Kinghorne.

ca. 1700
$2,700-3,100   SWO

An early-18thC "Stuart Crystal" miniature portrait, the faceted rock crystal over an ivory portrait miniature of a woman, possibly Queen Anne, within an openwork scroll frame, surmounted by a crown applied with enamel and set with a tiny diamond crystal, fittings deficient.

1¼in (3cm) high
$5,000-6,200   WW

An 18thC garnet slide floral pendant, with detachable lower section, mounted in silver.

2½in (6.5cm) long

$800-950   WW

A George III locket pendant, with a glazed miniature of a gentleman on front and verso, in a graduated border of blue enamel with white enameled borders, with half-seed pearl accents, signed with the initials "S.C. 1757," with possibly later triangular bale, light scratches.

Ivory Act certification no. RXULYS34Y

ca. 1790   1¾in (4.5cm) diam ⅝oz

$700-800   DN

A late-18thC Georgian ivory miniature navette brooch, with a glazed ivory miniature of a woman holding a basket of fruit, the basket intricately composed of seed pearls and gold, in a border of blue and white enamel banding, the reverse with a glazed compartment for hair, applied with intertwined initials, mounted in gold, later brooch fittings.

1¾in (4.5cm) high

$800-950   WW

A Wedgwood Jasperware abolitionist cameo, in black and white ceramic depicting a kneeling enslaved African, his hands and feet in chains, with a motto reading "Am I not a Man and a Brother?," on a plain gold mount.

ca. 1790   1½in (4cm) long

$3,100-3,700   WW

An 18thC Georgian garnet and hairwork pendant, converted from a ribbon slide, the glazed compartment set with a section of cardboard applied with hair arranged in the form of a ship at sea, within a border of cushion-shaped garnets, mounted in gold.

¾in (2cm) long

$2,100-2,500   WW

A rare French enamel, ruby, and diamond ring, designed as a pair of doves among flowering branches, applied with black, white, green, and deep blue enamel, set with rose-cut diamonds and cushion-shaped rubies, the reverse similarly enameled with an indistinct inscription in French, in a fluted gold shank.

See Hugh Tait ed., "The Art of the Jeweller: A Catalogue of the Hull Grundy Gift to the British Museum," British Museum (1984), page 77, no. 360 for an illustration of a ring of similar design, probably intended as a betrothal gift (British Museum accession no. 1978,1002.213). A similar design by the French jeweler Maria, published in Paris ca. 1765, is illustrated in Charlotte Gere, "Rings from 1500-1900," in A. Ward et al., "The Ring from Antiquity to the Twentieth Century," Thames & Hudson (1981), page 110-11.

ca. 1765   size L½

$25,000-31,000   WW

An 18thC gold, enamel, and diamond ring, the table-cut diamond within a domed square gold mount, accented with arches of black and pale blue enamel, on a shank with engraved shoulders.

size N½

$5,000-5,600   WW

A George III diamond cluster ring, the pear-shaped diamond within a diamond surround and stylized diamond coronet, closed-back gold setting, on a pierced and fluted gold shank.

size L½

$3,100-3,700   WW

A Georgian amethyst and diamond mourning ring, set with an oval amethyst within a closed-back setting, between rose-cut diamonds backed with green foil, mounted in gold, the shank applied with black enamel with the dedicatory inscription "MARY ROBINSON OB:24 MAR1785 AE43" in reserve.

ca. 1785   size S½

$1,500-1,900   WW

A late-18thC George III diamond cross pendant, set with rose-cut diamonds in foil-backed cut-down collet settings.

1½in (4cm) long

$625-750   WW

A late-18thC diamond pendant, comprising a stylized palmette and bow motif suspending a diamond cluster drop, closed-back silver setting, later pendant fittings and loop.

1½in (4cm) long

$4,000-4,300   WW

A late-18thC enamel and diamond brooch, set with a border of graduated old mine-cut diamonds surrounding a blue enamel plaque set with diamonds, in a silver and gold closed-back setting, folding pendant loop.

1½in (4cm) wide

$8,500-10,000   WW

A George III enamel mourning ring, with a blue and white urn on an opalescent ground beneath a glazed panel, with a black enamel coronet above the initials "EG," the reverse engraved "Elizabeth Viscountess Galloway Ob 2nd Jan.y 1792 aet 65," on a tapered polished shank, chips.

ca. 1792   *size T ¼oz*

$4,600-5,200   DN

A late-18th/early-19thC hardstone cameo ring, the carved agate cameo depicting a woman in profile, her hair elaborately styled, on a gold mount, restoration.

cameo 1¼in (3cm) long

$750-875   WW

A diamond brooch, set with rose-cut diamonds in a foliate spray issuing from a cluster, possibly intended as a stylized depiction of Halley's Comet, mounted in silver.

ca. 1800   *2¼in (5.5cm) high*

$1,700-2,200   WW

A George III garnet-set flower-head brooch, the flat-cut garnets in closed-back silver settings, later brooch fitting.

1½in (4cm) diam

$625-750   WW

An early-19thC Georgian gold and emerald locket brooch, designed as a ribbon bow intricately constructed from gold filigree, the center floral motif set with a step-cut emerald, the reverse with a glazed locket compartment for hair.

1½in (4cm) wide

$625-750   WW

A Georgian topaz cross pendant, the faceted topaz arms in gold cut-down collet settings, polished loop bale, on a later belcher link chain, chip in topaz, clasp broken.

ca. 1810   *1½in (4cm) long ¼oz*

$1,000-1,250   DN

ESSENTIAL REFERENCE—REGENCY & LATE GEORGIAN

Strictly speaking in terms of dates, the label "Regency" should be applied to artifacts made in Great Britain from 1811-20, the period when, due to his father King George III's (mental) illness, George, Prince of Wales, was appointed Prince Regent to discharge royal functions. However, for stylistic reasons, it is more often used for a longer period— namely, from 1811-30—to encompass the reign of the Prince of Wales who, on the death of his father in 1820, was elevated from Prince Regent to George IV. On occasions, "Regency" is also stretched to cover 1811-37, and thus include the reign of George IV's brother, William IV. However, primarily because of the stylistic changes that were gradually gaining traction, that period is more usefully described as "Late Georgian."

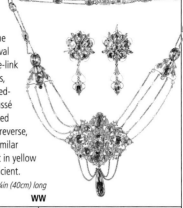

An early-19thC Regency topaz and gold necklace, the chain set with graduated oval topazes separated with fine-link neck chains and seed pearls, suspending a topaz and seed-pearl pendant within repoussé gold surrounds, with a glazed locket compartment in the reverse, later clasp, with a pair of similar Regency topaz earrings, set in yellow gold, one earring hook deficient.

necklace 15¾in (40cm) long
$5,000-6,200   **WW**

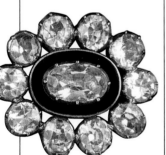

An early-19thC Regency gold guard chain, the circular links with engraved decoration and a gold cannetille barrel clasp.

14¼in (36cm) long ¾oz
$1,900-2,200   **WW**

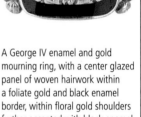

A Regency gold micromosaic necklace, the graduated oval micromosaics within yellow gold cannetille, French import mark on clasp, with matching earrings.

necklace 18in (46cm) long
$6,000-7,500   **WW**

A George IV enamel and gold mourning ring, with a center glazed panel of woven hairwork within a foliate gold and black enamel border, within floral gold shoulders further accented with black enamel, the reverse engraved "Sarah Slatter died 27th Jan 1822 Aged 36," British hallmark for 18ct gold, date letter for 1822.

ca. 1822   size O
$800-950   **WW**

A late Georgian chrysoberyl mourning brooch, designed as a cluster of oval chrysoberyls in foil-backed settings, accented with a band of black enamel, mounted in gold, the reverse inscribed "HIJ, Ob 23 Jan 1827."

ca. 1827   1¼in (3cm) wide
$1,900-2,200   **WW**

An early-19thC chalcedony intaglio and diamond brooch, set with a section of chalcedony engraved with an intaglio of Ceres in profile, within a silver scrollwork frame set with rose-cut diamonds, accented with blue enamel, later brooch fitting.

2¾in (7cm) high
$1,700-2,200   **WW**

A Regency three-color gold "giardinetti" brooch, with yellow, rose, and green gold textured and incised flower heads and leaves, with a cushion-cut sapphire, garnet, and ruby set among cabochon coral birds, above a woven basket, with a pin and "C" catch, chip on sapphire.

2in (5cm) wide ¼oz
$750-1,000   **SWO**

A gold cannetille "St. Esprit" brooch, the beaded cannetille dove in flight, set with oval-, cushion-, and pear-cut rubies and emeralds, suspending a ruby accented heart from its beak, with a glazed locket verso.

1830s   1½in (4cm) wide ¼oz
$3,000-3,500   **DN**

ESSENTIAL REFERENCE—ETRUSCAN REVIVAL

The ancient civilization of Etruria was centered on what became Tuscany and part of Umbria, in Italy, from the 7thC BC until about 200 BC, when it was supressed by the Romans. Artifacts discovered there during archaeological excavations in the 18thC, notably a number of black and red vases, were long thought to be Etruscan and, indeed, became the basis of the fashionable "Etruscan Style," especially in furniture, ceramics, and interior design, until the end of the 18thC— when it was realized that they were, in fact, Greek in origin! However, further archaeological digs in the early 19thC, most notably at Vulci on the estate of Lucien Bonaparte, unearthed authentic Etruscan gold and jewelry that provided patterns and templates for contemporary jewelers to produce pieces, such as the examples shown here. Accurately described as "Etruscan Revival," they were also often referred to as being "Archaeological" in style.

A Victorian Etruscan Revival brooch, with beaded and wirework detail throughout, set with three lapis lazuli beads, unmarked.

2½in (6.5cm) wide

$550-700   L&T

A mid- to late-19thC Etruscan Revival micromosaic brooch, depicting a woman holding a book, in a red dress and green and white shawls, with a beaded stylized border, unmarked.

1½in (4cm) diam

$2,500-3,100   L&T

A mid-Victorian shell cameo brooch, the cameo carved with a trio of cherubs in flight, after Thorvaldsen, within a gold rope-twist border, hairline cracks, repairs.

ca. 1860   1¾in (4.5cm) wide ⅜oz

$625-750   DN

An early-Victorian multi-gem brooch, with a center octagonal-cut sapphire in a claw setting, surrounded by pink foiled-back oval-cut stones, oval-cut chrysoberyls, and half pearls, set above radiating hooped wired settings, all with beaded surrounds, later brooch fitting, repairs, tarnishing.

ca. 1850   1¾in (4.5cm) high ½oz

$3,100-3,700   DN

A Royal enamel and pearl mourning brooch, attributed to Carlo Giuliano, containing a hand-colored photograph of Princess Alice of England (1843-78) behind a glazed panel, within a black and white enamel border of floral design and an outer border of pearls, mounted in gold, reverse inscribed "In remembrance of dear Alice Princess of England, Duchess of Hesse" and monogrammed "VRI" for Victoria Regina Imperatrix, later replaced brooch fitting partly obscuring inscription.

1880s   1½in (4cm) diam

$5,000-6,200   WW

A mid-19thC gem-set mourning brooch, of open scrolling design, the glazed panel with braided hair, in a border of color gems and scrolling braided hair motifs, engraved on reverse "W.T. 1861," unmarked.

1½in (4cm) wide

$450-500   L&T

A 19thC chrysolite and ruby brooch, designed as a bird with outstretched wings, its feathers set with variously shaped chrysolites, its eye set with a small ruby, mounted in silver on gold.

3in (7.5cm) wide

$3,500-4,000   WW

A 19thC topaz and diamond brooch, the center topaz in an openwork silver and gold mount of foliate design, set with rose-cut and cushion-shaped diamonds, later brooch fitting.

1¼in (3cm) wide

$3,100-3,500   WW

A Victorian gold locket brooch, with a polychrome enamel posy of flowers, the hinged and glazed locket compartment in yellow gold.

1½in (4cm) high

$350-400   WW

A Victorian diamond spray brooch, the flower head centered by an old-cut stone of approximately 0.30ct, in an unmarked white and yellow frame.

$1,500-1,900   HT

A Victorian gold, silver, and diamond target drop-pendant brooch, retailed by Carlo & Arthur Giuliano, cluster set with old round- and rose-cut diamonds, the center stone 0.65-0.70ct, with detachable attachments enabling it to be worn as a brooch or pendant, one tiny diamond missing, small area of lead solder, in a fitted C & A Giuliano gilt-tooled leather box.

3¼in (8.5cm) high ¾oz

$6,000-7,500   GORL

A Victorian pearl and diamond star brooch, the 12-point star set throughout with graduated pearls, with an old cushion-cut diamond in center, unmarked.

1½in (4cm) wide

$625-750   L&T

A 19thC multi-gem-set "giardinetti" brooch, the pierced gold basket with etched decoration, holding an array of gold-backed silver flower heads set with old mine- and rose-cut diamonds, with cabochon ruby and emerald accents, verso with engraved floral decoration and brooch fitting, clasp later.

1½in (4cm) wide ⅝oz

$4,300-5,000   DN

An onyx cameo, by Filippo Tignani, the black and white banded stone finely carved to depict Alexander the Great wearing a laureated helmet surmounted by a dragon, the reverse inscribed "Tignani Filipp Incisore Romano li 10 8bre 1870," cameo signed "F. Tignani Inc.."

The iconography of a handsome male figure with long curling hair wearing an elaborate dragon-crested helmet was especially popular in 19thC cameo carving and is commonly identified as Achilles (see British Museum, collection no. 1978,1002.1049 from the Hull Grundy Collection, by Luigi Rosi). However, the dragon-topped helmet is traditionally associated with depictions of Alexander the Great—for example, the relief of Alexander the Great in the National Gallery of Art, Washington, D.C., from the workshop of Andrea del Verrocchio (ca. 1435-88), accession no. 1956.2.1.

1870   *1½in (4cm) high*

$1,700-2,200   WW

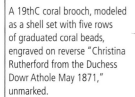

A 19thC coral brooch, modeled as a shell set with five rows of graduated coral beads, engraved on reverse "Christina Rutherford from the Duchess Dowr Athole May 1871," unmarked.

Anne Murray, Duchess of Atholl (1814-97), was wife to George Murray, 6th Duke of Atholl, and a close friend and Lady of the Bedchamber to Queen Victoria between 1854-97. It is believed that the Duchess was the first person Queen Victoria spoke to following the death of Prince Albert, leaving the bedroom where he had died and proclaiming "Oh, Duchess, he is dead!" The Duke and Duchess preferred the spelling Athole for their title and residence, hence the irregular spelling on the reverse of this brooch.

1¼in (3cm) wide

$550-625   L&T

A mid- to late-19thC brooch, of scrolling design with pendant detail, unmarked.

3½in (9cm) high

$3,100-3,700   L&T

A late-19thC French gold, pearl, and enamel brooch, with five raised claw-set pearls, within a blue-enameled quatrefoil border and blue-enameled hooped surround, the clasp stamped with French poinçon, enamel losses, small patches of lead solder.

ca. 1880   *1½in (4cm) diam ⅝oz*

$1,250-1,500   DN

A late-19thC hardstone cameo, the panel carved with Eros (Cupid) aiming his bow and arrow at a reclining deity, possibly Daphne, within an associated gold-color and half-pearl border, with brooch fitting, restorations, later backplate.

1¼in (3cm) wide ⅜oz

$480-520   DN

A late-19thC intaglio brooch, centering on a rock crystal cabochon carved to the reverse with a painted intaglio of a Maltese terrier, within a gilt frame, on a later gold bar brooch.

2in (5cm) wide

$875-1,100   WW

A late-19th/early-20thC cameo brooch, depicting a Classical beauty and her eagle.

2¼in (5.5cm) high ⅞oz

$590-650   WHP

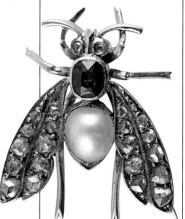

A late-Victorian gold bug brooch, set with a sapphire, baroque pearl, and rose-cut diamonds, one tiny eye diamond missing.

1in (2.5cm) wide ⅛oz

$800-950   GORL

A late-19thC gem-set butterfly brooch, set with circular-cut sapphires and rubies, rose-cut diamonds, and pearls, mounted in silver on gold.

1½in (4cm) wide

$1,000-1,500   WW

ESSENTIAL REFERENCE—MICHAEL PERKHIN

Russian jeweler Michael Evanipievich Perkhin (1860-1903) was born in Okulovskaya, in what is now the Republic of Karelia. On moving to St. Peterburg, he initially worked in one of the workshops of Erik August Kollin who, until 1886, was Fabergé's chief jeweler. Within two years of qualifying as a Master Craftsman himself, in 1884, Perkhin had replaced Kollin. His workshops not only produced all types of objets de vertu in gold, enamel, and hardstone, but also made all the most important Fabergé commissions of the late 19thC and early 20thC, including the iconic Imperial Fabergé eggs. Embracing a huge and diverse range of styles from Rococo to Renaissance, Perkhin's time as Fabergé's chief jeweler is generally acknowledged to be the company's most innovative.

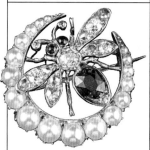

A late-19thC Victorian brooch, designed as a bee within a crescent moon, set with an oval sapphire, cushion-shaped diamonds, and half pearls, the eyes accented with cabochon rubies, mounted in gold, pearls untested.

1in (2.5cm) wide

$3,100-3,700   WW

A late-19thC brooch, with beaded detail throughout, glazed panel on the reverse, suspending a smaller drop with fringed detail, unmarked.

3¼in (8.5cm) high

$950-1,050   L&T

A Fabergé enamel and diamond brooch/button, maker's mark for Michael Perkhin, the translucent blue guilloché enamel over sunburst engine turning, center set with an old brilliant-cut diamond, within a rose-cut diamond border, numbered, Russian assay mark, detachable brooch fitting, later pin.

ca. 1895   *¾in (2cm) wide*

$7,500-8,500   CA

A Victorian emerald, diamond, and pearl locket, set with square step-cut emeralds, pearls, and rose-cut diamonds, unmarked, pearls untested.

2½in (6.5cm) long

$2,500-3,100   L&T

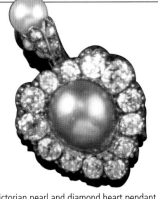

A Victorian pearl and diamond heart pendant, the center gray pearl within a surround of old cushion-shaped diamonds in silver and gold, with a pearl and diamond-set bail.

¾in (2cm) long

$3,100-3,700   WW

A Belle Époque platinum pendant necklace, the center cabochon emerald carved with a flower head, with a round-cut ruby above and millegrain-set diamond cluster drop below, the setting verso with engraved and millegrained decoration, emerald with surface abrasions and chips.

pendant 1¾in (4.5cm) long ⅜oz

$3,100-3,700   GORL

A 19thC Russian gold baptismal cross pendant, with lily-shaped arms finely enameled in black, with an Orthodox cross, floral scrolls, and lettering in reserve, accented with seed-pearl borders.

See a silver pendant of this traditional Russian design, dated to the 19thC, in the collection of the Victoria & Albert Museum, accession no. 508-1869.

1in (2.5cm) long

$800-950   WW

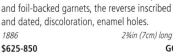

A Victorian gold, silver, and cloisonné enamel locket pendant, worked with a heron beneath wisteria, within a border mounted with pearls and foil-backed garnets, the reverse inscribed and dated, discoloration, enamel holes.

1886   *2¾in (7cm) long ⅞oz*

$625-850   GORL

A late-19thC black enamel and pearl locket, with a center star motif set with half pearls, the reverse with a glazed compartment holding a photograph, mounted in gold, pearls untested, one pearl replaced.

2¾in (7cm) long

$700-800   WW

A late-19thC pearl and diamond pendant, the pierced scrolling design set throughout with graduated old round- and eight-cut diamonds and five pearls, detachable bale and brooch fittings, unmarked, pearls untested.

1½in (4cm) long

$2,700-3,100   L&T

A late-19thC diamond star pendant, set with graduated cushion-shaped diamonds in silver and gold, with later plating.

1¼in (3cm) wide

$1,900-2,200   WW

A late-19thC Victorian diamond pendant, set with a centered old cushion-shaped diamond within a surround of further graduated old cushion-shaped diamonds, suspending from a detachable diamond-set bow in silver and gold.

2¼in (5.5cm) long

$7,000-8,000   WW

JEWELRY

A mid-19thC amethyst necklace, the amethysts in foliate gold borders, spaced by pearls, suspending a similar pear-shaped amethyst pendant, pearls untested.

pendant 2¼in (5.5cm) long

$5,000-6,200 **WW**

A late-Victorian seed-pearl necklace, the floral design set throughout with seed pearls, on a rope-twist chain, with a matching pendant/brooch, both unmarked.

16¼in (41cm) long

$2,500-3,100 **L&T**

A late-19thC French gold and sapphire pendant, the cabochon star sapphire within a polished gold border, with crossover detail and a bow surmount, stamped with French poinçon, on a rope-twist chain, some fractures in stone.

1¾in (4.5cm) long 1⅛oz

$2,500-3,100 **DN**

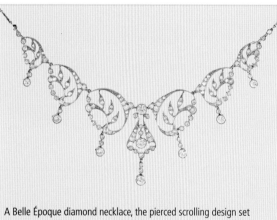

A Belle Époque diamond necklace, the pierced scrolling design set throughout with graduated old round- and rose-cut diamonds, unmarked.

center pendant 1½in (4cm) long

$7,500-8,500 **L&T**

A 19thC garnet articulated snake necklace, its body of gold linking, its head suspending a heart-shaped pendant from its mouth, decorated with various-color gold scrollwork, collet set with foil-backed oval garnets and cabochon garnet eyes.

15¼in (38.5cm) long

$2,500-3,100 **WW**

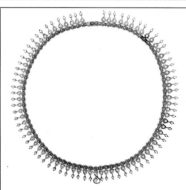

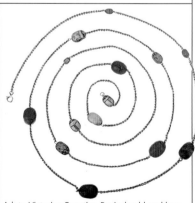

A Victorian coral and gold guard chain, formed of alternating gold twisted-rope links and coral anchorlinks.

34¾in (88cm) long

$2,500-3,100 **WW**

A Victorian pearl-set gold collar necklace, the fringe formed from small cannetille disks, each suspending two seed pearls in yellow gold, the center with a suspension loop.

16½in (42cm) long

$8,000-9,500 **WW**

A Victorian amethyst rivière necklace, the graduated amethysts in gold cut-down collets, suspending nine graduated pear-shaped amethysts.

14¼in (36cm) long

$5,000-6,200 **WW**

A late-Victorian Egyptian Revival gold necklace, set with 14 faience and hardstone scarboids on a fine oval-link yellow gold chain.

62¼in (158cm) long

$5,000-6,200 **WW**

A Victorian garnet and turquoise hinged bangle, modeled as two paws clasping a gem-set cluster, collet-set with an oval cabochon garnet and small cabochon turquoise details, unmarked.

2¼in (5.5cm) wide

$3,100-3,700 **L&T**

A Victorian hinged bangle, with three graduated blue enamel domes set with coral, with old brilliant- and rose-cut diamond star motifs in the center, in a surround of applied bead and rope-twist detailing, compartment in reverse.

ca. 1870   2¼in (5.5cm) diam 1¾oz

$4,300-5,000 **JON**

A late-19thC Victorian gem-set hinged bangle, the front set with graduated cat's-eye chrysoberyl cabochons, spaced by circular-cut diamonds, mounted in gold with a foliate scroll gallery.

2in (5cm) diam

$3,100-3,700 **WW**

A late-Victorian gem-set hinged bangle, the center fleur-de-lis panel set with old-cut diamonds and circular-cut sapphires, flanked by a sapphire trefoil motif and diamond accents, with safety chain, hand engraved "W.L to M.E.L 1897," two blue paste replacement stones.

2¼in (5.5cm) diam ⅜oz

$625-850 **DAWS**

A Victorian hardstone belt bracelet, comprising ten various agate panels including jasper, chalcedony, and agate, with an engraved buckle clasp, unmarked.

9in (23cm) long

$1,250-1,500 **L&T**

A mid-19thC composite pink topaz and emerald bracelet, the foliate center section in stamped gold, set with oval and pear-shaped topazes in pink foiled settings, accented with small cushion-shaped emeralds, on a gold bracelet composed of oval links.

6¾in (17cm) long

$1,250-1,500 **WW**

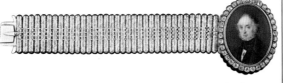

A mid-19thC portrait miniature in a gold and diamond bracelet, by Karl-August Schreinzer (1819-97), the clasp set with an ivory miniature reputedly depicting the engineer Charles Baird (1766-1843), within a border of cushion-shaped diamonds, on a gold cylindrical-link bracelet engraved on the front with Rococo-style scrollwork, miniature signed "Schreinzer."

7¼in (18.5cm) long

$5,500-6,000 **WW**

A Victorian 18ct-gold snake bracelet, the head, tail, and locket all with turquoise enamel, the head set with graduated split pearls and cabochon ruby eyes, suspending an enamel and seed-pearl locket from clasped jaws, with glazed hair panel in reverse, sinuous tapering link body, concealed push-button clasp, unmarked, enamel chips, one pearl missing.

7¾in (19.5cm) long ⅝oz

$2,500-3,100 **DAWS**

A mid-19thC French gold, garnet, and diamond bracelet, the pierced center quatrefoil panel with engraved scrolled decoration, with an octagonal step-cut rhodolite garnet and old mine-cut diamonds, on curved track links with engraved scrolled decoration, stamped with Paris post-1847 poinçons, an eagle head and a rhino head, unidentified maker's mark, light wear, large scratches.

ca. 1860   7in (18cm) long 1oz

$3,000-3,500 **DN**

A mid-Victorian star sapphire bracelet, the cabochon sapphire in a cut-down collet setting, between lion-paw shoulders, on a fancy link bracelet with beaded detail, the clasp with floral decoration and a small glazed locket panel verso, split in one lion claw.

ca. 1860   7in (18cm) long ⅝oz

$5,000-5,600 **DN**

An Archaeological Revival sapphire and pearl bracelet, by Niccola Marchesini, in Etruscan Revival style, the center line of oval-cut sapphires between courses of seed pearls, each in a corded wire surround, with granulation detail, with a similarly decorated clasp, signed "Marchesini Firenze Roma."

Following the huge popularity in Great Britain of Castellani's work, several contemporary jewelers also started creating jewels in the Archaeological Revival style to service the market created by Grand Tour-traveling Britons. Marchesini started on the Ponte Vecchio, in Florence, while the Murray's handbooks for Rome record the company as "Court Jewellers" at 138 Corso in 1875, and it was still flourishing in 1900.

ca. 1880   7in (18cm) long

$5,500-6,000 **CA**

A pair of early-Victorian amethyst earrings, each with three graduated chain-linked amethysts in yellow collet settings, with screw fittings.

1½in (4cm) long

$700-800 TEN

A pair of Victorian pearl and diamond drop earrings, each with an articulated fleur-de-lis and scroll top, grain and spitch set with graduated old European-cut and old Swiss-cut diamonds, a diamond and pearl suspended below, hook fittings, pearls untested and with substantial wear in the outer nacre.

1in (2.5cm) long ⅛oz

$1,700-2,200 SWO

A pair of Victorian drop earrings, each with three eliptical hoops with polished and textured decoration, a flower head in the center with bead border, arched bands above, on bead-and-hook fittings.

2¼in (5.5cm) long ¼oz

$550-700 SWO

A pair of Victorian drop earrings, with detachable pendant drops, each pear-cut citrine with an applied ruby-set flower head in the center and a split-pearl claw set on each side, textured pierced scrolls above with a center claw set in turquoise, an oval mixed-cut citrine above, on bead-and-hook fittings, one red paste replacement.

2¼in (5.5cm) long ⅜oz

$2,200-2,700 SWO

A pair of Victorian diamond drop earrings, each yellow plaque with a center cushion-shaped old-cut diamond in a star setting, in a rope-twist and beadwork border, surmounted by a smaller old-cut diamond, hook fittings, two diamond chips.

1¼in (3cm) long ¼oz

$1,900-2,200 WW

A pair of mid- to late-19thC turquoise earrings, the tassel drops set with circular cabochon turquoise, on polished surmounts with corded wire decoration, hook fittings.

1¾in (4.5cm) long

$3,100-3,500 CA

A pair of Victorian turquoise drop earrings, set in yellow gold.

1¼in (3cm) long

$625-750 WW

A pair of late Victorian diamond chandelier earrings, set with graduated old circular-cut diamonds in silver on gold, hook fittings.

1¾in (4.5cm) long

$12,500-15,000 WW

A late-Victorian gem-set quatrefoil pendant and matching earrings, set with opals within diamond borders, the pendant with a center square-shaped emerald in silver and gold.

earrings 1in (2.5cm) long

$2,500-3,000 WW

A late-19thC intaglio brooch and earrings, each set with a hardstone intaglio of a cherub playing a horn in a beaded border, the earrings each suspending three drop pendants, on post-and-butterfly fittings, unmarked.

earings 1½in (4cm) long

$1,250-1,500 L&T

A mid-19thC diamond cluster ring, collet set with nine graduated foil-backed rose-cut diamonds, the band with ribbed detail, unmarked.

size L

$2,500-3,000 **L&T**

A 19thC Archaeological Revival stone scarab ring, set with an Egyptian stone scarab, within a gold rope-twist mount, on an engraved and fluted shank, shank possibly later.

size S

$625-750 **WW**

A 19thC Archaeological Revival composite stone scarab ring, set with an Egyptian stone scarab, within a gold rope-twist mount, on a fluted shank, possibly converted from a bracelet link.

size O½

$625-750 **WW**

A mid-19thC Victorian diamond ring, pavé set with cushion-shaped diamonds, on a fluted shank, mounted in gold.

size P½

$2,100-2,500 **WW**

An unusual 19thC iron, gold, and diamond ring, the plain gold band overlaid with with a layer of iron, rubover set with a cushion-shaped diamond.

size K½

$1,700-2,000 **WW**

A Victorian sapphire and diamond ring, rubover set with a cushion-shaped diamond between cushion-shaped sapphires, mounted in gold, partly inscribed, dated "1885."

ca. 1885 *size O*

$375-500 **WW**

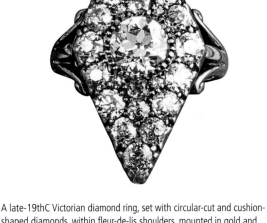

A late-19thC Victorian diamond ring, set with circular-cut and cushion-shaped diamonds, within fleur-de-lis shoulders, mounted in gold and silver, center antique diamond a later replacement.

size N½

$6,000-7,500 **WW**

A late-19thC pearl half-hoop ring, set with diamond pointers in a carved and pierced yellow gold mount, maker's mark "E.C," stamped "18."

size O½

$625-750 **WW**

A late-19thC Victorian emerald and diamond five-stone ring, set with three circular-cut emeralds spaced by a pair of circular-cut diamonds, on a gold mount with scrolled galleries, numbered "238."

size K½

$3,000-3,500 **WW**

A late-19thC citrine and diamond cluster ring, set with an oval citrine within a surround of old cushion-shaped diamonds in silver and gold.

size Q½

$1,700-2,000 **WW**

A late-Victorian diamond and emerald five-stone ring, with three old mine-cut diamonds, approximately 0.80ct total, interspaced by two step-cut emeralds with canted corners, with a pierced scrolled gallery, retipped claws, replacement shank, small chips in emeralds.

ca. 1900 *size O ⅛oz*

$2,100-2,500 **DN**

JEWELRY

An early-20thC Continental pendant, with a center step-cut ruby, in a foliate surround set with rose-cut diamonds and step-cut sapphires, with pearl accents, suspending a pearl drop, etched and pressed floral decoration verso, unmarked, suspended from a belcher-link chain, several sapphires reset, one diamond missing.

ca. 1910   2¾in (7cm) long ¾oz

$1,500-1,900   **DN**

An Edwardian aquamarine and seed-pearl pendant, millegrained set with an oval-cut aquamarine, in an open surround of seed pearls and rose-cut diamonds, unmarked, on a trace-link chain.

1¾in (4.5cm) long

$1,250-1,500   **L&T**

An early-20thC Indian tiger pendant, with an embossed tiger mask and front legs with etched decoration, circular cabochon garnet eyes, beaded and scrolled border, flower-head accents, vacant interior, suspended from a triangular red stone-set bale, with a French gold-color fancy-link chain, stamped with French poinçon.

pendant 2in (5cm) long 1½oz

$2,200-2,700   **DN**

An Edwardian diamond négligée necklace, the two old European-cut diamonds in collet settings, estimated 1.26ct and 1.61ct, color L, clarity VVS-VS, suspended from an oval hoop set with old-cut diamonds, on a fancy-link chain necklace.

ca. 1910   16½in (42cm) long ¼oz

$11,000-14,000   **DN**

A drop-shaped pendant, set with a pear-shaped pink tourmaline, within a wreath of rose-cut diamonds and circular-cut demantoid garnets, bordered by half pearls, mounted in gold and platinum, on a later gold chain.

ca. 1910   1½in (4cm) long

$1,000-1,250   **WW**

An early-20thC natural pearl and diamond necklace, composed of two strands of natural pearls, with a navette-shaped clasp pavé set with circular-cut diamonds.

17¼in (44cm) long

$5,500-6,000   **WW**

An Edwardian multi-gem fringed necklace, millegrained set throughout with various peridots and pink tourmalines, with seed-pearl detail, on a trace-link chain, unmarked.

center pendant 1in (2.5cm) long

$2,100-2,500   **L&T**

An early-20thC peridot necklace, the trace-link chain suspending 17 millegrain-set circular-cut peridots, unmarked, with a pair of associated seed-pearl and peridot pendant earrings, stamped "9ct."

necklace 15¼in (39cm) long

$875-1,100   **L&T**

An early-20thC amethyst rivière necklace, composed of a single row of graduated oval amethysts, unmarked.

14¾in (37.5cm) long

$2,200-2,700   **L&T**

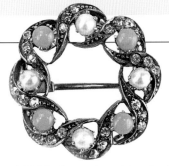

An early-20thC yellow metal wreath brooch, set with small diamonds, seed pearls, and coral.

¾in (2cm) diam ¼oz

$500-625   WHP

An early-20thC amethyst and seed-pearl brooch, millegrained set with an oval amethyst, in a pierced surround set with seed pearls, stamped "15ct."

1½in (4cm) wide

$375-500   L&T

An early-20thC amethyst, peridot, and pearl brooch, claw set with a cushion-cut amethyst and two cushion-cut peridots, in a border of seed pearls, unmarked.

1¼in (3cm) wide

$625-750   L&T

An early-20thC cameo pendant/brooch, set with a sardonyx cameo of a crowned woman in profile, within an openwork platinum and gold frame set with seed pearls and rose-cut diamonds.

1½in (4cm) high

$750-875   WW

An early-20thC cameo brooch, centering on a sardonyx cameo of a dancing Bacchante holding Bacchus' staff and a bunch of grapes, on a bar brooch with scrolled borders, set with cushion-shaped diamonds and two annular sections of sardonyx, mounted in gold.

3in (7.5cm) wide

$1,250-1,500   WW

An Edwardian ribbon-bow brooch, set with seed pearls and circular-cut diamonds in openwork platinum, centering on a cushion-shaped diamond.

ca. 1910   *2¾in (7cm) wide*

$1,500-1,700   WW

An early-20thC Dutch "giardinetti" ring, the urn, scrolled handles, flower heads, and leaves all set with foil-backed rose-cut diamonds, gold-backed silver closed-back settings, on a floral shank stamped with Netherlands 1906-53 revenue mark for domestic products.

panel ¾in (2cm) long ⅞oz

$4,600-5,200   DN

An early-20thC marquise panel ring, set with graduated old mine-cut diamonds, approximately 1.14ct total, centered with a circular cabochon turquoise in a millegrained setting, the shank stamped "18ct & Pt," slight thinning in shank.

size K ⅛oz

$1,250-1,500   DN

An Edwardian emerald and diamond ring, claw set with a mixed rectangular-cut emerald, flanked on each side by three old round-cut diamonds, modeled in 18ct gold.

size K

$1,500-1,700   L&T

An early-20thC 18ct-gold half-hoop ring, set with three diamonds and two emeralds, with carved setting and diamond chip spacers (one missing), the center diamond approximately 0.60ct, gold tarnished, small chips in stones.

size O ⅛oz

$3,100-3,500   GORL

An early-20thC 18ct-gold half-hoop ring, set with three oval-cut sapphires and four diamond spacers, wear, small chips in sapphires.

size O ⅛oz

$450-550   GORL

An early-20thC Art Nouveau silver necklace, set with clear and pink glass.

pendant 3¼in (8.5cm) long

$750-875   **WHP**

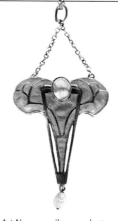

An Art Nouveau silver pendant necklace, cast in low relief with geometric foliate design, in blue and green enamel, set with abalone and drop, unsigned.

pendant 1¾in (4.5cm) long

$190-250   **WW**

A silver shield-shaped pendant, by Charles Horner, Chester, cast in low relief and with a green and blue enamel panel, stamped "CH."

1910   *½in (1.5cm) long*

$250-370   **WW**

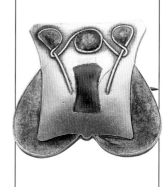

A Liberty & Co. silver and enamel brooch, designed by Archibald Knox (1864-1933), London, made by William H. Haseler, stamped "W.H.H./SILVER."

ca. 1900   *1¼in (3cm) high*

$1,100-1,500   **L&T**

An early-20thC Russian Art Nouveau ring, with a vertical row of two old-cut diamonds and a centered square cushion-cut sapphire, in claw settings, in scrolled crossover shoulders set with old European-cut diamonds, approximately 1.00ct total, the shank stamped with 56 Zolotnik mark and St. Petersburg mark, two further unidentified marks, surface wear in setting.

ca. 1910   *size M½ ⅛oz*

$2,500-3,100   **DN**

An Art Nouveau sapphire and diamond brooch, composed of foliate scrolls, mounted in platinum with millegrained borders.

ca. 1900   *2½in (6.5cm) wide*

$1,000-1,500   **WW**

An Art Nouveau gold bar brooch, retailed by Liberty, with two center rub-set circular cabochon opals, scroll and foliate stems on each side, each with a claw-set round mixed-cut demantoid garnet, with safety catch, pin and safety chain, marked "15ct," in a Liberty box, with receipt dated 1987, one garnet chipped, surface scratches.

⅛oz

$150-190   **SWO**

An Art Nouveau plique-à-jour enamel brooch, the sinuously modeled branch set with green plique-à-jour enamel and mother-of-pearl leaves, the stems highlighted by rose-cut diamonds, with bouton-pearl accents, later pin, pearls untested.

ca. 1900   *1½in (4cm) wide*

$1,500-1,900   **CA**

A Liberty & Co. Art Nouveau 18ct-gold ring, of swirling design, decorated with half-seed pearls and a circular cabochon opal, maker's mark "L&Co.," UK assay mark.

1901-02   *size O*

$875-1,000   **CA**

An Art Nouveau diamond brooch, by Henri Teterger, designed as the entwined initials "EL," set throughout with rose-cut diamonds, with green clover accents, signed "Hri. Teterger Fils."

ca. 1900   *1¼in (3cm) wide*

$1,000-1,250   **CA**

An early-20thC Arts and Crafts opal necklace, designed as a series of foliate links set with opal cabochons, suspending a similar pendant, stamped "18CT."

See Vivienne Becker, "Art Nouveau Jewelry," Thames & Hudson (1985), page 120, no. 191, for a closely comparable necklace designed by Carl Otto Czechka and made by Anton Pribil at the Wiener Werkstatte ca. 1905.

necklace 17¼in (44cm) long

$4,000-4,500 WW

An Arts and Crafts necklace, in the manner of Jessie Marion King, composed of floral and foliate motifs applied with green and blue enamel, set with cabochon moonstones and circular-cut synthetic rubies, mounted in silver, with filigree and rope-twist details, unsigned.

ca. 1905   *15¾in (40cm) long*

$5,000-5,600 WW

A Liberty & Co. Arts and Crafts pendant necklace, by Jessie Marion King (1875-1949), London, white metal with enamel, opal, and a seed pearl.

ca. 1900   pendant 1¾in (4.5cm) long

$750-1,000 L&T

A Liberty & Co. Arts and Crafts necklace, by Jessie Marion King (1875-1949), London, silver and enamel, stamped "L&Co./SILVER."

ca. 1900   18in (46cm) long

$750-1,000 L&T

ESSENTIAL REFERENCE—DORRIE NOSSITER

A jewelry designer born in Aston, Birmingham, Dorrie Nossiter (1893-1977) trained in the Arts and Crafts tradition at Birmingham's Municipal School of Art between 1910 and 1914. After her marriage in 1922, she moved to London, where she created some of her most famous designs. Between 1935 and 1939, her jewelry was shown at the "Art By Four Women" exhibition at Walker's Gallery. Popular themes in her work include flowers, peacocks, and organic patterns formed by wirework spirals and other repeating forms. Her work is also distinguished, as is immediately evident in this ring, by the incorporation of bright, polychrome gemstones.

An English Arts and Crafts necklace, white metal with enamel and moonstone cabochons.

ca. 1900   16¼in (41cm) long

$625-850 L&T

An Arts and Crafts silver and enamel bracelet, by Bernard Instone, composed of blue, pink, and yellow enamel flower heads, all joined by flat links, marked "SILVER B.I," damage and discoloration.

7¼in (18.5cm) long 1oz

$375-450 SWO

An Arts and Crafts haircomb terminal, by Henry Wilson (1864-1934), white metal with enamel and moonstone.

ca. 1905   3¼in (8.5cm) wide

$2,200-2,700 L&T

An Arts and Crafts silver ring, by Murrle Bennett & Co., London, with a turquoise cabochon, stamped "M.B.C/950."

ca. 1910

$625-750 L&T

An Arts and Crafts ring, by Dorrie Nossiter, with a centered square step-cut amethyst, between shoulders set with gemstone clusters, including step-cut emeralds, circular-cut amethysts, and seed pearls, within a beadwork and scrolled gallery, unsigned.

ca. 1940   *size R*

$6,000-7,500 CA

A white gold and jadeite dress ring, with foliate carved jadeite, bordered by millegrain-set round-cut diamonds.

1920s/1930s   *panel 1¼in (3cm) long ¼oz*

$1,600-1,900   **GORL**

A Cartier Art Deco jabot pin, both pointed terminals set with old brilliant-, single- and rose-cut diamonds and calibré-cut sapphires, diamonds approximately 0.30ct total, signed "Cartier," maker's mark, numbered, French assay marks, two sapphires deficient.

ca. 1920   *2½in (6.5cm) long*

$1,700-2,200   **CA**

An Art Deco diamond brooch, set with baguette-, old European-, old brilliant-, and eight-cut diamonds, approximately 8.40ct total, with a partial unidentified shield-shaped stamp, solder repairs to reverse.

ca. 1930   *2in (5cm) wide ¾oz*

$5,200-5,700   **DN**

A German Art Deco diamond brooch, millegrained set with 13 old round-cut diamonds, indistinctly marked.

ca. 1920   *1in (2.5cm) diam*

$750-875   **L&T**

An Art Deco jadeite clip brooch, set with a carved jadeite plaque, accented with single-cut diamonds in millegrain-bordered platinum, stamped "18CT PLAT."

ca. 1930   *1½in (4cm) high*

$1,000-1,250   **WW**

An Art Deco emerald and diamond brooch, set with circular- and single-cut diamonds, channel set with step-cut emeralds, mounted in platinum.

ca. 1920   *1½in (4cm) wide*

$1,700-2,200   **WW**

A Cartier Art Deco diamond clip brooch, designed as a stylized buckle with a wide ruyi motif, pavé set with circular-cut diamonds, accented by collet-set cushion-shaped and circular-cut diamonds, mounted in platinum, signed "Cartier London."

ca. 1930   *1¾in (4.5cm) wide*

$25,000-31,000   **WW**

An Art Deco double-clip geometric brooch, set with single-cut and baguette diamonds and calibré-cut aquamarines, along with a brooch mount enabling them to be worn together, stamped "18CT PT."

1930s   *2¼in (5.5cm) wide*

$8,500-10,000   **WW**

A French Art Deco geometric brooch, centered on a collet-set circular-cut diamond, on a bar brooch set with calibré-cut onyx and emeralds and circular-cut diamonds, numbered "95049," French assay marks for platinum and 18ct gold.

1920s   *3¼in (8.5cm) wide*

$8,000-9,500   **WW**

An Art Deco ruby and diamond brooch, designed as a trio of interlocking hoops set with calibré-cut rubies and rose-cut diamonds, French import assay marks for 18ct gold.

ca. 1920   *1½in (4cm) wide*

$1,000-1,250   **WW**

A Spaulding and Co. Art Deco diamond line bracelet, Chicago, with graduated millegrain-set old European-cut diamonds, approximately 4.74ct total, color mostly G-I, clarity varying VS-I, with scrolled foliate engraved gallery, concealed box clasp signed "SPAULDING & CO. CHICAGO," solder repairs.

Spaulding & Co. was established in Chicago in 1888 by Henry Abriam Spaulding. He had been Tiffany & Co.'s general representative in Europe during the 1870s and 1880s, responsible for introducing Tiffany & Co. to royalty and European nobility, and obtaining appointments for Tiffany to numerous royal households. In the late 1880s, Henry decided to move back to Chicago, where he wanted Tiffany to open a boutique. When it rejected the idea, Henry opened his own jewelry boutique in Chicago, with a showroom beneath the American Consulate in Paris. Spaulding & Co. soon became acknowledged as Chicago's rival to New York's Tiffany & Co., and it was renowned for both the style and quality of its jewelry.

An Art Deco emerald bead bracelet, the clasp and links set with polished onyx and single-cut diamonds, French assay marks for 18ct gold and platinum.

1920s   *7in (18cm) long*
$5,000-6,200   **WW**

ca. 1925   *6¾in (17cm) long ¾oz*
$10,000-11,000   **DN**

An Art Deco sapphire and diamond bracelet, composed of geometric links with millegrained borders pavé set with circular- and single-cut diamonds, connected by arches of calibré-cut sapphires and cylindrical links, each end capped with a cabochon sapphire, mounted in platinum, later British hallmarks and stamp "PT950."

1930s   *7in (18cm) long*
$25,000-31,000   **WW**

A pair of Art Deco jadeite earrings, composed of elongated platinum surmounts set with circular- and single-cut diamonds, suspending a carved jadeite drop, stamped "18CT PLAT," later post fittings.

ca. 1920   *2in (5cm) long*
$1,700-2,200   **WW**

A pair of Cartier Art Deco diamond clip brooches, each with a foliate ruyi motif, set with circular-cut and cushion-shaped diamonds, mounted in platinum, one signed "Cartier," the other "London."

ca. 1930   *1½in (4cm) high*
$31,000-37,000   **WW**

A pair of Art Deco pearl and diamond earrings, each bouton pearl surmount suspending an openwork drop millegrain set with rose-cut diamonds, suspending a bar terminating in a pearl, with a further pearl drop, pearls untested, later post fittings.

ca. 1925   *1½in (4cm) long*
$2,200-2,700   **CA**

An Art Deco ring, the center collet-set brilliant-cut diamond approximately 0.9ct, in point-set diamond and channel-set princess-cut ruby borders and shoulders, on a plain white shank stamped 18ct.

size L
$3,700-4,300   **HT**

An Art Deco ring, set with an oval ruby from Myanmar, Mogok region, 1.36ct, in stepped shoulders set with baguette diamonds, mounted in platinum.

1930s   *size M½*
$10,000-11,000   **WW**

An Art Deco panel ring, set with an old European-cut diamond in a millegrained collet, in an octagonal openwork surround set with Swiss- and single-cut diamond accents, bordered with rows of French-cut baguette sapphires and single-cut diamonds in the chenier shoulders, on a tapering D-section shank.

size K ⅛oz
$5,500-6,000   **DAWS**

An Art Deco stylized buckle dress ring, set with a center single old brilliant-cut diamond, the tapering precious white metal wrap-around shank terminating in a semicircular band of nine mixed rose-cut diamonds, unmarked, later sizing band applied in interior.

size G ¼oz
$375-450   **DAWS**

JEWELRY

Judith Picks

Well, here is more personal bias when it comes to picking out a particular piece. You may, however, be relieved to learn that on this occasion there is no Scottish connection. Basically, I have a Georg Jensen "Tulip" silver necklace by Harald Nielsen. It was originally designed ca. 1930 by Nielsen (1892-1977), who was the younger brother of the great Danish silversmith Georg Jensen's third wife, and one of the reasons I like it is because, first and foremost, it is eminently wearable. Indeed, over the years that I have had it, it has spent hardly any time dormant in a jewelry box! I also like it because Nielsen is primarily associated with Jensen's wonderful Art Deco hollowware and flatware patterns of the 1920s and 1930s (perhaps most notably the "Pyramid" pattern), and his jewelry designs are, therefore, rarer in comparison ... But I also like it specifically because of those wonderful tulips, and the fact that, although it was essentially conceived in the Art Deco style, it predates that period in the 1930s, when, as the French designer Paul Iribe observed, in streamlining and abstracting everything "they have sacrificed the flower on the altar of Cubism and the machine."

A Georg Jensen sterling silver "Tulip" necklace, by Harald Nielsen, stamped "GEORG JENSEN/925S/DENMARK/100B."

15in (38cm) long

$2,000-2,200   **L&T**

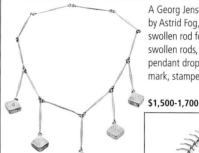

A Georg Jensen fringe necklace, designed by Henry Pilstrup, model no. 4, with five foliate pendants with patinated ground, collet set with oval malachite cabochons, on planished barrel links and a conforming clasp, maker's mark, stamped "925."

1933-44   *16¼in (41.5cm) long 2⅜oz*

$1,700-2,000   **DAWS**

A Georg Jensen necklace, designed by Astrid Fog, model no. 123, the swollen rod form suspending five swollen rods, each with square pendant drops, post-1945 maker's mark, stamped "925."

3oz

$1,500-1,700   **DAWS**

A Georg Jensen stylized coffee bean necklace, designed by Henning Koppel, model no. 270, with screw clasp, post-1945 maker's mark, stamped "925."

17¼in (44cm) long 4⅞oz

$1,700-2,000   **DAWS**

A Georg Jensen necklace and bracelet, by Bent Gabrielsen (1928-2014), each stamped "GEORG JENSEN/STERLING/DENMARK/115" with designer's monogram, necklace with import marks for 1969.

ca. 1969   necklace 14¼in (36cm) long

$3,100-3,700   **L&T**

A Georg Jensen silver cross pendant, design no. 89A, with scrollwork decoration, set with cabochon opals and a circular-cut ruby, signed "GJ" for Jensen, Swedish assay marks for silver.

1933-44   *2¾in (7cm) long*

$1,000-1,250   **WW**

A Georg Jensen sterling silver pendant, designed by Henning Koppel, deisgn no. 152, formed as an open heart, post-1945 maker's mark.

2in (5cm) long

$450-550   **WAD**

A Georg Jensen silver cross pendant, designed by Henning Koppel, model no. 151, with oval link bail, marked "Georg Jensen 925S Denmark 151," import mark for London 1987, scratches.

3¼in (8.5cm) long ⅞oz

$375-500   **SWO**

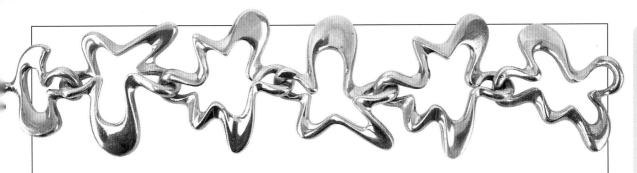

A Georg Jensen silver "Splash" bracelet, by Henning Koppel, composed of abstract silver links, signed "Georg Jensen," maker's mark "HK," British import marks for silver, with box stamped "Georg Jensen."
ca. 1956   *7¼in (18.5cm) long*
$2,100-2,500   **WW**

A Georg Jensen sterling silver bracelet, designed by Astrid Fog, design no. 169, composed of demilune disk links, post-1945 maker's mark.
7½in (19cm) long 4½oz
$800-950   **WAD**

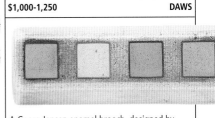

A Georg Jensen silver bracelet, designed by Ibe Dahlquist, model no. 197, with five stylized anchor links, connected to a T-bar closure, post-1945 maker's mark, London import marks "925," with original packaging and papers.
1970   *1¼in (3cm) wide 2¼oz*
$1,000-1,250   **DAWS**

A Georg Jensen openwork brooch, designed by Hugo Liisberg, model no. 300, with a duck flying above pond bulrushes, post-1945 maker's mark, stamped "Sterling Denmark."
2in (5cm) wide ½oz
$190-250   **DAWS**

A Georg Jensen openwork brooch, designed by Arno Malinowski, model no. 318, with a resting deer and squirrel in foliage, maker's mark, stamped "925S."
1933-44   *1½in (4cm) wide ½oz*
$250-310   **DAWS**

A Georg Jensen enamel brooch, designed by Nanna Ditzel, model no. 333A, with four squares of modulated teal enamel, post-1945 maker's mark, stamped "925."
1½in (4cm) wide ⅜oz
$250-310   **DAWS**

A Georg Jensen silver brooch, designed by Henning Koppel, model no. 324, stamped marks for London.
1965   *1¾in (4.5cm) wide*
$250-310   **WW**

A pair of Georg Jensen sterling silver flower-head stud earrings, designed by Georg Jensen, design no. 36, post-1945 maker's mark.
½in (1.5cm) diam
$500-550   **WAD**

A pair of Georg Jensen sterling silver cuff links, designed by O. Gundlach-Pedersen, design no. 42, post-1945 maker's mark.
¾in (2cm) diam ½oz
$100-150   **WAD**

ESSENTIAL REFERENCE—MID-CENTURY MODERN

A fundamental development in post-World War II design emerged with the "New Look," a term initially coined by Christian Dior to describe his extravagant, witty, and romantic haute couture collection of 1947. This reaction to the austerity of the war years and the functionalism of Modernism also infused other applied arts—with furniture, ceramics, glass, lighting, and, as here, jewelry, in general, becoming more curvaceous, sculptural, and organic in form and decoration. It was, however, a little later in the mid-20thC when the ghost of wartime sobriety was fully and finally laid to rest by the brightly colored, often outlandish designs of the 1960s—a decade in which the distinction between fine art (most notably Pop Art and Surrealism) and design was often blurred.

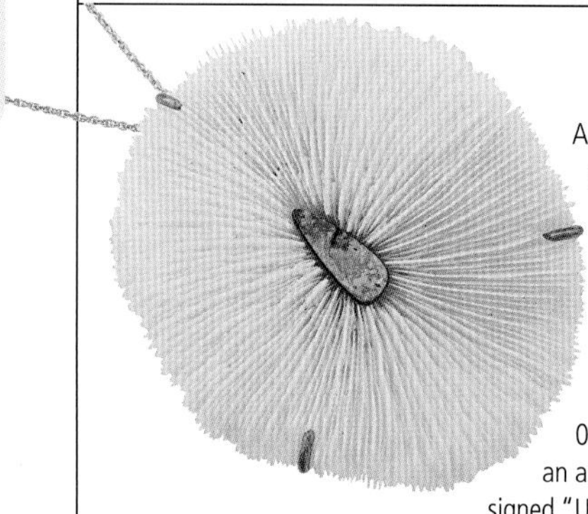

A white mushroom coral pendant, by Andrew Grima, the white mushroom coral (fungiidae) centered with a polished pear-shaped boulder opal, gold-color claw setting stamped "GRIMA 0.750," suspended from an associated rope-twist chain signed "Uno-A-Erre" and stamped "750," in a Grima London case, large opal chip.

Andrew Grima was a British society jeweler of the 1960s and 1970s, and his early clients included Queen Elizabeth II, Princess Margaret, and Jackie Kennedy Onassis. The entirely self-taught Grima joined his father-in-law's jewelry manufacturing business, H. J. Company, in 1946, and introduced new designs and techniques to the company, moving away from the more traditional and figural jewelry designs to organic and abstract jewel forms. Through his unique pieces, Grima has subsequently become known as the father of postwar jewelry design. His pieces have won numerous awards, including the DeBeers Diamonds International Awards a record-breaking 11 times, and they can be found in many of the most important museums in the world as well as in private collections. One of Andrew Grima's favorite stones to use was opal, and it featured in a number of his pieces throughout his career.

2¾in (7cm) long 1⅜oz

$4,700-5,200 **DN**

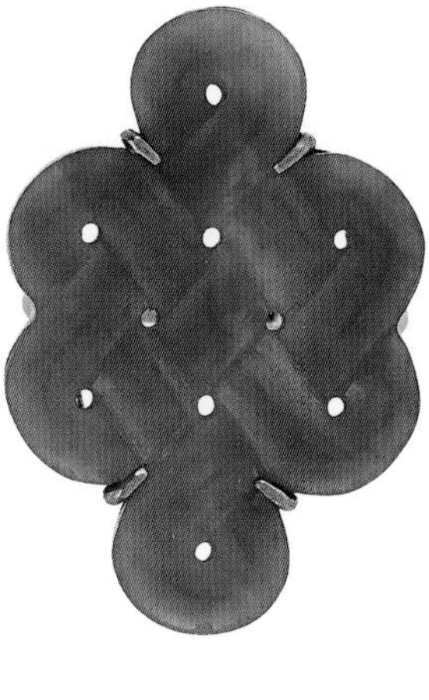

A mid-20thC natural jadeite endless knot dress ring, the carved, polished, and pierced knot jadeite panel claw set in a polished gallery with looped supports, on a polished shank, stamped "18CT," tiny chips.

panel 1¼in (3cm) long ⅜oz

$5,000-5,600 **DN**

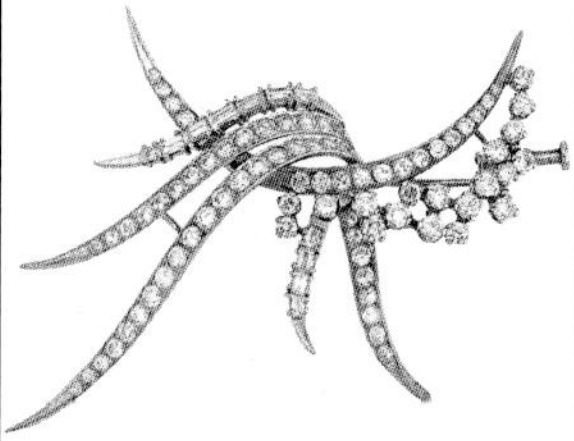

A diamond spray brooch, the intersecting diamond crescent and spray with a scattering of brilliant-cut diamond accents, approximately 2.82ct total, clarity mostly VS-SI, color H-J, unmarked.

1950s *2¼in (5.5cm) wide ⅜oz*

$1,400-1,600 **DN**

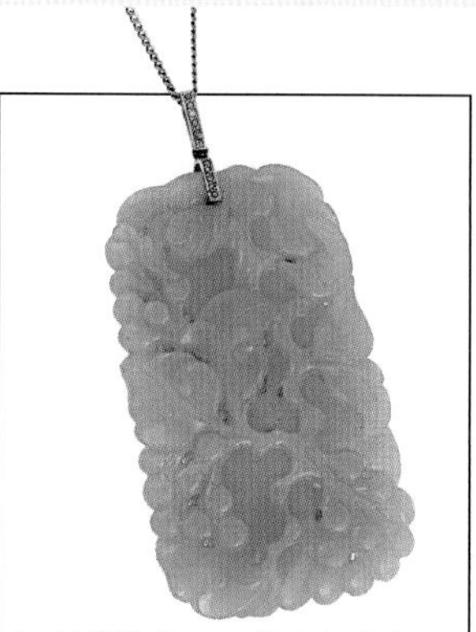

A mid-20thC natural jadeite jade pendant, the pierced jadeite jade panel carved with a bird among berries and coiling foliage, the bale set with rose-cut diamonds, on a French curb-link chain, small area of solder on the suspension loop.

2¼in (5.5cm) long 1⅜oz

$5,500-6,000 **DN**

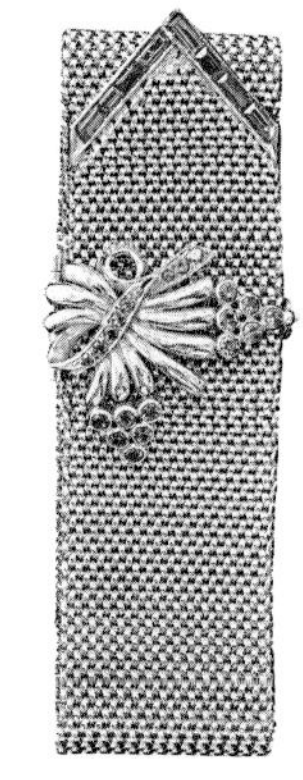

A mesh woven cocktail bracelet, the clasp surmounted by a hinged stylized flower spray pavé set with small rubies, the arrowhead end set with eight caliber-cut rubies, unmarked.

$3,700-4,200 **HT**

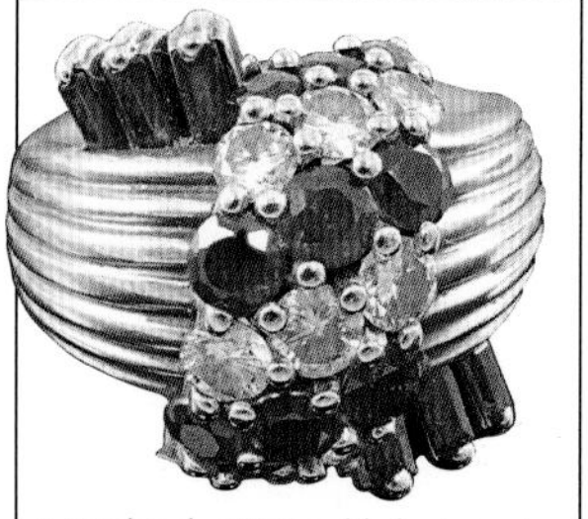

A Kutchinsky 18ct-gold cluster-set dress ring, set with 9 round-cut diamonds, 12 round-cut rubies, and 6 baguette-cut rubies, on a reeded shank, signed, small chip in one ruby.

early-1960s *size K ¼oz*

$2,500-3,100 **GORL**

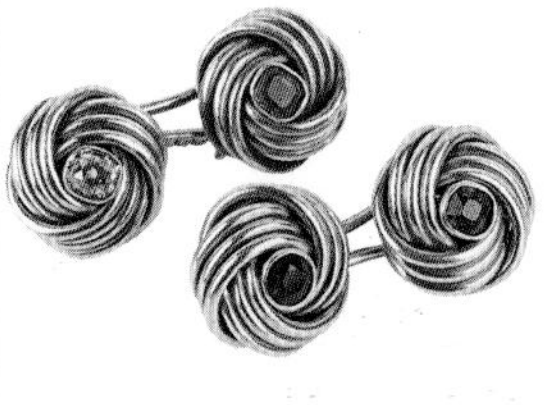

A pair of mid-20thC gold and gem-set cuff links, each end designed as a knot of gold wire, one set with a circular-cut sapphire and a cushion-shaped ruby, the other with an emerald and a diamond.

each end ½in (1.5cm) diam

$2,200-2,700 **WW**

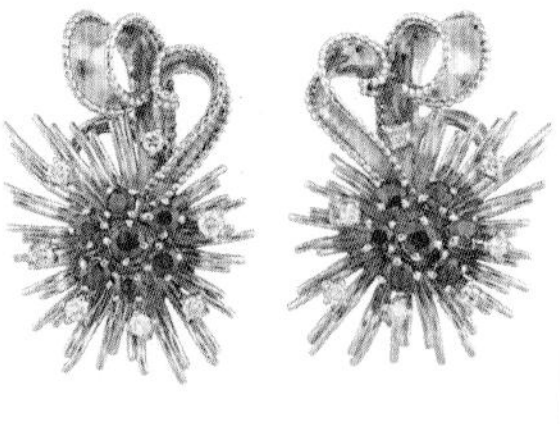

A pair of 18ct-gold earclips, by Ben Rosenfeld, each centered set with circular-cut rubies, accented with single- and brilliant-cut diamonds, approximately 0.55ct total, in a radiating mount surmounted by volutes, maker's marks "BRLd," London hallmarks, clip fittings.

1959 *1½in (4cm) long*

$1,600-1,900 **CA**

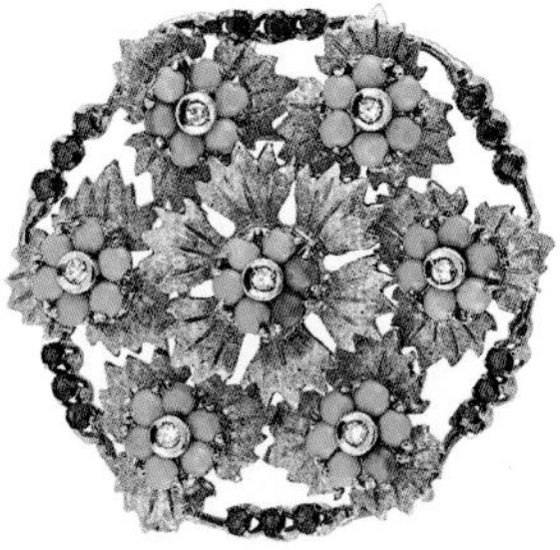

A floral cluster brooch, the center eight-cut diamond and circular cabochon turquoise cluster within a surround of textured leaves, in a surround of similarly set flower-head clusters, approximately 0.07ct total, with circular-cut sapphire borders, stamped "750 FP," restoration.

1960s *1½in (4cm) diam ½oz*

$750-875 **DN**

A lapis lazuli bead necklace, clasp stamped "18K."

17in (43cm) long

$1,250-1,500   WW

A mid-20thC oxidized metal "Shou" pendant, inset with oval-cut diamonds, approximately 0.29ct total, with a gold-color back, unmarked, suspended from a polished gold-color bale and belcher-link chain, stamped "9ct," scratches.

"Shou" is the traditional Chinese character that primarily symbolizes longevity.

1¼in (3cm) diam ½oz

$1,500-1,700   DN

A Missiaglia diamond and lapis lazuli bead necklace, with a reeded oval lapis lazuli and brilliant-cut diamond cluster clasp, approximately 0.72ct total, clasp signed "Missiaglia."

Missaglia was founded in Venice in 1846, and is now one of the oldest established jewelers in the city. The company is still family owned and employs its own designers and skilled craftsmen to make exceptional handmade "gioilelli alta" ("high-end jewelry").

20in (50.5cm) long 4oz

$2,000-2,200   DN

ESSENTIAL REFERENCE—LIZA SOTILIS

Known in artistic circles as "The Golden Greek," Liza Sotilis was born in Athens in 1939. Having studied there, and then at the Academy of Arts in Milan, Sotilis began working as an artist and sculptor, but she soon began making her own jewelry. Her first solo exhibition was at the age of 16 in Milan, with her first international exhibition two years later in Berlin. After the eminent international art dealer Alexander Iolas noticed her work, further exhibitions rapidly ensued, in which her pieces were often exhibited alongside iconic artists, such as René Magritte, Andy Warhol, and her great mentor, Giorgio de Chirico. Her pieces have been purchased by many in the contemporary art world, perhaps most notably Salvador Dalí, and frequent guests at her home in Via Dante in Milan included Warhol and Rudolph Nureyev. Sotilis once said of her work: "I sleep three hours a day because my creativity never ends. When I get tired of making jewelry, which I call 'micro-sculptures,' I paint, I design furniture. I do not make traditional jewels; they are different, my way, because I have to re-create what I see in my dreams."

A coiled snake bracelet, the scales with golden and blue enamel detail, the head set with nine graduated marquise-cut diamonds and round-cut ruby eyes, also can be worn as a necklace, stamped "750."

17in (43cm) long

$10,000-11,000   L&T

A Finnish silver pendant necklace, the open circular frame set with a center hardstone cabochon, stamped marks.

pendant 1¾in (4.5cm) long

$190-220   WW

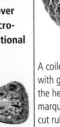

A quatrefoil pendant, attributed to Liza Sotilis, the textured panel with a center cultured pearl accent, loop fitting verso, in a Sotilis lozenge-shaped box.

1970s   2in (5cm) wide ⅜oz

$1,250-1,500   DN

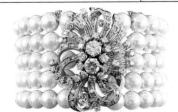

A mid- to late-20thC Continental five-strand cultured pearl bracelet, with white gold and diamond cluster-set scroll clasp and diamond-set line spacers, minor blisters in several pearls.

7½in (19cm) long 2⅞oz

$3,100-3,500   GORL

A Tiffany & Co. green nephrite jade and silver hinged bangle, "Feather Cuff," by Elsa Peretti, London, signed "TIFFANY & CO." with facsimile "Elsa Peretti" signature, stamped "925 HONG KONG," laser hallmark, in original Tiffany & Co. box and outer cardboard case, with original receipt, scratches.

2011   2¼in (5.5cm) wide 4⅛oz

$2,500-3,100   DN

A large Mexican sterling silver hinged bangle.

2¼in (5.5cm) wide (internal) 3⅝oz

$500-625   WAD

JEWELRY

An enamel and diamond brooch, by Leo de Vroomen, with blue, green, and yellow guilloché enamel and a scrolling detail of pavé-set round brilliant-cut diamonds, modeled in 18ct gold.

2in (5cm) diam

$6,000-7,500   **L&T**

A French birdhouse brooch, the two sitting birds with circular-cut ruby heads and circular cabochon turquoise bodies, within a textured gold-color birdhouse with a circular-cut sapphire- and ruby-accented branch, stamped with French eagle-head poinçon, light wear.

1960s   *1½in (4cm) wide ⅜oz*

$1,400-1,600   **DN**

A Cartier 18ct-yellow gold and silver brooch, in the form of a hawk resting on its trainer's gauntlet, its eye set with a small ruby, the glove decorated in black enamel and set with a small diamond and coral, signed verso and numbered "11513."

2in (5cm) high

$5,000-5,600   **WHP**

A Lalaounis gold brooch, designed as three entwined snakes, signature and maker's mark for Ilias Lalaounis, Greek assay marks.

ca. 1969   *2½in (6.5cm) high*

$4,000-4,500   **WW**

A mid-20thC citrine bow brooch, channel set in the center with caliber-cut citrines, stamped "585."

2¼in (5.5cm) wide

$500-625   **L&T**

A Scottish 9ct-gold thistle brooch, by Cairncross, Perth, set with a single Scottish freshwater pearl.

Granted a license from NatureScot, Cairncress made this brooch with freshwater pearls legally taken from the wild prior to March 27, 1991.

1¾in (4.5cm) wide

$375-500   **L&T**

A coral cherub brooch, the polished and carved cherub holding a sheaf of corn, with an applied diamond accented star on his forehead, two-color wings set with old-cut diamonds, approximately 0.98ct total, unmarked, some glue visible.

2¾in (7cm) wide 1⅝oz

$1,900-2,200   **DN**

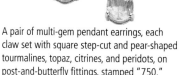

A pair of multi-gem pendant earrings, each claw set with square step-cut and pear-shaped tourmalines, topaz, citrines, and peridots, on post-and-butterfly fittings, stamped "750."

1¼in (3cm) long

$500-625   **L&T**

A pair of abstract ear pendants, the hooped gold-color wire orbs with claw-set circular-cut ruby accents, with oval lattice panels between with brilliant-cut diamond accents, approximately 0.38ct total, with post fittings, unmarked, light wear in settings.

1970s   *1½in (4cm) long ⅜oz*

$1,900-2,200   **DN**

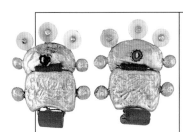

A pair of abstract earclips, by Liza Sotilis, each with two shaped and textured panels with gold-color disk sides, a trio of mother-of-pearl discs above, with (possibly ancient) bead accents, signed "Sotilis," with clip fittings, light wear.

See the Essential Reference for Liza Sotilis on page 437.

2in (5cm) long 1¼oz
$7,000-7,500   **DN**

A pair of ancient-style bead and gold-color ear clips, by Liza Sotilis, the reeded panels with circular glass antique-style (possibly ancient) bead bases, one embossed "Sotilis" on reverse, with clip fittings, light wear.

See the Essential Reference for Liza Sotilis on page 437.

1¾in (4.5cm) long 1⅞oz
$7,000-7,500   **DN**

A pair of Frascarolo and Cie. tiger cuff links, the striped enamel tiger masks set with brilliant-cut diamonds on the muzzle and ruff, approximately 0.92ct total, with circular-cut ruby eyes, stamped on reverse "Modele Deposse 750" and "FC Made in Italy," with Italian control marks "347 AL," with reeded baton swivel terminals, enamel chips.

Pierino "Rino" Frascarolo (1928-76) came from a wealthy Milanese family and set up Franscarolo & Cie. with two colleagues, Aldo Lenti (1910-82) and Daniele Valiera (1912-78). In the 1960s, the company became well known for fanciful enameled animal jewelry, and from 1966 Frascarolo's "Bestiario" collection gained worldwide acclaim, particularly in North America, where the company opened in New York in 1970 under the name Frascarolo & Co. Inc.

1970s   *¾in (2cm) wide ¾oz*
$2,200-2,700   **DN**

A rare Modernist silver ring, by Naum Slutzky, designed as a trio of partly articulated silver bars, on a silver band with paneled shoulders, maker's mark for Naum Slutzky.

Naum Slutzky (1894-1965) was born in Ukraine, the son of Gilel Slutzky, a goldsmith employed by Carl Fabergé. Naum trained as a goldsmith under Josef Hoffman at the Wiener Werkstatte before joining the Bauhaus. He fled to England in 1933, to escape the Nazis, and eventually took a series of posts as a lecturer in jewelry design in London and Birmingham, starting at the Center College of Art (now St. Martin's), and participating in the seminal 1961 International Jewelry Exhibition at Goldsmith's Hall. He initially planned to exhibit his early Bauhaus pieces, but instead exhibited recent designs in a strikingly Modernist style, which were subsequently purchased by the Goldsmith's Hall. See David Horton, "Naum Slutzky: Bauhaus Master Goldsmith," London (2017), page 11. An identical ring dated to 1965 can be found in the collection of the Victoria & Albert Museum, collection no. CIRC.412-1966.

1962   *size P*
$2,500-3,100   **WW**

A pair of 18ct-gold earrings, by Leo de Vroomen, each collet set with an oval-cut blue topaz within a green guilloché enamel border, clip fittings, signed.

1¼in (3cm) wide
$3,000-3,350   **L&T**

A 9ct-white gold dress ring, London, set with five small sapphires in an abstract bark design setting.

1974   *size R ¼oz*
$125-170   **WHP**

A silver square ring, by Dorothy Hogg, with beaded detail.

1970s   *size K/L*
$1,100-1,500   **L&T**

An 18ct-gold cluster ring, by Cropp & Farr, set with 3 oval-cut aquamarines and 12 round brilliant-cut diamonds.

1970s   *size M ⅛ oz*
$625-750   **GORL**

A platinum cluster ring, London, the oval conch pearl claw set within a surround of brilliant-cut diamonds, approximately 0.50ct total, maker's mark "NYA," small scratches on pearl.

2001   *size O ⅜oz*
$5,000-5,600   **DN**

An 18ct-gold cocktail ring, claw set with a cut-corner rectangular-cut fire opal, in a border of round brilliant-cut diamonds.

size Q
$2,700-3,100   **L&T**

JEWELRY

Judith Picks

I have picked out this "Queen Anne" parure, comprising a pendant necklace, bracelet, and earrings, for two reasons. The first is that most people new to costume jewelry assume it is essentially a 20thC and 21stC phenomenon, sparked by costume designers, such as Coco Chanel, in Paris after World War I, and fueled by the Great Depression of the late 1920s and 1930s—a development that incentivized jewelers to use materials significantly less expensive than precious metals and stones. These events undeniably promoted considerable growth in the costume jewelry market, but they certainly were not without historical precedent! For example, in the early 18thC, when this parure was made, a thriving costume-jewelry market had begun to develop in Europe for several reasons: the development and dissemination of high-quality paste stones from Gablonz, in Bohemia; the gradual introduction of finer machine cutting and faceting; and improvements in techniques, such as foil-backing paste and glass to enhance their brilliance and luster—and all the while the pieces produced were considerably more affordable than their precious equivalents. Which brings me to my second reason—perhaps that "affordability" is now in question: estimated to sell for under £620, this parure actually went under the hammer for a market-changing $32,000 (including a 30 percent buyer's premium). Just wow, but there again, if you look at it, closely you can see why!

A rare Georgian "Queen Anne" paste parure, comprising a necklace suspending a pendant, composed of faceted peacock blue paste in foiled settings, with hoops for a ribbon fastening, a similar bracelet and a pair of earrings, hook-and-clip fittings.

necklace 12½in (31.5cm) long
$31,000-37,000   **WW**

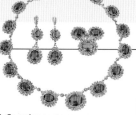

A Georgian paste parure, comprising a necklace, brooch, and pair of earrings, each set with oval pink paste stones and opaque blue paste cabochons imitating turquoise, in floral gilt-metal mounts.

1830s   necklace 16¾in (42.5cm) long
$5,000-6,200   **WW**

A French couture turquoise glass and gray rhinestone necklace and earrings set, probably by Francis Winter, the necklace arranged in Edwardian swag style, earrings stamped "FRANCE" on reverse.

Francis Winter, who made pieces for Dior, Balenciaga, and Chanel, among others, was particularly influenced by the styles of the Victorian and Edwardian eras. His designs also often featured unusual Austrian rhinestones, and often in the claw settings also employed by Mitchel Maer in his work for Dior.

1950s   necklace 15¾in (40cm) long
$1,000-1,250   **GRV**

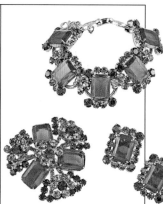

A Juliana four-piece gold-tone metal suite, comprising a bracelet, a brooch, and a pair of clip-back earrings, set with amber-tone rhinestones.

bracelet 6¾in (17cm) long
$220-275   **WAD**

A Ciner two-piece gold-tone metal set, comprising a necklace and a bracelet, decorated with enamel and clear rhinestones.

necklace 17½in (44.5cm) long
$350-400   **WAD**

A Kenneth Jay Lane gold-tone metal set, comprising a necklace and a pair of clip-back earrings, with a mat and hammered finish.

necklace 17½in (44.5cm) long
$150-190   **WAD**

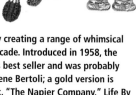

A Napier sterling silver-plated brass "Shangri-La" charm bracelet and earrings set, charms inspired by East Asia, featuring symbols, lanterns, dragons, Bhudda, and pagodas, accented with color glass beads, bracelet stamped "NAPIER."

In the 1950s, the charm bracelet became particularly popular. The Napier company catered for this by creating a range of whimsical charm bracelets throughout the decade. Introduced in 1958, the "Shangri-La" bracelet was Napier's best seller and was probably designed by its head designer, Eugene Bertoli; a gold version is featured in Melinda L. Lewis's book, "The Napier Company," Life By Design Publishing (2013).

1958   earrings 2in (5cm) long
$500-625   **GRV**

A Vrba three-piece blackened metal suite, comprising a brooch and a pair of clip-back earrings, set with blue glass cabochons and blue, green, and yellow rhinestones.

brooch 4in (10cm) high
$350-400   **WAD**

A rare 19thC glass and gilt-metal necklace, composed of links set with molded resin in gilt rope-twist borders and foil-backed glass cabochons, the center suspending a similar pendant fringed with gilt-metal drops.

pendant 3¼in (8.5cm) long

$1,900-2,200 **WW**

An Art Deco glass bead necklace, with alternating blue and frosted glass beads, with three larger clear glass textured beads in the center, the blue beads carved with floral patterns, separated by cut-metal rondelle beads.

1920s *27½in (70cm) long*

$300-375 **GRV**

A Bakelite, wood, and metal fringe necklace.

15in (38cm) long

$125-170 **WAD**

An Art Deco Bakelite flower necklace, with Bakelite cuboid beads and three floral motifs, interspersed with clear glass beads.

1930s *16¼in (41cm) long*

$220-275 **GRV**

A Weiss gold-tone metal necklace, set with blue rhinestones and cabochons, unsigned.

13½in (34.5cm) long

$350-400 **WAD**

A Miriam Haskell six-strand faux turquoise bead necklace, completed with a gold-tone metal filigree clasp set with faux turquoise and blue rhinestones.

16in (40.5cm) long

$450-500 **WAD**

ESSENTIAL REFERENCE—AURORA BOREALIS

The aurora borealis were named after Aurora, the Roman goddess of the dawn, and Boreas, the god of the north wind in Greek mythology. Also known as the northern lights, they comprise spectacular and brilliant displays of curtains, rays, spirals, and flickers of natural multicolor light in the sky. Caused by solar winds disturbing electrons and protons in the magnetosphere, and predominantly seen in high-latitude regions of the Arctic Circle, they provided the inspiration, and the name, for the similarly spectacular rhinestones that Swarovski developed in the mid-1950s, initially for Christian Dior. Swarovski created their shimmering iridescence by coating the crystal rhinestones with a polychrome metallic finish—one later used ingeniously by the American costume jewelry manufacturer Weiss, who inverted the stones in their settings to display their more densely color undersides.

A Christian Dior "Aurora Borealis" and green rhinestone necklace, by Henkel and Grossé, constructed from German Alpaca silver, unsigned, stamped "MADE IN GERMANY."

1961 *16½in (42cm) long*

$750-875 **GRV**

A Celine gold-tone metal heavy knot link necklace.

17in (43cm) long

$170-220 **WAD**

A Victorian gilt-metal locket and chain, the bar chain suspending a locket decorated with a wheat and sickle motif, set with small paste stones and seed pearls, lined with purple velvet.

The wheat sheaf was a popular motif in Victorian mourning and sentimental jewelry. Because wheat is harvested and then resown in the spring, it was used to symbolize the renewal or resurrection of the soul.

locket 2in (5cm) long

$300-375   **GRV**

A mid- to late-19thC Victorian silver heart pendant necklace, with clear paste stones around a turquoise glass heart-shaped cabochon, pendant probably silver, the flat-link chain stamped "STERLING."

As a piece of sentimental jewelry from the Victorian era, the heart in this necklace symbolizes love, charity, joy, and compassion. The color turquoise used in Victorian jewelry is intended to bring the wearer luck.

pendant 1in (2.5cm) long

$280-300   **GRV**

CLOSER LOOK—AN ART NOUVEAU PENDANT

The Art Nouveau style of the late19thC and early 20thC was, in a number of respects, a unique fusion of other earlier and contemporary styles. Evident here in the fuchsia stems and leaves are the curvaceous lines of the Rococo style, the strong return to Naturalism prompted by the Gothic Revival, and the Symbolist fascination with the forms of nature.

Carved from horn, the tubes, ovaries, petals, sepals, leaves, filaments, and anthers of the fuchsia are hand painted in shades of brown and green, not only for color, but also to enhance both the naturalism and the three-dimensionality of the composition.

The style and stigma of the fuchsia (collectively known as the pistil) are represented by a suitably elongated green glass bead drop. The pendant being almost certainly of French origin, the drop is, characteristically, chromatically en suite with the silk thread necklace and its pair of glass bead embellishments.

An Art Nouveau carved horn fuchsia pendant necklace, probably French.

ca. 1900   *pendant 3½in (9cm) long*

$1,100-1,350   **GRV**

A Murrle, Bennett & Co. Arts and Crafts enamel pendant necklace, of floral design with peacock-color gradient enamel, on a Figaro chain, white metal stamped "Silver" along with maker's mark.

pendant 2¾in (7cm) long ⅝oz

$1,250-1,500   **DAWS**

An Art Deco pink and black glass-bead flapper necklace, probably French, with rhinestone details, culminating in suspended tassels in a pendant form.

1920s   *27½in (70cm) long*

$700-750   **GRV**

A Givenchy gold-tone metal necklace, set with faux carnelian.

16in (40.5cm) long

$150-170   **WAD**

A Louis Vuitton gilt-metal monogram pendant necklace, modeled as a rope-twist heart with various monogram pendants, on a rope-twist chain and T-bar clasp, unmarked.

pendant 1¼in (3cm) long

$375-450   **L&T**

A Christian Lacroix silver-plated star pendant necklace, stamped "CL" on reverse.

1990s   *pendant 1in (2.5cm) wide*

$190-220   **GRV**

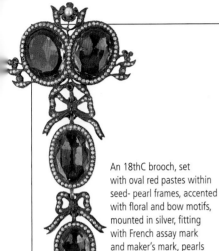

An 18thC brooch, set with oval red pastes within seed-pearl frames, accented with floral and bow motifs, mounted in silver, fitting with French assay mark and maker's mark, pearls untested.

3¼in (8.5cm) high

$750-875   **WW**

An Art Nouveau carved-horn bee brooch.

ca. 1900   *4in (10cm) wide*

$375-450   **GRV**

A Joseff of Hollywood Russian gold-plated lioness brooch, the roaring lioness motif set on a decorative panel suspending three looped rope chains and two medallions, each detailed with East Asian lettering, set with domed purple and topaz glass cabochons, stamped "Joseff" on reverse.

1940s   *6¾in (17cm) long*

$550-625   **GRV**

ESSENTIAL REFERENCE—"CLIP-MATES"

Double clips—matching pairs of clips that could be worn either separately or attached together on a hidden frame and worn as one—became particularly popular during the late 1920s and 1930s. This was in part, albeit not exclusively, fueled by a fashion for square-cut necklines, the shape of which could be emphasized and enhanced by wearing a dress clip on each side of the square. In 1927, the prestigious French jeweler Louis Cartier had patented a frame for attaching pairs of clips, and in 1931 Adolph Katz of the American costume jewelry manufacturer Coro followed suit with an interlocking catch mechanism and pair of clips patented as "Duettes." This, in turn, prompted equivalents from other costume-jewelry manufacturers, most notably Trifari's "Clip-Mates," created by their chief designer, Alfred Philippe, of which the clip shown here is an example.

A Miriam Haskell gold-tone metal heart brooch, set with beads and various color rhinestones.

2½in (6.5cm) high

$200-240   **WAD**

A Trifari "Clip-Mates" silver-tone metal duette, designed by Alfred Philippe, patent no. 2050804, set with clear rhinestones and faux pearls, one very small rhinestone absent.

2¾in (7cm) wide

$150-190   **WAD**

A pair of silver-tone paste and enamel ladybug brooches, unsigned.

In the 1940s, there was a craze for figural brooches and pins, such as these ladybugs. American costume jewelry creators, such as Coro, Trifari, and Marcel Boucher, in particular, cornered this market for figurals and produced numerous brooches in whimsical designs.

1940s   *1¼in (3cm) wide*

$80-110   **GRV**

A French silver brooch/pendant, by Henry Perichon, with square and round deep purple poured-glass cabochons, stamped "Henry."

Henri Perichon was based in Lyon, France, and worked primarily in bronze and silver, with his work strongly influenced by Medieval and Renaissance art. His jewelry was especially popular in the 1950s and 1960s, and, in part because of their rarity, his pieces are increasingly collectible today.

1960s

$375-450   **GRV**

An American gold-plated brooch, by Natasha Stambouli, set with round amethyst, green aventurine, amazonite, and rhodocrosite cabochons, detailed with round pink, green, and topaz rhinestones, stamped "NATASHA STAMBOULI."

1990s   *2¾in (7cm) wide*

$220-275   **GRV**

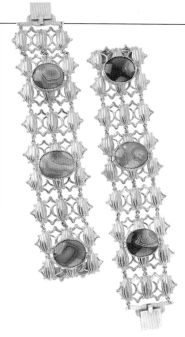

A pair of early-19thC gilt-metal bracelets, each composed of openwork panels set with agate cabochons.

7in (18cm) long

$1,000-1,100   **WW**

An unusual mid-19thC bog oak and gilt-metal bracelet, composed of links set with molded bog-oak fox faces, in gilt rope-twist borders.

See Shirley Bury, "Jewellery 1789-1910 Vol II: The International Era," Antique Collectors Club (1991), page 536, no. 277, for a comparable molded bog-oak parure and a discussion of the development of bog-oak jewels as part of the vogue for Irish jewels in the mid-19thC.

7in (18cm) long

$400-475   **WW**

A pair of mid-19thC gilt-metal bracelets, each composed of spiral linking, on a foliate clasp set with oval- and circular-cut purple pastes.

7¼in (18.5cm) long

$400-475   **WW**

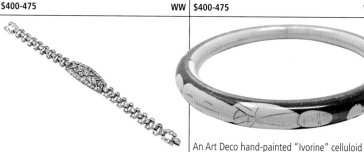

An Art Deco sterling silver and black Galalith bracelet, stamped "STERLING."

1920s   *7in (18cm) long*

$300-375   **GRV**

An American Trifari KTF Art Deco rhodium-plated paste bracelet, the center panel with a floral design, stamped "KTF."

This bracelet is stamped "KTF," which stands for Krussman, Trifari, and Fishel. Leo Krussman, Gustavo Trifari, and Carl Fishel ran the Trifari company together from 1925, and jewelry was stamped with their names until the mid-1930s. Examples of Trifari jewelry featuring the KTF stamp are very rare and highly collectible.

1930s   *7in (18cm) long*

$400-475   **GRV**

An Art Deco hand-painted "Ivorine" celluloid bangle, with an intricate East Asian-style design of two people and lettering.

Celluloid was a highly popular material in jewelry manufacture during the 1920s and 1930s. Newly pioneered injection-molding processes meant that cellulose could be used to produce many identical pieces at the same time. This resulted in the cost per piece being low and, therefore, well-suited to post-Great Depression and subsequent World War II austerity.

1920s   *3in (7.5cm) diam*

$125-170   **GRV**

A Sherman silver-tone metal hinged bangle, set with iridescent rhinestones.

2½in (6.5cm) diam

$350-400   **WAD**

A Chanel gold-tone turnlock bracelet, with Swarovski crystal "CC," date stamp "98A."

1998   *6¾in (17cm) long*

$1,600-1,900   **CA**

A Juicy Couture gold-tone metal hinged bangle, decorated with enamel and small rhinestones.

2½in (6.5cm) wide (internal)

$60-90   **WAD**

A pair of late-19thC French pâte-de-verre cameo earrings, hooks probably 9ct gold.

¾in (2cm) long

$220-275   **GRV**

A pair of Bohemian Art Nouveau gilt-metal flower earrings, with floral metal stampings on filigree-work panels, detailed with an array of foiled paste stones.

ca. 1900   3¼in (8.5cm) long

$290-325   **GRV**

A pair of Art Deco pressed Peking glass floral drop earrings, with screw backs.

1920s   1¾in (4.5cm) long

$220-250   **GRV**

A pair of Art Deco silver and pink Galalith drop earrings, the bullet-shaped beads carved with a linear and swirling design, with ornate screw backs, stamped "835."

1920s   2¼in (5.5cm) long

$250-290   **GRV**

A pair of "cocktail-style" couture rhinestone clip-on drop earrings, possibly by Max Müller, unsigned.

1950s   2¼in (5.5cm) long

$280-300   **GRV**

A pair of Christian Dior orange and blue rhinestone clip-on earrings, by Mitchel Maer, the reverse of one stamped "CHRISTIAN DIOR BY MITCHEL MAER."

These earrings can be dated to the 1950s, because the London-based designer Mitchel Maer produced jewelry for the House of Dior between 1952 and 1956. His bold rhinestone creations for the house were popular, because they complimented the couture evening wear designed by Dior during the decade, and they are particularly collectible today.

1952-56   1in (2.5cm) long

$375-420   **GRV**

A pair of Miriam Haskell faux baroque pearl and gilt-metal drop earrings, screw-back clip, signed "MIRIAM HASKELL."

The earrings were produced in the 1960s, when Robert Clark was head designer at Miriam Haskell. We can identify these earrings as being early-1960s, because their adjustable screw backs were utilized in the earliest part of the decade. Moreover, the screw-back clip on these particular earrings—which features a patent number—was produced exclusively for Haskell by the AroSac company; it can be tightened or slackened for the comfort of the wearer.

1960s   2in (5cm) long

$220-250   **GRV**

A pair of Kenneth Jay Lane gold-plated, turquoise acrylic, and rhinestone clip-on earrings, stamped "K.J.L." on clips.

1960s   2¼in (5.5cm) long

$450-475   **GRV**

A pair of Yves Saint Laurent gold-plated earrings, set with round- and square-cut green, gray, and pink glass cabochons, clip-on, both stamped "YSL" and "MADE IN FRANCE."

1980s   1½in (4cm) wide

$300-350   **GRV**

A pair of Christian Dior gold-tone metal clip-on earrings, each encasing a black sphere.

2¼in (5.5cm) long

$120-150   **WAD**

ARCHITECTURAL ANTIQUES

ESSENTIAL REFERENCE—CHIMNEYPIECES

Known more commonly nowadays as fireplace surrounds (or sometimes fireplace mantels), chimneypieces emerged in the late 15thC as the fireplace gradually transitioned from being an open hearth in the center or near one end of a room to a hearth enclosed within a wall. This enabled the smoke from the fire to be more efficiently dispersed upward through a wall-concealed flue to a rooftop chimney above. As Renaissance ideas on architecture and design permeated Europe, the within-a-wall fireplace became an increasingly substantial feature or focal point of a room, and the basic form—a projecting chimney breast with a decorative chimneypiece framing the hearth—has survived to this day.

Made from marble or other stones, plaster, wood, or, from the 19thC, cast iron, the basic configuration has remained fairly constant, comprising: a pair of columnar-like supports rising on each side of the hearth to support a lintel-like frieze spanning the top; above that there is often, but not always, a mantelshelf; and over that there can be a decorative over-mantel (sometimes, from the 18thC, incorporating a mirror). However, in contrast to the almost permanence of its basic construction, the manner in which the chimneypiece has been treated decoratively has constantly changed, and almost invariably reflects the prevailing historical style movement, spanning late Renaissance to Postmodern and all developments in between.

A George II pine fireplace surround, mid-18thC and later, the frieze carved with acanthus scrolls, top and mantel appear later, splits, losses, smoke darkening.

59¾in (152cm) wide

$4,300-5,000   SWO

An Irish George III carved pine fireplace surround, in Neoclassical style, with a molded platform top, above a frieze carved in relief with scrolling leaves and rosettes.

61in (155cm) wide

$1,000-1,250   ADA

A late-18thC George III brass fireplace surround, possibly Dublin, the brass front applied on cast-iron.

36¼in (92cm) wide

$2,500-3,100   DN

A late-18th/early-19thC George III carved white marble chimneypiece, the inverted breakfront mantel above ogee and stepped-edging moldings and a fluted frieze, the center lapis lazuli tablet with a carved marble figural panel depicting cavorting amorini in a roundel, within a drape hung from serpent-entwined uprights, flanked by jambs with flower heads above recessed panels of trailed bellflowers, on block feet.

Although this chimneypiece does not incorporate any scagliola—a technique that involves manipulating pigmented plaster to resemble pietra dura inlays in marble and ornamental hardstones, and for which the Italian craftsman Pietro Bossi (active in Ireland in the late 18thC) was well known—it is, nevertheless, much in the style of Bossi's work.

73½in (187cm) wide

$7,000-7,500   DUK

CLOSER LOOK—AN 18THC CARVED PINE CHIMNEYPIECE

The mantelshelf is a "breakfront." Less commonly referred to as a "broken front," it emerged in the early 18thC and is an overtly symmetrical configuration also used in furniture, most notably bookcases, in which a forward-projected section is centered between two recessed sections.

Derived from the Latin word for "tooth," dentil moldings are runs of small, spaced blocks that originated as a decorative device along the lower edge of a cornice in Classical Greek and Roman architecture. They began to appear on European furniture from around the early 17thC.

Also derived from the Classical vocabulary of ornament, scrolling foliage became a hugely popular and widely used form of carved, molded, or painted decoration in the various Classical Revival styles from the Renaissance onward. The Mediterranean "Acanthus spinosis," used here, was the most popular plant form, although not entirely dissimilar parsley, poppy, or thistle leaves were also often employed.

Just below the pair of scrolled, acanthus-carved brackets that support each end of the mantelshelf, and at the top of the pair of pilasters that rise up to meet the brackets, are what at first glance look like more acanthus forms—which they are, but they are also carved as grotesque foliate masks.

An 18thC Georgian carved pine fireplace surround, the breakfront shelf above a dentil-molded frieze, carved in relief with foliate scrolls and flowers, the jambs carved with trailing flower garlands and capped by scrolled brackets.

73¼in (186cm) wide

$2,700-3,100   L&T

An Irish blue limestone fireplace, with a frieze pediment on plain column supports, the surround with four-leaf clover, carved shamrocks, and síle na gíg (ancient Celtic female fertility symbols).

67in (170cm) wide

$20,000-22,000   ADA

A 19thC pine fireplace surround, decorated with chevrons and shamrocks.

41¾in (106cm) wide

$750-1,000   **ADA**

A 19thC painted pine fireplace surround, carved with diamond lozenge decoration.

56in (142cm) wide

$750-1,000   **ADA**

A 19thC French ormolu-mounted white marble fireplace surround/chimneypiece, the stop-fluted columns with acanthus leaf capitals, the frieze decorated with ribbon-tied laurel leaves.

57¾in (146.5cm) wide

$3,100-3,700   **WW**

A 19thC painted pine marriage fireplace surround, decorated with faux Cork red marble and Connemara faux mark panels, with chevrons and diamond lozenges.

59¾in (152cm) wide

$1,900-2,200   **ADA**

ESSENTIAL REFERENCE—RENAISSANCE REVIVAL

One of the major historical style revivals of the 19thC, along with the Gothic Revival, the Renaissance Revival flourished during the 1830s, 1840s, and 1850s, but it remained in vogue to varying degrees and on both sides of the Atlantic until the end of the 19thC. Fueled by a revival of the architectural Italian High Renaissance "palazzo" style—considered particularly appropriate not only for substantial residential homes but also public buildings, especially the new public libraries—it reintroduced numerous Renaissance forms and decorative motifs, most of which were derived/adapted from the Classical vocabulary of ornament. Particularly prominent among these were pilasters, family cyphers or emblems, scrolling foliate and floral forms, masks, and grotesques—most of which are employed on this Renaissance Revival oak chimneypiece, which dates from the end of the 19thC.

A large late-19thC Renaissance Revival carved oak fireplace surround, carved with C scrolls, cartouches, masks, and grotesques, dated "1895."

80in (203cm) wide

$1,000-1,250   **L&T**

A 20thC carved pine fireplace surround, in George II style, with egg-and-dart molding and foliate scrolls.

63in (160cm) wide

$7,500-8,500   **SWO**

An early-20thC carved pine fireplace surround, in George III style, with reeded decoration, applied with pressed metal appliques of Venus in her chariot surrounded by cherubs, paterae, and stiff leaves, above reeded columns.

65in (165cm) wide

$1,250-1,500   **WW**

A carved fireplace surround/chimneypiece, in Neoclassical style, the dentil cornice over a Classical carved frieze, with acanthus capitals and caryatids, losses and wear.

74in (188cm) wide

$450-500   **SWO**

ARCHITECTURAL ANTIQUES

An 18thC steel and brass fire grate, with a set of three 18thC brass fire tools.

22in (56cm) wide

$1,900-2,200 DN

A Regency cast-iron fire grate, in the manner of George Bullock, the cast back decorated with scrolling anthemion, with Thomas Hope-style leopard heads on the sides.

The design of this fire grate is based upon an unsigned drawing by the influential Regency period modeler, sculptor, cabinetmaker, and furniture designer George Bullock (1777-1818), at Tew Park, Great Tew, Oxfordshire, and inscribed "Plan of Stove in Dining room and Oak Study."

ca. 1820 *34¾in (88cm) wide*

$1,400-1,700 DN

A George IV brass and cast-iron fire grate, of slightly bowed design with reeded border supports, joined in the upper corners by square blocks with roundels, three-bar grill, with original detachable ashpan and a collection of brass fire irons and accessories.

32¾in (83cm) wide

$1,250-1,500 ADA

ESSENTIAL REFERENCE—REGISTER GRATES

By the turn of the 19thC, enclosed hob grates had, in general, superseded open dog grates in popularity in towns and cities. However, although elegant, hob grates were not efficient in terms of combustion and were, therefore soon replaced, again mostly in urban areas, by the new cast-iron "register" grate.

- **The register grate was significantly more efficient, incorporating a damper to control the supply of air to the fire, and usually supplemented with an additional damper in the throat of the chimney.**
- **Cast in one piece and forming the inner frame of the hearth, the mass-produced register was set as an insert within the fireplace surround—although from a functional viewpoint, it could be installed without the latter, and sometimes was.**
- **Apart from in particularly grand houses, and especially in their large entrance halls where open dog and hob grates remained popular, built-in register grates became almost universal in town houses during the course of the 19thC.**

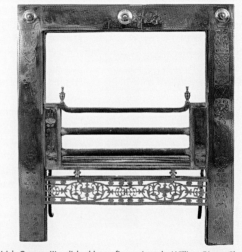

An Irish George III polished brass fire register, by William Binns, Church Street, Dublin, the three-bar grill surrounded by pierced and engraved brass borders, decorated with floral trails and circular bosses.

33¾in (86cm) wide

$8,500-10,000 ADA

A 19thC Victorian cast-iron "thistle" fire grate, the pointed fireback surmounted by a thistle, above a three-bar grate.

28¾in (73cm) high

$1,250-1,500 L&T

A late-19thC polished steel and iron fire grate, attributed to the Carron Foundry, in George III style, the fireback with a lunette fan top, fluted front legs surmounted by oval rosettes and topped with large urn finials, the front with fluted fan and dentil design, bowed bar burning area with conforming urns.

32in (81cm) wide

$2,500-3,100 DN

A late-19th/early-20thC brass and cast-iron fire grate, in George III style, in the manner of Thomas Elsley, the arched back decorated with an urn above a serpentine railed basket, the pierced front with engraved decoration and turned urn finials.

31¾in (80.5cm) wide

$875-1,250 WW

A wrought-iron fire basket, with scroll feet and open basket terminals, unsigned.

33½in (85cm) wide

$300-450 WW

Judith Picks

Sometimes a lot comes up at auction that, when the hammer finally comes down, blows its original estimate out of the water—in this case, roughly five-fold. For what it is worth, I can totally understand the presale estimate, given what the objects are—French chenets or firedogs—and given the prevailing state of the market ... but, but, 20/20 hindsight is a wonderfully accurate facility, and the more you look at them, in closer and closer detail, the more you really realize just how exquisitely they were conceived, sculpted, and cast. They really are things of beauty! Throw in the fact that they are in the form of a pair of "chevaux marins" (sea horses), derived from a drawing attributed to Lambert-Sigisbert Adam (1700-59) for a chenet designed with Triton astride a sea horse, and that chenets incorporating chevaux marins like these are recorded in an inventory at the Château de Passy, which belonged to the grandson of Samuel Bernard, King Louis XVI's banker, and it all goes a long way to explain it.

A rare pair of Louis XV ormolu sea horse chenets, "The Rothschild Chevaux Marins Chenets," French or German, each surmounted with a prancing horse with webbed hooves, on a Rococo scrolling leaf base, with chased and punched decoration, stamped "2," with bronze scroll supports.

ca. 1745-50   *17¼in (43.5cm) high*

$90,000-100,000   **WW**

A pair of 19thC gilt-bronze chenets, in Louis XVI style, each in the form of a quiver of arrows, decorated with swags of flowers and scrolling leaves.

22½in (57cm) high

$190-250   **WW**

A pair of mid-19thC French ormolu chenets, in Louis XV style, after Phillipe Caffieri, modeled as a young couple holding a ewer and a beaker, sitting on Rococo foliate C scrolls, each stamped with a "B."

11¾in (30cm) high

$1,100-1,500   **WW**

A pair of English cast-iron firedogs, stamped "COPYRIGHTED 1883/ C. A. WELLINGTON/4."

1883   *19¾in (50cm) high*

$250-370   **L&T**

A pair of wrought-iron firedogs, with ring handles over scroll supports.

36½in (93cm) high

$300-375   **CHOR**

A pair of large late-19thC Italian Venetian bronze andirons, in Renaissance style, each with a cherub finial above tiered balusters and urns cast with stiff leaves, masks, and swags, above triangular feet with winged satyrs and resting on dolphin's feet, on open scrollwork bases, each centered with a bearded mask.

74½in (189cm) high

$7,000-7,500   **WW**

A pair of firedogs, in Adam style, the urn standards with ram heads, raised on hoof feet.

ca. 1900   *18½in (47cm) high*

$625-750   **CHEF**

A 19thC French cast-brass fire fender and pair of chenets, the fender surmounted with opposing winged griffins, the pierced frieze cast with a row of balusters and a plinth base, the chenets with conforming decoration and scrollwork details.

$1,100-1,350   **ADA**

A George III brass serpentine fender, with pierced foliate decoration, patch repairs, rubbing, verdigris marks.

ca. 1780   *56in (142cm) wide*

$875-1,100   **DN**

A George III polished steel fender, surmounted by a pair of Classical urns upon fluted pedestals, the pierced front with a center oval rosette and lines of punched beading.

58¼in (148cm) wide

$625-750   **CHEF**

A George III pierced brass serpentine fender, decorated with a centered urn flanked by hippogriffs, latticework, and dragons.

56¾in (144cm) wide

$450-550   **CHEF**

An early-19thC Regency steel fire fender, with pierced decoration.

41¾in (106cm) wide

$300-375   **WW**

A French ormolu fire fender, in Louis XVI style, decorated with a pair of figures, a drummer boy and a young girl sharpening a knife.

ca. 1870-80   *53in (134.5cm) wide*

$300-450   **WW**

A 19thC wrought-iron fender, with scrolling decoration.

60¼in (153cm) wide

$375-450   **CHEF**

A 19thC Victorian wrought-iron club fender, with L-shaped wood seats on upright supports, divided by a center U shape, on a plinth base.

57¾in (147cm) wide

$1,000-1,250   **L&T**

A 20thC polished brass and steel club fender, with a red leather seat, on tubular supports.

74in (188cm) wide

$1,100-1,350   **CHEF**

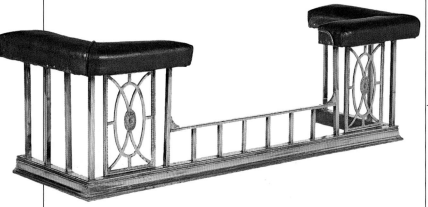

An early-20thC brass club fender, with leather seats, scratches, marks.

61in (155cm) wide

$3,100-3,700   **DN**

A 20thC steel club fender, with green leather padded seats.

62½in (159cm) wide

$1,250-1,500   **CHEF**

A large 20thC brass club fender, the padded seat upholstered in a red buttoned fabric.

76½in (194cm) wide

$1,500-1,900   **CHEF**

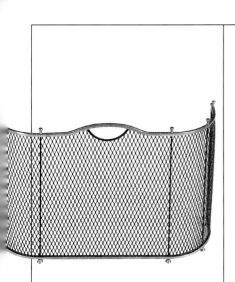

A George IV brass and wirework bowed fire screen.

30in (76cm) wide

$625-750   **ADA**

A French gilt-brass fire screen, with a ribbon-tied loop handle and draped swags, fitted with wire mesh, on splayed feet.

ca. 1900   *23¼in (59cm) wide*

$700-800   **ADA**

A French gilt-brass fire screen, with a cast scrollwork handle, the mesh wire with a centered medallion, raised on splayed scroll feet.

27½in (70cm) wide

$625-750   **ADA**

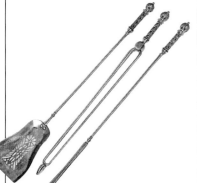

A set of three George III polished steel fire irons, the ball-finial handles decorated with a repeated rosette pattern, comprising a poker, tongs, and a shovel with pierced pan.

31½in (80cm) long

$500-625   **CHEF**

A set of three polished steel and brass fire irons, with shaped brass handles, comprising a shovel, tongs, and a poker.

ca. 1820   *32¾in (83cm) long*

$375-500   **CHEF**

A set of Georgian brass and oak mechanical bellows, lacking strap chain, knocks, wear.

24¾in (63cm) wide

$190-310   **SWO**

A pair of early-19thC tortoiseshell and mother-of-pearl bellows, inlaid with scrolling flowers and foliage.

13¼in (33.5cm) long

$125-190   **CHEF**

A pair of carved oak bellows, designed by Lewis F. Day, carved in low relief with "Lewis D and Temma Day," the reverse with "Wild Flowers," inside a floral border.

23¼in (59cm) long

$1,100-1,500   **WW**

A pair of late-19th/early 20thC beech and iron-bound bellows.

32¾in (83cm) long

$125-190   **CA**

ARCHITECTURAL ANTIQUES

A pair of 19thC patinated brass doorstops, in Empire style, each modeled as a large sphere on a rectangular plinth with an applied star.

9¾in (24.5cm) high

$625-850   **WW**

A 19thC brass doorstop, modeled as Saint George slaying the dragon, with a serpentine handle.

16¼in (41cm) high

$375-500   **CHEF**

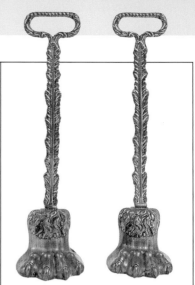

A pair of 19thC brass lion-paw doorstops, in Regency style, with foliate stems and handles.

15¼in (39cm) high

$700-800   **WW**

A pair of 19thC painted cast-iron lion door porters, scratches, pitting.

15in (38cm) high

$500-625   **SWO**

A late-19thC Victorian brass doorstop, cast as a stag standing before scrolling foliage.

15¾in (40cm) high

$250-370   **WW**

A Victorian painted cast-iron Punch doorstop, small paint chips.

13in (33cm) high

$125-190   **SWO**

A late-19thC Victorian brass doorstop, in the form of HMS "Victory," the pierced handle with a bust medallion of Admiral Nelson, on a lead weighted base.

18½in (47cm) high

$375-500   **WW**

A pair of gilt-metal doorstops, modeled as recumbent hounds, resting beside spiral-turned column supports, on stepped platform bases.

8¼in (21cm) wide

$625-750   **ADA**

A late-19th/early-20thC Cornish serpentine doorstop, with a brass ring handle.

10in (25.5cm) high

$875-1,000   **WW**

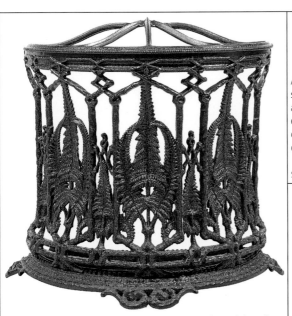

A 19thC Victorian Coalbrookdale cast-iron walking stick stand, "Fern" pattern, stamped "C-B-Dale," registration mark and serial no. "139688," areas of refinishing, wear, small losses.

24½in (62.5cm) high

$1,250-1,500   DN

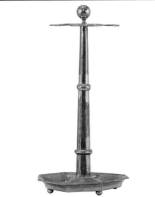

A Victorian cast-iron walking stick stand, with two divisions and a removable tray, cast diamond registration mark, column with movement, scuffs, oxidization.

28¼in (72cm) high

$100-150   SWO

A late Victorian brass walking stick stand, with four divisions and a spreading column, on a dished octagonal base.

30in (76cm) high

$300-350   SWO

A late-19thC cast-iron walking stick stand, with six divisions, the tapered column upon an octagonal tray, raised on lion-paw feet.

38½in (98cm) high

$375-500   CHEF

A Coalbrookdale cast-iron walking stick stand, mounted with 24 divisions, with pierced sides and two removable trays, repainted.

38¼in (97cm) wide

$450-550   SWO

An Italian novelty brass umbrella stand, modeled as a riding boot, with a brass spur and buckle joined by a leather strap, internally enameled, tarnishing, dents, scratches.

22in (56cm) high

$500-625   SWO

A Victorian cast-iron umbrella stand, in the manner of Coalbrookdale, decorated with trailing vines, with a removable tray, oxidization, wear, losses.

26in (66cm) high

$90-125   SWO

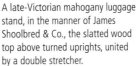

A late-Victorian mahogany luggage stand, in the manner of James Shoolbred & Co., the slatted wood top above turned uprights, united by a double stretcher.

23½in (60cm) wide

$750-875   CHEF

A 19thC faux bamboo cast-iron hall stand, with nine hooks over the walking stick/umbrella stand base, with a removable drip-tray, marked on the underside "N.14," mirror later and broken, rust, needs cleaning.

85¾in (218cm) high

$500-625   SWO

ARCHITECTURAL ANTIQUES

ESSENTIAL REFERENCE—COALBROOKDALE

Founded by Abraham Darby, ca. 1709, in the village of Coalbrookdale, Shropshire, the Coalbrookdale Company was at the forefront of the industrial revolution. Nowadays, it's best known for its Victorian cast-iron garden furniture, examples of which are included on this page.

● Underpinning Coalbrookdale's expansion was its use of locally mined coking coal, containing much lower than average levels of sulfur, to smelt iron ore, which produced much stronger, more durable iron that could be molded (cast) into more complex shapes than before.

● It initially produced domestic wares, such as cooking pots and kettles; the company expanded during the 18thC into cast-iron rails for the new railroads, cylinders for steam engines, and the world's first cast-iron bridge (at Ironbridge) in 1780.

● During the 19thC, the fashion for architectural cast iron, notably balconies, boomed, and was employed in the construction of the Crystal Palace for the Great Exhibition of 1851—Coalbrookdale exhibited a pair of ceremonial gates that were subsequently installed in London's Hyde Park.

● During the second half of the 19thC, Coalbrookdale's artifacts were exported around the world—the range of which can be seen in its colossal 1,032-page catalog of 1875 and included stoves, ranges, cast-iron beds, hall stands (some designed by Christopher Dresser), tables, chairs, and, as here, benches.

● Coupled with the Victorian taste for eclectic revival styles, it created a huge demand for garden furniture in the Gothic, Rococo, and Classical styles, and these were mostly configured in naturalistic plant-form patterns, some of which, again, are shown here.

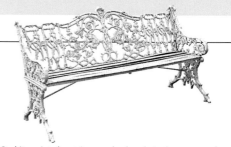

A 19thC white painted cast-iron garden bench, in the manner of Coalbrookdale, the pierced back and sides with naturalistic vine decoration, one arm detached but present, weakness in arm joints.

62¼in (158cm) wide

$500-625   CHEF

A 19thC cast-iron "Oak Leaf and Dog" garden bench, the pierced openwork back and arms with oak leaf panels, the arms with dog-head terminals.

67in (170cm) wide

$2,500-3,100   L&T

A late-19thC cast-iron "Peacock" garden seat, in the manner of Coalbrookdale, the center arched back pierced with foliate panels, over cast-iron slats.

72¾in (185cm) wide

$2,500-3,700   CHEF

A matched pair of painted metal "Fern and Blackberry" garden benches, in the manner of Coalbrookdale, one 19thC, the other later, the first cast iron and unmarked, the other in white metal with a design registration mark.

44½in (113cm) wide

$1,250-1,700   L&T

A late-19thC white painted cast-iron "Fern" garden bench, in the manner of Coalbrookdale, the back and sides pierced with various fern leaves, above a slatted wood seat, raised on conforming legs, "B165" mark on reverse.

55½in (141cm) wide

$625-750   CHEF

A late-19thC "Serpent and Grapes" garden bench, in the manner of Coalbrookdale, design no. 17597, the cast-iron end supports with dog-head arm terminals over a scrolling serpent, with diamond patent registry mark.

50½in (128cm) wide

$625-750   CHEF

A Victorian cast-iron park bench, slatted wood seat and back, the pierced and scrolled ends modeled with a centered crown among thistles and flowers.

75in (190.5cm) wide

$375-500   HT

A late-19thC Victorian Coalbrookdale cast-iron "Serpent and Grape" garden bench, the scrolling ends with dog-head terminals, with diamond registration marks and further rectangular plaques, later teak slats.

This design, no. 17597, is the second-oldest Coalbrookdale Foundry seat design. It was registered and patented at the Public Records Office on April 6, 1844. It appears as seat No. 9 in its 1875 Castings Catalogue, Section III, page 24.

63½in (161cm) wide

$2,700-3,200   WW

ESSENTIAL REFERENCE—VAL D'OSNE

The Val d'Osne cast-iron art foundry was founded in the town of that name in the Haute Marne, France, in 1835, by Jean Pierre-Victor André (1790-1851). Following rapid expansion, which included headquarters and a gallery on the Boulevard Voltaire in Paris, Val d'Osne became France's premier cast-iron maker during the 19thC and early 20thC, eventually being purchased in 1931 by a competitor, Sommevoire (today known as GHM). Known for its figural statues and busts, (often monumental) fountains, equestrian statues, diverse memorials, and garden furniture, as here, Val d'Osne won numerous awards for its work at both French and international exhibitions and expositions, most notably at: the Great Exhibition, in London in 1851; Paris in 1855; Santiago in 1875; Melbourne in 1879; and again in Paris, in 1878, 1889, and 1900. Its pieces remain admired and desirable today.

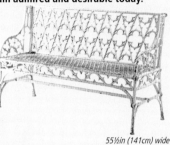

A late-19th/early-20thC French Val d'Osne cast-iron garden bench, in Gothic Revival style, with a pierced tracery back and arms, above a hexagonal latticework seat.

55½in (141cm) wide

$3,500-4,000 WW

A French polished metal garden bench, 19thC and later, the back with horizontal rails over a slatted seat, raised on tubular legs with stretchers.

66¼in (168cm) wide

$625-750 CHEF

A large wrought-iron country house gateway, probably 18thC, the center arched gate and smaller side panels surmounted by scrolled arch pediments, wear, minor rust, losses.

170in (432cm) high

$27,000-31,000 CHEF

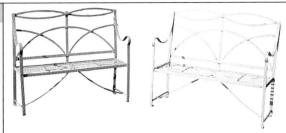

A pair of 19thC Regency wrought-iron garden benches, the backs with openwork reeded strapwork, above rib-slatted seats.

46in (117cm) wide

$6,000-7,500 DUK

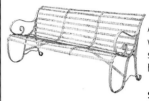

A late-19thC white painted wrought-iron garden bench, with scrolled end supports, united by horizontal splats.

71¾in (182cm) wide

$625-750 CHEF

A large wrought-iron country house gateway, probably 18thC, with a center-opening gate, flanked by two side panels, wear, minor rust, losses.

153in (389cm) high

$17,500-20,000 CHEF

A pair of late-19th/early-20thC iron gates, by S. Cowell, Norwich, with maker's raised nameplates on hinges, weathered, surface losses, no key, lock damaged.

103in (261.5cm) wide (each)

$2,000-2,500 DN

ESSENTIAL REFERENCE—CAMPANA URNS

The various revivals of the Greco-Roman vocabulary of architecture and ornament that spanned the Renaissance to the late 19thC promoted the production of numerous decorative forms from Classical Antiquity. Prominent among these was the urn—essentially a vaselike form with a foot or pedestal. Original urns, dating from the 5thC and 6thC BC, and discovered during archaeological digs in what is now Italy in the 14thC, took a number of forms. These included: the wide-neck and wide-body, bowl-like "calyx krater," used to mix wine; the "kylix," a low, shallow bowl for drinking wine; and the more overtly vaselike "amphora," for storing wine. During the Renaissance, these original shapes inspired a number of new forms, including the "tazza" or cup, derived from the "kylix" and, as with the 19thC example shown here and other examples elsewhere on this page, the "campana," which was derived from the "calyx krater" and translates from the Italian as "bell"—an inverted example of which it clearly resembles.

A 19thC French bronze campana urn, on a stepped square socle.

10¾in (27.5cm) high

$350-400   **TEN**

A pair of late-19thC cast-iron urns and pedestals, "Handyside" pattern, with later silver decoration, unmarked, signs of rust, urns not secured to bases.

55in (140cm) high

$2,000-2,500   **DN**

A pair of late-19thC white-painted cast-iron garden campana urns and pedestals, with fluted and part-lobed bodies on square socle bases, on tapered square pedestals.

50in (127cm) high

$1,900-2,200   **L&T**

A 19thC cast-iron Warwick vase garden urn, after the Antique, painted black, with entwined handles, decorated with busts.

22¾in (57.5cm) high

$1,500-1,900   **WW**

A pair of early-20thC cast-metal garden campana urns, the egg-and-dart molded rims over part-lobed bodies, each on a tapered and fluted foot, raised on square bases.

30in (76cm) wide

$375-500   **CHEF**

A late-19thC Japanese Meiji Period bronze garden fountain, the bowl on a scrolling naturalistic base, with an encircling water dragon, pale green verdigris patination, scuffs, possible losses.

33in (84cm) high

$7,500-8,500   **DN**

A pair of lead garden campana urns, probably early 20thC, the twin-handle bodies modeled with winged putti, color variation, knocks, restoration.

20¾in (53cm) high

$6,000-7,500   **DN**

A pair of large early-20thC wirework garden urns, each with a removable liner, traces of green paint.

35½in (90cm) high

$2,700-3,100   **WW**

A "Haddonstone" urn, the shallow bowl with latticework banding, leaf-molded socle and square base, raised on a paneled square plinth.

50½in (128.5cm) high

$750-875 HT

A pair of terra-cotta garden urns and covers, possibly 18thC, each with cast foliate decoration and wrythen finials, on foliate socle bases and stepped square feet, with remains of white painted decoration.

32¼in (82cm) high

$6,000-7,500 WW

A pair of large 19thC Scottish fireclay garden urns, molded with lilies of the valley.

38½in (98cm) high

$2,700-3,100 L&T

A Victorian cream-glazed earthenware birdbath, possibly Leeds LEFCO ware, the detachable bowl on a square tapering stem, flanked by four sitting elves, on a stepped square flower-molded base.

20in (51cm) high

$625-750 HT

A late-20thC composite stone copy of the Milton vase, the relief decoration depicting the expulsion of Adam and Eve from the garden of Eden.

46¾in (119cm) high

$625-1,000 CHEF

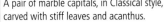

A pair of late-19thC lead garden planters, cast with scrolling foliate cartouches inside square frames.

33¾in (85.5cm) wide

$2,700-3,100 WW

A pair of marble capitals, in Classical style, carved with stiff leaves and acanthus.

15in (38cm) high

$3,500-4,000 TEN

A painted wood birdhouse, probably Edwardian, modeled as a cottage orné, scalloped lead roof with "pepper-pot" ends and baluster-turned finials, with center pediment over an arched opening.

32in (81.5cm) wide

$500-625 HT

ESSENTIAL REFERENCE—LEAD FIGURES

The tradition of casting statues in lead dates back to Roman times, but in Great Britain it became particularly prevalent during the late 17thC and 18thC, when lead figures increasingly began to feature in landscaped parks and gardens. The Flemish sculptor Jon Nost (d. 1710), who worked in England from the second half of the 17thC, founded the original lead figure manufactory in the Haymarket district of London ca. 1686 and received numerous prestigious commissions, including for Hampton Court Palace, Buckingham Palace, Chatsworth, and Castle Howard. During Nost's lifetime, the area stretching from the Haymarket down to the Hyde Park Corner end of Piccadilly became a center for both sculpture and lead figure production, with a number of lead yards springing up, including that of Nost's cousin, John Nost II (d. 1729), who took over the family business on Nost I's death before moving to Ireland.

A George II lead figural garden sundial, attributed to John Cheere, after John Nost, the solid gnomon and dial above the crouching figure of "Father Time" or Kronos, depicted with wings to represent how "time flies," the dial signed "B MARTIN, LONDON" and indistinctly engraved with the Boevey escutcheon of arms, repairs, weathering, color variation, markings are faint and rubbed.

It is possible that this sundial was made by Benjamin Martin, who worked between 1738 and 1777 from one address in Chichester and five in Fleet Street, and latterly as Benjamin Martin & Son until 1782, when the firm went bankrupt. Only two similar sundials of this particular kneeling form of "Time" have been noted. One at St. Osyth Priory, Essex, and another at Blair Castle, Perthshire, with a receipt dated for 1743 by John Cheere. Because the lead was piece molded, Cheere could assemble parts in new configurations; this was supposedly the case with the Blair Castle example, which is adapted from John Nost I's (fl.1677-1710) Indian sundial at Melbourne Hall, Derbyshire (I. Roscoe, "A Biographical Dictionary of Sculptors in Britain, 1660-1851," Yale University Press, 2009, page 262).

59¾in (152cm) high

$43,000-50,000 DN

A late-19thC carved Portland stone term statue of Pan, expressive and playing a pipe, a material-wrapped square-section column below, on a plinth base, weathering, lichen buildup, some losses.

78¾in (200cm) high

$6,000-7,500 DN

A large 20thC bronze garden statue of Apollo the Hunter, standing holding his bow, with faithful dog beneath.

52¾in (134cm) high

$3,500-4,000 CHEF

A set of four early- to mid-20thC lead garden figures, possibly by Crowther, emblematic of the Four Seasons, each in the form of a standing cherub on an octagonal base.

25¾in (65.5cm) high

$2,500-3,100 WW

One of a pair of 20thC composition stone sphinxes, after the model by Guelphi and Cheere, modeled opposing and saddled, color variation, minor chips, one with losses in detailing.

43in (109cm) wide

$17,500-20,000 the pair DN

A pair of mid- to late-19thC carved stone recumbent lions, modeled sphinxlike on rusticated oblong plinths.

35in (89cm) wide

$5,500-6,000 HT

One of a pair of 19thC carved stone recumbent hounds, variegated gray hardstone, on modern white painted plinths, minor repairs.

33¾in (86cm) wide

$4,700-5,200 the pair DN

One of a pair of 19th/20thC composition stone lions, each on a rectangular plinth.

13¾in (88cm) wide

$2,500-3,100 the pair DUK

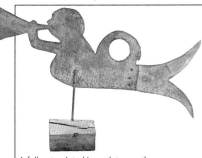

A folk art painted iron-plate weathervane, probably late 17thC, shaped as a flat section figure of Triton with a horn, mounted on an oak block, surface pitting, small area of corrosion damage.

35in (89cm) wide

$1,900-2,200   DAWS

An American yellow-painted sheet-iron "1819" weathervane, the flat body with a pierced date, openwork scroll back, wrought-iron scroll pointer, with a custom-made stand.

ca. 1819   35¾in (91cm) wide

$1,100-1,350   SK

A copper codfish weathervane, probably Massachusetts, the flattened form with molded scales, applied corrugated-sheet copper fins and a wire whisker, verdigris surface with traces of gilding and black painted details, with a custom-made iron stand, oxidation, minor seam separation, dent on one side.

ca. 1855   35¾in (91cm) wide

$4,200-4,600   SK

A small late-19thC American gilt sheet-copper bannerette weathervane, on a custom-made stand.

24¾in (63cm) wide

$750-1,000   SK

A large 19thC full-bodied copper running horse weathervane, with verdigris and gilt surface.

47in (119.5cm) wide

$22,000-27,000   POOK

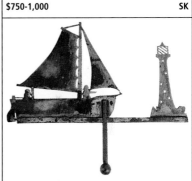

A late-19thC folk art marine copper weathervane, modeled as a boat sailing toward a lighthouse.

27¼in (69cm) wide

$1,600-2,200   WW

A late-19th/early-20thC folk art cat weathervane, the cat perched on a ball, mounted on a turned wood base.

21in (53.5cm) high

$875-1,250   WW

An early-20thC folk art naive copper rooster weathervane, painted green, on an ebonized wood plinth.

17¾in (45cm) wide

$1,500-1,900   WW

A 20thC sheet-copper flying duck weathervane, Delaware, stamped "F. Holzhauser Wil. DE," with Metal Artizan Co. Products logo, old repaired break at neck.

31in (78.5cm) wide

$1,000-1,250   POOK

TEXTILES

ESSENTIAL REFERENCE—PERSIAN/IRANIAN

A degree of confusion is sometimes encountered with rugs and carpets labeled as either "Persian" or "Iranian." Prior to the mid-1930s, and since the time of the Greek historian and geographer Herodotus (ca. 484-425 BC), the geographical area in which such carpets were and are made was known by most foreigners as Persia—derived from the Greek form of "Parsa," the name of the region that was homeland to the ancient Persians. In March 1935, Persia's then-ruler Rez Shah Pahlavi requested that the country be referred to from then on as Iran, in acknowledgment of the Iranian-, or "Airyan-," speaking peoples who both predated and were concurrent to the description Persian. Subsequently, rugs and carpets made prior to 1935 are mostly labeled Persian, and those made after 1935 Iranian.

However, the main centers of production, such as Tabriz, Mashad, Isfahan, Kashan, Kirman, Heriz, and Seneh, have remained largely unchanged, as have the tribes particularly associated with production, such as the Afshar, the Kashgai, and the Khamseh. Similarly, the historic distinction between town/city and village production for the most part still holds true. Towns and cities, in general, specialize in the production of carpets and rugs, typically fine woven with wool on cotton, or occasionally silk on silk, and patterns lean toward the curvilinear featuring flowers and foliage. Villages and tribal regions mainly produce rugs in wool on wool (carpets being fairly rare), and designs, in general, are individual, often geometric and/or stylized.

An Afshar rug, Southwest Iran, the cream field with two urns issuing flowers, flanked by stylized plants, enclosed by triple narrow borders.
ca. 1930   *63½in (161cm) wide*
$750-1,000   **TEN**

An Agra carpet, wear, color variation, losses.
268½in (682cm) long
$12,500-15,000   **DN**

A Bakshaish carpet, short pile, wear, losses, old repairs.
173½in   *(441cm) long*
$7,500-8,500   **DN**

An Azeri rug, Northwest Iran, woven with flower heads and a scrolling foliate pattern in cream, brown, red, pink, and black tones, against a blue ground, contained within a red/orange narrow border and guard stripes.
ca. 1950   *61in (155cm) long*
$1,500-1,900   **ADA**

A Bakhtiyari carpet, West Iran, the chestnut brown field of angular vines centered by an ivory medallion, framed by indigo spandrels and ivory palmette and vine borders, flanked by guard stripes.
ca. 1940   *156¼in (397cm) long*
$700-800   **TEN**

A Baluch prayer rug, Khorasan, the natural camel ground with the Tree of Life beneath the Mihrab, the upper spandrels with "Hands of Fatima," enclosed by narrow geometric borders and guard stripes, fraying on ends, binding cords missing, black dye corrosion.
1900   *63in (160cm) long*
$500-625   **TEN**

A Bidjar carpet, minor wear, fraying on fringing.
137¾in (350cm) long
$3,100-4,300   **DN**

A fine modern Ghom silk carpet, Central Iran, ivory lattice field of floral cartouches, enclosed by borders of birds and flowering plants, flanked by triple guard stripes, signed, very minor losses.
145in (368cm) long
$4,300-5,600   **TEN**

A Hamadan rug, West Iran, indigo "Herati" field, framed by pale blue spandrels and narrow borders.

ca. 1930
57in (145cm) long
$625-750
TEN

ESSENTIAL REFERENCE—HERIZ

Persian/Iranian carpet-producing towns situated away from the major city centers have historically been more prone to the influences of tribal or village weaving, and this has often resulted in a notably more angular style in the weaving of designs. The town of Heriz, for example, which lies to the northeast of Tabriz, has produced highly desirable and distinctive carpets with patterns based on formal town carpet designs. However, the main distinction between them is the more angular rendering of the design elements. Both allover and centered medallion designs are woven, the medallions often characterized by their starlike form. Such open, angular interpretations of the traditional themes vary in quality considerably, depending on the crispness of the outlines of the design and the combination of colors used.

A Heriz carpet, wear, losses, repairs.

128¼in (326cm) long
$7,000-8,000
DN

A large Heriz carpet, the madder ground with a large center indigo medallion, with mid-blue spandrels, moth damage, one tear.

ca. 1930
227in (577cm) long
$7,000-8,000
CHEF

A modern Heriz runner, Northwest Persia, the brick red field with a column of polychrome medallions, within a narrow indigo border.

298½in (758cm) long
$5,000-6,200
L&T

An Isfahan carpet, wear, replaced elements.

149½in (380cm) long
$3,700-5,000
DN

An Isfahan carpet, Central Persia, the ivory field with an asymmetrical design of large flower heads and vines, enclosed by borders of cartouches flanked by sky-blue meandering vine guard stripes, with two unusual inscribed panels in the upper border.

ca. 1925
185in (470cm) long
$10,000-12,500
WW

A mid- to late-20thC Isfahan carpet, Central Persia, the cream field with an allover palmette and vine pattern, within a red border.

175¼in (445cm) long
$4,700-5,600
L&T

An Isfahan carpet, Persia, with an allover design of swelling arabesques, tendrils, and foliage, with a center foliate medallion on an indigo ground, with conforming multiple borders.

222¾in (566cm) long
$8,500-10,000
DUK

A Kashan carpet, Central Iran, the field of vines centered by an ivory and indigo pole medallion, framed by spandrels and indigo floral borders.

ca. 1970   *132¾in (337cm) long*

$2,200-3,000   **TEN**

A mid-20thC Kashan carpet, Central Persia, the cream field with a light blue medallion suspending pendants, within a blue and polychrome shaped border.

175½in (446cm) long

$5,500-7,000   **L&T**

A late-19thC Kashan Mohtasham prayer rug, Central Persia, the abrash blue field with bird-filled foliage and a center vase, indigo spandrels, within a cream border.

Hajji Mollah Mohammed Hassan Mohtasham is generally regarded as probably the best of the master weavers who helped to reestablish Kashan as an important weaving center at the end of the 19thC. Few are signed, but the soft kurk lamb's wool, pale blue wefts, magenta silk selvages, and distinctive, more geometric, drawing style in subtle colors are typical characteristics of the high-quality production of his workshop.

78in (198cm) long

$8,000-9,500   **L&T**

A late-19th/early 20thC Khorassan carpet, East Persia, the bottle-green field with allover cypress tree and foliate pattern, within an indigo border.

175¼in (445cm) long

$1,250-1,500   **L&T**

A Mashad carpet, Northeast Iran, the soft strawberry field centered by an indigo medallion, framed by spandrels and indigo borders, flanked by guard stripes.

ca. 1960   *150in (381cm) long*

$1,250-1,500   **TEN**

A late-19th/early-20thC runner, Northwest Persia, the indigo field with allover foliate pattern, within a red border.

179¼in (455cm) long

$3,100-3,700   **L&T**

A Qum carpet, wear, losses, fading, restoration.

117¾in (299cm) long

$9,500-10,500   **DN**

An early-20thC carpet, Northwest Persia, the dark ground with a large center medallion, within a border populated with stylized flora.

138½in (352cm) long

$3,100-3,700   **DUK**

A Sarouk-Feraghan rug, with a center medallion and foliate motifs on a pale madder ground, areas of wear, strengthening.

ca. 1920   *82¾in (210cm) long*

$1,250-1,500   **CHEF**

A Serapi carpet, wear, broken strands, loose threads, old repairs.

145¾in (370cm) long

$4,200-4,600   **DN**

A 20thC Sultanabad carpet, West Iran, the raspberry field sparsely decorated with large serrated leafy vines, flower heads and vines, enclosed by indigo meandering vine borders and double guard stripes.

137¾in (350cm) long

$1,250-1,500   **TEN**

A Tabriz carpet, minor wear.

173¼in (440cm) long

$15,000-19,000   **DN**

A Tabriz carpet, made by order of his excellency Meskarzadeh, minor wear, marks, one edge rebound.

177¼in (450cm) long

$7,500-9,500   **DN**

A large Tabriz carpet, with allover design, wear, areas of low pile, losses, restoration, repairs.

246in (625cm) long

$15,000-19,000   **DN**

An early-20thC Tabriz pictorial carpet, Northwest Persia, with an allover design of a hunting scene, with mounted figures pursuing various wild animals amid foliage, with an indigo border woven with birds and kneeling female figures.

167in (424cm) wide

$7,500-8,500   **WW**

An early- to mid-20thC Tabriz carpet, signed "Javan Amir Khiz," Northwest Persia, the ivory field with an allover palmette and vine pattern, within a brown border.

167¼in (425cm) long

$4,000-4,700   **L&T**

A Tehran rug, short pile, repairs.

127¼in (323cm) long

$4,600-5,600   **DN**

A Ziegler Mahal carpet, the mustard field with columns of large serrated leaves and flower heads, enclosed by floral cartouche borders, flanked by guard stripes.

ca. 1890   *218in (554cm) long*

$12,500-15,000   **WW**

A kilim, Caucasus, the indigo field with four polychrome hooked medallions, enclosed by ivory borders of stylized flower heads and sawtooth guard stripes.

ca. 1900   *69½in (176.5cm) wide*

$800-950   **WW**

A Karabagh runner, South Caucasus, the indigo field with a column of polychrome medallions, flanked by zoomorphic and tribal motifs, enclosed by ivory borders of hooked devices and outer sawtooth guard stripes, repairs, dye corrosion.

ca. 1910   *46¾in (119cm) long*

$1,500-1,900   **TEN**

A late-19th/early-20thC Karabagh runner, South Caucasus, the dark indigo field with allover scroll and floral pattern, within a narrow brown border.

197in (500cm) long

$1,250-1,500   **L&T**

A Kazak rug, Central Caucasus, the mid-indigo field with five panels of hooked motifs, enclosed by ivory borders of stylized flower heads, flanked by barber poles and sawtooth guard stripes.

ca. 1890   *56in (142cm) wide*

$5,000-6,200   **WW**

A Shirvan rug, South East Caucasus, the indigo field with columns of angular stylized flower heads enclosed by Kufic borders, flanked by minor borders and arrowhead guard stripes.

ca. 1890   *47¼in (120cm) wide*

$3,100-3,700   **WW**

A Shirvan rug, Southeast Caucasus, the blood-red field with a column of hooked and cruciform guls surrounded by stylized rosettes and anthropomorphic devices, enclosed by ivory borders of indigo and madder hooked devices, flanked by guard stripes and barber poles, areas of low pile.

ca. 1890   *62¼in (158cm) long*

$2,200-2,700   **TEN**

A late-19thC Tashkent suzani, Central Asia, woven in sections on a linen base, the field centered by a large flower-head rondel, surrounded by smaller rondels and similar borders, with inner meandering vine guard stripes.

65in (165cm) wide

$1,700-2,200   **WW**

A 19thC Uzbek suzani, Central Asia, woven in panels on a linen ground, the field with center flower-head medallions flanked by urns, flowers, and a peacock, framed by borders of meandering serrated vines and flower heads.

39¼in (100cm) wide

$2,500-3,100   **WW**

A Zejwa rug, East Caucasus, the charcoal field with three serrated medallions containing and surrounded by zoomorphic devices, enclosed by narrow S and Z motifs, flanked by guard stripes.

ca. 1880   *45¼in (115cm) wide*

$1,100-1,500   **TEN**

A Bünyan wool rug, Central Turkey, the pale green ground with diagonal rows of flowers in yellow, blue, and cream tones, within broad pink borders with alternating floral and geometric motifs and guard stripes.

ca. 1950   118in (300cm) long

$2,000-2,500   ADA

A Dazkiri rug, West Turkey, the gray ground with a center geometric lozenge in red, yellow, and cream tones, within a cream border with a geometric pattern and orange guard stripes.

ca. 1950   56¾in (144cm) long

$625-750   ADA

A Hereke "Hummingbird's Eye" rug, Northwest Turkey, the cream ground with hummingbirds feeding from flowers in light green and pink tones, within a broad border of stylized foliate pattern and guard stripes, signed "HEREKE" on edge.

1940-50   132¾in (337cm) long

$7,500-8,500   ADA

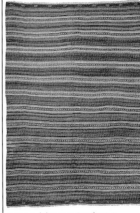

A Konya kilim rug, Southwest Turkey, the red/orange ground with broad horizontal cream stripes and narrow blue stripes.

ca. 1960   87½in (222cm) long

$1,400-1,700   ADA

A large Ushak carpet, West-Central Anatolia, the terra-cotta lattice field of angular vines, palmettes, and large flower heads, enclosed by aquamarine borders of angular vines, flanked by apple green guard stripes.

ca. 1900   190¼in (483cm) wide

$15,000-19,000   WW

A large mid-20thC Ushak carpet, the blue ground with a design of trees and wild animals, within a peach border.

210in (533cm) long

$2,700-3,200   CHEF

An early 20thC Dyers' Company Ushak carpet, West Anatolia, the camel field with allover palmette and foliate vine lattice pattern, within a blue border.

Chartered by King Henry VI in 1471, the Guild of Dyers acquired its first Hall in London in 1482 and has had several halls since. The current Dyers Hall stands at the corner of Dowgate Hill and College Street, and was completed 1839-41. The Dyers' Company's Gift Book records that this carpet was commissioned and presented in 1930 by Dr. Gerald Moody, who had joined in 1918 and became Prime Warden in 1935. It was installed in the Hall's "Court Room" (its principal room, used primarily for both meetings and dinners throughout the year). At the time when Dr. Moody was looking to commission a grand, custom-made carpet, the city of Ushak in the new Republic of Turkey would have been an obvious choice: back in the 15thC, Ushak had produced carpets for the Ottoman court in Istanbul and, from the 16thC onward, it became one of the largest producers of commercial carpets for Europe—enjoying a significant surge in demand from the late 19thC onward. Mary Beach Langton noted in her book, "How to Know Oriental Rugs," published by Sidney Appleton in 1904, that: "at Oushak [sic], alone, it is estimated that from five to six thousand weavers and dyers are employed. And here the best rugs are made … They are usually of good wool, often of permanent dyes" (page 177).

A late-19thC Ushak rug, West Anatolia, the light blue field with a cruciform red and orange medallion, within a narrow red border.

59in (150cm) long

$6,000-7,500   L&T

A large early-20thC Ushak carpet, West Anatolia, the plain orange field with an indigo and camel medallion, with similar spandrels, within an indigo border.

220½in (560cm) long

$3,700-5,000   L&T

396½in (1,007cm) long

$10,000-12,500   L&T

TEXTILES

ESSENTIAL REFERENCE—AFGHAN WAR RUGS

The tradition of weaving "War Rugs" in Afghanistan is of relatively recent origin, having emerged during the decade that followed the occupation of the country by the then Soviet Union in 1979. Indeed, Afghan rug makers began incorporating military motifs into their rug designs almost immediately after the Soviet Union invaded, and they have continued to do so after the Soviet withdrawal, and through the subsequent and numerous other military and political conflicts, including the United States' invasion of 2001. Conveying their maker's personal experiences and interpretations of war and conflict in the region, they are becoming increasingly desirable.

A Khotan rug, Chinese Turkestan, the field centered by a roundel surrounded by diamond medallions, framed by geometric spandrels and indigo borders of angular plants, flanked by guard stripes.

ca. 1930   63in (160cm) wide

$625-750   TEN

A modern Indian carpet, the pale mushroom field with vines, cloud bands, and palmettes, enclosed by wide floral borders and outer olive green guard stripes.

116in (295cm) wide

$1,250-1,500   TEN

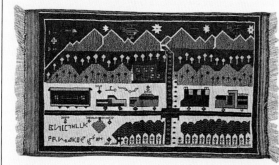

An Afghan "War Rug," woven in cream, claret, and indigo tones, the center field with war icons and symbols in a mountainous landscape, contained within side cords and fringes.

ca. 1980s   55in (140cm) wide

$450-550   ADA

One of a pair of Indian carpets, of classical design, the ivory field with allover design of palmettes and vines, enclosed by brick red meandering vine borders, flanked by guard stripes.

ca. 1980   184in (467cm) long

$3,100-3,700 the pair   WW

ESSENTIAL REFERENCE—TURKOMEN

The original Turkomen (or Turkmen) rugs were produced by the Turkomen tribes, who are the main ethnic group in Turkmenistan and are also found in Afghanistan and Iran. In the past, most Turkomen rugs were made by the nomadic Turkomen tribes, almost entirely with locally sourced materials: wool from the herds, and vegetable and other naturally occurring dyes from the land. They created geometric designs that varied from tribe to tribe, the best known of these being the Yomut, Ersari, Saryk, Salor, and Tekke. The size of these nomadic rugs was (and still is) limited to what can be woven on smaller, portable looms. However, larger rugs were produced on static looms in village communities, and, in more recent times, even larger rug workshops began to appear in towns and cities. Since about 1910, synthetic dyes have also been used along with natural ones. Collectors of Turkomen rugs particularly love the irregularities of the nomadically produced examples, created by variations in the locally sourced natural materials, and also the varying degrees of "Stretch" in woolen warps or wefts associated with small looms that are regularly folded up for transportation.

An Indian Kerman rug, minor wear.

ca. 1990   90½in (230cm) long

$750-1,000   WAD

A late-19th/early-20thC North Indian rug, of Turkomen engsi design, the purple field with a paneled and arched pattern, within a camel border and elem panel.

79½in (202cm) long

$500-625   L&T

A mid-20thC Moroccan Berber mixed-weave long rug.

126in (320cm) long

$400-475   WAD

A large Empire Savonnerie Neoclassical wool carpet, the center floral medallion with tulip-head detailing, within a rust red-brown field with scrolling acanthus leaves, fan-rosette, and floral garlands supporting Classical vases with floral displays, wear, slight color variation, repairs, later adaptions.

A wide range of imagery was employed on Savonnerie carpets during the first 20 years of the 19thC, initially under Napoleonic rule and then, from 1814-15, the restoration of the Bourbon monarchy. Prominent among these were the Neoclassical motifs popularized by Percier & Fontaine and iconography specific to Napoleon and his family—bee motifs being a particularly notable example. Almost equally in evidence was the more overtly martial imagery associated with Napoleon—this being especially evident in the earlier designs of Jacques-Louis de la Hamayde de Saint-Ange-Desmaison (better known as simply Saint-Ange), who studied under Percier. In contrast, however, this carpet, with its focus on sweeping floral splendor, suggests a commission for a room designed to reflect luxury and opulence—not political power, military might, and economic strength—and as such might be considered prescient in terms of the Bourbon Restoration.

ca. 1810 *238in (603cm) long*
$25,000-31,000 **DN**

ESSENTIAL REFERENCE—V'SOSKE CARPETS

In his "New York Times" obituary, Stanislav V'soske (1899-1983), cofounder of V'soske Inc. in the mid-1920s, was described as the "dean of American rug design." Based in Michigan, V'soske introduced hand-tufted, hand-carved rugs to the United States, and worked almost from the outset with a wide range of eminent architects and designers, from Frank Lloyd Wright, Stuart Davis, and Arshile Gorky to Michael Graves, Charles Gwathme, Richard Meier, and, as with this example, Oliver Messel (see the Essential Reference for Messel on page 210). From the late 1970s to the early 1990s, V'soske is credited with harnessing a rebellion in hand-tufted wool and silk against 1970s Minimalism (think industrial wall-to-wall gray carpeting), and the transition to a much more exuberant Postmodernism.

A V'soske machine-woven carpet, designed by Oliver Messel, of Aubusson style, the green ground with foliate spandrels and a center ivory medallion woven with further flower sprays and entwined flower heads, the crimson floral borders with yellow and pink latticework, small marks, stains, discoloration, worn threads.

258¼in (656cm) long
$20,000-25,000 **DN**

A needlework wool rug, designed by Augustus Welby Northmore Pugin (1812-52) or Edward Welby Pugin (1834-75), with panels bearing the cypher "M" with a coronet, section of a larger carpet, with later linen backing and cotton binding.

The remains of a medieval palace belonging to the archbishops of Canterbury in East Sussex was converted into a school, Mayfield School of the Holy Child Jesus, by Edward Welby Pugin 1863-66. This needlework rug originally ran the entire length of the chapel. Due to the sheer scale of the work, the rug was constructed in small paneled sections and later sewn together to form the carpet. Hand-stitched by the sisters of Mayfield Chapel, the carpet was produced for Mother Cornelia Connelly, founder of the Society of the Holy Child Jesus. As in other projects, E. W. Pugin continued to use the decorative designs of his father, of which this may be one.

ca. 1860 *88½in (225cm) long*
$5,000-6,200 **L&T**

A Spanish carpet, the mustard field with columns of cruciform motifs, enclosed by floral borders, signed and dated in outer guard stripes "STUYCK 1925" and "RF DE TAPICES."

ca. 1920 *138in (349cm) wide*
$2,500-3,100 **WW**

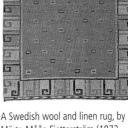

A Swedish wool and linen rug, by Märta Måås-Fjetterström (1873-1941), signed "MMF."

82¾in (210cm) long
$4,000-4,700 **L&T**

A kelim rug, possibly North European, wool on cotton.

ca. 1930-40 *51¼in (130cm) long*
$190-250 **WAD**

A large mid-20thC Donegal thick-pile carpet, woven in red, navy, and green tones, the large center field with three rows of geometric motifs and lozenges, contained within triple-line borders.

$2,200-2,700 **ADA**

Judith Picks

Provenance plays a considerable role when it comes to desirability and, therefore, value or price, as is most certainly the case with this splendid, 16thC Biblical-themed Brussels tapestry. Depicting the story of Abraham's servant Eliezer meeting Rebecca by a well, it is almost certainly from the same series as a tapestry depicting the departure of Jacob for the land of Canaan, and it is probably from the same set that was in the collection of Chevalier Alphonse de Stuers, once the Netherlands' Ambassador to France. Moreover, both of these tapestries have borders of the same design that compare with another Biblical tapestry, depicting "The Last Supper," in the Metropolitan Museum of Art, New York. Like this and the de Stuers tapestry, the example in the Met also has the same slightly unusual and distinctive depiction of owls in the side panels—an ornithological motif that would enable anyone to respond to an enquiry on how one knows about this tapestry's provenance with the straight-face reply: "a little bird told me!"

An early- to mid-16thC Brussels Biblical tapestry, depicting Rebecca and Eliezer at the well, woven in metal thread, wools, and silks, with maidens carrying water urns on the left, Eliezer's camels on the right with a penitent kneeling man, the borders decorated with fruit and flower clasps, meandering vine and interspersed by various animals, including a falcon, a peacock, owls, a monkey, and a dog, with a blue outer strip with a green top and bottom outer strip, surface wear, not backed, color muting and variation.

176in (447cm) wide

$37,000-50,000 **DN**

An early-18thC Brussels Biblical tapestry, "The Discovery of Moses," by the Frans Van Der Borght workshop, Brussels, probably after designs by Jan Van Orley and Augustin Coppens, woven in silk and wool, with Moses in a basket being saved by the Queen of Egypt, with attendant figures, a verdure setting and townscape beyond, Brussels town mark, signed in lower margin "F V D Borght," lacking original border, with signature and town mark dropped back in from the original, color muting.

While the figural designs are traditionally attributed to the Flemish artist Jan Van Orley, it would seem probable that the landscape setting may have been the work of Augustin Coppens. In this collaboration, they were echoing the work of Nicholas Poussin and Charles Le Brun at the royal tapestry works at Gobelins from the 1680s. This particular design is known to have been woven by various members of the Borght weaving dynasty, but signed examples are rare. A similar example, dated 1737, hangs in Maastricht Town Hall.

148in (376cm) wide

$31,000-37,000 **DN**

A mid- to late-16thC Brussels mythological tapestry, worked in silks and wool, depicting Pomona and probably Vertumnus, flanked by Classical figures, with a panel of urns issuing fruits and cornucopia beneath, a formal garden beyond, flanked by trees bearing fruits, animals, and birds, framed by borders of scrolling acanthus and further mythological figures.

The design for this tapestry is based on a cartoon, possibly by Jan Cornelisz Vermeyen (1500-59) and commissioned by Charles V. The cartoons were for a series of nine tapestries, one set of which is in the Spanish Royal Collection. Other similar tapestries, probably woven by Jan Raes, are also found in the Boston Museum of Fine Arts, having previously been in the Barberini Collection in Rome.

149½in (380cm) wide

$11,000-15,000 **WW**

A late-17thC Flemish Biblical tapestry, "The Departure of the Prodigal Son," in wool and silk, depicting a young man standing before a sitting older bearded man, gesturing to a city in the distance, a staff in his hand, within a border with fruit, flowers, birds, and putti.

124in (315cm) high

$8,000-9,500 **L&T**

A 16thC Spanish armorial tapestry, bearing the arms of Don Diego Fernandez De Cordova, 3rd Marquis of Comares, with the quartered arms of Aragón and Jerusalem, per pale; Castillea and León, per fesse; Aragón-Sicilia; folch de Cardona y Aragón-Prades; Aragón-Urgel; and Pallars; encircled by the collar of the Fleece and surmounted by a large ducal coronet, against a blue field within a foliate scroll border.

The coat of arms is for Don Diego Fernandez de Cordova, also known as "El Africano," born 1524 in Oran, on the northwest coast of present-day Algeria. Elected Knight of the Golden Fleece by Philip II in 1577, he died in 1601 after having been governor of Oran in 1573 and 1589-94. He is buried at the abbey of Poblet.

88¼in (224cm) high

$60,000-75,000 **L&T**

A late-17thC Aubusson verdure tapestry, Central France, woven in silks and wool, depicting a rural scene of birds and animals within a wooded landscape, with buildings beyond, enclosed by floral vine borders, modern linen backing, some corrosion, splits.

96½in (245cm) wide

$7,500-8,500 **TEN**

A late-17thC Flemish pastoral hunting tapestry fragment, with figures on horseback watching birds in flight and a standing figure with a dog, later border and backing.

99¼in (252cm) wide

$6,000-7,500   DN

A large late-17th/early-18thC Flemish verdure tapestry, depicting a castle as viewed through a wooded river landscape, with a unicorn, water bird, and camel in the middle ground, and two other birds, including an ostrich, within a repeating patterned border, old repairs, fading.

191¾in (487cm) wide

$15,000-17,500   CHEF

A late-17th/early-18thC Aubusson Biblical tapestry, "Christ Brought Before Herod," from a "Passion of Christ" series, depicting Christ standing and gesturing before Herod, who is sitting on a throne, attended by a soldier and three other figures.

121¼in (308cm) wide

$7,500-8,500   L&T

An early-18thC Flemish mythological tapestry, "Diana Resting," by the workshop of Judocus De Vos, Brussels, depicting the sitting goddess resting after the hunt and an attendant with a flaming torch, with sewn foldovers to accommodate wall height, Brussels town mark, signed "J. DE. VOS" in selvedge, part of a larger hanging, pulled threads, sun fading, later reverse backing.

106in (269cm) wide

$6,000-6,500   DN

A late-18thC French Louis XVI Aubusson tapestry, with a pair of ribbon-tied medallions and an amorous couple, within floral swags and agricultural trophies.

151½in (385cm) wide

$5,000-6,200   WW

A late-18th/early-19thC Aubusson chinoiserie verdure tapestry, after Jean Pillement, "A la pagode et au Carquois" (At the pagoda and the quiver), from the chinoiserie series, depicting flora and fauna in an exotic river landscape with a pagoda beyond, within a stylized border, signed "M. R. DAUBUSSON."

188¼in (478cm) wide

$15,000-17,500   CHEF

Two of a set of four mid-19thC French Aubusson tapestry entre-fenêtre panels, with center flower bouquets set within laurel wreaths and garlands against a cream ground, with rose pink borders.

156¾in (398cm) high

$8,000-9,500 the set   L&T

A 19thC French Aubusson tapestry portiere, with tasseled drapes and swags of flowers.

106in (269cm) high

$1,100-1,500   WW

TEXTILES

A mid-17thC needlework panel depicting Charles I and Queen Henrietta Maria, worked in color threads, the figures in landscape before a castle with beasts, birds, and trees, in a tortoiseshell frame, minor fading and staining.

12½in (32cm) wide

$12,500-15,000 **TEN**

A stumpwork panel depicting Charles II and Catherine of Braganza, in the manner of John Nelham, worked in color and metal threads, the pair wearing plumed helmets, a castle beyond, within a foliate cartouche on a foliate ground with figures and birds, in an ebonized wood and tortoiseshell frame, splits, stains, color loss, rippling.

John Nelham was a London embroidery designer and professional stitcher who was listed as a member of the Court of Assistance in the Court books of the Worshipful Company of Broderers from 1679, and he was associated with William Rutlish, embroiderer to King Charles II. An embroidery at Blair Castle, signed by Nelham, has a distinctive raised oval cartouche bordered by baroque stylized flowers and leaves, and it is this feature that has led to the attribution of panels bearing such cartouches to Nelham.

ca. 1660

19in (48cm) wide

$4,700-5,600 **TEN**

A mid-17thC stumpwork panel depicting Charles I and Queen Henrietta Maria, worked in color and metal threads with seed pearls, the royal couple with an attendant in a tent flanked by further attendants, animals, and trees, a castle beyond, initialed "AL," in a tortoiseshell frame, color loss, tiny holes, minor staining, and rippling.

12½in (32cm) wide

$7,500-10,000 **TEN**

A mid-17thC needlework panel depicting "Faith," "Hope," and "Charity," worked in color threads, Faith holding a book inscribed "FAITH," Charity nursing a baby, and Hope with an anchor in a landscape attended by two boys, beyond a castle, mythical beasts, insects, and flowers, in a tortoiseshell frame, color loss, stains, minor rippling.

15in (38cm) wide

$8,500-10,000 **TEN**

A Charles II stumpwork needlework picture depicting the Adoration of the Magi, worked in color silks and metallic threads, with a castle and a farmhouse, with birds, butterflies, and flowers, in an elaborate border decorated with a lion, a stag, a camel, a leopard, birds, flowers, and a dog chasing a hare, in an 18thC gilt and ebonized wood frame.

ca. 1670

21¼in (54cm) wide

$8,500-10,000 **WW**

A mid-17thC needlework panel depicting Rebekah and Izaac at the Well, worked in color threads, the figures in a landscape with further figures, animals, and insects among trees, a castle and further buildings beyond, in a tortoiseshell frame, fading, minor staining.

20in (51cm) wide

$5,500-7,000 **TEN**

A 17th/18thC needlework drawstring purse, the linen ground worked in color silks and silver metal thread, depicting the Salutation of the Virgin Mary on one side and Elijah fed by ravens on the other.

4¼in (11cm) high

$2,500-3,100 **L&T**

An 18thC Georgian fine needlework purse, the ivory ground embroidered in color silks with roses, hollyhocks, bluebells, and foxgloves, with a metal thread border and trim.

4¾in (12cm) high

$1,250-1,500 **L&T**

A mid- to late-17thC English beadwork pastoral panel, the linen ground worked with polychrome beading, depicting a female figure standing in a pastoral landscape, surrounded by wild fauna and flora.

20¾in (53cm) wide

$10,500-12,500 **CHEF**

A 17thC Charles II silkwork book or casket cover, the linen ground embroidered with color silks, depicting a gentleman and a woman within landscape settings, with buildings in the distance, in two parts.

4¾in (12cm) high

$1,250-1,900 **L&T**

A 17thC English stumpwork panel, the ivory silk satin ground embroidered in fine silk and polychrome threads, depicting a female figure holding flowers in a rural landscape, surrounded by flora and fauna, pastoral workers and a castle beyond, minor stains, minor losses.

11½in (29cm) wide

$3,700-5,000 **CHEF**

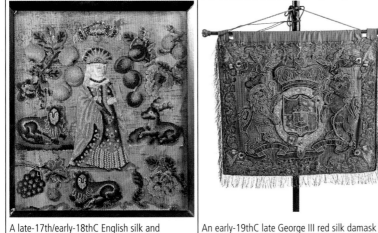

A late-17th/early-18thC English silk and beadwork panel, worked in polychrome beading on white silk, depicting a female figure dressed in blue robes, surrounded by flora and fauna, later backing, minor fraying, losses.

11¾in (30cm) high

$550-700 **CHEF**

An early-19thC late George III red silk damask and wirework pennant or banner, with an embroidered border and appliqué center royal coat of arms beneath a "GR" monogram, on a mahogany tripod stand.

21¼in (54cm) wide

$1,000-1,400 **WW**

One of three Italian embroidered velvet curtains, in Renaissance style, stamped with alternating circles and diamonds, the circles containing a hound and stag head, the diamonds with Tudor roses, the wide appliqué borders with interlocking raised work in gilt-bronze round linen couched threads, gilt-bronze wires, and tinsel curls, lined and interlined.

These curtains were formerly in the collection of Bernard Nevill (1930-2019). Nevill was a professor of textiles at the Royal College of Art, a textile designer, and a director of design at Liberty's, where he produced two exciting ranges of printed textiles: "Islamic" (1963) and "Jazz" (1964). He was an aesthete and a great collector, and felt he was rescuing beautiful objects when others appeared to have no use for them. The curtains featured in an article on Nevill in the "World of Interiors" magazine in February 2020.

ca. 1870   *161¾in (411cm) high*

$6,000-7,500 the set **WW**

One of a pair of French beadwork or sable pictures, depicting scenes from Aesop's Fable "The Fox and the Crow," each with a line from the fable.

ca. 1850   *9in (23cm) wide*

$300-450 the pair **WW**

A woolwork picture of HMS "Juno," Sebastopol, Crimea, worked in polychrome woolen threads, bearing the White Ensign and French Tricolore, discoloration.

1854   *24½in (62cm) wide*

$5,500-7,000 **CHEF**

A late-19thC woolwork picture of boats in an estuary, light staining.

14in (35.5cm) wide

$2,100-2,700 **CHEF**

TEXTILES

A George III needlework sampler, by Jane Hopkins, worked in colors, depicting plants, insects, cherubs, beasts, and Adam and Eve, with Biblical lines from Genesis III, 2, 3, 4, and inscribed "Jane Hopkins Finished this Sampler October ye 9 1783," in a later glazed walnut frame.

1783   *16½in (42cm) high*

$1,000-1,500   **WW**

A Georgian sampler, by Sarah Ann Steele, worked in two-ply silk in full cross-stitch, with two young ladies and their small dogs, a large tabby cat among two pigeons, a pair of gardeners, and a Queen Anne-style house with trees and two stags, within a stylized tulip border, in a mahogany frame.

ca. 1820   *20in (51cm) high*

$625-800   **HT**

A George IV sampler of "Burghley House near Stamford," by Ann Bailey, worked in colors, primarily in cross-stitch, with an oval garden at front and trees on each side, in a glazed gilt frame, inscribed "Burghley House near Stamford the seat of the Marquis of Exeter," signed "Ann Bailey aged 11 years 1821."

1821   *23½in (60cm) wide*

$4,200-5,000   **WW**

CLOSER LOOK—A LATE-18THC NEEDLEWORK SAMPLER

As much as anything else, samplers were multiple-learning tools for children, and here two of the basic educational building blocks—the alphabet and numbers 1-10—sit atop the composition.

Religion, and especially the Bible, was also a core component of education in the 18thC, and here Caleb and Joshua—2 of the 12 spies Moses despatched to scout the feasibility of the Israelites being able to live in the Land of Canaan (the "Promised Land")—are depicted returning with a favorable report.

A stylized but idyllic landscape, primarily comprising trees, bushes, and birds, probably represents not only the Biblical "Promised Land" but also the late-18thC Britain of King George III.

Patriotism and loyalty to the Crown and the Church are also clearly in evidence, and are particularly pointed in the latter half of the 18thC—a period often described as the Age of Revolution and Rebellion.

A small George III needlework sampler, by Ann Jackson, worked with color silks on a linen ground, dated "1787" and signed "Ann Jackson her Work," in a later glazed frame.

11in (28cm) high

$1,250-1,500   **WW**

A Scottish needlework sampler, by Elizabeth Stark, Edinburgh, worked in silk and linen on flax, with the alphabet and number series above a field with two large stags, a fruit tree, flowering urns, birds, rabbits, and a peacock, with a center reserve with the Lord's Prayer, dated, in a period rosewood frame.

1841   *21¾in (55.5cm) wide*

$450-550   **L&T**

An early-Victorian family sampler commemorating the marriage of William and Mary Sykes in 1814, by Selina Sykes (second child), worked in black silk in full cross-stitch, with a list of their 13 children (including two sets of twins), 6 of them also with their deaths recorded, over a Bible verse, framed and glazed.

1844   *21½in (54.5cm) wide*

$450-550   **HT**

An embroidered sampler, by Mary Ann Semple, with an extract from Carlos Wilcox's "The Cure for Melancholy," with flora and fauna set within a decorative border, on a later linen backing.

1851   *20½in (52cm) high*

$500-625   **CHEF**

A woolwork sampler, by Margaret Cottom Walmsley, worked in polychrome woolen threads, depicting a country house flanked by angelic figures, surrounded by a fruiting strawberry plant border.

1862   *24¼in (61.5cm) wide*

$210-275   **CHEF**

An English quilted coverlet, with a circlet of leaves and initials "SMS" encircling a conifer cone, the deep border with linked roundels with a carnation spray, each corner with a cone, embroidered with cream, green, and red silks in stem, chain, and satin stitches, lined.

ca. 1700 *55in (140cm) wide*

$2,200-2,700 **BON**

An early-20thC cotton patchwork quilt, with polychrome detail, in a Perspex box frame.

53½in (136cm) wide

$190-250 **SWO**

An unusual four-block cotton applique quilt, by Sarah Annie Maizey Marker Smith, Jackson/Scrabble, Frederick County, Maryland, with flowers and stuffed cherries.

ca. 1910 *90in (228.5cm) long*

$3,500-4,000 **POOK**

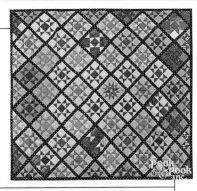

A large late-19thC "Ohio Star" patchwork quilt, minor stains, discoloration in white patches.

114in (289.5cm) wide

$1,900-2,500 **POOK**

An early-20thC Amish wool and cotton plain-weave pieced quilt, Lancaster County, Pennsylvania, in a double nine-patch pattern.

86in (218.5cm) wide

$8,000-9,500 **POOK**

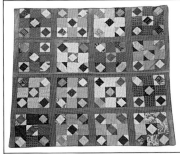

An early-20thC Canadian patchwork quilt, sun fading, stains.

78¾in (200cm) wide

$100-150 **WAD**

An Amish log cabin quilt, Lancaster, Pennsylvania.

ca. 1930 *85in (216cm) long*

$1,200-1,500 **POOK**

A floral pattern "Gone with the Wind" cotton quilt, "The Scarlett" pattern, with original tags attached, one Fruit of the Loom and one National Sure-Fit Quilting Co., bearing an image of Scarlett and Rhett, accompanied by a typescript contract agreement between Loew's Inc. and National Sure-Fit Quilting Co., dated January 22, 1940, regarding manufacturing of home textiles "which will represent characters in the said novel and/or motion picture," signed by both parties.

1940 *84in (213cm) long*

$2,200-2,700 **BON**

Judith Picks

This is an exceedingly rare and nearly complete first edition of the King James Bible. Once described as "the only literary masterpiece ever to have been produced by a committee," its publication was not only of huge religious and political importance, it also had significant linguistic and literary consequences, too. Commonly known as the "Authorised Version," it was commissioned in 1604 by King James I of England (and VI of Scotland), following a suggestion from the leader of the Puritan party and President of Corpus Christi College, John Reynolds. It was hoped that it would be a means of settling conflicts within the Church of England, between Puritans and Anglicans, and between the Bibles used by the clergy—the Bishop's Bible—and those used by laymen—the more compact and easier to read versions of the Geneva Bible.

The project was carried out by nearly 50 translators, divided into six companies, each tasked with translating certain sections of the Scriptures, and each consulting a variety of works, including Hebrew and Greek sources, as well as the Bishop's Bible for the basic English text, and the Tyndale and Coverdale versions of the Geneva Bible. Although not mentioned, they also borrowed freely from the Catholic translation of the New Testament published in Rheims in 1582. The primary work was completed 1607-09, and was then sent to a committee of six at Stationer's Hall in London for a final revision during 1610. Two editions of the Bible were then printed in 1611 and have come to be known as the "He" and "She" Bibles, for their respective readings in Ruth iii. 15: "he went into the citie," and "She went into the citie." These two versions were printed at two different offices, and the discrepancy probably lies more in the ambiguity of the passage than with any fault of one of the typesetters. Nowadays, bibliographers generally agree that the folio "He" Bible of 1611, of which this is an example, is the first impression.

Along with the publication of Shakespeare's First Folio, 12 years later in 1623, the King James Bible had a major impact on the development of the English language, helping to shape literary language for generations to come. There was no new English translation until the Revised Version of 1881, and the influence of the Authorised Version may best be described in the words of the historian G. M. Trevelyan: "For every Englishman who had read Sidney or Spenser, or had seen Shakespeare acted at the Globe, there were hundreds who had read or heard the Bible with close attention as the words of God. The effect of the continual domestic study of the book upon the national character, imagination, and intelligence for nearly three centuries to come, was greater than that of any literary movement in our annals, or any religious movement since the coming of St. Augustine." (Carter, "Printing and the Mind of Man," Cassell, 1967, page 69).

King James Bible, "The Holy Bible, Conteyning the Old Testament, and the New: Newly Translated out of the Originall Tongues ... by His Maiesties speciall Comandement," first edition, published by Robert Barker, London, with "he went into the citie" in Ruth iii. 15, Gothic and roman type, in two columns within a ruled border, calendar printed in red and black, illustrated throughout, bound to style in full modern brown calf, stamped in gilt, red morocco spine label, wear, tears, stains, repairs.

1611

$90,000-100,000

15in (38cm) high

FRE

Pico della Mirandola, Giovanni Francesco, "Libro detto Strega, o delle illusioni del Demonio," first edition in Italian, published in Bologna, translated by Leandro degli Alberti from the Latin, the title within a pictorial woodcut border, with 55 leaves plus errata, later vellum cover, part of leather lettering label to spine.

This is the first book in Italian dedicated to witchcraft. It reports the witchcraft (and antiwitchcraft) activity that struck the principalities of Mirandola and Concordia between 1522 and 1523.

1524

$10,000-12,500

CA

Hobbes, Thomas, "Leviathan," second edition, published by Andrew Crooke, with additional engraved allegorical title, printed title with woodcut device of a bear and foliage, folding table, contemporary calf cover, rebacked and recornered, paper repairs, discoloration.

The second and pirated edition, which had been banned in England by the censors.

1678

$2,000-2,500

CA

Browne, John, "A Compleat Treatise of the Muscles, As they appear in Humane Body, And arise in Dissection; With Diverse Anatomical Observations Not yet Discovered.," first edition, printed by Thomas Newcombe, with engraved portrait frontispiece of Browne, 37 engraved plates, contemporary mottle calf cover, later rebacked in lighter calf, original red leather lettering label, some pages with light marks.

1681

$1,900-2,200

CA

Camden, William, "Camden's Britannia," first translated edition, translated by Edmund Gibson, with eight plates of medals, 49 of 50 maps by Robert Morden, contemporary calf cover, lacking engraved portrait frontispiece, some damp and edge wear.

1695

$1,500-1,900

CA

The Qur'an, copied by Muhammad Muhsin al-Isfahani, Persia, Arabic manuscript on paper, with illuminated markers between verses, margins ruled in blue and gold, sura headings written in thuluth and gold, lacquer binding in the style of Razi, covers richly decorated with a diaper pattern of floral motifs in gold on a red ground, some smudging and discoloration, crude repairs, chips on edges.

1716   *4in (10cm) high*
$2,100-2,700   **CHEF**

Kidder, E., "E. Kidder's Receipts of Pastry and Cookery, For the Use of his Scholars ...," first edition, London, with engraved frontispiece portrait of Kidder by Robert Sheppard, engraved title page, 40 leaves of engraved recipes (printed only on rectos), eight engraved plates (three folding), full polished brown calf cover, stamped in blind and gilt, morocco spine label, ownership initials stamped in blind on front board, edges stained red, marbled endpapers, lacking advertisement leaf.

A scarce cookbook, probably produced by pastry master Edward Kidder (1665/66-1739) for his students, in conjunction with one of his cooking classes, at one of the earliest cooking schools in England to include the instruction of baked goods. There is some conjecture over when this edition was printed, because the volume is undated, with "English Short Title Catalogue" (or ESTC; T92423 and T92424) positing this as a 1740 reissue, yet, a copy of this edition sold at Swann in 2016 and included a 1733/34 ownership inscription, thus indicating otherwise. Virginia McLean offers a date of publication of about 1725, and Bitting slightly earlier. Another copy noted in ESTC (T92423) has a slightly different title page with the location of Kidder's school at St. Martin's instead of. St Thomas. This edition, with the S.t Thomas address, while more common, is still scarce.

ca. 1720-30s
$2,000-2,700   **FRE**

Shelley, Mary Wollstonecraft, "Frankenstein: or, The Modern Prometheus," first Bentley edition, later issue, published by Richard Bentley, London, revised, corrected, and illustrated with a new introduction by the author, engraved frontispiece dated 1831 showing Frankenstein and his monster, half title with Schiller, without the letterpress series title, engraved vignette title page or advertisement leaf found in the 1831 edition (see note), bound with "The Ghost-Seer! From the German of Schiller' as issued, tears, marks.

"Frankenstein" was first published in 1818 and a second edition in 1823. Bentley's edition, published in 1831 and incorporating extensive revisions by the author, was the third overall, the first illustrated edition, and the first edition in one volume. Copies are also noted with title pages dated 1832 and 1836; this 1839 issue is usually described as the fourth. The engraved vignette title page, not present here, is absent in other copies of the 1839 printing.

1839
$4,700-5,000   **L&T**

Dickens, Charles, "A Christmas Carol. In Prose. Being a Ghost Story of Christmas," first edition (text uncorrected), first issue, published by Chapman & Hall, London, with four hand-colored etched plates by John Leech, four wood-engraved illustrations in text, all edges gilt, original reddish-brown cloth, spine rolled, marks, fading, one plate loose.

In this copy, the period after "gloom" on page 21, line 22, is faint. According to Dickens scholar Grahame Smith, this is characteristic of the second edition, but otherwise all textual points agree with those listed for the first edition.

1843
$5,300-6,000   **L&T**

Darwin, Charles, "On the Origin of Species By Means of Natural Selection, or The Preservation of Favoured Races in the Struggle for Life," third edition, seventh thousand, published by John Murray, London, original wavy-grain green cloth, spine lettered and decorated in gilt, decorative blind panels on sides, brown coated endpapers, with folding lithographic table, slightly rolled, small sections of wear.

The third edition comprised 2,000 copies in total and was "extensively altered" from the second edition, including the addition of a historical sketch "written to satisfy complaints that Darwin had not sufficiently considered his predecessors in the general theory of evolution" (Freeman).

1861
$3,700-4,300   **L&T**

Beeton, Izabella, "Book of Household Management," first edition, with tinted frontispiece, engraved title with "18 Bouverie St" address, 12 color plates, slight staining, repairs.

1861
$625-1,000   **CHEF**

Stevenson, Robert Louis, "Strange Case of Dr Jekyll and Mr Hyde," first UK edition, published by Longmans, Green and Co., London, early-20thC green half calf gilt cover, spine sunned, joints and corners rubbed, penciled ownership inscription "H. S. Churchill" on title.

1886
$800-1,050   **L&T**

Marx, Karl and Engels, Friedrich, "Manifesto of the Communist Party," fifth edition, first authorised English translation, original printed paper wrappers, stapled as issued, ownership signature on verso of front cover, covers loose, fragile but complete.

Only one copy of this edition can be found in an institution, with no copies of this edition found at auction.

"Manifesto of the Communist Party" was subjected to a defective English translation in 1850, which rendered the famous opening line, "A spectre is haunting Europe," as "A frightful hobgoblin stalks throughout Europe." The present translation was overseen by Engels himself, with the assistance of Samuel Moore.

1888
$1,500-1,900   **CA**

Emilio, Luis F., "History of the Fifty-Fourth Regiment of Massachusetts Volunteer Infantry, 1863-1865," first edition, published by The Boston Book Company, Boston, illustrated frontispiece, one folding map, original blue-green cloth, titled in gilt "A Brave Black Regiment," spine lettered in gilt, wear on cover, light soiling and spotting in text.

The famous all-Black 54th Massachusetts Infantry Regiment, led by Robert Gould Shaw, was the second all-Black Union regiment to fight during the Civil War after the 1st Kansas Color Volunteer Infantry Regiment, and the first military unit consisting of Black soldiers recruited in the North. Prior to 1863 and the Emancipation Proclamation, little effort was made in the North to recruit Black soldiers for the war effort. This changed in February 1863, when abolitionist governor John Andrew assembled the unit after receiving authorization from Secretary of War Edwin Stanton. The unit is remembered for its courageous fighting and, in particular, its charge on Fort Wagner on July 18, 1863. The author, Luis F. Emilio, was a captain in the 54th Regiment, and later an acting commander after emerging as the highest-ranking surviving officer after the carnage at Fort Wagner. The story of the regiment was famously told in the award-winning 1989 movie "Glory."

1891

$3,000-3,500 FRE

Chaucer, Geoffrey, "The Works of Geoffrey Chaucer," published by Kelmscott Press, Hammersmith, text printed in red and black Chaucer type, double column, titles in Troy type, woodcut title-page, numerous woodcut initial letters and words, repeated foliate borders, all from designs by William Morris, with 87 woodcut illustrations by William Harcourt Hooper after drawings by R. Catterson-Smith from designs by Edward Burne-Jones, original holland-backed blue paper board, printed paper spine label, light spotting, disoloration on cover.

One of 425 copies on paper, a superb copy of the masterpiece of the private press movement and a work that had an unparalleled influence on book design and typography throughout the following century. Printing began in August 1894 and was not completed until nearly two years later, in May 1896. Morris had been in failing health for some time and died that October. Copies on paper were advertised at £20 (about $25) but, suitably for a book famous "long before it came off the press" (Peterson, "The Kelmscott Press," University of California Press, 1992, page 228), the price had already been rising among dealers before publication. Often compared in stature to the Gutenberg Bible, it is considered "not only the most important of the Kelmscott Press's productions; it is also one of the great books of the world. Its splendour … can hardly be matched among the books of its time" (Ray, "The Illustrator and the Book in England," The Pierpont Morgan Library, 1976).

1896

$75,000-90,000 L&T

Stoker, Bram, "Dracula," first edition, first issue, original yellow cloth, lettered in yellow, later ownership inscription on front, losses in spine and endpaper, marks, discoloration.

Bram Stoker's mother wrote on reading the book: "My dear, it is splendid, a thousand miles beyond anything you have written before, and I feel certain will place you very high in the writers of the day—the story and style being deeply sensational, exciting, and interesting … No book since Mrs. Shelley's Frankenstein or indeed any other at all has come near yours in originality, or terror."

1897

$6,600-7,200 CA

Baum, L. Frank, "The Wonderful Wizard of Oz," first edition, second state (including corrected text), published by Geo. M. Hill Co., Chicago and New York, illustrated by W. W. Denslow, original third state green pictorial cloth, with publisher's imprint at foot of spine stamped in red serifed type, boards stamped in green and red, contemporary ownership signatures, discoloration, soiling, wear.

1900

$2,700-3,200 FRE

Potter, Beatrix, "The Tale of Peter Rabbit," first trade edition, published by Frederick Warne & Co., London, color illustrations, gray leaf-patterned endpapers, original brown boards, expertly rebacked with original spine laid down, lettered in white with an inset image of Peter Rabbit on upper cover, with contemporary owner's presentation inscription on front endpaper.

1902

$1,100-1,500 CA

Austen, Jane, "Sense and Sensibility," with an introduction by Joseph Jacobs, illustrations by Chris Hammond, first edition thus, original decorative gilt cloth, all edges gilt, later ownership inscription on half title, spine rolled, some marks.

1899

$1,250-1,700 L&T

Du Bois, W. E. B., "The Souls of Black Folk: Essays and Sketches," first edition, first printing (with "18 April" printed on verso of title page), published by A. C. McClurg & Co., Chicago, original black cloth, stamped in blind and gilt, top edge gilt.

A beautiful example of one of Du Bois's most famous works, and a landmark in the history of sociology and African-American literature.

1903

$9,500-10,500 FRE

Sassoon, Siegfried, "An Ode for Music," first edition, published by Chiswick Press, 1 of only 50 or 60 copies printed, woodcut printer's device on final leaf, original brown wrappers, black title on front cover, some spotting.

Sassoon's very scarce privately printed first book.

1912

$1,700-2,200 CA

Hemingway, Ernest, "in our time," first and very limited edition, no. 8 of 170 numbered copies, printed at the Three Mountains Press, Paris, for sale at Shakespeare & Company, printed on Rives handmade paper, illustrated with a woodcut frontispiece portrait of Hemingway by Henry Strater, original tan paper-covered boards, printed in black and red, signed and inscribed by Hemingway on the front free endpaper to his soon-to-be editor at Charles Scribner's Sons, Maxwell Perkins, ca. June 1925, "For Maxwell E. Perkins/With very best wishes/from Ernest Hemingway/Paris 1925," scattered wear on extremities, discoloration on endpapers, ink stain on frontispiece.

Marking the beginning of one of the 20thC's most legendary literary relationships, this is perhaps the most consequential association copy of any Hemingway title: the author's presentation of his first collection of short stories to his future editor at Scribner's, the legendary Maxwell Perkins (1884-1947). The two had begun a professional courtship just eight weeks earlier, which would not only lead eight months later to the genesis of one of American literature's most significant editorial relationships, but also last until Perkins' death in 1947, and result in the publication of Hemingway's most enduring works, including "The Sun Also Rises" (1926), "A Farewell to Arms" (1929), and "For Whom the Bell Tolls" (1940).

1924
$275,000-350,000 FRE

Milne, A. A., "Winnie-the-Pooh," first edition, illustrations by Ernest Shepard, pictorial endpapers, original pictorial gilt cloth, first state dust jacket, some offsetting in endpapers, spot staining, spine losses.
1926
$2,200-2,700 CA

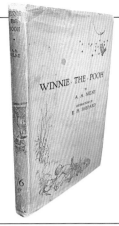

Woolf, Virginia, "Orlando: A Biography," first edition, published by Crosby Gaige, New York, one of 861 copies printed on rag paper and signed by the author in purple ink on verso of the half title, original black cloth, spine decorated in gilt, publisher's device gilt on front board, top edge gilt, with seven plates (including three showing Vita Sackville-West as Orlando), slightly faded.

The true first edition, preceding the Hogarth Press edition by nine days.
1928
$5,000-5,600 L&T

Orwell, George, "Animal Farm: A Fairy Story," first edition, first impression, published by Secker & Warburg, London, original green cloth, spine lettered in white, with dust jacket, spine and dust jacket wear.
1945
$4,700-5,500 L&T

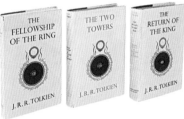

Tolkien, J. R. R., "The Lord of the Rings" trilogy, "The Fellowship of the Ring," "The Two Towers," and "The Return of the King," first editions, first impressions, published by George Allen & Unwin Ltd., London, each volume respectively 1 of only 3,000, 3,250, and 7,000 copies, original red cloth, spines lettered in gilt, top edges dyed red, folding map printed in red and black on rear of each work, with dust jackets, "Fellowship" with illustrations in text, "Return of the King" with signature mark "4" and sagging type on page 49, spotting, spines rolled, marks on dust jackets.
1954-55
$31,000-37,000 L&T

King, Martin Luther, Jr., "Stride Toward Freedom: The Montgomery Story," first edition, published by Harper & Brothers, New York, in original quarter black and blue cloth, stamped in silver, in contemporary price-clipped dust jacket, and with original tattered dust jacket, inscribed to early organizers of the Montgomery Bus Boycott, Alfonso and Lucy B. Campbell, "To:/Mr. & Mrs. A. L. Campbell/With best wishes/and warm Personal/Regards/Martin L. King Jr.," initialed "LBC" for Lucy B. Campbell, wear on corners and spine.
1958
$12,500-15,000 FRE

Fleming, Ian, "Dr. No," first edition, first impression, second-state binding, published by Jonathan Cape, London, original cloth with Honeychile silhouette in brown on front board, with dust jacket, slight wear.
1958
$950-1,050 L&T

Heller, Joseph, "Catch-22," first edition, first printing, published by Simon and Schuster, New York, original blue cloth, stamped in white, in original unclipped dust jacket, original preprinted Simon and Schuster "A Note to the Reader" postcard laid in, scattered edge wear.
1961
$2,500-3,100 FRE

Burgess, Anthony, "A Clockwork Orange," first edition, first printing, published by Heinemann, London, original black cloth, stamped in silver, in original illustrated unclipped first-state dust jacket, priced 16s Net, designed by Barry Trengrove.
1962
$4,000-4,700   FRE

Herbert, Frank, "Dune," first edition, first printing, published by Chilton Books, Philadelphia/New York, original light blue cloth, stamped in white, in original unclipped first-issue dust jacket ($5.95 price on front flap and four-line publisher's imprint on rear flap), designed by John Schoenherr, disoloration, wear.
1965
$8,000-9,500   FRE

Tolkien, J. R. R., "The Hobbit: or There and Back Again," third edition, second impression (sixteenth impression overall), published by George Allen & Unwin Ltd., London, illustrated by the author, original green boards lettered and decorated in blue, map endpapers, color frontispiece depicting Hobbiton, three further color plates ("Rivendel,l" "Bilbo comes to the Huts of the Raft-elves," "Conversation with Smaug"), illustrations in text, with dust jacket, discoloration and fading on spine.

Provenance: By descent from Ivan Chambers. Inscribed by the author "for Mr. I. Chambers, J. R. R. Tolkien" on the title page, with the bookplate of the recipient Ivan Chambers OBE (1902-98) on the front free endpaper. Chambers was a noted bookseller who worked for W. J. Bryce, which operated from a building on London's Museum Street owned by Stanley Unwin, Tolkien's publisher. "The success of Tolkien's writing, as well as his subsequent fanatical worldwide readership, was due in no small part to the author–publisher relationship that existed between Tolkien, Stanley Unwin, and later[Stanley's son] Rayner Unwin" (Oxford Dictionary of National Biography).
1966
$22,000-27,000   L&T

Kerr, Judith, "The Tiger who came to tea," first edition, first impression, published by Collins, London, color illustrations throughout, original mat pictorial boards, with dust jacket.

Rare, especially in the dust jacket. Now a children's classic, "The Tiger who came to Tea" was Judith Kerr's first book. Her preparatory sketches for the work are now held by the British Library.
1968
$4,300-5,000   L&T

Thompson, Hunter S., "Fear and Loathing in Las Vegas: A Savage Journey to the Heart of the American Dream," published by Random House, New York, a rare publisher's uncorrected page proof, original illustrated blue stiff wrappers, illustrated by Ralph Steadman, notations on front wrapper "Fiction, $5.95, Pub 6/72," "Thompson" in manuscript red ink along bottom edge, with a first edition copy, original black cloth, stamped in blind and silver, in original unclipped dust jacket, designed by Ralph Steadman, light wear on top edge.
1971
$4,000-4,500   FRE

Adams, Richard, "Watership Down," first edition, first impression, published by Rex Collings, London, original brown cloth gilt, folding map at rear, with dust jacket, inscribed by the author "Yours sincerely, Richard Adams, London February, 1983" on the title page, light rubbing on binding, endpapers renewed, small marks.
1972
$3,350-4,000   L&T

Hawking, Stephen, "A Brief History of Time," first edition, published by Bantam Press, with diagrams, original cloth, and dust jacket.
1988
$460-520   CA

Rowling, J. K. "Harry Potter and the Chamber of Secrets," first edition paperback, published by Bloomsbury, signed "J K Rowling" on dedication page, which is coming loose.
1998
$300-450   HT

Ortelius, Abraham, "Islandia" [Iceland], published in Antwerp, hand-colored engraved map, incorporating sea monsters, polar bears, and Hekla volcano, faint creases, minor staining.

Ortelius's path-breaking and richly imaginative map of Iceland first appeared in the 1587 French edition of the "Typis orbis terrarum." It was drawn by Danish priest and historian Anders Sorenson Vedel or Velleius (1542-1616) using the work of Icelandic bishop Gudbrandur Thorlaksson (1547-1621), and dedicated by Ortelius to Frederick II of Denmark.

ca. 1590 or later   *21¾in (55.5cm) wide*
$10,500-12,500   **L&T**

Tegg, Thomas, "Tegg's New Plan of London, &c. With 360 References to the Principal Streets, &c. 1826," hand-colored engraved map, with street key, dissected and laid on linen, with original slipcase with paper label, wear.
1826
$300-375   **CA**

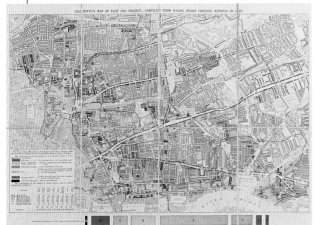

Booth, Charles, "Labour and Life of the People" Volumes I and II, published by Williams and Norgate, London, original green cloth, containing a collection of lithographic and color maps, including "Descriptive Map of East End Poverty, compiled from School Board Visitors' Reports in 1887" (pictured), bindings shaken and worn.
1889-91   *20in (50.5cm) wide*
$8,400-9,200   **L&T**

Speed, John, "The Kingdome of China newly augmented," first edition, published by George Humble, showing George Humble in Popshead Alley as the seller, hand-colored engraving, the only carte-à-figures map made of the region, also showing Korea, Japan, and India, four vignettes in the upper border, including "the manner of their execution," small repair verso, three small wormholes.
1626   *19¾in (50cm) wide*
$1,400-1,700   **CA**

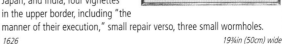

Beaufort, the Reverend Daniel Augustus, "A New Map of Ireland, Civil and Ecclesiastical," second edition, published by William Faden, London, engraved by Samuel John Neele (1758-1824), hand colored and dissected on 16 sheets laid down on linen, in an ebonized glazed frame.
1797   *38½in (98cm) high*
$1,500-2,000   **L&T**

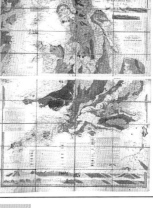

Knipe, J. A., "Geological & Mineralogical Map of England and Wales, with Parts of Scotland, Ireland & France," hand-colored engraved map, sectionalized and laid on linen in two halves, spotting, staining.
1838   *47¼in (120cm) high*
$1,250-1,700   **CA**

Boucher, Lucien (1889–1971), "Air France" Map, lithographic poster.
1948   *39in (99cm) wide*
$800-950   **L&T**

Garbutt, Paul E., "London Transport" Underground map, published by Waterlow & Sons Ltd., on industrial board, with an attached label stating "Pimlico station will open Autumn 1972."
ca. 1970   *81½in (207cm) wide*
$450-550   **CA**

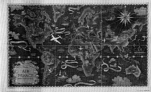

A wooden peg doll, late 18th/early 19thC and later, with inset glass eyes, the head with gesso and painted features, above a pigeon-chested body with replacement arms and legs, wearing a silk costume.

21¾in (55cm) high

$1,600-1,900 **WW**

A German papier-mâché shoulder-head doll, with painted features, molded and painted black Apollo knot hairstyle, sloped shoulders to a kid leather milliner-style body with carved lower arms and legs, with large feet and painted yellow slippers, wearing original cotton print dark blue dress with intricate flower pattern, white lace collar, long sleeves, and underclothes, slight paint loss on hair.

1830-40 *20in (51cm) high*

$1,500-1,900 **C&T**

A 19thC Italian carved wood doll, with glass eyes, the painted wood head and body with articulated arms and terra-cotta hands, wearing an 18thC embroidered silk costume.

14¼in (36cm) high

$625-750 **WW**

A mid-19thC German early pedlar papier-mâché shoulder-head doll, with painted features and black hair, on a cloth body with kid leather arms, wearing original cotton print dress with apron, red cape, and bonnet, holding a bunch of flowers in her left hand and basket of wares in her right, the wares include a small all-bisque Parian-type doll, pincushions, a comb, ribbons, fans, and more, standing on a wood stepped base within a glass case.

10¼in (26cm) high

$1,700-2,200 **C&T**

A French Portrait Jumeau almond-eyed bisque-head Bébé doll, with spiral blue glass paperweight eyes, painted lashes and feather brows, pierced ears, cork pate, and blonde shoulder-length wig, on a wood and composition eight-ball jointed body with fixed wrists and blue "Jumeau, Medaille D'or, Paris" stamp, wearing a blue and pale pink dress with lace, underclothes, socks, white leather shoes, and a straw bonnet decorated with summer flowers.

ca. 1880 *14¼in (36cm) high*

$12,500-15,000 **C&T**

A rare French "Queen of Hearts" bon-bonier wax shoulder-head doll, with glass eyes, white cardboard cylinder-shaped skirt with door for candies held by a gilt-metal clasp, wood arms with swivel wrists, wearing an ivory silk dress with red hearts, ornate headdress, and white silk bead necklace, the base with three metal wheels and original "Boissier, Paris" gold and white label, light crazing on face.

1880s *12½in (32cm) high*

$450-550 **C&T**

A French Depose Jumeau size 9 bisque-head Bébé doll, with fixed blue glass paperweight eyes, painted lashes and feather brows, and applied ears with pink glass bead earrings, cork pate with shoulder-length blonde wig, on a fully jointed wood and composition body with fixed wrists and "Jumeau, Medaille D'or, Paris" blue stamp, wearing original cream and maroon dress with pleated center panel and skirt, silk patterned maroon jacket with crochet buttons and matching bonnet, underclothes, and socks, marked "Jumeau," white leather shoes with rosettes, incised "Depose," "9," repairs.

ca. 1885 *20in (51cm) high*

$5,500-6,000 **C&T**

A French Leon Casimir Bru Jne size 9 bisque-head Bébé doll, with fixed brown glass paperweight eyes, painted lashes and feather brows, pierced ears, cork pate, and blonde wig, on a Bru fully jointed wood and composition body, wearing a cream dress with lace on collar, sleeves, and underclothes, incised "Bru Jne," "9," some small repairs.

ca. 1890 *19in (48cm) high*

$12,500-15,000 **C&T**

A French all-bisque "Mignonette" doll, with fixed brown glass eyes, painted mouth, original long blonde wig with decorative ribbons, jointed at the shoulders and hips, wearing painted black heeled shoes and original pink crepe dress with wings.

ca. 1890   *4¼in (11cm) high*

$625-750   **C&T**

A pair of German miniature all-bisque dolls, each with fixed blue glass eyes, painted lashes, brows, and mouths, original blonde wigs, swivel necks, jointed at the shoulders and hips, the girl with painted and molded pink socks and black sandals, the boy with white socks and brown shoes, wearing matching homemade pink shorts with shirts and jackets.

ca. 1890   *4¼in (11cm) high*

$1,500-1,900   **C&T**

A rare French Jules Steiner Figure A size 9 Black bisque-head Bébé doll, fixed brown glass paperweight eyes, painted lashes and feather brows, ears with pearl earrings, original pate and black wig, on a fully jointed composition body, wearing a red knitted dress with sailor-style collar and lace on cuffs, a beret, underclothes, red socks, and marked brown leather shoes, incised "Steiner," "Bt SGDG," "Paris," "A," "9."

ca. 1890   *16in (40.5cm) high*

$5,000-6,200   **C&T**

A French Steiner Figure A size 9 bisque-head Bébé doll, with fixed blue glass paperweight eyes, painted lashes and feather brows, pierced ears, original pate with sheep-skin wig, on a fully jointed composition body with fixed wrists, wearing a white cotton and lace dress with red flannel skirt, cape, and bonnet, with underclothes, socks, and shoes, incised "Steiner," "Paris," "Fre A," "9."

ca. 1890   *16in (40.5cm) high*

$2,500-3,100   **C&T**

ESSENTIAL REFERENCE—SERIES FANTASTIQUE

Cofounded in the early 1840s by Pierre-François Jumeau and Louis-Desire Belton, in Montreuil-sous-Bois, near Paris, Maison Jumeau gained a reputation for making dolls with beautiful faces and exquisite clothing that replicated contemporary fashions. After Pierre-François's son, Emile Jumeau, joined the company in 1867, Jumeau expanded significantly, most notably following the production, in 1877, of the first "Bébés." Made in the image of little girls, and characterized by realistic glass eyes and, again, fashionable clothes, they were mass-produced for a domestic and international market.

In 1892, the entrepreneurial Emile Jumeau introduced a much more exclusive range of dolls. Inspired by bisque heads with incredibly realistic facial expressions—ranging in emotion from laughing to crying—and the dramatic eyes that Jumeau had been originally commissioned to produce for automata maker Leopold Lambert, they were collectively named the "Series Fantastique." Made in very small numbers up until 1899—mostly as special commissions or for exhibitions—the series ran from mold number 201 to 221 (this example is a 203), and were mostly Bébés, although one, possibly two adult dolls were also made. Rare and of exceptional quality, they are very highly desirable, and invariably exchange hands for considerable sums.

A rare German Kestner 121 all-bisque doll, with fixed blue glass eyes, single stroke brows, open mouth with two square upper teeth, original blonde wig, swivel head, and jointed at the shoulders and hips, with painted and molded white socks and black heeled shoes, wearing a white dress and bonnet, tiny repair on leg.

ca. 1895   *5½in (14cm) high*

$450-550   **C&T**

A French Francois Gaultier bisque-head Bébé doll, with fixed blue glass paperweight eyes, painted lashes and brows, pierced ears, cork pate, and long brown wig, on a fully jointed wood and composition body, wearing a later pink silk dress with metallic thread and lace decoration, with underclothes, socks, and white shoes, flower garland in hair, incised "6," "FG" in scroll, some repainting.

ca. 1895   *17in (43cm) high*

$2,500-3,100   **C&T**

A very rare French Jumeau size 5 bisque-head character doll, mold no. 203, from the "Series Fantastique," with fixed brown glass paperweight eyes, painted lashes and feather brows, open/closed mouth with smile and molded upper teeth, accented tongue and molded laughter creases, pierced ears with coral bead earrings, cork pate and long auburn wig, on a fully jointed wood and composition body with paper "Bebe Jumeau, Diplome d'Honneur" label, wearing original blue cotton sailor-style dress with pleated skirt, underclothes, socks, and original Bébé Jumeau brown leather shoes, stamped "5" and with original paper "Au Louvre, Paris" label, and a straw boater, incised "203," "5," red stamp "DEPOSE, TETE JUMEAU, Bte SGDG," and painter's mark.

ca. 1895   *19in (48cm) high*

$17,500-20,000   **C&T**

A very rare English Lucy Peck poured-wax portrait doll of a young Queen Victoria, deep blue glass eyes, molded lids, and painted feathered brows, open mouth with tinted lips, molded ears, inserted light brown hair with original side braids held by blue and black ribbon rosettes, with a black glass bead and ribbon headdress, sloped shoulders on a cloth body with individually posed poured-wax lower arms, with molded hands, legs with molded toes, wearing original detailed blue plaid pure silk off-the-shoulder dress with black velvet and lace detail, bustle at rear and matching jacket, underclothes, and choker with original gold pendant incised "VR," stamped "From Mrs Peck, The Dollhouse, 131 Regent Street" on body.

Lucy Peck's doll shop specialized in Royal portrait dolls—including one of Queen Victoria as a young lady—that are extremely rare to find, this example being one of the best to be offered for sale at auction.

ca. 1900   *9¼in (74cm) high*

$6,000-6,700   **C&T**

A pair of German Simon & Halbig miniature bisque-head dolls, each with fixed blue glass eyes, original short wigs, composition bodies, jointed at the shoulders and hips, with painted black socks and molded brown sandals, wearing original red-and-blue striped rompers, one with a blue felt hat.

ca. 1910   *5in (12.5cm) high*
$300-375   **C&T**

A German J. D. Kestner miniature all-bisque jointed "Googly" doll, with weighted brown side-glancing eyes, short brown wig, fixed neck and jointed at the shoulders, elbows, hips, and knees, with painted white socks and brown shoes, wearing original red-and-white gingham dress, with white pinafore and underclothes.

ca. 1910   *4¾in (12cm) high*
$700-800   **C&T**

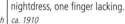

A German A.M 353 Asian bisque-head baby doll, with weighted brown glass eyes, painted hair, composition baby body, wearing a cream nightdress, one finger lacking.

ca. 1910   *17in (43cm) high*
$350-400   **C&T**

A rare German Hertwig all-bisque Goldilocks doll, with painted features and molded hair, fixed neck and jointed at the shoulders, with brown painted shoes, wearing original crochet dress.

ca. 1910   *1¾in (4.5cm) high*
$350-400   **C&T**

A rare German Kestner 111 all-bisque jointed "Googly" doll, with weighted blue glass eyes, painted lashes, brows, and mouth, original blonde wig, fixed neck and jointed at the shoulders, elbows, hips, and knees, with painted and molded white socks and brown sandals, wearing a knitted brown dress and white shirt.

ca. 1910   *5½in (14cm) high*
$1,100-1,500   **C&T**

A German Gebruder Kuhnlenz 34-28 Black bisque-head doll, with weighted brown glass eyes, open mouth with upper teeth, original black wig, on a fully jointed composition body, wearing original white silk dress with lace trim, bonnet, underclothes, socks, and leather shoes.

ca. 1910   *19in (48cm) high*
$1,500-1,700   **C&T**

An English Chad Valley "Bambino" cloth doll, the felt face with side-glancing glass eyes, painted lashes, brows, and smile, short brown hair and swivel head, velvet body, jointed at the shoulders and hips, wearing original red, white, and blue sailor-style dress with beret, socks, and shoes.

1920s   *14¼in (36cm) high*
$500-625   **C&T**

A German Kathe Kruse VII painted cloth doll, the young boy with molded and painted features, short brown hair, swivel head on a cloth body, jointed at the shoulders and hips, stitched fingers, wearing a gray flannel jacket and black pants, with later marked Kathe Kruse white sandals, minor paint loss on hair.

1920s   *14¼in (36cm) high*
$950-1,050   **C&T**

A Chad Valley cloth Snow White doll, brushed cotton face with painted features, wearing original outfit.

1930s   *15¾in (40cm) high*
$250-310   **FLD**

Judith Picks

There are various reasons why this dollhouse—known as "The Evans Baby House"—is special. First and foremost is that much of its excellent provenance is writ large within it—literally! On the top floor there is a wall plaque inscribed: "Miss Hancock has sent Anne a large old-fashioned baby house which was made for her great grandmother. It possesses little furniture but has given great delight"—"from Mrs Evans at Britwell Court, Burnham Beeches, to her sister Mrs Phelps in Madeira, May 6th 1825" ... and accompanying this, within the drawer in its plinth base, are various papers and other correspondence further recording the history of the house, including inventories, renovations, and additions. Such detailed provenance is very rare, as, indeed, is the fact that this enduringly loved house has survived some 300 years since its initial construction in the mid-18thC, when so many other houses from that period have not.

Provenance aside, the house is also special in terms of where it stands in the history of both the construction and the primary purpose of dollhouses. The earliest known examples date from the mid-16thC, mostly in Germany and the Netherlands, and were referred to as "baby" rather than "doll" houses, with the latter only becoming the more common description in the late 18thC. These early examples—the best known being the "Munich Baby House" made for Albert V, Duke of Bavaria—were essentially "cabinets of curiosities," serving largely as symbols of wealth and social status. By the early 18thC, however, when the concept had traveled from Continental Europe to England, the houses began to gradually evolve from elaborately furnished cabinets or cupboards to architecturally detailed models of actual houses and primarily intended as playthings, and in many respects the mid-18thC Evans Baby House, with its built-in plinth drawer, can be said to straddle these two forms.

An important early-Victorian cupboard dollhouse, "Gregson House," the pine cupboard opening to reveal three bedrooms above a music, dining, and drawing room; the lower floor with hallway flanked by kitchen and "stillroom," the rooms with brass-handle doors and marbled fireplaces, the carpets mainly of velvet, oilcloth, or baize, the walls with hand-painted or embossed color paper, the original furniture of wood, tin, and cardboard, the walls hung with watercolors, many by original owner Bessie Wilkinson, further fittings in ceramic, glass, alabaster, and lead, the whole house peopled with original dolls.

Originally named "Maryland Lodge," the house was commissioned, then furnished by MIss Elizabeth "Bessie" Wilkinson upon the death in childbirth of her sister Mary Anne Boulton, in an attempt to help Mary Anne's six children and newborn, also Mary, recover from this tragedy; after inheritance by Bessie's nephew Henry Gregson, following her death in 1857, it became known as the "Gregson House."

1830 and later   *80¼in (204cm) high*
$50,000-62,000   WW

An 18thC Georgian three-story dollhouse, "The Evans Baby House," with later 19thC adaptations and contents, ocher- and red-painted pine and other wood, the window front opening to three single-room floors, with painted walls and corner fireplaces with faux marble surrounds, with hand-tinted prints on the walls, the basement floor fitted with original Georgian dressers, all raised on a plinth base fitted with a single drawer.

57¼in (145.5cm) high
$59,500-67,000   L&T

A three-story wood dollhouse, "Idaville," by Percy Platnauer, gray-painted brick facade and sides, fenced front with opening gates, large double bay windows on each side, tiled pitched roof with four chimney stacks, the front opening to seven rooms on three levels, with turned balustrade staircases, original flooring, fireplaces, furniture, and wallpapers, and with working electric lighting.

ca. 1912   *41in (104cm) high*
$8,500-10,000   C&T

A large German Silber & Fleming dollhouse, painted wood with paper brick-effect facade, with glazed bay and arched windows, the front opening in two wings to six rooms, four with original fireplaces, all with original interior lace hangings and a variety of furniture, including a Waltershausen desk and a gilt grandfather clock.

ca. 1880   *43¾in (111cm) high*
$4,300-5,600   C&T

A large Anglesey three-story dollhouse, "Renouf," in Georgian style, with pillar-supported porch with balcony, glazed windows, Welsh slate roof with three gable dormer windows and widow's walk, opening in two wings to six rooms, hallway and landing on each floor, all with wallpaper, flooring, and curtains, hinged roof over three attic rooms, three further basement rooms, fully electrified.

The "Renouf" was first exhibited at the London Dolls House Festival in May 1997 and featured in "International Dolls' House News," Vol. 6, no. 7, in July that year.

61in (155cm) high
$2,500-3,100   C&T

A wood dollhouse, in Far East colonial style, with veranda front and removable shaped tin roof.

ca. 1930s   *37in (94cm) wide*
$1,000-1,500   CHEF

A German Steiff white mohair straw-filled teddy bear, with black boot-button eyes, pointed snout, and light brown stitched nose, mouth, and claws, swivel head, jointed at the shoulders and hips, with elongated arms, large feet, and felt paw pads, button on left ear, wearing navy pants and a white shirt, some holes in left paw pad.

ca. 1909   *13in (33cm) high*

$1,000-1,500   **C&T**

A German Steiff white teddy bear with growling mechanism, mohair body, felt paws, shoe-button eyes, button in ear, with great expression and hump to back.
ca. 1910

$8,000-9,500   **TMY**

A rare German Bing clockwork roller skater mohair teddy bear, black boot-button eyes, stitched nose, mouth, and claws, swivel neck and straw-filled body, with clockwork mechanism, lacks skates and stick.

ca. 1912   *8in (20.5cm) high*

$775-850   **C&T**

A Farnell World War I miniature soldier mohair teddy bear, with clear glass eyes, swivel head, jointed at the shoulders and hips, some wear.

These tiny bears where often given to soldiers as they left for war in 1914-18.

3½in (9cm) high

$500-625   **C&T**

An English J. K. Farnell golden mohair teddy bear, straw- and kapok-filled, with large brown glass eyes, clipped muzzle, stitched nose and mouth, swivel head, jointed at the shoulders and hips, cloth paw pads, wearing a leather collar, discoloration, pads recovered.

ca. 1920   *19in (48cm) high*

$700-800   **C&T**

A German Jopi golden mohair straw-filled teddy bear, with large red glass eyes, stitched nose, mouth, and claws, swivel head, jointed at the shoulders and hips, the long body with weighted growler (not working), felt paw pads, minor repairs.

1920s   *20in (51cm) high*

$350-420   **C&T**

A rare German Schuco Yes/No mohair teddy bear, with orange glass eyes, clipped muzzle and black stitched nose and mouth, swivel head, jointed at the shoulders and hips, felt paw pads, pink neck ribbon, tail operates the yes/no mechanism, with original paper label on chest and stock label on left wrist, some fading, neck ribbon frayed.

1920s   *12in (30.5cm) high*

$1,100-1,500   **C&T**

A rare German Helvetic lavender mohair teddy bear, with brown glass eyes, black batwing stitched nose and stitched claws, swivel head, jointed at the shoulders and hips, velvet pads, balding, fading.

1920s   *20½in (52cm) high*

$550-700   **C&T**

A rare German Helvetic musical mohair teddy bear, with black eyes, black horizontally stitched nose and mouth, stitched claws, swivel head, jointed at the shoulders and hips, felt pads, squeeze-operated musical mechanism in body, some small sparse areas.

ca. 1928   *17½in (44.5cm) high*

$750-875   **C&T**

A rare Farnell sitting open-mouth teddy bear, straw-filled cotton plush, with pink velvet plush in lower open mouth and inner ears, red glass eyes with black stitching, vertically stitched nose and upper mouth, arms with wire armature and shaped legs, wearing a red-and-white neck tie, bald area in upper body.

1930s   *10in (25.5cm) high*
$170-220   **C&T**

A Merrythought blonde mohair teddy bear, straw-filled articulated body, black paw stitching, wear, losses.

ca. 1930s   *13in (33cm) high*
$100-150   **SWO**

A Chad Valley teddy bear, with oversize legs, padded paws, and embroidered buttons on chest, label stitched on right leg, repairs, loose threads.

1930s   *13in (33cm) high*
$170-220   **SWO**

A wood straw-filled mohair humpback teddy bear, probably Steiff (lacking button in left ear), swivel head, boot button eyes, stitched snout and claws, jointed body with felt pads, some bald patches and wear.

17¼in (44cm) high
$1,250-1,600   **TOV**

An English Deans Rag Book polar bear group, "Ivy & Brumas," straw-filled white mohair Ivy, with brown plastic eyes, brown cloth nose, and black stitched claws, Brumus with shorter mohair, stitched nose, mouth, and felt pads, each with original label.

These polar bears where made to celebrate the first polar bear cub to be born at London Zoo in 1949.

ca. 1950   *Ivy 19in (48cm) high*
$350-420   **C&T**

A large Steiff limited-edition Winnie the Pooh, no. 149 of 500 released worldwide, sitting, with large tag in the ear, product no. 690600.

33½in (85cm) high
$450-500   **LSK**

A Charlie Bears "Pierre" panda bear, from the "Isabelle Collection," limited edition no. 11 of 300, cinnamon and cream mohair, wearing a clown's ruff and conical hat, with swing label certificate, dust bag and box, no. SJ3993B.

ca. 2008   *13in (33cm) high*
$625-750   **FLD**

A Steiff Rupert the Bear, limited edition no. 2,372 of 3,000, UK and Ireland exclusive, white alpaca, boxed with certificate, no. 653568.

2020   *11in (28cm) high*
$150-190   **FLD**

A large Hermann Teddy Original "Spectacle" bear, brown, white, and mid-brown hair, with original Hermann tag on chest.

31½in (80cm) high
$120-150   **LSK**

A Dinky Toys No. 110 Aston Martin DB3 sports car, green body, red hubs and interior, with driver figure and racing "22," in original cardboard box, crushing on box ends.
$150-190   LSK

A Dinky Toys Hong Kong issue No. 57/001 Buick Riviera, light blue body with white roof, red interior, detailed hubs, in original cardboard box, tape repair on box.
$120-150   LSK

A Dinky Toys No. 173 Nash Rambler, salmon pink with mid-blue side panels and silver trim, white tires, in original cardboard box.
$90-110   LSK

A Dinky Toys No. 156 Rover 75 sedan, cream lower body and mid-blue upper body, cream rigid hubs, in original cardboard box.
$190-220   LSK

A French Dinky Toys No. 1400 Peugeot 404 Taxi Radio G7, black body with red roof, tan interior, concave hubs, "G7" labels, with original antenna, in original yellow cardboard box, slight tear in box.
$300-350   LSK

A Dinky Toys No. 183 Morris Mini Minor, metallic red body, gloss black roof, and white interior, in original all-cardboard picture-sided box.
$120-150   LSK

A French Dinky Toys No. 587 Citroen H "Philips" display van, yellow and silver body, with red hubs and "Philips" livery, in original all-cardboard picture-sided box.
$250-310   LSK

A French Dinky Toys No. 589A Berliet tow truck, "Depannage/Autoroutes," orange body, red roof light, chrome concave hubs, black plastic antenna, with road sign in bag, picture-sided cardboard box, with correct folded leaflet.
$600-670   LSK

A French Dinky Toys No. 566 Citroën Police support vehicle, dark blue and white body, with battery box fitment in base, in original cardboard box.
$300-350   LSK

A French Dinky Toys No. 888 GBO Berliet Sahara recovery vehicle, light tan body with white roof, plastic tan hubs, with original Supertoys lift-up lid cardboard box and leaflet.
$250-300   LSK

A Dinky Toys No. 948 McLean articulated tractor trailer, red cab and chassis, gray trailer fitted with matching red plastic hubs, in original Supertoys box.
$190-220   **LSK**

A French Dinky Toys No. 569 Berliet open-back dump truck, turquoise cab and back, dark green chassis and hubs, with black plastic components, red interior, with original pictorial cardboard box and leaflet.
$200-240   **LSK**

A Dinky Toys No. 923 Big Bedford Heinz delivery van, red cab and chassis, yellow hubs, yellow back with Heinz Baked Beans can livery, in original Supertoys cardboard box, some wear.
$120-150   **LSK**

A Dinky Supertoys No. 642 "pressure refueller," with box.
$60-90   **WHP**

A Dinky Supertoys No. 503 Foden flatbed truck, blue and orange, with box.
$70-100   **WHP**

A French Dinky Toys No. 884 Brockway Bridgelayer six-wheeled truck, in military green, with plastic bridge sections and inflatable pontoons, in original Supertoys cardboard box, with river design paper play mat.
$200-240   **LSK**

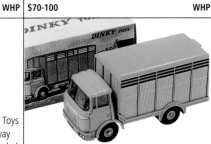

A French Dinky Toys No. 577 Berliet livestock trailer, yellow and green body, with yellow hubs and brown chassis, with two black-and-white cows, in original picture-sided cardboard box.
$150-190   **LSK**

A French Dinky Toys No. 570a Peugeot J7, "Autoroutes," orange body with concave hubs, amber roof light, complete with all accessories and figures, in original cardboard box.
$1,050-1,400   **LSK**

A Dinky Toys No. 300 Massey Harris tractor, red body with yellow hubs (rear cast, front plastic), with blue driver, in original yellow picture box.
$140-170   **LSK**

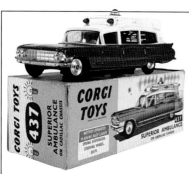

A Corgi Toys No. 437 Superior Ambulance, with box.

$90-110   WHP

A Corgi no. 448 B.M.C. Mini Police Van with Tracker Dog, dark blue with red interior, with policeman and dog, with inner pictorial stand and box.

$140-160   FLD

A Corgi Toys No. 210S Citroen DS19, with box.

$60-90   WHP

A Corgi Toys No. 261 James Bond Goldfinger Aston Martin DB5 diecast model car, gold body, wire wheels, silver trim, and red interior, with James Bond and Bandit figures, with secret instruction envelope containing instruction leaflet, spare Bandit figure and lapel badge, with catalog leaflet, all contained on inner pictorial stand in outer picture box.

$350-400   FLD

A Corgi no. 258 The Saint's Volvo P1800, white with white Saint label, red interior and spun hubs, with driver figure, in blue and yellow picture box.

$100-150   FLD

A Corgi Toys No. 1111 Massey Ferguson 780 combine harvester, red body with yellow tines and driver figure, yellow attachments with red plastic front and rear wheels, in original lift-off lid all-cardboard box, with packing pieces and Corgi club leaflet.

$275-310   LSK

A Spot-On Tri-ang No. 103 Rolls Royce Silver Wraith, light blue top, silver bottom, and red interior, in original cardboard box with correct color spot, along with leaflet and collectors card.

$700-750   LSK

A Spot-On No. 191 Sunbeam Alpine sports car, yellow body, pale cream interior and steering wheel, chrome front and rear bumpers, cast spun hubs, in original box with leaflet, collectors card, and packing piece.

$790-850   LSK

A Spot-On Tri-ang Models No. 118 B.M.W. Izetta, lilac body, with cream hubs and red steering wheel, in original cardboard box.

$210-250   LSK

A Spot-On No. 106a/1 Austin Prime Mover with open trailer, orange with cream interior, black chassis, orange trailer with silver inner back, cast hubs, in original cardboard box.

$550-625   LSK

A Spot-On No. 110/2b AEC "London Brick Co Ltd." truck, red body and black roof, bricks with "Phorpes Bricks" transfer, in original cardboard box, play wear.

$200-240   LSK

An early-20thC Carter Patterson & Co. painted wood model truck, paint loss, wheels mishapen and wobbly, back section loose on chasis.

21¾in (55cm) long

$625-750 CHEF

A large Tri-ang scale Magic Midget tinplate clockwork model, in racing green with driver figure, boxed with matched Meccano keys.

ca. 1937

$2,100-2,700 FLD

A Wells tinplate sedan car, maroon and cream livery, the sunroof opening to reveal its driver, with box.

1930s 14¼in (36cm) long

$700-800 WHP

A Scalextric Mercedes 190 3L, model no. C775.
$70-100 WHP

A Scalextric E3 Aston Martin GT, with box.
$90-110 WHP

A Japanese Aoshin The Monkees "Monkeemobile" tinplate battery-operated car, in red, with green lithographed interior and four sitting plastic band members, with box.
$625-750 FLD

A Lesney Matchbox Regular Wheels 22b Vauxhall Cresta, metallic dark pink body and turquoise side panels, with rear silver trim and red taillights, pale green windows, gloss black base, and 20-tread gray plastic wheels with rounded axles, with box.
$170-210 FLD

A Matchbox Lesney No. 27 Bedford Articulated Low-Loader, pale blue cab, dark blue trailer with metal wheels, in original box.

This is a rare color variation of this model.
$550-625 LSK

An ASAM Alan Smith Auto Models 1/48 scale white metal kit-built model of a Steetley Kenworth 8x4 Tractor unit, with six-axle low-loader and Submarine load, in original box.
$250-310 LSK

A Jimson No. 115 plastic and friction-drive model Land Rover, gray body with white roof and red interior, in original card box.
$250-300 LSK

A Lesney Products No. 1 745D Massey Harris tractor, No. 745D "Major Scale" series, red and cream body with cream hubs, in original cardboard box, an exhaust broken off but present.
$750-875 LSK

TOYS & MODELS

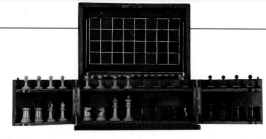

A Victorian mahogany games compendium, comprising a boxwood and ebony Staunton-pattern chess set and a three-part leather-covered board, boxwood and ebony dominoes, a cribbage board with bone accessories, four sets of playing cards and a whist marker, and a horse racing game and gavel, small losses, cribbage board possibly replaced.

12½in (32cm) wide

$625-750 SWO

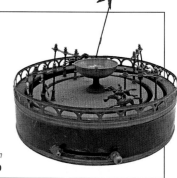

A French tinplate horse-racing game, cold-painted with circulating runners and riders, slightly bent rails and mounts.

ca. 1900   12¼in (31cm) diam

$450-500 SWO

A German Tipp & Co. tinplate "Graf" Zeppelin DLZ 127 airship, lithographed body, tinplate rear propeller, clockwork mechanism not working with fixed key.

13¾in (35cm) long

$875-1,000 C&T

A Marx Moon Rider Space Ship tinplate toy, lithographed with pilots and passengers, with three wheels and a yellow tail fin, with integral key and on/off switch.

ca. 1952   12¼in (31cm) long

$340-400 FLD

A Tri-ang Minic Kitty and Butterfly clockwork plastic toy, formed as a black-and-white cat with a butterfly, with box.

$40-50 FLD

A Sacul Rag, Tag, and Bobtail set of hollow-cast figures, with box.

ca. 1951

$170-220 FLD

A Subbuteo Table Speedway, with box.

Subbuteo issued a whole range of racing games, but these did not survive past the early 1960s, probably due to competition from slot cars, such as Scalextric.

1950s

$550-625 FLD

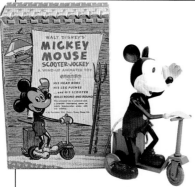

A Nurseryland Mickey Mouse Scooter Jockey, with plastic clockwork Mickey Mouse with wire tail on a plastic scooter, with integral key, in an illustrated box.

$150-170 FLD

A Pelham Puppets Gerry Anderson's Supercar Mike Mercury, with box.

$150-170 FLD

A Japanese Horikawa Gear Robot, battery-operated tinplate, gray body with clear chest revealing gears in red and green, with tinplate feet, no box.

$200-240 FLD

A Palitoy Action Man figure with Judo outfit, with painted hair, Judogi (top and pants), and all grading belts, comprising white with red tips, yellow, orange, green, blue, brown, and black, with partial information sheet.

This set from the Action Man Sports range is rare, assumed to be because of the lack of interest from toy retailers and resulting poor sales.

ca. 1970

$520-550   FLD

A Denys Fisher (Kenner) Six Million Dollar Man Maskatron action figure, complete with three masks and two special arms, with box.

$125-160   FLD

ESSENTIAL REFERENCE—THE TOY MARKET

"The toy market is primarily fueled by nostalgia," Kayleigh Davies, Toys and Models specialist at Fieldings Auctioneers, recently observed, "and so is ever changing." She adds, "One generation grows up and gets a little more disposable income and a hankering to revisit the toys of their childhood, while another is downsizing and clearing out. Toy fairs were once dominated by die-cast models, such as Dinky, Corgi, and Matchbox, Britains toy soldiers and Hornby trains, but Star Wars, Action Man, Masters of the Universe, and other action figures are now even more in evidence. The finest 0-gauge locomotives and die-cast models are still reaching dizzying heights at auction, but the lower end of the market is essentially static. Basically, the toys of the late 20thC are gradually taking over and we are seeing constant world record-breaking prices for action figures and video games; small pieces, such as weapons for action figures, that would often be lost in play are proving desirable and have a large impact on prices. In conclusion, it is an evolving market, but one that can generally be predicted by the fads of 40 years before, and I expect we will continue to see climbing prices for the 1970s and 1980s toys for quite some time."

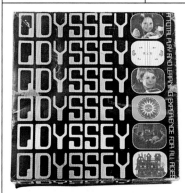

A Magnavox vintage 1972 Odyssey ITL200 electronic gaming system, comprising a console, controllers, and ephemera relating to various games, in original polystyrene two-tier display packaging with cardboard lid, near complete.

$190-220   LSK

A collection of assorted Kenner Star Wars weapons and accessories, including blue/black Imperial Blaster, Endor Blaster, black Rebel Blaster, blue Bespin Blaster, AT-AT Driver Rifle, Rebel Rifle, Princess Leia Boushh Rifle, Luke Skywalker Jedi Knight green lightsaber, Rebel Battle Staff, C-3PO limbs, cloaks, and more.

Weapons are a large part of the value of Star Wars figures—the items that were most likely to be lost during play.

$220-275   FLD

A Palitoy Star Wars Power of the Force Tri-Logo Endor Chase complete playpack, complete with inner packing tray, two baggies, instructions, and catalog leaflet.

$600-670   FLD

A GiG (Takara) Diaclone Dia-Train plastic transforming robot toy, with box.

The Diaclone series was an early range of transforming robot toys, and some of the figures were used as the basis for the first Transformers toys.

1980s

$275-325   FLD

An original Nintendo NES ROB Robotic Operating Buddy, comprising a robot with arms and Nintendo Gyro, no box, battery covers missing.

$90-125   LSK

An original Nintendo Virtual Boy 32-bit console system, complete with Mario's Tennis Game Pack included, in original cardboard box, complete with very little use.

$400-450   LSK

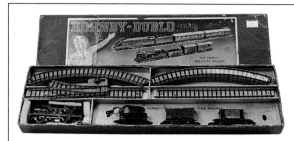

A prewar DG7 Hornby-Dublo clockwork 0-6-2 goods train set, comprising a LNER 2690 black locomotive with shadowed gold letters and numbers, NE open wagon, NE goods van, oval of track, original box base, replacement lid with original picture attached.
$350-420   **LSK**

A Hornby 20v ac loco and tender LMS 6201, "Princess Elizabeth," numbered on cab and "LMS" on tender, maroon cab interior, chips, box overpainted.
1938-40
$1,250-1,500   **LSK**

A Bassett-Lowke gauge-O electric 4-6-0 locomotive and tender 850, "Lord Nelson," in Southern green livery, in a reproduction box, restored.
$400-475   **TOV**

One of a set of four 2½in-gauge Nigerian Railway coaches, comprising two sleeping cars, a day car, and a luggage van, the hinged roofs revealing fitted interiors with bunk beds and bedding, a dining table, and other contents, to go with a Bassett-Lowke model locomotive, "The Emir of Zaria."
ca. 1920s
$300-350 the set   **LSK**

A No. E320 20vAC Riviera Blue Train locomotive and tender, gold-lined cab, red-lined brown deflectors, smokebox, smokebox door, running plate, and domes.
1938-41
$210-250   **LSK**

A Wrenn gauge-OO/HO locomotive and tender, "King George VI," with optional "City of Leeds" nameplates, with box, packing pieces, and instructions, box base stamped "Packer No 2, Ref No 911145."
$500-625   **TOV**

An ACE Trains 0-gauge electric 3-rail E/7 Castle Class locomotive and tender, "Earl of Mount Edgecumbe," in original box with leaflet.
$520-600   **LSK**

A Red Tree Models/ACE Trains 0-gauge "Warship" Bo-Bo diesel hydraulic loco D802, "Formidable," British Railways Locomotive green, small yellow warning panels on ends, box base complete, some scuffing.
$550-625   **LSK**

A set of three Ace Trains gauge-O C/4 LNER "teak" coaches, with "The Flying Scotsman" nameplates, with box.
$170-220   **TOV**

A brass 2½in-gauge live steam 4-6-2 locomotive and eight-wheel tender, the cab with pressure gauge, controls, and removable roof panel, within a tracked display case, along with a small quantity of track, spares, and paints.

$1,250-1,700 TOV

A Japanese Aster Hobbies gauge-1 live steam spirit-fired model of a British Railways Castle Class No. 5070 4-6-0 locomotive and tender, "Sir Daniel Gooch," finished in British Railways green, serial no. 216/280 with matching plaque on the underside of tender, in original cardboard box, with an Aster Hobbies manual and catalog.

ca. 2008

$3,350-4,000 LSK

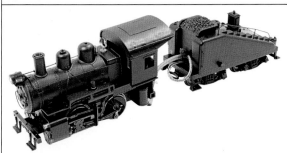

An Aristocraft gauge-1 ref. 84200-01 0-4-0 butane-gas-powered live steam locomotive and tender, USA switcher, finished in plain black, undecorated, in an aluminum-style flight case with instructions, transmitter, filler, syringes, and other tools, including power supply.

$800-875 LSK

A detailed 4in-gauge nickel-plated 4-4-0 live steam locomotive and tender, "Argentina," spirit fired with fittings, including a pressure gauge, marked "VER, B.Aires," sight glass, regulator, feed water pump, firebox door, and brake, external details include steam whistle, safety valve, sprung buffers, hinged front buffers, spring and brake detail, internal mechanism, full boiler tubing and burner detail, bell, headlight, Stephenson weighted reverse gear, cylinder drain cocks, water and spirit storage on tender, extensive rivet detail, and wood-clad cylinders, on a display track, in an oak-framed display case.

ca. 1900   *train and tender 31½in (80cm) long*

$8,500-10,000 SWO

A 5in-gauge live steam coal-fired model of a Great Western Railway Class 14XX tank locomotive, finished in green, with "GWR" on sides and "1439" to cab, hand painted, reworked from a Winson Engineering Kit.

30¼in (77cm) long

$3,500-4,200 LSK

A brass and steel 2½in-gauge live steam model of a 4-6-0 locomotive and tender, in "LNER" green and black livery, play wear, rust, losses.

$250-310 TOV

A Carette Model No. 692/3P portable steam engine, comprising spirit-fired boiler with single-cylinder mounted slide valve engine, chain-driven rear wheel, ball governor, Carette trademark on front of engine.

ca. 1895   *9in (23cm) long*

$1,100-1,500 LSK

A scale live steam model of a showman's traction engine, not in working order, rusted.

37¾in (96cm) long

$3,100-3,700 SWO

A Markie 1/10-scale spirit-fired model of a live steam traction engine, finished in maroon with brass detailing, fitted with road tires.

20in (51cm) long

$1,900-2,200 LSK

A model sailing pond yacht, with rigging, on a stand, traces of old paint.

ca. 1910   *31¼in (79.5cm) long*

$875-1,100   **SWO**

A large late-19thC model sailing pond yacht, clinker built, on a display stand, lacking masts and sails.

71¼in (181cm) long

$300-350   **SWO**

A large model sailing twin-masted pond yacht, with rigging bow sprit, brass fittings, general wear.

ca. 1910   *60¼in (153cm) long*

$160-220   **SWO**

A Bing two-funnel battleship, painted gray, with front, back, and side guns, two masts, lifeboats added, clockwork mechanism not working.

ca. 1912   *20in (51cm) long*

$1,100-1,500   **C&T**

A German Fleischmann tinplate clockwork single-funnel ocean liner, red and black painted hull, brown decks, and white superstructure, flags replaced.

1930s   *8½in (21.5cm) long*

$220-275   **C&T**

A Flower Class Corvette HMCS "Snowberry" model, hand built, with remote control unit.

33½in (85cm) long

$160-200   **C&T**

A Sutcliffe tinplate "Grenville" model destroyer, black hull and gray body, five deck guns, torpedo tubes embossed "Sutcliffe made in England," working clockwork motor, missing key and two masts, in original box.

13in (33cm) long

$475-550   **C&T**

A Royal Navy Gun Boat 488 model, hand built, with remote control unit.

36¼in (92cm) long

$250-310   **C&T**

A Japanese wood electric-drive model motor launch, black-and-red hull, unlabeled, missing back seat.

15¾in (40cm) long

$60-100   **SWO**

ROCKING HORSES 495

TOYS & MODELS

A Victorian carved and painted wood rocking horse, with glass eyes and partial leather saddle, mounted on curved rockers.

82¼in (209cm) wide

$6,000-6,700　　**L&T**

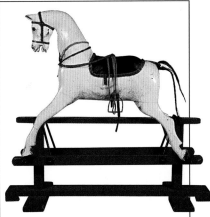

A Victorian painted wood rocking horse, on hinged swing support with pendulum movement.

44½in (113cm) wide

$475-550　　**ADA**

A painted wood rocking horse, refurbished by Stevenson Brothers, dapple gray with saddle and reins, on a wood trestle base.

ca. 1900　　*54in (137cm) high*

$2,500-3,100　　**CHEF**

An early-20thC F. H. Ayres small dapple gray rocking horse, with glass eyes, horsehair mane and tail, partial original leather tack, on a trestle support and turned columns, the base stamped "395 PATENTED JAN 29 1880" with metal plaque stamped "F.H. AYRES/MANUFACTURERS/ 111 ALDERGATE ST/LONDON."

32¼in (82cm) wide

$2,700-3,200　　**L&T**

An early-20thC dapple gray painted rocking horse, on stand.

62¼in (158cm) wide

$1,100-1,500　　**CHEF**

A small early-20thC rocking horse, probably by F. H. Ayres, with glass eyes, horsehair mane and tail, original leather saddle and replaced tack, on painted trestle support and turned columns.

31in (79cm) wide

$950-1,050　　**L&T**

A modern Stevenson Brothers carved oak rocking horse, fitted with leather and claret suede saddle, the stand with maker's label "Stevenson Brothers England 2006 6490."

56in (142cm) wide

$1,500-1,900　　**TOV**

A modern Stevenson Brothers black painted rocking horse, fitted with a leather and claret suede saddle, with maker's label "Stevenson Brothers England 2006 6488."

50in (127cm) wide

$1,400-1,700　　**TOV**

A late-20thC Kings Horses Thelwell pony rocking horse, with maker's label, with original "Thelwell's Grooming Box."

45¾in (116cm) wide

$1,400-1,700　　**TOV**

A Yoruba gelede mask, Nigeria, with a high forehead, scroll-top ears, navette eyes with square apertures, pierced nostrils, an open mouth, and vertical cheek scarifications, with a channeled and pierced edge for attachment, with a red pigment, on a stand.

6½in (16.5cm) high

$300-450 **WW**

ESSENTIAL REFERENCE—MOSSI KARANGA MASK

Masks made by the Mossi people of Burkina Faso often combine the stylized features of humans and animals (and sometimes even insects). This particular example, known as a "Karanga" mask, combines a humanlike face with a tall, concave superstructure (almost 3ft tall) representing the horns of a large antelope (Hippotragus koba)—a totemic animal to which not only the owner of the mask, but also his entire clan, are inextricably linked in terms of their life force. The mask would have originally been polychrome painted or stained (usually with geometric motifs), and there are remnants of black, white, and red pigments on the back of it. Karanga masks are traditionally used in various cultural celebrations, most notably ancestor worship, but also at funerals, when they play a prominent role in assuring a smooth transition to the afterlife. During burials, masks escort the body to the grave and ensure all burial procedures are correctly followed. At the conclusion of the rites, the spirit's union with clan ancestors is joyfully celebrated with dances in which performers imitate the motions of the animals their masks depict.

A Mende helmet mask, Sierra Leone, janus with aluminum mounts and two animal teeth.

15¼in (38.5cm) high

$750-1,000 **WW**

A Mossi "Karanga" mask, Burkina Faso, the face with incised outline triangles and fiber bindings, the curved horn crest pierced at the tip, on a stand.

40¼in (102cm) high

$1,250-1,500 **WW**

A Bamileke crocheted hat, Cameroon, cotton with rows of stiffened burls.

11¾in (30cm) wide

$170-220 **WW**

A Bamileke juju headdress, Cameroon, feathers, cloth, and fiber.

28¼in (72cm) diam

$1,000-1,250 **WW**

An Igbo bracelet currency, Nigeria, bronze with incised chevrons on the ends.

9in (23cm) long

$875-1,000 **WW**

An Ashanti woman's kente cloth, Ghana, silk and cotton, consisting of 13 strips.

64¼in (163cm) long

$750-875 **WW**

A late-19th/early 20thC Zulu knobkerrie, South Africa, rhinoceros horn, with a bulbous finial and tapering shaft.

28¼in (71.5cm) long 12½oz

$3,100-3,700 **WW**

ESSENTIAL REFERENCE—MUMUYE

The Mumuye people of Nigeria have a rich artistic tradition, much of which is in the form of figurative carving linked to religious practices and healing. Collectively known as "lagalagana," these figures, which can also serve as personal confidants, typically have elongated features and large earlobes—the latter due to the Mumuye practice of inserting decorative disks into their earlobes from an early age. The figures with these large lobes are almost invariably female, albeit genitalia are typically very understated or absent altogether. Another characteristic, almost always present—and evident on the figure shown here—is an exaggerated naval, often depicted protruding outward.

A Mumuye standing female figure, Nigeria, with a triangular nose and pursed lips, linear scarifications, circle eyes with pigment and a large pair of ears, with bent arms at the side, on a perspex base.

15¾in (40cm) high

$750-875   **WW**

A Nigeria post, carved with a female bust and with a U-shaped surmount support, on a stand.

58¾in (149.5cm) high

$300-450   **WW**

A Bembe spoon, Democratic Republic of the Congo, the handle carved as a figure astride a drum, with torso scarifications and a tall headdress.

7in (18cm) long

$500-625   **WW**

A 19thC West African carved ceremonial stool, probably Yoruba, Nigeria, carved overall with semicircular panels filled with notches and stick-carved bands, each side with a geometric pattern, one end carved with a warrior holding aloft a sword, the other end carved with two animals, with a square panel in the seat giving access to the void.

Maurice Stanley Cockin (1882-1961) was assistant district commissioner in Southern Nigeria between 1911 and 1914. During this time, he formed an important collection of African works of art, including many varied pieces and previously little-known styles from the tribes of the north of Benin. After being injured in World War I, Mr. Cockin did not return to Nigeria; however, he maintained a high level of interest in African affairs. At one point, he wrote an article on "Nigeria's need for a museum," in which he criticized British authorities for their failure in this regard (Journal of the Royal African Society, XXXVII, October 1938, pages 502-03). His collection expanded greatly, when, according to J. B. Donne, his wife was able to purchase a large part of the Sir Cecil Armitage collection. The story goes that, after Sir Cecil's death, some items were sold to the British Museum, "the remainder was sold sight unseen to Mrs Cockin for £100 [$125], as a result of a chance encounter with a dealer; the dealer had been on the point of putting all the woodwork on the bonfire in despair at not being able to sell it" (Donne, "The Celia Barclay collection of African art," The Connoisseur, 180, 1972, page 91). After the death of Maurice in 1961, the collection was inherited by his daughter Celia Barclay; much of it was then acquired by the British Museum in 1978 and 1984, respectively.

26in (66cm) wide

$2,500-3,700   **DUK**

A Maasai shield, Kenya, hide with painted geometric decoration, with a wood rib handle.

37¾in (96cm) high

$875-1,000   **WW**

A Gurunsi stool, Ivory Coast/Burkina Faso, the curved seat with end lifts, raised on four tapered legs.

22½in (57cm) wide

$800-950   **WW**

A Lega stool, Democratic Republic of the Congo, the top with stamped circle decoration.

15in (38cm) high

$625-750   **WW**

A Zulu headrest, South Africa, the long top on carved asumpa and block end supports, with a further open headrest profile between with ribbed, asumpa, and block decoration, the base with inscribed monogram "AZ."

20¾in (52.5cm) wide

$2,500-3,100   **WW**

TRIBAL ART

A stone figure, "Kneeling Man," by Maggie Ittuvik Tayarak (1898-1961), Kangiqsualujjuaq (George River), disk number inscribed.
4½in (11.5cm) high
$750-875 WAD

A pair of perched birds, stone with red marker inlay, ivory bases, unsigned.
2in (5cm) wide
$1,250-1,500 WAD

A stone carving, "Many Faces," by Miriam Marealik Qiyuk (b. 1933), Qamani'tuaq (Baker Lake), signed in Roman.
11in (28cm) high
$1,000-1,250 WAD

A stone and antler figure, "Musk Ox," by Mark Tungilik (1913-86), Naujaat (Repulse Bay), unsigned.
2in (5cm) wide
$1,050-1,200 WAD

A steel and paint figure, "Spirit Wolf," by Simon Tookoome (1934-2010), Qamani'tuaq (Baker Lake), made in collaboration with Joe Fafard, signed in syllabics, dated and numbered 15/20.
1997   9¼in (23.5cm) long
$875-1,000 WAD

A stone fish, unsigned.
ca. 1965   4in (10cm) wide
$450-500 WAD

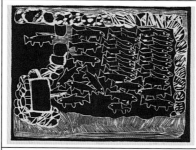

A woodcut, "Fishing Weir," by Janet Kigusiuq (1926-2005), Qamani'tuaq (Baker Lake), signed and titled in syllabics, dated "96," framed.
1996   21¾in (55cm) wide
$625-750 WAD

A textile, by Nancy Kangeryuaq Sevoga (b. 1936), Qamani'tuaq (Baker Lake), untitled, stroud, felt, thread and embroidery floss, signed in syllabics.
34½in (87.5cm) long
$550-700 WAD

An Inuit model kayak, Greenland, with a wood frame, sealskin cover, and marine ivory mounts.
24¼in (61.5cm) long
$500-625 WW

A Maya stucco head, Mexico, the finely modeled face with a roughly modeled headdress, covered with a white slip, on a porphyry plinth.

ca. AD 250-750   *11½in (29cm) high*

$3,500-4,200   **WW**

A Suriname stool, South America, the navette-shaped top with carved scrolling and notched decoration.

14½in (37cm) wide

$350-420   **WW**

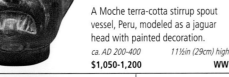

A Moche terra-cotta stirrup spout vessel, Peru, modeled as a jaguar head with painted decoration.

ca. AD 200-400   *11½in (29cm) high*

$1,050-1,200   **WW**

A Zia olla, New Mexico, earthenware with a white slip, polychrome decorated on two sides with a bird perched in a floral bough.

9½in (24cm) high

$1,050-1,200   **WW**

A Shipibo terra-cotta bowl, Peru, the exterior with painted linear and cross decoration.

14¼in (36cm) diam

$500-625   **WW**

A Mexican blue jade pendant, carved as a Mayan figure wearing a feather headdress, the sides pierced for suspension.

4½in (11.5cm) long

$1,900-2,200   **WW**

A Chancay textile, Peru, camelid fiber decorated with two deity figures, with outstretched arms and wearing ornate headdresses, surrounded by birds and horned animals, mounted on fabric.

ca. AD 1100-1400   *47¾in (121cm) wide*

$1,250-1,500   **WW**

A Pueblo turquoise boulder necklace.

29in (73.5cm) long 18oz

$950-1,050   **BON**

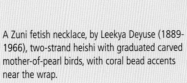
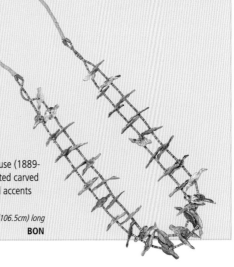

A Zuni fetish necklace, by Leekya Deyuse (1889-1966), two-strand heishi with graduated carved mother-of-pearl birds, with coral bead accents near the wrap.

42in (106.5cm) long

$6,000-7,500   **BON**

A Southern Plains shield cover, possibly Niuam (Comanche), the softly tanned cover gathered at the back and tied with a hide thong, the front decorated with a circular motif comprising five concentric rings of alternating colors, with remnants of earlier pictographic elements evident underneath, including depictions of quadruped and human figures, a painted hide tab pendant near the edge.

See J. Emmor Harston, "Comanche Land," The Naylor Company, San Antonio, TX (1963), page 123, where the frequent appearance of a sun motif on Niuam shields is discussed: "Each warrior feathered, painted and 'medicined' his shield to suit himself; but all were painted to represent the sun … The painting was done with cinnabar (scarlet quicksilver ore), of which they had an abundance in their Chisos Mountain camps." Harston further indicates that other colors appearing prominently on these shields are yellow ocher and various shades of blue.

20in (51cm) wide

$5,300-6,000   BON

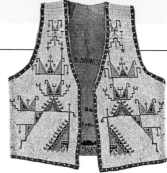

A Sioux beaded man's vest, sinew and thread sewn, fully beaded on hide, with four vertical arrangements of branching geometric devices on a white ground, stamped in the interior in ink "C. R. Darling."

21½in (54.5cm) long

$2,500-3,100   BON

A pair of Cheyenne moccasins, beaded with buffalo tracks on the toe, with geometric devices running about the sole.

10¼in (26cm) long

$1,100-1,350   BON

A Northern Plains or Plateau pipe bag, possibly Nez Perce, pigmented with ocher and beaded with vining foliate designs on each side, suspending hide fringe wrapped in yarn, string and/or ribbon.

35½in (90cm) long

$4,000-4,700   BON

ESSENTIAL REFERENCE—NAVAJO WEAVING

Descendants of the Athabascan race, the Navajo emerged in the southwest of what is now the United States in around the 15thC.

- **Originally a nomadic tribe of hunter-gatherers, they eventually began to settle, and in doing so adopted many of the farming and artistic practices of the Pueblo people.**
- **Alongside pottery, weaving skills learned from the Pueblo became the primary artistic medium of the Navajo, and toward the end of the 19thC their hitherto utilitarian blankets made for use as cloaks, dresses, and saddle blankets became increasingly sophisticated and featured—in both blankets and rugs—far more complex geometric designs.**
- **Moreover, as the commercial market for their weaving grew, the Navajo sometimes began to incorporate animal, human, and plant-form imagery into the patterns— particularly notable among these were representations of spirit figures ("Yeis"), corn, birds, livestock, and horses.**

A Navajo Yei tapestry, with a single standing Yei figure, framed within a stepped border with crosses, fringe at the corners.

56½in (143.5cm) high

$8,500-10,000   BON

A Navajo late classic child's blanket, with seven vertical zigzag bands in alternating indigo and cream, on an aniline-dyed red ground.

49in (124.5cm) long

$16,000-19,000   BON

A Navajo cuff bracelet, with five rows of ten square turquoise stones separated by silver drops, on five stamped bands.

2½in (6.5cm) wide 4¾oz

$2,000-2,500   BON

A Navajo ketoh, with stamped and repoussé decoration, with turquoise cabochons of various sizes.

3¾in (9.5cm) high 4½oz

$2,000-2,500   BON

A Navajo (Diné) belt, by Victor Moses Begay, with a rectangular buckle adorned with two concentric rows of teardrop and circular turquoise, six conformingly-designed oblong conchas and seven butterfly spacers, signed "VMB."

36½in (92.5cm) long 11⅞oz

$2,700-3,200   BON

A Kawaiisu polychrome bottleneck basket, with diamonds and hourglass forms, quill outlines on the shoulder, the body encircled by dual zigzag bands, with a paper G. A. Steiner Collection label on the underside inscribed "G24."

8¾in (22cm) diam

$17,500-20,000   **BON**

A 20thC Mono Lake Paiute degikup basket, by Lucy Telles, polychrome decorated with butterflies, diamond, and triangle pendants.

7in (18cm) diam

$7,000-8,000   **BON**

A Northwest Coast bentwood box, possibly Tlingit, with painted form-line animals on each face, including a beaver, a frog, and two others, the tapering lid with inset operculum shells, pigment loss, areas of overpaint, base replaced.

27¾in (70.5cm) high

$8,500-10,000   **BON**

A fine Northwest Coast wood pipe bowl, possibly Haida, the deep bowl lined with a thin copper barrier, the body relief carved with repeat registers of form-line beaver motifs, drilled through the side for a pipe stem, the underside with a rounded humanoid face framed by fine parallel grooves.

The style of fine grooving framing the face is an ancient Northwest Coast surface technique that appears to predate the development of form-line relief carving, and it can still be seen on the rims of some carved bowls and bent-corner dishes, along with frontlets and other objects. A pipe bowl sharing the same basic form as the present item can be found in the collection of the National Museum of the American Indian (object no. 2/8704), purchased by George Heye from George T. Emmons ca. 1911. The reproduction of the original catalog inventory card describes the object as a "Feast pipe representing a killer-whale. Haida workmanship."

3¾in (9.5cm) diam

$50,000-56,000   **BON**

A Northwest Coast horn ladle, probably Tlingit or Haida, the deep bowl attached by horn rivets to the separate handle, the shaft carved with a series of surmounted totemic avian, animal, and humanoid figures, terminating with the head of a raven, the eyes and other details accented with abalone shell inlay.

16½in (42cm) long

$4,300-5,600   **BON**

A Northwest Coast land otter effigy pendant, probably Tlingit or Tsimshian, carved from a large animal tooth, the crouching otter executed in relief with pronounced ribs and form-line details, a wide tongue emerging from the mouth and extending backward across the snout, pierced for suspension.

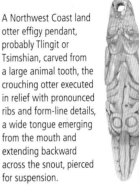

4¾in (12cm) long

$4,300-5,600   **BON**

ESSENTIAL REFERENCE—A TLINGIT NAAXEIN

The Tlingit are an indigenous people of the Pacific Northwest coast of North America. Art and spirituality are intertwined and play a substantial role in Tlingit culture, and even everyday objects, such as baskets, boxes, bowls, and spoons, feature sophisticated decoration and are imbued with spiritual power and other cultural beliefs. The Tlingit are, however, best known for their weaving and, especially, their "Naaxein" (Chilkat blankets). Made from cedar bark and wool—the latter mostly from mountain goats—they emerged in the early 19thC and were a radical departure from the hitherto geometric patterns on white grounds. They were replaced by bold, curvilinear clan crests woven in blacks and yellows (and sometimes a bluish green) on pentagonal-shaped fields. To achieve this, a complex and unique form of twining that was capable of reproducing the clan crests in the flowing style originally used on carved and painted regalia was invented. The weaving process, including the preparation of the materials, for just a single crested robe was purportedly more than a year, and so it is no surprise that these robes have become icons of the indigenous culture of the Pacific Northwest—a fact fully reflected in, as the example shown illustrates, the prices they can command when they come up for auction.

A Tlingit "Naaxein" (Chilkat blanket), yellow cedar bark, mountain goat wool, and dyes.

ca. 1880   70in (178cm) wide

$33,000-42,000   **WAD**

A Northwest Coast raven rattle, with wings partly outstretched, supporting a reclining human figure connected to a frog on its back, further carved with the face of a hawk and another creature on the underside, with repairs.

12½in (32cm) long

$31,000-37,000   **BON**

A Haida silver spoon, attributed to Charles Edenshaw/Da.a xiigang (1839-1920), with a form-line and hachured loon along the handle, the beak forming the terminal, with a similarly executed marine animal adorning the back of the bowl.

4¼in (11cm) long ⅜ oz

$5,500-7,000   **BON**

TRIBAL ART

Judith Picks

This particularly splendid 19thC "hudoq" (dance) mask was made by the indigenous Kayan Dayak people of Kalimantan, the Indonesian portion of the island of Borneo. It is decorated with red, white, and black pigments, with inset mirror eyes and hair, and adorned with a basketlike rattan headdress embellished with five black-and-white hornbill feathers. It would have been traditionally worn, along with an equally flamboyant banana leaf costume, during an agricultural ceremony—to mark planting, harvesting, or both. The Kayan people believe that rice, their staple food, has a soul that can be attacked by evil spirits, and the mask and costume were intended to scare those spirits away. Even just looking at it stationary on a stand, I am absolutely certain it would have worked every time!

A Kayan Dayak Hudoq mask, Kalimantan, Borneo, the back of the mask with a mouth stick, on a stand.

32in (81cm) high

$4,300-5,000   **WW**

A Solomon Islands Melanesia currency, clam shell tridacna.

7¾in (19.5m) wide

$1,000-1,250   **WW**

A Chambri Lakes suspension hook, Papua New Guinea, carved masks with cowrie shell inset eyes, with pigment decoration.

28¼in (71.5cm) long

$2,500-3,100   **WW**

A Marquesas Islands bowl and cover, Polynesia, with allover low-relief carved symbols, tiki-head handles, one pair with hands, raised on a short spreading foot.

15½in (39.5cm) wide

$4,300-5,000   **WW**

A Boiken dish, Papua New Guinea, with relief-carved decoration including two masks, pierced for attachment, on a stand.

17½in (44.5cm) diam

$500-625   **WW**

A basalt stone pounder, Marquesas Islands, French Polynesia, with a rounded base, patination on the handle from use, remnants of an old label on the reverse.

7¾in (19.5cm) high

$3,350-4,000   **L&T**

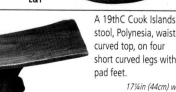

A 19thC Cook Islands stool, Polynesia, waisted curved top, on four short curved legs with pad feet.

17¼in (44cm) wide

$5,000-6,200   **WW**

A breastplate ornament, "Kap Kap," Nggela Sule, Solomon Islands, tridacna clam and turtle shell with coconut fibers, overlaid with an intricately carved filigree of shell featuring a series of six allover pattern bands, each with a differing wave motif, with a vegetal string linking the two parts terminating on the reverse with a series of disk-shaped shell beads.

5½in (14cm) diam

$1,250-1,700   **L&T**

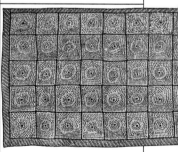

A Niue Island barkcloth, Polynesia, with 40 painted squares, each with a radiating dash design in blue and black pigment.

143¼in (364cm) wide

$10,000-12,500   **WW**

A Maori "Patu Onewa" club, New Zealand, graywacke, with a ribbed butt and a pierced handle.

12½in (32cm) long

$4,000-4,700   **WW**

A Maori "Patu Wahaika" hand club, New Zealand, with allover notch and linear carved decoration, with a standing tiki and a head, with haliotis shell eyes.

13½in (34cm) long

$800-1,050   **WW**

ESSENTIAL REFERENCE—"HEI-TIKI"

Hei-tiki (or just tiki) are traditional pendant ornaments crafted by the Maori, the Polynesian first settlers of New Zealand. In the form of a human fetus, they symbolize fertility, were primarily worn by women, and were handed down from generation to generation. They are mostly carved from "inanga," a hard nephrite related to jade, found on New Zealand's South Island, and which the Maori call "pounamu" after their name for the South Island: Te Wai Pounamu. It is also often referred to as "greenstone"—purportedly because, when Captain Cook "discovered" New Zealand in 1769, he documented noticing the Maori laboriously "working a green-color stone." Although essentially green in hue, it does display considerable tonal variations—from a pale, grayish green to a dark, mottled, almost brownish green, and many shades in between. It also can vary significantly in terms of translucency and opacity. Although the example shown here no longer has them, almost all hei-tiki were originally made with inlaid color eyes, usually fashioned from shells, such as haliotis (better known as abalone).

A Maori pendant, "Hei-Tiki," 19thC or earlier, New Zealand, carved and polished inanga pounamu, with carved features, the head angled with recessed eyes originally for the insertion of shell inlays, with two horizontal lozenges indicating the feet, successive tapering perforation holes, the original now worn through.

4¼in (10.5cm) high

$15,000-19,000   **L&T**

An Aboriginal carved wood shield, Western Australia, the front with grooved parallel bands running vertically and diagonally, with similar decoration on the reverse, the center section unadorned and bearing an integral handle.

25½in (64.5cm) high

$875-1,250   **L&T**

A 19thC Aboriginal Rainforest sword club, Queensland, Australia.

55in (140cm) long

$1,000-1,250   **WW**

An Aboriginal carved wood "Tjuringa," Australia, the front with incised geometric motifs, the reverse with incised emu tracks, covered in an ocher wash, raised on a custom-made mount.

28½in (72.5cm) high

$625-750   **L&T**

A 19thC Aboriginal "pineapple" head club, Queensland, Australia, with a spike finial, the shaft with fine carved grooves and with a cut textured grip.

29in (73.5cm) long

$625-750   **WW**

A 19thC Aboriginal spear thrower, "Woomera," Victoria, Australia, with stylized carving on both sides, the front with emu tracks and red pigment, the ends with gum, one with remains of the bone spike.

27¼in (69cm) long

$450-550   **WW**

A flintlock 16-bore land service pistol, the barrel molded on the breech, action with crown over "GR," brass trigger guard, brass butt cap, walnut stock, and steel swivel ram.

15¾in (40cm) long

$800-950 HT

A French 1786 pattern pistolet de bord, the lock plate stamped "J" and signed, the barrel stamped faintly "C.109," "MLE AN9," and "P" with a crown device over.

14in (35.5cm) wide

$1,050-1,250 CM

An English 1796 pattern 10-bore Tower flintlock heavy dragoon pistol, border engraved, rounded lock plate with crowned "GR" and "Tower" marks, iron ramrod below, no visible serial number.

barrel 9in (23cm) long

$1,500-1,900 CHEF

An East India Company (EIC) flintlock 16-bore holster pistol, round barrel with EIC lugs on top with proof marks, maker's stamp (crown over "I.R."), and "REA 1802," for John Rea working at 122 Minories making pistols for the Navy, EIC mark and "REA" on lock, unusual rounded grip with brass butt cap and trigger guard, minor fracture repairs.

This is a variation of the Short Cavalry pistol of 1778 to 1807.

1802

$875-1,000 LOCK

barrel 9in (23cm) long

An East India Company flintlock ship's store pistol, lock dated "1808" and with the EIC lion, brass furniture, steel ramrod, walnut stock with apron and "S" side plate.

1808　　*barrel 9in (23cm) long*

$750-875 LOCK

A flintlock dueling pistol, by H. Nock, octagonal barrel with London proof marks and "HN Patent" (for Nocks patent breech), gold line and gold poinçon marked "Nock London" beneath a crown, finely checkered grip with flat sides and spur trigger guard.

Henry Nock was a London gunmaker based at various addresses from 1770 to 1804, and at 10 Ludgate Street from 1784-1804. He was "Gunsmith-in-Ordinary" to King George III in 1789, and made Master of the Gunmakers' Company in 1802 (see Blackmore, "A Dictionary of London Gunmakers 1350-1850," Phaidon Christies, 1986).

ca. 1790　　*barrel 10in (25.5cm) long*

$3,700-4,300 LOCK

A flintlock dueling pistol, by H. Richards, octagonal barrel with gold line and platinum touch hole, rain-proof pan, roller on the frizzen spring, spur trigger guard and half-cock safety, engraved barrel tang and trigger guard bow, maker's address "39 Fish Street Hill, London" on barrel, with London proof marks below.

$2,900-3,350 LOCK

A pepperbox percussion pistol, by Liversidge Gainsbro, with a cluster of six barrels, overhammer action with fine foliate scrollwork, maker's name on the action tang, finely checkered walnut grip and patch box on the metal butt cap.

9½in (24cm) long

$450-550 HT

A 19thC French Novelle Fils rifled percussion target pistol, Limoges, octagonal barrel, the hammer, lock plates, tang, trigger guard, and butt cap with scroll engraving and the maker's name inlaid in gold.

barrel 9in (23cm) long

$500-625 CHEF

A Victorian percussion cap six-shot pepperbox pistol, the frame with scroll engraving.

barrels 4¼in (11cm) long

$500-625 CHEF

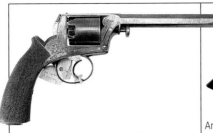

A percussion 5-shot revolver, the frame engraved "Imperial Patent Revolver," Adams Patent 1851 pattern, self-cocking revolver, unfluted cylinder, acanthus scrolling on frame, much original blue remaining, checkered walnut grip.

barrel 7in (18cm) long

$1,050-1,250   **LOCK**

An Allen & Wheelock .32 rim-fire revolver, the octagonal barrel with maker's name and address, windage-adjustable front sight, groove rear sight, front action stamped "JULY 3. 1860," side hammer, sheath trigger, six-shot cylinder, and two-piece walnut grip.

9¼in (23.5cm) long

$400-450   **HT**

A Smith & Wesson .32 rim-fire revolver, the barrel stamped with maker's name and address, fixed front sight, notch rear sight, top hinge-opening mechanism revealing a deeply fluted five-shot cylinder, sheath trigger and two-piece wood grip.

8¼in (21cm) long

$375-500   **HT**

A Smith & Wesson .32 rim-fire revolver, the barrel stamped with maker's name and address, fixed front sight, top hinge-opening mechanism revealing a deeply fluted five-shot cylinder, sheath trigger, and two-piece wood grip.

8¼in (21cm) long

$500-625   **HT**

A rare "True Blue" .32 rim-fire revolver, the barrel stamped with the name, fixed front sight, groove rear sight, side-loading groove, five-shot fluted cylinder, sheath trigger, and two-piece walnut grip.

7in (18cm) long

$290-340   **HT**

A flintlock blunderbuss, made from a "Brown Bess" musket, the barrel with English proof marks, bell mouth, large heavy lock, shortened handrail stock with brass furniture, lock marked "Tower" and with a crown, modern brass-tipped rammer "S" plate on reverse of stock.

barrel 9in (23cm) long

$410-475   **LOCK**

An 18thC French blunderbuss, the barrel with engraved tang, converted to percussion cap.

32¾in (83cm) long

$875-1,000   **CHEF**

A W. Jeffery & Son 20-bore side-plate side-by-side shotgun, the barrels with the maker's name, scroll etched action, ejectors, automatic safety, blued trigger guard, walnut stock, and shaped horn forend tip, in a fitted Brady case.

43¾in (111cm) long

$1,500-1,900   **HT**

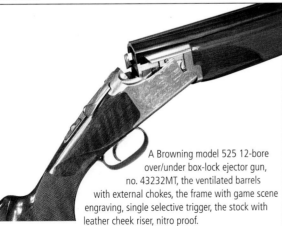

A Browning model 525 12-bore over/under box-lock ejector gun, no. 43232MT, the ventilated barrels with external chokes, the frame with game scene engraving, single selective trigger, the stock with leather cheek riser, nitro proof.

barrels 30in (76cm) long

$800-950   **CHEF**

A deactivated Inglis "Bren MK.II NO.5" .303 light machine gun, with wood carrying handle, removable magazine, adjustable rear sight, moving bolt, bipod, and wood rear stock, date stamped "1944," serial no. "12T7705," along with a spare magazine and EU certificate "170980."

1944   *46¼in (117.5cm) long*

$1,600-2,100   **HT**

A mid- to late-18thC Scottish basket-hilted cavalry officer's broadsword, the steel hilt of six panels decorated with lozenges and points, large wrist guard, the leather-covered grip with wire binding and red felt liner, bun-shaped pommel, double-edge blade applied with engraved gold plaque.

The applied 19thC gold plaque reads: "The claymore was once the property of the Unfortunate Prince Charles and worn by him at the Battle of Culloden, after his defeat it fell into the hands of CAPt DRUMMOND of his suite who gave it to the late ROBt GRAHAM of Gartmore Esq." Although the information on the plaque surely cannot be correct—this sword is neither a claymore nor a pattern known at the time of the '45—it demonstrates the great historical value placed on relics of this period by the early 19thC.

38¼in (97cm) long

$5,000-5,600   **L&T**

An 18th/19thC Turkish/Ottoman short sword, with studded chevron-grooved wood hilt, the metal guard with down-curved quillons, relief decorated with animal and leaf ornaments, slightly curved blade with partial double fuller on both sides.

32in (81.5cm) long

$1,500-1,900   **CHEF**

A 19thC Caucasian Russian silver and niello-mounted shashka, the curved engraved blade with a shaped grip and cloven pommel, within a leather-and silver-mounted scabbard, with two suspension loops, signed on each side within a lozenge, knocks, dents.

37½in (95.5cm) long

$3,000-3,500   **LOCK**

A Japanese mid-Muromachi Period wakizashi, attributed to Sukemitsu, Shimada, curved blade, gunome hamon with Suangashi, deep bohi on both sides, signed tang with two peg holes, copper habaki, lobed iron tsuba, shakudo fuchi with repeating wave pattern, butterfly menuki, horn kashira, signed kozuka with goose design, ribbed saya in red lacquer, with paperwork, wood blade copy, shirasaya and modern stand.

22in (56cm) long

$3,000-3,500   **HT**

ESSENTIAL REFERENCE—CHARLES JAMES FOX

Charles James Fox (1749-1806) was the leading British Whig party statesman of the late 18thC, and political opponent of the Tory party prime pinister William Pitt the Younger. Fox's political career lasted more than 38 years, during which he championed the causes of religious minorities, liberty, and the French Revolution, and was a fierce opponent of King George III. The king's eldest son George, Prince of Wales, was a Fox ally and regularly wore a buff-color vest, indicating his political support for the Whig party. Edmund Burke's eulogy of Fox, in the House of Commons, after he took on the tyranny of the East India Company, on December 1, 1783 reads: "He well knows what snares are spread about his path, from personal animosity … and possibly from popular delusion. But he has put to hazard his ease, his security, his interest, his power, even his … popularity … He is traduced and abused for his supposed motives. He will remember that obloquy is a necessary ingredient in the composition of all true glory: he will remember … that calumny and abuse are essential parts of triumph … He may live long, he may do much, but here is the summit. He never can exceed what he does this day." Some 170 years later this quotation was used by President (at the time Senator) John F. Kennedy as the frontispiece to his book "Profiles in Courage" (Harper, 1956).

A late-18th/early-19thC George III gilt-etched and blued-steel presentation sword, "Sword Of Prudence," wire-bound grip, gilt-metal vase-shaped pommel, with the original wood and gilt-metal scabbard, engraved on the gilt-metal quillons on one side "SWORD OF PRUDENCE," on the other "Presented to the Rt Hon.ble C. J. Fox, with the warmest respect/BY A BRITON & A LOVER of his COUNTRY," with double-edge blued steel and parcel-gilt blade, gilt etched on one side "Consider well weigh Strictly Right & Wrong,/ Resolve not quick, but once resolv'd be Strong," above a martial trophy and British emblem, the other side gilt etched with the figures of "Prudence," "Justice," and "Britannia," original crimson fabric covering worn.

$5,000-6,200   **DUK**

A Japanese Edo Period katana, attributed to Kawachi Daijo Fujiwara Masahiro, Hizen, curved blade, gunome hamon, signed tang with single peg hole, copper habaki, unryu fuchi, and kashira, dragon menuki, koshirae saya, and tsuka, with paperwork, wood blade copy, shirasaya, and stand.

40¼in (102cm) long

$8,000-9,500   **HT**

A fine Victorian London Scottish officer's dirk, bi knife marked "J MEARBECK SHEFFIELD," the finely carved black wood grip with studded decoration, the haunches applied with engraved mounts, pommel with engraved pin top, the single fullered blade with scalloped back edge and spear point, the leather-covered wood scabbard with engraved mounts, set with a bi knife and fork.

16½in (42cm) long

$2,900-3,350   **L&T**

A German SA dagger, by Richard Herder, with Rohm presentation etched blade, maker's mark, service wear.

$1,100-1,500   **LOCK**

A Naval General Service Medal 1793-1840, named to "Hon. G.G.Waldegrave. Capt. R.N.," with rare "AMANTHEA, 25 JULY 1810" clasp.

Vice Admiral Granville George Waldegrave, 2nd Baron Radstock CB (September 24, 1786-May 11 1857), joined the Royal Navy in 1798 and rose through the ranks, becoming a Captain in 1807, Rear Admiral in 1841, Vice Admiral of the White in 1853, and the Red in 1855. From 1831-37, he was a Naval Aide-de-Camp to King William IV, then to Queen Victoria from 1837-41.
$40,000-45,000   CHEF

A French Legion D'Honneur, early type, chips in white and blue enamel.

1816   *1¾in (4.5cm) long*
$250-310   LOCK

A Victoria Baltic Campaign (1854-55) medal, named to "Jules Deroy/Austerlistz," with a miniature Baltic medal.
$500-625   CHEF

An India General Service (1854-95) medal, with "PERSIA" clasp, named to "Lieut. R.P.Mainwaring 20th Regt. Bombay N.I.."
$700-800   CHEF

An Egypt (1882) medal, with "THE NILE 1884-85" bar, named for "1945 Pte R R Baxter 20th Husrs," undated.
$300-375   LOCK

A George V Military Cross, unnamed as issued, in original fitted case.
$780-830   LOCK

A Greek military dress uniform, belonging to Edward John Trelawny and worn during the Greek War of Independence, comprising a jacket, an embroidered linen vest, a scarlet wool sash, linen breeches, a scarlet felt cap, nickel bridle mounts, a circular cast-metal target brooch, and a cast-nickel sword hilt.

Edward John Trelawny (1792-1881) was an English gentleman and novelist, best known for his friendships with Romantic poets Percy Bysshe Shelley and Lord Byron. In 1823, Trelawny joined Byron in the Greek War of Independence, where he commanded a troop of 25 Albanian soldiers under the Eastern Greek warlord Odysseas Androutsos. Following his campaign in the mountains, Trelawny married Androutsos' half-sister. Upon his return to England in 1831, he documented his adventures in his semi-fictional autobiography "Adventures of a Younger Son."

1821-32
$21,000-25,000   SWO

A late-19thC 2nd Battalion Coldstream Guards side drum, the brass body painted on one side with crest and battle honors, the other side unpainted, stamped "HAWKES & SON MAKERS LONDON 2238," striped wood tension hoop, removable glass top with holes, raised on a 1930s walnut stand, chips, scratches.

20in (51cm) diam
$1,700-2,200   MART

An important World War II SOE Jolly Roger sailing standard, comprised of blue and white cotton fields separated by a red cross, each field embroidered with symbols: a yellow flower and a leafy branch, a caduceus, a constellation of dots over a wavey line, and a black skull and crossbones, the red cross centered with a white sailboat.

From the SOE vessel "Catina," part of the Force 133 flotilla called "the Levant Fishing Patrol," captained by Dr. Darrell Wilkinson, which carried out operations in the Adriatic during World War II. Its operations formed part of the basis for the 1961 movie "The Guns of Navarone." Formerly in the collection of Dr. Darrell Wilkinson.

35¾in (91cm) wide
$2,100-2,500   SWO

A Roman marble head of a youth, probably 2ndC AD, the head turned slightly to dexter, with tightly curled hair, on a turned dark metal column support, set into a square pedestal on a square plinth.

12¼in (31cm) high

$27,000-32,000   **DUK**

A pair of 1stC BC/1stC AD ancient Egyptian Roman Era eye inlays, Egypt, composed of white sclerae overlaid with dark glass to form the iris, framed by deep blue faience brows above, on a custom-made mount.

5¾in (14.5cm) wide

$3,100-3,700   **L&T**

A 3rd-5thC Gandharan stucco fragmentary face of Buddha, Northwest India, with serene downward gaze, traces of polychromy, chips, wear.

7¾in (19.5cm) high

$1,100-1,500   **CHEF**

A Khmer red sandstone head of Shiva, in Baphuon style, possibly 11thC, with fine detail and braided hair.

10¾in (27.5cm) high

$2,900-3,350   **CHEF**

A black stone Buddha head, in Northern Qi Sui Dynasty style.

10¼in (26cm) high

$4,300-5,000   **CHEF**

A Thai stucco head of Buddha, Haripunjaya School, probably 13thC, with soft gaze and tightly coiled hair., mounted on a stand

10¾in (27.5cm) high

$700-800   **CHEF**

A 1st-3rdC Gandharan gray schist-garlanded putti stair riser, of four infants beneath dogtooth molding.

9¼in (23.5cm) wide

$800-950   **CHEF**

A 2nd/3rdC Gandharan gray schist figure of a standing Buddha, with partial aureole, wearing robes, missing arm, chiseled at back.

8¼in (21cm) high

$450-550   **CHEF**

A 3rd-5thC Gandharan green schist figurative panel, arranged as three registers, each of two Buddhist figures in niches.

8in (20.5cm) high

$410-460   **CHEF**

A Bronze Age marble idol, Iberia, rendered with shallow chevron incisions, the eliptical head with single perforation in the center, raised on a custom-made mount.

ca. 2000-1800 BC   *7in (18cm) high*

$5,300-5,800   **L&T**

An obsidian and gold torpedo vase, Phoenician or Egyptian, Near East, with dual lugs below the shoulders overlaid with gold foil, the shoulders horizontal to the body and topped with the disk rim, also overlaid with thin gold sheet, on a custom-made mount (not pictured).

1000-500 BC   *5in (12.5cm) high*

$15,500-18,000   **L&T**

A Corinthian black figure terra-cotta juglet, Greece, attributed to the Brussels Painter, the teardrop-shaped body decorated with a black figure of a swan, trumpet mouth and miniature strap handle, on a rounded base.

ca. 620-590 BC   *3¼in (8.5cm) high*

$2,500-3,000   **L&T**

A 4thC BC Apulian red figure Pelike, painted with the portrait of a woman, the reverse with a nude man carrying a situla and staff, restored.

6in (15cm) high

$550-700   **GORL**

A mid-4thC BC ancient Greek terra-cotta hydria, Magna Graecia, with vertical ribbing on the body, an applied laurel wreath encircling the neck, dotted ovolo on the rim, dual upturned handles, and a single vertical handle reaching from the neck to the shoulder, on a disk foot.

14¾in (37.5cm) high

$4,000-4,500   **L&T**

A 1stC AD Roman glass perfume bottle, translucent purple with opaque white marbled mosaic pattern.

4¼in (11cm) high

$1,500-1,900   **L&T**

A 1stC AD Roman pale green glass "LotusBud" beaker, Eastern Mediterranean, probably Tyre, blown in a three-part mold with separate base section, on a flat base with concentric ring and dot, with five rows of eight almond-shaped "lotus bud" bosses in relief.

Although traditionally the nodules on these distinctive beakers are referred to as "lotus buds," it has been suggested (Stern, "Roman Mold-Blown Glass," L'Erma di Bretschneider, 1995) that, in fact, they represent the knots of Hercules' wooden club. As well as his legendary strength, the demigod was renowned for his drinking abilities. As such, it seems probable that the form of these beakers was a visual pun alluding to the drinker's own prowess with alcohol. For a similar example, see Detroit Institute of Arts, accession no. 44.4.

5in (12.5cm) high

$9,500-10,500   **L&T**

A 1stC BC/1stC AD ancient Egyptian Graeco-Roman Period glass inlay fragment of a comedy mask, Egypt, mosaic glass, on a turquoise ground, the white-faced figure with highly elaborate red coiffure tied with multicolor bands.

1in (2.5cm) high

$5,300-5,800   **L&T**

A 5th-7thC AD Sasanian glass bottle, Western Asia, cut and applied glass, the body with applied disks and profuse iridescence, on a disk foot.

3½in (9cm) high

$2,500-3,100   **L&T**

ESSENTIAL REFERENCE—UPRIGHT PIANOS

In marked contrast to their "grand" equivalents, for a long time upright pianos were, in general, perceived as being ungainly in appearance, and it was not until the mid-1890s that some designers began to reimagine the form. M. H. Baillie Scott's innovation, which was thought to derive from the form of an Elizabethan strongbox, was to enclose the keyboard, music stand, and candleholders behind broad doors that rationalized the shape of the instrument. The result was a piece of drawing room furniture that was, and is, both cleverly functional and aesthetically pleasing. Baillie Scott first exhibited the piano at the Arts and Crafts exhibition of 1896. Three years later he moved to the Isle of Man, and hence this form of the upright piano became known as the "Manxman."

A John Broadwood & Sons Arts and Crafts "Manxman" oak piano and stool, London, by Mackay Hugh Baillie Scott (1865-1945), ebonized and ivory keys, brass and wrought-steel candle sconces, oak stool with brass hinges, later but period upholstered seat, with ivorine label for "LIBERTY & CO," recently refurbished.
ca. 1904 58¼in (148cm) wide
$4,200-4,600 **L&T**

A Steinway & Sons Patent Grand Construction mahogany cased piano, New York, no. 157302, on squared tapered legs with spade feet and brass casters, repolished, possible repainting, sun bleaching, two hairline cracks in keys.
Ivory Act certification no. HHTJMZ93
58¼in (148cm) wide
$8,500-11,000 **GORL**

A mid-19thC giltwood, satinwood, and rosewood "Grecian" concert harp, by J. Schwieso, brass-mounted satinwood soundboard, fluted columnar pillar, relief-carved angels on the capital, eight pedals, five sound holes, 43 strings, with brass plaque signed on one side "Schwieso & Co., Improvement, No. 263 Regent Street London," the reverse with "Schwieso late foreman to S. Erard, No. 417," no stringing.
67in (170cm) high
$1,250-1,700 **GORL**

An English boxwood and ivory double flageolet, by Bainbridge, 85 Holborn Hill, London, New Patent, in a mahogany case.
Ivory Act certification no. R1KL7REG
$1,100-1,500 **GHOU**

A set of silver-plated bagpipes, black hardwood with ivory mounts and engraved plated collars, plain black velvet bag, chanter lacking.
CITES certification no. GQAT6YLS
$2,000-2,400 **L&T**

A Holton Professional Model gold-lacquered double French horn, model no. H181, with case, scratches.
$750-1,000 **GHOU**

A Henri Selmer MK VI gold-lacquered tenor saxophone, serial no. 105762, with case, crook, and mouthpiece, plating loss, pitting, pads worn.
1963
$5,500-6,700 **GHOU**

A 19th/20thC full-size violin, with a two-piece back and purfling on both sides, the bow stamped for "Jérome Thibouville Lamy," the stick with an ebony frog inset with mother-of-pearl eyes and a white metal mount, the ebony adjuster with two white metal bands, with a black lacquered shaped case.
23½in (60cm) long
$2,900-3,500 **DAWS**

An Italian cello, labeled "Officina Claudio Monteverde, Cremona," signed and dated "1923" on label, the two-piece back of medium/fine curl with similar wood on the sides and head, the table of a medium-width grain, the varnish of a dark plum-red color on a golden ground, with bow and soft case, minor repairs.
1923 29¾in (75.5cm) long
$11,000-15,000 **GHOU**

A 20thC violin, by Heinrich Th. Heberlein Jr., with a two-piece back, bearing labels in the interior for "Heinrich Th. Heberlein Jr., Markneukirchen 1930, Copie Ferdinandus Gagliano 1780," damages.
back 14¼in (36cm) long
$1,700-2,200 **CA**

A C. F. Martin Limited Edition HD-40MS Marty Stuart Signature acoustic guitar, made in USA, serial no. 594691, Indian rosewood back and sides, natural spruce top, autographed "To Doctor Steve - Thanks!, Marty Stuart," mahogany neck, ebony fretboard with Marty Stuart customized inlay, in original hard case, minor marks.

Number 230 of a limited-edition run of 250 Marty Stuart Signature guitars released worldwide.

1997

$4,200-4,700   GHOU

A C. F. Martin 000-28EC Eric Clapton Signature Model acoustic guitar, made in USA, serial no. 1xxxxx8, rosewood back and sides, natural spruce top, ebony fretboard, in original hard case, minor marks.

2006

$3,700-4,300   GHOU

A Santa Cruz H acoustic guitar, Indian rosewood back and sides, natural spruce top, mahogany neck, ebony fretboard, in original hard case, scratches.

1998

$3,100-3,700   GHOU

A C. F. Martin D-42JC Johnny Cash Signature Model limited-edition acoustic guitar, made in USA, serial no. 6xxxx7, 1 of 80 made, ebony finish body, ebony fretboard, in original hard case, surface marks.

While Martin initially anticipated 200 of this limited-edition model, only 80 were made. Hand signed by Johnny Cash and C. F. Martin IV on the soundhole label.

1998

$15,000-17,500   GHOU

A Fender Montego 1 hollow-body electric guitar, made in USA, light tobacco sunburst finish, maple back and sides, spruce top, maple neck, ebony fretboard, with original hard case.

A guitar designed by the renowned Roger Rossmeisl, fewer than 100 of the Fender Montego model were made.

1971

$9,500-11,000   GHOU

Pat Smear's personal Gretsch White Falcon hollow-body electric guitar, made in Japan, serial no. 906593-39, Classic White Falcon finish body with orange sparkle binding, ebony fretboard, modified Cadillac tailpiece, modified switching, the body with pillow-filling interior, in original hard case bearing white tape, one inscribed "Stays on the bus," the other "Falcon."

Used by Dave Grohl in the video for the Foo Fighters' 1997 single "Monkey Wrench," and used by Pat Smear on "The Color and the Shape" album recordings. The guitar was also used on various Foo Fighters tours.

1990

$59,500-67,000   GHOU

A Fender Telecaster electric guitar, made in USA, serial no. 0xxx2, Clive Brown butterscotch, lightly aged refinished body, '56 pencil date on bridge cavity, lightly aged maple neck with XA-5-56 pencil mark, decal probably replaced, maple fretboard, later switch and capacitors (originals retained), '56 dated potentiometers, in a later hard case.

1956

$21,000-25,000   GHOU

A Fender Precision Bass guitar, made in USA, serial no. 8xxx5, Olympic white refinished body (over Olympic white or blond), maple neck, rosewood fretboard, with contemporary hard case, missing bridge cover, scratch plate and bridge plate screws replaced with incorrect flathead type, checking, blemishes, light wear.

CITES certification no. 627180/02

1962

$7,000-7,500   GHOU

A Fender Custom Shop Dennis Galuszka Master Built Custom Stratocaster NOS electric guitar, made in USA, serial no. CZxxxxx9, shallow-carved gun-checkering on a natural walnut body, the neck walnut '56 light V profile with oil finish, in original hard case with certificate and tags.

A one-off by Galuszka, and named the "Guntar," because it was decorated like an antique gun.

2008

$14,000-17,500   GHOU

A Gibson Custom Shop Jimmy Page Signature EDS-1275 double-neck electric guitar, serial no. 0x0, cherry red finish, rosewood fretboards, with original hard case with tags, certificate, accessories, and original shipping box.

One of 250 Gibson master luthier-built re-creations of Page's original.

2007

$12,500-15,000   GHOU

A Gibson Les Paul Custom electric guitar, made in USA, serial no. 1xxxx0, black finish, ebony fretboard, in original Gibson hard case, refret, replacement bridge pickup (ca. 1990 Gibson humbucker pickup), bridge, control knobs, Grover tuners, and strap buttons, gold plating loss, case very worn.

Used by "Honest John Plain," formerly of the UK band "The Boys," and can be seen in the 2002 video single release of "Never Listen to Rumours."

1973

$6,000-7,500   GHOU

A red England vs. West Germany International Cap, red velvet with a white tassel and silvered braiding, embroidered with the England three-lion crest and "West Germany/1978," original recipient unknown.
1978
$800-950 GBA

George Best's blue Northern Ireland vs. Scotland, England, and Wales International Cap, blue velvet with a gilt tassel and gold-color braiding, embroidered "S/E/W/1969-70."

In George's 20th, 21st, and 22nd appearances for Northern Ireland, they lost 1-0 to Scotland, 3-1 to England, with George scoring, and 1-0 to Wales.
1969-70
$28,500-35,000 GBA

An England women's international soccer cap, awarded by the now defunct Women's Football Association, black, with WFA badge, undated, original recipient unknown.
$1,250-1,500 GBA

The MacGregor boxing trunks worn by Muhammad Ali during his match vs. Larry Holmes, "The Last Hurrah!" on October 2, 1980, white satin trunks with black trim, maker's label on the front elasticated waistband.

Provenance: From the collection of German sports reporter Hartmut Scherzer, who got them while in Ali's dressing room in Las Vegas after the fight. Ali's trainer Angelo Dundee was Mr. Scherzer's close friend and presented the trunks to him.
$8,500-10,000 CA

A Welsh International Rugby Union jersey, with embroidered Prince of Wales feathers, label to collar for "D L Davies, Swansea," and "J E Tucker."

Provenance: Consigned by the family of the England International hooker John Samuel "Sam" Tucker (1895-1973). The label on the interior refers to Sam Tucker's son, who swapped the jersey after one of six International matches with Wales in the 1920s.
1920s
$550-700 JON

Bobby Charlton's red No. 10 Manchester United vs. Real Madrid match worn short-sleeved jersey, Umbro collar labels, with V-neck collar.

This jersey was worn by Bobby Charlton in the friendly match against Real Madrid played on October 1, 1959, and was obtained by Ferenc Puskas as a swap with Charlton after the match. The clubs played five friendly matches over three years from 1959 to 1962, and were seen as vital parts of Matt Busby's rebuilding program at United after the Munich air crash.
1959
$47,000-55,000 GBA

Diego Maradona's blue-and-white striped Argentina No. 10 international jersey, Le Coq Sportif, short sleeved, with AFA badge.
ca. 1988
$10,000-12,500 GBA

Steven Gerrard's white, red, and blue No. 4 England vs. Slovakia match-worn long-sleeved jersey, Umbro, with button-up collar and embroidered three-lion badge inscribed "ENGLAND," with "England v. Slovakia 11.06.2003" decal, the reverse lettered "GERRARD," areas of pitch staining.
$1,900-2,200 GBA

A rare England vs. Ireland international program, played at West Bromwich Albion, October 21, 1922, internal paper brown, light vertical fold.
1922
$3,700-4,300 GBA

A program for the first UEFA European Cup final Real Madrid vs. Reims, played at the Parc des Princes, Paris, June 13, 1956.

The winners of the first UEFA European Cup were Real Madrid, who won the match 4-3.
1956
$4,700-5,600 GBA

A rare program printed for the possibility of a replay for the 1968 European Cup final Manchester United vs. Benfica, which would have been played at Arsenal FC if the final had ended in a draw.
1968
$12,500-15,000 GBA

A very rare autograph of British racing car driver Jim Clark, signed in ink on the back of a postcard depicting him with mechanics at the start of an international race on August 22, 1965, in a Ford Lotus.

Jim Clarke won World Championships 1963-65 and the Indianapolis 500 in 1965, but was tragically killed at the age of 32 in a Formula 2 race at Hockenheim.
$500-625 GBA

The 1996 NBA All-Star Game signed basketball, the official Spalding NBA ball signed by all 26 players and coaches, including Michael Jordan, Scottie Pippen, Shaquille O'Neal, and more.

The star-studded game was held on February 11, 1996, at the Alamodome in San Antonio, Texas, with Michael Jordon awarded the MVP.

1996

$3,500-4,200   **FRE**

The match ball used for the Argentina vs. Germany FIFA World Cup final played at the Estadio Azteca, Mexico City, June 29, 1986, autographed by Brazilian FIFA match referee Romualdo Arppi Filho and his assistants Erik Fredriksson and Bernylloa Morea, with a signed letter of provenance from Filho.

The white Adidas "Azteca" ball is formed of 32 pentagonal panels with a sinuous black-and-white design inspired by the architecture and murals of the Aztec civilization that flourished in center Mexico through the 14thC to the 16thC. Handsewn, it comprised an outer polyurethane layer and three inner layers, collectively intended to ensure the ball was hard-wearing, retained its shape, and was waterproof for a World Cup staged at high altitude on hard, sun-baked pitches and at a date in the calendar that coincided with Mexico's rainy season.

1986

$55,000-70,000   **GBA**

A Sandham Strudwick "Special" cricket bat autographed by the 1934 England and Australia Ashes teams, the front autographed by the Australia team, including Woodfull, O'Reilly, Fleetwood-Smith, Kippax, Bradman, Ponsford, Wall, Darling, and others, the England team including Wyatt, Hobbs, Ames, Hammond, Walters, Farnes, and others, the reverse of the bat autographed by the Surrey, Kent, Middlesex, Yorkshire, Sussex, and Lancashire cricket teams from the Australian tour.

$800-950   **GBA**

A rare winner's medal from first modern Olympics Games at Athens, designed by Jules Chaplain, signed, struck in silver for first place (second place medals were bronze), with a portrait of Zeus with the globe in his right hand, upon which stands the goddess of victory, Nike, holding an olive branch, on the left in Greek the script reads "OLYMPIA," the reverse with the Acropolis and the Parthenon, the inscription translated from the Greek reads "INTERNATIONAL OLYMPIC GAMES, ATHENS, 1896," original recipient unknown.

1896

$55,000-70,000   **GBA**

A Shane Warne signed red leather official cricket ball, with certificate of authenticity and photo proof of signing.

Autographed by the "King of Spin," who sadly passed away in 2022.

5½oz

$500-625   **GBA**

An Art Deco 1932-33 Bodyline Ashes Tour silver-cased traveling/fob watch, Birmingham, the wavy engine-turned square dial with black Arabic numerals enclosing subsidiary seconds dial, in a plain case with hanging loop, one side engraved "E PAYNTER FROM FERGY" (probably Bill Ferguson) and a kangaroo, the other "ASHES 1933" and Saint George and the Dragon.

Eddie Paynter (1901-79) hit the winning runs for England in the final test of the now infamous Bodyline Ashes Tour of 1932-33, and played with his controversial captain Douglas Jardine and fast bowlers Harold Larwood and Bill Voce. Bill Ferguson (1880-1957) acted as scorer and baggageman for England, and developed the radial "wagon-wheels" scoring chart.

1932   *1½in (4cm) wide*

$500-625   **HT**

A gilt-metal and enamel 1926 FA Cup steward's badge, inscribed "THE FOOTBALL ASSOCIATION, FINAL TIE 1926 STEWARD," with brooch fitting.

1926

$375-500   **GBA**

A rare cal. 262 split-second stopwatch chronograph used for the 1980 Olympic Games, movement numbered "14461XXX" twice (only used on movements that were sent to the Neuchâtel Observatory in Switzerland for chronometer testing and approval), in a Longines black leather protection case with a blued leather strap lanyard (to be used for hanging from the neck).

ca. 1970s   *2½in (6.5cm) diam*

$2,200-3,000   **CA**

A UEFA European Football Championship 1976 winner's medal, gilt-metal, inscribed "UEFA," the reverse with "CHAMPIONNAT D'EUROPE DE FOOTBALL 1976," recipient unknown, in a red fitted case.

Czechoslovakia defeated West Germany 5-3 on penalties, the winning kick and unforgettable penalty were by Panenka.

1976   *1¼in (3cm) diam*

$6,000-7,500   **GBA**

An early-20thC Mammoth Niblick golf club, with a hickory shaft, leather and whipped cord grip, retailed by Fortnum and Mason, molded marks for Fortnum Mason, Piccadilly, London, on the head.

35½in (90cm) long

$400-475   **SWO**

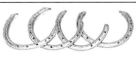

A silver and enamel match safe commemorating Tottenham Hotspur's achievement of winning the 1901 FA Cup as a nonleague team, with a portrait of a Tottenham soccer player circled by an inscription, hallmarked silver.

1¾in (4.5cm) high ½oz

$4,700-5,500   **GBA**

The aluminum racing plates worn by Desert Orchid when he won the Cheltenham Gold Cup, March 16, 1989, with letter of authentication from David Elsworth Racing dated March 17, 2010, slight wear.

The prerace favorite was ridden by Simon Sherwood, trained by David Elsworth and owned by Richard Burridge.

1989

$5,500-7,000   **GBA**

THE DECORATIVE ARTS MARKET

The market for Decorative Arts remains one of the leading sectors within the art and antiques market as a whole. From early Arts and Crafts, to Beaux Arts, to Art Nouveau, to later Arts and Crafts, and through Art Deco, these distinctive late-19thC to mid-20thC style movements continue to command the attention not only of already committed collectors, but also of a younger audience that is beginning to look around for alternatives to contemporary Modernism and, in many instances, are turning toward what their parents collected.

In a market as broad and diverse as Decorative Arts, there are inevitably variations in performance between and within its constituent parts. In early ceramics, for example, the Martin Brothers and William de Morgan continue to forge ahead on the price front, closely followed by Pilkingtons (especially its lusterwares) and Ruskin (particularly its high-fired and soufflé wares), while Doulton Lambeth and Moorcroft, after something of a recent downturn, seem to be on the up again.

Also of note is a newfound strength in all things Arts and Crafts. The market had softened earlier in the 21stC, but recently it has recovered ground and, in many instances, exceeded it: copper items, including decorative boxes, wall mirrors, and clocks, are proving particularly desirable, especially from the Newlyn, Cotswold, and Keswick schools, with their typical adornments of stylized floral and animal motifs—add Ruskin roundels or splashes of peacock enamel and the interest peaks.

There has also been a surge in demand for Arts and Crafts lighting: from table lamps to hall lanterns, those with original shades bringing in the strongest prices—as are the high-quality pieces by James Powell & Sons and the fluid designs of John Walsh Walsh. It is worth noting, too, that other iconic makers of both lighting and glass, and spanning Arts and Crafts, Art Nouveau, and Art Deco, continue to perform well—most notably Tiffany, Quezal, Loetz, and Daum.

Art Deco, with its distinctively clean lines, has also returned to form, especially among those looking for something "sharper" in style. It is also worth noting that, following a significant firming up in 2022 of laws banning or restricting the sale of ivory, there has been an upsurge in solid bronze and ceramic figures of the period. Classic Lorenzl figures, for example, showing slender female dancers in striking poses, appear to have filled that gap in the bronze and ivory market, while figures from the great Italian firms of Lenci and Essevi continue to smash auction records, and on their coat-tails a stream of other makers, such as Goldscheider, Katzhutte, and Keramos, offer equally daring figures for slightly more affordable sums.

As to Clarice Cliff—a perennial personal favorite—she continues to hold her position as the queen of Art Deco ceramics, with prices either holding or, in the case of the rarest examples, increasing. However, other makers contemporary to Cliff have also strengthened in the market over the last year or so. This has certainly been the case with, for example, Shelley—the clean, crisp lines and elegant forms of its Art Deco designs are enjoying a real resurgence of interest, especially among collectors in Japan buying through that ncreasingly important component of Decorative Arts sales: the Internet.

Will Farmer, Director, Fieldings Auctioneers

Top Left: A Loetz hand-blown glass "Cytisus" vase, with handles.

See Mergl, Ploil and Ricke, "Loetz Bohemian Glass 1880-1940," Hatje Cantz (2003), page 121.

ca. 1902   *4¾in (12cm) wide*

$6,000-6,700   **DRA**

Above: A Martin Brothers Pottery stoneware bird jar and cover, by Robert Wallace Martin, the rotund bird with claw feet, a short beak, blue feather eyebrows and wings, in shades of blue, tan, and green, highlighted with white, on an ebonized wood base, painted "Martin Bros 6-1892 London & Southall" to neck and indistinctly to base rim.

1892   *7½in (19cm) high*

$27,000-32,000   **WW**

ESSENTIAL REFERENCE—CLARICE CLIFF

Clarice Cliff (1899-1972) was born in Stoke-on-Trent, England. She started out on what was to become—especially for a woman at that time—a groundbreaking and prolific career by becoming an apprentice enameler at Linguard Webster & Co. in 1912. Four years later, she joined A. J. Wilkinson as an enameler and, by the mid-1920s, had been set up by them in her own studio: the Newport Pottery. Her trail-blazing "Bizarre" range was launched in 1927 and her "Fantasque" range soon after. Cliff's innovative, eye-catching, colorful patterns, applied to diverse table- and decorative wares of invariably complementary and often equally distinctive shape, encapsulated the spirit of the mid-1920s to the early 1930s. Popular at the time, and even more so among collectors nowadays, they were rendered even more desirable by the fact that they were all hand painted by a trained team of decorators—mostly women, and collectively known as the "Bizarre Girls"—who were given the artistic freedom to slightly vary the patterns as they saw fit, so one rendition of a pattern is never the same as another.

A Clarice Cliff circular dish-form plate, "Applique Windmill" pattern, hand painted with a stylized landscape, with a large and a smaller blue windmill below an orange sky, with red and black banding, hand-painted "APPLIQUE" and Bizarre mark.

ca. 1932   *9in (23cm) diam*

$2,700-3,100   **FLD**

A large Clarice Cliff ribbed charger, "Broth" pattern, hand-decorated around the border with abstract motifs and bubbles in orange, blue, and black, within black, orange, and green banding, Fantasque mark.

A 1928 Fantasque design, this pattern was derived from a section of a design by John Butler, who Clarice had worked under as an apprentice but was ultimately inspired by the image of fat floating on top of broth.

ca. 1929   *17¾in (45cm) diam*

$7,000-8,000   **FLD**

A Clarice Cliff octagonal side plate, "Applique Lucerne" pattern, hand painted with a stylized turreted castle landscape beneath a blue sky, hand-painted "Applique" and Bizarre mark, minor rubbing.

ca. 1930   *5½in (14cm) wide*

$1,100-1,350   **FLD**

A Clarice Cliff Bizarre ribbed charger, "Inspiration Caprice" pattern, painted with radial design in shades of blue, pink, sand, and black on a turquoise inspiration ground, printed and painted factory mark.

17¾in (45cm) diam

$3,100-3,700   **WW**

A small Clarice Cliff ribbed charger, "Rhodanthe" pattern, painted in colors, printed factory marks.

12¾in (32.5cm) diam

$375-500   **WW**

A Clarice Cliff dish-form wall plaque, "Tennis" pattern, hand painted in an abstract block-and-line design with a panel of stylized nets, with red, purple, and black banding, Bizarre mark.

ca. 1930   *10¼in (26cm) diam*

$3,700-5,000   **FLD**

A Clarice Cliff Fantasque Bizarre bowl, decorated in the "Carpet" pattern.

7¾in (19.5cm) diam

$350-420   **WHP**

A large Clarice Cliff "Holborn" fruit bowl, "May Avenue" pattern, hand painted with a stylized tree and cottage landscape, with black and blue banding, Bizarre mark.

ca. 1933   *7¾in (19.5cm) diam*

$1,400-1,700   **FLD**

A Clarice Cliff Bizarre preserve pot and cover, "Blue Firs" pattern, painted in colors, printed factory marks, old restoration to cover.

3¼in (8.5cm) high

$375-500   **WW**

A Clarice Cliff "Mei Ping" vase, "Fantasy Tree" pattern, shape no. 14, hand painted with a stylized tree in blue and green, with an orange trunk and matched banding, Fantasque mark, restored.

ca. 1929   *6in (15cm) high*

$625-750   **FLD**

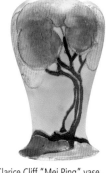

A Clarice Cliff "Mei Ping" vase, "Inspiration Autumn" pattern, shape no. 14, hand painted with a stylized tree landscape over a turquoise glazed ground, hand-painted "Inspiration" and Bizarre mark.

ca. 1930   *6in (15cm) high*

$1,900-2,200   **FLD**

A Clarice Cliff "Mei Ping" vase, "Orange House" pattern, shape no. 14, hand painted with a stylized cottage and trees, flowers on the reverse, between green and black banding, Fantasque mark, small chip on foot, surface scratches.

ca. 1930   *6in (15cm) high*

$1,000-1,250   **FLD**

A Clarice Cliff "Mei Ping" vase, "Seven Color Secrets" pattern, shape no. 14, hand painted with a stylized tree and cottage coastal landscape, between black and orange banding, Bizarre mark.

ca. 1932   *6in (15cm) high*

$800-1,000   **FLD**

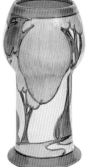

A pair of Clarice Cliff Bizarre vases, "Pastel Autumn" pattern, shape no. 269, painted in colors between pink bands, printed factory marks.

6in (15cm) high

$1,100-1,350   **WW**

A Clarice Cliff Bizarre vase, "Inspiration Clouvre" pattern, shape no. 358, enameled in colors on a mat blue ground, printed and painted marks.

7¾in (19.5cm) high

$1,250-1,500   **WW**

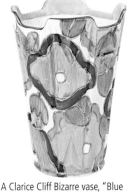

A Clarice Cliff Bizarre vase, "Blue Chintz" pattern, shape no. 451, painted in colors, printed factory marks.

6in (15cm) high

$375-500   **WW**

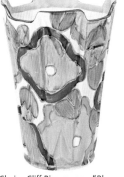

A Clarice Cliff "Isis" vase, "Applique Lugano" pattern, hand painted with a stylized landscape, with a watermill beneath a blue sky, with black and yellow banding, "FANTASQUE" and Bizarre mark.

ca. 1930   *9½in (24cm) high*

$3,500-4,000   **FLD**

A Clarice Cliff "Isis" vase, "Latona Red Roses" pattern, hand painted with large red flowers with black leaves over a white glazed ground, hand-painted "LATONA" and Bizarre mark.

ca. 1930   *9½in (24cm) high*

$3,500-4,000   **FLD**

A Clarice Cliff vase, "Applique Orange Avignon" pattern, shape no. 362, hand painted with a stylized bridge over a lake with water lilies beneath an orange sky, between red and black banding, hand-painted "Applique" and Bizarre mark.

ca. 1930   *7¾in (19.5cm) high*

$3,100-3,700   **FLD**

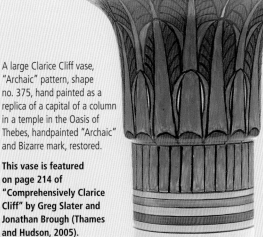

A large Clarice Cliff vase, "Archaic" pattern, shape no. 375, hand painted as a replica of a capital of a column in a temple in the Oasis of Thebes, handpainted "Archaic" and Bizarre mark, restored.

This vase is featured on page 214 of "Comprehensively Clarice Cliff" by Greg Slater and Jonathan Brough (Thames and Hudson, 2005).

ca. 1929   *9¾in (24.5cm) high*

$5,500-6,000   **FLD**

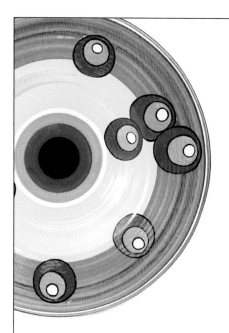

A Clarice Cliff single-handle "Lotus" pitcher, "Diamonds" pattern, hand painted with repeat panels of diamonds and geometric motifs, with orange, yellow, black, blue, and green banding, Fantasque mark, hairline crack.
ca. 1929   10in (25.5cm) high
$2,500-3,100   **FLD**

A Clarice Cliff Bizarre "Athens" pitcher, "Delecia Pansies" pattern, shape no. 30, polychrome painted, printed and painted factory mark.
    7in (18cm) high
$300-375   **WW**

A small Clarice Cliff "Eton" coffeepot, "Blue Autumn" pattern, with angular handle and spout, hand painted with a stylized tree and cottage landscape, with red, black, and yellow banding, red and black painted square-shaped cover, "FANTASQUE" and Bizarre mark.
ca. 1930   6in (15cm) high
$3,350-4,000   **FLD**

ESSENTIAL REFERENCE—SUGAR SIFTERS

One of Clarice Cliff's most recognizable designs, the conical sugar sifter (or caster) had two documented factory shape numbers—489 and 558. It was introduced in 1931 and made up until around 1938. Because it is such an eye-catching and pure geometric form, and because it was issued in a wide and diverse range of Clarice Cliff patterns, it has almost become something of a collecting field in itself. Notable among those patterns are: "Autumn," "Applique Avignon," "Blue Chintz," "Blue Firs," "Bridgewater Orange," "Farmhouse," "House and Bridge," "May Avenue," "Marguerite," "May Blossom," "Mountain," "Rudyard," "Solitude" (shown here), and "Tropic," but that is to name but a few. The one thing that collectors and would-be collectors really need to look out for is damage or restoration of damage on the rim of the base and/or, especially, on the tip of the cone: both detract from the value.

A Clarice Cliff conical sugar sifter, "Solitude" pattern, hand painted with a stylized tree and bridge landscape, between green, yellow, and black banding, "FANTASQUE" and Bizarre mark, restored.
ca. 1933   5½in (14cm) high
$1,250-1,600   **FLD**

CLOSER LOOK—MAY AVENUE PATTERN

After experimenting with pastel colors during 1931-32, Clarice Cliff returned to using a stronger palette with the "May Avenue" pattern, which was introduced in 1933. The vivid and unusual blue employed here for the banding and the sky is a particularly good example of this.

Clarice Cliff created numerous shapes for pitchers, but this—"Daffodill"—with its combination of elegantly flared and more stepped and angular curves—is one of the most overtly Art Deco in style.

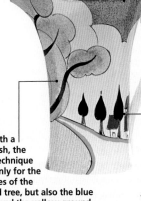

Applied with a special brush, the stippling technique used not only for the green leaves of the foreground tree, but also the blue sky above and the yellow ground below, lends the "May Avenue" pattern a painterly sophistication.

Clarice Cliff drew inspiration for the "May Avenue" pattern from Amedeo Modigliani's 1919 oil painting "Cagnes Landscape," and it showcases her ability to transform depictions in fine art into her own, unique, pottery designs.

A large Clarice Cliff "Daffodil" pitcher, "May Avenue" pattern, hand painted, "FANTASQUE" and Bizarre mark, restored.
ca. 1933   7in (18cm) high
$1,600-2,000   **FLD**

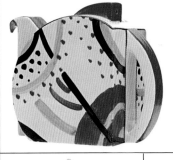

A Clarice Cliff "Stamford" teapot, "Carpet (Red)" pattern, hand painted with an abstract spot-and-line design in red, black, and gray, with red banding, Bizarre mark.
ca. 1930   4¾in (12cm) high
$4,300-5,000   **FLD**

A Clarice Cliff conical sugar sifter, "Crocus" pattern, painted in colors between yellow and brown bands, printed factory mark.
    5½in (14cm) high
$375-500   **WW**

A large Clarice Cliff umbrella stand, "Inspiration Caprice" pattern, hand painted with a stylized tree landscape with a pagoda on a hilltop in tonal turquoise, blue, and ocher glaze, handwritten ocher "Inspiration" and printed Bizarre backstamp, hairline cracks, minor crazing.
ca. 1930   24in (61cm) high
$2,700-3,100   **FLD**

ESSENTIAL REFERENCE—WILLIAM DE MORGAN

Son of a distinguished mathematician, William Frend De Morgan (1839-1917) studied to be an artist at the Royal Academy schools. While there he met William Morris, who became a lifelong friend, and switched his attention from fine art to the decorative arts.

- De Morgan initially designed furniture and stained glass—some examples were for Morris & Co.—and ventured into pottery in 1863. From 1872 onward, he focused entirely on ceramics, especially on highly decorative tiles.
- He worked from a number of locations, most notably a pottery he established in Chelsea (1872-81) and another in Fulham (1888-1907).
- He initially made extensive use of commercial tiles, bought in blank from companies, such as Wedgwood and Minton, before eventually developing a high-quality biscuit tile of his own, better resistant to frost and moisture. Other forms, notably vases and chargers, were also either bought in blank or made in his own potteries.
- Stylistically, De Morgan's primary inspiration lay in the Middle East—in what he referred to as "Persian ware"—but is nowadays more correctly described as 15thC and 16thC Iznik ware. The inspiration lay not only in the rich vocabulary of imagery but also the colors—notably dark blue, turquoise, green, yellow (especially a shade of lemon), manganese purple, and "Indian" red—and the glazes.
- In the early- to mid-1870s, De Morgan "rediscovered" the reflective-metallic technique of lusterware found in Hispano-Moresque pottery and Italian maiolica. The result was his own, instantly recognizable style in which fanciful subjects—ranging from extraordinary creatures to exotic plant forms and buoyant boats under sail—are rhythmically depicted under luxuriously luminous glazes.
- In 1906, De Morgan published a novel—the first of a number of best sellers. The following year he left the pottery, which was in financial difficulty. Production continued for a short while under his leading painters, Charles and Fred Passenger.

A William De Morgan ruby luster charger, centered with a merman with a fish on the end of his triton, within a sunburst border, surrounded by a band of dancing putti on a leaf ground, with a banded and circle border, the reverse centered with four fish and a wide band of stylized scrolling foliage, faint "Davis" stamp on the center, scratches.

See Martin Greenwood, "The Designs of William De Morgan," Richard Dennis (2007), plate 8, for a similar band of putti.

ca. 1875-80   *17¼in (43.5cm) diam*

$25,000-31,000   **SWO**

A William De Morgan luster bowl, by Charles Passenger, the interior decorated with an eagle battling a serpent in a tree, the exterior with concentric band decoration alternating in red and gilt, signed "C.P" in gilt on underside, probably on a Carter's commercial blank.

8¾in (22cm) diam

$5,000-6,200   **DUK**

A William De Morgan Arts and Crafts charger, glazed earthenware with ruby luster.

ca. 1885   *14¼in (36cm) diam*

$6,000-7,500   **L&T**

A William De Morgan charger, by Fred Passenger, painted with three comical scaly fish swimming amid scrolling waterweed, in ruby luster on a white ground, painted "FP" monogram.

14¼in (36cm) diam

$14,000-17,500   **WW**

A William De Morgan "Galleon" plate, painted with a galleon weighing anchor, in ruby luster on a white ground, the reverse with a foliate design, unsigned, broken and repaired.

For this design, see Martin Greenwood, "The Designs of William De Morgan," Richard Dennis (2007), page 51, catalog no. 1266.

8½in (21.5cm) diam

$550-700   **WW**

A William De Morgan solifleur vase, painted with carnation flowers, in ruby luster on a white ground, the neck ruby luster, impressed thistle mark, chips.

9in (23cm) high

$750-1,000   **WW**

A William De Morgan Arts and Crafts ruby luster tile, depicting a mountain goat leaping over a crescent moon.

For this design, see Martin Greenwood, "The Designs of William De Morgan," Richard Dennis (2007), page 122.

ca. 1890   *6in (15cm) wide*

$3,100-3,700   **L&T**

A William De Morgan "Prancing Lioness and Cub" tile, Merton Abbey period, painted with a large lioness above her cub, before grass clumps, in ruby luster on a white ground, impressed factory mark.

For the original design, see Martin Greenwood, "The Designs of William De Morgan," Richard Dennis (2007), page 122, figure 1015.

6in (15cm) wide

$4,300-5,000   **WW**

A William De Morgan luster-glazed "Fish" vase, allover decorated with fish against a scrolling ground, the interior rim with lustrous silver/blue glaze, inscriptions on base obscured by two later applied paper labels.

9¼in (23.5cm) high

$2,500-3,100   **DUK**

A William De Morgan Pottery vase, painted with "Tudor Rose" flowers in eggplant and green on a turquoise ground, the rim a blue band with turquoise interior, impressed factory mark, minor restoration on rim.

8in (20.5cm) high

$6,000-7,500   **WW**

A William De Morgan Pottery tulip vase, by Halsey Ricardo, the shoulder with six apertures, painted on the body with a frieze of alternating peacocks and snakes, before foliage sprays, the neck with geometric bands in blue, turquoise and yellow on a white ground, painted "HR" monogram, minor glaze chips.

7¼in (18.5cm) high

$6,000-7,500   **WW**

A fine William De Morgan vase and cover, by Halsey Ricardo, painted with classical dolphins, in shades of turquoise and green on a blue and purple calm water ground, the domed cover with a radiating star motif, impressed thistle mark, painted "HR" monogram, small restoration on rim, minor glaze chips.

9¾in (24.5cm) high

$12,500-15,000   **WW**

A William De Morgan Pottery vase, by Edward Porter, painted with hares among tufts of grass in blue, turquoise, and green on a pale green ground, impressed tulip mark, painted "EP" monogram, minor glaze loss on top rim.

For the original drawing of two of the hares, see Martin Greenwood, "The Designs of William De Morgan," Richard Dennis (2007), page 102, figure 1429.

5¼in (13.5cm) high

$5,500-6,000   **WW**

A William De Morgan "Persian" twin-handle vase, painted on one side with a dragon eating a yellow fruit, the reverse with a serpent among fruiting stems, in shades of eggplant, green, yellow, blue, and turquoise on a white ground, impressed Merton Abbey mark, painted "JB" monogram and "1890."

1890   *9¼in (23.5cm) high*

$12,500-15,000   **WW**

An early William De Morgan tile, painted in blue with a large scaly fish swimming in a shoal of smaller fish, unsigned.

6in (15cm) wide

$5,000-5,600   **WW**

An early William De Morgan tile, painted in blue with a swan catching a fish in a river with bulrush, unsigned.

6in (15cm) wide

$5,000-5,600   **WW**

A William De Morgan double carnation tile, glazed earthenware, impressed Sands End mark.

late 1890s   *8in (20.5cm) wide*

$1,000-1,500   **L&T**

A William De Morgan "Galleon" tile, impressed Sands End Pottery mark, crazing, small chips.

The Victoria & Albert Museum holds what appears to be the original design for this tile: no. E.819-1917.

6in (15cm) wide

$2,500-3,100   **SWO**

ESSENTIAL REFERENCE—DOULTON LAMBETH

The Doulton Factory was founded in Lambeth, London, in 1815 by John Doulton, Martha Jones, and John Watts, and it initially focused production on stoneware bottles and storage jars. When John Doulton's son Henry joined the firm in 1835, the business began to expand rapidly, making and supplying drainpipes and water filters to many cities, both in the UK and overseas. The commercial success of Doulton's sanitary wares enabled it to switch its focus to decorative wares, both domestic and architectural. In 1863, the pottery began to work with students at and graduates of the Lambeth School of Art—by the 1880s, it employed more than 200 artists and designers, many of them women. Names of particular note include the Tinworth brothers, Arthur and George, and the Barlow siblings, Hannah, Arthur, and Florence, as well as Mark Marshall, and the significant styles embraced included Arts and Crafts, Moorish, and Art Nouveau. In 1901, Doulton received a Royal Warrant, and thereafter became known as Royal Doulton (see pages 523-24).

A Doulton Lambeth stoneware jardinière, by George Tinworth, relief-decorated with fruiting raspberries in full bloom.

10in (25.5cm) high

$800-950   WHP

A Doulton Lambeth stoneware tyg, by Hannah Barlow, with a lobed panel incised with a sitting dog, with a raised verse "Most things have two handles – A wise man takes hold of the better," incised artist's monogram, impressed marks and numbered.

6in (15cm) high

$800-950   SWO

A Doulton Lambeth stoneware vase, by Florence Barlow, with incised scrolling leaves and roundels, the panels with pâte-sur-pâte birds on branches, incised on the rim with artist's monograms and numbered "327," impressed mark on base, mounted on a wrought-iron stand.

17¾in (45cm) high

$1,900-2,200   SWO

A pair of Doulton Lambeth stoneware vases, by Florence Barlow, each with a scrolled ground and pâte-sur-pâte panels of budgerigars, artist's monogram, impressed marks, numbered "990," and dated "1886," small chip on one.

1886   18½in (47cm) high

$1,250-1,700   SWO

A Doulton Lambeth stoneware pitcher, by Hannah Barlow, incised with donkeys and figures within a woodland scene, artist's monogram, impressed marks and dated "1875," firing crack.

1875   7¾in (19.5cm) high

$700-800   SWO

A Doulton Lambeth stoneware mouse group, "Play Goers," by George Tinworth, modeled as mice performing a Punch & Judy play, with three young mice watching, glazed in colors, incised "Play Goers," impressed Doulton Lambeth mark, incised "GT" monogram.

5½in (14cm) high

$4,300-5,000   WW

A Doulton stoneware mouse and frog group, "Lost and Serves them Right for Betting (Returning from the Derby)," by George Tinworth, modeled as a large mouse pulling a carriage with four frogs, a large frog riding the mouse, incised on the base rim "Lost and serves them right for betting," glazed green, buff, and brown, incised "GT" monogram, signpost missing.

6in (15cm) wide

$10,000-12,500   WW

A Doulton Lambeth stoneware grotesque, decorated by Mark V. Marshall, modeled as a foliate wild boar, in a green, brown, and blue glaze, incised artist's monogram, impressed marks, minor firing crack, fine chips.

8¼in (21cm) high

$1,050-1,400   SWO

ESSENTIAL REFERENCE—ROYAL DOULTON FIGURINES

Doulton (see page 522, facing page) became known as Royal Doulton after receiving a Royal Warrant in 1901. However, the figurines for which the latter is well known were actually first produced at Doulton in the 1880s, initially under the stewardship of George Tinworth, and then from 1889 onward under Charles Noke.

From 1912/13, all figurines were assigned a "HN" number, with the "HN" standing for Harry Nixon, who was in charge of the painting department. In total, more than 4,000 HN numbers were assigned, the first of which, HN1 "Darling," was allegedly named after Queen Mary called the figurine "a darling" on a visit to the factory in 1913.

Notable designers of Royal Doulton figurines have included: Leslie Harradine, from the 1920s-50s; Mary Nicholl and Peggy Davies, who designed the majority of the figurines during the 1950s and 1960s; and Alan Maslankowski from 1968-2006.

Figurines that were produced for only a short period of time are obviously rarer and, ergo, more valuable, as are those with unusual color combinations—many figurines were made in a range of colors and can vary significantly in price. As a rule of thumb, the most desirable and valuable figures are those produced before World War II.

Royal Doulton "Shakespeare" pitcher.

10¾in (27.5cm) high

$375-500   TEN

A Royal Doulton glazed stoneware model, "The Roman Galleon," by Gilbert Bayes (1872-1953), on an ebonized base.

See Louize Irvine and Paul Atterbury, "Gilbert Bayes: Sculptor 1872-1953," Richard Dennis (1998), pages 36-37 and 171.

1928   17in (43cm) high

$1,900-2,200   L&T

A Royal Doulton stoneware finial for a clothesline post, "Tudor Rose," by Gilbert Bayes FRBS, glazed in colors, one side a red rose, the other white, with later ebonized wood stand, unsigned.

See Louize Irvine and Paul Atterbury, "Gilbert Bayes: Sculptor 1872-1953," Richard Dennis (1998), pages 171 and 172.

13¼in (33.5cm) high

$1,000-1,400   WW

A Royal Doulton china figure, "A Jester," second version, wearing black and white motley, impressed "10.21," incised "171," green printed mark, no HN number.

1920   9¼in (23.5cm) high

$1,900-2,200   HT

An early prototype earthenware figure for Royal Doulton, "St George," by Stanley Thorogood, standing with a plumed helmet in his left hand, a dog at his feet, with polychrome decoration, incised signature, crazing, some flaking.

Stanley Thorogood (1873-1953) trained at Brighton School of Art, won a Gold Medal Travelling Scholarship to Italy, became superintendent of art instruction, Stoke-on-Trent, 1913-19, and from 1920 wasdDirector of Camberwell School of Art, in London. He is particularly known for his sculptures of knights and equestrian subjects, both largely informed by 19thC romantic literature of medieval chivalry.

15¾in (40cm) high

$5,000-6,200   SWO

A Royal Doulton china figural group, "Spooks," wearing a pink and purple robe and a green and red robe, impressed "1.24," incised "211," green printed mark, no HN number.

1924   7in (18cm) high

$10,000-12,500   HT

A Royal Doulton ceramic model, "Spook," by Harry Tittensor, with a black cap and a mottled red and blue cape, painted mark "Painted by Doulton and Co. Ltd., Spook," incised probably 714, printed Doulton stamp, crazing.

ca. 1916-36   4¼in (11cm) high

$1,700-2,200   SWO

A Royal Doulton figure, "Dulcinea," designed by Leslie Harradine, model no. HN1419, modeled as a young woman sat on a chaise lounge, wearing a pink and red dress, green printed factory mark, red painted "HN 1419 'Dulcinea' Potted by Doulton & Co," restored.

1930-38   5¼in (13.5cm) high

$950-1,050   TEN

A Royal Doulton glazed earthenware figure, "Motherhood," printed factory stamp, impressed "329/3.21" painted "H.N. 570," indistinctly signed "F. CLAYTON" on base.

ca. 1925   8¾in (22cm) high

$8,000-8,500   L&T

A Royal Doulton figure, "Molly Malone," by Leslie Harradine, model no. HN1455, green and red printed marks.

1931-37   7½in (19cm) high

$3,100-3,700   BELL

A Royal Doulton glazed earthenware figure, "St George and The Dragon," printed pottery mark and painted marks "HN2856/KW/ 17.7.87."

1987   *16¼in (41.5cm) high*

$2,100-2,500   **L&T**

An early prototype earthenware figure for Royal Doulton, "Elizabeth I on Horseback," by Stanley Thorogood, with polychrome decoration, incised signature on both sides, on an ebonized wood plinth, horse's ear missing, crazing.

12in (30.5cm) high

$1,900-2,200   **SWO**

A Royal Doulton parrot speaker cover, designed by Charles Noke, manufactured for Artandia Ltd., modeled as a cockatoo perched on a stone mound, printed marks.

Throughout the 1920s, Artandia Ltd. produced decorative speakers for luxury liners that were placed around the ships, in both communal areas and private cabins, to amplify music.

ca. 1927   *15¼in (39cm) high*

$300-350   **SWO**

A Royal Doulton stoneware figure of a goat, designed by Francis Pope, modeled sitting on a square plinth, impressed Doulton mark, minor losses.

See Desmond Eyles and Louise Irvine, "Doulton Lambeth Wares," Richard Dennis (2002), page 194, for a comparable figure illustrated, and page 195 for the original Doulton catalog for 1935 illustrating this model.

19¾in (50cm) high

$1,000-1,250   **WW**

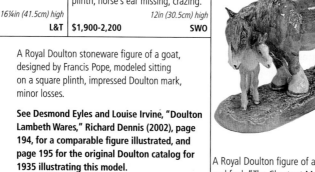

A Royal Doulton figure of a mare and foal, "The Chestnut Mare," model no. HN2533, on a plinth.

$190-250   **TEN**

A Royal Doulton glazed earthenware figure, "The Matador," printed factory stamp, painted "HN2324/DS/30.3.95/24106."

1995   *25½in (65cm) wide*

$1,000-1,250   **L&T**

A Royal Doulton figure, "Sitting Fox," model no. HN147, covered in a mat black glaze, printed factory mark.

5¾in (14.5cm) high

$375-500   **WW**

ESSENTIAL REFERENCE—CHARACTER PITCHERS

While pottery Toby jugs (aka pitchers), which date back to the mid-18thC, depict a sitting figure (mostly a heavily set, jovial man wearing a long coat and a tricorn hat, and holding a mug of beer in one hand and a pipe of tobacco in the other), Character pitchers depict just the head and shoulders of a person.

At Royal Doulton in the early-1900s, Charles Noke designed not only a number of traditional Toby jugs portraying various figures from politics, literature, and folklore, but also produced some Character pitchers of similar figures. Royal Doulton soon gained a reputation for the latter, and began to produce them in three different sizes: large, small, and miniature.

After Noke, Harry Fenton became a prominent designer, modeling 26 different Character pitchers (as well as 15 Tobies). After Fenton's death in 1953 other notable Character pitcher designers have included Mark Henk, Stanley J. Taylor, William K. Harper, David B. Biggs, and Caroline Dadd. Stylistically, one notable development has been the pitcher handle becoming a more integrated and prominent part of the overall design.

A small Royal Doulton character pitcher, "The Jester," made for Bentalls, green printed factory mark and "Souvenir from Bentalls, 1936."

1936   *3¼in (8.5cm) high*

$250-310   **BELL**

A large Royal Doulton ceramic character pitcher, "Goatee-beard Cavalier," printed backstamp and numbered "13" on reverse, crazing.

6in (15cm) high

$500-550   **LSK**

A Royal Doulton double-sided character pitcher, "Mephistopheles," printed lion and crown mark verso.

5¾in (14.5cm) high

$210-275   **LSK**

A Royal Doulton Winston Churchill Toby jug (or pitcher), with stamped factory marks to base.

1960s   *9in (23cm) high*

$160-220   **SWO**

A Goldscheider Art Deco pottery figure, by Stefan Dakon (1904-92), model no. 6757, modeled as a dancer in a floral skirt and spotted top, standing on a black base, impressed and painted marks "Dakon MADE IN AUSTRIA, 6757/116/6."

ca. 1933   *13in (33cm) high*
$950-1,050   **TEN**

A Goldscheider patinated terra-cotta figure, "Salome," by "Latour," impressed maker's marks "LATOUR/FRIEDRICH GOLDSCHEIDER/WIEN/3726/32/27."

See O. Pinhas, "Goldscheider," Richard Dennis Publications (2006), page 45.

ca. 1912   *31½in (80cm) high*
$950-1,050   **L&T**

CLOSER LOOK—AN ART DECO GIRL

This figure of a girl in a hatbox is by Stefan Dakon (1904-92). With fellow Austrian artist and sculptor Josef Lorenzl (1892-1950), his invariably dynamic and overtly Art Deco sculptures defined the "house style" of the Viennese ceramics manufacturer Goldscheider from the mid-1920s until the end of the 1930s.

The political and social emancipation of women, especially young women, after World War I and during the 1920s and 1930s is symbolized not only by the overall composition of a girl emerging from a hatbox, but also by the uncovered "acres" of bare flesh (legs and arms) on display.

Although Dakon's composition is characteristically bold and dynamic, it also incorporates subtleties and refinements, notably the pleats and folds in the girl's blue dress, that elevate it beyond frivolity to a sophisticated work of art.

While the black and white cross-hatched pattern on the box and lid are perfectly in keeping with the stylized, geometric angularity associated with the later Art Deco style, the subtle irregularity of its freehand-painted application is equally in tune with the more curvaceous and essentially naturalistic modeling of the girl.

A Goldscheider Art Deco pottery figure, by Stefan Dakon (1904-92), model no. 7200, modeled as a girl sitting in a hatbox, impressed and painted marks "Goldscheider Wien MADE IN AUSTRIA, Dakon, 7200/24/11."

ca. 1935   *6in (15cm) high*
$2,200-2,700   **TEN**

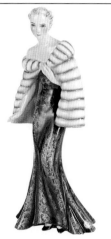

A Goldscheider Art Deco glazed earthenware figure, by Claire Herczeg (1906-97), traces of applied maker's label, printed factory marks, and artist signature, impressed "8204/177/10."

ca. 1935   *12¼in (31cm) high*
$950-1,050   **L&T**

A Goldscheider earthenware figure, by Stefan Dakon, model no. 5815, modeled as a girl standing with her hands in her pockets, wearing a checked scarf and shorts, signed "Dakon" on the plinth, printed and stamped marks "5815/487/10" and incised "16P," restored.

15¼in (38.5cm) high
$800-950   **SWO**

A Goldscheider Art Deco glazed earthenware figure, by Josef Lorenzl (1892-1950), printed factory marks, painted artist signature, impressed "7904."

ca. 1935   *10¾in (27.5cm) high*
$4,700-5,500   **L&T**

A Goldscheider bust of a girl, painted and glazed terra-cotta, printed and incised maker's marks "GOLDSCHEIDER/WIEN/MADE IN AUSTRIA/6305."

ca. 1930   *9in (23cm) high*
$800-950   **L&T**

A Goldscheider Pottery wall mask, model no. 6774, modeled as a woman with orange curly hair, holding an apple, glazed in colors, impressed and printed marks, restored neck, losses in hair.

8in (20.5cm) high
$60-120   **WW**

A Goldscheider wall mask, modeled as a lady with curled orange hair and a green scarf, holding a set of black beads, printed mark and impressed "7121," restored, chips in back.

12½in (31.5cm) high
$375-450   **FLD**

A Goldscheider wall mask, attributed to Ernest Webber, modeled as the face of a lady with curled blue hair, green eye makeup, and red lips, printed mark and impressed "6086 189 165."

5½in (14cm) high
$480-520   **FLD**

DECORATIVE ARTS

A Grueby Faience Company tall vase, by Ruth Erickson, glazed earthenware, with lilies, impressed on underside "Grueby Pottery Boston U.S.A." with lotus symbol, incised artist's initials and date "RE 10/4/9."

1909   *13¾in (35cm) high*
$16,000-21,000   DRA

An exceptional Grueby Faience Company floor vase, by Ruth Erickson, glazed earthenware, incised artist's initials "ER" on underside.

This vase was exhibited at the 1900 Exposition Universelle in Paris. See Clark, "The Arts and Crafts Movement in America 1876-1916," Princeton (1992), page 139.

1899-1910   *30¼in (77cm) high*
$20,000-25,000   DRA

A rare Grueby Faience Company vase, glazed earthenware, with calla lilies, impressed on underside "Grueby Pottery Boston U.S.A. 180," with lotus symbol.

Exhibited at: "The American Century: Art & Culture 1900-1950," May-August 1999, Whitney Museum of American Art, New York.

1898-1910   *18in (46cm) high*
$110,000-120,000   DRA

A rare Grueby Faience Company three-color vase, by Gertrude Stanwood, glazed earthenware, with cinquefoils, impressed "Grueby Faience Co. Boston U.S.A.," paper manufacturer's label on underside, "Grueby Pottery Boston U.S.A. Registered Trade Mark" with lotus symbol, incised artist's initial "St."

ca. 1904   *10in (25.5cm) diam*
$25,000-31,000   DRA

A rare early Grueby Faience Company bicolor gourd vase, glazed earthenware, with leaves, impressed "Grueby" signature on underside.

See "House Beautiful," December 1898, page 7.

ca. 1898   *8¼in (21cm) diam*
$40,000-45,000   DRA

A rare Grueby Faience Company vase, glazed earthenware, with irises, impressed on underside "Grueby Pottery Boston U.S.A." with obscured lotus symbol, incised unidentified artist's initials "J.E."

1898-1910   *7¼in (18.5cm) high*
$23,500-30,000   DRA

Judith Picks

As you can see from the surrounding images on this page, most of the highly desirable art pottery produced by the Grueby Faience Company around the turn of the 20thC was of organic form and then finished in an allover, mat cucumber and/or sandy yellow glaze. However, other decorative techniques were also employed. For example, when decorating their pictorial tiles "cuerda seca" (Spanish for "dry cord") was often employed, in which thin bands of waxy resin were used to separate different color glazes during firing in the kiln. Far, far rarer, however, was Grueby's use of the cloisonné technique on its art pottery. A French word for a technique introduced into China from Western Asia around the 14thC, and subsequently introduced into Japan in the 17thC (where it was primarily used on metal wares), cloisonné involves separating different color enamels within "cloisons" or fields formed by metal wires glued to the underlying surface prior to firing—in this case to create a ring of stylized moths around the shoulders of the vase. Along with this one, there are only four known examples of Grueby pottery decorated with this technique: one is in a private collection; one is in the Newark Museum of Art; and one was recently donated to the Metropolitan Museum of Art, New York. All in all, a rarity and a provenance that does much to explain this example's recent price at auction!

An important Grueby Faience Company covered jar, glazed earthenware decorated in cloisonné, with moths, glazed-over impressed manufacturer's mark on underside.

See Eidelberg (ed.), "From Our Native Clay: Art Pottery from the Collections of the American Ceramic Arts Society," Turn of the Century Editions (1987), page 43, no. 73 for this example.

1898-1910   *6¾in (17cm) high*
$140,000-150,000   DRA

A rare Grueby Faience Company "Jungle Book" tile, by Russell Crook, glazed earthenware, with elephant and child.

See Montgomery, "Arts & Crafts Tile from the Collection of the Two Red Roses Foundation," Lucia Marquand (2017), page 68.

ca. 1900   *16in (40.5cm) wide*
$6,000-8,000   DRA

A rare Grueby Faience Company tile, by Frederick Roth, glazed earthenware, with elephants, glazed "FW" mark verso.

ca. 1907-12   *8¾in (22cm) wide*
$12,500-15,000   DRA

ESSENTIAL REFERENCE—LENCI

The Lenci factory was established in 1919 in Turin, Italy, by Helen (Elena) König Scavini (1886-1974) and her husband Enrico. The name "Lenci" is thought to be a corruption of Helen's nickname: "Helenchen" or "Lenchen," but it is also an acronym of the company motto "Ludus Est Nobis Constanter Industria," which translates as "Play Is Our Constant Work."

The company started out as a maker of rag dolls, adding ceramics, primarily figures and busts, to its range in 1928. Many of the figures were designed by Helen König Scavini herself, although the factory also worked with other designers, notably: Abele Jacobi (1882-1957), Giovanni Grande (1887-1937), Sandro Vachetti (1889-1976), and Mario Sturani (1906-78). Helen König Scavini's highly expressive figures, in particular, perfectly captured the Art Deco style of the late 1920s and 1930s, and they were much admired by Walt Disney, who, allegedly, tried to persuade her to work for him.

The Lenci company was taken over in 1937, with ceramic production eventually ceasing in 1964.

A Lenci pot and cover, painted in black, orange, and red, with figures in 18thC costume bowing to each other within a garden, the cover with banding, inscribed "Lenci Made in Italy Torino XIIIV(?)," scratches, small chips.

6in (15cm) diam

$2,500-3,100   **SWO**

A Lenci porcelain figure group, of a gentleman doffing his hat to a lady, painted marks and incised "619."

12in (30.5cm) high

$375-500   **ECGW**

A Lenci wall mask, "Testa," by Helen König Scavini, modeled as the head of a young woman wearing a headscarf, paper label, black printed "Lenci Made in Italy Torino PM 1938," impressed model no. "561."

1938   *11¾in (30cm) high*

$300-450   **BELL**

A Lenci glazed earthenware figure, "Sul Mondo," by Mario Sturani and Helen König Scavini, glazed signature on underside "Lenci R.S. Made in Italy Torino," impressed "500."

See Panzetta, "Le Ceramiche Lenci," Allemandi (2003), page 107, no. 39.

ca. 1935   *19in (48cm) high*

$19,000-22,000   **DRA**

A Lenci pottery figure, "Nella," by Helen König Scavini, modeled sitting on a bench, an open book by her side, a frog resting on the back of the bench, enameled in colors, painted marks, lid restored.

See Alfonso Panzetta, "La Ceramiche Lenci," Allemandi (2003), page 163, catalog no. 323.

9in (23cm) high

$3,200-4,000   **ECGW**

An Ai Monti a Lenci Pottery figure, designed by Abele Jacopi, model no. 697, the young lady modeled standing, on a shaped rectangular base, with wooden ski poles, painted in colors, impressed number, painted mark and monogram, corner of base and figure at ankles reattached.

17¼in (43.5cm) high

$2,500-3,100   **WW**

A Lenci figural group of Madonna and child, by Paola Bologna (1898-1960, Italian), the child holding a dove, painted marks.

7½in (19cm) high

$190-250   **ECGW**

A Lenci figural group of Madonna with child, with detachable halo, painted marks and incised "586."

8¼in (21cm) high

$450-500   **ECGW**

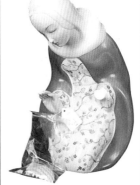

A Lenci figure of Madonna, by Paola Bologna, modeled kneeling with hands raised, painted marks and paper label numbered "432," incised "NC," damages.

10¾in (27cm) high

$160-220   **ECGW**

Freya THOUGHT HER ANTIQUE HUNTING DAYS WERE OVER . . .

Written in consultation with **Judith Miller**

'Who could resist a treasure hunt with murder at its core?'

SJ Bennett

Author of *The Windsor Knot*

A Martin Brothers stoneware bird jar and cover, by Robert Wallace Martin, modeled with webbed claw feet and a slender beak, glazed blue and green on a buff ground with white highlights, on an ebonized wood base, incised "3.1902, R W Martin & Bros London & Southall" on base and neck.

1902   *7¾in (19.5cm) high*
$31,000-37,000   **WW**

A Martin Brothers Pottery stoneware bird jar and cover, by Robert Wallace Martin, the rotund bird with claw feet, a short beak, blue feather eyebrows and wings, in shades of blue, tan, and green, highlighted with white, on an ebonized wood base, painted "Martin Bros 6-1892 London & Southall" on neck and indistinctly on base rim.

1892   *7½in (19cm) high*
$27,000-32,000   **WW**

A Martin Brothers Pottery "Snark" creature jar, by Robert Wallace Martin, salt-glazed stoneware, glazed signature and date on back "RW Martin London + Southall 1885," incised signature and date on inner collar "RW Martin + Brothers. London + Southall 5.1885," original paper label on underside "R.W. Martin & Bro's., Art Potters 16, Brownlow St., High Holborn."

1885   *9½in (24cm) high*
$25,000-31,000   **DRA**

A Martin Brothers stoneware bird jar and cover, "Monk," by Robert Wallace Martin, with a short broad beak, forward stare, and balding pate, wings tucked behind, glazed in shades of green, blue, and brown, with pale blue highlights on wings, on an ebonized wood base, incised on head "R W Martin & Bros London & Southall, 17.2.1912" and "5.8.1911" on base.

1912   *7½in (19cm) high*
$11,000-15,000   **WW**

Judith Picks

I have picked out a Martin Brothers salt-glazed stoneware bird jar in more than one previous edition of "Miller's Antiques Handbook and Price Guide," and I have absolutely no hesitation in doing so—this time with the splendidly named "Tall Wally"—again! Quirkily sculpted by Robert Wallace Martin (1843-1923), who had studied at the Lambeth School of Art, and in a palette of brown, yellow, cream, gray, and blue glazes developed by his brother Walter (1857-1912), they continue to command substantial, and seemingly continuously higher prices at auction. This should not be surprising: their remarkably humanlike, anthropomorphic expressions—ranging from supercilious to stern, and various enigmatic points in between (here "knowingly conspiratorial")—should ensure desirability beyond any point in time.

A Martin Brothers Pottery bird tobacco jar, "Tall Wally," salt-glazed stoneware, on an ebonized wood base, incised signature and date on inner collar and base "Martin Bros London + Southall 11-1895."

1895   *18½in (47cm) high*
$100,000-110,000   **DRA**

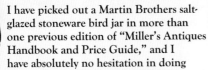

A Martin Brothers stoneware "Grotesque" spoon warmer, by Robert Wallace Martin, modeled as a dragonlike creature, with scaly skin, a gaping mouth and swept back feathers and tendrils, glazed in shades of green, blue, white, and brown, incised "49 2/80 R W Martin London & Southall," professional restoration.

See Malcolm Haslam, "The Martin Brothers Potters," Richard Dennis (1978), page 86, figure 113.

1880   *8in (20.5cm) high*
$4,300-5,000   **WW**

A Martin Brothers Pottery bird tobacco jar, "Wally," by Robert Wallace Martin, salt-glazed stoneware, on an ebonized wood base, incised signature and date on collar and foot "RW Martin London + Southall 19.9.81," paper exhibition label on collar "Richard Dennis Martin Brothers Pottery Exhibition 1978 109."

1881   *10½in (26.5cm) high*
$23,500-30,000   **DRA**

A Martin Brothers Pottery "Grotesque" spoon warmer, by Robert Wallace Martin, salt-glazed stoneware, incised signature and date on underside "RW Martin Bros London + Southall 7-1884."

See Malcolm Haslam, "The Martin Brothers Potters," Richard Dennis (1978), page 62, for this example.

1884   *7in (18cm) wide*
$37,000-43,000   **DRA**

A Martin Brothers stoneware "Grotesque" reptile creature, by Edwin and Walter Martin, modeled lying with front paws outstretched, his back with fur ruffles, incised decoration with white highlights, incised "4-1894, Martin Bros London & Southall."

1894   *4¼in (11cm) wide*
$8,000-9,500   **WW**

DECORATIVE ARTS

A rare and large Martin Brothers Pottery salt-glazed stoneware vase, with a carved marine scene of fish, octopuses, cuttlefish, eel, spotted ray, starfish, coral, and sea grass, incised signature and date on underside "Martin Brothers London + Southall 9.1891."

1891   *14½in (37cm) high*

$10,500-12,500   DRA

A Martin Brothers double gourd buttressed vase, glazed stoneware, incised on underside "Martin Bros, London + Southall, 2-1903."

1903   *6½in (16.5cm) high*

$4,700-5,200   FRE

A Martin Brothers glazed stoneware vase with prunts, by Edwin Martin (1860-1915), incised on underside "Martin Bros, London + Southall."

ca. 1900   *7½in (19cm) high*

$4,700-5,200   FRE

A Martin Brothers Pottery salt-glazed stoneware twin-handle vase, by Robert Wallace Martin (1843-1923), with cats, incised "RW Martin & Bros London + Southall 4-1883."

1883   *8¾in (22cm) high*

$1,000-1,500   FRE

Judith Picks

Whether in fine art or the decorative arts, it is usually reasonably easy to track the transmission of ideas and subsequent changes in style and/or fashion. At its simplest, the latter almost invariably comes about because, when an artist or a designer produces something innovative or new, other artists or designers then see it (whether in the flesh, in print, or nowadays on the Internet), and are inspired to reproduce it (closely or otherwise). Sometimes, however, there just doesn't seem to be any "paper trail"—simply, there is no obvious means of transmission. This crumpled and twisted, salt-glazed stoneware pot made by the Martin Brothers in 1884 is a case in point. As the inscription on the body reveals, it is a pot gone wrong; the potter has messed it up but had the presence of mind (probably in a "eureka" moment) to realize it is an "art form" in its own right. Interestingly, if we leave London and cross the Atlantic just a decade later, to a relatively remote location on the Mississippi, we find George Ohr—the "Mad Potter of Biloxi"—producing not at all dissimilar and equally avant garde crumpled and twisted shapes (see page 534). Perhaps George just picked up the idea from the ether?

A Martin Brothers salt-glazed stoneware crumpled vase, inscribed on the body "And the vessel that he made/of clay was marred in the hand/of the potter: Jer XVIII-4," incised on underside "10-84, Martin Bros, London & Southall."

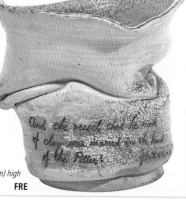

1884   *3½in (9cm) high*

$4,300-5,600   FRE

A Martin Brothers glazed stoneware pitcher, with swirl decoration, incised on underside "Martin Bros, London + Southall, 12-1895."

1895   *7in (18cm) high*

$1,100-1,500   FRE

A Martin Brothers salt-glazed stoneware double-sided face pitcher, incised on underside "5-1902, Martin Bros, London + Southall."

1902   *7½in (19cm) high*

$4,000-4,700   FRE

An early Martin Brothers stoneware "Owl" jar and cover, by Robert Wallace Martin, triangular section, modeled in relief with three owls, one asleep, two with eyes slightly open, the cover modeled with a white mouse, glazed in colors "12 77 R W Martin, London & Southall," numbered "3" on both cover and base, old damages.

1877   *5¼in (13.5cm) high*

$3,000-3,500   WW

A Martin Brothers salt-glazed stoneware double-sided face pitcher, incised on underside "R. W. Martin + Bros, Southall."

ca. 1900   *4¼in (11cm) high*

$4,700-5,500   FRE

ESSENTIAL REFERENCE—FLORIAN WARE

The earliest of the wares produced by William Moorcroft (1872-1945) were, from 1897, conceived while he was working as a designer for James Macintyre & Company of the Washington Works, Burslem. Launched by Macintyre in 1898, and produced until ca. 1906, Florian ware firmly established Moorcroft's reputation as an innovative designer and master craftsman.

The shapes of these ornamental wares—vases, chargers, plates, bowls, jardinières, etc.—were inspired by Middle and Far Eastern ceramics, and also, from ca. 1900, by Classical (especially Pompeiian) forms. Their decoration—a blend of Art Nouveau and Arts and Crafts, which was always sympathetic to the shapes employed—primarily comprised flowing floral patterns, in highly distinctive applied raised slip and underglaze colors.

Collectors have numerous floral patterns to choose from, based on, most notably, poppies, tulips, iris, violets, cornflowers, daisies, narcissi, roses, and forget-me-nots. However, there are also butterfly, peacock feather, and fish patterns, as well as some landscapes. Earlier color themes include pale blue and green grounds often (but not always) with the patterns in darker tones of the same color; later examples also include white and cream grounds with patterns in pinks, yellows, and brown, with some designs enriched with gilding.

Collectors should note that while all Florian wares bear a printed backstamp and are signed or initialed by Moorcroft, some versions—mostly those made for specific retailers—are known by and stamped with a different name. Notable examples include Hesperian ware (for Osler's), Burslem ware (some nonfloral designs for Liberty), and Butterfly ware.

An early 20thC Macintyre Moorcroft Pottery Florian ware vase, with two loop handles, tube lined and painted in shades of blue with poppies and cornflowers, printed mark in brown, signed in green, numbered "104(?) IW."

6½in (16.5cm) high

$450-550   HT

A Moorcroft Florian vase, "Yacht" pattern, of ship's decanter form.

9¼in (23.5cm) high

$125-170   WHP

An early 20thC Moorcroft Pottery Florian ware vase, tube lined and painted in shades of blue, green, and yellow with flowers, impressed "Moorcroft, Burslem, England," signed in green.

9in (23cm) high

$550-700   HT

A Moorcroft Pottery vase, "Moonlit Blue" pattern, tube lined and painted, with EPNS mount, impressed and signed in green.

1920s   7½in (19cm) high

$1,000-1,250   HT

A large Moorcroft Pottery vase, "Flambe Orchids" pattern, designed by William Moorcroft, tube-line decorated in colors with "Frilled and Slipper Orchids" before spring flowers, in colors under a flambé glaze, impressed factory marks, painted blue signature and date.

1939   12¾in (32.5cm) high

$1,050-1,250   WW

An early-20thC Moorcroft Pottery vase, "Pomegranate" pattern, tube lined and painted in typical palette, impressed "Moorcroft, Burslem, England, M32," signed in green.

7in (18cm) high

$500-625   HT

A rare Moorcroft Pottery luster vase, "Eventide" pattern, designed by William Moorcroft, tube-line decorated with a band of trees, covered in a bronze luster glaze, impressed factory marks.

8¾in (22.5cm) high

$500-625   WW

A large Moorcroft vase, "After The Storm" pattern, designed by Walter Moorcroft, limited-edition no. 98/200, tube lined and painted with a landscape with dark storm clouds in the background, signed and dated "16.VI.98" on underside, impressed factory marks and other painted marks.

1998   20½in (52cm) high

$1,050-1,250   DUK

A Moorcroft Pottery saucer, "Hazledene" pattern, designed by William Moorcroft, painted with a radial design of trees in blue and green on a pale celadon ground, impressed factory marks.

4¼in (11cm) diam

$300-375   WW

A small Moorcroft jar and cover, decorated with fruit and finches, on a shaded blue ground.

4¼in (11cm) high

$60-100   **WHP**

A miniature Moorcroft vase, typically decorated with flower heads, on a shaded blue/green ground.

2¾in (7cm) high

$70-100   **WHP**

A large modern Moorcroft Pottery trial vase, "Anemone" pattern, tube lined in colors on a blue ground, impressed and painted marks, dated.

1994   10¾in (27.5cm) high

$250-310   **WW**

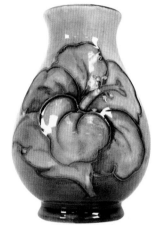

A miniature Moorcroft vase, typically decorated with pink hibiscus, on a shaded green ground, Queen Mary label.

3¾in (9.5cm) high

$60-90   **WHP**

A Moorcroft trial vase, decorated with stylized passionflowers and fruit, on a dark blue ground.

7in (18cm) high

$250-310   **WHP**

A Moorcroft Collectors Club vase, "Demeter" pattern, by Emma Bossons, decorated with stylized poppies on a cream ground, with box.

8½in (21.5cm) high

$160-210   **WHP**

A Moorcroft Pottery plate, "Carribean" pattern, designed by Walter Moorcroft, tube-line decorated in colors with exotic fish and sea horses among waterweed, under a light flambé glaze, impressed factory marks.

10¼in (26.5cm) diam

$300-375   **WW**

A Moorcroft Pottery plate, "Moonlit Blue" pattern, designed by William Moorcroft, painted in shades of blue and green on a blue ground, impressed factory marks, painted blue signature.

8¾in (22cm) diam

$500-550   **WW**

A Moorcroft Pottery footed bowl, "Dawn" pattern, designed by William Moorcroft, tube-line decorated with trees in a landscape, with a scallop border, in shades of blue, impressed marks, painted blue signature.

8in (20.5cm) diam

$300-375   **WW**

ESSENTIAL REFERENCE—NEWCOMB COLLEGE

Established in 1886 in New Orleans, Louisiana, Newcomb College (or, in full, the H. Sophie Newcomb Memorial College) was founded to instruct young Southern women in the liberal arts. Under the tuition of such art professors as William Woodward, Ellsworth Woodward, and Mary Given Sheerer, the Newcomb College potters produced a range of outstanding Arts and Crafts pottery until production ceased in 1940.

- The shapes of Newcomb College wares were mostly inspired by the soft, curvaceous forms of both indigenous rustic and traditional Asian pottery.
- Decorative inspiration came primarily from the flora and fauna indigenous to the southern United States; typical flora included tobacco and cotton plants, blossoms, and cacti.
- Sadie Irvine and A. F. Simpson were among many of the notable artist/designers.
- Along with marks denoting the pottery, the artist, and the date, the underside of Newcomb College wares also originally bore a label declaring that the "Designs are not duplicated."

An early tall Newcomb College Pottery glazed earthenware vase, by Mary Sheerer, with stylized lilies, impressed manufacturer's mark and date code "NC JM U" on underside, with incised artist's initials "MS."

1902   *11¼in (28.5cm) high*

$21,000-25,000   DRA

An early Newcomb College Pottery glazed earthenware covered jar, by Mazie Teresa Ryan, with cinquefoils, impressed and glazed manufacturer's mark "NC XX18 Q" on underside, with artist's signature and date "MTRyan 1904."

1904   *4¼in (11cm) high*

$8,500-12,500   DRA

A rare early Newcomb College Pottery glazed earthenware vase, by Mazie Teresa Ryan, with alligators, impressed and glazed manufacturer's mark and date code "NC VV83 JM Q" on underside, with artist's initials "M.T.R," paper manufacturer's label on underside "Newcomb Pottery New Orleans Subject Alligator Designs are not duplicated."

See Poesch, "Newcomb Pottery: An Enterprise for Southern Women, 1895-1940," Schiffer (1997), page 117, no. 72, where this example is illustrated.

1904   *9¼in (23.5cm) diam*

$150,000-160,000   DRA

An early Newcomb College Pottery glazed earthenware tyg, by Roberta B. Kennon, with tulips, inscribed on body "Tulip-beds of different shapes and dyes, bending beneath the invisible west-wind's sighs," impressed and glazed manufacturer's mark and date code "NC SS61 JM W" on underside, with glazed artist's initials "RBK."

1904   *6¾in (17cm) diam*

$11,000-15,000   DRA

An early Newcomb College Pottery glazed earthenware vase, by Leona Nicholson, with magnolias, impressed and glazed manufacturer's mark and date code "NC JM Q AH65" on underside, with artist's initials "LN."

1905   *14½in (37cm) high*

$100,000-110,000   DRA

A rare early Newcomb College Pottery glazed earthenware vase, by Sabina E. Wells, with dogs, impressed and glazed manufacturer's mark and date code "NC Q AB13" on underside, with artist's initials "SEW" and seconded mark.

1905   *9½in (24cm) high*

$14,000-17,500   DRA

An early tall Newcomb College Pottery glazed earthenware vase, by Leona Nicholson, with irises, impressed and glazed manufacturer's mark and date code "NC JM W CE2" on underside, with artist's initials "LN."

1908   *12½in (32cm) high*

$35,000-40,000   DRA

A rare Newcomb College Pottery glazed earthenware transitional covered jar, by Ora Reams, with MacIntosh roses, impressed manufacturer's mark "NC JM B" on underside, with glazed date code "FA60," incised date "1912," and incised artist's cipher "OR."

1912   *6in (15cm) high*

$7,500-8,500   DRA

A Newcomb College Pottery glazed earthenware vase, by Anna Frances Simpson, with tall pines and a full moon, impressed manufacturer's mark "NC 325 RB53" on underside, with artist's initials "AFS."

1929   *9¼in (23.5cm) high*

$7,500-8,500   DRA

ESSENTIAL REFERENCE—GEORGE OHR

Born in Biloxi, Mississippi, George Ohr (1857-1918) first worked as a blacksmith, then a file cutter, and then a tinker, before becoming a sailor. However, in 1879 his childhood friend Joseph Meyer invited him to New Orleans, Louisiana, to learn the art and craft of pottery.

Subsequently, back in Biloxi, Ohr established his own pottery, digging his own clay from the banks of the Tchoutacabouffa River, shaping vessels—mostly hollow wares—and then "misshaping" (folding, denting, crumpling, twisting, and squashing) them into unique forms that were in many respects as eccentric as his own appearance and, indeed, behavior!

The eccentricity of the vessels was not, however, confined to just their shapes. Ohr called all his pots his "mud babies," and his workshop the "Pot-Ohr-E." Indeed, he referred to himself at any given time as: "Geoerge Ohr M.D. (Mud Dauber)," "George Ohr P.M. (Pot Maker)," "The Unequaled Variety Potter," "The Pot-Ohr," or, as he is best known nowadays, "The Mad Potter of Biloxi."

Many examples of George Ohr's work are now displayed at the Ohr-O'Keefe Museum of Art in Biloxi, while privately owned pieces continue to change hands at seemingly increasingly high prices.

A small George Ohr earthenware pitcher, in olive, cobalt, and brown glaze, impressed "GEO. E. OHR, BILOXI" on underside.
ca. 1892-94   *4½in (11.5cm) wide*
$4,300-5,600   FRE

A George Ohr glazed earthenware vase, with a ruffled lip and in-body dimples, in an unusual orange, brown, raspberry, and green glaze, incised "GE Ohr Biloxi" on underside.

For this illustrated example, see Clark et. al., "The Mad Potter of Biloxi," Abbeville (1989), page 93.
ca. 1895-1900   *6¼in (16cm) high*
$15,000-19,000   DRA

A rare George Ohr bisque earthenware vase with face, with a crimped rim and in-body cat "face," incised script signature "G E Ohr" on underside.

Blasberg, "The Unknown Ohr," Peaceable Press (1989), page 45, illustrates a similar example.
1898-1910   *7in (18cm) high*
$10,000-12,500   DRA

A large George Ohr glazed earthenware vase, with in-body manipulations, ruffled rim, deep indigo glaze, impressed signature "G. E. OHR, Biloxi, Miss." on underside.
1897-1900   *6¼in (16cm) high*
$11,000-15,000   DRA

A George Ohr ribbed and folded glazed earthenware vessel, in brown and speckled ocher glaze, impressed "G.E. OHR, Biloxi, Miss" on underside.
ca. 1897-1900   *4¼in (11cm) wide*
$2,500-3,700   FRE

A George Ohr glazed earthenware vase, with a twisted neck and pinched rim, in olive green glaze, twice impressed signature "G.E. OHR. Biloxi, Miss.."
ca. 1897-1900   *6¼in (16cm) high*
$2,200-2,700   FRE

A George Ohr glazed earthenware pitcher, with a cutout handle and manipulated rim, mottled emerald, raspberry, and purple glaze, incised script signature "G E Ohr" on underside.
1898-1910   *4¾in (12cm) high*
$9,500-11,000   DRA

An exceptional George Ohr scroddled bisque earthenware vase, with a pinched and folded rim and body, inscribed "Alice E. Harrison Jan 3, 1907" on base, incised script signature "G E Ohr" on underside.
1907   *6½in (16.5cm) wide*
$14,000-17,500   DRA

A George Ohr glazed earthenware three-handle mug, in mat gunmetal glaze with a streaky olive interior, signed "G E Ohr" on underside under glaze.
ca. 1898-1910   *4¾in (12cm) high*
$5,000-6,200   FRE

An early Rookwood Pottery "Sea Green" glazed earthenware vase, by William P. McDonald, with Venus, impressed manufacturer's mark, date, and number "Flame mark 589F W G" on underside, with incised artist's initials "WPMD."

1894   *7¼in (18.5cm) high*
$4,700-5,500   **DRA**

A rare Rookwood Pottery "Standard Glaze" earthenware lamp base, by Kataro Shirayamadani, with tulips, electroplated copper and brass mount, impressed manufacturer's mark and number "Flame mark I T4250" on underside, with incised artist's cipher and paper auction label "The Glover Collection Cinncinati Art Galleries 0937."

1901   *12in (30.5cm) high*
$6,000-6,700   **DRA**

A rare Rookwood Pottery "Modeled Mat" glazed earthenware figural vase, by Anna Marie Valentien, impressed manufacturer's mark, date, and number "Flame mark I 128 Z" on underside, with incised artist's initials "A.M.V.."

1901   *6¼in (16cm) high*
$2,000-2,500   **DRA**

A Rookwood Pottery "Scenic Vellum" glazed earthenware vase, by Edward T. Hurley, impressed manufacturer's mark, date, and number "Flame mark IX 904C V" on underside, with incised artist's signature.

1909   *10½in (26.5cm) high*
$2,100-2,700   **DRA**

A rare Rookwood Pottery four-tile landscape frieze, glazed earthenware decorated in cuencaeach, impressed manufacturer's mark "Rookwood Faience" on underside of each example, and numbered "1226YC."

See Karlson, "American Art Tile 1876-1941," Rizzoli, (1998), pages 80 and 82; and Karlson, "The Encyclopedia of American Art Tiles Region 3," Schiffer (2005), page 147.

ca. 1910   *each tile 11¾in (30cm) wide*
$6,000-6,700   **DRA**

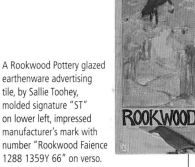

A Rookwood Pottery glazed earthenware advertising tile, by Sallie Toohey, molded signature "ST" on lower left, impressed manufacturer's mark with number "Rookwood Faience 1288 1359Y 66" on verso.

ca. 1910   *15in (38cm) high*
$19,000-22,000   **DRA**

A Rookwood Pottery "Scenic Vellum" glazed earthenware vase, by Lenore Asbury, impressed manufacturer's mark, date, and number "Flame mark XVII 1124E V" on underside, with incised artist's initials "L.A."

1917   *7in (18cm) high*
$2,000-2,500   **DRA**

A Rookwood Pottery "Winter Scenic Vellum" glazed earthenware vase, by Sallie Coyne, impressed manufacturer's mark, date, and number "Flame mark XVIII 271C" on underside, with incised artist's initials "SEC."

1918   *9½in (24cm) high*
$1,600-2,000   **DRA**

A tall Rookwood Pottery "Decorated Mat/ Double Vellum" glazed porcelain vase, impressed signature, date, and number "Flame mark XVIII 339B" on underside, with incised artist's initials "L.J.T.."

1928   *14½in (37cm) high*
$750-1,000   **DRA**

ESSENTIAL REFERENCE—ROSEVILLE

The Roseville Pottery was founded in Roseville, Ohio, in 1890. It initially produced utilitarian wares and launched its first art pottery range, "Rozane," in 1900. Frederick Hurten Rhead (1880-1942), son of Frederick Rhead and brother of Charlotte Rhead, worked at Roseville 1904-08 and created several ranges, including the popular "Della Robbia." Other notable designers included Frank Ferrell and glaze maker George Kraus. In 1908, Roseville introduced several mass-produced, molded ranges, many of which were inspired by forms from nature. The pottery closed in 1954.

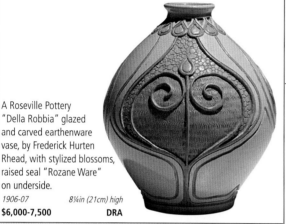

A Roseville Pottery "Della Robbia" glazed and carved earthenware vase, by Frederick Hurten Rhead, with stylized blossoms, raised seal "Rozane Ware" on underside.

1906-07   8¼in (21cm) high

$6,000-7,500   DRA

CLOSER LOOK—A DELLA ROBIA KRAKER

The shape of the vase is derived from the ancient Greek "krater," which translates as a "mixing vessel." Traditionally, it was of large, open-top, two-handle form, fashioned in either pottery or metal, and mostly used for mixing wine and water.

The vase is from Roseville's "Della Robbia" line of art pottery, which was introduced by the English-born ceramicist Frederick Hurten Rhead (1880-1942), and named after a family of eminent ceramic sculptors who lived and worked in Florence, Italy, during the Renaissance.

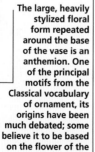

In addition to the use of decorative imagery from Classical Antiquity, for Roseville's "Della Robia" line, many of those figures and motifs were hand-carved, such as in this ancient Greek battle scene, which is in low relief.

The large, heavily stylized floral form repeated around the base of the vase is an anthemion. One of the principal motifs from the Classical vocabulary of ornament, its origins have been much debated; some believe it to be based on the flower of the acanthus, some on the honeysuckle, some on the sacred Assyrian hom, and others the Egyptian lotus. Confusingly, it is similar to the Classical palmette.

A rare Roseville Pottery "Della Robbia" glazed earthenware krater, incised "G.B." on body.

ca. 1910   17in (43cm) high

$7,000-8,000   FRE

A rare Roseville experimental glazed earthenware vase, by Frederick Hurten Rhead, squeeze-bag decoration, with applied paper label "From the White Pillars Museum" (De Pere Historical Society, De Pere, Wisconsin).

1904-08   9in (23cm) high

$7,500-10,000   FRE

A Roseville Pottery "Della Robbia" glazed and carved earthenware vase, by Frederick Hurten Rhead, with daffodils, raised seal "Rozane Ware Royal" on underside, with glazed decorator's signature "H. Smith."

1906-07   20½in (52cm) high

$17,500-20,000   DRA

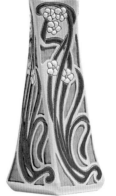

A Roseville Pottery "Della Robbia" glazed and carved earthenware vase, by Frederick Hurten Rhead, with flowers, raised seal "Rozane Ware" on underside, with incised decorator's initials "EC."

1906-07   9¾in (24.5cm) high

$7,500-10,000   DRA

A Roseville Pottery glazed earthenware peacock umbrella stand, by Frederick Hurten Rhead, squeeze-bag decoration, signed "HR" (for Harry Rhead, brother of Frederick Rhead).

ca. 1908   20½in (52cm) high

$10,000-12,500   FRE

A rare Roseville Pottery "Rozane Olympic" glazed earthenware hydria, marked "ROZANE "OLYMPIC" POTTERY, THE HOURS TAKING THE HORSES FROM JUNO's CAR" on underside.

ca. 1910   14¼in (36cm) high

$8,000-10,000   FRE

A Roseville Pottery "Carnelian II" glazed earthenware vase.

See Huxford, "The Collector's Encyclopedia of Roseville Pottery," Second Series (1980), pages 71-73.

ca. 1926   16in (40.5cm) high

$2,000-2,500   DRA

ESSENTIAL REFERENCE—RUSKIN

The Ruskin Pottery was founded in West Smethwick, near Birmingham, England, in 1898 by Edward Richard Taylor and his son William Howson Taylor. While the inspiration for the shapes and forms of their vessels came from traditional Chinese ceramics, the glazes and glazing techniques they used were highly innovative. For example, William Howson Taylor energetically studied the composition of luster, crystalline, and high-fired glazes (all lead-free) in diverse colors, as well as mastered the highly complex techniques employed in the application of soufflé and flambé glazes. Decoratively, the result was a series of abstract compositions that, when they come onto the market, continue to command the attention of collectors some 90 years after the factory closed its doors (and the records of the formulae of the glazes were destroyed) in 1935, following the economic downturn of the early 1930s.

A Ruskin Pottery high-fired stoneware vase, designed by William Howson Taylor, covered in a speckled apple-green glaze, with a speckled lavender and turquoise green neck, white running patches, impressed factory mark and date.

1906   *7¾in (19.5cm) high*
$4,700-5,200   **WW**

A Ruskin Pottery flambé-glazed earthenware vase, by William Howson Taylor, impressed manufacturer's stamp and date.

1906   *9in (23cm) high*
$1,100-1,500   **L&T**

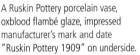

A Ruskin Pottery high-fired stoneware vase, designed by William Howson Taylor, mottled pale blue with purple and lavender, impressed marks and dated.

1907   *9¼in (23.5cm) high*
$2,100-2,700   **WW**

A Ruskin Pottery porcelain vase, oxblood flambé glaze, impressed manufacturer's mark and date "Ruskin Pottery 1909" on underside.

1909   *10¾in (27.5cm) high*
$3,500-4,200   **DRA**

A Ruskin Pottery potpourri bowl and cover, luster-glazed earthenware and ivory.

ca. 1910   *7¼in (18.5cm) diam*
$625-850   **L&T**

A Ruskin Pottery oxblood-glazed porcelain "Ginger" jar, impressed manufacturer's mark and date "Ruskin Pottery 1911" on underside, with partial paper manufacturer's mark "Ruskin Pottery This color scheme cannot be repeated."

1911   *8¼in (21cm) high*
$750-1,000   **DRA**

A Ruskin Pottery oxblood-glazed porcelain vase, impressed manufacturer's mark and date "Ruskin England 1922" on underside.

1922   *11in (28cm) high*
$2,100-2,700   **DRA**

A Ruskin Pottery high-fired stoneware vase, designed by William Howson Taylor, sang de boeuf glaze with lavender and silver on the shoulder, impressed "Ruskin England 1926."

1926   *8¾in (22cm) high*
$625-750   **WW**

A Ruskin Pottery stoneware soufflé glaze vase, designed by William Howson Taylor, mottled midnight blue over light blue, impressed marks, dated.

1927   *6¼in (16cm) high*
$250-310   **WW**

A Wedgwood & Sons Arts and Crafts wall charger, by Alfred Powell (1865-1960), decorated by Mabel Tatton, painted and glazed earthenware, impressed "WEDGWOOD," signed in gilt "M. TATTON" on rim.

The influence of William Morris and Edward Burne-Jones can be seen in Alfred Powell's design for this dish—the flora and fauna imagery are pariculary reminensicent of tapestries made by Morris & Co. at Merton Abbey. Mabel Tatton started decorating at Etruria for Wedgwood in 1907, then left in 1914 to study at Hornsey College, Middlesex, before returning to the factory as head of the painting and enameling department from 1920 until 1928. The appearance of Tatton's signature in gilt on the rim marks this piece as an exceptional example of her decorating skills.

1910-20   *18½in (47cm) diam*
$4,700-5,500   L&T

ESSENTIAL REFERENCE—ERIC RAVILIOUS

Eric William Ravilious (1903-42) was an English painter, designer, book illustrator, and wood engraver who grew up in East Sussex and is best known for his watercolor paintings of the South Downs. A war artist in World War II, he died at the age of 39 when an aircraft he was flying in was lost off Iceland. During his lifetime, Ravilious engraved more than 400 illustrations and drew over 40 lithographic designs for books and other publications, and in 1936 was commissioned by Wedgwood to design some ceramics. Popular Ravilious designs included: "Alphabet" (1937); "Afternoon Tea" (1938); "Travel" (1938); "Boat Race Day" (1938); and, as here, "Garden Implements" (1939). He also produced a commemorative mug for the aborted coronation of Edward VIII, which was revised for the coronation of George VI in 1937, then posthumously reworked for the coronation of Queen Elizabeth II in 1953, and again in 2023 for the coronation of King Charles III.

A Wedgwood beaker mug, "Garden Implements" pattern, designed by Eric Ravilious, printed with a vignette of garden tools in a barrel, in black and pink luster, printed factory mark.

4¼in (11cm) high
$450-500   WW

A rare Wedgwood Pottery bowl, "Boat Race" pattern, designed by Eric Ravilious, printed in colors with a boat race vignette on the exterior, the well with Piccadilly Circus, printed factory mark, fine star hairline on base.

12¼in (31cm) diam
$5,000-5,600   WW

A rare Wedgwood Pottery vase, designed by Keith Murray, shape no. 3765, ribbed body, covered in a mat blue-green glaze, printed factory mark, "KM" monogram.

7¼in (18.5cm) high
$500-625   WW

A rare Wedgwood glazed and gilt porcelain footed bowl, "Fairyland Lustre Nizami" pattern, by Daisy Makeig-Jones, pattern no. Z5485, with "The old woman complaining to Sultan Sunjar" scene in interior, stamped "Wedgwood Made in England" on underside, with glazed pattern number "Z5485."

See des Fontaines, "Wedgwood Fairyland Lustre," Richard Dennie (1976), page 259, for the interior pattern illustrated.

ca. 1925   *8¼in (21cm) diam*
$10,500-12,500   DRA

A Wedgwood glazed and gilt porcelain vase, "Fairyland Lustre Candlemas" pattern, by Daisy Makeig-Jones, pattern no. Z5157, gilt stamped "Wedgwood Made in England" on underside, with glazed pattern number "Z5157 A."

See des Fontaines, "Wedgwood Fairyland Lustre," Richard Dennie (1976), page 171.

ca. 1925   *7½in (19cm) high*
$5,500-7,000   DRA

A Wedgwood Pottery luster bowl, designed by Daisy Makeig-Jones, the exterior printed and painted with fish swimming amid waterweed, in colors and gilt on a streaked green ground, the interior with a band of waterweed on a pearl luster ground, printed Wedgwood mark.

10½in (26.5cm) diam
$1,600-2,000   WW

A Wedgwood meat platter, "Garden" pattern, designed by Eric Ravilious, printed with a vignette of a man diving into a pool, the rim with a stylized border, in blue and black, printed factory mark.

12¾in (32.5cm) wide
$625-750   WW

ESSENTIAL REFERENCE—KEITH MURRAY

Born in New Zealand in 1892, Keith Day Pearce Murray emigrated to England with his parents in 1906 and went on to train as an architect. In the late 1920s, however, his architectural career faltered in the recession and, inspired by the Modernist and Art Deco wares he had seen at the "Exposition Internationale des Arts Decoratifs et Industriel Modernes" in Paris, in 1925, he began designing glass and ceramics. It was a subsequent return to architectural practice, and a commission to design its new factory at Barlaston, that forged his links with Wedgwood—his Modernist vases, plates, bowls, and other tablewares, with their elegant geometric, lathe-turned, semi-mat monochromatic forms, putting him at the forefront of a revival in British ceramics during the 1930s and 1940s.

A Wedgwood Pottery vase, designed by Keith Murray, shape no. 3801, covered in a gray glaze, impressed and printed factory marks, facsimile signature.

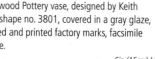

6in (15cm) high
$550-700   WW

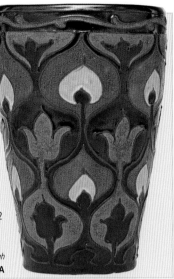

An important American Arequipa Pottery vase, by Frederick Hurten Rhead, glazed squeeze-bag-decorated earthenware, glazed manufacturer's mark, number and date "488 1912 AC" on underside, with pot under tree.

1912   7½in (19cm) high
$205,000-230,000   DRA

A 20thC Beswick Belted Galloway bull, no. 1746B, black and white gloss.

7¾in (19.5cm) wide
$1,250-1,500   L&T

An exceptional Danish Bing & Grøndahl reticulated covered vessel, by Fanny Garde, hand-carved and glazed porcelain, with roses, glazed signature, and number "F Garde 622" on underside, with stamped manufacturer's mark "B&G Kjøbenhavn Danish China Works B&G."

See Duncan, "The Paris Salons 1895-1914 Volume IV: Ceramics & Glass," ACC (1999), page 61, for a related example illustrated.

ca. 1900   11in (28cm) high
$21,000-25,000   DRA

A Boch Freres Art Deco vase, by Charles Catteau, decorated with seven penguins against a pale gray craquelure ground, printed mark and painted "D.110," poorly reattached break.

1930s   12½in (32cm) high
$1,000-1,250   FLD

A Burmantoft's Faience pottery jardinière and stand, model no. 2318, modeled in low relief with a galleon sailing before a rising sun, in colors between green bands, the base with cream, yellow, and green columns, impressed and painted marks.

39½in (100.5cm) high
$1,050-1,250   WW

A Carlton Ware toucan lamp, advertising Guinness, with original paper shade.

15¾in (40cm) high (including shade)
$250-310   WHP

A Carter's Poole Pottery tile panel, "Sea Tales," made for W. H. Smith retail store, decorated in colors with a galleon at full sail, title "Sea Tales" in Eric Gill's serif typeface, in an oak frame, marks concealed.

21in (53.5cm) high
$1,600-2,000   WW

A Chelsea Keramic Art Works redware kylix, by Hugh C. Robertson, with slip decoration, incised signature on underside "HCR."

ca. 1876   7in (18cm) diam
$700-950   DRA

An Art Deco "Hydrangeas" charger, decorated by Charlotte Rhead, centered with tube-lined flowers and leaves, inscribed with signature and numbered "3797."

12¾in (32.5cm) diam
$250-310   SWO

A Chelsea Keramic Art Works experimental vase, by Hugh C. Robertson, oxblood-glazed stoneware, impressed "CKAW" on underside.

1885-89   8in (20.5cm) high
$5,200-6,000   DRA

A luster-glazed earthenware vase, by Lucien Lévy-Dhurmer (1865-1953) for Clement Massier (1845-1917), painted "CLEMENT MASSIER," impressed "CLEMENT MASSIER/GOLFE/JUAN/(AM)/L. LEVY."

See B. Coleman, "The Best of British Arts & Crafts," Atglen (2004), page 213, for this vase illustrated.

ca. 1895   15in (38cm) high
$7,000-7,500   L&T

A rare large Cowan Pottery glazed earthenware plate, by Viktor Schreckengost, glazed signature "Viktor Schreckengost" on underside, with impressed manufacturer's mark "Cowan."

ca. 1930   *17in (43cm) diam*

$3,100-3,700   **DRA**

A pair of Cowan Pottery glazed earthenware "Pelican" bookends, by Albert Drexler Jacobson, impressed manufacturer's mark "Cowan" on each lower edge.

See Duncan, "American Art Deco," Thames and Hudson (1999), page 119.

1931   *5¼in (13.5cm) high*

$1,900-2,500   **DRA**

A rare Cowan Pottery glazed earthenware wall-hanging charger, "Danse Moderne Jazz" pattern, by Viktor Schreckengost, impressed manufacturer's mark "Cowan" on reverse.

See Adams, "Viktor Schreckengost: American Da Vinci," Tide-Mark (2006), pages 24-25 and 31.

ca. 1931   *11in (28cm) diam*

$8,000-9,500   **DRA**

A rare Cowan Pottery glazed earthenware equestrian wall-hanging charger, by Viktor Schreckengost, glazed signature "Viktor Schreckengost Cowan Pottery" on underside, with impressed manufacturer's mark "Cowan."

ca. 1931   *11½in (29cm) diam*

$1,250-1,700   **DRA**

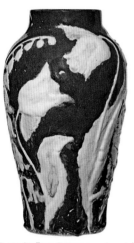

A rare Dedham Pottery experimental glazed stoneware vase, by Hugh C. Robertson, incised signature "Dedham Pottery HCR B.W." on underside.

1896-1908   *10½in (26.5cm) high*

$15,000-19,000   **DRA**

A large Della Robbia Pottery plaque, "Sea Sprites," designed by Ellen Mary Rope, worked on by Liz Wilkins and Marion de Caluwe, modeled in relief with two sea figures swimming in turbulent waters, glazed in blue, yellow, and cream, incised "Rope" signature and date bottom left, incised "Della Robbia, 184" and artist's monograms on reverse, in a wood frame, cracked.

This panel was originally known as "Water Babes," and is also known as "Water Sprites." A similar panel is held in the Victoria & Albert Museum collection (C.145-2018).

1902   *21¾in (55cm) wide*

$2,200-2,700   **WW**

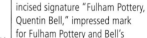

A Fulham Pottery painted table lamp and shade, by Quentin Bell (1910-96), decorated with nude male and female figures diving into water, contemporary hand-painted shade by the same artist, the base with incised signature "Fulham Pottery, Quentin Bell," impressed mark for Fulham Pottery and Bell's own stamp.

24¾in (63cm) high

$3,500-4,000   **DUK**

A rare Fulper Pottery vase, leopard skin crystalline on mahogany flambé-glazed stoneware, stamped rectangular manufacturer's mark "Fulper" on underside.

1910-16   *9¾in (24.5cm) high*

$7,000-8,000   **DRA**

A Gallé faience cat, painted with heart and circle patches in blue, on a yellow ground, with applied glass eyes, signed "E. Gallé, Nancy" on foot.

13½in (34cm) high

$1,000-1,250   **DUK**

A late-19thC George Jones majolica ewer, in Palissy style, the body applied with lizards and shells on a leaf-and-barkmolded ground, with green and brown glazes throughout, the handle formed as a serpent coiling around the shoulder, raised on a round socle foot, impressed "GJ" monogram.

17¾in (45cm) high

$1,700-2,200   **L&T**

A rare and exceptional American Grand Feu Art Pottery vase, moss agate-glazed stoneware, impressed manufacturer's mark "GRAND FEU POTTERY L.A. CAL TT" on underside, with incised "154."

1916-18   *8in (20.5cm) diam*

$6,000-8,000   **DRA**

A Grays Pottery Art Deco "Paris" pitcher, "Moon and Mountains" pattern, by Susie Cooper, printed mark, small chip in foot rim.

4in (10cm) high

$220-275 FLD

An important Arts and Crafts slipware pottery pitcher, by Horace Elliott, yellow glaze and brown slip, with an angel wing-form handle and wide curved spout, sgraffito feathers on wing, on the body "Here is a mixture, of Earth and Heaven, An Angel's wing to a pitcher given, Take hold of the wing, for a handle, pray! Or the vessel of earth may fly away," signed on foot "Copyright Horace Elliott" and on base "Elliott, London 1893," minor losses in glaze, crazing/stress marks, small chips.

1893   11in (28cm) high

$10,500-12,500 JON

A Linthorpe Art Pottery twin-handle Peruvian vessel, by Christopher Dresser, glazed earthenware, impressed facsimile signature "C. DRESSER (indistinct)/298."

See H. Lyons, "Christopher Dresser: The People's Designer, 1834-1904," Woodbridge (2004), page 98, plate 134, where this vase appears in a period advertisement for Linthorpe Art Pottery.

ca. 1880   8¼in (21cm) high

$4,700-5,500 L&T

A Lomonosov character pitcher, designed by Natalia Danko, modeled as a woman wearing a headdress, glazed in vivid colors and highlighted in gilt, printed factory marks.

5¼in (13.5cm) high

$190-250 WW

An important American Marblehead Pottery "Ipswich" vase, by Annie Aldrich and Sarah Tutt, glazed earthenware, impressed manufacturer's mark "MP" with ship symbol on underside, with incised artist's initials "AT."

This is one of only a few known examples. For further reference, see Clancy and Eidelberg, "Beauty in Common Things: American Arts & Crafts Pottery from The Two Red Roses Foundation," Two Red Roses Foundation (2008), page 88; and Kaplan, "The Art That is Life: The Arts & Crafts Movement in America 1875-1920," Little, Brown (1998), pages 256-57.

ca. 1909   8¾in (22cm) high

$250,000-285,000 DRA

A Louis Wain "Lucky Pig" spill vase, painted in colors, impressed factory marks, facsimile signature, professional restoration in ear.

4½in (11.5cm) high

$1,050-1,250 WW

A tall American Marblehead Pottery glazed earthenware vase, by Arthur Hennessey and Sarah Tutt, with stylized mistletoe, impressed manufacturer's mark "MP" with ship symbol on underside, with incised signature "HT."

1908-16   9in (23cm) high

$7,500-10,000 DRA

A rare American Marblehead Pottery glazed earthenware vase, by Arthur Hennessey and Sarah Tutt, with conventionalized roses, impressed manufacturer's mark "MP" with ship symbol on underside, with incised signature "HT."

The stylized form of the flowers may have been influenced by Charles Rennie Mackintosh's famous "Mackintosh Rose" design.

ca. 1910   8in (20.5cm) diam

$33,000-40,000 DRA

A rare American oxblood-glazed earthenware vase, by Maria Longworth Nichols Storer, with sea horses, glazed signature and date "MLS 97" on underside.

For this illustrated vase, see Clark, "The Arts and Crafts Movement in America 1876-1916,"Princeton (1992), page 133, no. 179.

1897   7in (18cm) high

$7,500-10,000 DRA

A Maw & Co. Pottery vase, "Divers (Mermaids)" pattern, by Walter Crane (1845-1915), the compressed body painted with spiraling sea maidens and alternating columns of scrolling foliage, in shades of ruby luster on a cream ground, unsigned, painted flower motif to base.

See P. G. Konody, "The Art of Walter Crane," George Bell & Sons (1902), for the complete range of seven vases designed by Walter Crane.

8¾in (22cm) high

$21,000-25,000 WW

A Merrimac Pottery glazed earthenware vase, with feathers, incised decorator's initials "EB" on underside.

ca. 1900   6¾in (17cm) high

$8,500-10,000 DRA

A Minton & Co. glazed earthenware vase, attributed to Christopher Dresser (1834-1904), with gilt and enamel highlights.

See W. Halén, "Christopher Dresser," Phaidon (1994), page 124, plate-131, where related Minton & Co. artwork is illustrated.

ca. 1870   *6in (15cm) high*

$3,500-4,200   **L&T**

A tall Minton's "Secessionist" ewer, designed by John Wadsworth and Leon Solon, slip-decorated with Art Nouveau flowers and foliage, in shades of mustard, green, turquoise, and blue, printed factory marks, stress hairline in neck.

14¼in (36cm) high

$250-310   **WW**

A pair of Minton's "Secessionist" vases, designed by John Wadsworth and Leon Solon, each tube lined with a stylized Art Nouveau flower, in green and yellow on a red ground, impressed and printed marks.

10¾in (27.5cm) high

$375-500   **WW**

A pair of late-19thC majolica plaques, in Palissy style, molded and applied in high relief with fish, including carp, eels, snails, shellfish, turtles, and frogs, on a "Straw mat" effect base, unmarked.

16½in (42cm) wide

$3,500-4,200   **HT**

A Pilkington's Tile & Pottery Co. Arts and Crafts tile, by C.F.A. Voysey (1857-1941), glazed earthenware.

See C. Blanchett, "20th Century British Tiles," Schiffer Publishing (2006), page 455, where a similar tile is illustrated; and K. Livingstone et. al., "C. F. A Voysey Arts and Crafts Designer," V&A Publishing (2016), page 292, plate 385, where designs for related tiles are illustrated.

ca. 1920   *6in (15cm) wide*

$2,000-2,500   **L&T**

A Pilkington's Royal Lancastrian pottery vase, by Richard Joyce, shape no. 2662, painted in silver luster with two medieval knights, each holding a shield and jousting pole, with two Tudor roses between, below a stylized anthemion rim and over a Maltese cross border, impressed monogram and date cypher (cross).

1917   *9¼in (23.5cm) high*

$1,250-1,700   **HT**

A Reissner, Stellmacher & Kessel "Amphora" porcelain portrait vase, polychrome glazed with gilt highlights, red printed "RStK TURIN TEPLITZ BOHEMIA," with impressed "139/28."

ca. 1900   *8¾in (22cm) high*

$3,500-4,200   **L&T**

A French Art Deco "Il Pleut, Il Pleut, Bergère" glazed earthenware vase, by Robert Lallemant (1902-54), signed "T R LALLEMANT, FRANCE" on underside.

ca. 1925-33   *7¼in (18.5cm) high*

$625-750   **FRE**

An early 20thC Royal Lancastrian pottery ewer, shape no. 3144, painted by Richard Joyce, with three carp swimming amid weeds, in copper luster on a mottled green ground, monogrammed "JR" under crown.

7in (18cm) high

$800-950   **HT**

A large Swedish Rörstrand vase, by Per Algot Erikson, hand-carved and glazed porcelain, with dandelions, stamped triple crown manufacturer's mark "Rörstrand" on underside, with artist's initials "AE" and numbered "20519 RR."

ca. 1900   *18¼in (46.5cm) high*

$8,000-9,500   **DRA**

A Saturday Evening Girls potpourri jar, by Albina Mangini, glazed earthenware decorated in cuerda seca, with Viking ships, glazed signature and date "AM 2-15 S.E.G." on underside.

1915   *5¼in (13.5cm) high*

$4,000-4,700   **DRA**

A rare Teco Pottery glazed earthenware buttressed vase, by William Day Gates, model no. 375, impressed manufacturer's mark "Teco" on underside.

See Darling, "Teco: Art Pottery of the Prairie School," Erie Art Museum (1989), page 154.

1902-20   *11in (28cm) high*

$4,700-5,500   **DRA**

An exceptional Tiffany Studios Favrile Pottery coupe, moss green-glazed earthenware, with frogs and water lilies, incised signature and number "P1031 L.C.Tiffany - Favrile Pottery" on underside.

See Eidelberg, "Tiffany Favrile Pottery and the Quest of Beauty," Lillian Nassau (2010), pages 28 and 96.

1904-14   *8¼in (21cm) diam*
$50,000-62,000   **DRA**

An important Van Briggle Pottery glazed earthenware vase, by Artus Van Briggle, with two handles and an Art Nouveau patinated bronze mount, incised signature and date "AA Van Briggle 1904" on underside, with incised Japanese artist's cipher.

This work was probably made for the 1904 St. Louis Exposition, the metal base designed and executed by R. Ito, one of two Japanese craftsmen hired by the company. See Eidelberg (ed.), "From Our Native Clay: Art Pottery from the Collections of the American Ceramic Arts Society," Turn of the Century (1987), page 62, no. 99, where this example is illustrated.

1904   *5¼in (13.5cm) high*
$10,500-12,500   **DRA**

A Weller Pottery Fru-Russett glazed earthenware vase, with Virginia creepers and male nude, incised signature "Weller" on underside and near base.

ca. 1904   *18in (46cm) high*
$6,000-7,500   **DRA**

A large Troika Pottery "Wheel" vase, by Avril Bennett, cast in low relief with geometric panels, glazed brown and blue, painted marks.

12½in (32cm) high
$1,250-1,700   **WW**

A Troika Pottery "Double Base" vase, cast in low relief with a geometric figure design, in tan and blue, painted factory marks, painted "CC" monogram.

14in (35.5cm) high
$1,500-1,900   **WW**

A pair of Wemyss Ware "Elgin" vases, "Cabbage Roses" pattern, decorated by James Sharp, painted and impressed "WEMYSS."

ca. 1900   *17¾in (45cm) high*
$1,500-1,900   **L&T**

A large Wemyss Ware cat, sponged black on white with applied green glass eyes, impressed "WEMYSS WARE/R.H.&S.," printed retailer's stamp "T. GOODE & CO."

ca. 1900   *12½in (32cm) high*
$6,600-7,200   **L&T**

A large Wemyss Ware pig, "Shamrocks" pattern, impressed "WEMYSS," printed retailer's stamp "T. GOODE & CO."

Unusually, the decoration on this pig features both three- and four-leaf clovers.

ca. 1900   *18in (46cm) wide*
$5,300-6,000   **L&T**

An early-20thC Wemyss Ware "Gordon" plate, "Raspberries" pattern, decorated by Edwin Sandland, on a black ground, painted and impressed "WEMYSS."

8in (20.5cm) diam
$950-1,250   **L&T**

A Wilkinson's Pottery vesta match safe, "Do Scratch my Back," modeled as a dog sitting with tongue out, painted in shades of yellow, red, and black, the oval base inscribed "Do scratch my back," retailed by Soane & Smith, London, stamped factory mark.

4¾in (12cm) high
$190-250   **WW**

A Hungarian Zsolnay eosin-glazed earthenware vase, with snails and flowers, raised five churches seal and impressed number "M 8079" on underside.

ca. 1900   *9in (23cm) high*
$17,500-22,000   **DRA**

A Daum Frères mottled glass "Tiger Lily" vase, overlaid and acid etched, cameo signature "DAUM NANCY, FRANCE," with Cross of Lorraine.

ca. 1900   *11¾in (30cm) high*

$4,000-4,700   **L&T**

A tall Daum vase, acid-etched, wheel-carved, and martelé cameo glass, with crocuses, etched and gilt signature "Daum Nancy" on underside.

See Buttiker, "Daum Nancy III," Hirmer Verlag (2009), pages 52-53.

ca. 1900   *11½in (29cm) high*

$4,300-5,000   **DRA**

A Daum "Poppies" vase, internally decorated, wheel-carved and acid-etched cameo glass, incised "Daum, Nancy, France" on base.

ca. 1900   *19in (48cm) high*

$4,000-4,700   **FRE**

A fine Daum vase, acid-etched, wheel-carved, and martelé cameo glass, with morning glories, etched and gilt signature "Daum Nancy" on underside, with Cross of Lorraine.

ca. 1900   *9½in (24cm) high*

$6,000-7,500   **DRA**

A Daum vase, acid-etched and wheel-carved cameo glass, with daisies, etched signature "Daum Nancy France" on base, with Cross of Lorraine.

See Blount and Blount, "French Cameo Glass," Gazelle (1980), page 74.

ca. 1900   *9¾in (24.5cm) high*

$3,500-4,200   **DRA**

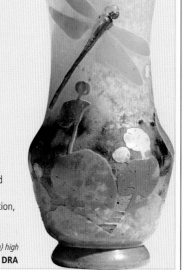

An exceptional Daum dragonfly vase, acid-etched and wheel-carved cameo glass, with applied decoration, etched signature "Daum Nancy" on underside.

ca. 1900   *7¾in (19.5cm) high*

$28,500-33,000   **DRA**

A Daum Frères painted cameo glass vase, decorated with flowering lilies, signed "DAUM/NANCY" on body, with Cross of Lorraine.

ca. 1900   *3¼in (8.5cm) high*

$800-950   **L&T**

A Daum "Paysage D'Hiver" glass vase, cut with a cameo and enameled winter landscape, painted signature "DAUM/NANCY" on base, with Cross of Lorraine, small losses.

ca. 1900   *4¾in (12cm) high*

$2,200-3,000   **CHOR**

A Daum vase, acid-etched, padded, vitrified, and wheel-carved cameo glass, with roses, etched signature "Daum Nancy" on underside, with Cross of Lorraine.

ca. 1900   *6¼in (16cm) wide*

$2,700-3,200   **DRA**

A Daum Frères cameo and overlaid glass vase, decorated with parrots, etched "DAUM NANCY FRANCE" on foot.

ca. 1930   *11¾in (30cm) high*

$10,000-12,500   **L&T**

ESSENTIAL REFERENCE—GALLÉ & ART NOUVEAU

Émile Gallé was born in Nancy, Lorraine, in 1846. From the early 1880s until his death in 1904, he was France's "Shining star" in the applied arts and a leading member of the Art Nouveau movement that emerged in Europe as a reaction to what its exponents considered to be the overbearing symmetry, rigidity, and prudishness of late-19thC Classicism.

Gallé's formative years included: studies in minerolgy, art history, and botany at Weimer University; the acquistion of glassmaking skills at his father's glass studio, and at Burgun, Schverer & Co. in Meizenthal; a close friendship with Tokuoso Takashima, a Japanese botanical artist studying at the Nancy School of Forestry; and a later acceptance among the literary and artistic elite of Paris, including a friendship with Marcel Proust.

These experiences led him inexorably to the heart of Art Nouveau, a new art for a new century, characterized by: a revival of the curvaceous and anti-Classical Rococo style; a belief that the potential of medieval Gothic ornament had never been fully realized prior to its eclipse by the Renaissance; the rediscovery of asymmetrical Japanese design; and, above all, a renewed fascination with the sinuous, curving lines inherent in nature, especially in flowers and insects, as a primary source of imagery.

Although he went on to design ceramics and furniture, Gallé was first and foremost a glassmaker and established his own studio in Nancy in 1873 (and subsequently, ca. 1890, the École de Nancy). Early pieces included classically shaped, clair-de-lune glass with Rococo-style enameled and gilt decoration as well as pastiches of late medieval Islamic-style glass. However, from the early 1880s, he began to develop the carved cameo Art Nouveau glass for which he became best known.

The rarest is the unique or limited edition "Studio" glass, each made with up to five different color layers of glass, the inner layers often mottled in imitation of hardstones, such as jade, quartz, and agate, the outer ones hand- or wheel-carved in deep relief, and some also incorporating gold, silver, or platinum foil between the layers to highlight details of the decoration.

Produced in far greater numbers, however, are the "commercial" pieces made from the late-1890s onward. The motifs and imagery are similar to those used on the Studio glass, but they are replicated with stencils and are "carved" in shallower relief (within only two or three layers of glass) by immersion in hydrofluoric acid baths. Although the most numerous, these commercial pieces—which include those known as "Gallé Industriel," made in the factory from his death in 1904 until its closure in 1931—are nevertheless also highly desirable by collectors.

A tall early Émile Gallé vase, acid-etched, enameled, and gilt glass, with chrysanthemums, gilt cameo signature "Gallé" on body.

ca. 1880   *14¼in (36cm) high*

$2,700-3,500   **DRA**

A Gallé "Clématites" cameo vase, double overlaid and acid-etched glass, signed in cameo "GALLÉ."

ca. 1910   *12¾in (32.5cm) high*

$1,900-2,500   **L&T**

An Émile Gallé reticulated gourd, enameled and gilt eggplant glass, with flowering vine.

See Arwas, "Glass: Art Nouveau to Art Deco," Papadakis (1997), page 144.

ca. 1900   *9½in (24cm) wide*

$12,500-15,000   **DRA**

An exceptional Émile Gallé marquetry vase, padded, wheel-carved, and hand-carved cameo glass, with crocuses, incised signature "Galle" on body, "déposé Ges-Gesch" on underside.

See Duncan, "The Paris Salons 1895-1914 Volume IV: Ceramics & Glass," ACC (1999), pages 202 and 204.

ca. 1900   *13¼in (33.5cm) high*

$14,000-16,000   **DRA**

An Émile Gallé "Clematis" vase, cased acid-etched cameo glass, with raised signature "Gallé."

ca. 1900   *12in (30.5cm) high*

$2,700-3,500   **FRE**

A tall Émile Gallé vase, acid-etched and fire-polished cameo glass, with mushrooms, snails, and spider web, signed "Gallé" in cameo on body.

ca. 1900   *12½in (32cm) high*

$9,500-11,000   **DRA**

An Émile Gallé perfume bottle, acid-etched cameo glass, with a water lily, signed "Gallé" in cameo on body.

ca. 1900   *4¼in (11cm) wide*

$3,100-4,000   **DRA**

A Lalique opalescent glass "Perruches" vase, etched "R. Lalique France" on underside.

See Marcilhac, "R. Lalique," Editions de l"Amateur (2005), page 410, no. 876.

ca. 1919 *9½in (24cm) diam*
$12,500-15,000 DRA

A Lalique "Poissons" vase, frosted and polished electric blue glass, molded "R. Lalique" on foot and underside, with etched "France."

See Marcilhac, "R. Lalique," Editions de l"Amateur (2005), page 422, no. 925.

1921 *10in (25.5cm) diam*
$40,000-47,000 DRA

A Lalique butterscotch glass "Chardons" vase, no. 929, molded "R. LALIQUE."

1922 *7¼in (18.5cm) high*
$6,000-7,500 L&T

A Lalique "Lièvres" vase, no. 942, clear, frosted, and blue stained glass, intaglio "R. LALIQUE."

1923 *6¼in (16cm) high*
$3,700-5,000 L&T

A Lalique deep amber glass "Serpent" vase, no. 896, intaglio "R. LALIQUE."

1924 *9¾in (24.5cm) high*
$22,000-27,000 L&T

A Lalique "Sophora" vase, no. 977, gray and white stained glass, intaglio "R. LALIQUE," engraved "R. Lalique France."

1926 *10¾in (27.5cm) high*
$3,700-5,000 L&T

A Lalique "Coqs et Raisins" vase, no. 1043, clear, frosted, and green stained glass, molded "R. LALIQUE," wheel-engraved "R. LALIQUE FRANCE."

1928 *6¼in (16cm) high*
$2,000-2,500 L&T

A Lalique "Languedoc" vase, no. 1021, cased jade and white stained glass, later engraved "R. Lalique France No. 1021."

1929 *9in (23cm) high*
$31,000-37,000 L&T

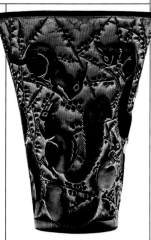

A Lalique "Senart" vase, no. 1098, deep amber and white stained glass, stenciled "R. LALIQUE FRANCE."

1934 *8½in (21.5cm) high*
$11,000-14,000 L&T

A Lalique "Amour Assis" box, no. 3, clear, frosted, and blue stained glass, molded "R. LALIQUE," engraved "France."

1919   *5¾in (14.5cm) high*

$4,700-5,500   **L&T**

A Lalique "Bacchante" liquor bottle, no. 1186/B, clear, frosted, and blue stained glass, stenciled "R. LALIQUE FRANCE."

1931   *8¾in (22cm) high*

$7,200-8,200   **L&T**

A Lalique "Vigne Cave À Liqueurs," no. 1189, clear and frosted glass, nickel-plated metal mount and key, bottles stenciled "R. LALIQUE," tantalus stamped "R. LALIQUE FRANCE BREVETÉ S.G.D.G.."

1931   *12in (30.5cm) high*

$22,000-30,000   **L&T**

A Lalique "Amphitrite" scent bottle, no. 514, electric blue glass, molded "LALIQUE," engraved "R. Lalique France No. 514."

1920   *4in (10cm) high*

$8,500-10,000   **L&T**

Judith Picks

I have picked this exquisite "Muguet" ("Lily-of-the-Valley") clear, frosted, and turquoise-stained glass scent bottle but, to be perfectly honest, I could just as easily have gone for any of the other wonderful Lalique scent bottles illustrated on this page. Essentially, this is because—and I think it is easy to see just by looking at them—many of the most desirable perfume or scent bottles made were designed by René Lalique (1860-1945) and the company that still bears his name.

The earliest examples date to the 1890s, and they include the exquisite "Amethyst" and "Silver Serpent" flaçons displayed at the Musée des Arts Décoratifs, in Paris. However, it was not until ca. 1906, when Lalique began to collaborate with the parfumier La Maison de Coty, that production began on a commercial scale. Employing the new technique of press-molding, which enabled bottles to be mass-produced and then hand-finished (mainly using etching and color staining for decoration), Lalique designed 16, mostly demi-crystal, flacons for Coty fragrances (until the early 1930s). These, however, are only the tip of the iceberg. Lalique has, over the course of the 20th and early 21stC, designed flacons for about 60 other leading parfumiers, such as Worth, D'Orsay, Bouchon, Roget et Gallet, Guerlain, Houbigant, Nina Ricci, and Maison Lalique itself.

Prices vary considerably, depending on a mixture of rarity, age, and uniqueness of design, but I can honestly say that I have never seen one that I did not like (and want).

A Lalique "Marquila" scent bottle, no. 515, blue and white stained glass, molded "R. LALIQUE FRANCE," engraved "R. Lalique France No. 515."

1927   *3¼in (8.5cm) high*

$2,700-3,200   **L&T**

A Lalique "Oreillles Lézards" scent bottle, no. 479, clear, frosted, and gray stained glass, engraved "R. LALIQUE."

1911   *4¼in (11cm) high*

$10,000-12,500   **L&T**

A Lalique opalescent glass "Suzanne" statuette, no. 833, molded "R. LALIQUE."

1925   *9in (23cm) high*

$15,000-17,500   **L&T**

A Lalique "Muguets" scent bottle, no. 525, clear, frosted and turquoise stained glass, stenciled "R. LALIQUE FRANCE."

1931   *4in (10cm) high*

$6,000-7,500   **L&T**

A Lalique "Caravelle" table centerpiece, clear and frosted glass with a hint of gray staining, engraved with three seagulls on the front and ten birds on the reverse, the rigging also engraved, nickel-plated illuminating mount, wheel-engraved "R. LALIQUE."

"Surtout de tables," or ornamental centerpieces, were an essential part of formal dining from the second half of the 18thC and throughout the 19thC. The design with the seagulls was created for the visit of King George VI and Queen Elizabeth to Paris in 1938 and was part of a large dinner service also featuring seagulls. The "Caravelle" centerpiece had been designed in 1931, but the seagulls were added for the gift. The galleon is an emblem on the coat of arms of Paris. The royal visit was intended to take place on June 29, but the Queen's mother died, so it was postponed until July. Only two other examples are known to exist—a version held in the Musée Lalique Collection and one in the British Royal Collection.

1938   *28½in (72.5cm) wide*

$95,000-110,000   **L&T**

ESSENTIAL REFERENCE—CAR MASCOTS

Lord Montagu of Beaulieu was purportedly, around the turn of the 20thC, the first person to mount a figurine—of Saint Christopher, the patron saint of travelers—on the radiator/hood of an automobile (his Daimler). Thereafter, the concept of the "car mascot" as a symbol of status and prestige took flight. By the mid- to late 1920s, the prestigious French glass maker René Lalique et Cie began to produce an exclusive range of them: 29 commercially available models in all, mostly in the form of animals, birds, and symbolic figures inspired by Classical Antiquity. The majority were made in colorless or tinted, satin-finish or frosted glass, and mostly in the prevailing sleek and dynamic Art Deco style. Also known as "figureheads" and, in French, "bouchons de radiateur," many of them were also marketed by Lalique as paperweights and bookends. The hood or radiator mounts, which enabled them to be internally illuminated at night, were commissioned directly by Lalique's British agents Breves Galleries, although they were also available from other third parties.

A Lalique "Tête De Paon" car mascot, no. 1140, clear and frosted glass, intaglio "R. LALIQUE," molded "FRANCE."

1928   *7in (18cm) high*

$4,700-5,600   L&T

A Lalique longchamp car mascot, no. 1152B, clear and frosted glass, molded "R. LALIQUE FRANCE."

1929   *5in (12.5cm) high*

$7,200-8,400   L&T

A Lalique "Victoire" car mascot, no. 1147, also known as "Spirit of the Wind," frosted and clear glass with strong Art Deco lines, molded "R.Lalique France" on base, the "Q" with a double tail.

ca. 1928   *7¾in (19.5cm) wide*

$22,000-27,000   MGO

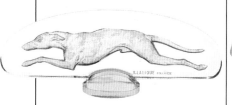

A Lalique "Levrier" ("Greyhound") car mascot, no. 1141, clear glass, inscribed "R.Lalique" and "FRANCE."

ca. 1928   *7¾in (19.5cm) wide*

$10,000-12,500   MGO

A Lalique "Tete De Belier" ("Ram Head") car mascot, no. 1136, embossed "R.Lalique France."

ca. 1928   *$8,500-11,000*   MGO

A Lalique "Sanglier" ("Wild Boar") car mascot, no. 1157, unusual black and gray finish, inscribed "R.Lalique."

ca. 1929   *3½in (9cm) wide*

$1,900-2,500   MGO

A Lalique "Grenouille" ("Frog") car mascot, no. 1146, acid etched "R. Lalique France," molded "France."

ca. 1928   *2½in (6.5cm) high*

$11,000-14,000   MGO

A Lalique "Comet" car mascot, molded "R. LALIQUE," the "Q" with a double tail, with original Breves mount with an ebonized wood base.

This is the third rarest of the 29 car mascots produced by René Lalique. The mascots were lit from within by a lightbulb, creating a beautiful, warm glow at night.

ca. 1925   *7¾in (19.5cm) wide*

$120,000-140,000   MGO

A Lalique Rolls Royce "Spirit of Ecstasy" car mascot, no. 34 of 200, etched "RR034" on base, with original presentation box and numbered certificate.

This rare Lalique Rolls Royce "Spirit of Ecstasy" was commissioned from Lalique by Rolls Royce Motor Cars Ltd. in 1994 to commemorate its 90th anniversary. The "Spirit of Ecstasy," designed by Charles Sykes, also known as the "Flying Lady," has adorned Rolls Royce car radiators in various sizes from 1911 to the present day.

ca. 1994   *7¾in (19.5cm) high*

$150,000-160,000   MGO

A Loetz hand-blown glass "Pampas" vase.

See Mergl, Ploil and Ricke, "Loetz Bohemian Glass 1880-1940," Hatje Cantz (2003), page 295.

ca. 1899   *4in (10cm) diam*

$1,100-1,500   **DRA**

A Loetz hand-blown glass "Norma" vase, etched signature "Loetz Austria" on underside.

See Mergl, Ploil and Ricke, "Loetz Bohemian Glass 1880-1940," Hatje Cantz (2003), page 290.

ca. 1899   *5¾in (14.5cm) high*

$2,400-2,700   **DRA**

A pair of Loetz Jugendstil twin-handle vases, iridescent glass and pewter.

ca. 1900   *7¾in (19.5cm) high*

$2,700-3,200   **L&T**

A Loetz Jugendstil "Papillon" twin-handle vase, iridescent glass and pewter, stamped on base "1680."

ca. 1900   *7¾in (19.5cm) high*

$2,000-2,500   **L&T**

A rare Loetz hand-blown glass "Phänomen" vase, no. Gre 388, by Franz Hofstötter, etched "Lötz" on underside, with crossed arrows mark.

Hofstötter designed this form and decoration for the 1900 Paris Exposition Universelle. See Mergl, Ploil and Ricke, "Loetz Bohemian Glass 1880-1940," Hatje Cantz (2003), page 94, no. 39.

1900   *18in (46cm) high*

$59,500-67,000   **DRA**

An early-20thC Loetz wrythen glass "Papillon" vase, with petrol iridescent mottled decoration over a deep-blue ground, with applied stylized flower silver overlay.

7in (18cm) high

$1,900-2,200   **FLD**

A Loetz hand-blown glass "Cytisus" vase, with handles.

See Mergl, Ploil and Ricke, "Loetz Bohemian Glass 1880-1940," Hatje Cantz (2003), page 121.

ca. 1902   *4¾in (12cm) wide*

$6,000-6,700   **DRA**

A rare Loetz hand-blown glass "Phänomen" vase, etched signature "Loetz Austria" on underside.

ca. 1901   *5½in (14cm) diam*

$15,000-19,000   **DRA**

A Loetz "Phänomen" glass vase, no. PG 5301, dimpled and decorated with undulating parallel bands of iridescent threads fused together over a Camelienrot (Carnelian red) ground, light surface wear.

ca. 1907   *7¾in (19.5cm) high*

$3,500-4,000   **FLD**

A Loetz orange tango glass "Ausfuehrung 157" vase, with applied black stripes and rim, on a raised foot below a black glass knop, light surface wear.

ca. 1914   *8¾in (22cm) high*

$250-310   **FLD**

A Loetz footed bowl, by Michael Powolny (1871-1954), cased orange glass with applied trailing decoration.

ca. 1920   *5in (12.5cm) diam*

$625-750   **L&T**

ESSENTIAL REFERENCE—MONART

Monart color glass was made at the Moncrieff Glassworks in Perthshire, Scotland, by an emigrant Spanish family versed in the traditions of turn-of-the-20thC French art glass. The first experimental piece was made ca. 1923 by glassworker Salvador Ysart. Encouraged by Mrs. Isabel Moncrieff, wife of glassworks owner John, production began soon after. The company name is a combination of "Mon" from Moncrieff and "art" from Ysart. Subsequently aided by Salvador's sons Paul, Vincent, Augustine, and Antoine, it continued until 1961—albeit interrupted by the war and, from 1946, without Salavador and two of his sons, who left to make their own and similar glass under the Vasart name.

Objects produced included fruit bowls, pitchers, plates, lemonade sets, and table lamps, but vases—in numerous shapes and sizes—comprised most of the range. Desirability ultimately resides in their distinctive, variegated coloring—primarily achieved by rolling or dabbing, and then manipulating fine-quality French or German enamels into the partly inflated vessel before fully inflating and, usually, encasing in a layer of clear glass. Favored colors included green, blue, pink, orange, red, yellow, and black. In many cases, however, other decorative elements were introduced, too, notably: flecks of aventurine or "goldstone" (imported from Paris); silver mica flakes (bought from a local Woolworths at Christmas time), and charcoal—the latter leaving entrapped bubbles when it evaporated. Individually handcrafted and with such diverse ingredients, no two pieces emerged identical.

Visual similarities with some Gray-Stan and Vasart glass means identification is not always straightforward, but helpful pointers include a raised disk on the underside, produced by grinding down the pontil mark; if you're lucky, it might still have its original, Monart adhesive label.

A John Moncrieff Ltd. Monart glass vase, with aventurine inclusions.
ca. 1930   *8½in (21.5cm) high*
$500-625   **L&T**

A Monart glass vase, shape no. KK, internally decorated with a fine blue spiral and swirl line over mottled green, with aventurine inclusions.
1930s   *11in (28cm) high*
$950-1,100   **FLD**

A Monart table lamp and shade, mottled green glass, in two pieces.
13in (33cm) high
$625-750   **DAWS**

A John Moncrieff Ltd. Monart vase, green and blue mottled glass, with aventurine inclusions, with maker's paper label.
ca. 1930   *9¼in (23.5cm) high*
$500-625   **L&T**

A John Moncrieff Ltd. Monart vase, pulled yellow glass with bubble inclusions, traces of maker's label on base.
ca. 1930   *14¼in (36cm) high*
$750-875   **L&T**

A large Monart vase, shape no. EF VI, internally decorated with a graduated deep to lighter orange, with color flecks throughout, wear.
11in (28cm) high
$1,250-1,500   **FLD**

A John Moncrieff Ltd. Monart vase, red and blue mottled glass, with bubble inclusions.
1930s   *10¾in (27.5cm) high*
$1,100-1,250   **L&T**

A large John Moncrieff Ltd. Monart glass table lamp and shade, the shade with associated painted metal fittings.
ca. 1930   *20½in (52cm) high*
$3,500-4,200   **L&T**

An early Tiffany Studios hand-blown Favrile glass vase, etched "L.C.T. B413" on underside.

ca. 1895   *12½in (32cm) high*
$7,500-8,500   **FRE**

A Tiffany Studios Favrile two-color cameo vase, hand-blown wheel-carved glass, with grapevine, amber iridescent interior, etched "3826B L.C. Tiffany-Favrile" on underside.

11in (28cm) high
$3,700-5,000   **FRE**

A Tiffany Studios hand-blown Favrile glass "King Tut" vase, etched signature and number "L.C.T. L59" on underside, with paper manufacturer's label "Tiffany Favrile Glass Registered Trademark."

ca. 1899   *9in (23cm) high*
$7,500-8,500   **DRA**

A small Tiffany Studios blue Favrile glass vase, etched "LOUIS C. TIFFANY/L. C. T./D531" on base.

See Duncan, "Louis C. Tiffany: The Garden Museum Collection," ACC (2004), page 233, where a similarly decorated vase is illustrated.

ca. 1899   *5in (12.5cm) high*
$1,500-2,000   **L&T**

A rare Tiffany Studios "Agate" vase, hand-blown and faceted Favrile glass, etched signature and number "V 295 L.C.T. Favrile" on underside.

ca. 1904   *8¾in (22cm) high*
$5,200-6,000   **DRA**

A rare Tiffany Studios "Floriform" vase, hand-blown and wheel-carved glass, etched signature and number "L.C.T. W6767" on underside.

A similar example was displayed on a false fireplace at Tiffany Furnaces in Corona. See Koch, "Louis C. Tiffany's Art Glass," Crown (1978), figure 120; Koch, "Louis C. Tiffany's Glass, Bronzes, Lamps," Crown (1989), page 31; and Grover, "Art Glass Nouveau," Tuttle (1989), page 86.

ca. 1905   *13½in (34cm) high*
$52,000-59,500   **DRA**

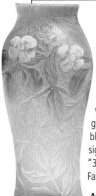

A Tiffany Studios cameo vase, hand-blown and wheel-carved Favrile glass, with dogwood blossoms, etched signature and number "3073 C L.C. Tiffany Favrile" on underside.

A similar example is held in the permanent collection of the Chrysler Museum of Art, Norfolk, Virginia.

ca. 1908   *10½in (26.5cm) high*
$6,500-7,500   **DRA**

A Tiffany Studios "Intaglio" chalice, hand-blown and wheel-carved Favrile glass, with grapes, etched signature and number "3409 E L.C.Tiffany-Favrile" on underside.

ca. 1910   *9in (23cm) high*
$2,200-3,000   **DRA**

A Tiffany Studios "Agate" cabinet vase, hand-blown Favrile glass, etched signature and number "L. C.Tiffany Favrile 7429 N" on underside.

ca. 1919   *2¼in (5.5cm) high*
$2,200-3,000   **DRA**

A set of two Tiffany Studios hand-blown Favrile glass vases, with patinated and gilt-bronze bases, impressed signature and number "TIFFANY STUDIOS 711" on underside of each.

13¼in (33.5cm) and
14¼in (36cm) high
ca. 1920
$2,500-3,100   **DRA**

A Gabriel Argy-Rousseau pâte-de-verre "Les Oizeaux" footed bowl, with molded "G. Argy-Rousseau."

See Bloch-Dermant, "G. Argy-Rousseau: Glassware as Art," Thames & Hudson (1991), page 205.

ca. 1925   *10¼in (26cm) diam*
$3,500-4,200   **DRA**

A Gray-Stan glass vase, with an internal blue and yellow feathered swirl, cased in clear glass, with two applied blue angular handles.

Provenance: From the family collection of the late James Manning, senior glass blower and designer for Elizabeth Graydon Stannus of Gray-Stan Glass.

1930s   *10¼in (26cm) high*
$2,000-2,500   **FLD**

A mid-19thC Baccarat cameo glass vase, cased in pink over opal, cut with repeat scrolling acanthus, with gilt details, between plain banded borders.

11¾in (30cm) high
$450-520   **FLD**

A Russian Imperial Glassworks green overlay blue vase, cut with ovolu and fluted bands within geometric borders, engraved Nicholas II monogram mark and date, very minor surface wear.

1915   *6¾in (17cm) high*
$3,100-4,000   **TEN**

An E. Bakalowits Söhne sherry decanter, Vienna, by Koloman Moser (1868-1918), cased and wheel-carved glass, with gilt-metal.

A similar decanter by Moser, with amber glass, is in the Saint Louis Museum, Missouri, object no. 41:1996.

ca. 1899   *9in (23cm) high*
$9,500-11,000   **L&T**

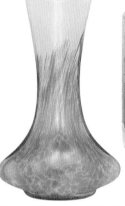

A Kralik irridescent glass "Helios" vase, unsigned.

ca. 1900   *11¾in (30cm) high*
$250-370   **ROS**

A James Couper & Sons green glass "Clutha" vase, Glasgow, by Christopher Dresser (1834-1904), with blue, aventurine, and opaque trailed inclusions.

See H. Lyons, "Christopher Dresser: The People's Designer," Woodbridge (2005), pages 164-65, plate 313, where a comparable example is illustrated.

ca. 1890   *8½in (21.5cm) high*
$1,000-1,250   **L&T**

A Legras "Winter Landscape" glass vase, enameled with trees in a snowy landscape, enameled "Legras" signature.

2¼in (5.5cm) high
$250-350   **WW**

An early 20thC Moser glass vase, Karlsbad, with internal optical ribbing, decorated with an orange stylized tulip and bud with cut leaves, over a clear to opalescent amber ground, signed, light surface wear.

5in (12.5cm) high
$950-1,050   **FLD**

A late-19thC Italian Salviati & Cie Murano glass ewer, slender S-form neck and fine scrolled handle in multicolor glass, with gold aventurine over a multicolor spotted body, over a white ground.

7¼in (18.5cm) high
$350-420   **FLD**

A Murano blue glass twin candlestick, attributed to Vittorio Zecchin, raised on a circular foot.

1920s   *9in (23cm) high*
$625-750   **SWO**

A Secessionist glass vase, possibly by Palme Konig, in mottled amber and pale blue, with sinuous copper overlays inset with a turquoise and tigereye cabochon, the lower copper section chased to imitate watered silk, unmarked.

4in (10cm) high
$750-875   **HT**

A Quezal hand-blown glass "Hooked-Feather" vase, etched signature and number "Quezal A 958" on underside, with paper retailer's label "The Bailey, Banks & Biddle Co. Phila."

ca. 1910   *7¼in (18.5cm) diam*

$2,200-3,000   **DRA**

A 19thC Richardson ruby crystal glass bowl, with scalloped rim, decorated with gilt scroll panels in the interior and on the domed foot, minor wear.

11¾in (30cm) diam

$1,000-1,500   **FLD**

A Charles Schneider mottled orange glass vase, manufactured for retail by Finnigans, Bond Street, with irregular blue spots, set in a wrought-iron open mount with columns and loop terminals, etched "Schneider Finnigans."

9½in (24cm) diam

$700-800   **WW**

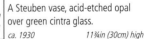

A Steuben vase, acid-etched opal over green cintra glass.

ca. 1930   *11¾in (30cm) high*

$1,000-1,100   **DRA**

A Steuben vase, "Hunting" pattern, by Frederick Carder (1863-1963), shape no. 2683, cased and acid-etched lead glass, mirror black over alabaster, unmarked.

ca. 1927-32   *12in (30.5cm) high*

$3,100-3,700   **FRE**

An early-20thC Stevens & Williams twin-handle vase, intaglio cut with flowers and butterflies in yellow over white over pink, unmarked.

9in (23cm) high

$3,100-3,700   **FLD**

A late-19thC double gourd cameo glass vase, possibly Stevens & Williams, cased in opal over blue, cut with a flowering bough between plain banded borders, engraved numerical code "437/3" on base.

10¼in (26cm) high

$1,400-1,700   **FLD**

A late-19thC Thomas Webb & Sons Burmese glass posy vase, decorated with floral gilt decoration in Japanese style, by Jules Barb, over a graduated pink to blush ground.

3½in (9cm) high

$625-750   **FLD**

A late-19thC Thomas Webb & Sons cameo glass vase, cased in opal over citron, cut with a large spray of flowers between plain banded borders, acid mark on base.

9¼in (23.5cm) high

$1,100-1,500   **FLD**

A late-19thC Thomas Webb & Sons cameo glass scent bottle, cased in opal over ruby, cut back with a flowering briar rose bough, silver-mounted collar and spherical screw cap, by Sampson Mordan & Co., dents in cap.

4in (10cm) high

$1,500-1,900   **FLD**

A WMF Art Nouveau claret pitcher and stopper, silver plate and green glass, the handle and mounts cast with sinuous fruit, two maidens on the base mount, with a hinged and pierced stopper, raised on pad feet, stamped marks, small surface scratches.

16¼in (41cm) high

$1,100-1,500   **SWO**

DECORATIVE ARTS

An Aesthetic Movement ebonized and parcel-gilt overmantel mirror, the original mirror plate within an arcaded frieze painted with floral sprays on a gilt ground, the sides with incised decoration, flanked by triangular panels, above a baluster balustrade, losses.

ca. 1890   *59¾in (152cm) high*

$1,400-1,700   **TEN**

An Aesthetic Movement maple and ebonized writing table, the molded top with green leather inset, with two frieze drawers, on twin turned and fluted column supports, raised on outswept legs, stamped "EDWARDS & ROBERTS."

48in (122cm) wide

$1,100-1,500   **CHEF**

A Victorian Aesthetic Movement ash triple wardrobe, with black painted foliate scrolls and geometric banding, the molded cornice over a mirrored door, flanked on each side by a paneled door with brass drop handles, enclosing hanging spaces and three drawers, on a molded plinth and bracket feet.

83in (211cm) high

$625-750   **HT**

An Art Nouveau walnut cabinet, by Louis Majorelle (1859-1926), with specimen wood marquetry inlay, poker-work signature "L. MAJORELLE/NANCY."

ca. 1900   *59in (150cm) high*

$15,000-19,000   **L&T**

A J. S. Henry Art Nouveau mahogany occasional table, London, attributed to George Montague Ellwood (1875-1955), inlaid with specimen woods and mother-of-pearl.

ca. 1910   *26¾in (68cm) diam*

$1,500-1,900   **L&T**

A J. S. Henry Art Nouveau carved oak armchair, London, with a velvet upholstered seat and armrests.

Established ca. 1880 and based in Old Street, London, J. S. Henry was a wholesale manufacturer of art furniture—mostly in the Art Nouveau style—in mahogany and satinwood with decorative inlay. It used designs by G. M. Ellwood, George Walton, W. A. S. Benson, C. F. A. Voysey, E. G. Punnett, and W. J. Neatby, although few were attributed. An example of this chair is held at the Kelvingrove Museum and Art Gallery in Glasgow, Scotland.

ca. 1910   *47¾in (121cm) high*

$1,100-1,500   **L&T**

ESSENTIAL REFERENCE—CAMILLE GAUTHIER

Camille Gauthier (1870-1963) began his career, ca. 1893, working as a draftsman for the great furniture designer and maker Louis Majorelle. As such, he accompanied Majorelle in his transition from producing reproductions of Louis XV furniture to fully embracing and developing the elegant and curvaceous Art Nouveau style. Having become a member of the steering committee of the École de Nancy—founded in 1890 by Majorelle, Émile Gallé, Jacques Gruber, and other Art Nouveau designers and craftsmen—Gauthier decided to set up, with the upholsterer Paul Poinsignon, his own furniture manufactury. In keeping with one of the center principles of the École de Nancy—"art for all"—the workshops married highly skilled craftsmen with the most up-to-date woodworking machines: a form of industrial production that successfully reduced the cost of production and, ergo, improved affordability, but without sacrificing the quality of construction.

An Art Nouveau tulipwood dining suite, attributed to Camille Gauthier (1870-1963), comprising a sideboard cabinet (pictured) with a marble top and cast bronze handles, an extending dining table, and seven dining chairs with later upholstery.

ca. 1900   *67¾in (172cm) wide*

$12,500-15,000 the set   **L&T**

An Art Nouveau walnut armchair, by Georges De Feure (1868-1943), with later close-nailed upholstery.

ca. 1900   *34¼in (87cm) high*

$2,900-3,500   **L&T**

An early-20thC Art Nouveau copper mirror, with a beveled surface, surmounted with a portrait relief of Hermes or Mercury set against an armorial, flanked on each side by brass flowers, indistinctly incised "Colin" on bottom.

17in (43cm) high

$190-250   **SWO**

An oak chair, by Charles Rennie Mackintosh (1868-1928), for Miss Cranston's Argyle Street Tea Rooms, with original drop-in rushed seat.

In 1898, early in the career of renowned Scottish architect Charles Rennie Mackintosh (1868-1928), entrepreneur Catherine Cranston—known simply as Miss Cranston—commissioned him to furnish her new tea rooms on Argyle Street, Glasgow, Scotland. The commission afforded Mackintosh a new freedom to experiment and led to further projects, including the Ingram Street Tea Rooms (1900) and the Willow Tea Rooms (1903). The work at Argyle Street followed his previous work at Miss Cranston's new Buchanan Street Tea Rooms, two years earlier in 1896, in collaboration with George Walton, who designed the furnishings. In this new undertaking, however, their roles were reversed, with Mackintosh in charge of the furnishings and Walton the interiors. The furniture Mackintosh designed for these new rooms exhibits a new, more robust evolution of his repertoire and established a style for much of his work up to 1900. Combining English Arts and Crafts and Scottish vernacular design, Mackintosh produced furniture in a bold and simple aesthetic that marked him out from his contemporaries. Indeed, his designs—in clear-varnished or more usually dark-stained oak and with an emphasis on broad, unmolded, rectangular planes—were in contrast to the more delicate refinement of Walton's interiors, and suggested that design-wise they were "moving away from one another." See R. Billcliffe, "Charles Rennie Mackintosh: The Complete Furniture," Furniture Drawings & Interior Designs, Cameron & Hollis (2009), pages 62-63, 1898.45, "Chair with curved top rail for the Argyle Street Tea Rooms."

1898   *39¼in (99.5cm) high*
$41,000-47,000   L&T

An oak writing table, by Charles Rennie Mackintosh (1868-1928), for Miss Cranston's Ingram Street Tea Rooms.

This table formed the base of a writing table made by Frances Smith for the Ladies' Rest Room at Miss Cranston's Ingram Street Tea Room in 1909. The desk originally had a superstructure with dividers that enabled four people to sit at it at any time, and may in any case have been removable.

Provenance: Messrs Coopers Tea Rooms (Ingram Street Tea Rooms), Glasgow, from whom purchased by the present owner, ca. 1960.

1909   *35¾in (91cm) diam*
$37,000-43,000   L&T

A pair of Arts and Crafts high-back oak armchairs, attributed to M. H. Baillie Scott (1865-1945), with leather upholstery.

An example of this chair is illustrated on the cover of the guidebook for Blackwell, Windermere, designed by Baillie Scott for Edward Holt in 1898-1900.

ca. 1895   *47½in (120.5cm) high*
$7,000-8,500   L&T

An Arts and Crafts triptych fire screen, by Arthur W. Simpson (1857-1922), Kendal, carved oak frame, with glazed embroidered panels, possibly by Annie Garnett.

Annie Garnett (1864-1942) was a key figure in the Arts and Crafts movement's revival of hand spinning and weaving in the English Lake District. Garnett was acquainted with the Simpson family through the Keswick School of Industrial Arts and based her geometric patterns on natural forms, notably exhibiting a peacock feather-embroidered screen at the Arts and Crafts Exhibition Society in 1903.

ca. 1900   *36¾in (93.5cm) wide*
$4,300-5,600   L&T

An Arts and Crafts oak bureau, by Arthur Simpson, Kendal, the drop front over two short and two long drawers, with heart escutcheons, on square block feet, the reverse with "The Handicrafts" badge.

35¾in (91cm) wide
$2,200-3,000   WHP

An Arts and Crafts copper and oak wall mirror, by John Pearson (1859-1930), with beveled mirror plate.

ca. 1898   *28½in (72.5cm) wide*
$3,500-4,200   L&T

A Heal & Son Arts and Crafts oak "Mansfield" press, London, by Ambrose Heal, no. "235," possibly made by the Guild of Handicraft, with copper fittings.

Ambrose Heal turned to C. R. Ashbee and the Guild of Handicraft workshops in Essex Road, Mile End, to produce much of his earliest bedroom furniture. The Guild produced 11 of these "Gentleman's Wardrobes" before production moved to its own workshops ca. 1899.

See Oliver S. Heal, "Sir Ambrose Heal and the Heal Cabinet Factory 1897-1939," Unicorn (2014).

ca. 1899   *92¼in (234cm) high*
$7,200-8,000   L&T

A Heal & Son chestnut chest-of-drawers, by Ambrose Heal (1872-1959), London.

ca. 1920   *48in (122cm) high*
$5,000-5,600   L&T

DECORATIVE ARTS

A rare early Gustav Stickley oak and patinated iron sideboard, model no. 961, with four drawers and two doors, each concealing a removable shelf, large red manufacturer's decal "Als Ik Kan Stickley" on reverse with joiner's compass.

ca. 1902-03   *69¾in (177cm) wide*
$25,000-31,000   **DRA**

A Gustav Stickley oak smoker's cabinet, Eastwood, New York, model no. 522, signed with red joiner's compass decal.

See Stephen Gray, "The Early Work of Gustav Stickley," page 92.
ca. 1902   *27in (68.5cm) high*
$5,500-7,000   **FRE**

A rare early Gustav Stickley oak "Eastwood" table, model no. 449, red manufacturer's decal "Als Ik Kan Stickley" on underside with joiner's compass.

ca. 1902   *23½in (60cm) diam*
$4,300-5,000   **DRA**

An early Gustav Stickley drop-front oak writing desk, model no. 518, with patinated iron, the drop-front writing surface concealing divided storage above a fixed shelf.

1902   *52¼in (133cm) high*
$5,000-6,200   **DRA**

A Gustav Stickley oak magazine cabinet, Eastwood, New York, model no. 548, signed with red joiner's compass decal.

See Stephen Gray, "The Early Works of Gustav Stickley," Turn of the Century (1987), page 99.
ca. 1902   *43¼in (110cm) high*
$2,500-3,100   **FRE**

A rare oak armchair, attributed to Harvey Ellis for Gustav Stickley, with pewter and copper inlay, red decal "Als Ik Kan Stickley" on arm, with joiner's compass.

See Cathers and Montgomery, "Arts and Crafts Furniture from the Collection of the Two Red Roses Foundation," Lucia Marquand (2017), page 220.
ca. 1903   *43¼in (110cm) high*
$19,000-22,000   **DRA**

A Gustav Stickley oak china cabinet, model no. 815, with glass and patinated iron, with two doors concealing three fixed shelves, remnants of paper manufacturer's label on reverse.

1907-12   *64¼in (163cm) high*
$6,000-7,500   **DRA**

ESSENTIAL REFERENCE—THE MORRIS CHAIR

The original version of what became known as the "Morris Chair" was produced by Morris & Co., the company established by William Morris (1834-96), the leading proponent of the British Arts and Crafts Movement. Inspired by a prototype made by carpenter Ephraim Colman, it was first marketed ca. 1866. Its main feature was an adjustable reclining back, and it also had a dark brown stained wood frame with curved armrests, barley twist-turned arm supports and leg stretchers, and plant-form pattern tapestry-covered upholstered seat and back cushions. The "Morris" chair here is a North American evolution of that original. Although it is named in honor of Morris, and despite retaining the original's adjustable reclining back, it is aesthetically different. Gone are the barley-twist arms supports and leg stretchers, as is the patterned tapestry upholstery, in favor of monochrome leather upholstery and an oak frame with arm supports and arms of chunkier square and rectangular sections. Encapsulating the "Craftsman" variant of the Arts and Crafts style, it was first produced by Gustav Stickley and copied by a number of other North American manufacturers thereafter.

A Gustav Stickley oak and leather flat-arm Morris chair, model no. 332.
ca. 1910   *39½in (100.5cm) high*
$6,000-7,500   **DRA**

A Gustav Stickley oak and hammered copper dresser, model no. 902, with six drawers, two paper "Craftsman" manufacturer's labels on underside of one drawer.
1912-16   *41in (104cm) wide*
$14,000-17,500   **DRA**

A Roycroft oak sideboard, model no. 01, with copper and mirrored glass, with two leaded glass doors concealing a fixed shelf, two silver drawers, two doors concealing open storage, all over one linen drawer, incised orb and cross mark on face of linen drawer.

ca. 1906   *66¼in (168cm) wide*
$10,500-12,500   **DRA**

A rare Roycroft oak server, model no. 9 variant, with mirrored glass and patinated iron, with five drawers, incised orb and cross mark on one edge.

ca. 1906   *56in (142cm) wide*
$9,500-11,000   **DRA**

A pair of Roycroft oak chairs, model no. 30, with leather and brass, incised orb and cross mark on both.

ca. 1906   *43¼in (110cm) high*
$1,900-2,500   **DRA**

A pair of Roycroft oak twin beds, incised "Roycroft" manufacturer's mark on each headboard.

ca. 1910   *80¾in (205cm) long*
$2,200-3,000   **DRA**

ESSENTIAL REFERENCE—CHARLES P. LIMBERT

Born in Linesville, Pennsylvania, Charles P. Limbert (1854-1923) was the son of a cabinetmaker and furniture dealer, had an early grounding in the furniture business working in his father's store, and, by the mid-1880s, had become a furniture salesman. He then began making chairs in Grand Rapids, Michigan, while continuing to distribute furniture made by others. After several major collaborations in the late 1880s, including the Klingman & Limbert Chair Co., he opened his own company, the Charles P. Limbert Furniture Co., in Grand Rapids in 1902. A custom-built furniture factory followed in Holland, Michigan, in 1906, where his team of craftsmen designed and built "Limbert's Holland Dutch Arts and Crafts Furniture." Limbert continued to manage the company until 1922, at which point poor health prompted him to sell his shares, and the company subsequently closed in 1944. The forms of Limbert furniture are comparable to those of Gustav Stickley (see page 556, facing page), but many pieces show the more direct influence of the Scottish designer Charles Rennie Mackintosh (1868-1928) and the Glasgow School. Prices are, in general, comparable to those commanded by Roycroft.

A Stickley Brothers oak tabouret, brass manufacturer's label "Quaint Furniture Stickley Brothers Co. Grand Rapids, Mich." on underside.

ca. 1902   *18¾in (47.5cm) high*
$1,250-1,500   **DRA**

An L. & J.G. Stickley upholstered oak reclining Morris rocking chair, model no. 831, with three adjustable positions for the backrest, unmarked.

ca. 1910   *35½in (90cm) high*
$550-700   **FRE**

A Limbert oak writing desk, with brass and glass, with a pull-out lidded writing surface, complete with an inkwell, pen tray, and storage, branded manufacturer's mark "Limberts Arts Crafts Furniture Made in Grand Rapids and Holland" on interior of drawer.

ca. 1920   *41¾in (106cm) wide*
$1,700-2,200   **DRA**

A Frank Lloyd Wright Taliesin mahogany occasional table, Heritage Henredon, slate top, incised manufacturer's mark "FLW" on leg.

1955   *22½in (57cm) diam*
$3,700-5,000   **DRA**

A Frank Lloyd Wright cypress plywood upholstered chair, for the Charles L. and Dorothy Manson House, Wausau, Wisconsin.

For further reading on the Manson House, see William Allin Storrer, "The Architecture of Frank Lloyd Wright, Fourth Edition: A Complete Catalog," University of Chicago Press (2017), page 271.

1938   *28in (71cm) high*
$12,500-15,000   **FRE**

A Rivington Art Deco "The Miramar" cocktail cabinet, London, walnut with ivorine handles, with a fitted interior.

ca. 1930   57¾in (147cm) high

$1,250-1,900   L&T

A Token Works Art Deco mahogany and cedar wardrobe, designed by Betty Joel, with a paneled front and sides, the top section with two veneered doors with stepped rectangular handles, opening to an arrangement of shelving and hanging space, over a parallel drawer base, raised on reeded block supports, labeled "Token Hand-made Furniture Designed by Betty Joel, made at Token Works 1929."

1929   78¼in (199cm) high

$550-700   SWO

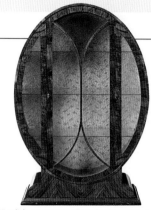

An English Art Deco walnut display cabinet, with removable glass shelves.

ca. 1930   57in (145cm) high

$550-700   L&T

ESSENTIAL REFERENCE—SERGE CHERMAYEFF

Born into a wealthy family in Grozny, in what was then part of the Russian Empire, and today is in the Chechen Republic, Serge Chermayeff (1900-96) moved to England at an early age and was educated at the Royal Drawing Society School (1910-13) and then at Harrow (1914-17), prior to his family losing its fortune during the Russian Revolution. While supporting himself as a journalist working for the Amalgamated Press (1918-23), he undertook a series of architectural and design courses at schools in Germany, Austria, France, and the Netherlands, before becoming chief designer (1924-27) at the decorating firm of E. Williams. In 1928, after becoming a British citizen, Chermayeff and the French designer Paul Follot were appointed to run the decorative arts department of the eminent English furniture makers Waring & Gillow, and it was during this period that he designed the Art Deco style cabinet illustrated here. Other work of note in the decorative arts included designing Bakelite radio cabinets for EKCO. From the mid-1930s, his focus shifted to Modernist architecture, initially in Great Britain (buildings of note include the Grade I listed De La Warr Pavilion in Bexhill, East Sussex), but after emigrating there in 1940, in the United States.

An Art Deco cabinet, attributed to Serge Chermayeff (1900-96) for Waring & Gillows, ripple sycamore veneer on mahogany, with silver, ebonized, and green lacquered detailing.

ca. 1928   66½in (169cm) high

$2,500-3,700   L&T

An Art Deco console table, in the manner of Edgar Brandt, marble and wrought steel.

ca. 1930   54in (137cm) wide

$2,200-3,000   L&T

An Art Deco ebonized wood occasional table, with D-shaped support on a rectangular base, unsigned.

58¼in (148cm) wide

$500-625   WW

An Art Deco walnut armchair, with a horizontal band on the barrel back, raised on fluted tapering legs, with later upholstery.

31½in (80cm) high

$625-750   SWO

An Art Deco giltwood stool, in the manner of Sue et Mare, with later silk upholstery and matching squab cushion.

ca. 1925   24¾in (63cm) diam

$500-625   L&T

A pair of Art Deco leather club armchairs, each with shaped arms with studded edges, raised on casters.

35in (89cm) high

$1,700-2,200   SWO

A Morris & Co. Arts and Crafts embroidered panel, by May Morris (1862-1938), color silks on a linen ground, in a glazed mahogany frame.

ca. 1890   22¾in (58cm) high

$1,100-1,500   L&T

A Tomkinson & Adam Ltd. carpet design, Kidderminster, by C. F. A. Voysey, watercolor and graphite on paper, with stylized bird-and-foliate repeat pattern, signed and dated, with Tomkinsons Carpets Ltd. stamp.

The stylized birds used in this design are found in many of Voysey's works. In an interview with "The Studio" magazine in 1893, he stated "I do not see why the forms of birds may not be used, provided they are reduced to mere symbols."

1900   22in (56cm) wide

$4,200-4,600   L&T

An Arts and Crafts hand-knotted wool carpet, after Gavin Morton and G. K. Robertson, the ivory field with allover decoration of bold palmettes and stiff leaves in blue, green, and pastel, enclosed by a conforming indigo palmette border.

See M. Haslam, "Arts and Crafts Carpets," Rizzoli (1991), page 106, figure 67, for a carpet of similar design.

256¾in (652cm) long

$30,000-35,000   L&T

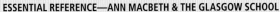

ESSENTIAL REFERENCE—ANN MACBETH & THE GLASGOW SCHOOL

In an age of rapid change and industrialization, Glasgow was becoming an increasingly prosperous city in the late 19thC—a model of pioneering design and manufacturing, especially within the shipbuilding and textile industries. In parallel, the Glasgow School of Art fostered young designers who could contribute to this transformation, and it was in the wake of this exciting atmosphere of creative experimentation that Ann Macbeth—born 1875 in Bolton, Lancashire—enrolled in the School in 1897.

Under Jessie Newbery, head of the embroidery department, Macbeth developed a striking organic style. Her embroideries were a regular feature in "The Studio" magazine, her work typically featuring young female figures encased within an array of stylized roundels and openwork banding. In 1908, Macbeth succeeded Newbery as head of the department and, as a teacher, she took inspiration from William Morris' Arts and Crafts ideals, encouraging students to be inspired by nature as a source of ideas and produce high-quality, stylistically distinctive work. Like Newbery before her, Macbeth strongly believed that art embroidery should be accessible to all classes, often encouraging the use of cheaper materials, such as burlap and less-expensive silk threads to facilitate this. Macbeth died in 1948, and this rare surviving collar, probably worn by her for a portrait taken in 1900, with its friezes of intertwined leaves, petals, and stylized rosebuds, captures the organic essence and vibrancy of both Macbeth and the Glasgow style.

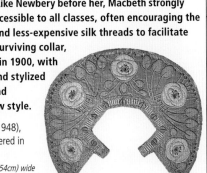

A Glasgow School collar, by Ann Macbeth (1875-1948), padded silk ground with appliqué of silk, embroidered in silk threads in satin stitch and couching.

ca. 1900   21¼in (54cm) wide

$15,000-19,000   L&T

A French Art Nouveau table cover, printed cotton plush velvet, with cotton fringing.

ca. 1900   66¼in (168cm) wide

$450-550   L&T

An Art Deco carpet, by Ashley Havinden, hand-knotted wool, with applied label verso.

When Ashley Havinden (1903-73) joined the London advertising agency W. S. Crawford in 1922, he had no formal training in the arts but subsequently took evening classes in design and drawing at the Centre School of Arts & Crafts (1922-23), and received private drawing lessons from Henry Moore in 1933. The London Gallery held Havinden's first solo exhibition in 1937, and he later featured in an exhibition of British abstract paintings at the Lefevre Gallery. He remained with W. S. Crawford for 45 years, becoming art director in 1929 (and vice chairman in 1960). He was given full freedom to develop his distinctive style, working on campaigns for Martini, Liberty's, and Chrysler, among others, and, at the same time, producing rug and textile designs for Duncan Miller Ltd. and Edinburgh Weavers. In 1951, Havinden received an OBE for services to British design.

ca. 1930

$3,000-3,500   L&T

An Art Deco circular wool pile floor rug, by Judith Found, with stylized geometric decoration, in shades of black, cream, and gray-green, artist's mark on side.

Judith Found (1944-2022) worked as a freelance fashion print designer. She went on to teach printed textiles on the fashion design course at St. Martin's School of Art in London (now Centre Saint Martins)—teaching successive generations of designers, including John Galliano, Katharine Hamnett, Matthew Williamson, Craig Green, and Richard Quinn. Earlier in her career, she sold designs to photographer Elsbeth Juda, who, with her husband Hans, ran "The Ambassador Magazine" for the promotion of British textiles and fashion; to Deryck Healey Associates in London; and to fashion design studios in New York, Paris, Italy, Japan, Canada, and Germany.

73½in (187cm) diam

$1,250-1,700   CA

Judith Picks

With its elongated, sinuously curvaceous, plant-formlike lines that instantly reference nature, the wooden case of this splendid clock is quintessential Art Nouveau. It was designed by one of the movement's leading furniture makers, Tony Selmersheim, and its shape works perfectly with its underlying mechanism. It is, however, the gilt-bronze sculptural elements of the clock that really elevate it into something special. Created by Alexandre Charpentier, they explore some of the core concerns of contemporary Symbolist poets, such as Charles Baudelaire and Paul Verlaine, whose raison d'être was to represent absolute truths symbolically through language or metaphorical images. In this case, that absolute truth is "La Fuite de L'Heure" ("the flight or passage of time")—the imagery in the surmount comprising a young man kissing his lover while protectively holding her aloft and grasping the scythe wielded by an old man to keep him at bay. As such, it is a powerful and poignant reminder of human mortality, and one augmented with the bas-relief panels below that depict the Fates from Greco-Roman mythology spinning the yarn for the cycle of life. All in all, and as the Symbolists intended, it is a composition that successfully elevates a "mere" (I use the word loosely) functional clock into a meaningful work of art.

A fine Art Nouveau padouk and gilt-bronze table clock, "La Fuite De L'heure," by Alexandre Charpentier (1856-1909) and Tony Selmersheim (1871-1971), the twin-train movement striking the hour and half hour, the surmount signed in the bronze "ALEXANDRE CHARPENTIER," side and front panels signed with monogram.

1898   *34¼in (87cm) high*
$32,000-37,000   **L&T**

An early-20thC Burmantofts Aesthetic Movement turquoise-glazed faience mantel clock, shape no. 1434, striking on a single bell, white enamel dial with black Roman numerals, gilt bezel, case surmounted by a sphinx, fascia molded with a heron amid bulrushes and lilies, impressed marks, with original label.

13½in (34.5cm) high
$1,000-1,250   **HT**

A late Foley "Tempus Fugit" mantel clock, "Intarsio" pattern, model no. 3676, printed with Art Nouveau foliate panels in colors, circular metal dial, printed factory marks, painted "3676."

9¾in (25cm) high
$1,000-1,250   **WW**

An Art Nouveau figural clock, by Friedrich Goldscheider (1845-97), gilt terra-cotta, with applied maker's seal verso and numbered, with incised artist's signature.

ca. 1900   *20½in (52cm) high*
$1,100-1,500   **CA**

A rare Liberty & Co. "Tudric" pewter and copper mantel clock, attributed to C. F. A. Voysey, French movement, the molded arch pediment over an offset copper chapter ring embossed with Arabic numerals, applied with five flying birds above, on a plain flat plinth, the underside stamped "Tudric 0101."

13½in (34.5cm) high
$15,000-19,000   **SWO**

A Liberty & Co. "Tudric" clock, by Archibald Knox (1864-1933), model no. 096, pewter and abalone, stamped on base "096."

See S. Martin, "Archibald Knox," Artmedia (2001), page 235, for an illustration of this clock.

ca. 1902-05   *11½in (29.5cm) high*
$23,500-30,000   **L&T**

A Liberty & Co. "Tudric" clock, London, model no. 0382, pewter and enamel, stamped under base "TUDRIC 0382."

ca. 1902-05   *10in (25.5cm) high*
$7,500-8,500   **L&T**

A Tiffany & Co. argentium repeater desk clock, gold engine-turned dial, Roman number markers, moon hands, cabochon push button, the case with vibrant royal blue and white enamel stripes, with wind-up key.

2½in (6.5cm) high
$7,500-8,500   **FRE**

An Art Deco Egyptian Revival polychrome enamel pocket watch, by Plojoux Geneve, Plojoux Geneve 17-jewel movement, manual winding, the signed champagne dial with Arabic numerals, ornate inner rail track and subsidiary seconds dial, the case decorated with stylized lotus flowers and scarabs in enamel, back of case signed and numbered.

$2,200-2,700   **WW**

A Jaeger-LeCoultre Art Deco double-sided desk clock, patinated metal, mirrored and clear glass, and slate, marked on the dial "JAEGER-LECOULTRE/8 DAYS/SWISS" on each side, with "JAEGER-LECOULTRE/SWISS" on the slate plinth on each side.

ca. 1930   *8¾in (22cm) wide*
$950-1,050   **L&T**

An early-20thC glass 11-light chandelier, of open scroll form, applied with flower heads and hung with drops and spheres.

28¾in (73cm) high

$800-950   **WW**

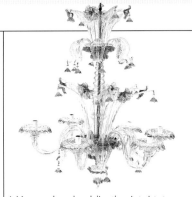

A Murano glass chandelier, the air-twist stem decorated with leaves and pink floral drops, leading to six lights, one dish chipped and cracked.

31½in (80cm) high

$220-300   **SWO**

An Art Nouveau copper and brass three-branch ceiling light, three copper foliate arms, with frosted glass bell shades, unsigned.

33½in (85cm) high

$700-800   **WW**

A rare Arts and Crafts patinated copper and glass center light, designed by Harold Stabler (1872-1945), made by Richard Llewellyn Benson Rathbone (1864-1939).

Harold Stabler initially trained in woodwork and stone-carving before being appointed Head of Metalwork at the Keswick School of Industrial Arts in 1898. After a short time there, and later Liverpool University, he moved to London in 1907 where he became Head of the John Cass Institute's Art School, until 1937, and in 1936 was appointed a Designer for Industry by the Royal Society of Arts. Working in a number of media, including enamels, metals, glass and ceramics, Stabler had a notable influence on the development of modern British design of the 1920s and "30s.

A relative of W.A.S. Benson, Richard Llewellyn Benson Rathbone initially trained in metalwork with Benson, before setting up his own workshop in 1908. He produced metalwork designs, in-keeping with the Arts & Crafts aesthetic, for Mackmurdo, Heywood Summner and C.F.A. Voysey, and also taught metalwork classes at Liverpool University, where he was joined by Harold Stabler in 1903. By 1905 he had moved to London to become Head of the Art School at the John Cass Institute.

ca. 1904   *40½in (103cm) wide*

$11,000-14,000   **L&T**

A rare Gustav Stickley lantern, model no. 203, from the Charles B. Evans House, Queens, hammered copper, iron, and hammered amber glass, impressed manufacturer's mark "Als Ik Kan" on ceiling cap with joiner's compass.

See Stubblebine, "Stickley's Craftsman Homes: Plans, Drawings, Photographs," Gibbs Smith (2006),pages 265 and 492, where this commission is discussed.

ca. 1914   *18in (46cm) high*

$43,000-50,000   **DRA**

An Arts and Crafts copper and brass table lamp, designed by W. A. S. Benson, with an adjustable mount, fitted with an opaline brocade-style shade, in the manner of John Walsh Walsh, with graduated straw on ruby opalescence, the tripod stand stamped "Benson."

14¼in (36cm) high

$1,050-1,250   **SWO**

An Arts and Crafts brass and copper extending standard lamp, by W. A. S. Benson (1854-1924), later converted to electricity, with later pleated silk shade, stamped "REG. NO.127090" on base.

ca. 1900 72¾in (185cm) high (fully extended)

$1,400-1,600   **L&T**

An Art Nouveau patinated metal table lamp, the base cast with a maiden standing above a stylized thistle panel, the flaring gilt-metal shade with red cast jewels and a tassel border, unsigned.

19in (48cm) high

$550-700   **WW**

An Art Nouveau "Amphora" porcelain table lamp, by Riessner, Stellmacher & Kessel, painted with a female head in profile, with tube lining and gilt, against a painted forest scene, with a two-light mount and a stepped base, stamped "Amphora" and numbered "631," remnants of printed mark, drilled.

28¼in (72cm) high

$800-950   **SWO**

A Continental Art Nouveau glass table lamp, with metal fittings, wired for electricity.

ca. 1910   *17¼in (44cm) high*

$950-1,050   **L&T**

DECORATIVE ARTS

A Tiffany Studios 18-light "Lily" table lamp, New York, Favrile glass shades, with etch-signed "L.C.T.," patinated bronze base, marked "Tiffany Studios, New York/383" on underside.

ca. 1900   21½in (54.5cm) high
$60,000-75,000   FRE

A rare Tiffany Studios table lamp, simple Indian patinated bronze base, Favrile glass, and glass hurricane shade with acid-etched three feather brand logo on top, impressed "TIFFANY STUDIOS NEW YORK 21448" on base, oil font impressed "TGDCO TIFFANY STUDIOS NEW YORK 21448," with original switches molded "TIFFANY STUDIOS," shade etched "L.C.T.."

See Duncan, "Tiffany Lamps and Metalware," ACC (2019), page 18, for this base illustrated, and pages 37-38 for similar shades.

ca. 1900   22in (56cm) high
$55,000-60,000   DRA

A Tiffany Studios and Rookwood Pottery geometric table lamp, the Rookwood Pottery base by Albert Munson, incised mat-glazed earthenware, with impressed manufacturer's mark "Flame mark I 191NZ" on underside, with incised artist's initials "AM," leaded glass shade, with impressed manufacturer's mark "TIFFANY STUDIOS NEW YORK 1913."

See Duncan, "Tiffany Lamps and Metalware," ACC (2019), page 152, where this shade is illustrated.

ca. 1901   22¾in (58cm) high
$8,000-9,500   DRA

A Tiffany Studios "Vine Border (Lemon Leaf)" table lamp, patinated bronze "Tyler" base, heavily modeled leaded glass shade, impressed "TIFFANY STUDIOS NEW YORK 1470" on shade, impressed "TIFFANY STUDIOS NEW YORK 203" on oil font and base.

See Duncan, "Tiffany Lamps and Metalware," ACC (2019), page 39, for the base illustrated and page 144 for the shade.

ca. 1905   25¾in (65.5cm) high
$26,000-30,000   DRA

A Tiffany Studios "Filigree" table lamp, adjustable patinated bronze "Villard" base with claw feet, Favrile glass, and patinated bronze shade, signed "TIFFANY STUDIOS NEW YORK" on base and shade, numbered "440" on leg.

See Duncan, "Tiffany Lamps and Metalware," ACC (2019), page 94, for the base illustrated and page 151 for the shade.

ca. 1910   25in (63.5cm) high
$40,000-45,000   DRA

A Tiffany Studios "Black-Eyed Susan" table lamp, leaded glass shade, patinated bronze "Crutch" base, impressed "TIFFANY STUDIOS NEW YORK 1447" on shade, impressed "TIFFANY STUDIOS NEW YORK 444"on base.

See Duncan, "Tiffany Lamps and Metalware," ACC (2019), page 96, for the base illiustrated and page 135 for the shade.

ca. 1910   22¼in (56.5cm) high
$31,000-37,000   DRA

A Tiffany Studios "Tulip" table lamp, patinated bronze library standard "Mushroom" base, leaded glass shade, impressed "TIFFANY STUDIOS 9943" on base, impressed "TIFFANY STUDIOS NEW YORK" on shade.

See Duncan, "Tiffany Lamps and Metalware," ACC (2019), page 84, for the base illustrated and page 137 for the shade.

ca. 1910   23in (58.5cm) high
$37,000-43,000   DRA

A rare Fulper Pottery Vasekraft table lamp, leopard skin crystalline-glazed stoneware, leaded glass shade, stamped rectangular manufacturer's mark "Fulper" on underside of base.

1909-17   17¼in (44cm) high
$8,000-9,500   DRA

An American boudoir lamp, by Dirk van Erp, hammered copper mica, with impressed open-box windmill mark "Dirk Van Erp San Francisco" on underside of base.

ca. 1915   10in (25.5cm) high
$11,000-14,000   DRA

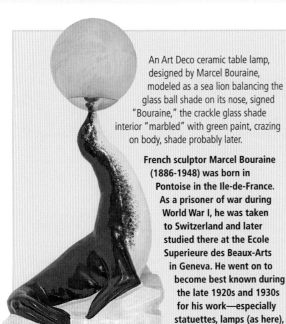

An Art Deco ceramic table lamp, designed by Marcel Bouraine, modeled as a sea lion balancing the glass ball shade on its nose, signed "Bouraine," the crackle glass shade interior "marbled" with green paint, crazing on body, shade probably later.

French sculptor Marcel Bouraine (1886-1948) was born in Pontoise in the Ile-de-France. As a prisoner of war during World War I, he was taken to Switzerland and later studied there at the Ecole Superieure des Beaux-Arts in Geneva. He went on to become best known during the late 1920s and 1930s for his work—especially statuettes, lamps (as here), bookends, and radiator figures—in the prevailing Art Deco style.

22in (56cm) high

$875-1,000   **SWO**

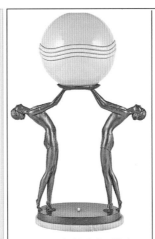

An Art Deco double lady table lamp, attributed to Josef Lorenzl (1892-1950), patinated metal, raised on an alabaster plinth, with an opaque glass shade.

ca. 1925   *20in (51cm) high*

$1,700-2,200   **L&T**

An Art Deco figural table lamp, by Josef Lorenzl, modeled as a nude holding a mottled jade-green globe, on an onyx plinth, refinished, rewired.

20½in (52cm) high

$1,250-1,500   **SWO**

An Art Deco opalescent glass table lamp, probably Sabino or Etling, modeled as a naked maiden offering up a pearl, before a large clamshell, unsigned.

10½in (26.5cm) high

$250-370   **WW**

A Daum Art Deco acid-etched and frosted glass table lamp, the shade of elongated domed form, cylindrical body with a spreading foot, the shade and base with etched chevron design, etched signature "Daum Nancy, France" on base and shade, with a Cross of Lorraine.

ca. 1925   *21¾in (55cm) high*

$3,700-5,000   **CA**

A French Art Deco bronze and marble figural lamp, by Jean Lormier, signed "J. Lormier" on lower edge.

ca. 1930   *18¼in (46.5cm) wide*

$700-800   **DRA**

A pair of Art Deco chrome "Skyscraper" table lamps, each with three branches, mounted on black plinths.

22in (56cm) high

$500-625   **SWO**

An Art Deco wrought-iron two-light lamp, in the manner of Edgar Brandt, the center clustered stem supporting a floriform terminal, the branches supporting frosted glass Muller Frères conical shades, the shades signed "Muller Frères Luneville."

24in (61cm) high

$375-500   **WW**

An Art Deco floor lamp, brass, and enameled steel, with a fabric shade.

ca. 1930   *61½in (156cm) high*

$1,500-1,900   **DRA**

DECORATIVE ARTS

ESSENTIAL REFERENCE—TIFFANY & CO.

Founded in New York in 1837 as "Tiffany, Young & Ellis," Tiffany & Co. (as it became in 1853) has long been better known as just Tiffany's. Initially a "Stationery and fancy goods emporium," the emphasis shifted away from stationery to jewelry after cofounder and jeweler-by-training Charles Lewis Tiffany took control. Then, during the second half of the 19thC, it spread further into other areas of the decorative arts—most notably, in addition to jewelry, glass (see page 551), lighting (see page 562), and, as here, metalware. This expansion was fueled in no small part by the establishment in 1885 of the design and production company Tiffany Studios by Charles Lewis's son Louis Comfort Tiffany. It continued for much of the 20thC—prior to Tiffany & Co. being sold to Avon Products, Inc. in 1978 and, after further changes of ownership, becoming part of the LVMH (Moet Hennessy Louis Vuitton) group in 2021.

A documentary Victorian Tiffany & Co. silver pepperette, in Aesthetic style, from the "Harlequin" set, pattern no. 5141, etching design no. 153, quatre-lobed form with lateral rib, engraved with foliage, pierced push-on cover with a copper knop, strap handle with a foliate pierced copper grille, raised on four short bracket feet, the base stamped "Tiffany & Co Sterling Silver and Other Metals," with engraved presentation inscription "GIVEN BY T.R.H. PRINCE & PRINCESS OF WALES, XMAS 1879," with a Tiffany research certificate dated November 2021.

Provenance: The inscription refers to Prince Albert Edward and Princess Alexandra of Denmark, later King Edward VII and his Queen Consort. The Tiffany Archive records the entry for order no. 9720 for a "5141" Pepper, in the Silver Manufacturing Ledger no. 3, costing 10.00 for making and 14.00 for etching. The etching design is illustrated in appendix 2 of the archive, and the "1879 Blue Book," page 89, documents H. R. H. the Prince of Wales at the top of the purchaser list.

1879   *3½in (9cm) high*
$12,500-15,000   **JON**

A Tiffany & Co. parcel-gilt silver "Japanesque" tea caddy, the body applied with a gilt flying dragonfly and a spider weaving an engraved web, the cover with chased gilt geometric square design, stamped "TIFFANY & CO/ STERLING-SILVER/3" and numbered "3683 M 8880."

ca. 1875   *6¾in (17cm) high*
$11,000-15,000   **L&T**

A late-19thC Tiffany & Co. silver caddy spoon, "American Chrysanthemum" pattern, the bowl with molded arch-shaped decoration, engraved foliate decoration on the handle, with engraved initials on the front terminal, marked "Pat. 1880 M."

4½in (11.5cm) long 1oz
$150-190   **WW**

ESSENTIAL REFERENCE—LIBERTY & CO.

Founded in 1875 by Arthur Lazenby Liberty (1843-1917) as a furniture and drapery store, originally known as East India House, in London's Regent Street, Liberty & Co. soon became better known simply as Liberty's. As the store's original name suggests, there was initially a strong emphasis on selling Middle Eastern and Asian artifacts. But this soon expanded to incorporate wares of European design and manufacture—initially traditional, but increasingly contemporary innovations, most notably from designers and craftspeople (often commissioned directly by Liberty's) working in the Aesthetic, Arts and Crafts, and Art Nouveau styles. In covering most categories of the decorative arts—from furniture to textiles and costume, from jewelry to metalware and lighting, and from ceramics to glass—Liberty's became as much an arbiter of late-19th and 20thC style and taste as the designers it patronized and supported. The store is still thriving and, since 2010, has been owned by a private equity firm.

A pair of English Liberty & Co. pewter candlesticks, by Archibald Knox, model no. 0221, marked on base, faults, scratches, discoloration.

ca. 1900   *5¾in (14.5cm) high*
$375-500   **CHOR**

A Liberty & Co. "Tudric" pewter footed bowl, by Oliver Baker, model no. 067, on four arched legs with flaring pad feet, set with four lapis stones at the top, stamped marks.

13in (33cm) wide
$450-550   **DUK**

A pair of Liberty & Co. pewter twin-handle "Tulip" vases, by Archibald Knox, both marked on base "Tudric, 029."

ca. 1903   *10in (25.5cm) high*
$1,250-1,500   **FRE**

A pair of Edwardian Liberty & Co. napkin rings, Glasgow, of D form on dolphin-head end supports, cast in low relief with Celtic knots enclosing bosses, engraved "JB" and "MB."

1911   *2¼in (5.5cm) wide 2oz*
$350-420   **HT**

A Liberty & Co. Art Nouveau silver and enamel belt buckle, Birmingham, of double-heart form, with spot-hammered decoration, deep blue and green enamel decoration.

1912   *3½in (9cm) wide 2oz*
$375-500   **WW**

ESSENTIAL REFERENCE—GEORG JENSEN

Son of a blacksmith and knife grinder, Georg Jensen was born in 1866 in Rådvid, Denmark. Prior to establishing the Georg Jensen Company, in Copenhagen in 1904, he had been apprenticed as a goldsmith, graduated in sculpture, and run a failed ceramics business. Some 31 years later, upon his death in 1935, the New York Herald's obituary saluted him as "the greatest silversmith of the last 300 years." Initial success with jewelry soon enabled expansion into the production of hollow ware and flatware, and stylistically his company have embraced all the great style movements of the 20th and 21stC (the company flourishes to this day): Arts and Crafts, Art Nouveau, Neoclassical, Art Deco, Modernism, Organic Modernism, Postmodernism, etc., but all somehow rendered quintessentially "Jensen." Much of this can be attributed to the company always—both before and after Georg Jensen's death—working with great and innovative designers, notable among whom, and in addition to Jensen himself, were: Johan Rohde (1865-1935), Gundorph Albertus (1887-1969), Harald Nielsen (1892-1977), Henning Koppel (1918-81), and Vivianna Torun Bülow-Hübe (1927-2014)—the latter best known as just Torun.

A Georg Jensen silver "Blossom" tureen, model no. 2C, with stamped manufacturer's mark and "925S/DENMARK/STERLING/2A," import marks for 1937.

design conceived 1905   *12½in (32cm) wide*

$3,500-4,200   **L&T**

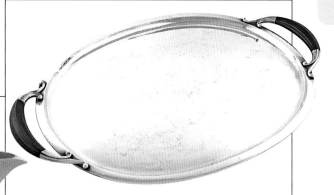

A Georg Jensen silver two-handle tray, design no. 787B, by Johan Rohde, with spot-hammered decoration, wood handles with scroll motifs.

20¾in (52.5cm) wide 57¼oz

$4,600-5,200   **WW**

A Georg Jensen "Louvre" bowl, lightly planished bowl, on berried branches and leaf stems, on a stepped domed foot, stamped "Sterling/925/17B."

5¼in (13.5cm) high 9oz

$875-1,000   **HT**

A Georg Jensen sugar basket, lightly planished bowl, with overhead fixed handle with berry terminals, on stylized berried surmounts and a stepped circular foot, stamped "925.S/Sterling/235B."

5¼in (13.5cm) wide 5oz

$700-800   **HT**

A Georg Jensen "Blossom" spoon, stamped "925 S/21," George Stockwell import marks for London, 1931.

5½in (14cm) long

$150-220   **HT**

A Georg Jensen bowl, deeply engraved with sparse stylized leaves, stamped "STERLING 925."

8½in (21.5cm) high 19oz

$1,250-1,500   **HT**

A set of six Georg Jensen "Acorn" teaspoons, stamped "Sterling."

4½in (11.5cm) long 2oz

$125-190   **HT**

A pair of Georg Jensen sterling silver sugar tongs, design no. 3, with a chrysoprase, stamped "GEORG JENSEN/ GJ 830S/3/14/826S."

ca. 1917   *5½in (14cm) long*

$1,050-1,250   **L&T**

A large Art Nouveau silver twin-handle vase, by William Hutton & Sons, London, with applied strap handles with foliate motifs, the body with applied floral panels, stamped marks.

1901 18½in (47cm) high 118½oz

$6,000-7,500 WW

An Art Nouveau Regimental presentation silver three-handle cup, with three scroll handles, on a circular foot, engraved with the regimental badge, and inscribed "2ND Battalion The Welch Regiment, Officers Cross Country Challenge Cup," and "Presented by Captain C. R. W. Allen Sept. 1906," marked with a lion head, maker's mark "C" and "K."

ca. 1906 9¼in (23.5cm) high 43oz

$1,100-1,350 WW

An Edwardian Art Nouveau silver pedestal fruit bowl, by Joseph Rodgers & Sons, Sheffield, with three stylized handles, minor scratches.

1908 10¾in (27.5cm) high 46oz

$1,250-1,500 GORL

An Austrian silver box and cover, by Otto Prutscher for the Wiener Werkstätte, executed by Alfred Mayer, with spot-hammered decoration, the pull-off cover with an ivory finial, on four ivory bun feet.

Ivory Act certification no. BADP857C

1908 5½in (14cm) high 9½oz

$25,000-31,000 WW

An Arts and Crafts silver and enamel caddy spoon, by Omar Ramsden, London, spot-hammered fig-shaped bowl, intertwined wirework handle, set with a triangular red enamel boss.

1927 3¼in (8.5cm) long 1⅜oz

$1,600-2,000 WW

A late Arts and Crafts silver-mounted coconut mazer, by Henry George Murphy, London, with a spot-hammered interior, the border with a rope-twist border and serpentine frieze with stylized lotus decoration, on three similarly decorated bun-type feet, cracks, repairs.

1929 4½in (11.5cm) diam

$450-550 DAWS

A pair of Arts and Crafts silver and enamel dishes, by Omar Ramsden, London, each with a 16-section batwing border, with ball motifs, spot-hammmed bodies, the centers with a coiled fish on a green enamel ground, with rope-work borders, engraved "OMAR RAMSDEN ME FECIT."

1933 6¾in (17cm) diam 16½oz

$2,900-3,350 WW

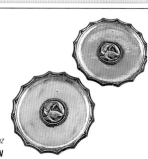

An Art Deco four-piece silver tea set, by Charles Boyton (1885-1958), London, with stylized scroll handles, raised hinged covers with knop finials, on raised lozenge bases, signed "Charles Boyton."

1931 7in (18cm) high 28oz

$2,700-3,100 WW

An Art Deco silver teapot, by Adie Bros, Birmingham.

1932 6¼in (16cm) high 25⅞oz

$480-550 CHOR

An Art Deco silver and enamel bowl, by Wakely and Wheeler, London, with three bands of cornflower-blue enamel decoration, on four bracket supports, on a circular foot.

1934 11¾in (30cm) diam 47oz

$3,500-4,200 WW

Judith Picks

Ever since I first encountered one of his designs, I have never had anything but bordering-on-incredulous admiration for Dr. Christopher Dresser. Born in 1834—he died 70 years later in 1904—his life spanned the Victorian age. Much of his working life coincided with a period in which many designers drew on a mishmash of older British and European styles for inspiration, resulting in a series of stylistic revivals collectively, and sometimes disparagingly, referred to as Victorian Eclecticism. In marked contrast, Dresser—like William Morris with the Arts and Crafts Movement and later Émile Gallé with Art Nouveau—looked elsewhere to create a new aesthetic. In Dresser's case, literally so, with his promotion of the Aesthetic Movement and ideas inspired by a range of cultures and, especially, his study of botany and his travels in Japan in the 1870s. More than that, however, and working in diverse mediums and with numerous companies, he fully embraced new mechanized production techniques in an effort to make high-quality and beautifully designed products more accessible—ergo affordable—to a much wider clientele than hitherto. Over and above that, however, it is the extraordinarily prescient modernity of Dresser's designs—witness this brass and copper flask—that really amaze: if it had been designed 100 years later, it would still look just as innovative and just as new!

A Benham & Froud Aesthetic Movement brass and copper flask, by Christopher Dresser, London, with original cork stopper and chain, stamped manufacturer's mark.

ca. 1885   12¾in (32.5cm) high
$7,000-8,000   **L&T**

An Arts and Crafts jardinière, by Clement Heaton (1861-1940), copper with applied cloisonné decoration.

Clement Heaton, an early member of A. H. Mackmurdo's Century Guild, set up his company Heatons Cloisonné-Mosaic Ltd. at 6 Berners Street, London, in 1887, a year after selling his share in his father's lucrative stained-glass business, Heaton, Butler & Bayne, for about $6,000 He patented his enameling technique in 1886, inspired by medieval techniques that precluded the firing process and instead used color cements: a mixture of resin, beeswax, sulfur, marble dust, and color pigments. Hardening over time, these cements could be polished to give the soft mat finish characteristic of Heaton's work, as seen in this example.

ca. 1890   7¾in (19.5cm) high
$1,400-1,700   **L&T**

A copper and brass chamberstick, by W. A. S. Benson (1854-1924), the repoussé engraved design by Heywood Sumner.

See I. Hamerton, "W. A. S. Benson, Arts & Crafts Luminary & Pioneer of Modern Design," Woodbridge (2005), page 253, plate 23, and page 125 for this example.

ca. 1900   8¾in (22cm) high
$410-475   **L&T**

A Newlyn two-handle copper vase, with embossed fish, stamped.

9½in (24cm) high
$250-310   **CHOR**

A set of four 20thC brass wall lights, in Arts and Crafts style, in the manner of the Cotswold School, each with a pierced foliate circular backplate and twin scrolling branches and sconces, discoloration, paint residue, splits, losses.

7in (18cm) diam
$750-875   **CHOR**

A Newlyn copper tray, embossed with a border of fish and shells, with two handles and a pierced gallery, bearing the inscription "For St Ives Choral Society 1923," impressed stamp, marks, glue residue, scratches.

20in (51cm) wide
$220-300   **CHOR**

A large copper box, by John Pearson, decorated with mythological beasts, signed with initials "JP" and dated "1905" on back, discoloration, dents, scratches, polish holes.

1905   15in (38cm) wide
$1,400-1,700   **CHOR**

A McVitie & Price brass and copper cookie box, with Ruskin ceramic roundels, stamped "MCVITIE & PRICE/LONDON AND EDINBURGH."

ca. 1910   7in (18cm) wide
$1,250-1,500   **L&T**

A French bronze of "Eve" or "Salambo," by Jean-Marie-Antoine Idrac (1849-84), the base signed "A Idrac" and stamped "Thiebaut Freres Fondeurs Paris."

28¼in (72cm) high

$4,200-4,600 **WW**

A French bronze of a dancer with a lyre, by Mathurin Moreau (1822-1912), the base signed "Math. Moreau/Hors. Concours."

27¾in (70.5cm) high

$3,200-4,000 **WW**

A late-19th/early-20thC bronze of Orpheus, cast by Barbedienne, after Raoul Charles Verlet (1857-1923), signed to cast and inscribed "F Barbedienne Fondeur," some patina rubbing.

Originally titled "LA DOULEUR D'ORPHÉE" ("Orpheus' Sorrow"), the work depicts the figure with a lyre and three-headed Cerberus at his feet, in the act of turning to look at his love Eurydice and, in the process, losing her forever. The plaster model for this work was first exhibited in 1887.

39¼in (99.5cm) high

$6,000-7,500 **DN**

A late-19thC French bronze of the Medici Venus, after the Antique, standing before a cherub riding a dolphin, on a shaped base, stamped "F Barbedienne. Fondeur" and with its foundry mark.

18in (45.5cm) high

$1,000-1,250 **WW**

A large late-19thC bronze bust of Dionysus, Naples, after the Antique, cast by Fonderia Sommer, inscribed on the reverse cast "Fonderia Georgio Sommer Calabritto 2-3 Napoli Made in Italy," later painted in red "26," "50," and three daisy marks, on a variegated yellow marble socle, restoration on base.

The original bust was excavated from the ash and lava-covered Villa Dei Papiri, on the outskirts of Herculaneum, in 1759. It is now housed in the Naples Archaeological Museum and has been previously identified as the Greek philosopher Plato.

26½in (67cm) high

$11,000-15,000 **DN**

A late-19thC large bronze group, "Perseus Freeing Andromeda," after Jean Louis Gregoire (1840-90), signed on the cast and dated, on a bronze-mounted hardstone revolving base, rubbing, small damages, marple plinth discolor.

1870 *41in (104cm) high*

$20,000-25,000 **DN**

A late-19thC French bronze group of the "Uffizi Wrestlers," after the Antique, on a naturalistic base, with dark brown patination.

The original sculpture, attributed to Lysippus, was found in 1583 in the Horti Lamiani on the Esquiline Hill in Rome. It was bought and restored by Cardinal Ferdinando de' Medici, before being put on exhibition in the Villa Medici. It is currently on view in the Gallerie degli Uffizi, Florence.

17in (43cm) high

$2,500-3,100 **WW**

A large late-19th/early-20thC bronze group, "Hercules, Athena, and Cerberus," after Ernest Rancoulet (1842-1915), signed on the cast.

34½in (87.5cm) high

$9,500-11,000 **DN**

A bronze group, "Two Mothers," after Eugeny Alexandrovich Lanceray (Evgeni Eugene Lanse) (1846-86), of a mother and child on a mare, a foal at their side, on a rounded rectangular mound base, signature and foundry mark in Cyrillic.

13in (33cm) wide

$14,000-17,500 **TEN**

ESSENTIAL REFERENCE—BERGMAN BRONZES

Born in Gablonz, Bohemia (from 1918 Czechoslovakia, then since 1993 the Czech Republic), Franz Bergman (1838-94) worked as a metal chaser and finisher, prior to founding a small bronze factory in Vienna in 1860. Upon his death, ownership of the company passed to his son, Franz Xavier Bergman (1861-1939). He set up a new foundry and, although not a sculptor himself, under his direction it gained a considerable reputation during the first half of the 20thC for the quality of its bronzes. Bergman bronzes are particularly notable for their impressive attention to detail and, in many cases, the vibrancy of their patinated and cold-painted finishes. Its bird and animal subjects, as illustrated here, are particularly desirable, but it also produced numerous Asian and erotic figures—with the latter sometimes stamped "Namgreb" (Bergman in reverse). The foundry closed in 1954, and its remaining stock and molds were sold to Karl Fuhrmann & Co.

A Bergman cold-painted bronze model of an English partridge, standing alert, its feathers in naturalistic colors.

9in (23cm) high

$3,500-4,200   CHEF

An early 20thC Austrian cold-painted bronze of a woodcock, possibly by Franz Xavier Bergman, with an indistinct mark on the underside, possibly a B within an amphora, paint chips, minor verdigris on legs, unable to stand up.

11¾in (30cm) wide

$2,500-3,100   BELL

An early-20thC Austrian cold-painted bronze model of a woodcock, probably by Bergman, no clear foundry mark, indistinct mark on underside, beak is bent, rubbing on paintwork.

9¼in (23.5cm) wide

$2,500-3,100   BELL

An early-20thC Austrian cold-painted bronze of a blackbird, by Bergman, Vienna, the underside stamped "GESCHUTZ/4465" and a "B" within a vase, some rubbing.

7½in (19cm) wide

$1,700-2,200   BELL

A cold-painted bronze model of a parrot, in the manner of Bergman, naturalistically painted, unmarked, paint losses, small hole in right wing.

6¼in (16cm) high

$875-1,250   CHEF

A small cold-painted bronze model of a woodcock, in the manner of Bergman, naturalistically painted.

3½in (9cm) high

$800-1,000   CHEF

An early-20thC Austrian cold-painted bronze figure of a greyhound, by the Bergman Foundry, stamped on the underside with a "B" within an urn and serial numbers, further indistinct numbers on collar.

4¾in (12cm) high

$1,400-1,700   BELL

A late-19th/early-20thC Austrian cold-painted bronze model of a cat, in the manner of Franz Bergman, stamped "Geschutzt."

7in (18cm) wide

$300-450   WW

An Art Deco figure, "The Disk Dancer," by Marcel-Andre Bouraine (1886-1948), modeled as a nude female holding two plastic disks, in patinated green Le Verrier art metal, signed "Derenne," on a tapering marble plinth, some wear, disks probably not original.

19¼in (49cm) high

$1,250-1,500   SWO

A patinated bronze sculpture, "Diana with Fawns (Diana the Huntress)," by Marcel-Andre Bouraine (1886-1948), on an angled base, signed "Bouraine."

29in (73.5cm) high

$8,000-9,500   WW

A patinated bronze figure, "Dancer of Lebanon," by Demetre H. Chiparus (1886-1947), on an onyx base, signed "CHIPARUS."

ca. 1925   14½in (37cm) high

$6,000-7,500   L&T

An Art Deco figure, "The Nimble Dancer," by Demetre H. Chiparus (1886-1947), patinated and cold-painted bronze, ivory, and inlaid onyx, the base indistinctly inscribed "D. H. CHIPARUS."

See Bryan Catley, "Art Deco and Other Figures," Antique Collectors Club (1978), page 91.

ca. 1925   18½in (47cm) high

$12,500-15,000   L&T

A French Art Deco patinated bronze figure, "Hindu Dancer," by Claire Jeanne Roberte Colinet (1880-1950), modeled as an exotic dancer poised on one leg with her right arm outstretched, raised on a cast bronze plinth molded with Hindu deity.

ca. 1930   17in (43cm) high

$2,200-2,700   DAWS

A French Art Deco patinated bronze figure, "Woman with birds of Paradise," signed "G. Daverny, Editions Reveyrolis Paris," impressed "Bronze Veritable" on rear foot, raised on a rectangular Nero Portoro marble-mounted base, wear, scratches, chips.

ca. 1930   28¼in (72cm) wide

$2,700-3,200   SWO

A bronze figure, "The Vine," by Harriet Whitney Frishmuth (1880-1980), incised signature and date "1921 Harriet W Frishmuth" on lower edge, with impressed foundry mark "Gorham Co. Founders OBWS."

This work was cast in an edition of 396, with 79 produced at the Gorham Company Foundry, Providence, Rhode Island.

1921   12½in (32cm) high

$10,500-12,000   DRA

ESSENTIAL REFERENCE—WERKSTÄTTE HAGENAUER WIEN

After training as a goldsmith, Carl Hageneauer (1872-1928) founded the Werkstätte Hagenauer Wien in Vienna, in 1898. It produced decorative figurines and utilitarian domestic artifacts to his own designs as well as those of others, such as Josef Hoffmann and Otto Prutscher. His eldest son, Karl Hagenauer (1898-1956), having studied with Josef Hoffman and created designs for the Wiener Werkstätte, joined the company in 1919. He gradually took managerial and artistic control—in the case of the latter, initially responding to the changes in public taste that accompanied the popularity of the Vienna Secession and then, from the mid-1920s and through the 1930s, being at the cutting edge of Art Deco style. Typical useful objects included mirrors, candlesticks, bookends, lamp bases, ashtrays, and, often in the form of athletes or animals, cigar cutters and corkscrews. Distinctively stylized, figurine-size human and animal sculptures also figured, and many of the latter were designed by Karl's younger brother, Franz Hagenauer (1906-86), who took over the company after Karl died. The Werkstätte Hagenauer Wien closed in 1987, but its retail premises on Vienna's Opernring survives as a museum and a shop.

A pair of bronze and painted figurines of African warriors, by Hagenauer, each modeled holding a spear and shield, stamped marks, gilt rubbing and losses.

4¾in (12cm) high

$500-625   CHOR

An Art Deco cold-painted "Scarf Dancer," by Josef Lorenzl, raised on an hexagonal onyx plinth, signed "Lorenzl," spotting, chips on base.

18¾in (47.5cm) high

$4,300-5,000 SWO

An Art Deco cold-painted bronze of a ballerina, by Josef Lorenzl, raised on an onyx plinth, impressed "Lorenzl," rubbing, chips on plinth.

9¼in (23.5cm) high

$1,900-2,200 SWO

CLOSER LOOK—A LORENZL DANCER

Female dancers, scantily clad or, as here, naked, were sculptor Joseph Lorenzl's favorite subject. The elegance of this dancer's long neck and face in profile are as characteristic of his style as the "boyish" modernity of her haircut.

There is invariably a precision of poise and movement inherent in Lorenzl's figures, and this is perfectly symbolized by the "just so" gesture of the dancer's thumbs and index fingers.

The athletic slimness of the dancer's torso, extending into similarly slim, elongated, and extended limbs, are also quintessential Lorenzl.

It may be by just one leg, and only by the tips of her toes, but the dancer is firmly rooted to the pedestal. The physical balance of the symmetry of the figure, and its stylized composition, is never in danger of being attributed to any Art Deco sculptor other than Lorenzl.

A bronze figure, "Dancer," by Josef Lorenzl (1892-1950), on an onyx base, signed "LORENZL" on base in the bronze.

ca. 1925 *23in (58.5cm) high*

$10,000-12,500 L&T

An Art Deco cold-painted bronze figure of a dancer wearing a ruff, by Josef Lorenzl, raised on an onyx plinth, signed "Lorenzl," minor rubbing.

8½in (21.5cm) high

$1,700-2,100 SWO

An Art Deco cold-painted figure, "The Flute Player," by Josef Lorenzl, raised on a chamfered onyx plinth, on a square base, signed "Lorenzl," minor chips and rubbing.

ca. 1930 *21¾in (55cm) high*

$6,000-7,500 SWO

A patinated bronze and ivory figure, "Cat Dancer," by Enrique Molins-Balleste (1893-1958), on a marble base, signed "H. MOLINS" on base.

Ivory Act certification no. AQGU9WNT

ca. 1925 *15¾in (40cm) high*

$5,000-6,200 L&T

A cold-painted bronze, ivory, and patinated ivory onyx figure, "Con Brio," by Ferdinand Preiss (1882-1943), signed "F. PREISS" in the bronze.

ca. 1925 *13½in (34.5cm) high*

$12,500-15,000 L&T

A patinated bronze, ivory, and onyx figure, "Cabaret Girl," by Ferdinand Preiss (1882-1943), foundry mark on base.

ca. 1925 *15¼in (38.5cm) high*

$12,500-15,000 L&T

THE MODERN MARKET

The years of COVID-19, while difficult for so many in myriad ways, have been a surprisingly robust period for art and design. This has been especially true of the post-World War II Modern market, and the (hopefully) post-COVID-19 question now is: Will these prices settle or continue to increase? Well, one constant over the last 50 years or so has been a seemingly relentless shift toward Modern design. Why? Plausible explanations range from "people don't want to collect what their parents collected" to "if you've chosen to hang postwar contemporary art on the wall, you're less inclined to put 18thC or 19thC furniture of almost any style or geographic origin underneath it." Regardless, it is altogether possible that tastes will shift yet again, and there might be what could be referred to as a "retro-retro" movement toward traditional furniture (see the Introduction to the Furniture market on page 166). However, in hard cash terms, it has yet to materialize.

More specifically, what I have seen from early 2023 onward is a leveling out of prices for some midrange and lower-end furniture, ceramics, lighting, and glass. However, this has not been at the expense of "Sell-through rates" at auction, which at Modern decorative arts sales have been running at about 88-92 percent—the commensurate DNS ("did not sell") of 8-12 per cent being significantly lower than the 15-20 percent it was running at even in what were considered successful sales prior to COVID-19. It is certainly possible that this increased sell-through is a result of many more online bidders participating in auctions, having become relatively comfortable with the process when COVID-19 restrictions made travel and on-site inspection more difficult or even impossible. Regardless of the underlying reason or reasons, however, the overall result has been a very solid market.

So, that leaves the perennial key question: Where might the next year or so take us? My expectation is that, at least for the near future, the desire for postwar furniture, ceramics, lighting, and glass will continue, and by its very nature the practice of collecting will in itself partly fuel that—to adapt a friend's astute observation, "You buy a china cabinet once … then 40 pieces [of glass or ceramics] to put in it!" It is important to remember, however, that the "ceramics market," for example, is really a term that extends to hundreds of makers, ranging from large factories to single-potter studios, each existing within micromarkets that can perform differently from one another at the same time.

Over and above all, perhaps the most telling phenomenon of recent years has been that of the pre-Modern (yet prescient of it) George Ohr, known as the Mad Potter of Biloxi, whose work continues to show almost unprecedented strength in the market, bolstered not only by collectors but also by museums with a Modernist bent. Of course, George Ohr was never just an art potter but more or a genius working clay in unconventional ways. This, perhaps more than anything else, explains the market, underscored by savvy, confident buyers completely aware that rare is always rare, great is always great, and, as I have often said from the podium while calling a sale, "better is always better"!

David Rago, President, Rago, Wright, LAMA, Toomey & Co.

Top Left: A Chanel quilted black medium double-flap purse, black leather with gold-tone hardware, with original dust bag and authentication card, light scratches.

1986-88 *9¾in (24.5cm) wide*

$5,000-6,200 **WW**

Above: A hand-built stoneware "Tulip" vase, by John Ward (b. 1938), with black and white panels, impressed seal mark.

10¾in (27.5cm) high

$14,000-17,500 **WW**

ESSENTIAL REFERENCE—ARNE JACOBSEN'S "EGG" CHAIR

The "Egg" armchair was originally designed in 1957-58 by the Danish architect Arne Jacobsen (1902-71) for the reception area of the SAS Royal Hotel in Copenhagen—for which he had designed not only the building but also all its other fixtures and fittings. The sculptural form of Jacobsen's decidedly modern take on the traditional "wing-back" armchair embraces the sitter, cocooning him or her in the plushest of comfort. Embracing then-new technologies that allowed for the creation of seats from a single mold, it consists of a fiberglass shell covered in a flexible foam that is molded to the shape of the human body and then covered in an upholstery fabric—in this instance leather. Raised on a steel, four-footed pedestal base, it also enables the sitter to both swivel and tilt for additional convenience and comfort. Originally produced by Fritz Hansen, the Danish furniture company, it is still produced by it under license to this day.

A Fritz Hansen "Egg" chair, by Arne Jacobsen, leather with steel frame, traces of manufacturer's label on frame.
1958   *41¾in (106cm) high*
$8,500-10,000   **L&T**

A pair of Chandigarh teak armchairs, "Cane and Teak Wood Armchair," by Pierre Jeanneret (1896-1967), no. PJ-010104T, with solid teak frames, braided canework seats and backrests, compass-type double side-leg assembly, the legs connected by two crosspieces and supporting the armrests, both with white painted identification code "A.I.I.M.S. ST. HOSTEL," one numbered "80," the other "24."

The lettering on the chair "A.I.I.M.S." relates to the All India Institute of Medical Sciences.

26in (66cm) high
$12,500-15,000   **DUK**

A Herman Miller high-back chair, "EA124," by Charles and Ray Eames (1907-78 and 1912-88), faux leather with aluminum frame, cast manufacturer's mark and serial number "683/84/938-011" on frame.
ca. 1960   *38¼in (97cm) high*
$1,250-1,500   **L&T**

An Artifort armchair, model no. F444, by Pierre Paulin, with a tan leather slung seat and tubular frame, label on underside.
$2,200-3,000   **WHP**

An early Artifort "Groovy" chair, by Pierre Paulin (1927-2009), model no. F-580, painted aluminum with purple upholstery, unmarked.
1960s   *26½in (67.5cm) high*
$2,000-2,700   **FRE**

An Edra red velvet rose chair, by Masanori Umeda, on polished aluminum splayed legs.
1990   *34½in (87.5cm) high*
$1,500-1,900   **HT**

An R&Y Agousti armchair, model no. F05, covered with shagreen panels, lifting, rubbing.
$700-950   **CHOR**

A Moroso brown leather armchair, "Doodle," by Front, the shape reminiscent of a folded blanket.

Moroso's marketing for this chair reads: "Sitting on the echo of a thought ... From the hand which unconsciously doodles during a phone call, lines of thought sprint out." The three members of Front merged their absent-minded doodles from design meetings to form the inspiration for this chair.
2013
$1,250-1,900   **WHP**

A chrome and leather "Aviator" armchair, the chrome frame with cutout side panels, overstuffed brown leather seat and backrest.
27½in (70cm) high
$550-700   **DUK**

A Poltronova black leather armchair, "Joe," by Jonathan De Pas, Donato D'Urbino, and Paolo Lomazzi, first edition, in the form of a baseball glove, with embossed star on right-hand side.

Designed in 1970 and inspired by the Pop Art movement, the "Joe" chair is a homage to the legendary American baseball star Joe DiMaggio.

early-1970s
$3,500-4,200 WHP

ESSENTIAL REFERENCE—EAMES'S LOUNGE CHAIR & OTTOMAN

The Eames lounge chair (No. 670) and matching ottoman (No. 671) has long been one of the most instantly recognizable creations of the American husband-and-wife design team, Charles and Ray Eames (1907–78 and 1912–88, respectively). Comfortable like an old-fashioned club sofa, it is essentially the mid-20thC answer to the Victorian daybed, and one that looks equally appropriate in an executive office, a home study, or a sitting room. Charles Eames said he wanted the chair to have "the warm receptive look of a well-used first baseman's mitt," so they opted for molded plywood veneered with rich, warm rosewood and combined it with supple leather upholstery. For the base, tubular steel and plywood were tested and rejected in favor of black enamel and polished aluminum, and while the chair's five-prong base swivels, the four-prong base of the ottoman does not. The final prototype was produced in 1956 as a birthday gift for their friend, the Hollywood movie director Billy Wilder. The furniture manufacturer Herman Miller put it into production in 1957, the same year that it won first prize at the prestigious design exhibition the Milan Triennial, and it has been in continuous production since.

A lounge chair and ottoman, by Charles and Ray Eames, model no. 670 and 671, molded plywood, rosewood veneer, enameled aluminum, and enameled steel, with leather upholstery, manufacturer's label on stool.

CITES certificate no. 627403/01
1956
$3,100-3,700 *chair 32¼in (82cm) high* **L&T**

A Stokke adjustable armchair, "Varier Peel," by Olav Eldoy, in black on a circular beech base, shaped to represent a falling orange peel, along with a matching footstool.
$700-950 WHP

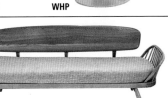

An Ercol elm and beech studio couch, "Surfboard," model no. 355.
$1,100-1,500 WHP

An American Leather "Dot Com" sofa, by Vladimir Kagan (1927-2016), unmarked.
ca. 1997 *79in (200.5cm) wide*
$6,000-7,500 FRE

A Hille Furniture modular sofa or seating arrangement, "Form Group," by Robin Day, comprising two single seats with cream leather loose upholstery and metal framework.
1960
$1,100-1,500 WHP

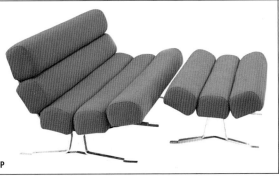

A William Plunkett three-seater sofa, "Kingston," along with a matching ottoman, with aluminum frames, both upholstered in orange Kvadrat fabric, designed by Nanna Ditzel, label on underside of sofa.
$3,200-4,000 WHP

A Ligne Roset two-seater orange sofa, "Togo," by Michel Ducaroy, with tag and marks on underside.
50in (127cm) wide
$1,400-1,700 WHP

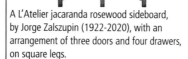

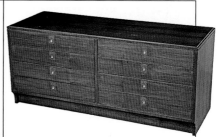

A Fornasetti "Strumenti Musicali" four-leaf screen, designed by Piero Fornasetti, lithographic print on lacquered wood, the reverse lacquered black, on casters, painted "NO2 DI.6/1990 NR SS" on base of one panel.

81in (206cm) high

$3,200-4,000 **WW**

A L'Atelier jacaranda rosewood sideboard, by Jorge Zalszupin (1922-2020), with an arrangement of three doors and four drawers, on square legs.

As a Polish Jew, Jorge Zalszupin was forced to flee to Romania during World War II; it was there that he trained as an architect. Following the war, he worked in France for a time, but wanted a fresh start far away from Europe. In 1949, he arrived in Rio de Janeiro and began collaborating with other designers who were involved with the beginnings of Brazilian Modernism. In 1959, he founded L'Atelier, which went on to become a famous and respected design brand.

1960s

$2,700-3,350 **WHP**

A Heal's Furniture rosewood low chest-of-drawers, by Archie Shine Design, with eight short drawers, with flush brass ring handles and escutcheons, above a shaped apron.

50in (127cm) wide

$1,400-1,700 **DUK**

An exceptional cherry and rosewood double-pedestal desk, by George Nakashima (1905-90), New Hope, Pennsylvania, book-matched top with three butterflies, signed and dated "George Nakashima Feb 9, 1985," inscribed with client's name.

1985 *71in (180.5cm) wide*

$35,000-42,000 **FRE**

A David Linley dining table, London, contemporary inlaid oak.

94½in (240cm) long

$6,000-7,500 **L&T**

ESSENTIAL REFERENCE—PAUL EVANS

Having trained as a silversmith at the Cranbook Academy of Art, in Bloomfield Hills, Michigan, Paul Evans (1931-87) moved to New Hope, Pennsylvania, in 1955, where he met fellow craftsman Phillip Lloyd Powell. Sharing a showroom for the next ten years, together they created a range of unique pieces, many of which involved using techniques Evans had learned as a silversmith and involved welding or fusing together materials as diverse as stone, wood, glass, and metal. In 1966 Evans relocated to Plumsteadville, also in Pennsylvania, where he established his own studio, and consolidated his reputation as one of the 20thC's most important studio furniture makers. However, prior to his retirement and death in Massachusetts in 1987, he also designed pieces for the American furniture company Directional, of which the "PE400 Cityscape" table shown here is an example.

A "Boston" table, by Wendell Castle (1932-2018), stack-laminated and carved cherry, incised date and signature "W. Castle 80."

1980 *41¼in (105cm) wide*

$25,000-31,000 **FRE**

A G-Plan coffee table, "Spider," by Victor Wilkins, circular glass panel top, on splayed supports.

1960s *35½in (90cm) diam*

$450-550 **CHOR**

A Directional dining table, "PE 400 Cityscape," by Paul Evans, olive ash burl, polished chrome, and glass, unsigned.

ca. 1970s *96in (244cm) long*

$3,100-4,300 **FRE**

An Italian Rinnovel umbrella stand, designed by Ettore Sottsass, Milan, with a conical turquoise barrel, internal division, raised on a brass-finished stand, scratches, wear.

ca. 1955 *21¾in (55cm) high*

$1,250-1,700 **SWO**

A Swedish Kasthall jacquard woven rya rug, "Pine - America U.N. Rug," by Astrid Sampe, leather manufacturer's label "Kasthall Pine Astrid Sampe 1961 Made for Dag Hammarskjöld Library, UN Headquarters, NY Made in Sweden" on underside.

1961   *59in (150cm) long*
$1,600-2,100   **DRA**

A pair of Chiesa Della Salute curtains, screen-printed "Sanderlin" cotton fabric, designed in 1960 by John Piper for Arthur Sanderson & Co., the original artwork commissioned in 1959 by Arthur Jeffress Gallery.

                              63in (160cm) wide (each)
$1,250-1,700   **SWO**

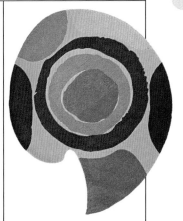

A Danish Halling-Koch Design Center tufted wool rug, "Windmill," by Nanna Ditzel (1923-2005), Copenhagen.

ca. 1965   *96¾in (246cm) diam*
$5,000-6,200   **L&T**

A hand-hooked wool tapestry, "Prayer Mat," by Alan Davie (1920-2014), signed, labeled, and numbered "3/8" on bottom left and right corners, pile darkening.

1976   *76in (193cm) wide*
$6,000-7,500   **SWO**

A Missoni floral rug, "Luanda," labeled, color slightly muted.

                                   118in (300cm) long
$3,100-3,700   **SWO**

A wool rug, "Panacée," by Shiro Kuramata (1934-91), from the edition of 50 produced by Paul Hughes Fine Art.

1989   *79½in (202cm) long*
$6,000-7,500   **L&T**

A custom wool carpet, by Vladimir Kagan, Kagan by Carpet Creation, hand-tufted New Zealand wool and felted wool, cotton canvas backing.

2009   *88in (223.5cm) wide*
$7,000-8,000   **FRE**

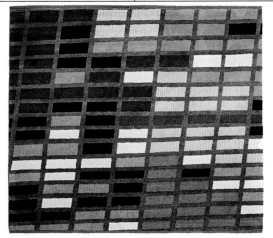

A Christopher Farr rug, "Mid Town Condé Nast," by Sarah Morris (b. 1967), 1 of 25, hand-knotted and hand-spun wool, inscribed in pen on "Christopher Farr" label.

2001   *96in (244cm) wide*
$4,300-5,600   **L&T**

A wool rug, by Peter Collingwood (1922-2008), in shades of blue, with braided ends.

                                   54¼in (138cm) long
$5,000-6,200   **L&T**

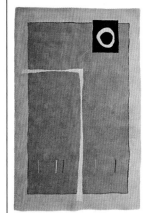

A wool and linen rug, by Helen Yardley (b.1954), stenciled "HELEN YARDLEY/LONDON" and numbered "147" on reverse.

                                   118in (300cm) long
$1,500-1,900   **L&T**

A large two-handle melon teapot, by Richard Batterham (1936-2021), decorated with a broad chattering band, glazed in ash.

10¼in (26cm) high

$1,250-1,500 **WW**

A stoneware medium bottle, by Richard Batterham (1936-2021), beaten, covered to the foot with an ash glaze, unsigned.

17in (43cm) high

$2,200-2,700 **WW**

A blue wax-resist thrown vessel, by Peter Beard (b. 1951), decorated with a geometric pattern, impressed seal marks.

8¾in (22cm) high

$4,500-5,500 **WW**

An Aldermaston pottery charger, by Andrew Hazelden, depicting Adam and Eve and the Tree of Knowledge, dated and initialed label on base.

1995 *18½in (47cm) diam*

$340-400 **CHOR**

An "Extra Large Moon Jar," by Akiko Hirai (b. 1970), encrusted stoneware with cherry ash glaze, painted monogram.

See Victoria & Albert Museum, catalog no. C33-2019 for a comparable form.

2019 *25½in (65cm) high*

$31,000-37,000 **WW**

ESSENTIAL REFERENCE—EMMANUEL COOPER

Emmanuel Cooper (1938-2012) was a distinguished craftsman, teacher, writer, and editor. A potter of international standing, his work is represented in many public and private collections, both in the UK and overseas. The author of nearly 30 books, he was also the founder and editor of "Ceramic Review," one of the world's leading craft magazines. For over a decade, Cooper was visiting professor on the Ceramics and Glass program at London's Royal College of Art, and was awarded an OBE for "Services to art" in the 2002 New Year Honours list. In his own words: "My work is influenced by the urban city environment, by such things as hard, textured surfaces, by street lighting, neon, endless movement and a sense of urgency. Colours are those of roads, pavements [sidewalks] and buildings, textures are those we encounter in the metropolis."

A volcanic glaze porcelain bowl, "White Highway I," by Emmanuel Cooper, with impressed artist's seal.

2002 *6in (15cm) diam*

$2,000-2,500 **DUK**

A stoneware spade-form vessel, by Philip Evans (b. 1959), russet and white stripes with gold detail, with a textured surface.

4½in (11.5cm) high

$150-190 **CHOR**

A large celadon crackle glaze bowl, by Chris Keenan (b. 1960), the exterior with a continuous meandering line design, impressed mark on base.

12in (30.5cm) diam

$500-625 **DUK**

A stoneware bowl, "Pale bowl with gray/green speckled band," by Jennifer Lee (b. 1956), with oxides.

This work is recorded in the artist's archives as JL-401/303.

1986 *12½in (32cm) diam*

$37,000-43,000 **FRE**

MODERN DESIGN

A Madoura Pottery Edition Picasso limited-edition tile, "Mask (Ramie 311)," by Pablo Picasso (1881-1973), framed, with a painted inscription.
1956   *7¾in (19.5cm) wide*
$4,200-4,600   **WW**

A "Baby Bud Alice Topiary Vase," by Kate Malone (b. 1959), no. KM1854, crystalline-glazed stoneware and porcelain, incised signature and date.
2016   *3¾in (9.5cm) high*
$800-1,050   **WW**

A hand-built stoneware footed vessel, by John Maltby (1936-2020), decorated with a stylized star, moon, and lines, signed on underside.
5¼in (13.5cm) high
$625-750   **DUK**

A hand-built stoneware vessel, by John Maltby (1936-2020), with a loop handle, decorated on one side with flowers under a red sun, the reverse with splashes of color against a dark brown glaze, signed on underside.
10¼in (26cm) high
$750-1,000   **DUK**

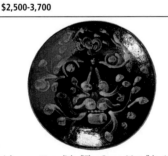

A thick-walled glazed earthenware turquoise bowl, by Gertrud and Otto Natzler (1908-71 and 1908-2007), Los Angeles, California, signed "Natzler" on underside, with applied original label "M082."
1962   *6½in (16.5cm) diam*
$2,500-3,700   **FRE**

A Richard Parkinson Pottery "Judge" bust, designed by Susan Parkinson, model no. 87, modeled in relief and painted in shades of blue/gray, the base painted with Ionic pillars and a cartouche with "SP RP" monogram, impressed factory marks on base.
13¼in (33.5cm) high
$450-550   **WW**

A large Fulham Pottery vase, by John Piper (1903-92), decorated with a stylized female figure in profile, with an arm outstretched to pluck a petal from a sunflower, on a multicolor ground with bold brushstrokes, the base signed "John Piper, VIII/82, Fulham Pottery."
11¾in (30cm) high
$9,500-12,000   **DUK**

A large pottery dish, "The Green Man," by John Piper (1903-92), decorated with the foliate pagan symbol against a deep blue/black ground, signed "J. P. 1981" on underside, surrounded by foliate brushstrokes.

"The Green Man" was a recurrent theme in Piper's work, the artist finding inspiration from medieval church roof bosses and column capitals. The symbol of spring and rebirth was used in his paintings, prints, and ceramics, including a collaboration with Wedgwood commissioned by the Art Fund, and which saw Piper designing a collection of plates alongside other contemporary artists, such as Peter Blake, Patrick Caulfield, Patrick Heron, Bruce McLean, and Eduardo Paolozzi.
1981   *15½in (39.5cm) diam*
$4,500-5,200   **DUK**

A globular stoneware vase, by Katherine Pleydell-Bouverie (1895-1985), with repeating ribbed decoration against a celadon-type glaze, impressed mark on base rim.
8in (20.5cm) high
$2,500-3,100   **DUK**

A large slipware pitcher, by John Pollex (b. 1941), with polychrome patchwork decoration, impressed "JP" mark.

9½in (24cm) high

$250-310 CHOR

A Poole Pottery studio wall charger, by Tony Morris, depicting a clown, minor glaze loss, scratches.

Tony Morris designed artwork and a series of plates depicting circus clowns in 2004. These were the first pieces made in Tony's studio at Upton.

16½in (42cm) diam

$2,200-3,000 CHOR

A Poole Pottery vase, "Atlantis," by Guy Sydenham (1916-2005), the black body with allover trailing slip decoration in green, impressed and incised marks on base.

10¾in (27.5cm) high

$1,000-1,250 DUK

A large Poole Pottery table bowl, by Guy Sydenham (1916-2005), the wide rim with incised decoration, the interior with a center spiral and radiating color from red to orange, with impressed and incised marks on underside.

15in (38cm) diam

$375-500 DUK

A fine porcelain bowl, by Dame Lucie Rie (1902-95), white interior with inlaid manganese radiating lines between a center manganese roundel and rim band, the exterior with incised sgraffito radiating lines against a manganese glaze, impressed seal on base.

9in (23cm) diam

$55,000-70,000 DUK

A flaring conical bowl, by Dame Lucie Rie (1902-95), covered in a pitted lemon-yellow mat glaze, the rim with a controlled bronze band, impressed seal mark.

7in (18cm) diam

$16,000-20,000 WW

A glazed stoneware vase, by Peter Voulkos (1924-2002), signed "Voulkos."

ca. 1952   *11in (28cm) high*

$3,700-5,000 FRE

A stoneware vase, by Philip Smeale Wadsworth (1910-91), with brushwork bamboo against an earthy green glaze, incised monogram on base.

14in (35.5cm) high

$875-1,100 DUK

A hand-built stoneware "Tulip" vase, by John Ward (b. 1938), with black and white panels, impressed seal mark.

10¾in (27.5cm) high

$14,000-17,500 WW

A modern Baccarat gilt-metal-mounted glass champagne cooler, "Harcourt" pattern, with scroll handles and detachable liner, etched mark, with remains of paper label, scratches, wear.

9¾in (24.5cm) high

$1,500-1,900 **TEN**

A tall Italian glass vase, by Afro Celotto, with blue, yellow, and red spiraling stripes, with frosted hammered surface decoration, cased in clear glass, etched signature.

19¼in (49cm) high

$625-750 **WW**

A fluted bowl and center flower stem, "Persian Set," by Dale Chihuly (b. 1941), no. PP01, yellow and blue bands with thin eggplant veins and applied red rim, with Perspex display box and cover, etched "PP01" on flower stem, for Portland Press 2001 studio edition.

2001 *12¼in (31cm) wide*

$4,500-5,200 **WW**

A blown glass "Tabac" basket, by Dale Chihuly (b. 1941), signed and dated "Chihuly "79."

1979 *7½in (19cm) wide*

$4,700-5,700 **FRE**

A large postwar glass "Head" vase, by Sam Herman, decorated with mottled iridescent gold whiplash lines over a mottled blue ground, signed and dated, with paper label.

1978 *12¼in (31cm) high*

$3,500-4,200 **FLD**

ESSENTIAL REFERENCE—AMANDA BRISBANE

Amanda Brisbane (1964-2016) took an art foundation course at London's Center School of Art and Design (1982-83), a BA Hons in 3D glass at the West Surrey College of Art and Design (1983-86), and also studied at Philadelphia's Tyler School of Art (1985) and the Massachusetts College of Art in Boston (1986). In 1987, she established "Amanda Brisbane Glass," near Ludlow, Shropshire, and worked for a company specializing in the development of composite materials from 1993-99, before opening her own glass studio again in 2000, from which she worked until her death in 2016.

Brisbane specialized in sand-casting glass, a technique in which hot molten glass is poured into a precarved sand mold. Traditionally, the sand is removed once the glass has cooled and solidified, but Brisbane's approach—in addition to developing her own oxides to color the glass—was to intervene before the glass had fully solidified, manipulating it with her hands to coax changes in the shape and color—a fluid technique that ensured no two sculptures were ever identical. Favored subjects included butterflies, as shown here, fish and other aquatic forms, flowers, and natural phenomena, such as skies, rainbows, fires, and frozen water. Examples of her work are displayed in many museums worldwide, including the Corning in New York, the Ebeltoft Glasmuseet in Denmark, and the Stourbridge Glass Museum in England.

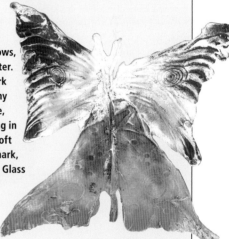

A sand-cast glass sculpture, "Butterfly," by Amanda Brisbane, signed.

19¾in (50cm) high

$2,500-3,100 **WW**

A Kosta glass vase, designed by Vicke Lindstrand, with a thick cased wall over a blue interior, the blue etched away with an interpretation of "Air" with stylized birds in flight, engraved mark and "LG 2499," with original label, small nibble in rim.

1950s *6½in (16.5cm) high*

$950-1,050 **FLD**

A Kosta glass vase, designed by Vicke Lindstrand, with a thick cased wall over a magenta interior, the magenta etched away with an interpretation of "Earth" with stylized figures, unmarked.

1950s *4¼in (11cm) high*

$875-1,000 **FLD**

A Kraków Glass Institute hand-formed cylindrical glass vase, designed by Jerzy Słuczan-Orkusz, model no. W-525/72, graduated red fading to yellow, decorated with applied scroll applications.

An example of this design was exhibited at the 2019 exhibition "Pursuing Color—Glass Art of Jerzy Słuczan-Orkusz." The exhibition was the outcome of a joint collaboration by the National Museum in Wrocław and the Ceramics and Glass Center in Kraków to research the history of 20thC Polish design.

ca. 1972 *9¾in (24.5cm) high*

$190-250 **FLD**

ESSENTIAL REFERENCE—LITTLETON & VOGEL

Studio glass artists John Littleton (b. 1957) and Kate Vogel (b. 1956) have worked collaboratively since 1979 (and married in 1985). Born in Madison, Wisconsin, and son of Harvey Littleton, a founder of the American Studio Glass movement, John Littleton originally studied photography at the University of Wisconsin before beginning to create glass with another student, Cambridgeshire, UK-born Kate Vogel, who had started studying fine art.

Moving to, and establishing a studio, in Bakersfield, North Carolina, in 1979, their earliest collaborations were the "Bag" forms: blown-glass bubbles, sometimes sandblasted or acid etched to create a soft-textured, satiny sheen, and shaped to look like soft fabric bundles "tied" at the neck with a loop of glass and terminating in a flared ruff, for which they remain well known. Other ensuing forms include: "Handkerchiefs,"with soft, inverted cones with flared, undulating lips; and "Favors," comprising ovoid or lobed forms with two flared frills of glass on each side and resembling candies twisted in colorful paper. Since 2000, their work has also included a series of arms and hands cast in amber-color glass, with the hands holding objects, such as river stones; large faceted glass "jewels"; and colorful cast glass leaves.

A frosted hand-blown glass sculpture, "Seven Sacks," by John Littleton and Kate Vogel, etched signature and date "John Littleton Kate Vogel © 2000" on underside.

2000　　　　　　*19in (48cm) high*
$6,000-7,200　　　　　　**DRA**

A hand-blown, cut, and polished glass sculpture, by Harvey Littleton, untitled, etched signature and date "Harvey K. Littleton 1977 ©" near base.

1977　　　　　　*13in (33cm) high*
$2,700-3,350　　　　　　**DRA**

A Mdina Fish glass vase, the disk-form body with polished front, mottled blue, red and white glass cased in clear, etched "Mdina 1978" on base.

1978　　　　　　*9¾in (24.5cm) high*
$400-475　　　　　　**WW**

An Orrefors "Ariel" glass vase, designed by Olle Alberius, with a heavy cased wall in clear crystal over a lilac to pink, cut with a running frieze of birds flying among clouds, with engraved signature and number "521-E7."

1980s　　　　　　*7in (18cm) high*
$550-700　　　　　　**FLD**

A Orrefors "Kraka" glass vase, designed by Sven Palmqvist, decorated with a graduated blue to green to clear tint, over a fine air-bubble mesh ground, full engraved signature.

1950s　　　　　　*11¾in (30cm) high*
$460-520　　　　　　**FLD**

A Nuutajarvi Notsjo "Maljakko" glass vase, by Kaj Franck, model no. KF 239, the sommerso-style body cased in clear crystal over tonal olive green and red, unsigned.

1950s
$450-625　　　　　　**FLD**

A cylindrical vase, by Josef Soukup, with cut and polished edge, green and blue glass, etched "Soukup" on base.

12in (30.5cm) high
$300-350　　　　　　**WW**

An Italian hand-blown glass vase, by Lino Tagliapietra (b. 1934), etched "Lino Tagliapietra 93" on underside.

1993　　　　　　*21in (53.5cm) high*
$6,000-7,500　　　　　　**FRE**

An Italian hand-blown glass sculpture, "Dinosaur," by Lino Tagliapietra, partial battuto and inciso surface, etched signature and date "Lino Tagliapietra 2006" on underside, with a digital certificate of authenticity from Schantz Galleries.

2006　　　　　　*51½in (131cm) high*
$45,000-54,500　　　　　　**DRA**

A Venini Murano glass "VVV" vase, designed by Gianni Versace, with black and white squares and one red square, cased in clear glass, applied Venini label, etched "Venini 99 Gianni Versace," with paper certificate.

1999   *10¾in (27.5cm) high*

$1,500-1,900   **WW**

A Venini "Inciso" sommerso glass vase, by Paolo Venini, cased in clear over deep citron and blue, with a finely engraved horizontal band, three-line acid mark, minor scratches.

ca. 1956   *6½in (16.5cm) high*

$1,500-2,000   **FLD**

A Vistosi "Pulcini" glass bird, by Alessandro Pianon, internally decorated glass, murrine and copper.

ca. 1963   *9½in (24cm) high*

$10,000-12,500   **DRA**

A Vistosi "Pulcini" glass bird, by Alessandro Pianon, glass and copper.

ca. 1963   *12¼in (31cm) high*

$5,000-6,200   **WRI**

A 20thC Whitefriars textured range "Drunken Bricklayer" vase, designed by Geoffrey Baxter, pattern no. 9672, in meadow green.

13in (33cm) high

$1,250-1,500   **FLD**

A Whitefriars "Cinnamon" glass vase, designed by Geoffrey Baxter, cast in low relief with a star motif, unsigned.

6in (15cm) high

$250-310   **WW**

A 20thC Whitefriars textured range "Banjo" vase, designed by Geoffrey Baxter, pattern no. 9681, in tangerine, with original paper label.

12½in (32cm) high

$2,200-3,000   **FLD**

A Whitefriars "Kingfisher" blue glass vase, designed by Geoffrey Baxter, with textured body, unsigned.

7in (18cm) high

$350-420   **WW**

A large vessel, by Toots Zynsky, untitled, filet de verre fused and thermo-formed glass threads, signed "Z" on underside.

Born in Boston, Massachusetts, Mary Ann Zynsky (b. 1951)—better known as "Toots" Zynsky—studied at the Rhode Island School of Design, where she was one of the first students of eminent glass artist Dale Chihuly. In 1971, she was part of a group, including Chihuly, who founded the soon-to-be highly influential Pilchuck Glass School, in Washington State. A pioneer of the studio glass movement, she drew from the traditions of painting, sculpture, and the decorative arts to inspire her innovative, intricate vessels, in which "filet-de-verre"—the pulling and manipulation of fine color threads from glass canes—within distinctive, undulating forms is a recurring theme. Examples of her work can be found in numerous museums, including the Seattle Art Museum and the Smithsonian American Art Museum in Washington.

18½in (47cm) wide

$25,000-31,000   **DRA**

An Artemide Area 160/120 floor lamp, designed by Mario Bellini, white parchment shade on a white column, on a square base, labeled "Milano Artemide spa Modello Area 160/120 Design Mario Bellini Made in Italy Patent Pending."

1970s *67¼in (171cm) high*
$625-750 **TEN**

A Martinelli Luce "Pipistrello" lamp, by Gae Aulenti (1927-2012), model no. 620, designed in 1965, stainless steel, chrome, lacquered aluminum, and opalescent thermoplastic, embossed manufacturer's plaque on underside of base.

ca. 1970s *28in (71cm) high*
$4,700-5,500 **FRE**

A "Molar" lamp, by Dan Dailey (b. 1947), chromed steel, clear and sandblasted glass, electric fittings, unmarked.

1970s *13in (33cm) high*
$1,400-1,700 **FRE**

A "PH Artichoke" light, designed by Poul Henningsen, designed in 1958 and produced by Louis Poulson, copper petal diffusers, unsigned.

30in (76cm) high
$3,200-4,000 **WW**

A Kagan-Dreyfuss Inc. three-light ceiling lamp, by Vladimir Kagan (1927-2016), patinated brass and enameled aluminum, with three downlights and three uplights, unmarked.

ca. 1960 *45in (114.5cm) high*
$5,500-7,000 **FRE**

A pair of 20thC French crystal glass and gilt-metal wall lights, attributed to Maison Bagues, each modeled with a parrot perched on a tapering plinth, with leaf and flower scroll arms and twin lights.

25¾in (65.5cm) high
$6,000-7,500 **WW**

A Parzinger Originals floor lamp, by Tommi Parzinger, silver-gilt and lacquered wood, enameled aluminum, and parchment.

ca. 1955 *64¾in (164.5cm) high*
$1,700-2,200 **DRA**

An Italian Poliarte floor lamp, by Albano Poli, the aluminum shaft supporting three circles, relief-decorated with color Perspex and three spots.

1970s
$1,000-1,500 **WHP**

An Italian VeArt Murano glass floor lamp, designed by Toni Zuccheri, the chromed stem with six textured cubical glass shades, terminating on a round foot, scratches, spotting.

ca. 1969 *43¼in (110cm) high*
$1,700-2,200 **SWO**

A VeArt Murano glass chandelier, by Örni Halloween, with chrome-plated steel, applied manufacturer's label "VeArt Hand Crafted Made in Italy" on one glass sconce and on center dome.

ca. 1980 *32in (81cm) diam*
$2,000-2,500 **DRA**

A pair of Venini blown glass pendant lamps, by Massimo Vignelli (1931-2014), aluminum ceiling cap, unmarked, wired for American use.

ca. 1960s *10½in (26.5cm) high*
$3,700-4,300 **FRE**

A bronze sculpture, "Maquette for Stranger," by Lynn Chadwick (1914-2003), six of six, model no. 340, with green/brown patina, signed and numbered.

The subject of the "Stranger" occupied Chadwick from 1954 to 1969—a theme which also informed his contemporary "Winged Figure" works. As Alan Bowness explained in his 1962 monograph of his work: the stimulus was Chadwick's commission, in 1957, from the Air League of the British Empire to create a memorial to the 1919 double-crossing of the Atlantic by the airship R34. Having served as a pilot in the Fleet Air Arm of the Navy during World War II, Chadwick had a deeply personal link to flight and, ergo, the concept of a winged figure—itself embedded in the myth of Icarus. In 1961, shortly after its creation, a cast of "Maquette for Stranger" was declared Hors Concours ("beyond competition") at the VI Bienal de São Paulo of 1961.

1961

12½in (31.5cm) high

$72,000-80,000

L&T

A bronze of flying swans, by John Cox (1952-2014).

67in (170cm) high

$5,000-6,200

SWO

ESSENTIAL REFERENCE—STUART DEVLIN

Born in Geelong, Australia, Stuart Devlin (1931-2018) trained at the Royal Melbourne Institute of Technology, won a silversmithing scholarship at the Royal College of Art in London in 1958, then accepted a two-year fellowship at Columbia University in New York before returning to Australia to teach. In 1964, he designed Australia's first decimal coinage (he subsequently designed coinage and medallions for more than 36 countries worldwide). In 1965, he returned to London, set up a small workshop in Clerkenwell, and began to create his own distinctive style of jewelry and metalware, which he intended to "delight, surprise, intrigue, and even amuse." In 1966, he was made a freeman of the Goldsmiths' Company, and elected a liveryman in 1972. In 1979, with the Duke of Westminster, he set up a prestigious showroom in Conduit Street. Subsequent awards included being made a Companion of the Order of St. Michael and St. George "for services to the art of design" in 1980; the Royal Warrant of Appointment as Goldsmith and Jeweller to Queen Elizabeth II in 1982; and from 1996-97, Prime Warden of the Worshipful Company of Goldsmiths, who acclaimed him as "the designer with the Midas touch."

A pair of Stuart Devlin silver and silver-gilt candlesticks, London, each with a removable cylindrical openwork shade, polished textured stem, and plain circular foot.

1973

13½in (34cm) high 30¾oz

$5,000-6,200

JON

An Italian silver-plated brass and Murano glass ostrich, by Gabriella Crespi, impressed signature "Gabriella Crespi" on base.

ca. 1970

18in (46cm) high

$3,000-3,500

WRI

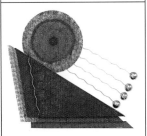

A rods sculpture, by Curtis Jere, signed "C Jere 1993."

1993

40¼in (102cm) wide

$1,100-1,500

SWO

A sculpture, "Boar," by Elizabeth Frink (1930-93), modeled midstride on a naturalistic base, raised on a serpentine marble base, signed and numbered "5/7."

Commissioned by the Zoological Society of London as the Stamford Raffles Award for Contributions to Zoology, 1971, and awarded by Prince Philip, Duke of Edinburgh, to Beryl Patricia Hall (1917-2010) for her work on the taxonomy and zoogeography of African birds.

1967-8

9½in (24cm) wide

$33,000-42,000

DUK

A unique verdigris and polished bronze sculpture, "Pointing Figure," by Bernard Meadows (1915-2005, British).

In the 1960s, Meadows left the commercially sucessful "Geometry of Fear" furrow he had been plowing and, like his contemporary Kenneth Armitage, looked for a new sculptural vocabulary that spoke to the nascent optimism of the 1960s. An element of joy returned, and sculptures, such as "Pointing Figure," are classic Meadows of this period. Although superficially abstract, their strong anthropomorphism is clear: the rounded forms being heads (with eyes), although slippery enough to also connote bellies or even an entire body reduced to a singular form. This shifting nature of what the forms could be is enhanced by the smooth surfaces. In contrast to his 1950s sculpture, there are no jagged edges to arrest the eye, to turn you back on yourself. Instead, Meadows' sculpture flows with you and the space surrounding it, and in this way he returns to the conceptual world occupied by his former employer and mentor, Henry Moore.

1967

22¾in (57.5cm) wide

$6,000-7,500

L&T

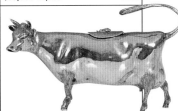

A Channel Islands silver cow creamer, by Bruce Russell, with textured fur finish on back and legs, gilt gadfly on the hinged cover, with original cardboard box and Bruce Russell & Son receipt.

ca. 2001

6¼in (16cm) wide 6⅜oz

$1,900-2,500

MART

MODERN DESIGN

A rare complete Alexander McQueen tartan ensemble, "Joan" collection, comprising a fitted bodice with cap sleeves, a tight curved skirt, and matching boots of black leather with insert of tartan wool, labeled.

"British Vogue" photographed a model in Wellington boots wearing a similar McQueen tartan ensemble for its December 1998 issue.

Fall-Winter 1998-99
$11,000-12,500 KT

A rare Antony Price men's futuristic quilted suit, glossy yellow synthetic fabric with curved quilting, zipper fastened, the fitted pants similarly worked with particular emphasis on the crotch and seat areas, labeled.

Believed to be the showpiece modeled by the late Nick Kamen at the Camden Palace and Hippodrome shows in 1983. However, an identical jacket was worn on stage by Mick Jagger as early as 1981 for the Rolling Stones European tour of that year, and he also wore a blue version onstage. An identical ensemble was also featured in "New Sounds, New Styles" magazine, December 1981. Presumably Price used the 1983 fashion shows as an opportunity to retrospectively showcase previous collections. See Steve Strange interviewed by Annie Nightingale, YouTube, in which they discuss the Camden Palace "Fashion Extravaganza" show. Strange describes Price: "He's got a certain eye–it's called class … He's had a huge influence on the Paris catwalk but he doesn"t get the credit for it."

1981-83   size L
$22,000-27,000 KT

A Biba quilted and printed brown cotton two-piece ensemble, with overall floral-spray repeats, the long-line jacket with square self-covered buttons, matching wide-flared pants, woven label.

late-1960s   26in (66cm) waist
$3,000-3,500 KT

A Chanel black faille cocktail suit, by Karl Lagerfeld, the jacket with pronounced full, curved sleeves, gilt coin buttons, matching skirt, labeled.

Fall-Winter 1988   size 40
$1,100-1,250 KT

A Christian Dior red straw "Rose" toque, "Licence Chapeaux," the crown with a center rosebud, the brim formed from overlapping straw petals, labeled.

ca. 1958   8in (20.5cm) wide
$1,000-1,250 KT

A Christian Dior London beaded pink crêpe minidress, the collar, front closure, and cuffs with large pink and yellow blister beads, with textured and plain gold sequins and beads, Boutique labeled, no. "51195."

ca. 1968   36in (91.5cm) bust
$6,000-6,700 KT

A Christian Dior couture soutache braid frock-coat, "Marquis de Botanique," by John Galliano, "A Poetic Tribute to the Marchesa Casati," in 18thC style with tails at rear, decorative "pockets," and self-covered buttons, entirely formed from intricately stitched off-white braid in flower-head and foliate repeats, couture labeled, typed Bolduc numbered "19920."

This coat was one of the opening looks (No. 8) and shown in ecru on the runway. Each ensemble in this opening passage was named after marquises with floral/ garden references.

Spring/Summer 1998   34in (86cm) bust
$40,000-45,000 KT

A Christian Dior sequined beret, with stiffened "Stalk," comb in interior grosgrain band, Licence Chapeaux labeled, made in England.

1960s/early-1970s
$500-625 KT

A Dior Swarovski crystal logo belt, designed by John Galliano, the white leather belt with bold Swarovski crystal "DIOR" motif, with pendant chains and crystal clips, leather tie and D-ring closures, signed and numbered.

2003   35½in (90cm) long
$4,700-5,500 L&T

A Christian Dior couture scarlet cocktail dress, by Yves Saint Laurent, "Longue" line, of scarlet slubbed silk with integral boned ivory mesh corset, also part-lined in chiffon, the upper bodice part-lined in red silk, the fitted bodice with faux button closure above a full skirt of knife pleats, two further graduated pleated silk layers alternated with crin-stiffened and tulle petticoats with silk underslip, concealed rear zipper fastening, labeled and numbered "98618."

This model is very similar to the "Hazel" model but has a slightly more revealing décolleté (the top button is open) and has three layers of pleats instead of one, emphasizing the fullness and sculptural silhouette of the gown.

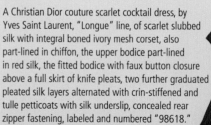

Spring/Summer 1959   24in (61cm) waist
$25,000-31,000 KT

A Fendi printed hide coat, by Karl Lagerfeld, probably late 1970s, printed with giraffe patterns, edged in dark brown fox, labeled and embroidered "Flora" in lining.

34in (86.5cm) bust

$650-750   KT

A John Galliano bias-cut red satin-backed crêpe evening gown, woven with motocross print and "John Galliano" repeats, slip-on style, no fastenings, commercial collection, Paris label.

Spring/Summer 2002   size UK8

$5,000-6,200   KT

A rare Karl Lagerfeld surrealist hat, made by Kirstin Woodward, the scarlet satin boudoir chair trimmed with box pleats at the base, gold tassels on chair back, elastic head strap, labeled.

A similar hat was featured in the "British Vogue" "New Hattiness" article, November 1985, and was modeled by Isabelle Pascoe and photographed by Paolo Roversi.

Exhibited: FIT Fashion & Surrealism, October 30, 1987, to January 23, 1988.

1985   9½in (24cm) high

$2,500-3,100   KT

A rare Jeanne Lanvin couture medieval-inspired black wool-crêpe evening jacket, large woven label with gold date stamp, emblazoned with a geometric lattice of layered and domed, faceted silver sequins.

Jeanne Lanvin produced an evening gown in black crêpe with an identical sequined motif for her Fall-Winter 1936-37 collection. A jacket featuring almost identical embellishment is seen in the October 28 issue of "British Vogue," described as: "Lanvin's sheer black wool jacket, armed with silver paillette circles, and short circular skirt."

Spring-Summer 1936   36in (91.5cm) chest

$4,300-5,000   KT

A Paco Rabanne chain-linked bodice, probably 1990s, formed from joined gilt-metal disks, with clasp on halterneck and rear waist, signed.

26in (66cm) long

$2,000-2,700   KT

A Yves Saint Laurent fully sequined silk evening gown, by Tom Ford, with cheongsam-style neckline, the sequined design inspired by traditional Chinese embroidery motifs, including fish jumping among waves, blooms, and floral roundels, fully lined in sea-green silk and with chain-weighted hem, "Rive Gauche" labeled, F40, made in France, with original retail tag bearing RRP of "$23,995.00."

This was Tom Ford's final collection for Yves Saint Laurent (he began his tenure at the house in 1999, his first collection being Spring-Summer 2001 for the Rive Gauche line). Ford sought archival inspiration from Saint Laurent's 1977 "Chinoises" collection, and this design was one of three dazzling fully sequined finale gowns shown on the runway for the collection. The yellow version included in this finale was exhibited in "China: Through the Looking Glass" at the Metropolitan Museum of Art, May 7 to August 16, 2015.

A Pierre Cardin minidress, Paris, quilted black cotton with three circular cutouts and metal disks, concealed zipper at rear, New York labeled.

ca. 1969   32in (81cm) bust

$22,000-27,000   KT

A Vivienne Westwood corset, "Portrait" collection, the front satin panel printed with a detail from François Boucher's painting, "Daphnis and Chloe" (1743), side gold mesh panels, and zipper on rear, yellow on red label.

An identical corset was featured in the September 1990 issue of "Vogue," page 347, with a retail price of £280 ($350), accessorized with a pearl choker, eye patch, and sword. It was featured again in the June 1991 issue, worn with a yellow striped ballgown skirt.

Fall/Winter 1990-91 34in (86.5cm) bust

$4,700-5,500   KT

An Yves Saint Laurent couture metallic brocade evening coat, woven with large-scale interlocking palmettes in steel gray, black, and golden threads, edged in dark brown mink and lined in black silk, labeled and numbered "24109."

Spring-Summer 1969   34in (86.5cm) bust

$4,300-5,000   KT

Fall-Winter 2004   30in (76cm) waist

$16,000-19,000   KT

MODERN DESIGN

A Chanel quilted black medium double-flap purse, black leather with gold-tone hardware, with original dust bag and authentication card, light scratches.

1986-88 9¾in (24.5cm) wide
$5,000-6,200 **WW**

A Christian Dior fuschia pink medium "Lady Dior" purse, cannage quilted lamb leather, "DIOR" charm, gold-tone hardware, date code "15-BO-0113," with detachable strap, authenticity card, dust bag, and box.

2013 9¼in (23.5cm) wide
$2,900-3,350 **CA**

A Christian Dior Les Sacs monogram purse, with double gold-tone chain, leather body with black fabric exterior, with Christian Dior gold lamé detailing and trim, stamped "Christian Dior, Made in France" on interior, with original Christian Dior Les Sacs gray box, original tissue paper, and original Christian Dior tag.

1970s 10¼in (26cm) wide
$625-1,000 **BOG**

ESSENTIAL REFERENCE—WILARDY ORIGINALS

"Handbag Specialities" was founded 1946 in New York by father and son Charles and William Hardy. In 1953, the company moved to Union City, New Jersey, while retaining showrooms in Manhattan, and was fully taken over by William in the 1960s (it eventually ceased trading in 1977). Much of its commercial success—the handbags were sold through exclusive outlets in Hollywood, Miami, New York, Paris, and London, and carried by iconic stars, such as Marilyn Monroe—can be attributed to its main division known as "Wilardy Originals" and, more specifically, William Hardy's innovative designs in Lucite—a lightweight, transparent synthetic polymer sometimes referred to as acrylic glass.

Hardy originally used Lucite to design a jewelry box, but when he showed it to buyers at Saks Fifth Avenue, New York, they were so enamored, they suggested adding a carry handle, and thus the Wilardy Lucite handbag was born. Although Lucite can be color with dyes, these were initially very limited and consequently Wilardy often experimented in the early days with materials bonded in-between layers of clear Lucite—notable examples including: white lace and gold ("stardust"); black lace and gold ("Gold Dust"); and gold lamé.

An Hermès Electric Blue Togo leather Birkin 35 purse, calfskin leather exterior, with dual rolled leather handles, silver-tone hardware, turn-lock fastening, detachable clochette with padlock, keys, and four protective base studs, leather lined interior with one slip and zipper pocket, date code "R," with dust bag, light scratches.

2014 13¾in (35cm) wide
$14,000-17,500 **FELL**

An Hermès canvas and natural leather Retourné Kelly 28 purse, with gilt hardware, padlock, clochette, and two keys, signed, blind stamp "I," with dust bag.

1979 11in (28cm) wide
$6,500-7,000 **KT**

A Louis Vuitton monogrammed leather vanity case, with tan leather carry handle, luggage tag, and monogrammed trim with gold hardware, cream leather interior with double row of tan leather straps, riveted to support bottles, interior serial plate numbered "1035671" and the lock stamped "1241218," with key and inner tray, monogrammed "R. J. D," scuffs, stains.

15¾in (40cm) wide
$1,400-1,700 **FLD**

A Wilardy clear Lucite bag, decorated with diamantés.

1950s 7¾in (20cm) wide
$950-1,250 **BOG**

An early 20thC Louis Vuitton steamer trunk, wood with monogram canvas covering, embossed monogram leather trim, engraved brass hardware, raised on four metal casters, interior with three large removable organizers and further removable compartments, all with cloth ties, back painted monogram "C. O. M." on exterior, with original labels for Louis Vuitton and Saks & Company, New York, and stamped "776581," lock marked "70 Champs Élysées/Paris/Louis Vuitton/London/149 New Bond Street," with "Made in France" and "063609" below.

Louis Vuitton was born in Anchay in eastern France in 1824. At the age of 14, he headed to Paris to serve an apprenticeship with luggage maker M. Maréchal, and he opened his own firm in 1854. His principal innovation was the application of waterproof canvas to the lid of his trunks, eliminating the need for water-repelling and dome-shaped lids, which allowed trunks to be stacked in transit. His son Georges eventually took over the firm, and two of his trademark inventions are evident here: the five-tumbler lock, introduced in 1890, which resisted picking and enabled each client to have the same combination for all their luggage; and the monogram canvas (1896), conceived to repel counterfeiters and designed in the prevailing Japonisme style of the time. It was the latter in particular that made Vuitton trunks one of the Gilded Age's most recognizable luxury goods—a status they retain to this day.

44in (112cm) wide
$19,000-22,000 **FRE**

A large Louis Vuitton "Alzer" hard case suitcase trunk, monogrammed leather with gold hardware, with luggage strap and key, lock plate stamped "H6," monogrammed "R. J. D," lacks interior tray, dents, wear.

$1,700-2,200 **FLD**

Every antique illustrated in Miller's Antiques has a letter code, which identifies the dealer or auction house that sold it. The list below is a key to these codes. In the list, auction houses are shown by the letter A and dealers by the letter D.

Inclusion in this book in no way constitutes or implies a contract or a binding offer on the part of any of our contributors to supply or sell the goods illustrated, or similar items, at the prices stated.

ADA Ⓐ
ADAM'S
www.adams.ie

BE Ⓐ
BEARNES HAMPTON & LITTLEWOOD
www.bhandl.co.uk

BELL Ⓐ
BELLMANS
www.bellmans.co.uk

BOG Ⓓ
BAGS OF GLAMOUR
www.bagsofglamour.co.uk

BON Ⓐ
BONHAMS
www.bonhams.com

C&T Ⓐ
C&T AUCTIONEERS & VALUERS
www.candtauctions.co.uk

CA Ⓐ
CHISWICK AUCTIONS
www.chiswickauctions.co.uk

CHEF Ⓐ
CHEFFINS
www.cheffins.co.uk

CHOR Ⓐ
CHORLEY'S
www.chorleys.com

CM Ⓐ
CHARLES MILLER LTD.
www.charlesmillerltd.com

DAWS Ⓐ
DAWSON'S
www.dawsonsauctions.co.uk

DN Ⓐ
DREWEATTS
www.dreweatts.com

DOY Ⓐ
DOYLE
doyle.com

DRA Ⓐ
RAGO ARTS
www.ragoarts.com

DUK Ⓐ
DUKE'S
www.dukes-auctions.com

ECGW Ⓐ
EWBANK'S
www.ewbankauctions.co.uk

FELL Ⓐ
FELLOWS
www.fellows.co.uk

FLD Ⓐ
FIELDINGS
www.fieldingsauctioneers.co.uk

FRE Ⓐ
FREEMAN'S
www.freemansauction.com

GBA Ⓐ
GRAHAM BUDD
www.grahambuddauctions.co.uk

GHOU Ⓐ
GARDINER HOULGATE
www.gardinerhoulgate.co.uk

GORL Ⓐ
GORRINGE'S
www.gorringes.co.uk

GRV Ⓓ
GEMMA REDMOND VINTAGE
www.gemmaredmondvintage.co.uk

HT Ⓐ
HARTLEYS
www.hartleysauctions.co.uk

JON Ⓐ
ROGERS JONES & CO.
www.rogersjones.co.uk

KT Ⓐ
KERRY TAYLOR AUCTIONS
www.kerrytaylorauctions.com

L&T Ⓐ
LYON & TURNBULL
www.lyonandturnbull.com

LC Ⓐ
LAWRENCES AUCTIONEERS
(CREWKERNE)
www.lawrences.co.uk

LOCK Ⓐ
LOCKDALES
www.lockdales.com

LSK Ⓐ
LACY SCOTT & KNIGHT
www.lsk.co.uk

MART Ⓐ
MARTEL MAIDES AUCTIONS
www.martelmaidesauctions.com

MGO Ⓓ
MARK GOODGER ANTIQUES
markgoodger.co.uk

POOK Ⓐ
POOK & POOK INC.
www.pookandpook.com

PW Ⓐ
WILSON55
www.wilson55.com

RMA Ⓐ
ROB MICHIELS AUCTIONS
www.rm-auctions.com

ROS Ⓐ
ROSEBERYS
www.roseberys.co.uk

SK Ⓐ
BONHAMS SKINNER
skinner.bonhams.com

SOU Ⓐ
CATHERINE SOUTHON
www.catherinesouthon.co.uk

SWO Ⓐ
SWORDERS
www.sworder.co.uk

TEN Ⓐ
TENNANTS
www.tennants.co.uk

TMY Ⓐ
TOOMEY & CO.
www.toomeyco.com

TOV Ⓐ
TOOVEY'S
www.tooveys.com

WAD Ⓐ
WADDINGTON'S, TORONTO
www.waddingtons.ca

WHP Ⓐ
W&H PEACOCK
www.peacockauction.co.uk

WRI Ⓐ
WRIGHT
www.wright20.com

WW Ⓐ
WOOLLEY & WALLIS
www.woolleyandwallis.co.uk

This is a list of auctioneers that conduct regular sales. Auction houses that would like to be included in the next edition should contact us at *publisher@octopusbooks.co.uk*.

ARKANSAS
Ponders Auctions
www.pondersauctions.com

BOSTON
Bonhams Skinner
skinner.bonhams.com

CALIFORNIA
Bonhams
www.bonhams.com

I M Chait Gallery
www.chait.com

eBay, Inc.
www.ebay.com

Michaan's
www.michaans.com

San Rafael Auction Gallery
www.sanrafaelauction.com

Slawinski Auction Co.
www.slawinski.com

Sotheby's
www.sothebys.com

NORTH CAROLINA
Robert S Brunk Auction Services Inc.
www.brunkauctions.com

Raynors' Historical Collectible Auctions
www.hcaauctions.com

SOUTH CAROLINA
Charlton Hall Galleries Inc.
www.charltonhallauctions.com

COLORADO
Pacific Auction
www.pacificauction.com

CONNECTICUT
Norman C Heckler & Company
www.hecklerauction.com

Lloyd Ralston Toys
www.lloydralstontoys.com

Winter Associates Inc.
www.auctionsappraisers.com

SOUTH DAKOTA
Fischer Auction Company
fischerauctionandrealestate.com

FLORIDA
Auctions Neapolitan
www.auctionsneapolitan.com

Burchard Galleries/Auctioneers
www.burchardgalleries.com

Kincaid Auction Company
www.kincaid.com

TreasureQuest Auction Galleries Inc.
www.tqag.com

GEORGIA
Arwood Auctions & Appraisers
Tel: 770 423 0110

Great Gatsby's
www.greatgatsbys.com

Red Baron's Auction Gallery
www.redbaronsantiques.com

IDAHO
The Coeur d'Alene Art Auction
www.cdaartauction.com

INDIANA
AAA Historical Auction Service
aaaauctionservice.com

Lawson & Co.
www.lawsonandco.com

Schrader Auction
www.schraderauction.com

Stout Auctions
www.stoutauctions.com

Strawser Auctions
www.strawserauctions.com

ILLINOIS
The Chicago Wine Company
www.tcwc.com

Hack's Auction Center
www.hacksauction.com

Leslie Hindman Inc.
www.hindmanauctions.com

L H Selman Ltd.
www.theglassgallery.com

Sotheby's
www.sothebys.com

Toomey & Co.
www.toomeyco.com

IOWA
Jackson's Auctioneers & Appraisers
www.jacksonsauction.com

KENTUCKY
Hays Auctions
www.haysauction.com

LOUISIANA
New Orleans Auction Galleries
www.neworleansauction.com

MAINE
Thomaston Place Auction Galleries
www.thomastonauction.com

MARYLAND
Hantman's Auctioneers & Appraisers
www.hantmans.com

Richard Opfer Auctioneering Inc.
www.opferauction.com

Sloans & Kenyon
www.sloansandkenyon.com

Theriault's
www.theriaults.com

Weschler's
www.weschlers.com

MASSACHUSETTS
Douglas Auctioneers
www.douglasauctioneers.com

Eldred's
www.eldreds.com

Grogan & Company Auctioneers
www.groganco.com

Bonhams Skinner
skinner.bonhams.com

White's Auctions
www.whitesauctions.com

Willis Henry Auctions Inc.
www.willishenry.com

MICHIGAN
DuMouchelle Art Galleries Co.
www.dumouchelles.com

MINNESOTA
Tracy Luther Auctions
www.lutherauctions.com

MISSOURI
Selkirk Auctioneers
www.selkirkauctions.com

Simmons & Company Auctioneers
www.simmonsauction.com

NEW HAMPSHIRE
The Great Atlantic Auction Company
www.atlanticauctioncompany.com

Paul McInnis Inc.
www.paulmcinnis.com

Schmitt Horan & Co.
www.schmitt-horan.com

NEW JERSEY
Bertoia Auctions
www.bertoiaauctions.com

Nye & Co.
www.nyeandcompany.com

Rago Arts & Auction Center
www.ragoarts.com

NEW YORK
Bonhams
www.bonhams.com

Christie's
www.christies.com

Copake Auction Inc.
www.copakeauction.com

Samuel Cottone Auctions
www.cottoneauctions.com

Doyle
www.doyle.com

Guernsey's Auction
www.guernseys.com

H. R. Harmer
www.hrharmer.com

Keno Auctions
www.kenoauctions.com

Mapes Auction Gallery
www.mapesauction.com

Phillips
www.phillips.com

Sotheby's
www.sothebys.com

Stair Galleries
www.stairgalleries.com

Swann Galleries
www.swanngalleries.com

OHIO
Belhorn Auction Services
www.belhorn.com

Cincinnati Art Galleries LLC.
www.cincyart.com

Cowan's Historic Americana Auctions
www.cowanauctions.com

Garth's Auction Inc.
www.garths.com

Treadway Toomey
www.treadwaygallery.com

Wolf's Auction Gallery
wolfsgallery.com

OREGON
O'Gallery
www.ogallerie.com

PENNSYLVANIA
Noel Barrett
www.noelbarrett.com

William Bunch Auctions
www.bunchauctions.com

Concept Art Gallery
www.conceptgallery.com

Freeman's
www.freemansauction.com

Hunt Auctions
www.huntauctions.com

Pook & Pook Inc.
www.pookandpook.com

Sanford Alderfer Auction Co.
www.alderferauction.com

Stout Auctions
www.stoutauctions.com

TENNESSEE
Kimball M Sterling Inc.
www.sterlingsold.com

TEXAS
Austin Auctions
www.austinauction.com

Dallas Auction Gallery
www.dallasauctiongallery.com

Heritage Auction Galleries
www.ha.com

VIRGINIA
Old World Mail Auctions
www.oldworldauctions.com

Green Valley Auctions Inc.
www.greenvalleyauctions.com

Ken Farmer Auctions & Estates
www.kenfarmerllc.com

Phoebus Auction Gallery
www.phoebusauction.com

CANADA

ALBERTA
Hall's Auction Services Ltd.
www.hallsauction.com

Hodgins Art Auctions Ltd.
www.hodginsauction.com

Lando Art Auctions
www.landoauctions.com

BRITISH COLUMBIA
Maynards Fine Art Auction House
www.maynards.com

Waddington's
www.waddingtons.ca

Heffel Fine Art Auction House
www.heffel.com

ONTARIO
A Touch of Class
www.atouchofclassauctions.com

Waddington's
www.waddingtons.ca

Robert Deveau Galleries
robertdeveaugalleries.com

Heffel Fine Art Auction House
www.heffel.com

Sotheby's
www.sothebys.com

QUEBEC
Empire Auctions
www.empireauctions.com

Iegor - Hôtel des Encans
www.iegor.net

Specialists who would like to be listed in the next edition, or have a new address or telephone number, should contact us at *publisher@octopusbooks.co.uk*. Readers should contact dealers before visiting to avoid a wasted journey.

AMERICAN PAINTINGS
Bakker Gallery
www.bakkerproject.com

Jeffrey W Cooley
www.cooleygallery.com

AMERICANA & FOLK ART
Elle Shushan
elleshushan.com

Bucks County Antique Center
Tel: (215) 794-9180

Garthoeffner Gallery Antiques
www.garthoeffnerantiques.com

Allan Katz Americana
www.allankatzamericana.com

Olde Hope Antiques Inc.
www.oldehope.com

Pantry & Hearth
www.pantryandhearth.com

Patricia Stauble Antiques
www.patriciastaubleantiques.com

Throckmorton Fine Art
www.throckmorton-nyc.com

Jeffrey Tillou Antiques
www.tillouantiques.com

ARCHITECTURAL ANTIQUES
Garden Antiques
www.bi-gardenantiques.com

Cecilia B. Williams
cbwantiques@gmail.com

ARMS & MILITARIA
Faganarms
www.faganarms.com

BAROMETERS
Barometer Fair
www.barometerfair.com

BOOKS
Bauman Rare Books
www.baumanrarebooks.com

CARPETS & RUGS
Douglas Stock Gallery
douglasstockgallery.com

CERAMICS
Charles & Barbara Adams
Tel: (508) 760-3290
Email: adams_2430@msn.com

Jill Fenichell
www.jillfenichellinc.com

COSTUME JEWELRY
Deco Jewels Inc.
www.decojewelsny.com

CLOCKS
Kirtland H. Crump
www.kirtlandcrumpclocks.com

Schmitt Horan & Co.
www.schmitt-horan.com

DECORATIVE ARTS
HL Chalfant Antiques
www.hlchalfant.com

Brian Cullity
www.briancullity.com

Peter Eaton Antiques
www.petereaton.com

Leah Gordon Antiques
www.leahgordon.com

Samuel Herrup Antiques
www.samuelherrup.com

High Style Deco
www.highstyledeco.com

R. Jorgensen Antiques
www.rjorgensen.com

Bettina Krainin Antiques
www.bettinakraininantiques.com

Macklowe Gallery
www.macklowegallery.com

Lillian Nassau
www.lilliannassau.com

Rago Arts & Auction Center
www.ragoarts.com

Sumpter Priddy Inc.
www.sumpterpriddy.com

James L Price Antiques
priceantiques.com

RJG Antiques
www.rjgantiques.com

John Keith Russell Antiques Inc.
www.jkrantiques.com

Israel Sack
www.israelsack.com

Kathy Schoemer American Antiques
www.kathyschoemerantiques.com

Van Tassel/Baumann American Antiques
Tel: 610 647 3339

DOLLS
Sara Bernstein Antique Dolls & Bears
www.rubylane.com/shop/sarabernstein-dolls

Theriault's
www.theriaults.com

FURNITURE
Antique Associates
www.aaawt.com

Artemis Gallery
www.artemisantiques.com

Boym Partners Inc.
www.boym.com

Carswell Rush Berlin Inc.
www.american-antiques.net

Evergreen Antiques
www.evergreenantiques.com

Eileen Lane Antiques
www.eileenlaneantiques.com

Lost City Arts
www.lostcityarts.com

GENERAL
Bucks County Antiques Center
Tel: 215 794 9180

Manhatten Arts & Antiques Center
www.the-maac.com

GLASS
William Pitt Paperweights & Art Glass
www.wpitt.com

Holsten Galleries
www.holstengalleries.com

JEWELRY
Ark Antiques
www.arkantiques.org

LIGHTING
Chameleon Fine Lighting
chameleonhome.com

MARINE ANTIQUES
Hyland Granby Antiques
www.hylandgranby.com

METALWARE
Wayne & Phyllis Hilt
www.hiltpewter.com

ASIAN
Mimi's Antiques
Tel: 443 250 0930

PAPERWEIGHTS
The Dunlop Collection
www.glasspaperweights.com

SILVER
Chicago Silver
www.chicagosilver.com

Imperial Half Bushel
www.imperialhalfbushel.com

TEXTILES
Pandora de Balthazar
www.pandoradebalthazar.com

M Finkel & Daughter
www.samplings.com

Cora Ginsburg
www.coraginsburg.com

Stephen & Carol Huber
www.antiquesamplers.com

TRIBAL ART
Arte Primitivo
www.arteprimitivo.com

Marcy Burns American Indian Arts
www.marcyburns.com

Morning Star Gallery
www.morningstargallery.com

Elliott & Grace Snyder
www.elliottandgracesnyder.com

Trotta-Bono American Indian Art
www.trottabono.com

20THC DESIGN
Mix Gallery
Tel: (609) 773-0777

Moderne Gallery
www.modernegallery.com

Modernism Gallery
www.modernisminc.com

CANADIAN SPECIALISTS

CERAMICS
Cynthia Findlay
www.cynthiafindlay.com

Pam Ferrazzutti Antiques
Tel: (905) 639-2608

FURNITURE
Faith Grant
www.faithgrantantiques.com

Maus Park Antiques
www.mausparkantiques.ca

Milord Antiques
www.milordantiques.com

Richard Rumi & Co. Antiques
www.rumiantiques.com

GENERAL
Toronto Antiques on King
www.torontoantiquesonking.com

JEWELRY
Cynthia Findlay
www.cynthiafindlay.com

Fraleigh Jewellers
www.fraleigh.ca

Fiona Kenny Antiques
www.fionakennyantiques.com

SILVER
Louis Wine Ltd.
www.louiswine.com

INDEX

INDEX